International Directory of
COMPANY HISTORIES

International Directory of

COMPANY HISTORIES

VOLUME 29

Editor

Tina Grant

St. James Press

AN IMPRINT OF THE GALE GROUP

DETROIT • SAN FRANCISCO • LONDON
BOSTON • WOODBRIDGE, CT

STAFF

Tina Grant, *Editor*

Miranda H. Ferrara, *Project Manager*

Laura S. Berger, Joann Cerrito, David J. Collins, Steve Cusack,
Nicolet V. Elert, Jamie C. FitzGerald, Kristin Hart, Laura S. Kryhoski,
Margaret Mazurkiewicz, Michael J. Tyrkus, *St. James Press Editorial Staff*

Peter M. Gareffa, *Managing Editor, St. James Press*

Library of Congress Catalog Number: 89-190943

British Library Cataloguing in Publication Data

International directory of company histories. Vol. 29
I. Tina Grant
338.7409

ISBN 1-55862-388-4

Printed in the United States of America
Published simultaneously in the United Kingdom

St. James Press is an imprint of The Gale Group

Cover photograph: Entrance Hall of the Helsinki Exchange
(courtesy Helsinki Exchanges of Finland)

10 9 8 7 6 5 4 3 2 1

CONTENTS _____

Preface . . . . page vii
List of Abbreviations ix

Company Histories

PREFACE

The St. James Press series *The International Directory of Company Histories (IDCH)* is intended for reference use by students, business people, librarians, historians, economists, investors, job candidates, and others who seek to learn more about the historical development of the world's most important companies. To date, *IDCH* has covered over 3,900 companies in 29 volumes.

Inclusion Criteria

Most companies chosen for inclusion in *IDCH* have achieved a minimum of US$50 million in annual sales and are leading influences in their industries or geographical locations. Companies may be publicly held, private, or nonprofit. State-owned companies that are important in their industries and that may operate much like public or private companies also are included. Wholly owned subsidiaries and divisions are profiled if they meet the requirements for inclusion. Entries on companies that have had major changes since they were last profiled may be selected for updating.

The *IDCH* series highlights 10% private and nonprofit companies, and features updated entries on approximately 45 companies per volume.

Entry Format

Each entry begins with the company's legal name, the address of its headquarters, its telephone, toll-free, and fax numbers, and its web site. A statement of public, private, state, or parent ownership follows. A company with a legal name in both English and the language of its headquarters country is listed by the English name, with the native-language name in parentheses.

The company's founding or earliest incorporation date, the number of employees, and the most recent available sales figures follow. Sales figures are given in local currencies with equivalents in U.S. dollars. For some private companies, sales figures are estimates and indicated by the abbreviation *est.* The entry lists the exchanges on which a company's stock is traded and its ticker symbol, as well as the company's principal North American Industry Classification codes.

Entries generally contain a *Company Perspectives* box which provides a short summary of the company's mission, goals, and ideals, a list of *Principal Subsidiaries, Principal Divisions, Principal Operating Units,* and articles for *Further Reading.*

American spelling is used throughout *IDCH*, and the word ''billion'' is used in its U.S. sense of one thousand million.

Sources

Entries have been compiled from publicly accessible sources both in print and on the Internet such as general and academic periodicals, books, annual reports, and material supplied by the companies themselves.

Cumulative Indexes

IDCH contains two indexes: the **Index to Companies**, which provides an alphabetical index to companies discussed in the text as well as to companies profiled, and the **Index to Industries**, which allows researchers to locate companies by their principal industry. Both indexes are cumulative and specific instructions for using them are found immediately preceding each index.

Suggestions Welcome

Comments and suggestions from users of *IDCH* on any aspect of the product as well as suggestions for companies to be included or updated are cordially invited. Please write:

The Editor
International Directory of Company Histories
St. James Press
27500 Drake Rd.
Farmington Hills, Michigan 48331-3535

ABBREVIATIONS FOR FORMS OF COMPANY INCORPORATION

A.B.	Aktiebolaget (Sweden)
A.G.	Aktiengesellschaft (Germany, Switzerland)
A.S.	Atieselskab (Denmark)
A.S.	Aksjeselskap (Denmark, Norway)
A.Ş.	Anomin Şirket (Turkey)
B.V.	Besloten Vennootschap met beperkte, Aansprakelijkheid (The Netherlands)
Co.	Company (United Kingdom, United States)
Corp.	Corporation (United States)
G.I.E.	Groupement d'Intérêt Economique (France)
GmbH	Gesellschaft mit beschränkter Haftung (Germany)
H.B.	Handelsbolaget (Sweden)
Inc.	Incorporated (United States)
KGaA	Kommanditgesellschaft auf Aktien (Germany)
K.K.	Kabushiki Kaisha (Japan)
LLC	Limited Liability Company (Middle East)
Ltd.	Limited (Canada, Japan, United Kingdom, United States)
N.V.	Naamloze Vennootschap (The Netherlands)
OY	Osakeyhtiöt (Finland)
PLC	Public Limited Company (United Kingdom)
PTY.	Proprietary (Australia, Hong Kong, South Africa)
S.A.	Société Anonyme (Belgium, France, Switzerland)
SpA	Società per Azioni (Italy)

ABBREVIATIONS FOR CURRENCY

DA	Algerian dinar	Dfl	Netherlands florin
A$	Australian dollar	Nfl	Netherlands florin
Sch	Austrian schilling	NZ$	New Zealand dollar
BFr	Belgian franc	N	Nigerian naira
Cr	Brazilian cruzado	NKr	Norwegian krone
C$	Canadian dollar	RO	Omani rial
RMB	Chinese renminbi	P	Philippine peso
DKr	Danish krone	Esc	Portuguese escudo
E£	Egyptian pound	Ru	Russian ruble
Fmk	Finnish markka	SRls	Saudi Arabian riyal
FFr	French franc	S$	Singapore dollar
DM	German mark	R	South African rand
HK$	Hong Kong dollar	W	South Korean won
HUF	Hungarian forint	Pta	Spanish peseta
Rs	Indian rupee	SKr	Swedish krona
Rp	Indonesian rupiah	SFr	Swiss franc
IR£	Irish pound	NT$	Taiwanese dollar
L	Italian lira	B	Thai baht
¥	Japanese yen	£	United Kingdom pound
W	Korean won	$	United States dollar
KD	Kuwaiti dinar	B	Venezuelan bolivar
LuxFr	Luxembourgian franc	K	Zambian kwacha
M$	Malaysian ringgit		

International Directory of

COMPANY
HISTORIES

Aavid Thermal Technologies, Inc.

1 Eagle Square, Suite 509
Concord, New Hampshire 03301
U.S.A
(603) 224-1117
(800) 366-2843
Fax: (603) 224-6673
Web site: http://www.aatt.com

Public Company
Incorporated: 1993
Employees: 2,245
Sales: $209.1 million (1998)
Stock Exchanges: NASDAQ
Ticker Symbol: AATT
NAIC: 331315 Aluminum Sheet, Plate & Foil
   Manufacturing; 332116 Metal Stamping; 551112
   Offices of Other Holding Companies; 54133
   Engineering Services

Aavid Thermal Technologies, Inc., founded in 1993, is the world's technology and market leader in thermal management. Headquartered in Concord, New Hampshire, Aavid and its three subsidiaries provide thermal management products that dissipate unwanted heat in electronic and electrical components and systems—such as microprocessors and integrated circuits (ICs) for digital and power applications. The company is the oldest and largest business devoted exclusively to solving thermal problems and carries the broadest range of products in the thermal management industry; Aavid holds approximately 25 percent of the North American market. The company's products include computational-fluid-dynamics (CFD) software, aluminum and copper heat sinks and fan combinations, heat pipes, conductive adhesives, compliant interface materials, and liquid-cooled cold plates. Aavid supports its customers with an experienced applications and thermal engineering staff that analyzes customer thermal problems, recommends design changes in the customer's product, and designs a thermal solution. Through its highly integrated network of software, development, manufac-

turing, sales, and distribution centers located throughout North America, Europe, and the Far East, Aavid services a highly diversified base of more than 4,000 national and international customers, among which are original equipment manufacturers (OEMs), distributors, and contract manufacturers. The company operates manufacturing facilities in New Hampshire, California, Texas, Canada, China, Taiwan, and the United Kingdom. Aavid also supports an advanced research development center in Texas and another in New Hampshire. The company's total sales soared from $37.61 million in 1992, to $61.62 million in 1994, to $107 million in 1996 (the year Aavid went public), and to $209.1 million in 1998.

The Early Years: 1964–95

During the second half of the 20th century, designers of electronic systems responded to consumer demands and increasing competition by offering new products in smaller form factors having improved performance (functionality and speed), greater reliability, and lower prices. System designers relied principally on system integration, a strategy that necessitated overall system designs with fewer, smaller, and lighter components, circuit boards, and structural components. In fact, successful system integration for electronics was enabled in large part by increasing levels of silicon-circuit integration that, in turn, generated high levels of heat and created significant challenges for thermal management. Excessive heat degraded system performance and reliability and could cause system failure.

At first many engineers selected off-the-shelf fans and heat sinks (simple aluminum devices that helped dissipate heat from electronic devices, much as radiators do for automobile engines) to treat "hot spots" that occurred around electrical components. These after-the-fact designs of thermal management, however, were not very efficient at shedding heat; finished products had to operate at a fraction of their peak capability to minimize failure-causing heat loads. Major challenges surfaced for solutions to heat generated by digital products, power supplies, motor controls, and traction drives as well as methods to guarantee uninterruptable power supplies. It was in this challenging technological climate that Aavid Thermal Technologies made its first appearance.

According to Laurie Ann Toupin's story "Hot Company in the Cooling Business," published in the November 16, 1998 issue of *Design News,* Aavid Thermal Technologies' roots go back to the early 1960s when Ken St. Jacques and an associate interviewed engineers at Digital Equipment Corp. to discuss thermal problems. After several months of working through weekends, Ken and his partner designed a special heat sink that removed heat from semiconductors by providing a cooler temperature for the heat to flow upward, a success that in 1964 led to the formation of Aavid Engineering Co. Toupin said that the founders had "named the company Arvid Engineering, using a family name," but the printer who prepared materials to announce the company's opening substituted an *a* for the *r*. There was no time for a reprint before the scheduled market release—and Aavid Engineering remained the company's name.

In 1985 entrepreneur Alan F. Beane, who later served as president and chief executive officer at Aavid Thermal Technologies, bought Aavid Engineering and began to implement a national expansion plan. By 1993, however, Aavid Engineering was highly leveraged, suffered severe liquidity problems, and could not pay scheduled principal and certain interest obligations on its subordinated debt. In October 1993, Alan Beane and Sterling, Oak Investment Partners, in a leveraged buyout, acquired Aavid Engineering, which became a wholly owned subsidiary of newly formed Aavid Thermal Technologies, Inc.

In 1992 Aavid implemented a Synchronous Flow and Constraint Management system that significantly shortened the time of manufacturing cycles. Furthermore, in 1994 the company opened its advanced thermal laboratory for characterizing the thermal properties of products and prototypes. In this laboratory, the company's proprietary modeling software analyzed thermal conditions in three dimensions in just minutes; a wind tunnel simulated air flow in customer applications; and an isothermal bath facilitated and characterized liquid cooling, thereby providing real-time testing of a customer's thermal solutions.

The company's international expansion accelerated in August 1995 when Aavid acquired Lebanon, New Hampshire-based Fluent Inc., a leading developer and marketer of computational-fluid-dynamics (CFD) software. Fluent became Aavid's second wholly owned subsidiary (the first was Aavid Thermal Products), and the company planned to leverage Fluent's international presence to accelerate penetration into international markets. Fluent's international sales were 56.2 percent of its total revenues.

Microchip Explosion and Market Expansion: 1996

On January 29, 1996, Aavid completed its initial public offering (IPO) by completing the sale of an aggregate of 2,645,000 shares of common stock at $9.50 per share. The company then was traded on the NASDAQ national market under the symbol AATT and began an aggressive campaign for national and international expansion.

On May 16, 1996, the company purchased all the stock of Chicago-based Fluid Dynamics International Inc. (FDI) and absorbed it into the Fluent subsidiary. Prior to the acquisition, FDI had been a major competitor of Aavid's software operations. FDI was a provider of computerized design and simulation software used to predict fluid flow, heat and mass transfer, chemical reaction, and related phenomena. Also in May came Aavid's purchase of Polyflow S.A., a small Belgian software company focusing on the flow of polymers (naturally occurring or synthetic substances consisting of giant molecules formed from polymerization) in the plastics industry. Then, on September 16, 1996, Aavid acquired substantially all of the assets of Franklin, New Hampshire-based Alumax Extrusion's aluminum-extrusion manufacturing facility. During the same month, Aavid established a joint venture with Birchtek Engineering Co. Limited, located in Taiwan. In September 1996 Aavid also unveiled its United Kingdom headquarters for sales and manufacturing.

Next, on December 24, 1996, Aavid purchased all of the assets of Toronto-based Beaver Precision Products, Inc. According to a *Business Wire* issued May 5, 1997, this acquisition "paired Aavid's extensive array of heat-dissipation products and advanced technology development capabilities with Beaver's turn-part manufacturing capabilities and established a Canadian distribution network for thermal products." Aavid's Canadian branch moved into a new facility in Ontario and thereby was enabled to expand not only its "fabrication and precision-manufacturing capabilities" but also to "respond more rapidly and flexibly to regional-product and delivery demands," commented Robert Soucy, general manager of the branch.

As new generations of microprocessors—such as Intel's Pentium and Pentium Pro chips and the IBM/Motorola Power PC chip—became faster and more complex they generated more heat. Likewise, advancements in semiconductor packaging (for example, area array and flip-chip technologies), smaller form factors, more sophisticated power requirements, and other advances in chip technology created excessive heat in microprocessors and ICs in electronic and electrical components and systems. Heat was an absolute constraint in electronic system design because microprocessors and ICs operated efficiently only in a narrow temperature band. The excessive heat generated within the component not only degraded semiconductor and system performance and reliability, but also could cause semiconductor and system failure.

In short, the problems caused by excessive heat drove the demand for innovative thermal solutions and products for digital electronics applications. This "turning point in the computer industry 'validated' Aavid's importance. Although Aavid had, all along, been providing heat solutions for digital electronics, the industry at large was reluctant to admit that heat generation was 'a limiting factor' in production," said Stephen Eldred, Aavid's chief financial officer, when interviewed by Hope Jordan for a story in the March/April 1998 issue of *Northeast Export Magazine.* But that changed, wrote Jordan, "when the November 28, 1996 issue of *Electric News* quoted Andrew Grove, Intel's president and chief executive officer, as saying 'Problems facing the industry include testing, validating and heat generation.'"

By year-end 1996, Aavid believed it had the broadest range of products in the thermal management industry. The company's customers included Allen-Bradley, AT&T, Chrysler, General Electric, Hewlett-Packard, IBM, Intel, Motorola, COMPAQ, and Packard Bell. Net revenues increased by 47.6 percent from $61.62 million in 1994 to $90.94 million in 1995 and, in 1996, increased by 17.6 percent to $107.0 million.

Engineering, Outsourcing, Globalization: 1997

Aavid's method of product design incorporated thermal engineering, that is, engineers incorporated cooling solutions from the very start of the product's development process. The result was maximum cooling performance, increased flexibility in finished product design, and increased revenue resulting from elimination of late-stage changes to deal with "hot spots." Many electronics manufacturers did not have the internal resources to solve their complex thermal management problems and turned to third parties to design thermal solutions.

To create solutions applicable to these thermal dissipation situations and to capitalize on the trend to outsourcing thermal management problems, Aavid defined a six-point strategy: 1) focus on leading markets and leading customers; 2) development of a more flexible, lower-cost infrastructure that would allow the company to make good profits as the market leader in heat dissipation for electronics; 3) forward integrate to increase value; 4) backwards integrate, sometimes, to lower costs; 5) international expansion; and 6) domestic expansion. Aavid positioned itself to be the Total Integrated Solution for Cooling Electronics by delivering world-class thermal design services, thermal-flow analysis software, and worldwide, quick-ramp, high-volume manufacturing—in short, Thermal Design, Thermal Analysis, Global Fabrication. Each one of Aavid's three wholly owned subsidiaries—Aavid Thermal Products, Fluent, and Applied Thermal Technologies—played its special part to implement this strategy.

At the center of the Total Integrated Solution was Aavid Thermal Products, with nearly 700,000 square feet worldwide dedicated to manufacturing and distributing thermal solutions. This subsidiary's experienced teams brought thermal solutions from CAD/CAM systems to loading docks in record time, implementing the most advanced methods in heat-sink manufacturing every step of the way. Their thermal management products—which operated by conducting, convecting, and radiating away unwanted heat—helped to maintain system performance and reliability and also helped to avoid premature component and system failure. Substantial engineering was required in the design of these products to maximize heat dissipation while minimizing assembly costs for customers. Aavid Products

placed the company in a unique leadership position to provide its clients in the electronics and communications industries with the broadest available range of products in the thermal management industry. Aavid Thermal Products' customers included Allen-Bradley, Chrysler, COMPAQ, General Electric, Hewlett-Packard, IBM, Intel, Lucent, Motorola, and Packard Bell.

Fluent, the world leader in CFD software, enabled design engineers to produce virtual models of their products on their computers through a detailed simulation of fluid flow and heat transfer. Its software was used to predict fluid flow, heat and mass transfer, chemical reaction, and related phenomena. Fluent's software products and services helped engineers with detailed product development, design optimization, troubleshooting, scale-up, and retrofitting. They significantly reduced engineering costs while improving the final design of products in applications ranging from design of electronic components and systems to automotive engineering, and from combustion system design to process plant troubleshooting. Fluent, headquartered in Lebanon, New Hampshire, had offices throughout the United States. Its European headquarters were located in Sheffield, England, with local offices in France and Germany. Fluent's software also was available around the world through joint ventures, partnerships, and distributors in Australia, Brazil, China, Japan, Korea, Taiwan, the Czech Republic, and most European countries. Fluent licensed its software to more than 1,800 customers worldwide, including Allen-Bradley, AT&T, Boeing, British Aerospace, Chrysler, Ford, Fujitsu, General Electric, Hewlett-Packard, IBM, Intel, Motorola, Packard Bell, and StorageTek.

California-based Applied Thermal Technologies' design center, established in the first quarter of 1997, integrated Aavid's technical strengths to solicit customer-funded research and development and to provide consulting and cutting-edge design. This subsidiary acted as a catalyst for technology and business development for Aavid's two other subsidiaries. Applied Thermal Technologies—leveraging on technical capabilities gained from both Aavid Thermal Products and Fluent to develop, test, and validate thermal solutions—worked as an extension of its clients' team for product design. Aavid believed that design centers would enhance its visibility as a technology leader and create earlier and closer ties to new and existing customers. Among Applied Thermal Technologies' clients were the following: Applied Materials, Bay Networks, Cisco Systems, Hewlett-Packard, Sony, Sun Microsystems, and many other high-level clients in Silicon Valley.

Among Aavid's other major accomplishments in 1997 were the following: the opening of a Manchester, New Hampshire plant (47,000 square feet) for high-volume thermal management products for the computer and networking markets; acquisition of the remaining 49 percent of Aavid Taiwan and launch of a 40,000-square-foot manufacturing operation in the Guang Dong Province of China; introduction of IcePak thermal analysis software for analyzing cooling problems at the component, board, and systems level; acquisition of the remaining 50 percent of Belgian-based Polyflow; and the successful integration of FDI into Fluent, thereby strengthening Aavid's CFD product offerings. In 1997 Aavid's sales jumped 57 percent to $167.75 million, earnings per share increased 106 percent to $0.97

per share, and shareholder value increased 156 percent to $218 million.

Toward the 21st Century: 1998 and Beyond

One of Aavid's first products was a specially designed heat sink that became the precursor of the many heat sinks that would follow as PC manufacturers and other designers of electronic products enhanced their products with an ever-increasing number of transistors. Performance rapidly improved, but so did the amount of heat generated by superfast and dense PC processors and other electronic components. None of the three basic approaches in use for thermal management—whether they were heat spreaders, heat sinks, or fans and blowers—produced the desired results. For instance, as Aavid Thermal Products' Christopher Chapman commented in an interview with newswriter Mark Hachman, writing for the August 16, 1998 issue of *Electronic Buyers News,* "A well-designed PC will use a fluted or straight fin, channeling the air directly down the path of the air delivered by the intake fan. However, a heat sink extending 6 inches or more above any surface will create a nonuniform air flow." In June 1998 Aavid introduced "Pocket Coolers," a new family of fan-heat sinks designed to cool chips packaged in ball-grid arrays. These heat sinks were light and small, measuring 7 to 15 millimeters, and the fan had a minimum life of 50,000 hours at 25 degrees Celsius. Then in December, Fluent announced that IcePak, its thermal analysis and design software for cooling electronics, supported a direct interface with Pro/ Engineer mechanical design software. With this interface users could export the IcePak model from within Pro/Engineer and avoid repetitive modeling.

Indeed, as Aavid Chairman and CEO Ronald F. Borelli had pointed out in his "1997 Letter to Shareholders," all indicators reflected that "heat dissipation as a persistent and growing problem for all sectors of the electronics industry" would intensify in the years ahead. Aavid's continuous initiatives to expand its capability for thermal analysis and thermal design—as well as its continuing global expansion—established the company as the world's technology and market leader in thermal management.

For fiscal 1998 Aavid reported record sales of $209.1 million, an increase of 24.7 percent over 1997 sales of $168.75 million. Net income for 1998 was $11.7 million, that is, 37 percent ahead of 1997 net income of $8.5 million. Earnings per share were $1.23 for 1998, an increase of 26 percent over the $0.97 per share for 1997.

As the 21st century drew near, Aavid Thermal Technologies, Inc. looked to the future with guarded confidence (increased competition from relatively large providers of thermal management products, interruption or reduction of raw materials, especially of the aluminum extrusion required for heat sinks, and so on, might prevent the company from meeting delivery schedules to clients) and creative enthusiasm based on its past and current performance. The company validated its technological expertise when it agreed to participate in *EDN Magazine's* Hands-on-Project to explore the thermal engineering aspects of a projected future desktop computer, dubbed the Year 2003 Computer. *EDN* Senior Technical Editor Bill Travis led the project and reported on it in a story titled "Keeping HAL Cool in 2003," published in *EDN Magazine's* October 8, 1998 issue.

To carry out this Hands-on-Project, Travis enlisted the help of system packaging experts from Palo Alto Products International, Inc. (Palo Alto) and of engineers from Aavid's three subsidiaries. Palo Alto designed "the Year 2003 Computer chassis and case, based on projections of the form factors of the various computer subsections." Aavid's Applied Thermal Technologies—staying within stipulated overall system constraints—generated possible cooling system models that used various fan, heat-sink, vent, and baffle configurations. Aavid Thermal Products "generated projected designs for the cooling-system hardware, including heat sinks, interfaces, fans, and attachment methods." Fluent used its CFD software to provide thermal analyses—or temperature profiles—of the various cooling configurations from Applied Thermal Technologies and from Aavid Thermal Products.

The Aavid Thermal Products/Fluent contributions were interactive. Without using CFD software it would have been necessary "to construct physical models . . . and then use sensors, temperature-indicating wax or stick-ons, or infrared instrumentation to measure the local temperatures," Travis emphasized. He added that perhaps the most important result of the Hands-on-Project was that today's cooling techniques and devices could "be applied to tomorrow's systems in a cost-efficient way and that the simulation and thermal-engineering principles applied during the project would remain valid, regardless of the form assumed by future computers." In sum, Aavid Thermal Technologies, Inc. was developing the technology needed for thermal management in the upcoming millennium.

Principal Subsidiaries

Aavid Thermal Products, Inc.; Applied Thermal Technologies, Inc.; Fluent, Inc.

Further Reading

Hachman, Mark, "Heat Wave!—Today's Dense PC Chips Require Lots of Cool," *Electronic Buyers News,* August 16, 1998.

Jordan, Hope, "Heating Up the Market in Global Cooling," *Northeast Export Magazine,* March/April 1998.

Roos, Gina, "Thermal Management Plan Lights a Fire Under Aavid," *Electric Buyers News,* October 7, 1996, p. 34.

Toupin, Laurie Ann, "Hot Company in the Cooling Business," *Design News,* November 16, 1998.

Travis, Bill, "Keeping HAL Cool in 2003," *EDN Magazine,* October 8, 1998, cover story.

—Gloria A. Lemieux

АЭРОФЛОТ

Aeroflot—Russian International Airlines

37 Leningradsky Prospect
Korpus 9
Moscow
125167
Russian Federation
(095) 155-66-48
Fax: (095) 155-66-47
Web site: http://www.aeroflot.org

Public Company (51% State-Owned)
Incorporated: 1923 as Dobrolet
Employees: 14,500
Sales: $1.4 billion (1997)
Stock Exchanges: Russia
NAIC: 481111 Scheduled Passenger Air Transportation

Once the largest airline in the world, during the days of the Soviet Empire, Aeroflot—Russian International Airlines is now the largest remnant of the former Aeroflot—Soviet Airlines. In June 1992, Aeroflot—Soviet Airlines was reorganized, and the national carrier became known as Aeroflot—Russian International Airlines. Valery Okulov was appointed the airlines' General Director, and the company was designated a public joint-stock company, with 51 percent of the stock being owned by the government and the remaining 49 percent belonging to the employees. The new Aeroflot flies to 150 destinations in 93 countries and provides 70 percent of all the international air transport in and out of Russia. Although it has had to struggle with unending financial difficulties, safety mishaps, and scandals, Aeroflot somehow keeps flying and remains important as Russia's national carrier.

Soviet Origins

Before 1920 Russian air enthusiasts had experimented with aircraft development, and in 1920 and 1921, as the Russian Civil War drew to a close, small-scale experiments with air transport were made under both private and state initiative.

Flights to the Nizhni Novgorod fair, a traditional trade fair, engendered a more systematic approach toward aviation. The Chief Administration of the Civil Air Fleet was soon established, and one of its first acts was to develop in 1921 a joint venture with German interests to create the Deutsch-Russiche Luftverkehrs A.G. (Deruluft). Specializing in flights to the West, Deruluft's regular services began from Königsberg in eastern Germany to Moscow on May Day, 1927. In its tenth year of operation it had two main routes—from Berlin to Moscow and from Königsberg to Leningrad—and it carried 3,600 passengers and 145 tons of post and goods.

Systemic domestic aviation developed at approximately the same time, with the state playing a more significant role. In March 1923 the first Soviet airline, Dobrolet, was created as a joint state and commercially based organization and the first regular service was introduced in July 1923 from Moscow to Nizhni Novgorod. The Russian people shared the West's interest in aviation, and an attempt was made to formalize this in March 1923 with the creation of a large public organization—the ODVF, or Friends of the Air Fleet, under the slogan "working people build the air fleet." Aviation could be portrayed as an exciting diversion from the real difficulties of the New Economic Policy as well as a potential source of future international conflict. At the 13th Party Congress in May 1924 it was noted that "the rapid growth of military and civil aviation in capitalist countries makes it necessary to strengthen and develop our own."

The actual scale of activities, however, was still very small. In 1923 Georgian and Ukrainian based airlines were also created, backed by banks and commercial enterprises. During the 1920s, Dobrolet began to expand its activities across Russia, forming subdivisions as it did so, and in September 1926, it was made into an all-union organization. International flights to Mongolia and Afghanistan were initiated, but the main airlink to the West was still by Deruluft.

In 1928 a general consolidation began. The Ukrainian airline was merged with Dobrolet, and between 1930–32 a succession of organizational changes culminated in all Soviet civil aviation being subsumed under the title Aeroflot in March 1932. Henceforth all internal civil flying activity was under the control of Aeroflot. The new airline did not become fully responsible for international flights to the West until the agreement with Deruluft expired in 1937, when the latter's routes were either suspended because of the growing hostility between Nazi Germany and Stalin's Russia or taken over by Aeroflot.

In this way, Aeroflot emerged as the monopoly carrier in the USSR, with a structure essentially unchanged until the breakup of the Soviet Union in 1991–92. During this long period Aeroflot experienced sustained expansion, interrupted only by World War II, when it played an important military role. By the end of the 1930s Aeroflot had become the world's largest airline. After 1945 the Soviet state made a deliberate attempt to direct medium- and long-distance travelers within the USSR onto Aeroflot. By 1990 Aeroflot connected 3,600 cities and towns in the USSR and flew to 102 countries, carrying 138 million passengers and three million tons of cargo and mail (five million passengers and 100,000 tons of freight on its international routes). No American airline could compete at this level. However, as the Deputy Director of Aeroflot said in 1963, "a true comparison between ourselves and the United States would not be with their largest airline but with all their airlines put together. . . . We do not expect to be larger in total carrying than all those airlines for a few years yet." In fact, despite this optimism, Soviet aviation has always taken second place to American aviation on a world scale.

Aeroflot's fleet has had to evolve rapidly to sustain this expansion, though lead times for the introduction of new planes have usually been longer than in the West, especially as technology became more sophisticated. Early planes were imported or built under license in the USSR, but their long-term development was closely tied to the creation of an independent Soviet aircraft industry. In 1929, 61 percent of new planes used by Dobrolet were foreign, but after 1934, apart from the war years, Aeroflot's fleet remained essentially Soviet-built until the purchase of Airbuses at the end of the 1980s. This fleet was a product of the famous design teams led by Antonov, Tupolev, and Ilyushin.

Aeroflot's activities went far beyond those associated with Western airlines. A primary function was the transportation of domestic passengers and freight. In addition, Aeroflot acted as the international Soviet flag carrier. International flights always had a high prestige, but they never made up more than a small part of the passenger or ton miles flown by Aeroflot (usually well under five percent). Moreover, Aeroflot was also responsible for agricultural aviation, including fertilizer and pesticide dusting, some air sowing, attempts at climate modification to assist agriculture, forest patrols, and fish spotting for Soviet fishing fleets. The important work of air surveying and prospecting in the remoter areas of the USSR and the airborne movement of construction materials to new sites was also organized through Aeroflot, as was the Soviet air ambulance service.

Aeroflot was also responsible for its own ground services and airport development. Systematic airport development was begun in the 1930s under Aeroflot's control, and this became especially important after 1945 when the decision was made to link all the significant towns and cities by air. This led Aeroflot into building both airports and hotels to ensure the availability of adequate accommodation for its crews and passengers.

Cold War Competition

Aeroflot's organizational structure has been based on proliferating territorial divisions. In 1964 the organization of its international flights was turned into an independent division within Aeroflot under the trade name Aeroflot-International Airlines. Each territorial division (of which there were over 30 in 1990) was responsible for the full range of Aeroflot's work within its defined area. Aeroflot was overseen by the Chief Directorate of the Civil Air Fleet which became the Ministry of Civil Aviation in 1964. As Aeroflot grew in size, this structure became unwieldy and problems of overlap developed. It was nevertheless maintained, possibly because it suited local political purposes. The manner in which this system actually functioned was still obscure into the 1990s, given the USSR's past secrecy. In the 1930s Aeroflot, and aviation generally, had been affected by the Stalinist purges. It was typical of the time that the designer Tupolev should be arrested for "betraying secrets," and then be made to lead a research team of aircraft designers in the prison camps. Real public light in the West was first thrown on Aeroflot's internal organization in 1957, when a highly qualified British airlines trade union team led by Clive Jenkins was given a detailed insight into Aeroflot's working and when Jenkins updated his report in 1963. These early reports, which were later confirmed as secrecy diminished, suggested a reasonably efficient organization, but one which was struggling to keep up with its rapid, underplanned expansion. Senior staff also appeared to lack a good overview of Aeroflot's functioning or have a realistic idea of its economic status.

To understand Aeroflot, it is important to appreciate that the needs of the state were paramount, and aviation was vital to the state's survival. In this, of course, Aeroflot was not alone, since in the West too, governments played a key role in the development of civil aviation. Aeroflot, however, represented an extreme case of this trend.

Soviet policy was geared to rapid industrial development in conjunction with shortages of capital. Because transport generally involved high infrastructure costs, policy involved squeezing the maximum output from minimum inputs. This was also true of Aeroflot. Especially after World War II, domestic travel by air was encouraged in preference to rail and road. But this did not mean that Aeroflot had unlimited resources. It too was squeezed with high load factors of some 80 percent for freight and 75 percent for passengers, in addition to a "mottled pattern" of technology in the sense that while modern planes were used on the main services, smaller feeder services had to put up with older planes than similar services in the West. Domestic services in planes were also on a no-frills basis, with the late development of seat belts, and refreshments often limited to salted water in well-used plastic beakers. Ground services were also underdeveloped with low levels of mechanization. This excited much negative comment from foreigners, and after 1985 it became apparent that many Soviet citizens were also dissatisfied. However, this pattern made considerable sense given the state's objectives. Because the overall level of the Soviet economy was low, it was inevitable that the attempt to develop a national airline on the scale of Aeroflot would mean that considerable quality sacrifices would have to be made. In particular, this meant that on Aeroflot's international services, where it was competing with Western airlines, it had to offer comparable levels of service.

The strategic role given to Aeroflot in transport was informed by more than solely economic considerations. One was geography. It was inevitable that in the USSR, the largest country in the world, air travel would play a decisive role in linking population centers separated by distance, inhospitable terrain and climate. Beyond this, Aeroflot was also heavily influenced by the state's defense priorities. In the early 1930s civil and military planes were broadly interchangeable, but even when specialist air forces developed, civilian airlines were included in military planning for troop movements, and Aeroflot was no exception. Civilian pilots and many air crews were always considered part of the military reserve. The importance to the state of these aspects of Aeroflot's role was reflected in the presence of military figures in its top management.

Another feature of Aeroflot's development was its service to four political objectives of the Soviet state. One was the conscious use of Aeroflot's successes to boost the prestige of the Soviet state with its own people. A second, more specific political function was the role given to Aeroflot in transporting the "matrices" of central newspapers, like *Pravda,* from Moscow on a daily basis so that they could be published on the same day throughout the USSR. A third political role involved direct agitation in the 1930s. For a period Aeroflot had its own fleet of airplanes which carried propagandists and experts across the country. At the center was the biggest plane in the world at the time, the *Maxim Gorky*—in the words of Mikhail Kolstov, "a steel-engined stormbird, a winged agitator, which will bring culture, knowledge, light and political learning to the most distant parts of the country." Finally, Aeroflot played an important role in enabling the KGB and its predecessors to keep close control of their own empire and the country at large.

Political imperatives played a comparable role in Aeroflot's development as an international carrier. Soviet leaders such as Khrushchev attached great importance to carrying the national flag abroad. They felt personally humiliated when the planes they landed in appeared inferior to their Western counterparts. By the same token, triumphs such as Khrushchev's nonstop flight to Washington in an Aeroflot TU-114, and the subsequent embarrassment of the Americans in not having a large enough moving stairway to fit it, were widely appreciated.

These competitive international political pressures also affected Aeroflot's technical choices. In the 1930s the general world trend to build larger planes coincided with what was called "gigantomania" in the USSR—the idea that "biggest is best." The huge *Maxim Gorky* propaganda plane was seen as an early triumph. After the war the drive was to develop jet planes, and the widespread early use of the TU-104 jet on passenger services was seen as a similar triumph. Such a politico-technological drive, however, did not necessarily serve Aeroflot well. In the 1960s the pressure was on to build a supersonic airliner to match the Concorde. Unfortunately this made little economic sense, for this project meant that resources had to be taken away from other areas. Aeroflot suffered increasingly in the late 1970s and 1980s from its lack of large capacity transport planes of the Jumbo, airbus types. Indeed, its problems here may well have been one of the many signals received by the Soviet leadership at this time which made them realize that they were beginning to fall behind the West.

Political considerations also influenced Aeroflot's international route development. The latter was expected to help give the Soviet bloc an appearance of unity by its route planning and its long distance flights to Beijing (before the Sino-Soviet split) and to Havana from the 1960s. Moreover, Aeroflot was "a Soviet ambassador" to the Third World as Moscow attempted to compete with Western interests there.

Aeroflot under Gorbachev

It was inevitable that Aeroflot would be heavily affected by the political and economic turmoil in the USSR after 1985. At first *glasnost* and *perestroika* seemed beneficial. As Aeroflot became subject to searching criticism, information about its safety record became available and passengers became more vocal about poor service and lack of reliability, even to the extent of staging sit-ins on heavily delayed planes. The management of Aeroflot initially appeared to assume that the reorganization of the Soviet economy would be to their advantage, ridding them of excessive state control and allowing them to develop joint ventures with Western airlines such as Aer Lingus and Lufthansa. They did not appreciate the extent to which Aeroflot's own accounting had obscured the levels of state subsidy, nor did they anticipate the increasing dislocation that would occur in the economy after 1989, plunging internal flights into greater chaos.

Internal organizational change at this time emphasized the increasing autonomy of Aeroflot's territorial divisions, especially in the republics. The fallout from the failed August 1991 political coup in Moscow, however, took this process even further. In the first instance the breakup of the USSR pushed the new states to begin to try to divide up Aeroflot. The speeding up of economic reform also created serious disturbances in the Aeroflot organization. Effective management "buy-outs" or privatization of parts of the organization took place. These moves tentatively began a process pushing post-Soviet aviation in the successor states toward a pattern more typical of the West, with separate companies providing different parts of the total provision of air services. This transition, however, was made more difficult by the removal of some subsidies which forced Aeroflot away from its cheap fares policy, thus creating further economic difficulties.

Far from being a flagship, Aeroflot began to look like a white elephant for the new states, with an aging fleet and no obvious source for the massive new investment needed to renovate the civilian air structure as a whole. However, throughout the world, governments have continued to give direct and indirect support to airlines, and the successor states in the former USSR appeared no less anxious to ensure that their "bit" of Aeroflot did not go under. Beneath the turmoil, therefore, it seemed likely that Aeroflot and its former parts would still be a major factor in world aviation, albeit in a reduced form.

The New Aeroflot: 1990s

In 1989, Aeroflot reported Ru1.19 billion in revenues. *Air Transport World* reported that before the Soviet break-up, Aeroflot had 2,500 jetliners, even more turboprops, an armada of 9,000 helicopters and smaller planes, and employed half a million people. By 1992, following the breakup of the USSR, about 70 airlines were flying in the Commonwealth of Independent States, nearly half of them former divisions of Aeroflot.

After flying under the name "PKO Aeroflot, Soviet Airlines" briefly during the summer of 1992, Aeroflot became known as "Aeroflot—Russian International Airlines" (ARIA), still the 25th largest in the world, with 20,500 employees and 104 passenger aircraft. Tellingly, Russian International Airlines made its first flight on leased Airbus A310s. The carrier hoped to meet Western standards of service; some personnel were trained by Lufthansa.

In order to improve decision-making flexibility, Aeroflot established three separate subsidiaries, divided by the type of aircraft operated: Golden Star (Tu-154), Moscow Airways (Il-62), and Russky Vityaz (Il-76 and Tu-154); the Airbuses were operated by a separate division.

In 1993, ARIA reported income of R 900 billion, much of it in hard currency. Traffic for the year was up 18 percent at ARIA and the 30 other airlines carrying Aeroflot markings, according to *Aviation Week & Space Technology*. ARIA worked with British Airways to create a new airline to exploit new routes from Europe to the Orient. Air Russia planned to fly Boeing 767s from London, Paris, and Rome to Tokyo via Moscow. Aeroflot also entered into a U.S.-based cargo joint venture, North American Aeroflot.

Violent Crash in 1994

Whatever confidence Aeroflot's new partners were placing in it must have been severely tested by the bizarre and tragic events of March 22, 1994. An Aeroflot pilot on the "elite" Airbus A310 service between Moscow and Hong Kong reportedly allowed his teenage son to attempt to fly the airplane. Instead of taking over the controls immediately when the plane began to descend, the pilot coached the boy in how to recover the aircraft. The resulting crash over Siberia killed 75 people.

While pilots were mishandling the planes, it appeared managers were mishandling the money. In October 1995, Marshal Evgeni Shaposhnikov was appointed general director of 51 percent state-owned ARIA (it had became a joint stock company on June 21, 1994) in response to criticism of the carrier's business practices. Although Shaposhnikov was a military man, his forward-thinking Western-styled business ideas ruffled many feathers in the Russian aviation community. ARIA's revenues were at R 4.67 billion in 1995, and employment had been pared to about 15,000. Shaposhnikov was replaced in March 1997 by Valery Okulov, Boris Yeltsin's son-in-law.

Under Okulov, the airline sought to enhance its fleet. With the help of a loan from a New York finance group, ARIA bought two new Boeing 777s for its Los Angeles-Moscow service in 1998. Also during this time, the Export-Import Bank of the United States (Eximbank) backed another purchase of ten Boeing 737s and committed to finance $1 billion worth of Pratt & Whitney engines and equipment for use in Ilyushin jets to be flown by Aeroflot.

Challenges ensued in the late 1990s, as Russia's prosecutor general began investigating Aeroflot for currency law viola-

tions. According to a March 1999 article in *Forbes* magazine, Aeroflot was possibly connected to the byzantine financial network of Russian tycoon Boris Berezovsky, whose business practices were also under investigation.

Aeroflot reportedly lost $93 million in 1997 and had an airliner briefly impounded by Canadian authorities over a $6 million debt to a hotel company. With financial challenges and doubts about its efficiency and safety at the forefront as it headed into a new century, Aeroflot occupied a unique and perhaps tenuous place among world airlines, a place, however, to which it seemed accustomed throughout its history.

Further Reading

Brady, Rose, "Aeroflot Takes Off for Joint-Ventureland," *Business Week,* October 30, 1989, pp. 48–49.
——, Air Russia: Civilizing the Wild Red Yonder," *Business Week,* November 5, 1990, p. 110.
Bugaeva, B.P., ed., *Istoriya grazdanskoi aviatsii SSSR,* Moscow, 1983.
Covault, Craig, "Aeroflot Crash Probe Reveals Violent Descent," *Aviation Week & Space Technology,* April 11, 1994, p. 33.
Davies, R.E.G., *Aeroflot: An Airline and Its Aircraft,* Rockville, Md.: Paladwr Press, 1993.
Douglas Campbell, C., and M. Miller, "Aviation in Soviet Russia," *Journal of the Institute of Transport,* Vol. 16, No. 7, May 1935.
Duffy, Paul, "Aeroflot—Times Set to Change," *Air Transport World,* September 1996, pp. 39–46.
——, "In the Aftermath of Aeroflot," *Air Transport World,* July 1992, pp. 36–41.
Fraser, Hugh, "Carve-Up at Aeroflot," *International Management,* October 1992, pp. 75–77.
French, F., "Aeroflot in the Seventies," *Flight International,* Vol. 97, No. 3190, April 30, 1970.
Grazhdanskaya aviatsiya SSSR, 1917–1967, Moscow, 1967.
Jenkins, Clive, "Aeroflot," *Flight International,* Vol. 84, No. 2856, December 5, 1963.
——, "Aeroflot," *Flight International,* Vol. 72, Nos. 2,533–2,535, August 9, 1957.
Klebnikov, Paul, "The Day They Raided Aeroflot," *Forbes,* March 22, 1999, pp. 106–10.
MacDonald, Hugh, *Aeroflot: Soviet Air Transport since 1923,* London: Putnam, 1973.
Melcher, Richard, "Soviet Breakup? Coup? That's Minor Turbulence," *Business Week,* February 17, 1992.
Nelms, Douglas W., "Air Russia: Grinding to a Start," *Air Transport World,* November 1992, p. 88.
Novichkov, Nicolay, "Aeroflot Faces Survival Struggle," *Aviation Week & Space Technology,* January 12, 1998, p. 400.
——, "Aeroflot Moves Ahead with Fleet Expansion," *Aviation Week & Space Technology,* April 20, 1998, p. 39.
Ott, James, "Aeroflot, Marriott Cooperate on In-Flight Catering Service," *Aviation Week & Space Technology,* January 23, 1989, pp. 64–65.
"Perestroika Spurs Aeroflot to Begin Major Changes in Business Operations," *Aviation Week & Space Technology,* June 5, 1989, pp. 84–87.
"Russia's 'New' Aeroflot Seeks Own Identity," *Aviation Week & Space Technology,* February 7, 1994, pp. 39–41.
Talbott, Strobe, ed., *Khrushchev Remembers. The Last Testament,* London: Andre Deutsch, 1974.
USSR in Construction, No. 6, June 1932, and No. 1, January 1935.

—Mike Haynes
—updated by Frederick C. Ingram

Alaska Air Group, Inc.

19300 Pacific Highway South
P.O. Box 68947
Seattle, Washington 98168-0947
U.S.A.
(206) 431-7040
Fax: (206) 433-3379
Web site: http://www.alaskaair.com

Public Company
Incorporated: 1932 as Star Air Service
Employees: 12,464
Sales: $1.89 billion (1998)
Stock Exchanges: New York
Ticker Symbol: ALK
NAIC: 481111 Scheduled Passenger Air Transportation;
   551112 Offices of Other Holding Companies

Alaska Air Group, Inc. is the holding company for Alaska Air, the tenth largest U.S. airline with the country's youngest fleet of aircraft. More than 12 million passengers a year fly Alaska Air, and nearly four million its sister airline, the group's subsidiary Horizon Air. Alaska Air maintains marketing agreements with Northwest Airlines, American Eagle, KLM, Quantas, and several small commuter carriers, and is also the largest wholesaler of Disneyland vacation packages in the United States.

1930s Origins

The company that eventually became Alaska Air was founded in 1932 by Linious "Mac" McGee, a veteran of several failed business ventures who had traveled to Alaska in 1929 and set himself up as a fur buyer. In 1931, McGee and a pilot friend, Harvey W. Barnhill, purchased a used three-passenger Stinson prop plane in San Francisco and shipped it to Alaska for use on McGee's fur-buying forays. By January 1932, "Barnhill & McGee Airways" were offering charter flights in advertisements in the Anchorage daily newspaper. Barnhill and McGee dissolved their partnership shortly afterward, and McGee took over the business.

Anchorage in the early 1930s was a frontier town with an economy based largely on credit. With pilots working on commission, ferrying freight and passengers across Alaska, McGee was able to build up a fleet of seven identical Stinson planes painted with the black-and-white "McGee Airways" logo. Battered by the worldwide Depression and the seasonal nature of the Alaskan economy, however, the business was constantly on the brink of failure.

In 1934, McGee merged his struggling airline with another Anchorage airline, Star Air Service, which had a fleet of eight planes. This company had gotten its start in April 1932, when two aviators from Seattle, Steven E. Mills and Jack Waterworth, who were backed by a friend who put up the money, arrived in Anchorage with a Deluxe Fleet B-5 two-seater plane and set up shop as flight instructors. With a combined fleet of 15 planes, Star was now Alaska's dominant airline, but the business, beset by high repair costs to its fragile wood and fabric planes, continued to struggle throughout the mid-1930s.

The era of high-risk Alaska bush flying began to wind down in the late 1930s, when Star Air Service started de-emphasizing charter flights in favor of more regularly scheduled service. In 1937, in an effort to stabilize its finances, the company was incorporated as Star Air Lines. The following year, Congress passed a bill creating the Civil Aeronautics Authority to regulate the growing commercial airline industry.

Competing under CAB in the 1940s

In preparation for the advent of governmental regulation, Star began paying pilots a salary, rather than allowing them to compete for commissions, painted its 15 planes a uniform orange with a black logo, and tried to stick to semi-regular schedules for its flights. In 1940, the Civil Aeronautics Board (CAB) held hearings in Anchorage. As a result of these, Star was awarded temporary certificates in 1942 for most of the routes it desired, including many flights from Anchorage to other points. However, the airline's petition for the crucial route between Seattle and Anchorage was denied in favor of politically well-connected Pan Am.

In 1941, the financially vulnerable Star was purchased by New York businessman Raymond Willett Marshall, who had interests in other transportation companies and saw that ownership of Star could be profitable for him. The following year, vice-president and board member Homer Robinson arranged to enlarge Star by purchasing three other Alaska airlines—Lavery Air Service, Mirow Air Service, and Pollack Flying Service—as well as a hangar at the Anchorage air field. In light of these additions, the company's name was changed to Alaska Star Airlines in mid-1942, and then, in 1943, to Alaska Airlines, Inc.

The most significant change to the airline during this time, however, came after America's entry into World War II in December 1941; the war resulted in a severe shortage of pilots. Nevertheless, the airline purchased its first multiengine plane, a Lockheed Lodestar, in 1943. In that same year, the company's stock was first traded on the American Stock Exchange.

Because Alaska Air was owned by an outsider, meetings of the Alaska Air board were moved to New York in the 1940s, and a series of somewhat powerless company presidents was hired and fired in the ensuing years. The airline was chronically short on equipment, funds, and reliability, and pilots were frequently forced to purchase fuel for their planes out of their own pockets.

In 1945, with the war winding to a close, the airline hired its first stewardesses. With the arrival of James A. Wooten as president in 1947, Alaska Airlines began a rapid postwar expansion. Wooten's professional background was in air freight, and his strategy was to buy up surplus planes, engines, and parts from the government, which was selling off vast amounts of equipment left over from the war. The airline's fleet increased dramatically, and to keep the planes busy, Alaska Air expanded its charter business. The federal government had liberalized the airline industry, and Alaska Airlines planes began flying everywhere, hauling almost anything, including live cattle. The company flew rice to Chiang Kai-shek's troops under siege by Mao Tse-tung's Communist forces in China and brought back Chinese laborers to work in Canada. Alaska Airlines planes flew Jewish refugees to Israel and 11 loads of German war brides to America. During the Berlin airlift, the company made 87 flights into Germany. All of this helped Alaska Airlines to become the world's largest charter airline by 1948.

Closer to home, in the late 1940s the airline added popular charter flights from Anchorage to Honolulu and also began regular, though technically "nonscheduled" flights, that originated in Chicago and passed through Seattle on their way to Alaska. The frantic pace of charter flights mandated by Wooten put Alaska Air into the black, and finally the airline outgrew its facilities in Alaska, moving its base of operations to Paine Field in Everett, Washington, and making Anchorage a branch office.

However, the lax state of federal regulations that had made this flourishing activity possible was coming to an end. In 1949, the CAB shut down Alaska Airlines entirely for a short period for safety violations and levied heavy fines. Subsequently, the airline was completely prohibited from engaging in its worldwide charter business and allowed just eight trips a year between Alaska and the continental United States. Wooten left his post as president shortly thereafter, and the airline's second era of high-flying adventure came to a close.

Retrenching in the 1950s

With its sphere of activity restricted to Alaska, the company turned its attention to consolidation of its standing within the state, buying two smaller airlines, Al Jones Airways and Collins Air Service, in 1950. Throughout his tenure as owner of Alaska Air, Raymond Marshall had run the company with an eye to his own financial gain, rather than the long-term welfare of the airline itself. In 1951, with continued financial improprieties crippling the company's operations, the CAB forced Marshall out of day-to-day control over the airline by compelling him to place his stock in a five-year voting trust. In that year as well, the CAB granted Alaska Air a temporary certificate for a route outside Alaska, the long-coveted Seattle-Alaska run.

In 1952, Nelson David, a CAB-appointed president, took over, and a period of rebuilding financial and operational stability within the airline ensued. By 1957, the airline was in functional shape, and David and his cohorts departed to make way for the arrival of Charles F. Willis, Jr., a decorated World War II pilot who took over as president and chief executive officer by purchasing most of Marshall's stock in the company.

Under Willis's direction, Alaska Airlines began to make up in personality what it lacked in capital. The company became the first to show movies on planes in the late 1950s, and with the inauguration of service on its first pressurized plane, a DC-6 that allowed pilots to fly above rough weather rather than through or around it, Alaska Air introduced "Golden Nugget" service, which included an on-board honky-tonk saloon with a piano.

In 1960, the company was allowed to shuck its cumbersome bush routes to tiny towns in the interior of Alaska, and the following year the airline entered the jet age with the purchase of a Convair 880. Locked in tough competition with Pan Am, Northwest, and another regional carrier, Pacific Northern, Alaska Air turned to cheap and imaginative gimmicks to try to set itself apart from the competition throughout the 1960s. In addition to the "Golden Nugget" promotion, the company offered safety instructions read in rhyme ("A life vest is beneath each seat / They're stored so we won't lose 'em. / Now fix your eyes on the stewardies / They'll show you how to use 'em."), fashion shows in the aisles of the planes, and bingo games en route. The airline also worked to promote tourism within Alaska, organizing charters from the continental United States to the frozen north. In 1963, the company conducted a promotional tour of Japan in an effort to further expand the state's appeal.

In 1964, the company was finally given a permanent certificate from the CAB for its most important route, the nonstop flight from Seattle to Anchorage. During this time Alaska Air also added two important new planes to its fleet: the Lockheed

Hercules, a massive cargo plane which it used to fly oil-drilling equipment to Alaska's North Slope and, in the early 1970s, to South America; and the Boeing 727, which would become the company's signature passenger aircraft.

Celebrating the Alaska Centennial in 1967

In 1967, as Alaska celebrated its centennial, the company adopted a "Gay Nineties" promotional theme with stewardesses dressed in Edwardian garb. In the same year, the airline expanded its coverage of Alaska to include exclusive service to the Southeast corner of the state with the opening of an airport in Sitka, Alaska. This led to the acquisition, in the following year, of two smaller airlines: Alaska Coastal Ellis and Cordova Airlines. The "Gay Nineties" theme gave way in 1970 to "Golden Samovar" service, complete with Cossack costumes and beverages served from giant Russian samovars, in recognition of the company's introduction of charter service to Siberia. After many years of diplomatic wrangling, the airline was able to win permission for more than two dozen flights in 1970, 1971, and 1972.

Despite the promotional fanfare service to the Soviet Union brought, the airline as a whole was in difficult straits. Throughout the first two years of the 1970s, company cargo planes sat idle, sapping revenues as work on the Alaska pipeline was held up. A further blow came on September 4, 1971, when an Alaska Air jet crashed on landing in Juneau with a loss of 111 lives. It was the worst single-plane domestic air disaster to date. Financially, despite the CAB's award of exclusive rights to serve Southeast Alaska, the airline was struggling badly. Finally, president and chief executive officer Willis was deposed in 1972 by the airline's board and replaced by Ronald F. Cosgrave, a board member who had gotten his start in business providing Alaskans with mobile homes.

When Cosgrave took over, Alaska Air was $22 million in debt to its creditors. In an effort to salvage the company, the airline cut flights and employees and dropped its freight business entirely. The new management also set out to improve the airline's punctuality in hopes of banishing its unflattering image as "Elastic Airlines." By 1973, the airline's performance had improved and it was turning a small profit. In this new, less-flamboyant phase, symbolized by the more sober logo of a native Alaskan that was painted on the tail of the company's planes, the airline remained profitable throughout the mid-1970s.

With the passage of the Airline Deregulation Act of 1978, the American airline industry underwent a radical transformation. Alaska Airlines also underwent a transformation of sorts at the start of the new era. The real estate arm of the company was broken off into a separate company. Cosgrave became chairman of the new firm, relinquishing the reins of the airline to his close associate, Bruce R. Kennedy. In alliance with Alaska Air, Cosgrave then launched a failed campaign to take over one of the airline's competitors, Wien Air Alaska, that later resulted in federal fines for Alaska Airlines and its leaders for improprieties during the attempt.

Kennedy's role as leader of Alaska Air was to shepherd the airline through the marked expansion of the brave new unregu-

lated world of the 1980s. Immediately, the company placed two more continental American cities on its route map: Portland, Oregon, and San Francisco, California. The Arctic cities of Nome and Kotzebue, and then Palm Springs, California, were added shortly; and Burbank and Ontario, California, came on line in 1981.

By 1985, Alaska Air was serving cities in Southern California, Idaho, and Arizona as well, and profits were up. The company was able to settle a three-month-long strike by its machinists in June, part of an overall strategy to pare labor costs to the bone and maintain peace with its unions. In November, the company introduced a popular daily air freight service from Alaska called "Gold Streak."

Anticipating further expansion, the airline formed Alaska Air Group as a holding company in 1985. Horizon Air, a Seattle-based regional commuter airline serving the Pacific Northwest, was purchased in 1986. A year later, the company bought California-based Jet America Airlines, which was merged into Alaska Airlines after getting slammed by larger airlines on its East-West routes from Southern California to the Midwest. Despite this setback, Alaska Air pressed ahead with its expansion into the hotly contested California market.

In an effort to compensate for the seasonal imbalance in travel to Alaska, much of which takes place during the summer, the airline in 1988 inaugurated service to the Mexican resort cities of Mazatlan and Puerto Vallarta, whose high season is the winter. By 1989, the company served 30 cities in six western states outside Alaska, and 70 percent of its passengers flew south of Seattle. The airline had successfully used its base in Alaska as a springboard to profitable performance in larger markets. Alaska Air continued its emphasis on customer service as its calling card, stressing higher-quality food and more leg room on its flights than on other airlines.

New Vision for the 1990s

In 1990, the company unveiled a strategic plan that included lease orders for 24 new Boeing 737-400 aircraft. One provision of the transaction was the company's sale of a $60 million preferred stock position to International Lease Finance Corporation (ILFC), lessor of the airplanes. A creative feature of the stock transaction was that the conversion rights were purchased by a large group of Alaska's management employees, who were to redeem the stock from ILFC and convert it to common stock no later than 1997. The conversion feature was structured to create an incentive for management to achieve strong stock performance through operating results. At the same time, Alaska announced a large repurchase of shares, using proceeds of the preferred stock sale, and began an employee stock purchase plan.

The airline further expanded its route map in 1991, adding the international destinations of Magadan and Khabarovsk in the Russian far east, and Toronto, its first city served north of the American border and east of the Rockies. (Toronto was eventually dropped in July 1992.) As the company notched awards for customer service and marked its 19th consecutive year of profits in a turbulent industry, Kennedy retired in May 1991 and was succeeded by Raymond J. Vecci.

Furious competition descended on Alaska Air's home turf after the carrier declined to buy its rival MarkAir Inc. in the fall of 1991. Since it began carrying passengers in 1984, MarkAir had worked out feeder arrangements with Alaska Air that kept competition to a minimum. However, after the buyout offer was refused, it unleashed low-cost service on the Anchorage-to-Seattle market and others within Alaska, where Alaska Air earned nearly one-third of its revenues.

In 1992, Alaska Air posted its first loss—$121 million—in 20 years. Under Vecci, the carrier canceled two planned maintenance facilities and deferred a massive $2 billion aircraft purchase; it was able to increase utilization of its existing planes, however. The company cut back on unprofitable routes and even tampered with its award-winning customer service formula, economizing on in-flight meals and other amenities. Attempting to reduce costs on labor resulted in predictably tense relations with the unions. The strict fiscal regimen produced prompt results; Alaska's losses fell to $45 million in 1993 and produced a $40 million profit in 1994. Record-setting cargo operations accounted for about eight percent of these revenues.

In 1993, competition heated up, as the legendary low-cost airline Southwest Airlines entered the Pacific Northwest market by acquiring regional carrier Morris Air. United Airlines simultaneously transferred many competing routes to its less expensive shuttles. Alaska Air was able to reduce its costs, while maintaining a level of customer service that helped make it the leading carrier out of Seattle, Portland, and Anchorage. Alaska Air billed itself as "the last great airline." Still, analysts argued that Alaska Air was in need of deeper cuts, and the company was also plagued by union strikes by flight attendants.

In early 1995, Vecci was dismissed and replaced by John Kelly, formerly CEO of Horizon Air. Alaska and Horizon expanded West Coast routes to capitalize upon a new "open skies" agreement between the United States and Canada. Alaska Air also added a new Russian destination. Its competitor MarkAir had by then centered its jet service on Denver.

In 1996, Alaska Air conducted the first commercial passenger flight using Global Position System (GPS) navigation technology. It announced plans to become the first airline in the world to integrate GPS and Enhanced Ground Proximity Warning System (EGPWS) technology, adding a real-time, three-dimensional display of terrain. The system was scheduled to be operational in all the carrier's Boeing 737-400s by April 1999.

Innovation was important to the company. In 1989, Alaska Air had become the first airline to use head-up guidance systems to operate in foggy conditions. In 1995, it became the first U.S. carrier to sell tickets over the Internet. The airline installed self-service "Instant Travel Machines" that printed boarding passes and allowed customers to bypass the traditional ticket counter. The addition of an X-ray device to the unit was being tested in Anchorage in the spring of 1999, which would allow passengers to check their own baggage. For in-flight emergencies, the carrier also planned to provided automatic external defibrillators in all planes by the year 2000.

Alaska Air's operating revenues were $1.59 billion in 1996, and increased to $1.74 billion the next year. The impressive revenue growth of 1998—profits were up 49 percent to $190.5 million—continued into 1999. Alaska Air had evolved into a lean, low-cost carrier. As it approached a new century, the airline again looked to expand, buying Bombardier regional jets and Boeing 737s and adding new training and maintenance facilities.

Principal Subsidiaries

Alaska Airlines, Inc.; Horizon Air Industries, Inc.

Further Reading

Alaska Airlines: General Information and History, Seattle: Alaska Airlines, 1992.

Beauchamp, Marc, "... We're Vulnerable," *Forbes,* March 6, 1989.

Benton, Hal, and Andrea Rothman, "Is Alaska Big Enough for These Two?," *Business Week,* April 13, 1992, pp. 74–76.

Kernstock, Nicholas C., "Alaska Air Prospers by Focusing on Niche Markets, Profitability," *Aviation Week and Space Technology,* September 25, 1989, pp. 110–11.

Levine, Jonathan B., "Alaska Air: Is It California Dreamin'?," *Business Week,* November 30, 1987, p. 150.

Miller, Bettye Wells, "High Flyer," *Managing Service Quality,* March 1992, pp. 153–56.

Nelms, Douglas W., "Alaska Turnaround," *Air Transport World,* May 1996, pp. 49–55.

O'Lone, Richard G., "Alaska Buoyed by Initial Response to Its Soviet Far East Service," *Aviation Week and Space Technology,* July 29, 1991, pp. 34–35.

Proctor, Paul, "Alaska Expansion Yields Gains, Growing Pains," *Aviation Week and Space Technology,* November 27, 1995, pp. 36–37.

Satterfield, Archie, *The Alaska Airlines Story,* Anchorage: Northwest Publishing Company, 1981.

—Elizabeth Rourke
—updated by Frederick C. Ingram

Alitalia

Alitalia-Linee Aeree Italiana, S.p.A.

111, Viale Alessandro Marchetti
00148 Rome
Italy
+39-0665621
Fax: +39-0665624416
Web site: http://www.alitalia.it

Public Company (53% State-Owned)
Incorporated: 1946 as Alitalia-Aerolinee Italiana
  Internazionali
Employees: 19,600
Sales: L9.08 trillion (1998)
Stock Exchanges: Milan
Ticker Symbol: AZA
NAIC: 481111 Scheduled Passenger Air Transportation

Alitalia-Linee Aeree Italiana, S.p.A is the national airline of Italy. It has been consistently working to transform itself into a modern, low-cost airline. Alitalia has more than 20 partner airlines; in 1998 the carrier teamed with KLM Royal Dutch Airlines in a strategic alliance with far-reaching implications. The Italian government was scheduled to divest its holdings in Alitalia entirely by 2000.

Roman Origins

Alitalia was established in September 1946 as Alitalia-Aerolinee Italiana Internazionali, with British financial assistance consisting of an initial capital investment of L900 million and an additional investment of L1.5 billion by the start of 1947. The company began operations in the spring of that year with two three-engine Fiat G.12s flying routes from Turin to Rome and from Rome to Catania.

During its first year of operation Alitalia expanded its airliner inventory through the acquisition of two G.12s, four Siai Marchetti SM.95s, and three Avro Lancastrians; by year's end it had transported a total of 10,306 passengers and 110 tons of cargo. Furthermore, in its first year of scheduled air services, the airline covered a network of over 9,000 kilometers and employed just under 300 personnel, 55 of whom were flight crew. By 1948 the airline was able to offer its first intercontinental service, introducing flights from Rome to Buenos Aires, and by 1950 it had substantially modernized its fleet with the addition of Douglas DC-4s and DC-3s. Expansion continued throughout the 1950s; by the tenth anniversary of the airline in 1956, its planes had traveled a total of 48,630 kilometers and had transported a total of 116,394 passengers. The number of employees had risen to 1,120 and the company's capital to L4.5 billion.

Major Merger in 1957

In 1957 Alitalia-Aerolinee Italiana Internazionali merged with Linee Aeree Italiana (LAI), a regional operator 40 percent owned by the U.S. airline Trans World Airways (TWA), to become Alitalia-Linee Aeree Italiana, SpA, the single Italian domestic and international airline. The merger helped to centralize air transport operations in Italy, and the new entity was able to compete more effectively with other national carriers in Europe. The new company was also substantially larger, with a net capital of L10 billion, an expanded network, and a staff of over 3,000. By the end of 1957 over 478,000 passengers had been carried by the fleet which had been expanded to include Convair-Metropolitans and Viscount 785s.

The year of the Rome Olympics, 1960, was a milestone for Alitalia. Chosen as the official carrier for the games, the company introduced its first jet airliners: French-made Caravelle SE210s, which served medium-haul routes, and larger DC-8s, which were put into service on the intercontinental routes. These additions to the Alitalia inventory helped the airline achieve its goal of carrying one million passengers in one year. One year later, to facilitate the airline's expansion, company headquarters was moved from Ciampino to the recently completed Leonardo da Vinci International Airport at Fiumicino. In 1967, the same year that it introduced its new tricolored ''A'' on the tail fins of its aircraft, Alitalia purchased several DC-9s for its medium-haul routes in Europe and the Middle East. The following year, with the retirement of the aging Viscount turboprop powered aircraft, Alitalia had completed its transformation into an all-jet fleet consisting of 19 DC-8s, 24 DC-9s, and 19 Caravelles.

During this period, dramatic developments were taking place in aircraft manufacturing. In 1969 Boeing introduced the Boeing 747 ''jumbo jet,'' an aircraft that had virtually twice the passenger capacity of the other aircraft, promising an increase in revenue for the airlines. Alitalia placed an order with Boeing and received its first 747 in May 1970. The aircraft was immediately put to work on high density long-haul routes. In 1973 Alitalia expanded its wide-bodied fleet and took delivery of its first 275-seat DC-10/30.

A Decade of Crisis: 1970s

During the 1970s Alitalia experienced increasingly difficult financial circumstances. The price of crude oil quadrupled, the western economies entered a period of recession, and airlines experienced a sharp decrease in demand. For Alitalia, as well as its competitors, one solution was to furnish its fleets with more fuel-efficient aircraft. Alitalia's gas-guzzling DC-8s and Caravelles were replaced by more efficient Boeing 727s, the first of which was put into service in 1976. Inflation and political instability in Italy during the latter half of the decade left the airline facing large debts, persistent losses, and falling revenues.

By 1980, despite the partial re-equipment program of the past few years, the airline's fleet had become outdated and inefficient; the average age of their aircraft ranged from six to eight years, generally older than those of the company's European competitors. In 1982 the company was able to order McDonnell Douglas Super 80s to replace the aging Boeing 727s on medium-haul routes and also made plans to purchase more Boeing 747s to replace their fleet of DC-10s, the safety of which had been questioned following several accidents involving other airlines.

In order to maximize its potential for profit, Alitalia began to diversify its business interests by creating separate support companies that would provide travel services and information. These companies included Societa Italiana Gestione Sistemi Multi Accesso (SIGMA), which focused on the development and management of information services in the tourist sector, Italiatour, developed to promote tourism in Italy, and Alidata, a software marketing company.

Also during this time, Alitalia went through a substantial restructuring at the hands of Luciano Sartoretti, the managing director of finance. By 1986 Sartoretti had trimmed and reshaped the company's debts. In 1987 Alitalia returned a profit of over L73 billion following a period that had seen a healthy expansion across much of the European airline business. Nevertheless, the airline still faced several problems. First, although the company's performance was considered adequate, it was losing market share—both within Europe and on the transatlantic routes—to its closest rivals, Air France and Lufthansa A.G. of West Germany. These two competitors had been pursuing aggressive expansion plans through major re-equipment programs and allowing for greater passenger capacity on profitable routes. Alitalia, however, had spent the past five years diversifying its interests and had failed to expand its fleet of about 123 aircraft. Alitalia was therefore less able to benefit from a number of generally profitable years in the airline business in the 1980s.

Late 1980s Labor Unrest

Beginning in September 1987 Alitalia was plagued by a series of disruptive strikes by pilots, cabin staff, and ground crew—an occurrence some thought reflected both senior management's inability to deal effectively with its employees and a general weakness in their long-term planning. The following year, in an attempt to resolve some of its structural problems and intractable disputes, Alitalia recruited Carlo Verri from the executive committee of the Swedish group Electrolux A.B. The appointment of Verri, a businessperson from the private sector with no previous experience in the airline business, was designed to provide Alitalia with free market know-how and top management expertise. His primary concerns were to resolve the chronic labor problems and to develop a long-term growth strategy. By May 1989, Verri had reached an agreement with the cabin crew which ran for 20 months, and in July of the same year he reached a four-year agreement with the pilots. In October he announced a plan to finance a long-term re-equipment program for both aircraft and ground equipment. Verri's plans for the rejuvenation of Alitalia, however, were brought to an abrupt end in November 1989, when he was killed in an automobile accident.

Despite Alitalia's losses from the interruption of its Mediterranean and Middle East routes during the war in the Persian Gulf in 1991, and despite its reputation for, in the words of *Forbes* writer Peter Fuhrman, ''slovenly service, poisonous labor relations, and antiquated equipment,'' the airline experienced some financial recovery in the early 1990s. Aggressive marketing and competitive pricing in 1991 resulted in unexpectedly good results, including a 5.3 percent growth in its cargo operations against an average decrease of 2.7 percent for other European national carriers. Alitalia briefly participated in an innovative ''air bridge,'' shipping bodies for the short-lived Cadillac Allanté from Turin to Detroit. Demand from India was expected to create the most growth for freight services.

Although sales rose by eight percent in 1991, Alitalia posted a loss like everyone else in the business during one of the industry's most catastrophic years. Alitalia relocated its headquarters to a new office complex outside Rome in 1991. At this time, the airline employed nearly 20,000; the group as a whole employed nearly 30,000.

In March 1992 Alitalia announced an ambitious five-year investment plan calling for an allocation of over L4.4 trillion for expansion of the Alitalia fleet to 165 aircraft. The plan also called for the purchase of five new planes for intercontinental routes and 14 more for operations within Europe. According to Alitalia chief executive Giovanni Bisignani, the expansion plan—at a time of retrenchment in the international airline business—was designed to enable the company to survive by ''moving to achieve a critical mass, but staying fast and flexible.''

Alitalia entered into an equity partnership with Hungarian carrier Malév in December 1992. The US$77 million investment gave 30 percent of Malév shares to Alitalia and five percent to SIMEST S.p.A., an Italian government unit. The expectation was to develop Budapest's role as a gateway between Eastern and Western Europe. The two airlines together served 122 cities on five continents.

The carrier lost US$203 million in 1993. Lean and effective competition from British Airways and KLM forced incoming CEO Roberto Schisano to cut about 1,500 jobs at Alitalia. The company struggled with debts of US$1.8 billion. On the plus side, Alitalia inked a quite lucrative marketing deal with U.S.-based Continental Airlines in May 1994.

In November 1995, an ambitious regional start-up began competing with Alitalia on the Milan-Rome route. Air One was one of many budget carriers launched on the wings of the economical Boeing 737, although it was the first operator of that type in Italy.

The new entrants, which also included AZZURRAair and Air Sicilia, lacked Alitalia's access to government subsidies (although AZZURRA was to become a franchisee of Alitalia). European Union (EU) commissioners, eager to promote a free market, were beginning to place a great deal of scrutiny on bailouts. Tense negotiations resulted in a L2.75 billion recapitalization in 1997, pared from L3.3 billion. As conditions for its approval, the EU required Alitalia to divest various holdings, including its stake in Malév. The airline also had to trim operations and lay off another 1,200 employees.

Domenico Cempella was named managing director and CEO after Schisano departed in 1995. He and chairman Fausto Cereti succeeded in wringing productivity concessions for the unions in return for some equity. Part of their recovery package included forming Alitalia TEAM, a sister company to hire ''B''-scale workers. The regional subsidiary Alitalia Express was also formed. After losing US$683 million in 1996, Alitalia posted its first profit (L438 billion, US$243 million) in nine years in 1997.

The KLM-Alitalia alliance was expected to capture 20 percent of the European passenger market by 2001, more than doubling each carrier's respective market share. Since KLM also had a close alliance with Northwest Airlines, and Alitalia an agreement with Continental, the global implications ran deep as the United States and Italy neared agreement on an ''open skies'' agreement.

The alliance proved that Alitalia still had considerable clout left among world airlines. Alitalia's profit of L539 billion on L9.08 trillion in 1998 revenue demonstrated it was on the right track management-wise. Alitalia continued to invest in marketing and equipment in order to capture a larger market share. The airline was planning to implement a SABRE yield management system in 1999. In 1998 the state holding company, Istituto per la Recostruzione Industriale, owned 53 percent of Alitalia shares and was scheduled to divest its holdings entirely by 2000.

Principal Subsidiaries

Alitalia Team; Alitalia Express (98%); Sisam (60%); Eurofly (45%); Italiatour (99.6%); Racom-Teledata (94%); Aviofin (95%); Alitech.

Further Reading

Airline Business 100, London: Reed Business Publishing, 1992.
Alitalia Forty-Five Years, Rome: Gruppo Alitalia, 1992.
''Alitalia Relies on Asian Pivot,'' *Asian Finance,* September 1989, pp. 26–27.
''Alitalia Unveils Huge Investment for 1992,'' *Flight International,* March 18, 1992.
Cook, James, ''Italy's Flying Banker,'' *Forbes,* July 22, 1991, p. 86.
Cottrill, Ken, ''KLM, Alitalia Join Forces,'' *Trafficworld,* December 7, 1998, pp. 37–38.
European Equity Research, London: Salomon Brothers, November 1989.
Feldman, Joan M., ''Booting Up Competition,'' *Air Transport World,* October 1996, pp. 89–90.
Flint, Perry, ''Alitalia's Trial by Fire,'' *Air Transport World,* May 1992, pp. 78–79.
——, ''End of the Roman Holiday,'' *Air Transport World,* September 1991, pp. 22–26.
''Head of Troubled Alitalia Killed in Automobile Crash,'' *Reuters,* November 8, 1989.
Hill, Leonard, ''Malév/Alitalia: Synergies for Survival,'' *Air Transport World,* March 1993, pp. 90–95.
——, ''Roman Remake,'' *Air Transport World,* December 1998, pp. 37–41, 70.
——, ''Taxiing Toward Recovery,'' *Air Transport World,* September 1997, pp. 51–53.
''The Italian Factor,'' *Flight International,* April 26, 1992.
Lefer, Henry, ''Alitalia Cargo Pulls Its Weight,'' *Air Transport World,* June 1993, pp. 195–96.
Rossant, John, ''Captain to Alitalia: 'We Have No Choice','' *Business Week,* June 20, 1994, p. 166.
Sparaco, Pierre, ''Alitalia Pursues Strict Recovery Plan,'' *Aviation Week and Space Technology,* November 21, 1994, p. 91.
——, ''Alitalia Targets Short-Term Recovery,'' *Aviation Week and Space Technology,* May 15, 1995, p. 38.
''A World Class Airline for World Cup Soccer?,'' *Forbes,* March 5, 1990.

—Stephen Kremer
—updated by Frederick C. Ingram

Allied Domecq PLC

24 Portland Place
London WIN 4BB
United Kingdom
(44) 171-323-9000
Fax: (44) 171-323-1742
Web site: http://www.allieddomecq.co.uk

Public Company
Incorporated: 1961 as Allied Breweries
Employees: 49,700
Sales: $7.24 billion (1998)
Stock Exchanges: London Amsterdam Brussels
Ticker Symbols: ALDCY
NAIC: 551112 Offices of Other Holding Companies;
    31214 Distilleries; 31213 Wineries; 722213 Snack &
    Nonalcoholic Beverage Bars; 72241 Drinking Places
    (Alcoholic Beverages)

Allied Domecq PLC is the second largest distiller of wine and spirits in the world, second only to industry leader Diageo. In addition to its major international beverage brands, the company also has holdings in the food and retailing sector. Allied Domecq's Wine & Spirits division generates approximately 60 percent of the company's annual revenue, while its Retailing division is responsible for the other 40 percent or so. The company's brand name spirits include Beefeater, Ballantine's, Courvoisier, Kahlua, and Sauza. It also owns retail operations such as the Baskin-Robbins ice cream chain, Dunkin Donuts, Togo's Eatery franchises, and numerous pubs in the United Kingdom such as Big Steak Pub with Wacky Warehouse, Mr. Q's, and Firkin. In total, Allied Domecq operates over 14,000 such locations in over 60 countries throughout the world.

The Early Years

The beginnings of Allied Domecq PLC can be traced to 1961, when three UK-based brewing companies merged to form a larger company, which was named Allied Breweries. Prior to the merger, the three companies—Ind Coope, Tetley Walker, and Ansells—had operated independently for years, each gradually becoming a major presence in the brewing and pub-operating business throughout the years. In 1968, Allied Breweries merged once again, this time with Showerings, Vine Products and Whiteways, which owned Harveys of Bristol.

A decade later, the still-growing company acquired J Lyons, a company whose holdings included the United States-based Baskin-Robbins ice cream chain. Three years later, in 1981, the company name was changed to reflect this addition, and Allied Breweries became Allied-Lyons plc.

After its name change, Allied-Lyons set about restructuring its business operations and holdings. The company was separated into three main divisions, each with its main focus in a different area. The name Allied Breweries re-emerged as one of the new divisions, which was responsible for the brewing and pub-operating portion of the company's business. Additionally, Allied Vintners was formed as the company's new wine and spirits division, with two of its main brand name products being Teacher's and Harveys. The third division was J Lyons, which was responsible for the company's retail operations—such as the Baskin-Robbins chain.

Mid-80s through Mid-1990s: Growth through Acquisition

In 1987, a year after it completed its corporate restructuring, Allied-Lyons scored big with the acquisition of the Canadian-based company Hiram Walker-Gooderham & Worts Ltd. The purchase gave Allied-Lyons control of Hiram Walker's well-known brand name product lines, such as Ballantine's, Canadian Club, Courvoisier, and Kahlua. Although Hiram Walker's overall operations were merged into those of Allied-Lyons, the newly acquired brand names remained unchanged.

Two years later, Allied-Lyons made another major purchase, adding the Whitbread spirits division to its Allied Vintners holdings. The Whitbread acquisition brought the brand names Beefeater, Long John, and Laphroaig to the Allied-Lyons family. Also in 1989, Allied-Lyons completed the purchase of the

Company Perspectives:

Providing outstanding customer service lies at the heart of all Allied Domecq and to ensure that its formidable range of spirit and retail brands meet all customer and consumer demands, the company has developed an extensive network of either wholly owned, joint venture, third party operations and franchised outlets around the world. Stretching from Canada to Australia, be it a Baskin-Robbins factory in Moscow or a distillery producing Sauza tequila in Mexico, the focus on delivering top quality consumer brands and excellence in service is paramount.

Dunkin Donuts store chain, and added the entity to its J Lyons retail operations division.

As the company entered the 1990s, the string of successful acquisitions continued, and the company's expansion plans were furthered. By 1993, Allied-Lyons had also inked a brewing joint venture deal with Carlsberg A/S, naming the venture Carlsberg-Tetley.

The year 1994 brought with it an extremely notable development in Allied-Lyons' history, as the company purchased Pedro Domecq—the top marketer of spirits in Spain and Mexico. The addition of Pedro Domecq gave Allied-Lyons control of some very well known brand name spirits, and greatly bolstered its portfolio. Most notably, Pedro Domecq brought with it two of the world's top three brandies—Presidente and Don Pedro—as well as the two leading Spanish brandies—Fundador and Centenario. Also acquired with the purchase were Sauza—the number two brand of tequila in the world—and La Ina, a well-known brand of sherry. As a result of the Pedro Domecq acquisition, in September 1994 Allied-Lyons once again changed its name—this time to Allied Domecq PLC—and began publicly trading its stocks under that name.

The Mid-1990s: Another Reorganization

After Allied-Lyons' transition into Allied Domecq, the company decided to focus solely on its spirits, wine, and retailing operations. The food manufacturing holdings were divested in 1994 and 1995, except for the company's 50 percent interest in Panrico, a Spanish bakery business. The remaining holdings were separated into two divisions: Allied Domecq Spirits & Wine, and Allied Domecq Retailing.

The company's pub-operating business was reorganized in 1995 as well, into two United Kingdom-based operations: Allied Domecq Leisure and Allied Domecq Inns. These two new divisions replaced the four regional pub companies that had been in action—Tetley, Ansells, Ind Coope, and Taylor Walker. Allied Domecq Inns became the umbrella under which approximately 1,470 pub locations continued to operate. Another aspect of the realignment of this area of the company was the creation of Allied Domecq Restaurants and Bars, an arm that was formed to manage the locations where food sales were

prominent. Allied Domecq Restaurants and Bars was composed of over 560 pubs, including all Big Steak Pubs.

Allied Domecq also sold off its tea and coffee interests in 1996, including Tetley Tea and Lyons Irish Tea. Tetley was sold to Karand Limited and the Lyons tea business was transferred to Unilever, Ireland. Also divested was Allied Domecq's 50 percent interest in the Carlsberg-Tetley joint venture.

In 1997, Allied Domecq added yet another food-related retail operation to its portfolio when it purchased the Togo's Eatery chain. Togo's was a deli-style sandwich shop. Soon after the addition, Allied Domecq initiated a new marketing strategy involving Togo's and its Dunkin Donuts and Baskin-Robbins chains. Company officials had noticed that while Dunkin Donuts did the majority of its business in the morning hours, Baskin-Robbins generated most of its own in the evening. Upon bringing Togo's underneath the corporate umbrella—a chain which was busiest during lunchtime—Allied Domecq decided to try saving money on real estate by opening new locations that combined all three chains. In addition to offsetting real estate costs, the co-branding concept also made it possible for Allied Domecq to introduce its lesser-known brands into an area where one of its better-known chains was already dominant.

The End of the Century and Beyond

By mid-1998, Allied Domecq was continuing to build its Spirits & Wine division, and had worked out a deal with a subsidiary of industry giant Diageo PLC. The subsidiary in question was the well-known Guinness Ireland Group Limited, from whom Allied Domecq purchased a 49.6 percent minority stake in Guinness's Irish drinks company Cantrell & Cochrane Group Limited.

The Spirits & Wine division also spent time restructuring its spirits business in the United States, so as to cut costs and make its operations more efficient. The sales, marketing, and administrative operations of Hiram Walker and Allied Domecq's import arm (Domecq Importers) were combined, with Allied Domecq Spirits, USA being the result.

The Spirits & Wine operation also revamped its marketing strategies, and began attempting to target younger customers than it had been in the recent past. It was noted that consumption of spirits in the United States, for example—as opposed to that of beer or wine—had decreased throughout the 1980s and 1990s, especially in the young adult demographic. Allied Domecq made an effort to win back this consumer group by offering interesting and often exotic drink options, while also reeducating its customers about its products and their merits.

Meanwhile, Allied Domecq's retailing division was being bolstered by the merger of its United Kingdom off-license interests—Victoria Wine and Thresher—with those of Whitbread PLC. After the deal was closed both Allied Domecq and Whitbread owned 50 percent each of the new entity, named First Quench Retailing.

As the end of the twentieth century approached, Allied Domecq continued reevaluating and streamlining its operations in an attempt to earn a solid return on its shareholders' equity. The company made history in early January 1999, when it completed the first major business transaction ever to use the new European currency, the euro. The transaction occurred when Allied Domecq reviewed its Cantrell & Cochrane Group (C&C) operation and determined that ownership of C&C did not fit Allied Domecq's long-term strategies.

In June 1999, Allied Domecq began the process of selling its over 3,500 United Kingdom-based pubs to Whitbread. The move was made in order to enable Allied Domecq to focus more intently on its core businesses in the Wine & Spirits and Retailing divisions. Soon thereafter, rumors began to circulate that Pernod Ricard was planning on initiating a bid to take over Allied Domecq's Wine & Spirits division, although the company's officials refused to confirm the rumor.

By late 1999, Allied Domecq was generating solid sales figures and was ranked second worldwide in its industry. It was producing either the number one or two-ranked product in seven different international spirits and wine categories. Its annual income was experiencing a growth spurt, to the point that the company attracted the attention of U.S. investment guru Warren Buffett, who had a reputation of selecting undervalued companies' stocks that had potential to deliver huge returns in the future. With Buffett and others seemingly hooked, Allied Domecq's future success rested on its ability to ensure that its operations continued to be efficient and well managed.

Principal Divisions

Allied Domecq Spirits & Wine; Allied Domecq Retailing; Allied Domecq Spirits, USA; Allied Domecq Retailing, USA; Allied Domecq Leisure; Allied Domecq Inns; Allied Domecq Restaurants and Bars.

Further Reading

Beck, Ernest, "Allied Domecq Reaches Accord to Sell Pubs Unit to Whitbread for $3.84 Billion," *Wall Street Journal,* May 26, 1999.

Boyd, Terry, "Franchising Facts," *Business First—Louisville,* December 21, 1998.

"Business: The Company File—Buffett Takes a Sip of Allied Domecq," *BBC News,* May 18, 1999.

Goodway, Nick, "Talk Grows of Deal Between Spirits Firm Allied Domecq and Pernod Ricard," *Evening Standard,* June 1, 1999.

Marquand, Barbara, "Co-Branding Brings Cafes to Banks, Pizza to Kmart," *Sacramento Business Journal,* December 18, 1998.

O'Brien, George, "This Franchisee is Making Serious Dough," *Business West,* January 1999.

Sinton, Peter, "Double Dipping: Family Sells then Buys Back Gelato Business," *San Francisco Chronicle,* March 3, 1999.

Sledge, Ann, "Beverage Marketers Capitalize on Changing Tastes," *Fairfield County Business Journal,* April 5, 1999.

—Laura E. Whiteley

A S C A P

The American Society of Composers, Authors and Publishers (ASCAP)

ASCAP Building
One Lincoln Plaza
New York, New York 10023
(212) 621-6000
Fax: (212) 724-9064
Web site: http://www.ascap.com

Nonprofit Company
Incorporated: 1914
Employees: 500
Sales: $508.3 million (1998)
NAIC: 81392 Professional Organizations

The American Society of Composers, Authors and Publishers (ASCAP) collects songwriting royalties for its 80,000 members. ASCAP's constituency encompasses music publishers and songwriters including some of the best-known names in the business: Bruce Springsteen, Stevie Wonder, Garth Brooks, Madonna, Wynton Marsalis. More obscure writers and classical composers, lyricists, and publishers are also represented by the group. John Philip Sousa, Irving Berlin, and George M. Cohan were among the charter members. Besides distributing about 84 percent of its revenues to members, ASCAP also provides access to various types of insurance and benefits.

Tin-Pan Alley Origins

By the end of the 19th century, urbanization in the United States had brought entertainment out of the home and into nightclubs and cabarets. Performance had become more the domain of professional musicians, which dampened sheet music sales, the traditional income stream for music publishers. Meanwhile, some clubs were earning staggering profits on these performances while paying the publishers only the cost of the printed musical scores.

The U.S. copyright law of 1909 provided the basis for ASCAP's existence. This law gave artists rights to how their work was used just as patents protected inventors of more tangible creations. The 1909 law applied to public performance of musical works as well.

A nostalgic version of ASCAP's birth recounts composer Victor Herbert hearing one of his songs being slaughtered in a New York cabaret and thereby becoming inspired to stop illegal infringements. Herbert was apparently one of a group of nine who met in a New York restaurant in October 1913 to create a performing rights organization. Nathan Burkan, an entertainment lawyer, and Englishman George Maxwell were also in attendance. ASCAP's first official meeting was held on February 13, 1914, whereupon Maxwell was named its first president. The group started out with about 100 members.

ASCAP's mission was essentially to enforce the 1909 copyright law by compiling member works into a catalog and hiring personnel to monitor their public performance. ASCAP licensed its entire catalog as a whole, not individual pieces.

Since restaurants and clubs had been accustomed to using this music for free, ASCAP met resistance from the beginning. The venues threatened to stop musical performances altogether, which panicked the local musicians' union, which also believed it would have to pay licensing fees.

ASCAP won a few critical court victories that ensured its position, however. The U.S. Supreme Court ruled that performances need not be ticketed to count as for-profit, and therefore subject to copyright law. At the end of its first year, 85 hotels were paying the Society $8.23 per week to license its catalog.

ASCAP did not try to license vaudeville performers; rather it used their personnel as collection agents while pressuring publishers to join for fear of losing out on the supreme promotional avenue that vaudeville presented.

Company Perspectives:

ASCAP is its members—creative people who write the music and lyrics that enrich lives in every corner of the world. The members of ASCAP are where music begins. ASCAP is home to the greatest names in American music, past and present—from Duke Ellington to Beck, from George Gershwin to Stevie Wonder, from Leonard Bernstein to Madonna, from Garth Brooks to Tito Puente, from Henry Mancini to James Horner—as well as thousands of writers in the earlier stages of their careers. ASCAP represents every kind of music. ASCAP's repertory includes pop, rock, alternative, country, R&B, rap, hip hop, film and television music, folk and roots, jazz, gospel, contemporary Christian, Latin, new age, theater and cabaret, symphonic and concert—the entire musical spectrum.

The Golden Age of Cinema: 1920s

In December 1920, the Society rearranged its compensation and representation structures to reflect the growing importance of popular music publishers. Rather than receive a third of royalties, lyricists and composers together had to split half while the publishers now received the other half. The composition of the board was restructured in similar proportions.

Motion picture exhibitors were more organized in their resistance to ASCAP's demands. The Motion Picture Exhibitors League of America (MPELA) began a nationwide boycott of ASCAP in 1917 and also lobbied Congress for amended regulations. At the same time, ASCAP won significant lawsuits against various theaters.

However, these victories were so expensive they prompted ASCAP to consider doubling its rates in order to cover legal expenses, which amounted to more than $40,000 in 1921–22. ASCAP billed about $380,000 in 1922; two-thirds came from movie theaters.

The Motion Picture Theater Owners Association (MPTOA) attempted to set up a rival organization in 1922. However, it failed to win the support of either producers or publishers. Although the MPTOA resistance soon died down, its confrontation aroused the interest of the Justice Department, prompting a lengthy investigation.

ASCAP was working to license sound motion pictures by the time *The Jazz Singer* proved the commercial viability of the medium in 1927. In spite of some consolidation among the music publishers that supplied the motion picture industry, ASCAP held on to this market as well.

Meanwhile, yet another medium was competing for the public's attention: radio. This one would not be so conveniently managed for ASCAP. Radio interests resisted in the courts and through the National Association of Broadcasters (NAB), which sought to supply a royalty-free source of music. A 1924 FCC ruling and several court cases legitimized ASCAP's operation, however, and ASCAP also found public sympathy lay with its

artists. Unsuccessful legislation had simultaneously attempted to exempt radio broadcasts from the 1909 copyright law.

The Great Depression and World Domination

While writers, publishers, and users more or less reached a détente with the Society, the austerity of the Depression would strain their relationships. A round of anti-ASCAP legislation circulated and became law in seven states. Montana even issued arrest warrants charging ASCAP officers with extortion, costing president Gene Buck six hours in an Arizona jail.

In 1931 ASCAP received fees of $960,000 from the radio industry. The next year, ASCAP required radio users take out blanket licenses exclusively. Fees were set based on percentages of each station's income. Interestingly, newspaper-owned radio stations were given generous fee breaks, for obvious PR purposes, according to one author.

ASCAP also required stations to log all compositions played during one quarter of the year, while only providing the stations lists of ASCAP members, not ASCAP-controlled songs. Commercial establishments such as restaurants playing the ASCAP tunes on their radios also had to pay licensing fees.

Not only had ASCAP brought radio in line, according to the Justice Department, its board of directors had ''absolute control of the entire music industry.'' Everybody needed ASCAP to survive. The department's lengthy investigation culminated in a trial in 1935 and the signing of a consent decree in 1945.

ASCAP also encountered some criticism for its exclusive policies that kept popular and lesser-known jazz and country singers out of the fold, and compensated them less once finally admitted. In addition, prospective members needed to establish themselves commercially in order to become eligible, creating something of a Catch-22 situation. Since blanket licenses removed any incentive for users to play music from nonmembers, that group found itself increasingly redundant.

Birth of BMI: 1939

In the late 1930s, NAB was still casting about for alternate sources of music. While preparing to enter yet another round of negotiations with ASCAP in 1939, Broadcast Music International (BMI) was incorporated in New York. BMI soon acquired the catalog of one major publisher—E.B. Marks—and was ready to challenge ASCAP.

Besides favoring the interests of broadcasters, BMI also became the champion of newer genres such as rhythm and blues and rock 'n' roll. Its search for new material led it to thousands of songs composed by Argentinean, Mexican, Jewish, Italian, and Native American writers.

In 1940 ASCAP collected $7.3 million, $4 million from radio. A new ASCAP contract proposed to effectively double radio's rates, largely at the expense of the networks such as NBC and CBS—two that had together bought a 40 percent interest in BMI. This resulted in a boycott of ASCAP by most radio stations—in January 1941, BMI radio subscribers outnumbered its competitors by three to one.

By the time ASCAP had come to terms with the stations in 1941, it had lost a considerable amount of money during the boycott, and bargaining power as well. The new contract with radio was actually less lucrative than the old one. ASCAP had overplayed its hand and lost its monopoly.

The federal case against ASCAP resulted in the Society signing a consent decree which allowed members to share nonexclusive rights to license their works. ASCAP also agreed to license music on a program-by-program basis. Other provisions curtailed ASCAP's control. In addition, the self-perpetuating board system was ended, revenues distributed more evenly, and membership criteria relaxed. The Society and its officers paid $35,250 in fines.

Continued Resistance: 1970s–90s

After Wyoming passed one restrictive law in the 1970s, ASCAP withdrew from the state entirely. Music users there in principle then had to license music directly from the individual copyright holders. The law was eventually repealed. The U.S. copyright law of 1976 included a "Homestyle Exemption" allowing establishments to operate small radios and TVs free of licensing fees.

In the late 1980s both ASCAP and BMI targeted professional associations which used music at their conventions. In 1990 both charged a maximum per-event fee of $4,000. ASCAP's live music fees for groups of 250 or less started at $25 per day.

The American Society of Association Executives accused ASCAP and BMI of harassment and intimidation in implementing these licenses. They also protested ambiguous wording in the agreements, failure to disclose their repertory, and "double dipping" in the case of meetings held at hotels, which were also required to be licensed. In addition, an association had to sign a multiyear agreement before it could play even one bar of music at a single event.

ASCAP reached a settlement with TV broadcasters over a decade-old fee dispute in 1993. The new lower per-program fees could be applied retroactively. ASCAP collected $390 million in 1992.

Advancements in entertainment technology brought big-screen TVs and satellite dishes to restaurants around the same time, spawning sports bars and similar concepts. Restaurateurs became the subject of increased music licensor attention. In an article in *Restaurant Business*, they compared ASCAP representatives to Biblical tax collectors and to the "Syndicate." They were furious at being forced to take out licenses in order to display television broadcasts of football games and the like, and being forced to pay for music broadcast during commercials. They also accused ASCAP of devious collection practices.

Food-service businesses pushed for legislation to curb the music licensors and contemplated class-action lawsuits. They complained about ASCAP's bewildering form, which contained 594 license categories (compared to 98 for BMI). They also complained of tactics of intimidation. At the time, ASCAP and BMI were filing up to nearly 1,000 lawsuits per year.

The Fairness in Musical Licensing Act of 1995 circulated through Congress on behalf of the associations. The act sought to have the licensors disclose their repertory and to exempt incidental music. At the same time, Governor Christine Todd Whitman vetoed a similar New Jersey bill. Legislation was also pending in 20 other states, however. Most of these at least passed code-of-conduct laws for performing rights organization's agents.

Oscar-winning (Barbra Streisand's "The Way We Were") songwriter Marilyn Bergman became ASCAP's first female chair in 1995. She contended that although royalties only amounted to one percent of a restaurant's expenses, that provided nearly a third of an artist's income. ASCAP had 70,000 members at the time.

In 1996 ASCAP proposed dramatically lower per-program rates for news, talk, and religious television stations. These broadcasters had complained that their program fees were in some cases more expensive than other stations' blanket licenses.

In 1997 bills proposing to reform music licensing circulated through Congress for the third year in a row. One finally passed in 1998, and it exempted small restaurants from fees for televisions and radios. Eleven other circuit courts around the country became able to hear complaints; this had been the exclusive province of the Southern District Court of New York. The principle of vicarious liability for trade show operators was preserved, although in 1994 a U.S. District Court ruled that associations were not responsible for policing the music used by individual exhibitors.

Coping in the Digital Age

In the late 1990s, ASCAP worked on coping with the licensing issues that new Internet technologies presented. MP3 was the best-known format for downloading digital audio, and bootleg MP3 web sites threatened to become a major worry. ASCAP teamed with European licensors MCPS/PRS (UK) and BUMA/STEMRA (Holland) in the International Music Joint Venture created to process licensing requests.

The Internet provided ASCAP a new way to serve. Besides posting a listing of its repertoire on the web, in 1998 ASCAP launched Rate Calc, an interactive tool for calculating fees. The company's EZ-Seeker program searched web sites for sound files, identified with electronic "watermarks." ASCAP licensed almost 1,000 web sites, and made royalty payments to writers based on Internet performances.

In 1998 ASCAP distributed nearly $425 million of its $508 million gross to writers; both were records. However, the Fairness in Music Act was expected to impact future earnings. ASCAP had reciprocal agreements with 55 similar organizations in foreign countries; foreign performances accounted for over $130 million.

Further Reading

Besen, Stanley M., et al., "An Economic Analysis of Copyright Collectives," *Virginia Law Review* 78, February 1992, pp. 383–419.
Breuhaus, Brian, "Dinner Music," *Restaurant Business,* November 1, 1998.

Brooks, Steve, "All Keyed Up," *Restaurant Business,* October 10, 1993.

——, "ASCAP and BMI Are Turning Up the Volume," *Restaurant Business,* July 1, 1995.

Conlin, Joseph, "Paying the Piper," *Successful Meetings,* October 1992, p. 26.

Foisie, Geoffrey, "Music Accord Is Upbeat for TV Profit," *Broadcasting and Cable,* November 8, 1993.

Jensen, Melinda, "Congress Could Turn Table on Music Licensers," *Successful Meetings,* April 1995.

Petrozzello, Donna, "ASCAP Restructuring Rates," *Broadcasting and Cable,* August 12, 1996.

Ryan, John, *The Production of Culture in the Music Industry: The ASCAP-BMI Controversy,* Lanham, Md.; London: University Press of America, 1985.

Taylor, R. William, "ASAE Interim Report on Music Licensing," *Association Management,* March 1992.

—Frederick C. Ingram

Andersen Worldwide

1345 Avenue of the Americas
New York, New York 10105
U.S.A.
(212) 708-6530
(800) 698-7258
Fax: (212) 245-3034
Web site: http://www.arthurandersen.com

Private Company
Incorporated: 1918 as Arthur Andersen & Company
Employees: 123,791
Sales: $13.9 billion (1998)
NAIC: 541211 Offices of Certified Public Accountants

Andersen Worldwide, the second-largest accounting and business services firm in the world, was established to manage and coordinate the worldwide operations of Arthur Andersen and Company and Andersen Consulting. The two units were created in 1989, with Arthur Andersen and Co. providing auditing and tax services as well as specialty business and corporate services, and Andersen Consulting providing management consulting services in technology, systems integration, and application software products; system designs for customer service, securities trading, and Internet sales; and various business consulting services.

Early History

The founder and guiding force behind the early years of the accounting firm was Arthur Edward Andersen. Born in Plano, Illinois, in 1885, Andersen was the son of a Norwegian couple who had immigrated to the United States four years earlier. At a young age, Andersen displayed a propensity for mathematics. Upon graduating from high school, he worked in the office of the comptroller at Allis-Chalmers Company in Chicago, while attending classes at the University of Illinois. In 1908, he received a degree in accounting from the university and at 23 years old became the youngest certified public accountant in Illinois.

From 1907 to 1911, Andersen served as senior accountant for Price Waterhouse in Chicago. Following a one-year term as comp-troller for the Uihlein business interests in Milwaukee, primarily Schlitz Brewing Company, Andersen was appointed chairperson of Northwestern University's accounting department. Soon thereafter, however, in 1913, Andersen decided to establish his own accounting firm. At the age of 28, he founded the public accounting firm of Andersen, DeLany & Company in Chicago.

Andersen's small company began to grow rapidly, as demand for auditing and accounting services increased dramatically following Congress's establishment of federal income tax and the Federal Reserve in 1913. One of Arthur Andersen's first clients was Schlitz Brewing, and the company's client list soon expanded to include International Telephone & Telegraph, Colgate-Palmolive, Parker Pen, and Briggs & Stratton. However, the company's primary business consisted of numerous utility companies throughout the Midwest, including Cincinnati Gas & Electric Company, Detroit Natural Gas Company, Milwaukee Gas Light Company, and Kansas City Power & Light Company. Into the 1920s, work for utility companies comprised about 50 percent of Andersen's total revenues, and the company became known as a "utility firm," a dubious distinction in accounting circles. In 1917, Andersen was awarded the degree of B.B.A. from Northwestern University, and, the following year, when DeLany left the partnership, his firm became known as Arthur Andersen & Company.

Licensed as accountants and auditors in many states across the country, the company grew rapidly during the 1920s. The firm opened six offices nationwide, the most important of which were located in New York (1921), Kansas City (1923), and Los Angeles (1926). Serving as auditor for many large industrial corporations, Arthur Andersen also began providing financial and industrial investigation services during this time. In 1927, company representatives testified as expert witnesses in the Ford Motor Company tax case. However, the company's most important investigation, a milestone in the history of Arthur Andersen & Company, involved Samuel Insull's financial empire.

Managing the Insull Empire in the 1930s

Samuel Insull emigrated from England to the United States in 1892. Hired as a secretary by Thomas Edison, Insull would soon prove to be an adept entrepreneur. During this time, the

Company Perspectives:

Arthur Andersen is a global, multidisciplinary professional services organization that provides clients, large and small, all over the world, the thing they need most to succeed: knowledge. *Our work is to* acquire knowledge *and to* share knowledge—*knowledge of how to improve performance in management, business processes, operations, information technology, finance, and change navigation—so that our clients can grow and profit. This* knowledge *comes from these sources: experience, education, and research. In all three, Arthur Andersen excels.*

use of Edison's incandescent lights was provided only to licensed utility companies, which became known as "Edison Companies." As many of Chicago's utilities approached bankruptcy early in the 20th century, Edison sought someone to organize them and keep them solvent. Insull volunteered for the job and immediately began to acquire and manage his own utility companies. In a few years, Insull had built an empire of utility companies, including the first utility to construct a generator with a capacity more than 12,000 kilowatts. In 1907, Insull created Commonwealth Edison, which was formed by the merger of two Insull holdings, Commonwealth Electric and Chicago Edison.

By the early 1930s, Insull's utilities, many of which had suffered during the Great Depression, represented a complicated network of holdings nearly $40 million in debt and badly in need of reorganization. When the Chicago banking community—on which Insull had always relied exclusively—was unable to provide the required cash, Insull was forced to turn to the East Coast banks for help. The East Coast banks refused to extend financial assistance, but, rather than forcing Insull into bankruptcy, they chose Arthur Andersen to act as their representative and manage the reorganization and refinancing of Insull's business holdings.

In 1932, the firm was placed in charge of supervising all the Insull utility companies' income and expenditures and was also involved in the subsequent financial reorganization of all the Edison companies within Insull's empire. To Arthur Andersen's credit, none of the utility companies went bankrupt; the firm maintained a firm control on all the assets during the period of refinancing. Moreover, Arthur Andersen not only increased its gross revenues by 20 percent through the Insull account but also garnered a reputation for honesty and independence that heightened its stature in the business community across the country. Thereafter, the company had no difficulty attracting large corporate clients. The incident also gave rise to the company's self-proclaimed role as watchdog of the accounting industry's methods and procedures.

Andersen not only provided direction for his company and personally approved of all the firm's clients, he remained involved in nearly every aspect and detail of company business. Until the day he died, he paid himself 50 percent of the firm's profits, while the other 50 percent was distributed among the rest of the partners. As he grew older, and as the company grew

increasingly successful, Andersen became less tolerant of those within the firm who disagreed with him or began to eclipse his leadership, and he tended to fire or drive out those with whom he wasn't compatible. Nevertheless, he had an uncanny sense of hiring particularly talented accountants, and many of the individuals hired during the 1920s and 1930s would play prominent roles in the company's development years later.

Under the watchful eye of its founder, Arthur Andersen and Company brought in many new accounts during the 1930s, including Montgomery Ward, one of the most sought-after clients during the decade. By 1928, the company employed approximately 400 people, and, by 1940, that figure had increased to 700. To provide greater accessibility to its clients, the firm opened new offices in Boston and Houston (1937) and in Atlanta and Minneapolis (1940).

During World War II Andersen himself reached the pinnacle of his success. His numerous writings on accounting—including "Duties and Responsibilities of the Comptroller" and "Present Day Problems Affecting the Presentation and Interpretation of Financial Statements"—prompted a growing admiration and respect for him in financial, industrial, and academic circles. Andersen served as president of the board of Trustees at Northwestern University and as a faculty member in accounting at the school. In recognition of his contribution to the field of accounting, and also for his devotion to preserving Norwegian history, he was awarded honorary degrees by Luther College, St. Olaf College, and Northwestern.

New Leadership After World War II

During this time, Andersen began grooming his associate, Leonard Spacek, for the company's leadership position. Spacek joined the company in 1928 and was named a partner in 1940, becoming one of Andersen's closest and most trusted confidants. Upon Andersen's death in January 1947, Spacek took over the company, remaining committed to the regimented management style of the founder. During Spacek's tenure, the firm grew from a regional operation located in Chicago with satellite offices across the United States into an international organization with one-stop, total service offices located around the world. Most importantly, however, Spacek began to focus on Andersen's idea that the company serve the public role of industry policeman.

Until the 1950s, the accounting profession was generally regarded as a club, with its own principles, methods, and procedures that had developed over the years without any standardization. Spacek began a campaign to improve accounting methods and practice by emphasizing the importance of implementing uniform accounting principles that would ensure "fairness." Spacek argued that accounting principles should be fair to the consumer, to labor, to the investor, to management, and to the public. Spacek hoped that his concept of fairness would serve as a foundation for accounting principles that the whole profession would ultimately find acceptable.

Most business historians agree that Spacek did the profession a service by initiating the standardization movement within the industry and by bringing public attention to the fact that existing auditing practices varied with each company. However, like Andersen before him, Spacek drew considerable criticism from the profession. Unable to change the prevailing attitudes of those within the industry, Spacek focused on his own company, creating Andersen University, with its Center for Professional Education. A training center located in St. Charles, Illinois, the university provided company employees with the opportunity to attend courses in a variety of accounting subjects.

Growing Consulting Services in the 1970s–80s

By the time Spacek retired from the company in 1973, Arthur Andersen & Company had opened 18 new offices in the United States and over 25 offices in countries throughout the world. With a staff of over 12,000 and an increase of revenues from $6.5 million to over $51 million during the period from 1947 to 1973, Andersen had grown into one of the world's preeminent accounting firms. The company also featured a profitable consulting service, helping large corporations install and use their first computer systems in the 1950s and branching out into production control, cost accounting, and operations research in the 1960s. Moreover, with audit and accounting revenues reaching a plateau due to the maturity of the industry, the company's consulting services began to represent an increasing share of Andersen's income. In the 1970s, Arthur Andersen became involved in a host of consulting activities, including systems integration services, strategic services, development of software application products, and a variety of additional technological services.

Under the aggressive leadership of Spacek's successor, Harvey Kapnick, the consulting services developed rapidly, and by 1979, its fees represented over 20 percent of Andersen's total revenues. Anticipating the importance of the burgeoning market for consulting services, Kapnick proposed to split the company into two separate firms, one to oversee auditing and another to focus on consulting as a comprehensive service business. When he presented this proposal to the company's partners, however, he met with protest. The auditors summarily rejected Kapnick's strategy, demanding proprietary control over all aspects of the company's managerial and financial affairs.

Kapnick resigned in October 1979 and was replaced by Duane Kullberg, who had joined the company in 1954 as an auditor. Reassuring the auditors that he would not take any action to split the company along operational lines, Kullberg nevertheless gave more operating control to the consulting side of the business, where employees were becoming increasingly irritated with the centralized control of the auditors. Kullberg's strategy seemed to work; internal discord subsided and both the auditing partners and the consulting principals (who were not called partners until later) devoted themselves to their respective businesses.

However, other problems arose for Arthur Andersen. In the mid-1980s, the company was the subject of several lawsuits filed by creditors and shareholders of bankrupt companies the firm had audited. These companies—including DeLorean Motors Company, Financial Corporation of American (American Savings & Loan), Drysdale Government Securities, and others—claimed that Arthur Andersen had failed to realize the extent of their financial struggles, and, moreover, had failed to inform the public of their findings. In 1984, Arthur Andersen

was forced to pay settlements amounting to $65 million within a two-month period.

Nevertheless, Arthur Andersen's business continued to thrive, particularly in the field of consulting services. By 1988, 40 percent of the company's total revenues were generated from consulting fees, making Arthur Andersen the largest consulting firm in the world. During this time, conflict between the auditors and the consultants flared up again, centering on discrepancies in the pay scale and disagreement over the control of consulting operations. Specifically, consultants questioned why they should earn less than auditors, when typical auditing projects brought in $4 million in fees in 1988, and consulting jobs garnered as much as $25 million. Furthermore, consultants took issue with the company's practice of allowing accounting partners to manage the consulting business.

Restructuring in the Late 1980s

Tensions continued to increase; when the firm's disgruntled consulting partners resigned, management filed lawsuits and infiltrated meetings held by the consultants. Finally, in an effort to end the chaos, Kullberg agreed to restructure the company. Under Kullberg's plan, Arthur Andersen was divided into two entities, an auditing and tax firm known as Arthur Andersen & Company and a consulting firm dubbed Andersen Consulting. Each of these firms then became separate financial entities under the Swiss-based Arthur Andersen Societe Cooperative, the ruling body of the company's worldwide organization, which would coordinate the activities of the entire firm's operations. In addition, the traditional management hierarchy, in which consultants reported to auditors, was altered, allowing consultants to report to managers in their field all the way up through the level of consulting partner.

In 1989, Lawrence A. Weinbach replaced Kullberg as chief executive officer. Upon graduating from the Wharton Business School, Weinbach had joined Arthur Andersen and had become a partner after nine years. Known for his diplomacy, Weinbach helped smooth over the harsh feelings among auditing and consulting partners, encouraging everyone to concentrate on increasing business. Under his leadership, Arthur Andersen's revenues skyrocketed. Between 1988 and 1992, Andersen's revenues increased from just under $3 billion to almost $5.6 billion, an increase of nearly 50 percent brought on mostly by the company's burgeoning consulting activities. During these years, revenue from Andersen Consulting grew by 89 percent while revenue from Arthur Andersen & Company's accounting and tax services grew by 38 percent. Clearly, Weinbach recognized the importance of the company's position as the largest management consultant firm in the world.

In the early 1990s, Arthur Andersen was beset with lawsuits from creditors of thrifts that had collapsed during the 1980s. Furthermore, in 1992, the company was sued by the government's watchdog Resolution Trust Corporation for negligence in its auditing of the failed Ben Franklin Savings & Trust. Nevertheless, the company weathered these difficulties, renewing its commitment to high-quality, irreproachable auditing services and focusing on improving and developing both its auditing and consulting services. With a settlement in 1993 Arthur Andersen resolved the lawsuits relating to the failed savings and loans and was released from any further liability.

The firm grew more cautious after this debacle, turning down more clients and even dropping several existing ones. However, outstanding lawsuits continued to plague the Big Six accounting firms, making insurance coverage more difficult for these firms to acquire. The cost of insurance and settlements for the Big Six was estimated at 12 percent of local fee income in the United States and eight percent in Britain. Arthur Andersen considered incorporation as a shield for the personal assets of partners not found directly negligent. The Big Six firms also pursued legislative changes that would limit their liability.

Increasing Income in the 1990s

Arthur Andersen's fee income rose steadily in the mid-1990s, as did that of the other Big Six accounting firms. The general accounting prosperity had several causes: an economic boom in the United States, the growth of the accounting firms in Asia and Eastern Europe, and especially an increase in management consulting fees. Total revenues for Arthur Andersen surpassed the $6 billion mark in 1993, rose to $6.7 billion in 1994, and jumped to $8.1 billion in 1995. Half of the firm's $9.5 billion in fees in 1996 came from consulting. Arthur Andersen led the industry in fee income per partner in the mid-1990s.

With the consulting branch enjoying the greatest rise in profits, the accounting branch began offering its own consulting services in the early 1990s to companies with less than $175 million in annual sales. Placing themselves in competition with the consulting partners did nothing to heal the animosity that had led to the division of the company in the first place. Consulting partners argued for total independence from the parent company in the late 1990s, citing the vast disparity in fee contributions between the two subsidiaries. The accounting partners alleged that the consulting business would never have taken off without their initial support, referrals, and subsidies.

Managing partner and chief executive officer Lawrence Weinbach retired in 1997, throwing the divided firm into chaos as a search for a successor led to heated disagreements. One nominee came from consulting, and another came from accounting. Both were rejected in a vote by all company partners. An acting CEO was named by the board: W. Robert Grafton, an accounting partner. Soon thereafter, Andersen Consulting, as the result of a unanimous vote by its partners, sought an arbitrator to gain their firm's complete independence from Andersen Worldwide.

In 1999 Andersen Worldwide continued to oversee its two squabbling operating units and continued to lead the world in providing business consulting services. Its revenues reached almost $14 billion in 1998, and the firm boasted 382 offices in 81 countries around the world.

Principal Operating Units

Arthur Andersen and Co.; Andersen Consulting.

Further Reading

"Accountancy Mergers: Double Entries," *Economist,* December 13, 1997.
"British Accountants' Liability: Big Six PLC," *Economist,* October 7, 1995.
"A Glimmer of Hope," *Economist,* April 1, 1995.
"Finance and Economics: Disciplinary Measures," *Economist,* March 6, 1999.
Spacek, Leonard, *The Growth of Arthur Andersen and Company, 1928–1973: An Oral History,* New York: Garland, 1989.
Stevens, Mark, *The Big Six,* New York: Simon & Schuster, 1991.

—Thomas Derdak
—updated by Susan Windisch Brown

Archway Cookies, Inc.

5451 W. Dickman Road
Battle Creek, Michigan 49015
U.S.A.
(616) 962-4031
(888) 427-2492
Fax: (616) 962-8149
Web site: http://www.archwaycookies.com

*Wholly Owned Subsidiary of Specialty Foods
    Corporation*
Incorporated: 1936 as Swanson Home Style Cookies
Employees: 180
Sales: $160 million (1998 est.)
NAIC: 311821 Cookie & Cracker Manufacturing

Archway Cookies, Inc. is one of the top cookie makers in the United States. The company's biggest sellers are variations on its original oatmeal cookie, which together account for more than 40 percent of sales. Archway's line of over 60 varieties also includes fat-free, low-fat, and sugar-free types, as well as holiday cookies sold at the end of the year. The company makes soft-baked cookies, which have a shorter shelf life than the ''hard'' brands and are generally preferred by consumers over the age of 50. In the late 1940s the company began selling baking franchises in order to expand nationwide, but it bought most of them back in the 1960s. By the late 1990s only four franchise bakers were left, with two company-owned bakeries supplying the bulk of the country. In 1998 Archway was purchased by Specialty Foods Corporation, which also owned California-based Mother's Cake & Cookie. The combined companies made Specialty Foods the number-three cookie maker in the country.

Early Years

Archway's origins date to 1936, when the husband and wife team of Harold and Ruth Swanson began baking soft oatmeal cookies and doughnuts in their garage in Battle Creek, Michigan. In the company's early days the cookies were distributed only locally, packaged from the start in clear wrappers that

helped stimulate both appetites and sales. During World War II, with baking ingredients in short supply, the Swansons decided to concentrate exclusively on cookies. Swanson Home Style Cookies, as they were known, grew into a line of 15 different varieties by the late 1940s.

Seeking to expand outside of Michigan, the Swansons decided to license their cookie recipes and brand name to franchisees in neighboring states. The first franchise was sold in December 1949 to Ellison Bakery of Fort Wayne, Indiana, and a year later the family-owned Ellison company purchased a second Archway license for Wisconsin. Other franchise sales followed, and the company began to expand its reach throughout the country and into Canada. In 1954 the Swansons changed the brand and company names to Archway Cookies, as the name Swanson was already recognized nationally in association with a popular brand of frozen dinners. Growth continued throughout the 1950s. In addition to selling franchises, the company built plants of its own in Ashland, Ohio, and Boone, Iowa, with only the company headquarters remaining in Battle Creek. In 1962 the Swansons sold Archway to George Markham, a company vice-president. Over the next two years, under Markham's leadership, Archway bought back the majority of its franchises, which then numbered 22, and gained control over most of its production. Franchises were still important to the company, however, providing a source of new cookie varieties that were popular in different regions of the country. The Ellison Bakery in Indiana, for example, developed the company's Ruth's Oatmeal and Rocky Road recipes, which it discovered through a series of baking contests that it sponsored at state fairs. Although most of Archway's cookies were available in every market, some types were only offered regionally if the varieties were not popular outside of a particular area. This and other factors helped keep the company's national profile relatively low, as it focused its energies on regional competitors, rather than national brands such as Keebler and Nabisco.

Key to the company's success was the quality of its soft-baked cookies. These were much less common in the cookie market, but at the same time were perceived to be closer to homemade than other cookies. Soft-baked cookies had higher moisture content than ones that were dry and relatively hard,

Company Perspectives:

Commitment to traditional quality and guaranteed freshness is the foundation of Archway cookies and its more than 60 Home Style, Gourmet, Fat Free, Sugar Free, Bag, and Holiday cookie varieties. It has also led the Company to become the nation's leading producer of oatmeal-based cookie varieties.

and thus had a much shorter shelf life. To compensate for this, the company developed a system of baking cookies only after orders for them were received, allowing it to keep store stocks fresh and minimize waste. Archway's goal was for stores to sell half of the cookies on display each week, ensuring that the vast majority would be purchased well before the six-week ''sell-by'' date was reached.

Over time the company also came to offer a number of different holiday varieties, which were marketed primarily during the Christmas season. As many as 15 to 20 additional types of cookies were produced during this time of year, and the company took on extra employees to keep up with the demand. Archway's primary market was consumers over the age of 50, and the company focused its marketing and advertising on this customer base, rather than children. During the late 1960s and into the 1970s, sales continued to grow as Archway distribution expanded. Stores were serviced by independent distributors, which the company felt could best reach the wide range of businesses that sold its products. These ranged from large supermarkets to small mom-and-pop stores.

New Ownership and ''Healthier'' Cookies in the 1980s

In 1983 George Markham sold Archway to senior executives Thomas Olin and Eugene McKay, Jr. Both had been with the company since the 1960s, Olin having managed the Ashland, Ohio, baking plant and later serving as national vice-president and general manager of the company's eastern baking operations. The two new owners each took the titles of co-president and co-CEO.

During this time, what the industry referred to as ''The Great Cookie War'' began when the major food companies began to introduce their own lines of soft-baked cookies. With the large-scale advertising campaigns and national clout of Procter & Gamble, Frito-Lay, Nabisco, and Keebler targeting Archway's market niche, the company was forced to fight back with a ''buy one, get one free'' offer and other marketing strategies. Although sales of the new soft cookie brands started out strong, they quickly crumbled as consumers found taste to be disappointing, and the companies discovered they were displacing sales of their original brands. Within several years the majors withdrew from the soft cookie business, leaving Archway holding its own.

In the late 1980s, as Americans grew increasingly health-conscious, Archway responded to concerns about saturated fat

by removing the ingredient from all of the company's products. Studies showing that oat bran was an especially beneficial dietary fiber were also published around this time, and sales of Archway's oatmeal cookies grew as a result. In 1988 the company's date-oatmeal cookies were lauded as the most healthful cookies on the market by a consumer watchdog organization, and four other Archway varieties finished near the top of the ranking of 250 cookie brands.

Over the next several years Archway also rolled out a line of fat-free cookies, as a wave of studies that exposed the harmful effects of fat in the diet were published. Annual sales, which were not disclosed by the privately held company, reached an estimated $68 million in 1993, and grew an astounding 138 percent the following year with the success of Archway's fat-free cookies.

Controversy arose in 1994 when the company canceled the Illinois franchise of Oak State Products, Inc., after it discovered that Oak State had been making fat-free cookies for Nabisco. The 38-year franchisee Oak State sued to have the license reinstated, and a judge issued a temporary injunction against Archway. Archway argued that the agreement with its franchisees required them to get permission from the company before baking cookies for a competitor. Oak State had in fact informed Archway when Nabisco approached it in 1992 to help with an unspecified product, but Archway had not learned until August 1993 that Oak State was baking, and had helped develop, Nabisco's new SnackWells fat-free cookie line. Not only was SnackWells an instant and major success, but it competed directly with existing Archway products. Ironically, Oak State had helped Archway develop its own fat-free line. The issue was settled before it went to court, when Oak State sold its franchise back to Archway. The two companies also agreed to coordinate the change in distribution for Illinois, which would now be supplied from Archway's Boone, Iowa, plant.

1995 Alliance with Kellogg's Boosts Sales

In 1995 Archway entered into an agreement with the Battle Creek-based Kellogg Company to use Kellogg's All-Bran cereal in a line of low-fat cookies. This represented the first time Kellogg's would allow another company to market a co-branded product. The new cookies were a success, and propelled Archway for the first time into the number three spot in U.S. cookie sales, though it slipped back to number four after a time.

Archway owners Thomas Olin and Eugene McKay, Jr., stepped down from day-to-day management of the company in 1996, letting their sons Thomas Olin, Jr., and Eugene McKay III take over their roles as co-president and co-CEO, while remaining joint chairmen of the company board. When Thomas Olin Sr. died a few months later, his widow, Gloria Olin, was given his co-chairman position.

The year 1996 also saw Archway initiate a new television advertising campaign which featured an animated ''spokes-cow'' character and the tagline ''Classic Cookie Jar Material.'' Moreover, the company upgraded its packaging during this time, redesigning logos and adding product identification to package ends. Most Archway cookies were still packaged in clear wrappers as they had been since the 1930s, with the exception of larger-size bags and certain holiday varieties. In a national promotion launched in 1997, "The Big Cookie Tour," the company gave away over one million free cookies in cities across the United States. A special "cookie mobile" showcased a costumed character named Archie the Baker who entertained and gave away cookies. The tour was produced in conjunction with a sweepstakes contest advertised on cookie packages that offered trips, luggage, and other travel-related prizes.

Early the next year the company introduced a new line of sugar-free cookies, including such varieties as Chocolate Chip, Oatmeal, Rocky Road, and Shortbread. These cookies used Sorbitol and Maltitol as sweeteners, and although they were not low in calories, they were popular among diabetics because they did not increase blood sugar levels. The packages displayed the logo of the American Diabetes Association, and Archway pledged five cents from each sale to that organization.

In October 1998 Archway was sold to Specialty Foods Corporation of Deerfield, Illinois, in a deal reportedly worth close to $100 million. Archway joined the Oakland, California-based Mother's Cake & Cookie Co. in the Specialty Foods portfolio, making Specialty Foods the third largest cookie baker in the United States. Archway management remained the same, and the company did not announce any major changes in direction.

Reshuffling among leading cookie makers had been taking place for several years, with number two Keebler being purchased by Inflo Holdings, Inc. in 1996 and subsequently merging with number three Sunshine. Market leader Nabisco also announced a major restructuring in 1998. Cookie sales had been stagnant or dropping slightly for several years, and consumers had lost interest in the fat-free varieties that had initially been highly successful. Nabisco's SnackWells, once the number two cookie brand, had seen sales drop by almost two-thirds, and the company had added fat back to most of the brand's varieties, changing its advertising to emphasize flavor over fat content. Archway was also affected by these changes, with supermarket sales of its cookies slipping from $159 million in 1997 to $152 million in 1998.

Nevertheless, after more than 60 years Archway cookies were still an American favorite, and the company that produced them was solidly ensconced in the top ranks of cookie makers. Though it maintained many traditions such as its clear packaging and the emphasis on soft-baked oatmeal cookies, the com-

pany was frequently adding new varieties and using new marketing methods to keep up with the times. Despite the turbulence brought on by shifting marketplace trends and the changes taking place within many top cookie companies, Archway had maintained its position as the leading maker of oatmeal cookies and remained a major player in its field.

Further Reading

"Archway Bakes Into No. 3 After Introducing Low-Fat Treats," *Associated Press,* August 29, 1995.

"Archway Cookies, Kellogg Co-Brand Low-Fat Cookie," *Food & Drink Daily,* May 9, 1995.

"Archway Cookies Meets Increased Product Demand," *Industrial Engineering,* September 1, 1992, p. 18.

"Archway Seeks to Sever 38-Year Relationship over Nabisco Fat Free Cookie Contract," *Milling & Baking News,* May 3, 1994, p. 10.

Campbell, Tom, "Wyoming County Bakery Finds Success is Sweet with Cookies," *Business-First Buffalo,* September 16, 1991, p. 1.

Culloton, Dan, "Specialty Foods Corp. Buying its Way to Top," *Chicago Daily Herald,* October 15, 1998, p. 2.

Gorton, Laurie, "A New Twist on Productivity—Changes in Material Handling Enable Archway Cookies to Ship and Sell its Products in Fresher Condition," *Baking & Snack,* October 1998.

Harmon, Linda, "It Takes a Smart Cookie to Run a Successful Bakery," *Business Digest of Greater Fort Wayne,* December 1, 1989, p. 2.

Hickman, Beth, "Marketing Strategies Remain Key in Battle for Cookie Dollar," *Milling & Baking News,* April 2, 1996, p. 1.

Littman, Margaret, "See is for Cookie," *Bakery Production and Marketing,* June 15, 1997, p. 40.

McWard, Christine, "Cookie-Cracker Sales Are in a Slump, but Industry Leaders Are Revved Up to Restructure, Revamp & Revitalize," *Baking & Snack,* October 1998.

"Oak State, Archway Settlement Includes Sale of Franchise," *Milling & Baking News,* August 9, 1994, p. 14.

Sanchez, Jesus, "Firms Tell How Soft-Cookie Sales Crumbled After a Heated Battle," *Los Angeles Times,* July 6, 1987, p. 1.

Scherer, Colleen, "Package of the Month—The Low Fat Challenge," *Baking & Snack,* August 1995.

Smith, Gary, "Cookie War Ends, 'New Era' Begins: Wenona Bakery Parts Company with Archway but Expects to Expand," *Peoria Journal Star,* July 27, 1994, p. B1.

Steel, Susan, "Cookie Monster," *Columbus Dispatch,* December 12, 1994, p. 1.

Stratton, Lee, "Commercial Gives Voice to Bovine Brouhaha," *Columbus Dispatch,* November 15, 1995, p. 1B.

—Frank Uhle

Arden Group, Inc.

2020 South Central Avenue
Compton, California 90220
U.S.A.
(310) 628-2842
Fax: (310) 631-0950

Public Company
Incorporated: 1940 as Arden Farm Company
Employees: 1,856
Sales: $ 296.5 million (1998)
Stock Exchanges: NASDAQ
Ticker Symbol: ARDNA
NAIC: 44511 Supermarkets & Other Grocery (Except
    Convenience) Stores; 551112 Offices of Other
    Holding Companies

The Arden Group, Inc. is a holding company whose main subsidiary, Arden-Mayfair, Inc., operates 13 supermarkets in and around Los Angeles, California. Ten markets operate under the name Gelson's and three under the name Mayfair. The stores serve the upper end of the consumer spectrum. In addition to traditional groceries, they stock a wide range of specialty and gourmet items: imported foods, sushi, unusual produce, fresh seafood and meat, wine and liquor, flowers, delicatessen and bakery items, and health and natural food products. Some Gelson's stores provide fresh pizza and pasta preparation and coffee bars and even offer banking and pharmacy services through third parties. Mayfair markets are smaller than Gelson's and their variety is not as broad. Customer service is a high priority at both stores. Staff are scheduled to keep waiting times to a minimum; they assist customers in finding and carrying out their purchases. Gelson's and Mayfair credit cards are available to qualified customers. The Arden Group had total sales of $296.48 million in 1998, up from $274.35 million in 1997, a 53-week fiscal year.

Origins

The company's history may be traced as far back as the 1933 incorporation of Western Dairies, Inc., a small California dairy operation that gradually expanded its geographic scope and product line to become a grocery retailer known as the Arden Farm Company beginning in 1940. By 1964, Arden Farms was ready for growth through acquisition.

In October of that year Arden acquired Mayfair Markets, a chain of supermarkets in Los Angeles, creating Arden-Mayfair, Inc., later a subsidiary of the Arden Group. At the same time, Arden acquired a small chain of supermarkets from the Gelson Brothers. The Gelsons had opened their first store in North Hollywood in the late 1940s. The new company enjoyed $455 million in sales in 1965. In April 1966 it made a preliminary application for listing on the New York Stock Exchange, and management predicted that trading would begin on October first of the same year. In April 1967 an innocuously worded statement to the press announced that J. Earl Garrett, Arden-Mayfair president and chief executive officer for less than a year, had asked to retire from all company positions, effective at month's end.

In April 1967 scandal struck Arden-Mayfair. L. David Callahan, a stockholder and company director, brought suit in federal court to prevent the company's annual meeting from being held. Callahan charged that company executives had been involved in serious conflicts of interest and that the annual proxy statement issued by the company withheld information about them, in violation of Securities and Exchange Commission (SEC) rules. A federal district judge denied the request to postpone the meeting, but acknowledged that the company's proxy statement was "insufficient as required by law." Instead, the Arden-Mayfair board postponed the meeting on its own, telling the *Wall Street Journal* it was "in order to enable the company to set the record straight and to give shareholders all available information in view of the publicity given this litigation."

In the wake of Callahan's suit it was revealed that Garrett's abrupt request to resign had been occasioned by a meeting Callahan had with another company director, Luther Anderson, in August 1966. Callahan had described nine potential conflicts of interest in which Garrett was involved. Anderson believed that if the allegations were true they warranted Garrett's removal. About six weeks after Callahan's revelations, Garrett wrote to the New York Stock Exchange (NYSE) asking that the company's application for listing on the exchange be put on hold, citing an expected drop in Arden-Mayfair earnings and questions regarding the voting rights of holders of Arden-Mayfair preferred stock. In the meantime company directors formed a conflict of interest committee and, in January 1967, voted in favor of Garrett's resignation. As planned by the board, Garrett would resign in stages: first he would take a six-month leave-of-absence, then quietly resign—after the annual shareholders' meeting in April. The board also decided to require Garrett to repay the funds from at least one of the questionable transactions. When Garrett finally did ask to resign, he did not specify the date he meant to leave. In response, Callahan brought his suit.

Arden-Mayfair's revised proxy statement detailed nine conflicts of interest, a number the *Wall Street Journal* claimed was not exhaustive. They included questionable sales to Garrett, the leasing of buildings owned by Garrett to Arden-Mayfair, and real estate commissions on Arden-Mayfair transactions paid to Garrett's sons. When the proxy statement was issued, the *Journal* reported that the company intended to press charges against Garrett.

The 1967 meeting eventually was held in late June. After assuring stockholders that it was doing everything possible to clear up the conflicts of interest, the new president, Luther Anderson, announced that the company finally had turned the corner after a difficult period with earnings in 1966 of approximately $4.24 million. Company expansion would be trimmed back to 16 new store openings from 21 the previous year, and as soon as the situation had stabilized, the company would renew its application for a NYSE listing.

The company suffered a loss of more than $600,000 for the first half of 1967 but rebounded in the second half and was able to report net income of about $400,000 for the entire year. As a result, it suspended dividend payments to shareholders in summer 1967. They were not resumed until early 1969 after Arden-Mayfair's strong performance in 1968 with a net profit of $2.73 million. In May 1968 President and CEO Luther Anderson announced that the company was reactivating its application for listing on the NYSE.

Financial and Legal Woes in the 1970s

Arden-Mayfair entered the 1970s falling afoul of the Federal Trade Commission (FTC). In January 1970 the FTC accused the company of receiving illegal brokerage services, from the Chambosse Brokerage Co. Arden-Mayfair purchased grocery products from Chambosse that were then marketed under the company's own brands. According to the *Wall Street Journal,* "a substantial portion of [Chambosse's] business consists of arranging sales of such products to Arden-Mayfair." The FTC maintained that Arden-Mayfair had accepted the services without paying a brokerage fee. Chambosse had passed the cost onto its own suppliers, according to the FTC, "when in fact it is acting for Arden-Mayfair or had been or is now subject to the control of Arden-Mayfair." In April Arden-Mayfair agreed to a FTC consent order barring the company from accepting illegal brokerage services.

One year later, in January 1971, TelAutograph Corporation, a manufacturer of message transmission equipment, announced that it was going to purchase 85,000 shares of Arden-Mayfair, bringing its stake to 300,900 shares in all and making it the largest single Arden-Mayfair shareholder. In July 1971 TelAutograph and Arden-Mayfair agreed to merge the two companies. Under the terms of the agreement, TelAutograph became a fully owned subsidiary of Arden-Mayfair. In December 1971, after the shareholders of both companies had approved the deal, the Arden-Mayfair board of directors elected Bernard Briskin company CEO and chairman of its board's executive committee. Briskin was the former president and CEO of TelAutograph.

In September 1971, while the merger was being ironed out, a federal grand jury accused Arden-Mayfair and three other dairies of violating antitrust laws by conspiring to fix prices in Washington State and Alaska. According to the indictment, the companies, which sold more than $70 million of dairy products annually in the two states, allegedly had maintained prices at artificial and noncompetitive levels since before 1965. The suit was resolved when the Justice Department recommended a consent decree that barred the four companies from conspiring to fix prices. Arden-Mayfair called the consent decree "a satisfactory conclusion," according to the *Wall Street Journal.*

Arden-Mayfair's financial performance was disappointing in the decade of the 1970s. Following its profit in 1969, the company had a net loss of $2.82 million in 1971, a net income of $42.12 million in 1971, a net loss of $1.1 million in 1972, a net income of $2.38 million in 1974 (in part the result of the sale of 16 stores to the Lucky chain), another loss of about $1.5 million in 1975, and a loss of $3.5 million in 1976. Briskin left his position as CEO during this period and was replaced by Bruce Krysiak.

Arden-Mayfair's financial woes came to a head in 1976 with a stockholder revolt led by the Louart Corporation, the major shareholder in the company, with 18 percent of Arden-Mayfair stock. Before the annual shareholders' meeting, Louart fielded its own slate of candidates for the board, charging that Arden-Mayfair's management was responsible for $18 million in losses between 1970 and 1976. Arden-Mayfair management laid the blame at the door of past directors and the former president, Bruce Krysiak. Krysiak had resigned in 1976 after only two years on the job, according to him because of policy differences with other directors and according to the board because of $1.5 million in losses. After the meeting one director revealed that the board considered liquidating the company at one point. Eventually, they concluded that the operation could be salvaged, in part by aggressively closing many of the nonperforming Mayfair markets in southern California. The Louart challenge ultimately was defeated by a 72.4 percent margin.

In July 1977 the Arden-Mayfair board announced a restructuring plan that would create a brand new company, with Arden-Mayfair as its subsidiary. Later that summer, however, two suits were brought against Arden-Mayfair, by the SEC and the Louart Corporation. Both charged the company and 14 past and current directors with fraud and waste. According to a report in the *Wall Street Journal,* Louart maintained that Arden-Mayfair directors had wasted company assets to "maintain themselves in their positions of power and financial advantage." It also accused directors of conspiring to sell 560,000 unissued shares of Arden-Mayfair stock to friendly investors to maintain control of the company during the power struggle at the annual meeting the previous year. Louart claimed that it had not been informed of the stock offering.

The suits dragged on through 1977. Arden-Mayfair held no annual meeting that year because the corporation counsel in California had failed to approve the company's restructuring plan. In May 1978 it presented a brand new restructuring proposal, one similar to the earlier plan in that it created a new holding company, called Arden Group Inc., which would be the parent company of Arden-Mayfair. It differed from the original plan in the way it redistributed common and preferred shares and bonuses. Louart, however, opposed the revised plan for reorganization as well and, before the 1978 annual meeting, it again mounted an alternative slate of candidates for the board of directors. Summer 1978 saw a round of suits and countersuits. By late July, though, it was clear that Louart would not prevail. A superior court judge rejected a Louart motion to bar holders of recently issued stock from voting at the meeting; the judge also refused to interfere with Arden-Mayfair's revised restructuring proposal. At the meeting on August 1, 1978, Arden-Mayfair shareholders supported company management completely, electing its slate of directors and approving the formation of Arden Group. A year later, in July 1979, Arden Group and Louart reached an agreement under which Arden agreed to buy shares held by Louart for $2.6 million and to pay an additional $650,000 in exchange for Louart's dropping all suits against Arden.

Turnaround in the 1980s

Arden's financial situation improved during the 1980s. After a record net income of $15.83 million in 1979, the company turned a profit every year through 1991, including $4.2 million in 1981, $4.2 million in 1982, $5.2 million in 1985, $5.6 million in 1986, $4.6 million in 1986, $7.37 million in 1987, $10.2 million in 1989, $11.8 million in 1990, and $11.5 million in 1991. By 1984, Arden's seven-store chain, Gelson's, had sales of $120 million and was called "one of the most prosperous small grocers in the United States," by *Chain Store Age Executive*. One cause of Arden's turnaround in the 1980s was its aggressive paring away of unprofitable stores. In 1986 the company put 17 of its 39 stores on the sales block, and by 1993 it had disposed of all but 12, five Mayfair Markets and seven Gelson's.

In June 1986 Arden became involved in a new controversy when it announced a plan to create two separate classes of common stock. The new Class A common stock would pay higher dividends; Class B would have super-voting powers, with ten votes per share instead of one. Almost immediately the plan was attacked by stockholders as undemocratic. Two shareholders brought suit in Delaware court, claiming that the plan would concentrate control of the company in the hands of Bernard Briskin, Arden's president and CEO, and its largest shareholder, with a 21.1 percent stake. The Delaware Chancery Court issued a preliminary injunction that blocked the implementation of the plan. Arden finally settled the lawsuit by agreeing to purchase the plaintiffs' shares for a total of about $7.4 million. The plaintiffs agreed not to purchase Arden voting stock for 18 months, and no more than ten percent of Arden's

voting stock for eight years. The day after the suit was settled, Arden applied to the SEC for permission to introduce the new class of common stock. In August 1987 344,000 Class A shares were exchanged for the new Class B shares.

Growth in the 1990s

In December 1992 Arden announced plans to spin off TelAutograph and GPS Pool Supply, its communications and swimming pool supply subsidiaries, which accounted for about $77 million of the company's $315.9 million in annual sales. Arden CFO Ernest Klinger told the *Wall Street Journal,* "It's been confusing to existing shareholders, potential shareholders and analysts to look at a company whose results include retail operations, communications equipment and pool supplies." GPS Pool Supply was sold in May 1994 for $4.6 million. TelAutograph had been sold to Danka Business Systems in September 1993 for $35.5 million. In May 1997, however, an arbitrator adjusted the purchase price because the valuation of certain parts of TelAutograph's inventory had been incorrect. As a result Arden was required to pay Danka nearly $1.9 million.

In November 1993 Arden purchased a neighborhood shopping center in Calabasas, California. It built and developed a shopping center on the site and opened a new Gelson's in January 1996. The store extended the services already offered by Gelson's—gourmet food, produce, deli products, coffee bars, fine bakeries—and introduced third-party banking and pharmacy services. The store was expensive and depressed Arden profits in 1995 while it was being built. But once completed the store proved a bigger success than the company had hoped. In both 1997 and 1998 the store saw sales rise and expenses as a percent of sales drop. Encouraged by the results, Arden opened a similar store in Northridge, California in November 1997. That store, unfortunately, did not perform up to company projections. In 1998 Arden canceled plans for a similar store on a site in Santa Barbara. That same year Arden signed a long-term deal with a developer for a Gelson's in Beverly Hills.

Arden's net income remained healthy throughout the latter half of the 1990s. It rose from $3.52 million in 1996, to $5.95 million in 1997, to $10 million in 1998. In July 1998 the Arden board of directors executed a four-for-one stock split, raising the number of Class A common shares from five million to ten million, and the Class B common shares from 500,000 to 1.5 million.

Principal Subsidiaries

Arden-Mayfair, Inc.

Further Reading

"Arden Group to Offer Class A Shareholders Three Choices in Swap," *Wall Street Journal,* June 30, 1987, p. 68.

"Arden-Mayfair Agrees to FTC Consent Order on Grocery Brokerage," *Wall Street Journal,* April 28, 1970, p. 18.

"Arden-Mayfair Board Votes Restructuring to Create New Firm," *Wall Street Journal,* February 23, 1977, p. 16.

"Arden-Mayfair Cancels Annual Meeting, Slates Special Session June 27," *Wall Street Journal,* April 22, 1967, p. 19.

"Arden-Mayfair Got Food-Broker Services Illegally, FTC Asserts," *Wall Street Journal,* January 7, 1970, p. 8.

"Arden-Mayfair Inc. Is Target of Lawsuit Citing Fraud, Waste," *Wall Street Journal,* August 30, 1977, p. 10.

"Arden-Mayfair Says It Has Revised Plan of Reorganization," *Wall Street Journal,* May 23, 1978, p. 45.

"Arden-Mayfair, Two Aides Are Charged by SEC with Fraud and False Reporting," *Wall Street Journal,* August, 19, 1977, p. 34.

"Arden Sells Telautograph Unit," *Supermarket News,* October 18, 1993.

"Consent Decree Filed in Price-Fixing Suit Against 4 Milk Firms," *Wall Street Journal,* February 21, 1971, p. 11.

"Court Enjoins Swap Offer for Arden Group Shares," Dow Jones News Service, August 1, 1986.

"Director Suit Charges Arden-Mayfair Failed to Tell Holders Enough," *Wall Street Journal,* April 12, 1967, p. 10.

"Gelson's, Los Angeles Gucci of Groceries," *Chain Store Age Executive with Shopping Center Age,* January 1984, p. 114.

Hill, G. Christian, "Arden-Mayfair Inc. Meeting Is Wracked by 3-Pronged Battle," *Wall Street Journal,* April 21, 1976, p. 17.

Pinkerton, Stewart, and Peter Kann, "Arden-Mayfair Faces Shareholder Meeting Amidst Conflicts-of-Interest Controversy," *Wall Street Journal,* June 26, 1967, p. 4.

"Supermarket Operator Arden Group Sets 4-for-1 Stock Split," Dow Jones Online News, June 17, 1998.

"TelAutograph Acquires 85,000 Common Shares of Arden-Mayfair Inc.," *Wall Street Journal,* January 25, 1971, p. 5.

"Two Arden Holders Oppose Plan to Create 2 Classes of Common Stock," *Wall Street Journal,* September 10, 1986, p. 1.

—Gerald E. Brennan

The Art Institute of Chicago

111 S. Michigan Avenue
Chicago, Illinois 60603-6110
U.S.A.
(312) 443-3600
Fax: (312) 443-0849
Web site: http://www.artic.edu

Nonprofit Organization
Founded: 1882 as the Chicago Academy of Fine Arts
Employees: 1,772
Sales: $161 million (1998)
NAIC: 71211 Museums

Chicago's premier cultural institution and one of the greatest art museums in the world, The Art Institute of Chicago welcomed more than 1.7 million visitors in 1998. Its collection holds more than 300,000 objects, including an important set of European paintings, a wealth of antiquities, a wide variety of non-Western art, and a substantial archive of architectural sketches and drawings. In addition to the permanent collection, the museum presents revolving exhibits in the largest temporary exhibition space in the country. The School of the Art Institute of Chicago is often regarded as the best art education program in the country. The Art Institute's theater in residence, the Goodman, is a prominent cultural attraction in its own right.

Early History

In 1866, the Chicago Academy of Design was formed by a group of artists. When this organization foundered, the businessmen who made up its board of trustees set up a parallel organization, the Chicago Academy of Fine Arts, which was incorporated in 1879. The creation of an art museum was vital to a city that was recovering from a disastrous fire eight years earlier and struggling to rebuild itself as a great American metropolis. By 1885, when the museum's first quarters were built, by John Wellborn Root of the firm (Daniel) Burnham and Root, the name had changed to The Art Institute of Chicago.

The year 1893 saw Chicago's World Columbian Exposition, a major fair designed to show off the reborn, rebuilt Chicago. Afterwards, The Art Institute moved into the "World's Congresses" hall, a structure built for the exposition by the firm of Shepley, Rutan and Coolidge, where it has remained ever since. This Michigan Avenue structure, with its two bronze lions standing guard out front, is one of the city's most recognizable sights. The lions, sculpted by Edward Kerney, were added in 1894. The Ryerson and Burnham libraries were added in 1901, confirming the institution's educational and archival commitment.

Building a Collection in the Early 1900s

In 1906, on the recommendation of the American Impressionist Mary Cassatt, the museum paid $40,000 for El Greco's *Assumption of the Virgin,* a 13-foot-high canvas dated 1577 that went a long way towards establishing the museum's reputation. In 1922 Bertha Palmer, widow of the merchant Potter Palmer, left a collection that included an early Monet titled *The River.* This bequest would form the core of the Art Institute's Impressionist catalogue. Four years later, Frederic Clay Bartlett donated a trove of paintings that included Vincent van Gogh's *Bedroom at Arles* as well as Georges Seurat's *Afternoon on the Island of the Grand Jatte,* which would later become perhaps the single most popular picture in the Art Institute. Another close contender for this distinction, however, was Grant Wood's *American Gothic,* depicting a stern-looking farm couple, which came into the collection in 1930, the same year it was painted. Martin Antoine Ryerson, who served as vice-president of the Art Institute and who has been called the single greatest benefactor of the museum, died in 1932, willing his diverse collection to it.

Chicago banker Charles L. Hutchinson served as president of the Art Institute's board of trustees from 1882 to 1924, and during his tenure he helped the museum move beyond its origins as a provincial organization, in the direction of a world-class institution. Hutchinson saw social reform and improvement as an essential component of the museum's mission, and during his tenure he saw to it that the Art Institute would find its place in the public life of the city. William M. R. French worked alongside Hutchinson, serving as director, curator of painting and sculpture, and director of the School of the Art Institute. French's most significant action was organizing the International Exhibition of Modern Art (also known as the Armory Show) in 1913, a show intended to introduce modern European art to the relatively unreceptive Chicago audience. The futurists and cubists included in the exhibition were branded degenerates and charlatans in the local press, and from that moment on the Art Institute struggled with how best to present challenging art without alienating the public.

When Robert B. Harshe took over as director in 1921, he remarked, "Our present policy of acquiring works of art, depending as it does on what is offered us . . . leads us into casual and haphazard acquisitions." The 1920s were a prosperous time in America, and while the acquisitions overseen by Harshe may have been "haphazard," they helped to attract legions of museumgoers. By 1933, due to nationwide economic troubles, several programs sponsored by the museum had to be curtailed. Nevertheless, Chicago mounted another spectacular international exposition in 1933, the Century of Progress, and the Art Institute's parallel exhibition attracted 1.5 million visitors between June 1 and November 1. One of the highlights of the show was James Whistler's *Arrangement in Gray and Black: The Artist's Mother,* on loan from the Louvre.

Educating the Public under Daniel Rich: 1938–58

Harshe's successor, Daniel Catton Rich, joined the museum staff as editor of its *Bulletin.* When he took over as director in 1938, he vowed to strengthen the museum's educational programs and its curatorial staff. A renewed effort to connect to the public—via lectures, tours, and film programs—characterized Rich's tenure. Rich hired Katharine Kuh, one of the first important women in American museum history, and she oversaw the Gallery of Art Interpretation and eventually became the Art Institute's first curator of modern painting and sculpture. In 1947, the museum held the first major Georgia O'Keeffe retrospective, and in similar exhibits it helped broaden the canon of Western Art. Daniel Catton Rich also saw the importance of diversifying the type of art on exhibition; the Department of Primitive Art (which would later be renamed the Department of Africa, Oceania, and the Americas) opened in 1957.

The postwar years saw a series of expansive exhibitions focusing on themes including French tapestry, art from Vienna, and religious art, as well as single-artist retrospectives of van

Gogh, Cézanne, and Seurat. These shows were the forerunners of the "blockbuster" extravaganzas that came to characterize American museum life and economics in the 1980s and 1990s.

In presenting both "hard" and "easy" art, Rich's Art Institute of Chicago managed to challenge the public without ever losing its favor, though an exhibition of "Abstract and Surrealist American Art" in 1947 became a lightning rod for reactionary criticism, and Rich was even accused of communist tendencies. Such obstacles appear not have interfered with the museum's successful campaign of 1951–52, during which $2 million was raised. This was the first time the Art Institute appealed directly to the public for financial support. In 1958, his last year as director, in addition to mounting the Seurat retrospective, Rich also declined to exhibit a selection of watercolors by Winston Churchill. The museum, he explained, was not in the business of exhibiting work by amateurs.

By this time, the Art Institute's painting collection was impressive. Its greatest strengths were in nineteenth-century French paintings and old Flemish and old Italian works. As John Maxon wrote in his introductory essay to a 1970 catalogue, "The collection does not cover the whole history of Western painting with equal emphasis. But what it covers, it covers gloriously."

Expanding the Institute's Reach: 1970s–80s

In the 1970s, the Art Institute undertook construction of a large addition, extending the building eastward to Columbus Avenue. This addition was completed in 1977 by Skidmore, Owings & Merrill, the city's most famous architectural firm. Expansion of another kind continued as James N. Wood became director of the Art Institute in 1980 and made it his mission to broaden the historical scope of the Art Institute's exhibition program, moving beyond the now-familiar strengths of the European painting collection. Departments of photography and architecture were also formed during his tenure. In an afterword to the catalogue of an exhibition commemorating the 100th anniversary of the museum's relocation to the Michigan Avenue address, Wood gave an eloquent summary of his vision as director: "I am convinced that a democratic society will and must always demand equal access to the experience of original works of art."

Whatever else Wood accomplished as director, it is likely that he will be best remembered for the Claude Monet retrospective of 1995. Monet had long been one of the museum's most popular artists, and the advertising campaign and celebration of the exhibit in the media created a furious demand for tickets. Nearly a million people came to see the show in a four-month period, and it had an substantial impact on the Art Institute, on the city of Chicago, and on art museums all over the world. Sales to the public of year-long memberships to the Art Institute skyrocketed from 90,000 to more than 150,000, and the gift shop netted $1.5 million—a four-month total that approximately equaled the shop's net of the entire previous year. Monet posters, umbrellas, and coffee mugs sold in incredible numbers, inspiring other museums to market their own blockbuster exhibits in similar ways.

While memberships and gift shop sales were important to the Art Institute's financial health, donations continued to be the museum's primary avenue for acquiring works. The Japanese government presented the Art Institute with $1 million in 1989, a gift that assisted in the remodeling of the Galleries of Chinese, Japanese, and Korean Art, and in the construction of an unusually serene gallery for Japanese screens, which was designed by Tadao Ando. Corporate donors also became increasingly important to the Institute. The Sara Lee Corporation, for example, would make a sizable gift in 1998 of a selection of late 19th-century and early 20-century art, including important works by Edgar Degas, Camille Pissarro, Henri Matisse, and Alberto Giacometti.

While painting was the Art Institute's forte, it offered many other attractions, and the specializations tended to reflect the interests of its benefactors. A partial listing of its deepest reserves would include West African sculpture, Japanese woodblock prints donated by the Buckingham family, decorative paperweights donated by Arthur Rubloff, and a reconstruction of the trading room from the Chicago Stock Exchange (designed in 1893–94 by Dankmar Adler and Louis Sullivan).

Also during this time, the museum followed a national trend of catering to children with the Kraft General Foods Education Center designed, according to the Institute, "to present accessible art experiences to young people"; the center opened in time for the first day of school in the fall of 1992.

The Late 1990s and Beyond

American museums welcomed 225 million visitors in 1997. This figure seemed to contradict the idea that Americans had become a stay-at-home culture in which television and the Internet represented the sole forms of entertainment. Nevertheless, the museum did face the challenge of staying relevant at the turn of the century, balancing its obligation to enlighten the public with concessions to its short attention spans and diminished cultural literacy. The Art Institute took a leadership role in determining this new course, maintaining a sense of its own legacy as it did. The historian Neil Harris wrote, "The Art Institute's deep identification with the life of Chicago and the Midwest, the fierce pride it has elicited (and demanded) from donors and supporters, its characteristic self-promotion, and its efforts, more than once in every generation, to reinvent its mission and methods, are among the ingredients that have supplied its special character."

In 1999, The Art Institute of Chicago announced plans for a sculpture garden and another expansion, to be designed by internationally famous architect Renzo Piano. This announcement made the Art Institute one of 60 museums in the country enlarging their quarters at the end of the 20th century. This museum boom has been attributed to steady increases in the stock market and to the aging of the population, not to mention a general atmosphere of public-spiritedness that has particularly benefited museums. Architecture critic Herbert Muschamp has analyzed the phenomenon, writing, "No longer merely the ornament of power, culture is a power in its own right." After listing such cultural locales as concert halls and botanic gardens, he asserted, "The museum occupies a privileged place in the hierarchical scheme of things."

Further Reading

The Art Institute of Chicago Museum Studies, Special Issue, One Hundred Years at the Art Institute: A Centennial Celebration, Chicago: Art Institute of Chicago, 1993.

Dobrzynsky, Judith H. "They're Building a Lot More Than Their Collections," *New York Times,* April 21, 1999, p. D13.

Harris, Neil, *Chicago's Dream, A World's Treasure: The Art Institute, 1893–1993,* Chicago: The Art Institute of Chicago, 1993.

Maxon, John, *The Art Institute of Chicago,* New York: Thames and Hudson, 1970.

Muschamp, Herbert M. "Culture's Power Houses: The Museum Becomes the Engine of Urban Redesign," *New York Times,* April 21, 1999, p. D1.

—Mark Swartz

AT&T Corporation

32 Avenue of the Americas
New York, New York 10013
U.S.A.
(212) 387-5400
(800) 222-0300
Fax: (212) 387-5695
Web site: http://www.att.com

Public Company
Incorporated: 1885 as American Telephone and
     Telegraph Company
Employees: 107,800
Sales: $53.22 billion (1998)
Stock Exchanges: New York Philadelphia Boston
     Midwest Pacific Tokyo London Paris Geneva Brussels
Ticker Symbol: T
NAIC: 51331 Wired Telecommunications Carriers;
     513322 Cellular & Other Wireless Telecommunica-
     tions; 51334 Satellite Telecommunications; 541611
     Administrative Management & General Management
     Consulting Services; 522210 Credit Card Issuing;
     514191 Internet Access Providers; 513210 Cable
     Broadcasting Networks

The predecessor of AT&T Corporation, the American Telephone and Telegraph Company, was the largest corporation in the world for much of the 20th century. A government-regulated monopoly for most of its existence, it built most of the U.S. telephone system and was the standard of the worldwide telecommunications industry. It was dismembered in 1984 as a consequence of an action by the U.S. Department of Justice (DOJ) and through a consent decree signed that year. Its local operating companies became separate entities, leaving AT&T with the long-distance segment of the business, the only remaining government-regulated aspect of the company. In 1995 it was divided into three more parts, with only the long-distance and other service-oriented businesses left under the name AT&T. Under new

CEO C. Michael Armstrong, the reconfigured company began moving toward offering a combination of telephone, television, and Internet services following the acquisitions of major cable providers TCI Communications and MediaOne.

Beginnings

AT&T had its origin in the invention of the telephone in 1876 by Alexander Graham Bell. In 1877 Bell and several financial partners formed the Bell Telephone Company, and in 1878 they formed the New England Telephone Company to license telephone exchanges in New England. The two companies licensed local operating companies in Chicago, New York, and Boston. Over the next year Bell and his backers sold a controlling interest in the companies to a group of Boston financiers.

The companies were soon embroiled in patent disputes with Western Union Telegraph Company, the world's largest telegraph company. During the dispute, the two Bell companies were consolidated into the National Bell Telephone Company, and Theodore J. Vail was named general manager. In November 1879, the patent suit was settled out of court. Western Union left the telephone business and sold its system of 56,000 telephones in 55 cities to Bell. Bell agreed to stay out of the telegraph business, and paid Western Union a 20 percent royalty on telephone equipment leases for the next 17 years. Between 1877 and 1881, Bell licensed numerous local operating companies as a way to promote the telephone without having to raise capital. The companies signed five- to ten-year contracts, under which Bell got $20 per telephone per year and the right to buy the licensee's property when the contract expired.

National became the American Bell Telephone Company in 1880 and obtained more capital at that time. Starting in 1881 Bell urged the locals to make the contracts permanent, rescinding Bell's right to buy the respective properties, but giving Bell variously 30 to 50 percent ownership of the operating companies. The companies could build long-distance lines to connect exchanges in their territories, but they were prohibited from connecting them with those of other operating companies or independent phone companies. Bell thus became a partner in the local telephone business, allowing Bell to influence the locals and conserve

Company Perspectives:

We aspire to be the most admired and valuable company in the world. Our goal is to enrich our customers' personal lives and to make their businesses more successful by bringing to market exciting and useful communications services, building shareowner value in the process.

capital for long-distance operations. American Bell needed large amounts of equipment, and in 1881 it acquired Western Electric, a major Western Union supplier, to serve as its manufacturer. Bell then consolidated into Western Electric several other manufacturers it had licensed to make telephones.

More long-distance lines were being built as telephone technology improved. In 1884 Bell built an experimental line between Boston and New York. The next year it added a Philadelphia—New York line. To construct, finance, and operate its long-distance system, Bell established the American Telephone and Telegraph Company in 1885 to operate as its long-distance subsidiary. At that time the nascent U.S. telephone system was primarily a series of unconnected local networks. Vail, who was named AT&T president, wanted to get a long-distance network in place before Bell's basic patents expired in 1894. By the time it established AT&T, Bell was in firm control of the telephone business. It regulated the operating companies' long-distance lines and Western Electric, their major supplier. It also had the right to take over their property if they violated their contracts.

In 1888 a huge blizzard in New England knocked most telephones out of service. The company responded by pushing to put more cables underground. Later that year it became clear that a long-distance network would cost more than planned, and AT&T floated $2 million in bonds to raise capital. The company returned to public investors frequently throughout its history to finance its ever-expanding enterprises. For decades AT&T stock was the most widely held in the world. To attract investors so often, AT&T was forced to be efficient, even though it lacked real competition for much of its history.

Technical advances came regularly. The first coin-operated public telephone was installed in 1889. During 1891 two-party and four-party service was introduced, and the first automatic dial system was patented. A New York-Chicago long-distance line opened in 1892, and Boston-Chicago and New York-Cincinnati lines were initiated in 1893.

Bell initially had a monopoly on the telephone because of its patents, but in 1894 its patent expired. Rather than compete by providing better and less expensive service, Bell often took the growing independent phone companies to court, claiming patent infringements. As Western Electric would not sell equipment to the independents, new manufacturers sprung up to accommodate them. The independents were particularly successful in rural areas in the West and Midwest where Bell did not provide service. By 1898 some cities had two unconnected phone systems, one Bell and one independent. This competition

forced Bell to expand faster than it otherwise would have. It jumped from 240,000 phones in 1892 to 800,000 in 1899.

The company needed capital to keep up with this expansion, and Massachusetts, where American Bell was based, presented far more regulatory interference than New York, where AT&T was based. As a result, AT&T in 1899 became the parent company of the Bell System until the breakup in 1984. AT&T's capital jumped from $20 million to more than $70 million. By 1900 AT&T was organizing itself into the vertical structure that characterized it for decades thereafter. It had assets of $120 million compared with a total of $55 million for the independents, but its finances were run overly conservatively and its service was reputedly poor.

Meanwhile, the telephone was having a dramatic impact on the United States, where large numbers of people still lived in the relative isolation of farms or small towns. The telephone lessened their isolation, and the response to the new invention was enthusiastic. The number of rural telephones shot from 267,000 in 1902 to 1.4 million in 1907. The telephone was coming to be viewed as indispensable by virtually all businesses and most private homes.

The Early 1900s: Fighting the Independents

Competition from independents continued to mount. Their rates were sometimes half of Bell's, and the United States was in an antimonopoly mood. Many rural communities started their own not-for-profit phone companies that were later sold to independents or Bell. By 1907 the independents operated 51 percent of all phones. AT&T was fighting back, having made the decision to take on the independents when it moved and changed its name. The company's first and most effective move was to slash rates. The arrogance of early company officials was replaced by a desire to please customers. AT&T also bought out independents, set up its own "independents," and used its political and financial clout to strangle competitors. AT&T's greatest advantage was its virtual monopoly of long-distance service—which it refused to let independents use.

The invention of a certain electric device, the loading coil, in 1899 gave long-distance service a push by allowing smaller-diameter wires to be used, which made underground long-distance cables feasible. They were implemented for an underground New York—Philadelphia line in 1906, but long-distance signals remained weak and difficult to hear until the invention of the vacuum-tube repeater in 1912.

Competition had given AT&T a necessary push, forcing it to expand and grow, but it also weakened its finances. Between 1902 and 1906 debt grew from $60 million to $200 million. Through a series of bond purchases starting in 1903, financier J. P. Morgan tried to wrest control of the company from the Boston capitalists, beginning a free-for-all that lasted several years. When the dust cleared in 1907, Morgan and his New York and London backers had won, and they brought back Vail as president. Vail had left in 1887 because of differences with the Bostonians, whose view was focused narrowly on short-term profit. Vail and his backers had a wider vision than the Bostonians, believing they should create a comprehensive, nationwide communications system.

In 1907 AT&T boasted 3.12 million telephones in service, but had a terrible public image, low staff morale, poor service, serious debts, and a bevy of technological problems. Within a decade Vail turned the company around, making it a model of corporate success. He soon sold millions of dollars in bonds by offering them at a discount to shareholders, which reestablished confidence in the company. He also dramatically increased research and development, hiring talented young scientists and laying the foundation for what would, in 1925, become Bell Labs. Vail concentrated the company's visionaries into central management and left day-to-day network decisions to workers more interested in practical questions. For its first two decades AT&T had put profits for its shareholders above service for its customers; Vail was one of the first U.S. business leaders to balance profit with customer satisfaction.

At the same time, Vail was a monopolist, believing competition had no place in the telephone industry. He and Morgan set out to make AT&T the sole supplier of U.S. telecommunications services. In 1910 Vail became president of Western Union after AT&T bought 30 percent of Western's stock. For the first time telegrams could be sent and delivered by phone. Telephone and telegraph lines could back each other up in emergencies. AT&T gobbled up independent phone companies at an ever-increasing rate. When Morgan found an independent in financial trouble, he used his power as a leading banker to squeeze its credit, often forcing it to sell to AT&T. By 1911 AT&T had bought so many small independents that Vail consolidated them into a smaller number of state and regional companies. AT&T's ownership was motivated partly by profit, but also by the desire to ensure good service.

Antimonopoly pressures from consumers and government began to mount on AT&T well before then. A crucial turning point came in 1913, after Morgan's death, when Vail decided to sell Western Union and allow independents access to AT&T's long-distance lines. The move cost $10 million and ended AT&T's dream of a national telecommunications monopoly, but it won AT&T respect and ended growing pressure to dismember it.

Coast to Coast Long Distance Achieved in 1915

By that time AT&T was working on the first coast-to-coast telephone line, using loading coils and repeaters. On January 25, 1915, Alexander Graham Bell, in New York, and former collaborator, Thomas Watson, in San Francisco, engaged in a coast-to-coast repeat of the first-ever telephone conversation 39 years earlier. AT&T was also making important progress in automatic switching systems and sent the first transatlantic radio message in 1915. As the telephone became a matter of national interest, pressure for federal regulation mounted, and Vail welcomed it as long as regulators were independent.

During World War I the AT&T network was used for domestic military communications. AT&T also set up extensive radio and telephone communications lines in France. The war pushed AT&T's resources to the limit, with a $118 million construction budget for 1917. In 1918, a year in which AT&T had ten million phones in service, the U.S. government took over the telephone system. The government set rates and put AT&T under a branch of the post office, although the company

continued to be run by its board of directors. One of the government's first decisions was to start a service connection charge. It then raised both local and long distance rates. Lower rates had been touted as a major benefit of public ownership. When the rates went up, support for government ownership collapsed, and in August 1919 the government gave up its control of AT&T. Vail retired in the same year, leaving the presidency to Harry Bates Thayer, and died in 1920.

AT&T grew rapidly as a regulated monopoly during the laissez-faire 1920s. The Graham Act of 1921 exempted telephony from the Sherman Antitrust Act. Of almost 14 million telephones in the United States in 1921, the Bell System controlled 64 percent; and 32 percent, although owned by independents, were plugged into the AT&T network. Commercial radio boomed, and AT&T entered cross-licensing patent agreements with General Electric, Westinghouse, and Radio Corporation of America, with which it was soon embroiled in legal disputes. By the end of 1925, AT&T had a national network of 17 radio stations. AT&T put its first submarine cable into service between Key West, Florida, and Havana, Cuba, in 1921. In 1925 Bell Labs became a separate company, jointly funded by AT&T and Western Electric. The same year, Thayer retired and was succeeded by Walter S. Gifford, who served for the next 23 years. His influence on the U.S. telephone industry was second only to Vail's.

Gifford quickly got AT&T out of radio and other side ventures, although it tried to establish a controlling interest in motion picture sound technology in the late 1920s. He reduced the fee licensees paid from the 4.5 percent of gross revenue established in 1902, to four percent in 1926, and two percent in 1928. AT&T stockholders grew from 250,000 in 1922 to nearly 500,000 in 1929. In 1929 Bell Labs gave the first U.S. demonstration of color television. By 1932 AT&T had the second largest financial interest in the film industry, but sold it in 1936.

The first years of the Great Depression badly hurt AT&T. Many subscribers could no longer afford telephones. AT&T sales for 1929 were $1.05 billion; by 1933 they were $853 million. Western Electric sales in 1929 were $411 million; 1933 sales were $70 million. Western Electric laid off 80 percent of its employees, and AT&T laid off 20 percent.

By 1933 telephone use began growing again, and by 1937 it exceeded pre-Depression levels. During the late 1930s the newly formed Federal Communications Commission (FCC) conducted a long, damaging investigation of AT&T's competitive practices that reopened the battle over AT&T as a monopoly. In 1939 AT&T had assets of $5 billion, by far the largest amount of capital ever controlled by a corporation up to that time. It controlled 83 percent of all U.S. telephones and 98 percent of long-distance wires. Subsidiary Western Electric manufactured 90 percent of all U.S. telephone equipment. The FCC's final report was initially ignored due to the outbreak of World War II but had significant impact later.

Growth During World War II

Telephone use, particularly long distance, grew tremendously during World War II, with 1.4 million new telephones installed in 1941 alone. Western Electric and Bell Labs devoted themselves primarily to military work from 1942 to 1945, filling thousands of government contracts and making technological innovations. The most important work was in radar, the experience that gave AT&T a huge lead when microwave radio relay became the principal means of transmitting long-distance telephone and television signals in the postwar period.

The FCC forced AT&T to lower rates during the war, and its plants and infrastructure were worn out by wartime production. AT&T's business boomed after the war, as population and prosperity increased, and the habit of long-distance telephoning acquired during the war continued. The company installed more than three million telephones in 1946. Benefits of wartime technology were many. Moving vehicles were brought into the telephone system by radio in 1946. Coaxial cable was first used to take television signals over long distances in 1946. Microwave radio began transmitting long-distance calls in 1947. Bell Labs brought out the transistor, a replacement for the vacuum tube and one of the important inventions of the 20th century, in 1948; its inventors won the Nobel Prize in 1956.

The end of the war brought serious labor trouble. AT&T and the National Federation of Telephone Workers faced off over wages, working conditions, and benefits, producing a nationwide strike in 1947. Public opinion went against the strikers, and the eventual compromise favored AT&T.

Gifford retired in 1948 and Leroy A. Wilson became president. His first task was to push a rate increase past government regulators. He got one in 1949 that helped AT&T sell more stock to raise needed capital. As an outgrowth of the 1930s FCC investigation, the U.S. Department of Justice filed suit in 1949, seeking to split Western Electric from AT&T. AT&T succeeded in delaying the case until the Eisenhower administration, which was not as interested in regulation, took power. In the meantime the government talked Western Electric into taking over the management of an advanced weapons research laboratory. It formed Sandia Corp. in 1949 to do so. In the 1950s Western Electric worked on the Nike antiaircraft missiles, making $112.5 million on the venture. Western and Bell Labs worked with others on a huge air-defense radar system. These defense projects gave AT&T a powerful lever against the antitrust suit. In a consent decree in 1956 AT&T agreed to limit its business to providing common-carrier services and to limit Western Electric's to providing equipment for the Bell System, except for government contracts. The antitrust case was settled on this basis.

In 1951 Wilson died and Cleo Craig became president. In the next few years AT&T made it possible to dial directly to other cities without using an operator. This and ensuing developments enabled long-distance charges to be repeatedly reduced. In 1955 AT&T laid the first transatlantic telephone cable, jointly owned with the British Post Office and the Canadian Overseas Telecommunications Corporation. Craig retired in 1956, and Frederick R. Kappel became president.

AT&T was in enviable financial shape by the late 1950s, although some accused it of getting there by overcharging subscribers. The booming U.S. economy led to unprecedented calling volumes—particularly from teenagers, many of whom were getting their own telephones. Telephones moved from shared party lines to private lines, and telephone services like weather and time announcements became widespread, adding

further revenue. AT&T split its stock three-for-one in 1959 and two-for-one in 1964. By 1966 AT&T had three million stockholders and nearly one million employees. In 1954 AT&T began offering telephones in colors other than black. In 1961 it developed Centrex, a system in which an office maintained its own automatic switching exchange; in 1963 it offered the first Touch-Tone service; in 1968 it brought out the Trimline phone, with the dial built into the handset. By 1965 the Bell System served 85 percent of all households in the areas in which it operated, compared with 50 percent in 1945, and was providing a vast array of services at a variety of rates.

Expanding into Space: Bellcom and Telstar

AT&T formed Bellcom to supply most of the communications and guidance systems for the U.S. space program from 1958 to 1969. Bell Labs worked intensively on satellite communications, and the first AT&T satellite, *Telstar,* was launched in 1962. Comsat, a half-public, half-private company handling U.S. satellite communications, was founded in 1962, with AT&T owning 27.5 percent at a cost of $58 million.

AT&T worked on an electronic switching system throughout the 1950s and 1960s. The project was more complicated than expected, and by the time the first electronic equipment was installed in 1965, AT&T had spent about $500 million on the project. The speed and automation that electronic switches gave the phone system, however, made possible the vast increases in traffic volume in the 1970s and 1980s, as the United States moved to an information-based society.

In the 1950s and 1960s other companies began trying to capture specific portions of AT&T's business. The Hush-a-Phone Company marketed a plastic telephone attachment that reduced background noise. Microwave Communications Inc. (MCI) tried to establish private-line service between Chicago and St. Louis. Carter Electronics Corporation marketed a device that connected two-way radios with the telephone system. AT&T responded by forbidding the connection of competitors' equipment to the Bell System. Several FCC investigations followed, with decisions that created competition for terminal equipment and intercity private-line service. AT&T began to face serious competition for the first time in 50 years.

Kappel retired in 1967 and was replaced by H. I. Romnes, a former president of Western Electric. AT&T's earnings were leveling off after tremendous growth in the early 1960s. There also were service problems in 1969 and 1970, with numerous consumer complaints in New York. Similar predicaments followed in Boston, Denver, and Houston. AT&T borrowed money and raised rates to pay for repairs.

More serious problems were beginning for AT&T. In the early 1970s sales by the interconnect industry were growing, and businesses were buying telephone equipment from AT&T competitors. The U.S. Equal Employment Opportunity Commission accused AT&T of discriminating against women and minorities. AT&T, without admitting it had done so, signed consent decrees under which it agreed to increase the hiring, promotion, and salaries of women and minorities.

MCI claimed AT&T was still preventing it from competing and filed an antitrust lawsuit in 1974. The situation became disastrous when the DOJ filed another antitrust suit later in 1974, this time asking for the dismemberment of AT&T. The DOJ charged that AT&T had used its dominant position to suppress competition. The suit dragged on for years.

During the years of the suit, AT&T continued to grow. Both 1980 and 1981 were years of record profits. The $6.9 billion AT&T made in 1981 was the highest profit for any company to that time.

The Breakup of the Bell System

The DOJ suit finally came to trial in 1981. By then AT&T and the government both wanted to settle the case. AT&T longed to get into computers and information services, but was prevented by its 1956 agreement. In 1982 the FCC required AT&T to set up a separate, unregulated subsidiary called American Bell to sell equipment and enhanced services. In January 1982 AT&T and the DOJ jointly announced a deal to break up the Bell System, while freeing the remainder of AT&T to compete in non-long-distance areas such as computers.

Federal Judge Harold Greene gave final approval for the AT&T breakup in August 1983. At that time AT&T was the largest corporation in the world; its $155 billion in assets made it larger than General Motors, Mobil, and Exxon combined. After the breakup, on January 1, 1984, AT&T had $34 billion in assets. Its net income dropped from $7.1 billion to $2.1 billion, and its workforce from 1.09 million to 385,000. Its 22 regional operating companies were split off into seven regional holding companies, and AT&T lost the right to use the Bell name. AT&T stockholders received one share in each of the regional companies for every ten AT&T shares they owned. AT&T also lost the highly profitable Yellow Pages, which went to the regional companies.

The new AT&T consisted of two primary parts: AT&T Communications, the long-distance business, and AT&T Technologies, a group of other businesses that mainly involved the manufacture and sale of telecommunications equipment for consumers and businesses. Western Electric was broken up and folded into AT&T Technologies. Long distance was expected to provide the bulk of short-term revenue for the new AT&T, but the unregulated technologies group, backed by Bell Labs, was expected to quickly blossom. AT&T Technologies initially concentrated on switching and transmissions systems for telephone companies. AT&T was losing ground to competitors in that sector and wanted to fight back. The company also worked on telephone-equipment sales, sold through AT&T phone centers and such retailers as Sears. American Bell changed its name to AT&T Information Systems and began pushing computers. AT&T International quickly signed a deal with the Dutch company N.V. Philips to sell switching equipment throughout the world, setting up AT&T Network Systems International.

To help pay for the breakup, AT&T took a fourth-quarter charge of $5.2 billion in 1984, the largest to that time. AT&T, however, was now free to go into computers, a field it had longed to get into since the 1956 consent decree, and the company began spending hundreds of millions of dollars to develop and market a line of computers. James E. Olson became president of AT&T in 1985, cutting 24,000 jobs from the infor-

mation division later that year to improve its profits. In 1986 Olson became chairman, and Robert E. Allen became president. Olson concentrated on centralizing management and refocusing company strategy around the idea of managing the flow of information.

The company chose Brussels, Belgium, as the site for its regional headquarters serving Europe, the Middle East, and Africa. It also began joint ventures with companies in Spain, Italy, Ireland, Denmark, South Korea, and Taiwan to get its telecommunications products into foreign markets. Still, foreign revenues accounted for only ten percent of company earnings, compared with 40 percent for many other U.S.-based multinationals. Company earnings declined because of a slumping business equipment market and greater than expected reorganization costs. Earnings also suffered from a drop in rental revenues as more AT&T customers decided to buy their telecommunications equipment outright.

Meanwhile AT&T's computer operations were in trouble. The company had developed a new operating system, Unix, for its computers. Unix had some advantages; but the users of personal computers were not familiar with it, manufacturers of larger computers were committed to their own proprietary systems, and buyers stayed away. AT&T computer operations lost $1.2 billion in 1986 alone. At the end of the year the company restructured its computer operations to concentrate on telecommunications-based computers and computer systems. It custom designed a system for American Express that automatically phoned customers while putting customer information on a terminal screen. At the end of 1986 AT&T cut another 27,400 jobs and took a $3.2 billion charge. Income for the year was only $139 million.

In 1987 the DOJ recommended that the regional operating companies be allowed to compete with AT&T in long distance and telecommunications equipment manufacturing—its two core businesses. The idea was unacceptable to Judge Harold Greene, overseer of the AT&T breakup. Because of fierce competition from MCI and other companies, AT&T retained 76 percent of the long-distance market, down from 91 percent in 1983.

Unix made some gains in 1986 and 1987, and AT&T formed the Archer Group, a consortium of computer makers manufacturing Unix systems. It included Unisys and Sun Microsystems. After nearly $2 billion in losses in computers, the data systems group finally signed a major contract with the U.S Air Force in 1988. The $929 million contract for minicomputers provided only a slim profit margin, but AT&T hoped that the deal would push its computers over the top, make Unix an industry standard, and lead to further government sales. Olson died in 1988, and Allen became chairman.

More Changes in the Late 1980s

MCI and others continued to erode AT&T's share of the $50 billion long-distance market, which stood at 68 percent at the end of 1988. To fight back, AT&T redeployed 2,500 employees to sales positions and aggressively tackled the business communications market. AT&T also took a $6.7 billion charge to modernize its telephone network and cut 16,000 positions. As a result, the company lost $1.7 billion in 1988, its first-ever loss for the year.

Some industry analysts, however, felt the company was finally turning around after four years of confusion and drift. It won two major government contracts that year. One, expected to earn AT&T $15 billion by 1989, was to build a new government telephone system. Competitor US Sprint Communications won a $10 billion contract for a second part of the same system. Regulators finally gave AT&T the right to match the low prices of MCI and US Sprint, leading to the end of the long-distance price wars waged since the AT&T breakup. AT&T showed a $2.7 billion profit for 1989, its largest since the breakup.

In mid-1990 AT&T raised its long-distance rates after low second-quarter earnings. It had been hurt by declining long-distance revenue and slow equipment sales. The company, however, soon made several important sales. It received an extension of a $100 million personal computer sale to American Airlines's Sabre Travel Information Network and signed an agreement to upgrade China's international communications system. AT&T made its first entry into Mexico's communications market, winning a $130 million contract from Mexico's national telephone company, Teléfonos de Mexico. It signed a $157 million contract to build an undersea fiber-optic cable between Hawaii and the U.S. mainland, and announced that it planned to build a high-capacity undersea cable between Germany and the United States, with Deutsche Bundespost Telekom. It also won a $600 million contract from GTE Corporation to build cellular network equipment.

Hoping to make money from its financial and information resources, AT&T launched a credit card, Universal Card, in early 1990. By late 1990 it was the eighth leading credit card in the United States, with revenue of $750 million. Wall Street analysts, however, expected the credit card's startup costs to hold back AT&T earnings until at least 1992. Bell Labs announced important breakthroughs in computer technology in 1990, including the world's first computer using light. Products based on the new technologies were years off, but AT&T continued to manufacture computers. AT&T signed an agreement with Japan's Mitsubishi Electric Corporation to share memory-chip technology, and licensed technology from Japan's NEC Corporation to make semiconductors. Late in the year, Philips, under financial pressure, sold back its 15 percent stake in AT&T Network Systems International.

In the early 1990s AT&T's overseas ventures began bearing fruit. About 15 percent of its revenue, more than $5 billion yearly, came from international calling and sales to foreign buyers of equipment and services. In 1991 AT&T made a major acquisition in the computer industry, buying NCR Corporation through an exchange of stock valued at $7.4 million. AT&T officials believed the purchase of NCR, which accounted for about 60 percent of its sales in international markets, would put AT&T on the path to becoming a truly global company and a leader in networked computing. NCR had introduced more new products than any other computer company in the preceding year. NCR officials saw advantages of the merger to be an increased customer base, access to the research and development capabilities of Bell Labs, and the addition of AT&T's technical, marketing, and sales resources.

AT&T's fortunes looked solid following the NCR acquisition. The company's stock price was climbing, and several of its previously sluggish operations posted their best earnings figures in years. One area in which AT&T needed market presence was cellular telephone service, though the company was the largest manufacturer of cell phone system switching devices. In August 1993 the company acquired McCaw Cellular Communications for $12.8 billion in stock. The Kirkland, Washington-based McCaw operated one of the largest cellular systems in the United States, with coverage of a third of the country.

Division into Three Companies

Despite these positive developments, AT&T was still having problems. NCR in particular was not earning its keep and lost $600 million in 1994. AT&T's long-distance service profits were accounting for the bulk of the corporation's income, but competition was growing ever fiercer. On September 20, 1995 the company announced it was splitting up yet again, this time into three separate entities. The largest would be known as AT&T Corporation and consist primarily of the long distance businesses, AT&T Wireless, the Universal Credit Card, and AT&T Labs. The next largest would be Lucent Technologies, which would consist of the company's consumer and business products operations and Bell Labs. The smallest would be NCR Corporation, consisting more or less of what it had been when AT&T purchased it four years earlier. The breakup, the largest corporate restructuring in history, was accomplished by means of a spin-off of stock to AT&T shareholders. Some 40,000 of the company's employees were also expected to lose their jobs.

Other developments at this time included AT&T's first foray into the world of cyberspace, with the introduction of an array of business and home Internet access services. Also, in February 1996, Congress passed a new telecommunications act which ended monopolies for providers of local phone service. AT&T vowed to become a presence in the local service arena again, though this would entail leasing lines from the largely unfriendly Baby Bells.

In the months following the company's restructuring, corporate morale and investor confidence ebbed as AT&T's efforts to fine-tune the reconfiguration proceeded slowly. CEO Bob Allen, nearing his planned retirement date of January 1998, saw his chosen successor rejected by the board in mid-1997. Finally, on November 1, Hughes Electronics CEO C. Michael Armstrong was approved to take over the reins at AT&T, and Allen stepped down.

Armstrong quickly set about cutting fat and implementing new strategies. He sold the company's credit card unit to Citibank for $3.5 billion, and its communications outsourcing business to Cincinnati Bell for $625 million. He purchased Teleport Communications Group, a local exchange business-service carrier in New York and 65 other cities, for $11.3 billion. International efforts, always a weak point with AT&T, were boosted by the formation of a joint venture with British Telecom. Advertising expenses were cut for a second time in two years, and an additional 18,000 layoffs were announced. Armstrong's biggest move during his first year came in the summer, when he cut a deal to purchase cable television giant TCI for $53.5 billion in stock.

In October the company merged its Wireless Services division with Vanguard Cellular Systems, a Northeast U.S.-based cell phone company with 625,000 subscribers. AT&T also started its own "dial-around" service, Lucky Dog. A host of new competitors had emerged who were offering low residential long-distance rates via special 7-digit access numbers. The heavily advertised Lucky Dog was an attempt to tap into this market, and was promoted with no mention of its corporate owner. In December, a deal worth $5 billion was reached to buy IBM's Global Network Internet access business, which was expected to provide a starting point for the joint venture with British Telecom.

Armstrong's first year performance was winning rave reviews, and he continued at full throttle in 1999 with the $60 billion acquisition of a second major cable provider, MediaOne. In a heated battle, AT&T had outbid both Comcast and Microsoft. As a sop to the latter, an agreement was reached to sell the computer giant $5 billion in AT&T stock, and to use Microsoft products in the company's new cable boxes. Deals with Comcast and Time Warner also brought more cable subscribers to the company. Armstrong's vision for AT&T's future was to offer both telephone and Internet services through the newly acquired cable TV networks, taking advantage of the large data-transmission capacity they offered. This would eliminate the slow download speed experienced by Internet users who connected via telephone line and modem. Billions of dollars would have to be invested to retrofit cable systems for interactivity and telephone use for the plan to succeed.

This new direction would take AT&T full circle, back into the direct-wired residential telecommunications business it had consisted of before the 1984 breakup. The company's big gamble would take years to pay off, but many were betting on AT&T to succeed. For the first time since the breakup of the Bell System, AT&T seemed to be coming to grips with both its past and its future, as it began to gird for the challenges of the changing telecommunications market of the 21st century.

Principal Subsidiaries

AT&T Campuswide Access Solutions, Inc.; AT&T Capital Holdings, Inc.; AT&T Communications Americas, Inc.; AT&T Communications of Illinois, Inc.; AT&T Communications of Indiana, Inc.; AT&T Communications of New Jersey, Inc.; AT&T Communications of Ohio, Inc.; AT&T Communications of Pennsylvania, Inc.; AT&T Communications of the Midwest, Inc.; AT&T Communications of the Mountain States, Inc.; AT&T Communications of the South Central States, Inc.; AT&T Communications of the Southern States, Inc.; AT&T Communications of the Southwest, Inc.; AT&T Communications of Virginia, Inc.; AT&T Communications of Washington, D.C., Inc.; AT&T Communications of West Virginia, Inc.; AT&T Communications of Wisconsin, Inc.; AT&T Global Network Services; AT&T Microelectronica de España S.A.

(Spain); AT&T Network Systems International B.V. (Netherlands); AT&T of Puerto Rico, Inc.; AT&T of Tampa, Inc.; AT&T of the Virgin Islands, Inc.; AT&T Solutions, Inc.; AT&T Web Site Services; AT&T Wireless Services, Inc.; AT&T WorldNet Service; Actuarial Sciences Associates, Inc.; Alascom, Inc.; Istel Group, Ltd. (U.K.); Liberty Media Group; Liberty Media International; Lucky Dog Phone Co.; Transoceanic Communications, Inc.

Principal Divisions

Consumer Markets Division; Business Services; AT&T Solutions; AT&T Wireless Services; AT&T Local Services Division; Network Services; AT&T Labs.

Further Reading

Brooks, John, *Telephone: The First Hundred Years,* New York: Harper and Row, 1976.

Evans, David S., ed., *Breaking Up Bell: Essays on Industrial Organization and Regulation,* New York: Elsevier Science Publishing Co., 1983.

Finneran, Michael, "The AT&T Breakup: A New Model for a Global Telecom Colossus," *Business Communications Review,* November 1995, pp. 78–9.

Goldblatt, Henry, "AT&T Finally Has an Operator," *Fortune,* February 16, 1998, pp. 79–80.

Greenfield, Karl Taro, "Ma Everything!," *Time,* May 17, 1999, pp. 58–60.

Greenwald, John, "AT&T's Power Shake," *Time,* July 6, 1998, pp. 76–8.

Kirkpatrick, David, "AT&T Has the Plan," *Fortune,* October 16, 1995, pp. 84–6.

——, "Could AT&T Rule the World?," *Fortune,* May 17, 1993, p. 54.

Kupfer, Andrew, "AT&T Gets Lucky," *Fortune,* November 9, 1998, pp. 108–10.

——, "AT&T: Ready to Run, Nowhere to Hide," *Fortune,* April 29, 1996, pp. 116–18.

——, "AT&T's $12 Billion Cellular Dream," *Fortune,* December 12, 1994, p. 100.

Loomis, Carol J., "AT&T Has No Clothes," *Fortune,* February 5, 1996, pp. 78–80.

McCarroll, Thomas, "How AT&T Plans to Reach Out and Touch Everyone," *Time,* July 5, 1993, p. 44.

Scheisel, Seth, "AT&T Conjures Up Its Vision for Cable, But Can It Deliver?," *New York Times,* May 7, 1999, p. 1C.

Sims, Calvin, "AT&T's New Call to Arms," *New York Times,* January 22, 1989.

Slutsker, Gary, "The Tortoise and the Hare," *Forbes,* February 1, 1993, p. 66.

Snyder, Beth, "AT&T Joins Wave of Marketers Hiding IDs Behind New Brands: Lucky Dog Dial-Around Service Aims for Value-Conscious Crowd," *Advertising Age,* November 2, 1998, p. 17.

Trager, Louis, "AT&T Sticks to Consumer Path," *Interactive Week Online,* May 3, 1999.

—Scott M. Lewis
—updated by Frank Uhle

Barry Callebaut AG

Seefeldquai 17
CH-8034 Zurich
Switzerland
(41) 1 3886161
Web site: http://www.barry-callebaut.com

Public Company
Incorporated: 1850 as Callebaut; 1842 as Cacoa Barry
Employees: 3,543
Sales: SFr 2.16 billion (US $1.58 billion) (1998)
Stock Exchanges: Zürich
NAIC: 31132 Chocolate & Confectionery Manufacturing
from Cacao Beans

Franco-Belgo-Swiss Barry Callebaut AG is the world's leading manufacturer of chocolate and cocoa products for industrial and consumer use. A publicly traded subsidiary of Klaus J. Jacobs Holdings (KJJ), which owns some 67 percent of the company, Barry Callebaut has its corporate headquarters in Zurich, Switzerland, while maintaining its French and Belgian roots. Barry Callebaut operates some 20 cocoa processing and chocolate production facilities worldwide, including four factories in the United States and Canada and ten facilities in Europe, including The Netherlands, the United Kingdom, and Italy, as well as France and Belgium. The company also has entered new markets in the 1990s, opening a factory in Lodz, Poland to serve the Eastern European market and a state-of-the-art facility in Singapore, from which the company hopes to gain access to the potentially huge chocolate markets in Asia—that is, if the company can succeed in converting Asian taste buds to its products.

Barry Callebaut also is well represented in the Ivory Coast—the world's largest single producer of cocoa beans. The company operates four cocoa processing and refining plants, as well as holding a share of that country's cocoa crop. In all, Barry Callebaut transforms between 11 and 15 percent of the total worldwide cocoa crop. Along with its Ivory Coast plants, Barry Callebaut operates two cocoa bean processing factories in Cameroon. Barry Callebaut also operates, in addition to its production facilities, six Chocolate Schools—in Saint Hyacinthe, Quebec, Canada; Pennsauken, Pennsylvania; Meulan, France; Wieze, Belgium; Nervi, Italy; and in Singapore.

Product of a merger between Callebaut and Cacao Barry in 1996, Barry Callebaut provides a more or less complete range of *couverture* chocolates and other industrial use chocolates to the confectionery, ice cream, baked goods, dairy, and gourmet chocolate markets. Industrial cocoa and chocolates account for the majority of Barry Callebaut's revenues—in 1998 the industrial market represented 94 percent of the company's total sales of SFr 2.16 billion. Barry Callebaut also produces confectionery products for the consumer market; these sales represent the remaining six percent of the company's total sales.

Barry Callebaut went public in June 1998, listing on the Zurich Stock Exchange. The company remains controlled at nearly 67 percent by Swiss magnate Klaus J. Jacobs, architect of the consumer chocolate giant Jacobs Suchard, which was acquired by Philip Morris in the early 1990s. Jacobs, a former Olympic horseman and one of the wealthiest people in Switzerland, also holds 24 percent of Adecco, a European leader in the recruitment and temporary employment service market, as well the financial services company Allgemeine Finanzgesellschaft, in Germany.

300 Years of Chocolate History

The combined Barry and Callebaut operation represented some 300 years of chocolate history when Callebaut bought rival Barry in 1996. Led by Klaus J. Jacobs, the renamed Barry Callebaut became the world's single largest producer of industrial use chocolate and cocoa products, processing as much as 15 percent of the world's supply of raw cocoa.

Both companies traced their origins to the 19th century, yet both companies entered their respective core markets—cocoa and chocolate production—in the early decades of the 20th century. Cacao Barry was founded in 1842 by Charles Barry in Meulan, France. The Barry family entered cocoa production in 1920, building a facility in Meulan that would remain one of Cacao Barry's most important production facilities through the end of the century.

Company Perspectives:

The Core Values Of Barry Callebaut are Consistent Quality: *The uniformity of our production sites, together with the most up-to-date equipment and the know-how of our teams, guarantee a consistent quality throughout the world and thereby an unequalled security of supply.* Just In Time Delivery: *The geographical spread of our production units and the uniformity of production sites guarantee a just-in-time delivery in Europe, North America and Asia. This allows our customers to maintain a minimum stock, thereby reducing the risks of deterioration of the quality.* Ability and Support in Research & Development: *We are going to combine and substantially reinforce our worldwide know-how in the production sector while continuing to intensify the product development in order to allow our customers to better adapt to the changing needs of the consumers.* Technical Assistance: *Our experience in the cocoa and chocolate industry must be used for the benefits of our customers. Our teams will be at our customers' disposal in order to develop new products as well as assisting them with the start-up of new equipment so as to avoid any production difficulties.*

Belgium's Callebaut family entered the trade in 1850, operating a brewery, malt, and dairy company, before turning to chocolate production in 1911. The Callebaut family's original chocolate products were chocolate bars; chocolate *couverture,* or covering, products—extending the company's production of industrial use chocolate—were introduced in 1925. By then the Barry family company had been taken over by another family, the LaCarre family. The LaCarres would keep the Cacao Barry name, however.

Barry and Callebaut would operate, in large part, complementary product lines throughout the century, with the former processing raw cocoa for use by chocolate producers such as the latter. Nevertheless, Barry would gain a reputation for its own fine quality chocolate products—and especially its industrial use chocolates. Meanwhile, Callebaut's small family-run operation would benefit from the increasing worldwide interest in Belgian chocolates, considered by many to be the finest chocolates in the world. Callebaut began exporting its products in 1950, building up the Callebaut name in the European and North American markets.

During this time Barry began imposing itself as one of the world's premier cocoa products producers. Seeking to extend its activity to complete control of the cocoa production process, Barry initiated partnerships with the principal cocoa-producing countries. This course would lead the company to implant itself on the African continent. In 1952 Barry opened production facilities in Cameroon and in the chief cocoa bean producing nation of the Ivory Coast.

Barry's expanding grip on cocoa processing and cocoa products manufacturing would lead the company to withdraw from the consumer products segment in the mid-1960s in favor of continuing to boost its share of the industrial use cocoa market.

At the same time, Barry sought to expand its presence in the chief cocoa consuming markets, principally the European and North American markets. This expansion would lead the company to build or acquire factories in England, Canada, and in the United States, where the company acquired US Cocoa, one of the United States' leading cocoa powder producers.

Mergers and Acquisitions: 1970s–90s

Barry's expansion continued in the 1970s, including the acquisition of Italy's Sicao. Callebaut also was extending its presence in Italy, building a plant and opening one of its Chocolate Schools there. Meanwhile, Barry's control of the cocoa market increased with the acquisition of Cacao Processing United in Louviers, France; under Barry's leadership, the Louviers plant specialized in cocoa bean processing, grinding, and pressing, for the production of the principal cocoa products: cocoa powder, cocoa liquor, and cocoa butter. In 1974, Barry would take over one of its chief domestic competitors, with the acquisition of Belgium's Goemaere.

The 1980s, however, would see changes in ownership for both Barry and Callebaut. The Callebaut family business was taken over by Interfood, a subsidiary of Tobler-Suchard, maker of chocolate and cocoa consumer products. The Callebaut family did not withdraw from chocolate-making entirely: in 1982 Bernard Callebaut moved to Canada, where he founded Chocolaterie Bernard Callebaut. In 1983 Interfood was in turn bought up by Klaus J. Jacobs, then in the process of building a consumer chocolate empire. The resulting Jacobs Suchard became one of the world's leading chocolate manufacturers.

Barry, too, had lost its independence. In 1982 the company was taken over by fellow French concern Sacré et Denrées. Nevertheless, Barry, like Callebaut, continued operations under its own name. A crucial step in Barry's expansion was taken in 1985, when the company acquired Bensdorp, of Bussum in The Netherlands. The Bensdorp name was already known worldwide. Founded in 1840 by Gerard Bernadus Bensdorp, this company built its success on two processes that became important for the overall cocoa trade. These processes were the alkalization—or "Dutching"—of cocoa, and the separation of cocoa butter from the cocoa mass. The main Bussum facility was established in 1884, and it remained in operation through the 20th century. Under Barry's ownership, Bensdorp continued to produce its own branded cocoa products.

Jacobs Suchard continued its own expansion drive, acquiring the United Kingdom's S&A Lesne in 1985. In 1987 Jacobs Suchard purchased the Brach candy company, based in Chicago, Illinois, a move intended to enable Jacobs Suchard, by then with annual sales topping US $3 billion, to move into the U.S. consumer candy market. This acquisition, however, proved somewhat disastrous and would lead Jacobs into a retreat from the consumer chocolate market. Soon after the Brach acquisition, Klaus J. Jacobs Holdings announced its agreement to sell off its consumer candy holdings to the Philip Morris Group for a purchase price worth nearly US $2 billion. These operations were combined with Philip Morris's Kraft foods subsidiary to form the Kraft-Jacobs-Suchard division.

Klaus Jacobs, however, would retain Jacobs Suchard's industrial chocolates divisions. Jacobs would also be left holding the Brach candy subsidiary, which later merged with Tennessee-based rival Brock's in the 1990s. With his chocolate holdings pared down, Jacobs once again consolidated around the Callebaut industrial use chocolates operation. Jacobs would retain 100 percent control of Callebaut, keeping the company private until after its late 1990s merger with Cacao Barry.

In 1987 Barry added a new cocoa processing plant in its Meulan, France base. Not long after, the company found itself under new ownership. In 1992 the Société Centrale d'Investissement (SCI) acquired control of Cacao Barry. Under SCI's ownership, Barry expanded in the United Kingdom, adding a chocolate production unit there. SCI's losses—which reached FFr 8.3 billion in 1994—would, however, lead the investment group to bring in a new partner in that year, selling 49 percent of Cacao Barry to the Compagnie Nationale à Portefeuille (CNP), an investment vehicle held by the Albert Frère group.

Two years later, Klaus Jacobs gained access to Barry by purchasing, through Callebaut, CNP's share of Barry, before acquiring complete control from SCI. The purchase price was reportedly near US $400 million. The merger—which was named Barry Callebaut, with headquarters at Jacobs' Zurich base—created the world's leading producer of industrial use cocoa and chocolate. The merger also brought Jacobs back into the ranks of the world's leading chocolate manufacturers.

The company's existing operations underwent a restructuring, reinforcing the two companies' mostly complementary operations, while combining the two companies' brand recognition. Barry Callebaut's brand lines now included the Bensdorp brand of cocoa powders; the Barry and Callebaut brands of gourmet chocolate and cocoa products; and the new Barry Callebaut brand of industrial use cocoa powder, butter, liquor, and chocolate.

The merger nearly fell through, however. The company's extensive international implantation required it to receive clearance from the antitrust review boards of the countries concerned. The company met the most resistance in Callebaut's Belgian home, where the merger was, in fact, rejected. Barry Callebaut won out, however, on a technicality (the review board handed down their decision too late), and the merger was allowed to be completed. As part of the merger, Barry Callebaut agreed to sell off part of its Goemaere cocoa production unit.

Barry Callebaut's antitrust difficulties forced it to postpone a planned public offering. This was finally achieved in June 1998, when Barry Callebaut placed a listing on the Zurich Stock Exchange. Klaus Jacobs remained in control of the company, with nearly 70 percent of its shares. The public offering gave Barry Callebaut further impetus for a newly revigorated expansion campaign.

Barry Callebaut sought to extend its dominance of the Western European and North American chocolate markets—the primary chocolate markets worldwide—to those of other parts of the globe. On the Barry side, the company already had entered the Eastern European market in 1995, with the construction of Cacao Barry Polska, a chocolate production facility. Callebaut, meanwhile, had been looking to expand in the booming Asian market—where chocolate was beginning to find some popularity—by opening sales offices in Singapore and Hong Kong. In 1997 the company began construction on a state-of-the-art chocolate production facility in Singapore, with plans to extend distribution from there to such markets as Vietnam, China, Hong Kong, the Philippines, and Japan, as well as covering the New Zealand and Australian markets.

Barry Callebaut also moved to consolidate its main markets. In 1998 the company acquired Van Leer Chocolate, based in the United States. This acquisition was followed by the acquisition of Carma-Pfister AG, a Swiss-based chocolate company, in January 1999. These moves were followed soon after by the acquisition of Chadler Industrial de Bahia. Based in Brazil, the February 1999 purchase was aimed at enabling Barry Callebaut to enter the South American market. With a presence on nearly all the continents, and with ownership of nearly 15 percent of the world's cocoa supply, Barry Callebaut was certain to continue leading the world's cocoa and chocolate industries.

Principal Divisions

Barry Callebaut France; Barry Callebaut Belgium; Barry Callebaut United Kingdom; Barry Callebaut The Netherlands; Barry Callebaut Italy; Barry Callebaut Poland; Barry Callebaut Canada; Barry Callebaut United States; Barry Callebaut Ivory Coast; Barry Callebaut Singapore; Barry Callebaut Cameroon.

Further Reading

Forcino, Hallie, "Joining Strengths: Merger Synergies Benefit Barry Callebaut," *Candy Industry,* June 1, 1997, p. 72.

Hall, William, "Wraps Come Off of Chocolate's Best-Kept Secret," *Financial Times,* June 5, 1998.

"Le groupe chocolatier Barry Callebaut reprend le suisse Carma-Pfister," *Les Echoes,* January 19, 1999.

Parry, John, "Chocolate Man Won't Melt Away," *The European,* July 11, 1996, p. 21.

Tiffany, Susan, "Cacao Barry Accepts Challenge of an Emerging Market," *Candy Industry,* May 1, 1996, p. 32.

"Swiss Financier in Pounds 250m Cocoa Deal," *Financial Times,* July 10, 1996.

—M.L. Cohen

BDF ●●●●
Beiersdorf

Beiersdorf AG

Unnastrasse 48
D-20245 Hamburg
Germany
(49) (40) 49 09 0
Fax: (49) (40) 49 09 34 34
Web site: http://www.beiersdorf.com

Public Company
Incorporated: 1882 as P. Beiersdorf & Co.
Employees: 16,447
Sales: DM 6.28 billion (1997)
Stock Exchanges: Frankfurt
NAIC: 32562 Toilet Preparation Manufacturing; 325412
　　Pharmaceutical Preparation Manufacturing; 339113
　　Adhesive Tape, Medical, Manufacturing; 322222
　　Adhesive Tape (Except Medical)

Beiersdorf AG is an international company based in Hamburg, Germany, that develops, manufactures and distributes products in the areas of skin care, wound dressings, and sticking tapes. Beiersdorf reported international sales of over DM 6.2 billion in 1997, up over DM 500 million from its 1996 results. Cosmetic and personal care products accounted for 54.4 percent of the company's sales that year, led by its famous Nivea line of skincare products. The Medical Division, producer of Hansaplast and Curad bandages and Eucerin medicinal creams and salves, accounted for 23.4 percent of sales, while the tesa division, producer of a broad variety of tesa tapes and adhesive products, made up 22.1 percent of 1997 sales. Although concentrated in Germany and Europe, Beiersdorf was active in over 100 markets around the world.

Origins in the 1880s

The roots of Beiersdorf AG lie in the pharmacy that Paul C. Beiersdorf opened in Hamburg in the fall of 1880. After a while Beiersdorf began working with dermatologist Paul Gerson Unna on the development of a medicated adhesive bandage.

Unna had created salves that were effective in promoting the healing of damaged skin. However, no one had been able to develop an effective way to use them on a bandage; the secretions from the skin mixed with the salve and broke it down quickly, ruining its medical efficacy. Beiersdorf solved the problem by spreading a solution of gutta-percha, a substance similar to rubber, on gauze, making it impervious to the skin's moisture. It was a completely new product, a bandage that made possible a precise treatment of skin problems using exact dosages of medication. He gave it the unwieldy name Guttapercha-Pflastermulle, which was eventually shortened to Guttaplaste.

Beiersdorf received a patent for his invention on March 28, 1882, the date considered the founding of Beiersdorf AG. Dr. Unna told fellow physicians about Guttaplaste and described it frequently in his publications, and the bandages caught on quickly. Prescriptions for Guttaplaste soon outstripped Beiersdorf's ability to produce them in his pharmacy. In the summer of 1883, he closed it and established a small facility in Altona, a town just outside Hamburg where he could concentrate exclusively on his bandage business. By that time, Beiersdorf was manufacturing 54 different types of bandages. They were manufactured in the literal sense: nine workers produced the materials and medications by hand, then two other employees cut and packaged the bandages and wrote out the labels. Between 1882 and 1890 P. Beiersdorf & Co. began making other products as well: stick-salves, paste sticks, and medicinal soaps. But the adhesive bandage line, which soon grew to include 100 types, remained his bestselling and most important product.

In 1890 Beiersdorf's 16-year-old son committed suicide. So shaken was Beiersdorf that in May 1890 he decided to give up his business. The buyer he settled on was a 27-year-old pharmacist from Silesia, Oscar Troplowitz. According to their deal, Troplowitz would pay 60,000 Marks and take over sole ownership in July 1891 after working for a year as Beiersdorf's partner. When Troplowitz arrived in Altona in August 1890 to begin work, however, it was obvious that he and Beiersdorf would have difficulties working together. Troplowitz offered an

Company Perspectives:

Beiersdorf Company Principles: We direct all our efforts in all parts of the world to the needs of our customers and the demands of the market. We develop, manufacture, and distribute brand products of reliable quality and of high benefit to the consumer. Our company is uniform throughout the world, while at the same time it takes into account the requirements of each of our diverse markets. We concentrate our activities on areas in which we possess mature competence with the goal of being among the world's leading suppliers. We believe in fair, aggressive competition. We work continually for good profits, because they are a precondition for the company's successful long-term development. We believe that creative, needs-oriented research and development is a critical element for the company's security in the future. We do business in an ecologically responsible manner to protect the environment and natural conditions of our life. We cultivate open communication and reliable, long-term cooperation with our business partners and other social groups. We consider the qualifications, involvement and performance of our employees to be the decisive elements in Beiersdorf's success. As a result, we have a responsibility towards our employees.

extra 10,000 Marks to take over immediately and the company changed hands on October 1, 1890.

Developing New Products: The 1890s and 1900s

One of the first things Troplowitz did was to modernize Beiersdorf's primitive facilities. In 1892, he purchased a large parcel of land in Hamburg, built a factory, and introduced machine production—in particular for printing labels—which began on November 1, 1892. Troplowitz continued to work closely with Dr. Unna. One of their developments was a refinement of Guttaplaste, another medicated bandage called Paraplast, whose stiff cotton gauze made the gutta-percha solution unnecessary. Troplowitz also set out to create a surgical tape. The problem he faced was developing one that would adhere but without irritating the skin. His solution was to use zinc oxide, which counteracted the irritating effects of resin, the primary ingredient in bandage adhesives. The new medical tape was marketed under the name Leukoplast—from *leukos,* the Greek word for "white"—in 1901. Within a decade the tape was being used in hospitals throughout the world.

Working on Leukoplast led the Beiersdorf company into completely new product lines. Along the way, in 1897, Troplowitz had developed a brand new, self-adhering tape which was however not suitable for use on human skin. He marketed it instead, as a mechanic's tape under the names Citoplast and Lassoplast. Beiersdorf advertised for repairing bicycle tires and other mechanical uses, the first such tapes in the world. Another new product, developed around 1900, was a paste made from the powder Troplowitz's dentist gave to patients to clean their teeth. Troplowitz arranged to have it packaged in tin tubes to preserve its shelf life and began manufactur-

ing the world's first commercial toothpaste. On Dr. Unna's recommendation, calcium chloride was added to the recipe to make the new product effective against infections and inflammations of the mouth. The toothpaste was called Pebeco and its first ads urged daily dental hygiene. Within five years Pebeco was Beiersdorf's bestselling product, and eventually became the first to sell more than one million units.

Beiersdorf manufactured a wide range of products during the first decade of the 20th century, including soaps, depilatories, mouthwashes, pomades, and shaving soaps. A lip balm in stick form, called Lobello, became one of Beiersdorf's most popular products of all time. First sold in 1909, it remains the market leader in many countries. In 1911 Beiersdorf purchased the patent for a material called Eucerit. Developed by Dr. Isaac Lifschütz, Eucerit was created as a stable, water-soluble foundation for medicinal salves. Beiersdorf took over the manufacture of Eucerit, but Troplowitz had the idea to use it as the base for a new skin product, called Nivea Creme. The name—which comes from the Latin word for snow—was not new at Beiersdorf. The company had begun selling a Nivea soap in 1905. That soap, long forgotten, bequeathed its name to Nivea Creme, which evolved into the world's best selling skin cream. At first packaged in Art Nouveau-style cans, a simple yet elegant blue and white design was introduced in the middle 1920s. That essential design is still used today.

Beiersdorf expanded quickly to foreign markets. It signed an exclusive distribution contract with the New York firm Lehn & Fink in 1892. In 1898 it began exporting its products to Austria-Hungary. By 1909 Austrian revenues reached 218,000 Marks annually; by 1913 they had reached 556,000 Marks. Business in Austria was so good that Beiersdorf opened a branch in Vienna in January 1914. The company opened a London office together with a warehouse for distribution in the United Kingdom in 1909. By the start of World War I, there were production facilities in Buenos Aires, Copenhagen, Mexico, Moscow, New York, Paris, and Sydney Australia, and sales representatives in 29 countries around the world.

Troplowitz reinvested Beiersdorf profits in improved facilities. Two years after it opened, the Hamburg factory was too small for Beiersdorf's needs and had to be expanded. Every two to three years afterwards, until the start of World War I, a new facility was built. By 1913 the company's total production area was 30 times larger than that in Troplowitz's original plant. Between 1900 and 1914 Beiersdorf's product line tripled in size and its revenues increased 12fold. To help him manage his burgeoning enterprise, Troplowitz in 1906 made a partner of his brother-in-law Otto Hanns Mankiewicz. Troplowitz supervised company research and production; Mankiewicz, an attorney, oversaw sales, distribution, legal matters, and other external business.

Organizational Turmoil: The 1920s

World War I ended Beiersdorf's expansion abruptly. In 1918, the final year of the war, Beiersdorf was struck by two crippling circumstances. In April, Oscar Troplowitz died suddenly of a stroke at the age of 55. Just six months later his 47-year-old partner, Otto Mankiewicz, died of a heart attack. Neither man left an heir. Together with Germany's loss of the war and the collapse of the government of Kaiser Wilhelm, the two deaths created nearly insurmountable problems for Beiersdorf. Control passed into the hands of Frau Troplowitz, who was both Oscar's wife and Mankiewicz's sister; an advisory board, comprised of Max Warburg and Dr. Carl Joseph Melchior, from Beiersdorf's bank, was created at the same time to oversee company operations. To make company management more efficient, the legal form of the company was changed to a GmbH in February 1920 and the official name was changed to P. Beiersdorf & Co. GmbH. Frau Troplowitz owned the property and machinery; the bank invested 300,000 Marks and was given majority voting shares.

Then, in August 1920, Frau Troplowitz passed away suddenly and the company was once again thrown into turmoil. The crisis was overcome quickly, however, and within a month the land, buildings, and equipment held by Frau Troplowitz's estate were transferred to the GmbH. During the runaway inflation of 1921–22, the company's legal form was changed again and it became P. Beiersdorf & Co. AG on June 1, 1922. The change was not without problems, however. During the war, nations who fought against Germany had seized Beiersdorf holdings, patents, and trademarks. Afterwards they were reinstated to the GmbH, and successor corporations were prohibited from taking the patents and trademarks over. Thus, the GmbH maintained its separate existence as the holder of all rights and property, which it leased to the Aktiengesellschaft (AG).

Beiersdorf's foreign trade was ruined by the war. In 1913, foreign sales accounted for 42 percent of revenues; in 1919 there were no foreign sales. Furthermore, the nations that had been at war with Germany often seized all German holdings, including property, patents, and trademark rights. In the United States, Beiersdorf retained John Foster Dulles, who later served as secretary of state under Dwight Eisenhower, who regained its U.S. rights. The war and inflation put a temporary halt to Beiersdorf's new product development programs; a more pressing concern was finding replacements for raw materials which were no longer available or affordable.

During the 1920s, however, the company brought out some 70 new or significantly modified products. About half were personal care items such as tooth powders, hair products, children's creams, lavender soaps, hair removal creams, sunburn creams, and insect bite salves. In 1921 Hansaplast adhesive bandages for cuts, scrapes, and other wounds appeared on the market. It was a product that would remain an important part of Beiersdorf's line for the remainder of the century. In 1929 Beiersdorf marketed the first deodorant in salve form. The company's former leading product, Pebeco toothpaste, went into decline in the 1920s as the public's preference changed from medicinal to minty flavors. The introduction of Nivea toothpaste in 1933 was an unsuccessful attempt to win back the market.

Beiersdorf researchers working with Dr. Carl Mannich made a major breakthrough when they developed a reliable heart medication from digitalis. Digitalis, a plant derivative, was known to regulate the heartbeat, but it had to be administered in precise dosages: under-medication was ineffective but over-medication was fatal. Mannich isolated the active chemical in a stable form from the *Digitalis lanata* plant. Beiersdorf took over the production and marketing of the medicine, called Pandigal, in 1927. The drug became the foundation of the company's pharmaceutical division.

Depression and Dictatorship: The 1930s and 1940s

The German economy finally stabilized between 1924 and 1930, and Beiersdorf's growth resumed. Its German revenues during that period increased 300 percent—one third of its sales at the time were made directly to retail outlets such as pharmacies and cosmetics stores. A second production facility was built in Hamburg, and other plants were enlarged. The company's workforce grew from about 300 just after the war and reached 1,000 for the first time in 1929. Remarkably, during the Great Depression, which left six million without jobs in Germany between 1930 and 1933, Beiersdorf did not lay off a single worker.

When the Nazis came to power in 1933 Beiersdorf was attacked as a Jewish company and Germans were exhorted by government media to buy from its ''German'' competitors instead. Board members and executives with backgrounds the Nazis considered non-Aryan resigned in the interest of the company. Carl Claussen, a non-Jewish member of the Beiersdorf board of directors, took over as head of the company, a position he would hold until the mid-1950s. Some former Beiersdorf executives left Germany to oversee the company's foreign subsidiaries.

A consortium of foreign companies was established, companies whose debts of approximately 2.7 million Reichmarks had been paid off by Beiersdorf, creating a steady stream of foreign currency into Germany, as well as raw materials which were not available to the German parent company. Despite the regime's hate campaign, which continued throughout the 1930s, the number of Beiersdorf employees and its revenues both more than doubled. The company's most significant new product of the decade was a transparent tape that could be used in the office or home. Called Beiersdorfs Klebefilm, the tape was first released in 1935 and renamed tesafilm in 1941, a name it still goes by today. It quickly developed into one of the world's bestselling tapes and a major product line for Beiersdorf.

Shortages and Rebuilding: The 1950s and 1960s

In the years immediately following World War II, Beiersdorf production was blocked by severe shortages of materials and energy, as well as regulations promulgated by the Allied military government. However, even though no cosmetics could be produced or sold in 1946, the company took out ads to keep its brands in the public eye. Finally, in 1947 it received permission from the military government to resume production of Nivea Creme and toothpaste, but raw materials were in such short supply that only limited quantities could be produced.

The economy took a turn for the better after 1949 and the company slowly returned to normal development and production. In 1951 8x4 Seife, Europe's first deodorant soap, was introduced; it became the largest revenue producer of the company's Body Care division. Other new products for Beiersdorf in the 1950s included a pH-balanced skin cream called pH5-Eucerin and Atrix, a glycerin-based hand cream. Atrix helped the company regain foreign markets where the rights to the Nivea brand name had been lost during the war. By 1957, Beiersdorf's rebuilding program was running at full steam. Some 30 percent of revenues were from products that had been developed after 1949. Two major factories in Hamburg were rebuilt and expanded in the middle 1950s. The high demand for tesafilm, in particular industrial tapes, necessitated a brand new facility which was built in 1961 in Offenburg, in southeastern Baden-Württemberg.

In 1952 Allianz Versicherung AG acquired more than 25 percent of Beiersdorf's shares, the largest number in the hands of a single stockholder. The company expanded its executive board from four to six members in the early 1960s and, in 1967, shortened its name to Beiersdorf AG. It continued to expand its manufacturing capabilities through the 1960s and 1970s. In 1967 a 40,000-square-meter piece of land in Hamburg was acquired; in May 1971 a central laboratory and technology center was opened. In August 1969 negotiations for additional land for future expansion were concluded with the Hamburg city government. A new facility for the manufacture of industrial tapes was also completed in 1971.

New products were developed and product lines expanded in the 1960s. In 1965, the pharmaceutical division developed the first digitalis medication in tablet form. The new pills were just as effective as intravenous administration and by the mid-1970s the medication Novodigal was one of the most prescribed medicines in Germany. Tesafilm revenues swelled, spurred by worldwide automation of industry and the subsequent demand for industrial tape. New kinds of tape were continually introduced, including electrical tapes and watertight tapes made with plastic foam. The company was developing new bandages and adhesive strips as well and in the early 1970s a special line of bandages and medical products was formed. Despite tougher competition and market consolidation of the personal care area, Nivea solidified its position as the most popular skin cream in the world. By the early 1970s most company product lines—Nivea, tesa, and Hansaplast, in particular—were the European market leaders.

Reorganization: The 1970s and 1980s

In the early 1970s, Georg W. Claussen, who had succeeded his father Carl Claussen as Beiersdorf president, proposed that the company's management structure be altered to reflect its current circumstances. In 1973 a large U.S. consultant company was hired to study the question and in 1974 a new organizational structure was introduced at Beiersdorf based on its recommendations. The division of Development, Production, and Sales departments into separate domestic and foreign areas was done away with. In its place, four market-oriented divisions were set up to cover Europe and North America, and a fifth division for all products was set up for the rest of the world. Two umbrella divisions were placed over the other five: one for finance and administration, and another to coordinate the work of the executive board. The head of each division was given an additional area of responsibility for the entire company, for example personnel, sales, or material purchasing. Responsibility for the performance of Beiersdorf's foreign subsidiaries was divided among executive board members at the same time. In 1978, the Tchibo Frisch-Rost Kaffee AG acquired a 25 percent

share in the company, essentially enabling it to share control with Allianz. The same year a new company logo was adopted, the initials BDF followed by four dots meant to represent the companies product divisions.

From the mid-1970s until the mid-1980s Beiersdorf experienced a period of growth and new product development, in particular of its Nivea line. By the mid-1970s the foundation for the Nivea name—care, gentleness, and a reasonable price—had been laid. It released Nivea Pflege Schaumbad (bubble bath) in 1977, Nivea Duschbad (shower gel) in 1978, Nivea After Shave Balsam in 1980, and a bath oil, face cream, shampoo, and conditioning rinse between 1982 and 1984. Nivea's combination of quality and value caught on with consumers: annual sales grew from DM 180 million in 1970, to DM 500 million in 1981. By 1990 they had passed DM 1 billion, and in 1998 they reached DM 3 billion for the first time. New Nivea products moved quickly into leading market positions. Within five years of its introduction, Nivea Visage had sales of over DM 500 million and had become the most successful Nivea product after Nivea Creme.

Beiersdorf restructured its strategic approach in three important respects during the 1980s and 1990s. First, it narrowed the focus of its operations to areas of core competence, skin care, tape, and medical supplies. Second, it began the systematic development of comprehensive Nivea and tesa product lines. Third, it set about making strategic acquisitions and mergers. In 1983 the company acquired Bode Chemie, a chemical manufacturer, and incorporated it into the Beiersdorf medical division. In 1984 Beiersdorf shut down its soap manufacturing facility and delegated production to newly acquired subsidiary Hirtler GmbH, which had greater expertise and state-of-the-art equipment. The acquisition of Futuro strengthened the company's presence in the market for therapeutic hosiery.

Conquering International Cosmetic Markets: The 1990s

Beiersdorf carried out other internal reorganizations in the 1990s. It created a unified international marketing and production concept for its various product lines. It linked planning and production units and standardized product formulas, production, and packaging across the company and all its subsidiaries. In the 1990s Beiersdorf sales were fueled by its powerful line of Nivea cosmetics, a line that expanded constantly during the decade, building a seemingly never-ending variety of skin creams (including those for men), sun care creams, antiwrinkle creams, baby creams, shower products, and deodorants. In 1993 Nivea's worldwide sales reached US$1.47 billion. Helping Nivea results for 1993 was Beiersdorf's reacquisition of the rights to the Nivea brand name in the United Kingdom, rights that had been held by an English company since World War II. So successful was Nivea—it accounted for 70 percent of sales for the company's Cosmed division—that Rolf Kunisch, named Beiersdorf's president and CEO in 1993, predicted that Nivea's annual international sales would reach US$3 billion by 2000. Nivea's growth was exceptionally strong in Germany that year; sales increased more than three times faster than general consumer expenditures on toiletries and cosmetics.

Those results helped offset losses incurred by Beiersdorf's costly restructuring of the tesa tape division, which was experiencing economic difficulties, primarily because of a downturn in the automobile industry. There were rumors early in the decade that the company might sell off the tesa division entirely. Nonetheless, tesa continued to pioneer new processes and materials. The result was a number of new industrial tapes, including Bodyguard for cars and tesa Klarsichtfilm (transparent film), for computer data storage, with a capacity equal to 15 CD-ROMs.

Nivea sales increased worldwide. In 1996 international sales accounted for 60 percent of the company's total turnover. U.S. sales increased by over 11 percent that year, reaching US$147.9 million; the United Kingdom, Turkey, Greece, Scandinavia, the Czech Republic, Hungary, and Portugal all reported double-digit sales increases; Eastern Europe sales grew by 20 percent. The year 1997 was Nivea's seventh consecutive year of double-digit growth, climbing to US$1.38 billion. Increases were especially phenomenal in some Asian markets: 25 percent in Thailand and 40 percent in Indonesia. In 1998 Nivea's annual sales reached an all-time high of DM 3.87 billion, an increase of 13.1 percent; DM 2.6 billion of that came from sales outside Germany. Nivea products outsold all the company's other products combined.

Principal Subsidiaries

Juvena Produits de Beauty GmbH; La Prairie GmbH; Cosmed-Produktions GmbH; J0BST GmbH, Medical Stockings; Bode Chemie GmbH & Co; NOPI GmbH; Hirtler GmbH; tesa-Werke Offenburg GmbH; Beiersdorf Gesellschaft m.b.H. SA (Austria); Beiersdorf NV (Belgium); Beiersdorf spol. sr.o. (Czech Republic); Beiersdorf s.a. (France); Beiersdorf SpA (Italy); Juvena (International) AG (Switzerland); BDF México, S.A. de C.V. (Mexico); Beiersdorf, Inc. (USA); Futuro Inc. (U.S.A.); Beiersdorf Australia Ltd.; BDF Nivea Ltda. (Brazil); Beiersdorf SA (Chile); Beiersdorf S.A. (Columbia); PT. Beiersdorf Indonesia; Nivea-Kao Co., Ltd. (Japan).

Principal Divisions

Cosmed; Medical; Tesa.

Further Reading

"Beiersdorf Beauty Sales Get a Boost from Nivea," *WWD,* March 1, 1996.

"Beiersdorf Cosmetics Sales up 12% in '93," *WWD,* February 25, 1994.

"Beiersdorf Taps Kunisch As CEO and President," *WWD,* February 4, 1994.

Dang, Kim-Van, "Beiersdorf Aiming for Growth in U.S.," *WWD,* November 1, 1996.

Drier, Melissa, "Beiersdorf's Growth Bolstered by Nivea" (Beauty Report 2), *WWD,* February 28, 1997.

"New Developments for Nivea Sun Reflect Market Trends," *Cosmetics International,* January 10, 1994.

"Nivea Is Key to Beiersdorf Success," *Cosmetics International,* July 25, 1994.

100 Jahre Beiersdorf: 1882–1982, Hamburg: Beiersdorf AG, 1982.

"Optimale Launch Continues Beiersdorf Innovation Policy," *Cosmetics International,* July 10, 1995.

Schwammthal, Daniel, "Beiersdorf's Restructuring Expected to Fuel '98 Gain," *Wall Street Journal (Europe),* February 4, 1998.

Steenhuysen, Julie, "Bandage Makers Fight It Out with High-Tech Products," *Reuters Business Report,* April 2, 1997.

—Gerald E. Brennan

BELL⊕HOWELL

Bell and Howell Company

5215 Old Orchard Road
Skokie, Illinois 60077
U.S.A.
(847) 470-7100
Fax: (847) 470-9425
Web site: http://www.bellhowell.com

Public Company
Incorporated: 1907
Employees: 5,926
Sales: $900.2 million (1998)
Stock Exchanges: New York
Ticker Symbol: BHW
NAIC: 514191 On-Line Information Services; 51421
    Data Processing Services; 54199 All Other
    Professional, Scientific & Technical Services

Bell and Howell Company is one of the leading suppliers of equipment and services for information-related services and products, including online research databases, digital imaging systems, mail and messaging technologies, e-commerce solutions, and a wide range of other software applications. From the time of its original involvement in motion picture technology at the beginning of the 20th century, the company has been at the forefront of technological development.

Early Years: Serving the Motion Picture Industry

During the early 1900s, when Chicago was the center of the motion picture industry, Donald J. Bell worked as a projectionist in theaters around northern Illinois, where he became well acquainted with the equipment used for showing movies. As his interest in films and equipment grew, a friend helped secure him permission to use the machinist tools in the powerhouse of Chicago's Northwestern Railway, where Bell remodeled an Optoscope projector and later modified a Kinodrome projector. Bell met Albert S. Howell at the Crary Machine Works, where many of the parts for projectors were manufactured.

Howell was born in Michigan and traveled to Chicago to work in a machine shop that built and repaired motion picture projectors. In 1906 he applied for his first patent, a device that improved framing for 35mm Kinodrome motion picture projectors. With Bell's experience as a movie projectionist, contacts in the movie industry, and ready cash, and Howell's inventive genius and mechanical aptitude, the two men decided to start their own business. Incorporated with a capitalization of $5,000 in February 1907, Bell and Howell Company entered the business of manufacturing, jobbing, leasing, and repairing machines.

During its first year of business, over 50 percent of the new company's business involved repairing movie equipment made by other manufacturers. What made the company famous, however, was its development of equipment that addressed the two most important problems plaguing the movie industry at the time: flickering and standardization. Flickering in the early movies was due to the effects of hand-cranked film, which made the speed erratic. Standardization was needed as divergences in film width during these years made it nearly impossible to show the same film in any two cities within the United States. By 1908, Bell and Howell refined the Kinodrome projector, the film perforator, and the camera and continuous printer, all for the 35mm film width. With the development of this complete system, and the company's refusal to either manufacture or service products of any other size than the 35mm width, Bell and Howell forced film standardization within the motion picture industry.

In 1910, the company made a cinematograph camera entirely of wood and leather. When the two men learned that their camera had been damaged by termites and mildew during an exploration trip in Africa, they designed the first all metal camera. Introduced in 1912, the design 2709 soon garnered the reputation as ''the most precision film mechanism ever made'' and was produced for 46 continuous years. Following the relocation of the motion picture industry from Chicago to Hollywood, Bell and Howell's first movie camera was used in Southern California in 1912. By 1919, nearly 100 percent of the equipment used to make movies in Hollywood was manufactured by Bell and Howell.

With business expanding rapidly, the number of employees at Bell and Howell increased from 18 to 85 over a few years. In

Company Perspectives:

We are a leading information services and solutions provider to a select range of industries around the world. In each of our businesses, we transform information through software and services, helping our customers operate more effectively and efficiently. We concentrate on market niches where our leadership, experience, and customer focus enable us to anticipate customer needs and develop practical, cost-effective solutions that bring value to the marketplace. We continually look for opportunities with strong recurring revenues and high customer retention and renewal rates. This strengthens our leadership position, makes us more predictable, and allows us to make prudent use of financial leverage.

1914, Bell and Howell decided to permanently locate its offices on Larchmont Avenue in Chicago. In the midst of the company's success, however, internal problems began to emerge. While Howell supervised production, Bell acted as a company salesperson, a job that required many long trips. In order to meet the needs of a growing business during his absences, Bell hired Joseph McNabb as both bookkeeper and general manager in 1916. When Bell returned from one of his trips, he discovered that McNabb had made drastic changes in the operation of the company. While confronting McNabb, Bell accused Howell of acting as McNabb's accomplice. Bell gave them their last paychecks and fired them.

The following day, McNabb and Howell returned to the office and offered to purchase Bell's holdings in the company. McNabb brought with him Rufus J. Kittredge and Charles A. Ziebarth. Kittredge, McNabb's father-in-law, was head of a label manufacturing firm, and Ziebarth had been a former employee at Bell and Howell and a superintendent at the Chicago laboratory of the American Film Company. Both men had significant capital to invest in the company and years of management experience.

The purchase of Bell's interests in Bell and Howell amounted to $183,895. Having contributed an initial investment of $3,500 a little over ten years earlier, Bell was satisfied with the purchase price. Nevertheless, as he left, Bell told McNabb that the company was "a milked cow." Bell moved first to New York and then to California and was never again associated with the company except in name. With Bell's resignation as director and chairperson, four new officers were elected: Rufus Kittredge as president, Albert Howell as vice-president, Joseph McNabb as treasurer, and Charles Ziebarth as secretary.

By the 1920s, Bell and Howell's business was widely dispersed; two-thirds of all revenue came from the sale of cameras, camera accessories, punches, pilots and dies, and perforators. Hollywood was still equipped with mostly Bell and Howell products, and net sales had increased from $10,000 in 1907 to $338,500 by 1923, while profits were erratic. Nevertheless, the company opened branch offices in both New York and Los Angeles, and a new building was established in Hollywood.

Bell and Howell had expanded into the amateur movie market in 1919 when the company began developing 17.5mm equipment. In 1921 McNabb and Howell were invited to Rochester, New York, by George Eastman of Eastman Kodak to observe experiments using 16mm reversal material. McNabb and Howell were impressed with the results and redesigned all the company's 17.5mm equipment to use the 16mm film. In 1923 Bell and Howell manufactured the first spring-driven 16mm camera, beating Eastman Kodak by two years. The demand for this camera was so great that, even at a price of $175, it was on back order until 1930. Over the next 20 years, almost two-thirds of all company developments were in the amateur field, and Bell and Howell equipment became prized for its lifetime guarantees.

Kittredge resigned as president in 1923, remaining to chair the board of directors until 1930. McNabb succeeded his father-in-law as president and led the company through the prosperity of the 1920s. Bell and Howell's growth necessitated larger facilities. Accordingly, the plant on Larchmont was doubled in size, and the company also opened its Rockwell Engineering Laboratory. From 1923 to 1929, the firm's net sales increased annually with a high point in 1925 when the percentage of profits to sales reached 39.9 percent.

After the financial collapse on Wall Street in 1929, Bell and Howell was forced to adapt its products and change its price structure to meet the economic conditions of the Great Depression. Net sales decreased between 1930 and 1933, and the company was operating at a deficit in 1932.

In spite of this financial setback, the company's department of product development and improvement remained highly active. In 1932, the Filmosound 16mm sound-on-film projector was introduced, and the company pioneered a zoom lens called the "Varo." Also that year, the automatic production printer as well as the motor drive and magazines on Eyemo cameras first appeared. Both a 16mm and 8mm perforator were manufactured in 1934, along with the 16mm continuous sound printer and the 8mm projector. In 1935, both the spool camera and the Bell and Howell developing machine were produced, while the turret camera and a title writer were brought to market in 1938. The following year, the 35mm non-slip sound printer was introduced. As a result of these product developments, Bell and Howell net sales rose to $2.7 million in 1936 and $4.8 million by 1939. Disappointingly, however, net profits generally remained unchanged.

World War II: Production and Managerial Changes

The fortunes of the company improved dramatically with the onset of World War II. Contracts were made with the U.S. Army, Navy, and Air Force for defense materials. During these years, Bell and Howell developed the gun camera used to assess the accuracy of machine guns, the retriflector sight used in B-29 bombers, the flight simulator employed in training pilots, bombardiers, and navigators to use radar, and an adaptation of the Eyemo camera for military purposes. By 1945, sales amounted to $21.9 million, the highest in the company's history, while the number of employees increased to over 2,500.

The war years also ushered in changes for the company's management and employees. Howell had resigned as chief engineer in 1939 and was appointed to chair the board of directors, where he served until his death in 1951. Charles Ziebarth remained with the company until his death in 1942. One year later, the company created the Bell and Howell Employees Trust to provide for the retirement of its workers, and in the spring of 1945 the company decided to go public.

At the end of the war, Bell and Howell experienced a sudden drop in production for war materials, losing government contracts worth $9 million in 1945. Even though the company retooled its manufacturing lines for civilian products and introduced 12 new items from 1947 to 1949, including the Foton camera and various microfilm equipment, Bell and Howell was hit hard by a 40 percent decline in sales for the U.S. photographic industry. Net sales decreased from over $21 million in 1945 to $13 million in 1949, and the number of employees dropped by 30 percent.

One fortunate occurrence during these years was the purchase of the microfilm division of Pathe Manufacturing Company in 1946. This purchase provided the company with new product lines of microfilm equipment, including recorders, readers, and automatic feeders. Two years later, the Microfilm Division was selling products to Harris Trust, Firestone, Federal Reserve Bank of Chicago, and Continental Illinois National Bank.

After a long tenure as president of Bell and Howell, Joseph McNabb died in January of 1949 and was replaced by his hand-chosen successor Charles Percy. Percy, a graduate of the University of Chicago, had held a variety of positions in the company beginning in 1938. When he assumed the position of president and chief executive office at Bell and Howell he was 29 years old.

The new president represented a marked departure from the past in both administration and public relations. As owner and president, McNabb had run the company as he chose; his word on financial matters and product development was final. Percy, on the other hand, was the first among equals in a newly created executive committee. Charged with the responsibility of making recommendations on policy, salaries, promotions, dividends, acquisitions, and a host of other issues, Percy did not possess sole authority to make decisions. In addition, not many people outside Bell and Howell knew who McNabb was or what he did. When the company went public, it was clear there was a need for someone with a flair for dealing with the media. Percy's speeches, interviews, and articles over the years of his presidency led to a rise in personal prestige and, consequently, a comparable rise in public esteem for Bell and Howell.

1950–70: Expansion and Diversification

During the 1950s, the company continued to emphasize development and expansion of its product line, which eventually included inexpensive amateur equipment, tape recorders, and hi-fi phonographs. In 1951, Bell and Howell was awarded its first Oscar by the Academy of Motion Picture Arts and Sciences for technical achievement. Four years later, the 16mm Filmo 70 camera was adapted for Admiral Richard E. Byrd's journey to the South Pole. Other developments included the electric eye camera in 1956 and the first zoom lens to fit 8mm projectors in 1957.

Under Percy's direction, Bell and Howell also initiated an aggressive acquisition strategy. Its first purchase was the Three Dimension Company, a manufacturer of stereo equipment, slide projectors, and tape recorders. DeVry Corporation, a projector company, was also purchased during this time. The Inserting and Mailing Machine Company, maker of equipment for mail-order firms, insurance companies, and banks, was acquired in 1958. With the purchase of Consolidated Electrodynamics Corporation, a research and development firm involved in aviation equipment, control systems, and electronic instrumentation, Bell and Howell sales increased to $114 million by 1960, while its staff grew to 7,590.

In 1960, the company's International Division was reorganized. Major acquisitions, manufacturing contracts, and licensing agreements during this time led to the sale and servicing of Bell and Howell products in 99 countries around the world. The success of the International Division was indisputable: in 1963 cumulative sales from the division jumped an amazing 67 percent over the previous year.

Increasingly active in public life and service, Percy resigned as president in 1963 but remained as chairperson until he was elected to the U.S. Senate in 1966. Peter G. Peterson assumed Percy's responsibilities in 1963 and became company chair when Percy relinquished that title. Since 1958, Peterson had served as the company's executive vice-president, head of the Photo Products Division, and chair of the Bell and Howell corporate research board.

Continuing Percy's strategy of expanding the company's product lines through acquisitions, in 1966 management purchased DeVry Technical Institute, Inc., a training school for students in motion pictures, radio, television, and electronics. The following year, Charles E. Merrill Publishing Company was acquired, as was KEL Corporation, a manufacturer of radio communications equipment. New products were also coming from Bell and Howell's own research and development programs. A thermal spirit copier-duplicator was developing in 1964, and a Super 8mm movie camera was completely automated and introduced in 1965. One year later, a zoom lens system was designed for the *Surveyor I* spacecraft, and language materials that facilitated instruction in speech correction and remedial reading were developed in conjunction with Bell and Howell Language Master equipment.

Under Peterson, the company's accomplishments rivaled those recorded during Percy's leadership. Developments in photographic equipment and business machines, work in software materials for the educational field, expansion into space exploration technology and instrumentation, and the growth of the international operation led to a 1970 sales figure of $297.7 million with net profits of approximately $11 million. However, profit margins for many products were much lower than expected, and the aggressive diversification strategy resulted in an assortment of entirely unrelated holdings—over 20 divisions were offering products and services that ranged from high-tech vocational classes to military binoculars.

1970–90: Divestiture and Privatization

In January 1971, Peterson joined the Republican administration of President Nixon and was soon appointed Secretary of Commerce. His successor was Donald N. Frey, who held a Ph.D. in metallurgical engineering from the University of Michigan and represented the first engineer to hold the position of chief executive officer at Bell and Howell. Charged with the responsibility of pruning the company into a more efficient and profitable shape, Frey got rid of Bell and Howell's movie camera business and its consumer products business, including its trademark sound/slide projectors and famous 8mm cameras, as well as a host of other marginally profitable businesses. He then made microimagery and mail sorting, two previously tangential operations, the focus of Bell and Howell's product development.

By the early 1980s, Frey was confident he had turned the company around; from 1983 to 1984 operating earnings increased 33 percent to $24.6 million, and sales grew 11 percent to $679.2 million. Bell and Howell's mail-handling equipment operation and its vocational schools, especially DeVry Institute of Technology, expanded and generated significant sales. Furthermore, Bell and Howell had received Academy Awards for its motion picture program tape punch and modular film printer in 1975 and 1981, respectively. However, the company's microimagery division, which provided nearly 30 percent of the company's total sales, had developed into a cash cow with a projected annual sales growth rate of five percent; the market for microfilm had reached its peak and was saturated with competing products. Moreover, Frey had mistakenly held on to many businesses long after they had lost their profitability. Most importantly, however, by 1986 Frey had made 37 acquisitions, only one of which he could point to with satisfaction. Despite Bell and Howell's growing financial problems, compounded by 15 years of continuous acquisitions and divestitures and the high turnover of its management, Frey predicted that his restructuring strategy would succeed.

In 1986, however, Gerald Schultz, trained as the successor to Frey, was named president of the company, and as revenues stalled in 1988 at $600 million, Schultz became part of the management group that joined forces with Texas financier Robert M. Bass to undertake a $678.4 million leveraged buyout of Bell and Howell. Contributing $82.3 million of the funds for the buyout, Bass assumed control of the company, appointed Schultz chief executive officer, and privatized the entire operation. After the acquisition, the company immediately began to sell what it regarded as non-core businesses in order to raise the money necessary to pay off the buyout debt. In September 1989, the company sold its textbook publishing division, Merrill Publishing, formerly one of its core businesses, for $260 million to Macmillan, Inc.

1990s and Beyond

Bell and Howell remained under Bass' control for seven years, during which time it changed direction and evolved into an entirely new company. By 1995, the one-time leader in cameras and projection equipment had morphed into an information management business, with an emphasis on manufacturing mail processing systems and providing micrographics ser-vices as a republisher of newspapers, periodicals, dissertations, and books on microfilm. In early May 1995, Bell and Howell once again went public, trading on the New York Stock Exchange under the ticker symbol BHW.

Two years later, the company once again saw a change in leadership. James Roemer, who had joined Bell and Howell in 1991 as president of the Publication Systems division, was named CEO of the parent company in February 1997. In January of the following year, he became the company's chairman as well.

By the time Roemer took the helm, Bell and Howell was operating in three business segments: Mail and Messaging Technologies; Information Access; and Imaging. The Mail and Messaging Technologies, which made up approximately 45 percent of the company's revenue, provided software-driven mail processing functions including collating, cutting, bursting, folding, inserting, scanning, encoding, and sorting. Its customers included organizations with high-volume mailing needs such as financial institutions, direct mail marketers, credit card companies, and others.

The Information Access segment, comprised of Bell and Howell Information and Learning and Bell and Howell Publishing Services, was the second largest segment, bringing in approximately 36 percent of the company's total revenue. The Information and Learning business collected information found in magazines, newspapers, out-of-print books, and dissertations and transformed it into digital format, selling it via Internet and CD-ROM to universities, schools, and libraries. Bell and Howell's Publishing Services unit provided software, services, and e-commerce systems to manufacturers, dealerships, and service networks. The bulk of Publishing Services' business was in providing electronic parts catalogs to auto, marine, and motorcycle dealerships around the world.

Bell and Howell's final and smallest business segment was its Imaging Unit, a manufacturer of scanners that transformed paper documents into electronic or microfilm format. The Imaging business's primary markets were financial services, health care, insurance, government, and transportation.

Looking toward the future, Bell and Howell expected to continue a steady rate of growth, with a focus on Internet-related opportunities. The company anticipated an increasing use of the Internet in new product development in all of its core business units. According to the company's 1998 annual report, this new product development was expected to be a major element in the company's growth. "We aim to stay so close to the markets we serve that we develop and introduce leading-edge products and services before our customers even recognize those needs themselves," James Roemer wrote in his 1998 letter to shareholders. Another growth strategy involved strengthening Bell and Howell's overseas presence. As of 1999, most of the company's international business was confined to Western Europe; however, the company had plans to begin shipping mail processing equipment into Japan and China as well. The company also planned to enhance its growth by continuing to make strategic acquisitions based upon the needs of each of the business units.

Principal Subsidiaries

Bell & Howell A-V Limited (U.K.); Bell & Howell Information Publications International Limited (U.K.); Bell & Howell Cope Company; Bell & Howell Document Management Products Company; Bell & Howell Financial Services Company; BHAC Leasing Corporation; Bell & Howell Foreign Sales Corporation (Barbados); Bell & Howell France S.A.; Bell & Howell GmbH (Germany); Bell & Howell AG (Switzerland); Bell & Howell Ges.m.b.H. (Austria); Bell & Howell International Services Company; Bell & Howell Japan Ltd. Co.; Bell & Howell Limited (U.K.); Micromedia Limited (U.K.); Paragon Technical Services Limited (U.K.); International Imaging Limited (U.K.); Bell & Howell Ltd. (Canada); Bell & Howell Mail Processing Systems Company; Blue Lake Software, Inc.; Bell & Howell Mailmobile Company; Bell & Howell Europa BV (Netherlands); Bell & Howell Nederlands B.V. (Netherlands); Bell & Howell Postal Systems Inc.; Bell & Howell Publication Systems Company; Bell & Howell Paperwise Company; Bell & Howell PW Licensing Company; Bell & Howell (Singapore) Pte Ltd.; UMI Company; DataTimes Corporation.

Further Reading

Elliott, Alan, "Bell & Howell Co: Making Archived Works Available on Internet," *Investor's Business Daily,* March 5, 1999.

O'Hanlon, John, "World Leader in Information Services and Solutions," *Wall Street Corporate Reporter,* April 5–11, 1999.

Robinson, Jack, *Bell and Howell Company: A 75-Year History,* Chicago: Bell and Howell, 1982.

Schaff, William, "Bell & Howell Reinvented," *InformationWeek,* January 25, 1999.

Simon, Ruth, "What, All Kidding Aside, Is New," *Forbes,* October 20, 1986, pp. 88–91.

Toy, Stewart, and Zachary Schiller, "Bob Bass May Have to Settle for a Quick Profit on This One," *Business Week,* October 9, 1989, pp. 48–50.

—Thomas Derdak
—updated by Shawna Brynildssen

BELLSOUTH

BellSouth Corporation

1155 Peachtree Street N.E.
Atlanta, Georgia 30309
U.S.A.
(404) 249-2000
Fax: (404) 249-5599
Web Site: http://www/bellsouth.com

Public Company
Incorporated: 1983
Employees: 88,450
Sales: $23.1 billion (1998)
Stock Exchanges: New York
Ticker Symbol: BLS
NAIC: 51333 Telecommunications Resellers; 33421
    Telephone Apparatus Manufacturing; 551112 Offices
    of Other Holding Companies

BellSouth Corporation is one of the world's largest communications companies, serving close to 34 million customers in the United States and in 18 other countries, with a particularly large market in Latin America. The company provides local telecommunications as well as wireless local and long distance service, long distance access, cable and digital television, Internet access, and other electronic commerce. In addition, BellSouth is a leading advertising and publishing company, putting out many advertising directories, including The Real Yellow Pages ONLINE. The company began as a so-called Baby Bell company with a market in the southeastern United States. Though this region remains a core market for the company, it is in no way a strictly regional entity. Approximately 40 percent of BellSouth's revenues come from providing traditional local telephone service in its region, with the rest coming from other services both in and outside the South.

1980s Origins from Bell Breakup

BellSouth was formed in 1983 as part of the court-ordered breakup of the American Telephone and Telegraph Company (AT&T), at that time the world's largest corporation. AT&T had built most of the U.S. phone system but was frequently accused of suppressing competition through unfair trade practices. It was broken up in keeping with a consent decree to settle a lawsuit brought by the U.S. Department of Justice. AT&T left the operation of local telephone service in the United States to 22 local telephone companies, all operating under AT&T's umbrella. The breakup divided the 22 locals among seven regional holding companies (RHCs). BellSouth was formed from the combination of Southern Bell Telephone and Telegraph Co. and South Central Bell Telephone Co. Its territory was composed of Florida, Georgia, South Carolina, North Carolina, Kentucky, Tennessee, Alabama, Mississippi, and Louisiana. BellSouth and the other RHCs were not free to enter any business they chose. The consent decree prohibited them from using their monopoly power to their advantage and from entering certain businesses, including long-distance telephone service. At that time the new corporation named John L. Clendenin chairman.

BellSouth began as the 12th-largest corporation in the United States, with $11 billion in assets, 13.4 million telephone lines, and 131,500 employees. It was also the most profitable of the seven regionals, with a promising future because it was located in one of the fastest-growing areas of the country. Six of the ten fastest-growing counties in the United States were in BellSouth's territory. Southern and South Central already were prospering, their combined assets having grown 47 percent and their combined net income having grown 65 percent in the four years before the AT&T breakup. Collectively they had spent $15 billion on plant modernization and new facilities in the five years before BellSouth's creation.

AT&T had often used the South as the testing ground for new technologies, which gave BellSouth a lead in high-technology services, such as using telephone lines to monitor gas meters. Shortly before the breakup, Southern Bell began a joint videotex project, which enabled subscribers to use home computers for banking and shopping. BellSouth continued that push into new technologies, starting a mobile phone subsidiary, BellSouth Mobility Inc., in its first year of business. In March 1984 BellSouth Mobility started a cellular telephone system in Chattanooga, Tennessee, in a joint venture with Cellular Radio of Chattanooga,

Inc., and Chattanooga-Northwest Georgia Cellular Radio Inc. It then began a $5.2 million cellular system in Memphis, Tennessee. In May 1984 it agreed to develop a $3.3 million cellular network in Baton Rouge, Louisiana, with East Ascension Telephone Co. and Star Telephone Co., and a $4.8 million cellular system in Orlando, Florida. Plans were laid to expand many of these cellular networks even as they were being built. South Central Bell offered fiber optic lines, completing the first direct customer hookup for Amsouth Bancorp late in 1984. Also in 1984 South Central began offering WatchAlert, a system that allowed a security-alarm signal to be transmitted even if a phone line was busy or cut. To promote these technologies to multi-tenant business offices, BellSouth Enterprises, Inc. formed BellSouth Systems Technology in 1984. The subsidiary focused on directory publishing and advertising, mobile communications, and computer systems. BellSouth made $1.26 billion in 1984.

BellSouth, along with five other RHCs, began trading on the London Stock Exchange within its first few months of business, to gain access to European capital. In the rapidly changing telecommunications market, BellSouth could not count on all of its large customers continuing to use it for long-distance access. Advances in technology meant that large companies could bypass the local network and tie directly into the long-distance system through microwave antennas. BellSouth hired market researchers to develop profiles of the company's major customers. It then established special teams to work with the top 200 customers and to encourage them to continue using the BellSouth network for long-distance access. The residential market was split into groups based on income and phone-use patterns, with services pitched to the customer groups that would be most interested in them.

In 1985 BellSouth signed a four-year contract to buy telecommunications equipment from Canada's Northern Telecom Inc. In the same year the Georgia Public Service Commission approved a $27 million rate increase for Southern Bell. The FCC ended its requirement that all Bell operating companies sell cellular telephones through a separate subsidiary. BellSouth earned $1.42 billion in 1985.

In February 1986 BellSouth Enterprises increased its presence in the lucrative cellular telephone market when it bought 15 percent of Mobile Communications Corp. of America for $107.5 million. The following year BellSouth Enterprises bought almost all the assets of Universal Communications Systems Inc. for $79.1 million.

By 1986 the national Yellow Pages market had reached $6.8 billion, and BellSouth was expanding its Yellow Pages services out of its area of operation in search of greater profits. In February 1986 the company bought L.M. Berry & Co., a large,

independent Yellow Pages publisher whose 1985 revenues topped $780 million. That acquisition made BellSouth a world leader in the profitable directory publishing business and the largest Yellow Pages publisher in the United States. The company, however, faced stiff competition for the Yellow Pages market from other companies, particularly Southwestern Bell, which was also trying to expand Yellow Pages services.

In 1987 BellSouth began offering an information gateway service that let customers access databases using a personal computer. By dialing a number in the Atlanta area, customers could get stock quotes and make airline reservations. Customers with cellular phones could also dial a number to get local traffic reports. BellSouth continued foreign expansion by buying an Australian telephone answering machine company.

BellSouth and the other regional holding companies were dealt a major legal setback in 1987 when Justice Harold Greene, who was overseeing the breakup of AT&T, ruled that the companies still could not enter the long-distance telephone business in the United States, offer advanced information services, or manufacture phone equipment. Greene ruled that removing the restrictions would impede competition and violate antitrust laws. BellSouth and the other regionals appealed. Greene's ruling, however, prevented the regionals from transmitting only information they collected themselves. The regionals could not own or develop their own databases, but they were allowed to transmit third parties' databases. BellSouth was, therefore, able to sign an agreement with Telenet Corporation to link some of its local and national communications networks.

Still, BellSouth hoped to increase the use of online information services and increase the revenue from its local network. In 1987 BellSouth's government systems division won a $25 million contract from the U.S. Army to modernize telecommunications systems at six installations in Alaska, Arizona, Colorado, and Texas.

Growth in the Late 1980s

By 1988 BellSouth was the fastest growing regional holding company, with an impressive use of new technologies and services and the addition of 600,000 new telephone lines to the network every year. That growth allowed BellSouth to install new switches and fiber-optic cables without having to tear out old equipment before it was fully depreciated. Of all the RHCs in 1988, BellSouth had the largest sales at $13.6 billion, the most assets at $28.5 billion, and highest profits at $1.7 billion. Part of the growth came from the Southeast's rapid expansion. The area's population had grown 4.3 percent since 1984, adding 4.5 percent to annual phone-line growth. The growth also came partly because BellSouth's network was the most technologically advanced in the United States, with 95.3 percent of its switching offices using electronic controls and nearly 98 percent of its major trunk lines using high-capacity fiber-optic cable. Profits were enhanced by the fact that BellSouth had avoided the ill-fated diversification pursued by most other RHCs, sticking instead to telephone-related businesses. Moreover, while most other RHCs suffered demoralizing employee strikes over health care costs in 1988, BellSouth had kept down health care costs and avoided confrontation. In 1989 *Fortune* magazine labeled the company "the most admired utility" for these reasons.

In 1988 BellSouth spent $3.2 billion on advanced digital switching and transmissions systems to improve communications and lay the groundwork for new telecommunications services. CEO Clendenin wanted to use BellSouth's advanced network to transmit a great variety of voice, data, and television programs into millions of homes for far less money than the cost of using conventional copper lines. BellSouth was the first RHC to bring fiber-optic cables directly to homes, hoping to use them to transmit security and energy-management information and cable television, in addition to voices.

BellSouth won a $55 million telephone-switch contract from the U.S. government in late 1987. The following year, however, amid accusations that it had improperly obtained information from a government employee in the process of bidding on the contract, BellSouth withdrew its bid, and the government awarded the contract to AT&T.

Despite its early entry into cellular systems, BellSouth lost several cellular phone deals to rival RHCs. Cellular service was an area in which the regionals were allowed to compete outside of their local territory, and the lost deals meant lost opportunities to expand BellSouth's reach in a rapidly growing telecommunications market. In 1988 BellSouth reversed the trend, buying Mobile Communications Corp. outright for $710 million in stock. The acquisition made BellSouth the third-largest U.S. cellular telephone company, with 345,000 subscribers. It also brought BellSouth into the paging services business. When the Republican and Democratic conventions of 1988 were both held in BellSouth's market area, the company displayed its latest technology at both conventions, hoping to influence government officials to ease restrictions. Profits in 1988 were $1.67 billion.

The year 1989 began with a disappointment when Bell Atlantic beat out BellSouth in the competition for a $220 million, ten-year contract to build an advanced phone system to link government agencies in the Washington, D.C., area. Nevertheless, business was flourishing for BellSouth and for telecommunications in general. Telecommunications was a bigger business than computers or aerospace in 1989, and telephone use was growing three times faster than the population. Industry observers agreed that BellSouth, along with the other regionals, was running and selling basic local phone service better than it had as part of AT&T.

In 1989 BellSouth bought the 60 percent of Air Call Communications that it did not already own for $34.5 million. At the time, BellSouth wanted to offer electronic Yellow Pages, but the idea was rejected in 1989 by Justice Greene, who ruled it would violate the consent decree that broke up AT&T. BellSouth moved toward further expansion of its cellular network when it formed a consortium with two British companies—General Electric Company plc and Plessey Company plc—to bid on one of the mobile-telephone network licenses being offered by the British government. BellSouth then agreed to merge its cellular properties with LIN Broadcasting Corp., which would have created the second-largest cellular network in the United States. Rival McCaw Cellular Communications Inc., the largest cellular firm in the United States, however, raised its offer for LIN and ended up buying the company after a long battle. McCaw paid BellSouth $66.5 million in merger termination fees and other expenses.

BellSouth's local phone earnings, along with those of the other regional holding companies, were regulated by state commissions that allowed only a certain rate of return, about 12 percent to 15 percent by 1989. When earnings exceeded those rates, BellSouth had to give refunds. BellSouth pushed for incentive-based rate plans that would allow the company to keep a percentage of profits it earned above the allowed rate of return. It argued that the incentives would make the company more efficient and lead to better service. Three BellSouth states—Alabama, Florida, and Kentucky—passed such laws, but regulatory commissions then cut the rates BellSouth could earn. The rate cuts were expected to cost BellSouth $690 million in the early 1990s.

Continuing its interest in advancing technology, in 1990 BellSouth won FCC permission to test a wireless telephone system at the University of Georgia in Athens with the Sony Corporation. As part of a cost-cutting program, the company offered an early retirement incentive to nearly 3,000 executives.

By 1990 BellSouth had invested $550 million in overseas operations and was the only regional offering mobile communications on four continents. Telephone services that had been nationalized in many countries were being privatized, presenting huge business opportunities. BellSouth pushed its services in the Caribbean and Latin America. It had cellular telephone interests in Argentina, Uruguay, France, Britain, Switzerland, and Mexico; paging interests in Australia, Britain, and Switzerland; and it started a joint venture in India to create telecommunications software products and services. The Australian company, Link Telecommunications, boasted that country's largest independent paging and telephone-answering services. In August 1990 BellSouth announced plans to develop a digital cellular phone system in New Zealand by mid-1992. BellSouth executives scrambled to learn foreign business practices. In Argentina they billed customers every ten days to keep pace with that country's steep inflation.

Competition in the Mid-1990s

Until 1992, regulations stemming from the AT&T breakup had kept BellSouth and the other Baby Bells from expanding into a broader range of information services. However, a federal court ruling in February 1992 allowed the Bell offspring to begin offering new services, such as special fax retrieval systems and interactive video and data networks for businesses. The ruling set off a surge of competition, with the big telecommunications companies vying for new territory and new information services. Of the Baby Bells, BellSouth was widely referred to as the most conservative, being unwilling to offer new, untested technology. By 1994, many other companies had moved into BellSouth's southern territory, with MCI stringing fiber optic cable in Atlanta itself, and U S West spending $300 million to upgrade its cable and multimedia networks in Georgia, for example. BellSouth moved cautiously to repel the onslaught.

In 1995 the company invested $500 million in a joint venture with Disney and two other partners to produce innovative entertainment programs carried by phone as well as cable lines. This was BellSouth's first step into the media and entertainment world. The company also built a trial interactive multimedia network in 1995, limiting it to the Atlanta suburb of Chamblee. Chamblee residents were able to download video games and movies and do home shopping over special high-capacity phone wires. Furthermore, in partnership with Sprint and GTE, Bell-South pioneered a North Carolina Information Superhighway. This was a high-speed network that allowed hospitals, schools, and businesses to transmit data and video across the state, so that patient records, for example, including x rays, could be zapped in seconds from one institution to another. While Bell-South spent money to expand into these new service areas, it also moved to cut costs, aggressively trimming its workforce. Some 10,200 BellSouth workers were laid off between 1993 and 1995.

In 1997, BellSouth got a new CEO, Duane Ackerman, who girded the company to face even more competition, as relaxed regulations finally permitted other phone companies to offer local phone service in BellSouth's territory. The company expected to lose as much as 20 percent of its local telephone business, as other companies vied to get a piece of the booming southern market. Yet BellSouth was still in good shape. Its revenues from overseas markets had blossomed to $1.2 billion in 1996, a significant boost to its profits. Moreover, the competition in the local phone market finally undid some of the regulation that the company had long lobbied to overturn. While the old system had required BellSouth to return a portion of its profits to its customers, the law changed in 1996 to let the company respond more nimbly to the competitors flocking into its territory.

New competition was not entirely bad for business. Even as BellSouth lost individual accounts, it picked up money by selling wholesale access to its lines to the new competitors, who did not want to build networks of their own. BellSouth was also a keen marketer. Among all the Baby Bells, it offered the only 24-hour, seven-day customer service, and it also trumpeted its brand name reputation for reliability by spending heavily on television and print advertising. The company sold both wireless and regular telephone service to customers in the South through 250 stores or kiosks that it owned, many of them situated inside chain stores such as Office Depot, Radio Shack, and Circuit City.

BellSouth continued to flourish in spite of the rapid changes in the communications industry and the sharpening battle for customers in its prime market. Its business strategy had three parts: to provide premium local service in the Southeast, to maintain its substantial wireless communications business across the rest of the country, and to continue to expand into the booming Latin American communications market. Growth was steady and profitable in the late 1990s, with revenues rising steadily from $16.8 billion in 1994 to over $23 billion in 1998. Net income rose as well, and the company had record cash flow from operations in 1998.

The communications industry was again changing drastically in the late 1990s, as companies consolidated. By May 1998, there were only four Baby Bells left, and BellSouth, which had long been the biggest of the regional phone companies, was now the second smallest. After the acquisition of Ameritech by San Antonio, Texas-based SBC Communications, industry analysts generally predicted that more mergers would follow until only three or four companies were left. BellSouth had suddenly become a much smaller company, as its competitors became so much bigger. Nevertheless, it continued to grow, both in revenues and services offered, with strong sales of its data, wireless, and regular phone services leading to an almost 40 percent earnings increase for the last quarter of 1998.

Principal Subsidiaries

BellSouth Enterprises; BellSouth Communications Group; BellSouth Telecommunications, Inc.

Further Reading

"BellSouth's Earnings Increase 38%, Helped by Gain, Sales Growth," *Wall Street Journal,* January 26, 1999, p. A8.

Gannes, Stuart, "BellSouth Is on a Ringing Streak," *Fortune,* October 9, 1989.

Greising, David, and Kathy Rebello, "Is BellSouth Really 'Ready to Get It On'?," *Business Week,* May 8, 1995, pp. 80–82.

Hayes, John R., "Focused," *Forbes,* May 19, 1997, pp. 124–26.

Kanell, Michael E., "Once-Largest of Baby Bells Faces Tougher Road if SBC's Plans Go Through," *Knight-Ridder/Tribune Business News,* May 11, 1998.

Lazo, Shirley A., "Long-Awaited Call from BellSouth," *Barron's,* October 2, 1995, p. 46.

Le Carnevale, Mary, "BellSouth to Drop 8,000 Employees; More Cuts at Phone Firms Are Likely," *Wall Street Journal,* November 9, 1992, p. A4.

Mason, Charles, "Is the Bloom off the BellSouth Rose?," *Telephony,* October 21, 1991, pp. 18–24.

Ramirez, Anthony, "BellSouth Taps Experience for Move into New Services," *New York Times,* February 6, 1992, p. D4.

Schmidt, William E., "BellSouth Eager for Kickoff," *New York Times,* November 15, 1983.

Ward, Judy, "Belle of the Brawl," *Financial World,* June 6, 1995, p. 49.

—Scott M. Lewis
—updated by A. Woodward

Blue Mountain Arts, Inc.

P.O. Box 4549
Boulder, Colorado 80306
U.S.A.
(303) 449-0536
Fax: (303) 417-6496
Web site: http//:www.bluemountain.com

Private Company
Incorporated: 1972 as Hartford House, Ltd.
Employees: 120
Sales: $60 million (1998 est.)
NAIC: 511191 Greeting Card Publishers

Blue Mountain Arts, Inc. publishes cards, books, calendars, prints, and other gift items which feature the company's signature style: poetry and prose printed on a backdrop of colorful nature illustrations. The company offers over 1,000 designs of everyday, all-occasion greeting cards in addition to holiday and special day greeting cards. In addition, over 1,000 Blue Mountain card designs are deliverable through electronic mail from the company's Internet domain. By the late 1990s, Blue Mountain Arts had sold more than 350 million greeting cards and 16 million books of prose and poetry. Their products, sold worldwide, have been translated into French, German, Spanish, Russian, Dutch, Finnish, Japanese, Korean, Chinese, Hebrew, and Afrikaans.

Togetherness Creates a Business in the 1970s

Blue Mountain Arts combines the complementary creative abilities of artist Stephen Schutz and poet Susan Polis Schutz. Before founding the company Stephen was employed as a physicist at an atmospheric research center in Boulder, Colorado, while Susan taught English and pursued free-lance writing. The initial intention was not to develop a business, but to unite their hobbies as a catalyst for togetherness. Stephen superimposed Susan's free-form poems on his watercolor paintings of mountain and human silhouettes. Stephen and Susan created posters that expressed their thoughts about life, love, and nature, which reflected the hippie stylings of the early 1970s.

Upon seeing the pictures in the couple's home, friends commented on their salability. The business took hold when the two convinced the manager of a local Boulder bookseller to offer a dozen posters for sale on a consignment basis. The posters sold quickly and other stores began to carry the posters as well.

When Stephen and Susan transferred their poster designs to greeting cards, they innovated the all-occasion greeting card in two ways. The first innovation was their development of an all-occasion card which was blank inside, in which personal messages could be written. The second innovation was the inclusion of Susan's poetry, which was intimate and sentimental. Previously, standard greeting card messages included poetry of a rhymed, more formal style. Susan's emotional, free-form poetry reflected an era that rejected such conventions in favor of heartfelt self-expression.

Stephen and Susan transformed their creative aspirations into a business in 1971 when the couple founded Blue Mountain Arts. The Schutzes rented the main floor of the home in which they lived to support the business, while they lived in the basement. The two traveled around the United States, in a pick-up truck with a camper shell on the back, and sold their artwork at stores and trade shows along the way.

Blue Mountain Arts products found a loyal customer base, and business expanded accordingly. The product line expanded to include calendars, stationery, and gift books. Moreover, Susan wrote a book of poetry entitled, *Come into the Mountains, Dear Friend,* which Blue Mountain Arts published in 1972. The book was highly successful and others books followed, including *Peace Flows from the Sky* (1974) and *Someone Else to Love* (1976). Greeting cards and another gift book, published in 1974, contained prose quoted from such diverse authors as Mark Twain, Kahlil Gibran, and Helen Keller. As with the cards and posters, the written contents of the books were complemented with Stephen Schutz's illustrations.

After five years, the company had achieved great success; Blue Mountain Arts had grown to approximately $7 million in sales in 1976. The company's product line included 24 poster and stationery designs, 120 card designs, eight calendars, and 40 inspirational scrolls, sold through over 12,000 retail outlets.

Company Perspectives:

Blue Mountain Arts is helping the world communicate.

The company had also published 16 books of poetry and inspirational prose. Many of their products were available in several languages. Having employed several kindred artists and writers, Blue Mountain Arts soon entered the business of traditional greeting cards as well, providing holiday, birthday, and other special day cards for the first time in 1981.

During this time, their innovation and success attracted attention to the Schutzes and Blue Mountain Arts. Popular magazines including *Time, American Home, Marriage Encounter, Family Weekly,* and *People,* featured stories on the company. The business also attracted the attention of Hallmark Cards, Inc., the largest company in the greeting card industry. In 1985 Hallmark approached Blue Mountain Arts with an offer to acquire it or to engage in joint ventures. Stephen and Susan Schutz refused, however, deciding that their company embodied their values and a partner or parent might cramp their style.

1986–88 Legal Dispute with Hallmark

In April 1986, while shopping in a California card store, Susan Polis Schutz was surprised to mistake Hallmark's Personal Touch line of greeting cards for her own company's Airbrush Feelings and Watercolor Feelings line of greetings cards. Blue Mountain Arts contacted Hallmark by letter, noting the similarity and asking the latter to forgo production and distribution of the Personal Touch line. When Hallmark refused, Blue Mountain Arts hired a specialist in intellectual property rights and filed a lawsuit in U.S. District Court in Denver for violation of the company's trade dress and copyright. In November 1986 Blue Mountain Arts won a preliminary injunction which required Hallmark to remove 83 of the 90 offending cards from stores until the dispute was resolved. Hallmark followed the court order but distributed 83 new, similar card designs in the meantime.

While Hallmark conceded that it had copied the Blue Mountain Arts style, it did not view the practice as illegal and appealed to higher courts. In August 1987, Hallmark filed a brief in the Tenth Circuit Court of Appeals which contained the expert opinion of the Society of Illustrators, a prestigious, non-profit organization in New York City. The opinion stated that a monopoly on a particular artistic style should not allowed. Upon examining the brief, however, Blue Mountain Arts lawyers found the words ''Property of Hallmark Cards Creative Department'' stamped on the back of an exhibit. The lawyers then submitted a plea to the U.S. Court of Appeals to reject the brief based on Hallmark's obvious association with the Society of Illustrators. Eventually, the Court rejected the brief and upheld the injunction in May 1988.

The following August Hallmark retaliated, requesting the Supreme Court review the case on the basis that the injunction conflicted with the Copyright Act and arguing that to give an artist special claims on a style was unconstitutional. The *Wall Street Journal,* on September 22, 1988, quoted Blue Mountain Arts' response which termed Hallmark's imitation of the trade dress as an act of ''counterfeit.'' Blue Mountain Arts argued that, ''Contrary to Hallmark's assertion, Hallmark does not need to copy Blue Mountain's cards in order to compete.'' A company was recognized by its trade dress, they contended, and costumers could be confused by an imitation and that could have a negative impact on a company that had succeeded through its distinctive style.

The Supreme Court again upheld the preliminary injunction in October 1988, and Hallmark settled with Blue Mountain Arts. In the consent decree Hallmark agreed to repurchase the Personal Touch line of cards from retail outlets. The line would be discarded and replaced with a new concept which did not copy Blue Mountain Arts's trade dress. An admission of fault or liability was not required by either party. Also, Hallmark agreed not to block sales of Blue Mountain Arts products in its stores. The case was considered a landmark for the protection of intellectual property rights for creative entrepreneurs.

The lawsuit against Hallmark hampered productivity at Blue Mountain Arts, diverting time and energy away from the company's creative rhythm. Nevertheless, the company had garnered significant national media attention, as articles about it appeared in the *Wall Street Journal,* the *New York Times,* and *Life* magazine; in 1987, the Schutzes were interviewed for ABC's *20/20* television show. Despite a slight lull in creative efforts during this time, the Schutzes did publish a bestselling book in 1986, *To My Daughter, with Love, on the Important Things in Life. To My Son With Love* followed in 1988 and *Love, Love, Love* in 1989, all of the books being illustrated by Stephen Schutz. Moreover, bookmarks and coffee mugs were added to the Blue Mountain Arts product line.

Blue Mountain Arts in the Computer Age

The early 1990s at Blue Mountain Arts were characterized by a more high-tech approach to greeting cards. One significant computer-based innovation was Stephen Schutz's trademarked 5-D Stereogram, an application of technology to art that used a random-dot system and accounted for the span between human eyes in producing the visual sensation of a three-dimensional picture. Stereogram pictures were not immediately recognizable to the viewer, but at first glance looked like a melange of color. To see the image, a person had to look very close at the picture, nose almost touching it, and then pull it away from the eyes, at which point a three-dimensional image became apparent. The designs were created and transferred into a computer, which generated the multi-dimensional picture.

The computer program took Stephen Schutz, a Princeton-trained physicist, six months to write. Blue Mountain Arts produced one million cards which sold so quickly that a reprint was necessary a month later. The company sold the popular pictures as posters, cards, and collected in a book, *Endangered Species in 5-D Stereograms*, published in 1994.

When Blue Mountain Arts launched its web site offering free electronic greetings in September 1996, the Schutzes saw the Internet version of its greetings as another extension of their mission to help people communicate their feelings. The idea originated when their son Jared, later Director of Business Development at Blue Mountain Arts, went to college at Princeton, and the family began keeping in touch by electronic mail. The Schutzes' children began writing birthday and other special greetings by e-mail, leading to the development of e-mail greeting cards.

Blue Mountain Arts started with 35 card designs for birthdays, graduation, emotional support, thank you, and all-occasion greetings of love and friendship. The recipient of an online greeting received an e-mail notification which included a link to the company's web site. The recipient then accessed the greeting from the "Card Pickup Window" on the company's web site. The cards featured animated animals, some of which sang or spoke, and danced or moved in some manner when the viewer clicked a computer mouse on the image. By the 1996 winter holidays 100 different greeting card designs were available on the Internet from Blue Mountain Arts.

The company's electronic greetings were unique in several ways. True to the company's mission of helping people communicate, the greetings were free of charge, and personal messages could be added by the sender. Moreover, Blue Mountain Arts did not require that personal questions be answered before a greeting could be delivered. By contrast, other online greetings routinely charged about $2.50 for an online card and required demographic surveys be answered by the sender, with questions about gender, age, and mailing address. Having approximately 20,000 retail outlets throughout the United States and in several foreign countries, Blue Mountain Arts decided not to sell its printed products online, believing that to do so would be disloyal to their vendors.

Blue Mountain Arts succeeded without advertising on other web sites and without extensive advertising on its own web site. The company was concerned that advertising banners would interfere with the more intimate experience customers had come to expect from the company. It did, however, experiment with subtle, less invasive forms of advertising to cover the costs of maintaining and developing online greetings. For example, at the web site proflowers.com, an online flower delivery company founded by Jared Schutz, a Blue Mountain Arts banner would appear on the screen only after that PC user had already sent a greeting card and was familiar with the company.

By the late 1980s Blue Mountain Arts had expanded its online offerings to over 1,000 online card designs, available for every known and obscure holiday in the United States as well as worldwide cultures and religions. Moreover, the web site incorporated French and Spanish language accessibility. The French language cards, found under *Arts Mont Bleu,* supplied greetings for French holidays, such as Bastille Day, while Spanish language cards for Spanish holidays could be found under *Monte Azul.* German language cards and holidays were expected to be launched in 1999 under *Die Kunst der Blauen Berge.*

By the end of 1997 the company's web site was among the ten most visited Internet domains, with more than 12 million people having visited the site. In April 1999 alone more than five million people accessed www.bluemountain.com. Through word-of-mouth as well as through the access of greeting card

recipients, Blue Mountain Arts reached an estimated 21 percent of Internet users. Annual retail sales of their printed products has increased 20 percent since the web site was launched.

Blue Mountain Arts v. Microsoft in 1998

In November 1998, Blue Mountain Arts found evidence that the junk e-mail filter on Microsoft's new Internet browser, Internet Explorer, transferred electronic greetings sent from Blue Mountain Arts customers to junk mail trash. When the company contacted Microsoft they were informed that a bug in the software caused the problem, and that no definitive date for resolving the problem could be forecast. Further, on November 27 of that year, Blue Mountain Arts found evidence that WebTV, a subsidiary of Microsoft as well as its Internet service provider, had obstructed thousands of the company's e-mail greetings to WebTV customers.

Microsoft had recently issued an updated test software, Outlook Express 5 Beta, an electronic mail software program that detected junk e-mail and diverted it to a junk mail folder before an Outlook Express e-mail user would see it. The filter determined junk e-mail by particular characteristics, such as multiple exclamation points and words in all capital letters, as well as by a statistical formula that analyzed the frequency with which those characteristics were found.

Several coincidences raised suspicions of unfair business practices on the part of Microsoft. Blue Mountain Arts had never had any problems over the past two years in providing electronic greeting cards, and Microsoft had launched its own greeting card service about the time the problems began. Also, the timing of the obstruction coincided with peak holiday greeting season, from Thanksgiving through Valentine's Day. Blue Mountain Arts was naturally concerned about a potential loss of credibility and goodwill with its customers and advertisers.

In December 1998 Blue Mountain Arts filed for a restraining order to stop Microsoft and WebTV from obstructing the transfer of its e-mail greetings on the Internet. WebTV promptly altered its filtering process to allow the greetings to proceed to their recipients. Moreover, a temporary restraining order was issued against Microsoft by a California Superior Court, which required Microsoft to cooperate with Blue Mountain Arts to redesign the greeting cards so that they would not be diverted to the junk mail folder by the junk mail filter.

On February 2, 1999 the California Superior Court ruled in favor of Blue Mountain Arts, transferring the temporary restraining order to a preliminary injunction. The Court found that Microsoft's assistance to Blue Mountain Arts under the temporary restraining order had not effectively resolved the problem. The injunction required Microsoft to allow the effective delivery of the company's electronic greetings by altering the software itself.

Judge Robert Baines acknowledged Microsoft and Blue Mountain Arts as competitors in the electronic greeting card business and found it inconceivable that the Microsoft engineers who developed the filter had no knowledge of the competitive electronic greeting card business. The judge considered a variety of factors which led him to conclude that Microsoft had, "some concern if not outright targeting of Blue Mountain Arts or similar outfits.'' Having won the preliminary injunction, Blue Mountain Arts hoped to settle the case out of court as it moved into a new century of business.

Further Reading

''Card Concern Battles Hallmark's Request to Supreme Court,'' *Wall Street Journal,* September 22, 1988, p. 32.

Cuff, Daniel F., ''Blue Mountain Owners Hail Ruling on Cards,'' *New York Times,* May 25, 1988, p. 28.

Espe, Erik, ''Greetings from Microsoft,'' *Business Journal,* December 21, 1998, p. 1.

Greim, Lisa, ''Card Firm Accuses Microsoft of Blocking Software maker Says Filter Halts Even Own E-Greetings,'' *Denver Rocky Mountain News,* December 22, 1998, p. 1B.

——, ''Judge Agrees with Boulder Firm, Slaps Microsoft,'' *Denver Rocky Mountain News,* January 30, 1999, p. 3B.

''Hallmark Deal Ends Suit,'' *New York Times,* October 25, 1988, p. 52.

''Hallmark Ordered to Pull Card Line,'' *New York Times,* November 22, 1986, p. 18.

Hamilton, Anita, ''Online Greetings,'' *Time,* March 22, 1999, p. 116.

''Injunction Against Company is Upheld by Appeals Court,'' *Wall Street Journal,* May 26, 1988, p. 6.

Jackson, Tim, ''Card Wars Result in Some Bitter Messages,'' *Financial Times,* December 28, 1998, p. 10.

Johnston, Stuart, ''Piling On Microsoft,'' *Information Week,* December 21, 1998, p. 131.

——, ''You're Invited to Stop, At Least Temporarily,'' *Information Week,* January 4, 1999, p. 16.

''Judge to Microsoft: Don't Block E-Cards,'' *Newsbytes,* December 22, 1998.

Kadlececk, John, ''Stephen and Susan Polis-Schutz, Blue Mountain Arts,'' *Boulder County Business Report,* December 1988, p. 31.

Kaufman, Leslie, ''60s Messages in a 90s Medium,'' *New York Times,* January 23, 1999, p. C1.

Kelley, Tina, ''A Small Card Maker Finds Itself Atop the Web,'' *New York Times,* June 4, 1998, p. D3.

Kreck, Dick, ''There's Magic in Those Spots Before Your Eyes,'' *Denver Post,* March 28, 1994, p. 8E.

Lambert, Eileen, ''Low-Key Blue Mountain Arts Plays Hardball,'' *Boulder Planet,* March 10–16, 1999, p. 7.

Long, Bill, ''Colorado's Blue Mountain Arts Offers Electronic Greeting Cards via Web,'' *Knight-Ridder/Tribune Business News,* September 26, 1996.

''Microsoft Must Alter Software in Blue Mountain Suit,'' *Newsbytes,* January 29, 1999.

''Poetic Justice,'' *Life,* August 1988, p. 8.

Riedman, Patricia, ''Electronic Greetings Competition Intensifies Ads Bolster Blue Mountain and E-Greetings,'' *Advertising Age,* October 19, 1998, p. 48.

''Rocky Mountain High: Greeting Card Company Scores Big on Internet,'' *Tulsa World,* April 11, 1999, p. 53.

Rowland, Mary, ''Tales of Triumph: Three Small Companies Decided to Put Up their Dukes and Fight the Big Guys who Stole their Ideas,'' *Working Woman,* February 1988, p. 76.

Stricharchuk, Gregory, '' 'Friend of Court' Rebuffed,'' *Wall Street Journal,* December 24, 1987, p. 9.

Thomas, Cynthia, ''Hallmark is in David-and-Goliath Battle,'' *Wall Street Journal,* July 18, 1986, p. 6.

Trott, Bob, ''Microsoft Gets It from All Sides,'' *InfoWorld,* December 21, 1998, p. 8.

Wang, Penelope, ''A Not-So-Nice Greeting: Hallmark Challenges Competitors with Look-Alikes,'' *Newsweek,* November 3, 1986, p. 54.

Williams, Mary Jo, ''Caring Enough to Copy the Very Best,'' *Fortune,* June 20, 1988, p. 12.

—Mary Tradii

Bonneville International Corporation

Broadcast House, 55 North 300 West
Salt Lake City, Utah 84110-1160
U.S.A.
(801) 575-7500
Fax: (801) 575-7548
Web site: http://www.bonneville.com

*Wholly Owned Subsidiary of Deseret Management
    Corporation*
Incorporated: 1964
Employees: 1,300
Sales: $90.5 million (1998 est.)
NAIC: 513111 Radio Networks; 513112 Radio Stations;
    51312 Television Broadcasting; 51211 Motion Picture
    & Video Production

Bonneville International Corporation operates Salt Lake City's KSL-TV and also KCSG-TV in St. George, Utah, in addition to 15 radio stations in Salt Lake City, Chicago, San Francisco, Los Angeles, and Washington, D.C. The company is a subsidiary of Deseret Management Corporation, a holding company owned by the Church of Jesus Christ of Latter-day Saints (LDS). Bonneville's own subsidiary Bonneville Communications produces award-winning spots promoting family values and the LDS church. Those "Homefront" ads shown worldwide on many commercial stations and many other Bonneville productions have received numerous professional awards. Bonneville also produces music and entertainment specials, educational programs, and television movies. Through satellite technology, Bonneville broadcasts church and Brigham Young University sports programs to audiences in many nations.

Origins

Although radio was invented by Marconi around the turn of the century, commercial radio stations were not started until the Roaring Twenties. In 1922 the LDS church started one of the nation's first radio stations when church President Heber J. Grant spoke on station KZN from a tin shack on top of Salt Lake City's Deseret News Building. The church-owned newspaper had responded to the federal government's encouragement of newspapers to enter the new broadcasting industry.

In 1923 KZN began a tradition carried on by its radio and television successors when it broadcast part of the LDS General Conference held in the Tabernacle in historic Temple Square. The following year KZN was split off into a separate firm from the *Deseret News*, and in 1925 KZN became KSL to remind listeners that it was based in Salt Lake City.

Another landmark occurred on July 15, 1929, when KSL first broadcast a performance of the Mormon Tabernacle Choir. That weekly event became "the longest-lasting continuous regular program in broadcast history, celebrating 65 years of continuous broadcasts in July of 1994," according to Dr. Rodney H. Brady.

During the Great Depression, KSL in 1932 became one of the first 50,000-watt clear channel AM stations in the United States and also became part of the Columbia Broadcasting Network, later renamed the CBS Network. President Franklin D. Roosevelt made radio history in the 1930s by using his "radio chats" to encourage Americans to stay optimistic in the midst of troubled times.

Americans bought more radios as the number of stations proliferated in the 1920s and 1930s. In 1929 just over ten million households owned at least one radio; that number jumped to 27.5 million in 1939 as radio became a major source of information and entertainment.

In 1946 KSL started Utah's first FM radio station, and three years later KSL Television began broadcasting in black and white. TV in the 1950s featured family-oriented programs, such as *Father Knows Best* and *The Ed Sullivan Show*.

Bonneville International: The Arch L. Madsen Era

In 1961 LDS Church President David O. McKay recruited Arch L. Madsen to leave Washington, D.C., for Salt Lake City and become KSL's general manager. Madsen's leadership and

67

Company Perspectives:

Bonneville International Corporation is a values-driven company composed of values-driven people making a difference through mass communications. We make a difference by serving and improving individuals, families, communities, and society through quality entertainment, information, news, and values-oriented products. We make a difference by satisfying our customers' communications needs through superior programming, creative marketing, advanced technology, and skillful use of our resources. We make a difference by providing professional and personal growth opportunities for our colleagues, by enhancing positive feelings of self-worth, and by exerting positive leadership in the communications industry. Central to the achievement of our mission are these core values: integrity, excellence, service, profitability, leadership, and sensitivity.

years of experience in the broadcast industry helped KSL purchase Seattle-based KIRO television and radio stations in January 1964, which led to the organization of Bonneville International Corporation five months later.

In the 1960s broadcast companies were restricted to owning no more than seven stations of each kind—AM radio, FM radio, and television. Under those regulations, Bonneville decided to expand into selected major markets. In 1966 Bonneville made its first acquisition—an FM radio station later named WMXV that broadcast from New York City's Empire State Building. In 1969 Bonneville purchased KBIG-FM, a major station located on Sunset Boulevard in Los Angeles. Under Arch Madsen, Bonneville also acquired Kansas City's KMBZ-AM and KLTH-FM in the 1960s.

Also in the 1960s Bonneville was one of the first independent broadcast companies to start its own news section in the nation's capital when it organized its Washington News Bureau. Using the latest electronic devices, the bureau provided Bonneville's radio and TV stations with the latest reports about politics and government.

Bonneville continued in the 1960s to increase Mormons' access to their church headquarters by starting to broadcast LDS General Conferences on nationwide television and using satellite technology to broadcast General Conferences to other nations.

In January 1972 Bonneville began distributing its first "Homefront" spots designed to build family solidarity and to increase awareness of the LDS church. The first campaign, "Your Children Need More of You," featured ten different radio and three TV spots shown on 1,297 radio and 141 TV stations.

The success of these spots was shown in a 1985 Opinion Research Corporation survey that found 54 percent of Americans, when aided, could recall an LDS advertising message. The next highest was 18 percent who could recall a Catholic ad message.

In 1975 Bonneville organized Bonneville Communications, a full-service advertising and creative services firm to handle U.S. and international broadcasts of General Conferences and Mormon Tabernacle Choir performances.

Bonneville under Arch Madsen in the 1970s acquired San Francisco's KOIT-FM and later KOIT-AM. In 1978 it acquired Dallas-based KZPS-FM and later KZPS-AM.

Bonneville's expansion in the 1960s and 1970s led to its relocation in the early 1980s to the Broadcast House, a key component of downtown Salt Lake City's Triad Center. Three Saudi Arabian brothers named Adnan, Essam, and Asil Khashoggi, who had made fortunes as arms dealers, decided to invest in Salt Lake City when they created a Utah subsidiary called Triad Utah. Despite the Khashoggis being investigated by the U.S. Securities and Exchange Commission, their playboy reputations, and the reservations of some Bonneville board members, the LDS church cooperated by selling six key acres to Triad to construct the new building. "Bonneville's Broadcast House became the first, most visible part of the Triad package," wrote Robert Gottlieb and Peter Wiley in their 1984 book *America's Saints.*

Bonneville International's President Arch Madsen retired in 1985 after reaching the company's mandatory retirement age of 72. In a 1989 *Deseret News* article, Madsen said that because of Bonneville's numerous awards, "I don't want to brag, but I built the company and it's built a very good reputation. . . . We purchased (the radio and television stations) for a song compared to their present value."

Bonneville Under Dr. Rodney Brady in the Late 20th Century

Bonneville's Board Chairman Gordon B. Hinckley, first counselor in the LDS Church's First Presidency, in 1985 asked Dr. Rodney H. Brady to replace Madsen as Bonneville International's president. Although he had no broadcasting experience, Brady accepted the offer to build on the foundation set by Arch Madsen.

A Utah native, Brady had received B.S. and M.B.A. degrees from the University of Utah before earning a doctorate in business administration from the Harvard Business School. He then spent three years as an Air Force officer, followed by serving as vice-president of Management Systems Corporation and in the mid-1960s as a vice-president of Hughes Tool Company's Aircraft Division. Beginning in 1970, Brady was the assistant secretary for administration and management at the U.S. Department of Health, Education, and Welfare. Next, he became an executive vice-president and board member of Bergen Brunswig Corporation, and in 1978 was chosen as the president of Weber State College in Ogden, Utah.

Brady in the late 1980s maintained Bonneville's standards. For example, in 1988 the company rejected a new fall TV show called *Dirty Dancing* offered by CBS to its affiliates "because it lacked values and quality," according to a 1989 *Deseret News* article. Brady was pleased when CBS canceled the show after just a few weeks into the new season.

"We're not happy with the quality of network programming, but it's important to be affiliated with the networks," said Brady, who realized that some network programs were fine and that Bonneville's presence might "bring others up to higher ground in programming."

In 1988 the LDS church and several other Protestant, Catholic, and Jewish churches sponsored the creation of the new Vision Interfaith Satellite Network (VISN), a cable television channel operated by the nonprofit National Interfaith Cable Coalition. Although not a member of the coalition, the LDS church provided various programs for its allocated time periods. "VISN initially provides the Church an opportunity to disseminate to millions of viewers—both members and nonmembers—many of the programs the Church has produced over the years," said Richard P. Lindsay, the LDS church's managing director of public communications in the November 1988 *Ensign,* a church magazine. "It will help those of other faiths understand our strong moral and family values." Unlike some other religious channels, VISN did not include direct proselytizing, money requests, or criticism of other churches.

Brady also faced financial challenges as the entire broadcast industry in the 1980s no longer enjoyed double-digit growth due to competition from cable television, independent producers, more radio stations, and the growing number of Americans watching rented movies on their VCRs. CBS, ABC, and NBC remained important, but consumers gained a diversity of new options for media entertainment and education.

In response, Brady made many changes at Bonneville International to keep the firm profitable. "The company's other values come before profitability, but profitability is necessary to achieve the other values," said Brady. Some employees were disappointed when some fellow workers lost their jobs, but in 1988 Brady reported that Bonneville enjoyed its most profitable year without divulging details of the private company.

In 1989 Bonneville International owned and operated two TV stations: Salt Lake City's KSL-TV Channel 5, a 36,000-watt station with 22 percent market share; and Seattle's KIRO-TV Channel 7, a 316,000-watt station with 20.4 percent market share. By the mid-1990s Bonneville also ran 15 radio stations, including Salt Lake City's KSL-AM; KIRO-AM and KIRO-FM in Seattle; San Francisco's KOIT-AM and KOIT-FM; KBIG-FM in Los Angeles; Kansas City's KMBZ-AM, KLTH-FM, KCMO-AM, and KCMO-FM; Chicago's WTMX-FM; KPSN-FM and KIDR-AM in Phoenix; KZPS-FM in Dallas; and New York City's WMXV-FM.

By the mid-1990s Bonneville subsidiary Bonneville Communications had earned about 400 awards, including 15 Clios for advertising excellence, three Emmys, and a Bronze Lion from the Cannes Film Festival. Bonneville Communications used what it called "Heart Sell" emotional advertising to promote the LDS church and also other clients, including Foot Locker, Kinney Shoe Corporation, Wilson's Leather, B. Dalton Booksellers, The Salvation Army, Charter Medical Corporation, and The American Cancer Society. A company publication in the mid-1990s stated, "As one of the pioneers of high-quality public service advertising, Bonneville Communications clears more free air time for its clients than any other agency in the world."

Bonneville's "Homefront" ads, started in the early 1970s, had by 1994 been shown on over 5,000 radio and 800 television stations on NBC, CBS, ABC, CBC, and several cable channels in the United States and Canada, plus over 6,550 radio and 1,300 TV stations in Latin America, Australia, Spain, New Zealand, Italy, Portugal, Russia, and the Czech Republic. A 1994 Bonneville fact sheet stated that "Homefront is the longest running, most broadcast, highest awarded public service campaign in the world."

Those spots, some of which introduced listeners or viewers to *The Book of Mormon,* played a role in the church's worldwide missionary program. A 1993 Church Missionary Department survey of 13,000 new converts found that 57 percent had seen Homefront ads, and 69 percent of those who had seen the ads said they had helped in their decision to join the church.

The Late 1990s

In 1995 Bonneville sold KIRO-TV in Seattle to A.H. Belo Corporation of Dallas for $162.5 million. By the end of 1998 Bonneville no longer had any TV or radio stations in Kansas City, Phoenix, Dallas, Seattle, or New York. Bonneville's sale of at least 14 radio stations and purchase of several others resulted from the 1996 Telecommunications Act that allowed firms to increase their ownership in one market from two AM and two FM stations to a total of eight stations. Bonneville's President Bruce Reese, who replaced Rodney Brady in June 1996, in 1997 reported that the firm's strategy was to concentrate its radio stations in major markets preferred by large advertisers.

In 1998 Bonneville International in Salt Lake City continued to operate KSL-TV (which had switched network affiliation from CBS to NBC), KSL-AM, Bonneville Communications, Bonneville LDS Radio Network, Bonneville Satellite, Bonneville Worldwide Entertainment, and Video West Productions. Bonneville also operated WNND-FM, WTMX-FM, and WLUP-FM in Chicago; KOIT-FM, KOIT-AM, KDFC-FM, and KZOZ-FM in San Francisco; KZLA-FM in Los Angeles; and KCSG-TV in St. George, Utah. Bonneville in Washington, D.C., continued to operate its News Bureau and also owned three radio stations: WGMS-FM, WTOP-FM, and WTOP-AM. In addition, Bonneville operated three stations in nearby Arlington, Virginia: WWVZ-FM, WWZZ-FM (formerly WXTR-FM), and WXTR-AM.

In late 1998 a new entity called DTV Utah announced its plans to build a $7 million tower near Salt Lake City to broadcast digital signals. KSL-TV managed this operation, but it was supported by seven other TV stations in the area: KTVX, KUTV, KUED, KBYU, KULC, KUWB, and KJZZ. This move, part of the nationwide transition from analog to digital technology, was stimulated by the Federal Communications Commission's requirement that all commercial TV stations must broadcast digital signals by May 1, 2002 and all television broadcasts must be digital by 2006.

In May 1999 the Deseret Management Corporation announced the creation of its new subsidiary called World Media

Inc. to coordinate the electronic and Internet activities of Bonneville International and other Deseret Management companies, along with those of Brigham Young University and other LDS-owned organizations. Rodney Brady served as the president and chief executive officer of the new firm.

Bonneville International's development reflected the expansion of Mormonism from a primarily Intermountain West church before World War II to a widespread national and international religion in the second half of the 20th century. For example, from 1980 to 1990 church membership in the United States grew from 3.2 million to 4.2 million, an increase of 30 percent, compared to the overall U.S. population increase in the same decade of ten percent. In 1990, eight states had at least 100,000 Mormons. The church's growth continued in the 1990s, with its worldwide membership reaching about ten million by the end of the decade.

The bottom line was that Bonneville International played an important part of the worldwide growth of Mormon influence, along with Zion's Security Corporation, Deseret Book Company, and Beneficial Life Insurance, all part of the Deseret Management Corporation.

To expand its international capabilities, Bonneville in 1996 signed its first agreement with Loral Orion Network Systems, a subsidiary of New York-based Loral Space & Communications. The 1996 deal allowed the church to use Loral Orion's first satellite, *Orion 1,* to broadcast its programs to European cities. In 1998 Bonneville signed a second contract that granted the firm rights to use *Orion 2,* scheduled to be launched in the summer of 1999, to broadcast to Latin America. The Bonneville-Loral Orion agreements were quite significant, especially in light of Loral's plans to launch satellites that eventually would reach 85 percent of the world's population.

Unlike religions that rejected much modern technology due to an either-or perspective, the LDS church and Bonneville International embraced many of the latest discoveries. Bonneville integrated faith and finances, reason and revelation, and computers and community values in a way that served both church members and commercial clients while impressing broadcast professionals. Combining Bonneville International's high-tech capabilities and professional business management with its core values based on religious ideals proved to be a successful method of running a corporation.

Principal Subsidiaries

Bonneville Worldwide Entertainment; Bonneville Communications; Video West Productions; Bonneville LDS Radio Network; Bonneville Satellite; Bonneville Washington News Bureau; World Media Inc.

Further Reading

Brady, Rodney H., *Bonneville at Thirty: A Values-Driven Company Composed of Values-Driven People,* New York: Newcomen Society of the United States, 1994.

Brown, Matthew, ''Bonneville International,'' *Deseret News,* October 1, 1989, pp. M1–M2.

Carricaburu, Lisa, ''Digital TV Hits Utah Years Early . . . ,'' *Salt Lake Tribune,* October 21, 1998, p. A1.

''Church Helps Form Cable TV Network,'' *Ensign,* November 1988, p. 109.

Goldfisher, Alastair, ''Radio Deals Create Static for Listeners,'' *Business Journal—San Jose,* July 14, 1997, p. 1.

Gottlieb, Robert, and Peter Wiley, *America's Saints: The Rise of Mormon Power,* New York: G. P. Putnam's Sons, 1984.

——, ''The Search for Mormon Influence,'' *Utah Holiday,* August 1986, pp. 28, 30, 32.

Hart, John L., ''LDS in West Increase; South, East Also Grow,'' *LDS Church News,* June 8, 1991, pp. 3–4.

Jenkins, Carri, ''Outmigration: Making Home Away from Home,'' *BYU Today,* May 1989, pp. 39–43.

''Loral Orion to Expand Bonneville International's Broadcasting into South America,'' *Business Wire,* April 7, 1998, p. 1.

Taylor, Chuck, ''KIRO-TV to Be Sold As Result of Merger,'' *Seattle Times,* September 27, 1996, p. A11.

Walden, David, ''Kirton & McConkie,'' in *Centennial Utah,* edited by by G. Wesley Johnson and Marian Ashby Johnson, Encino, Calif.: Cherbo Publishing Group, 1995, pp. 64–65.

—David M. Walden

The Boyds Collection, Ltd.

350 South Street
McSherrystown, Pennsylvania 17344
U.S.A.
(717) 633-9898
Fax: (717) 633-5511

Public Company
Founded: 1979
Employees: 203
Sales: $197 million (1998)
Stock Exchanges: New York
Ticker Symbol: FOB
NAIC: 42299 Other Miscellaneous Nondurable Goods
Wholesalers

The Boyds Collection, Ltd. is a leading American designer, importer, and distributor of handcrafted collectibles. While Boyds is perhaps best known for its lines of plush bears and resin figurines, the company also offers such gift items as glass ornaments and doll accessories. Boyds products are generally recognized for their quality craftsmanship, low prices, and designs characterized as "Folksy with Attitude." The company offers 430 different plush animals, which range in price from $4 to $95 each. Most Boyds animals are fully jointed with movable arms, legs, and heads, and their outer coverings are fashioned from a variety of fabrics, ranging from acrylic plush to custom-dyed chenille wool. The company's founder and CEO, Gary Lowenthal, designs each of the plush animals along with a team of artists. Once Lowenthal creates a pattern and prototype, the animals are taken to a seamstress in China, who produces a working model. Each animal is stuffed and embroidered by hand.

Boyds' three major resin products are marketed under the names Bearstones, Folkstones, and Dollstones, figurine lines that include small resin bears—similar in look to the plush animals—resin angels, faeries, and snowpeople, and resin dolls, frogs, and penguins. Each resin piece, retailing anywhere from $9 to $60 apiece, is inscribed with a hidden bear paw—a symbol of authenticity—while the bottom of each piece is stamped with the name, edition, and piece number. Boyds' success is attributed in part to its niche distribution; Boyds sells its products through a network of 23,000 independent gift and collectible retailers, premier department stores, selected catalogue retailers, and televised QVC showcases. Moreover, Boyds selectively licenses its images; for example, its popular Bearstones® images are licensed to Sunrise Stationery, a division of Hallmark Cards, for use on paper products. Kohlberg Kravis Roberts (KKR) owns 56 percent of Boyds.

Modest Beginnings in 1979

Boyds Collection, Ltd. originated in 1979 when Bloomingdale managers Gary (G.M.) and Justina (Tina) Lowenthal left their jobs and moved to Boyds, Maryland, to open a small antique shop out of their "semi-restored" Victorian home. However, the Lowenthals found the antique business expensive and confining. They later moved on to other ventures, such as the making of decorative dried wreaths and split oak tables, neither of which proved profitable. The couple next started buying and selling antique reproductions, which were much more affordable than antiques.

By 1982, the Lowenthals began to wholesale some of their own reproductions, including their very successful duck decoys. The decoys were hand-painted and available in many different sizes and styles, including a nine-inch teal and a giant three-foot whistling swan. Word of the beautiful ducks spread quickly, and the Lowenthals began filling orders for three dozen ducks a day. Gary, who designed the ducks, later estimated that they painted about 40,000 ducks altogether.

In 1984, the Lowenthals produced their first resin sculptures of minutely detailed miniature houses. These "Gnomes Homes" were a combination of American architecture and Gary Lowenthal's imagination. Around the same time, the Lowenthals' created their first plush teddy bear, which they named Matthew after their newborn son. The merlino-wool teddy bear was a hit, and Boyds was on its way to becoming a leader in the collectibles industry.

The company quickly outgrew its space in the Lowenthal home, and the couple moved operations to an old Sunday school

Company Perspectives:

The Boyds Collection Ltd. has received many Awards and a whole lotta Recognition from the Gift Industry and Collectors alike, for which we are not-too-Humbly Grateful! Our wonderful Whimsical and ''Slightly Off-Centered'' designs speak to the Heart and Soul ... a bit of Ol'Fashioned Appeal in a slick and fast-moving world.

on the same street. When the ''Boyds Bears'' proved extremely popular, the need for greater space again arose. In 1987, the Boyds company was relocated from Maryland to McSherrystown, Pennsylvania, near Gettysburg, to take advantage of much-needed space and favorable labor markets. The young company also expanded its product line to include hares, moose, and cats in addition to bears.

The 1980s: Carving Out a Niche and Building a Name

Boyds decided against selling its products to major discount stores and toys chains, preferring to distribute them instead to upscale department stores and retailers. This decision helped Boyds develop close relationships with its retailers, as well as to occupy a strong market niche and establish a distinct brand identity. Gary Lowenthal, who referred to himself as ''The Head Bean,'' believed the company's close relationship with its retailers helped it identify market trends, predict customer demand, and shorten the lead time for new products.

The company also steered away from mass producing its plush animals, deciding instead to continue making each product by hand. Lowenthal went to great lengths to ensure that the company's products were meticulously handcrafted, modifying some of his designs 30 times before completion. Each pattern was either cut by hand or machine, depending on its design, and then hand-stuffed. The plush animals' noses, eyebrows, pawpads and other features were also embroidered by hand. Before being shipped to retailers, each plush animal was hand-brushed and inspected three times.

Ironically, while collectors were delighted with the high quality of Boyds products, they were dismayed with the low price. Most collectors equated higher prices with enhanced value. However, Lowenthal disagreed, believing that an item's cost did not necessarily reflect its worth. He refused to inflate the price of an item to make it more collectible. Lowenthal claimed that it was more important to put Boyds bears in the hands of kids than to make them more desirable to collectors. He did manage to sustain collectors' interest by retiring about 40 percent of the company's products each year in addition to introducing new lines. New lines had a similar ''look'' that made them easily recognizable as Boyds.

New Product Lines in the 1990s

In 1992, the immensely popular T.J.'s Best Dressed line made its debut. The line featured fully jointed bears, cats,

moose, and other animals dressed in handmade stylish clothing, including homespun rompers and hats trimmed with silk flowers. T.J.'s Best Dressed quickly became Boyds most desired collection, with each piece retailing for between $11 and $52.

However, it was The Bearstone Collection®, unveiled in 1993, that made Boyds a major contender in the collectibles market. The Bearstone Collection, a line of small resin teddy bear figurines, became so sought-after that some retailers claimed the line earned twice its projected sales in its first year.

In 1994, Boyds unveiled The Folkstone Collection, a line of nontraditional whimsical figurines with folk art themes. The Folkstones Collection was later divided into three lines: The Folkstones and Wee Folkstones, two lines of ''pencil-style'' santas, snowpeople, faeries, angels, and animals; Ribbit and Company, a line of distinguished-looking frogs; and The Tuxedo Gang, a line of sophisticated penguins.

Yesterday's Child ... the Dollstone Collection, a series of little girl figurines from different eras with companion dolls or teddy bears, was introduced in 1996. Like the Bearstones and Folkstones, the Dollstones were handmade, handpainted, and handboxed. The limited-edition dolls were 16 inches tall and came with a six-inch plush companion and special accessories.

During the same year, the Loyal Order of Friends of Boyds (LOFB) was formed to further enhance product identity. The club grew quickly and had over 100,000 members in 1996. Members paid an annual fee of $32.50 and received a special product kit that contained a resin figurine, a plush animal, and a resin pin. The items found in the kit were limited editions, not sold in stores. Members also had the opportunity to purchase additional limited editions offered only to members.

In the fall of 1997, Boyds expanded the Dollstone Collection and introduced its first two porcelain dolls. Dissatisfied with the look of the hands and feet on most porcelain dolls, Lowenthal developed a new sculpting technique that allowed for more intricate details. The resultant Boyds porcelain dolls had finely crafted hands, which could hold watering cans and cookie trays, and wear textured socks and shoes with real shoelaces. The dolls were poseable and finely dressed. A series of 12-inch dolls was made available in unlimited editions that sold for $33 to $34.

Boyds also produced a line of accessories for its plush animals and dolls called The Bear Necessities. The line included upholstered chairs and sofas, wooden cabinets, and garden furniture. In 1998, one of Boyds' porcelain dolls was a runner-up in the NALED (National Association of Limited Edition Dealers) Achievement Awards. Boyds' dolls later received a DOTY (Doll of the Year) award.

A Buyout in 1998

By 1998, Boyds' distribution network included over 19,350 independent gift and collectible retailers, which represented over 23,500 individual stores. A specially selected network of resin dealers—about 6,050 accounts—generated most of the sales. Because of the high sales volume of Boyds products, resin dealers were carefully selected. In order to be granted dealership status, resin dealers had to meet an annual performance criteria. In 1998,

Boyds had a waiting list of about 5,500 resin dealers, most of whom were already plush dealers who had expressed an interest in selling Boyds resin figurines. Boyds divided its resin dealers into Gold, Silver, and Bronze Paw distinctions, based on the amount of merchandise the dealers ordered annually from the company. Dealers maintaining the highest Paw distinctions enjoyed benefits such as priority delivery of products and special consideration when ordering limited editions.

With Boyds having grown from a small home business to a major competitor in the collectibles market, Gary and Justina Lowenthal found themselves back in the rat race they had tried to escape when they left Bloomingdale's almost 20 years earlier. Gary Lowenthal, in particular, longed to spend more time developing designs and nurturing the creative side of the business and less time with administrative affairs. In April 1998, Kohlberg Kravis Roberts (KKR), a private investment firm and one of the oldest buyout firms in New York, invested over $600 million in the company.

After the buyout, KKR owned 56 percent of Boyds. Industry experts considered the move a risky one for KKR. Even though Boyds was extremely profitable, the company was young and had few hard assets. Moreover, because its products were theme-oriented and selectively retired, its future depended upon the popularity of its upcoming designs. Boyds was also highly leveraged at the time of the buyout, with a debt equaling 100 percent of its capitalization. In fact, the KKR buyout panicked many collectors who felt Boyds' success depended upon Gary Lowenthal's designs. To alleviate their fears, Lowenthal issued a public statement in which he promised to stay involved with the creative aspects of the company. Lowenthal said he hoped KKR would handle much of the business and legal operations that had been taking up too much of his time.

The year after the KKR buyout was a good one. The company posted a 52 percent rise in revenue growth to $197.8 million from $129.8 million, and this growth enabled Boyds to go public. On February 26, 1999, Boyds began trading on the New York Stock Exchange under the symbol FOB—an acronym for Friends of Boyds—with an initial offering of $18 a share. The company sold approximately 9.25 million shares, and shareholders sold another 6.75 million. Boyds' offering thus totaled 16 million shares and generated approximately $288 million. The company used the proceeds to redeem part of its outstanding notes and to reduce its bank debt.

The year 1999 also marked the introduction of some new Boyds lines. With the unveiling of its Jodibears line (named for its designer, Jody Battaglia), Boyds added puppets to its lineup. To satisfy collector demand for high-end Boyds products, the company introduced its Uptown Collection, a three-bear series limited to 12,000 pieces each. The Uptown bears retailed for about $60 and sold for as high as $120 on the secondary market.

While Boyds plush animals and resin figurines comprised 97 percent of its sales in 1998, the company licensed its images for other products as well, such as clothing, home textiles, stationery, and rubber stamps. As it moved toward a new century, the company planned to increase this licensing, as well as to unveil new products, including a line of "millennium bears" and a piece to celebrate its 20th anniversary. Moreover, the company was also planning to expand into Asia, Europe, and Canada.

Further Reading

"The Boyds Collection Announces Initial Public Offering," *Business Wire,* December 23, 1998.

"The Boyds Collection Begins Trading on the NYSE," *PR Newswire,* March 5, 1999.

Dochat, Tom, "McSherrystown, PA-Based Marketer of Boyds Bears Goes Public," *Knight-Ridder/Tribune Business News,* March 5, 1999.

"KKR Makes Quick Profit by Bringing Boyds to IPO," *Buyouts,* March 8, 1999.

"KKR to Make Equity Investment in Boyds," *PR Newswire,* April 2, 1998.

"Store Promotions Bear-ly and More," *Playthings,* February, 1995, p. 50.

Tuttle, Denis, "Boy, Oh, Boyds!," *Beans and Bears,* June 1999, p. 61.

—Tracey Vasil Biscontini

Broderbund Software

500 Redwood Boulevard
Novato, California 94947-6921
U.S.A.
(415) 382-4400
Fax: (415) 382-4582
Web site: http://www.broderbund.com

Wholly Owned Division of Mattel, Inc.
Incorporated: 1981 as Broderbund Software, Inc.
Employees: 550
Sales: $290 million (1998 est.)
NAIC: 42143 Computer & Computer Peripheral
Equipment & Software Wholesalers; 51121 Software
Publishers

Broderbund Software, which became a division of Mattel, Inc. in 1999, develops, publishes, and markets consumer software for home, school, and small business use. Recognized as a pioneer and leading producer of educational software, the company also became well known for its personal productivity and entertainment software. Through a series of mergers and acquisitions, the Broderbund software line has changed through the years, and its lineup in the late 1990s was overseen first by The Learning Company and then by ultimate parent company Mattel. Popular software titles available under the Broderbund brand name have included various versions of *The Print Shop, Cosmopolitan Fashion Makeover, Mavis Beacon Teaches Typing, Compton's Encyclopedia, Totally MAD* (the total collection of *MAD Magazine*), and *Calendar Creator*; the popular software series *3D Home Architect, American Greetings Cards,* and *National Geographic*; and *Family Lawyer, Business Lawyer,* and *Family Tree Maker* (formerly marketed under the Quicken brandname). This lineup of products was shuffled by Mattel when it acquired The Learning Company, and Broderbund along with it. Some original Broderbund titles, such as *Myst* and *Riven* are now published under other brand names and divisions in the Mattel corporate structure.

1980s Origins

Broderbund Software traces its heritage to two brothers, Douglas and Gary Carlston, who founded the company during the computer software industry's infancy in 1980 in order to market computer game programs the elder Douglas had created. Douglas Carlston was first exposed to computers during the 1960s. As a college student he worked as a part-time programmer in Harvard's Aiken Computation Laboratory. Carlston's interests were myriad, however. During the 1960s and 1970s he also spent a year in Botswana teaching geography and math, returned to the United States to write *Beginning Swahili,* graduated magna cum laude from Harvard, wrote language texts for American Express, studied economics at Johns Hopkins School of Advanced International Studies, returned to Harvard and earned a law degree, and started a two-partner law firm in Maine where he resumed computer programming in his spare time. Utilizing a Radio Shack computer, Carlston developed his first two software games, *Galactic Empire* and *Galactic Trader,* which found commercial success after being published by outside companies.

By 1979 Douglas Carlston was earning more as a programmer than as an attorney. He then left his law practice and drove a ten-year-old car across country to Eugene, Oregon, where his younger brother Gary lived. The cross-country trip was apparently too much for the vehicle, given what Douglas Carlston later told *Forbes:* "We started the company because I was stuck without a car and didn't have the money to buy a new one." The name for the Carlston brothers' new company was derived by adding the contrived word "broder" (a blend of Swedish and Danish words meaning "brothers") to the German word "bund" (which in English means "alliance").

With working capital of $7,000 obtained from family members, the "brothers' alliance" was thus formed to market Douglas Carlston's computer game software directly to retailers rather than through other publishers. By mid-1980, after establishing an alliance with StarCraft, a Japanese software house, the company began marketing home entertainment software. In 1981 Broderbund Software, Inc. was incorporated as a California company.

Company Perspectives:

Brøderbund Software, a division of Mattel, develops, publishes and markets a broad line of interactive software for use in homes, schools and small businesses. Since its founding in 1980, the Company has repeatedly broken new ground, conceiving and developing families of software products with enduring customer appeal based on creativity, innovation and ease-of-use. Brøderbund is committed to providing its customers with engaging products that set quality standards and take advantage of the latest technologies.

Douglas Carlston became Broderbund's first president, and Gary Carlston was named chief executive officer. In 1981 the brothers were joined by a sister, Cathy Carlston, who became vice-president of educational market planning and was later instrumental in marketing software to schools. The company quickly grew to include more than 40 employees and sell millions of dollars worth of software annually. Broderbund relocated its operations from Eugene to California's Marin County in 1982.

During the early 1980s Broderbund published and distributed what was principally entertainment software, developed in conjunction with freelance programmers. Concerned that the company have adequate back-up capital on hand during its infancy, Douglas Carlston courted a number of outside investors between 1982 and 1984. He raised $3 million, and while the funds were never needed, these investors later played a role in Broderbund's initial public offering.

In 1984 Broderbund diversified, adding productivity and educational programs that the Carlstons believed consumers would want after computers gained widespread acceptance. In 1984 Broderbund scored its first major hit in the category of personal productivity with the release of *The Print Shop,* a pioneering "home creativity" program that enabled users with little computer knowledge to create calendars, greeting cards, fliers, posters, and signs.

Broderbund's first educational software success came after the Carlstons observed increasing numbers of schools purchasing computers despite the limited availability of educational software. The company responded by developing and releasing *Where in the World is Carmen Sandiego?* in 1985. The program, the first of many Carmen Sandiego titles destined to become hits, was credited as the industry's first "edutainment" software, blending both education and entertainment qualities. Based on a geography game the Carlston brothers had invented and played as children, the program was created in conjunction with Broderbund's in-house developers. It soon gained widespread admiration and acceptance from parents and teachers. The educational value of the game was found in its entertaining goal: to piece together geographical and historical clues in order to track Carmen Sandiego, an international jewel thief traveling through time and around the world.

The early 1980s was a largely unregulated period for software developers. Recognizing that upstart companies sometimes created computer versions of arcade games without great consideration for royalties and copyrights, Broderbund utilized a private investigator to seek out those pirating the company's software. The company's efforts to protect its programs translated into several copyright infringement lawsuits during the mid-1980s, and in 1986 Broderbund won a groundbreaking suit that found that software maker Unison World Inc. had infringed on Broderbund's copyright of *The Print Shop.* A federal court ruled that Unison had copied the "overall appearance, structure, and sequence" of Broderbund's software. Broderbund won an undisclosed settlement, and the decision was later cited by other software companies claiming copyright law covered the appearance of a software program as well as a program's basic computer code.

Reorganizing in the Late 1980s

In 1987 Broderbund was reincorporated in Delaware and announced intentions for an initial public offering of stock. However, a mid-year industry concern regarding the impact of a new IBM "personal computer" on the then-dominant "microcomputer" industry resulted in a major sell-off of computer stocks. About the same time, Broderbund earnings came in below projections, and the public offering was postponed.

In 1989 Broderbund released a software program called *The Playroom.* This program, which later became part of the company's Early Learning Products group, featured two mice that taught preschoolers reading and math fundamentals. That same year Gary Carlston and Cathy Carlston left the company, while Douglas Carlston assumed his brother's former titles of chairman and chief executive. Ed Auer, who had joined Broderbund in 1987 after 23 years at CBS, Inc., was promoted from chief operating officer and senior vice-president to president.

In 1990 Broderbund surpassed the $50 million mark in annual revenues, earning $6.2 million on sales of $50.4 million. In 1991 Broderbund flirted with the idea of merging with Sierra On-Line Inc. in a deal that would have made Broderbund a wholly owned subsidiary of Sierra, an entertainment software publisher. In March of that year the two companies signed a merger agreement for a stock swap worth nearly $90 million, but soon afterwards the deal was called off.

In 1991 Broderbund debuted *Kid Pix,* a children's drawing and painting program initially developed by an Oregon art professor for his son. The program proved to be an affiliated-label hit for Broderbund, which had identified a market need for such a product. For Broderbund's 1991 fiscal year (ending August 31, 1991), sales climbed to $55.7 million as earnings inched up to $7 million.

With some of Broderbund's venture capitalists seeking to cash in their investments, in November 1991 the company went public. Investors sold a 36 percent stake in Broderbund for $11 a share. One month later the stock was selling for nearly twice its initial offering price.

In the early 1990s Broderbund benefited from widespread interest in Carmen Sandiego in the form of numerous licensing agreements and marketing opportunities. In 1991 the company signed an agreement with Western Publishing Company, Inc. to use the Carmen Sandiego adventures to market various printed materials, including books and puzzles. That same year PBS premiered a weekday quiz show that, while it did not garner any licensing fees, exposed a daily audience of one million viewers to the Carmen chase. In 1992 Broderbund sold the live-action film rights for Carmen Sandiego and began discussions with the California company University Games to develop a board game based on the exploits of Carmen Sandiego. A year later, the Fox network debuted an animated Carmen Sandiego show. Video games, clothing, albums, and a calendar also joined the growing list of licensed Carmen Sandiego merchandise.

Broderbund's programs continued to demonstrate their staying power through sales records. In 1992 Carmen Sandiego titles surpassed 2.5 million in sales, while sales of *The Print Shop* titles eclipsed the four-million-unit mark. Conversely, the products offered by most of Broderbund's competitors had a shelf life of less than a year.

New Products and Markets in the 1990s

In 1992 Broderbund made several moves to expand its product line and marketing opportunities. In July 1992 Broderbund acquired PC Globe, Inc., an Arizona-based manufacturer of electronic maps and atlases, for $1.5 million. As a Broderbund subsidiary, PC Globe went on to publish *Maps 'n' Facts,* a family atlas and geographical information program. The company also added mainstream retailers like Wal-Mart to its established retail base of computer specialty stores, and the expansion of merchandising channels helped accelerate sales; for the 1992 fiscal year Broderbund's revenues rose to $75 million while earnings climbed to $9.65 million.

Gambling on the belief that CD-ROM drives would become commonplace on computer drives, Broderbund committed its future product line to CD-ROM platforms in the early 1990s. In February 1992 Broderbund released its first CD-ROM title, *Where in the World is Carmen Sandiego?.* In the spring of 1992, Broderbund released another product that reflected their belief that parents would pay in the neighborhood of $50 for an interactive storybook. *Just Grandma and Me,* Broderbund's second CD-ROM product, was its first interactive children's storybook designed to be read on computers.

Broderbund's success during this time was noticed by the nation's leading business periodicals. Both *Fortune* and *Forbes* lauded the company, and the latter labeled Broderbund ''the country's most successful maker of educational software.'' For the 1992 holiday season, Broderbund's titles dominated the computer software charts. Five of its programs claimed spots in the list of the top ten best-selling software programs. Broderbund's holiday hits included three of the company's six Carmen Sandiego titles as well as *Kid Pix* and *The Playroom.*

In March 1993 Broderbund's affiliated-label program was dealt a blow when its largest affiliated label, the California developer Maxis Software, went independent after recording more than $10 million in annual sales; Maxis had been partnered with Broderbund since 1988. Nevertheless, Broderbund's own revenues for the 1993 fiscal year mushroomed to $95.6 million, garnering the company $13.6 million in earnings.

Broderbund took important strides to expand beyond its traditional market of 10- to 14-year-olds in 1993. Targeting an older teenage audience, Broderbund debuted *Myst,* a nonviolent adventure-exploration game that encouraged players to employ puzzle-solving skills in a surrealistic world. Also introduced during this time was *3D Home Architect,* a program designed to assist amateur home designers and remodelers in creating rooms or houses. The company also adopted the moniker Early Learning Products for its growing line of educational software programs for children aged three to ten.

Between 1991 and 1993 the number of CD-ROM software titles in the nation grew from about 20 to 400, and CD-ROM software grew to claim about a ten percent stake in the $750 million consumer software market. Broderbund's gamble on CD-ROM technology began yielding concrete dividends in 1993. By the latter part of that year, the company's first two CD-ROM interactive storybooks—*Just Grandma and Me* and *Arthur's Teacher Trouble*—were among the top ten best-selling CD-ROM titles nationally.

To further expand on and accelerate its publication of interactive storybooks, Broderbund agreed in September 1993 to a joint venture with Random House, Inc. to create interactive multimedia storybooks. The storybook series, called Living Books, represented one of the first ventures between a leading consumer software publisher of interactive children's books and a large print publishing house. Living Books was designed to expand existing distribution networks for both companies, capitalize on the growing market for interactive software for children, and accelerate development of each company's electronic book plans. In attempting to captivate young readers while at the same time allowing for an interactive multimedia experience, Living Books titles adopted such features as animated illustrations, multimedia sound effects, and options for the reader. Objects on the screen could be activated through use of a mouse or stories could be narrated, with text simultaneously displayed in English, Spanish, or Japanese.

In December 1993 Broderbund stock—like the stock of a handful of other software makers—dropped precipitously, Broderbund's $6 per share to $34.50, after the company announced it was taking a cautious view towards future growth. The announcement came at a time when the personal computer software market as a whole was making a transition from floppy disk to CD-ROM format. Concerns about Broderbund's future stemmed from a decline in sales of Broderbund's older software titles on floppy disks as well as the entrance of Microsoft Corporation into the home software market with programs similar to Broderbund's *Kid Pix* and *The Print Shop.* During the 1993 holiday season, Broderbund's sales of CD-ROM products rose, while sales of floppy disk products and affiliated-label programs fell.

A Failed Merger Attempt in the Mid-1990s

The company's stock eventually rebounded into the $41 range, and in February 1994 Broderbund agreed to be acquired in a $400 million stock swap by one of its largest competitors, Electronic Arts Inc., which boasted three times the sales of Broderbund. The merger was expected to create one of the nation's largest consumer software production companies. The company would serve the home entertainment-education market for both computers and video game players by combining Broderbund's high technology and expertise in interactive software with Electronic Arts Hollywood productions skills and experience providing entertainment and video games for such companies as Sega, Nintendo, and 3DO. The merger also aimed to bolster each company's durability against growing competitive threats: Microsoft, which was impinging on Broderbund's turf, and Acclaim Entertainment, a video game manufacturer and Electronic Arts competitor. Broderbund also hoped that the merger would encourage international expansion opportunities and additional hardware platforms for its software.

As merger negotiations proceeded, Ed Auer retired his position at Broderbund and was replaced by William McDonagh, who had joined the company in 1982 as controller and had advanced through the ranks to the positions of chief financial officer and senior vice-president before becoming president. During this time, Broderbund created a new business development department to pursue alliances with other companies and increase international sales, which at the time represented less than ten percent of all revenues. Internal reorganizations resulted in Broderbund partitioning its program development operations into three separate segments designed to address the company's principal market categories: early learning, entertainment and education, and personal productivity.

In the spring of 1994 the joint-venture Living Books took substantial steps to expand its available titles. It outmaneuvered its competition to acquire the multimedia rights to the books of Dr. Seuss (Theodore Geisel) from the author's widow. Random House, Broderbund's partner in Living Books, had been the exclusive publisher of the 48 Dr. Seuss print books, which had sold over a total of 200 million copies. That same month Living Books also acquired world multimedia rights to the "First Time" series of The Berenstain Bears preschooler stories, which had sold over 165 million copies since debuting in 1982.

In May 1994 Broderbund pulled out of its merger agreement with Electronic Arts after the stock value of both companies took a sizable drop. The devalued Electronic Arts stock reduced Broderbund's take in the deal by nearly $100 million. Broderbund agreed to pay Electronic Arts $10 million to terminate the merger; nonetheless, Broderbund stockholders welcomed the move and the Broderbund's stock value rose $6.50 to $41.25, approximately the level it had been trading at prior to the merger announcement.

During the 1994 fiscal year, Broderbund published 68 new products—50 percent more than the previous year—in part because of the need to address the diverse platform needs of its customers. Broderbund's revenues for the year rose to $111.7 million while profits slid to $11 million. The company's bottom line suffered from the more than $10 million in charges related to the terminated merger with Electronic Arts. Earnings were bolstered, however, by sales of CD-ROM software, which proved less expensive to produce and yielded a higher profit margin than floppy disk programs.

By the beginning of its 1995 fiscal year (September 1994), Broderbund had released a full line of CD-ROM software. A CD-ROM version of *Myst* that featured 2,500 original 3-D graphics and an original soundtrack became the company's most popular product that year. Broderbund hailed it as the first ever blockbuster CD-ROM entertainment software program. By October 1994 the company's stock had risen to $57.50 on the strength of the popularity of CD-ROM-driven computers and Broderbund's Living Books, Early Learning, and *Myst* programs. *Myst* was credited by some analysts as an important reason for the substantial increase in sales of CD-ROM-based computers during the 1994 holiday season.

Broderbund entered 1995 with new generations of popular software, including *The Print Shop Deluxe CD Ensemble* and *3D Home Architect.* The company also announced plans to release its first Berenstain Bears interactive storybook and other new entertainment titles. Its *Myst II* sequel to the original *Myst* program was targeted for release in 1996. For the first six months of fiscal 1995, Broderbund posted revenues of $98 million—better than all of 1993's sales—and earnings of $21.9 million—better than earnings from any preceding full year. Named a *Business Week* "Hot Growth" company back in 1993, the magazine noted that by early 1995 Broderbund had brought investors a two-year return of better than 180 percent.

Settling In in the Late 1990s:

The "hot growth" slowed in 1997, however, when revenues increased to $190 million but net income fell below $10 million. As a consequence, Broderbund stock fell from a high of $76 a share in 1995 to a low of $17.75 a share in 1997. Once a haven for the creative, known for the demarcation between creators and "the suits," Broderbund was forced to institute a system of cost controls more closely resembling traditional management models.

The end of the decade for Broderbund was characterized by acquisitions and mergers. In 1996 Broderbund acquired Banner Blue Software and T/Maker, Inc. In 1997 the company purchased the remaining 50 percent of the Living Books series from Random House, as well as Parsons Technology, Inc. Also that year Broderbund created its own in-house Red Orb Entertainment to develop games and entertainment. Acquisitions continued into 1998 with the purchase of the *This Home* and *Designers Vision* series from manufacturer Autodesk.

In 1998 the acquisition cycle reversed when The Learning Company merged with Broderbund, and Broderbund became a fully-owned subsidiary of The Learning Company. Under its new owners, Broderbund felt two effects instantly. In early September 1998, The Learning Company announced a planned campaign—"Broderbund is Back"—in an effort to return Broderbund to a position of leadership in the consumer software industry. This campaign was directed at improving national and international sales in its educational and OEM (Original Equipment Manufacturers) channels, among others. Later in September 1998, The Learning Company revealed the second effect of the acquisition, its plans to lay off 500 employees from Broderbund and to close the production facility in Petaluma, California. These maneuvers streamlined the operation of the two companies, reducing overlap and positioning the new company to challenge Simon and Schuster as the largest electronic publisher selling to K-12 schools. By March 1999, The Learning Company had captured more Codie Awards than any other company at the Information Industry Association's 1999 Codie Awards ceremony; several Broderbund titles such *3D Home Design* and *Family Tree Maker* were among the winners.

In an ironic twist to the merger/acquisition frenzy, The Learning Company itself was purchased by Mattel, Inc., in 1999. As a result, The Learning Company and its Broderbund unit joined Mattel's $1 billion software division, bringing under one roof such popular software product brands as *Reader Rabbit, Barbie, Carmen Sandiego, Hot Wheels, Matchbox, Family Tree Maker, The Oregon Trail, American Girl,* and *Fisher Price,* among others.

Further Reading

Adelson, Andrea, "Random House Children's Books Headed for PC's," *New York Times,* September 11, 1993, p. 39.

Bulkeley, William M., "Courts Expand the Copyright Protection of Software, but Many Questions Remain, *Wall Street Journal,* November 18, 1986, p. 35.

Cox, Meg, "Living Books Receives Rights To Seuss Books," *Wall Street Journal,* April 21, 1994, p. B7.

Dolan, Carrie, and Don Clark, "Electronic Arts Sets Acquisition of Broderbund," *Wall Street Journal,* February 10, 1994, p. 5.

——, "Small Software Companies Crack the Educational Market: Childish Pursuits Pay at Broderbund, Home Of Carmen Sandiego," *Wall Street Journal,* March 10, 1993, pp. B1–B2.

Fisher, Lawrence M., "Broderbund Stock Tumbles on Growth Concerns," *New York Times,* December 24, 1993, p. D3.

——, "CD-ROM Sales Propel Profit At Broderbund," *New York Times,* March 23, 1995, p. C6.

——, "Demand for CD-ROM Titles Lifts Broderbund Earnings," *New York Times,* October 8, 1994, pp. 39, 41.

——, "2 Companies in Software Drop Merger: No Broderbund Deal with Electronic Arts," *New York Times,* May 4, 1994, p. D5.

Giltenan, Edward, "Who in the World is Doug Carlston?," *Forbes,* April 27, 1992, pp. 100–102.

King, Ralph T., Jr., "Broderbund Jilts Electronic Arts; Scraps Agreement to Be Acquired," *Wall Street Journal,* May 4, 1994, p. B5.

Kupfer, Andrew, "Identify a Need, Turn a Profit," *Fortune,* November 30, 1992, pp. 78–79.

"Learning Co. Hopes to Be Building a Mystery with Broderbund Acquisition," *Weekly Corporate Growth Report,* June 29, 1998, p. 9685.

"The Learning Co. Lays Off 500 from Broderbund in an Effort to Streamline Operations and Reduce Expenses," *Electronic Education Report,* September 30, 1998.

Markoff, John, "Electronic Arts' Move Reflects Industry Trend," *New York Times,* February 11, 1994.

"Mattel Completes Merger with The Learning Company," *PR Newswire,* http://www.prnewswire.com/comp/540363.html.

Ricadela, Aaron, "Broderbund Buy Gets TLC a Clean Slate, Strong Titles," *Computer Retail Week,* July 6, 1998, pp. 3–5.

——, "Small Publishers Stay Sharply Focused," *Computer Retail Week,* August 17, 1998, p. 3.

Rifkin, Glenn, "Competing Through Innovation: The Case of Broderbund," http://www.strategy-business.com/casestudy/98205/page1.html.

—Roger W. Rouland
—updated by Shannon and Terry Hughes

CABOT

Cabot Corporation

75 State Street
Boston, Massachusetts 02109-1806
U.S.A.
(617) 345-0100
Fax: (617) 342-6103
Web site: http://www.cabot-corp.com

Public Company
Incorporated: 1922 as Godfrey L. Cabot, Inc.
Employees: 4,800
Sales: $1.64 billion (1998)
Stock Exchanges: New York Boston Pacific
Ticker Symbol: CBT
NAIC: 325182 Carbon Black Manufacturing; 326113
   Unsupported Plastics Film & Sheet (Except
   Packaging) Manufacturing; 331419 Primary Smelting
   & Refining of Nonferrous Metals, Except Copper &
   Aluminum; 42272 Petroleum & Petroleum Products
   Wholesalers, Except Bulk Stations & Terminals;
   42152 Coal & Other Mineral & Ore Wholesalers

Cabot Corporation is a diversified, global chemical and plastics manufacturer with industry leadership in such areas as carbon black, fumed silica, tantalum powder production, and plastics compounds. It is also involved in liquified natural gas importation and distribution and the manufacture of industrial safety products.

Early Days: Cabots and Carbon

Godfrey Lowell Cabot, the founder of Cabot Corporation, lived to be 101, and the choices he made early in his career set much of the company's course to the present day. Born in 1861, he was both a Cabot and a Lowell, a son of two of the most powerful and prestigious old Boston Brahmin merchant families. After graduating from Harvard in 1882, he went to the oil and gas fields of western Pennsylvania to start a business. There he found that the industry produced huge amounts of carbon debris, waste products of gas blow-offs and refining.

Godfrey's older brother Samuel had founded a paint and stain business, using coal tars to make black pigment. Godfrey decided to build his business around carbon black, the very substance that was fouling the oil fields. Distinct from soot, this substance, a form of carbon sometimes called lamp black, had been around for a long time. Prehistoric cave dwellers used it to draw animals on cave walls, and the Egyptian pharaohs used it as a pigment. The Cabots saw similar applications for it.

The Cabots built a plant in Buffalo Mills, Pennsylvania, that used natural gas to produce carbon black in 1882, and in 1884 Godfrey patented a carbon black production process that used stationary plates and rotating burners. In 1887 Godfrey bought out Samuel's interest in the business.

At about this time, a glut developed in the carbon black market; at the same time, new uses were being found for natural gas, which was the raw material for carbon black. Cabot's response was to purchase gas leases and drill on the sites, drilling his first successful gas well in Saxonburg, Pennsylvania, in 1888. He continued, despite the glut, to buy up small carbon black factories as well, and by 1897 he was probably the largest producer in the industry.

In 1898, with the exhaustion of the Pennsylvania gas fields, Cabot moved his operation to West Virginia, where he acquired oil and gas leases, which he drilled successfully. He continued to add gas sites in West Virginia, consolidating his holdings, and building a natural gasoline extraction plant near Elizabeth, West Virginia, in 1914. These holdings were the forerunners of Cabot's natural gas processing plants in the Southwest.

World War I and New Carbon Black Applications

While the advent and spread of high-speed presses and similar applications greatly expanded Cabot's business, World War I demonstrated the potential for carbon black in the modern economy. It had been known for a while that carbon black could inhibit damage to materials caused by the sun; a few years before the war, the India Rubber Gutta-Percha and Telegraph Works Co. of Silvertown, England, began to manufacture automobile tires using carbon black as a stabilizing or reinforcing agent. During World War I the United States began using carbon black, and its superior properties became evident in

---

Company Perspectives:

Cabot will be a great company—the best company in all markets that it serves, best particularly in safety, quality and innovation; employee, customer and community satisfaction; and shareholder return. Cabot will become a great company by striving for excellence in everything it does, through: highly motivated employees; a values-based organization; surpassing customers' needs and earning their admiration; and expanding the use of core technologies.

---

improved tread wear and lower rates of tire failure. After the war, its use spread throughout the tire industry, providing a tremendous burst of growth to Cabot and other suppliers. The company came to excel in producing different grades and types of carbon black for different applications.

In 1922 Cabot's company was incorporated as Godfrey L. Cabot, Inc. At about this time, the locus of carbon black production was shifted out of West Virginia, first, unsuccessfully, to Louisiana, and then to Texas. Carbon black plants in the East were sold; gas production and distribution continued, though it was cut back. Thomas Cabot, Godfrey's son, opened Cabot's Southwestern Division, headquartered in Breckenridge, Texas, in 1925. Two years later, headquarters were moved to Pampa, Texas.

By 1930 Cabot had built eight carbon black plants in Texas and one in Oklahoma. In the early 1930s Cabot used a new technique to develop a pelletized, dustless carbon black, which was tradenamed SPHERON. Bulk sales of this easily transportable product fueled Cabot's growth in the mid-1930s, in spite of the Great Depression. This in turn led to the construction of other carbon black plants in 1937 and 1938.

As was the case from the very beginning of Godfrey Cabot's enterprise, carbon black production and energy were developed in tandem. Cabot formed Cabot Shops, Inc., in 1930 to construct the carbon black plants. It also made oil well pumping units. In 1935 Cabot began drilling for oil and gas in Texas and built two natural gas processing plants in West Texas near two of its carbon black plants. Residue from the gas process was delivered to the carbon black plants and used as raw material.

Although Godfrey L. Cabot, Inc. was able to stay afloat, the period from 1925 to 1939 was not a boom period for the company. The Depression greatly cut back demand for gas as well as carbon black. In fact, the carbon black facilities in the Southwest experienced losses that were barely balanced by gas and gas distribution profits from West Virginia, Pennsylvania, and New York.

World War II: Rubber Shortage and Governmental Support

By 1939 Cabot had sales of nearly $7 million. Natural gas accounted for more than 50 percent of sales, while carbon black yielded about 35 percent. In that year, too, war changed the nature of the business. As Japan spread its control over the rubber plantations in Malaya and the East Indies, the United

States was faced with a cutoff of shipments of natural rubber. The government responded by imposing restrictions on the use of natural rubber and by constructing synthetic rubber plants. Cabot stockpiled 100 million pounds of carbon black at its own expense when it anticipated shortages for 1943 to 1945. The substance was considered so important to the war effort that a governmental interagency carbon black committee was set up when production lagged in 1942, and funds were made available to producers. Among the facilities built or added to by Cabot during this period, with government support, included plants in McCoy, Louisiana; Borger, Texas; Guymon, Oklahoma; and Wickett, Texas.

After the war, Cabot converted several of its carbon black plants from gas process to oil process. This move helped set the stage for Cabot to become an international company later, as oil did not need to be piped and plants could be built closer to their markets.

By 1950 the company had become the largest producer of carbon black and reaped the benefits of a general upsurge in worldwide demand. Also, as GIs returned home, automobiles were sold in increasing numbers, and those automobiles needed tires. In 1950 Cabot built its first carbon black plant in Europe, near Liverpool, England. Plants followed in Canada (1953), France (1958), and Italy (1960). In addition, plants partially owned by Cabot were opened in Australia (1959) and in the Netherlands (1960); both of these facilities relied heavily on Cabot technology.

Diversification and Expansion: 1950–80

During this period Cabot continued to perform research that improved carbon black processes and products, opening a research facility in Cambridge, Massachusetts. The company also began to branch out. In 1952 Cabot began importing fumed silica and in 1957 began production of the substance in the United States under the name Cab-O-Sil. Fumed silica is an ultra-fine high purity silica that is used to provide reinforcement, viscosity control, and free flow properties to a variety of products, including silicones, adhesives and sealants, reinforced plastics, and coatings. It is used extensively in the automotive, cosmetics, paint and ink, construction, and pharmaceutical industries. Cab-O-Sil would become the leading producer of fumed silica in North America.

At this time, Cabot also became involved in a study group on liquified natural gas (LNG). This involvement led to the opening in 1971 of Distrigas in Everett, Massachusetts, the only LNG terminal and distribution center in New England. Cabot LNG Corporation supplies between 5 percent and 25 percent of New England's liquified natural gas needs, including those of power companies, in the late 1990s.

In 1960 all of the various Cabot businesses and subsidiaries were united into Cabot Corporation. The company went public in 1963 with the sale of 12 percent of its common stock. In 1962 founder Godfrey Cabot died.

Expansion continued throughout the 1960s, particularly overseas. Subsidiaries and plants were opened in Argentina, Colombia, Germany, and Spain. In 1963 Cabot entered into two completely new arenas. The company began experiments on plastic polymers and compounds and in 1963 began producing titanium, a high-performance metal, at its facility in Ashtabula, Ohio. The company also launched considerable research in the area of experimental plastic polymers and compounds. It eventually became a world leader in the production of thermoplastics used in films as well as in injection-molded and extruded plastic products. By the end of the 1960s, it was clear to Cabot that production of high-performance materials was a high-growth area.

To this end, the company, under CEO Robert A. Charpie, acquired the Stellite Division from Union Carbide in 1970. According to the 1970 annual report, Stellite "profoundly changed the nature of the Company by launching Cabot in a new direction, that of high performance materials, by providing major diversification strength, and by broadening our technological base in a way that is complementary to the technical skills we have in the performance chemical field."

The main business of this new division consisted of nickel- and cobalt-based alloys that were designed to withstand extreme heat, corrosion, and wear. Such materials were used in gas turbine engines, electrical power generating stations, chemical processes equipment, and other like applications. In 1978 Cabot acquired Kawecki Berylco Industries, which enabled the company to produce beryllium-copper, tantalum, and columbium products as well as aluminum alloys. Tantalum in particular was used extensively by computer and electronics manufacturers, as well as in aerospace, ballistic munitions, and various chemical processes.

Apart from gains made by entry into the high-performance metals business, Cabot's energy component experienced major growth in the 1970s as a result of the energy crisis of 1973–74. The value of Cabot's oil and gas reserves shot up, and this provided a major impetus to step up exploration, particularly in the Gulf of Mexico and mid-continent. The company withdrew from exploration outside the United States. In addition, the company undertook further development in West Virginia, and the pipeline and distribution systems there were upgraded.

The company also expanded its gas processing and pipeline business in the 1970s. It acquired further industrial gas pipelines in West Virginia and completed another gas processing plant in Texas. Most significantly, it acquired TUCO, Inc. in 1979, which added about 500 miles of pipeline and two gas processing plants to its holdings in the Southwest.

Although Cabot's energy holdings increased in value, the energy crisis also negatively affected Cabot. The cost of the type of oil needed for carbon black production tripled, putting a severe squeeze on profits. Cabot invested heavily in new, more efficient technology and instituted programs to reduce raw material costs.

However, in the 1970s, Cabot, on the advice of the Boston Consulting Group, came to see its chemical businesses, including carbon black, as "cash cows." In essence, cash was extracted from this vital area of the business and put into diversification into metals manufacturing, ceramics, semiconductors, and other businesses in which Cabot had little expertise. Chemical plants were ignored and allowed to deteriorate. This destabilized the entire company. On top of this, gas prices collapsed in the 1980s, leaving Cabot with vast liabilities from acquisitions and plant investment, but much reduced income.

Late 1980s: New Leadership

In 1987 the Cabot family, which owned 30 percent of the company, replaced Charpie and tapped Samuel Bodman as CEO in hopes of turning the company around. Among other things, Bodman stopped the slide of the chemicals side of the business by investing $500 million to upgrade the plants. Bodman also divested the metals and ceramics businesses and got out of energy exploration and production in order to concentrate the company on its strong suits in organic industrial chemicals, such as carbon black, fumed silica, high-performance materials, and plastics. The result was that through the early 1990s, the company consistently had operating revenues around $1.5 billion, and in 1992 earned 12.5 percent on equity.

In 1993, Cabot purchased the Tantalum Mining Corporation in Manitoba, Canada. The mine was North America's only significant producer of tantalum, a rare, anti-corrosive hard metal. It was also one of two major suppliers of spodumene, a mineral used primarily in the pyroceramic industry, and for cesium, a rare, highly reactive metal with various uses. Cabot acquired the mine with an eye toward using its tantalum reserves to further expansion of the company's high-performance materials business, which began with the acquisition of Union Carbide's Stellite Division in 1870.

Also in 1993, Cabot began to experiment with developing inkjet colorants. Building upon its long-time experience in working with carbon black, the company was able to develop colorants that offered enhanced color, stability, ink formulation flexibility, and print quality. In 1996, Cabot formally established a new division—the Inkjet Colorants Division—to oversee development, production, and marketing of this new product line. In 1998, the Cabot's Inkjet Colorants' products were used for the first time in new inkjet printers being produced by the printer manufacturers. By 1999, the Inkjet Colorants Division had four facilities located in Massachusetts, Germany, and Japan.

Another operating division was added to the Cabot stable in 1995. The Aurora, Illinois-headquartered Microelectronics Materials Division (MMD) was established to develop and manufacture high-performance products for the semiconductor industry. MMD's major products were chemical-mechanical planarization slurries—liquid suspensions with an abrasive component used to microscopically polish and plane down tiny layers of semiconductor chips. Within four years of its inception, the division had grown to include manufacturing operations in Hammond, Indiana, and Barry, Wales, and was serving customers in North America, Japan, Europe, Taiwan, Korea, and the South Asia Pacific.

Meanwhile, Cabot had discovered a new use for the rare metal cesium, which was abundant in the Manitoba mine the company had purchased in 1993. The company's researchers developed a cesium-based formula that could be used to decrease clogging during oil drilling, thereby speeding up the process substantially. In 1996, Cabot formed the Cabot Specialty Fluids business unit to oversee development and marketing of these new cesium-based drilling and completion fluids. This same year, it sold its TUCO operation for $77 million.

Cabot's new divisions got off to a somewhat slow start, causing a 54 percent decrease in the company's net income between fiscal 1996 and 1997. However, in 1998 Cabot regained some of its lost ground, posting a 35 percent net gain—up to $122 million from the previous year's $93 million.

Looking Ahead

In 1998 Cabot began the lengthy process of revamping its corporate structure. The company's goal was to move from a product-focused structure to a market-focused structure, in which business units would be defined by the markets they served. Toward this end, plans were underway to replace the company's eight traditional business units—Fumed Silica, Carbon Black, Plastics, Microelectronics Materials, Performance Materials, Specialty Fluids, Inkjet Colorants, and Liquefied Natural Gas—with 20 new, more market-specific business units.

The company also had plans for expansion in several of its divisions. A natural gas liquefaction plant was scheduled for opening in Trinidad in mid-1999. In addition, a new fumed silica manufacturing facility in Midland, Michigan, and a Microelectronics Materials slurry manufacturing plant in Geino, Japan, were both expected to be operational by the close of the millennium. Cabot also expected to maintain a rapid pace in new product development and applications. According to a February 22, 1999 article in *Forbes,* the company was spending $83 million annually—almost a full third of its pretax income—on research and development.

Principal Subsidiaries

Cabot LNG Corporation.

Principal Divisions

Carbon Black; Inkjet Colorants; Fumed Silica; Microelectronics Materials; Plastics; Performance Materials; Specialty Fluids.

Further Reading

Berlin, Rosalind Klein, "The Smutty Story of Cabot Corp.," *Fortune,* December 5, 1988, p. 133.
"Cabot CEO Looks to Future Growth," *Chemical Marketing Reporter,* March 8, 1993, p. 9.
Chakavarty, Subrata N., "White Slacks and Carbon Black," *Forbes,* October 26, 1992, p. 122.
Condon, Bernard, "The Soot King," *Forbes,* February 22, 1999.
Plishner, Emily S., "Cabot Concentrates on Microparticulate Growth," *Chemical Week,* March 10, 1993, p. 14.

—Kenneth F. Kronenberg
—updated by Shawna Brynildssen

Carlsberg A/S

100 Ny Carlsberg Vej
DK-1799 Copenhagen V
Denmark
(45) 33 27 33 27
Fax: (45) 33 27 47 11

Public Company
Incorporated: 1970 as United Breweries, Ltd.
Employees: 20,589
Sales: DKK 32.9 billion (US $4.6 billion)
Stock Exchanges: Copenhagen
NAIC: 31212 Breweries; 312111 Soft Drink
 Manufacturing; 312112 Bottled Water Manufacturing

Carlsberg A/S is one of the world's largest brewing companies. Its two principal brands, Carlsberg and Tuborg, are the leading beers in Denmark and are also two of the most widely sold beers in the global market. More than three-quarters of the brewery's sales come from outside Denmark. The company operates brewing facilities in Singapore, Malawi, Germany, Italy, Hong Kong, Cyprus, and a number of other countries and maintains licensing agreements for distribution of its brands in others, so that Carlsberg and Tuborg can be found in 150 different countries altogether. Carlsberg A/S has interests in a few businesses outside brewing as well. Most notably, the company owns Royal Scandinavia A/S, makers of renowned fine porcelain, silverware, and glassware. Carlsberg also owns a 43 percent interest in Tivoli Gardens, a well-known amusement park in Copenhagen.

1873–1900: Carlsberg and Tuborg

Carlsberg A/S was formed from the merger of two venerable Danish breweries, Carlsberg and Tuborg. The original Carlsberg brewery was founded in Copenhagen in 1847 by Captain J. C. Jacobsen. The captain was interested in brewing technology, and he studied modern brewing methods extensively before he opened his shop, which he named for his son Carl. His constant work to improve the quality of his beer soon made his lager very popular. Carl Jacobsen carried on his father's passion for beer making, and he studied brewing both in Denmark and abroad before taking his place in the family business in 1871. Carl eventually established his own brewery, called New Carlsberg. New Carlsberg and Old Carlsberg were united in 1906, as both father and son willed their breweries to a charitable foundation J. C. Jacobsen had established in 1876. The Carlsberg Foundation assumed the running of the breweries, carried on scientific research in beer making through its Carlsberg Laboratory, and supported Danish history and the arts through the establishment of several museums.

Tuborg was founded in 1873 by a group of Danish businessmen headed by Phillip Heyman. The Tuborgs Fabrikker first included a glass factory and a sulfuric acid works, but Heyman spun off all but the brewery in 1880. Tuborg's Green Label pilsner quickly established a strong reputation in Denmark. By 1894 Tuborg was the major partner in an affiliation of 11 Copenhagen breweries.

1900–1980s: Penetrating Foreign Markets

Carlsberg and Tuborg signed an operating agreement as early as 1903, stating that they would share profits and deficits and contribute equally to financing new plants and installations. The two brands dominated the Danish beer market. Though Danes were dedicated beer drinkers, the market was relatively small, as the total Danish population was only around five million people. Carlsberg and Tuborg eventually decided to expand their sales outside the country. After World War II, the two breweries began intensive marketing campaigns abroad. As a result, their exports tripled between 1958 and 1972, and the two companies established breweries in other European countries and in Asia. To reinforce their growing export presence, Carlsberg and Tuborg combined under one name in 1970, becoming United Breweries Ltd. Under the terms of the charter, the Carlsberg Foundation was awarded a mandatory ownership of at least 51 percent of the shares of the new company.

United Breweries continued to expand its business by penetrating foreign markets. One of its most important markets was Great Britain. In 1970 the company set up a partnership with the British beer maker Watney to build a lager brewery at Northampton. This was United's biggest operation outside Denmark.

By 1975 the Carlsberg brand lager produced there accounted for about 14 percent of British lager sales. The Grand Metropolitan group took over Watney in 1972, and in 1975 it sold its 49 percent interest in Carlsberg U.K. back to United Breweries, leaving the Danish parent with 100 percent control. Grand Metropolitan continued to distribute Carlsberg lager through its 7,500 pub outlets.

United Breweries took a different tack with its Tuborg brand, however. The largest British brewer, Bass Charington, distributed Tuborg, which was at first all imported directly from Denmark. Tuborg then was brewed under license at four Bass breweries, but that agreement ended in 1981. United took back independent control of Tuborg marketing in Britain, hoping to increase sales. The company also intensified its drive to market Tuborg internationally and in 1981 licensed a Hungarian brewery to produce the lager there.

United Brewery's two main brands were available in almost every European capital by the middle 1980s. About 70 percent of United's beer was sold abroad, through direct exports, through licensed foreign breweries, or through breweries that the company owned. Despite its growing success in Europe, Asia, and Africa, United faced problems in its native Denmark. That country ranked eighth in the world in per capita beer consumption, and United had an 80 percent market share, but sales were stagnant. United worked under a fixed price system in Denmark, where it sold its products for the same price everywhere, regardless of volume. Some Danish supermarkets began to fight against what they considered United's monopolistic practices, by slashing beer prices to less than wholesale. United resorted to threatening to halt deliveries of Carlsberg and Tuborg to stores that discounted. Another problem with the Danish market was that younger drinkers were turning increasingly to wine. In an effort to win back its young customers, United entered into a distribution agreement with American brewer Anheuser-Busch to sell its Budweiser brand in Denmark. Younger people were interested in American imports and more apt to experiment with a new brand than older drinkers. Anheuser-Busch also began to import the Carlsberg brand to the United States for United.

United Breweries diversified somewhat in the 1980s. It formed Carlsberg Biotechnology in 1983 and acquired interests in firms that made such things as ventilation plants and fishing industry equipment. The company acquired 83 percent of a German brewery in 1988, the Hannen Brauerei GmbH, and also bought Vingaarden A/S, a Danish wine and spirit maker. A separate financial branch, Carlsberg Finans A/S, was estab-lished in 1989 to manage the parent company's stock portfolios and pension funds. But by the end of the 1980s the company decided to sell off much of its nonbeverage business. United Brewery's name had been changed in December 1987 to Carlsberg A/S to give the firm a more distinct business profile. The renamed company consolidated its operations and gradually began to pare down its workforce to cope with what it perceived to be a mature beer market. Sales grew steadily throughout the 1980s, from DKK 6.31 billion in 1982 to DKK 10.48 billion in 1990.

1990s: Strategic Alliances

Carlsberg A/S continued to make investments in international markets in the 1990s. The company acquired a controlling interest in Unicer, the largest brewery in Portugal, in April 1991. Carlsberg subsequently sold its stake in a Spanish brewery, Union Cervecera, which had been losing money. Guinness bought out Carlsberg's 60 percent share, and then Carlsberg acquired ten percent of Guinness's interest in a larger Spanish brewery, La Cruz del Campo S.A. Carlsberg also moved to secure its crucial British market by forming an alliance with Allied-Lyons, a large brewing and wholesale company. Britain provided almost half of Carlsberg's worldwide profit by the early 1990s, and competition among brewers there had become increasingly stiff. Previous to the 1991 merger with Allied-Lyons, Carlsberg had only a four percent share of the British beer market, with 1990 sales of DKK 1.31 billion. The new firm, a 50-50 joint venture called Carlsberg-Tetley P.L.C., had an 18 percent market share, just behind market leaders Bass, with 23 percent, and Courage, with 21 percent. The alliance gave Carlsberg access to Allied's six breweries, its strong distribution network, and a larger brand portfolio. Carlsberg had to wait almost a year for the British antitrust agency to approve the deal, but when Carlsberg-Tetley began operations in early 1993, it had a secure place among the top three British brewers.

The situation in Britain, where three large companies including Carlsberg-Tetley controlled about two-thirds of the beer market, seemed a model to Carlsberg for what the global market was becoming. Global consumption of beer for 1991–92 was down, reflecting the European economic recession, and competition escalated among increasingly large international brewing companies. Carlsberg continued to strengthen its ties with foreign breweries, as it anticipated negative growth in beer consumption in the 1990s. Some of Carlsberg's slow growth in Europe was offset, however, by increased sales in Asia. Carlsberg had become the leading international beer brand in the Far East by the early 1990s, and Singapore, Malaysia, and Hong Kong were particularly good markets for the company. Carlsberg A/S also had modest sales in South Korea, Japan, Indonesia, and Nepal. Carlsberg's subsidiary Danbrew worked on construction of a Carlsberg brewery in Thailand in the early 1990s, and by 1992 Carlsberg beer was introduced to China and Sri Lanka.

In Denmark, Carlsberg undertook a major restructuring of its beer production facilities. In 1992 the company began to phase out its Tuborg brewery and transferred production to two other existing plants, in the interest of long-term operating economy. Carlsberg had been cutting its workforce since the mid-1980s, and this move further reduced the company's personnel. Carlsberg took another significant action concerning its home market in 1992, acquiring 80 percent of A/S Dadeko, the company in charge of the bottling and sale of Coca-Cola, Fanta, Sprite, and other soft drinks in Denmark.

Throughout the early 1990s, Carlsberg's British joint venture, Carlsberg-Tetley, was faced with intense competition and declining market share and profits. In 1996 Allied Domecq PLC, Carlsberg's partner in Carlsberg-Tetley, decided to exit the business, selling its 50 percent interest to the company's strongest rival, Bass Brewers. Carlsberg and Bass planned to merge the two companies, with Bass owning 80 percent and Carlsberg owning the remaining 20 percent. In 1997, however, Britain's Department of Trade and Industry blocked the merger on the grounds that it would operate against the public interest. Subsequently, the Department of Trade ordered Bass to divest itself of the Carlsberg-Tetley shares. Carlsberg bought the shares from Bass for approximately $183 million.

In 1997 the company ended its partnership with St. Louis-based Anheuser-Busch, which for 12 years had been the sole U.S. distributor for Carlsberg products. Subsequently, Carlsberg handed over U.S. distribution rights to Labatt USA, a subsidiary of Labatt Breweries of Canada. Carlsberg also became more firmly entrenched in the soft drink market in 1997, when it entered into a joint venture with the Coca-Cola Company. The partnership, named Coca-Cola Nordic Beverages, was developed to bottle, sell, and distribute Coca-Cola soft drink products in Denmark and Sweden. To obtain European Union Commission approval for the joint venture, however, Carlsberg was ordered to sell off its interests in Bryggerigruppen A/S, the Danish bottler of PepsiCo soft drink brands, and A/S Dansk Coladrik, the maker of Jolly Cola. In 1998 Coca-Cola Nordic Beverages expanded its activities to include Norway and Finland.

In 1998 Carlsberg acquired 50 percent of the shares of the Finnish brewing operation, Oy Sinebrychoff AB, of which it already owned ten percent. A Swedish subsidiary of Oy Sinebrychoff, Falcon Breweries, then assumed responsibility for brewing and marketing Tuborg beer in Sweden. The company's growth campaign continued in early 1999. In January, Carlsberg agreed to acquire full ownership of another of its joint ventures, Danish Malting Group, A/S. Under the agreement, Carlsberg purchased the 50 percent shareholdings owned by its partner in the operation, the U.S.-based ConAgra, Inc.

Carlsberg added to its already-strong Asian presence in the spring of 1999 when it signed an agreement to invest in the Hite Brewery, Korea's largest brewery. The Hite Brewery had a market share of approximately 50 percent in Korea, which ranked in the top 20 beer markets in the world. Once the transaction was completed, Carlsberg would become the second largest holder of voting shares, owning 15 to 20 percent of issued share capital. Also in the spring of 1999, Carlsberg announced its plans to sell off its Vingaarden A/S, the Danish wine and spirit producer it had purchased in 1988.

Looking Forward

Carlsberg A/S achieved modest but steady growth in sales and profits through the 1990s, despite an intensely competitive international beer market. The company was poised to move into the new century with approximately 100 subsidiaries and associated companies and a presence in 150 markets. Due to declining beer consumption and increasing competition in many of the markets Carlsberg served, however, the company faced the possibility of lower profits in the years to come.

Principal Subsidiaries

A/S Kjøbenhavns Sommer-Tivoli (Denmark; 43%); Carlsberg Brewery Hong Kong Limited (51%); Carlsberg Brewery Malaysia Berhad (Malaysia; 27.6%); Carlsberg Brewery (Thailand) Co., Ltd. (8%); Carlsberg Finans A/S (Denmark); Carlsberg France S.A.; Carlsberg Importers S.A.-N.V. (Belgium; 10%); Carlsberg Italia S.P.A. (75%); Carlsberg Malawi Brewery Limited (Malawi; 49%); Carlsberg-Tetley Brewing Ltd. (United Kingdom); Ceylon Brewery Ltd. (Sri Lanka; 8%); Coca-Cola Nordic Beverages A/S (Denmark; 51%); Danbrew Ltd. A/S (Denmark); Danish Malting Group A/S (50%); Falcon Holding AB (Sweden); Gorkha Brewery Limited (Nepal; 48.3%); Grupo Cruzcampo, S.A. (Spain; 11%); Hannen Brauerei GmbH (Germany); Hue Brewery Ltd. (Vietnam; 35%); Israel Beer Breweries Ltd. (20%); J.C. Bentzen A/S (Denmark); Nuuk Imeq A/S (Greenland; 23.68%); Okocimskie Zaklady Piwowarskie S.A. (Poland; 43.5%); Oy Sinebrychoff AB (Finland; 60%); Panonska Pivovara D.O.O. (Croatia; 40%); Royal Scandinavia A/S (Denmark; 60.96%); South-East Asia Brewery Ltd. (Vietnam; 35%); Tuborg Nord BCD: (Denmark); Türk Tuborg Bira Ve Malt Sanayii A.S. (Turkey; 2.2%); Unicer S.A.-União Cervejeira S.A. (Portugal; 31%); United Romanian Breweries Bereprod SRL; Vingaarden A/S (Denmark).

Further Reading

Barnes, Hilary, "Improvement at Danish Brewer," *Financial Times,* November 27, 1979, p. 34.
——, "United Breweries Holds Dividend, Plans Scrip," *Financial Times,* November 25, 1987, p. 28.
"Bass and Tuborg End Lager Agreement," *Financial Times,* April 6, 1981, p. 4.
"Brewers in the Snug Bar," *Financial Times,* October 23, 1991, p. 22.
"Brewers Merging British Operations," *New York Times,* October 23, 1991, p. D3.
"Brewing Up a Qualified Success," *Marketing,* October 31, 1991, p. 16.
Glamann, Kristof, *Jacobsen of Carlsberg: Brewer and Philanthropist,* Copenhagen: Gyldendal, 1991.
Gooding, Kenneth, "Grand Met. Ends Brewing Link with Carlsberg," *Financial Times,* September 13, 1975, p. 10.
Guttman, Robert, "Danish Business Goes Global," *Europe,* September 1994, p. 10.
"Lager Clout," *Marketing,* March 8, 1990, p. 35.
Navarro, Valerie, ". . . While A-B Gets Ready to Bring Bud to Denmark," *Advertising Age,* February 3, 1986, pp. 40–42.
Rawstorne, Philip, "Allied and Carlsberg To Merge UK Beer Interests," *Financial Times,* October 23, 1991, p. 1.
Ridlake, Suzanne, "Beer Giants Merge," *Marketing,* October 24, 1991, p. 2.

—A. Woodward
—updated by Shawna Brynildssen

CARQUEST Corporation

12596 W. Bayaud Avenue, Suite 400
Lakewood, Colorado 80228
U.S.A.
(303) 984-2000
Fax: (303) 984-2001
Web site: http://www.carquest.com

Private Company
Incorporated: 1974
Employees: 35,000 (est.)
Sales: $1.4 billion (1997 est.)
NAIC: 44131 Automotive Parts & Accessories Stores

CARQUEST Corporation is an alliance of warehouse distributors (WDs) and "jobber-stores" that sell automotive replacement parts to professional technicians and retail buyers. The company's participation in the automotive aftermarket includes replacement parts for almost all automobile makes and models as well as truck, farm, and recreational vehicles. CARQUEST-brand products are distributed through more than 60 distribution centers and 3,400 stores throughout the United States as well as Canada and Mexico.

Competitive 1970s Activates Alliance

O. Temple Sloan, owner of General Parts Inc. (GPI) in Raleigh, North Carolina, provided the impetus in founding CARQUEST with Joe Hughes of Indiana Parts and Warehouse in Indianapolis and Dan M. Bock of Bobro Products in the Bronx, New York. In 1974 the three auto parts companies joined together in response to competition from high-volume retail stores. Sloan had studied Genuine Parts, the company that initiated the National Automotive Parts Association (NAPA), and decided that programmed distribution through a cooperative alliance would be the most effective means to remain competitive. Programmed distribution connected warehouses and jobbers in a process of automotive parts distribution that would allow overnight delivery of any item. Through this three-step distribution, an alliance of jobber-store affiliates and WDs would provide the best customer service to professional repair shops, commercial users, car fleets, and farmers, as well as Do-It-Yourself (DIY) retail buyers, through accessible, well-stocked distribution centers. The CARQUEST founders agreed that three-step, programmed distribution would be the best strategy in the automotive "aftermarket" of replacement parts, and they were determined to help jobbers get a reasonable share of that market, including DIY retail business.

With 100 auto parts stores selling wholesale replacement parts, tools, and equipment, CARQUEST generated $29 million in sales in its first year of business. As the umbrella company CARQUEST developed private label brands—products not manufactured by the company, but packaged with the company name. CARQUEST-brand name recognition was sought through television advertising with Johnny Rutherford as spokesman and through product catalogs that were produced for wholesale as well as retail use. Within five years CARQUEST had almost 1,500 jobbers successfully retailing auto parts throughout the United States. Straus-Frank Company in San Antonio became a member wholesale distributor in 1976, and A.E. Lottes in St. Louis and Hatch Grinding in Denver joined in 1980.

Sloan, always the ambitious go-getter, was instrumental in much of the growth at CARQUEST. In 1980 the owner of General Trading Company in St. Paul was ready to retire and approached Sloan to purchase his company. The acquisition was the first of more than a dozen such transactions in the following years. In 1983 GPI entered large-scale retail merchandising with the purchase of Valley Motor Supply in Havre, Montana, which included 35 stores in Montana and Wyoming. By 1984 sales for the CARQUEST alliance had reached $600 million.

Expansion of the CARQUEST alliance in the mid-1980s continued under then-president Dan Bock, former owner/president of Bobro Products, which was sold and renamed BWP Distributors in 1984. CARQUEST obtained three new WD memberships: Autoparts Warehouse in Honolulu; Muffler Warehouse in Pocatello, Idaho; and World Supply in Lemont, Illinois. GPI expanded into Kentucky when it acquired a WD in Lexington. In addition, two CARQUEST WD members, Parts Distribution in Memphis and Parts Warehouse in Bay City, Michigan, merged with GPI. By 1990 CARQUEST had 15 member WDs, 2,300 jobbers, 62 distribution centers, and more

Company Perspectives:

CARQUEST is committed to providing the finest quality parts in the automotive aftermarket. All of the parts in the CARQUEST-brand line are produced to exacting standards of performance and dependability, by the best manufacturer in the industry, to meet or exceed OEM specifications. CARQUEST is committed to the three-step distribution process: moving the product from the manufacturer, to the distribution center, to the CARQUEST Auto Parts Store, for final distribution to automotive technicians and do-it-yourselfers across the country.

than 43,000 dealer accounts. CARQUEST sales reached a plateau of approximately $600 million, with a 70 percent professional installer and 30 percent retailer sales distribution.

Mission Renewed in the Late 1980s

CARQUEST sales reached a plateau, and CARQUEST leadership found that the company had lost sight of its tradition of jobber marketing to the professional user. Competition for DIY retail business had diverted the company from its primary customer base in professional repair technicians. In the 1980s inventory requirements proliferated with increased numbers of foreign-made automobiles and the more complex technology in domestic vehicles. These new challenges required individual service and an abundant inventory at each distribution center. CARQUEST responded by improving its relationship with jobbers and by helping jobbers create better relationships with professional repair technicians.

Moreover, the following mission, as reprinted in the April 1996 *Automotive Marketing* magazine, was created to facilitate renewed focus at CARQUEST: "(1) Establish CARQUEST auto parts stores as the most recognizable supplier of quality products and services to the aftermarket nationwide. (2) Make a total commitment to provide the most complete service, supply, and marketing programs to enable CARQUEST jobbers to effectively compete on a profitable basis. (3) Each WD pledges to commit its total marketing efforts and direction to achieve 100% distribution through CARQUEST jobbers and support CARQUEST programs and products in a unified fashion. (4) Move with practical speed toward CARQUEST branded products."

CARQUEST sought to create a brand-name product line and new partnership with its jobbers through exclusive distribution of CARQUEST products. Previous to brand development, CARQUEST had offered short line, retail-oriented DIY products, such as oils and filters, under the brand "Proven Value" (PV). The company decided to expand the number of product lines using both PV and CARQUEST for full line coverage, and it added Bravo, a limited product line for the economical buyer. Through regional member councils, CARQUEST gathered information that determined the product lines to be manufactured. In accordance with jobber input, market-based decisions led to the development of several product lines as well as marketing programs to support brand recognition. Areas of strong growth

for professional users included rack and pinion steering, emission control, fuel injection, brake systems, temperature control/heating, and air conditioning. Manufacturers included Moog Automotive, Dana, and others.

CARQUEST began to focus its distribution exclusively through CARQUEST Auto Parts Stores. Though the company lost some business to accounts that offered other product lines, the company gained through exclusive distribution at affiliated auto parts stores. With increased competition from large volume retailers, AutoZone in particular, who impinged on sales to professional users, CARQUEST continued to endorse three-step distribution in partnership with store jobbers. Two-step distribution—from manufacturer to retailer to end-user—could not respond to the complex, immediate needs of professional repair mechanics with a large inventory at distribution centers. Exclusive distribution allowed CARQUEST to focus on the traditional aftermarket with well-trained jobbers serving professional installers. CARQUEST prided itself on its ability to supply the hard-to-find part.

CARQUEST initiated the Technician's Network, or TECH-NET, which sought to improve public respect for automotive repair professionals while it emphasized a code of ethics for quality assurance through high standards of ability, such as Automotive Service Excellence (ASE) certification. TECH-NET provided technical training videos as well as printed materials to improve and update skills of professional installers, aligning quality of product with quality repair service. A toll-free telephone help-line with trained technicians, supported by a database of automotive repair information, offered technical assistance for automotive repair diagnosis. In 1989 more than 2,000 professional automotive repair technicians subscribed to the program.

CARQUEST's commitment to jobber success led the company to develop four levels of training. The first level was the library of how-to videotapes with more than 100 titles available on loan for two-day checkout through a jobber or distribution center. Through seminars and printed materials, Counterman Training covered technical information as well as customer relations skills. Hands-on technical training was made available for professional installers, and management seminars, the fourth level of training, provided jobbers with a variety of business skills.

CARQUEST supported its new products lines as well as its commitment to jobbers with national and local advertising strategies. Advertising on national television served to establish CARQUEST as a national, brand-name automotive replacement parts distributor. Televisions commercials featured country singer Roy Clark as the company spokesman beginning in 1988. Catalogs of CARQUEST products for the DIY market were made available for local use in direct mail advertising or as newspaper inserts. More than 33 million catalogs per year have been printed for member use. CARQUEST also provided wholesale catalogs as well as farm and agriculture catalogs.

In 1990 CARQUEST began to advertise during car-related events on ESPN, such as NASCAR and USAC auto racing competitions, to stimulate brand recognition and brand support among the general public. CARQUEST's sponsorship agreement for the 1991 USAC Prime Thunder Series provided a mini-camera installed in race cars. Televised filming from inside the race cars featured the CARQUEST logo, as "CARQUEST Auto Parts Stores Cage Cam" appeared on television screens. In 1992 CARQUEST sponsorship of the race included two mini-cameras. On the local level CARQUEST members also promoted the company through sponsorship of racing and other motor sports events and auto shows. In Boston, Virginia CARQUEST Auto Parts stores distributed discount coupons to racing fans for the CARQUEST Autoparts Stores 300. The CARQUEST Bowl, a collegiate postseason football game, stagnated under the shadow of better known and more popular bowl games, however.

Overall, the company's activities supported its four goals, and by 1993 CARQUEST brand sales had increased to 40 percent of sales, up from 20 percent to 25 percent of sales in 1980s. In 1994 the company's fourth goal was reworded as: "Continually improve the quality, coverage, and competitive position of CARQUEST branded products." By April 1996 CARQUEST had developed 31 product lines and CARQUEST-brand sales had risen to more than 70 percent of the total. CARQUEST directed its marketing programs to specific CARQUEST products and vendors. The company remained committed to programmed distribution, which the leadership believed allowed for better customer service and sustained the company's competitive standing in the auto parts market.

Consolidation and Mergers in the 1990s

Much of the growth and change at CARQUEST in the first years of the 1990s can be attributed to competitive forces that made consolidation, mergers, and acquisitions an automotive aftermarket trend. New WD members at CARQUEST included PSC in Phoenix and Parts Wholesalers in Bangor, which joined in 1989 and later merged with GPI. CAP Warehouse in Las Vegas joined in 1991, extending CARQUEST's reach to a region of rapid growth. Pacific Wholesalers in Portland, Oregon joined in 1990 and merged with GPI the same year. Service Parts in Albany, Georgia merged with GPI in 1990; CARQUEST member World Supply merged with GPI in 1991 as did founding member Indiana Parts and Warehouse. CARQUEST member Straus-Frank Co. purchased the Pettigrew-Smith chain of 27 auto parts stores in Houston in 1992. Automotive Parts Wholesale in Bakersfield joined in 1993. Mergers with GPI also included Freemont Electric in Seattle in 1993 and ADI in St. Louis in 1994. In 1996 WD member Sussen of Cleveland, which had merged with Buffalo, New York member Avro earlier, merged with GPI.

Leadership changes at CARQUEST intertwined with changes in the aftermarket. Mergers and bankruptcies reduced the number of member WDs from 18 in 1986 to ten in 1996, also reducing the Board of Directors to ten members. Peter Kornafel, owner and president of Denver CARQUEST member WD, Hatch Grinding, became president of CARQUEST in 1996. Hatch Grinding, which had been family-owned and -operated since 1951 and served 110 CARQUEST jobbers in the Rocky Mountain Region, merged with GPI the same year. Kornafel based his decision to merge as the best strategy for growth at Hatch Grinding. As president, Kornafel pinpointed jobber success as the sole mission of CARQUEST. In correlation with change of leadership, CARQUEST relocated its headquarters from Tarrytown, New York to Lakewood, Colorado, a suburb of Denver. The company streamlined and restructured operations for more effective communication between departments with functions more clearly delineated.

CARQUEST's stated goals proved to be in alignment with the automotive aftermarket trend toward affiliation and consolidation. Independent jobbers increasingly became members of programmed distribution companies such as CARQUEST. Although CARQUEST's member WDs tended to own more auto parts stores than in the past, approximately two thirds of CARQUEST jobber-stores were independent sellers. The benefits of affiliation were similar to those enjoyed by chain stores, such as national and regional advertising, brand recognition, and training. In 1996 CARQUEST disseminated an eight-page brochure describing its training program through automotive trade publications. That the strong response required a reprint of the brochure demonstrated the demand for training to update skills with new automobile technologies.

GPI Continued To Lead in the Late 1990s

As the largest member of the CARQUEST alliance GPI continued to provide the buttress for a national network of distribution. In May 1997 GPI expanded into Canada through the partial purchase of Acktion Corporation, a joint venture in which GPI acquired four distribution centers in eastern Canada. GPI acquired 15 Art's Auto Parts stores in eastern Nebraska and western Iowa in July 1997. Assets of Big A Auto Parts Warehouse in Omaha were acquired by GPI and CARQUEST member BWP Distributors in September 1998. While going through bankruptcy proceedings, Big A Auto Parts sold eight distribution centers and the Omaha warehouse to GPI, along with assets of 125 Big A Auto Parts stores that those distribution centers served. Through the transaction GPI expanded into Albuquerque, Denver, Phoenix, Salt Lake City, and other cities. Later, in October 1998, GPI purchased two Colorado Springs stores from Big A Auto Parts stores.

BWP established a CARQUEST market in Pennsylvania with two acquisitions. From Big A Auto Parts, BWP acquired a warehouse in Philadelphia and assets of the 17 stores it supplies. About the same time, in September 1998, BWP Distributors acquired warehouses in Philadelphia from Motor Masters, which added $25 million value in annual sales and established CARQUEST in the automotive parts aftermarket in Philadelphia and southeastern Pennsylvania.

In November 1998 GPI purchased Republic Automotive Parts, Inc. from Keystone Automotive Industries. The acquisition included mechanical parts operations and nine warehouse distribution centers. The 88 auto parts stores included in the deal generated $110 million in revenue in 1997, revenue that would become CARQUEST revenue in the years that followed. The stores were located in Alaska, Arizona, California, Iowa, Illinois, Indiana, Michigan, Mississippi, and Pennsylvania. In March 1999, The Parts Source, Inc. merged with GPI. That transaction affected 41 stores and a distribution center in Ocala, Florida. At $3 per share and 3.4 million outstanding shares of common stock, the merger cost GPI $10.2 million. With 27 distribution centers in the United States and four in Canada,

CARQUEST sales under GPI alone amounted to approximately $1 billion in annual sales in the late 1990s.

Programmed Distribution Refined in the Late 1990s

With national expansion through CARQUEST jobber-stores and distribution centers, CARQUEST continued to provide the benefits of affiliation to its members. CARQUEST supported jobber success in its efforts to build name-brand support through sponsorship of sporting events. In 1998 CARQUEST entered a three-year agreement with the Grand Prix Association-Long Beach to be the title sponsor to the NASCAR Busch Series Grand National Division at Gateway International Raceway in St. Louis. The CARQUEST Auto Parts 250 would be nationally televised on CBS. Also under CARQUEST sponsorship, Paul Romine won the IHRA Top Fuel Dragster World Championship in 1997 and 1998; CARQUEST renewed its sponsorship for 1999. Paul Romine and CARQUEST also co-operated to raise funding for the 1999 Special Olympics World Games held in major cities in North Carolina. Local GPI involvement included volunteers and transportation support. In addition, CARQUEST was involved in The History Channel Great Race, a 14-day, pre-1951 vintage car rally race, traveling through 40 cities coast-to-coast in 1999. CARQUEST provided stopover points for race participants.

CARQUEST continued to apply its formula for jobber success through a focus on the success of the professional technician. TECH-NET evolved to include financial assistance and advice, and an annual Excellence Award, which would be granted to foremost repair facilities with prizes valued at $15,000. A Technical Advisory Council comprising award winners and finalists participated in the formulation of CARQUEST programs. Up-to-date technician training developed with on-site manufacturer clinics that covered specific car part systems such as a brake system or fuel injection system. The training video library grew to more than 150 titles, and CD ROM training was being discussed.

In 1998 CARQUEST launched the TECH-NET Professional Auto Service Program, a complete marketing program for automotive repair professionals, with the goal to enhance the experience of automotive repair for consumers. More than 1,200 automotive repair businesses enrolled in the program. In connection with the marketing program CARQUEST also introduced the CARQUEST Credit Card program, which offered 90 days' same as cash and no annual fee to individuals and repair shops. CARQUEST offered repair shops the opportunity to have their business name on the card as well to encourage repeat business and name recognition.

CARQUEST leaders found that three-step distribution continued to support the immediate and broad needs of the professional repair facility. Complex vehicle technology and more female car owners shifted the automotive aftermarket away from DIY retail toward greater reliance on professional repair facilities. Sales to national dealer accounts rose to $100 million in 1998, up from $34 million in 1996. CARQUEST gained 30 new national accounts in 1998 and CARQUEST products experienced sales growth at approximately double the automotive aftermarket industry average in 1998.

Principal Operating Units

CARQUEST Warehouse Distributor Members: Auto Parts Wholesale; Automotive Warehouse, Inc.; BWP Distributors, Inc.; CAP Warehouse; CARQUEST Canada, Ltd.; General Parts, Inc.; A.E. Lottes Company; Muffler Warehouse; Straus-Frank Company.

Further Reading

"Aggressive Is CARQUEST's Plan for 1992," *Aftermarket Business,* January 1, 1992, p. 7.

"The Auxer Group, Inc. Announces a Licensing Agreement with CARQUEST," *PR Newswire,* October 14, 1998, p. 1589.

"CARQUEST Meets Goals To Boost Sales, Market, and Brand Presence," *Automotive Marketing,* April 1996, p. 17.

"CARQUEST Names Kornafel New President, Moves HQ," *Automotive Marketing,* July 1996, p. 12.

"CARQUEST 1992 Marketing Strategy Means Business," *Automotive Marketing,* December 1991, p. 45.

"CARQUEST Strongly Supports Three-Step Distribution," *Automotive Marketing,* October 1991, p. 48.

"CARQUEST Takes Viewers for a Ride," *Aftermarket Business,* May 1, 1992, p. 18.

Dooms, Tracy M., "CARQUEST Move To West Side Park Will Leave South Street," *Indianapolis Business Journal,* August 26, 1991, p. 9.

Eyerdam, Rick, "Bowl Congestion Restricted Carquest," *South Florida Business Journal,* January 14, 1994, p. 1A.

"Gateway International Names CARQUEST New Title Sponsor for NASCAR Busch Race; Raceway Receives Long-Term Commitment from Auto-Parts Firm," *Business Wire,* January 15, 1998, p. 01150196.

Gray, Tim, "Distributor Cap'n: With Temple Sloan at the Helm, General Parts Sells to the Top of North Carolina 100," *Business North Carolina,* October 1997, p. 58.

"How To Build a Private Label Brand Successfully," *Automotive Marketing,* November 1995, p. 35.

"In-Store Focus," *Automotive Marketing,* May 1990, p. 10.

Jordan, Steve, "Houston Company To Sell Omaha, Nebraska Auto Parts Warehouse, Store Assets," *Knight-Ridder/Tribune Business News,* September 17, 1998, p. OKRB982590F6.

"Keystone Finalizes Sale of Republic Auto Operations," *Aftermarket Business,* November 1, 1998, p. 32.

"The Parts Source Buys APS Ocala DC as CARQUEST Snaps Up More APS DCs," *Automotive Marketing,* October 1998, p. 2.

"The Parts Source, Inc.," *Aftermarket Business,* March 1999, p. 8.

"Program Distribution . . . Reaching Down To Embrace the Service Dealer," *Motor Age,* September 1989, p. 72.

Simon, Jeremy, "Competitor Buys Two Colorado Springs, CO Auto Parts Stores," *Knight-Ridder/Tribune Business News,* October 21, 1998, p. OKBR9829407E.

Tucker, Randy, "Omaha Nebraska, Auto Parts Stores Gird for Borders Bookstores-Type War," *Knight-Ridder/Tribune Business News,* July 7, 1997, p. 707B1141.

Wirebach, John, "Big Three Now Serve Half the Jobbers. What Will They Do in 1997?," *Automotive Marketing,* January 1997, p. 5.

——, "1994: The Year in Review: The Future of the Aftermarket Became a Little Clearer This Year," *Automotive Marketing,* December 1994, p. 16.

——, "Programmed Distribution: 93. Does Every Other Programmed Group Want To Be NAPA?," *Automotive Marketing,* April 1993, p. 53.

—Mary Tradii

Cartier Monde

27 Nightsbridge
London SW1X 7WB
England
(44) 171 838 8500
Fax: (44) 171 838 8555
Web site: http://www.cartier.com

Division of Vendome Luxury Group PLC
Founded: 1847
Sales: $2.38 billion (Vendome Luxury Group 1997)
NAIC: 33991 Jewelry (Except Costume) Manufacturing;
   44831 Jewelry Stores

One of the most revered names in jewelry, Cartier Monde (French for "World") is also the world's largest luxury jeweler, operating nearly 200 retail stores in more than 125 countries. The centerpiece of Vendome Luxury Group PLC—the London-based luxury goods subsidiary of Swiss-based, South African-controlled Compagnie Financière de Richemont AG, former owner of the Rothmans tobacco empire—Cartier accounts for the greatest share of the Vendome group's annual sales, which reached US $2.38 billion in 1997, Vendome's last reported yearly results as a public company. Joining Cartier in the Vendome stable are such luxury brands as Alfred Dunhill, Vacheron & Constantin, Lancel, Mont Blanc, Piaget, and Chloe. Through Cartier, Vendome has continued adding to its stable, with the acquisition of Italy's Van Cleef & Arpels in May 1999.

Cartier operates its own chain of nearly 200 retail stores, including the company's flagship locations in Paris, New York, and London; during the 1990s the company made strong expansion moves, opening in such mid-level markets as St. Louis and Seattle. Nonetheless, Cartier's retail growth remains purposefully restrained. The company has been well placed to capture a leading share of the luxury goods market, which boomed in the late 1990s, despite economic troubles in the Asian region.

Even though Cartier continues to be synonymous with fine jewelry and exclusive wristwatches, the company has developed a strong portfolio of so-called wholesale items, including cigarette lighters, scarves, and other relatively low-priced accessory items. These products, sold at the Cartier stores and through third party retails, account for more than two-thirds of total Cartier sales.

Cartier—through Vendome—ended a period as a public company in 1998, when main Vendome shareholder Richemont offered to buy out Vendome's minority shareholder. The offer, which paid some 26 percent above the stock price for a total of some US $1.7 billion, valued Vendome at US $5.7 billion.

Cartier is led by Allain Dominique Perrin, chief architect of the company's development for nearly 20 years. Another major Cartier figure is Micheline Kanoui, the company's lead designer and wife to Joseph Kanoui, chairman of the Vendome group.

Symbol of Elegance at the Turn of the Century

Born in 1819, Louis François Cartier entered the goldsmith and jewelry trade as an apprentice under the Parisian jeweler Adolphe Picard. When Picard retired, Cartier bought his master's business on consignment, establishing the house of Cartier in 1847 on Paris's Rue Montorgueil. Cartier's jewelry designs—which presented simplified versions of the era's ornate fashions—quickly made a mark on Parisian society. Cartier soon was adopted by royalty, finding his first notable champion and patron in Princess Mathilde, a cousin to Napoleon. Princess Mathilde was said to have been the arbiter of the Second Empire's sense of elegance and fashion.

Mathilde's patronage helped ensure Cartier's early success. By 1853, the young company could afford to move its quarters, to the Rue Neuve-des-Petits-Champs. By the end of that decade, Cartier was once again on the move, now to the Boulevard des Italiens. It would not be until the end of the century, however, that Cartier moved to the exclusive Rue de la Paix. In the meantime, Cartier's list of nobles and notables continued to grow—as did the number of Cartier's private commissions.

From the beginning, Cartier's designs extended beyond jewelry to embrace a variety of objects—including early attempts at creating wristwatches—primarily in the neoclassic vein. Cartier also introduced a design theme that would remain a constant with the Cartier house throughout the 20th century, introducing jewelry and other objects inspired by animal motifs. These designs, which began to appear in the 1870s, were produced in part in collaboration with jewelry designer Alphonse Fouquet.

Such design collaborations would take on even more importance for the firm in succeeding generations. Louis François Cartier was joined by son Louis Alfred, born in 1841. In 1898, Alfred brought his own son, Louis Joseph into the firm, changing its name to Alfred Cartier & fils. The following year, Cartier took up residence on the prestigious Rue de la Paix, the center of Parisian elegance, a location the company would keep throughout the 20th century.

Under Louis Alfred, Cartier's fame spread farther and farther beyond Paris. Before long, Alfred's two other sons joined the jewelry house. Youngest son Jacques-Theodule was sent to London, to open the company's Cartier London branch. Pierre-Camille traveled to the United States, where he opened Cartier New York in 1908. The opening of the London branch office corresponded with an important commission, received from Queen Alexandra of England, for 27 tiaras in honor of the coronation of King Edward VII in 1902. Two years later, Edward appointed Cartier a royal warrant as supplier to the Royal Court of England.

The rest of European royalty quickly followed suit. By the end of the decade, Cartier had been named royal supplier of jewelry to most of Europe's royal houses, from Spain, Portugal, Russia, Greece, Serbia, Belgium, Romania, and Albania, as well as the principality of Monaco and the former French royal House of Orleans. Cartier's standing among royalty had become so secure that the Prince of Wales would refer to the Parisian jewelers as the "Jeweller to Kings, King to Jewellers." Cartier designs for the time were marked by an adherence to the Guirland style, tempering that style's ornate designs with the Cartier hallmark of simplicity, eschewing somewhat the Art Nouveau style then popular. Instead, Cartier would adopt—and help impose—a new artistic style that would have a strong impact on much of pre-World War II culture: Art Deco.

Jeweller to Kings, Kings to Jewellers in the 20th Century

Under the leadership of Louis in Paris, Jacques in London, and Pierre in New York, Cartier entered its period of greatest achievement, a period in which its influence came to be felt on the jewelry industry worldwide. As Jacques and Pierre built the firm's overseas branches, each pursuing their own passions—Jacques traveling frequently to India and the Persian Gulf in search of the finest pearls; Pierre courting the McLeans, to whom Cartier sold the famed Hope diamond, and the Rockefellers, Whitneys, Astors, Vanderbilts, and others of the U.S. powerful industrial elite—Louis Cartier was busy creating the Cartier legend from his Paris base.

Possessed of a fine artistic sense and a correspondingly shrewd aptitude for business, Louis Cartier would be credited with raising the Cartier name to the rank of the world's most prestigious jewelry house. Louis Cartier was among the first to use the rare metal platinum, which, lighter than gold, enabled the invention of the so-called "invisible" setting. Louis Cartier also continued his grandfather's interest in jeweled wristwatches. Teaming up with watchmaker Edmond Jaeger, Cartier introduced, in 1904, what would be considered the first modern wristwatch, the Santos, created in honor of Cartier's friend, the Brazilian aviator Alberto Santos-Dumont. The Santos was followed by other wristwatch designs, including the Tonneau in 1906 and the famed Tank watch, in honor of the Allied victory to end World War I in 1918.

Cartier's interest in wristwatches led to the formation of the European Watch and Clock Company in 1919. By then, Cartier's Paris location also had grown, extending its facade from the original number 13 address to the number 11 in 1912. Five years later, in 1917, the company had installed its New York branch in its permanent Fifth Avenue location—having bought the building with a string of pearls worth $1 million. Another new division, the S (for silver) division, was created in 1923. The following year, the company would produce one of its greatest artistic triumphs, the Rolling Ring, developed by Jean Cocteau and Louis Cartier and made up of three interlocked bands of white gold, yellow gold, and pink gold, which would remain a worldwide bestseller for the company through the end of the century.

An important addition to Cartier arrived at the end of the 1920s as the company continued its tradition of design collaborations—the arrival of Jeanne Toussaint, who was named president of the company's "haute joaillerie" division in 1933, heralded Cartier's most exalted era. Unable to draw herself, Toussaint—considered the arbiter of taste of the era—instead guided a team of artists to create some of Cartier's most well-known designs and launch the world firmly into the Art Deco era.

After Louis and Jacques Cartier died in 1942, Pierre became the company's sole president. The company would continue to mark the fashion world with successes, such as the watches Baignoires in the 1950s and the Crash watch of the mid-1960s. When Pierre Cartier died in 1964, however, the company had been in slow financial (if not artistic) decline. By the end of the 1960s, Cartier's empire had become dissipated, bought up by a number of investors.

World Leader for the 1990s

In 1973 the industrialist Robert Hocq, assisted by financier Joseph Kanoui, led a group of investors—including South Africa's Rupert family, founders of the growing Rothman/Richemont dynasty—to buy up Cartier's New York branch. By the end of the decade, the group had moved to buy up the rest of the Cartier divisions, reorganizing the company as Cartier World. At the start of the 1980s, the Kruger family bought out the rest of the Cartier investors, adding the company to its Richemont holdings, which already included Alfred Dunhill.

Hocq, Kanoui, and, especially, Allain Dominique Perrin, named CEO of Cartier World, were credited not merely with saving Cartier's dwindling fortunes, but with raising it to the ranks of the largest jewelry concerns in the world. This process originated in the early 1970s as the company introduced a series of nonjewelry items bearing the Cartier name—and the Cartier cachet. Hocq and company also dared to break beyond the traditionally closed circuit of high fashion jewelry to sell these new products, including the Cartier cigarette lighter, in certain retail stores, such as the Civette tobacco shops in Paris.

By the end of the 1970s, the company had developed its "wholesale" products concept under the trademarked name "Le Must de Cartier." The spinoff products, primarily accessories with modest prices, brought the Cartier name within reach of every consumer, without sacrificing the grandeur and reputation of the Cartier jewelry line. In the early 1980s, Cartier extended the Must line to include Cartier-branded perfumes. At the same time, the company moved aggressively to protect its brand against counterfeits.

The Must line of wholesale products, sold both in Cartier stores and in third-party stores, would grow to form more than 60 percent of the company's sales, which topped the US $1 billion mark in the mid-1980s. The company then looked toward expanding its empire, making a number of acquisitions—either under its own name or through parent Richemont—to build a portfolio of some of the world's most exclusive names. These acquisitions, including Beaume et Mercier in 1988 and Piaget and Alderbert in 1989, joined the fashion house Chloe and world famous pen maker Mont Blanc, all owned by Richemont.

In 1993 the various luxury goods holdings of the Richemont holding group were reorganized as a new, publicly traded company, the Vendôme Luxury Group PLC. Cartier formed the centerpiece of that company, providing more than half of it sales. Perrin remained CEO of Cartier, continuing an expansion drive begun during the 1980s, but stepped up for the 1990s. Cartier began adding retail locations, building up a worldwide chain of nearly 175 stores by the late 1990s.

Despite the crushing economic climate during much of the 1990s, including an extended U.S. and European recession in the early part of the decade and the collapse of much of the Asian market in the latter half of the decade, Cartier maintained steady growth—in part because the Cartier name provided a cushion against the general decline in the luxury goods market. Nevertheless, the difficult economic climate was punishing Vendome's share price. In 1998 Vendome's parent and principal shareholder Richemont announced that it was willing to buy up all minority shares in Vendome.

The newly private Vendome continued to add to its luxury goods portfolio, buying the Lancel leather goods brand in 1998 and adding to the Cartier group with the acquisition of Van Cleef & Arpels in 1999. Cartier, which celebrated its 150-year anniversary in 1997, remained under the inspired leadership of Allain Dominique Perrin and chief designer Michelline Kanoui, certain to extend the Cartier legacy into the 21st century.

Further Reading

"Fabulous Jewelry from the House of Cartier," *USA Today Magazine,* May 1, 1997.

Okun, Stacey, "The Legend and the Legacy: The House of Cartier Celebrates 150 Years of History and Romance," *Town & Country Monthly,* March 1, 1997, p. 122.

—M.L. Cohen

Centex Corporation

2728 North Harwood
Dallas, Texas 75201-1516
U.S.A.
(214) 981-5000
(800) 566-3229
Fax: (214) 981-6400
Web site: http://www.centex.com

Public Company
Incorporated: 1950 as Centex Construction Company
Employees: 10,259
Sales: $3.98 billion (1998)
Stock Exchanges: New York London
Ticker Symbol: CTX
NAIC: 23321 Single-Family Housing Construction

Centex Corporation is one of the most successful diversified building companies in the United States, with products and services ranging from new home construction, manufactured housing, and industrial construction, to mortgage lending, pest control, and construction contracting. Centex protected itself from the cyclical nature of building construction not only through diversification but also through geographical expansion. As of the late 1990s, the company was involved in construction in 20 states across the nation.

Early History

The company got its start just after World War II, a time characterized in the United States by growth and consumerism. In 1945 Texas native Tom Lively ''scraped together $500 and drew up his 5 feet 6 inches to talk business with Ira Rupley, a successful Dallas land developer,'' as a 1956 *Newsweek* article related. A young entrepreneur, Lively had ''left his home town of Whitewrite, Texas, in 1937, and for years had scraped along selling clothing and hardware and 'a little of this and that' before settling on real estate.''

Rupley, who had made his name in home construction, entered into partnership with Lively on a still-unnamed building company. They began ''modestly enough with a scattering of single and double houses around Dallas,'' noted *Newsweek*. In 1949 they undertook their first major project, a large subdivision of 300 houses that sole for $6,500 each. The success of the subdivision led to the 1950 formation of the Centex Construction Company.

For its first few years, the company concentrated its building efforts exclusively in Texas. However, by the mid-1950s Centex was ready to expand. One of the company's early projects was also an historic one. Centex built Elk Grove Village near Chicago, America's first master-planned community. This was the forerunner of modern master-planned areas, and boasted some 7,000 homes, all built by Centex, by the 1990s.

Diversification and Expansion: 1960s–70s

By 1960 Centex Construction Company had produced some 25,000 residences in several states. The company began expanding its operations to include the production of housing materials. Centex opened a cement manufacturing business with facilities in Texas and Nevada, then bought out a Dallas contractor, J.W. Bateson, which had specialized in commercial buildings. Reflecting its new diversification, the company changed its name during the 1960s to Centex Corporation.

In 1969 Centex went public, selling 500,000 shares of common stock. By this time the builder's net worth stood at about $10 million, with gross revenues of almost $100 million. By the 1990s, its stock would be traded both nationally and internationally.

As Centex moved into the 1970s, it increased its scope of operations. The company acquired two leading builders, one in Chicago, the other Dallas-based Fox & Jacobs, then the largest builder of single-family homes in the Southwest. Fox & Jacobs' strategy for producing affordable housing seemed to be working. A 1976 *Fortune* article noted that the Centex subsidiary was able to ''turn over its $1 million inventory of building materials 15 times a year. The extraordinarily fast turnover is the key to the company's ability to hold down prices and still keep profit margins healthy on houses in a wide variety of sizes.'' Expansion continued as Centex acquired Frank J. Rooney, Inc., Florida's largest general contractor.

The 1970s became a peak time for building, and as need dictated, Centex expanded its cement business in Texas and became a partner in another cement plant in Illinois. Centex also opened an oil-and-gas plant that would come to be named Cenergy. However, for all its diversification efforts, Centex was still primarily associated with one region of the United States. Explained William Barrett in a 1990 *Forbes* article, "In fiscal 1979, 72 percent of the company's . . . homes were built in Texas, a dangerously high concentration. Centex executives started cutting back there and expanding elsewhere before the economic bust set in, but not nearly fast enough." Per-share profits subsequently fell 59 percent, from $3.44 for the fiscal year ending March 1981 to $1.41 the following fiscal year.

Beyond Texas in the 1980s

A crash in Texas construction followed the plummet in oil prices in 1986 and the subsequent failure of a number of Texas savings and loans. Although Centex was affected, its home construction in other parts of the United States kept the company afloat. However, the company owned $76 million worth of land that it was not practical to develop in the collapsed Texas market. In 1987 Centex established a new subsidiary, Centex Development Company, to oversee the land. The same year, Centex invested in further diversification, moving into medical facility construction with the subsidiary Centex-Rodgers Construction.

A rebound of sorts began by the late 1980s, with Centex's homes numbering more than 100,000. That decade saw the company increase its market from eight cities to 35 (by 1992 that number would rise to 39) through a combination of new business launches and acquisitions. One particularly key acquisition was that of the John Crosland Company, a major name in the Carolinas.

At the same time, Centex was also trimming and consolidating its forces to build a stronger organization. The oil-and-gas subsidiary Cenergy, for example, was spun off as a separate company in 1984; this divestment more firmly planted Centex in the construction business.

By the early 1990s, Centex operated several subsidiaries, all aimed at supporting the building business. One offshoot was Centex Mortgage Banking, which by 1985 had changed its name to CTX Mortgage Company and had expanded into all of the builder's major markets. Its purpose was to establish home prices and facilitate mortgages for Centex customers. According to company history, CTX initiated title and insurance operations, thus clearing the way to develop real estate as well as build on it. That development subsidiary made its debut in 1987 as Centex Development Company. By fiscal 1992, CTX Mortgage Co. had cleared $2.5 billion in home loans.

Centex banking interests did not end there, however. The corporation ran its own savings and loan institution, Texas Trust Savings Bank, FSB. The smaller interest provided just one percent of Centex's total 1992 revenues, with the bulk of incoming money (53 percent) coming from the building and mortgage banking subsidiaries. Contracting and construction services were also a big part of Centex's subsidiary interests. With Centex Cement Enterprises, which later changed its name to Centex Construction Products, the company had the ability to produce and deliver not only cement but also ready-mix concrete and gypsum boarding.

It was the homes themselves, however, that brought Centex into the public eye. A typical Centex home was somewhat unique; a staff of three in-house architects would trek to different building sites around the United States to determine just the kind of residence that would fit the development best. With the architects designing upward of 300 home concepts each year, there were plenty of options from which to choose. Thus, a "typical" Centex home could span from 900 to over 5,000 square feet, and cost from as little as $50,000 to as much as $1.1 million. (The higher-end projects were sold under the name Centex Custom Homes.)

Centex also involved itself with "Homes Across America," a building initiative of Habitat for Humanity. Habitat was formed to provide volunteer-constructed, low-cost homes for those who otherwise could not afford housing. Centex participation resulted in activity in all of its markets; the company announced in 1992 that 23 Habitat homes would be built in the following year.

Though its primary focus was on residential homes, Centex had a hand in the development of some public buildings. Contracts for 1992 included Veterans Administration medical centers in Detroit and Indianapolis; hospital expansions in San Diego and Miami; a wastewater treatment plant in Hot Springs, Arkansas; and even a Wal-Mart store in Paducah, Kentucky. Other high-profile Centex projects included Cinderella's Castle, EPCOT Center's Land Pavilion, and the Grand Floridian Beach Resort, all built for Disney World in Orlando, Florida.

The company's success could be attributed in part to the team-building attitude demonstrated by its top managers. Indeed, "in an industry famous for its flamboyant, ego-driven characters, CEO Larry Hirsch and his crew are quiet, low-key types who keep pretty much to themselves," reported Barrett. When CEO successor William J. Gillian was introduced, a *New York Times* article quoted a securities analyst as remarking, "One of the beauties of Centex is that they are decentralized. The company has demonstrated its ability to grow and to build its markets without running into the control problems that have plagued others." Centex described its business plan as based on a "3-D" strategy: diversify, decentralize, and differentiate.

Industry Leader in the Early 1990s

Whatever the strategy, it resulted in top scores for Centex. A *Builder* survey of America's top 100 building manufacturers ranked by closings rated Centex number one in 1992. Its unit output (9,184) easily outdistanced second-place, Michigan-based Pulte Homes (6,493). As *Builder* reported, Centex also posted a 29 percent increase in closings over 1991, as well as a ten percent increase in gross revenues covering the same period.

Although the early 1990s was not a banner period for the home building industry, conditions had begun to improve. While hardly recession-proof, Centex took advantage of the times. Then-CEO Larry Hirsch even remarked to *Forbes*, "I think a national recession would be a tremendous opportunity for Centex." As *Forbes* writer Barrett explained, Hirsch meant that a recession would "drive down the cost of land and interest rates—the bread of life for home builders—and would almost certainly weed out some smaller, highly leveraged competitors."

These predictions proved correct. By late 1992, with a slow recovery in the works, housing interest rates dropped to new lows and sales began to take flight. "Wall Street has started to appreciate home builders as manufacturers of a basic consumer product," a securities analyst told *Builder*. Centex benefited, posting 1992 revenues of $2.3 billion, with the high margins attributed to improvements in both the home-building and mortgage banking areas. (The company claimed the distinction of never having reported either a quarterly or an annual loss since becoming a public company.)

For all Centex's success in Texas, Florida, and other areas, one important region proved difficult for the company to penetrate. The company entered highly competitive Southern California several years before, but the area proved "a tough market to crack," as Centex president Tim Eller told *Builder*. Eller noted, however, that the shaky economy "has given us an opening we needed. We expect to increase our volumes there significantly."

Centex Construction Products benefited from an increase in demand for cement, aggregate, concrete, and wallboard in the mid-1990s. Its revenues nearly doubled in 1994. That year Centex took the subsidiary public, although it retained 56 percent of the stock after the initial public offering. In a somewhat unusual set-up for an IPO, Centex Corporation not only retained all of the offering proceeds, it left Centex Construction with an increased debt load. With the company's strong cash flow, the increased debt was not seen as a problem by analysts.

Although rising interest rates had slowed new home construction and had affected the company's mortgage banking subsidiary in the early 1990s, Centex enjoyed a leap in net income in 1993, from $35 million in 1992 to $61 million. In 1994 net income had risen to $85 million on revenues of $3.2 billion.

In the mid-1990s the company made several changes in its stable of subsidiaries. In 1994 Centex sold its remaining savings and loans operations. The same year, it began a joint venture that would build assisted living centers for Alzheimer's sufferers, as well as luxury homes in the United Kingdom. In 1995 the company purchased Vista Properties Inc., a $115 million acquisition that provided 3,500 acres of land in seven states to Centex for residential, commercial, and industrial development.

Centex diversified into two new industries in 1996: pest control, with the purchase of Environmental Safety Systems, and security systems, with the purchase of portions of Advanced Protection Systems. Although both acquisitions moved Centex into new areas, the company tied them into its traditional business by selling the services to its new home buyers.

Centex's expansion and diversification continued into the late 1990s. In 1998 the company purchased 80 percent of Cavco Industries, a maker and retailer of manufactured housing based in Phoenix. Cavco homes generally were priced between $60,000 and $110,000 and sold in the western United States. The $75 million deal gave Centex an entrée into an area of housing construction that chairman Bill Gillian characterized in *Builder* as "a profitable business with a high return on revenue and assets." Centex followed up on its move into this new industry by purchasing in 1998 AAA Homes, a retailer of manufactured homes with approximately 260 retail outlets in the United States, Japan, and Canada. Centex also planned on using the manufactured housing in its own developments rather than selling them solely to customers with their own land.

Expanding on the idea of selling housing related products, such as security systems, to its home buyers, Centex opened two retail stores that sold a variety of products for use in the home. Dubbed Life Solutions, the stores offered products ranging from walking shoes to medical devices to foot massagers, and services ranging from delivery and installation to gift wrapping to notary service. The stores opened in suburbs of Chicago and Washington, D.C., and enjoyed very good sales their first year, according to Mike Albright, chairman and CEO of Centex Life Solutions. In addition to its plans for a third store, the company was investigating the possibility of using mail order and Internet sales.

Although Centex had diversified into several new industries in the 1990s, it remained primarily a home construction company. In 1998 it purchased Wayne Homes, a construction company that specialized in building on buyer-owned land. In 1999 Centex began selling lower-priced homes under the brand name Fox & Jacobs. At $90,000 to $134,000, the homes were targeted at first-time home buyers, although the company also saw interest from empty-nesters. In addition, the company planned to purchase Chicago-based Sundance Homes' suburban operating assets. Centex's revenues and net income rose steadily throughout the mid- to late 1990s. By 1998 the company was earning $145 million on revenues of $3.98 billion.

Principal Subsidiaries

Centex Construction Group, Inc.; Centex-Rodgers Construction Company; Centex-Rooney Construction Co. Inc.; Centex Real Estate Corp.; The Mangano Company, Inc.; Mountain Cement Company.

Further Reading

Barrett, William P., "A Tremendous Opportunity," *Forbes,* May 28, 1990, pp. 72–76.
"Builder 100," *Builder,* May 1993, p. 172.
"Centex Climbs in Chicago Market," *Professional Builder,* March 1999, p. 48.
"Centex Enters Manufactured Arena," *Builder,* January 1998, pp. 15–17.

Cochran, Thomas N., "Offerings in the Offing: Centex Construction Products," *Barron's,* March 28, 1994, p. 50.

"How a Texas Outfit Builds a Good Cheap House," *Fortune,* April 1976, p. 164.

Hylton, Richard D., "Home Building Is Good for Some," *New York Times,* April 27, 1990.

"Lively's the Name," *Newsweek,* March 26, 1956.

Maynard, Roberta, "Centex Goes Retail," *Builder,* May 1998, p. 40.

"New Operating Chief Is Selected at Centex," *New York Times,* January 8, 1990.

O'Malley, Sharon, "Centex Goes Back to Basics," *Builder,* January/February 1999, p. 10.

—Susan Salter
—updated by Susan Windisch Brown

Central Sprinkler Corporation

451 North Cannon Avenue
Lansdale, Pennsylvania 19446
U.S.A.
(215) 362-0700
Fax: (215) 362-4731
Web site: http://www.centralsprinkler.com

Public Company
Incorporated: 1972
Employees: 1,300
Sales: $225 million (1998)
Stock Exchanges: NASDAQ
Ticker Symbol: CNSP
NAIC: 332919 Other Metal Valve & Pipe Fitting
Manufacturing; 326122 Plastics Pipe & Pipe Fitting
Manufacturing

Central Sprinkler Corporation, through its wholly owned subsidiary Central Sprinkler Company, is one of the largest manufacturers and distributors of automatic fire sprinkler systems and sprinkler components in the United States. The company not only makes sprinkler heads, but a wide array of component parts for sprinkler systems, including valves, grooved couplings and fittings, CPVC plastic pipe and fittings, and steel pipe. In addition, the company is one of the leading distributors of automatic fire sprinkler systems and parts, with numerous distribution centers located across the United States, and one each in the United Kingdom, Singapore, and China. During the last 25 years, sales have been on a continual increase, due in large part to the fact that federal and state regulations require sprinkler systems in both commercial and multi-residential buildings, and that similar regulations require sprinkler systems for older commercial constructions to meet the local building codes.

Early History

Central Sprinkler Company opened its doors for business in 1972. The company was established so that it could meet the growing need for automatic fire sprinkler systems, which had become part of the federal and state regulations requiring such sprinkler systems in commercial and larger, multi-residential buildings. One of the company's first products, and the one that became its best-selling product during the middle and late 1970s, was the design and manufacture of the standard commercial sprinkler head.

The sprinkler head itself is the part of a sprinkler system that is activated by heat and, consequently, discharges a powerful and steady stream of water. The materials that comprise a sprinkler head include brass, copper, and various other types of corrosion resistant materials. A standard commercial sprinkler head is put in place on or near the ceiling of a room and is made up of a fusible alloy pellet that is contained in a bronze center strut by the use of a ball that is stainless steel. As the alloy melts at its activating temperature, the ball is pushed into the center strut and releases ejector springs, which, in turn, initiates the activity of the sprinkler head and discharges a strong steam of water according to a prescribed flow path. Most of the company's commercial sprinkler heads are designed to be activated at temperatures normally ranging between 136 and 286 degrees Fahrenheit.

The company grew steadily but slowly on sales of its standard commercial sprinkler head and system, and management was cautious in its strategic plan for future growth. By the 1980s, Central Sprinkler Company looked attractive to many other firms and groups of independent financiers as a prospective acquisition, since it was financially stable with a good cash flow. In the acquisition-crazed period of the time, no company seemed immune from being purchased, no matter how good their balance sheet looked and how talented their management. Thus the company was purchased by a group of investors. The group assumed the name of Central Sprinkler Company when it was purchased in May of 1984 and it conducted the operations of the firm under the same name. Previous to the actual purchase of Central Sprinkler, the investment group did not list any assets or liabilities, nor had it engaged in any other activity or operation other than the acquisition of Central Sprinkler Company. The highest level of management within the company remained to direct its operations and in doing so bought a portion of the firm's stock, with the rest of it purchased by the independent investment group.

With the impetus of leadership from the outside investment group, Central Sprinkler Company initiated an aggressive ac-

Company Perspectives:

Central Sprinkler is a leader in the fire sprinkler systems industry. The Company is a leading designer, manufacturer and distributor of the most diverse line of fire sprinklers available, a complete line of valves and accessories, CPVC pipe and fittings, steel pipe, and ductile iron grooved fittings. Management is confident that strong market fundamentals combined with the Company's diverse line of quality sprinklers, innovative research and development programs, strong relationships with installation contractors and continued development of cost cutting programs should be major contributing factors to expected sales and profit improvements going forward.

quisitions program of its own. The company's first purchase was that of Spraysafe, one of the leading manufacturers and distributors of sprinkler heads and sprinkler systems in the United Kingdom. Its first foray into the international arena was regarded as a success not only by company management but by industry analysts who began to recommend that investors purchase Central Sprinkler stock. With one purchase, top executives at the firm not only managed to significantly expand their product line to include glass bulb sprinkler heads, one of the items for which Spraysafe was known, but also had arranged the start of a distribution network for marketing Central Sprinkler products throughout Europe.

By the end of the 1980s the company was manufacturing and marketing an impressive variety of sprinkler system valves that were used as component parts in fire sprinkler installations. The valve is the device that controls the water supply within an automated sprinkler system, so that when a system is activated at a certain temperature, the valve triggers the flow of water through the system. In addition, the company also was garnering a reputation for its proprietary product line of steel sprinkler pipes. The pipe, which is used to carry the water from its source to the fire sprinklers when activated, received approval that is Underwriters Laboratory Listed and Factory Mutual Approved.

The 1990s and Beyond

During the early and mid-1990s the company expanded its product line to make a concerted effort to capture a larger part of the market. In late 1989 Central Sprinkler designed and manufactured a residential/life-safety sprinkler that it reworked during the early 1990s. The sprinkler was meant to provide a quick response and react to a fire before it could spread, which, in turn, significantly reduces the smoke and toxic fumes released by the fire. Designers added a glass bulb activating mechanism, which made the sprinkler even more effective, and the product soon gained the reputation as one of the best means for the protection of life during a fire.

In 1993 the company introduced another type of sprinkler head, the extended coverage commercial sprinkler. A revolution in sprinkler technology, this type of sprinkler head extended the water spray from 130 square feet to an amazing 400 square feet.

Introduced and marketed under the trademark name of Optima, management at Central Sprinkler soon discovered that this sprinkler was one of the company's most profitable products. In addition to the extended coverage commercial sprinkler, during the same year the company introduced the early suppression response sprinkler, designed for use in special and uniquely hazardous environments. Designed specifically to protect large storage areas where a quick response sprinkler with a high density of water spray is needed, the company included a larger orifice in the design of the sprinkler head to reduce the amount of pressure required for the spray. In 1995 Central Sprinkler continued its innovative designs with the introduction of a specific application series made to provide improved fire protection while at the same time keeping installation costs to a minimum.

Aside from expanding Central Sprinkler's product line, management decided to embark on a vertical integration program that included strategic acquisitions to expand its market share. In July of 1994, management created a new company, Castings, Inc., through the purchase of a foundry located in the southeastern United States. The foundry manufactured piping system components and significantly enhanced Central Sprinkler's desire to provide corrosion resistant piping for its sprinklers. Purchased for $1.8 million, Castings, Inc. soon was fully integrated within its parent company's production facilities and distribution network. The acquisition of a ductile iron factory shortly afterward by Castings provided the company with the ability to make its own grooved fittings and couplings and other piping systems component parts. In May of 1995 management formed another new company, Central CPVC, to manufacture CPVC plastic pipe and fittings. The company began building a new facility in Huntsville, Alabama, and production started in 1997. All of these developments were meant to provide Central Sprinkler with the ability to compete more readily, not only in the fire protection market, but in the mechanical, industrial, original equipment manufacturing, and heating and air-conditioning markets, where management saw the most promising opportunities for growth.

During this time the company began to expand its distribution network and provided a host of different parts normally used in sprinkler system installations. Fittings, electric switches, control valves, and hangers were sold to contractors. In keeping abreast of the technological developments that impacted its business, Central Sprinkler began to market and sell computer-aided design systems to architects and contractors for use in the installation of highly sophisticated commercial and multi-residential sprinkler systems.

Unfortunately, for all its success during the early and mid-1990s, Central Sprinkler was hard hit by a series of lawsuits filed against it in August of 1997 and March of 1998. The class action lawsuit filed in 1997 by the State of California was on behalf of a number of building owners who had installed the company's brand-name Omega sprinkler system in their buildings. The lawsuit brought against the company in 1998 was filed by the U.S. Consumer Product Safety Commission, also focusing on the Omega sprinklers. Both suits charged that the sprinklers were faulty and would not work properly during a fire. Although the company discontinued the manufacture and sale of the Omega sprinkler in 1998, Central Sprinkler was forced to reach an agreement with both plaintiffs such that it would provide for a free replacement sprinkler and its component parts, and that a separate account would be established for payment to the owners of the Omega sprinkler, the administration of a recall program, and an extensive notification program related to the recall of the Omega sprinkler.

During the summer of 1998 Central Sprinkler announced that it would recall more than eight million Omega sprinkler heads and systems and that any homeowner or commercial property owners who responded to the recall notice would receive a free replacement sprinkler system. In addition, the company announced that it had set aside $38 million to pay for both the replacement sprinklers and for a portion of the charges that customers incurred during the installation of the sprinklers. In spite of the settlement, many people remained unsatisfied with the terms of repayment, and a number of individuals chose to file individual lawsuits against the company. As a representative of the Building Owners and Managers Association International argued, the $38 million set aside by Central Sprinkler was inadequate since it represented "less than five bucks a sprinkler."

Responding to the likelihood of greater financial problems because of the litigation, in April of 1999 management at Central Sprinkler hired Mathias J. Barton to act as chief financial officer and senior vice-president of finance. Barton, although a young man of 39, brought with him considerable experience in finance, accounting, information systems, purchasing, and customer service operations. He had worked previ-ously at Rapidforms, Inc., a New Jersey-based manufacturer of business forms and other products. The hope was that Barton could steer the company's ship through the reefs of impeding lawsuits that were potentially damaging to the continuance of its operations.

During the first quarter of 1999, sales for the company declined about five percent. This was due to the discontinuance of the Omega sprinkler systems and the increased competition within the marketplace. Yet Central Sprinkler forged ahead in its research and development program, confident in its ability to maintain a position of technological leadership and its market share within the sprinkler system industry.

Further Reading

Ceniceros, Roberto, "Sprinkler Heads Under Fire," *Business Insurance,* August 18, 1997, p. 1.
——, "Sprinkler Maker Suing Insurers for Recall Cover," *Business Insurance,* October 19, 1998, p. 1.
——, "Sprinkler Settlement Gets Preliminary OK," *Business Insurance,* November 2, 1998, p. 3.
"Central Sprinkler Corporation," *Wall Street Journal,* June 3, 1998, p. B12(E).
"Central Sprinkler Doesn't See Recall Adding More Charges," *Wall Street Journal,* October 15, 1998, p. B4(E).
"Firm Had 3rd Period Loss: $26.6 Million Charge Cited," *Wall Street Journal,* September 22, 1998, p. B17(E).

—Thomas Derdak

Centrica plc

Charter Court
50 Windsor Road
Slough, Berkshire SL1 2HA
United Kingdom
(071) 821-1444
Fax: (071) 821-1870
Web site: http://www.centrica.co.uk

Public Company
Incorporated: 1997
Employees: 15,423
Sales: £7.5 billion (US$12.4 billion) (1998)
Stock Exchanges: London Tokyo New York Toronto
NAIC: 22121 Natural Gas Distribution

Centrica plc is the largest gas supplier in the United Kingdom, serving 16 million households, and a growing force in that country's electric industry. Formed during the 1997 breakup of British Gas, Centrica inherited the gas supply portion of the business and the rights to the British Gas name. British Gas plc was incorporated in 1986 when the state-owned British Gas Corporation was privatized, and more than 4,025 million shares were issued by the British government. This privatization of the gas industry reversed the nationalization of 1949, when more than 1,000 separate private or municipally owned companies were taken into state ownership. As the inheritor of this vast and established network, Centrica acted from a position of strength when Britain introduced competition into the gas industry and used the well-known British Gas name to capture electric customers when that industry was deregulated as well in the late 1990s.

Company Precursors

Experiments using coal gas for lighting were performed in the late 18th century in England. William Murdock reportedly lit his home in Redruth, Cornwall, with gas in 1792, and in the early years of the 19th century, when Britain was the world's first industrial nation, several factories made their own gas for lighting. The first gas company in the world to provide a public supply was the Gas Light and Coke Company of London, which received its charter in 1812. Gas for lighting proved both popular and profitable; by 1829, around 200 gas companies had been set up. Almost all of these companies relied on private capital, and the first municipal gas department was set up in Manchester in 1817 by the police commissioners and was taken over by Manchester Corporation in 1843.

The first gas companies were established in a competitive climate; there were no restrictions on where a company might set up in business if the organizers could raise the capital and thought they could make a profit. In the early days it was by no means unheard of for two companies to serve the same street; in one notable case in South London no less than four competing companies had mains in the same street. However, people soon recognized that unbridled competition served neither the interests of gas companies nor their customers. Within London, where the problem was most severe, the Metropolis Gas Act of 1860 allocated each company its own district within which it had a monopoly. To prevent exploitation of captive customers, a statutory limit of ten percent on dividends had been imposed by the Gasworks Clauses Act of 1847, but this limitation did not satisfy customers. Companies were enjoying monopoly powers and already earning the maximum dividend; there was little incentive for them to cut prices despite increasing sales and improved technology. This form of statutory regulation thus proved ineffective in protecting the interests of the public.

In the mid-1870s competition began to offer customers the prospects of a better deal. At first the competition came from lighting oil. Persistent overproduction in the Pennsylvania oil fields in the United States meant there was a surplus over U.S. needs, which would then be shipped out and dumped cheaply on world markets, especially in the early 1870s. Oil lamps proved a popular alternative to gas. By the late 1870s, electricity was also beginning to emerge as a competitor for the gas lighting business. A practical arc lamp was produced in 1876, and Thomas Edison in the United States and Sir Joseph Swan in Britain independently produced the first incandescent light bulbs in 1879–80. The gas industry responded in three ways; it attempted to improve the efficiency of its lamps, it looked for alternative markets, and it looked to its pricing structure.

At the suggestion of George Livesey, chief engineer of the British South Metropolitan Gas Company and the foremost gas engineer of his generation, the sliding scale was introduced in 1875. Under his system, dividends and prices were linked inversely; that is, increased dividends could be paid if the price of gas came down, but if the price of gas rose, dividends had to be cut. Individual companies sought private legislation to permit them to introduce the sliding scale; by the year 1900, two-thirds of all gas sold was covered by this arrangement. Its fairness to customers depended crucially on the datum price, or the price from which variations would be calculated. It was the good fortune of the gas companies that many technical improvements to cut costs were made after they adopted the sliding scale. Shares in the major gas companies were regarded as a very sound investment. Livesey also introduced a profit-sharing scheme for his workers in 1889; the bonus was linked to reductions in the price of gas. Similar co-partnership schemes were set up by several of the larger gas companies, but few outside the industry adopted the concept.

When gas companies were looking for alternative uses for gas, they began to consider its use for cooking and heating in the home. The first geyser water heater was invented in 1868, and gas fires to heat individual rooms were developed in the 1880s. However, gas companies were more interested in persuading customers to use gas for cooking. Experimental gas stoves had been shown at the Great Exhibition of 1851, but they had made no headway against the popular coal-fired kitchen ranges that provided heat and hot water as well as facilities for cooking. By the 1870s there were gas stoves recognizably similar in layout to most modern stoves, with an oven below and burners above. As far as the gas managers of the time were concerned, the special advantage of the stove was that it was likely to be used more during the day than at night; it would therefore use off-peak gas. Lighting, of course, was still the predominant load. For rational, promotional, and financial reasons, the installation of stoves could be subsidized from the profits on gas sales. As customers were disinclined to buy, they were supplied with basic, robust cast-iron stoves on cheap rental terms. By contrast, in the United States stoves were offered for sale, not rent, and were of lighter construction, well-finished, and with attractive trim. This policy of supplying subsidized stoves was developed more extensively in Britain between 1890 and the 1920s than anywhere else in the world, and British companies sold more gas than the rest of Europe put together.

Despite the excitement engendered by the first incandescent electric light bulbs, customers soon found them costly and unreliable. Gas saw a strong return to popularity in the 1890s, following the invention by an Austrian chemist of the Welsbach incandescent mantle, which increased fivefold the efficiency of gas for lighting. Gas was still very much a middle-class fuel; poorer people living in rented homes used coal, oil, and candles, and they could not afford to have gas installed, even if they wanted to use it. This situation, however, was about to change dramatically.

The change was generally attributed to the invention in 1888 of the prepayment, penny-in-the-slot meter. This alone would not have brought about the spread of gas into working-class homes, however. The manager of the municipal Ramsgate gas undertaking, W. A. Valon, noted that half the houses in the town had no gas supply. He decided that instead of offering to provide just the stove on easy terms, he would provide the whole gas installation—pipes, stove, and lights. As his new customers would pay for their gas in advance through a prepayment meter, there was no need to ask for a deposit as security. The profit on gas sales to poor homes was unlikely to be sufficient to pay for the installation costs, so there was a surcharge on the gas price for such customers, typically 25 percent—the prepayment supplement. The scheme spread like wildfire. In the words of George Livesey, ''this extension of gas supply to weekly tenants is the most extraordinary and remarkable development of the business that has ever been known.'' Between 1892 and 1912 the number of gas customers increased from two and one-half million to seven million, and sales doubled. The use of gas for cooking became more important than gas for lighting, as virtually all new customers were supplied with a stove.

This expansion of the industry was not accompanied by any structural change; it was still extremely fragmented. In 1914 there were some 1,500 suppliers of gas, two-thirds of whom had statutory monopoly powers within their areas of gas supply. There was little pressure toward amalgamation, in part because of high legal and consultancy fees, and also because of geography since supply networks could not easily be linked to achieve economies of scale. Another major factor was the split between the municipal and privately owned companies; about one-third of the industry was municipally owned. Each company could set its own technical standards and, because subsidized rental of appliances was almost universal, there was no independent appliance retailing network that might have encouraged harmonization of standards and appliance innovation.

The interwar period was a difficult time for the gas industry. At the outbreak of World War I in 1914, ten times more homes had a gas supply than electricity. Although the number of gas customers continued to rise until 1939, the increase in gas sales slowed, while electricity sales grew sharply. The prepayment supplement had paid for so many homes to be equipped with gas lighting that the defense of the lighting business was a major preoccupation; it was feared that if electricity displaced gas for lighting, it would soon displace gas stoves and heaters. As a consequence, the industry was distracted and could not concentrate its efforts fully on displacing the huge stock of obsolete rented appliances and selling modern stoves, heaters, and water heaters in their place. The real value of the prepayment supplement—fixed in cash terms before 1914—fell, and cost increases meant there was no surplus for upgrading appliances.

Electric stoves were attractive and modern by contrast with the traditional rented gas stoves. Moreover, the gas industry had no answer to new types of electric appliances—vacuum cleaners, irons, and radios—which were sold aggressively through retailers and by door-to-door salesmen. These popular new items, and the convenience and cleanliness of electric lighting, ensured that householders came to regard electricity as a necessity. Many builders and customers, attracted by the idea of the all-electric house, saw no need to install gas; some councils with their own municipal electricity undertakings even sought to ban their tenants from using gas. In the right market, however, gas could hold its own. The Ascot instantaneous water heater, developed in Germany by Junkers, was efficient and stylish; it provided a service where electricity could not compete. Its makers targeted their main promotional efforts at architects and builders rather than at gas companies and achieved conspicuous success. The Ascot became synonymous with gas water heating in Britain as the Hoover did with vacuum cleaning.

Restructuring the Gas Industry in the Mid-20th Century

The Electricity (Supply) Act of 1926 brought about the restructuring of the electrical industry, which until then had been as fragmented as gas. The government-appointed Central Electricity Board was charged with building a national grid. This initiative during the worst years of the Great Depression might suggest that electricity was the key to a prosperous national future, and politicians of all parties were keen to jump on the electrical bandwagon. Nothing comparable was planned for gas. Under the leadership of David Milne-Watson of the Gas Light & Coke Company, the gas industry lobbied strongly for a ''level playing field,'' but its pleas fell on deaf ears. By the late 1930s, people both within and outside the industry realized the existing structure could not survive without radical change. There was a need for some form of national framework for gas; those in the industry hoped that this would not mean state control.

These rumblings were muted during World War II, but thoughts on the future of the industry continued. A government committee under Geoffrey Heyworth proposed the compulsory purchase of all gas companies and the establishment of ten regions; regulation would be undertaken by commissioners, following the analogy of the electricity industry. His report was published in 1945, but by then a Labour government committed to the nationalization of the industry had been elected. There was little public concern or controversy, unlike the debates on the nationalization of coal, transport, electricity, or steel. Few may have given the industry much chance of survival, let alone expansion. Opposition came more from Conservative members of Parliament than from the industry, whose senior leaders gave an undertaking to cooperate with the government's plans ''to maintain an efficient gas service to the public,'' in the words of the British Gas Council.

Under the Gas Act of 1948, the industry passed into public ownership on May 1, 1949. Some £220 million of British Gas three percent stock—three percent annual interest was payable on the face value of the stock—was issued as compensation to the former owners; 1,037 separate undertakings, previously under private or municipal ownership, were amalgamated into 12 area gas boards. Scotland and Wales each had their own board; Northern Ireland was outside the scope of the act. The Gas Council, a small central coordinating body, was established. Apart from its chairman and vice-chairman, this comprised the 12 area board chairmen. Most had held senior positions in the

industry although other interests were presented; for example, one had a trade union and one a local government background. The duties of the Gas Council were to advise the minister on gas matters and to promote the efficient exercise of their functions by the area boards; the central body had a small secretariat, of 159 members, one-third of whom dealt with publicity and another third with purchase of coal and the sale of coke. The main executive power rested with the boards, though capital investment programs had to be submitted through the council to the minister for approval. There were national arrangements for wage-bargaining; close cooperation soon brought a measure of voluntary harmonization between the various boards over technical standards, commercial policy, and other areas of common interest. The industry was legally bound to take account of the interests of both workforce and customers through consultative arrangements.

The new area boards settled down quickly but faced two long-term problems. Their public image was still that of an old-fashioned if not immediately moribund industry, and they were losing the battle for the domestic load to electricity. In the ten years from 1948, sales of gas increased by 20 percent; over the same period, sales of electricity more than doubled. Old rented stoves, heaters, and water heaters were not being replaced quickly with modern equipment, and the sales efforts of the boards were hindered at first by postwar material shortages and the export drive, and also by government purchase tax and restrictions on renting. The other problem was the price of gas, which no longer enjoyed its traditional advantage over electricity. While the price of electricity rose by 17 percent between 1950 and 1957, gas rose by 51 percent. The cost of high-grade coal for gas-making doubled between 1947 and 1957, whereas power stations could use cheaper grades.

Efforts to rebuild the market for gas appliances were urgently needed but less important than the need to reduce the relative price of gas, and the industry began to search for alternative methods of gas production. One path explored was the total gasification of coal, a process developed in Germany before the war. Another alternative which seemed to offer better prospects was the use of oil feedstocks for gas-making, either as an enricher of gas made by other processes or later by direct catalytic conversion of oil into gas. Britain, and notably the Gas Council's own scientists, were pioneers in the intense research efforts that resulted in several processes that could take any oil feedstock available in large quantity at low cost, especially naphtha and refinery waste gas, and convert it direct into usable gas. Major contracts were signed with oil companies to secure long-term supplies. For the first time in its history, the gas industry's fortunes were unshackled from coal, during the 1960s.

Marketing Efforts in the 1960s

This technical breakthrough was matched by a change, of course, in marketing. Market research showed that gas still had a negative image by contrast with the strong modern image of electricity. W. K. Hutchison, the deputy chairman of the Gas Council, put himself at the head of the campaign to change the image of gas. In the words of the advertising agents, ''The amiable, innocuous figure of 'Mr. Therm' around which the Gas Council's advertising had for many a year revolved, seemed too bland, too typecast to take up the challenge. . . . And so it was that 'High Speed Gas, Heat That Obeys You'. . . invited newspaper readers to realize how 'with it' they were to be using gas.'' This coincided with the arrival on the market of a new generation of stoves with timers and automatic ignition, and stylish and efficient gas heaters that quickly took over from coal the main task of heating living rooms. Showrooms were modernized and moved to prime high-street locations.

The next stage was to attack the domestic central heating market, which was at the time being vigorously promoted by the oil companies. Gas was helped both by the arrival of natural gas and the OPEC oil price rises from 1973. It was also helped by the introduction of the Clean Air Act in 1956, which aimed to reduce the air pollution caused by coal-burning domestic fires. Natural gas enabled a significant reduction of smoke in the atmosphere. By 1989 more than 70 percent of all gas customers had gas central heating, a clear indication of the success of this campaign.

The 1960s saw other momentous changes that were to have even more far-reaching effects. Natural gas arrived in quantity for the first time in Britain. In its early days the Gas Council commissioned British Petroleum to act as operator to prospect for natural gas onshore; this search proved unsuccessful. The Gas Council was therefore particularly interested to hear of U.S. plans to ship liquefied natural gas (LNG) by tanker; cooling to very low temperatures reduces methane to a liquid, the volume of which is 1/600th of its gaseous state. The British government gave its approval to a trial to assess the practicality of the scheme, and the first experimental shipment arrived at Canvey Island in the Thames estuary in 1959. Gas Council proposals to proceed with import of LNG on a large scale ran into fierce opposition in government, predictably from the coal and oil lobbies. Approval was finally given by the British cabinet to a 15-year contract to buy gas from Algeria; two tankers shuttling to and fro would carry the equivalent of ten percent of British gas output at that time. The two vessels came into service in 1964. To enable all parts of the country to take advantage of these supplies of natural gas, a high-pressure national grid was constructed, at first linking eight boards to Canvey Island. The grid network was 320 miles long in 1966–67; by 1976–77 the network extended 2,915 miles, and all boards were connected.

1967–77: Conversion to Undiluted Natural Gas

The liquefied methane project was running in parallel with another natural gas project. A huge discovery of natural gas in Holland in 1959 led to speculation that more might be discovered under the North Sea. The Gas Council was very keen to participate in the search and joined in partnership with experienced U.S. operators to explore, drill, and subsequently to produce gas and oil. The necessity for Gas Council involvement was questioned at the time as, under British law, all gas found and landed in the United Kingdom had to be offered for sale to the council. The election of a Labour government in 1964 strengthened the hand of the Gas Council; it was positively encouraged to participate in North Sea activities.

It was fortunate that some of the early acreage allotted contained the huge Leman gas field. The council thus had invaluable information on the actual costs of finding and producing gas; it was able to negotiate prices based more on the costs of production

(then two pence per therm; 240 pence = £1) than on average revenue (16.5 pence) or the cost of seaborne gas from Algeria (6.5 pence). A whole series of discoveries soon proved that supplies of natural gas from the North Sea would meet British needs for a few decades at least. This raised the question of how best to use it. Up until then, natural gas had been converted into a coal-gas equivalent of only half the heat value of methane, volume for volume. There were enormous advantages of distributing methane without dilution; processing costs would be minimal, and the capacity of gas mains would be effectively doubled. Against this had to be set the cost of converting every appliance so that it could burn methane instead of coal gas. A survey of several thousand customers round the Canvey Island terminal in 1966 showed the great variety of equipment to be converted, three or four appliances per home on average. A large proportion were 15 years old or more. Ways had to be found to convert all these old appliances or to persuade customers, by offering generous terms, to buy new ones.

Despite the cost and potential problems, the advantages of complete conversion were overwhelming. This was an enormous technical, marketing, and public relations exercise. There was undoubted inconvenience, but considering the opportunities for error and complaint, most customers accepted the conversion with good will; it gave them a direct and personal opportunity to share in the excitement of the North Sea discoveries. Conversion was free and, for many, it gave an opportunity for old appliances to be brought up to scratch or replaced cheaply; besides, North Sea gas was cheaper. The conversion exercise was, in the words of Sir Denis Rooke, chairman of British Gas from 1976 until 1989, "perhaps the greatest peacetime operation in the nation's history." The main conversion program began in 1967 and, 13 million customers later, the last home was converted in 1977. From 1912 until nationalization in 1940, sales had more than doubled. Between 1949 and the end of the conversion program they increased sixfold.

Until the early 1960s, the gas industry had managed to avoid the relentless tinkering by politicians that had bedeviled the other nationalized industries: coal, steel, transport, and electricity. It had not been perceived as having any long-term significance and had neither failed nor succeeded dramatically. With its involvement in North Sea exploration and consequently higher public profile, this situation changed. Now the government thought seriously about establishing a production board along the lines of the Central Electricity Generating Board. The Gas Council persuaded the government that the existing arrangements were working harmoniously and suited the needs of the industry. As a consequence the 1965 Gas Act, essential to clarify the powers of the Council to buy gas in bulk and sell to its area board customers, left the basic structure untouched. It was clear, however, that strong central leadership was necessary to enable the company to cope with the changes brought by natural gas; new headquarters departments were set up covering production and supply, marketing, and economic planning. Rooke, who had been a member of the team working on the import of LNG from its inception in 1957, became development engineer, responsible for new production processes and planning an integrated supply system. Later, as member for production and supply, he played a crucial role in the technical changes in gas manufacture and distribution in the 1960s and 1970s. The arrangements under the 1965 Act were temporary; a restructuring was necessary to place overall responsibility at the center. In 1973 the Gas Council was replaced by the British Gas Corporation (BGC), still state-owned, and the area boards set up in 1949 became regions under direct control of the BGC.

One outcome of the success of the North Sea search for gas was that the BGC became a producer of oil and thus became involved in international fuel markets. This situation did not survive the election of the Conservatives to power in 1979. BGC was required to sell its oil assets, spun off as Enterprise Oil; the proceeds went not to the industry but to the government. At this time the government also became concerned at the dominant position enjoyed by BGC in the business of retail sale of appliances. The matter was referred to the Monopolies and Mergers Commission, which ruled that BGC's position in the market was against the public interest. The government drew back from enforcing a withdrawal from appliance trading; gas showrooms served to deal with accounts and service queries as well as selling. Independent retailers began playing a larger part in appliance retailing than ever before in the history of the industry; even so, British Gas still had a turnover of £300 million from appliance trading in the early 1990s.

Privatization in the Mid–1980s

When the privatization of the industry was under consideration, some ministers were keen to introduce an element of competition and to break up the unified structure of the industry that had evolved since nationalization, largely in response to the availability of natural gas. Any breakup was opposed by Rooke, who lobbied strongly for the retention of the unified structure that had served the nation so well; his views ultimately prevailed, although the nationalized electricity industry was to be split up in its subsequent privatization. The BGC was privatized as a whole by the Gas Act of 1986 and returned to private ownership in what was then the largest company flotation ever undertaken. After a vigorous television advertising campaign to "Tell Sid" to buy shares, three million people became owners of British Gas plc shares. The advertising alone cost £25 million, much of it paid by the government; the total cost of the privatization, including fees, underwriting, and value-added tax, was £347 million.

As a private company, British Gas was no longer geographically restricted to the United Kingdom and U.K. offshore waters. The government, however still preferred it to purchase its supplies from the U.K. sector of the North Sea for strategic and balance of payments reasons. Rooke retired in 1989 and was succeeded as chairman and chief executive by Robert Evans. The company made substantial investments in foreign oil and gas assets to strengthen its business worldwide. After its privatization, British Gas acquired interests in four exploration and production companies: Acre Oil and part of Texas Eastern North Sea were acquired to strengthen the company's oil and gas holdings in the North Sea's U.K. sector; some of Tenneco's subsidiaries were purchased, with exploration and production interests in a number of countries around the world; a 51 percent stake in Canada's Bow Valley Industries gave exposure to the North American energy market; and British Gas also bought Consumers Gas, Canada's largest natural gas distributor. It also continued to offer a consultancy service so that others could benefit from its expertise.

With privatization came the need to reinstate a regulatory organization to safeguard the public from the misuse of British Gas's monopoly position. The Office of Gas Supply (OFGAS), under a director general, monitored tariffs and commercial practices. In 1989 British Gas was obliged to formalize its charging structure for large non-domestic customers. It was also obliged to make its transmission network available to carry gas not sold directly; this allowed producers of gas to contract directly with customers for the sale of large quantities of gas. This regulatory change removed the monopoly of gas distribution that had been enjoyed by gas undertakings since the middle of the 19th century.

In the postwar years the position of the gas industry in the British fuel market was totally transformed. From its perceived role as a minor player, it emerged as a major force in not only the United Kingdom but also in world energy markets. In the early 1990s it supplied more than half the energy used in British homes. It made enormous technical and commercial strides and demonstrated that the question of state ownership of the business for much of the period was irrelevant to its record of dynamism and success.

In the first years after privatization, British Gas enjoyed growing profits; its profit after tax in 1991 was £916 million. However, competition steadily ate away at the company's market share, and regulation curbed earnings in the early 1990s. By 1995 British Gas held only 35 percent of the gas market for industrial and commercial customers, down from 100 percent in 1990. The company's residential market share was in jeopardy with its opening to full competition to be completed in 1998.

Although customers' gas bills had fallen after British Gas was placed in the private sector, public sentiment had shifted in the mid-1990s against privatizing utilities. The utilities' high profits were criticized, and in 1995 the Labour Party proposed a one-time "windfall" tax, which would be taken only out of profits already realized. Adding fuel to the fire of the public's disapproval was the 67 percent pay raise given to British Gas's chief executive, Cedric Brown, in 1994. Continued criticism of Brown led to his retirement in 1996.

Demerger in 1997

British Gas announced in 1996 its plan to split into two separate companies. One, eventually named BG plc, would take over the pipeline business, all foreign ventures, and the vast majority of British Gas's exploration and production assets. The other, dubbed Centrica plc, would control the retail business in the United Kingdom, two large gas fields off the coast of England, and the rights to the British Gas name. At the time, BG plc seemed to get the stronger end of the deal. The storage and pipeline business had been generating two-thirds of British Gas's profits and the international exploration assets were considered valuable.

Although the company cited a desire to better focus on specific businesses as the reason for the split, speculation was raised that the company was trying to force contract renegotiations with gas producers. Locked into contracts made in the 1980s, British Gas was paying almost double the going rate for gas in the mid-1990s, when BG's market share was falling. All of these contracts went to the cash-poor Centrica, effectively forcing renegotiation of these contracts. Indeed, by the end of 1997, Centrica had renegotiated all its major high-priced contracts, winning lower rates from such gas suppliers as Conoco and Elf Exploration.

Centrica's financial results for 1996 highlighted its weak position relative to its counterpart, BG. Profits after one-time charges relating to gas contract renegotiation and restructuring were $886 million for BG, whereas Centrica posted a loss of $1.2 billion. Although the company still saw a loss of £791 million after one-time charges in 1997, its renegotiated contracts and new products were encouraging. Centrica began a joint venture with Household Finance Corporation in creating a new financial product, the credit card Goldfish, which was well received. Centrica also created a new division to investigate possible new products and services, including savings accounts and home security. All non-energy businesses, such as British Gas Trading, British Gas Services, and Home Energy Centres, were grouped in the new division.

In 1998 Centrica lost approximately one million households to 20 independent suppliers when its gas market was opened fully to competition. Centrica had new opportunities, however, from the partial opening of the European Union (EU) to gas competition, brought on by a 1997 directive from the EU energy ministers. Further opportunities had arisen by late 1998 when the British electricity market opened to competition. Centrica, with the well-known British Gas name, was in a good position to compete with the regional electric utilities. Advance transfers to British Gas Trading, Centrica's domestic gas supply subsidiary, numbered 400,000. By the end of 1998 the company had 850,000 electricity customers, and a few months later that number had climbed to nearly 1.5 million.

For the first time since its breakup, Centrica reported a profit in 1998: £89 million after exceptional charges. The company expanded its gas and oil field portfolio with the purchase in 1998 of PowerGen North Sea Limited. Further purchases of oil and gas assets were announced in 1999, from Dana Petroleum plc and British Borneo.

Principal Subsidiaries

British Gas Trading Ltd.; British Gas Services Ltd.; British Gas Energy Centres Ltd.; Accord Energy Ltd.; Hydrocarbon Resources Ltd.; Centrica Financial Services.

Further Reading

Barty-King, Hugh, *New Flame,* Tavistock: Graphmitre, 1984.

"BGT Powers Up for New Assault," *Marketing Week,* September 10, 1998, p. 3.

"British Gas. Hot Air?," *Economist,* February 10, 1996.

"British Gas Marks End of Restructuring," *Oil and Gas Journal,* March 10, 1997, p. 26.

Chantler, Philip, *The British Gas Industry: An Economic Study,* Manchester: Manchester University Press, 1938.

Elliott, Charles, *The History of Natural Gas Conversion in Great Britain,* Royston: Cambridge Info. & Research Services with BGC, 1980.

Everard, Stirling, *The History of the Gas Light and Coke Company 1812–1949,* London: Benn, 1949.

Falkus, Malcolm, *Always under Pressure: A History of North Thames Gas since 1949,* London: Macmillan, 1988.

Hutchison, Sir Kenneth, *High-Speed Gas: An Autobiography,* London: Duckworth, 1987.

Report on the Gas Industry in Great Britain, London: Political and Economic Planning, 1939.

Rogers, Danny, "British Gas Unit Takes on Banks," *Marketing,* November 6, 1997, p. 1.

"A Tempting Target," *Economist,* December 9, 1995.

Williams, Trevor I., *A History of the British Gas Industry,* Oxford: Oxford University Press, 1981.

—Francis Goodall
—updated by Susan Windisch Brown

Chadwick's of Boston, Ltd.

35 United Drive
West Bridgewater, Massachusetts
U.S.A.
(508) 583-8110
(800) 525-6650
Fax: (508) 587-1398

Wholly Owned Subsidiary of Brylane Inc.
Founded: 1983
Employees: 2,500
Sales: $534 million (1997 est.)
NAIC: 45411 Electronic Shopping & Mail-Order Houses;
44815 Clothing Accessories Stores; 44819 Other
Clothing Stores

Chadwick's of Boston, Ltd. is the largest off-price catalog retailer of women's apparel in the United States. Although it markets clothing for the entire family in all sizes, in addition to accessories, gifts, and cosmetics, women between the ages of 25 and 55 are the company's primary customers. Chadwick's sells women's clothing under private labels as well as such name brands as Pierre Cardin, Herman Geist, JG Hook, and Blassport. Established in 1983 by retailer Zayre Corporation, Chadwick's was sold to Brylane Inc. in 1996. Chadwick's boasts a mailing list of 11 million names and claims 4.8 million active buyers. The company also owns and operates two outlet stores in New England.

Emerging in the 1980s

Chadwick's of Boston made its debut in 1983 as an off-price mail-order company offering specialty women's apparel brand names and prices similar to those in the Zayre Corp.'s Hit or Miss chain of stores. Hit or Miss outlets were at the time selling brand-name apparel at 20 to 50 percent off regular prices, and the close correspondence between Hit or Miss merchandise and that offered in Chadwick's catalogs allowed customers to handle and judge the products before trusting to catalog shopping from home. Originally considered an experimental project, Chadwick's had sales of $3 million in fiscal 1984 (the year

ended in January 1984), $21 million in 1985, and $24 million in 1986, when Zayre's management decided that Chadwick's had achieved its goals and proven a viable operation.

In 1987 Zayre spun off its off-price segment, consisting of its T.J. Maxx, Hit or Miss, and Chadwick's of Boston units, to a new subsidiary named The TJX Companies, Inc. As a division of TJX, Chadwick's function remained to feature off-price specialty items of women's apparel, much of which was also carried in the Hit or Miss stores, at prices significantly below conventional retailers and other mail-order catalogs. These items were said to consist of first-quality current-fashion and classic merchandise, including sportswear, casual wear, dresses, suits, and accessories, in a mix of brand names and private labels, targeting 20-to-50-year-old women, including housewives as well as career women, who were interested in moderately-to-upper-moderately-priced merchandise. Chadwick's delivered 23.7 million catalogs in 1987, an increase of 35 percent over the previous year. The division also developed an independent merchandising group during this time.

Chadwick's of Boston's sales grew from $33 million in 1987 to $43 million in 1988 and $47 million in 1989, when TJX's annual report declared that the division was selling "moderately-priced merchandise substantially below regular department store prices to a customer whose profile is similar to that of the Hit or Miss customer." This report said that the size of a typical Chadwick's catalog was about 56 pages and that nine mailings had been made during the fiscal year, including a focus book, or smaller book highlighting the best-selling items. About 35 percent of the goods sold were private label and 65 percent branded.

Chadwick's mailed 39 million catalogs during 1989. The TJX division also moved its base of operations from Stoughton, Massachusetts, to a new 175,000-square-foot fulfillment center in West Bridgewater. This state-of-the-art facility offered the long-term capacity of shipping four million orders per year. In addition, Chadwick's developed an independent buying staff for the organization.

Chadwick's fall 1989 catalog was redesigned to offer a more fashionable, visually appealing, and lifestyle-oriented presentation. Management considered the results encouraging and carried the new design into the winter and holiday catalogs, both of which were deemed successful. In response to what TJX's annual report called "the extremely promotional retail environment as well as specific promotions by other apparel catalogs," Chadwick's also successfully introduced an end-of-season promotional sales catalog. In addition, during 1989 the division conducted market research in order to keep abreast of shifts in customer lifestyles. The number of Chadwick's catalogs reached 50 million in 1989. Sales in 1990—the year ended January 27, 1990—reached $77 million.

Dramatic Growth in the Early 1990s

The calendar year 1990 was marketed by dramatic expansion and other changes. Chadwick's mailed catalogs 20 times for a total distribution of about 67 million catalogs. TJX's annual report described it as "America's first company to offer the off-price concept in women's apparel nationally through the convenience of a mail-order catalog." The Chadwick's target customer was now described as the working woman between 20 and 45, a group of women "who are interested in attractively priced merchandise and who enjoy the convenience of catalog shopping." A heavy focus was placed on career wear, including current fashions and classic styles in dresses and suits. Weekend apparel was also featured, and Chadwick's increased its assortment in petite sizes. Net sales reached $112.7 million in 1991.

During 1991 Chadwick's reported "resounding success" in shifting its focus quickly in response to an increase in demand for casual wear by mailing a casual-wear focus book. The company also reported improvement in order fulfillment through better forecasting and more aggressive buying and furthered strengthened product quality-control programs, leading to reduced merchandise returns. Moreover, Chadwick's purchased its formerly leased West Bridgewater facility. Sales totaled $173.4 million in 1992, an increase of 56 percent over the previous year. Operating income rose by 44 percent, despite considerable increases in postal and United Parcel Service costs, as well as a national economic recession.

During this time Chadwick's took steps to improve its merchandise quality, an initiative it was hoped would attract more customers and reduce the volume of returned merchandise. The company also increased its telemarketing capacity and upgraded the existing system to improve the ordering process. This quality assurance program also focused on ensuring that merchandise orders were packed correctly. Finally, the company began test-marketing a line of menswear. Distribution capacity at Chadwick's more than doubled with the expansion of its fulfillment center from 175,000 square feet to more than 400,000 square feet. Chadwick's sales reached $291 million in 1993.

By the end of 1994 Chadwick's had added menswear to certain of its catalog offerings and had expanded its offerings in large and petite sizes for women. Its target customers again included homemakers as well as working women. A further expansion of the fulfillment center completed that year brought the West Bridgewater facility to 676,000 square feet of space, while the company also leased 127,000 square feet nearby for offices and warehouse space. The Chadwick's customer database was proving valuable to its parent company, providing data

for TJX's store siting, micromarketing, and promotional strategies. Chadwick's also was planning a new catalog bearing the Cosmopolitan name, of magazine fame, geared toward young working women and offering the latest fashion trends at affordable prices.

A 1995 *Discount Store News* article declared that "Chadwick's appeals to the customer who needs to dress like she got it at Talbot's, but whose budget is more sensitive to discount values." Chadwick's sales volume grew so rapidly in 1994—passing more than $420 million for 1995—that it experienced difficulty in filling orders. As a result, sales barely grew the next year, and profits fell from four to three percent of revenues, and then to a nominal level.

Nevertheless, Chadwick's rebounded in 1996, registering sales of $472.4 million, operating profit of $26.6 million, and net income of $8.3 million. In fact, its operating profit comprised about 84 percent of parent TJX's that year. The cataloger's fulfillment rate—the percentage of customers who actually received the apparel they wanted to order—improved significantly during this time. However, because of rising paper costs, Chadwick's reduced its mailings by more than 16 percent, to 196 million catalogs.

TJX, in order to focus attention on its store-based retailing and pay down some of its debt, decided in 1996 to spin off Chadwick's of Boston as a separate company. Its plan was to sell 61 percent of the company in a $158-million initial public stock offering. The prospectus called Chadwick's "the nation's first and largest catalog retailer of off-price women's apparel," concentrating on careers, casual, and social wear at prices 25 to 50 percent below regular department stores. The company's six million active customers were said to be typically "middle- to upper-middle-income women between the age of 25 and 55." (The company had narrowed the upper limit of its target customer's age back to 50 years in 1995.) Chadwick's also began publishing Bridgewater, a new catalog that included men's as well as women's off-price apparel.

Becoming a Brylane Subsidiary

In July 1996, TJX postponed plans to spin off Chadwick's, citing a recent downturn in the stock market as exercising a dampening effect on new issues. Instead, three months later, it announced plans to sell the company to Brylane LP for an estimated $328 million in cash, notes, and receivables. Brylane, a rival catalog company, had an annual sales volume one-third larger than that of Chadwick's and specialized in plus-sized apparel for women as well as big-and-tall apparel for men. Interviewed for *Catalog Age* by Melissa Dowling, Brylane chairman and chief executive officer Peter Canzone observed that both enterprises had been "going after the same value-oriented apparel catalog customer" and added that "Chadwick's has some of the best merchandise negotiators in the catalog business." Chadwick's recorded sales of $451.5 million and net income of $10.9 million in 1996.

Brylane made its initial public offering the following year, becoming Brylane Inc., while its new acquisition, Chadwick's of Boston, retained its identity as an independent subsidiary still based in West Bridgewater, Massachusetts. In March 1997

Chadwick's introduced the Jessica London catalog, a new catalog for larger-sized women. Two million copies were mailed to potential customers derived from a mailing list of those who had purchased larger-size clothing from Brylane in the past. A Chadwick's executive told Shannon Oberndorf of *Catalog Age,* "We've been building up our plus-size file for the past year after seeing the growth in orders of our regularly featured large sizes. We're not trying to go after the Brylane customer, but targeting a segment of our own buyers." The Jessica London catalog offered prices sharply below those of department and specialty stores and targeted younger, career-oriented women sizes 14W to 26W.

Under its new ownership, the Chadwick's catalog continued to target women between the ages of 25 and 55 who wore regular-sized apparel (sizes 4 to 20.) In addition, Chadwick's had expanded its merchandise offerings to target women who wore petite and special-size apparel (sizes 2 to 26). Private labels, including brand names such as Savannah, Fads, Stephanie Andrews, and JL Plum, accounted for 53 percent of Chadwick's net sales in 1997. Men's and children's apparel, women's special-size apparel, and accessories, gifts, and cosmetics—tested and offered on a limited basis—accounted for 22 percent of net sales. The company offered 73,000 stockkeeping units of merchandise at an average of about $27. The average order was $87. In its 1997 annual report, Brylane described Chadwick's market segment as about one-third—or 33 million—of all U.S. adult women. The medium age of the Chadwick's customer was said to be 42, with typical income equal to, or above, the national average.

Chadwick's announced plans in August 1997 to build a 330,000-square-foot distribution and customer-service center in an industrial park in Taunton, Massachusetts, where the company had received property tax concessions. A portion of the company's ready-to-wear women's-apparel catalog operations was moved to this location in the spring of the following year. The remainder of Chadwick's operations were still located in the Boston suburb of West Bridgewater. The company's overstock was marketed through retail outlet stores in Brockton, Massachusetts, and Nashua, New Hampshire. As it moved toward a new century, the company was reportedly planning to broaden its product line through the introduction of a bed and bath furnishings catalog.

Further Reading

Bailey, Steve, and Steven Syre, "Chadwick's Preparing Its IPO in Buyer's Market," *Boston Globe,* May 24, 1996, p. 52.

Bushnell, Davis, "Tax Incentives Draw Complaints," *Boston Globe,* January 11, 1998, South Weekly/Business Section, p. 10.

Cochrane, Thomas M., "Catalog Couture," *Barron's,* February 10, 1997, p. 53.

Dowling, Melissa, "A Fitting Acquisition," *Catalog Age,* December 1996, p. 6.

"Mail Order Proves a Strategic Fit," *Discount Store News,* February 20, 1995, p. 20.

Oberndorf, Shannon, "A Plus-Size Chadwick's," *Catalog Age,* June 1997, p. 12.

Reidy, Chris, "TJX to Sell Chadwick's for $328m to Brylane," *Boston Globe,* October 22, 1996, p. C2.

—Robert Halasz

Chelsea Milling Company

201 W. North Street
Chelsea, Michigan 48118
U.S.A.
(734) 475-1361
Fax: (734) 475-7577
Web site: http://www.jiffymix.com

Private Company
Incorporated: 1901
Employees: 350
Sales: $100 million (1998 est.)
NAIC: 311211 Flour Milling

The Chelsea Milling Company is the number four maker of prepackaged baking mixes in the United States. The family-owned and run business has been making the Jiffy line of mixes since 1930, when Mabel Holmes created the country's first commercially marketed biscuit mix in her kitchen in Chelsea, Michigan. Adhering to its original philosophy of using high quality ingredients, keeping prices low, and spending no money on advertising, the company has held its position as a sales leader in the ensuing decades against competitors such as General Mills and Pillsbury. In the 1990s the company began to hire professional outside management personnel for the first time, successfully boosting operating efficiency and revenues while maintaining traditional values and goals.

Roots in the 19th Century

The Chelsea Milling Company's beginnings date to a time when nearly every town had a mill that ground the wheat of area farmers for local use. The company was founded in 1887 when E. K. White, whose relatives had been milling flour in Michigan, Indiana, and Kansas as early as 1802, purchased the mill in the small Michigan town of Chelsea. In 1901 the business was incorporated as the Chelsea Milling Company, and in 1908 it was sold to Harmon S. Holmes, White's daughter Mabel's father-in-law. Mabel White Holmes's husband, Howard Holmes, was given the job of managing the mill.

The company continued to grind flour for local consumption, like hundreds of other Michigan mills, until 1930, when Mabel Holmes had an experience which inspired her to create a new product, a premixed blend of flour, baking powder, and other ingredients. Legend has it that one day when her twin sons had brought two friends home from school for lunch, she noticed the hard biscuits the motherless boys' father had made and decided to formulate a blend of biscuit ingredients that "even a man could prepare." After a number of attempts, she hit upon a formula that was reliable and could be manufactured at the family mill. The multi-purpose baking mix was given its name soon thereafter when Mabel and her husband were driving to Chelsea from Chicago. Thinking back to her childhood, she remembered the phrase her family's cook had used when preparing biscuits for dinner, "They'll be ready in a jiffy!"

Taking the name Jiffy for the new mix, the company began marketing it locally, soon gaining more sales when the C. F. Smith supermarket chain in Detroit decided to stock it. Although General Mills' Bisquick and a host of others quickly followed Jiffy to market, its quality and low price kept it on store shelves as other brands came and went. From the beginning the company spent no money on advertising, preferring to let sales build by word of mouth. This also cut overhead and allowed Jiffy mixes to be priced significantly lower than most competing brands.

In 1936 tragedy struck when Howard Holmes fell to his death from a malfunctioning grain elevator inside one of the company's silos. His twin sons Dudley and Howard, Jr., the latter being an engineering student at nearby University of Michigan, immediately decided to help run the company, with Mabel assuming the position of president. In 1940 Howard Jr. took over that job, also utilizing his engineering training to oversee equipment design and maintenance. Dudley became the company's secretary-treasurer and took responsibility for developing new products, purchasing raw materials, and managing the mill. At this time Chelsea Milling also introduced its second Jiffy mix, for pie crust.

The early 1940s saw significant sales growth as the large number of women entering the workforce during the Second World War created a surge in demand for convenience foods.

Company Perspectives:

Our mission is to provide the consumer with the best possible value. "Jiffy" Value is defined as the highest quality ingredients at the best price. We use only the highest quality ingredients for our mixes and formulate our products so that the consumer doesn't have to add additional ingredients to bake an excellent product. Our dedication to the consumer in terms of quality and value is the driving force behind our commitment that a satisfied customer is our first concern.

By the end of the decade Jiffy mixes were being distributed nationally, though still manufactured at the single plant in Chelsea. The company introduced another new product in 1950, one that would prove to be its most successful, a corn muffin mix. Although Chelsea Milling had continued to grind flour for sale to the public, this was phased out by 1957, with all of the mill's output henceforth utilized solely in its mixes. Wheat bran, a by-product of the milling process, was sold to the Battle Creek, Michigan-based Kellogg Co.

Plant Expansion in the Wake of Jiffy Mix Success

Over the years the company made a number of additions to its facilities and equipment, starting in the early 1930s when it purchased the adjacent home of an elderly widow. The woman had left her husband's dilapidated workshop standing, out of respect for his memory, and the Holmes family reached an agreement with her to purchase the land, but let the buildings stand until she died. They also gave her new plumbing and kept her lawn cut as part of the bargain. The image of Chelsea Milling's large grain silos standing directly behind her weathered house was captured by artist Jonathan Taylor in an etching that achieved some degree of fame at the time. In the 1940s the company purchased and installed its automated packaging equipment, built to Howard Holmes' specifications. This design was so efficient that the company later bought and put into storage a number of additional machines to use for future expansion and spare parts.

In the mid-1960s Chelsea Milling undertook its most ambitious construction project to date, building a new flour mill that more than doubled production capacity. Milling in the new six-level structure was more efficient and enabled greater quality control than had previously been possible. As it had done since the beginning, the company purchased "soft" wheat from Michigan farmers, cleaned and ground it at the plant, then mixed it with other ingredients to create the 15 different mixes now being sold under the Jiffy banner. These ranged from Mabel's original biscuit mix to a variety of different muffin, cake, and frosting mixes, plus others for brownies and pie crust. Packaging materials were manufactured at a company-owned facility in Marshall, Michigan, and shipped to Chelsea. Capacity of the new plant was one million packages per day, with production frequently taking place around the clock.

In 1970 Chelsea Milling added a 36,000 square foot warehouse, and by mid-decade it was announcing plans for further expansion of its manufacturing and storage capacity, though this was put off several times and not completed until the mid-1990s. The company's line of products stood at 19 by 1976, with each ranking first, second, or third in its category against the mixes of such competitors as General Mills, General Foods, and Pillsbury. With the exception of the larger size of Mabel's original baking mix, these were packaged in six to nine ounce boxes, proportioned such that the average family of four could make enough servings for a single meal. Prices, which had started out at ten cents a box for the larger-size original mix in 1930, were well under 50 cents each for the muffin and cake mixes, one-third to one-half less than the competition. 225 people were employed by the company, an increase of ten percent from a decade earlier. Products were distributed throughout the Midwest by a fleet of Jiffy-owned trucks and to the rest of the country by commercial carriers. Some sales were made to overseas U.S. military bases, but widespread distribution overseas, though experimented with, never took off and was ultimately abandoned.

In 1984 controversy briefly surfaced when two states removed Jiffy corn muffin mix from store shelves after they were found to contain higher amounts of EDB, a grain insecticide, than each state allowed. The amounts found were below federal standards, and the company defended its products' quality, asserting that the two states were setting limits far below what was necessary for safety. After a brief period of media interest, the EDB scare blew over without permanent damage to Jiffy's reputation.

Management Changes in the Late 1980s

Throughout the years president and CEO Howard Holmes, Jr., had continued to run the company, while his brother Dudley Holmes had left and returned several times as he pursued different career paths. Jiffy mix creator Mabel White Holmes passed away in 1977, and in 1984 Dudley announced his retirement and sold back his ownership shares. Although Howard Holmes Jr. was now in his 70s, no plan had been made for transferring the company's presidency to a new leader. Without officially declaring a successor, Howard began in 1987 to cede some authority to his eldest son Howard Holmes III.

Howard III, who was known as "Howdy," had spent the previous 20 years involved in automobile racing. His successful career had included six Indianapolis 500 races, where he had been named Rookie of the Year and had set a track record for high average finish position. He had also managed a sports marketing firm and written a book and a number of magazine articles. His racing career had given him a great deal of experience in the world of public relations, marketing, and management. When he joined "team Jiffy," as he came to call it, he brought these diverse experiences to the table, much to the discomfort of some family members who believed that the company should not deviate from tradition. Howdy's brother Bill, who had been with the company since 1981, was particularly unhappy with the direction he was beginning to take Chelsea Milling.

By the late 1980s, the company's profits were reportedly declining, and it was suffering from a number of inefficiencies that had become institutionalized over time. These included scheduling workers for large amounts of overtime and using a local accounting firm that both kept and audited the books. Mix sales had also begun to stagnate as Americans increasingly favored pre-cooked convenience foods and restaurant meals. Howdy Holmes was convinced that the only way to get back on track was to hire outside, professional management staff to run critical areas of the business such as finance, human resources, and plant operations. However, he was persistently clashing with his brother about these ideas, to the point of having several fistfights with him on company premises.

After a long period of conflict, in 1991 William Holmes decided to leave the company's day-to-day operations, though he remained on its board of directors, and took up the career of pilot that he had trained for in the Air National Guard. Howdy Holmes soon oversaw the hiring of a team of management professionals drawn from top companies such as Ocean Spray and Unisys. The company began to institute much-needed changes which included replacing its accountant with top firm Deloitte and Touche, restructuring workers' shifts to eliminate excess overtime, tending to some overlooked environmental problems, and instituting a preventative maintenance program for plant equipment.

Though there had been initial resistance to the changes, the new programs soon proved successful, and many of the hard feelings between family members began to heal as the wisdom of Howdy's moves became apparent. Howdy Holmes officially became president and CEO in 1995, when his father gave up everything but the position of chairman of the board. Other family members were also involved in the business, including Howdy's sister Kathryn, who worked in sales on the West Coast, and their cousin Dudley Jr., vice-president of procurement. In 1997 a long-anticipated 125,000 square foot plant expansion was completed, greatly increasing storage capacity and eliminating the need for leased space, which the company had relied on for years. A new $300,000 machine was also purchased that wrapped Jiffy mix boxes into six-packs for distribution to warehouse clubs and other bulk-sales stores.

Although Chelsea Milling still did not advertise, it launched a World Wide Web site, which Holmes considered to be more of a "word-of-mouth" approach than actual advertising. He also implemented small changes to Jiffy mix boxes, adding pictures of other products to the backs. The company retained its conservative approach to introducing new mixes, adding only two new muffin flavors and a buttermilk pancake mix in the mid-1990s. While many competitors believed that the constant introduction of faddish spin-off products helped build a brand, Chelsea Milling preferred to focus on staples which would not go in and out of fashion, a credo which also yielded savings in product development and marketing costs. Commenting on the company's disinterest in creating low-fat ver-

sions of its mixes, CEO Holmes told *Milling and Baking News,* "It is an interesting fact that some of the fastest-growing foods in our country are hamburgers and French fries." By the end of the 1990s the company was turning out 1.4 million boxes of Jiffy mixes per day. Annual sales reached an estimated $100 million in 1998, up from approximately $65 million a decade earlier.

With the difficult transition to a new generation of leadership finally over, the Chelsea Milling Company approached the start of its second century with its traditions intact, but having also set in motion the modernization it needed to remain competitive and profitable. Still eschewing advertising, and with packaging designs only slightly changed since the 1930s, the company's original vision of offering quality baking mixes at a fair price was one which still met with widespread public approval. Jiffy remained among the top three sellers in every category of mix the company made, capturing an astounding 85 percent of corn muffin mix sales nationwide.

Further Reading

Bacon, John U., "Jiffy's Success Mixes Family, Change," *Detroit News,* February 21, 1999.

Belcher, Denise R., "Taste, Sight Mix Well in a Jiffy," *Jackson (Michigan) Citizen-Patriot,* January 29, 1973, p. 17.

Child, Charles, "Jiffy Mix Official Says Some States are Overreacting to Scare," *Ann Arbor News,* February 24, 1984, p. A4.

Grantham, Russell, "Milling it Over: Jiffy Mix Maker Renovates Plant—Slowly," *Ann Arbor News,* June 18, 1995, p. 1C.

Hickman, Beth, "Consumer Mixes: New Products Stir Up Category Sales," *Milling & Baking News,* December 17, 1996, p. 32.

Koselka, Rita, "A Family Affair (Chelsea Milling)," *Forbes,* June 11, 1990, p. 83.

Lindquist, Ellen, "Ready in a Jiffy," *Ann Arbor News,* March 19, 1989, p. 1E.

Malan, Allan, and Deanna Malan, "Mabel's Magic Mixes," *Michigan History Magazine,* January-February, 1998.

"Production at Chelsea Milling Moves in a Jiffy from Wheat . . . to Flour . . . to Packaged Mixes," *American Miller & Processor,* April 1966, pp. 14–19.

Stearns, Patty LaNoue, "Good Ol' Days—In a Box," *Detroit Free Press,* November 8, 1995, p. 1F.

Stern, Gabriella, "Against the Grain: Race-Car Driver Goes Home, Sets New Course for Bake-Mix Concern," *Wall Street Journal,* February 19, 1997, p. 1A.

Strange, Clara, "She Discovered How to Make a Fortune in a 'Jiffy'," *Detroit Free Press,* February 26, 1967, p. 4B.

Watkins, Doug, "Chelsea Milling Company Giant in its Field," *Ann Arbor News,* February 27, 1972.

Zdrojewski, Ed, "Changing Times in Jiffyville," *Milling Journal,* July/August/September, 1998, pp. 12–14.

—Frank Uhle

Church & Dwight Co., Inc.

469 North Harrison Street
Princeton, New Jersey 08543-5297
U.S.A.
(609) 683-5900
(800) 332-5424
Fax: (609) 497-7269

Public Company
Incorporated: 1925
Employees: 1,127
Sales: $684.4 million (1998)
Stock Exchanges: New York
Ticker Symbol: CHD
NAIC: 325181 Alkalies & Chlorine Manufacturing;
325611 Soap & Other Detergent Manufacturing;
325612 Polish & Other Sanitation Good
Manufacturing

Church & Dwight Co., Inc. is the world's leading producer of sodium bicarbonate (baking soda), a chemical that performs a broad range of functions, including cleaning, deodorizing, leavening, and buffering. It manufactures and sells products based on sodium bicarbonate, mainly under the Arm & Hammer trademark. These products, aside from baking soda itself, include toothpaste, deodorant, and laundry detergent. Church & Dwight also makes Brillo scouring pads and other consumer products, as well as specialty products for industrial customers.

Century-Old American Tradition:
Beginnings in 1846

The company was founded in New York City in 1846 as John Dwight & Co. by Dr. Austin Church and his brother-in-law John E. Dwight, who had begun processing and packaging baking soda in powdered form in his kitchen. It was marketed for use in home baking. In 1867 two sons of Church formed Church & Co. to compete with John Dwight & Co. The Arm & Hammer trademark derives from that year, in which Church &

Co. acquired a spice and mustard business named Vulcan Spice Mills that used an arm and hammer—presumably about to descend on an anvil—as its trademark because Vulcan, the Roman god of fire, was associated with the forging of metals.

Church & Co. began, in 1888, issuing trading cards bearing the Arm & Hammer trademark to publicize its baking soda and saleratus (potassium bicarbonate) products. In 1896 it merged with John Dwight & Co., which also was issuing trading cards for its "Cow" brand of baking soda, to form Church Dwight Co. The merged firm continued to market baking soda under both the Arm & Hammer and Cow trademarks for some time. Arm & Hammer Super Washing Soda was introduced in the 19th century as a heavy-duty laundry and household cleaning product. About 1915 Church Dwight began suggesting that baking soda could serve as medicine, offering a booklet titled "Home Remedies for Simple Ailments." Soon it was also advertising baking soda as a tooth cleaner and a cleaner and freshener for laundry and for kitchen surfaces. The firm was incorporated as Church & Dwight Co. in 1925.

Church & Dwight was run by family members in highly conservative fashion for the next four decades—so much so that the company earned more in some years from its investment portfolio than from operations. When its methods of producing baking soda became obsolete, it turned to outside suppliers for the product. When the output of these suppliers proved insufficient, Church & Dwight, in 1968, completed what soon became the world's largest facility for the production of sodium bicarbonate, in Green River, Wyoming.

In 1968 Church & Dwight was producing nearly half of the sodium bicarbonate and borax in the United States, in collaboration with Allied Chemical Co., a major producer of the sodium carbonate (soda ash) used—along with carbon dioxide—as the raw material for baking soda. Its production plants, in Syracuse, New York (for consumer products) and Green River (for industrial products), were receiving soda ash from Allied's own adjacent plants and turning out about 100,000 tons of sodium bicarbonate a year. Nearly half was going to bulk industrial users, such as baking, pharmaceutical, and fire extinguisher companies. The rest was processed into granules, placed in yellow boxes bearing the Arm & Hammer trademark, and sold to the public. Church & Dwight was accounting for at least 90 percent of U.S. consumer sales of baking soda. Washing soda (also manufactured by the company) and borax (purchased from suppliers) was accounting for about 40 percent of the company's total sales volume.

Exploiting the Arm & Hammer Name Through the 1980s

About this time company management belatedly realized that housewives who, traditionally, had used Arm & Hammer baking soda as an all-purpose problem solver—to bake bread, clean stains, eliminate odors, relieve indigestion, and alleviate the pain of minor burns and abrasions—had turned to an array of specialized products for all of these uses. Accordingly, under Dwight C. Minton, a fifth-generation descendant of Austin Church who succeeded his father as Church & Dwight's president in 1969, and Robert A. Davies III, vice-president of Arm & Hammer marketing, the company itself began to specialize.

Church & Dwight exploited the venerable Arm & Hammer name to market baking soda tablets for indigestion and mint-flavored ones as a mouth freshener. It also began marketing a phosphate-free laundry detergent based on soda ash and introduced an underarm deodorant (which failed) and oven cleaner, all under the Arm & Hammer name. Net sales rose from $22.4 million in 1969 to $77 million in 1975, and net income increased more than fourfold to $3.8 million during that time period.

In addition, a brilliantly successful advertising campaign begun in 1972 persuaded housewives to open the basic yellow box and place it in the refrigerator for use as a deodorant/freshener. Sales of the box rose 72 percent within three years. To stimulate sales even more, a follow-up campaign advised consumers to remove the contents after a while and pour them down the kitchen drain to deodorize it, too. Yet another ad campaign impelled consumers to store the box in the freezer for the same purpose. "There are at least 10 guys running around New York claiming some credit for the refrigerator campaign idea," adman Gerald Schoenfeld told Jack J. Honomichl of *Advertising Age* in 1982. The company also added a bigger box of Arm & Hammer baking soda for heavy-duty applications, such as use in swimming pools and septic tanks, and created new packaging for use as cat litter deodorizer.

Davies became president of Church & Dwight in 1981, although Minton remained chief executive officer. That year the basic yellow box of baking soda accounted for about one-third of the company's sales volume of $127.1 million. Its main end use now was to deodorize refrigerator air. (In 1970 the main use had been the cleaning of refrigerator surfaces.) The second most important use was general household cleaning. Other uses in 1981 included water treatment; cleaning refrigerator surfaces; skin rash treatment; deodorizer for rugs, kitchen drains, septic tanks, or cat box litter; and swimming pool treatment. The product's use in home baking now appeared to be negligible. Arm & Hammer had unaided recognition among 97 percent of U.S. female heads of households. Almost all grocery stores stocked the yellow box, and surveys found that, at any point in time, about 95 percent of all U.S. households had one or more packages in use in the home.

Church & Dwight opened another manufacturing plant in Old Fort, Ohio, in 1980. Four years later it purchased the Syracuse plant of Allied Corp. (formerly Allied Chemical Co.) for $14 million. The company's Canadian subsidiary also owned a plant in Ontario. Church & Dwight moved its headquarters from New York City to Piscataway, New Jersey, in the late 1970s, and to Princeton, New Jersey, in 1985.

Church & Dwight reformulated and reintroduced its dry laundry detergent at a lower price in 1981 and introduced a carpet and room deodorizer in 1981 and an oven cleaner containing no sodium in 1982. Liquid detergent was introduced to the metropolitan New York City area in 1984. In the same year the company began testing its own toothpaste and tooth powder, both with baking soda. In addition, Church & Dwight started marketing a deodorizing spray and a carpet freshener containing baking soda and a bleach and a fabric softener for sheets without baking soda. All of its consumer products, including washing soda, continued to bear the Arm & Hammer name. Although shares of company stock were being traded over the counter, most were held by descendants of the founders or employees.

Church & Dwight's Chemicals Division was producing two-thirds of all sodium bicarbonate sold to U.S. industrial customers in 1986. The division had found a recent customer in the animal feed industry, which applied it as an antacid supplement for dairy cattle. Church & Dwight purchased a 40 percent share of a British firm, Brotherton Chemicals, in 1985, for the industrial sector of its business and increased its stake to 80 percent in 1987. Of the firm's $231.4 million in sales that year, however, 78 percent came from consumer products marketed by the Arm & Hammer Division.

In 1986 Church & Dwight acquired and absorbed DeWitt International Corp., a producer of over-the-counter pharmaceuticals and health and beauty aids. Also that year, the company began a relationship with Armand Hammer, the flamboyant chairman of Occidental Petroleum Corp. Tired of having to reply in the negative when asked if he was the "baking-soda king" because of the resemblance between his name and the Arm & Hammer trademark, Hammer purchased about five percent of Church & Dwight's shares for about $15 million, receiving a seat on the company board, so he could reply in the affirmative. As part of the transaction, Occidental and Church & Dwight formed a joint venture to continue the manufacture and marketing of potassium carbonate products at an Occidental-acquired plant in Muscle Shoals, Alabama, whose customers included Church & Dwight. In 1991, after Hammer's death, his successor sold Occidental's stake in Church & Dwight for $19 million, but the joint venture remained in effect.

Church & Dwight in the 1990s

Church & Dwight's net sales of $428.5 million in 1990 was an increase of more than fourfold in a decade, and its net income of $22.5 million was about three times the 1980 figure. The company now had 12 facilities, including three in England and one each in Australia, Malaysia, and Singapore. Its laundry detergent now accounted for one-third of all revenues and ranked third in the United States after Tide and Surf. The company also held 60 percent of the world market for sodium bicarbonate. Arm & Hammer Dental Care toothpaste, introduced nationally in 1988, held 11 percent of the U.S. toothpaste market in 1993. Specialty products included ArmaKleen, a baking soda-based cleanser of computer circuit boards. In 1994 Church & Dwight established a division within its specialty products group to develop industrial cleaning solutions based on baking soda, and two years later it began selling cleaning products to the metal cleaning industry.

In 1994 Church & Dwight introduced a line of stick and roll-on deodorants in major U.S. markets under the name Arm & Hammer Deodorant Anti-Perspirant with Baking Soda. It also purchased the remaining share of Brotherton Chemicals. But sales dipped by $17 million that year, and the company's profits fell 77 percent. Minton attributed the poor results to introducing too many new products. One of these was a liquid detergent more concentrated than other leading brands that fared poorly in the marketplace and had to be reformulated because consumers thought they were being offered less for their money. Another was Peroxicare, a toothpaste with peroxide as well as baking soda that may have been competing, to the detriment of both, with Arm & Hammer Dental Care in the fiercely competitive dentifrice market.

Church & Dwight was still struggling to regain its momentum when Davies, who had left the company in 1984, was renamed president in 1995. He also was named chief executive officer, succeeding Minton, in November of that year. Although sales dropped again in 1995, the company took in record revenues of $527.8 million the next year and more than doubled its net income. That year the company also introduced sensitive-formula, extra-whitening, and smooth spearmint toothpaste variants and stick underarm deodorants. Results were even better in 1997. That year Church & Dwight acquired a group of five household cleaning brands from The Dial Corp. Among these was Brillo scouring pads. It also introduced nationally an aerosol deodorant antiperspirant.

In 1998 Church & Dwight acquired the Toss 'n Soft brand of fabric softener dryer sheets from Dial and combined it with Arm & Hammer Fabric Softener Sheets under the Arm & Hammer Fresh & Soft brand name. The company also was offering more differentiated baking soda products, such as Arm & Hammer Super Scoop, an anticlumping cat litter introduced nationally in 1997, and Arm & Hammer Dental Care Gum, a baking soda-based oral care product introduced in 1998 in three flavors. Church & Dwight had record revenues of $684.4 million and record net income of $30.3 million in 1998.

In 1999 Church & Dwight launched a multimillion-dollar advertising campaign intended to "reeducate America on the benefits of deodorizing the fridge, and offer added convenience," according to a company executive quoted by Christine Bittar in *Brandweek*. Spots to air in the spring and fall were to encourage seasonal replacement of a new baking soda box dominated by the color blue rather than the familiar yellow package. The company also introduced an Arm & Hammer Advance White line of dentifrices in early 1999. Also in 1999, Church & Dwight formed a joint venture with Safety-Kleen Corp. called ArmaKleen Co. to distribute Church & Dwight's proprietary line of aqueous cleaners.

In 1998 Church & Dwight was still manufacturing sodium bicarbonate at Green River and Old Fort and still retained its partnership agreement with General Chemical Corp. (formerly Allied). The company's liquid laundry detergent, previously contract manufactured, was moved to the Syracuse plant in 1995. The manufacture of powdered detergent, also being produced in Syracuse from light soda ash, was to move to Green River in 1999. Cat litter was being manufactured in both Green River and Syracuse. A Lakewood, New Jersey plant acquired in 1998 was manufacturing the underarm deodorant line and was to begin producing dentifrice products in 1999. The Brillo product line and the dryer sheets were being produced at the London, Ohio plant acquired from Dial Corp. Other company products were being manufactured by contractors.

Church & Dwight, in early 1999, also owned, through subsidiaries, a distribution center in Ontario, Canada, and a manufacturing facility in Wakefield, England. The Canadian subsidiary was leasing offices in Toronto. A Venezuelan subsidiary was closed in 1998. Church & Dwight still had a half-interest in the Armand Products potassium carbonate manufacturing plant in Muscle Shoals. Its executive offices and research and development facilities, owned by the company, were in Princeton, and it was leasing space in two buildings adjacent to this facility.

Consumer products accounted for 82 percent of Church & Dwight's revenues in 1998. Among these were Arm & Hammer Dental Care toothpaste, tooth powder, gel, tartar-control formula and gel, Peroxicare, and tartar-control Peroxicare. Two underarm deodorants were available in various scented and unscented stick, aerosol, and roll-on forms. Its line of specialty products consisted of sodium bicarbonate for commercial baked goods and as an antacid in pharmaceuticals, a carbon dioxide release agent in fire extinguishers, an alkaline agent in swimming pool chemicals, and an agent in kidney dialysis. Sodium sesquicarbonate and a special grade of sodium bicarbonate were being sold to the animal feed market as a food additive for use by dairymen as a buffer, or antiacid, for dairy cattle.

Church & Dwight's largest shareholders at the beginning of 1999 were Gabelli Foods, Inc., which held 8.4 percent, and FMR Corp., which held seven percent. Company debt of $48.8 million at the end of 1998 compared with only $7.5 million at the end of 1996.

Principal Subsidiaries

Armand Products Co. (50%); Brotherton Specialty Products Ltd. (Great Britain); C&D Chemical Products, Inc.; Church & Dwight Ltd./Ltee; DeWitt International Corp.

Principal Divisions

Arm & Hammer Division; Arm & Hammer International; Specialty Products Division.

Further Reading

"Arm & Hammer: Taking the Cure," *Sales Management,* February 15, 1970, pp. 59–60.

Bittar, Christine, "In-the-Box Thinking," *Brandweek,* January 25, 1999, p. 3.

Gordon, Mitchell, ''Profitable Pairing,'' *Barron's,* September 6, 1982, pp. 37–38.

Honomichl, Jack J., ''The Ongoing Saga of 'Mother Baking Soda','' *Advertising Age,* September 20, 1982, pp. M2–3, M-22.

Jacobs, Sanford L., ''And Now We Discover a Miracle Product That's Not So New,'' *Wall Street Journal,* March 21, 1973, p. 1.

Marinelli, Tom, ''A 'Soda' Supplier for 140 Years Is Diversifying,'' *Chemical Week,* May 7, 1986, pp. 78–79.

Montana, Constanza, ''Armand Hammer and Arm & Hammer Finally Arm in Arm,'' *Wall Street Journal,* September 23, 1986, pp. 3, 18.

''The New Face of Arm & Hammer,'' *Business Week,* April 12, 1976, p. 60.

Nulty, Peter, ''No Product Is Too Dull To Shine,'' *Fortune,* July 27, 1992, p. 96.

''A Smell-Less Story,'' *Forbes,* August 15, 1974, p. 29.

''Sodium Bicarb Expansions Put C&D on the Offensive,'' *Chemical Market Reporter,* July 22, 1996, pp. 3, 18.

Somasundaram, Meera, ''Missteps Mar Church & Dwight's Plans,'' *Wall Street Journal,* April 28, 1995 (on ProQuest database).

Treadwell, T.K., ''The Legacy of . . . Church & Dwight Trade Cards,'' *Antiques & Collecting,* January 1991, pp. 26–28.

Weisz, Pam, ''Church & Dwight in Need of Next Big Idea,'' *Brandweek,* November 13, 1995, p. 8.

—Robert Halasz

Churchill Downs Incorporated

700 Central Avenue
Louisville, Kentucky 40208
U.S.A.
(502) 636-4400
Fax: (502) 636-4430
Web site: http://www.kentuckyderby.com

Public Company
Incorporated: 1874 as Louisville Jockey Club and
    Driving Park Association
Employees: 2,925
Sales: $147.3 million (1998)
Stock Exchanges: NASDAQ
Ticker Symbol: CHDN
NAIC: 711212 Racetracks

Churchill Downs Incorporated is a horse racing company best known for hosting the Kentucky Derby, America's most prestigious horse race. The Derby, which is more than 125 years old, is held annually at the company's flagship track, Churchill Downs, in Louisville, Kentucky. Churchill Downs' other racetracks include Ellis Park Race Course in Henderson, Kentucky; Calder Race Course in Miami, Florida; a majority interest in Hoosier Park of Anderson, Indiana; and a minority interest in Kentucky Downs Race Course located in Franklin, Kentucky. The company also operates the Kentucky Horse Center in Lexington, Kentucky, a thoroughbred training and boarding facility.

Simulcast wagering is also a segment of Churchill Downs' business. The company has full ownership of the Sports Spectrum, a simulcast wagering facility in Louisville, and majority ownership of similar facilities in Indianapolis, Merrillville, and Fort Wayne, Indiana. It also holds a majority interest in Charlson Broadcast Technologies, LLC, a software and video services company catering to racetracks and simulcast-wagering facilities, and a minority interest in Kentucky Off-Track Betting Inc., an alliance of Kentucky racetracks that operates simulcast-wagering facilities in four Kentucky locations.

Late 1800s: Birth of a Legend

Churchill Downs was founded by an ambitious 26-year-old Kentuckian, Col. Meriwether Lewis Clark, Jr. Clark, the grandson of William Clark, one-half of the famous Lewis and Clark expedition team, hatched the idea for the racetrack while traveling in England and France in the early 1870s.

Horse racing in Clark's native state was by no means a new idea at that time; the first known Kentucky racecourse had been established almost 90 years earlier in Lexington. The Bluegrass State, with its reputation for thoroughbred horses, was a natural hotbed for this form of sport. By the time Clark was traveling in Europe, however, both horse racing and breeding were in decline in Kentucky, damaged by the ravages of the Civil War. An avid racing fan, Clark sought a way to revive the sagging industries. Lacking experience in racetrack management, he used his trip abroad to research several successful European racing establishments. When Clark returned to Kentucky, he broached a plan to a number of prominent and moneyed Louisville gentlemen: to build a track, hold a championship race, and establish a Jockey Club with memberships offered to high-society subscribers. The proposal was agreed upon, and in June 1874 the Louisville Jockey Club and Driving Park Association was incorporated. Clark leased 80 acres of land from his uncles, John and Henry Churchill, on which to build the new track—and sold 320 subscriptions to the track at $100 each to fund its construction.

On May 17, 1875, Clark's racetrack was ready for its debut. Its inaugural meet included four races: the Kentucky Derby, Kentucky Oats, Clark Handicap, and Falls City. The Derby, which was modeled after England's Epsom Derby, was the headliner, drawing a crowd of 10,000 spectators. Attendees wagered approximately $50,000 on the four races run that day, but the track itself did not oversee the betting. Instead, the wagering concessions were operated by an outside organization. Despite the popularity of gambling at the track, the race was more than just a sporting or wagering event. Due to Clark's excellent promotional skills, it was an important social event as well—and for the next two decades, Churchill Downs was the place to be for the wealthy society set.

Unfortunately, the popularity and social cachet of the Derby were not enough to make the track a financial success. Although Clark covered thousands of dollars of company expenses from his own funds, Churchill Downs drifted deeper into debt. In 1894, a group of investors headed by Louisville racehorse owner and bookmaker William F. Schulte purchased the failed track, incorporating as the New Louisville Jockey Club. Clark was kept on as the track's presiding judge until 1899, when he committed suicide.

One of the first things Schulte did was order construction of a new 1,500-seat, $100,000 grandstand on the opposite side of the track from the original stands. The new grandstand was topped by two twin spires, which were to become the hallmark of Churchill Downs and the Kentucky Derby. Schulte's efforts did little to boost the financial condition of the enterprise, however, and the track continued to lose money through the end of the 1800s.

Turn of the Century: New Leadership

In 1902, Schulte's group of investors began looking for someone to take over the track, and in October of that year, they found their successors: Louisvillians Charles Grainger, Charlie Price, and Matt J. Winn. Grainger, a former mayor of Louisville, was named president, Winn vice-president, and Price racing secretary. The real leader of the group was Winn, a former tailor with no racetrack management experience but a keen business sense. Winn's motivation for taking on the track was partly personal; since watching the very first running of the Derby as a boy in the infield, he had been an unrelenting fan and attendee of the race.

Winn turned out to be a top-notch public relations man. Concerned that the track was not receiving the patronage it once had from the Louisville society set, he made personal appeals to various individuals, offering them choice seats for the coming Derby. A $20,000 clubhouse was built to accommodate these elite Louisville gentry, who paid $100 each for a membership. Under Winn's and his colleagues' determined leadership, the track—which had failed to make money for 28 years—turned its first profit in 1903. That year, Grainger and the others asked Winn to become Churchill Downs' general manager.

A few years later, Winn had another battle to face, this time with the government. An anti-gambling reform movement, which had been gathering steam across the nation, swept into Louisville in 1907 when a new, reformist mayor was elected. The city's administration placed a ban on bookmaking, which was the only form of betting at Churchill Downs. Winn responded by tracking down a handful of old pari-mutuel machines—a type of wagering machine used in France, which divided up the total pool of money bet and calculated winners' returns based on what they had wagered. Although Louisville had a prohibition against machine betting, an amendment exempted pari-mutuel machines from the law, making them a viable option. The machines proved to be very popular when they were unveiled; five times more money was wagered on the 1908 Derby than on the previous year's race. Ironically, the government's bookmaking ban had only served to increase the very activity it was trying to restrict.

The Derby continued to increase in popularity. Winn aggressively courted race participants from the eastern states, ensuring that the event would garner national attention. His cause was furthered in the early 1910s, with the setting of three successive track records that thrust the race into the news. In 1913, Donerail became the longest shot to win the Derby, paying $184.90 for a $2 bet. In 1914, Old Rosebud set a track speed record; and in 1915, Regret became the first filly to win the Derby. The publicity generated by the successive three records served to firmly establish the Kentucky Derby as a preeminent American sporting event.

1919–50: Acquisitions and Divestitures

In 1919, a group composed of Churchill Downs owners and the owners of three other Kentucky racetracks joined together to form the Kentucky Jockey Club as a holding company for the four tracks. Winn retained his position as vice-president and general manager of Churchill Downs.

The Kentucky Jockey Club set about expanding its racing empire beyond the state line, building a new track in Crete, Illinois, and acquiring two existing properties also in Illinois. In 1927, the group reorganized as the American Turf Association, a holding company for all seven tracks. With the subsequent onset of the Great Depression, however, the business began to unload its holdings, selling two of its Illinois tracks and shutting down racing at two of its Kentucky operations. For economic purposes, the remaining three tracks—Churchill Downs, Latonia, and Lincoln Fields—were divided into two separate corporate entities: Churchill Downs-Latonia Inc. and the Lincoln Fields Jockey Club. Despite the reshuffling, the three tracks remained under the ownership of the American Turf Association. Matt Winn moved from his position as vice-president and general manger to president of Churchill Downs in 1938, the year after the reorganization.

In 1942, Churchill Downs-Latonia Inc. sold off its Latonia track and changed its name to Churchill Downs Incorporated. The American Turf Association's remaining holding, Lincoln Fields, was sold in 1947, and three years later, the Turf Association dissolved. Shareholders exchanged their shares one-for-one for Churchill Downs Inc. stock. Winn had died the previous year at the age of 88.

1950s–70s: Renovations

Winn was succeeded as Churchill Downs' president by Bill Corum, a former *New York Times* sports columnist. During Corum's reign, Churchill Downs and the Kentucky Derby continued to develop, drawing more attention and more attendees. A major milestone occurred in 1952, when a CBS affiliate aired the first national telecast of the Derby. For the first time, people all over the nation were able to watch what came to be called the "most exciting two minutes in sports." Other, less dramatic, advances made under Corum's leadership included the addition of more seating boxes in the grandstand and clubhouse; installation of film patrol to provide racing officials with replays; and the addition of an automatic sprinkler system in the grandstand and clubhouse.

Corum died in 1958, and his position was filled by Wathen Knebelkamp. The aggressive and business-minded Knebelkamp immediately initiated an extensive building and renovation program. His improvements included new jockeys' quarters, a new press box, and 1,000 additional seats on the north end of the grandstand. One of Knebelkamp's best-known additions to the track was the Skye Terrace, a posh box seat area on the fourth and fifth floors of the clubhouse that came to be nicknamed "Millionaire's Row."

In 1960, speculation that Churchill Downs was targeted for a hostile stock takeover developed. Attempting to forestall this, track directors drafted a proposal to have the city purchase the track via a bond issue. The proposal, however, was rejected, and the threat of a takeover continued to mount. Finally, in 1969, when a company called National Industries made a serious play for the track, a group of Churchill Downs board members banded together to establish the "Derby Protection Group." The group outbid National Industries for control of the track, pushing its stock price up from $22 to $35.

The 1970s ushered in a new Churchill Downs president. Lynn Stone, who had previously served as the track's vice-president and general manager, replaced the retiring Knebelkamp in early 1970. The ongoing modernization of the track facilities that had marked Corum's and Knebelkamp's administrations continued unabated under Stone's direction, with the construction of steel emergency stairways in the stands and the refurbishing of the stable areas. By 1980, the extensive renovation program that had been initiated by Knebelkamp in the early 1960s was almost complete. More than $10 million had been pumped into the track over about 15 years, in the form of various improvements.

In 1982, the track's board of directors voted to add racing days to the Spring Meet, extending it from 55 days to 93 days. Despite its efforts, however, both the 1983 and 1984 racing seasons were disastrously bad, resulting in enormous losses.

Defeated, Stone resigned from his position in late summer of 1984, and was replaced by Thomas Meeker as acting president.

1984–99: Growth and Diversification

The 40-year-old Meeker, a Louisville lawyer who had formerly served as general counsel to Churchill Downs, was the youngest to hold the president's position since Clark founded it at age 29. Determined to revive waning interest in the track, Meeker launched a new marketing plan, the linchpin of which was a five-year, $25 million renovation program. The program included core renovations, construction of a new turf course and paddock complex, improvements to the clubhouse and barn areas, and upgrading of the Skye Terrace.

Meeker's campaign had the desired results. With the track once again pulling in record numbers of guests, Churchill Downs was chosen to host the 1988 Breeders' Cup—a much-publicized championship race begun four years earlier. More than 71,000 spectators turned out for the Breeders' Cup, setting an attendance record for the event. Churchill Downs would play host to the Breeders' Cup again in 1991, 1994, and 1998.

The track thrived under Meeker's leadership, showing growth on virtually all fronts. In the 1990s, the company began to grow beyond the boundaries imposed by the Churchill Downs property. The first major diversification came in 1992, when the company opened the Sports Spectrum, a simulcast wagering facility located just seven miles from the track. Although Kentucky law prohibited the Sports Spectrum from operating during race days at Churchill Downs, the facility offered visitors the chance to bet on races around the nation at all other times. Two years later, the company gained a majority interest in a second racetrack—Hoosier Park, in Anderson, Indiana. Under its Hoosier Park license, the company also began operating simulcast wagering centers in three other Indiana locations.

More acquisitions were soon to follow. In 1998, the company purchased Ellis Park Race Course, located in Henderson, Kentucky, and the Kentucky Horse Center training facility in Lexington, Kentucky. Another deal was closed in January 1999, for Calder Race Course in Miami, Florida. In May 1999, the company announced an agreement to purchase the Hollywood Park Race Track and Hollywood Park Casino, located in Inglewood Park, California. In addition, Churchill Downs acquired stakes in two companies that provided video services and telecommunications for the pari-mutuel betting industry. This diversification was partially in response to Kentucky's mid-1990s legalization of riverboat gambling, which was likely to encroach on the race track's revenues. A second reason for the aggressive acquisition pattern was that because its race tracks operated for only three months of the year, Churchill Downs needed to add sources of year-round income. With its simulcast facilities and its interests in the video and telecom businesses, the company was attempting to offset the seasonality of its core racing business.

Racing Into the New Century

As Churchill Downs closed out the 1900s, it planned to move into the new century with a four-point growth strategy.

The four initiatives included promoting and enhancing the live racing product; increasing its share in the interstate simulcast market; becoming a leader in the consolidation and development of the racing industry; and integrating alternative forms of gaming into existing racing operations. Toward these ends, Churchill Downs planned to actively seek other racing businesses for acquisition and to meanwhile improve the race programs at all of its existing tracks. The company also intended to pursue growth in the simulcast market by packaging a year-round racing signal to sell nationally. Other phases of this simulcast growth initiative were to include testing of in-home simulcast wagering and a Television Games Network, with round-the-clock sports programming.

Principal Subsidiaries

Calder Race Course, Inc.; Charlson Broadcast Technologies, LLC (60%); Churchill Downs Investment Company; Churchill Downs Management Company; Ellis Park Race Course; Hoosier Park L.P. (77%); Kentucky Horse Center; Kentucky Off-Track Betting, Inc. (25%); Louisville Sports Spectrum.

Further Reading

Beyer, Andrew, "Churchill Downs Takes Care of Itself," *Washington Post,* April 26, 1999, p. D1.

Chew, Peter, *The Kentucky Derby, the First 100 Years,* Boston: Houghton Mifflin, 1974.

Churchill Downs 100th Kentucky Derby, Louisville: Churchill Downs Incorporated, 1973.

Doolittle, Bill, *The Kentucky Derby: Run for the Roses,* New York: Time-Life Books, 1998.

Hillenbrandt, Laura, "The Derby," *American Heritage,* May/June 1999, p. 98.

Hirsch, Jim, and Jim Bolus, *Kentucky Derby: The Chance of a Lifetime,* New York: McGraw-Hill Book Company, 1988.

Klein, Frederick, "Winn, Place and Show," *Wall Street Journal,* April 30, 1999, p. W7.

Levy, William, *The Derby,* Cleveland: World Publications Co., 1967.

Privman, Jay, "Churchill Downs: A Run for Roses, a Race for Profits," *New York Times,* April 27, 1999, Sec. 8, p. 2.

—Shawna Brynildssen

CIRCUIT CITY.

Circuit City Stores, Inc.

9950 Mayland Drive
Richmond, Virginia 23233-1464
U.S.A.
(804) 527-4000
Fax: (804) 527-4194
Web site: http://www.circuitcity.com

Public Company
Incorporated: 1949 as Wards Company
Employees: 46,562
Sales: $10.8 billion (1999)
Stock Exchanges: New York
Ticker Symbol: CC
NAIC: 443112 Radio, Television & Other Electronics
    Stores; 443111 Household Appliance Stores

Circuit City Stores, Inc., is the nation's second largest retailer of consumer electronics, with more than 540 stores located throughout the United States. The company trails only Best Buy in consumer electronics sales. Aside from its signature superstores, Circuit City also operates some smaller stores, including several consumer-electronics-only stores and a chain of approximately 50 mall-based stores called Circuit City Express. Circuit City also runs a chain of car lots called CarMax. CarMax, a public company launched by Circuit City and still 75 percent owned by it, has roughly 30 used car superstores as well as 17 new car franchises. Circuit City is also behind the promotion of a video movie disk format called Divx, and it sells both Divx players and disks at its Circuit City stores. The company, based in Virginia, pioneered the concept of the electronics superstore, providing a broad variety of products in a cavernous setting. In perfecting this formula, the company became the dominant marketer in many of the areas into which it expanded.

Ushering In the Television Era

Circuit City was founded by Samuel S. Wurtzel, an importer-exporter who owned a business in New York. Wurtzel had sold his business and was vacationing in Richmond, Virginia in 1949 when he went to get a haircut and, while chatting with the barber, learned that the first commercial television station in the South would shortly go on the air in Richmond. Learning this, Wurtzel got the idea that it would be a good business proposition to open a store to sell television sets, reasoning that sales in the area would increase because of consumer interest in the new station's local broadcasts.

Wurtzel moved his family to Richmond and opened a store named "Wards," an acronym of its founder's family's names: "W" for Wurtzel, "A" for his son Alan, "R" for his wife Ruth, "D" for his son David, and "S" for his own name, Samuel. In addition, Wurtzel took a partner, Abraham L. Hecht. From its base in retailing televisions, Wurtzel soon branched out his business to include other home appliances. Within ten years, the business had expanded to encompass a chain of four stores, all of which were located in Richmond. Combined sales volume was about $1 million a year.

In 1960 Wards started to expand in another direction, as it began to operate licensed television departments within larger discount mass merchandisers in different areas of the country. The company ran television and other audio equipment sales operations in G.E.M., G.E.S., and G.E.X. stores. In the following year, Wards offered stock to the public for the first time, selling 110,000 shares in the company for $5.375 through a Baltimore stock broker.

In 1962 Wards increased its commitment to customer service by implementing a new service plan that included a free loan of a television set if a customer's television could not be repaired in the home. Two years later, the company opened its fifth television and appliance store, in Richmond's Southside Plaza Shopping Center. This, along with the company's earlier stock offering, signaled a period of quick expansion for the company.

In 1965 Wards made its first moves to grow through acquisition. The company purchased the Richmond Carousel Corporation, a discount department store in Richmond, from the T.G. Stores company. By taking over this company, Wards moved into the sale of automotive supplies, gasoline, household supplies, clothing, and children's toys, as well as appliances. In

Company Perspectives:

Moving forward with continued innovation and superior customer service: Sam Wurtzel started a tradition in 1949 when he identified a new product—the television—and delivered it door-to-door. We extended the tradition when we developed the Circuit City Superstore, providing low prices and knowledgeable sales assistance. Through CarMax and Divx, we are bringing new consumer benefits to the automotive and home video industries as well. By delivering superior customer service—at Circuit City and in these new businesses—we believe that we can produce outstanding returns for stockholders.

addition, in September 1965 Wards purchased Murmic, Inc., a Delaware company that operated hardware and housewares sales areas in department stores located in the Southeast.

The following year, Wards opened its sixth Virginia store, this one located in the Walnut Mall Shopping Center in Petersburg. Each of the company's stores featured 5,000 to 8,000 square feet of space in which to display and sell televisions, audio equipment, and other household appliances. With the additional revenue from this facility, company sales reached $23 million. Also in 1966, one of Samuel Wurtzel's sons, Alan, a lawyer, returned to Richmond to take a role in the family business, in preparation for eventually taking over the reins from his father.

Geographic Expansion in the 1970s

In 1968 Wards offered additional stock to the public, selling 1,700 shares on the American Stock Exchange. With the revenue generated by this offering, in May 1969 the company purchased Custom Electronics, Inc., an outfit that sold audio and hi-fi equipment. The company owned four stores in the Washington, D.C. area, as well as a mail order audio supplies operation called Dixie Hi-Fi; it also ran nine stereo departments in department stores located in an area stretching from Mobile, Alabama to Albany, New York. Five months later, Wards continued its rapid expansion in the Mid-Atlantic states by buying the Certified TV and Appliance Company of Virginia Beach, Virginia, which operated three stores in the Tidewater area. The company also opened an additional Carousel store in the Richmond area.

One month later, Wards branched out from its familiar geographical area and its core business of appliance retailing when it purchased The Mart, located in Indianapolis, Indiana. This company had as one of its major components the tire retailing operations of the Rose Tire Company and its affiliates, but it also sold televisions, appliances, and furniture. In its furthest geographical leap, Wards also signed a contract to operate licensed television departments in Zody's Department Stores in Los Angeles.

The company's rapid expansion continued in 1970. Wards bought Woodville Appliances, Inc., which ran five television and appliance stores in Toledo, Ohio. Also in the Midwest, it acquired the operations of the Frank Dry Goods Company, which ran a television, appliance, and furniture store in Fort Wayne, Indiana.

By this time, Wards' rapid growth had brought it to a new era, and this was symbolized in 1970 by the transfer of power from the founders of the company to a younger generation. Samuel Wurtzel, its founder, stepped down as president, although he remained chairman of the board, and Abraham Hecht, his partner, retired. In their stead, Alan Wurtzel was named president of the company.

Among the first moves made by the new president was the opening of two specialty stores in Richmond, called Sight 'N Sound, that sold only audio equipment. These outlets were designed to take advantage of the boom in demand for high-tech stereo equipment.

In 1972 Alan Wurtzel, still president, assumed the responsibilities of chief executive officer of Wards. In an effort to eliminate weaker areas of the company, he closed the Franks of Fort Wayne store that Wards had purchased two years earlier and shut down three stores formerly run by Certified in Virginia. Following this consolidation, the company began to expand in the next year. Five audio stores were opened: three in the east, in Washington, D.C.; Richmond, Virginia; and Charlottesville, Virginia; and two in California. In the following year, Wards began to suffer the adverse effects of its rapid expansion and diversification into areas not related to its core business of television and appliance retailing. In 1974 the company lost $3 million on overall sales of $69 million. In an effort to stem the red ink, Wurtzel withdrew Wards from areas in which it was not turning a profit, such as tire sales. In addition, Wards was losing a large amount of money on its licensed appliance departments in three discount department store chains that were doing very badly. To cut its losses, the company began to move out of its leased audio and television operations in department stores, retaining only its involvement in the California Zody's stores.

Birth of the Superstore in the Mid-1970s

In a shift in direction, Wards also closed two of its original stores in Richmond, opting instead to risk half the company's net worth opening a $2 million electronics superstore. With this move, Wards began to shift its focus from appliances in general to the growing market in consumer electronics. The company called its pioneering venture "The Wards Loading Dock." With 40,000 square feet, the warehouse store displayed and sold a very large selection of video and audio equipment and major appliances. This enormous facility, with its exceptionally broad offerings of more than 2,000 products, enabled Wards to take a strong lead against its competitors. In addition, the superstore's high volume of sales meant that the company could afford to offer lower prices than its smaller competitors, as well as such amenities as home delivery and in-store repairs. In this way, by locating its stores in medium-sized markets otherwise served only by smaller, mom-and-pop operations, Wards was able to exploit growing consumer interest in new electronics products. The successful superstore concept became the innovation upon which Wards built its future growth.

Also during this time, Wards expanded its Dixie Hi-Fi line of discount audio stores, adding nine new properties. In the next year, as its Richmond superstore showed promising returns, Wards began to streamline its operations. The company sold its four Woodville television and appliance stores in Toledo, Ohio, and also shuttered four of its five Mart stores in Indianapolis. In addition, the company shed its two Carousel stores in Richmond.

Two years later, in 1977, anticipating that the boom in stereo sales would eventually slow, Wards began to broaden the offerings of its Dixie Hi-Fi and Custom Hi-Fi discount audio equipment stores, transforming them into full-service electronics specialty markets. With this new concept, Wards changed the name of the stores to "Circuit City," opening six of the new facilities in the Washington, D.C. area. With 6,000 to 7,000 square feet of space, the new stores featured video and audio equipment made by well known brand names, as well as in-store service capabilities and a pick-up area for people to load purchases into their cars.

To shift its operations toward the Circuit City concept, Wards continued to streamline in 1978. The company left the mail order electronics business, which it ran under the name "Dixie," and also closed its four Richmond Sight 'N Sound stores. In the following year, the company continued its progress toward large retail outlets, opening a second Wards Loading Dock in Richmond. The company ended 1979 with $120 million in sales.

In 1981 Wards made its first incursion into a significant and challenging new market when it merged with the Lafayette Radio Electronics Corporation, which ran eight consumer electronics stores in the New York City metropolitan area. The company paid $6.6 million for the bankrupt retailer, earning $36.5 million in tax credits as a result of the acquisition, a benefit that observers predicted would drive up its own earnings. Lafayette's reputation within the highly competitive New York market was that of a small specialty seller that provided obscure, high-priced brand name goods to hi-fi hobbyists. Wards faced an uphill battle in its struggle to broaden the chain's appeal and return it to profitability, especially since other New York electronics retailers routinely discounted items 50 percent or permitted haggling over the price of their products.

At the same time that Wards moved into the New York market, the company began to expand its Loading Dock superstore concept in the geographical areas where it already had a presence. Capitalizing on its other name, the company christened its new outlets Circuit City Superstores. The first four stores under this name opened in Raleigh, Greensboro, Durham, and Winston-Salem, North Carolina. In the following year, Wards simplified the naming of its outlets by changing the names of its Richmond Wards Loading Dock stores to Circuit City Superstores.

By 1982 Wards was operating four retail chains, including Circuit City stores, larger Circuit City Superstores, its Lafayette properties in New York, and its operations in Zody discount stores in California. Altogether, the company ran 100 outlets, twice the number it had owned just seven years earlier. A total of 80 percent of Wards' revenue was derived from sales of consumer electronics, and the company reaped solid profits from its marketing of Sony Betamax videocassette recorders and Pioneer stereo equipment. In Washington, D.C., Wards' Circuit City stores held the largest market share, garnering 11 percent of the sales of consumer electronics. By the end of 1983, Wards' pattern of consistent growth through its marketing decision to emphasize large retail outlets had led to sales of $246 million for the fiscal year.

Boosting Circuit City in the 1980s

As a sign of its shifting identity, Wards changed its corporate name to Circuit City Stores, Inc., in 1984. Also in this year, its stock was listed on the New York Stock Exchange for the first time. Although the leadership of the company changed hands—Alan Wurtzel stepped up to the post of chairman of the board, to be succeeded by Richard Sharp—its basic direction did not. Sharp's background was in computers, not retailing, and he had first come into contact with Circuit City when he installed a computer system to control sales and inventory in some of its stores. Under Sharp, the company continued to consolidate its operations in very large stores, replacing regular Circuit City stores with Circuit City Superstores. This process began in Knoxville, Tennessee; Charleston, South Carolina; and Hampton, Virginia.

These stores, some of which contained nearly an acre of floor space, used their grand scope to bring a theatrical flair to retailing consumer electronics. The stores featured solid walls of television sets, all tuned to the same channel. Customers entered by walking past the service department, a visible symbol that the company serviced what it sold. The stores were laid out like baseball diamonds, and customers were led around the displays by a red tile walkway. Particularly popular items were located at the back of the store, to encourage impulse purchasing on the way. By 1984 Circuit City was operating 113 stores, which made it the leading specialty retailer of brand name consumer electronics. The company's growth continued briskly, fed by innovative new electronics products such as cordless telephones, microwave ovens, and videocassette recorders (VCRs), for which initial demand was high. Its Superstores contributed the largest part of its earnings, while the company's New York operations continued to lose money. To fuel continued growth, Circuit City further expanded its operations. In 1984 the company planned a large expansion around Atlanta and opened 15 new stores in Florida. In locating stores, Circuit City adhered to a policy of clustering them together in the same geographic area, which allowed for economies of scale in advertising and promotion.

In 1986 Circuit City took the final step in consolidating its operations. The company closed down its 15 unprofitable stores in the New York area, run under the Lafayette name, after a five-year, $20 million struggle to crack this tough market. In addition, Circuit City withdrew from its arrangement with the 50-store Zody's discount department store chain in California. This low-rent retailer, which had long been suffering financial troubles, provided an inhospitable home to Circuit City's operations and contributed no earnings to its bottom line. Instead, the company decided to put the resources previously used to run these operations into further Circuit City Superstores, concentrating expansion in the Southeast and in California, where it planned to open its own free-standing stores. In moving into a new area, Circuit City methodically set out to win the lion's share of sales in that market. The company typically opened a large number of very large stores all at once, advertised heavily, and distributed products efficiently.

These efforts bore fruit in February 1987, when Circuit City's annual sales hit the $1 billion mark for the first time, driven in large part by the demand for VCRs, which also pushed up demand for new televisions and other audio equipment. The company faced a challenging future, however, as demand for this core product cooled and competition from other electronics superstores heated up. Despite these adverse circumstances, by 1988 the company owned 105 stores, 32 of which were located in California.

Armed with the nation's largest market share, Circuit City planned to add 20 new outlets. Among these new outlets were several that featured a new format. Called Impulse, these stores were tested by the company in Baltimore, Maryland; Richmond, Virginia; and McLean, Virginia. These stores, designed for malls, sold small electronic products for personal use or to be given as gifts. Three years later, the company announced that its test of this concept had been successful, and that it planned to open 50 more such outlets.

By 1989 Circuit City's profits had tripled in just three years to reach $69.5 million, despite a general recession in the consumer electronics retailing industry. Observers attributed the company's success to strong management and a merchandising formula that had been honed and refined for many years. That formula was adjusted further in 1989 when Circuit City began opening mini-Superstores in markets too small for a full-fledged massive outlet. Claiming that the mini-store offered the same service and selection as a larger outlet, the company opened a test site in Asheville, North Carolina. By the following year, sales overall had hit $2 billion, and earnings were up as well.

Competition and New Ideas for the 1990s

Circuit City surged ahead in the early 1990s, with strong sales growth and steady expansion into new markets. By 1994 it had close to 300 stores and had plans to open almost 200 more. But growing competition, particularly with the similar electronics superstore chain Best Buy, caused the company to fight harder for market share and to search for new ways to make money. In late 1993, Circuit City announced it would cut prices in markets it shared with Best Buy, sparking a grueling price war. The firm differed from Best Buy in offering a high-service, hard-sell sales environment, with sales people working for commission. Best Buy was more of a help-yourself retailer. Circuit City publicly defended its more aggressive style, broadcasting the results of a survey in 1994 that claimed that consumers preferred its level of service. By 1995, half its stores were in markets shared by Best Buy, and 70 percent of its markets were classified by analysts as highly competitive. Despite the competition, Circuit City had sales of about $7 billion by 1995, and sales and earnings were rising by 20 percent annually.

The company went in a new direction in 1993, opening the first of what became a chain of used car lots. Two years later, Circuit City was trumpeting its new chain, CarMax. Circuit City's CEO Sharp moved the company into used cars because he saw that the existing market was lucrative, fragmented, and not well run. Customers hated the haggling and distrusted sales people, as a rule, in the traditional used car lot. CarMax offered a huge, clean lot of cars marked with bar codes so that customers could easily locate the vehicles in which they were interested from a central computer listing. Prices were fixed, so the dreadful bargaining was out. CarMax lots held 500 to 1,000 cars, all no more than five years old, and with less than 70,000 miles on them. Each car went through a 110-point inspection, and CarMax offered a 30-day warranty. The aim was to bring Circuit City's retailing experience into this new industry and make the buying process easier on the customer. Though Circuit City was cautious about releasing sales figures for its first CarMax stores, one analyst estimated that its Richmond, Virginia lot was bringing in about $55 million after being open one year.

Used cars seemed like an odd leap for an electronics retailer, yet it was clear Circuit City needed something to keep it going, as the electronics market became saturated. Best Buy passed up Circuit City in the mid-1990s and won the title of number-one electronics retailer, and competition between the rivals did not let up. In 1998 Circuit City trotted out a new product, a digital movie disk called Divx, hoping to get in on a ground floor technology. Divx was pitched to Circuit City by a Los Angeles legal firm, and Circuit City threw money at it. Divx originally stood for digital video express, but it soon became known just by the acronym. It was a disk digitally encoded with a movie, and consumers could purchase it for between $4 and $5, watch the movie within 48 hours, and then throw it away. Divx players were hooked by phone line to a central computer, which registered when the movie was watched, and billed the customer an additional three dollars if the disk was used after the initial two-day period. It competed directly with another digital movie format called DVD, which were disks offered for rent, like traditional videocassette movies. Both these technologies were struggling for consumers' attention, with each format offering only a few hundred titles as they rolled out in the fall of 1998. The large video rental chains refused to sell Divx disks, fearing they would undermine their business, and only Circuit City and another chain called Good Guys initially sold Divx.

By 1999 Circuit City was enjoying strong sales in its core electronics business, but its used car and Divx ventures were not doing well. CarMax lost $23.5 million in 1998, on sales of $1.5 billion. The chain had grown to more than 30 locations, but Circuit City CEO Sharp halted further expansion in 1999, as sales declined. Competition with a copycat chain, AutoNation, had left CarMax struggling. Some new stores were way too big, and advertising costs were heavy. By 1999 Divx, too, seemed to have lost out to the competition. An estimated 10,000 retailers were selling DVD disks, the reusable digital movies that could either be rented like movies on video or purchased for about $20. Only about 740 of these 10,000 retailers also dealt with Divx, and most of these retailers were actually Circuit City stores. Both Sony's film studios and Warner Brothers declared they would not make their movies available on Divx, and the technology seemed to be getting squeezed out. Circuit City's core business was still robust, and it remained to be seen if the company would find new directions as some of its experiments fizzled.

Principal Subsidiaries

CarMax (75%).

Further Reading

Andrews, Edmund L., "Struggling for Profits in Electronics," *New York Times,* September 10, 1989.

Bautz, Mark, "How a Straight-Arrow Company Makes Out Like a Bandit," *Money,* October 1995, p. 68.

Brinkley, Joel, "DVD Leads Race for TV Disks, But It Is Looking Over Its Shoulder," *New York Times,* July 6, 1998, pp. D1, D4.

Brown, Paul R., "Some People Don't Like To Haggle," *Forbes,* August 27, 1984.

Carpenter, Kimberly, "Circuit City Lays an Egg and Hatches a Strategy," *Business Week,* April 21, 1986.

"Circuit City Expansion," *Television Digest,* April 17, 1995, p. 17.

"Circuit City Fires Back at Critics," *Discount Store News,* September 19, 1994, p. 5.

Cochran, Thomas N., "Circuit City Stores, Inc.," *Barron's,* January 2, 1989.

Foust, Dean, "Circuit City's Wires Are Sizzling," *Business Week,* April 27, 1992.

King, Sharon R., "Circuit City Is Learning the High Price of New Video Technology," *New York Times,* April 6, 1999, p. C9.

Lavin, Douglas, "Cars Are Sold Like Stereos by Circuit City," *Wall Street Journal,* June 8, 1994, pp. B1, B6.

Merwin, John, "Execution," *Forbes,* April 18, 1988.

Rudnitsky, Howard, "Would You Buy a Used Car from This Man?," *Forbes,* October 23, 1995, pp. 52–54.

Spiegel, Peter, "Car Crash," *Forbes,* May 17, 1999, pp. 130–32.

—Elizabeth Rourke
—updated by A. Woodward

Cirque du Soleil Inc.

8400 Second Avenue
Montréal, Quebec H1Z 4M6
Canada
(514) 722-2324
(800) 678-2119
Fax: (514) 722-3692
Web site: http://www.cirquedusoleil.com

Private Company
Incorporated: 1984
Employees: 1,300
Sales: $204 million (1998)
NAIC: 71119 Other Performing Arts Companies

Part circus, part theater, Cirque du Soleil Inc. produces avant-garde entertainment shows staged at permanent locations and presented to a worldwide audience through an extensive touring schedule. In 1999 Cirque du Soleil (Circus of the Sun) had four productions touring throughout North America, Asia, Europe, and the Pacific region, and four productions appearing at permanent locations in Las Vegas; Orlando, Florida; and Biloxi, Mississippi. Headquartered in Montréal, the company operated offices in Las Vegas, Amsterdam, and Singapore. During the late 1990s, the company was diversifying into new business areas, including operating retail locations that sold Cirque du Soleil merchandise, producing films and television shows, and negotiating for licensing agreements.

Origins

Cirque du Soleil came from the street, its creation the inspiration of a group of street performers gathered in Baie Saint-Paul in the province of Québec. Among the street performers entertaining passersby in the rural Canadian town were fire-eaters, mime artists, jugglers, and stilt-walkers, who banded together in 1982 to form the "Club des Talons Hauts," or the "High-Heels Club." The troupe, who chose their name because most of the members performed on stilts, decided to organize a festival that could serve as a forum for the exchange of ideas

and techniques among street performers. The festival, called the "Fête Foraine de Baie St-Paul" (Baie Saint-Paul Fair) was the precursor to Cirque du Soleil, which was organized two years later with Guy Laliberte, a fire-eater, as its founding president.

Founded as a nonprofit organization, Cirque du Soleil received financial backing from the Québec government, which was sponsoring celebrations for the 450th anniversary of Jacques Cartier's arrival in Canada. Cirque du Soleil's first performance was held in 1984 in the small Québec town of Gaspé, where patrons entered a blue-and-yellow big top tent and witnessed a unique form of circus entertainment. More theater than circus, Cirque du Soleil purposely strayed from the conventions of a traditional circus, blending the talents of street performers with original music, extravagant costumes, and special lighting effects. There were no animals in any of the acts and the show did not depend on the talents of a star performer, both of which were common characteristics of traditional circuses. Further, the militaristic marches and fanfares heard at traditional circuses were replaced with an original music score, providing a sometimes haunting, sometimes ethereal soundtrack that threaded the performances together. Cirque du Soleil was intent on being different, and from its start the organization achieved its goal. A Cirque du Soleil performance was "utterly otherly," as one theater reviewer described it; another characterized it as "*commedia dell'arte* as restaged by surrealists in a birthday-party mood." The public, drawn to the curious spectacle, applauded, their numbers increasing as the performers took their show on the road and developed Cirque du Soleil into a global phenomenon.

After first being staged in Gaspé, Cirque du Soleil traveled throughout Québec in 1984, appearing in ten cities and playing to audiences of 800 at each performance. The following year, the troupe took its first steps outside its home province and began performing in neighboring Ontario, where audience reception provided further impetus to expand Cirque du Soleil's touring schedule. By 1986, the seating capacity of Cirque du Soleil's big top tent had been expanded to 1,500, during a year in which the troupe earned national and international attention. The company performed at Vancouver, British Columbia's Children's Festival and at Expo '86, the World's Fair hosted by

Vancouver. Internationally, Cirque du Soleil earned accolades and awards at several competitions and festivals held overseas. By the end of 1986, Cirque du Soleil officials were convinced of the concept's broad-based appeal. Two years after its birth in the small town of Gaspé, Cirque du Soleil's avant-garde form of entertainment was primed for exportation on a broad scale.

1987: Touring Begins in Earnest

In 1987 Cirque du Soleil made its debut in the United States, creating a themed production named *Le Cirque Reinvente,* which earned the company its first major critical acclaim. The company performed at the Los Angeles Festival and appeared in San Diego and Santa Monica, attracting crowds that prompted company executives back in Montréal to quickly organize a second tour in the United States. For the second tour, Cirque du Soleil returned to Santa Monica and added performance dates in San Francisco, Washington, D.C., and New York City, where among other unusual acts, audiences witnessed the spectacle of a Cirque du Soleil performer conduct the *1812 Overture* in ski boots while strapped to a trampoline.

While audiences collected under Cirque du Soleil's performing tent in New York City's Battery Park, in Montréal the company's choreographers, costume designers, and other artists were developing new conceptualized formats to take on tour. The goal was to create new productions to stimulate and to perpetuate audience appeal. Thematic, the productions ranged from lighthearted to somber, each distinctly different and each distinctly Cirque du Soleil. The company's managers were forward-thinking and objective-oriented, formulating and then pursuing successive five-year plans. The shows themselves were expressions of artistic and athletic ability, but the stewardship of the company was conducted in a businesslike way. This approach fueled the geographic expansion of Cirque du Soleil's touring schedule, diversified the company's activities into new revenue-generating areas, and, eventually, developed the strength of the Cirque du Soleil name to a force equal to a popular consumer brand. Although the maturation of the Cirque du Soleil concept into an eccentric yet formidable marketing force did not gain momentum until the mid-1990s, some lucrative projects were started during the late 1980s. In 1988 the company began negotiations that would proceed for the next four years for an Asian tour. In 1989 Cirque du Soleil sold its

concept for European performances to Circus Knie, which subsequently began producing its own version in Europe.

By 1990, the seating capacity for Cirque du Soleil performances had been increased to 2,500. Prices ranged between $6 and $33.50 per ticket, accounting for nearly all of the company's annual revenue. The company's touring schedule had been expanded greatly by this point, with a number of different troupes performing a 214-show tour, typically stopping in cities for a four- or five-week stay. The tour launched in 1990—covering 13 cities in the United States and Canada—started in Montréal, where the company's new production debuted. Called *Nouvelle Expérience,* the new production was greeted enthusiastically by audiences throughout the 19-month tour, by far eclipsing all previous ticket sales records. By the end of the tour, 1.3 million people had seen *Nouvelle Expérience,* while audiences in London and Paris were introduced to the genuine Cirque du Soleil through a tour of *Le Cirque Reinvente.*

At the end of the 1990–91 tour, preparations had already begun for what would prove to be a year of significant achievement. After years of negotiations, Cirque du Soleil embarked on its first tour of Asia, financed by a $40 million investment by Fuji Televisions Network, which handled ticket sales and promotion for the tour. The production, whose budget rivaled that of a major Broadway musical, featured 72 international artists and musicians, their performances a collage of previous Cirque du Soleil shows, particularly the company's groundbreaking *Le Cirque Reinvente.* Called *Fascination,* the production debuted in Tokyo, beginning a 118-performance, eight-city tour that was staged in venues with seating capacities ranging between 4,500 and 9,000. While the four-month tour in Asia was under way, Cirque du Soleil also began a tour organized in partnership with Circus Knie that presented shows in 60 towns in Switzerland. Busy on all fronts, the company also appeared in Las Vegas for the first time, bringing *Nouvelle Expérience* to the Mirage Hotel for a year-long engagement in a tent behind the hotel. The year also saw Cirque du Soleil add to its portfolio of productions with the creation of *Saltimbanco,* Italian for "street performer," which began a 19-month North American tour after its debut in Montréal in April.

Of the numerous achievements in 1992, perhaps none was more important to the company's financial well-being than the one-year engagement at the Mirage Hotel. The success of *Nouvelle Expérience* enraptured casino owner Steve Wynn, turning the one-year engagement into a permanent engagement. Further, Wynn agreed to construct a more than $20 million permanent facility for Cirque du Soleil at the new Treasure Island resort, scheduled to open in 1994. The addition of its first permanently placed production was a dramatic change for the otherwise peripatetic Cirque du Soleil, but it provided the company with a major and reliable stream of revenue. Moreover, the relationship with Wynn proved to be highly advantageous for Cirque du Soleil, leading to other arrangements for permanently placed productions in the years ahead. In addition to this budding success story, the company could claim victory with its new *Saltimbanco* production, in the midst of its 19-month North American tour in 1993. The $20 million production, featuring 40 artists and a traveling company of 110, was attracting near-capacity audiences. For the production to break even financially, 70 percent of the 2,500-seat big top needed to be filled, a percentage *Saltimbanco* far surpassed by averaging nearly 93 percent of capacity in paid attendance and 98 percent of capacity in total attendance. By the time *Saltimbanco* had finished its North American tour, 1.4 million people had seen the production, with more to come, as the production embarked on a six-month run in Tokyo in 1994. On top of the revenue obtained from ticket sales, the company also was gaining revenue from its merchandise line sold at the performances and through a mail-order catalogue, which was attached to the program for individual performances. Cirque du Soleil's growing legions of fans could buy CDs of the production's music, as well as a full range of merchandise that included inexpensive items, such as $5 buttons, and decidedly more expensive items, such as a $350 Cirque du Soleil leather jacket. As Cirque du Soleil developed into a recognizable brand name, the marketing forces behind the company were becoming increasingly ambitious.

Diversification and Expansion in the 1990s

Cirque du Soleil celebrated its tenth anniversary in 1994, its management having devised and fulfilled two, five-year plans. For the next five years, management laid out a diversified blueprint for growth, the implementation of which would greatly increase the company's financial stature. Construction of a $10 million "creation studio" in Montréal was planned to serve as an elaborate rehearsal space, an extensive European tour was planned, and, significantly, a television series was planned. The *Saltimbanco* production was slated for the European tour, but continuing with its tradition, the company debuted two new productions before the European tour got under way. Completion of the permanent theater in Las Vegas included the debut of *Mystére* in 1994, marking the beginning of a ten-year contract signed with Mirage Resorts. During its first year, the 1,541-seat theater registered an impressive sellout ratio of 98 percent, attracting more than 660,000 spectators. While *Mystére* settled into its permanent home in Las Vegas, the company finished development of a new touring show, *Alegria,* which began a two-year North American tour in Montréal in 1994.

Testament to Cirque du Soleil's widespread recognition and appeal arrived in an unusual fashion in 1995, when the Canadian government asked the company to create a show for the G7 Summit in Halifax, Nova Scotia. While the company entertained the heads of state from the most economically powerful countries in the world, it launched its first, full-fledged European tour in Amsterdam, where the company established its European head office. From Amsterdam, the *Saltimbanco* production took to the road, appearing in major metropolitan cities in five countries. *Saltimbanco* stopped its run in London in early 1997, five years after its debut, and was replaced by *Alegria,* which began another two-year tour in Europe. Back in Montréal, meanwhile, yet another production had been unveiled in Cirque du Soleil's home city, the company's ninth production. Debuting in April 1996, *Quidam,* "anybody" in Latin, was intended to illuminate, in the show's director's words, "our frailty and angst at the dawn of a new century." The production began a longer-than-usual, three-year North American tour after its opening in Montréal, appearing in 14 cities and attracting more than 2.5 million spectators.

The enormous attendance total for the *Quidam* production was representative of Cirque du Soleil's overall growth, which began to accelerate rapidly as the company's productions fanned out across the globe and new areas of growth were explored. Sales for the company were $30 million in 1994; by 1996, Cirque du Soleil was collecting $110 million, an increase achieved substantially by revenue obtained from its permanent production in Las Vegas. *Mystére,* by itself, generated $40 million in revenue in 1996, convincing Wynn to construct a second theater for Cirque du Soleil. In 1997, Wynn devoted $60 million for a new theater at his new Las Vegas resort, Bellagio. A third permanent site for Cirque du Soleil also was under construction in 1997, located at Walt Disney World, near Orlando, Florida. To meet the creative demands required to stage new productions at these theaters, and to create new shows for touring productions, the company had a new complex for its rehearsal and costume-design activities, the "creation studio" that had been planned several years earlier. Opened in February 1997, the $22 million facility in Montréal measured 150,000 square feet, serving as the company's headquarters and the site where all Cirque du Soleil productions were developed.

The construction activity in 1997 translated into the debut of several new productions in 1998 and 1999. In October 1998, Cirque du Soleil's second permanent production debuted at Wynn's Bellagio. Named *O*—a play on the French word, "eau," for water—the production was unique, even for the innovative Cirque du Soleil. The production was staged in, around, and above a 1.5 million-gallon pool, which, through a series of lifts, could rapidly be transformed into a dry stage. A $90 million production, *O* became the most expensive ticket in Las Vegas, with a seat in the 1,800-seat theater selling for $100. Two months later, another new production opened at a permanent Cirque du Soleil theater, *La Nouba,* staged at the Walt Disney World Resort. Concurrent with the start of the company's second and third permanent productions, construction for a fourth permanent theater was under way, again sponsored by Steve Wynn. *Alegria,* back from its European tour, found a permanent home at Wynn's $600 million, Biloxi, Mississippi-based Beau Rivage resort, debuting in 1999. Elsewhere, Cirque du Soleil was busy touring, unveiling a new production, called *Dralion,* for a three-year North American tour, and dispatching *Saltimbanco* for a three-year tour of Asia and the Pacific, which began in January 1999.

Cirque du Soleil ended the 1990s with seven productions performing in 22 countries in Asia, the Pacific, North America, and Europe. Looking ahead, the company intended to use its worldwide exposure to build the Cirque du Soleil name into an internationally recognized brand. Toward this end, the company released its first feature film, called *Alegria,* distributed by Sony Pictures Classics. The film was expected to open in theaters in late 1999 or early 2000. The company also completed a large-format (IMAX) film entitled *Journey of Man* in 1999. For the future, Cirque du Soleil, displaying a penchant for market saturation, planned to produce television specials and, perhaps, establish a chain of merchandise stores, based on prototype units tested in Florida in 1998.

Further Reading

Barry, David, "Cirque du Soleil Wows San Jose, Could Come Back," *Business Journal—San Jose,* October 1, 1990, p. 5.
"Big Tent," *Fortune,* April 28, 1997, p. 363.

Cohen, Joyce, "Cirque du Soleil's Production 'O' Making Quite a Splash in Las Vegas," *Amusement Business,* November 23, 1998, p. 16.

Corliss, Richard, "A Show That Soars—and Swims," *Time,* October 26, 1998, p. 82.

——, "Cirque du Soleil," *Time,* April 19, 1993, p. 65.

Deckard, Linda, "Cirque du Soleil Tops 600,000 in First Half of North American Tour," *Amusement Business,* March 1, 1993, p. 1.

Fingersh, Julie, "Cirque du Soleil's $40 Mil TV Deal Opens Asian Mkt.," *Amusement Business,* January 13, 1992, p. 36.

Fitzgerald, Kate, "Cirque on a Search: Show Looks for New Sponsors To Join in Global Growth," *Advertising Age,* December 7, 1998, p. 28.

Harvey, Dennis, "O," *Variety,* December 21, 1998, p. 87.

Jaeger, Lauren, "Cirque du Soleil Tour To Play 2.5 Mil.," *Amusement Business,* June 15, 1998, p. 1.

Munk, Nina, "A High-Wire Act," *Forbes,* September 22, 1997, p. 192.

Oppen, Larry, "Cirque du Soleil's 'Mystere' Production a Hit at Las Vegas' Treasure Island," *Amusement Business,* June 5, 1995, p. 14.

Paxman, Andrew, "Cirque Enters Mouse's Big Top," *Variety,* January 25, 1999, p. 79.

Skow, John, "Pree-senn-ting the Circus of the Sun; a Brash New Troupe Fills Its Tent with Fresh Ideas," *Time,* May 30, 1988, p. 66.

Stevenson, William, "Cirque du Soleil's 'Alegria,' " *Back Stage,* April 21, 1995, p. 52.

Zink, Jack, "La Nouba," *Variety,* February 8, 1999, p. 88.

Zoltak, James, "Cirque du Soleil's 'Quidam' Averages a $3 to $4 Merchandise Per Cap.," *Amusement Business,* June 2, 1997, p. 5.

—Jeffrey L. Covell

The Connell Company

45 Cardinal Drive
Westfield, New Jersey 07090-1099
U.S.A.
(908) 233-0700
(888) 343-2231
Fax: (908) 233-1070
Web site: http://www.connellco.com

Private Company
Incorporated: 1926 as Connell Rice & Sugar Co.
Employees: 125
Sales: $1.5 billion (1997 est.)
NAIC: 551112 Offices of Other Holding Companies;
42241 General Line Grocery Wholesalers; 532411
Commercial Air, Rail & Water Transportation
Equipment Rental & Leasing; 52231 Mortgage &
Nonmortgage Loan Brokers; 532412 Construction,
Mining & Forestry Machinery & Equipment Rental
and Leasing; 23331 Manufacturing & Industrial
Building Construction

Originally and perhaps best known as a major broker of rice, The Connell Company has grown to become one of the largest and most diversified privately held corporations in the United States. Through its several subsidiaries, Connell is involved in exporting rice; exporting food-processing equipment and supplies; importing, brokering, selling, and distributing canned food products; developing office buildings; leasing, distributing, and selling construction equipment; arranging financing of leased equipment and commercial property development; and offering asset management services to the technology sector. With three generations of the Connell family active in the company at the end of the 20th century, the New Jersey-based Connell Company had estimated sales of well over $1 billion in the late 1990s. Grover Connell, the company's president and chief executive officer since 1950 had an estimated net worth of $500 million in 1998.

Origins as a Rice Broker

The Connell Company traces its origins to the 1926 founding of the Connell Rice & Sugar Co. The senior Grover Connell was a native of Texas who moved to New York City, where he established headquarters for his thriving rice distribution and export business. When Connell died in 1950, and was succeeded by a son who bore the same name, company sales had reached $10 million a year. Connell Rice headquarters were moved in 1958 from New York to a modern building in Westfield, New Jersey, near the Connell family residence. From there, the company exported bagged rice via ship to companies around the world. The company's executives had developed their own interests in rice farms by the 1960s.

The primary business of Connell Rice & Sugar was, according to a 1967 Federal Trade Commission (FTC) document, buying and reselling commodities for its own account and acting as a broker for transactions in refined sugar, corn products, and other commodities. In addition, the company was receiving monthly fees for studies of commodity prices and market conditions that it circulated to various industrial organizations.

In 1974, Connell Rice & Sugar, under the leadership of Grover Connell, Jr., became involved in urging Congress to repeal certain legislation, in force since the Great Depression of the 1930s, designed to support rice prices by restricting production in the United States. Discussing the legislation, as well as the nature of the rice business in general, Connell told Elizabeth M. Fowler of the *New York Times* that year that the United States produced about two percent of the world's rice, yet was the world's largest exporter of the product. Connell attributed this irony to the fact that the world's largest rice-producing nations, such as China, Japan, and India, were also experiencing sharp rises in population and thus needed even more rice to feed themselves. Connell's company was exporting rice to about 100 countries at this time, while also importing some rice and selling it domestically. All told, rice was accounting for about 85 percent of the company's annual sales volume of $350 million, and Connell was reported to be the nation's largest rice exporter.

The Politically Charged 1970s

Grover Connell's ties to two U.S. House of Representatives members became an issue during this time, when reporters revealed that Department of Justice officials were investigating charges that South Koreans were attempting to influence U.S. policies regarding rice and other export programs by bribing congressmen. According to the final report of a House investigation, Representative Otto Passman of Louisiana told a federal investigator that he forced the Koreans to hire a Connell shipping company by threatening to cut off foreign aid otherwise.

Moreover, in 1977 a Department of Agriculture officer recommended suspending Grover Connell from doing business under the department's Food for Peace program, charging that he had concealed ownership of a shipping agency representing foreign governments in the chartering of vessels carrying these food shipments. According to this official, Connell Rice & Sugar shipped 72 percent of all rice moved under the program in 1976.

Finally, Grover Connell was indicted in 1978 on six counts of violating federal law by illegally using a Korean rice dealer with ties to the South Korean government as his agent for sales to the government under the Food for Peace program. He was alleged to have paid the dealer, Tongun Park, $600,000 in commissions and then covered up the payments by sending them to the offshore bank account of a Korean company. The firm itself was reported to have paid Park $8 million in commissions on rice sales to Korea. The charges against Connell were dismissed in 1979 after Park, who was now a prosecution witness, changed his testimony, according to the Department of Justice.

The South Korean government subsequently sought to reduce its dependence on Connell Rice & Sugar for imports of its main food staple. However, according to a *Wall Street Journal* story in 1983, Grover Connell and his allies in Congress and the U.S. rice trade were making it difficult for South Korea to buy rice from rival exporters. Korean officials attributed their problems to Connell's campaign donations to a number of Democrats in the House of Representatives, many from rice-producing states. In 1982 a State Department official told Congress that Connell had threatened to use his influence to cut off foreign aid to South Korea unless the country bought his rice.

Connell Rice & Sugar's business allies in the United States included two California growers' cooperatives that were handling about 75 percent of the state's rice crop. Virtually all of the export portion of this crop was being brokered by Connell and sent to South Korea. According to a 1984 *Forbes* story, when the South Korean government ordered a shipment from another company, the cooperatives declined to sell except through Connell, which charged $35 a ton more than the other company's contract price. In 1992 Connell was cleared of allegations that it conspired to monopolize California's rice trade. The jury, however, could not agree on the broader issue of whether the company was guilty of restraint of trade. The U.S. Court of Appeals reinstated, in 1996, this part of the lawsuit by 70 rice growers against Connell.

Extending the Company's Scope in the 1980s

Grover Connell continued to foster ties with members of Congress in the 1980s. In 1989 his company distributed more honoraria, or speaking fees, to members than any other firm: about $100,000 in all. Most of the money was being paid to members of the House and Senate agricultural committees or members from major rice- and sugar-growing states, but congressional staff members also received such payments. According to a 1990 *Washington Post* story, at least once a week Grover Connell would invite a member of Congress to company headquarters for a report on what the legislative body was doing and then pay a fee of $2,000. Connell said he and his wife were also each making the maximum $25,000 a year in personal political donations to federal campaigns. Some $200,000 in corporate funds were donated to help build a media center for the Democratic Congressional Campaign Committee.

By this time the firm, having extended its scope of operations, had become The Connell Company, a holding company for its diverse activities. A 1988 *Forbes* story reported that Connell's expansion had begun in 1973 with leasing. In 1987 the company leased $600-million worth of railroad hopper cars, coal barges, shipping containers, aircraft, and office buildings. Connell reduced the risks of such a venture by leasing only to reliable corporate clients, handling goods with no risk of rapid depreciation, and taking payment in the form of an equity interest in the equipment at the end of the lease. Meanwhile, the lessee paid property taxes, maintenance, and insurance but realized its own benefit in the form of lower taxes.

The government of Zaire, long a client for rice shipments from Connell under the Food for Peace program, began leasing equipment for its government-run mining company, Gecamines, in the 1980s. In 1987 Connell became Gecamines' authorized supplier in the United States, with 12 U.S. companies and their subsidiaries required to sell through Connell. Grover Connell defended the country's ruler, Mobutu Sese Seko, against charges of massive human-rights abuses and corruption and, when Mobutu came to the United States during 1988–89, arranged for about 50 members of Congress to attend receptions for the visitor. Some members of Congress also visited Zaire under Connell's auspices. The company lost its contract with Gecamines later in 1990 under pressure from the World Bank, which argued that its fees were excessive. Nevertheless, Connell was said to be grossing more than $15 million a year from its dealings with Mobutu before he was overthrown in 1997.

Connell Realty & Development Co., a subsidiary, erected two office buildings in the 1980s on 107 acres in the township of Berkeley Heights, New Jersey. In 1997 this arm of the operations began construction of another office structure on an adjacent 63-acre parcel of this corporate park, with completion scheduled by the end of 1998. Plans called for more three more buildings at some future date, depending on leasing activity and demand. Connell Realty & Development had estimated operating revenue of $20 million in 1994.

The 1990s and Beyond

Connell Rice & Sugar Co. was exporting domestically grown rice, as well as rice grown in the Far East and other areas, to more than 100 countries in 1999. Within the United States, it was distributing rice to the brewing industry, wholesalers, food processors, and retail chains. It also had long-standing relationships for handling its storage, toll milling, and transportation.

Connell Rice & Sugar held an estimated share of more than 20 percent of the sugar and rice export market in 1998.

Subsidiary Connell International Co. was exporting a wide range of equipment and supplies to food-processing businesses in more than 100 countries. It also was serving as exclusive distributor for many of its suppliers and handling additional equipment and supplies on a private-label basis. These activities were being served by offices in Malaysia, Senegal, Taiwan, and Thailand.

The Connell & Co. subsidiary was the largest industrial refined sugar and flour broker in the United States, providing brokerage and sales services to food companies processing and marketing sugar, flour, cocoa and chocolate, vegetable oils, and bakery seeds, and engaged in packaging and bread-bag manufacturing. The sales service was operating out of Westfield; Oak Brook, Illinois; and Omaha, Nebraska. The purchasing service was operating out of Oak Brook.

Connell Foods, Inc. was importing canned food products from more than 50 countries for distribution throughout the United States to supermarkets, cooperatives, wholesale grocers, institutional distributors, food processors, and drug and restaurant chains. It maintained offices in Taiwan and Thailand.

Connell Finance Co., Inc. was active in virtually all aspects of equipment, project, and real-estate financing, with a portfolio of equipment having an original cost of over $800 million. The company had arranged over $10 billion of lease financings.

Connell Equipment Leasing Co., which became a division of Connell Finance in 1997, had been providing single-investor lease financing and equipment advisory services since 1982. It was financing all types of long-lived, durable assets, having completed over $125 million of financing of equipment such as forklift trucks, cranes, tractors, and front-end loaders.

Connell Gatco Co. was working directly with mining, quarrying, and construction companies, supplying them with parts, components, and equipment, such as bearings and loading, hauling, and dumping vehicles. It was also acting as an exclusive distributor for several leading manufacturers and providing marketing, technical, and after-sales support.

Connell Realty & Development Co. was developing corporate headquarters office buildings for both single and multiple tenants, arranging for both construction and permanent financing of these assets through its own funding. It had ownership positions in, or had arranged leasing financing for, more than 9 million square feet of commercial property space.

Connell Technologies Co. was providing equipment, real-estate financing, and asset-management services to the technology sector. It had acted as financial adviser to a large institutional investor for a $43-million lease of semiconductor manufacturing equipment with a major computer-chip manufacturer. Offices were in Westfield and California's Silicon Valley.

As the decade drew to a close, the parent Connell Company was firmly ensconced as the country's largest independent rice and sugar broker, while its heavy equipment leasing business was doing record business as well. Despite some negative press generated by the sometimes controversial political interests and lobbying of CEO Grover Connell, the company seemed assured of maintaining its hold on the markets it served into the next century.

Principal Subsidiaries

Connell Rice & Sugar Co.; Connell & Co.; Connell Foods, Inc.; Connell Finance Company, Inc.; Connell Equipment Leasing Company; Connell Gatco Company; Connell Realty & Development Co.; Connell Technologies Company.

Further Reading

"Appeals Court Resurrects Suit," *San Francisco Chronicle,* December 3, 1996, p. E2.

Babcock, Charles R., "Controversial Rice Broker Provides Plentiful Hill Speech Fees," *Washington Post,* July 11, 1989, p. A5.

——, "The Corporate King of Honoraria," *Washington Post,* March 20, 1990, pp. A1, A9.

Cloply, Michael, " 'Somebody Took the Profits'," *Forbes,* January 16, 1984, pp. 67–68.

"Foremost-McKesson, Connell Rice Accept FTC Orders on Commodity Transactions," *Wall Street Journal,* April 19, 1968, p. 12.

Fowler, Elizabeth M., "Easing of U.S. Curbs on Rice Is Sought by Exporter," *New York Times,* November 4, 1974, pp. 59, 61.

Garbarine, Rachelle, "Developer Stays the Course for a Bigger Office Park," *New York Times,* June 29, 1997, Sec. 9, p. 9.

King, Ralph, Jr., "A New Way to Beat Inflation," *Forbes,* January 11, 1988, pp. 264–65.

Lachica, Eduardo, "Seoul Runs Afoul of U.S. Rice Trader," *Wall Street Journal,* July 7, 1983, p. 26.

Pound, Edward T., "Connell Loses Lucrative Contract to Supply a Mining Firm in Zaire," *Wall Street Journal,* November 26, 1990, p. B5.

"Rice Trader Indicted in Dealing with Park," *New York Times,* May 27, 1976, p. 6.

Robbins, William, "Ex-U.S. Aide Scores Main Rice Exporter," *New York Times,* May 1, 1977, p. 23.

——, "Korean Link Hinted in New U.S. Inquiry," *New York Times,* November 1, 1976, p. 3.

—Robert Halasz

Conso International Corporation

513 North Duncan Bypass
Union, South Carolina 29379
U.S.A.
(864) 427-9004
Fax: (864) 427-8820
Web site: http://www.conso.com

Public Company
Incorporated: 1993
Employees: 1,550
Sales: $125.51 million (1998)
Stock Exchanges: NASDAQ
Ticker Symbol: CNSO
NAIC: 313221 Narrow Fabric Mills; 314999 All Other
    Miscellaneous Textile

Conso International Corporation is the world's largest manufacturer of decorative trimmings for the home furnishings industry. Along with its subsidiaries, including the popularly known operations of Simplicity Patterns and British Trimmings, Conso produces and sells a full range of knitted and woven fringes, decorative cords, tasseled accessories, jacquard and other woven braids and apparel trims, sewing tapes, and supplies and instructional material for home sewing of apparel and decorative items. Conso also distributes decorative window accoutrements and other home furnishings accessories. Through a worldwide sales force, its products are marketed to manufacturers, distributors, and retailers. Manufacturing facilities are located in the United States, the United Kingdom, Mexico, and India.

Origins

The Conso Co. began manufacturing millinery trimmings for both men's and ladies' hats in 1867, right after the Civil War. It maintained a steady presence in the domestic decorative products market for much of its first 125 years. By the middle of the 20th century, the company was branching out into the manufacture of curtain ties and window shade fringes sold through such mass merchants as Kmart and Sears, as well as about 300 small drapery stores and distributors. Sales swelled to about $55 million a year during this time, and the company was employing a workforce of 1,200 people.

Conso was shuttled among a string of corporate parents beginning the 1960s: Sara Lee in 1968; Consolidated Foods in the early 1970s; and Springs Industries in 1979. Neither Conso nor its two major competitors, Holyoke, Massachusetts-based Mastex Industries and Lending Textiles of Montgomery, Pennsylvania, seemed to focus on new products or marketing approaches. In fact, Consolidated Foods all but shut down Conso's product development and marketing departments in order to save money. Conso languished under its various owners, and by 1985 only 200 employees labored in its approximately 220,000-square-foot plant in a depressed part of the textile town of Union, South Carolina. Sales fell to around $12 million, while productivity reached a new low, with orders taking up to ten weeks to fill.

New Start As an Independent: 1980s

Enter Cary Findlay, Jr., an accountant with the Charlotte, North Carolina office of Deloitte Haskins & Sells, who, in the mid-1980s, was doing research for top buyout specialists. In 1986, at age 47, Findlay quit his job and teamed up with old friend Warren Pollock, a retired textile executive, to form Carolinas Capital Funds Group, their own buyout firm. They scraped together some capital, and began to search for unwanted subsidiaries of big corporations and individual, privately owned companies looking to sell.

The partners bought the struggling Conso Products for just over $5 million, financing most of the deal with $5 million in asset-based financing and a personal note belonging to Findlay and his wife, also an ex-Deloitte accountant. For equity, the Carolinas Group had just $55,000 from the Findlays, $55,000 from Pollock, $140,000 from two Conso managers, and a vision. They would inject new capital into the business, add new products and a sales effort, and, making use of the already existing distribution network, create a splash in the trimmings market.

The Findlays contracted with Wesley Mancini, a well-known furniture fabric designer, to create a new trimming and tassel line suitable for high-end furniture, their Empress line, which debuted in 1987. Together they compiled a color catalogue and binders of sample cards showing the company's approximately 2,000 possible combinations of styles and colors and printed a 28-page brochure with step-by-step lessons to teach decorators, salespeople, and retail customers how cords, fringes, and tassels could be used, simultaneously creating demand for their product. They also instituted a four-point plan: Conso would produce goods of consistently high quality, offer hundreds of colors and styles grouped into collections, charge reasonable prices, and offer rapid delivery.

Their timing could not have been better. The trim market follows a feast or famine cycle, and in 1987 sales were beginning to rise as graying baby boomers were nestling deeper into their homes, and Victorian-era symbols of warmth and comfort were enjoying renewed popularity. Sales increased to $15 million by the end of that first year. In order to expand its customer base in the Midwest in 1987, Conso acquired R. Nyren Company of Chicago, a division of Lea & Sachs, Inc. that specialized in the manufacture and sale of industrial trimmings, primarily for flag companies. It also purchased Hamilton Web, a manufacturer of woven braids and jacquards, based in Providence, Rhode Island, and in 1988 bought Lorina Embroideries of Guttenberg, New Jersey. All operations were transplanted to Union in a move to manufacture all goods in-house. By 1989, with the use of decorative trim on a decided upswing, and C&A Home Fabrics, a large domestic upholstery mill, selling Conso trim, Conso's sales had doubled to about $23 million. Eighty jobbers now offered the Empress line, up from ten in 1987, and the company was experiencing a delivery crunch. Moreover, as Findlay noted in an article in *HFD*, Conso was in the practice of allowing its customers to place special orders for specific colors, requiring no minimum for an order. Soon everyone wanted to come out with their own colors, Findlay recalled, adding that "with so many special orders, it bogged down delivery." In response, the company began setting increased minimum orders. Based on the success of the Empress collection, Conso introduced its more upscale Imperial line for the 1989 market year and increased its minimum yardage for orders along with its color range.

By 1992, Conso was recognized as the leading producer of decorative trimmings for draperies and upholstered furniture, controlling approximately 75 percent of its market. It had a sales staff of 15 regional sales managers, sales offices in New York and Hickory, North Carolina, and a 25,000-square-foot handwork *maquiladora* in Juarez, Mexico. The company had introduced a

third line, the Duchess Collection, in 1991, available exclusively to the furniture trade. It now sold directly to most of the Carolina upholstered furniture manufacturers, including Drexel Heritage, Hickory, Baker, and Sherrill, and to textile retailers Hancock's, Calico Corners, and Fabric Bonanza. In the drapery segment, major mills customers included Burlington Industries, Springs Mills, J.P. Stevens, and WestPoint Pepperell. The Conso product line had expanded to include laces and jacquard trimmings for the craft and apparel market, and the company's non-wovens department was making some of the decorative strapping used in the automotive business.

Expansion Overseas: 1990s

Conso had another big growth year in 1993. It made its first public offering of common stock, becoming the only publicly traded company to specialize in decorative trimmings, and simultaneously acquired British Trimmings, the largest producer of similar products in the United Kingdom, for $3.3 million cash and 115,900 of Conso's unregistered shares. British Trimmings had opened its doors for business in 1929, and had a history not unlike Conso's. Founded in England at a time when the hat trade was flourishing, it quickly outgrew its original plant and continued to expand at a steady pace, despite a period of recession, to become a woven and knitted trimmings manufacturer for upholstery and garments. Further growth through takeovers of competitors and suppliers followed, until British Trimmings was itself bought and sold several times during the 1970s and 1980s. Following its merger with Conso Products in 1993, British Trimmings was assigned the role of sales for the joint companies in continental Europe, the Pacific Rim, and the Middle East.

Conso continued its growth in the United Kingdom in 1994 with the purchase that June of Wendy Cushing Trimmings, Ltd. of London, a privately owned company which enjoyed sales of $800,000 during the year preceding its purchase. Cushing, who ran the company, was a highly regarded designer of original and restoration decoration trimmings and tassels; she had previously had designs in a number of the Collections marketed by both Conso and British Trimmings and now joined the Conso staff. Following the addition of Wendy Cushing Trimmings, Conso undertook to expand its foreign sales base beyond the United Kingdom by opening a new export sales office in England in 1994 to serve continental Europe and the Middle East, and a similar office in Miami that same year to serve the Caribbean and Latin America. At the time, Conso exported about ten percent of its sales. In early 1995, the company also opened an office in Thailand to serve its Pacific Rim customers, and British Trimmings produced its first wholesale catalogue, which doubled in size during the next four years.

British Trimmings significantly increased Conso's revenues. In fiscal 1994, the company's sales totaled $41.6 million—an increase of 81 percent in one quarter alone. Findlay stepped down as chief executive officer and president in May 1995 in order, according to his publicly delivered statement, to devote his attention primarily to the company's strategic goals in the areas of acquisitions, expansion of product lines, and international operations. Findlay, who maintained control of 53 percent of Conso's stock and stayed on as chair, was rumored locally to have resigned for other reasons as well: negative press surrounding the well-publicized murder of two young boys by their mother, a Union resident and Conso employee with ties to the Findlay family.

However, within half a year of Findlay's change of status, Conso had purchased a new production and distribution facility in London to house the operations of Wendy Cushing Trimmings and a subsidiary of British Trimmings. The company as a whole had sales of $63 million in 1995, one third of which came from British Trimmings, and was filling 95 percent of its orders in three days. And the trend toward fringe showed no signs of abating. In the 1980s, upholstered furniture accounted for 36 percent of average annual furniture sales of $24 billion in the United States. By the mid-1990s, that figure was up to 46 percent of annual sales of $31 billion. British Trimmings enjoyed a prestigious decorating coup when, in early 1996, the British Royal Family hired its Wendy Cushing Trimmings subsidiary to consult in the restoration of Windsor Castle. Following this, Cary Findlay registered to sell about a quarter of the shares of his 52.4 percent stake in Conso in the over-the-counter market.

Further Acquisitions

Conso's next move was in the direction of further acquisitions. In March 1996, for $385,962, it purchased the assets of the Claesson Company, an innovative design company of window accessory products, owned by Margareta Claesson, who became manager of Conso's U.S.-based Decorative Accessories Division. The Claesson Company, whose sales were more than $800,000 in 1995, moved to Union, South Carolina, where it joined Conso's existing decorative brassware and tiebacks operations. In September 1997, for $262,000, Conso added the assets of HFDC, Inc., whose products included design rings and brackets, and thereby broadened Conso's decorative accessory products. Two years later, it acquired Simplicity Patterns Company for $33 million in cash plus liabilities of about $21.5 million. Simplicity, a fully integrated design, manufacturing, distribution, and marketing organization, founded in 1927, was one of the world's largest producers of instructional patterns and catalogues and had net sales of $55 million for its fiscal year ended January 1998.

When Cary Findlay reassumed the position of president and chief executive of Conso in August 1998, the company was clearly the industry leader with a new 86,000-square-foot distribution center adjacent to its plant in Union. Conso's fiscal 1996 return on equity had been 21 percent and its return on assets 14—two to three times the average for the Russell 2000 index of small companies. Conso's net income for that year increased 39 percent to $6.4 million from $5.5 million in the prior year; net sales increased 18.6 percent to $70.7 million from $59.6 million. In fiscal 1997, that figure rose 3.9 percent to $73.4 million and the total stock market value of the company reached $70 million. British Trimmings continued to hold its share of the British wholesale market, and catalogue sales continued to expand as the company instituted plans to introduce two new collections. In addition, while the trimmings market continued to grow at a rate of six to ten percent each year, Conso's growth was even greater because of its ever-larger share of the pie, a situation assured it as the sole owner, operator, and stockpiler of the no-longer built machinery necessary to fabricate its many varieties of trim.

Yet company gains were modest overall, and by September 1998, Conso was reporting a shrinking gross margin for the past two years as a result of pricing pressures at low and medium price points. Sales results for fiscal 1998 were well below the strong gains reported in 1995 and 1996 and the four percent gain reported in 1997. Despite an upturn in fourth quarter earnings, net sales were down slightly at $72 million while earnings dropped to $5 million from the prior year's $7 million. In fact, though export sales increased from 11.5 to 11.9 percent, European operations were harder hit than domestic, an outcome due to the strong pound sterling and high interest rates, which created difficult trading conditions for United Kingdom manufacturers.

In response, Conso took measures in 1998 to reduce production and overhead costs; it began production at a new hand assembly plant in India, India Trimmings, reduced 13.8 percent of its personnel in the United States and 25.6 percent of its workers in the United Kingdom, and undertook construction of a new 33,000-square-foot dye house facility in Union, which, when complete, would more than double its capacity to dye yarn in the United States, reducing yarn inventory levels and outside dying costs. Management viewed Conso as a consumer products company and turned its attention to further acquisitions, with special interest given to home decorating companies that would expand Conso's existing product lines. The company's name was changed to Conso International Corporation as it pursued a global growth strategy that also included: consolidating certain British Trimmings operations into domestic operations; cross-merchandising among units; expanding the customer base; and expanding international production and distribution operations and export sales.

Principal Subsidiaries

British Trimmings Ltd.; Wendy Cushing Trimmings Ltd.; India Trimmings Limited; Val-Mex, S.A. de C.V.; Simplicity Capital Corporation; Simplicity Holdings; Simplicity Patterns Co., Inc.

Further Reading

Block, Toddi Gutner, "On the Fringes," *Forbes,* October 23, 1995, p. 314.

Burritt, Chris, "Around the South: Top Company in Union Hit with Scandal Amid Trial," *Atlanta Journal and Constitution,* July 21, 1995, p. 5D.

"Carolinas Capital Funds Group, Inc. and Springs Industries Announce Sale of the Conso Products Division of Graber Industries," *Business Wire,* October 6, 1986.

Cohne, Marci, "Renascent Conso Blossoms," *HFD—The Weekly Home Furnishings Newspaper,* May 8, 1989, p. 19.

"Conso Products Company Expands in London," *PR Newswire,* December 28, 1995.

"Conso to Purchase Simplicity Patterns," *Spartanburg (South Carolina) Herald,* June 11, 1998, p. B4.

"Keeping in Trim," *Home Furnishings,* September 1998, p. 22.

Lankford, Kimberly, "Simple Things," *Kiplinger's Personal Finance Magazine,* July 1997, p. 57.

Treiser, C. Kinou, "In Trim," *Investor's Business Daily,* January 19, 1996, p. A3.

"With All the Trimmings," *Spartanburg (South Carolina) Herald,* February 16, 1997, p. E1.

Wyman, Lissa, "Conso: Trimmings Sail As Sails Swell," *HFD—The Weekly Home Furnishings Newspaper,* April 6, 1992, p. 88.

—Carrie Rothburd

CROWN Vantage

Crown Vantage Inc.

300 Lakeside Drive
Oakland, California 94612-3592
U.S.A.
(510) 874-3400
(800) 421-8289
Fax: (510) 874-3531
Web site: http://www.crownvantage.com

Public Company
Incorporated: 1995
Employees: 3,550
Sales: $851 million (1998)
Stock Exchanges: NASDAQ
Ticker Symbol: CVAN
NAIC: 322121 Paper (Except Newsprint) Mills

Crown Vantage Inc., a relatively new company in the U.S. paper industry, produces and markets paper products tailored to meet the special needs of niche markets for a diverse array of end uses, including specialty magazines and catalogs, books and computer manuals, financial printing and corporate communications, as well as packaging and labels for food and retail products, coffee filters, and disposable medical garments. Operating through two segments—printing and publishing papers and specialty papers—Crown Vantage has three pulp mills that produce about three-quarters of its internal pulp needs and 31 paper machines located at eight mills in the United States and two mills in Scotland. The company has the capacity to manufacture more than one million tons a year of value-added paper products.

A Mid-1990s Spin-Off

In August 1995, the James River Corporation, a Richmond-based maker of Dixie disposable dishware and Brawny paper towels, created a new spin-off company to assume its communications papers business and part of its packaging business, and to leave it free to concentrate on producing consumer tissue and paperboard. James River had grown from a one-mill specialty paper operation in 1969 to become one of the world's largest specialty paper and paper products companies by the mid-1990s with extensive operations in both the United States and Europe. However, beginning in 1993, the market for printing papers began to loosen up, with prices heavily discounted and inventories high. As a result, James River was eager to turn its attention to consumer products as a means of paying down its heavy load of long-term debt. James River created the spin-off, Crown Vantage Inc., in order to take over its printing, writing, and specialty paper operations, thereby leveraging $580 million to reduce its debt.

At the time of the spin-off, Crown Vantage's business operations were organized into four divisions: specialty packaging and converting papers in Michigan, New Jersey, and Louisiana; coated groundwood papers in Louisiana; business publishing papers in New Hampshire; and the Curtis Fine Papers Group in Massachusetts, Delaware, Virginia, and Scotland. James River shareholders were given all the stock in the new holding company.

The Crown Vantage name recalled the Crown Zellerbach Corporation of San Francisco, from whom James River had purchased its paper-related assets in 1986. Spun off from James River, the new operation known as Crown Vantage, located in Oakland, California, began business in 1995. It had a production capacity of one million tons of paper and more than 500,000 tons of pulp, 33 machines on 11 sites, about 4,100 employees, $1 billion in sales, and $625 million in debt. Approximately 120,000 acres of managed forest were also included in the transfer to the new company.

The new company's declared business strategy was to shift a major portion of its production away from commodity grade papers to higher value-added products. Toward that end, it immediately began to implement a capital spending program to support to upgrade its value-added mix of products, reduce costs, improve productivity and invest in customer service. Under the direction of chairman and chief executive officer Ernest S. Leopold, who had been James River's executive vice-president for communications papers, Crown Vantage set up a capital expenditure budget of $485 million for 1995 through 1999, with $350 million targeted for maintenance and environmental projects and $135 million earmarked for profit-enhancement projects. In 1996, the company spent approximately $40 million to rebuild one of the

Company Perspectives:

Crown Vantage's strategic focus is to develop, manufacture and market printing, publishing and specialty packaging and converting papers. The company takes pride in the development of committed, long-term relationships with customers as well as in its innovative products and service. Its strategy is to differentiate itself from the rest of the industry by focusing on specialty markets and niches—the higher value-added grades of papers: text and cover stock, for instance, used for annual reports and other high-end printing, and the coated publication papers for special interest magazines, catalogs and covers.

machines at its Louisiana coated groundwood mill. This modernization effort gave the mill ten percent more capacity in the production of catalog and magazine grade papers at the lower end of the 45- to 70-lb. range. It also reduced its per-ton costs and improved manufacturing quality. As a result of both of these advantages, Crown Vantage was able in 1996 to corner about five percent of the North American coated groundwood market. Recognizing these accomplishments, the *Los Angeles Times* named Crown Vantage to its list of the 100 best-performing companies in California in 1996.

The middle to late 1990s continued to be a very rocky time for the North American paper industry as a whole. In 1995, sales were strong across the board, and Crown Vantage, one of the industry leaders, achieved revenues in excess of $1 billion. However, beginning in 1996 and continuing through 1998, the industry's fortunes declined steeply. This decline was the result of the Asian economic crisis that sent paper imports into the United States to record-level highs and deflated paper prices across the board. Despite these weak market conditions, Crown Vantage achieved and maintained a sold-out position on coated publication papers from 1996 to 1998; yet the company's sales base was far from certain, and management felt it necessary to implement strategic, cost-cutting moves.

In mid-1997, the company decided to close its smallest mill in Newark, Delaware. The two-machine, non-integrated operation had the capacity to make 10,000 tons per year of uncoated premium printing papers, but since January 1997, it had produced only very short runs of specialty grade papers with the yearly total stopping short of 2,000 tons. Management consolidated premium specialty grade production at its Massachusetts and Ypsilanti, Michigan, mills as well, moving economy text and cover production from those mills to its New Hampshire base. The company also sold 108,000 acres of timberland in New England and the Southeast for $36 million to pay off some of its long-term bank debt. Yet even with such efforts, Crown Vantage experienced losses for the year totaling $32 million, due largely to the continued low price of paper products in North America.

In 1998, the demand for paper in the United States remained strong, but imports continued to flood the market, and the industry continued to suffer from the ongoing influx of cheap imported papers, which covered a range of paper grades and product markets. The price of Crown Vantage stock plunged 63 percent to reach a low of $3.25 per share, lower than the minimum $5 maintenance standard required for Nasdaq listing. The company lost $8.8 million in the first half of 1998, roughly $8 million more than it had lost the year before. By year's end, it reported a net loss of $140.5 million or $14.79 per share, which, after a major fixed asset write-down and other one-time charges, translated to an operating loss of $8.3 million. In order to maintain its competitiveness, Crown Vantage asked and was allowed to continue its Nasdaq listing pending improvement of share value. The company also implemented additional moves to cut operating expenses. Per ton costs, helped along by a decline in the price of natural gas and more favorable energy contracts, fell 3.6 percent due to lowered pulp costs and lower energy costs, as well as from lower chemical usage and improved operating expenses. As a result, company costs fell 12 percent during the next 12 months.

The company also changed its orientation to focus its efforts, realigning operations into two major businesses: Specialty Papers and Printing and Publishing Papers. It combined its coated and uncoated printing papers into a single business and assigned each of its two new business divisions a vice-president of manufacturing and a second vice-president for sales and marketing. At the same time, it reduced its workforce by seven percent. With the retirement of Leopold and the election of Robert Olah to the post of chief executive officer in early 1999, Crown Vantage instituted the organizational changes necessary to focus on becoming a marketing-driven company with the goal of increasing its top-line revenues.

The Future: Capitalizing on Upticks in the Market

Management also focused on initiatives to improve the company's financial structure and reduce its debt. In 1998, after reaching an agreement with James River, by this time known as Fort James Corporation, to drop mutual monetary claims dating back to the spin off, Crown Vantage received $33 million in pay-in-kind notes. It was simultaneously successful in settling a six-year property tax dispute it had engaged in with the town of Berlin, New Hampshire, concerning the taxability of factory machinery. The settlement of this suit, which held that machinery was not assessable, reduced the company's tax bill by $2 million per year and allowed it to reverse accruals for withheld taxes in the amount of $9 million.

However, even such positive turns of events could not stem the slump in the paper industry. In early 1999, with prices of paper and pulp near historical lows, the company decided to divest its most commodity-oriented paper and pulp mills, those in Berlin and Gorham, New Hampshire, for about $45 million in order to raise money to pay down its debt. The sale of the mill to American Tissue Company, a New York-based papermaker with Wisconsin operations, was also part of a move to explore new supply chain relationships, to build on sales and marketing while outsourcing manufacturing operations. The agreement with American Tissue created a strategic alliance to produce some of Crown Vantage's high value-added brands. At the same time, Crown Vantage began to outsource distribution and warehousing operations in New Jersey, Chicago, and Los Angeles. It also developed a web site to promote sales and service to a new market—the small-quantity consumer—which had been underserved traditionally through existing distribution channels. Lastly, Crown Vantage expanded its efforts to take advantage of its relationships with multinational companies to expand it sales of packaging papers worldwide.

Because of the diversity of Crown Vantage's markets and the broad range of its product lines, it had never had large-scale production numbers in specific markets. In fact, by reconfiguring its operations, Crown Vantage hoped to buffer itself from declines in the non-specialty, mass-produced paper markets. Thus, while analysts looked for improvement in the paper industry to begin in the second half of 1999, projecting a yet stronger outlook for 2000, Crown Vantage management hoped for the balance of supply and demand to tip in its favor earlier and entered 1999 ready to market its products aggressively. Fortunately, customer demand remained strong, and no competitors had announced the development of new paper mills in North America. Crown Vantage's top priorities thus included: paying down its debt and growing in profitable segments, as well as edging its share price back upward. In order to reach its goals, it planned to engage in product development to further shift its base to higher value-added products and to replace the sales volume in specialty paper it had lost during the last two years. As it celebrated the 125th anniversary of its Guardbridge

facilities in Scotland and the 75th anniversary of its Port Huron, Michigan, plant mid-year, Crown Vantage also targeted markets for its specialty packaging and converted papers, including: food service, label, multi-wall bag, technical and industrial, flexible packaging, paperboard packaging, and gift wrap. The company's target strategies included sending sales and product specialists out to serve these specialized niches.

Principal Operating Units

Specialty Papers; Printing and Publishing Papers.

Further Reading

"CEO Interview," *Wall Street Transcript,* May 10, 1999, p. 32.

Guest, David, "Guardbridge Crowns Changes with a New Standard: Paper Mill Located in Scotland," *Pulp & Paper International,* October 1995, p. 23.

"James River Plans Debt Offering; James River Corp. Spinning Off New Paper Company," *Pulp & Paper,* August 1995, p. 23.

Jimenez, Ralph, "Mill Town faces Uncertain Future," *Boston Globe,* October 25, 1998, p. 1.

Swann, Charles E., "Crown Vantage: Company Profile," *American Papermaker,* January 1996, p. 25.

—Carrie Rothburd

CULP

Culp, Inc.

101 South Main Street
Post Office Box 2686
High Point, North Carolina 27261
U.S.A.
(336) 889-5161
Fax: (336) 889-8339
Web site: http://www.culpinc.com

Public Company
Incorporated: 1972 as R.G. Culp and Associates
Employees: 4,300
Sales: $477 million (1998)
Stock Exchanges: New York
Ticker Symbol: CFI
NAIC: 31321 Broadwoven Fabric Mills

Culp, Inc. is a world leader in the manufacture and marketing of upholstery fabrics for furniture, as well as a leading producer of mattress fabrics known as tickings. Over 3,000 of the company's upholstery fabrics are used in residential and commercial furniture applications by such manufacturers as Furniture Brands International, Bassett, Flexsteel, La-Z-Boy, LADD, Hon Industries, Herman Miller, and Steelcase. The company's 1,000 mattress ticking styles are sold to manufacturers Sealy, Serta, Simmons, and Spring Air. The company focuses on fabrics that have broad appeal in the promotional and popular-priced categories of furniture and bedding. Culp operates three regional distribution and 17 manufacturing facilities, which include a variety of weaving, printing and finishing operations, as well as yarn and greige (unfinished base fabric) production. These operations enable Culp to have one of the broadest product lines in its industry.

1970s Origins as a Fabric Converter

Culp has long been known as an aggressive mill that combines a breadth of offerings at a variety of price points. The company's commitment never to turn away a customer—and to treat even the smallest as if it were the most important—was established by Robert Culp, Jr. Culp founded R.G. Culp and Associates in 1972 after a successful career in the upholstery fabrics business.

At age 55, having worked for 30 years for Golding Brothers, a mattress ticking, upholstery, and drapery fabrics supplier, Culp, Jr., leased a portion of a knitting mill in High Point, North Carolina, and converted it to offices and a warehouse. He used much of his personal savings to finance the new company and appealed to several friends for additional investments. Howard Dunn, a former colleague at Golding, joined Culp in starting the company, as did Culp's son, Robert III, who, at 25, had a master's degree from the Wharton School of Business at the University of Pennsylvania.

Culp, Jr., maintained leadership of the company until the late 1980s, at which point, Robert Culp III took over as chief executive officer in 1988 and chairman in 1990. The business continued to adhere to Culp's philosophy of "winning the ties," influencing customers to do business with Culp because of the company's commitment to serve customers.

Originally the company was strictly a fabric converter, something of a wholesaler in the fabric world. Specifically, R.G. Culp and Associates took orders from furniture and mattress makers and arranged to have different mills make the necessary cloth. One of the company's first big customers was Stuart Furniture, forerunner of Klaussner Furniture in Asheboro, North Carolina, to whom Culp sold a cloth originally designed to line caskets when Stuart asked for a fabric to cover sofas and chairs. The company had first-year sales of $1.4 million.

A Full-Line, Full-Service Manufacturer in the 1980s

The furniture industry made a dramatic shift in the late 1970s when furniture makers began to buy fabric directly from upholstery fabric manufacturers. As a result, R. G. Culp and Associates, with sales of $22 million as a converter, moved into the manufacturing arena in 1978. It leased its first plant, Upholstery Prints, in Burlington, North Carolina, where it successfully pioneered the method of transferring prints onto upholstery fabric using heat, the same method used to print designs on t-shirts. In the early 1980s, flock fabrics were becoming popular for the first time, and Culp's method of transfer printing proved less expensive than the traditional wet printing. The innovation thus created a niche for the company and fueled its growth.

As a manufacturer, Bob Culp dreamed of seeing the newly renamed Culp, Inc. become a full-line, full-service producer capable of fulfilling a broad range of customer needs. Yet of the three men who ran the company in the late 1970s, only Howard Dunn had any experience in manufacturing. Nonetheless, in 1979, the company opened Culp Ticking to convert mattress ticking, and, by 1983, was manufacturing the majority of its product line.

Culp also reasoned that by having a stake in several market segments, such as residential furniture and bedding, and manufacturing a broad range of fabrics types at various price points, his company could withstand the cyclical nature of fabric sales. "That way no matter what is hot, we have products in that area," Culp observed. To achieve this end, the company embarked upon a determined capital investment program with the long-term goal of becoming a vertically integrated producer of a broad range of goods serving a variety of upholstery markets. In the early 1980s, Culp made several acquisitions: a former Cannon Mills fabric plant that produced jacquard and dobby woven fabrics in Graham, North Carolina (1982); a dyeing and finishing plant formerly operated by Dan River in Burlington, North Carolina (1983); and in 1985, it purchased the Baxter Kelly plant in Anderson, South Carolina, which produced woven velvets. Culp also invested $27 million in new equipment between 1983 and 1986. To help pay for its acquisitions, reduce its bank borrowing and finance further growth, the company went public in 1983, offering about one million shares of common stock for sale.

Culp was well on its way to becoming a major player in the upholstery market by the mid-1980s with a reputation not just for good value, but for service as well. By 1985, sales were at $100 million; by 1986, they totaled $150 million—$113 million from upholstery fabric, $22 million from mattress ticking, and $15 million from industrial fabrics. Yet in spite of its

growth, the company continued to employ a tight-knit, family business management structure. Almost all of the sales and management personnel in the company came up through its ranks, and when people left key positions, they were replaced from the ranks.

A major part of Culp's development program was its increased reliance on a distinctive "stock distribution system" that it had established at its inception. Beginning in the 1980s, Culp committed a set level of production each month to popular fabric styles and colors, which were kept in stock for immediate distribution to small furniture manufacturers from its warehouses around the country. At the same time, the company's special order system was set in place to attend to the needs of its larger manufacturers. All fabrics went to central distribution centers, which shipped directly to the large customers, while warehouses around the country served the smaller customers.

Aggressive Spending and Acquisitions in the Late 1980s

By the mid- to late 1980s, Culp was set to expand again, launching a program aimed at reducing lead times to customers and making it the foremost manufacturer of textured and jacquard upholstery fabric. It began plans to expand its mattress ticking division, purchasing a printing plant in Stokesdale, North Carolina, in 1986 from Fieldcrest Cannon where it began to process all of its printed ticking. The following year, Culp contracted with a company in Germany for a large number of jacquard looms for its plant in Graham and installed 90 state-of-the-art dobby looms in a new 100,000 square foot plant it constructed in Pageland, South Carolina. In 1988, it bought the tufting and flocking business of Quaker fabric.

While Culp was expanding product lines and services, becoming a vertically integrated firm, it was also changing its business organization, reorganizing along product lines as part of an effort to dispel the image of Culp as a producer of converted goods and seconds. In 1987, its upholstery business was still divided into a textured and prints division and a tufted and woven pile fabrics division. In place of these two divisions, it began to market upscale and contemporary patterns, regardless of price point, with the Culp Decorative Fabrics label, while country and commercial designs were assigned the Culp name. Culp also undertook in 1987 to become known as a producer of original, innovative fabrics, expanding its design staff significantly to implement a new emphasis on design.

Culp now manufactured velvets, flocks, wovens, and jacquards as well as mattress ticking, and business was strong in the midst of a persistently sluggish home furnishings market. The company also had a growing overseas market, long before exports became a popular catchword in American textile circles, accounting in 1989 for $5.3 million of Culp sales. The company reported a 27 percent gain in net income for fiscal 1991, attributing its steady growth to three primary factors: increased exports, increased domestic shipments to existing accounts, and its diversity of offerings. Despite its heavy emphasis on acquisitions and capital investment during the late 1980s, the company had no substantial long-term debt. At the close of fiscal 1991, a year during which its capital spending totaled $11 million (capping off a five-year period during which capital expenses totaled $46 million), Culp's long-term debt amounted to less than $17 million on a total capital base of approximately $66 million. Yet the company was experiencing growing pains as a result of its flurry of acquisitions and decided to halt growth in order to fine tune its manufacturing expertise, upgrade facilities, and "learn the business."

In fact, Culp was at the leading edge of its market in its move toward vertical integration. Beginning in the early 1990s, consolidation became common among upholstery fabric makers as a means of accommodating customers. As furniture manufacturers and retailers got larger, suppliers had to increase in size to serve them. Large, vertical mills had the advantage over small ones because they could meet the volume and delivery requirements of large furniture manufacturers and retailers. Culp thus continued to increase its vertical capacities, beginning with its 1993 acquisition of Rossville Mills, Chromatex, and Rossville Velours for $34 million. In 1995, it bought Rayonese Textile, Inc. and then invested $13 million to add 72 air-jet jacquard looms to this subsidiary to triple production of bedding and furnishing fabrics. It added privately held Phillips Mills for $47 million in 1997, giving it additional velvet and printing capacity. Later that year, it bought out its supplier, Artee Industries, a yarn manufacturer, for $17 million and capped off the year by purchasing Dan River's spun yarn operation in Wetumpka, Alabama.

In 1994, Culp reorganized its management structure again to accommodate its greater capacity. Led by a five-person team of executive officers who made business decisions collectively, the company was divided into six business units which handled day-to-day operations: Velvets/Prints, Culp Textures, Rossville/Chromatex, Culp Home Fashions, Phillips Mills, and Artee Industries. Each unit was run independently by a team comprised of a representative from manufacturing, marketing, finance, human resources, and design. Each unit also had its own sales force. The new structure was intended to allow the company to work more closely with customers on product development and to foster a focused effort on selling. It would also allow for an emphasis on internal operations. In fact, general and administrative expenses declined while on-time deliveries increased, and between 1989 and 1996, workplace accidents decreased by 86 percent while labor turnover dropped 25 percent, attendance improved 20 percent, and the company gave its employees a yearly wage increase.

Niche Markets and Exports in the 1990s

By 1996, Culp's overseas market had taken off with sales to Canada and Mexico, Europe, the Middle East, Asia, and Australia. Between 1989 and 1996, international sales increased at a rate of 47 percent annually from $5.3 million to $70 million, or 25 percent of sales. The emphasis on overseas selling meant that even when the domestic market in upholstery fabric was down, Culp could continue to grow. As a group at that time, upholstery manufacturers were among the most prolific exporters in the American textile industry with many companies exporting 15 to 30 percent of their fabrics. Culp was perhaps the segment's largest exporter with exports totaling about 29 percent of sales for fiscal 1998. Estimates for the year put the domestic residential fabric market at about $2.2 billion and the international market at about twice that.

However, shaky economies in many important international markets began to temper Culp's export success. Business also began to slow in the United States in 1997, although the company still achieved a more than five percent gain in domestic sales due primarily to significantly higher sales and shipments of mattress ticking. Culp's streak of 21 quarters during which it posted consistently higher earnings ended that year. During 1998, weak international sales of printed flock upholstery fabrics and Culp's recent spate of acquisitions led the company once again to decide to take a breather to unify related products and marketing programs. It further streamlined operations by cutting back to four divisions, which encompassed all of its manufacturing and marketing operations: Culp Decorative Fabrics, Culp Home Fashions; Culp Velvets/Prints, and Culp Yarns. The company also began to direct efforts toward specialty markets: fabrics for infant car seats, strollers, and cribs; RVs and van conversions; slip-on automotive seat covers; marine applications; and outdoor furniture. Culp also returned its focus to its strength—customer service—investing in a proprietary software, CulpLink, which allowed customers to view information online concerning their current and past orders. Finally, Culp opened its Howard L. Dunn Design Center, a state-of-the-art facility where customers were invited to view new products and participate in product development.

Principal Subsidiaries

Rayonese Textile, Inc. (Canada); Culp International, Inc.

Principal Divisions

Phillips Weaving; Artee Yarns.

Principal Operating Units

Culp Decorative Fabrics; Culp Home Fashions; Culp Velvets/Prints; Culp Yarns.

Further Reading

Duff, Mike, "Culp, Inc.; Ready for the Big Leagues," *HFD—The Weekly Home Furnishings Newspaper,* April 13, 1987, p. 1.
Krouse, Peter, "Textile Tiger," *News & Record,* September, 7, 1997, p. E1.
McCurry, John W., "Culp Contends for Upholstery's Crown," *Textile World,* March 1996, p. 56.
——, "Upholstery Mills Chase Soft Fabric," *Textile World,* November 1998, p. 76.
Williams, Christopher, "Culp's Performance Goes Against Fabric of Textiles," *News and Observer (North Carolina),* November 1997, p. 22.

—Carrie R. Rothburd

dELiA*s Inc.

435 Hudson Street
New York, New York 10014
U.S.A.
(212) 807-9060
Fax: (212) 807-9060
Web site: http://www.delias.com

Public Company
Incorporated: 1993 as dELiA*s LLC
Employees: 1,700
Sales: $158.4 million (1998)
Stock Exchanges: NASDAQ
Ticker Symbol: DLIA
NAIC: 45411 Electronic Shopping & Mail-Order Houses

dELiA*s Inc. sells apparel, accessories, athletic gear, footwear, and home furnishings through several direct-mail catalogs, web sites, and retail outlets. Its target market is the segment of population often known as Generation Y—young men and women aged ten to 24 in the late 1990s. The company's flagship catalog operation, dELiA*s, offers trendy clothing, cosmetics, footwear, and accessories designed to appeal to girls and young women. Other catalogs offer apparel and accessories targeting teenage boys, teen-oriented home furnishings, clothing, and accessories for pre-teen girls, and soccer equipment and apparel. Under its subsidiary, iTurf Inc., dELiA*s also maintains a collection of web sites, which offer the same merchandise found in the various catalogs. The e-commerce sites are linked to an entertainment and community web site geared to teen girls, which is also owned and operated by iTurf. In addition to its catalog and e-commerce operations, dELiA*s owns more than 40 retail outlets under dELiA*s, TSI Soccer Corp., Screeem!, and Jean Country names.

dELiA*s Inception: Targeting an Underserved Market

dELiA*s was launched in September 1993 from the New York apartment of Stephan Kahn, a former Wall Street analyst with a string of degrees from Yale College, Oxford University, and Columbia Business School. Kahn hatched the idea with his former Yale roommate, Christopher Edgar, a doctoral student in comparative literature with previous experience as a journalist and securities analyst.

Kahn and Edgar became aware that the growing population of young Americans known as Generation Y was becoming a major segment of the consumer market. The partners' research revealed that these offspring of the baby boom generation were spending billions of dollars annually, much of it on apparel. More significantly, very few apparel retailers were exclusively targeting this age group, despite its obvious buying power. Kahn and Edgar saw a ready-made niche with very little competition. Potential investors were less enthusiastic, however, and the pair's petitions for seed money were rejected. Undeterred, Kahn laid out $100,000 of his own savings and obtained additional startup capital from family and friends.

After studying such popular teen magazines as *Mademoiselle* and *Seventeen*, Kahn and Edgar hired designers and fashion consultants to create an apparel catalog for Generation Y girls. The catalog, which they called dELiA*s, combined creative layouts and editorial content with the latest styles from more than 50 brand-name vendors and emerging designers. Offering more than the traditional mail-order catalog, dELiA*s was actually a "magalog"—a hybrid catalog and fashion magazine. The publication was first distributed in March 1994 through a network of on-campus college representatives, and in its first year earned $139,000 in sales. Orders were taken by in-house phone representatives—many of whom were college aged—who were specially trained to understand and communicate with teen and young adult customers. Order fulfillment was handled by an independent third-party contractor.

In early 1995, Kahn and Edgar changed dELiA*s method of catalog distribution to a direct mail approach. In addition to using rented mailing lists, the company placed ads for free catalogs in the back pages of popular teen magazines. The response was overwhelming. Within days, dELiA*s received thousands of calls, most of them from high schoolers. These young girls quickly became captivated by dELiA*s distinctive design and cutting-edge, urban-look fashions. Referrals and word of mouth produced more requests for catalogs, and the company's mailing list bulked up rapidly. By the end of fiscal

1995, dELiA*s maintained a database of 290,000 house names—that is, customers who had either made purchases or requested a catalog. Sales increased to more than $5 million. In late 1996, with more than one million names in its database, catalog distribution in the United States and Japan, and sales at more than $30 million, Kahn and Edgar took dELiA*s public. The IPO raised approximately $20 million. Six months later, a secondary offering brought in another $20 million.

1997: Breaking into New Markets

With working capital generated from its public offerings, dELiA*s was ready to expand. It did so in 1997, in several different ways. In late autumn, the company opened its first dELiA*s retail outlet store in Reading, Pennsylvania, and signed leases for two additional outlets in New York State. Two months after opening the Pennsylvania outlet, dELiA*s made its first two acquisitions.

On December 10, the company acquired TSI Soccer Corporation, a privately held direct marketer of specialty soccer apparel and equipment. The North Carolina-based TSI operated 13 retail stores located in Georgia, Maryland, North Carolina, and Virginia, but the majority of its sales were made through a direct-mail catalog operation. Because the U.S. soccer market was primarily composed of Generation Y youth, TSI's target market dovetailed perfectly with dELiA*s. The acquisition added one million names to dELiA*s existing house list, making it the largest database of teenage shoppers in the United States. It also provided dELiA*s with access to the other half of the Generation Y market: teen boys. "This gives us a big list of customers with proven boy buyers and new girl buyers, as well as a young, aggressive management team," said dELiA*s CFO Evan Guillemin in a December 1997 interview with *Women's Wear Daily.*

Just one week after completing the TSI acquisition, dELiA*s made another purchase. The company acquired gURL Interactive Inc. gURL Interactive was the owner of gURL.com, an entertainment web site for girls that featured magazine-style articles, interactive games, bulletin boards, and chat rooms. The popular gURL site, which had been developed by three female students in New York University's Interactive Telecommunications Program, had a loyal following of young women just the right age for dELiA*s fashions. The company planned to use its newly acquired web site as the cornerstone for a whole teenage Web community.

In late 1997, dELiA*s also began offering a line of teen-oriented home furnishings through a new catalog called Contents. Contents, first mailed as a dELiA*s catalog insert, contained furniture accessories and bedding for bedrooms and dorm rooms, as well as decorating ideas and advice.

1998: Continued Growth

In early 1998, Kahn and Edgar began adding to their Web presence with the launch of a dELiA*s web site. The site, which had a prominent link on the gURL.com site, initially allowed visitors only to order catalogs and get a feel for the dELiA*s style. Within a few months, however, the site was equipped with e-commerce capabilities, so visitors could view and order merchandise online. Like the popular catalog, dELiA*s web site offered more than just shopping. With contests, games, advice columns, and "fashion horoscopes" sprinkled throughout, the site became a destination spot, an up-to-the-minute source of fashion advice and entertainment. The company also built up its gURL.com site to include several new features.

dELia*s continued to build its online community with the May 1998 launch of discountdomain.com, a subscription site that offered deeply discounted merchandise to members in exchange for a monthly fee. dELiA*s also took its home furnishings business to the Web with contentsonline.com, the electronic version of the Contents catalog. For operational purposes, all of the company's Internet properties were rolled into a newly formed subsidiary—iTurf Inc. dELiA*s made good use of cross-promotion by advertising the iTurf sites in its print catalogs, thereby greatly increasing traffic to the sites.

A few months later, dELiA*s added another business to its retail stable with the purchase of two New York-based clothing store chains. The chains—Screeem! and Jean Country—consisted of 26 locations in New York and New Jersey. Both catered to young men and women, carrying the sort of trendy apparel favored by dELiA*s followers. The Screeem! stores were also known for their unique, high-energy shopping environment, which featured live deejays, fashion shows, and promotional appearances. Like the 1997 purchase of TSI Soccer, the acquisition of Screeem! and Jean Country furthered dELiA*s growth in two key ways. Because the stores' product mix contained about 60 percent young men's apparel, they strengthened the company's base in the male market. The chains also gave dELiA*s further entry into the full-priced retail store business, an opportunity Kahn intended to fully leverage. In a June 1998 interview with *Women's Wear Daily,* he remarked that he planned to expand the Screeem! chain at a 40 percent pace for the next three to five years.

In the fall of 1998, dELiA*s expanded its catalog operations by purchasing selected assets of Fulcrum Direct, Inc., a catalog company targeting pre-teens. The $4.75 million purchase included trademarks and customer lists for five catalogs, the largest existing database of pre-teen buyers and catalog requesters and the largest collection of catalogs geared to this age group. The company also launched a brand new catalog called Droog, which offered apparel and footwear for boys and young men. Droog, the male counterpart to dELiA*s, was the first catalog in the United States to specifically target Generation Y boys. A Droog web site was launched in tandem with the catalog, becoming another building block in dELiA*s Internet community.

The company's two years of aggressive expansion resulted in 1998 sales of $158.3 million and a profit of almost $80 million. The company boasted an impressive mailing database of almost 11 million names at the end of 1998—a 175 percent increase from 1997—and unsolicited catalog requests were pouring in at the rate of more than 100,000 per month. The Internet segment of dELiA*s business was thriving as well. "We are now registering well over 20 million monthly page views on our combined sites and have several hundred thousand participants in our gURL community site," Kahn was quoted as saying in a December 2, 1998, *Business Wire* release.

1999: New Customers, New Stores, and an IPO

dELiA*s maintained a steadily rapid rate of growth as it entered 1999. It kicked off the year with a January re-launch of one of the catalogs purchased from Fulcrum Direct. The catalog, Storybook Heirlooms, targeted girls aged 4 to 11. It offered upscale special occasion clothing, as well as casual apparel and accessories. In March, the company launched a similar catalog—called dot dot dash—aimed at girls aged 7 to 11. Corresponding web sites for both Storybook Heirlooms and dot dot dash were created and linked to dELiA*s iTurf e-commerce hub. The addition of the two merchandise lines for younger girls, sometimes called "tweens," gave the company a female customer base ranging in age from 4 to 24.

February 1999 marked the opening of the first full-price retail dELiA*s store. Located in a White Plains, New York, mall, the 3,000 square foot store offered apparel, accessories, gifts, and entertainment merchandise in a shopping environment that typified dELiA*s hip style. A second store followed in June, located in Wayne, New Jersey. The company also opened two more TSI Soccer stores and signed several new leases for both dELiA*s and TSI units.

In April 1999, dELiA*s took its Internet subsidiary, iTurf, public in an offering of 4.2 million shares, which represented approximately 28 percent of its value. iTurf consisted of two main segments: the gURL community network and a collection of e-commerce sites. The gURL community was essentially an expanded version of the gURL.com site Kahn and Edgar had purchased in 1997. It offered magazine-style articles and columns, chat rooms, and posting boards, as well as an e-mail service called gURLmail and a collection of gURLpages— more than 103,000 personal Web pages designed by users of the gURL network. iTurf's e-commerce segment consisted of online versions of dELiA*s various catalogs. Both the gURL network sites and the e-commerce sites were linked together in the iTurf.com gateway site. The IPO generated enormous interest, and iTurf's stock immediately skyrocketed, reaching a high of $66 per share within just a few days.

ITurf's newsmaking did not end with its IPO. Near the middle of May, the company announced a two-year strategic marketing alliance with America Online, Inc., the world leader in interactive services, Web communities, and e-commerce services. The iTurf-AOL partnership gave iTurf properties prominent positions in various areas of the America Online Internet community. It was expected that iTurf's presence on AOL, which served more than 17 million members, would greatly increase traffic to the iTurf sites. "This alliance will give iTurf the opportunity to reach the largest consumer audience in cyberspace," Kahn said in a May 12, 1999, press release. He elaborated, "AOL is the leader in creating and managing online communities and providing online shopping opportuni-

ties, which positions us well as we look to offer six of our e-commerce sites to AOL's members and Web-based users."

In early June, iTurf forged another important relationship when it partnered with RocketCash Corporation, a shopping gateway web site that allowed parents to create an online spending account for their children. Parents using RocketCash established pre-set spending accounts for their children via credit card and approved their access to specific merchants' sites. This gave teens the ability to make online purchases in a secure environment, without using a credit card or providing any personal information. Under the terms of the iTurf-RocketCash alliance, the two companies agreed to develop cross-promotional initiatives designed to drive traffic to one another's sites.

Full Speed Ahead

As it prepared to enter a new century, dELiA*s had various projects scheduled. The company planned to add ten more dELiA*s retail stores by the end of 1999, located in major cities in the Northeast and Midwest. An additional seven to ten TSI Soccer stores were also scheduled for opening. In addition, the company planned to convert most of its Screeem! locations to dELiA*s stores, and close the remaining locations. The company's iTurf subsidiary was likewise gearing up for new ventures. One of its major projects was a book for teen girls based on editorial content from the gURL.com site. The book, tentatively entitled *Deal with It,* was scheduled to be published by Scholastic in late 1999. dELiA*s also expected to begin publishing and marketing gURL-branded calendars for the year 2000.

It appeared that dELiA*s' growth in the years to come would continue, based on an essential yet simple premise: to serve the Generation Y market in as many ways as possible. The company believed it had barely scratched the surface of the Generation Y market possibilities and was planning to pursue new product lines, such as books and music. Another key tenet of the company's strategy was to follow its prized customers as they advanced through life. "As the Gen Y population grows, so will dELiA*s," the 1998 annual report asserted. "We'll track our customers from preadolescence to young adulthood, providing them with a wide array of products and services and developing new, innovative strategies that will increasingly define the way an entire generation communicates, interacts and shops."

Principal Subsidiaries

iTurf Inc.; TSI Soccer Corporation.

Further Reading

Choi, Soozhana, "Funky Fashions for Teen-Age Girls," *Gannett News Service,* March 16, 1999.

Gould, Lance, "How 2 Grown Men Mastered Girl Talk," *Crain's New York Business,* October 27, 1997, p. 4.

Gyr, Diane, "Teen Idol: dELiA*s Creates—and Conquers—the High School Catalog Market," *Direct,* August, 1998, p. 41.

Joseph, Regina, "gURLy Style," *Adweek Online,* March 16, 1998.

Morgan, Kendall, ''Where the Girls Are: Small Catalogs Use a Direct Approach to Capture a Trend-Savvy Youth Market,'' *Dallas Morning News,* September 2, 1998, p. 4E.

Much, Marilyn, ''Cataloger Turns New Page in Retail Business,'' *Investor's Business Daily,* February 9, 1998.

Murphy, David, ''dELiA*s Next Big Step,'' *Fortune,* February 15, 1999.

Neuborne, Ellen, ''We Are Going to Own this Generation,'' *Business Week,* February 15, 1999.

Steinhauer, Jennifer, ''Mail Order: Like Mother Like Daughter,'' *New York Times,* July 6, 1997, p. 21.

''Stores with Sizzle,'' *Chain Store Age,* September 1998, p. 74.

—Shawna Brynildssen

Deloitte Touche Tohmatsu International

1633 Broadway
New York, New York 10019-6754
U.S.A.
(212) 492-4000
(800) 335-6488
Fax: (212) 492-4111
Web site: http://www.deloitte.com

Private Company
Founded: 1989 as Deloitte & Touche
Employees: 82,087
Sales: $9 billion (1998)
NAIC: 541211 Offices of Certified Public Accountants

Deloitte Touche Tohmatsu International (DTTI) is the fifth-largest accounting and business services firm in the world, and one of the prestigious Big Five accounting firms that dominate public accounting. The partnership was created as a result of the 1989 merger between two of what were then the ''Big Eight'' accounting firms—Touche Ross and Deloitte, Haskins, and Sells. The two firms were roughly the same size before the merger; the newly combined firm could boast of revenues of nearly $5 billion, with such clients as General Motors, Procter & Gamble, Nabisco, Sears Roebuck and Company, and other Fortune 500 companies. The Tohmatsu name was added to reflect the business of Tohmatsu Avoiki & Sanwa, Japan's largest audit firm, which was part of Touche Ross at the time of the merger. By 1999, Deloitte Touche Tohmatsu was providing 132 countries worldwide with a host of professional services that included accounting, auditing, and tax services; management consulting; and financial and tax advice. The merger between Touche Ross and Deloitte, Haskins, and Sells was thought by many industry experts to be an unlikely match, given their radically different styles. Still, the accounting industry as a whole had a long history of mergers and acquisitions; over the years more and more partners have become concentrated in a shrinking number of firms. The genealogy of Deloitte Touche Tohmatsu looks much like a large family tree stretching back over 100 years to the rise of the multinational corporation and its need for standardized accounting procedures.

History of Deloitte, Haskins and Sells

Each of the two predecessor firms to Deloitte & Touche has a long history of growth. Deloitte, Haskins and Sells traces its history back to the mid-1800s in England, when William Welch Deloitte devised the double entry accounting system to help the Great Western Railway to deal with its large capital stock. In those days, as companies grew, due to their size and complexity, new problems were presented over how to depreciate fixed capital. For example, some imagined that as the cost of replacement of locomotives rose, then the value of a firm's assets rose by the same amount, ignoring depreciation. The system devised by Deloitte solved this problem and was instrumental in the passage in 1844 of the Joint Stock Banking Act in England, which required firms to provide balance sheets and income statements. A number of leading firms were established at this time, including Deloitte in 1845 and Price Waterhouse. Changes in tax legislation, such as the introduction of an income tax in the United States in 1913, were critical for the growth of accounting as a profession. Thus, as Archibald Richards pointed out in his historical account of the company, the evolution of accounting as a profession can only be understood in the context of the developing business community. In other words, accountancy became indispensable to any well-run business, and the practice of accountants has roughly paralleled business trends.

Deloitte evolved for this entire period, moving with the needs of business. For example, in the late 1970s and early 1980s Deloitte began offering administration services for 401(k) retirement plans for companies. Using leased software, Deloitte administered 20 investment funds, offered myriad services for participants, and provided consultants in such areas as legal issues, plan design issues, employee communications, and compliance issues. The service was set up nationwide and administered through regional consulting offices in over 15 offices with a staff of over 250 people. The company also moved increasingly toward management consulting.

History of Touche Ross

The origins of Touche Ross, the other partner in the Deloitte Touche marriage, can also be traced back to England. Founded in 1899, the firm initially provided services needed by investment trust companies. Starting with a staff of 11 that included

Company Perspectives:

Deloitte Touche Tohmatsu is dedicated to delivering world-class service to its world-class clients, and we do this in over 130 countries. Our mission is to help our clients and our people excel. These two forces come together in a powerful combination of wide-ranging services in every major business center in the world. Our services include assurance and advisory, management consulting, and tax advice to hundreds of the world's biggest and most respected companies, including the world's largest manufacturer, 5 of the 25 largest banks and four of the largest trading companies. Our people also listen in over 100 languages; beyond the major economies many of our professionals serve and assist the emerging markets, advising governments and institutions throughout Central Europe and Asia Pacific.

only two accountants, the firm grew rapidly through directorships, receiverships, and reconstruction, rather than by additional audits. The 1930s were rough years for the company, but by the end of World War II, the firm had a staff of 67 and was called George A. Touche & Co., then a small- to medium-sized firm. Expansion continued in America, Canada, and overseas, both through internal expansion and by merger. The firm eventually assumed its position as one of the Big Eight.

By the 1970s Touche Ross was the third largest accounting firm in the United Kingdom. By 1972 the firm included 74 offices, 450 partners, and 5,000 staff in the United States and, through Touche Ross International, offices in 45 countries.

Prior to the merger of 1989, Touche Ross had garnered a reputation as a maverick in the industry and the least stuffy member of what was then known as the Big Eight. Deloitte, Haskins, and Sells, however, was known as the industry's ''creaky old man.''

Pre-Merger Period

The climate in the industry during this time was somewhat unstable. Contributing to this was a problem that large all accounting firms shared; that is, many of the economic disasters of the 1980s, specifically leveraged buyouts and the savings and loan scandal, took place under the watch of Big Eight accounting firms. With Deloitte's corporate culture, thought to be slow and steady, and Touche's reputation as an aggressive auditor, many at the time thought the marriage of Deloitte and Touche to be one of strange bedfellows.

Moreover, competition had created an environment in which the accounting industry was no longer a bunch of bookkeepers but a broad-based consulting practice serving a network of multinational organizations that included corporate, governmental, and financial institutions. This created the background for Deloitte's involvement in the savings and loan fiasco—with a pressure to retain clients so strong that by the 1980s, a government accounting office study of 11 bankrupt thrifts found that a number of accounting audits, including some completed

by Deloitte, Haskins, and Sells, failed to meet professional standards. The long held view that these accounting firms played a disinterested neutral advisory role was burst asunder. The competition for clients had obviously intensified in the deregulated savings and loan (S&L) environment of the 1980s. During this time, Touche made headlines when two of its employees were accused of insider trading. In 1989 three accountants in the firm's London office were charged with having profited from information obtained illegally from a Touche audit of a British industrial conglomerate.

Despite some negative publicity and skepticism from analysts, and through the work of J. Michael Cook from Deloitte and Ed Kangos at Touche, the firms were able to hammer out an agreement. Together the companies would seem to have Fortune 500 clients locked up: Touche had Chrysler, while Deloitte had General Motors; Touche had retail giants Sears, Macy's, Litton Industries, and Pillsbury, while Deloitte had the Wall Street buyout powerhouse of Kohlberg Kravis Roberts as well as Kimberly Clark, Monsanto, and Procter & Gamble. After the merger, the Deloitte contingent largely took control of the new firm, with long-time Deloitte chief J. Michael Cook taking over as chairman and chief executive officer. The merger took place the same year that another major merger between Big Eight firms, Ernst & Whinney and Arthur Young, reduced the Big Eight to the Big Six.

Diversification in the Early 1990s

As the company moved into the 1990s, it ventured into complementary services with data processing applications to ease out of the slide in its management consulting business, while still trying to recover from its ill-fated involvement (along with other Big Six firms) in the disastrous S&L slide. This effort, coupled with the recession at the beginning of the decade, made the period a difficult one for DTTI. In the glory days of management consulting of the 1980s, when mergers and acquisitions were running wild, Deloitte & Touche had reported double digit annual growth rates in its consulting business. In 1991, however, Deloitte's New York consulting business plunged 30 to 40 percent, due mainly to the slumping financial services sector. In response to the slump, Deloitte slashed its own costs, or as Alan Breznick, writing in *Crain's* in 1992, put it: ''Instead of just cutting other people's jobs these days, high-priced management consultants are cutting their own for the first time.'' Deloitte also began revamping its other business services as well and in turn cut its consulting rates.

To expand its management consulting services, Deloitte & Touche entered into an operating agreement with Software 2000 of Hyannis, Massachusetts, to offer customers complementary services. The agreement combined Deloitte's personnel and training knowledge with Software 2000's software expertise. The software products were installed in Deloitte's joint technology centers in New York and Charlotte, North Carolina, and offered software applications, such as audits, tax management, and consulting services for various management problems.

In other software ventures, Deloitte & Touche joined with Brightwork Development and Egghead Discount Software in July 1992 to provide a software license auditing service to find and eliminate illegal software copies. The service cost $10,000 to $30,000 for a 500-workstation site. The need for the service was apparent since, in 1991 alone, the Software Publishers Association collected $3 million in litigation involving pirated software. In another venture in July 1992, Deloitte launched Microcomputer Asset Management Services, which also helped companies comply with software-licensing laws.

The U.S. firm Deloitte & Touche L.L.P. had 1992 revenues that rose sharply over 1991, with gross revenues for the year of $2 billion, 50 percent of which was derived from environmental risk management consulting services—manufacturing plant audits, waste minimization plans, regulatory and public policy analysis, risk financing, and design of management systems, among other services. Deloitte & Touche's international parent, DTTI, also had a big year, reporting global fee income up seven percent to $4.8 billion (U.S. dollars) in fiscal year ending September 1992.

In the late 1980s and early 1990s, however, the company continued to devote a substantial portion of its resources to settling matters related to the S&L crisis. In December 1992 the firm, according to chairman and chief executive officer Cook, began negotiating with the federal government to resolve an estimated $1.4 billion in claims from the failure of the federally insured thrifts. In general, many of the Big Six were accused of negligent auditing practices that may have overstated the value of failing thrifts. The firm was also embroiled in several suits relating to clients that had declared bankruptcy and to its association with Michael Milken, the Drexel Burnham Lambert junk-bond dealer.

Deloitte Touche Tohmatsu's risk management consulting services continued to grow as well, posting a 12.7 percent increase in revenues to $13.3 million for 1992. Overseas growth was also being fueled; the government of Russia enlisted the aid of an international group of Western advisers, including DTTI, to guide it through its privatization program. The firm was also seeing growth prospects in Asia, especially Korea. Growth, however, was slower in the company's more traditional financial services businesses like insurance program reviews, but the company noted that these areas were expected to rebound.

Growth continued slowly but steadily into the mid-1990s, with revenues rising to $5 billion in 1993, $5.2 billion in 1994, and $5.9 billion in 1995. The firm's strong presence in Asia was a factor, as it benefited from that area's booming economy. In addition, DTTI followed the path of the other Big Six firms by focusing on its consulting business rather than its lawsuit-prone auditing practice. To promote the growth of its consulting practice, the firm created a new operating unit, Deloitte & Touche Consulting, in 1995 that combined its consulting business from the United States and the United Kingdom.

In 1996 DTTI diversified its service offerings further by creating a corporate fraud unit, with a subfocus on the Internet. The same year it purchased the largest facilities and location consulting company in the United States, PHH Fantus. Renamed Deloitte & Touche Fantus Consulting, the company became part of the firm's real estate group. DTTI began NetDox in 1997, a joint venture with the Chicago-based bank Thurston

Group. The new company delivered financial, legal, and insurance documents over the Internet.

The firm grew rapidly in 1996 and 1997, with revenues rising to $6.5 billion and $7.4 billion, respectively. Its staff also grew to 65,000 in 1997 as the firm expanded its services and its international presence. Nevertheless, the firm fell to last place in the rankings of the major accounting firms as further consolidation in the industry created new mega-firms. That year Price Waterhouse and Coopers & Lybrand agreed to merge, making the Big Six into the Big Five. Now the smallest of the Big Five, DTTI began an aggressive new advertising campaign. Stating its intention not to merge with any other Big Five firms, DTTI continued its pursuit of growth through internal expansion and the acquisition of smaller practices.

In 1997, the consulting practice was integrated with the firm's operations in South America, Canada, Europe, Asia Pacific, and Africa, and was reorganized into three units, divided according to the size and purpose of the client. Deloitte Consulting served multinational and global clients; Management Solutions served mid-sized companies; and Emerging Markets Group provided consulting to sovereign governments in emerging economies and international lending agencies. In 1998 the global consulting group had revenues of $3.2 billion and could boast the fastest growth rate in the industry: more than 40 percent in the past year.

The growth in the consulting group contributed to a year of record growth for the firm as a whole. With revenue of $9 billion in 1998, DTTI grew at a rate of 22 percent for the year. The firm's tax practice expanded significantly, winning new clients and acquiring new practices, to total its revenues at more than $3 billion. Its work environment was praised in several surveys and rankings in the late 1990s, including *Fortune*'s "100 Best Companies to Work for in America," which ranked DTTI 14th in 1998. No doubt this reputation helped with the firm's recruiting, which added 8,500 professionals in 1998, bringing its total staff to more than 82,000 in 1999.

In 1999 the partners of DTTI elected James E. Copeland as its new global chief executive officer. During his four-year term, Copeland would oversee the implementation of a new global management structure. Encouraged by the success of its 1997 integration of its consulting practices, the firm had decided to integrate its other practices. As the smallest of the Big Five, DTTI would have to make the most of its global practices and continue its aggressive growth strategy to maintain its footing in the increasingly consolidated accounting and business consulting industry.

Principal Divisions

Deloitte & Touche L.L.P.; Deloitte and Touche Real Estate Group; Deloitte Consulting; Management Solutions; Emerging Markets Group.

Further Reading

"Agency Sues 2 Audit Firms," *New York Times National Edition,* March 7, 1992.
Breznick, Alan, "Big Six Consultants Called to Account Deloitte & Touche," *Crain's New York Business,* February 23, 1992.

"Deloitte & Touche Offers Software-Auditing Service," *PC-Week,* July 20, 1992.

"Deloitte Wants More Women For Top Posts in Accounting," *Wall Street Journal,* April 28, 1993.

"Finance and Economics: Disciplinary Measures," *Economist,* March 6, 1999.

"A Glimmer of Hope," *Economist,* April 1, 1995.

Jones, Edgar, *Accountancy and the British Economy 1840–1980: The Evolution of Ernst & Whinney,* London: B.T. Batsford, Ltd., 1981.

Kettle, Sir Russell, *Deloitte & Co., 1845–1956,* New York: Garland Publishing Inc., 1982.

Rees, David, "Merged Accounting Firms See Shakeups Rather Than Benefits," *Los Angeles Business Journal,* May 20, 1991.

Richards, Archibald B., *Touche Ross & Co. 1899–1981: The Origins and Growth of the United Kingdom Firm,* Touche Ross & Co., 1983.

"Russia Has Enlisted the Aid of an International Group of Western Advisers to Guide it Through Privatization," *Oil and Gas Journal,* August 3, 1992.

"S&L Agency Sues Deloitte, Peat Marwick, Seeking Total of $250 Million in Damages," *Wall Street Journal,* March 9, 1992.

"Software 2000 Signs with Big-6 Firm," *Midrange Systems,* February 18, 1992.

Stevens, Mark, *The Accounting Wars,* New York: Macmillan Publishing Company, 1985.

——, *The Big Eight,* New York: Macmillan Publishing Company, Inc., 1981.

——, *The Big Six: The Selling Out of America's Top Accounting Firms,* New York: Simon & Schuster, 1991.

Swanson, Theodor, *Touche Ross: A Biography,* Touche Ross & Co., 1972.

"Too Few Accountants," *Economist,* January 31, 1998.

Woo, Junda, "Big Six Accounting Firms Join Forces for Legal Change," *Wall Street Journal,* September 1, 1992.

—John A. Sarich
—updated by Susan Windisch Brown

DenAmerica Corporation

7373 North Scottsdale
Scottsdale, Arizona 85253
U.S.A.
(602) 483-7055
Fax: (602) 905-9797

Public Company
Incorporated: 1996
Employees: 10,000
Sales: $256 million
Stock Exchanges: American
Ticker Symbol: DEN
NAIC: 72211 Full-Service Restaurants

DenAmerica Corporation operates 200 full-service family restaurants, most of them branded, in about 25 states. The company is the largest franchisee of Denny's restaurants in the nation, with 99 Denny's restaurants in 18 states. These 24-hour-a-day units offer traditional, family-style fare and are perhaps best known for their popular breakfast menu. DenAmerica also owns 101 Black-Eyed Pea restaurants in 13 states, including 73 in Texas, Oklahoma, and Arizona. Black-Eyed Pea units are known for their home style menu, which includes pot roast, chicken-fried steak, and roast turkey entrees.

1990s Origins from a Reverse Merger

DenAmerica Corp. was formed in 1996 when DenWest Restaurant Corp. of Scottsdale, Arizona, acquired Georgia-based America Family Restaurants in a reverse merger. American Family, which had gone public in 1994 with an initial offering of 2.9 million common shares, operated 78 Denny's and 56 non-branded restaurants at the time of the merger. American Family's annual sales had increased about 47.4 percent, from $72.5 million in 1993 to $106.9 million in 1995. DenWest had more than doubled its restaurant sales during the same time period, from $32.6 million to about $75 million, and had acquired an additional 26 Denny's restaurants in 1994 for a total of 72 Denny's units west of the Mississippi. Combined, the two companies operated more than 200 restaurants in 27 states and accounted for about ten percent of Denny's U.S.-based system.

The decision to merge was driven by both companies' need to decrease overhead expenses and by each one's appetite for growth. Consolidating into a single headquarters shaved millions off annual operating expenses and allowed for other efficiencies, such as eliminating staff, closing some regional offices, and installing more efficient insurance and purchasing programs.

Prior to the merger, each company had pursued a somewhat different growth strategy. American Family Restaurants, which had been in existence since 1986, under the direction of its chairman and chief executive officer, Jeffrey Miller, had focused on acquiring smaller regional chains of family restaurants which it then converted to the Denny's concept. DenWest, formed by the 1995 consolidation of several related companies under the stewardship of Jack Lloyd, pursued the acquisition of existing Denny's from other operators and constructed entirely new units.

Under the terms of the merger agreement, shareholders of the privately held DenWest received almost seven million common shares of American Family, $24.3 million in bonds and warrants, and control of DenAmerica's board of directors. American Family shareholders controlled another approximately six million shares of DenAmerica Corp. Even before the deal had closed, news of the organizational change resulted in improvement in the share price of American Family. The companies, too, felt optimistic about the new entity and worked to strengthen its market position. Within a month of the announcement of merger in mid-1995, DenWest acquired 25 properties in Texas, Oklahoma, Colorado, Alabama, Virginia, Florida, Georgia, and North and South Carolina from Kettle Restaurants, Inc. and began implementing its plan to fill in the gaps in its southeast base, thereby strengthening DenAmerica's position in one of its existing areas of operation. Days later, American Family acquired 11 Mr. Fable's Restaurants in western Michigan for approximately $2.7 million. Taken together, these acquisitions increased the soon-to-be-created DenAmerica's overall restaurant base by almost 17 percent and brought its number of restaurants to somewhere in the vicinity of 250. Four months after the decision to merge had been announced, American Family's stock had risen 44 percent.

Going Beyond the Denny's Concept

According to Jeffrey Miller, the new president and chief executive officer of DenAmerica, the new company chose to target the family-dining segment because this portion of the dining-out market was fragmented and underdeveloped at the time. It picked the 1,600-unit Denny's because this particular restaurant concept had a national presence but relatively sparse market penetration. Denny's units typically yielded higher sales and operating margins than the company's smaller, lesser known brands. Following the merger, DenAmerica strategically focused its efforts upon limiting the number of chains that it franchised and narrowing its geographic base. It also undertook a store-by-store review, with the aim of maximizing the return on investment from each restaurant.

As a result of this refocusing and reevaluation, the company made the decision in 1996 to sell 23 Ike's restaurants and Jerry's restaurants in Ohio, Indiana, Kentucky, and Illinois for $4.6 million and to convert 22 of its non-branded restaurants to the Denny's concept. It also sold 33 of its non-branded restaurants. Shortly thereafter, in a move conceived as a means of growing beyond the Denny's concept, DenAmerica purchased the Black-Eyed Pea restaurant chain, the 92nd-largest family dining chain in the nation, from Unigate P.L.C., a British food manufacturer and distributor, for $65 million in early 1997. The Black-Eyed Pea chain consisted of 130 restaurants, 30 of which were franchises, in Texas, Oklahoma, Georgia, and Washington, D.C. The acquisition boosted the number of restaurants operated by DenAmerica to more than 300.

The Black-Eyed Pea restaurant acquisition added about $75 million in revenues to the company for fiscal 1996, generating an earnings increase in the vicinity of $11.5 million before administrative expenses, interest, taxes, depreciation, and amortization were taken into account. DenAmerica's overall net income for 1996 was $1.1 million compared with only $200,000 for the year before. Restaurant sales for 1996 were $241.5 million, considerably more than the $74.7 million totaled for 1995. Good times notwithstanding, however, Miller made the decision in July 1996 to leave DenAmerica to pursue other business interests. The company was next led by Jack Lloyd and Bill Howard as president and executive vice-president, respectively.

Streamlining Denny's, Expanding Black-Eyed Peas

The company's revenues continued to rise—39 percent throughout the first nine months of 1997—but then sales plummeted $9.1 million in the third quarter of the year. By mid- to late-1997, same-store sales were suffering across the board at DenAmerica, down 4.6 percent at the Black-Eyed Pea and down 5.8 percent at Denny's; the company's share price had tumbled from $5.25 to $2.25. DenAmerica, which then ranked tenth among the nation's restaurant franchisees based on revenue, closed out the quarter ended July 2, 1997, with a loss of $350,000. This turn of events prompted the management to sue the former owner of the Black-Eyed Pea for damages that included loss of franchise royalties and the lessening of business value, claiming that it had supplied DenAmerica with false and misleading information at the time of the purchase. By the end of the third quarter, DenAmerica reported a loss of $408,000 on revenues of $227.79 million compared with a gain

of $1.31 million on revenues of $163.77 million for the year before. The company finished the year with a net loss of nearly $21 million, although this upset was due in part to reserves taken in preparation for the upcoming sale of some of its properties.

Management responded to the downswing in DenAmerica's fortunes by reexamining its position. The company had recently fallen out of compliance with certain of its debt covenants, and although it received waivers to defer interest from bondholders, it began to sell more Denny's to alleviate its debt. In a July 1997 move to reduce the number of its Denny's inherited from American Family, DenAmerica sold off two other non-branded restaurants and 14 non-performing Denny's units east of the Mississippi where the chain had been underperforming. DenAmerica also made plans to sell another ten non-branded restaurants and 61 Denny's formerly owned by American Family Restaurants. Since Denny's units in the western United States and Florida were performing well, the company planned to expand the chain in those regions at the same time that it launched an expansion of its Black-Eyed Pea chain.

In 1998, DenAmerica sold 71 of its lowest-volume restaurants, including 63 Denny's, to Houston-based Olajuwon Holdings for $28.7 million. With the completion of this sale, which enabled DenAmerica to pay off more of its still remaining $60 million debt, DenAmerica now operated 103 Denny's and 104 Black-eyed Peas restaurants, and licensed three Black-eyed Peas. Since the 1996 merger, DenAmerica had sold 145 restaurants, most of them Denny's. DenAmerica then went ahead to purchase nine formerly franchised Black-Eyed Peas, adding to the four new units it had built in 1997. During 1998, same store sales at DenAmerica's Denny's gained about three percent in the first nine months, while Black-Eyed Pea sales decreased 1.5 percent for the year.

Franchise-Related Stresses

DenAmerica appeared to be suffering in large part from challenges specific to franchising. Denny's parent firm, Flagstar Cos., was itself emerging from a Chapter 11 bankruptcy reorganization in 1998 as the newly formed Advantica. Having been beset by 12 years of over-leveraging and racial discrimination claims, Flagstar had not had the time to devote any of its resources to marketing Denny's. Nor did it appear to be making Denny's its priority. Instead, Advantica opened units of its Coco's and Carrows chains, direct competitors in the family dining-out market, within close proximity of many Denny's restaurants. When Advantica initiated a price-slashing campaign as part of its effort to market Denny's, DenAmerica initially refused to go along with the strategy, insisting that Advantica's "value-priced" menus conflicted with the Denny's concept's focus on providing full service to customers. Pressured from above, however, DenAmerica eventually had to comply with Advantica's plan.

DenAmerica entered 1999 determined to continue to do business as usual, improving sales, investing where profitable, and selling off underperforming properties as needed. Its liabilities totaled $169 million compared with assets of $170 million, and its revenues had declined $44.6 million to $256 million in 1998 with a net loss of $4.7 million. However, management derived optimism from the fact that the company's same store sales at both its Denny's and Black-Eyed Pea restaurants were improving, with its Denny's units as a group outperforming those of Advantica. The company even had made plans for building another four new restaurants. Yet, at the same time, DenAmerica was considering the possibility of a buy-out. After the failure to complete a purchase offer of $158 million by the New York computer company, Tech Electro, DenAmerica secured $17.1 million in new financing of which 7.5 million went to repay debt, including some failed senior debt covenants.

Further Reading

Alva, Marilyn, "Life in the Fast Lane," *Restaurant Business,* November 1, 1995, p. 16.

Bertagnoli, Lisa, "POSitively Remarkable Point-of-Sale Systems," *Restaurants & Institutions,* August 15, 1995, p. 20.
"DenAmerica Posts $1.118 Million in Yearly Profits after Charges," *Nation's Restaurant News,* April 7, 1997, p.14.
Hamstra, Mark, "Denny's Largest Franchisee Looks to Other Concepts," *Nation's Restaurant News,* September 8, 1997, p. 3.
——, "Merged Denny's Franchisees Combine Strategies, Headquarters," *Nation's Restaurant News,* April 22, 1996, p. 11.
Jarman, Max, "Scottsdale Firm Expands to No. 2 Denny's Franchisee," *Arizona Business Gazette,* November 17, 1994, p. 7.
Martin, Richard, "The Franchisees: DenAmerica Corp.," *Nation's Restaurant News,* January 1, 1998, p. 64.
Ruggless, Ron, "DenAmerica Buys Good Eats Chain in $5 Million Stock Swap," *Nation's Restaurant News,* March 3, 1997, p. 3.

—Carrie Rothburd

Deutsche Post 🦢

Deutsche Post AG

Heinrich-von-Stephan-Strasse 1
D-53175 Bonn
Germany
(49) (228) 182-0
Fax: (49) (228) 182-7099
Web site: http://www.deutschepost.de

Government-Owned Company
Incorporated: 1490 as Kaiserliche Reichspost
Employees: 261,000
Sales: DM 28.7 billion (1998)
NAIC: 49211 Couriers; 45321 Office Supplies &
    Stationery Stores; 52211 Commercial Banking

The Deutsche Post AG is the largest provider of postal services in Europe. The company offers domestic and international letter and parcel delivery services for the general public, as well as direct mail management, mail process outsourcing, and logistics consulting for businesses. Deutsche Post is owned by the German government and planned to go public late in the year 2000. It operates 173 subsidiaries and 14,000 post offices in Germany, delivering approximately 70 million letters every workday in 1998. Deutsche Post holds majority shares in private international delivery services and shipping carriers in Austria, Belgium, France, Italy, Poland, Switzerland, and the United States, as well as a 50 percent share in the British Securicor Omega Express Distribution division and a 22.5 percent share in the express delivery service DHL International Ltd. Deutsche Post is also active in the stationery retail and direct mail advertising markets through its private subsidiaries McPaper AG and Merkur Direktwerbegesellschaft. The Deutsche Postbank AG, a commercial bank formerly part of the old Deutsche Bundespost and owned by the German government, was taken over by the Deutsche Post in 1999 for DM 4.3 billion.

Origins of Postal Services in Germany: 1490–1800

The year 1490 is considered the founding year of the German post office, when German emperor Maximilian I ordered that a regular messenger service be established from Austria to the Netherlands, France and Rome, so that he would be able to efficiently reign from his Innsbruck headquarters over his realm, including the new possessions he gained through marriage. The first post line between Innsbruck and Mechelen in Belgium was established in the same year. Maximilian I assigned the organization of this network to the noble family of the Tassis (later spelled Taxis) from Bergano, North Italy, who had already experience in providing messenger services to various courts.

A relay system was established in which post riders traveled five miles between posts and communicated with each other by blowing a horn. They rode without interruption to the next post at an assigned location where they handed over the mail. Thereby a letter could be delivered the 920 kilometers from Brussels to Innsbruck in five days during the summer, and in six days during the winter. In the 15th and 16th centuries members of the von Taxis family settled in the main cities of Europe as their postal system was steadily enlarged.

In exchange for running the postal service system, the von Taxis family was paid an annual reimbursement by the different royal courts. However, due to weak state finances, wartime losses, and the failure of noble families to settle their debts, the von Taxis were not always paid properly, and they started looking for additional sources of income. Although not technically allowed to deliver anything but "royal mail," the Taxis posts also delivered for private customers beginning at the latest in 1506. Financial difficulties were accompanied by tough competition from already existing messenger systems, primarily those between specific cities and the so-called "butcher posts." Since butchers often had to travel to buy livestock, they traditionally served as mail deliverers and charged their clientele by the piece. When emperor Rudolf II made the messenger business an imperial monopoly in 1597 these conflicts were only partially resolved, since some of his local opponents ignored his edicts. Beginning in June 1600, the general post master Leonard de Tassis was officially permitted to collect fees for mail delivery from private persons. The head of the imperial post was always appointed by the emperor. In 1615, however, Lamoral von Taxis persuaded German emperor Matthias to grant him the right to provide imperial postal service and to make it inherit-

Company Perspectives:

The Deutsche Post is developing into one of the leading mail communication and logistics concerns in the world. We offer our clients services of the highest quality at competitive prices. We match the expectations of a competitive market as well as the needs of a comprehensive national and international infrastructure. By further developing established products we solidify the trust put in us and establish a basis for introducing innovative services and expanding into strongly growing markets. Our entire value production is based on and regulated by state-of-the-art information technology.

able. With this security, the von Taxis family had an incentive to invest into the system's extension.

As early as 1516 the postal system was used to transport people as well as to deliver information. The Taxis postal system initiated a postal ride system from Leipzig to Hamburg in 1660 and additional routes were added soon after. However, traveling with the postal coach was anything but comfortable and secure. Like the horse riding posts, the postal coaches were used regularly to transport money and other valuables in addition to the mail and were often a target for highwaymen.

The time it took to deliver mail did not change much between 1500 and 1765. However, innovations such as the introduction of home mail delivery, drop-off mail boxes, and postal stamps improved the service. The first regulation regarding mail delivery personnel was enacted in Prussia in 1770. Improvements in the postal infrastructure, such as improved roads, were often interrupted by wars and slowed down by disputes between the various regional governors until well into the 19th century.

Peak and End of the Taxis Post: 1806–67

At the peak of its success in the 18th century just before the French Revolution, the Kaiserliche Reichspost, run by the Thurn und Taxis family as it was then known, was the leading postal system in the Holy Roman Empire, serving 11.3 million people in an area of over 222,000 square kilometers. Transit postal routes also connected the empire to France, England, Scandinavia, Poland, Russia, and to the court of the Turkish Sultan. However, the Holy Roman Empire was dissolved as a result of Napoleon's campaigns at the beginning of the 18th century. When emperor Franz II renounced the crown of the Holy Roman Empire in 1806, the scene was set for a series of wars of liberation throughout Europe which made it increasingly difficult for the Thurn und Taxis postal system to survive.

The Southern German states, which had collaborated with Napoleon, dropped out of the Reichspost after the German Confederation of the Rhine was founded in 1806. In 1810, 43 different postal administrations were fighting for share of the territory of the former Reichspost. This competition at times even took the form of ''postal wars,'' such as occurred in the state of Baden. Efforts to unify the German postal system at the

Congress of Vienna, where the new European order was worked out after the defeat of Napoleon, failed. A newly established confederation consisted of 39 independent German states, many of which had their own weights and measures, currencies, and tariffs. By 1824, the Thurn und Taxis principality had reached almost 80 separate agreements and treaties with members of the new German states and other countries.

The two leading powers of the German confederation, Austria and Prussia, proposed the basic guidelines for a German postal association established in 1847. However, no agreement could be reached, and in 1850 the two states founded the German-Austrian Postverein, a postal association which other German states eventually joined. Thurn und Taxis negotiated new agreements with Prussia and Austria in 1850 and 1851, and between 1851 and 1865, five postal congresses were held to update already existing agreements which developed into a sophisticated system of postal law. After Austria's defeat by Prussia in 1866, the German confederation was dissolved and a number of formerly independent postal administrations were integrated into the Prussian system. This marked the end of the almost 400-year-old Thurn und Taxis postal empire. On January 28, 1867, an agreement was concluded in Berlin between the Thurn und Taxis principality and Prussia according to which Prince Maximilian Karl von Thurn und Taxis surrendered all his postal rights and possessions to Prussia, making the Prussian post office the largest German postal system.

Groundbreaking Technologies and World War I: 1868–1932

Although the history of the German post office was greatly influenced by the sweeping political change and man-made catastrophes of this period, it was most affected by the development of revolutionary new technologies that led to fundamental change in how messages were exchanged. Worldwide mail delivery was greatly enhanced, for example, by the introduction of steam ships. In 1886 the first postal ship left for the German colonies in East Asia. In 1870 it took mail from 25 to 30 days to travel from Western Europe to Shanghai, and about seven days to North America. However, one of the most important inventions—the electric telegraph, first used in Germany around 1844 and introduced as a postal service in the following decade—made it possible to cut those times down to two days and two hours respectively. Under the leadership of Heinrich Stephan, who became German Postmaster General in 1876, the new technologies were quickly utilized by the German Reichspost. Beginning in 1876, telegraph cable connections were set up between Berlin and 221 German cities, and by 1896 there were about 17,000 public telegraph offices in Germany. At the same time, realizing the immense potential of the new medium of the telephone for the exchange of messages, Stephan pushed through ambitious plans to introduce telephone service on a large scale. With two Bell telephones which he had received as a personal gift, he began experiments in Berlin and contracted his acquaintance, entrepreneur Werner Siemens, to begin manufacturing German telephones as early as 1877 when as yet no public telephone network existed. Three years later, when only a single city in the United States over 15,000 inhabitants was without long-distance telephone service, the first long-distance telephone center with eight users was opened in Berlin. However, the Berlin business world was slow to embrace the novelty and in 1888 the network only had about 9,100 partici-pants. In the same year Stephan managed to secure the monop-oly for the establishment and maintenance of telephone net-works for the German Reichspost.

In 1870 the German Reich was established, and the new postal administration, the Reichspostverwaltung, began issuing postage stamps valid in all of Germany. Under the Bismarck's chancellorship, Prussian-dominated Germany underwent a pe-riod of fundamental political, technological, and social change which crucially affected the nation's postal system. Bismarck's struggle against the socialist movement by means of extremely restrictive legislation was accompanied by the establishment of a revolutionary system of social welfare which radically im-proved the lot of the common people. The Reichspost became the institution through which welfare payments were channeled and with the rising number of benefits such as disability insur-ance, pensions for the elderly, and later the benefits for survi-ving dependents, the postal system had to adapt to meet the new demand. This service was offered free of charge until 1921 and was performed by the post office until the 1950s and 1960s, when cash-free transactions replaced the cash payments. De-spite protests by the banking lobby, in 1912 the Reichspost was also granted the right to offer money deposit accounts and accompanying services. By 1920, before postwar hyperinflation hit the German economy, the number of the so-called postal check accounts exceeded 620,000 with deposits of 4.7 billion German Marks.

Beginning in the middle of the 19th century, railway trans-portation had become more and more popular and successively replaced horse carriers. Mail could be sorted en route, and dropped off without stopping, thereby cutting delivery times. The second wave of innovation was brought about by the automobile. In 1903 the German Reichspost used cars for the first time to deliver packages in the city of Cologne. Bavaria, which maintained its political independence and its own postal administration, established the first cross-country motorized line for the transportation of mail and people in June 1905. By 1914 the Bavarian postal administration was running a total of 127 lines with 155 vehicles and 136 trailers. In other German cities, battery-powered electric delivery vehicles were in ser-vice as early as 1911. The third invention which had a funda-mental impact was the airplane. In 1912 the first German air mail was delivered in a demonstration show between Darmstadt and Frankfurt. Beginning in 1912, zeppelins, huge gas-filled balloons operated by the Deutsche Luftschiffahrts Aktiengesell-schaft (Delag), were used regularly for both mail and passenger transportation.

World War I interrupted these developments: vehicles were needed for the war effort and gasoline supplies were limited. Regular domestic air mail lines in Germany were opened again in 1919. International air mail delivery was difficult for the Reichspost after the war because the Treaty of Versailles banned it from using former military airplanes outside Germany. How-ever, since the Versailles Treaty also forbid Germany from build-ing new airplanes, those planes were used to expand the domestic air mail system. After those restrictions were lifted in 1926, international air mail took off. In 1928, the German postal air mail system consisted of over 100 connections over a 33,000-kilometer network. The number of air mail letters, packages, and

newspapers grew 16-fold between 1919 and 1925, and had dou-bled again by 1933. Because early airplanes were not able to cross the Atlantic Ocean, mail was sorted on ships at sea and when they were close enough to the American continent, airplanes took off from the ships to speed the arrival of the mail.

After World War I, various transportation enterprises com-peted for shares of the postal market. However, the position of the Reichspost was considered secure since its wide network insured that mail would be delivered even in difficult-to reach areas. It further expanded its capacity by purchasing private transportation businesses. An agreement was reached with its main competitor, the Reichsbahn, the German railways, which in general gave the Reichsbahn the right the long-distance traffic on highways, lines parallel to railways, and the railway replacement lines (schienenersatzverkehr), while the Reichspost was given the right to all additional cross-country traffic.

Another 1920s innovation for the Deutsche Reichspost was radio and television transmission. The first public radio show was broadcast in Germany in 1923 and the first television transmission in 1928. While other institutions were soon given the right to produce content for the new media, the Reichspost established and maintained the technical infrastructure and pro-vided the transmission services. In 1920 the Postreklame—a business which offered advertising on postal vehicles, etc.—was integrated into the Reichspost to increase its income.

The Reichspost Under the Nazi Regime: 1933–45

The German postal system was used intensively for propa-ganda of Hitler's nationalist ideology after he came to power in 1933, in particular through postage stamps and radio broad-casts. The Deutsche Reichspost achieved a measure of indepen-dence under the Weimar Republic after it was taken out of the national budget but still required as a government-owned busi-ness to contribute significantly to the Weimar Republic. The Nazi government, however, reintegrated it as a ministry in 1934. Wilhelm Ohnesorge became postal minister in February 1937 and was a supporter of the Nazi regime until 1945. The post office not only paid Adolf Hitler considerable amounts of money to use his picture on numerous postal stamps, it also carried out Nazi policies by introducing special hours when Jews were allowed to use postal services, cutting them off from services such as newspaper delivery and long-distance tele-phone service, and not hiring them as employees. Ohnesorge illegally loaned money from the Reichspost budget to high Nazi officials and constantly monitored mail and phone messages, such as the long-distance telephone traffic between the United States and England, beginning in 1942.

In the first half of World War II, while Germany was con-quering new territory, the main challenge for the Reichspost was to get close to the battle fields and deal with the increasing amount of mail and freight being delivered to increasingly distant locations. The amount of work done by the Reichspost grew by 50 percent between 1938 and 1943. At the same time, the number of Reichspost personnel lost to the army and war production rose steadily from about 50,000 in 1940 to 450,000 in the first half of 1945. Nonetheless, the number of post office employees, includ-ing those working part time, rose from 565,000 in 1940 to a high of 631,000 by July 1944. Over 6,000 postal drivers and vehicles had to actively support the SS in 1943. Towards the end of the war when the German army was in retreat, more and more civil servants from the post office were required to support the defense effort, and more and more services were cut back in the homeland. Beginning in the second half of 1944, when the "total war" was proclaimed, most of the postal services were no longer available, and a rising number of postal facilities and the necessary transportation infrastructure was destroyed as Allied troops entered Germany. At the end of the war, the German postal system collapsed completely.

Two German States and Cold Postal Wars: 1946–89

After the Third Reich was defeated, the victors formed the Allierten Kontrollrat, consisting of representatives from the United States, Great Britain, France, and the Soviet Union, to govern the country. This group ruled that the borders separating the four zones of occupation were equivalent to postal zones. The exchange of private messages was forbidden for several months, and all the mail delivered later by the new Deutsche Post and all other forms of communication was censored. The June 1948 currency reform in the three Western German zones and the establishment of two separate German states in 1949 led to two separate German postal systems: the Deutsche Post in the German Democratic Republic (East Germany—GDR) and the Deutsche Bundespost in the Federal Republic of German (West Germany—FRG).

The Deutsche Post in East Germany had a monopoly of the delivery of messages in any form—radio and television broadcasts and the distribution of newspapers and magazines. It was headed by a ministry and had a service agreement with the government-owned lottery founded in 1954. The mail distribution was neither mechanized nor very well maintained because investment funding was lacking. Thus postal employees worked under ever more difficult conditions while their pay dropped toward the lower end of the scale. The quality of service declined too as the scarcity of workers became chronic. Home delivery was abolished and mail was delivered to mailbox-complexes on sidewalks in front of buildings while packages had to be picked up at the post office. The reputation of the Deutsche Post declined even more when otherwise unemployable people had to be hired, and cases of theft subsequently increased.

The Deutsche Post was used intensively by the GDR government as a source of "hard currency." After the Berlin Wall was built in 1961, East German authorities issued more and more restrictive regulations for gift parcels from the FRG to the GDR. The number of refused and confiscated packages rose steadily. Later the Stasi, the GDR secret service, systematically scanned packages for money and other valuables, which were then removed and sold. The same department organized the sale of postage stamps to collectors in the FRG through the VEB Philatelie Wermsdorf. Among their bestsellers were stamps from the Third Reich which the GDR "inherited" in great numbers. All together income from the trade in collectible stamps was estimated at 8 to 12 million Deutschmark annually. Another source of money for the GDR was the so called "Postpauschale," a sum collected from the West German government in exchange for opening and maintaining communication channels to West Germany and West Berlin. The last Postpauschale agreement from

November 15, 1983 increased the amount collected from DM 85 million to DM 200 million annually.

Because the East German government distrusted its citizens, it maintained its own telephone connections and mail delivery system. The carrier firm Zentraler Kurierdienst (ZKD), which shared space with certain post offices, delivered mail and packages between government-owned companies and authorities, and was largely used for secret messages and supplies. In the 1980s economic problems worsened; raw materials were so scarce that the print runs for magazines were rationed and the Deutsche Post, which delivered about three periodicals to every customer, refused to take new subscriptions. Specially trained civil servants at the post ministry were assigned to answer the flood of complaints. Ten percent of all Deutsche Post employees quit their jobs the year before the Berlin Wall came down.

After the founding of the FRG, the Deutsche Bundespost became the "special property" of the West German government and was required to carry out government orders. Under the Postverwaltungsgesetz, the postal law of 1953, the postal minister was simultaneously the chief executive of the Bundespost and the organization was required to transfer about ten percent of its total annual revenues—not profits—to the federal budget. Ironically, the Bundespost was already in the red itself, partly because postal rates were considered politically sensitive and thus were not adjusted to match costs. As a result, the Bundespost had to take out loans to cover its operating costs as well as to make the required contributions to the federal budget. Changes were recommended by a number of expert commissions, but these were abandoned or ignored by the changing governments in Bonn.

Change did not finally occur until the early 1980s. When the FRG fell behind other countries in terms of competitiveness, primarily due to the telecommunication monopoly of the Bundespost, Christan Schwarz-Schilling, a former entrepreneur who had been postal minister since 1982, initiated postal reform. A new law, the Poststrukturgesetz, went into effect on June 8, 1989. The Bundespost was transformed into three government-owned businesses which were managed independently according to market-oriented principles: the Deutsche Bundespost Telekom for the telecommunications sector, the Deutsche Bundespost Postbank for the banking, and the Deutsche Bundespost Postdienst for the postal service. The ministry still approved short- and long-term plans and salary levels for those three enterprises.

From 1950 onward, the Deutsche Bundespost in West Germany ran advertising campaigns encouraging people to help their "brothers and sisters" in the Eastern part of the country by sending them parcels of food and other items scarce in the GDR. Bundespost employees were granted the status of civil servants, who could not be laid off. Their number rose from 260,000 in 1952 to 360,000 a decade later. In 1954 the Bundespost initiated a modernization program for the sorting of letters. The number of letter centers was cut from 3,600 to just 350 in 1970. The centralization of mail logistics was accompanied by mechanization of letter sorting which was eventually applied to parcel post sorting as well. In fall 1961, a night air mail transportation system was established, carried out by the airline Deutsche Lufthansa. At the end of the 1960s and beginning of the 1970s, the Deutsche

Bundespost was the largest user of automatic data processing in the FRG, according to former executive manager Franz Schöll. However, another traditional part of the German postal system—the transportation of people—was finally abandoned. After World War II, the allied forces ruled that transportation services had to be run by local businesses; government-owned companies were no longer allowed to offer those services. The postal Kraftpost bus lines were re-established in the 1950s and in service until the early 1980s when the business was finally taken over by the new railway company Deutsche Bundesbahn.

The Postal Reunification in Germany: 1990–94

Just as the Deutsche Bundespost was about to realize far-reaching reforms, it was overwhelmed by a real revolution. On the evening of November 9, 1989, the government of the GDR—under immense political pressure—announced that citizens would be granted unrestricted rights to travel, and visas would begin being issued immediately. A few hours later, the first East Germans arrived at post offices in West Berlin to call their relatives from the other side of the Wall. Approximately four weeks later, the two postal ministers discussed cooperation between the Deutsche Bundespost and the Deutsche Post. The treaty that brought about the currency, economic, and social reunion of the two German states also reunited the two postal systems, and the two postal ministers ratified the agreement on May 17, 1990. The territory of the Deutsche Bundespost was suddenly enlarged by 44 percent, 26 percent more people had to be provided with service, the number of employees went up by 30 percent, and the number of branches grew by 68 percent.

Thereafter, the East German postal system was integrated into the Deutsche Bundespost and completely reorganized. This, however, was easier said than done. Numerous obstacles had to be overcome. For example, the Deutsche Post, like the Bundespost, had developed a four-digit system of postal codes. Many of these were codes were the same for two different cities; for example, 5300 was the code for both Bonn in West Germany and Weimar in East Germany. This problem was resolved temporarily by adding a capital letter to each postal code: O for East and W for West.

There were other challenges as well. East German post office facilities could not be taken over immediately, because of unresolved ownership issues. Then, the first appointed head of the Bundespost in East Germany was outed as a former Stasi informant. Moreover, postage fees were significantly lower in East Germany, reflecting the lower personal income in East Germany. This issue in particular created tension in Berlin post offices where employees from both parts of the city worked together but were paid different wages. West German businesses and even government-owned institutions took advantage of the lower rates in East Germany and mailed a great deal of their correspondence through East German subsidiaries, or just by dropping it off at post offices in East Germany.

After the communication borders had fallen and the West German Deutschmark had been introduced to the so-called new German Länder, the eastern part of Germany was flooded with mail, in particular advertising and catalogues from mail order businesses wanting to expand into the new market. The number of letters sent from West to East Germany rose by 300 to 500 percent between 1989 and 1990 while the amount of packages—due to mail order buying—grew five to tenfold. The East German postal infrastructure was completely unprepared for the increases. At some locations, warehouses had to be rented to accommodate the overwhelming volume of packages. Moreover, two out of three pieces of postal machinery in use at the time were completely worn out. The Bundespost helped immediately, offering 5,000 used vehicles and other desperately needed equipment. Spontaneously formed partnerships between postal workers from the East and West were followed by an exchange program where some 4,500 West German managers helped reorganize and modernize facilities in the east while East German post office employees were trained on the job in West German locations. However, it took until 1993–94 before the service quality in the Eastern post offices was equal to Western standards.

The integration of the east, along with the first Bundespost reforms, left the company with a deficit of DM 1.5 billion in 1990. At the same time, chaos of reunification hurt the quality of Bundespost service in the West as well, and the backlog of undelivered mail increased. The Bundespost started a publicity campaign in December 1991 to improve its image and stop the loss of business to private carriers. That was followed by a well-received advertising campaign worth DM 80 million publicizing the new five-digit postal codes, which were introduced on July 1, 1993. By the end of 1994, the Deutsche Bundespost Postdienst employed 342,413 people—14 percent less than it had in 1990. Between 1990 and 1994, investments totaled DM 10 billion. Although modernization had made considerable progress, personnel costs made up about 73 percent of all costs in 1994. That year, however, the company also realized a profit of DM 256.7 million out of DM 28.8 billion total revenues—its first profitable year since German reunification.

On the Way to Privatization: 1995–99

The second phase of the postal reform was the biggest privatization project in FRG history. The Deutsche Bundespost Postdienst was transformed into the Deutsche Post AG and officially registered in Bonn on January 2, 1995. Chairman of the Executive Board was Dr. Klaus Zumwinkel, a Wharton Business School graduate, former senior partner at McKinsey & Company Inc., and CEO of Quelle, Europe's biggest mail-order retailer, who had successfully led the Deutsche Bundespost since 1990. Under the new organizational structure, the executive board, which consisted of experienced managers from the private sector, made most decisions. However, Deutsche Post—like the other two Bundespost offspring—was overseen by the government holding company Bundesanstalt für Post und Telekommunikation, which was responsible for the overall payment agreements with the postal union. The holding company was supervised by the Ministry for Post and Telecommunication and supported by an advisory board comprised of 16 representatives from the federal and state parliaments which regulated the market and established rules for competition. Politicians were placed on the advisory board of Deutsche Post. The 1994 loss of DM 2.9 billion was made up by transfers from Deutsche Telekom AG, and from 1996 on the company was taxed like any other business. At the same time the markets for mail delivery and telecommunication were gradually opened to increased competition. For example, beginning in 1995 private companies were eligible to deliver mass mailings weighing over 250 grams.

In January 1998, the new postal law went into effect in Germany. It renewed the constitutional obligation to provide postal infrastructure by means of appropriate services and within an economic framework and granted Deutsche Post the exclusive right to deliver letters and addressed catalogues weighing less than 200 grams, with certain exceptions, until the end of 2002. The same year, however, 155 businesses were granted licenses to deliver certain kinds of letters under 200 grams, a move that prompted Deutsche Post to sue the government agency that had issued the licenses. One case was settled against the Deutsche Post in July 1999, as the now 170 messenger firms were offering same-day delivery, a service Deutsche Post did not offer.

In 1995 a new organizational structure was introduced, reducing the number of local offices from 385 to 172. The former 23 directorates were organized under the umbrella of five branches: Frachtpost (freight post), Briefpost (letter post), Postfilialen (post offices), Internationale Post (international mail), and Postphilatelie (postage stamps). Besides the efficient organizational structure, large-scale rationalization was at the core of the new business strategy. Deutsche Post had already invested heavily in new technologies during the first half of the 1990s to become competitive. In July 1995, the last of 33 brand-new logistic centers worth DM 4 billion for freight turnover went into service, accompanied by a new normative package format and a tracking and tracing system. In the mail delivery branch, which generated about 70 percent of all revenues, the concept ''letter 2000'' was inaugurated which significantly cut delivery times for letters. In 1998, 95 percent of all letters reached their destiny one day after being dropped off at a post office, in comparison to 86 percent in 1994. About DM 4 billion was invested for 83 new logistic centers for letter turnover, which replaced about 1,000 locations where letters at the beginning of the 1990s had been sorted mostly by hand.

A new concept for the country's 14,000 post offices was developed with the Deutsche Postbank AG, the former financial services arm of the Deutsche Bundespost. Bundespost had been privatized, but the German government later decided to let Deutsche Post take it over for DM 4.3 billion in January 1999. About one-third of all transactions in German post offices were Postbank transactions, and the fusion of the two companies gave Deutsche Post the opportunity to better utilize its network of post offices—the biggest and most concentrated branch network in Germany. The strategic goal of making the Postbank attractive for a public offering was to gain influence in the retail banking market. In addition, it was planned that new financial services such as construction loans, investment banking, and life insurance would be added beginning in 1999.

At the same time, new ways of offering postal services were explored. Inefficient post offices were closed, and retail businesses such as grocery stores and gas stations were allowed to offer postal services for longer hours. Moreover, 17,000 mail carriers offered a growing number of mobile services which spared people in rural areas the inconvenience of driving to the nearest post office. A shop-in-shop cooperation with the stationery retailer McPaper & Co. was so successful that the Deutsche Post acquired the company from the parent company Herlitz AG in January 1998, and to improve service quality it was regularly monitored by anonymous testers from a market research institute.

To increase its competitiveness in the market, Deutsche Post began expanding into new markets. In the domestic market, new business opportunities were explored in the fields of direct marketing, in-house postal services for big corporations, electronic transfer of letters from financial institutions which were then printed out and delivered from a post office branch close to the addressee, and online-shopping. However, the most pressing demand from existing clients was to handle mail throughout Europe and beyond, since the formation of the European Community and economic globalization. Within three years, Deutsche Post acquired major shares of ground parcel delivery companies in Austria, France, Poland, Belgium, Italy, Spain, Portugal, and the United States. The largest deal was the takeover in early 1999 of the Swiss logistics concern DANZAS with 16,000 employees and CHF 7 billion annual revenues.

Financial results for the second half of the 1990s at Deutsche Post were very promising. Although annual revenues increased only slightly from DM 27.4 billion in 1995 to DM 28.7 billion in 1998, profits rose by 450 percent from DM 282 million to DM 1.27 billion during the same period. Moreover, the percentage of personnel costs went down from 70.6 percent in 1995 to 66.2 percent in 1998, when Deutsche Post employed 233,863 people. The company planned to go public in fall 2000.

Principal Subsidiaries

Deutsche Post Express GmbH; Deutsche Post Service-und Vertriebsgesellschaft mbH; Deutsche Post Transport GmbH (75.2%); Deutsche Post Kontrakt Logistik GmbH; McPaper AG; Deutsche Post Direkt GmbH; Deutsche Post Adress GmbH (51%); Deutsche Post Consult GmbH; Deutsche Post Consult International GmbH; GMS Deutsche Post Logistik GmbH; Merkur Direktwerbegesellschaft mbh u. Co. KG (51.1%); IMS International Mail Service GmbH; Danzas (Switzerland; 99%); DHL International (Bahamas; 25%); DTZ Zadelhoff GmbH; trans-o-flex Schnell-Lieferdienst GmbH (24.8%); Belgian Parcel Distribution N.V. (98%); Ducros Services Rapides SA (France; 68.3%); Global Mail Ltd. (United States); IPP Paketbeförderung Gesellschaft m.b.H. (Austria); ITG Internationale Spedition (Germany; 80%); Qualipac AG (Switzerland); quickstep parcel service AG (Switzerland); Servisco Sp. z o.o. (Poland; 60%); Yellowstone International Corp. (United States); Van Gend & Loos (Netherlands); Selektvracht (Netherlands).

Further Reading

''Deal in the Post,'' *Banker,* December 1995, p. 15.
''Deutsche Post: Im Jahr 2000 auf's Parkett,'' *Spiegel Online Aktuell,* February 12, 1999.
''Deutsche Post on Buying Spree,'' *American Shipper,* June 1999, p. 20.
''Deutsche Post Scraps Trans-O-Flex Takeover Plans in Face of Commission Objections,'' *European Report,* May 13, 1999.
''Deutsche Post to Purchase Danzas,'' *Transportation & Distribution,* January 1999, p. 14.

Dohmen, Frank, and Ulrich Schäfer, "Post Modern," *Spiegel,* July 19, 1999.

Echikson, William, et. al., "Privatization: Posts with the Most," *Business Week International,* August 17, 1998, p. 18.

"Festakt mit Intrigen," *Spiegel,* December 23, 1994.

Glaser, Hermann, and Thomas Werner, *Die Post in ihrer Zeit,* Heidelberg: R. v. Decker's Verlag, G. Schenk, 1990.

"Kein Briefmonopol für Post AG," *Focus Online,* July 6, 1999.

Lotz, Wolfgang, *Deutsche Postgeschichte,* Berlin: Nicolaische Verlagsbuchhandlung Beuermann, 1989.

"Mit mehr Technik und weniger Personal in schwarze Zahlen," *Handelsblatt,* December 19, 1994.

"Post kauft weiteren Expressdienst," *Die Welt* (online edition), January 8, 1999.

Schmitz, Heinz, "Der Einfluß der Politiker bleibt," *Handelsblatt,* December 20, 1994.

Schöll, Franz, ed., *Einheitsfarbe Ginstergelb,* Berlin: Edition Hentrich, 1995.

—Evelyn Hauser

DeVry Incorporated

One Tower Lane
Oakbrook Terrace, Illinois 60181
U.S.A.
(800) 225-8000
Fax: (630) 571-0317
Web site: http://www.devry.com

Public Company
Founded: 1931 as DeVry Institutes
Employees: 2,850
Sales: $353.5 million (1998)
Stock Exchanges: New York
Ticker Symbol: DV
NAIC: 61141 Business & Secretarial Schools; 61151 Technical & Trade Schools; 611691 Exam Preparation & Tutoring

DeVry Incorporated operates one of the largest and most successful for-profit group of business and technical schools in the country, offering associate's, bachelor's, and post-graduate degrees in subjects ranging from engineering and electronics to accounting and business administration. DeVry Incorporated owns three separate higher-education companies, each of which has several national, and in some cases international, locations. The DeVry Institutes offer associate's and bachelor's degrees with an emphasis on engineering and technology; the Keller Graduate School of Management, to which the Center for Corporate Education (CCE) is connected, offers master's degrees with a focus on business management and accounting; and Becker CPA Review prepares accounting students for the Certified Public Accountant and Certified Management Accountant exams. DeVry holds a unique place in the field of education: it is a publicly traded, for-profit company, and as such treats its primarily older adult student body as not simply students seeking a general education, but as customers seeking particular, career specific services.

Beginnings: Convergence of Keller and DeVry

DeVry Institutes was created in 1931 by Herman DeVry. Originally founded as a mail-order electronics repair school,

DeVry later branched out into computers and accounting, and built campuses in the Chicago and Toronto areas. In 1967 Bell & Howell Company, best known perhaps for its role in inventing movie cameras, acquired the school and implemented a fast-paced, nationwide expansion program. Throughout the 1970s Bell & Howell developed a technology-based curriculum which focused on preparing students for careers in the burgeoning engineering and computer industry. By 1983 DeVry had an enrollment of 30,000 students nationwide.

The real success of DeVry Institutes, however, was owed not to Bell & Howell but to two men who met while working for the company in the early 1970s. Dennis Keller, a Princeton and University of Chicago graduate, and Ronald Taylor, who earned degrees from Harvard and Stanford, were working for DeVry in Chicago when they decided in 1973 to form their own post-graduate school of business. After raising just over $150,000 dollars from friends and family, the two entrepreneurs opened a non-accredited day school which offered certificates (not degrees, as the school was not accredited) in business administration. Calling the business the Keller Graduate School of Management, Keller and Taylor at first performed all the work the school required themselves, from moving furniture into a rented school room to teaching and balancing the books. By the end of 1974, the company had a staff of five, fewer than 30 students, and almost no money in the bank. Unless a new track could be found, Keller and Taylor knew they would be bankrupt within the year.

Because the school was unaccredited and ineligible for federal loans many potential students could not afford to enroll, even though Keller and Taylor kept tuition lower than other nonprofit institutions. So, instead of continuing to compete with such schools as a full-time day school with a traditional student body, the company switched its focus and began offering evening classes to working adults. By offering evening classes, the school's students had the option of continuing to concentrate on their careers while at the same time attending classes, a formula which has become increasingly effective to a broad range of students over the past few decades. The new emphasis proved to be quite profitable for the fledgling business: within two years the school was offering M.B.A. certification, and the year after that, in 1977, the Keller Graduate School was fully accredited.

Accreditation was traditionally a contentious issue between the academic establishment and for-profit institutions. According to Leslie Spencer, writing in *Forbes* magazine, the "educational establishment has long thrown roadblocks in the way of for-profit schools by withholding accreditation—the seal of approval required for a school to receive student loans and grants. Any school seeking to make a profit was automatically denied the seal." Because of the Keller Graduate School's success with its students, however, the company was able to throw over that tradition. Spencer, in the same article, noted that the "Keller Graduate School was the first for-profit school the North Central Association of Colleges & Schools ever accepted for membership."

Being granted accreditation enabled the school to overcome many obstacles: the school's academic reputation automatically and dramatically improved, making competition with other schools more feasible; federal loans became available to the school's students; and, most importantly, the school could offer degrees instead of certificates. By 1987, the Keller Graduate School was a true financial success, grossing $5 million a year with an enrollment of about 1,300 students.

While the Keller Graduate School saw increases in both profits and enrollment in the 1980s, DeVry Institutes was facing just the opposite: after its peak year of enrollment in 1983, the business began losing students as more and more people began looking towards business education, as opposed to technological training, to increase their career opportunities. As a result of this negative turn in DeVry's financial outlook, Bell & Howell, having owned DeVry since 1967, decided to divest its 85 percent stake in the company.

1980s: DeVry and the Keller Grad School Come Together

Keller and Taylor, buoyed by the steady growth of the Keller Graduate School, realized that acquiring the company owned by their former employers presented a unique and somewhat risky opportunity for expansion. Many analysts in the industry questioned why a small but vibrantly successful company like the Keller Graduate School would choose to saddle itself with a business which, despite being many times the size of the Keller Graduate School, was slowing in growth and losing profits. Keller and Taylor, however, saw that if DeVry's curriculum could be changed to meet the needs of the modern computer and technological industry, the two schools conjoined could benefit one another, offering training and educational services to an even broader range of students.

However, Keller and Taylor did not have the financial backing necessary to make such an acquisition. Thus, in 1987, the two men approached Citicorp, and a group of insurers headed up by Massachusetts Mutual Life Insurance Company, and borrowed the necessary funds to purchase the DeVry Institutes. Equity investors, Frontenac Venture Company of Chicago among them, also contributed to the effort, loaning Keller and Taylor over $16 million dollars. By the year's end, Keller and Taylor had purchased both Bell & Howell's 85 percent stake in the school as well as the 15 percent that was publicly owned for about $182 million dollars.

The two businesses, the Keller Graduate School and the DeVry Institutes, were conjoined under DeVry Incorporated, with Keller acting as chairman and CEO and Taylor acting as president and COO. Until its acquisition of DeVry, the Keller Graduate School was a Chicago institution, where five of its six campuses were housed. Suddenly, as leaders of DeVry Incorporated, Keller and Taylor had to contend with a cluster of DeVry campuses sprinkled around the United States and in Canada. Such tremendous, overnight growth offered not only an opportunity for the Keller Graduate School's expansion, but also presented many organizational and bureaucratic challenges. Keller and Taylor soon found that they needed to amend the DeVry Institutes' curriculum. They also had to face a potentially crippling debt.

To attract more students, Keller and Taylor treated the DeVry Institutes in much the same manner as they had handled the Keller Graduate School's needs: they began offering not only engineering and technical training to the Institutes' undergraduates, but added a business curriculum which complemented the post-graduate programs at Keller as well. Recognizing that most students who attended the DeVry Institutes in all likelihood needed to work while in school, Keller and Taylor expanded the hours and availability of DeVry's courses, making it possible for students to attend part-time and during the evening. Another important feature which helped to attract students, and draw them away from more traditional higher-education institutions, was the development of the year-round school year. Offering classes year-round enabled students to complete their programs in a fraction of the time it would otherwise take them, an important factor when considering that the typical DeVry student was attending courses for reasons of practical career advancement.

The curriculum at the DeVry Institutes in the late 1980s and early 1990s branched out to include a wide range of educational services, including courses on electronics engineering technology, computer information systems, telecommunications management, accounting technical management, and business administration.

Most DeVry students were first generation students, coming from low-income households and eligible for both federal and state student loans. To appeal to potential students, DeVry Institutes developed ways in which to make payment plans flexible and less rigid than those at rival institutions, allowing people previously priced out of the higher-education establishment an opportunity to earn degrees.

Keller and Taylor's efforts to turn the DeVry Institutes around worked; by 1992, after only five years of debt, DeVry Incorporated had paid off its creditors and was in the black, claiming a net worth of $1.3 million. It was not only DeVry's increased growth that saved the company, however. In 1991, DeVry Incorporated went public, with an initial public offering of 20 million shares of stock, priced at $1.25 per share. Since then, DeVry's stocks have continued to increase in value, with initial proceeds from the offering being used to pull the company out of debt.

1990s Expansion: Taking Advantage of Educational Trends

By the early 1990s two things became clear to analysts in the educational industry: students were graduating from high school in record numbers, and, of those graduates, more and more individuals were seeking training in higher education which would put them on a fast track to technological or business-oriented careers. DeVry Incorporated was in the right place at the right time, offering undergraduate training in technical fields and graduate programs for business people. Moreover, in doing away with such traditional collegiate frills as secluded, landscaped campuses and sports teams, DeVry managed to keep costs low, further bucking the higher educational trend of skyrocketing tuition.

As DeVry Institutes was shaped in the late 1990s into a school well-equipped for the needs of both the business and technology student, Keller and Taylor continued to refine the Keller Graduate School's curriculum. By 1999, the school was offering masters degrees in business administration, project management, human resource management, telecommunications management, accounting and financial management, as well as information systems management. The goal of having each school complement the other was complete, making Dennis Keller's 1988 prediction that "DeVry will be the brand name for our undergraduate degrees and Keller the brand of our postbaccalaureate degrees" a reality.

DeVry's positive reputation grew from several sources, the most powerful of which was the fact that a DeVry graduate in all likelihood was not going to be left upon graduation with a degree and no job. According to DeVry sources, in the 1990s, "of the more than 44,000 graduates who actively pursued employment or were already employed, more than 93 percent held positions in their chosen field of study within six months of graduation." The company also aggressively advertised its success, sending more than 300 recruiters annually to businesses and high schools across the country.

While tuition was lower at DeVry than at private colleges, many public universities still offered similar degrees for less money. What kept DeVry's enrollment up was the company's promotion of the fact that an individual with a DeVry degree could almost be guaranteed a position in his or her desired area. Taking into consideration DeVry's flexible payment plans and class schedules, DeVry's steadily increasing enrollment figures, almost every year in the 1990s, was not surprising.

The company did, however, have its detractors. Some in the education industry questioned the quality of DeVry's instructors, claiming that because most of them did not have PhD's in their fields that they were less qualified than professors found at more traditional universities. DeVry instructors were also usually hired part-time, in order to keep costs down, and had jobs outside of teaching, making one-on-one student-teacher interaction something of a rarity on DeVry campuses. DeVry responded to this criticism by pointing out that their instructors had the most important quality a DeVry student needed to complete meaningful training: hands-on experience in technological or business fields.

In the mid-1990s DeVry was financially strong enough to consider branching out and in 1996 acquired Becker CPA Review, a company which helped students prepare for accounting certification. With over 150 locations across the United States, the Middle East, Canada and the Pacific Rim, Becker truly represented to DeVry an international expansion. By the late 1990s DeVry could claim 16 campuses for the DeVry Institutes, 31 locations for the Keller Graduate School, and an enrollment of over 42,000 students, making the company one of the most successful and high profile for-profit schools in the nation. At decade's end, DeVry's future looked bright, with plans to open at least one new campus a year, as well as extensive on-line programs being developed to complement more traditional instruction.

Principal Divisions

DeVry Institutes; Keller Graduate School of Management (KGSM); Becker CPA Review.

Further Reading

Byrne, Harlan S., "Trends Favor Chain of Job-Training Schools," *Barron's Investment News & Views,* February 8, 1993.
Hofmeister, Sallie, "A Touch of Class," *Venture,* January 1988.
Murphy, Lee H., "DeVry's Classes Go Online: Competition, Convenience Push Internet Offerings," *Crain's Chicago Business,* November 30, 1998.
Spencer, Leslie, "Competition? Heaven Forbid," *Forbes,* January 2, 1995.
——, "Good School Story," *Forbes,* May 27, 1991.

—Rachel Martin

Dylex Limited

637 Lake Shore Boulevard West
Toronto, Ontario M5V 1A8
Canada
(416) 586-7000
Fax: (416) 586-7277
Web site: http://www.dylex.com

Public Company
Incorporated: 1967 as Dylex Diversified
Employees: 11,500
Sales: C$1.07 billion (1998)
Stock Exchanges: Toronto Montreal
Ticker Symbol: DLX
NAIC: 45211 Department Stores

One of the leading specialty retailers in Canada, Dylex Limited operates five retail chains that cater to distinct market segments. In 1999, the five chains comprised 640 stores, including 284 BiWay units, 113 Thrifty's units, 109 Tip Top units, 74 Fairweather units, and 60 Braemar units. Additionally, Dylex operated two menswear manufacturing businesses, Weston Apparel and San Remo Knitting Mills, as a facet of its Tip Top business. The company recorded explosive growth during the 1970s and 1980s, operating 17 chains and more than 2,700 stores in the United States and Canada at its peak. By the mid-1990s, however, Dylex was staving off bankruptcy and had confined its presence within the borders of Canada. One of the company's signature traits throughout its history was an emphasis on maintaining sharply focused, niche-oriented stores that catered to a specific market segment. This characteristic endured into the late 1990s. BiWay operated as a neighborhood-based discount concept offering a narrow range of general merchandise, food, health-and-beauty aids, and family apparel. Braemar sold classically styled fashions targeted for career women over 35 years old. Thrifty's ranked as Canada's leading jeanswear chain, selling moderately priced casual denim and denim-related clothing. Fairweather stocked fashion apparel for younger, contemporary working women. Tip Top, Dylex's original chain, sold men's clothing, suits, sportswear, and accessories. More than half of Dylex's stores were located in Ontario, with the remainder scattered among the country's other provinces.

Origins

The first discussions concerning the formation of Dylex took place during a lunchtime meeting in December 1966. On one side of the table sat Jimmy Kay, a Toronto-based entrepreneur with business interests in housewares, plastics, and lighting. On the other side sat representatives of the Posluns family, who for three generations had been involved in the Toronto garment industry. The Posluns and Kay had never met each other prior to the meeting—an auditor who worked for both Kay and the Posluns had arranged the meeting—but they were both interested in acquiring the same company, Tip Top Tailors. Founded in 1909, Tip Top Tailors was a once healthy chain of men's apparel stores that had lost its luster by the late 1960s, deteriorating into "an old, broken-down chain," according to Toronto broker Donald Tigert. From their perspective, the Posluns had little interest in whether Tip Top Tailors was profitable or not—they were interested in the company's five-story building. They had approached Tip Top Tailor's owners, the Dunkleman family, about buying the building, but the Dunklemans declined the offer, wishing to sell the entire business if they sold it at all. Kay was more interested in buying the chain of stores than he was in purchasing the headquarters building, a proposition the Dunklemans also rejected. Separately, each side had failed in their bid to acquire Tip Top Tailors, but during the course of lunch they agreed to pool their efforts and offer the Dunklemans what they wanted. Thus began a business relationship that would endure for the next quarter century.

The Dunklemans agreed to the joint bid by the Posluns and Kay, who formed a new company named Dylex, which concurrently went public, to serve as the holding company for Tip Top Tailors. The name Dylex, which had once been used by Kay for one of his holding companies, was an acronym for "damn your lousy excuses," a phrase that reflected the mentality of the company's new management. Kay and the dominant Posluns family member, Wilfred Posluns, established a reputation for acquiring ailing retail chains and injecting them with new life, a characteristic of their jointly controlled company as it developed into a retail giant. Tip Top Tailors was the first example of a rapid turnaround, a company whose former executives offered numerous reasons for its anemic performance, none of which were accepted by Kay or Posluns. Instead, Dylex management applied what one industry pundit characterized as a "don't-stand-for-any-nonsense" style of management, sharpening the chain's focus on its target clientele. In its first year under Dylex control, the floundering 52-store chain regained its lost vitality, registering C$37 million in sales by the end of 1967.

Tip Top Tailors was the first instance of Dylex's healing touch, the first of many to follow, but behind the numerous success stories of retail chains turned into market winners was an important, often overlooked, component of Dylex's business. From the start, the company was diversified, maintaining retail and manufacturing operations. Although the manufacturing segment of Dylex kept a low profile because it produced clothes for both Dylex chains and competing chains, it was a significant contributor to the holding company's financial health, accounting for approximately 25 percent of Dylex's revenue volume. Perhaps more importantly, the manufacturing side insulated the company from the cyclicality of its retail operations, a function the retail segment also performed when apparel manufacturing experienced a downturn. Equally as important to the company's early success was the acquisition strategy employed by Kay and Posluns. The pair prided themselves on not only acquiring the physical assets of retail chains but also the executives who managed the chains. "We wanted to bring in dynamic, entrepreneurial types," Kay explained, "who were inventive and had a good knowledge of the local market." By retaining quality executives gained through acquisitions and giving them considerable managerial freedom, Dylex developed an autonomous corporate structure, with each of the chains managed like entrepreneurial businesses. Dylex, operating in the background, gave each of its chains the benefits of a large corporate sponsor, providing capital and corporate services, but chains were largely responsible for using such services to their advantage.

The effect of a diversified presence in both manufacturing and retailing and delegating responsibility directly to store managers made for a balanced corporation unfettered by superfluous layers of management. Operating as such, Dylex recorded explosive growth during the 1970s, adding new chains through acquisitions during an era when the number of urban shopping centers in Canada proliferated. By the end of the 1970s, an estimated C$12 of every C$100 spent on clothing in Canada went to a Dylex-controlled store or manufacturer.

The acquisitions completed during Dylex's first decade of operation added a number of different retail chains to a portfolio anchored by Tip Top Tailors. The Dylex chains included Fairweather, Braemar, Suzy Shier, Thrifty's, Ruby's, Town and Country, Harry Rosen, Big Steel Man, and BiWay. Dylex's manufacturing operations included Manchester Children's Wear, Nu-Mode Dress, Paulman International, Forsyth Group, Canadian Clothiers, Tobias Kotzin, and Target Apparel. Combined, the entire Dylex empire generated more than C$650 million a year during the early 1980s, representing a prodigious leap from the total collected in 1967. The company ranked as Canada's premier retailer, but was largely unknown to many consumers, operating as the anonymous giant overseeing a stable of profitable chains. Apparel industry experts were aware of Dylex, however, attributing the success of Tip Top Tailors and its sister companies to the watchful eyes of Kay and Posluns. Although the Dylex chiefs granted their subsidiary companies considerable freedom, they were adamant that specific rules were obeyed. First, Kay and Posluns set specific sales goals, establishing benchmark figures that store managers were duty-bound to meet—with no excuses accepted. Second, and perhaps most importantly, Kay and Posluns demanded that each of its chains identify a specific, narrowly defined customer base and tailor their stores for such potential customers. Big Steel Man, for example, catered exclusively to 18- to 22-year-old males who were either college students or first-job young professionals. By maintaining a tight, niche-oriented focus for each of its chains, Dylex management had blanketed the Canadian retail market in little more than a decade, reaching nearly every demographic sector. Because of this successful approach, projections called for the company to reach C$1 billion in annual sales by 1987.

Expansion into the United States in the 1980s

With its position secure in a variety of market segments, Dylex turned its sights southward as the mid-1980s began and plotted a move into the United States. The potential rewards for such a foray were enticing, by far eclipsing what the company could glean in Canada, no matter how many stores it operated. In Canada, the specialty apparel and accessories industry registered C$8.2 billion in sales a year. In the United States, the same industry boasted $70 billion annually, presenting Kay and Posluns with a potentially lucrative challenge. They made their entry into the United States in a typical manner, acquiring the floundering Foxmoor women's apparel chain from Melville Corporation, a large U.S. specialty retailer, in 1984. Dylex paid C$49 million for the 614-store chain and quickly applied its restorative touch. The stores were redesigned and stocked with all new merchandise in an effort to refocus the chain on its specific market segment: young women who preferred color-coordinated apparel and accessories. After a year, sales increased 30 percent, and Dylex had secured a sizeable presence in the vast U.S. market.

Expansion, from the start, had been financed by mid-term debt and substantial cash flow, enabling the company to purchase one chain after another. The widening breadth of Dylex also had been aided by the company's practice of only acquiring a portion of its investments, preferring to enter into a partnership that gave Dylex a 50 percent interest in a particular chain. The remaining half of the business was generally owned by the executives in charge, an arrangement that strengthened the entrepreneurial backbone of the company. Chains such as Tip Top, Braemar, and Fairweather were wholly owned by Dylex, but most of the company's subsidiaries were partnerships by the mid-1980s. As the company moved forward after its acquisition of Foxmoor, it increased its presence in the United States by acquiring retail chains in partnership with other parties. The Foxmoor purchase was followed by the acquisition of 50 percent of National Brands Outlet (NBO), a 14-unit, men's discount clothing chain located in the New York metropolitan market. Next, Dylex invested in Wet Seal, a California-based junior fashion chain. The stake in Wet Seal was followed by an acquisition no one in the U.S. retail apparel industry could ignore. Dylex, still relatively unknown in the United States, purchased one of the leading specialty chains in the country, acquiring Brooks Fashion, a national chain with 670 stores operating under the names Brooks, T. Edwards, and Onstage. Entering the late 1980s, Dylex was an unmitigated retail giant. The company owned or partly owned 17 chains that operated more than 2,700 stores in the United States and Canada. Kay, who served as chairman, was brimming with confidence, projecting that Dylex would be a "C$4- or C$5-billion company by the end of the 1980s."

Tumultuous 1990s

For Kay and Posluns, who served as president and chief executive officer, the mid-1980s would be remembered as Dylex's golden years. Following their triumphant invasion of the U.S. market, the company began to suffer, at first only acutely, and then chronically. Problems quickly surfaced with the company's stake in Brooks Fashion, one of the few acquisitions in the company's history in which Dylex held a minority interest. Brooks was controlled by managers who, according to one analyst, "became very wealthy and weren't that interested in running the business." Profitability plunged and debt mounted at Brooks Fashion, its affect on Dylex exacerbated by other disappointing results registered by some of the company's other chains. At first, industry pundits brushed aside any concern of profound problems at Dylex. "The Dylex people have been through this many times," remarked one analyst, "if anyone can turn it around, they can." The problems persisted, however, aggravated by the pernicious economic conditions that emerged as the 1990s began. Kay departed, and Posluns was left at the helm of what was regarded as a sinking ship.

The recessive economic climate of the early 1990s inflicted significant damage upon the retail industry as a whole, and delivered a particularly harsh blow to Dylex. Between 1989 and 1994, the company accumulated losses of roughly C$150 million, putting Posluns, who served as chairman and chief executive officer, in an untenable position. Shareholders were distressed, particularly one group of U.S. investors who de-

manded a change in the directorship of Dylex, which was dominated by members of the Posluns family. By the end of 1994, the sprawling mass of Dylex had been winnowed down to 879 units in Canada and 174 units in the United States through divestitures and store closures, with further reductions in the offing. NBO, which had grown to 34 stores, was sold in early 1995 to Essex Holding, Inc., a divestiture that was indicative of a company in retreat. The sale of NBO, according to a Dylex official, was "consistent with [Dylex's] view that it can achieve more attractive returns by investing in its Canadian operations." Roughly a week later, the company hit bottom. Saddled with C$235 million of debt to creditors, Dylex filed for protection from creditors while it reorganized, declaring bankruptcy a decade after it had promised to dominate the North American specialty retail industry. Several days later, Posluns announced the closure of 200 stores in Canada as part of a sweeping restructuring.

After filing for the equivalent of a Chapter 11 in the United States in January 1995, Dylex emerged from bankruptcy in April 1995, ready to embark on the long road toward recovery. In July 1995, the expected change in management occurred. Wilfred Posluns as well as David Posluns, the company's chief financial officer, stepped down, making room for a new era of management. Elliott Wahle was named president and chief executive officer. Wahle, a former director of player personnel for the Toronto Blue Jays, had served as president of Toys 'R' Us (Canada) Ltd. before taking on the task of leading Dylex toward recovery. Under Wahle's direction, the company focused on improving its infrastructure, which had deteriorated after years of neglect. In effect, Dylex attempted to do to itself what it had done to numerous other retail chains throughout its 30-year history. Underperforming units were closed, several divestitures were completed, and funds were directed toward capital improvements. By March 1997, there was tangible evidence that Wahle had succeeded. During the previous year, the company had registered C$22.8 million in profits, nearly eight times the total it posted in March 1996. The results represented Dylex's most profitable performance since 1988.

As Dylex prepared for the 21st century, it did so from a solid financial foundation that positioned the company for growth. Although the company did not contemplate completing any acquisitions during the late 1990s, growth—achieved internally—stood as its primary objective. In 1998 Dylex spent more than C$44 million on its continuing effort to upgrade stores and to expand its existing chains. In 1999 the company anticipated devoting an equivalent sum to enhancing its portfolio, particularly its BiWay and Thrifty's chains, which were slated for renovation. Although the company had been forced to reduce its size considerably during the 1990s—paring down to 640 stores in 1999—it continued to rank as one of Canada's largest retail concerns, a stature Wahle intended to maintain in the future.

Principal Divisions

BiWay; Braemar; Thrifty's; Fairweather; Tip Top; Women's Wear Group.

Further Reading

Brauer, Molly, "What Is Dylex and Why Is It Looking at U.S.?," *Chain Store Age Executive with Shopping Center Age,* October 1984, p. 31.

"Cashing Out in Monaco," *WWD,* March 13, 1997, p. 30.

"Dylex Names Wahle President," *WWD,* July 31, 1995, p. 12.

Palmieri, Jean E., "Canada's Dylex Sells NBO Chain to Group Headed by Wm. Taggart," *Daily News Record,* January 4, 1995, p. 2.

Ryval, Michael, "Material Wealth," *Metropolitan Toronto Business Journal,* May 1982, p. 20.

Socha, Miles, "Dylex Revamp Plan Will Shut 200 Stores, Eliminate 1,800 Jobs," *WWD,* January 12, 1995, p. 14.

——, "U.S. Investors Seek Changes in Dylex Board of Directors," *Daily News Record,* December 15, 1994, p. 12.

Stern, Aimee, "The Intrapreneurs of Retailing," *Dun's Business Month,* September 1986, p. 54.

—Jeffrey L. Covell

EG&G Incorporated

45 William Street
Wellesley, Massachusetts 02181
U.S.A.
(781) 237-5100
Fax: (781) 431-4255
Web site: http://www.egginc.com

Public Company
Incorporated: 1947 as Edgerton, Germehausen & Grier,
   Inc.
Employees: 13,000
Sales: $1.41 billion (1998)
Stock Exchanges: New York
Ticker Symbol: EGG
NAIC: 334413 Semiconductor & Related Device
   Manufacturing; 334419 Other Electronic Component
   Manufacturing; 334513 Instruments & Related
   Product Manufacturing for Measuring, Displaying &
   Controlling Industrial Process Variables; 334519
   Other Measuring & Controlling Device
   Manufacturing; 54133 Engineering Services; 54199
   All Other Professional, Scientific, & Technical
   Services; 54171 Research & Development in the
   Physical, Engineering & Life Sciences

EG&G Incorporated is a diversified technology company that develops and provides products for public and private customers in the medical, aerospace, telecommunications, semiconductor, photographic, and other industries. The company's operations are broken into five business units: Instruments; Life Sciences; Engineered Products; Optoelectronics; and Technical Services. Its Instruments operation is based on x-ray imaging systems and provides screening and inspection systems for use in airport and industrial security, and environmental, food, and nuclear industry monitoring. The Life Sciences unit develops systems for biochemical research and medical diagnostics. The Engineered Products unit designs and produces pneumatic systems, seals, and bellows for aerospace, semiconductor, and

power generation markets. EG&G's Optoelectronics division specializes in optical sensing devices for industrial and medical applications. The company's final unit, Technical Services, provides engineering, research, management, and support services to governmental and industrial clients.

Nuclear Management and Monitoring: 1940s–50s

EG&G was established by three nuclear engineers from the Massachusetts Institute of Technology shortly after the end of World War II. These engineers, Harold E. Edgerton, Kenneth J. Germehausen, and Herbert E. Grier, had been involved in the American effort to construct an atomic bomb during the war. So valued were their contributions that after the war the government asked them to establish a company to manage further development of the country's nuclear weapons. The three established a small partnership called Edgerton, Germehausen & Grier on November 13, 1947, and quickly began collecting contracts to advise the government on nuclear tests in Nevada and on South Pacific islands.

One of the first employees of the new company was Bernard J. O'Keefe, another MIT graduate who had worked for Dr. Grier during the war. O'Keefe served with the 21st Bomber Command in the Mariana Islands during the war, and is said to have personally wired the bomb that later destroyed the Japanese city of Nagasaki. O'Keefe was sent to Japan after its surrender to investigate that country's progress with nuclear technology and recruit promising Japanese scientists for other atomic projects. A specialist in the design and development of electronic instrumentation and controls, O'Keefe quickly gained an important position in the growing firm.

Inconvenienced by the length of the company's name, employees soon began to rely on the simple acronym EG&G, which later became its official name. In order to maintain close contact with MIT and its excellent nuclear and electronic engineering programs, EG&G set up its headquarters in Bedford, Massachusetts, in northwest suburban Boston.

EG&G was involved in the U.S. effort to build a more powerful nuclear weapon, the hydrogen bomb. That year, Grier and O'Keefe were present at a Nevada test site to personally

Company Perspectives:

Our vision is that we can create value in an environment of ever-accelerating change. Value creation is our singular aim and ultimate measure of success. We believe that the increasing drive to create value represents the surest and most consistent avenue for us to benefit our customers, employees, stockholders and constituent communities. Our value creation model focuses on growth primarily derived from internal development.

witness an H-bomb detonation. After the weapon failed to explode, Grier and O'Keefe flipped a coin to determine who should scale the 300-foot test tower and disarm the bomb. Although O'Keefe lost, he won the special distinction of being the first man to disarm a live H-bomb.

O'Keefe had a second brush with disaster in 1958 when he witnessed an H-bomb detonation at Bikini Atoll in the South Pacific. There, shifting winds in the upper atmosphere caused a radioactive cloud of fallout to shower his bunker.

These experiences taught O'Keefe the awesome destructive power of nuclear weaponry and the dangers of radioactive fallout. As an engineer and manager he was bound to perform his company's contracts, but grew personally opposed to the use of nuclear weapons. This sharpened his sense of responsibility toward the emerging form of warfare, a quality that was not lost upon the government's Atomic Energy Commission.

As a result of EG&G's experience with detonations, and O'Keefe's concern for nuclear non-proliferation, the company became increasingly involved in distant monitoring projects, particularly as they related to Soviet nuclear tests. By observing changes in the atmosphere, EG&G was able to determine the incidence and strength of Soviet tests and provide important data on the progress of Moscow's weapons program. In the process, EG&G gained highly specialized knowledge in environmental sciences. These skills had numerous applications outside the weapons industry, in such areas as pollution control and environmental management.

Exploring Commercial Markets: 1960s

As early as 1960, O'Keefe and the company's three founders had considered establishing a new environmental analysis business, which would lessen EG&G's dependence on low-margin government contracts and permit the company to enter new commercial markets. But at the time, neither public concern nor legislation placed a high value on such endeavors.

Three years later, the United States, the Soviet Union, and the United Kingdom signed a protocol that banned nuclear tests in the atmosphere, above ground, in the water, or in outer space. With this document, EG&G appeared to lose a major portion of its business. However, the protocol did not prevent underground tests, which were far more complicated. EG&G remained the only company with the proper supervisory credentials to manage this type of nuclear testing. The company was forced to

develop geologic analytical capabilities and become a tunneling and mining operation as well.

Furthermore, the government had also laid plans to establish a kind of oceanographic equivalent to NASA. Eager to take a place in this organization, EG&G invested heavily in oceanographic research. While the underwater NASA never materialized, the efforts enabled O'Keefe to further cultivate new commercial markets for EG&G, including excavation and water transmission.

During this time the company's three founders moved further into retirement, taking ceremonial "executive chairman emeritus" positions. As a result, O'Keefe became the de facto head of the company. EG&G also pursued a strong acquisition campaign, taking over 13 companies between 1964 and 1967.

By 1967 a strong environmental movement began to form in the United States. With legislation still years away, EG&G began laying plans to play an important role in the environmental projects it was sure would result.

EG&G was divided into four main operating divisions. The smallest of these was EG&G International, which was primarily concerned with oceanography. The standard products and equipment division, which grew fastest during the 1960s, produced a variety of machines and electronic devices. EG&G's largest segment remained its nuclear detonation and monitoring business. But perhaps the most innovative and interesting division was the nuclear technology group, which was involved in the design of nuclear rocket engines for interplanetary propulsion.

Other noncombat nuclear projects included "nuclear landscaping" projects, in which controlled nuclear explosions could carve out harbors, canals, and other types of passages. EG&G's CER Geonuclear unit participated in tests wherein nuclear explosions were used to fracture layers of rock so that otherwise inaccessible gas and oil reserves could be exploited. These public works projects, while feasible, failed to gain public support. In fact, opposition to nuclear technology in general increased as people grew wary of the safety of nuclear energy. In addition, nuclear excavation would have required an unlikely waiver of the 1963 Nuclear Test Ban Treaty.

With the evaporation of good commercial prospects for its nuclear engineering expertise, EG&G was forced to rely again on military projects. Despite efforts to step up mechanical and electrical engineering work (partly by acquiring a spate of small research companies), EG&G mustered only four percent annual growth during the late 1960s.

Failed Initiatives: 1970–75

Interest in nuclear power increased dramatically during the 1973–74 Arab oil embargo, in which Americans sought to reduce their costly dependence on imported oil. Realizing that the world's oil exporting nations stood to permanently lose their largest customer, the United States, King Faisal of Saudi Arabia promptly called for an end to the embargo. Nonetheless, while Americans regained access to Arab oil, the end of the embargo was disastrous for the U.S. nuclear energy industry—and for EG&G. The end of the embargo removed one of the great justifications for nuclear power, and gave anti-nuclear activists time to properly organize legislative battles.

While EG&G was being locked out of yet another promising commercial application of its technologies, it attempted projects in other fields. Some years earlier, in an effort to develop a new process for purifying nuclear isotopes, EG&G developed a flash tube that was ideal for photocopiers. However, by the time an application could be developed, Xerox had already saturated the market with conventional designs. In another ill-timed move, the company bet that environmental laws would cause demand for the unconventional Wankel engine to rise. EG&G purchased a Texas automobile testing agency in hopes of winning large emission monitoring contracts. However, the oil embargo destroyed the market for the clean, but gas-eating Wankel, and automobile environmental legislation was abandoned.

During this time, with the encouragement of the government, EG&G established a minority-dominated subsidiary, EG&G Roxbury, in a neighborhood of Boston, hoping to help strengthen the economic structure of the community. The project floundered, however, when bureaucrats failed to properly support the program, causing only a few sales to be made from the subsidiary. After a few years of disastrous results, the entire program was wound up.

On the Upswing: 1976–80s

EG&G's environmental division, which languished after the oil embargo, finally began to take off in 1976. Rather than concentrating on environmental compliance, the group evolved into a comprehensive resource efficiency operation that could provide complete oceanographic, atmospheric, and geophysical analysis. By conserving resources, operations could more easily achieve pollution and waste reduction targets.

Another area of success was in port development. Although unable to blast out custom designed harbors with nuclear devices, EG&G was a world leader in oceanographic studies and channel engineering. The company designed numerous tanker ports in the Persian Gulf and bauxite harbors in South America.

In 1979 President Jimmy Carter asked Bernard O'Keefe to serve as chairperson of the government's synthetic fuels corporation. Having already been asked to serve on a transition team for then presidential candidate Ronald Reagan, however, O'Keefe refused Carter's offer.

With the election of Reagan in 1980, the United States took a sudden turn toward military armament programs. EG&G experienced a resurgence in its flagging nuclear testing business and was tapped to develop a number of new nuclear weapons systems, including the MX missile and the Strategic Defense Initiative. A self-described ''card carrying member of the military-industrial complex,'' Bernard O'Keefe wrote in his book *Nuclear Hostages* that the United States and the Soviet Union were locked in an arms race that neither of them could control. Ironically, EG&G remained deeply involved in a number of Reagan administration projects O'Keefe opposed, including the MX, the neutron bomb, and stationing of nuclear missiles in Europe. Nevertheless, EG&G's pretax operating profit doubled from the new business.

EG&G also became involved in the space shuttle program, checking the spacecraft's electrical components, loading its fuel, and managing the Cape Canaveral space center during shuttle missions. EG&G's site management abilities won it a position with the Department of Energy's elite Nuclear Emergency Search Team which investigated nuclear extortion threats. The company also won a contract to manage the government's troubled Rocky Flats installation outside Denver. This facility, which manufactured nuclear weapon triggers, was widely criticized for mismanagement under Rockwell International.

EG&G maintained its momentum throughout the 1980s, winning contracts from diverse governmental agencies, including the Department of Energy, the Army, the Air Force, the Department of Defense, and U.S. Customs. In 1988 the company hit a record high for both sales and earnings. O'Keefe retired from EG&G during this period of strong growth, and was succeeded by John M. Kucharski.

Rapid Diversification: 1990s

Under U.S. President George Bush, and with the subsequent collapse of the Soviet military threat, the number of EG&G nuclear test projects decreased significantly. As such, EG&G was under pressure to cultivate profitable new commercial ventures to offset the loss of revenue from military contracts. The company responded rapidly, entering new commercial markets via a series of acquisitions. One of the first acquisitions of the 1990s was Electro-Optics, the optoelectronics business of General Electric Canada. Electro-Optics designed and produced advanced semiconductor emitters and detectors for defense, space, telecommunications, and industrial applications. Other new ventures followed quickly: the Finland-based WALLAC Group, which produced analytical and diagnostic systems; IC Sensors, a maker of sensing devices for industrial, automotive, medical, and aerospace uses; and NoVOCs, Inc., an environmental remediation specialist.

In 1994, facing legal pressure from activists' groups, EG&G announced that it would discontinue its nuclear-related endeavors as its various existing contracts expired. That same year, the company undertook a major reorganization to accommodate its newly acquired interests and the discontinuation of its nuclear business. One important area of focus for the company was its Instruments division, which was rapidly becoming a leader in the field of weapons and explosives screening systems. After providing x-ray machines and metal detectors for the Democratic and Republican national conventions in 1992, the company won a contract to supply state-of-the-art explosives detection systems for federal courthouses across the nation. A subsequent contract with the Federal Aviation Administration called for ten of EG&G's most advanced explosives detection systems for screening checked baggage in airports.

In 1998 Gregory Summe replaced Kucharski as EG&G's president and CEO. Summe, formerly the president of AlliedSignal Inc.'s Automotive Products Group, was known for his ability to streamline and consolidate technology businesses. He assumed his new position with the twin goals of improving operational efficiency and restructuring EG&G's portfolio to sharpen the company's focus on identified high-growth markets. One of his first efforts toward better operational efficiency was to consolidate all EG&G's business into five independent strategic business units: Life Sciences, Instruments, Engineered Products, Optoelectronics, and Technical Services. The company also began repositioning its portfolio by liquidating assets that fell outside these growth areas and making acquisitions that strengthened EG&G's position within its identified markets. This strategy led to the largest acquisition in the company's history: Lumen Technologies. Lumen, purchased for $250 million in December 1998, was known globally as a producer of specialty lighting. The Lumen acquisition served to strengthen the company's existing position in the medical lighting market, while at the same time allowing it entry into the areas of video and entertainment lighting.

Looking to the Future

The consolidation efforts that Summe's management team initiated in 1998 were expected to continue, with the goal of streamlining sites, functions, and processes so as to reduce operating costs and improve quality, consistency, and response time.

The company intended to continue its focused acquisition strategy. It also planned to continue aggressively developing and marketing new products in its various divisions. Some of the products expected to be introduced were high-volume, cost-effective systems for drug screening, and a Point of Care system that allowed diagnosticians to determine whether or not a patient had suffered a heart attack in just 15 minutes. In addition to introducing new products, the company also anticipated an increased emphasis on product line extensions and renewals.

Principal Subsidiaries

EG&G Alabama, Inc.; EG&G Astrophysics (England); EG&G ATP GmbH (Germany); EG&G ATP GmbH & Co. Automotive Testing Papenburg KG (Germany); EG&G Automotive Research, Inc.; EG&G California, Inc.; EG&G Benelux BV (Netherlands); EG&G Canada Investments, Inc.; EG&G Canada Limited; EG&G Defense Materials, Inc.; EG&G do Brasil Ltda.; EG&G E.C. (U.K.); EG&G Emissions Testing Services, Inc.; EG&G Energy Measurements, Inc.; EG&G Exporters Ltd. (U.S. Virgin Islands); EG&G Florida, Inc.; EG&G GmbH. (Germany); EG&G Holdings, Inc.; EG&G Hong Kong, Ltd.; EG&G IC Sensors, Inc.; EG&G Idaho, Inc.; EG&G Information Technologies, Inc.; EG&G Instruments GmbH. (Germany); EG&G Instruments International Ltd.; EG&G Instruments, Inc.; EG&G International Ltd.; EG&G Japan, Inc.

(U.S.A.); EG&G Judson Infared, Inc.; EG&G KT Aerofab, Inc.; EG&G Langley, Inc.; EG&G Ltd. (U.K.); EG&G Management Services of San Antonio, Inc.; EG&G Management Systems, Inc.; EG&G Missouri Metals Shaping Company, Inc.; EG&G Mound Applied Technologies, Inc.; EG&G Omni, Inc.; EG&G Pressure Science, Inc.; EG&G Singapore Pte Ltd.; EG&G Special Projects, Inc.; EG&G Star City, Inc.; EG&G S.A. (France); EG&G SpA (Italy); EG&G Technical Services of West Virginia, Inc.; EG&G Vactec Philippines, Ltd.; EG&G Ventures, Inc.; EG&G Watertown, Inc.; Antarctic Support Associates (Columbia); B.A.I. GmbH. (Germany); Benelux Analytical Instruments S.A. (Belgium; 92.3%); Berthold A.G. (Switzerland); Berthold Analytical Instruments, Inc.; Berthold France S.A. (80%); Berthold GmbH & Co. KG (Germany); Biozone Oy (Finland); EC III, Inc. (Mexico; 49%); Eagle EG&G, Inc.; Eagle EG&G Aerospace Co. Ltd.; Heimann Optoelectronics GmbH (Germany); Heimann Shenzhen Optoelectronics Co. Ltd. (China); NOK EG&G Optoelectronics Corp. (Japan; 49%); Pribori Oy (Russia); PT EG&G Heimann Optoelectronics (Singapore); Reticon Corp.; Reynolds Electrical & Engineering, Inc.; Science Support Corporation; Seiko EG&G Co., Ltd. (Japan; 49%); Shanghai EG&G Reticon Optoelectronics Co. Ltd.; Societe Civile Immoiliere (France; 82.5%); The Launch Support Company, L.C.; Vactec, Inc.; WALLAC ADL AG (Germany); WALLAC ADL GmbH (Germany); WALLAC A/S; WALLAC Holding GmbH (Germany); WALLAC Norge AS (Norway); WALLAC Oy (Finland); WALLAC Sverige AB (Sweden); WALLAC, Inc.; Wellesley B.V. (Netherlands); Wright Components, Inc.; ZAO Pribori.

Further Reading

"Bombs for Peace," *Forbes,* September 15, 1969, pp. 71–72.
"EG&G Plays Big Role in Nuclear Weaponry, Other Defense Work," *Wall Street Journal,* May 21, 1984, pp. 1–21.
"Hope for the Wild Ones—But Don't Count on Them," *Forbes,* May 15, 1975, pp. 110–14.
"One-Stop Environmental Aid," *Business Week,* July 19, 1976, pp. 44–47.
"Personality: A Pioneer of the Nuclear Age," *New York Times,* January 15, 1967, p. F3.
"Pounds of Plutonium in the Ventilation Ducts," *New York Times,* December 12, 1989, p. 12.
"Spread Eagle Champ," *Forbes,* April 17, 1978, pp. 83–85.

—John Simley
—updated by Shawna Brynildssen

EINSTEIN BAGEL CORP. NOAH

Einstein/Noah Bagel Corporation

14103 Denver West Parkway
Golden, Colorado 80401
U.S.A.
(303) 215-9300
Fax: (303) 216-3403
Web site: http://www.einsteinbros.com

Public Company
Incorporated: 1995 as Progressive Bagel Concepts, Inc.
Employees: 11,700
Sales: $371.9 million (1998)
Stock Exchanges: NASDAQ
Ticker Symbol: ENBX
NAIC: 311811 Retail Bakeries; 722211 Limited-Service
    Restaurants

Einstein/Noah Bagel Corporation is the number one chain of retail bagel stores, with more than 433 Einstein Brothers Bagel stores and 112 Noah's New York Bagels stores in 29 states and Washington, D.C. The eateries offer a variety of creative bagel breakfast and lunch specialties, as well as complementary menu selections such as soups, salads, and baked sweets, and the company's own coffee brand, Melvyn's Darn Good Coffee. The bagel shops highlight the welcoming atmosphere of a neighborhood café, where customers are encouraged to relax and linger.

An Ambitious Conception

Einstein/Noah Bagel Corporation originated as Progressive Bagel Concepts, Inc. (PBCI) in March 1995 when Boston Chicken, Inc. acquired three of the foremost retail bagel companies located in diverse regions of the country. The owners of Offerdahl's Bagel Gourmet, Inc. of Fort Lauderdale, Bagel & Bagel, Inc. of Kansas City, and Brackman Brothers, Inc. of Salt Lake City, found that their store concepts were compatible in that they offered creative bagel flavors in an upscale, neighborhood setting. They joined together for the purpose of creating a national retail chain specializing in baked bagels and complementary products. PBCI began as a chain of 24 bagel shops, ten

Offerdahl's stores, five Bagel & Bagel stores, and nine Brackman Brothers stores. Also, five additional Brackman Brothers stores were in various stages of development.

Boston Chicken supported its new bagel operation both structurally and financially. To promote rapid development of bagel franchises, PBCI modeled Boston Chicken's structure of franchise area developers for the Boston Market chain of restaurants. Under that arrangement the company provided loans convertible to equity interest to regional franchisees for store development. The owners of the original bagel chains became franchise developers for their regions, and shared resources with Boston Chicken's area developers. PBCI benefited from Boston Chicken's basic infrastructure such as computer and communications systems, administration, and real estate for offices and bagel shops. Boston Chicken supported the new bagel company with an $80 million senior secured loan, convertible to majority stock equity interest. PBCI gathered additional financial resources through a private stock offering, which garnered $20 million.

PBCI opened its first Einstein Brothers bagel store in Ogden, Utah, in June 1995. The store featured bagels baked fresh all day, and served in a neighborhood café atmosphere, often with an outdoor patio, and decorated with warm earth tones and wood trim in the interior. Bagels and cream cheese "schmears" were offered in traditional as well as new, inventive flavors. Mass production techniques and inexpensive ingredients allowed the company to offer bagels at 45 cents a piece. After some experimentation at the Ogden store, PBCI decided to launch the Einstein Brothers Bagels brand on a large scale and Einstein Brothers was registered for trademark status.

The company sought rapid expansion of the Einstein Brothers Bagels brand through the acquisition and conversion of bagel stores, as well as through new store development. In August 1995 PBCI acquired Baltimore Bagel Company, a chain of 13 stores in San Diego, and two stores in Orange County, California. Nine Bagel Stop stores in Denver were acquired and converted to the Einstein Brothers brand concept. The Brackman Brothers stores completed their change to the Einstein Brothers concept in January 1996. Targets for franchise development included Chicago; Detroit; Milwaukee and Madison,

Wisconsin; Albuquerque; Las Vegas; Denver; and Tucson, and Phoenix, Arizona. PBCI became Einstein Brothers Bagels, Inc. (EBBI) in December 1995.

Though retail bagel store sales were strong, financial success was elusive. At the end of the first year, EBBI reportedly lost $68.1 million on revenues of $70.4 million. The loss was attributed to initial investment costs such as furniture, fixtures, franchise fees, grand opening promotions, and other expenses. Start-up expenses ranged from $269,000 to $592,000 per unit. EBBI ended 1995 with almost 60 stores.

EBBI became the number two bagel retailer in the United States, behind Bruegger's Bagel Bakery, with the acquisition of Noah's New York Bagels, Inc. (NNYB) of Alameda, California. Boston Chicken increased its earlier loan to EBBI to $120 million in February 1996 to fund the purchase. NNYB stores, founded in 1989, featured kosher bagels and other kosher deli products in the atmosphere of a New York bagel shop at the turn of the 20th century. The acquisition included 37 stores in California and Seattle, while negotiations for development of an additional 40 to 50 stores all along the West Coast were underway. Starbucks owned a 20 percent interest in NNYB, which was transferred to an undisclosed level of ownership in EBBI. NNYB founder Noah Alper became vice-chairman of EBBI. The NNYB brand store expanded to 57 stores in three states by July 1996.

In March 1996, EBBI entered the New England bagel market when it purchased Finagle A Bagel, a chain of three stores in Boston. Finagle A Bagel President Larry Smith was named head of the EBBI team that would develop Einstein Brothers Bagels franchises in New England.

1996 Stock Offerings Feed Expansion

EBBI had franchised more than 152 retail bagel eateries in 15 states when it filed with the Securities and Exchange Commission for an initial public offering and two private offerings of stock in May 1996. In conjunction with the IPO, the company changed its name to Einstein/Noah Bagel Corp (ENBC). ENBC expected to raise about $80 million through the offerings. The actual public offering took place on August 2, 1996 with 2.7 million shares offered at $17 per share. The value of ENBC stock rose to $21.25 per share and ended its first day of trading at $20.50 per share, a 21 percent increase in value. The public offering raised $46 million for debt repayment and franchise expansion. A separate public offering comprised 425,000 shares purchased by company officers, employees, and board directors. Moreover, Boston Chicken converted a $120 million loan into two million shares of ENBC, a 60 percent majority stock interest.

With new funds available the company's goal was to have between 275 and 300 stores in operation by the end of 1996. ENBC continued to follow the Boston Chicken franchising model to replicate Einstein Brothers and Noah's New York Bagel brand concepts quickly. A September 1996 distribution agreement with Marriott Distribution Services would facilitate expansion through its capacity for wide distribution of supplies and materials. In October 1996 Lone Star Bagels L.P. signed a development pact in which it agreed to develop more than 100 Einstein Brothers Bagels stores in Dallas-Fort Worth, Houston, and Austin, Texas. Peter Tucker, head of Lone Star Bagels,

opened the first store in Dallas that month and planned five more stores by the end of 1996. ENBC had 315 stores in operation in 26 states and Washington, D.C., at the end of 1996.

ENBC made a secondary stock offering in December 1996. That offering raised more than $85 million when ENBC sold three million shares at $30 per share. Though Boston Chicken purchased 500,000 shares, its majority interest was reduced to 53 percent ownership of ENBC. The new source of funding and information from area developers prompted ENBC to increase the 1997 estimate of new franchises from a possible 300 stores to as many as 350 stores. Five regional franchise developers committed to operate a total of 668 stores by the end of 1998.

Proceeds from the stock offering provided $32 million to Gulfstream Bagels, area developer for Florida. A 2,200-square-foot store would cost from $350,000 to $425,000 to develop, but bagel stores in Florida generated more than $15,000 average weekly sales. Gulfstream planned to open more than 20 Einstein Brothers stores in South Florida markets, such as Tampa, Naples, Palm Beach, and Miami in 1997. With a goal to open 100 to 150 stores, Steve Messing, chief development officer for Gulfstream, also considered Pensacola, Jacksonville, and Tallahassee. Gulfstream also owned and operated Melvyn & Elmo's Bagels, another ENBC brand which opened in Atlanta in May 1997, with 20 new stores planned to open by the end of 1997.

On August 17, 1997, EBBI opened its 500th bagel shop, and became the number one retail bagel company in the nation, surpassing Bruegger's at 473 stores. As of October 1997 ENBC had 546 bagel stores in 29 states and Washington, D.C., operated under various brand names, primarily Einstein Brothers and Noah's New York Bagels.

New products were introduced to attract lunch business such as sourdough baguettes, and focaccia sandwiches, tortilla roll-ups, and a pizza bagel. For St. Patrick's Day, ENBC introduced the Lucky Green bagel, made with "magic Irish green flour that imparts the Luck O the Irish on anyone who eats it." The company created its own coffee brand, Melvyn's Darn Good Coffee, sold fresh brewed in five daily variations, or in whole bags.

Despite some success at the store level, ENBC's stock values tended to perform poorly. In January 1997 the stock peaked at $33 per share, but declined significantly thereafter. In August the stock had dropped to $11 per share, resulting from an expectation that expansion would slow down. On October 30, 1997, ENBC stock fell further, to $10.25 per share. Financial considerations led to the closure of five of the ten regional franchise offices.

Conversion to Company Ownership

In November 1997 the board and management decided to reorganize its structure, changing all of its outlets from franchisee ownership to company ownership. ENBC did not own any of the 546 restaurants, but received royalties and earned interest on loans to franchisees. Company ownership shifted store profits to ENBC. Under the plan four area developers merged into the fifth, Einstein/Noah Bagel Partners, L.P. Area franchisees retained a 23 percent equity interest under Bagel Store Development Funding,

L.L.C., while loans made to area developers were converted into a 77 percent ownership in the retail bagel stores.

1998 Focus: Store-Level Improvement

Conversion to company ownership of the bagel stores reflected ENBC's objective to reorient its strategy. The company focused on improving sales and reducing operating costs at stores already succeeding, rather than continuing to open new stores. By March 1998 ENBC closed 25 stores with inadequate performance. Some did not fit the brand concept of a community-oriented, neighborhood cafe. The closures resulted in a $2.4 million write-down. ENBC changed its original projection of 150 to 200 store openings in 1998, and reduced the number to 25 to 50 new stores for the year.

In February 1998 Robert Hartnett was named CEO of the company. Hartnett had successfully led Gulfstream Bagels, area developer for Florida and the southeastern United States. Einstein Brothers stores in Florida generated ten percent higher sales than an average Einstein store. Under Hartnett those stores had successfully implemented local marketing programs and introduced new products. Also, Hartnett originated an effective compensation package for store managers. Similar strategies were implemented throughout the company in 1998, such as improvement of hiring and training practices, and measurements of store-level performance on a weekly basis. An incentive plan for store managers was launched systemwide. To increase revenues, ENBC enhanced in-store merchandising and raised menu prices.

ENBC strategy to improve sales led to the introduction of seasonal menus and catering services. New cream cheese schmears included mango in the summer and cappuccino in the fall. The fall lunch menu added soups, bean salad, and sourdough baguette sandwiches with such ingredients as goat cheese and kalamata olive spread. Winter holiday offerings included bagel buckets, with a baker's dozen of bagels and two varieties of cream cheese. Holiday specialty items included spiced cranberry lite cream cheese, gingerbread cookies, and cranberry walnut poundcake. Due to its popularity in 1997 the company offered Mel's Holiday Brew again in 1998.

ENBC sought corporate business when it introduced its, "Fancy Schmancy Catering" in November 1998. The program offered Breakfast Nosh Boxes of cinnamon rolls, scones, and muffins as well as bagels and cream cheese. Lunch Nosh Boxes featured baguette or bagel sandwiches, including napkins and utensils. Nosh boxes were designed to serve 15 or more people. Individual box lunches and assorted sweets were also available.

An Unknown Future

Creditor demands on parent company Boston Chicken led it to place a majority interest in ENBC up for sale in May 1998. While no one stepped forward to purchase ENBC and the offer for sale was withdrawn, Boston Chicken remained open to unsolicited offers. After Boston Chicken filed for Chapter 11 Bankruptcy reorganization in October 1998, ENBC distinguished itself from Boston Chicken, stating in an October 7, 1998 *Denver Post* article that, "Our operations are separate and our concepts are distinctively different." Nevertheless, finan-

cial problems at Boston Chicken affected stock values at ENBC which declined to $1 per share on October 21, 1998.

In August 1998 ENBC petitioned the NASDAQ National Market to remain listed on its stock exchange. ENBC was no longer in compliance with that market's criteria, a $5.00 per share price for 90 days and minimum net tangible assets of $4 million. ENBC's bid to remain on the National Market was based on a disagreement as to the net worth of the company. The NASDAQ defined a $70 million "minority interest" on its ENBC balance sheet as a liability. ENBC defined that amount as an asset in the acquisition of the area franchises. The NASDAQ National Market transferred ENBC to the NASDAQ Small Cap Market, and the company retained its stock symbol, ENBX.

Despite its financial tribulations, ENBC continued to succeed at the store level. A one-time charge of $212 million for goodwill in purchasing area franchise developers for more than their book value led to a loss of $31.8 million in 1998, but systemwide revenue increased 23 percent to $371.9 million in 1998. Previously, average store sales suffered from heavy use of coupons and discounts, but store weekly average sales reached $13,103 in 1998.

In March 1999 Einstein Brothers Bagels won an award from the Restaurant and Institutions Magazine. The 19th Annual Choice in Chains Award was presented to Einstein Brothers Bagels for First Place, Platinum, in the Bread/Bakery category. Winners were determined through consumer surveys commissioned by *Restaurants and Institutions* magazine, which rates more than 100 regional and national chains on attributes such as the quality of food, customer service, convenience, menu, atmosphere, value and cleanliness. More than 2,800 adults participated in the survey.

At the end of 1998 and the beginning of 1999 ENBC continued to reorganize for profitability. High overhead expenses led to the closure of company field offices, while staff at the Golden, Colorado headquarters dwindled from 350 employees to 160 employees. Executive positions were slashed from 24 positions to ten. By the end of 1998, ENBC closed 43 stores and opened 15 new stores. In early 1999, ENBC closed ten stores, opened five new stores, and only planned another five openings. CEO Hartnett expected franchise development to resume in 2000 under direct company supervision, rather than the elaborate financial arrangements which led to Boston Chicken's difficulties.

In 1999, Boston Chicken began looking to sell its interest in ENBC, but no buyers were immediately forthcoming. A new chief financial officer for ENBC, Paula Manley, was appointed in June of that year, and she was able to report encouraging financial results for the early quarters of the year. Revenues were increasing and net losses decreasing, attributable to increases in per store sales and reductions in the work force. Despite its troubled relationship with majority shareholder Boston Chicken, ENBC remained the company's top bagel shop as a new century approached.

Principal Subsidiaries

Einstein/Noah Bagel Partners, Inc.; Einstein/Noah Bagel Partners, L.P. (77%).

Further Reading

"Bagel Rebound," *Rocky Mountain News,* July 16, 1997, p. B2.

"The Bagel Went Down to Georgia: Melvyn & Elmo's Opens 1st Unit," *Nation's Restaurant News,* May 5, 1997, p. 53.

"Boston Chicken May Sell Stake in Einstein/Noah Bagel," *New York Times,* May 28, 1998, p. C3.

"Boston Chicken's Bagel Company Has Been Operating in the Hole," *Wall Street Journal,* July 30, 1996, p. B2.

Browning, E. S., "More Bagel Chains Go Public, But Is There Enough Dough?," *Wall Street Journal,* September 3, 1996, p. C1.

Bunn, Dina, "Einstein/Noah Bagel Ends Year Deep in Hole," *Rocky Mountain News,* February 18, 1999, p. 16B.

——, "Einstein Predicts Brighter Times," *Rocky Mountain News,* May 25, 1999, p. 16B.

"Einstein Broadens Bagel Chain," *Denver Post,* March 21, 1996, p. C2.

"Einstein/Noah Bagel Corp. Completes Offering of 3.0 Million Shares of Common Stock," *Business Wire,* November 27, 1996.

"Einstein/Noah IPO Raises $46 Million," *Nation's Restaurant News,* August 12, 1996, p. 2.

Gibson, Richard, "For Bagel Chains, Investments May Be Money in the Hole," *Wall Street Journal,* December 30, 1997, p. B8.

"Hot IPO: Investors Eat Up Einstein/Noah Bagel Shares," *Knight-Ridder/Tribune Business News,* August 4, 1996.

Kalisher, Jesse, "Art of Noise," *Brandweek,* June 29, 1998, p. 46.

Lewis, Al, "Einstein Stock Soars 57%," *Rocky Mountain News,* October 28, 1998, p. 1B.

Meres Kroskey, Carol, "Einstein's Evolution into Eatery," *Bakery Production and Marketing,* March 15, 1998, p. 32.

Oberbeck, Steven, "Bagel Wars Heat Up Across Utah As More Stores Open," *Knight-Ridder/Tribune Business News,* November 29, 1995.

Papiernik, Richard L., "Boston Chicken Takes Einstein Bros. Public," *Nation's Restaurant News,* June 10, 1996, p. 3.

——, "Einstein/Noah Chain Is No. 1 But Investors Remain Wary," *Nation's Restaurant News,* August 25, 1997, p. 12.

Parker, Penny, "Einstein Atop Bagel Heap As It Opens 500th Outlet," *Denver Post,* August 26, 1997, p. C1.

——, "Einstein Faces Nasdaq Hearing; Disagreement over Net Worth," *Denver Post,* July 30, 1998, p. C1.

——, "Einstein/Noah Scales Back Aggressive Growth Strategy," *Denver Post,* February 18, 1998, p. C10.

——, "Getting Big on Bagels," *Denver Post,* October 22, 1995, p. G1.

"PBCI Names Concept Einstein Brothers Bagels," *Nation's Restaurant News,* October 16, 1995, p. 54.

Trollinger, Amy, "Bagel & Bagel Parent Company Heads to Chicago." *Kansas City Business Journal,* August 1, 1997, p. 1.

Waters, Jennifer, "Bagel BUST," *Restaurants and Institutions,* June 1, 1998, p. 77.

—Mary Tradii

Ernst & Young

787 Seventh Avenue
New York, New York 10019
U.S.A.
(212) 773-3000
(800) 688-3677
Fax: (212) 773-6350
Web site: http://www.eyi.com

Private Company
Incorporated: 1989
Employees: 85,000
Sales: $10.9 billion (1998)
NAIC: 541211 Offices of Certified Public Accountants

Ernst & Young is the fourth largest public accounting firm in the world. The firm was formed in 1989 when the third largest accounting firm at the time, Ernst & Whinney (based in Cleveland, Ohio), merged with the sixth largest firm, Arthur Young (headquartered in New York), forming what, at the time, was the world's largest accounting firm. As of 1999 Ernst & Young stood as one of the "Big Five" accounting firms that dominated the accounting business. A private partnership, Ernst & Young was owned by its senior partners. Ernst & Young provided auditing services primarily to the world's largest corporations. In addition, it specialized in tax advice for multinational firms. In recent years, the firm increasingly moved into the business of management consulting, providing guidance to clients in such areas as risk management, mergers and acquisitions, and recent trends in worker-management relations. Other service areas included consulting on information technology and legal services.

Company Origins

The roots of Ernst & Young can be traced back well over 100 years to the formation of the auditing business and the development of generally accepted accounting practices, rules that became increasingly necessary with the rise of the multinational corporation and the intrusion of complicated taxes into private business. Prior to the 1989 merger, each of the two firms

had enjoyed rich histories. Both rose from very small beginnings by capitalizing on the enterprise potential of accounting in its early years. Pioneer Arthur Young founded and headed the original Arthur Young firm back in 1895 in Kansas City after breaking from an earlier union of the firm of Stuart and Young in Chicago. In 1896 Young formed the firm of Arthur Young and Company with his brother Stanley, but by 1906 Young had completely terminated his unsatisfactory partnership with Stuart. Arthur Young and Company flourished for many years, slowly developing its reputation as "old reliable" for auditing, adding more and more partners throughout the years.

The other half of the marriage, Ernst & Whinney, can be traced back to 1906, when Ernst & Ernst was founded in Cleveland, Ohio, as a partnership between Alwin C. Ernst and his older brother, Theodore C. Ernst. The firm took on its first additional partners in 1910 and from there the family tree expanded by immense and unforeseen proportions. By 1913, when income taxes began to be levied in the United States, the need for accountants swelled dramatically. By the 1980s the firm had become one of the largest members of the Big Eight. In one of its more publicized actions, Ernst & Whinney's audit paved the way for the 1979 government bailout of the Chrysler Corporation.

Meanwhile, the Arthur Young firm endured a rocky decade in the 1980s. Long known for its reliable auditing practice and a clean, conservative interpretation of tax law, the company image was tarnished by events of the 1980s, many in the area of the national savings and loan scandal. For instance, Arthur Young was sued for $560 million for allegedly allowing Western Savings Association of Dallas to overstate its net worth by more than $400 million. In 1988 the Bank of England sued Arthur Young and collected $44 million after a bank that Young audited collapsed.

In contrast to the struggles of Arthur Young prior to the merger, Ernst & Whinney's business had thrived, with its management consulting practice growing faster than its audit and tax practice. In fact, at the time of the merger, consulting fees accounted for 24 percent of Ernst & Whinney's revenues, whereas only 17 percent of Arthur Young's revenues came from consulting.

Company Perspectives:

Ernst & Young, one of the world's leading professional services organizations, helps companies across the globe to identify and capitalize on business opportunities. We deliver the value that clients care about; we provide ideas and solutions tailored to meet clients' needs; and we produce tangible results. Ernst & Young's depth and breadth of service and our global reach mean that we have the resources to serve any client, anywhere in the world.

1989 Merger

In general, both firms thought that a merger represented a comparative advantage for each. Although both had heavy hitters for clients, Arthur Young's clients were mostly investment banks and high-tech firms on the East and West Coasts, while Ernst & Whinney had more healthcare and manufacturing industry clients concentrated in the Midwest and South. Internationally, Arthur Young had more clients in Europe, while Ernst & Whinney had established a presence in the Pacific Rim countries. Arthur Young's clients included American Express, Mobil, and Texas Instruments, while Ernst & Whinney had BankAmerica, Time, Inc., and Eli Lilly.

Although touted as a merger, the evidence suggests that the 1989 transaction that created the firm Ernst & Young was, in fact, an acquisition in disguise, with the stronger Ernst & Whinney swallowing up the floundering Arthur Young practice. Arthur Young had established a strong reputation over many years, although it was generally seen as a cautious and stodgy practice. But by the 1980s, after much of its traditional audit practice started to collapse and massive leveraged buyouts became an increasingly common practice in the business world, Arthur Young had difficulty competing in the cutthroat environment of the accounting arena.

Historically, the accounting business has seen increasing numbers of partners concentrated in a decreasing number of firms. In this respect, the birth of Ernst & Young in 1989 was the natural outcome of the cycle of competition that breeds concentration and expansion, thus leading to further rounds of competition. But for over half a century previous to the creation of Ernst & Young, eight firms had dominated the accounting business. The elite group was dubbed the ''Big Eight'' by *Fortune* magazine.

Following two major mergers in the 1980s (the Ernst & Young deal and the merger the same year between Deloitte, Haskins & Sells and Touche Ross), the Big Eight became the Big Six. All of the Big Six were private partnerships, meaning that all were owned by the firm's senior executives, which also meant that none of the firms were required to report their profits.

The Ernst & Young merger created a firm with 6,100 partners and two chief executive officers, Ray Groves from Ernst & Whinney and William Gladstone from Arthur Young. The newly formed firm had world revenues in 1989 of $4.27 billion, and its total sales eclipsed that established by a merger in 1987 of Peat Marwick and KMG Main Hurdman.

The actual merger in 1989 was essentially viewed as a smart competitive move, although some observers thought the merger might be difficult due to perceived differences in management styles, with Ernst & Whinney governed from the top and Arthur Young favoring a more decentralized management system. At the time of the merger Ernst & Whinney had 1,276 partners and 14,739 total personnel in 118 U.S. offices as well as 3,159 partners and 35,600 total personnel in 89 countries. The smaller Arthur Young had 829 U.S.-based partners and 10,652 total U.S. personnel in 93 offices; worldwide they had 2,900 partners and 33,000 total personnel in 74 countries.

There was a conflict at the time of the merger over each firm's ''cola'' clients. A conflict of interest existed in that PepsiCo had been an Arthur Young client since 1965, while Coca-Cola had been an Ernst & Whinney client since 1924. Coca-Cola forced the firm to dump PepsiCo, as Ernst & Young noted that Coca-Cola had been a client for a longer time and that Coke's annual audit fee was $14 million, a much higher figure than Pepsi's $8.8 million audit fee.

In one of its first business decisions following the merger, Ernst & Young began to move into computer-aided software engineering. This step reflected Ernst & Young's diversification into management systems and strategic planning services for businesses. Under the general heading of Development Effectiveness, these services capped a string of moves into computer-aided software engineering. The general thrust of the project incorporated management consulting, Total Quality Management, and process innovation. The process innovation services were sold worldwide, primarily to the insurance and banking industries.

Paying for the S&L Scandal

However, as the newly formed firm faced the 1990s, it was steeped in the controversy surrounding the crisis of the savings and loan industry. Ernst & Young's audits of 23 failed savings and loans were investigated by the Office of Thrift Supervision (OTS) under a subpoena issued in June 1991. OTS was formed by the federal government to recover losses from accounting firms that should have discovered improprieties during S&L audits and to impose fines on auditors for violations of accounting rules. Some of the thrifts that Ernst & Young audited included Charles Keating's failed Lincoln Savings & Loan (Irvine, California), Silverado Banking (Denver, Colorado), Vernon Savings & Loan (Vernon, Texas), and Western Federal Savings & Loan (Dallas, Texas), all of which experienced total losses of over $5.5 billion. The OTS subpoena required that Ernst & Young surrender one million documents from its work for the 23 failed S&Ls.

Several judgments were rendered against Ernst & Young in connection with the investigation. In July 1992, for instance, the firm paid a fine of $1.66 million to settle accusations that it helped Charles H. Keating, Jr., deceive the federal government about the health of his failing S&L. Moreover, former Ernst & Young partner Jack D. Atchison's license was suspended for four years by the accounting board of Arizona. He was accused of helping persuade five U.S. senators to intervene with federal regulators on Keating's behalf. In connection with this settlement, Ernst & Young paid $63 million to settle charges of wrongdoing in the Keating affair. Ernst & Young did not admit guilt, however, and the claim was paid largely by insurance. In total, some $204 million in fines were paid in this civil suit.

In another settlement, Ernst & Young paid $400 million to the federal government in compliance with a federal ruling against the company. The settlement secured recovery of losses attributable to audit failures. In addition, the settlement avoided huge litigation costs and assured that future audits of insured institutions would be conducted according to the highest professional standards. With potential claims that could have mounted to an estimated $1 billion, the ruling relieved Ernst & Young of concerns regarding future penalties involving S&L auditing improprieties. Ernst & Young also agreed to change its accounting practices and ensure that its partners meet federal guidelines for working with federally insured financial institutions. Some of Ernst & Young's partners were barred from doing such work and changes in banking laws required accounting firms to be legally responsible for sharing with regulators reports prepared for bank management.

Expansion in the 1990s

Despite these troubles, Ernst & Young defied the rumors that it would fold. To eliminate overlap created by the merger and to reduce its payroll expenses, the firm cut its staff in 1991 and eliminated many partner positions. Although revenues had fallen slightly in the late 1980s, by the early 1990s revenues were modestly but steadily rising. Sales from Ernst & Young's risk management and actuarial services group rose 7.4 percent from 1990 to 1991, from $9.5 million to $10.2 million. Overall revenues rose from $5 billion in 1990 to $5.4 billion in 1991 and $5.7 billion in 1992.

The company garnered an increasing number of clients, and their involvement in such large projects as municipal insurance and environmental risk management consulting continued to grow. Revenues in risk management consulting went from $10.3 million in 1991 to $10.9 million in 1992. This increase reflected a growing market for these kinds of services. Moreover, major restructuring was taking place in hospitals and in the healthcare industry in general, creating a need for consultants. The traditional Ernst & Young mainstay, auditing, still fared quite well in the new firm's early years. By 1992, in fact, Ernst & Young performed the most audits of large publicly held multinational companies. It audited 3,231 companies with a total value audited of $10.228 trillion (based on asset figures for financial companies and sales for all other firms audited).

Ernst & Young's costly legal battles encouraged several changes in the mid-1990s. First, the firm hired a new general legal counsel, Kathryn Oberly, who reputedly made keeping costs down a higher priority than battling on principle. Second, the firm stepped up its expansion into consulting, an area much less fraught with legal responsibilities and their concomitant lawsuits than auditing. In addition to increasing its consulting in risk management, the company moved into information software products.

Ernst & Young also entered new business areas in the mid-1990s by developing alliances and by acquiring smaller

companies. In 1996 the firm forged an alliance with Tata Consulting, headquartered in India. The same year, its alliance with ISD/Shaw gave the firm an entree into banking industry consulting. The firm moved into the petroleum and petrochemical consulting business in 1996 when it purchased Wright Kellen & Co. Ernst & Young created a new subsidiary with the Houston-based company, which they named Ernst & Young Wright Killen.

Failed Merger with KPMG

In 1997 Ernst & Young forged an agreement to merge with KPMG International, another Big Six accounting firm. The agreement came only weeks after the announcement of a merger between Price Waterhouse and Coopers & Lybrand, which would have created the world's biggest accounting firm, with $12 billion in revenues and a staff of 135,000. However, the Ernst & Young-KPMG International merger overshadowed that, with combined revenues of $16 billion and 160,000 people. According to Ernst & Young, the deal was designed to satisfy multinational clients who wanted an auditor and consultant with offices in every city in which the client had offices. In addition, the merger would have limited the risk of a liability suit severely damaging earnings and would have made greater economies of scale for developing new products or services.

Combining the two huge companies presented a formidable task, particularly because they were intense competitors. Between 1991 and 1997 KPMG had lost approximately 60 of its auditing clients in the United States to Ernst & Young. A larger problem than overcoming historic rivalries, however, was gaining regulatory approval. The Ernst & Young-KPMG International merger and the Price Waterhouse-Coopers & Lybrand merger would have furthered the consolidation of the major accounting firms into the Big Four, an outcome disturbing to many industry analysts. Along with fears that the relative lack of choice would encourage a rise in prices, there were fears among clients that the combined firms would make company secrets vulnerable to rivals using the same firm.

Citing the high cost of pursuing the merger and the uncertain regulatory outcome, Ernst & Young suggested in early 1998 that the two firms abandon their merger plans. Some analysts thought that the money and attention required to integrate the firms, at a time when all Big Six firms were expanding rapidly, also discouraged the merger.

Ernst & Young experienced substantial growth in 1997, despite being hit by a $4 billion lawsuit alleging the firm mishandled the restructuring of Merry-Go-Round Enterprises in 1993. Overall revenues rose from $7.8 billion in 1996 to $9.1 billion in 1997. A substantial amount of this growth was fueled by a 30 percent surge in tax advice revenues and an 18 percent increase in worldwide tax revenues, an area in which Ernst & Young led the Big Six. The firm also boosted its efficiency in 1997, raising its revenue per employee ten percent that year, to $238,360. Revenues continued to rise spectacularly in 1998, reaching $10.9 billion, a jump of almost 20 percent.

The Big Five, as they were called with the completion of the Price Waterhouse-Coopers & Lybrand merger in 1998, continued to diversify their services in the late 1990s. Revenues from consulting on tax issues, personnel, management, property, and personal finance swamped revenues from auditing for Ernst & Young. In 1999 the firm had plans to add a worldwide law practice to its stable of services. Ernst & Young already had associated law practices in several countries by the end of the century and planned to build a global staff of 4,000 by the year 2005.

Further Reading

"Bean-Counters Unite," *Economist,* October 25, 1997, pp. 67–68.

Berton, Lee, "Arthur Young, and Ernst Firm Plan to Merge," *Wall Street Journal,* May 19, 1989.

Burton, J. C., ed., *Arthur Young and the Business He Founded,* New York: Arthur Young & Company, 1948.

Cannon, Phillippa, "Ernst & Young Tax Breaks $2 Billion Barrier," *International Tax Review,* February 1998, p. 9.

"Entrepreneurial Services: Ernst & Young's Territory," *Emerson's Professional Services Review,* November 1991.

"E&W, AY, DH&S, and TR Financial Data Creates Public Stir," *Emerson's Professional Services Review,* March, 1990.

"E&Y: The Masters of Total Quality Management," *Emerson's Professional Services Review,* March 1992.

Ernst & Ernst: A History of the Firm, Cleveland: Ernst & Ernst, 1960.

"Ernst & Young: Driving for Specialization and Service Integration Leadership," *Emerson's Professional Services Review,* March 1990.

"Ernst & Young Settles Lincoln Savings Case," *New York Times,* July 15, 1992.

"Finance and Economics: Disciplinary Measures," *Economist,* March 6, 1999, pp. 68–69.

Jones, Edgar, *Accountancy and the British Economy 1840–1980: The Evolution of Ernst & Whinney,* London: B.T. Batsford, Ltd., 1981.

Labaton, Stephen, "$400 Million Bargain for Ernst," *New York Times,* November 25, 1992.

Law, Donald M., "Business Tycoon Arthur Young Loved Life in Aiken at Crossways," *Aiken Standard,* April 19, 1987.

Moskowitz, Milton, et al., *Everybody's Business: A Field Guide to the 400 Leading Companies in America,* New York: Doubleday, 1990.

Stevens, Mark, *The Accounting Wars,* New York: Macmillan, 1985.

——, *The Big Eight,* New York: Macmillan, 1981.

——, *The Big Six: The Selling Out of America's Top Accounting Firms,* New York: Simon & Schuster, 1991.

Willis, Clint, "How Winners Do It," *Forbes,* August 24, 1998, pp. 88–92.

—John A. Sarich
—updated by Susan Windisch Brown

Esprit de Corp.

900 Minnesota Avenue
San Francisco, California 94107
U.S.A.
(415) 648-6900
Fax: (415) 415-550-3951
Web site: http://www.esprit.com

Private Company
Incorporated: 1970
Sales: $350 million (1998)
Employees: 1,300
NAIC: 315212 Women's, Girls' & Infants' Cut & Sew
   Apparel Contractors; 42233 Women's, Children's &
   Infants' Clothing & Accessories Wholesalers

Esprit de Corp. designs, manufactures, and distributes a wide variety of apparel and fashion accessories for women and children. Renowned for fostering a sense of social responsibility among its employees and customers, the company built its image on commitment to such causes as AIDS awareness and environmental conservation. Having soared to high-profile success from the mid-1970s to the late 1980s, by 1992 the company had plummeted to a state of financial ill-repute where it remained until the late 1990s, when the company launched a comeback under new leadership that freely capitalized on the brand recognition won during Esprit's glory days. The Esprit brand is marketed in 44 countries and is available in department stores, specialty stores and over 350 freestanding Esprit retail stores. The late 1990s saw the addition of a web site and a reinstated catalog as important alternative marketing venues.

Early History

Esprit was built primarily by Doug Tompkins and Susie Tompkins, a husband-and-wife team whose personal and political values informed the company's early business strategy. The couple met outside Lake Tahoe in 1963, when Susie Russell offered the hitchhiking Doug Tompkins a ride in her Volkswagen. Both Susie and Doug were from wealthy backgrounds and had dropped out of high school to explore more Bohemian lifestyles. After several months of travel together in Mexico and the western United States, they married and settled in San Francisco. There they embraced the social causes and fashions of that city's active counterculture.

In 1964 Doug, an enthusiastic skier and rock climber, invested $5,000 to start a retail business devoted to mountaineering equipment. Called North Face, the store was established in a prime location across from San Francisco's popular City Lights Book Store, and it quickly achieved success. Because of his capable staff, who oversaw daily operations, Doug was able to spend much of the year on international rock climbing and skiing expeditions. Susie remained in San Francisco, raising the couple's two children and occasionally assisting at the North Face store.

During this time, Susie Tompkins became interested in a business venture proposed by her friend Jane Tise. Together they formed the Plain Jane Dress Company, which offered puffed-sleeve, acrylic minidresses that Tise designed and Susie distributed. After the Plain Jane dress line became successful locally, it was marketed to New York department stores by Allan Schwartz, a salesperson who became a partner in the company.

Late in the 1960s, having sold the North Face operation for approximately $50,000, Doug Tompkins joined Plain Jane as a partner. While Tise and Susie designed the product and added new designs and labels to their popular line, Doug and Schwartz handled the marketing and sales responsibilities, targeting affluent California households with colorful, oversized catalogs.

Growth in the 1970s

By 1970 Plain Jane had sales exceeding $1 million a year. Doug and Susie Tompkins owned roughly 45 percent of the company, while Tise and Schwartz held the other 55 percent. At this time, some observers allege, Doug Tompkins stepped up his interest in the company, making bold decisions concerning the company's direction and professing an interest in taking charge. He was instrumental in steering the company's focus to more contemporary designs as the American ''hippie'' look

Company Perspectives:

There is no one perfect Esprit woman. Because Esprit is about the individuality of many. About what's on the outside and what's on the inside. About variety of sizes, shapes, colors, faces. There is no one perfect Esprit woman. There are many. She is the woman everyone wants to be. She was born a woman and just keeps getting younger. She doesn't lead and she doesn't follow, she's just out there if you can catch up with her. She believes that if you believe it, it will come. She believes that words haven't lost their meaning, like love and desire, like forever and a day, like different but the same, like life is what you make it.

subsided. In 1972, after he and Susie visited several countries in Asia, Doug decided to move manufacturing operations to Hong Kong, where clothing could be produced less expensively.

Schwartz and Tise sold their shares to the Tompkinses in 1976. Although Schwartz left the company immediately thereafter, Tise remained as chief fashion designer until 1979, when she reportedly became dissatisfied—as Schwartz had—with the lack of input allowed her by the Tompkinses. That year Susie took charge of the design department. By this time the company had expanded its product line under several different labels to include pants, blouses, and skirts. These different divisions of the company were soon reorganized and consolidated, and Plain Jane was renamed Esprit de Corp. The company's trademark loose-fitting casual designs in bold colors caught on, and Esprit rapidly evolved into one of the most popular clothing companies among 18- to 24-year-old women.

The Brand Becomes an Image in the 1980s

During the early 1980s Esprit swiftly expanded and distinguished itself in the business community through both its sales and the way in which it reflected the eclectic tastes of Susie and Doug Tompkins. An art and architecture enthusiast, Doug Tompkins spent a great deal of time and money to renovate the San Francisco winery that would become the company's new headquarters. Featuring skylights, wood floors, and Amish quilts on the walls, the brick building gained national recognition among architects and interior designers. The facility offered Esprit employees access to tennis courts, a running track, and a trendy café. Seeking to create an enjoyable work atmosphere to match the spirit of Esprit clothing, the Tompkinses encouraged employees to dress fashionably yet casually; high heels were not permitted on the easily scuffed wood floors of the headquarters building. Furthermore, the Tompkinses offered a unique benefits package. In addition to a 52 percent discount on Esprit clothing, employees received subsidized tickets to the theater, ballet, and opera, as well as free vacations in the mountains and foreign language lessons. Employees came to refer to their workplace as "Camp Esprit" and "Little Utopia."

From 1979 to 1985 the company's sales grew from $120 million to $700 million. As design director, Susie approved all drawings and fabrics, while Doug held the titles of president

and "image director." During this time, Esprit became the first clothing company to require department stores to relegate a part of their sportswear section specifically for use as a "shop within a shop." While the concept called for a relatively large amount of floor space, expensive track lighting, and special signage, many department stores complied because of the Esprit line's high sales volume. Catalogs also served as an important marketing strategy in the early 1980s. Oversized, glossy booklets featured pictures of employees and other "real people" modeling Esprit clothes, alongside written personal statements. In an interview, Doug Tompkins asserted that the Esprit customer is of "above-average intelligence and knows the difference between 'substance and superficiality'." "Women who wear Esprit," he concluded, "are the new feminists."

Between 1984 and 1986 the company borrowed nearly $75 million to open several retail stores, the first of which was a superstore in Los Angeles that showcased Doug Tompkins's design taste. The store cost about $15 million to build. Subsequent stores were established in New Orleans, San Francisco, and Aspen, Colorado, and by 1987 there were 14 Esprit retail stores nationwide. While owners of department stores that carried Esprit clothing protested that these retail outlets represented unfair competition, company executives disagreed.

Fiscal Stumbling in the Late 1980s

As Esprit grew, some critics charged that the company was overextending itself. In late 1986 and 1987, Esprit experienced losses for the first time in its history. Earnings fell from $62 million to $10 million, representing an 83 percent downturn. Several reasons were given for the abrupt reversal. The *San Francisco Examiner* suggested that competitors were copying Esprit designs and offering them at lower prices and further reported that some retailers were complaining of inferior quality and design in new Esprit lines. The Tompkinses maintained that while the company may have tried to expand too rapidly, its spring lines were selling well. They pointed to the decline of the U.S. dollar as the primary reason for the company's losses. Furthermore, they maintained, while international sales were escalating, Esprit's foreign operations were jointly owned with local investors so that profits were reinvested in the foreign market.

In 1986 Doug Tompkins turned Esprit over to Corrado Federico, who became the company's president, while Doug remained as Esprit's CEO and chairperson. Exploring ways to cut the company's costs and consolidate its operations, Federico implemented a freeze on hiring and bonuses that year. Although employees were soon required to pay for coffee and phone calls made in the office, the Tompkinses ensured that some of the unique benefits that made up Esprit's image as a fun, creative workplace remained. The following year the Esprit work force was cut by 30 percent, and Doug Tompkins brought in experts from rival fashion companies to manage the newly consolidated divisions.

It soon became apparent, however, that Esprit's downturns were more than just temporary. Critics cited both Esprit's failure to stay abreast of fashion trends, as well as irreconcilable differences that had developed between Susie and Doug Tompkins, as reasons for the company's troubles. Specifically, the Tompkinses had begun to argue about the direction the company should take. Susie regarded the company's image as too young, maintaining that customers were seeking a more sophisticated look. She believed Esprit's original customers had grown up, and she suggested introducing a line of corporate wear for the loyal Esprit buyer. Doug, on the other hand, argued that the company's youthful image was too important to change and that corporate women would not purchase Esprit.

In March 1988 the *Wall Street Journal* reported on the rift between the Tompkinses. While the column focused on the couple's relationship and Doug's alleged extramarital affairs with women in the company, it also reported that weak financial management and the design department's failure to note the fashion world's shift to a more traditional look were hurting business. In addition, interviews with former Esprit employees revealed that tension in the workplace was being fostered by two factions—those who sided with Doug and those in Susie's camp. The article also revealed that Doug was seeking minority equity partners to help maintain the struggling Esprit retail stores.

Doug Tompkins Takes Over in the Late 1980s

When Susie Tompkins petitioned a San Francisco court to appoint a third director to help run Esprit in March 1988, a judge advised that she and her husband resolve the situation without legal intervention. The following month, hoping to reverse the stalemate, the Tompkinses appointed three new directors—Peter Buckley, Isaac Stein, and Robert Bartlett—to turn Esprit around. By May of that year the new board recommended that Susie and Doug each remain 50-percent owners of Esprit but that they give up their operating control of the company. Under the plan Esprit president Federico became chief executive officer. Doug was given the title of chief executive officer of Esprit International operations and was required to abandon the idea of expanding Esprit's retail establishments through outside financiers. While many of Doug's duties at Esprit remained the same, Susie's role at the company changed dramatically. No longer the chief fashion designer, she was effectively out of the business. As a "fashion consultant" to Esprit she kept in close contact with the management team but announced that she would also spend time away from Esprit, concentrating on her volunteer work for such social causes as AIDS awareness. Early in 1989, Susie and Doug Tompkins filed for divorce.

That year Doug pursued his growing interest in environmental conservation within the parameters of the fashion industry by instituting a new marketing strategy in which the company actually advised the customer not to buy Esprit clothing if she did not need it. Doug argued that consumerism in general, and especially in the fashion industry, was leading to the destruction of natural resources and that Esprit should thus introduce clothing that would outlast the seasonal fads. Doug's "buy only what you need" campaign included hang tags with the warning on each article of clothing, as well as a new line of fashions in more traditional, muted colors. Initially the line was profitable, but it eventually declined, and, during this time, critics noted that Doug seemed to be more interested in ecology than fashion.

While Esprit had recovered from the previous two years' losses, the company was still regarded as unsteady and lacking a corporate vision. In July 1989 Esprit announced a new plan to refocus Esprit under one Tompkins. Doug was given the option to buy out Susie's 50 percent within 120 days of the agreement. If he did not, both halves of the company would go up for sale at auction. Clothing and footwear manufacturing giants Benetton and Reebok became interested in acquiring Esprit, when, after the requisite 120 days, Doug had not exercised his option.

Analysts speculated that by forcing the auction of the company Doug had initially hoped to acquire Esprit for a lower price than he would have paid to buy out Susie's share. However, as Reebok and Benetton became interested in purchasing Esprit, the price would have escalated. Furthermore, during this time, Susie was recruiting financial backing from the venture capitalist Bruce Katz, Esprit's head of Far East operations Michael Ying, and Isaac Stein. One day before the bidding on Esprit was to close, Doug and Susie worked out a deal, and Esprit never went to auction. Industry observers believed that Doug had been concerned that both he and Susie would lose the company to higher bidders, and, in order to keep Esprit in the family, he accepted Susie's offer in return for some interest in the company's international division.

Susie Tompkins: Solo in the Early 1990s

Susie Tompkins returned to head Esprit amid much publicity. Trade journals, newspapers, and magazines depicted her as the victor in the war to control Esprit. Some observed, however, that the recession of the early 1990s could prove particularly challenging for the company and her leadership. Under Susie's ownership, Stein was named Esprit's chairperson. Federico remained president until his resignation in April of the following year; Stein subsequently assumed the presidency. Appointing herself creative director, Susie brought back the design team with which she had worked before leaving Esprit in 1988. Expressing the desire to produce casual fashions that exuded social awareness, she stated that her mission was to ensure "that Esprit inspire good values."

In 1991 the recently appointed "image director," Neil Kraft, produced the "What would you do?" advertising campaign that surveyed young people about how they would like to change the world. The $8 million campaign featured quotes from America's young people on such issues as racism and abortion. Although the advertisements won several awards and generated a great deal of media attention, sales figures were nevertheless disappointing. The following year Kraft left Esprit, and his duties were taken over by Fritz Ammann, who was named chief executive officer while Stein remained chairperson.

Pursuing her goal of promoting a socially responsible work force, Susie Tompkins replaced the employees' free vacation program with a lunchtime lecture series featuring controversial figures speaking on current issues. She also established a volunteer program that paid Esprit employees for working ten hours per month at a nonprofit organization, providing that the employee matched that amount of time on his own. Furthermore, the ecological soundness of Esprit's manufacturing practices was monitored by a new environmental and community affairs department in the company called the "Eco Desk."

The Ecollection line of Esprit clothing and accessories, touted as both ecologically sound and fashionable, was introduced early in 1992. The line featured buttons made from reconstituted glass or carved from nuts, organically grown or vegetable dyed cloth, and purses handwoven in a Mexican cooperative. Also that year Susie introduced the adult clothing line she had conceived years before. Tompkins referred to the designs as "creative career" wear for the Esprit customer who had matured. The tailored trousers, sophisticated, pleated skirts, jackets, and vests were manufactured in earth tones such as plum, green, brown, and burgundy. Tompkins maintained that these clothes were functional as well as fun and appropriate for the business world. The unconventional fashion show at which the Susie Tompkins collection debuted received mixed reviews. Rather than provide a runway and models, Susie commissioned Reverend Cecil Williams of San Francisco's popular Glide Memorial Church to give a sermon on the troubled lives and deplorable living conditions of youth in America's inner cities. The show, featuring videotape and choral accompaniment, cost more than $5 million to create. While some reviewers were entertained, others reportedly were offended by Esprit's tactics. Nevertheless, the company reported that the line had generated $13 million in sales.

Financial Struggles and New Leadership

Soon thereafter, however, Susie Tompkins stepped down, or was forced out, as creative director of Esprit. In formal statements both she and the company contended that she was leaving—as her ex-husband Doug had—to focus on her outside interests. Despite her lack of corporate title at Esprit, Susie remained involved as an advisor and consultant. From a public perspective, Esprit may have fumbled, but the damage was recoverable. More telling of things to come was the state of the financial end, which was described as a disaster by industry analysts and insiders.

Forced to restructure its loans in 1992, Esprit saw a succession of CEOs and fashion failures. In 1993, the company made a short-lived foray back into the mail-order business with a catalog devoted to the Esprit Ecollection. Although loyal Esprit buyers seemed willing to spend $18 for an organic cotton t-shirt, the catalog alone was not enough to change the company's fortunes. In 1994, on a whim, the company picked up the master apparel license for Dr. Seuss and produced a few t-shirts and hats to sell in Esprit boutiques during the holiday season. Intended for the children's market, the Dr. Seuss items were wildly popular among adults and served as the one bright spot in the company's mid-1990s slump. Meanwhile, Esprit's U.S. sales shriveled from $360 million a year to about $200 million.

Then, in 1996, Jay Margolis, a former vice-chairman at both Tommy Hilfiger and Liz Claiborne, came to the helm. Backed by Oaktree Capital of Los Angeles and Cerberus Partners of New York, he bought Esprit's defaulted loans for $80 million dollars, severing Susie Tomkins's fiscal ties to the company. Although Tomkins and Esprit de Corp. would wrangle over tax indemnities issues in legal battles drawn out for years, the Margolis era had begun. Bolstered by a *Women's Wear Daily* poll which ranked Esprit as 28th in a list of 100 most recognized fashion brands, Margolis refocused marketing to attract a slightly older clientele, moving to more expensive fabrics and quality control. At the end of Margolis' first year, Esprit had added ten "shop-in shops" in departments stores around the country and two retail stores, and, more significantly, had shown a profit for seven straight months.

In 1997, Margolis stepped up the pace of Esprit's turnaround even further. The company started by announcing a new catalog, a tool for consolidating Esprit's made-over image as "modern and sophisticated, yet distinctly fun." Margolis expressed hope that the catalog might follow in the footsteps of Esprit's ground-breaking catalog of the 1980s. Unafraid to use what had proved to work in the past, the company added 14 new retail stores that retained signature design elements, such as exposed ceilings, industrial lighting, and stained concrete floors. In a bold, new move, however, Esprit de Corp. purchased Moonstone Mountaineering, Inc., a manufacturer and distributor of technical performance apparel and sleeping bags. Further consolidating its active-oriented sportswear products, Esprit also made a licensing pact with Beach Patrol Inc., to gain immediate entry into the highly specialized swimwear industry.

The late 1990s saw further diversification of Esprit's product line as the company looked into adding menswear, sleepwear, and intimate apparel. The end of the decade also saw market diversification as Esprit established itself in e-commerce. In celebration of its 30th year anniversary in 1998, Esprit launched an on-line store. The Dr. Seuss merchandise earned an Internet site of its own, at www.seusswear.com, and Esprit's subsidiary, Moonstone Mountain Equipment, earned a "Gold Award" in the World Wide Web/On-Line Advertising category from SF Interactive, a digital marketing agency.

Esprit stepped up efforts to diversify the age of its consumer base as well. In 1999, it launched the "I Am Esprit" advertising campaign, a series of close-up shots of customers ranging from women in their 40s to 12-month-old infants. The ads were featured in established trade publications and in "wild postings," on construction sites and vacant store fronts to reach middle-aged and junior consumers. The campaign was well-received as were most of Esprit's attempts to reinvigorate itself under Margolis' tutelage. By the end of the 1990s, Esprit de Corp. seemed to have recovered its lost market share and to have assured its place among a new generation of buyers. The company continued to open new stores, and the speed with which the new Esprit catalog grew to become a $15 million dollar operation left even the tongue-wagging fashion industry speechless.

Principal Subsidiaries

Moonstone Mountain Equipment.

Further Reading

Benson, Heidi, "Reinventing Esprit," *San Francisco Focus*, February 1991.
"Catching the Spirit at Esprit: The Tompkinses Go to Riches with Rags," *Money*, July 1986, pp. 56–57.
Carlsen, Clifford, "Esprit Dressed to Thrill," *San Francisco Business Times*, January 27, 1997.
——, "Suiting Up: Esprit Dives into Swimwear Market," *San Francisco Business Times*, December 8, 1997.
Dorrans Saeks, Diane, "Always True in Her Fashion," *Metropolitan Home*, September 1992.
Dobbin, Muriel, "Fashion by Esprit," *Baltimore Sun*, May 30, 1985.

"Esprit back on the Catalog Scene," *Catalog Age,* June, 1993, p. 39.

Ginsberg, Steve, "Getting Serious," *Los Angeles Times,* March 6, 1992.

——, "Susie Tompkins Battles Esprit," *San Francisco Business Times,* September 15, 1997.

Greenberg, Freddi, "The Greening of Esprit," *Working Woman,* October 1985, p. 110.

Itow, Laurie, "The New Color at Esprit: Red," *San Francisco Examiner,* March 1, 1987.

"Joi d'Esprit?," *California Business,* May 1, 1987.

King, Ralph, Jr., "How Esprit de Corp. Lost Its Esprit," *Forbes,* March 21, 1988, pp. 91, 94.

Klensch, Elsa, "Making It Work! Susie Tompkins, the Spirit in Esprit: An Interview," *Vogue,* August 1987, pp. 344, 376.

Marlow, Michael, "Susie's Esprit: New Looks, New Outlook," *Women's Wear Daily,* September 10, 1990, pp. 1, 6–7.

McGrath, Ellie, "Esprit: The Sequel," *Working Woman,* September 1991, pp. 67–69.

Miller, Cyndee, "Seuss Characters Leap from Page into Licensing World," *Marketing News,* April 14, 1997, p. 2.

Miller, Paul, "The Return of a Catalog Icon," *Catalog Age,* September 1, 1997, pp. 6, 38.

Rapp, Ellen, "The War of the Bosses," *Working Woman,* June 1990, pp. 57–59.

Rapaport, Richard, "Goodbye Susie: The Rise, Fall and Repositioning of Esprit and Its Founders," *California Business,* September 1, 1992.

Smith, Matt, "Esprit de Court," http://www.sfweekly.com, October 8, 1997.

Underwood, Elaine, "Reinventing Esprit's Core," *Brandweek,* May 13, 1996, p. 35.

Waldman, Peter, "Flagging Spirit: Esprit's Fortunes Sag as Couple at the Helm Battle Over Its Image," *Wall Street Journal,* March 16, 1988, pp. 1, 17.

White, Constance C. R., "Susie Tompkins: Crossing a New Bridge," *Women's Wear Daily,* March 10, 1993.

——, "Tompkins Gets Her Line," *Women's Wear Daily,* March 2, 1992.

—Tina Grant
—updated by Shannon Hughes

Family Golf Centers, Inc.

538 Broadhollow Road
Melville, New York 11747
U.S.A.
(516) 694-1666
Fax: (516) 694-0918
Web site: http://www.familygolf.com

Public Company
Incorporated: 1994
Employees: 3,719
Sales: $122.2 million (1998)
Stock Exchanges: NASDAQ
Ticker Symbol: FGCI
NAIC: 71391 Golf Courses & Country Clubs; 71399 All
   Other Amusement & Recreation Industries

Only six years after its founding in 1992, Family Golf Centers, Inc. is the leading consolidator and operator of golf centers (driving ranges) in North America, with 109 courses in operation at the end of 1998. The company also operates eight stand-alone ice rinks and manages 16 additional ice-rink facilities. Family Golf also operates three "Family Sports Supercenters," which included at least one golf center or ice rink and might include another sports-related attraction, such as a bowling center, soccer facilities, and batting cages, as well as a variety of family entertainment activities. The company was founded by Dominic Chang, a native of Taiwan and a Long Island resident who worked for a New York City bank for 18 years before starting his own business.

The Concept: Family Oriented Driving Ranges

Chang left Taiwan in the mid-1960s to attend college in New York and eventually settled into a career at Irving Trust Co., which later merged with the Bank of New York, where Chang rose to the rank of senior vice-president, entrusted with managing more than seven million square feet of real estate and overseeing a staff of 1,000.

By the 1990s, however, he felt he had advanced as far as possible at the bank and yearned to satisfy a long-time desire to own his own company. Because he was a self-confessed compulsive golfer who was neglecting his wife and children to play the game on weekends and practice on weeknights, his idea was to open a golf facility for the whole family. Children, he realized, didn't have the patience to play an entire course, but a driving range and other attractions, he believed, would hold their interest.

Chang got nowhere in turning to U.S. banks for financing, but after he offered to put up $1 million of his own and family money, one Taiwanese bank—China Trust—that had previously invested in Japanese golf centers, extended him about a quarter of the $2.7 million that he calculated he needed to open his first driving range. He then received a $750,000 loan from the Small Business Administration through the Long Island Development Corp. "He had done his homework," the corporation's executive director later told James Bernstein of *Newsday,* adding, "He backed up everything with research and statistics and material we could independently verify." The research confirmed, for example, that many driving ranges had been converted into shopping malls and condominiums in recent years, leaving golfers desperate for space to practice their shots.

Chang opened the first driving range near his home, in the Long Island community of Farmingdale, in March 1992. Included in the dual level, climate-controlled facility was a miniature golf course and other amenities. Originally called Sky Drive, this facility was renamed the Golden Bear Golf Center when Chang negotiated a license agreement with a company owned by Jack Nicklaus, the famed "Golden Bear" of golf. Chang eschewed the term "driving range," preferring "golf center" to emphasize the family aspect. He planned to build one new center each year, but the Farmingdale facility was such a hit that by early 1995 cash flow had enabled him to open four more Golden Bear Golf Centers: in Douglaston (a community in New York City's borough of Queens); Wayne, New Jersey; Elmsford, Long Island; and Clay, New York, as well as a non-Golden Bear in Utica, New York. All of these centers included miniature golf courses.

Although there were some 2,100 driving ranges in the United States in 1996, most were little or nothing more than caged-in plots of open ground. Chang's facilities offered much more. The Elmsford center had 80 driving stalls—half warmed by infrared heaters—a practice area including a sand trap, a chipping area, a putting green, a video training studio, instructors certified by the Professional Golf Association, and two miniature-golf courses. Children too young even for, or uninterested in, miniature golf could spend time in a small video-game center.

Selling Stock to Finance Acquisitions

In November 1994 Chang took his enterprise, which he had incorporated as Family Golf Centers, public, raising $5.4 million by selling 24 percent of the stock at $5 a share. Revenues rose from $2 million in 1993, when the company lost $763,000, to $6.4 million in 1994, with net income of $488,000. Chang used the money to buy open ten more centers, mostly from existing driving range owner-operators, but including an 18 hole championship golf course in Queensbury, New York. He generally paid a figure four times cash flow, plus the appraised value of the underlying real estate. Chang also became the exclusive licensee for Golden Bear in New York, New Jersey, Connecticut, California, and the Pittsburgh and Philadelphia areas. Although he had hired 12 former bank colleagues to help him run the business, Chang personally selected every site. In Bernstein's 1996 *Newsday* story, he lamented, "I don't call myself a golfer anymore. I don't practice enough. I don't get time to hit the ball."

Family Golf Centers's 15 facilities garnered net income of $1.1 million on revenues of $12.4 million in 1995. A second stock offering at $15 a share raised nearly $42 million for the company in December 1995. Only seven months later, the company received $81 million for yet another offering, at $27 a share. Now trading at 135 times earnings, Family Golf Centers seemed a bit too pricey to some investors, but one stock analyst told Bernstein that Chang "was the guy who really brought a business view to an industry where this didn't exist." The founder still held one-quarter of the publicly traded stock, shares worth $83 million on paper.

By this time Family Golf Centers consisted of 25 facilities. Seventeen were essentially driving ranges but most had such additions as miniature golf, practice putting and chipping areas, video games, snack bars or restaurants, clubhouses with locker rooms and meeting rooms, and pro shops with a variety of apparel and personnel who offered clinics and private lessons. Seven included par 3 golf courses. The company also opened a summer golf camp catering to children. Seven units continued to be Golden Bear licensees, but Family Golf had lost the right to open new ones, and Golden Bear had reclaimed the right to open or license facilities in competition with Family Golf's own units.

Family Golf Centers acquired 11 more facilities in September 1996. The company posted revenues of $28.1 million and net income of $4.3 million for the year. It was running 35 centers at the end of 1996 and 44 by May 1997. After reaching a peak of $32 a share in November 1996, the company's stock dropped to $17 a share in April 1997, following disappointing quarterly earnings. A new surge of investor support, however, followed the victory of Tiger Woods that month in the Masters Tournament. "Since the Tiger Woods explosion, the driving-

range business has been off the charts," a money manager told *Business Week.*

There were 51 Family Golf Centers in August 1997, when the company acquired Leisure Complexes Inc. for $46 million in cash and stock. Leisure Complexes was the owner of a Sports Plus entertainment complex including bowling alleys, ice rinks, and indoor game arcades; an 18 hole golf course; and seven bowling centers (six of them subsequently sold), all on Long Island. The company became a subsidiary of Family Golf, run—at least initially—by the current management.

The Leisure Complexes acquisition indicated that Family Golf Centers was moving to raise its revenues in the comparatively fallow fall and winter seasons. A month later, the company purchased the Long Island Skating Academy (practice home of hockey's New York Islanders), renamed it Ice Works, and affiliated it with the Sports Plus complex. Family Golf recorded revenues of $73 million and net income of $3.3 million in 1997. It was operating 57 golf-related facilities in 18 states at the end of the year.

Further Expansion in 1998

In February 1998 Family Golf Centers acquired Metro Golf Inc., operators of eight facilities in five states. Family Golf was the nation's largest operator of golf facilities in April 1998, when it acquired Eagle Quest Golf Center Inc., the second-largest owner, operator, and manager of driving ranges in North America, for stock valued at about $46.1 million. Eagle Quest's locations in Texas, Washington, and western Canada geographically expanded Family Golf's own network, which by this time extended to 19 states.

Two months later, Family Golf purchased Golden Bear Golf Centers Inc. from parent Golden Bear Golf Inc., a company controlled by Nicklaus, for $32 million in cash and the assumption of debt, thereby adding 14 more golf facilities in ten states. With this acquisition Family Golf gained entry into three more large markets: Detroit, Pittsburgh, and Portland, Oregon, raising its roster to 81 facilities in 23 states and 25 of the nation's 30 largest markets. The company also signed a new ten-year licensing agreement with Golden Bear Golf for its existing seven Golden Bear Golf Centers as well as the 14 acquired ones.

Chang and his associates saw no end to the golf boom. According to a *Newsday* article, the number of driving ranges being built each year was growing by 100, all rapidly being filled with experienced players practicing their swings or beginners learning to play. "America is graying," the company's chief financial officer told Bernstein in 1998, explaining that "People have more disposable income. They're getting out and whacking golf balls more and more and more as they get older." Chang observed, "Women want to play the game now. Kids want to play the game." He said he had hired 200 professionals to work at the ranges and added "If we do our job and train them, the opportunities will be unbelievable." In a 1997 *New York Times* interview, Chang said his ranges were averaging 800 customers every weekday, and 1,200 on Saturdays and Sundays.

To finance its continuing expansion, Family Golf Centers made its fourth public offering in July 1998, raising $105 million in net proceeds by selling 4.6 million shares. Shortly before the year ended, the company closed on a previously announced $100 million line of credit from a bank syndicate led by Chase Manhattan Bank. At about the same time, Family Golf acquired Skate Nation Inc. for $17 million in cash and the assumption of a $12 million debt. This company was operating six ice rinks and managing 17 additional facilities in 11 states.

In November 1998 Alpha-BET Entertainment signed a contract to provide games and games operations on an exclusive basis to Family Golf Centers' three Sports Plus supercenters: the one in Lake Grove, Long Island, and two others, in Evandale, Ohio (near Cincinnati) and Denver. Another Sports Plus facility was to open in New Rochelle, New York, in May 1999. Alpha-BET, a joint venture partnership between Betson Enterprises and Alpha-Omega Amusements, had been operating and servicing the more than 225 games at Lake Grove since that facility opened in 1996.

Family Golf Centers ended 1998 with 119 golf facilities, including ten under construction. It also was operating eight stand-alone ice rink facilities, managing 16 additional ice rink facilities, and operating three Family Sports Plus Supercenters. Two more ice and family entertainment centers were under construction. Family Golf Centers was operation four regulation 18-hole golf courses and 26 par 3 or executive golf courses. The company was a presence in 25 states, three Canadian provinces, and 28 of the top metropolitan areas in the United States.

In general, Family Golf Centers' ranges were lighted to permit night play, and the hitting tees were enclosed or sheltered from above and from the rear in a climate-controlled environment. In certain cases, all or a portion of the range was enclosed under an air-inflated dome to allow all-weather play. Two-tier ranges had about 80 to 100 hitting tees and smaller golf centers about 30 to 60. The company's pro shops were stocked with clubs, bags, shoes, apparel, videos, and golf-related accessories from a number of suppliers. It was also selling private label products at these shops, including balls, gloves, and other merchandise bearing the company's logo. Family Golf Centers' instructional facilities included the Colbert-Ballard Golf School and the Golf Academy of Hilton Head Island, Inc. Similarly, the company's ice rinks included such amenities as pro shops, video games, and restaurants and snack bars.

Family Golf Centers' revenues reached $122.2 million in 1998—a 67 percent increase for the year—though the company lost nearly $5 million, which included a $2 million accounting change. As a result, its stock price fell to $7 a share in the spring of 1999, compared to a high of more than $32 the previous spring. Chief Financial Officer Jeffrey Key said the company would continue to build driving ranges under construction but had postponed further acquisitions. Its long term debt had climbed from $22 million at the end of 1996 to $249.6 million at the end of 1998. Chang remained the largest stockholder, with 14.3 percent of the shares of common stock in March 1999. Despite the financial challenges it faced as the century drew to a close, following rapid growth through acquisition, golf appeared to maintaining its hold on the American leisure seeker and Family Golf occupied a unique niche in providing quality facilities for all ages and skill levels.

Principal Subsidiaries

Orient Associates International, Inc.; Skydrive Alley Pond Company, Inc.; Skycon Construction Co., Inc.; Skydrive Co., Inc.; The Practice Tee, Inc.; Rivarization Plus, Inc.; The Seven Iron, Inc.; Skate Nation Inc.; Eagle Quest Golf Centers, Inc.

Further Reading

Barkow, Al, "The Driving Range Becomes Big Business," *New York Times,* September 4, 1997, p. B15.

Bernstein, James, "Driving Force," *Newsday,* July 22, 1996, pp. C1, C5.

——, "Family Golf: Above Par," *Newsday,* June 8, 1998, p. C7.

Hadad, Herbert, "Golf Centers Start on L.I. and Grow," *New York Times,* January 1, 1995, Long Island Weekly, p. 13.

Hayes, John R., "The Guilty Golfer," *Forbes,* June 17, 1996, pp. 90, 93, 95.

Marcial, Gene G., "Tiger's Power at the Driving Range," *Business Week,* May 5, 1997, p. 126.

O'Brien, Tim, "Alpha-BET to Operate Games at Family Golf Centers," *Amusement Business,* November 16, 1998, p. 30.

Stapleton, Tara, "Skating Academy Gets New Name, New Owner," *Newsday,* October 28, 1997, p. A44.

Strugach, Warren, "Family Golf Centers Hit One Fat," *Long Island Business News,* April 2, 1999, p. 5A.

Wax, Alan J., "Family Golf Buys Golden Bear Units," *Newsday,* June 18, 1998, p. A60.

——, "Family Golf Closes on Line of Credit," *Newsday,* December 4, 1998, p. A74.

——, "Family Golf Expands, Acquires Eagle Quest," *Newsday,* April 3, 1998, p. A68.

——, "Indoor and Outdoor Merge on LI," *Newsday,* August 1, 1997, p. A55.

Welling, Kathryn M., "Maximum Frustration," *Barron's,* July 29, 1996, pp. 3–4.

—Robert Halasz

The Finish Line, Inc.

3308 N. Mitthoeffer Road
Indianapolis, Indiana 46236
U.S.A.
(317) 899-1022
Fax: (317) 899-0237
Web site: http://www.thefinishline.com

Public Company
Incorporated: 1976
Employees: 7,370
Sales: $522.6 million (1999)
Stock Exchanges: NASDAQ
Ticker Symbol: FINL
NAIC: 44821 Shoe Stores; 44819 Other Clothing Stores;
   45111 Sporting Goods Stores

The Finish Line, Inc. is an athletic specialty retailer, carrying men's, women's, and children's brand name footwear, apparel, and accessories. The company operates more than 350 stores, which are located primarily in malls, in 39 states throughout the Midwest, Southeast, and South. The average size of a Finish Line store is more than 5,000 square feet, which is substantially larger than its competitors and which allows for a broader and deeper merchandise mix. Sales of footwear bring in approximately 70 percent of the company's total revenue, with apparel and accessories making up the remainder.

1976–86: Franchise Beginnings

The Finish Line's founders, David Klapper and Alan Cohen, first became involved in athletic retailing in 1976 when they opened an Athlete's Foot franchise on Monument Circle in downtown Indianapolis. The Athlete's Foot was a Pittsburgh-based athletic footwear retailer that had begun franchising in 1972. By 1976, when Klapper and Cohen signed their ten-year franchise agreement, there were almost 100 Athlete's Foot stores located in malls throughout the country. Although athletic wear was not a major retail force at the time, Cohen and Klapper, long-time friends and fervent athletes, both believed in the potential of the nascent market.

Under the terms of the franchise arrangement, the duo had a ten-year license with the Athlete's Foot for the state of Indiana. Within four to five years, Klapper and Cohen had added nine more stores, located in the state's larger malls, to their operation. It was at that point they decided it was time for a change. As franchisees, Cohen and Klapper were constrained by the dictates of the Athlete's Foot on every front—from product mix to store size to merchandise presentation. The partners, however, believed that the athletic specialty business was taking a new shape, and they wanted the latitude to respond to the changing market. They decided to start their own company—the Finish Line.

To begin the new venture, Cohen and Klapper brought in two more full partners: Larry Sablonsky and David Fagin. Sablonsky, who was also from Indiana, had a department store background, and Fagin had previously been a sales rep for an athletic wear manufacturer. From its first days, the Finish Line was conceptually different from the Athlete's Foot. Whereas the standard Athlete's Foot store was fairly small—between 1,500 and 2,000 square feet—and located in an enclosed mall, the early Finish Line stores were located in strip malls and outlet centers and, at 3,000 to 4,000 square feet, were substantially larger than the norm. While the smaller Athlete's Foot stores had focused almost exclusively on athletic shoes, the Finish Line's extra space allowed for a much broader mix of merchandise, specifically apparel and accessories. This broader product mix let Finish Line target a broader market, offering shoes and apparel for the whole family, whereas athletic retailing had catered traditionally to young males aged 12 to 24.

Another difference between the Finish Line and the Athlete's Foot was the *type* of merchandise they carried. The Athlete's Foot focused on new, high-profile merchandise from big-name athletic vendors. As an unproven entity, the Finish Line could not always stock the latest, hottest products carried by its competitor and instead often carried value or closeout merchandise. Although begun out of necessity, this merchandise mix proved to be serendipitous, as it mirrored a trend toward closeout and outlet shopping that was just then taking shape in the United States.

Company Perspectives:

Finish Line's mission is to create and operate a superior athletic specialty retail entity—by combining conceptual innovation which includes an entertaining and exciting retail environment, the most current information technologies and systems, capable and focused management, and a dedicated and motivated work force empowered with the proper resources—in order to provide customers a beneficial and unique shopping experience.

Although the partners continued to operate their existing ten Athlete's Foot stores through the term of their ten-year agreement, the lion's share of their energies were focused on growing their Finish Line chain. By 1986, when Klapper and Cohen's franchise with the Athlete's Foot expired, they already had established between 25 and 30 Finish Line stores. The stores were concentrated in areas where the outlet shopping craze was most deeply rooted, such as North Carolina, Texas, and upstate New York.

1986–94: Gathering Speed

With the expiration of the Athlete's Foot franchise agreement, the partners had to decide whether to renew the contract or to convert their existing Athlete's Foot stores into Finish Line stores. They opted for the latter. Applying what they had learned from operating the two types of stores, the foursome determined to combine the best of both concepts for future expansion. They believed that the Athlete's Foot's strongest points were its high-profile products and its mall-based location strategy. The Finish Line's strengths lay in its larger store size and its combination of new and value merchandise. Blending the concepts, Klapper, Cohen, Sablosky, and Fagin decided to take their stores back into the malls, but to make them much larger and to carry a wider variety of merchandise, including both the latest, high-profile products and discounted, value items. Little by little, the company began closing its strip and outlet mall stores, becoming ever more entrenched in enclosed malls.

Meanwhile, the U.S. market for athletic footwear was booming. From 1982 through 1991, retail sales of athletic footwear had climbed from $3.88 billion to $10.73 billion. Much of this growth was directly attributable to an Oregon-based athletic shoe manufacturer named after a Greek goddess—Nike, Inc. Throughout the 1980s, the popular Nike shoes—characterized by the signature "swoosh"—took the nation by storm, showing up on feet of every age. When its footwear proved so wildly popular, Nike built a line of apparel and accessories that met with a similar consumer response. Soon, Nike was the Finish Line's largest vendor.

By 1991, there were 105 Finish Line stores operating primarily in the Midwest and Southeastern states. In June of the following year, with 120 stores up and running and sales at $98 million, the four partners took the company public. Then, using the IPO-generated capital and a concept that was proving highly successful, the company expanded rapidly for the next several years.

With the steady addition of more stores, revenues rose predictably each year, climbing to $129.5 million in 1993 and $157 million in 1994. By the end of fiscal 1994, Finish Line had 164 stores located in 22 states stretching from New York to Texas.

1994–96: Bigger Is Better

Not only was the company growing the number of its stores—it also was growing its store size. Of the 30 new stores opened in the company's fiscal 1995 (February 1994 to February 1995), the average size was 4,100 square feet. This brought the overall average store size up to 3,641 square feet, a 5.6 percent increase from the previous year's average. "Our stores are getting bigger, a strategy we believe will allow us to maintain a competitive edge against our mall competition, and better position us to compete against large box athletic retailers located outside of malls," wrote Alan Cohen in the company's 1995 annual report. These larger stores were laid out with a "track" around the perimeter, which served to draw customers through the various categories of shoes. Apparel and accessories were displayed inside the track.

The company also rolled out three new large-format stores for testing. Sprawling over 7,000 to 9,500 square feet, the monster stores were divided into separate departments for men's, women's, children's, licensed product, and activewear. The flashy new stores also incorporated new color schemes, lighting, signage, and video and audio screens. Aside from the three new formats, all Finish Line stores were formatted as either "rack" or "backroom" stores. The 33 rack stores, which ranged in size from 3,000 to 5,500 square feet, were the older store designs, with stock stored on the sales floor in original boxes. The more common backroom format had a sales floor with display and try-on areas and an adjacent stockroom used to store inventory. The stores became known for their trademark "wall of shoes," a large, often curving wall display holding hundreds of shoe styles.

Cohen's team followed through on the larger store strategy in fiscal 1996 and 1997, opening 69 stores over the course of the two years, with an average square footage of almost 5,000. At the end of fiscal 1997, the company's 251 stores had an overall average size of 4,336 square feet, as compared with 1994's average of 3,449 square feet. In addition to the overall jump up in size, the company unveiled a "large format" store in fiscal 1996, which dwarfed virtually all of its other stores. Located in downtown Indianapolis, the 20,000-square-foot behemoth was stocked with approximately 1,300 styles and 30,000 pairs of athletic shoes, as well as large lines of apparel and accessories. The store was an immediate success, reaffirming the partners' belief in their superstore concept. Based on the encouraging performance of the Indianapolis store, the company began to plan for a 1997 opening of three more large-format outlets—in Buffalo, New York; Denver, Colorado; and Memphis, Tennessee.

Because the larger stores cost $1.7 million, as opposed to the $375,000 needed to build an average-sized store, the company needed extra capital. It raised it in a 1996 secondary stock offering, selling 1.3 million newly created shares and grossing more than $35 million. In addition, Cohen, Klapper, Sablosky, and Fagin together sold 1.3 million shares of their own stock.

For categorization purposes, the company began to characterize its stores by size. Stores smaller than 10,000 square feet, which included the majority of locations, were classified as "traditional format" stores. These traditional format stores generally carried 600 to 700 shoe styles. "Medium format" stores were those ranging from 10,000 to 15,000 square feet, stocked with approximately 1,000 shoe styles. Stores that were larger than 15,000 square feet were designated as "large format" stores.

Size and quantity were not the only points of focus for the Finish Line during the mid-1990s. The company also was working to improve efficiency in its warehousing and distribution systems. In 1995 the Indianapolis distribution center was expanded to more than double its previous size. Shortly thereafter, new management software was implemented in the center to allow for more accurate tracking of inventory.

1997–98: Market Downturn

For most sports retailers, the second half of 1997 and all of 1998 were somewhat less than ideal. Sales growth of both athletic footwear and apparel slowed industrywide, resulting in overstocked inventories and collapsing profits for both retailers and wholesalers. Many of the Finish Line's mall retail competitors lost ground. Even the superpower Nike, which by that time accounted for more than 60 percent of the Finish Line's merchandise, had disappointing numbers.

The Finish Line initially fared better than most of its competitors, closing its fiscal year in February 1998 with a 32 percent increase in total sales and a 42 percent increase in net income. While the Woolworth Corp., the operator of the Foot Locker, Lady Foot Locker, and Champs retail chains, posted a four percent drop in same-store sales, the Finish Line reported a six percent gain. The company's management believed it was their larger store sizes that allowed them to prosper while other athletic retailers hit the skids. Whatever the reason, investors responded favorably, and the company's stock price skyrocketed—climbing more than 100 percent between February and July of 1998.

The company maintained its momentum through the spring of 1998, but stumbled during the summer months and was unable to recover. Same-store sales declined throughout the remainder of the year, as did net income. Finish Line's CEO Alan Cohen pointed to a sharp drop off in apparel and accessories sales as the culprit. "During this period, apparel fashion trends appear to have moved away from the athletic brands to other contemporary brands, which is evident by the recent sales strength of many non-athletic specialty retailers," he said in a September 29, 1998 press release. With approximately one-third of Finish Line's total sales coming from apparel and accessories, the company was harder hit by this particular decline than some of its competitors, who carried only 12 to 20 percent apparel and accessories.

Despite disappointing sales, the company continued to expand, opening 59 new stores in the fiscal year ending February 27, 1999, and remodeling or expanding 26 existing stores. At fiscal year-end, there were 358 Finish Line stores—a 19 percent increase over the previous year's total. In addition, the company's total retail square footage jumped up 32 percent to 2,095,000 square feet, as opposed to fiscal 1998's 1,587,000 square feet.

1999 Forward

Despite its slump, the Finish Line entered 1999 determined to move ahead with expansion plans, which were to include opening between 40 and 60 new stores and remodeling another 20. The company planned to continue with its strategy of opening larger stores and carrying broader and deeper product lines than most athletic specialty retailers. This, management believed, would allow them to continue reaching a broader demographic market and to maintain operating margins that were larger than traditional stores. Although apparel sales were in a slump, management expected them to rebound. "We feel apparel is in a down cycle. It will not remain down forever," Steven Schneider, the company's vice-president of finance, said, citing the cyclical nature of sports clothing retailing.

The company also planned to slightly alter its marketing tack in the coming years by moving from a local level approach to a more regional and national focus. In addition, plans were under way for marketing initiatives that specifically targeted female consumers, one of the most rapidly growing segments of the athletic retail market.

Further Reading

Andrews, Greg, "Finish Line Shares in Step with Hot Sector," *Indianapolis Star/News,* July 6, 1998.

"Finish Line Bets on Mega-Stores," *Indianapolis Business Journal,* June 3, 1996, p. 8A.

"Finish Line Company History," http://www.thefinishline.com/company/our_com.asp

McFeely, Dan, "Finish Line Hits Stride as Olympics Approach," *Indianapolis Business Journal,* February 13, 1995, p. 5.

Retting, Ellen, "Coaxing Women to the Finish Line," *Indianapolis Business Journal,* July 13, 1998, p. 1A.

—Shawna Brynildssen

FlightSafety
international

FlightSafety International, Inc.

Marine Air Terminal
LaGuardia Airport
Flushing, New York 11371
U.S.A.
(718) 565-4100
Fax: (718) 565-4134
Web site: http://www.flightsafety.com

Wholly Owned Subsidiary of Berkshire Hathaway Inc.
Incorporated: 1951 as Flight Safety, Inc.
Employees: 3,125
Sales: $410.9 million (1997)
NAIC: 611512 Flight Training

FlightSafety International, Inc. (FSI) is the largest provider of pilot training services to the general aviation, corporate, military, and commercial airline markets. The company operates simulation centers worldwide and manufactures flight simulators. It has few major competitors. FSI trains military personnel through its FlightSafety Services Corp. subsidiary. FlightSafety Academy in Vero Beach, Florida, provides primarily flight training to potential airline pilots. MarineSafety International trains ships' crews.

Origins

The need for the kinds of services that FSI provides can be traced to the fact that an estimated 65 percent of airline accidents may be attributed to human error. Independent providers of pilot training emerged because of cost considerations as well; simulator training was far less expensive and, of course, less risky than doing the training in the aircraft itself. FSI founder Albert Ueltschi tells a story of teaching an army pilot, in 1939, how to do snap rolls in an open cockpit plane. Apparently, when the plane rolled, Ueltschi's seat broke free from the plane, and he was unable to get his parachute open. Nevertheless, he was able to walk away from the accident. The flight training his company would offer would be far less risky. Flight simulators would enable pilot trainees to practice both normal and emergency procedures under controlled conditions.

FSI got in on the ground floor of an emerging airline industry in the 1940s and 1950s. In 1942 Albert Ueltschi hired on with Pan American Airlines, operating "flying boats" that flew out of Flushing Bay. Four years later he began working as the personal pilot for Pan Am founder Juan Trippe. At that time, corporations were buying up military planes left over from World War II and converting them for their own private uses. Many of the pilots, however, did not have any specific training on the planes they were being hired to fly. Sensing the opening of a profitable business specializing in flight training, Ueltschi started Flight Safety, Inc. in 1951.

Initially, Ueltschi was strictly a service provider, hiring moonlighting pilots from the major commercial airlines to train pilots flying private planes for corporate executives. Training was generally done in the clients' aircraft, along with some instrument trainers rented from United Airlines. Operating out of Pan Am's LaGuardia Terminal, some early clients included Eastman Kodak, Burlington Industries, National Distillers, and other companies that required training for the pilots of their corporate fleets—the dominant segment of airline traffic at the time. Perceiving that a demand might later exist for updated training services, Ueltschi mortgaged his house for capital.

The company grew by stops and starts, and, with the firm's future uncertain, Ueltschi kept his job at Pan Am. He would fly as Trippe's personal pilot for 17 years. Using his salary at Pan Am for living expenses, Ueltschi plowed all of FSI's profits back into the company. This high rate of reinvestment strategy was vital to keeping the company afloat in its early years and eventually led to large profits and strong sales growth.

Nevertheless, Ueltschi took some big risks to get the company off the ground. For instance, he raised $69,750 in investment capital by convincing some of his early clients to put up the money as prepayment for five years of training services for the crews of their corporate fleets. This gave Ueltschi the cash, without the debt load, to buy his first Link Trainer. The Link Trainer, a flight simulation machine used by the army in the 1930s and later to train pilots during World War II, was a

Company Perspectives:

Since the very beginning, the corporate mission of FlightSafety International has been kept clearly in focus. We are a training company, which means that training is our service, our area of specialization, our reason for being. Training is our business. A commitment to high-tech, high quality training has made FlightSafety a leader in the effective preparation of individuals who must accept the responsibility of uncompromised proficiency. With our roots firmly planted in aviation, FlightSafety is known around the world for the training of pilots in all categories—private, commercial, airline and military. The training of aircraft maintenance technicians, dispatchers and additional aircraft support teams has added to FlightSafety's reputation as an all-encompassing aviation training company.

mechanically controlled flight trainer designed to teach mail-carrying pilots how to "fly blind" on an instrument panel.

Soaring Safely Through the 1970s

After nearly 20 years, FSI achieved stable growth rates, and Ueltschi's growth prospects and markets hinged in large part on his success at training pilots. Essentially, he had to convince aircraft manufacturers that he could do a better job of training pilots for their own aircraft than they could themselves, and for less money. Prior to the development of the "training industry," the aircraft manufacturers generally had included the cost of initial flight training in the price of a new plane. Gradually, the manufacturers looked toward specialization on production and opportunities arose for companies like FSI to develop and specialize in the training business. For example, companies like Learjet realized, after a couple of bad accidents, that they should specialize in production and design and leave the training to experts. Learjet, in fact, became the first corporate jet manufacturer to sign up with FSI, which set up a training center with a Learjet flight simulator at the company's factory, providing initial and updating of training of pilots for new models.

This success led to other contracts with the airline manufacturers, and by the late 1970s Ueltschi's company had signed similar deals with 12 other plane makers, including Airbus Industrie in France. The business arrangement was the same for all clients: Flight Safety provided the initial training for the buyers of the new planes and trained their pilots at both a company training center and using simulators near the manufacturing facilities. Furthermore, pilots returned periodically for refresher courses, thereby creating more revenue and new markets for the company.

Flight Safety had become very successful, allowing Ueltschi to take the company public in 1968, although he maintained control of 34 percent of its outstanding common stock. From 1973 to 1977 the company's revenues rose by an average annual compound rate of 22 percent and earnings by 35 percent. Return on equity was 23.2 percent in 1978, and its stock price nearly doubled that year.

Markets also were expanding rapidly for Flight Safety. Even the commercial and commuter airlines, which, in large part, trained their own pilots, began to give some of their spillover business to the company. In addition, to ensure a steady supply of simulators, with demand growing for training services, Flight Safety purchased its own simulation systems division out of Tulsa, Oklahoma. The division built simulators for use by Flight Safety as well as for sale to the airlines.

With the large growth in new business in the 1970s Ueltschi changed the name of his company, adding "International" to create FlightSafety International, Inc. The company grew continuously from the late 1970s, virtually unimpeded. Continuing his high reinvestment policy, Ueltschi invested in a marine simulator at LaGuardia Airport to train operators of supertankers, or natural gas carriers. Ueltschi then launched agreements with 16 companies, including Texaco, to train ship crews.

With the company in solid competitive position at the onset of the 1980s, Ueltschi was poised to take further risks. Moreover, the aviation industry was expanding rapidly, pulling much of the airline services industry up with it. FSI branched out into military pilot training and, later, began to challenge commercial airlines for a portion of their pilot training market.

In 1984 the company successfully competed for an Air Force contract. The Air Force had begun to contract out flight training at Fort Rucker in Daleville, Alabama. To get a jump on the competition, Ueltschi bought land next to the base and installed a flight simulator. With this move Ueltschi usurped the contract bidding process and immediately won business from the nearby base. By the time the official contract competition was under way, FSI easily won the contract.

During this time, FSI had virtually monopolized the corporate pilot training market, prompting its main competitor, Singer Company (whose SimuFlite division ran a training center in Dallas, Texas), to sue FSI in 1984 for anticompetitive practices. Singer's suit claimed that FSI maintained too close a relationship with airplane manufacturers, allowing FSI to overtake the industry and exclude others from entering the market. Singer eventually dropped the suit, however.

Competition in the 1980s came mainly from the airline companies as FSI focused on the commercial airlines market. To penetrate the passenger airlines market, FSI needed to convince the commercial carriers that it would be cost-effective to purchase training services rather than to train pilots in-house. One of FSI's first moves into commercial industry pilot training was launched in 1989 through an agreement with Trans World Airlines (TWA). This new venture would make FSI the main source of trained pilots for TWA. Working out of a St. Louis-based training center, FSI began its Advanced Flight Crew Training Program. This project was part of a major capital spending program aimed mainly at the commuter aircraft training market. Furthermore, as government and the military further privatized, FSI won more contracts. The MarineSafety International and PowerSafety International divisions also expanded. Record earnings in 1989 reflected the boom: revenues were up $168.15 million, and net income grew 29 percent to $46.7 million.

Outsourcing in Vogue in the 1990s

As FSI entered the 1990s, it maintained its hold over the flight training industry with more than 100 simulators around the world and close connections with virtually all airplane manufacturers to train their customers. The company had a healthy cash flow and annual earnings growth of more than 15 percent from 1986 through 1990. Its closest competitor, SimuFlite, fell victim to a corporate raider, a casualty of the 1980s.

The commercial airlines also seemed to realized the cost-cutting potential of specialization by tapping FSI to conduct flight crew training. Furthermore, insurance companies writing policies for the airlines began to reduce premiums on those pilots who attended refresher courses to keep in top form on the latest equipment. All these factors pointed toward an increasing demand for flight training.

FSI not only sold its services to carriers in the United States but also to airlines in Europe and Asia. By early 1992 the company prepared to tap into the Latin American airline carriers markets. According to James Waugh, FSI's vice-president of marketing, the company was able to support Latin American carriers that had not achieved the critical mass necessary to support in-house training facilities. To support this move, FSI began relocating several transport category full-flight simulators to a newly acquired Miami site to serve the Latin American airlines that were upgrading their fleets. In addition, FSI continued its practice of opening up simulators near manufacturing plants. For example, the company opened a training center, equipped with Boeing simulators, near a Boeing plant in Seattle.

The increasing trend toward contracting out of airlines' technical services boded well for FSI's future commercial carrier business as more airlines sought services such as crew training from outside contractors. Furthermore, while most labor union agreements previously kept such services in-house, the airlines successfully applied leverage over new agreements to slash costs by contracting out. FSI evolved along with this trend, seizing an increasing share of the crew training business. In fact, the share of FSI's revenues from commercial and commuter airlines customers rose steadily throughout the early 1990s. With this shift in focus, the company looked to build new facilities close to airline markets, mostly near airports.

FSI expanded its business worldwide and rapidly increased its share of the commercial airline training business. In fact, 20 percent of FSI's revenues was derived from contracts with U.S., European, and Asian airlines. At its Vero Beach, Florida facility, FSI trained pilots for Air Afrique, All Nippon Airways, Asiana Airlines of Korea, Swissair, Australia's Tyrolean Airways, Air France affiliates Air Inter and UTA, and others. FSI also signed a contract with Taiwan's China Airlines to develop a cockpit resources management training system. Further solidifying FSI's competitive position was the purchase of the visual systems division of McDonnell Douglas. This allowed FSI more direct control over the production of visual systems as well. Pointing to its capital expansion plan (which called for development of not only the Miami training center but also centers in Texas, Arizona, and Hong Kong), its solid cash flow position, and its large orders from government agencies, analysts considered FSI well positioned to continue its lead in the industry.

FSI also manufactured simulators, which accounted for $52 million of its $297 million in revenues in 1993. By the mid-1990s, consolidation transformed the simulator market as it had the aircraft manufacturing industry. CAE Electronics and Thomson Training and Simulation both sold more airliner simulators than FSI, which manufactured more business jet and regional aircraft simulators. It delivered about a dozen full-motion simulators a year, only three of which were for airliners.

Revenues were about $326 million in 1995. At the time, about 1,000 FlightSafety instructors were training 50,000 pilots and maintenance technicians on 100 simulators for 50 different aircraft types. FSI continued to expand, planning a training center at Kunming Airport in southern China.

Life Under Berkshire Hathaway in the Late 1990s

As the airline's rising fortunes promised more aircraft orders, FlightSafety became an attractive target for Warren Buffet's Berkshire Hathaway Inc. holding company. FSI became part of the $8 billion a year conglomerate in 1997. The sale was worth $1.5 billion in cash and stock.

Boeing also had considered buying FSI, as the aircraft manufacturer had long provided introductory training for its customers. The two did enter into a joint venture, firmly establishing FSI in the training market for large airliners. Flight-Safety Boeing Training International focused on aircraft with 100 seats and more. Like FSI itself, the joint venture saw training of maintenance personnel as an important growth area.

FlightSafety exploited new PC capabilities by delivering additional training materials in the form of its LearnLinc software. The program had the capacity to link to the Internet. FSI also delivered simulator training at Florida's Embry-Riddle Aeronautical University.

FlightSafety Boeing planned to open an $85 million facility in London in 2000. In March 1999, FlightSafety Boeing broke ground on a $100 training center in Miami expected to attract 7,000 pilots and 3,000 maintenance a year, many from Latin American airlines. FSI also opened facilities in Houston, Fort Worth, Cincinnati, and Memphis in the United States and in Manchester, England. MarineSafety International had grown as well, training crews for 100 different types of vessels in Newport, San Diego, and Rotterdam.

Principal Subsidiaries

FlightSafety Services Corp.; MarineSafety International, Inc.; FlightSafety Boeing Training International (51%).

Principal Divisions

Simulation Systems Division.

Further Reading

Feldman, Joan M., ''Airlines Lighten the Load,'' *Air Transport World*, November 1992, pp. 32–36.
''FlightSafety International Will Invest Over $150 Million in Development and Training Facilities,'' *Wall Street Journal*, September 21, 1992.

"FlightSafety Marches into Europe," *Interavia Aerospace World,* October 1992.

"FlightSafety Orders MDC Vital VII Systems," *Flight International,* September 15, 1992.

Kernstock, Nicholas C., "FlightSafety Rides Boom in Airline, Military Training To Record Earnings," *Aviation Week & Space Technology,* November 27, 1989, pp. 89–91.

"McDonnell-Douglas Agrees To Sell Image Display Unit to FlightSafety," *Aerospace Daily,* November 25, 1992.

McKenna, James, "FlightSafety Moves Simulators to Miami Facility to Serve Latin American Airlines," *Aviation Week & Space Technology,* June 1, 1992, p. 31.

——, "FlightSafety Sees Airlines as Important Growth Market," *Aviation Week & Space Technology,* September 2, 1991, pp. 52–53.

Meeks, Fleming, "The Pilots' Pilot," *Forbes,* November 13, 1989, pp. 198–202.

Morner, Aimee L., "Training Pilots of Corporate Jets Is Down-to-Earth Business," *Fortune,* May 22, 1978.

Nelms, Douglas W., "And Then, There Were Four," *Air Transport World,* November 1994, pp. 99–104.

——, "Coalition of Giants," *Air Transport World,* October 1997, pp. 69–71.

Pacey, Margaret D., "Ground Support Take-Off: Aviation Specialists Prosper by Servicing Planes, Training Staff," *Barron's,* June 5, 1972.

Phillips, Edward H., "Business Flying: Costs, Limits of Flight Training Prompt," *Aviation Week & Space Technology,* October 17, 1988.

"A Simulating Experience: FlightSafety International Lead in Market for Flight-Training Services Could Boost Stock Value," *Forbes,* January 20, 1992.

Sweetman, Bill, "Contractors Innovate to Prosper," *Air Transport World,* December 1993, pp. 79–86.

Ueltschi, A.L., *The History and Future of FlightSafety International,* New York: FlightSafety International, 1999.

Velocci, Anthony L., Jr., "FlightSafety Eyes Future as Berkshire Subsidiary," *Aviation Week & Space Technology,* October 21, 1996, p. 31.

Zipser, Andy, "Fond of FlightSafety," *Barron's,* December 3, 1990, p. 40.

—John A. Sarich
—updated by Frederick C. Ingram

FORTUNE BRANDS

Fortune Brands, Inc.

1700 East Putnam Avenue
Old Greenwich, Connecticut 06870
U.S.A.
(203) 698-5000
Fax: (203) 698-0706
Web site: http://www.fortunebrands.com

Public Company
Incorporated: 1904 as The American Tobacco Company
Employees: 24,900
Sales: $5.24 billion
Stock Exchanges: New York
Ticker Symbol: FO
NAIC: 5551112 Offices of Other Holding Companes;
31214 Distilleries; 33711 Wood Cabinet &
Countertop Manufacturing; 323116 Manifold Business
Forms Printing; 332116 Metal Stamping; 333313
Office Machinery Manufacturing; 33992 Sporting &
Athletic Goods Manufacturing; 332913 Plumbing
Fixture Fitting & Trim Manufacturing; 332919 Other
Metal Valve & Pipe Fitting Manufacturing; 42234
Footwear Wholesalers

Fortune Brands, Inc., known until 1996 as American Brands, is a widely diversified conglomerate with principal businesses in distilled spirits, home products, hardware, office supplies, and golf equipment. Most of its brands are either number one or number two in their market categories. Fortune's brands include Jim Beam, the world's best-selling bourbon, Swingline staplers, Acco paper clips, Master Lock padlocks, Moen faucets, and Titleist and Pinnacle golf balls. Fortune was a major player in the tobacco industry until the late 1990s, when it sold its domestic and foreign tobacco interests and got out of that business entirely. The company sells its products worldwide, and 40 percent of sales as of 1999 come from outside the United States.

Early History

Fortune Brands traces its origin to the remarkable career of James Buchanan (Buck) Duke, founder of The American To-

bacco Company. Duke was born in 1856 on a small farm outside Durham, North Carolina, where his father, Washington Duke, raised crops and livestock. The Duke farm was ravaged by armies of both North and South at the end of the Civil War, and upon his release from a military prison Washington Duke found that his sole remaining asset was a small barn full of bright leaf tobacco. Bright leaf, so called because of its golden color, only recently had been introduced, but its smooth smoking characteristics already were making it a favorite, and its fame soon was spread by the returning soldiers. Duke set out to peddle what leaf he had, and, pleased with the response, he quickly converted his land to tobacco culture, selling his wares under the name Pro Bono Publico, meaning "for the public good" in Latin. In its first year of operation, W. Duke & Sons sold 15,000 pounds of tobacco and netted a very handsome $5,000.

Along with his father, his brother Benjamin, and half-brother Brodie, Buck Duke labored to make the family business succeed, working long hours from childhood and learning every aspect of the tobacco business from crop to smoke. Duke's timing was fortuitous—bright leaf tobacco became the most prized of all U.S. varieties, and Durham was the epicenter of bright leaf country. By far the best-known brand of bright leaf was Bull Durham, the label of William T. Blackwell & Company. Blackwell gained a long lead on the rest of the Durham tobacco merchants, including the Dukes, who did not establish their first true factory in Durham until 1873. The Dukes chose to concentrate their energies on the manufacture and sale of tobacco rather than on raising the crop, which was notoriously erratic in quality and quantity. Buying their leaf from local farmers, the Dukes would cure and then shred or compress the tobacco to form, respectively, smoking or chewing tobacco. As cigarettes were yet hardly known, tobacco smoking was accomplished with a pipe or in cigars, the latter not being made by the Dukes.

Buck Duke attended a business school for six months in 1874, when he was 18, and became an increasingly dominant figure in the family business. Intensely ambitious, single-minded, and aggressive, Duke had no interest in anything less than mastery of the tobacco business. In 1878 Buck, Washington, and Ben Duke formed a partnership with businessman George Watts of Baltimore, Maryland, each contributing equally to the capital base of $70,000. Richard H. Wright joined the partnership two years later. The company was profitable and expanding, but Buck Duke was dissatisfied with its role in second place to Blackwell's Bull Durham, and in 1881 he decided to enter the new and relatively small field of cigarettes. At the time, there were only four major producers of cigarettes in the United States, and none of them had yet understood the potential importance of mechanized rolling machines and widespread advertising. Duke appreciated the power of both, and he set out to catch the four leaders.

Duke located and leased two of the new automatic rollers invented by James Bonsack of Virginia, who agreed to give Duke a permanent discount in exchange for taking a chance on the untested machines. After some adjustments, the machine proved capable of rolling about 200 cigarettes per minute, or 50 times the production of the best hand-rollers. Duke next revamped his packaging, devising the slide and shell box to offer better protection against crushing; and he then marketed his Duke of Durham cigarettes at ten for 5¢, or half of the usual price. This combination of excellent bright leaf tobacco, smart packaging, and discount price was an immediate success, and to these tangible virtues Duke soon added the intangible power of advertising. He very early recognized that advertising would determine success in the cigarette business and throughout the 1880s spent unprecedented amounts of money on promotional gimmicks of every stripe, much to the astonishment, ridicule, and—later—regret of his rivals.

While Richard Wright handled marketing overseas and Edward F. Small built up the western U.S. trade, Duke himself decided in 1884 to meet his competitors head on in New York City, the largest market and manufacturing center of the cigarette business. He moved to the city, established a local factory, and commenced an all-out war against the four leading companies—Allen & Ginter, Kinney Brothers, and Goodwin, all of New York City, and Kimball of Rochester, New York. The Big Four sold 80 percent of the nation's 409 million cigarettes in 1880; after a few years of Duke's relentless campaign, the total market had swollen to 2.2 billion, and W. Duke & Sons owned 38 percent of it. The Duke name appeared on billboards, storefront windows, and the sides of barns around the country, as well as on some 380,000 chairs Duke distributed free of charge to tobacconists, and by 1889 company sales reached $4.25 million and net income was one-tenth of that. Duke had grown to dominance of the cigarette business in a single decade and, shortly, was to duplicate the feat worldwide.

Though triumphant, Duke was faced with the prospect of continuing bitter competition and restricted profits. The 32-year-old veteran thereupon proposed a solution that was startling in scope: to merge all five of the competitors and, by joining forces, bring to an end the wasteful price warfare. His fellow manufacturers at first balked at the initiative, but they eventually agreed and in January 1890 formed The American Tobacco Company, its $25 million in capital divided among ten incorporators, with J. B. Duke named president. The new company, one of the first true combinations in the history of U.S. business, controlled 80 percent of the nation's cigarette business and showed a net profit of $3 million in its first year.

Whereas American Tobacco was a large concern, it was by no means the entire tobacco industry, and having once captured the cigarette business Duke set to work on the rest of the tobacco world. In 1891 American bought out 80 percent of the relatively minor snuff business; four years later Duke launched what has come to be known as the "plug wars." Between 1895 and 1898 American Tobacco waged a prolonged struggle to enter the field of plug, or chewing, tobacco, the largest of the various tobacco markets. With this move Duke made clear the extent of his ambitions, and a number of the original American Tobacco incorporators saw fit to sell their stock rather than join him in what they saw as a foolhardy battle against superior odds. Duke's ambition proved to be realistic, however, and after three short years of price wars and buyouts he had secured more than 60 percent of the vast plug market, including such later giants as Lorillard, Liggett & Meyers, and Drummond. Duke's methods in doing so were much like those he used in the snuff, smoking tobacco, and cigar segments of the industry. Selective price wars were followed by acquisitions, followed by the return of prices to a more profitable and unchallenged level. Many of these practices were in violation of the Sherman Antitrust Act, one of whose more spectacular victims would later be J. B. Duke. For a long time the extent of American Tobacco's holdings was not obvious, as many of Duke's 250 acquisitions managed to maintain secrecy about their new affiliation; neither Congress nor the executive branch of government became interested in taking on the combinations until the first decade of the next century.

At the conclusion of the plug wars in 1898, Duke united his various plug companies into a new holding company called Continental Tobacco Company, most of whose stock was in turn owned by American Tobacco. In 1901 American Tobacco bought itself the largest share of the cigar industry, which, however, frustrated all efforts at monopoly because of the difficulty and variety of cigar manufacture; in the same year American Tobacco acquired a controlling interest in what would become the dominant retailer of tobacco in the country, United Cigar Stores Company. Having thus finished off nearly the entire domestic tobacco industry, Duke tightened his grip on his family of holdings, in 1901 forming and retaining the largest shareholding in Consolidated Tobacco Company, which in turn bought up the assets of the former American and Continental companies in a transaction that netted him a tidy profit while also providing more direct corporate control. Finally, Duke began to expand internationally. After a nationwide price war in England against a coalition of the leading British tobacco men, the two sides agreed not to compete in each other's countries and to pursue jointly the rest of the world's markets through a company called British-American Tobacco Company, two-thirds of which was won by James Duke and his allies. Even at this early date the overseas retail trade was significant; British-American soon employed some 25,000 salesmen in Asia alone, all of them working under Duke's director of foreign sales, James A. Thomas.

Duke's control of United Cigar Stores' more than 500 outlets gave the public a clearer picture of the extent of Duke's domain, and his company soon faced rising criticism and opposition, some of it violent. Those in both the industry and the public had reason to dislike Duke and his cartel; Kentucky tobacco growers, for example, their prices repeatedly lowered by the single large buyer in town, banded together in 1906 to burn down a number of the trust's large tobacco warehouses. More serious was the increasing pressure brought to bear by the U.S. Department of Justice, which took heart under the administration of President Theodore Roosevelt and began a series of antitrust actions against the industrial combines. In 1907 the department filed suit against Duke's creation, now once again called American Tobacco Company, and in 1911 the Supreme Court agreed that the trust must be dissolved to restore competition to the tobacco industry. Total corporate assets were estimated at more than $500 million.

From the complex dissolution of American Tobacco, designed and overseen by James Duke himself, came the elements of the modern tobacco industry. Spun off as new corporate entities were Liggett & Meyers, Lorillard, R.J. Reynolds, and a new, smaller American Tobacco Company. Each of these four except Reynolds was given assets in all phases of the tobacco business, and Reynolds, the youngest and most aggressive of the companies, soon acquired what it lacked. Control of British-American Tobacco was lost to the British, where it has remained. Duke turned over direction of American Tobacco to Percival S. Hill, one of his veteran lieutenants, and himself went with British-American as chairman and one of its directors. The founder retained large holdings of stock in each of the newly formed spin-offs and, upon his death, left a great deal of money to the eponymous Duke University and a score of other charitable causes.

Growth Through World War II

At the time of dissolution, the tobacco industry still exhibited two characteristics soon to be swept aside by modern advertising and changing tastes. The business continued to be dominated by chewing tobacco, and it featured a plethora of brands. In 1903, for example, no fewer than 12,600 brands of chewing tobacco were listed by an industry catalog, along with 2,124 types of cigarettes. In 1913 Joshua Reynolds, founder of R.J. Reynolds, introduced the era of nationally known cigarette brands with his new Camel, a blend of bright leaf and sweet burley tobacco that took the country by storm. Camel was probably the most successful cigarette ever launched, and in 1916 American Tobacco answered with Lucky Strike, while Liggett & Meyers pushed its Chesterfield; together the blitz of advertising caused an enormous upsurge in national consumption, from 25 billion cigarettes in 1916 to 53 billion three years later. By 1923 cigarettes had passed chewing tobacco as America's favorite form of nicotine, an evolution helped immeasurably by the growing acceptance of women smokers, for whom the cigarette was the only fashionable smoke.

Under the leadership of Percival Hill and, after 1926, his son George Washington Hill, American Tobacco battled Reynolds for decades in the race for cigarette dominance. Each of the Big Four manufacturers settled on one or, at most, a few brands and spent inordinate amounts of money on advertising in both print and radio formats. The Great Depression years were not as bad for the tobacco companies as they were for many industries. Consumption in 1940 was nevertheless no higher than it had been ten years before, with Lucky Strike sales hovering at around 40 billion cigarettes annually. World War II and its attendant anxieties provided an instant sales boost, however, pushing Lucky Strike totals to 60 billion by 1945 and 100 billion a few years later. American Tobacco also found a winner in Pall Mall, which ushered in the "king size," 85-millimeter, era in 1939 and soon was challenging Lucky Strike and Camel for the top spot. So complete was the triumph of the cigarette that when American Tobacco's sales reached $764 million in 1946, fully 95 percent of it was generated by cigarettes.

Postwar Years

The immediate postwar years were good for American Tobacco, which upped its overall share of the domestic tobacco market to 32.6 percent in 1953. But that would prove to be the high-water mark for the company's cigarette business. The year before, R.J. Reynolds introduced Winston, the first filtered cigarette, and inaugurated the trend toward lighter and less harmful smokes. American Tobacco replied with its Herbert Tareyton Filters in 1954, but with both Lucky and Pall Mall among the top three sellers overall it felt no urgency about the filter business and did not spend the money and effort needed to establish its brands in the new category. This failure would be crucial in determining the subsequent development of American Tobacco, which never did catch up to its competitors and eventually assumed a minor role in the cigarette world. While Reynolds and later Philip Morris reaped fortunes with Winston and Marlboro, American Tobacco belatedly pushed losers such as Hit Parade, a cigarette so unpopular that the company was reportedly unable to give away free samples.

In the long run, however, American Tobacco's relative failure in cigarettes may have been a blessing. Beginning in the mid-1960s, the company used the steady cash flow from its remaining tobacco business to make a number of promising acquisitions. Chief among these were Gallagher Limited, one of the United Kingdom's largest tobacco companies; James B. Beam Distilling Company; Sunshine Biscuits; Duffy-Mott; and several makers of office products. In recognition of the company's changing profile it was renamed American Brands in 1969, by which date its share of the domestic tobacco market had slipped to 20 percent and continued to decline. After a handful of other minor acquisitions, American Brands made its largest purchase in 1979, buying The Franklin Life Insurance Company, the tenth largest life insurer in the United States. By that time nontobacco assets were generating one-third of American Brands' operating income of $364 million, and the company's diversification program generally was regarded as a modest success.

American Brands, however, was weakest in the most lucrative of its markets, domestic tobacco. The increasing stigma attached to tobacco sales and the threat of government restrictions have ensured immense profits for those few companies still in the U.S. tobacco business, as no new potential competitors are both willing and able to venture into such troubled waters. Even as the cigarette makers diversify, therefore, domestic tobacco continues to pay up to 35 percent on every sales dollar, providing cash needed to diversify further out of tobacco. In domestic tobacco, American Brands' share of the market eventually fell to the neighborhood of ten percent. The $1.6 billion in sales generated there in 1990, however, returned more operating income than did the company's $6.4 billion in overseas tobacco business, where margins were much tighter, and equaled the return of all of the nontobacco divisions taken together.

American Brands fought off a takeover bid by E-II Holdings in the late 1980s and significantly strengthened its position in liquor and office products. Its liquor division was the United States' third largest seller of spirits, its office products division was billed as the world's largest, and Gallagher Limited had grown into the leading U.K. tobacco company, far outstripping its parent company's tobacco sales. Earnings growth had been steady for years at American Brands, whose balanced revenue structure rendered the company relatively immune to sudden downturns in any one area.

Without Tobacco in the 1990s

In 1991 American Brands strengthened its hold on the distilled spirits market by acquiring seven brands from the Seagram Company. American spent $372.5 million for the brands, which represented approximately one-quarter of giant Seagram's sales in the United States. In the midst of a turndown in liquor consumption, Seagram had decided that those who were drinking less should drink better. Thus it wanted to unload some of its less prestigious brands. American, however, was deliberately pursuing the opposite tack, aiming for more budget-conscious consumers. The brands it took over from Seagram were the American whiskies Calvert Extra and Kessler, Canadian whisky Lord Calvert, Calvert gin, Ronrico rum, Wolfschmidt vodka, and Leroux liquor. The acquisition made American's subsidiary Jim Beam Brand Company the third largest spirits company in the United States. American's strategy seemed profitable. Though its new liquor brands and its tobacco brands lacked both snob appeal and great market share, they did make money. Profits rose to record levels in 1991, with a rise of almost 40 percent for the year. Liquor sales, bucked by the Seagram acquisition, rose 12 percent, and tobacco sales rose all of one percent. This small rise, however, was the first increase for American since 1965.

By mid-1992 American Brands was confident that it had found a way to hang on to its tobacco business despite hard times for the industry. The threat of lawsuits and overall decline in smoking made conditions harsh domestically, and U.S. tobacco sales overall were declining by about three percent annually. But American energetically pursued a low-price strategy. It introduced several new brands, all priced at several dollars less per carton than leading brands like Marlboro and Winston. Though American's Pall Mall was fading, with sales dropping almost 20 percent in 1991, its new Misty and Montclair racked up sales. Extensive advertising trumpeted the new brands' principal virtue: they were cheap. Similarly, in its spirits division,

American's marketers claimed that its brands were just as good as the ones that cost more. The company seemed to have hit on a winning strategy, so it was somewhat of a surprise when in April 1994 American sold off all its American tobacco business. B.A.T. Industries, long ago the British sister of Duke's American Tobacco, bought up American Brands' holdings for $1 billion. Tobacco had made up 58 percent of revenues and 66 percent of profits for American in 1991. Now it was out of tobacco altogether except for one British cigarette manufacturer, Gallagher.

Six months after B.A.T. bought the tobacco division, American also sold off its profitable insurance subsidiary, Franklin Life Insurance Co. Franklin was bought by American General Corp. in a deal estimated to be worth $1.2 billion. Franklin had assets of $6.2 billion and had a strong market share principally in small towns and with middle-income blue-collar customers. The company was a money-maker for its parent, yet it was American's only financial service unit, and in many ways American looked better without it. It was focused on consumer goods after divesting Franklin, though these goods still were fairly mixed, from golf shoes to gin.

The company then changed its name in 1996, from American Brands to Fortune Brands. This came after the company sold the last vestige of its tobacco business, its British unit, Gallagher. The company was concerned that investors still associated its old name with a tobacco company. For example, when a smoker in Florida won a substantial jury award against another tobacco company in August 1995, American's stock suffered. The newly named company's CEO, Thomas Hays, explained the rationale behind the choice, saying, ''People talk a lot about something being fortunate or making a fortune, which is certainly what we want to do for our shareholders'' (from a December 9, 1996 interview in *Fortune* magazine).

By the late 1990s, Fortune was rather different from what it had been ten years earlier. After getting rid of its tobacco holdings, Fortune began buying up companies in the home and office products area, such as Schrock Cabinet Co. and Apollo Presentation Products, a maker of overhead projectors. It also bought in the liquor area, picking up Geyser Peak Winery in 1998 and in 1999 entering an agreement with two European liquor companies to jointly distribute their spirits worldwide. Fortune also vowed to manage the brands in its portfolio better, and in 1999 took a charge of $1.2 billion to restructure and write down goodwill. The company also announced it would cut costs by reducing its corporate staff by one-third and moving headquarters to Lincolnshire, Illinois, where its office products division already was located.

Principal Subsidiaries

Acco World Corporation; Masterbrand Industries, Inc.; Jim Beam Brands Worldwide, Inc.; Acushnet Company.

Further Reading

''American Brands' Net Fell 93% in 4th Period,'' *Wall Street Journal,* January 28, 1991, p. C8.
''American Brands Profit Sets Record,'' *New York Times,* January 25, 1992, p. 39.

Barrett, Amy, and Ernest Beck, "Fortune in Pact with Remy and Highland," *Wall Street Journal,* March 31, 1999, p. B4.

Fairclough, George, "Fortune Brands To Take Charge of $1.2 Billion," *Wall Street Journal,* April 28, 1999, p. C24.

Lieber, Ronald B., " 'What? Fortune Makes Golf Balls?,' " *Fortune,* December 9, 1996, p. 40.

Rice, Fay, "How To Win with a Value Strategy," *Fortune,* July 27, 1992, pp. 94–95.

Saporito, Bill, "Who'll Drink What Post-Recession?," *Fortune,* December 2, 1991, p. 13.

Scism, Leslie, "American General Corp. Seeks To Buy Life-Insurance Unit of American Brands," *Wall Street Journal,* November 29, 1994, p. A3.

Shapiro, Eben, "Seagram Is Selling 7 Liquor Brands," *New York Times,* November 1, 1991, p. D1.

"Sold American!"—The First Fifty Years, New York: American Tobacco Company, 1954.

Steinmetz, Greg, "B.A.T. To Buy Rival American Brands Division," *Wall Street Journal,* April 27, 1994, pp. A3, A4.

Winkler, John K., *Tobacco Tycoon: The Story of James Buchanan Duke,* New York: Random House, 1942.

—Jonathan Martin
—updated by A. Woodward

FOUR SEASONS
Hotels and Resorts

Four Seasons Hotels Inc.

1165 Leslie Street
Toronto
Ontario M3C 2K8
Canada
(416) 449-1750
Fax: (416) 441-4414
Web site: http://www.fshr.com

Public Company
Incorporated: 1961
Employees: 22,000
Sales: C$248.8 million (US$160.7 million) (1998)
Stock Exchanges: Toronto Montreal New York
Ticker Symbol: FS
NAIC: 72111 Hotels (Except Casino Hotels) & Motels

Four Seasons Hotels Inc. is one of the world's leading hotel management companies specializing in luxury and resort properties. The company manages over 40 hotels and resorts in North America, Europe, Asia, the Middle East, Australia and the Caribbean, with an additional approximately 20 more under construction as of 1998. The company owns its own hotels, principally under the Four Seasons and Regent names, as well as some others, including the Ritz-Carlton in Chicago and the Pierre in New York. About half the company's earnings come from management fees, and half from properties it owns directly.

Humble Beginnings

Four Seasons Hotels was founded by Isadore ''Issy'' Sharp. Sharp's father, Max, emigrated from Poland to Palestine in 1920, where he helped build one of the first kibbutzim. Relocating to Toronto five years later, Max worked for a few years as a journeyman plasterer; he married and began a family that would include his son Issy and three daughters. Drawing on his home renovation experience, Max Sharp soon began purchasing houses, repairing and decorating them, and then selling them at a profit. Issy Sharp had lived in 15 houses by the time he was 16 years old.

Sharp attended Toronto's Ryerson Polytechnical Institute and won high marks in architecture while distinguishing himself in athletics. After graduating, he worked alongside his father building small apartment buildings and houses. Determined to build a hotel on his own, Sharp struggled for five years to find the money in order to fulfill his dream. Unable to convince banks and venture capitalists that his hotel would succeed, Sharp finally turned to his brother-in-law, Eddie Creed, owner of a high fashion emporium in Toronto, and Creed's best friend, Murray Koffler, founder and chair of the Shoppers Drug Mart chain. These two men contributed $150,000 each to Sharp's project.

Still requiring over $700,000 in capital, Sharp approached one of his father's business acquaintances, Cecil Forsyth, who managed the mortgage department at Great West Life Insurance Company. Sharp's plan was to raise the rest of the necessary funds through a mortgage. Skeptical of Sharp's business acumen, Forsyth initially refused the application. However, he eventually yielded to Sharp's persistent requests, agreeing to provide the rest of the money.

Sharp's hotel cost nearly $1.5 million to establish and featured 126 rooms that would garner premium prices. Opening on the first day of spring in 1961, the Four Seasons Motor Hotel was an immediate success. Despite the hotel's location in a downtown Toronto area known for its prostitutes and indigent population, patrons were attracted to the structure's casual but upscale atmosphere, as well as its innovative inner courtyard surrounding a swimming pool. Soon the employees of the Canadian Broadcast System, located across the street, adopted the hotel as their after work watering hole, signalling the beginning of the hotel's celebrity association.

From the time the Four Seasons opened for business, Sharp created a climate that fostered professionalism and devotion among his employees. He initiated a profit-sharing plan, scheduled two ''stress breaks'' every day, and paid his front desk clerks twice the average rate, asserting their importance in providing the public with its first impression of the hotel. One of the more notable examples of employee dedication involved Roy Dyment, a bellboy at Four Seasons since 1967. Dyment discovered that a dignitary had left his briefcase behind after checking out, and he felt responsible since he hadn't placed the briefcase in the limousine trunk. When the worried guest phoned from Washington, stating that the material in the briefcase was essential for an upcoming meeting, Dyment purchased a plane ticket at his own expense and delivered the briefcase personally.

Sharp's second venture in the hotel business proved even riskier than his first. Launched in 1963, Toronto's Inn on the Park was built on 17 acres in a desolate area north of the city, where the only nearby business was a large garbage dump. Short $1 million before the start of construction, Sharp and his father again approached the obdurate Cecil Forsyth, this time for a loan. Forsyth, impressed by Sharp's instant success with the motor hotel, didn't hesitate in providing the money. Despite its location, Sharp's second hotel was also successful, and the area he had chosen for the 569-room resort hotel quickly grew into a sprawling corporate suburbia.

Growth Abroad in the 1970s

Next, Sharp sought to establish a hotel overlooking London's historic Hyde Park. In doing so, he ignored market research indicating that a new luxury hotel in that location would have trouble competing with such established first class hotels as the Dorchester, Claridge, and Savoy. Sharp opened his 227-room Inn on the Park in 1970. Despite its higher rates and the overcrowded market, the Inn on the Park enjoyed a 95 percent occupancy rate and became one of the most profitable hotels in the world. Its small size, luxurious appointments, and impeccable service were all elements that had become Sharp's personal trademark.

In the early 1970s, Sharp began developing hotels in smaller, less urban areas. He opened an inn in Belleville, Ontario, whose population was 35,000, and spent a year operating a resort in Nassau. Shortly thereafter, he built a luxury condo hotel in Israel that was marginally profitable but experienced difficulties maintaining staff, owing largely to the Israeli draft for military service. Plans for hotel projects in Europe were postponed due to disagreements with potential partners from Paris and Athens; when construction finally started on a hotel in Rome, workers kept uncovering Roman artifacts, and preservationists were able to block further construction on the site. Hoping to develop residential and office buildings in both Canada and Florida, Sharp was continually thwarted by civic officials, who placed restrictions on commercial development.

Undismayed by his setbacks, in 1972 Sharp approached the Sheraton division of ITT Corporation and proposed a joint Four Seasons-Sheraton partnership. The result was the Toronto Four-Seasons Sheraton, a 1,450-room establishment whose first year of operation was plagued by cost overruns, disagreements with city building inspectors, and a singles event which resulted in a temporary suspension of the hotel's liquor license. Although Sharp was hired as assistant manager of the property, he had no real authority to make decisions. In 1976, he finally sold his 49 percent interest for $18.5 million and decided to return to what he did best: developing and operating mid-sized hotels that catered to the luxury market.

That year Sharp purchased his first American property, The Clift, an elegant but aging hotel in San Francisco. Moreover, he opened the Four Seasons Hotel in Vancouver, and, one year later, won a bidding war to manage the new Ritz-Carlton in Chicago. In 1978, Sharp bought a property from Hyatt Hotels in Toronto and remodeled it to suit the Four Seasons style. This Four Seasons Hotel offered service to the wealthy, who frequented Yorkville, Toronto's most exclusive shopping district. In 1979, the Four Seasons Hotel in Washington began operations, and a short time later Sharp opened the first of several hotel and resort properties in Texas. One of Sharp's most successful moves came in 1981 with The Pierre, a landmark hotel in New York frequently cited as one of the best in the city. With a multimillion dollar renovation, The Pierre developed into a showcase of Four Seasons' style and service.

Financial Ups and Downs in the 1980s

Many hoteliers, Sharp included, followed Conrad Hilton's strategy of managing properties rather than owning them. From 1980 to 1985, Four Seasons opened hotels with a value of over $500 million at a cost of only $15 million. Nevertheless, Four Seasons also owned many properties, and in the early 1980s Sharp initiated an expensive renovation drive of the hotels in which it was owner or part-owner. By 1982, the hotel chain had approximately $116 million in long-term debt.

In order to lessen this debt, Four Seasons began selling its assets. Between 1980 and 1985, nearly $31.2 million worth of assets were sold, including equity in Montreal, Toronto, and San Francisco. Nevertheless, Four Seasons continued to manage these hotels under long-term contracts. When Sharp, Creed, and Koffler, the three original investors, created a new company to manage such non-hotel assets as development property and a laundry, another $22 million in debt was eliminated. The company's final tactic was to apply $30 million of an initial $60 million raised from a stock offering to reducing the remainder of the debt. Through these three moves, Four Seasons' debt-equity ratio was reduced to a comfortable 1:1 ratio by 1986.

When Four Seasons first publicly issued shares in the company in 1969, stock shares climbed as high as $22. However, after the erratic management and declining profits of the early and mid-1970s, Four Seasons stock had plummeted to only four dollars per share by 1977. Sharp and his partners then decided that it was in their best interest to turn Four Seasons into a private company. In 1985, when they decided to take Four Seasons public again, both Creed and Koffler retained an eight percent stake in the company but sold $8.5 million worth of stock. Sharp agreed to the public offering on the condition that a class of "multiple voting shares" be created for him. As a result of this arrangement, Sharp tightened his grip on Four Seasons; while the public had one vote for each share, Sharp's multiple voting shares carried 12 votes for each share. With a 29 percent share of Four Seasons equity and 83 percent of the votes, Sharp planned to thwart any takeover threat in the future.

Rapid Growth into the 1990s

During the late 1980s, Four Seasons began examining the world's financial centers, such as Tokyo, Paris, and Frankfurt, for future development sites. Expansion proceeded slowly as Sharp wanted only premium locations and refused to settle for less. From 1988 onward however, the acquisition, development, and building of properties was rapid.

By 1992, with the acquisition of Regent International Hotels Limited, a leading operator of luxury hotels in Asia and Australia, Sharp had created the largest network of luxury hotels in the world. Together Four Seasons and Regent International Hotels owned and operated 45 medium-sized luxury properties and resorts in 19 countries around the world. In 1992 and 1993, Four Seasons opened hotels in Bali, Milan, and London. New construction and development was ongoing in Singapore, New York, Mexico City, Paris, Berlin, Jakarta, and Prague, and resort properties were under development in Hawaii and California.

With a one-to-one employee-guest ratio, gourmet cuisine, and sumptuous decor resulting in accolades from such diverse publications as *Consumer Reports, Mobil Travel Guide,* and *Condé Nast Traveler Magazine,* Sharp nevertheless strove to improve his properties. His goal was to transform the name Four Seasons into a common phrase for high-quality hotels, and, during the early 1990s, he believed this goal was well within his reach. Nevertheless, the company was plagued by debt, leading almost to paralysis in the mid-1990s. A downturn that struck the hotel industry from 1990 to 1992 had made the company turn more to management at that time, because it was both more profitable and more stable in the long run than owning hotels. The chain typically bought a small equity stake in hotels it hoped to manage, however, as a way of opening the door to a successful management contract. Because of its debt burden, the company had been kept from bidding on some of the hotels it wanted to control. By 1994 it had 15 contracts under negotiation, and a company analyst expected Four Seasons to win just five of them.

To the rescue came an outside investor, the Saudi Prince Al-Waleed Bin Tala Bin Abdufaziz al Saud. He bought up 25 percent of the company's stock in 1994, and set aside C$100 million to fund further expansion of the chain. Al-Waleed was an international investor who had previously bailed out Euro Disney SCA, the floundering French Disneyland. The prince was reportedly impressed with the Four Seasons brand and service, and wanted to provide financial backing for long-term growth. With Al-Waleed's deep pockets, the company was able to complete its bids on management properties, and soon Four Seasons began building and buying worldwide.

Another mid-1990s development was the teaming up with Carlson Hospitality Worldwide, a Minnesota-based hotel management company. Carlson was known for its formidable development of mid-priced hotels and restaurants. It had brokered deals for more than 1,000 hotels and restaurants around the globe, which it managed through franchise and partnership agreements. Four Seasons entered a joint agreement with Carlson to develop its Regent brand of hotels. Four Seasons ran only nine Regents, which were revered in Asia, though there was only one in North America, in Beverly Hills. The company wanted to expand the brand, and turned to Carlson to manage this project. Four Seasons finished 1995 in the red, losing a reported $74.6 million, but Moody's upgraded its debt in 1996, and the company was clearly on the mend.

By 1997, *Business Week* declared that the company had never been healthier. Sales and profits were on the rise, and Four Seasons planned to run almost 20 more hotels over the next few years. Al-Waleed had helped the company get into lucrative Middle Eastern markets, and the chain also angled for properties in Paris, Las Vegas, and Caracas. Moreover, the luxury hotel industry in general had picked up remarkably from its early-1990s slump, and occupancy rates at some prime Four Seasons hotels were running better than 90 percent. The company continued to impress clients with its dedication to service, and stories abounded of dedicated employees going the limit to please. The chain was preferred by many famous people, from rock stars to politicians. While a sudden economic downturn in Asia in 1998 sent Four Season's Asian earnings way down, the hotels in the rest of the world seemed in fine condition, with average revenues per room rate rising significantly. The company was profitable and prospering despite the shock to its Asian markets, and its long-term goals centered on building its reputation worldwide through dedication to customer service. This was an area in which Four Seasons had always excelled. Into the next century the company hoped to build on its reputation for luxury and service, casting the Four Seasons name as a brand that signified excellence.

Principal Subsidiaries

Four Seasons Hotels Limited; Four Seasons Resorts B.V. (Netherlands); Four Seasons Hotel Berlin Gmbh (Germany); Four Seasons Hotels (Barbados) Ltd.; FSR International Hotels Limited (Hong Kong); Eurasia Hotel Limited (Hong Kong; 25%).

Further Reading

Byrne, Harlan S., "The Secret: Service," *Barron's,* May 11, 1998, pp. 20–22.

Greenberg, Larry M., and Peter Truell, "Saudi Investor Seeks to Buy 25% of Four Seasons," *Wall Street Journal,* September 28, 1994, p. A14.

"Issy: Quality Innkeeper—Quality Gentleman," *Report on Business Magazine,* June 1986, pp. 612.

Iverson, Doug, "Minnesota-Based Carlson Hospitality Worldwide Strikes Luxurious Deal," *Knight-Ridder/Tribune Business News,* December 4, 1996.

Kummer, Corby, et al., "Does Isadore Sharp Run the Best Hotels Anywhere?," *Connoisseur,* February 1990, pp. 72–76.

Olive, David, "Puttin' on the Ritz," *Report on Business Magazine,* June 1986, pp. 28–35.

Weber, Joseph, with John Rossant, "The Whirlwind at the Four Seasons," *Business Week,* October 13, 1997, pp. 82–84.

—Thomas Derdak
—updated by A. Woodward

Fresh Foods, Inc.

3437 East Main Street
Claremont, North Carolina 28610
U.S.A.
(828) 459-7626
Fax: (828) 459-3131
Web site: http://www.freshfoodsinc.com

Public Company
Incorporated: 1970 as Mom 'n' Pops Ham House
Employees: 3,800
Sales: $158.41 million (1998)
Stock Exchanges: NASDAQ
Ticker Symbol: FOOD
NAIC: 72211 Full Service Restaurants; 311812
    Commercial Bakeries; 311613 Rendering & Meat
    Byproduct Processing

North Carolina-based Fresh Foods, Inc., formerly known as WSMP, Inc., is a holding company for a variety of food preparation and restaurant businesses primarily in the Southeast, including: Pierre Foods, which prepares precooked red meats; Claremont Restaurant Group, which is responsible for all restaurant activities; and Mom 'n' Pop's Country Ham, which is one of the nation's largest ham producers. The company sells its value-added products through various distribution channels, such as supermarkets, convenience stores, vending machines, warehouse clubs, schools and healthcare providers. In its prepared foods operations, Fresh Foods produces more than 4.5 million microwaveable sandwiches per week, sold under several nationally recognized labels as well as under its own Pierre, Fast Choice, and Mom 'n' Pop's brand names. Fresh Foods' restaurant division owns and operates Sagebrush Steakhouse restaurants, Western Steer restaurants, Prime Sirloin restaurants, and Bennett's Smokehouse and Saloon restaurants.

A 1960s Start in Country Cooking

The company's history may be traced to the 1966 founding of Mom 'n' Pop's Ham House by Charles Conner and Marshall Digh. The restaurant was a success, popular for its sugar-cured ham, and the two men eventually incorporated and expanded the company. By 1970, Mom 'n' Pops Ham House had gone public, consisting of a handful of restaurants that specialized in "country" cooking in several North Carolina cities. The concept of homestyle cooking available at affordable prices would serve the company well into the 1990s.

Digh and Conner next made the decision to build upon the success of certain of their food items. In 1972, they opened a bakery division in a corner of their main office building, where they produced homemade-style biscuits for consumption in Mom 'n' Pops restaurants. At the same time, a ham curing facility was established at the company's Claremont, North Carolina, headquarters.

By the mid-1970s, demand for Mom 'n' Pop's biscuits was such that the company had added an automated line to roll, cut, bake, cool, and package biscuits. Future plant expansions in 1981 brought production capacity to 3,500 cases of biscuits per three-shift day by the early 1980s. Also during this time, the company shifted gears slightly to test the idea of creating and franchising family steakhouse restaurants, and the first Western Steer Family Steakhouse made its debut in 1975.

Mom 'n' Pop's and Western Steer expanded hand in hand, and Conner and Digh renamed their company Western Steer-Mom 'n' Pop's in 1981. The company found an outlet for its biscuits and cured hams in institutional and retail markets in addition to the restaurants where they were regularly served.

In addition to adding gift shops with a country store theme to its Mom 'n' Pops restaurants, the company also enhanced its restaurants with the late 1980s addition of an "All American Food Bar" that included 65 hot items and salad. Customers could buy unlimited trips to the food bar for $3.99 a person or $1.89 with the purchase of an entree. The concept proved popular, and by 1987 the food bar was accounting for some 40 percent of the menu mix and 20 to 25 percent of average store sales. This was not an unmediated boon, however, as the food bar involved an increase in the cost of both food and labor for the chain. By fiscal 1987, the company was reporting annual revenues of $62.9 million with earnings of $1.7 million, a figure considered disappointing by some analysts when compared to that of similar concept restaurants.

Changes in Leadership in the Late 1980s

Fiscal softness was compounded by uncertainty involving the company's ownership and identity when, early in 1987, Chairman, President, and CEO Marshall Digh announced that he wanted to retire and sell off his share of the company. Speculations abounded about a hostile takeover, and in fact, corporate raider E.W. Kelley of Kelley & Partners attempted to buy out the company, but wound up instead with a seat on the board and ownership of the promising, seven-unit Mom 'n' Pop's country store and coffee shop chain for $6.1 million. Western Steer representatives said in a news release at the time that ceding the unit to Kelley would enable the company to devote more of its time and resources to the continued development of its steakhouse restaurants.

Meanwhile, co-founder Conner, the company's new president and treasurer, called upon Richard Howard, an early Western Steer executive, to provide much of the $4.9 million needed to buy Digh's share of Western Steer-Mom 'n' Pop's in December 1987. Management rallied together under Conner and Howard to purchase Digh's approximately 15 percent stake in the company, increasing their holdings to a combined 40 percent and renaming the company WSMP, Inc. in 1988. Howard assumed the roles of chairman and chief executive after the purchase, and the two men promised to stay with the company for the long haul.

Surprisingly, then, in April 1988, Howard and Conner suddenly sold a $25,000 option to buy their 20 percent stake to a group of senior executives of the Wes-Mar Group, a food distributor based in Columbia, South Carolina, led by James C. Richardson, Jr., and Cecil Hash and including Howard's son. The transaction, which Howard and Conner agreed to help finance, cost $12.9 million and raised the buying group's stake in WSMP to 47.3 percent. Howard, Miller and Conner resigned immediately after completing the sale of their 917,000 shares, although Conner assumed the Tennessee and Virginia franchise rights of Prime Sirloin Steak and Seafood, an 11-unit steak house chain purchased by Western Steer shortly after he and Howard took control. He also maintained ownership of 18 properties, including seven Western Steer units.

Hash, who had himself been an operator of 31 franchised Western Steer units in North Carolina, became the new president and chief executive of WSMP, and immediately led the new management group in an attempt to take WSMP private in a $14.6 million leveraged buyout option presented to the board. However, the group withdrew its offer after a special committee of the board of directors indicated it would not recommend the proposed merger. Hash stayed with the company until 1993, when he was replaced by James Richardson as chair and chief executive officer.

The Search for a New Niche in the Early 1990s

The new group settled down to redefining the Western Steer concept as that of a value-added steakhouse. After limiting the sale of new franchises, it rewrote the franchise package to include training programs, marketing support, equipment deals, and product, site, and building specifications. With Western Steer the second smallest of the nation's eight major steakhouse chains, averaging $933,000 a unit in fiscal 1989, the group decided to undertake aggressive marketing to combat over-

competition on the one hand and high food costs on the other. From 1988 to 1990, at a time when the entire budget steak house segment was being hit by a slowing economy, Western Steer revamped its food bar, which now accounted for 45 percent of its sales, and slashed menu items. Addressing concerns about nutrition, it added a USDA choice beef product called MorLean. Plans called for 25 new units in 1990, part of a move to strengthen regional franchise dominance and expand into a national chain capable of competing with leader Bonanza/Sizzler. WSMP also began to experiment with converting its Western Steers to a table service, rather than buffet, concept.

In 1992, with 29 Western Steers and nine Prime Sirloin Steak and Seafood restaurants to its name, WSMP grossed $150 million from its underperforming dining establishments. Still casting about for a way in which to occupy the niche between the casual and budget steakhouse, the company made the decision to try adding onto its Prime Sirloin concept to create Prime Sirloin Buffet, Bakery, Steaks. The revamped restaurant, which offered a $4.99 lunch and dinner, was a success. By mid-year, there were eight Prime Sirloins in operation, while at the same time Western Steer had introduced an upgrade package, including an expanded buffet and in-store bakery.

Meanwhile Mom 'n' Pop's Bakery was generating the best revenue within the company, the division having grown to $30 million by 1993 from $10 million five years prior. No longer producing bakery goods for Western Steer restaurants, which preferred to cook on site, WSMP sold its food products to foodservice accounts and large food-processing companies. Among its most notable products was an assembled sandwich delivered frozen for distribution. The company was also making sandwiches sold under the Mom 'n' Pop's brand name.

However, the mid-1990s were a difficult time for steakhouses across the nation as Americans sought to eat less red meat, and WSMP's earnings zigzagged more than most. The company lost 21 cents a share in fiscal 1994, earned 38 cents a share the next year, then lost 55 cents a share in 1996. In 1994, in another attempt to branch out beyond the family steakhouse theme, WSMP teamed up with the Denver-based Bennett's Bar-B-Que to launch Bennett's Smokehouse & Saloon. The new chain represented a Texas roadhouse-themed merger of steaks and barbecue in a casual dining atmosphere. Under the partnership, WSMP began to operate four Bennett's units, in addition to its 33 company-owned restaurants, with exclusive development rights for Bennett's in Tennessee, North Carolina, and Virginia. Along with the Sagebrush Steak & Saloon restaurants, which WSMP agreed to acquire in late 1997 in a deal worth $40 million, Bennett's represented another step in WSMP's move away from its buffet-style restaurants to table service.

By 1997, the processed foods business totaled $58.6 million nationwide, and WSMP was on solid ground again. With 1997 revenues of $87.75 million and profits of $1.12 million, the company purchased back 14 of its restaurants from former president Hash and privately placed new shares of common stock for sale. In order to pay for its acquisitions, WSMP entered into a $13.5 million debt refinancing agreement arranged through a consortium of banks which allowed it to repay $11.5 million in existing debt and provided an additional $2 million in working capital. By the third quarter of the year, it found itself listed as one of the top stock performers for 1997 in

Nation's Restaurant News, posting profits of $616,853, which more than tripled its earnings of a year earlier, and increased its price per share 178 percent.

The Late 1990s and Beyond

The trend toward growth continued into 1998. Revenues reached $158.4 million, up from $87.5 million in 1996, while net income growth was up 109 percent. However, the price of WSMP's stock, which had risen 236 percent in 1997 after stagnating at $5 for most of the past 20 years, took a freakish turn in the middle of 1998. A stockbroker at the only brokerage firm to have an analyst assigned to WSMP, St. Louis-based Pauli & Company, died suddenly, and his clients began selling their shares, causing the stock price to sink 34 percent from $28 to $18.50 before it began to bounce back and hover around $21 a few months later.

At this point, WSMP undertook an initiative to expand into the branded sandwich field, making a concerted effort to establish its line of private label, ready-to-eat meal components. In addition, a new division, Mom 'n' Pop's Home Meal Replacement, marketed single-serve, modified atmosphere, packaged entrees and side dishes which were produced under custom manufacturing agreements with retailers and sold fresh-frozen. Since late 1996, WSMP had been supplying retailer Food Lion of Salisbury, North Carolina, with meal components, and in late 1997, it began to test market sausage, steak, chicken, and ham biscuits under the Hardee's label for CKE Restaurants, Inc. It also began to prepare chilled entrees, side dishes, and shelf-stable desserts for Ingles Markets, a North Carolina-based chain of supermarkets, in a move which reflected another trend in American dining, the growing desire of consumers to purchase prepared meals.

Since shoppers apparently preferred branded items to generics, WSMP focused its efforts in 1998 on creating a national network of restaurant brand sandwich lines for distribution to grocery stores, convenience stores, discount club stores, and coin-operated vending machines. The company signed a series of licensing agreements with CKE Restaurants, the parent of Hardee's chain, and with other entities affiliated with CKE—GB Foods Corporation, Checkers Drive-In Restaurants, Inc., and Rally's Hamburgers, Inc.—to offer refrigerated and frozen biscuits, biscuit sandwiches, hamburgers, and burritos through several channels in various markets throughout the country.

WSMP also entered into a pair of important acquisitions. In early 1998, it completed the purchase of Sagebrush, Inc. in a stock for stock merger and began plans to convert its remaining Western Steer properties to the Sagebrush theme. In June 1998, it acquired Pierre Foods for $122 million cash after issuing $155 million of senior unsecured notes and securing a $75 million syndicated bank loan. This Arkansas-based subsidiary of Tyson Foods. Inc., sold processed meats under the Pierre and Fast Foods labels, and supplied on-site foodservice items to schools and healthcare facilities. Its annual revenue totaled $150 million. WSMP already had a co-packaging agreement with Pierre to cook and process sandwich meats, which it shipped to Mom 'n' Pop's Bakery for assembly into sandwiches; in fact, it had been Pierre's largest customer for the past ten years. Although the Pierre brand had limited distribution in grocery stores, the acquisition of Pierre meant that WSMP now controlled its own

protein processing unit; it was a fully integrated producer and marketer of cooked, branded, and private label meat products and packaged microwaveable sandwiches.

In order to integrate its new purchases, WSMP adopted a new corporate structure and changed its name to Fresh Foods, Inc., a name chosen to be broad in scope and allow easy integration of future acquisitions and new brands by the company. As the parent of several wholly-owned subsidiaries, Fresh Foods expanded its board of directors and named three foodservice industry leaders to the new posts. As the company entered 1999, it was optimistic about its future despite the fact the growth had slowed toward the end of 1998, and by January 1999, stock prices had once again dropped to $4.88. Pierre's Jumbo Cheeseburger captured the 1998 Readers Choice Award for Food Product of the Year from Automatic Merchandiser, the top ten vote getter among all competition categories, and Pierre Foods was named as one of the nation's top suppliers to SYSCO, the largest foodservice marketing and distribution organization in North America. The company's board of directors authorized the repurchase of up to $1.5 million of its common stock, believing its stock to be an "excellent investment" under current market conditions.

Principal Subsidiaries

Pierre Foods, LLC; Claremont Restaurant Group, LLC; Mom 'n' Pop's Country Ham, LLC

Principal Divisions

Ham Curing Division; Mom 'n' Pop's Bakery Division.

Further Reading

"Fresh Foods, Inc., New Name for NC-Based Prepared Foods/Restaurant Company," *Business Wire,* May 7, 1998.

Hamstra, Mark, "WSMP Readies National Launch of Branded Sandwiches," *Nation's Restaurant News,* March 23, 1998, p. 1.

Hayes, Jack, "BBQ, Steakhouse Chains Partner in Smokehouse," *Nation's Restaurant News,* August 15, 1994, p. 12.

——, "Western Steer Founders Saddle Up New Sagebrush," *Nation's Restaurant News,* July 20, 1992, p. 3.

——, "Western Steer Vies for National Market," *Nation's Restaurant News,* July 16, 1990, p. 3.

Papiernik, Richard, "Meal Solutions Draw a Wider Following in Supermarkets," *Nation's Restaurant News,* October 13, 1997, p. 3.

Reynolds, Pat, "Pan-Free Baking," *Bakery Production and Marketing,* November 24, 1993, p. 154.

——, "Why WSMP Owns the Market," *Bakery Production and Marketing,* November 24, 1993, p. 148.

Romeo, Peter J., "After a Difficult Year, Western Steer Charts New Course," *Nation's Restaurant News,* January 25, 1988, p. F28.

——, "Management Group Tries to Take Western Steer Private at $14.6 M LBO," *Nation's Restaurant News,* September 5, 1988, p. 4.

——, "New Roster at Western Steer," *Nation's Restaurant News,* May 16, 1988, p. 1.

——, "Western Steer's 'Rescuers' Set to Sell Stake," *Nation's Restaurant News,* April 18, 1988, p. 4.

Williams, Christopher C., "Will Deals Whet Investors' Appetite for WSMP shares?" *Business North Carolina,* June 1998, p. 20.

—Carrie Rothburd

Friedman's Inc.

4 West State Street
Savannah, Georgia 31401
U.S.A.
(912) 233-9333
Fax: (912) 238-4873

Public Company
Incorporated: 1920
Employees: 3,071
Sales: $287.3 million (1998)
Stock Exchanges: NASDAQ
Ticker Symbol: FRDM
NAIC: 44831 Jewelry Stores

Friedman's Inc. is a chain of some 470 specialty retail jewelry stores throughout the southeastern United States and adjoining areas. Based in Savannah, Georgia, it has stores in 22 states, and sells to a low- to middle-income clientele in the 18-to-45 age bracket. The company maintains its position as "The Value Leader" (a registered trademark) among specialty retail jewelers by offering a wide selection of merchandise, prices comparable to those of such principal competitors as Zale's, and strong customer service. Founded in 1920, Friedman's remained outside the limelight until its purchase by the Morgan Schiff & Co. investment firm in 1990. Since then it has experienced explosive growth, in the process employing a strategy that focuses on "power strip centers" (or power strip malls) as opposed to large upscale shopping malls. This allowed it to operate at considerably lower overhead than jewelers selling from more prestigious locations, and during the mid-1990s Friedman's rapid expansion elicited a great deal of interest in the financial community. By the latter part of the decade, however, it had experienced growing pains which led to a shuffle of upper-level management.

A Tale of Two Brothers in the 1920s

The history of Friedman's may be traced to two brothers, Abraham and Benjamin Friedman, in south Georgia. In 1909, a merchant named Sam Segall came to the town of Savannah on the coast of Georgia, where he founded a jewelry store. In 1920, he died, and his two nephews Abraham and Benjamin took over the business. Because their name was Friedman, they changed the name of Segall's store. At some point Abraham moved away from Savannah, heading north to Augusta, on the Georgia–South Carolina line. Benjamin stayed behind, and in time they split up their holdings, which consisted of seven stores.

By all appearances the parting was amicable, and the two agreed that neither would interfere in the other's territory until their companies had grown more. Thus out of the line of Abraham came A. A. Friedman, an Augusta-based jewelry chain with 127 stores in 1997; and from the line of Benjamin came Friedman's Inc. For generations, it appeared that there would be no conflict between the descendants of Abraham and the descendants of Benjamin, because both were family-owned businesses.

However, by the late 1990s, Benjamin's former stores would no longer belonged to Benjamin's children. By contrast, A. A. Friedman remained under the control of the Augusta, Georgia Friedmans. Ultimately the two companies would clash over the right to the Friedman name, but before the owners of Friedman's took their troops into the fray, an empire would have to be built.

Seventy Quiet Years

For 70 years, the store founded by Benjamin Friedman remained well outside the limelight. As with many a private company later acquired by an outside investment firm, most of Friedman's early history is all but forgotten, with one notable exception. Having built its business, with mall-based retail stores—as is typical of most jewelers—Friedman's in 1979 found itself in a difficult position. It already had one store in a certain mall, and desired to open a second one for reasons that are no longer clear. Friedman's management did not want to confuse customers by operating both stores under the same name, so they developed the "Regency Jewelers" tradename.

According to the company's 1998 annual report, "Since then, the company has continued the use of the name when it deems it to be advantageous for advertising or marketing purposes. The company also uses the 'Regency Jewelers' tradename in 37 locations as of September 30, 1998. With the acquisition of all the rights of A.A. Friedman Co., Inc. of Augusta, Georgia . . . to the Friedman's Jewelers tradename, the company plans to change substantially all of the Regency Jewelers stores to Friedman's Jewelers stores during January 1999.'' Conflict over names—Friedman's and Regency—would be a recurring theme for the company.

1990: Morgan Schiff Acquires Friedman's

In a 1995 profile of Friedman's, Scott Thurston of the *Atlanta Journal and Constitution* described it as ''no newcomer.'' Over the course of its first 70 years, he wrote, it had become a ''quietly profitable family-run company'' which by 1990 had 48 mostly mall-based stores. In the latter year New York investor Philip Cohen and his investment firm of Morgan Schiff & Co. formed a partnership and purchased Friedman's for $50 million from the Friedman family.

Morgan Schiff already owned a similar company, Crescent Jewelers of California, and perhaps its experience prepared it for the vicissitudes of the industry. Certainly its first two years as owner of Friedman's would have been disappointing to any owner lacking in a long view: ''Initial results were dismal,'' wrote Thurston, ''as the recession and buyouts drove Friedman's into the red in 1991 and 1992.''

The turning point for the company came in 1993, when Morgan Schiff brought in Bradley Stinn as chief executive officer. Just 27 years old when he became a managing director for Morgan Schiff in 1986, Stinn had served as chief financial officer for Crescent Jewelers from 1990 to 1992. When he arrived in Savannah to take over Friedman's, he was only 33.

Stinn, in turn, attributed the company's turning point to a visit he made in 1992, when he was driving through south Georgia with Robert Morris, executive vice-president for store operations. On their way to Florida to visit Friedman's outlets there, they stopped at the coastal town of St. Mary's, a city with a mushrooming economy thanks to the flow of purchasing dollars from Navy personnel stationed at the nearby Kings Bay Submarine Support Base. Stopping at a strip mall with a Wal-Mart as its anchor store, Stinn offhandedly asked Morris, ''Think you could do business with a store here?'' Morris answered, ''I could do business out of my trunk here.'' The rest, as Thurston reported, was company history: ''Before leaving town they tracked down the shopping center's owner and signed a lease on the hood of his car. That episode—and the subsequent success of the St. Mary's store—prompted Stinn to go

full-bore with what he calls a 'Wal-Mart vapor trail' expansion strategy. So far, the results have been lustrous.''

The Power Strip Mall Strategy of the Mid-1990s

Thus was born what would become Friedman's strategy in the mid-1990s, as it defied tradition and embarked on a pattern of wild growth. Historically, jewelry retailers had established their locations in elegant-looking mall stores—which carried a hefty price tag. Stinn, on the other hand, proposed to put Friedman's stores in ''power strip malls'' like the one in St. Mary's. Whereas malls were collections of stores under one roof, their doors opening into a common area, strip malls were strings of separate stores with doors all facing toward a vast parking lot. The strip mall's ''anchor'' (or primary store in the group) drew customers who would presumably visit other stores as a result of stopping at the anchor, usually either a supermarket or a discount retailer such as Wal-Mart. The ''power'' designation simply suggests the great volume of shoppers drawn in by the anchor.

Certainly power strip malls lacked the cachet associated with traditional shopping malls, but they also lacked the costs as well. According to Pablo Galarza of *Investor's Business Daily*, a retailer could in 1994 set up a store in a power strip mall for about $225,000. If the owner then chose to ''walk away'' and cancel his lease, he would pay a penalty of perhaps $40,000. By contrast, in a large indoor shopping mall a retailer would shell out $400,000 just to get started, and a whopping $490,000 if he chose to walk away.

In the words of Craig Weichmann, an analyst for Morgan Keegan & Co., ''Schiff ran the numbers and the light bulb went of. Power strip malls offer attractive economics compared to large mall stores. Not only is competition less intense in power malls, there are more of them.'' Referring to two extremely upscale jewelry stores, Stinn told Galarza, ''We aren't looking to be Tiffany's or Cartier. We're interested in selling to the average working person.''

From 48 stores in 1990, the number of Friedman's retail outlets grew more than threefold in the next several years. As Phillip Carter wrote in 1995 in *Investor's Business Daily*, ''Company officials said Friedman's has just begun growing. Of the 750 retail stores it hopes to acquire in the Southeast, it has only purchased 158.'' Among the factors contributing to this runaway growth were the installment of a new computer system, of which CFO John Call said, ''Prior to the installation of that system, the company was operated manually, if you will. It allowed us the platform from which to control growth—that was a big add.''

This facilitated a change in the way the company offered credit, allowing point-of-sale credit agreements. By contrast, Carter wrote, ''At Zale's, customers fill out credit applications. These are electronically processed at a central location while the customer waits in the store. If these requests for credit lines are rejected, customers can be embarrassed. . . . Friedman's policy gives the local employee and store manager the power to issue credit up to certain limits at the store level.''

Thus technology helped the chain put into practice its policy of giving managers greater power over individual stores. With this freedom came greater responsibility, and Friedman's likewise compensated its "partners" (as Stinn began calling managers) on the basis of their store's sales and rate of collection. It was a system that, according to Stinn, "attracts people who want to stand on their feet."

The Late 1990s and Beyond

In the year that ended September 30, 1997, Friedman's opened a staggering 83 locations. By then it had become the third-largest jewelry retailer in the country, and in the seven months between the end of the 1997's fiscal year and an April 1998 interview with Stinn in *Jewelers Circular Keystone,* the company had added 40 more locations while net income rose by a phenomenal 39 percent. However, the company's rapid expansion came with a pricetag.

There had been a drop in comparable store sales and return on investment, while the ratio of bad debt levels to total revenues had increased. As a result, the company had shuffled its top management. Stinn, who remained as chairman, had turned over the CEO position to former Blockbuster Entertainment executive Richard Ungaro. Taking a controversial step, Friedman's had sunk $25 million into its privately owned sister corporation, Crescent (of which Stinn would thenceforth be CEO), in just 18 months. "Friedman's executives," Glen Beres reported in *Jewelers Circular Keystone,* "say that Crescent, which has struggled in recent years, is back on a positive track with expansion plans as ambitious as its East Coast counterpart."

Then there was the dispute with the descendants of Abraham Friedman. For some time, Friedman's and A. A. Friedman had been locked in a struggle over the name—a struggle initiated by Friedman's. In 1997 the two parties agreed that A. A. Friedman would turn over the rights to the name in exchange for $7 million. "It's kind of sad," one Augustan told the hometown *Chronicle,* adding "It won't seem the same without the name Friedman's." Under the terms of the agreement, A. A. Friedman would be able to continue using the name for two more Christmas seasons before Friedman's could enter its territory with its own name. In the meantime, A. A. Friedman would be phasing in the name it already used for some of its stores, Marks & Morgan. (Marks was the maiden name of Betty Friedman, the recently deceased A. A. Friedman chairwoman.)

Ironically, the name change seemed to hurt Friedman's in the short run. As Stinn told Beres, "we haven't gotten the full benefit of the agreement yet, because we don't have unrestricted freedom of operation in those markets until January 1999. In fact, there might have been some detriment, because [A. A. Friedman] advertised they were changing their name. We had a lot of people walk into our stores at Christmastime and say, 'I thought you were changing the name of your store'." In a further irony, the 1998 annual report stated that "The Company has received a letter from Service Merchandise"—one of its leading competitors—"alleging that Service Merchandise owns an incontestable federal registration for the trademark 'The Helbros Regency & Design' and that the Company's use of the service mark 'Regency Jewelers' infringes this mark. Service Merchandise has only requested that the Company halt further use of its Regency Jewelers mark. The matter is close to settlement."

Another thing that remained to be settled was the future of Friedman's relationship with Crescent. Asked if he thought the large investment in the sister corporation "could come back to haunt Friedman's," Stinn was emphatic in the negative: "The number-one fallacy is that the Crescent investment has kept Friedman's from doing something it would have otherwise done. That is flat-out wrong. If that money didn't go into Crescent, it would be in the bank now, earning interest." With regard to the possibility of a future merger between Crescent and Friedman's, however, he left it up to discerning readers to draw their own conclusions: "It's been 10 years since the leveraged buyout, and Crescent shareholders need to see a financial return. So Crescent has two considerations: to get liquidity for the investors by going public as an independent company or by merging into some other entity, Friedman's being most likely."

Further Reading

Beres, Glen A., "Friedman's Looks to Easy Growing Pains: Interview with Friedman's Chmn. Bradley J. Stinn," *Jewelers Circular Keystone,* April 1998, p. 184.

Bond, Patti, "Friedman's Shuffles Management Again," *Atlanta Journal and Constitution,* September 12, 1998, p. 1C.

Carter, Phillip, "Friedman's Inc.," *Investor's Business Daily,* February 10, 1995, p. A4.

Galarza, Pablo, "Friedman's Inc.," *Investor's Business Daily,* July 22, 1994, p. A4.

Luke, Robert, "Stock in Savannah Jeweler Has Been Hot Item All Year," *Atlanta Journal and Constitution,* December 5, 1994, p. E6.

Rogers, Donna W., "Friedman's Settlement: Name Changes Not Uncommon," *Augusta (Georgia) Chronicle,* May 25, 1997, p. F1.

Thurston, Scott, "Jewelry Chain Finds Successful Niche in 'Power Strip' Stores," *Atlanta Journal and Constitution,* May 21, 1995, p. 12T.

—Judson Knight

Fubu

350 5th Avenue Suite #6617
New York, New York 10118
U.S.A.
(212) 273-3300
Fax: (212) 629-0232
Web site: http://fubu.com

Private Company
Founded: 1992
Employees: 55
Sales: $200 million (1998 est.)
NAIC: 315211 Men's & Boys' Cut & Sew Apparel
  Contractors; 315212 Women's, Girls' & Infants' Cut
  & Sew Apparel Contractors

Fubu is one of the fastest growing apparel companies in the American fashion industry, producing a variety of clothing and accessories ranging from baseball caps and sweatshirts to men's semi-formal suits. The company was conceived and founded by Daymond John, a native of Queens, New York, in conjunction with three childhood friends, each of whom continue to play a role in Fubu's management. Fubu, an acronym for "for us, by us," gears its product line to young men, and the label's designs reflect the style of the music and fashion phenomenon known as hip-hop.

Company Origins

Daymond John, CEO of Fubu, entered the retail industry after becoming frustrated with what he perceived as a paucity of street-smart, fashionable clothing in the menswear industry. After having his mother teach him to sew, the 24-year-old began selling tie-top hats and other small accessories on the streets of New York. The venture quickly took on a life of its own, with John's mother reportedly taking out a $100,000 mortgage on her home to help finance the business. The family house was transformed into a small factory devoted to the production of hats and rugby-style t-shirts. Soon John, who was then also waiting tables at a Red Lobster restaurant in addition to designing clothes, had more orders than he could fill and so turned his energies full time to the fledgling business.

In 1994 Fubu saw its first real expansion. That year, John took his designs to the Men's Apparel Guild in California (MAGIC), an annual retail event held in Las Vegas, and, unable to afford a booth at the show, sold his wares from a hotel room. Within a couple of days, John, with irrepressible energy and salesmanship, had made Fubu's presence felt: every accessory and piece of clothing brought to the show had been sold, and John returned to Queens with over $300,000 worth of orders to be filled.

Soon after Fubu's success at the MAGIC event, the Asian conglomerate Samsung offered to distribute Fubu's collection, enabling the business to increase both production and the variety of its designs. What had begun with tie-top hats and t-shirts now expanded, with John and a small team of designers creating jackets, baggy "hip-hop" style pants, and oversized "bubble" coats, all of which were emblazoned with Fubu's distinctive, outsized logo. Within two years of striking its distribution deal with Samsung, the Fubu collection was picked up by the Macy's chain of retail stores, making the label more accessible nationwide.

From the business's inception, Fubu was intimately allied, both in its designs and its advertising, with the hip-hop music industry. "For us, by us" was a phrase invented by John to indicate to the consumer that his was a business devoted to fulfilling the fashion needs of young African-American men. According to industry analysts, such a customer demographic tended to adopt its apparel trends primarily from two sources: sports and rap stars. The best way, therefore, for a new urbanwear company to make its mark with its targeted consumer base was to have a high-profile representative of one of these industries involved in the promotion of that company's merchandise. According to Joel Stein, writing in *Time* magazine, "the trick to hip-hop fashion money, even more than offering slick styles, is somehow to get a rapper—preferably one on heavy rotation on MTV—to wear your stuff."

This form of promotion became especially important for a company when, as was the case with Fubu, advertising dollars

Company Perspectives:

Fubu is about Pride and Respect in what you wear and who you are.

were in short supply. After Fubu's breakthrough at the MAGIC show in Las Vegas, the company soon began canvasing the rap star LL Cool J, offering him free Fubu clothing in hopes that he would wear it to public functions. In 1994 LL Cool J wore some Fubu gear in concert, and soon thereafter he became a company spokesperson, giving the small label a high-profile image shared by few of its competitors.

The Right Concept at the Right Time: Menswear Takes Off

The early 1990s saw an explosion of growth in the menswear industry, particularly in sportswear. Suddenly, designers such as Ralph Lauren, Donna Karan, and Tommy Hilfiger saw skyrocketing sales in their casual menswear lines, as the young men's *de rigueur* uniform of slim-fitted jeans and t-shirts transformed into a more silhouette- and label-conscious look. The style to be imitated during this time, for young men of all backgrounds, was known in the industry as urban streetwear. According to Lauren Goldstein, in *Fortune* magazine, "In 1990 there were fewer than five urban booths at the MAGIC show. Last August (1998) there were at least 140." The burgeoning interest in urban wear not only offered an increase in sales to already established designers such as Lauren, but created an opportunity for small businesses to fill a growing niche market.

What fueled and inspired this market was rap music; Goldstein went so far as to note that "urbanwear companies have ridden in on the coattails—and jacket backs, and baseball caps, and shoes—of rap musicians." This marriage of musical tastes and fashion trends made the urbanwear market huge. Just as the 1980s saw a proliferation of suburban kids turning their tastes and pocketbooks to the urban sounds of hip-hop and gangsta' rap, so was the case in the retail industry in the 1990s, with urbanwear becoming a "crossover" point at which tastes from the suburbs and the city converged.

CEO John was aware of this convergence and used it to his company's advantage. Fubu's marketing efforts began to focus on broadening the concept of urban, making it more about attitude and style and less about ethnicity. According to John at the time, Fubu was "a sportswear company. Calling us 'urban' is like saying we come from the street and immediately labels us as something we don't necessarily want to be."

However, this style of the street was exactly what sold Fubu; and it was the label's genius to transform "the street"—and all the term entailed—into a concept readily recognizable and desirable to a broader consumer base. John acknowledged that the Fubu name represented a complete lifestyle: "The people who buy our clothes know that we're 'down.' They know that we don't just make the clothes, we wear the clothes. And we are part of the culture."

As rap music found a multicultural audience, so did Fubu in the mid-1990s. Commenting on the company's successful marketing to America's youth, Peter Ferraro, advertising director of *The Source* magazine, contended that "Fubu is no more hip-hop than the Gap, but by using the language of hip-hop, which is the language of youth in the United States and around the world, they have had success in expanding their brand from the inner city into the suburbs. Hip-hop is the one art form that has cohesion in youth culture. They have understood that hip-hop gets the gear out there on the right kids."

The "right kids" were of course more accessible when a label was broadly visible and available in many places. Fubu's distribution deal with Samsung gave the company exactly this sort of exposure, with Fubu lines being picked up by over 100 Macy's stores and over 300 J.C. Penney stores nationwide. Even while Fubu went more commercial, independently owned specialty stores continued to carry the label, making Fubu by 1998 a ubiquitous force in the hip-hop fashion industry.

From Fubu's inception, competition was fierce, particularly from other new labels. As hip-hop fashion grew in popularity with young men, so did the desire to wear clothes representative of a new urban ethos, an ethos to which established designers such as Lauren and Karan could stake no claim. The mid- and late 1990s thus saw a flourishing of small, independent labels which were carried by boutiques and, with big distribution deals, large department stores. Dexter Wimberly, an executive of the marketing firm August Bishop, noted in 1998 that "In the last three years, there has been more entrepreneurial spirit shown from African-American and Latino-owned upstart clothing companies than ever before."

Fubu found itself competing with such brands as Phat Farm, a label owned and begun by Russell Simmons, founder of Def Jam Records, as well as Wu-Wear, a company started by the rap group Wu-Tang Clan. Given the similar ties to the music industry of Fubu's competitors, it became necessary for Fubu to step up its own celebrity exposure. By 1998, Fubu was not only represented by LL Cool J (who even insisted on wearing a Fubu cap while filming an ad for retailer The Gap), but could also be seen on such music stars as Mariah Carey, Will Smith, Whitney Houston, and Brandy. In sales, too, Fubu trumped its competitors, with its wholesale volume jumping from $75 million in 1997 to $200 million in 1998, an increase far ahead those reported by other small labels.

Broadening Appeal: Womenswear and Beyond

Part of Fubu's contract with Samsung required the sportswear company to gross at least $5 million in sales within three years. John's company exceeded that figure in less than one year, making it possible for the company to look with confidence to its financial future. Fubu's early success made the company an appealing investment to other names in the retail industry, and soon Fubu formed licensing contracts which allowed its name to appear on a broad range of womenswear, accessories and loungewear.

In early 1999 Fubu formed a licensing deal with Pietrafesa Corporation, a producer of upscale, formal clothes, which allowed Fubu its first experiment with tailored, higher priced men's suits. In charge of the designing of the line was Pietrafesa, with Fubu heading up the line's sizing and form. The line included both single and double breasted suits, tuxedos, and a "country" suit modeled after vintage British designs. Prices for the suits ranged from $395 to $1,500.

While it might have seemed strategically incongruous for the casualwear company to attempt a formal, more conservative line of clothing, Fubu's deal with Pietrafesa actually reflected a growing demand among young consumers for stylish, tailored clothes. As a Fubu spokesperson put it, "Our customer is beginning to dress up and we want to be there with our own classics." Moreover, as Fubu's customer base grew older, and entered a work place in which formal clothing was required, Fubu's move to corner the tailored clothing market revealed a shrewd marketing sensibility.

Also during this time, Fubu's expansion plans resulted in a licensing deal in the winter of 1999 with the National Basketball Association. Urbanwear took many of its style cues from the sports world, and basketball, with its players outfitted in knee-length baggy shorts and loose jerseys, had a particularly strong influence over the retail industry. In its deal with the NBA, Fubu created a new line, called Fubu NBA, which focused on 40 pieces of sportswear, from sweatshirts and pants to shooting shirts and headgear. Prices ranged from $45 to $100, and each item carried both the NBA and Fubu logo. In designing the line, particular attention was given by Fubu to the most popular teams in the NBA: the Los Angeles Lakers, the Chicago Bulls, and the New York Knicks. In explaining Fubu's marketing approach with Fubu NBA, the company's vice-president, Phil Pabon, stated that "Our alliance with the NBA brings a whole legitimacy to our line—not just in numbers and sales but in that we are a true sportswear collection whether you want to call us urban, suburban, indifferent. . . . This opens a whole new segment of an existing market."

Just as Fubu looked towards increasing its sales with tailored clothing and licensing deals with the NBA, the company realized that its core line of clothing—bubble jackets, baggy jeans, and oversized t-shirts—had become quite popular with women as well. As a result, the company developed a line of women's clothing called Fubu Ladies. The collection, licensed in conjunction with Jordache, consisted of both form-fitting, tailored dresses and skirts, as well as clothing similar to that of the company's menswear, such as loosely cut shirts and oversized jeans. Competing against such brands as XOXO, Guess, and Tommy Jeans, the Fubu Ladies line was designed to attract younger, style conscious women, with prices ranging from $25 to $180.

In 1999 Fubu revealed its most ambitious plans for expansion, making the decision to open 45 retail stores overseas. Its first store was slated to open in the fall of 1999 in South Africa, where Fubu had already become a coveted brand name. The store, over 3,500 square feet of space, was slated by Fubu to carry all the company's major lines, including Fubu NBA and Fubu Ladies. Other targeted countries include Greece, Cyprus, Turkey, and three locations in Eastern Europe. Fubu had avoided opening stores in the United States because, according to John, "Here in the U.S. we have strong distribution and putting up freestanding stores would affect our relationship with our current department and specialty store accounts. But because we have no strong distribution overseas, rolling out stores is a good way to display our product."

A young company which experienced phenomenal rapid expansion, the future for Fubu looked bright, though some analysts found fault with the company's occasionally disorganized distribution system, probably attributable to that fact that Fubu became popular so quickly that at times it took on more orders than it could fill. However, with a menswear market which grossed in the late 1990s over $5 billion dollars, Fubu remained a singular success story. From the company's inception its founders took advantage of an exploding niche market in urbanwear, and it would likely continue to create new ways to grow.

Further Reading

Gellers, Stan, "Fubu Close to Signing Tailored Clothing License with Pietrafesa," *Daily News Record,* January 25, 1999, p. 2.

Goldstein, Lauren, "Urban Wear Goes Suburban," *Fortune,* December 21, 1998.

Hunter, Karen, "Fubu Challenges Rivals in Urban Apparel Industry," *Knight-Ridder/Tribune Business News,* November 11, 1996.

Redecker, Cynthia, "Fubu's Move to the Suburbs," *Women's Wear Daily,* January 14, 1999, p. 14.

Romero, Elena, "Fubu Gets Ball Rolling with NBA License," *Daily News Record,* January 25, 1999, p. 14.

——, "Fubu Unveils Plan to Open Overseas Retail Stores," *Daily News Record,* April 19, 1999, p. 2.

Stein, Joel, "Getting Giggy with a Hoodie: Young Black Designers are Giving Urban Fashions Street Appeal," *Time,* January 19, 1998.

Wax, Emily, "Clothes to Queens: Putting their Home Borough on Apparel Put Three Makers of Urban Clothing on the Map," *Newsday,* April 19, 1998.

—Rachel Martin

GNC Live Well.

General Nutrition Companies, Inc.

300 Sixth Avenue
Pittsburgh, Pennsylvania 15222
U.S.A.
(412) 288-4600
Fax: (412) 288-2099
Web site: http://www.gnc.com

Public Company
Founded: 1935
Employees: 13,834
Sales: $1.42 billion (1998)
Stock Exchanges: NASDAQ
Ticker Symbol: GNCI
NAIC: 551112 Offices of Other Holding Companies;
446110 Pharmacies & Drug Stores

General Nutrition Companies, Inc., is the largest specialty retailer of vitamin, mineral, and sports nutrition supplements in the world. It is also a leading supplier of personal care, fitness, and other health-related products. The holding company garners most of its earnings from its General Nutrition, Inc. subsidiary, which operates more than 4,000 retail stores internationally. Proprietary products manufactured by subsidiary General Nutrition Products account for more than half of the company's revenues. After sporadic growth since its inception in 1935, GNC turned around in the late 1980s and experienced explosive growth in the 1990s.

50 Years of Growth under Company Founder

David Shakarian, in 1935, opened the first of what would eventually become a successful chain of health food and vitamin stores called General Nutrition. His innovative health concept flourished in the steel-making town of Pittsburgh during the 1950s, prompting him to eventually open 30 other stores in that city. He also began adding vitamins and other health supplements to his product line, and expanding operations into other cities, such as New York.

Shakarian's success peaked during the 1970s. Demand for vitamins and a new generation of "miracle products," which claimed to improve both body and mind, emerged, and General Nutrition Inc. (GNI) experienced rampant expansion across the United States. As sales of the store's original core health food offerings continued to rise during the 1970s, shipments of vitamins and other supplements ballooned to represent about 50 percent of company sales. GNI's move into shopping malls bolstered its bottom line and gave the company a more progressive image. The lack of any competitors in GNI's niche, moreover, allowed the company to expand unfettered throughout the decade.

Shakarian profited handsomely during the 1970s by expanding the number and size of his stores, emphasizing an evolving line of trendy products, and developing and manufacturing his own proprietary products. He opened factories in Pennsylvania, North Dakota, South Carolina, and Minnesota. He also began selling his products by mail-order, substantially boosting access to less-populated areas and bolstering recognition of his specialty stores. By the early 1980s, Shakarian had grown the GNI chain from a single shop to a national network of 1,300 outlets. Although his Fortune 500 enterprise was publicly owned, Shakarian controlled about 80 percent of the stock, and he and many of his relatives amassed sizable fortunes.

Waning Profitability: 1980s

GNI's profitability began to wane in the early 1980s for a variety of reasons. GNI began to face stiff competition from supermarkets and drug stores. Supermarkets cut into GNI's food business by capitalizing on the increased demand for health food. Whole wheat bread, rice cakes, tofu, and other items popular with the health crowd became commonplace in most grocery stores, thus eliminating much of GNI's singularity. Likewise, both supermarkets and drug stores vastly increased their vitamin offerings, which diminished GNI's sales and profit margins on nonproprietary supplements.

In addition to increased competition, GNI was also hampered by questionable management decisions that it had made during the 1970s. It had over-expanded its product line to include a huge number of goods, many of which were performing poorly or were cannibalizing sales of related offerings. In addition, its stores were still dedicating a disproportionately large share of their floor space to relatively low-margin food items. In fact, many stores in the chain were unprofitable and had become a drag on GNI's bottom line. In some instances GNI had placed stores too close to one another. GNI also failed to capitalize on the emerging fitness boom that would dominate the market for health-related products during the 1980s, and it ignored younger, health-conscious consumers.

Augmenting GNI's woes were numerous lawsuits and complaints that had surfaced during the previous ten to 15 years, ranging from allegations of false claims about its vitamins to fiscal impropriety. Its public image was out of step with a more upbeat, energetic 1980s mentality—GNI was suffering from its reputation as a hard-sell, hippie-style granola shop that, on the side, pedaled a dubious mix of new-age snake oil cures. "In the 1960s and 1970s, it was our classic situation," said Gary M. Giblen, industry analyst, in an August 1993 issue of the *Pittsburgh Post-Gazette*. "You went in and everybody looked unhealthy. The biggest joke about health stores was that the help there looked like they were dying from starvation."

Shakarian died in 1984, just as the company was reaching a historic slump. Although GNI's stock price had vacillated wildly during the past few decades, often rising after the introduction of a faddish new vitamin supplement, it was selling for a pitiful $5 per share when its founder died—$25 less than its price 12 months earlier. And problems continued to mount. GNI's factories were operating at only 30 percent capacity, and Shakarian's will, which included much of GNI's stock, was contested by his survivors. The company fired long-time president Gary Daum and fellow manager Bart Shakarian (David's brother) and brought in Jerry Horn in 1985 to clean up the mess.

Return to Health: Late 1980s

Analysts questioned Jerry Horn's sanity when he, in 1985, accepted an invitation to serve as president of the troubled General Nutrition Inc. Horn had just performed an impressive six-year stint as president of Seattle-based Recreational Equipment, Inc. (REI), and had previously completed 20 successful years with Sears. In short order, Horn had virtually turned REI around, essentially obliterating its debt problems and boosting the company's profits 40 percent within three years, to $10.8 million. At his last assignment with Sears, moreover, Horn had revived the retailer's ailing San Francisco store, increasing its sales by 23 percent and making it the top profit contributor in Sears' western region—all within one year.

Now, having paid his dues and positioned himself to assume a number of high-profile, well-paid positions, Horn had chosen to attach himself to a lagging health food and vitamin retail chain of relatively ill repute. Indeed, national news publications of the early 1980s carried such headlines as "Under Attack: General Nutrition Inc. Is Besieged with Suits Over Bold Sales Tactics," and "Reliance on Fads Take Toll." The federal Food and Drug Administration (FDA) had become a regular detractor of the organization's vitamin offerings, and the Federal Trade Commission (FTC) was pressuring the organization about alleged false advertising claims related to its diet supplements. Furthermore, one of several lawsuits against GNI was filed by a group of shareholders, who claimed that the company was artificially inflating its stock price through questionable sales of faddish products.

Although GNI lost more than $15 million in 1985, Horn believed that the enterprise was a sleeper that offered excellent potential for long-term growth. He would build a new GNI based on its strengths of manufacturing and dominance of the U.S. "self-care" market. He also planned to change the focus of the company from products to consumers, and transform GNI outlets from health stores into "health management centers." "What's happened at GNI is very normal, it's classical," explained Horn in the July 1986 issue of *Executive Report*. "We were product-driven as opposed to customer-driven.... GNI tended to seize the latest fad. It was part of the original entrepreneurial spirit that built the company . . . but this sort of zeal was becoming its undoing."

One of Horn's first moves was to dump the chain's languishing stores. He also earmarked $20 million to renovate its profitable outlets and change their layout and product mix to reflect consumer preferences. Although GNI would still emphasize the development and sale of new items, Horn eliminated 30 percent of GNI's offerings and established a system of routing out nonperformers. GNI's confusing array of food products was organized into eight major categories, defined by their health attributes; high fiber, low sodium, low calorie, and low cholesterol products, for example, were arranged in identifiable groups.

Virtually every item sold in GNI stores, including vitamins, was repackaged in an effort to streamline its products. Floor plans were changed to appear cleaner and less cluttered, and new sections were added to exploit a growing demand for nonedible health products, such as skin and hair care goods. The company also bolstered offerings to body-builders and other serious athletes with over-the-counter energy and weight-gain supplements. To generate cash for expansion, the company sold its mail-order business and spotlighted its retail outlets.

Horn also made a concerted effort to appease critical federal regulators and to clean up the company's reputation. He initiated communication with the FDA, for example, seeking to establish a collaborative relationship. In addition, the company kicked off a new advertising campaign targeted more toward fitness-conscious consumers, including body-builders. Although Horn closed nearly 200 GNI stores in 1986, he opened 30 new ones and was planning to open many more before the close of the decade. Horn also set a goal of utilizing 88 percent of the company's manufacturing capacity, a strategy that would be achieved by augmenting sales through GNI stores with shipments to third-party retailers.

Horn's most prolific strategic initiative was a franchising program. Started in 1987, the program was created to help finance expansion and to infuse a new spirit of entrepreneurialism in the organization. GNI helped its franchisees, many of whom were former employees, by financing the stores and supporting owners with a high-quality marketing program. Existing stores that had been converted to franchises typically experienced sales increases of 60 percent during their first year of private ownership. As a result, GNI stepped up its franchising efforts throughout the late 1980s and early 1990s.

Although GNI struggled to regain profitability during the late 1980s, Horn had successfully put the company on a new path toward growth and prosperity. After closing down more than 300 stores and spending $46 million to settle lawsuits between 1985 and 1989, the GNI organization comprised over 1,100 outlets and was ringing up annual sales of more than $300 million. The streamlined nature of the new GNI reflected Horn's personality and management style. Out of the gym and behind his desk by 7:45 a.m., Horn stressed effort, teamwork, and a customer orientation.

Ownership Changes and Aggressive Growth: 1990s

William E. Watts replaced Jerry Horn as president of GNI in late 1988. Horn retained his position as chief executive officer and was later elected chairman of the board. In 1989 Watts, Horn, and other GNI executives accomplished a leveraged buyout of the company with the help of Boston-based investment firm Thomas H. Lee Company. A new company, General Nutrition Companies, Inc. (GNC), was created to operate GNI as its major subsidiary.

Although GNC was saddled with $360 million in debt following the leveraged buyout, its management sustained the efforts initiated by Horn and was able to slowly boost sales. By 1992, the first year in which GNC showed a quarterly profit, GNC was operating about 1,125 stores and generating over $380 million in annual sales. After strong earnings performances in 1991 and 1992, it was decided to take the company public again. The initial public offering generated $81 million, with a secondary offering in 1993 raising another $57 million. Proceeds were applied to reducing the company's debt.

With its new cache of capital, GNC began aggressively pursuing an aggressive growth strategy. Having successfully restructured its organization and cut much of the fat from the old GNI, GNC was prepared to concentrate on replicating its proven manufacturing, distribution, and retail strategy. GNC planned to expand its retail store base and boost market share by opening stores in new metropolitan areas and by stepping up its franchise efforts. Between 1992 and 1998 it would open more than 2,000 stores, making it one of the fastest growing retail chains in the nation during the 1990s.

GNC retained its emphasis on vitamins and minerals (which represented about 40 percent of revenues) and sports nutrition supplements (30 percent of sales), but it also began adding new lines of apparel and exercise equipment. In addition, the company significantly increased its marketing budget, with expenditures on television advertising more than doubling during 1992. Among several new advertising and marketing promotions was the newly introduced Gold Card membership, which originally cost $15 annually and gave customers 20 percent discounts on the first Tuesday of each month. The Gold Card program developed into a key component of the company's marketing strategy and had a membership of 3.1 million customers by 1998.

While most other retailers struggled to retain sales and profits during a lingering recession, GNC expanded its organization to include 1,216 stores by the end of 1992 and 1,553 by the end of 1993. Revenue gains ensued, as receipts shot up to $454 million and $546 million in 1992 and 1993, respectively. Furthermore, the average total floor space and sales-per-square-foot of its outlets soared as GNC continued to emphasize the development of self-care ''SuperStores.'' SuperStores consisted of a series of boutiques within the shop, each of which sported separate product categories, such as herbs, vitamins, apparel, or food.

Franchising, Acquisitions, and Demographics Fuel Growth, 1995–99

In 1994 GNC opened 172 company and 224 franchise stores and added another 207 units by acquiring Nature Food Centers for $61 million. Sales for fiscal 1994 were $672.9 million, up from $546 million in 1993. In 1994 *Success* magazine named GNC the top franchise opportunity in America, and in May 1995 GNC awarded its 1,000th franchise. Nearly half of GNC's more than 2,000 stores were franchises. The format worked well, and the company was able to successfully roll out new stores.

The company's biggest international presence at the time was in Mexico, where there were 63 GNC stores in 1995. It also had franchises in numerous other countries, including the Bahamas, Peru, Guatemala, the Philippine Islands, Trinidad, and Guam. Franchising was the company's main vehicle for international growth.

GNC established a foundation for expansion into the United Kingdom in 1995 by acquiring the U.K.'s second-largest, vertically-integrated self-care company, the Health and Diet Group, which operated 22 retail stores. GNC planned to open another 15 stores in the United Kingdom by the end of 1996 and saw a potential for 300–400 new locations there. In 1997, 24 GNC centers were opened in Canada.

In 1996 GNC launched the concept of Live Well stores, which were about one-third larger than traditional GNC outlets and included some of the details from prototype stores being tested in the Pacific Northwest that offered gourmet and health food products as well as upscale health and beauty products. The Live Well stores featured a different look and layout than traditional GNC stores. By mid-1998 the company had 15 Live Well stores in operation and planned to convert 55 existing stores and add another ten by the end of the year.

Continuing the ''Live Well'' theme, GNC launched ''Live Well'' as an advertising slogan in 1997 with a $50 million national television and print advertising campaign. The ad campaign was part of GNC's strategic shift from a specialty retailer to a branded retailer focused on wellness and self-care.

In August 1996 GNC acquired Nature's Northwest, which sold gourmet and health food products. During the summer of

1998 GNC created new $6 million stores that added upscale health and beauty products sold by its Amphora chain in Seattle to Nature's Northwest line. The first was opened in Lake Oswego near Portland, Oregon, in August 1998; it combined a natural foods supermarket with a pharmacy, spa, salon, and resource center.

To support its growth GNC had invested some $1.9 million in advanced logistics software and integrated bar code and hardware technology in 1997. The investment resulted in a 60 percent increase in distribution capacity and improved order accuracy to an astounding 99.9 percent.

For 1997 GNC reported net earnings of $103.4 million on revenues of nearly $1.2 billion, compared to earnings of $3.9 million on revenues of $990.8 million in 1996. The company estimated that it controlled 15 percent of the $7 billion vitamin/fitness market and was the biggest player in that category.

In addition to Live Well, the company was experimenting with other niche concepts, including two natural food stores called Nature Food Centre and Nature's Fresh, and Amphora, which specialized in bath and home fragrance products including aromatherapy products. The Amphora brand was also used for aromatherapy products carried in the Live Well stores.

GNC was also pursuing a strategy of partnering with outside firms to develop new health products that it would sell exclusively in its stores. It had established six partnerships since 1996. By mid-1998 only one such product was available in GNC stores, a shark cartilage extract developed by Aeterna Laboratories of Quebec, Canada. Another product, a plant oil extract linked to cardiovascular health developed by Monsanto, was due later in 1998. GNC's goal was to provide more scientifically validated proprietary products.

The strategy hit a snag in July 1998, however, when GNC filed suit against Humanetics Corporation, a Minnesota-based research company, for breaching its contract to allow GNC to exclusively market Humanetics' dietary supplement, 7-Keto. GNC charged that Humanetics had entered into another agreement with a Wisconsin distributor for the product.

GNC continued to open company-owned and franchised stores during 1998, and by the end of the year it had 2,566 company-owned and 1,332 franchised stores in all 50 states and 19 foreign countries. Although the company's net profit rose at an 83 percent annual rate from fiscal 1993 through fiscal 1997, *The Value Line Investment Survey* noted that GNC stock was under pressure during 1998 and had lost a substantial amount of its value. This was due to several external factors, including heightened competition through the proliferation of vitamins and other nutritional supplements and a growing number of discount chains. As a result, GNC saw its same-store sales weaken during 1998, when for the first time since 1993 it reported a negative year-over-year earnings comparison. For the fiscal year ending February 6, 1999, GNC reported net revenue of $1.42 billion, up 19 percent from the previous year, but net income declined seven percent to $98.0 million.

GNC's response was to slash the prices of some of its most popular commodity products in its company-owned stores. In other cases it offered special discounts to meet store-specific competition, and it launched a chain of outlet stores carrying a full range of products at a discount.

At the beginning of 1999 GNC entered into an alliance with Rite Aid drug stores under which Rite Aid would open full-line GNC stores within 1,500 Rite Aid locations. GNC would also manufacture a new line of vitamins and nutritional supplements called PharmAssure that would be jointly marketed by Rite Aid and GNC beginning in fall 1999. Rite Aid's 1,400 other stores would carry the PharmAssure product line, as would GNC's U.S. stores. Under the agreement GNC would also become the exclusive manufacturer of Rite Aid's private label vitamin line, and the two companies would launch a joint consumer Web site to provide nutritional information.

In April 1999 GNC announced it was ending its experiment with "wellness" grocery stores. It sold its Nature's Northwest, consisting of six stores located in the Portland, Oregon, area, for $57 million to Wild Oats Markets Inc., a Colorado-based chain of natural foods supermarkets. GNC was also negotiating to provide Wild Oats with a line of private label health supplements.

GNC's long-term strategy as it prepared for the 21st century was to position itself as the primary source of vitamins, nutritional supplements, and other health and fitness products for America's aging population. Demographically, GNC would serve the booming market of aging Americans. By 2005 there would be 150 million people over the age of 35. The dietary supplement market had grown from around $5 billion in 1994 to over $7 billion in 1998. With an aging baby-boom generation, it was predicted that the national market for vitamins and dietary supplements might exceed $12 billion by 2002.

Principal Subsidiaries

General Nutrition, Inc.; General Nutrition Corporation; General Nutrition Products, Inc.; General Nutrition Investment Company; GNC (U.K.) Holding Company; GNC Franchising, Inc.

Principal Divisions

Nature's Fresh; Amphora; General Nutrition Centres; Health and Diet Centres (United Kingdom).

Further Reading

"Amphora's All-Natural Design," *Chain Store Age Executive with Shopping Center Age,* July 1997, p. 118.

Callan, Katherine, "Success/E&Y Franchise Gold 100," *Success,* November 1994, p. 74.

Carlsen, Clifford, "GNC Pepping Up Expansion; Bay Fit for 10 More Stores," *San Francisco Business Times,* October 29, 1993, p. 8.

Elliott, Suzanne, "GNC President Pushing Franchise Growth," *Pittsburgh Business Times,* June 6, 1994, p. 9.

"Franchising Program in High Gear," *Chain Store Age Executive,* September 1993, pp. 26–27.

Fleming, Harris, "Two in One," *Drug Topics,* January 18, 1999, p. 15.

"General Nutrition Cos. Inc.," *Pittsburgh Business Times,* September 4, 1998, p. 33.

"GNC's Horn Opts for New Marketing Plan," *Pittsburgh Post-Gazette,* July 22, 1985, p. 13.

Kamen, Robin, "Nutrition Chain Getting Physical in New York," *Crain's New York Business,* October 19, 1992, p. 3.

Lindeman, Teresa F., "Pittsburgh-Based General Nutrition Companies Sells 'Wellness' Stores," *Knight-Ridder/Tribune Business News,* April 28, 1999.

Lo Bosco, Maryellen, "General Nutrition Opens its First Wellness Unit," *Supermarket News,* September 7, 1998, p. 41.

Marano, Ray, "Saudi Venture a Go for GNC," *Pittsburgh Business,* August 20, 1990, p. 1.

"More Than Granola as General Nutrition Revamps Merchandise and Store Design," *Pittsburgh Post-Gazette,* August 31, 1993, p. B8.

Reda, Susan, "GNC Logistics Restructuring Achieves Dramatic Gains in Speed and Accuracy," *Stores,* August 1997, p. 56.

Rouvalis, Cristina, "Ephedrine Scare Hits Pittsburgh-Based General Nutrition Companies Inc. Stock," *Knight-Ridder/Tribune Business News,* April 28, 1997.

——, "Studies Giving General Nutrition Healthy Outlook," *Pittsburgh Post-Gazette,* September 19, 1993, p. J8.

Slezak, Michael, "GNCs to Open in Rite Aid Stores," *American Druggist,* February 1999, p. 35.

Slom, Stanley H., "GNC to Pull More Weight in the 90s," *Chain Store Age Executive,* June 1992, pp. 21–22.

Tascarella, Patty, "GNC Ad Campaign to Cost $30 Million," *Pittsburgh Business Times,* December 9, 1996, p. 1.

——, "GNC Discovers Healthy Growth with Franchise Strategy," *Pittsburgh Business Times,* May 29, 1995, p. 3.

——, "GNC Sues Dietary Supplement Maker," *Pittsburgh Business Times,* July 3, 1998, p. 3.

——, "New 'Softer' GNC to Convert 55 More Stores to 'Live Well' Retail Concept," *Pittsburgh Business Times,* April 3, 1998, p. 4.

——, "The Son Also Rises," *Pittsburgh Business Times,* June 2, 1997, p. 10.

——, "Will Jerry Horn's Prescriptions Cure GNC?," *Executive Report,* July 1986, p. 20.

Varnas, Carol, "General Nutrition Announces National Expansion Plan for 1993," *Business Wire,* September 14, 1992.

—Dave Mote
—updated by David Bianco

Koch Enterprises, Inc.

10 South 11th Avenue
Evansville, Indiana 47744
U.S.A.
(812) 465-9600
Fax: (812) 465-9724
Web site: http://www.kochg.com

Private Company
Founded: 1873
Employees: 2,800
Sales: $520 million (1998)
NAIC: 331521 Aluminum Die-Casting Foundries; 332999 All Other Miscellaneous Metal Product Manufacturing; 422690 Adhesives & Sealants Wholesaling; 42173 Warm Air Heating & Air-Conditioning Equipment & Supplies Wholesalers; 541330 Engineering Services

Koch Enterprises, Inc. is a family-owned holding company that operates through several wholly owned subsidiaries. George Koch Sons, LLC, engineers, installs, and services various types of finishing systems for automotive and other industries. Koch Air, LLC, distributes Carrier heating, ventilating, and air conditioner equipment and provides design equipment selection and engineering assistance. The company's UniSeal, Inc. subsidiary manufacturers specialty sealant, adhesive, and low-density cellular rubber products for automotive, appliance and communications applications. Koch's Brake Supply Co. Inc. provides engineering services on hydraulic and pneumatic components, air compressors, and lubrication systems. Gibbs Die Casting Corp., located in Henderson, Kentucky, provides die casting to Toyota Motor Manufacturing and Toyota Motor Corporation.

George Koch: First Generation of a Family Business

George Koch (pronounced ''cook''), founder of Koch Enterprises, was four years old when he left Germany with his parents and three brothers to settle in Evansville, Indiana, where relatives already awaited them. Arriving in Indiana in 1843, Koch's father first tried his hand at farming before opening a successful brewery in Evansville. Although three of his brothers followed their father into the brewing business, Koch opted instead to join his cousins' business—a foundry that built steam engines and boilers, as well as saw and grist mill machinery. At 19, after a five-year apprenticeship at the foundry, he set off on a flatboat bound for New Orleans with a family friend. That the boat made it only as far as Vicksburg, Mississippi, did not seem to bother Koch, who decided to stay in Vicksburg. With his foundry training, he was easily able to find work as a tinsmith.

With the onset of the Civil War in 1861, Koch enlisted in the Confederate Army, serving for the duration of the war before returning to Vicksburg. Reverting to his prewar profession, he opened a tin shop, which ran successfully until it was destroyed by fire in 1872. After the fire, he went back home to Indiana, bringing with him his wife and two children. In Evansville, as in Vicksburg, Koch opened his own shop—the George Koch Tin Shop—with the help of his younger brother, William. Although there was not a large demand for tin work, the business kept afloat by doing repair work and manufacturing cookware and cistern covers. Soon, however, the resourceful Koch diversified into making stove venting, tin roofs, and guttering. In 1888, ready for expansion, he purchased property just down the street from his original shop and built a new two-story brick building. The shop, which was decorated with Koch's own decorative metalwork, housed a showroom, a tin shop, and the family's residence.

Koch's three sons—George, Louis, and Albert—all worked in the tin shop as teenagers and joined the business on a full-time basis as they became old enough. When George Koch died in 1903, the three brothers assumed responsibility for running the shop, with Louis becoming the general manager. The Koch brothers changed the name of the company to George Koch Sons to reflect its new ownership. In the 1920s, the company was joined by yet another Koch: Malcolm Koch, the oldest son of George's brother Ralph. Shortly after Malcolm came on board, the Kochs purchased machine shop equipment and began providing tooling services for various Evansville businesses.

Soon, the shop was busy turning out equipment for the various industries that were springing up in and around Evansville.

1930–40s: New Divisions

With the dawn of the 1930s, the Kochs began to turn their metalworking talents toward different ends. One of the first endeavors was the production of ornamental metalcraft pieces for the home. This new venture was begun on a small scale, by manufacturing decorative flower containers. When the flower containers proved well-received, the company followed up with an increasingly broad line of metal products. By the late 1930s, the company's decorative metalcraft department was operating in its own 100,000-square foot plant and producing more than 500 different articles, including wall and window shelves, coffee tables, magazine racks, hurricane lamps, and fireplace screens. A 25-person sales force marketed Koch's wares to every state in the United States. The metalcraft line continued to grow in popularity throughout the 1940s. Between 1940 and 1950, sales for the division increased by 300 percent, and its sales force doubled in size. The company also developed a Floral Metalcraft Division, which produced baskets, planters, candelabra, wedding accessories, and flower carts.

Another diversification in the Koch business came in 1936, when the company teamed up with Carrier Air Conditioning Corp. to form an air conditioning division. Carrier had been founded by Willis Carrier, the inventor of modern air conditioning, and was easily the leader in the air emerging air conditioning field. Koch Air, the company's new subsidiary, agreed to sell, distribute, install, and service Carrier products. In the late 1930s and early 1940s, air conditioning for both residential and commercial uses was only gradually became more common. Koch Air grew slowly but steadily during these years, capitalizing on the relative lack of competition.

At the same time the company was exploring new avenues of business, it was also nurturing and growing its core business, which had, by that time, become the making of heavy industrial equipment for various manufacturers. By 1940, Koch had garnered a national reputation as a maker of drying and baking ovens for industrial uses. Throughout the 40s, the company extended its capabilities to include the production of air handling and dust collecting equipment, spray painting booths, exhaust systems, and material handling conveyors. The company was considered a leading maker of conveyor-type finishing systems for wood and metal products, and had customers throughout the country.

1950s: Steady Growth

Business grew steadily in all of Koch's divisions throughout the 1940s and into the 1950s. Koch Air especially was boosted by the growing use of air conditioning both in homes and in commercial and industrial settings. Increasingly, builders were installing central air in new homes as a matter of course. In addition, many owners of existing homes were retrofitting their heating systems to accommodate add-on air conditioning units. As production of air conditioners increased, their prices dropped, making them a viable option for more and more consumers. In 1953, Koch Air expanded its distributorship area by approximately 30 percent and began to turn its focus toward

industrial air conditioning applications. Koch also worked quickly to bulk up its work force, increasing employment by 25 percent in 1955. "We of George Koch Sons concur in the belief of the national forecasters that business is going to continue on the up-grade for the next several years, particularly in the air conditioning field," Robert Koch, secretary-treasurer of the company, said in a November 1955 interview with the *Evansville Courier,* adding that "In order to keep abreast of this increased business and to retain our leadership in the field, we are increasing our personnel as rapidly as we can absorb them into our organization."

Air conditioning sales continued to swell through the second half of the decade, spurring still more expansions. At the close of 1957, anticipating a 25 percent increase in business for 1958, the company once again added employees. It also began renovating and expanding its service department and general office space. By the close of the 1950s, Koch had largely moved away from residential air conditioning, and was primarily targeting industrial and commercial customers.

A series of lucrative contracts in the early 1950s enhanced the performance of Koch's industrial division, as well. In April of 1953, the company was awarded a $30 million contract to design, fabricate, and install all of the ductwork for a new Portsmouth, Ohio, atomic energy plant. Koch was also awarded a contract to modernize the painting and processing equipment at the Fisher Body Company plant in Flint, Michigan. Other contracts for Koch included installation of a ventilation system for Ford Motor Company foundry in Ohio and installation of a finishing system for a Chrysler plant in Los Angeles.

In 1958, Koch's industrial division entered into a joint venture with the Memphis, Tennessee-based Wilco Machine Works, Inc., a woodworking machinery distributor. Under the terms of the agreement Koch and Wilco together began to manufacture and sell the patented Steinemann Coating Machine, an innovative high-speed fluid-coating system often used in the woodworking industries. At the end of the first year, the agreement was modified to split up the manufacturing and sales functions: Koch assumed responsibility for producing the machines, while Wilco took on the sales operation. In addition, Koch expanded its industrial product line by agreeing to carry Wilco's line of refuse burners. The burners were used for disposing of industrial waste, wood pulp, and agricultural refuse.

Koch's metalcraft division also grew during the 1950s, becoming one of the U.S. leaders in decorative metal furniture. In 1956, after steady increases in yearly sales, the company added both production equipment and personnel to accommodate increased orders. Annual sales continued to swell through the late 1950s, and in 1958 the company substantially expanded its sales force. By the end of the decade, Koch Metalcraft had established permanent showrooms in the Chicago Merchandise Mart and the Home Furnishings Mart in Dallas, Texas.

1960s–90s: Acquisitions and Expansions

In the early 1960s, Koch expanded and diversified again, purchasing the Chicago-based Bloomlife Floral Chemicals as a complement to its Floral Metalcraft Division. The new company produced chemicals used in the floral industry to lengthen the life of cut flowers. Koch moved the operation from Chicago to Evansville, purchasing a new building to house it.

Business continued apace, and by 1980 Koch was once again aggressively growing its business. In 1984 the company acquired Uniseal, Inc., a manufacturer specialty sealant, adhesive, and cellular rubber products for automotive, industrial, and communications companies. The following year, Uniseal, which had been in operation in Evansville since 1961, opened a second facility in St. Louis. Another of Koch's acquisitions was Brake Supply Co. Inc., a provider of hydraulic and pneumatic components and systems, application engineering services, and contract maintenance and repair. Brake Supply, also located in Evansville, had been in business for more than 30 years. Gibbs Die Casting Corp. was Koch's third acquisition and its first business to be headquartered outside Evansville. Gibbs, which was founded in 1966, was located in Henderson, Kentucky, and provided machined aluminum die casting, machining, assembly, and die building.

Focusing its energies more completely on industrial applications, Koch spun off its furniture and floral metalcraft divisions in 1988. The new company—Koch Originals—was headed by Louis J. Koch, a descendant of the company's founder. It remained in Evansville and continued to flourish throughout the 1990s.

In the mid-1990s, Koch and its subsidiaries kicked off another major growth initiative. In 1994, Koch Air acquired Carrier Midwest, a Carrier equipment distributor with offices in Indianapolis and Louisville. A similar acquisition followed in 1997 when the company purchased Marco Sales, a St. Louis-based Carrier distributor. With these two additions, Koch Air expanded its sales territory to cover almost all of Indiana and Kentucky, 80 percent of Illinois, and most of Missouri.

In the spring of 1995, Gibbs Die Casting announced that it was planning a $44 million expansion of its facilities, which would eventually add 250 jobs. The expansion was to include a 20,000 square foot addition to its existing facility and the construction of a new 60,000 square foot die casting plant with 10 casting presses and six melting furnaces. Just a few months later, Koch's Uniseal subsidiary, which had doubled in sales since Koch acquired it, purchased a 130,000 square foot building in Evansville. The company used the additional space to move its St. Louis operations to Evansville and combine the two operations.

In 1996, Koch partnered with a Cincinnati company to form a joint venture known as Audubon Metals, LLC. Koch's partner in the venture was the Cincinnati-based David J. Joseph Co., an automobile-shredding facility. Audubon Metals, which pro-

cessed aluminum alloy from scrap metal, was built in Henderson, Kentucky, next to Gibbs Die Casting.

Two years later, George Koch Sons began a $4 million project to add 42,000 square feet to its existing facility. The expansion, once complete, would allow Koch to consolidate its operations and thereby lower its overhead. "The rationale behind this is to become more competitive on the world market," said the company's purchasing manager, Jim Russell, in an August 1998 interview with the *Evansville Courier*.

Future Plans

On January 1, 1999, Koch completed a reorganization of its corporate structure, creating a new entity—Koch Enterprises, Inc.—to serve as a parent company for all of the company's subsidiaries. George Koch Sons, which had previously been the parent company, then became a subsidiary of Koch Enterprises.

According to a June 1998 article in the *Evansville Courier*, the company was striving toward a goal of reaching $1 billion in sales. Given this goal, it appeared likely that Koch would continue its growth efforts into the new century, both by acquiring new businesses and by expanding upon existing subsidiaries. Tapping new geographic markets was another likely avenue of growth. As suggested by its 1998 and 1999 consolidation efforts, Koch appeared to be angling for an expanded and strengthened position both in domestic and overseas markets.

Principal Subsidiaries

George Koch Sons, LLC; Koch Air, LLC; Gibbs Die Casting Corp.; Uniseal, Inc.; Brake Supply Co. Inc.

Further Reading

"George Koch Sons Begins Making Peacetime Products," *Evansville Courier*, August 28, 1945.
"Local Plant Enjoys Wide Success," *Evansville Courier*, February 12, 1939.
McKinney, Margaret, *Founding Families*, Indianapolis: News & Features Press, 1982.
Moss, Ed, "George Koch Sons Sees Business Continuing at 56 Million Dollar Pace," *Evansville Courier*, October 26, 1954.
Patry, Robert P., *City of the Four Freedoms: A History of Evansville, Indiana*, Evansville, Ind.: Friends of Willard Library, 1996.
Raithel, Tom, "Hot Weather Makes Company Growth Sizzle," *Evansville Courier*, June 29, 1997, p. E1.
——, "Koch Expansion Aims at Global Sales," *Evansville Courier*, August 13, 1998, p. C5.
——, "Koch Named Entrepreneur of Year," *Evansville Courier*, June 13, 1998, p. C5.

—Shawna Brynildssen

Grupo Modelo, S.A. de C.V.

Campos Eliseos 400
1100 Mexico City, D.F.
Mexico
(52) 5-282-2122
Fax: (52) 5-281-1308
Web site: http://www.gmodelo.com.mx

Public Company
Incorporated: 1925 as Cervecería Modelo, S.A.
Employees: 41,149
Sales: 15.52 billion pesos ($1.93 billion) (1997)
Stock Exchanges: Mexican
Ticker Symbol: GMODELOC
NAIC: 31212 Breweries; 322212 Folding Paperboard Box
    Manufacturing; 311213 Malt Manufacturing; 327213
    Glass Container Manufacturing; 332431 Metal Can
    Manufacturing

Grupo Modelo, S.A. de C.V. is the largest beermaker in Mexico, holding 55 percent of the national market in 1998, when it was the 12th-largest beer producer in the world and the most profitable brewer in Latin America. Its best known brand is Corona Extra, a light brew that ranked first in sales among beers imported to the United States in 1997 and fifth in the world in total production. The company also produces nine other brands of beer. A holding company, it is vertically integrated, beginning with its overseeing of the selection of seeds and germination of hops, and including brewing and bottling plants and distribution by trucks and ships. Grupo Modelo was, in the late 1990s, 50.2 percent owned by Anheuser-Busch Cos., the world's largest beer-producing company, and it was the exclusive importer of Anheuser-Busch's products in Mexico, including Budweiser and Bud Light. Anheuser-Busch did not, however, hold a majority of Grupo Modelo's voting shares.

The First Fifty Years

Beer was the basis for the holdings of the Sada and Garza extended families, whose Monterrey Group became the most powerful business combine in Mexico. Cervecería Cuauhtemoc was founded in Monterrey in 1890. Its chief rival was Cervecería Moctezuma, founded in 1894. Cervecería Modelo, which eventually outstripped the other two in production and sales, was founded in 1925 in Mexico City by Braulio Iriarte, with the help of President Plutarco Elias Calles.

Cervecería Modelo soon came under the control of Pablo Díez Fernández, who became its director general in 1930 and its majority stockholder in 1936. Born in Spain in 1884, Díez Fernández emigrated to Mexico at the age of 21 with money he borrowed from the Dominican fathers under whom he studied. He first worked as an accountant for a bakery, established the first mechanized bakery in Mexico, and then became part-owner of the first yeast factory for bread in Mexico. He went on to become co-founder and major stockholder of Celanese Mexicana in 1944 and a director of Banamex, one of Mexico's largest banks,

Diez Fernandez kept Modelo a private company that financed its expansion into producing malt, bottles, bottle caps and corks, and cartons through earnings rather than borrowing. He also acquired the regional breweries producing Victoria (1935), Estrella (1954), and Pacífico (1954). Modelo spent heavily on advertising during the late 1940s and early 1950s, much more so than its rivals. By 1956 it was the leading brewer, passing Cerveceria Cuauhtemoc and Moctezuma, with 31.6 percent of total beer production in Mexico. Modelo established plants in Ciudad Obregón (1960), Guadalajara (1964), and Torreón (1966) and created a national distribution network. Antonio Fernández Rodríguez, also Spanish-born, succeeded Díez Fernández as director general of the firm in 1971. Under his leadership, Modelo's share of the Mexican market grew from 39 percent in 1977 to 45 percent in 1985.

Seizing the U.S. Market in the 1980s

Fernández Rodríguez set his sights on the U.S. market by adopting a U.S.-style bottle for Corona, but the brand ran into trouble because a Puerto Rican beer of the same name held the trademark for the Corona name. The legal issue was not settled until 1985. In 1977 Modelo held only one percent of the market abroad for Mexican beers. Ironically, Corona's sales in the United States did not grow until it readopted the traditional clear bottle, with its long neck and brand name in raised letters painted on the glass. Modelo also repositioned the beer in the U.S. marketplace by ending discounting, in order to upgrade its image, and it conceded to importers the right to make promotional objects such as t-shirts and key chains with the Corona label.

Barton Beers, Ltd., Modelo's Chicago-based importer for the 24 states west of the Mississippi, was largely credited with spurring Corona's growth in the United States by targeting students, some of whom had sampled the brew on spring break at the Mexican resorts of Cancún and Cabo San Lucas. Barton's television commercials featured attractive young people chilling out with bottles of Corona on sun-drenched tropical beaches fringed with palm trees. Often served in bars and restaurants with a wedge of lime, Corona appealed to a yen for the exotic, while its light flavor—similar to U.S. beers—offered a comforting taste of familiarity. Meanwhile, Corona's other U.S.-based importer, Gambrinus Co. of San Antonio, was targeting millions of Mexicans with Spanish-language commercials linking the beer to evocative sounds and images intended to inspire nostalgia for the mother country.

Corona's U.S. sales rocketed from 1.8 million cases in 1984 to 13.5 million in 1986, passing Beck's and Molson to rank behind only Heineken among imports. Sales soared again in 1987, to 22 million cases. Then Corona hit a snag, attributed to a bizarre rumor that the brew was contaminated by urine. In addition, Gambrinus reportedly created resentment in northeastern markets by signing agreements with disreputable distributors who jacked up prices and provided shoddy service. In 1992 Corona regained its Number Two ranking north of the border, with 15 million cases sold. Moreover, the beach-party advertising was working in other parts of the world, including Australia and New Zealand, where Corona was the top imported beer, and Japan, where it ranked second.

Results in Mexico itself were not as good, even though Corona was the top beer. Modelo's sales in the home country dropped in 1982 and 1983 because of the nation's economic crisis, and the 1981 level of consumption was not surpassed until 1987. When Valores Industriales, S.A. (Visa), the holding company for Cervecería Cuauhtemoc, acquired Moctezuma in bankruptcy court in 1985, Modelo lost its top ranking in sales. Nevertheless, the company continued to make money, and it plowed the profits back into new investment instead of borrowing from the banks. In 1984 it opened its own plant in the state of Tlaxcala for producing barley malt. A decade later, this complex included 63 grain silos and was turning out 100,000 tons of malt a year. In 1991 Modelo's sales volume forged ahead of the beer division of Fomento Económico Mexicano (Femsa), Visa's beverage subsidiary and now Mexico's only other brewer.

Despite Modelo's prosperity, its large labor force was receiving only an estimated eight percent of the company's net value in 1990. Workers were averaging three to four times Mexico's minimum wage, but the latter sum was extremely meager (about $3 a day in 1998). Modelo had a long history of labor unrest, with the manufacturing and services division having sustained seven strikes and seven illegal stoppages between 1944 and 1994, including a 48-day walkout at the Mexico City plant in 1987, following which almost one-third of the 5,000 workers immediately lost their jobs. In 1998 Grupo Modelo was employing nearly 42,000 people directly and 180,000 indirectly.

Cervecería Modelo changed its name to Grupo Modelo in 1991 and went public in 1994, offering 13 percent of its shares on Mexico City's stock exchange. Because the company had virtually no debt and was earning large quantities of dollars and other hard currencies, its shares even rose during the severe recession that gripped Mexico following the sudden and devastating devaluation of the peso in December 1994. In 1998 the stock increased 24 percent in price even though all shares on Mexico City's stock exchange fell an average of 24 percent during the year.

Fernández Rodríguez's nephew Carlos Fernández González, a great-nephew of the founder, succeeded his uncle as director general of the firm in 1997, when he was only 31. He had started as a office boy at the age of 11. After receiving a degree in industrial engineering, he held posts in almost every area of the company. Fernández González initiated a program calling for company executives to meet with their staffs regularly, communicating Modelo's market position, mission, and strategy for reaching planned objectives. Quality control was being based on Japanese and U.S. "just in time" methods).

In 1997 Grupo Modelo accounted for 55 percent of all beer sales in Mexico and produced 35 million hectoliters. Corona Extra itself held 32.5 percent of the national market. During the year Corona passed Heineken to become the leading imported beer in the United States. Grupo Modelo held 80 percent of the export market for Mexican beers and was distributing its brands in 143 countries. Besides Corona Extra, its brands were Corona Light, Modelo Especial (mainly sold in cans and the company's second-leading brand), Light Modelo, Victoria, Negro Modelo, Pacífico, Estrella, Leon Negra, and Montejo.

Grupo Modelo's eighth plant, completed in Zacatecas in 1997, was scheduled to become the biggest in Latin America. The company (in 1996) had 644 distribution agencies and subagencies, all centrally administered except for 183 affiliates. Grupo Modelo was, in 1997, operating 33 companies, which owned approximately 1,394 facilities, including one factory each for producing metal cans, plastic caps, glass bottles, and cardboard boxes, and convenience stores under the names Modeloramas, Super Flash, Circle K, and Stores 12 + 12. Other subsidiaries were involved in the production of ice and machinery and the operation and maintenance of warehouses and distribution centers, real-estate properties, a shipping fleet, and even a soccer stadium in Torreón. Grupo Modelo also owned 9,910 vehicles. Net sales came to 15.52 billion pesos ($1.93 billion) and consolidated net profit to 2.36 billion pesos ($293.5 million) in 1997. The company's debt was only 2.8 percent of net sales.

A Troubled Partnership in the 1990s

With the advent of the North American Free Trade Area and eventual elimination of trade barriers, including tariffs, Grupo Modelo decided to protect itself from an invasion of U.S. beers into the Mexican market by forming a partnership with Anheuser-Busch Cos. It sold a 17.7-percent stake in the company (and a similar share of its unlisted operating subsidiary, Diblo, S.A. de C.V.) in 1993 to Anheuser-Busch for $447 million. Modelo remained the exclusive distributor of Anheuser-Busch's products in Mexico, a position it had secured in 1989. Four Modelo beers, including Corona, continued to be imported and distributed in the United States by Barton Beers and Gambrinus, rather than Anheuser-Busch. The two enterprises agreed not to open breweries or bottling plants in each other's country. Anheuser-Busch received an option to raise its stake in Modelo and Diblo to 50 percent within four years.

Anheuser-Busch appeared to fare poorly under the partnership, because in the late 1990s Budweiser and Bud Light were selling well only in tourist areas of Mexico. Nevertheless, the U.S. company exercised its option by raising its equity holding in Grupo Modelo to 37 percent in 1995 and 50.2 percent in 1997, bringing its total investment to about $1.6 billion. The sale price was in dispute, however, since the pact called for it to be 19 times earnings. With Modelo's stock trading at 38 times earnings in early 1998, its shareholders demanded more money, insisting that the valuation of Diblo's earnings should include profits from nonçonsolidated subsidiaries as well as companies in which Diblo held majority control. The matter was referred to international arbitration, which, in September 1998, ruled in favor of Anheuser-Busch.

Although Anheuser-Busch won this round, the company was angered by Grupo Modelo's decision in 1996 to renew its alliances with importers Barton Beers and Gambrinus for another ten years. In 1998 Anheuser-Busch was marketing what a *Wall Street Journal* article called "Corona clones" in southern Florida and Virginia, with at least one of the three beers scheduled for national distribution. Wholesalers were said to suspect that the introduction of these beverages had resulted from the giant U.S. brewer's failure to win distribution rights for Corona. Regardless of this troubled and rumor-laden partnership, Grupo Modelo remained the top Latin America beermaker, and its Corona Extra product remained a leading import in the United States. Its future as a partner of Anheuser-Busch was unsteady, but its reputation and popularity seemed assured.

Principal Subsidiaries

Cebadas y Maltas, S.A. de C.V.; Cervecería Modelo, S.A. de C.V.; Cervecería Modelo de Guadalajara, S.A. de C.V.; Cervecería Modelo de Noroeste; S.A. de C.V.; Cervecería Modelo de Torreón, S.A. de C.V.; Cervecería Modelo de Yucateca, S.A. de C.V.; Compañia Cervecería de Trópico, S.A. de C.V.; Compañia Cervecería de Zacatecas, S.A. de C.V.; Diblo, S.A. de C.V.

Further Reading

Adelson, Andrea, "A Workers' Beer Gains Status," *New York Times,* July 11, 1987, pp. 39, 43.

Crawford, Leslie, "Anheuser's Cross-Border Marriage on the Rocks," *Financial Times,* March 18, 1998, p. 46.

DePalma, Anthony, "Anheuser in Mexican Beer Deal," *New York Times,* March 23, 1993, pp. D1–D2.

Estrada, Teresa, *La industria cerveza en Mexico,* Mexico City: Universidad Autonoma de Mexico thesis, 1957.

Friedland, Jonathan, and Rekha Balu, "For Mighty Anheuser, No Rival Is Too Small—Even One It Owns," *Wall Street Journal,* October 22, 1998, pp. A1, A10.

Peterson, Jonathan, "Brewer Will Battle False Rumor About Its Product," *Los Angeles Times,* July 28, 1987, Part IV, pp. 1–2.

Solis, Dianna, "The Rio Grande Is Mainstream for Today's U.S. Palates," *Wall Street Journal,* January 19, 1993, pp. B1, B7.

Van Munching, Philip, *Beer Blast,* New York: Times Books, 1997, pp. 132–47.

Walsh, Mary Williams, "A Mexican Beer, A Hit in U.S., Exemplifies Export Hopes," *Wall Street Journal,* December 17, 1986, p. 26.

Wills, Rick, "The King of Imported Beers," *New York Times,* May 28, 1999, pp. D1, D2.

—Robert Halasz

Guitar Center, Inc.

5155 Clareton Drive
Agoura Hills, California 91301
U.S.A.
(818) 735-8800
Fax: (818) 735-4923
Web site: http://www.guitarcenter.com

Public Company
Incorporated: 1964
Employees: 1,727
Sales: $391.66 million (1998)
Stock Exchanges: NASDAQ
Ticker Symbol: GTRC
NAIC: 45114 Musical Instrument & Supplies Stores

Guitar Center, Inc. is the nation's leading retailer of musical instruments. In 1998 it recorded sales totaling $391.66 million. That was up nearly $100 million from 1997 figures when the company was number one in sales on the *Music Trades* 1998 Top 200, outstripping its nearest competitor by nearly $100 million. In 1998 the *Music Trades* also reported that Guitar Center had the highest dollar increase in sales, $166.7 million, between 1993 and 1997. In 1998 Guitar Center had a 6.7 percent share of the national market for musical instruments, up from 5.12 percent the previous year. Its 1998 annual report estimated that 68 percent of its sales are made to professional musicians or musicians who aspire to become professional. At the beginning of 1999, Guitar Center operated 48 stores in 24 major U.S. markets. Stores range in area from 12,000 to 20,000 square feet, much larger than the industry average of 3,200 square feet. In addition to 300 to 500 guitars, every Guitar Center location offers a broad selection of percussion instruments, amplifiers, keyboards, and accessories. Customers are attracted by Guitar Center's low prices as well as its hands-on atmosphere and its friendly, knowledgeable sales staff. The company's flagship store in Hollywood, which measures 36,000 square feet, features one of the nation's largest selections of used and vintage instruments as well as the famous "Rock Walk," an area that commemorates leading innovators and performers of popular music. With its purchase in summer 1999 of Musician's Friend, the country's largest online musical instrument retailer, Guitar Center poised itself to leap into the potentially lucrative Internet market.

1960s Origins

Guitar Center, Inc. was born, almost by accident, in 1964. Wayne Mitchell was managing the Organ Center, a 21-store chain of music stores in southern California. The store specialized in keyboards, organs in particular, the instrument that dominated music sales at the time. In 1964 the Thomas Organ Company acquired Vox, a manufacturer of guitars and amplifiers. Unfortunately, its sales reps knew next to nothing about the new products and had no idea how they should be sold. The Thomas representative approached Mitchell at Organ Center and—possibly through the application of subtle or outright pressure—persuaded him to take on the Vox line. A deal was reached: Mitchell would rent a storefront in Hollywood and Thomas would provide the sign. When it arrived it read "Vox Guitar Center," which later was shortened to Guitar Center.

Mitchell quickly discovered that his new store was a gold mine. Rock 'n Roll was taking off, the British Invasion was at its height, and bands like the Beatles, Rolling Stones, and Kinks had sparked an unprecedented demand for guitars and amps. When Mitchell realized how much better guitars were selling than organs, he started closing his Organ Centers to concentrate on the new business.

Not all of Guitar Center's early success can be explained by Mitchell's remarkably good timing. By all accounts, he was a born salesman and a charismatic personality. He brought the savvy and technique he had developed as an automobile salesman and put it to work at Guitar Center. He knew, for example, that auto dealerships rely on their parts and service departments to pay the bills, enabling salesmen to cut margins on car sales to a minimum and offer customers the best deal possible. Mitchell decided that the equivalent at Guitar Center was the accessories department. Its products—cords, straps, picks, and effects, for example—helped stores cover their expenses. Mitchell cut costs to the bone and invested little in the look of his store, an expense he considered not directly linked to profits. The early

Company Perspectives:

Guitar Center's mission is to build a vehicle that allows all associates and customers to achieve their goals, pursue their dreams, and reach their destiny.

Guitar Center stores showed it: old carpets mended with duct tape and racks purchased at closeout or bankruptcy sales gave them a bargain basement look.

One point that Mitchell insisted on was that Guitar Center pay all bills promptly. It used the reputation it developed, one unusual in music retailing, to win price concessions from manufacturers. Mitchell also created a hungry, aggressive sales atmosphere by putting his sales staff on straight commission. "If you didn't work," Chief Operating Officer Marty Albertson later recalled, "you didn't eat." A "hustle" atmosphere was created, which helped fuel Guitar Center's early growth, but which was consciously abandoned in the mid-1970s.

Mitchell used a series of gimmicks, described in company literature as "Barnum & Bailey-style sales promotions," to draw customers into his new store. He set a record, for keeping a store open longest (11 days), which made it into the Guinness Book of World Records. He created the world's largest Les Paul guitar cake. He mounted 36-hour-long sales extravaganzas in which the store opened at ten in the morning one day and did not close until ten in the evening the following day. He continued to rely on those events throughout Guitar Center's first 20 years.

By the end of the 1960s, Mitchell's combination of low prices, attention-grabbing promotions, and timely paying of suppliers had made Guitar Center one of the most profitable stores in southern California. In contrast to the staid, old-fashioned, department store style of the established music stores, the Guitar Center on Sunset Blvd. had a distinctly counterculture feel. Its salespeople were usually musicians themselves, with long hair, who while making their hard-sell pitch, encouraged customers to handle the merchandise, to pick it up and play it.

Expansion in the 1970s

Mitchell had the ultimate vision of 50 Guitar Center stores across the country. He opened a second store in San Francisco in 1972, and a third in San Diego the following year. Mitchell kept Guitar Center decentralized as it expanded, to cut overhead. The new stores were semiautonomous, run as a partnership. Mitchell was the majority partner to the store manager. Mitchell instilled all his employees with a sense of what Guitar Center *could* become, that it *could* grow. The positive attitude that Mitchell created manifested itself in the group that later evolved into the company's senior management. Mitchell began hiring them, as salesmen, in the mid-1970s: in 1975 Ray Scherr, who later took over the company; in 1977 Larry Thomas, later president and CEO; in 1979 Marty Albertson, later executive vice-president and COO. Guitar Center, historically, has had more than average staff turnover at the entry level, but the company has had nearly no turnover at the management level. Store managers remain an average eight years. By the late

1990s, most senior management had been with Guitar Center from ten to 15 years.

Ray Scherr moved rapidly from the sales floor, became a store manager, and then became a sort of junior partner to Wayne Mitchell. Scherr became a major force for innovation at the company in the 1970s and 1980s. It was Scherr's idea, for example, to centralize Guitar Center operations and thereby increase the company's buying power with vendors. Initially, Mitchell resisted the added expense of central administration until he could be shown that the money saved in vendor discounts would pay for it. Scherr also instituted the direct mail campaign that is still an important element of Guitar Center marketing. The Guitar Center of the late 1990s is the common product of the vision of both men. "Wayne [Mitchell] built a lot of the value culture of Guitar Center," Albertson said, "while Ray [Scherr] built the operating structure."

In 1979 the company received information that a bank was about to foreclose on a music store in Chicago. Guitar Center moved quickly and later that year opened its first Chicago store, the company's first outside California. Moving into the Chicago market forced Guitar Center to confront its weaknesses and to rethink its entire approach. It discovered it could not simply enter the Chicago market and conquer it. Chicago, Guitar Center learned, was dominated by local independent retailers who commanded fierce loyalty from their customers. What was more, Chicagoans were put off by the company's tried and true hard sell tactics as well as its radio ads, ads that had worked well in California for five years or more. "Chicago was where we cut out teeth on expansion," said Larry Taylor. "It changed the way we did business." The experience led Guitar Center to become more customer service oriented, working to win customer confidence and earn repeat business, a priority that had never been high previously.

Changes and Continued Growth in the 1980s

In 1980 Mitchell inaugurated an Employee Stock Ownership Plan (ESOP), a stock-sharing program for Guitar Center workers. The ESOP transformed the company from a sole proprietorship to one owned jointly by management and employees and helped increase employee commitment to company growth. Because of the transient nature of the company's entry-level sales force, however, the ESOP was later converted to a profit sharing plan.

For a short period around 1980, Guitar Center became involved in guitar manufacture when it purchased Kramer Guitar. Kramer eventually produced a full range of guitars for beginners to professionals and its popularity was increased substantially at the time by its association with guitarist Eddie van Halen. Kramer's head Dennis Berardi was, in Larry Thomas's words, "a very young, inspirational, undisciplined kind of guy." Berardi's management style clashed with Mitchell's, which was considerably more conservative. Running Kramer came to be so stressful for Mitchell that Guitar Center, Inc. decided to pull out. Mitchell already had heart problems and other members of senior management were afraid he would suffer a heart attack.

In 1983, at the age of 57, Wayne Mitchell did die of a heart attack. Mitchell's family sold half of his share of the company to the ESOP and half to Ray Scherr. Scherr, who had been Guitar Center president for several years, became the majority shareholder and took over the running of the company. The Guitar Center chain had, in the meantime, grown to nine stores and under Scherr the chain continued to grow, adding an average of one store a year for the next decade.

In 1985 the Hollywood store inaugurated the "Rock Walk," where the greats of popular music have pressed their hand prints in the sidewalk. It has gone on to become a popular tourist attraction in Los Angeles. More important, the chain had 12 stores that year and it had become obvious that an effective infrastructure was urgently needed that would enable the company to effectively control inventory and sales. As a result, Guitar Center interrupted its expansion drive for a couple of years to concentrate on computerizing its existing stores and introducing bar coding for its entire line of merchandise. The work lasted a year and a half, but when it was completed the company had a state-of-the-art system that was far ahead of its competitors in the music retail industry. Once in place, the system laid the foundation for Guitar Center's explosive growth during the 1990s.

Becoming a Public Company in the 1990s

Guitar Center had another short-lived involvement in manufacturing when it acquired amplifier producer Acoustic Amplification in 1987. It sold Acoustic only two years later. In 1991, Larry Thomas—after working as a salesman, a store manager, a regional manager, corporate general manager, and chief operating officer—became Guitar Center president. By 1993 the company had 17 stores across the United States, with annual sales of approximately $100 million.

In 1996 Ray Scherr decided to leave Guitar Center, Inc. As a result, senior Guitar Center management, led by Larry Thomas and Marty Albertson, borrowed $100 million and, together with three California venture capital companies, bought most of Scherr's stock in the company. Not long afterward, the company made a high yield bond offering to convert the $100 million loan to long-term debt. The added burden of that large debt, together with the new involvement of the venture capitalists who were counting on stepped-up, national growth, led to the decision to make an initial public offering in March 1997. The company had a scare the day the stock was priced when the market plunged 157 points and some of the banks involved almost pulled out. The stock, however, after being offered at $15, closed the first day of trading at $18 and about $90 million was raised. Guitar Center became the first publicly traded company in the music retail industry.

Going public raised some difficult issues for Guitar Center. The stock offering was predicated on the assumption that the company would expand quickly. It was accustomed, though, to opening one store at a time, then closely monitoring developments before moving on to the next opening. Suddenly it had to move efficiently at a much faster pace: in 1997 it opened five new stores, in 1998 it opened 12, and it planned 12 for 1999 and 16 for 2000. The company foresaw a network that would ultimately number 150, including a new smaller store format in

small- and middle-sized markets, across the United States. Another important question mark was whether manufacturers would be able to supply a much larger Guitar Center with the large volume of product it required. Most suppliers were able to adapt to Guitar Center's new needs. Still a common complaint of smaller music retailers is that they are often not able to take shipment on items because most have been allotted to Guitar Center. Its first year as a public company was a successful one. In spring 1998 it reported that sales had increased 39 percent and net income increased 60 percent to $11 million.

In May 1999 Guitar Center, Inc. acquired Musician's Friend in a stock transaction valued at approximately $50 million. Musician's Friend, based in Medford, Oregon, was the world's largest mail order and e-commerce retailer of musical instruments, with $97 million in revenue in 1998. Its acquisition made Guitar Center the leader in Internet as well as traditional musical instrument retailing. The Internet business was to remain headquartered in Medford under the name Musician's Friend. Most of its music stores were converted into Guitar Center stores. Guitar Center intended to use the stores, located in smaller markets, to create its new smaller store format.

Principal Subsidiaries

Musician's Friend.

Further Reading

Booth, Jason, "Guitar Center Earnings Are Music to Ears of Analysts," *Los Angeles Times,* December 14, 1998, p. 40.

"California Guitar Center Agrees to Buy Musician's Friend Mergers," *Los Angeles Times,* May 14, 1999, p. C2.

"Guitar Center Celebrates 35 Years," *Musical Merchandise Review,* January 1999.

"Guitar Center Expands with Stores in Chicago, Northern California," *Music Trades,* November 1996, p. 69.

"Guitar Center Merges with Musician's Friend," *Los Angeles Times,* June 8, 1997.

"Guitar Center's Profits To Miss Estimates," *Los Angeles Times,* June 5, 1999.

"Inside Guitar Center: A Look at the Financial Workings of the Nation's Largest Music Products Retailer," *Music Trades,* August 1996, p. 198.

"Is Guitar Center Worth $251.0 Million?," *Music Trades,* July 1996, p. 169.

"Meltdown in Miami: Showdown Between Guitar Center and Sam Ash Music," *Music Trades,* July 1997, p. 102.

Proctor, Lisa Steen, "Wall Street, Get Ready to Rock," *Los Angeles Business Journal,* March 17, 1997, p. 17.

"Record Sales at Guitar Center," *Music Trades,* April 1997, p. 50.

"Revenge of the Store," *Music Trades,* August 1997, p. 168.

Scally, Richard, "Guitar Center Packs Coffers in 97," *Discount Store News,* May 25, 1998. p. 8.

Strauss, Neil, "Coddling Musicians' Dreams: Selling the Stairway to Heaven, and Instruments Too," *New York Times,* February 3, 1999, p. 1E.

"The Top 200," *Music Trades,* August 1998.

Vrana, Debora, "Ready To Rock Guitar Center Going Public, Cranking Up for Nationwide Expansion," *Los Angeles Times,* March 14, 1997, p. D1.

—Gerald E. Brennan

H&R BLOCK®

H & R Block, Incorporated

4410 Main Street
Kansas City, Missouri 64111
U.S.A.
(816) 753-6900
Fax: (816) 753-5346
Web site: http://www.handrblock.com

Public Company
Incorporated: 1955
Employees: 2,600
Sales: $1.3 billion (1998)
Stock Exchanges: New York
Ticker Symbol: HRB
NAIC: 541213 Tax Preparation Services; 51121 Software
   Publishers; 522292 Real Estate Credit

The name of H & R Block, Incorporated has become synonymous with the business of preparing income tax returns, and justifiably so. The company is far and away the largest in this field with more than 10,000 offices in the United States, the United Kingdom, Australia, and Canada. During the 1998 income tax filing season it prepared 14.8 million U.S. tax returns, representing about 13 percent of all U.S. tax returns filed, and 2.4 million international returns. After diversifying in the late 1970s and 1980s into online information services through its acquisition of CompuServe Corporation and into temporary personnel services through its acquisitions of Personnel Pool of America and Interim Services, the company refocused in the 1990s to become a provider of diversified financial services.

Tax Preparation Evolved from Accounting Services Begun in the 1940s

H & R Block was founded in Kansas City, Missouri by Henry and Richard Bloch. The two brothers had followed slightly different paths: Henry Bloch had received his degree in math at the University of Michigan and served as a bomber crewman during World War II, whereas Richard studied eco-

nomics at the University of Pennsylvania's Wharton School of Finance. In 1946, while still in their early 20s, Henry and Richard teamed up and formed in their hometown a business services company called United Business. They offered bookkeeping, collections, advertising, and other forms of assistance to local businesses. Tax preparation was one of those services, but the Bloch brothers considered it so marginal that they offered it free of charge to their customers. Within eight years, they were running the largest bookkeeping firm in Kansas City. They also made a sideline out of preparing individual tax returns for people who worked in the building in which they were headquartered.

Preparing individual returns might have remained a mere sideline if the Internal Revenue Service (IRS) had not stopped offering such assistance to the public in 1955. Ironically, Henry and Richard Bloch wanted to get out of that line of work at the time, feeling that it was distracting them from their core operations for little profit. But one of their individual clients, an advertising salesman for the *Kansas City Star* named John White, persuaded them to give tax preparation more of a try—and to take out two advertisements in his newspaper. On the first day that the ads ran, the Blochs found their office flooded with customers.

Thirty-two years later, Henry Bloch would recall: "I can distinctly remember thinking, 'This tax thing is tremendous—it is really going to help our accounting business, what with the advertising and the referrals and all.' But it had the opposite effect. . . . Because my brother and I began devoting so much of our time and energies to the tax side, we didn't give our business clients the type of service they wanted. . . . We found that they were quitting on us."

Therefore, the Bloch brothers divested their accounting business by selling it to their employees. They reincorporated in 1955, setting up shop under the H & R Block name, and devoted themselves to preparing tax returns for the "little guy" full-time. The Bloch brothers also chose to deliberately misspell their last name in christening their new venture. Two similar, though distinct, reasons for why they did this have been given. According to one story they dropped the "h" in favor of the more phonetic "k" to make sure people would not mispronounce the name; in another, they simply assumed that people would misspell it phonetically anyway.

However they felt about the new company's name, customers were quick to pony up for its services. In its first year H & R Block generated $20,000 in revenues, enough to pique the Blochs' interest in expansion. In 1956 they opened seven storefront offices in New York City to see if they could duplicate their success. These new offices generated $67,000 in revenues in their first year, but the Bloch brothers grew homesick for Kansas City and did not want to stay in the Big Apple or shuttle between the two cities to keep tabs on business in both. Anxious to sell, they agreed to hand over their New York operations to two local accountants for only $10,000 and a percentage of future revenues. For that, H & R Block would be hailed as a pioneer in franchising, even though, as Henry Bloch later admitted, the company more or less backed into it. "When we first franchised," he said, "we didn't even know what the word meant."

The company's first experience in franchising also would turn out to be an unhappy one. Concerned by unscrupulous practices on the part of the New York franchisees, H & R Block would initiate legal action against them in 1964, charging violation of the company's pricing and advertising arrangements. The two parties settled out of court in 1966, and as a result H & R Block bought back the franchises for more than $1 million.

Dazzling Growth in the 1960s

More immediately, however, the New York experiment proved to the Bloch brothers that tax preparation would be a viable business outside of their hometown. In 1957 H & R Block opened offices in Topeka and in Columbia, Missouri. The next year, it added offices in Des Moines, Oklahoma City, and Little Rock to the roster. From there, the company grew at a dazzling rate. It went public in 1962, and by 1967 it could boast of having nearly 1,700 offices in 1,000 cities in 44 states. During the 1967 tax season H & R Block estimated that it would prepare a total of 2.5 million tax returns by the April 15th filing deadline. The company operated only 35 percent of these offices itself; the rest were franchised. At first, franchises were granted for a mere two percent of gross receipts. "We didn't sell franchises; we gave them away," Henry Bloch would later recall. "An employee would come in and ask us to help him open an H & R Block office in Chicago or Detroit or someplace. We gave him a little spending money and loaned him enough to rent a store and buy some desks. These guys were on their own, and in almost every case they have become wealthy men." In

the 1960s, however, H & R Block wised up and raised its price to ten percent, then about 30 percent of gross receipts.

Of course, the company needed legions of trained personnel to keep up with such rapid expansion. In many respects, this proved to be a more substantial problem than drawing customers. To cope with it, H & R Block set up its own training program, which operated more or less as a trade school for tax preparers. In exchange for a small fee, trainees would enroll in an eight-week course taught by company managers. At the conclusion of the course, trainees might receive employment with the company, but they were also free to work for competitors or use their expertise on their own returns. In 1967, for instance, more than 10,000 students enrolled in H & R Block's tax school, but less than half of them went to work for the company at the conclusion of the course. Even so, H & R Block gained 5,000 new employees to staff its storefronts that year.

The tax preparers themselves were and still are seasonal employees, the demand for their services being limited to the first four months of the year. Many of them are housewives, retirees, or people with day jobs looking for a second source of income. In recent years, the company has drawn many working mothers, who like the flexible hours that come with the job. Despite the seasonal nature of the job, most of them return the next year for another round of grappling with the IRS. In 1987 Henry Bloch stated that 75 percent of the company's preparers come back the following year, no doubt because the company rewards its veterans with higher commission rates.

With a virtual headlock on its market, no capital costs except for the leases on its storefront offices and a few dollars for furniture and coffee, and labor costs limited to a fixed percentage of revenues, H & R Block proved wildly successful in the 1960s. In an average year, profits increased by 50 percent over the previous year. In 1969 and 1971, however, changes in the federal tax code reduced the overall number of taxpayers, thus shrinking the company's customer base. Even worse, in 1972 the IRS went to war against tax preparation firms. It cracked down on fraudulent preparers, resumed helping taxpayers prepare their returns, and launched a massive advertising campaign encouraging them not to use commercial preparation services. The IRS campaign, aided by the press, succeeded in tarring legitimate preparation services like H & R Block as well as dishonest ones. That year, the company's profits fell for the first time in its history.

Solidified Its Position and Accumulated Cash Reserves in the 1970s

The IRS campaign eventually collapsed after some public relations debacles of its own. After IRS Commissioner Johnnie Walters declared that the 1040 form was so simple a fifth-grader could complete it, his claim was subjected to various acts of scrutiny that proved it was far more complex than that. An experiment conducted by the *Wall Street Journal* also suggested that the IRS's preparers were no more reliable than most commercial services. H & R Block not only weathered the firestorm but came out of it in better shape than before, because the IRS's crusade had weeded out its weaker competitors. It was, in fact, the only profitable tax preparation firm of consequential size left in the nation. H & R Block solidified its overwhelming position in 1972 when it opened outlets in 147 Sears department stores—an entirely appropriate move for a company that Richard Bloch once had described as ''the Sears, Roebuck of taxes.''

Once the crisis had passed, the company found itself faced with a happy dilemma, one that the Bloch brothers had begun to contemplate in the late 1960s. Because its capital costs were so small for a business of its size, and because most of its revenues came in the form of cash, H & R Block had been able to accumulate vast cash reserves. It also found itself unburdened by long-term debt. Because the tax preparation business seemed ready to mature and slow its rate of growth, it was only logical that the company should diversify through acquisition to keep its revenues pumped up. H & R Block spent most of the 1970s searching for likely acquisition targets, but it was limited by a lack of companies that were both available and potentially profitable as well as by Henry Bloch's reluctance to pull the trigger. ''A guy told me that two out of three acquisitions fail,'' he said in 1974. ''I just don't want to make a mistake the first time out.''

Diversification and Acquisition in the 1980s

H & R Block finally took its first major plunge in 1978, when it acquired Personnel Pool of America, a temporary personnel agency specializing in health care, for $22.5 million. The move seemed to make sense, as H & R Block already had some expertise regarding temporary personnel; after all, the core of its work force at the time was made up of temps. Indeed, the acquisition worked out well: In two years, Personnel Pool of America jumped from the sixth largest to the third largest company in the temporary help field.

The 1980 acquisition of CompuServe also proved quite successful. H & R Block paid $23 million for the information services company, which provided computer time-sharing for corporations and government agencies. Soon after it was acquired by H & R Block, however, CompuServe entered the burgeoning field of providing information services such as software forums, electronic bulletin boards, electronic mail, and interactive games for personal computer users. In doing so, it made its new parent company look positively brilliant. CompuServe's earnings tripled between 1983 and 1985, and its subscriber base quadrupled. It was growing so fast that CompuServe chairman and cofounder Jeffrey Wilkins resigned in 1985 when H & R Block refused to allow him and some of his managers to purchase CompuServe stock. Wilkins subsequently headed an investor group that offered to buy CompuServe for $72.5 million, but H & R Block refused to sell. Wilkins's departure may have seemed like a setback to H & R Block, which considered it wise to keep its acquisitions' existing management teams intact, but CompuServe continued to grow without him. In the early 1990s it was the largest commercial online service, with one million subscribers.

Also in 1980, the Bloch brothers entered into a joint venture with Ohio attorney and entrepreneur (as well as son-in-law of U.S. Senator Howard Metzenbaum) Joel Hyatt, who wanted to set up his own chain of discount law offices patterned after the Los Angeles-based firm of Jacoby & Myers. Hyatt's idea was to tap into the same middle-income market for basic legal services, but to stake out his own geographic territory before Jacoby & Myers could expand beyond its California base. He had opened nine offices between 1977 and 1980, when H & Block approached him with the idea of partnership. For Hyatt, such a

deal would provide him with the capital he needed for rapid and widespread expansion. The two parties set up a separate company called Block Management to operate Hyatt Legal Services to comply with American Bar Association rules forbidding anyone but lawyers to directly own a law firm. H & R Block took an 80 percent stake in the company, with Hyatt and his other partners taking the remaining 20 percent.

Both parties in this deal hoped that H & R Block's marketing resources would boost Hyatt Legal Services past archrival Jacoby & Myers. Before long, however, they realized that the synergies they had expected to create between tax preparation and legal services simply were not happening. In 1987 H & R Block sold its interest in Block Management to Joel Hyatt for $20 million in what was described as a friendly parting of ways.

The 1985 acquisition of Path Management Industries, a business seminar company, also proved that, for all of Henry Bloch's prudence, H & R Block's touch was not always golden when it came to acquisitions. The 1988 postal rate increase hurt Path Management by hiking the cost of its direct mail advertising, and the recession of the late 1980s depressed sales. Having paid $35 million for the company, H & R Block sold it to the American Management Association in 1990 for $20 million.

In the meantime, Richard Bloch had become less involved with the running of the company after he was diagnosed with lung cancer in 1978. Bloch battled his illness successfully, but after his recovery he devoted much of his time to sponsoring cancer research and treatment. He retired in the early 1980s. At about the same time, Henry's son Thomas M. Bloch began to work his way up through the ranks. Thomas M. Bloch became president and COO in 1988, and in 1992 he succeeded his father as CEO. Henry Bloch remained as chairman.

Of course, the business of preparing tax returns remained profitable for the company. Tax preparation did in fact represent a mature line of business for H & R Block in the 1980s, and the company's rapid diversification reduced its contribution to the overall bottom line to just more than half of total earnings by the decade's end. But when the IRS began allowing electronic filing of tax returns in 1986, it opened up a brand new opportunity for H & R Block. The opportunity to receive an early refund inspired many who prepared their own returns to come to H & R Block to file electronically. Providing the service was relatively easy for the company, because it used CompuServe's existing communications links to transmit the returns through cyberspace. H & R Block also began offering advances on refunds, or refund anticipation loans (RALs), through agreements with several different banks. In return for a service charge, a participating bank would loan the amount of the refund to an H & R Block client, accepting direct deposit of the refund check as repayment. Electronic filing gave the company's core business a needed boost; within five years it was handling an annual volume of 4.3 million electronic returns—nearly two-thirds of all returns filed electronically.

More Acquisitions, Divestitures, and Refocusing in the 1990s

For all the adventures that it encountered in the 1980s, H & R Block entered the 1990s still in the market for acquisitions. In 1991 it purchased Interim Systems, a temporary personnel agency, for $49.5 million and merged its assets with those of Personnel Pool of America. The resulting merged subsidiary then was renamed Interim Services. Interim Services was spun off in January 1994 through an initial public offering (IPO). Net proceeds to H & R Block were $200 million, with an additional $28 million going to Interim. Block sold its interest in the temporary staffing firm to focus on its tax preparation and computer information service businesses.

With $400 million earmarked for further acquisitions, the company had three main businesses. For 1991 its tax preparation service accounted for $700 million in revenue, its temporary personnel company Interim Services had $385 million in revenue, and CompuServe brought in another $280 million. H & R Block entered the personal financial software market in late 1993 with the purchase of MECA Software, which was best known for its "Managing Your Money" program. Block decided, however, to sell MECA in March 1995 for $35,000, while retaining the right to publish tax preparation software under the name TaxCut. By 1998 its subsidiary, Block Financial Corporation, was the second largest publisher of personal financial software, with record sales of Kiplinger TaxCut, as more people were using their computer and the Internet to prepare their own tax returns.

In April 1994 Thomas M. Bloch resigned as CEO of H & R Block. He wanted to spend more time with his family and teach at an inner city school. In September 1995 Richard H. Brown, former vice-chairman of telecommunications company Ameritech, was named president and CEO of H & R Block to succeed Thomas M. Bloch. He became the first nonfamily member to head the firm. Brown, with his high-tech background and interest in investing more in CompuServe, lasted less than a year. In April 1996 H & R Block spun off CompuServe with an IPO of 18.4 million shares that raised barely more than $500,000 and reduced H & R Block's ownership to 80 percent.

Series of Strategic Acquisitions in the Late 1990s

In June 1996 Frank Salizzoni, formerly president and chief operating officer of USAir Group, Inc., was named CEO and president of H & R Block. Salizzoni's plan was to transform the company into an integrated financial services business offering not only tax preparation help, but also such services as mortgage loans, financial planning, and investment advisory services. Over the next two and one-half years Block acquired two of its franchises and 251 independent tax preparation firms as well as mortgage businesses and a string of accounting firms. As a result of acquisitions, the company's total assets increased from $1.7 billion in 1997 to $2.9 billion in 1998.

In June 1997 H & R Block acquired the California-based firm Option One Mortgage Corporation, which controlled more than 5,000 mortgage brokers in 46 states. During 1997 H & R Block launched its mortgage service, H & R Block Mortgage Company, on a trial basis in 31 offices in four states. The mortgage service began by selling only second mortgage loans, then it introduced new mortgage products at offices in 15 states. As a result, H & R Block Mortgage Company accounted for $135.8 million of the company's 1998 revenues of $1.307 billion, or slightly more than ten percent. In February 1999 the company acquired Assurance Mortgage Corp. of America to further enhance its mortgage-related product offerings.

During the 1997–98 tax season H & R Block experimented with offering a wider range of financial services, including auto insurance, mortgages, and investment advice. It had 14 "premium" offices that featured enclosed offices rather than cubicles and sold mutual funds, annuities, stocks, and bonds. Some 30 offices also sold mortgages. Throughout 1998 and early 1999 the company opened prototype financial planning centers on a trial basis. These centers included investment advisors and mortgage representatives in addition to tax preparers. The company also tested a telemarketing approach to sell other financial products to its tax service customers though telemarketing call centers located in Florida and California.

In January 1998 the company divested CompuServe, selling its 80 percent interest to Internet access provider WorldCom Inc. in a stock-for-stock transaction valued at about $1.3 billion. Following the transaction, WorldCom sold CompuServe's online service and 2.6 million subscriber base to America Online (AOL) in exchange for AOL's ANS Communication division, which provided Internet access mainly for large businesses. AOL also committed to make WorldCom its largest network access provider.

As part of its strategy to provide a fuller range of financial services, H & R Block launched HRB Business Services, a national accounting and consulting business, in 1998. It had acquired several CPA firms during the year, including the Kansas City-based Donnelly Meiners Jordan Kline, Chicago-based Friedman Eisenstein Raemer & Schwartz and three of its affiliates, and Katz Sapper & Miller of Indianapolis. A fourth firm, Sigman Page & Curry, merged with Donnelly Meiners in September 1998, and two more firms were acquired by the end of the year. HRB Business Services was headed by Terrence E. Putney, the former president of Donnelly Meiners.

Block's strategy was to acquire CPA firms to strengthen its position in the tax preparation market. The addition of CPA firms was intended to attract more high-income individuals who would normally seek out their own CPA firm. One analyst estimated in 1998 that CPA firms controlled about one-fourth of the tax preparation market. H & R Block's share of the tax preparation market at the end of 1998 was 13 percent, and it could increase its share by acquiring CPA firms. By mid-1999, H & R Block was in the process of acquiring Olde Discount.

Without a doubt, the business odyssey of the Bloch brothers has been an astoundingly successful one. Richard Bloch once compared his company to Sears, and a journalist once called it "the McDonald's of tax preparation"; the fact that neither analogy seems absurd is a testament to H & R Block's standing in its part of the service economy. All three of these companies have dominated their respective markets so thoroughly that they have not only become synonymous in the public mind with what they sell, but their names have entered the annals of American popular culture.

It is also impressive that the company has managed to maintain a steep earnings curve. A $10,000 investment in H & R Block stock when the company went public in 1962 would have been worth $12.3 million in 1992. In 30 years the stock had split 120:1, dividends and revenues had increased every year, and earnings rose every year except one. With the company focused on becoming a provider of diversified financial services for an expanding market, the odyssey of H & R Block should continue to be successful.

Principal Subsidiaries

H & R Block Tax Services, Inc.; Block Financial Corp.; Option One Mortgage Corp.; HRB Investments, Inc.; HRB Business Services, Inc.; Franchise Partner, Inc.; H & R Block Canada Ltd.; H & R Block Ltd. (Australia); H & R Block Tax and Financial Services Ltd. (United Kingdom).

Further Reading

Butcher, Lola, "$400 Million in Hand, Block Hunts Deals," *Kansas City Business Journal,* September 4, 1992, p. 1.

Demery, Paul, "New Directions for H & R Block?," *Practical Accountant,* September 1995, p. 12.

Ellis, James E., "H & R Block Expands Its Base," *Business Week,* April 29, 1991.

Epper, Karen, "Block's Exit from Personal Finance Software Underscores Intense Competition in the Field," *American Banker,* April 6, 1995, p. 1.

"H & R Block Enters the Fray; AmEx Continues Acquisitions," *Practical Accountant,* July 1998, p. 8.

Hayes, David, "H & R Block Looks Ahead To Expand Financial Services," *Knight-Ridder/Tribune Business News,* September 11, 1997.

"A Jewel's Lost Luster," *Forbes,* March 24, 1997, p. 16.

Karp, Richard, "The Bewilderment of Henry Bloch," *Dun's Review,* September 1974.

Mannes, George, "One of Three Firms May Buy Ailing CompuServe," *Knight-Ridder/Tribune Business News,* September 5, 1997.

Nicolova, Rossitsa, "Block Acquisitions Promote Goals," *Kansas City Business Journal,* December 25, 1998, p. 10.

——, "Block's CPA Empire Growing," *Kansas City Business Journal,* December 11, 1998, p. 1.

Palmeri, Christopher, "Watch Out, Merrill Lynch," *Forbes,* May 4, 1998, p. 45.

Phillips, Dana, "Interim Share Price Stays Up After January IPO," *South Florida Business Journal,* February 18, 1994, p. 19.

Razzi, Elizabeth, "This Job Is Less Taxing," *Kiplinger's Personal Finance Magazine,* February 1997, p. 134.

Serres, Christopher, "H & R Block's Venture Passing Test," *Crain's Cleveland Business,* August 10, 1998, p. 3.

Silverman, Robin, and Christine Riccelli, "Henry W. Bloch," *Ingram's,* September 1990, p. 27.

Stodghill, Ron, II, "Tom Bloch's No. 1 Reason for Leaving the Field," *Business Week,* June 26, 1995, p. 127.

"Storefront Tax Service Earns a Good Return," *Business Week,* March 25, 1967.

"Taxman Henry Bloch," *Inc.,* December 1987.

Timmons, Heather, "H & R Block Still Hoping To Unlock Treasure Chest of Customers," *American Banker,* April 19, 1999, p. 23.

Wasserman, Elizabeth, "WorldCom Deal Brings Change to America Online as Well as CompuServe," *Knight-Ridder/Tribune Business News,* September 9, 1997.

—Douglas Sun
—updated by David Bianco

Hastings Entertainment, Inc.

<table>
<tr><td>

3601 Plains Boulevard, Suite 1
Amarillo, Texas 79102
U.S.A.
(806) 351-2300
Fax: (806) 351-2424
Web site: http://www.gohastings.com

Public Company
Incorporated: 1968 as Hastings Books and Music, Inc.
Employees: 5,3330
Sales: $398.7 million (1999)
Stock Exchanges: NASDAQ
Ticker Symbol: HAST
NAIC: 451211 Book Stores; 45122 Prerecorded Tape,
    Compact Disc & Record Stores; 44312 Computer &
    Software Stores

</td></tr>
</table>

Operator of a fast-growing chain of multimedia superstores, Hastings Entertainment, Inc. retails books, music, videos, and computer software through a network of stores predominately located in small towns in the western half of the United States. By the end of the 1990s, Hastings operated 130 stores in 18 states. The company's mix of product categories was the inspiration of Sam Marmaduke, regarded as a pioneer in cross-merchandising. Marmaduke's son John led the chain during the 1990s, when expansion picked up pace, particularly after the company's 1998 initial public offering. Further expansion was expected during the 21st century, with 500 potential sites for additional stores identified by the company's management. In mid-1999 Hastings launched a new site on the Internet to sell a broad selection of multimedia software to the electronic global marketplace.

Wholesale Origins

Hastings developed from an enterprise named Western Merchandisers, Inc., founded by Sam Marmaduke. Regarded as an pioneer in the wholesale industry, Marmaduke started his career as a rackjobber in 1946 when he arrived in Amarillo, Texas, to take over the wholesale business left to him by his late father. In his mid-20s at the time, Marmaduke transformed his father's small business, West Texas News Agency, into a family fortune, creating an expansive wholesaling business that later spawned Hastings, the retail arm of his wholesale business. Initially, Marmaduke achieved success by keeping operating costs down, an important aspect of his managerial approach and a characteristic Hastings would later inherit. More significantly, it was Marmaduke's diversification into other product categories that propelled his wholesaling company forward and cemented his reputation as an industry maverick. "They said I was crazy," Marmaduke recalled, describing his colleagues' reaction when he diversified into wholesaling record albums in 1959. The bold, innovative move succeeded, however, leading to the incorporation of Western Merchandising, Inc. in 1961, the book and music wholesaling enterprise from which Hastings developed.

Hastings was formed in 1968 when the first Hastings Books & Music retail store opened in Amarillo. Marmaduke, who later confessed he made a belated entry into retail, succeeded in retail as he had in wholesale, cross-merchandising decades before other bookstores or music retailers. Along with Tower Records, Hastings was among the first chains to offer books and music within it stores. Marmaduke's unique approach was emulated by his son John, who was named president of the Hastings business in 1973 and watched over the company's first decade of expansion. By the end of the 1970s, there were 22 Hastings stores in Oklahoma, Texas, Arkansas, and Kansas, all situated in small towns—a trademark of Hastings that the company employed as its expansion strategy in the years to come. Growth picked up pace for Hastings at end of the 1970s as John Marmaduke and his father decided to expand by acquiring other retail chains. In 1979 Hastings purchased 29 stores that sold music exclusively and that were located in regional shopping malls. Converted to the company's cross-merchandising strategy, the stores acquired in 1979 were followed by other acquisitions in 1981, 1983, and 1985. Expansion through acquisitions was coupled with internal expansion, as the Marmadukes used their profits to establish additional retail outlets, both freestanding units and stripmall stores. The first chapter of Hastings's corporate history ended at this point, with dozens of retail units located in small towns scattered throughout the Southwest and

Midwest. The next era began in the mid-1980s, when strategic changes were implemented that altered Hastings's business philosophy and changed the characteristics of the chain that had developed between 1968 and 1985. The strategic repositioning of the company stemmed from the influence of Western Merchandisers' biggest customer, Wal-Mart.

As Hastings developed into a regional retail chain, Western Merchandisers achieved prominence and robust financial growth by becoming a primary supplier to the Wal-Mart chain of discount retail stores. Hastings was similar to Wal-Mart in that both formats sold a variety of merchandise rather than a single product category, although Wal-Mart's merchandise diversity was greater, to be sure. In 1985, however, Hastings increased the breadth of its cross-merchandising approach, adding video rentals to the books and music it retailed. The addition of a video department led to a new name, Hastings Books, Music & Video, Inc., and, more importantly, signaled the company's decision to embrace the entertainment superstore concept. The first store to offer the three product categories, touted as the company's first "triple combo" unit, opened in 1985 in Amarillo's Wolfin Village Shopping Center. Equally as important as the foray into videos was a change in the company's pricing strategy, an alteration that underscored the chain's similarity to Wal-Mart. In 1986, searching for ways to beat back mounting competition, Hastings began discounting its merchandise. The experiment worked wonders, driving sales upward and convincing the Marmadukes that Hastings's future lay as a discount chain. By the end of the 1980s, the company's strategy was firmly set. The larger, all-media discount units the company was operating were realizing greater profits and sales. In response, the Marmadukes turned away from adding any more mall-based stores. Mall store leases were allowed to expire, directing management's focus on Hastings's blueprint for the 1990s: discount, triple combo, superstores.

With a prototype for future expansion established, the company pursued physical growth in its unique way. The prevailing characteristic of the chain was the location of its stores, nearly all of which were situated in small towns with populations ranging between 10,000 and 50,000. The company's niche was in towns such as Warrensburg, Missouri, Marshalltown, Iowa, and Stephenville, Texas, communities where competition was limited and residents often were delighted to have the opportunity to purchase a broad selection of books, music, and videos close to home. "When we go to open a new store in a small town," John Marmaduke explained, "and the people learn we are from headquarters, they don't just want to meet us—they want to hug us!" For these small rural towns, isolated from the wealth of merchandise showered upon their urban counterparts, Hastings offered what one company official described as "discovery opportunities" by cross-merchandising. From a practical standpoint, the intent was simple, effective, and profitable: "We want to sell mysteries to people who come in and buy music, and we want to sell music to people who come in to by mysteries," explained John Marmaduke.

1991: Marmadukes Forge Agreement with Wal-Mart

Although Hastings operated a number of stores in larger metropolitan areas with populations in excess of 250,000, the majority of the chain's stores were in small towns, which represented the basis of the company's strategy for expansion. The company used this approach to expand rapidly during the 1990s, a decade that began with Hastings's sister company, Western Merchandisers, falling under the control of another company. Although separate companies, Hastings and Western Merchandisers were woven closely together, with the fate of one company having an equal effect on the other. Accordingly, when Wal-Mart acquired Western Merchandising in 1991, the corporate life of Hastings was affected as well.

Following Wal-Mart's acquisition of its primary wholesaler, Hastings remained under the ownership of its founder and chairman, Sam Marmaduke, but both companies shared the same president and chief executive officer, John Marmaduke. Western Merchandisers and Hastings also shared overhead, distribution services, and headquarter support, and held their annual conventions together. Under this arrangement, the two companies prospered in the shadow of the sprawling Wal-Mart chain, but the close-knit relationship between Western Merchandisers and Hastings did not last. The numerous ties connecting the two companies were strained not from poor performance by either company, but from the success of each. Under the agreement reached with Wal-Mart in 1991, John Marmaduke was supposed to divide his time evenly between Western Merchandisers and Hastings. As Wal-Mart expanded its operations vigorously during the early 1990s, however, Western Merchandisers was forced to keep pace with the distribution demands of a fast-growing retail chain, which required an increasing amount of Marmaduke's attention. He was spending two-thirds of his time matching the gallop of Wal-Mart, leaving Hastings, whose all-media superstore concept was demonstrating encouraging success, without the full attention it required. "When you dance with an 800-pound gorilla," Marmaduke remarked, "the gorilla leads." After several years, the two sister companies could no longer effectively share the familial ties that had characterized their relationship since Hastings's creation in 1968. By the end of 1993, several months after Sam Marmaduke died of a massive heart attack, John Marmaduke decided not to renew his contract with Western Merchandisers and Wal-Mart. For the first time in its history, Hastings was going to be a truly independent entity.

In the wake of Marmaduke's decision to forgo stewarding both companies, Wal-Mart sold Western Merchandisers to Anderson News Corp., one of the country's largest distributors of consumer magazines. The divestiture was completed in August 1994, giving Hastings the freedom to pursue its own path. The chain, at this critical juncture in its history, comprised 95 stores spread throughout 13 states in the Southwest and the Rockies. Together, the stores generated approximately $300 million in revenue a year. With all his attention focused on this enterprise for the first time in years, Marmaduke faced a fundamental, pressing problem as he severed ties with Western Merchandisers (renamed Anderson Merchandisers). Hastings lacked sufficient infrastructure to support its existing operations and future expansion, having shared centralized functions with Western Merchandisers. To resolve this dilemma, Marmaduke organized a new purchasing staff, spent roughly $3 million to develop a management information system, and replaced other services and support previously provided by Western Merchandisers. Undaunted by this essential undertaking, Marmaduke concurrently announced expansion plans, targeting markets in

Missouri and Nebraska as sites for future Hastings stores. Immediate plans called for the establishment of 20 new stores in 1995, as well as the expansion of 12 existing stores. The success of this initial expansion and the trouble-free separation from Western Merchandising instilled confidence for more ambitious expansion to follow.

Independence Fans 1990s Expansion

As Hastings pushed forward into secondary markets with limited competition—"running to daylight," as Marmaduke described it—the company did so in a low-cost manner, continuing to embrace Sam Marmaduke's focus on keeping operating costs to a minimum. Instead of buying property or constructing new stores, the company expanded by taking on shorter-term leases on vacant buildings. The strategy increased flexibility, allowing the company to move from one location to another with greater ease, and it reduced the capital required for expansion. Following this mode of expansion, Hastings fleshed out its presence in the western half of the United States during the mid-1990s, establishing nearly a dozen new stores a year. All expansion was financed internally, using the profits gleaned from existing stores. Between 1995 and 1997, Hastings opened 23 new stores, giving the chain 114 stores scattered among 15 states. Some units measured as much as 47,000 square feet, generally the stores located in areas with populations in excess of 250,000, but most averaged between 20,000 square feet and 25,000 square feet, representative of the typical, small-town Hastings store.

In 1997 Marmaduke accelerated Hastings's expansion plans for the remainder of the 1990s. He announced plans to double the chain's size to 200 by 2000, with immediate plans calling for the establishment of 20 units in 1998—the most in one year in the company's history. As this expansion program was laid out, the company also began an extensive remodeling program scheduled to renovate all existing Hastings stores during the ensuing two years. For the resources to implement his expansion plans, Marmaduke turned to Wall Street through an initial public offering (IPO) of stock in June 1998. Although he had previously vowed to keep Hastings a private company, the financial demands of his proposed expansion campaign could not be met without a substantial infusion of cash. The IPO netted the company $36 million, with Hastings's stock debuting on the NASDAQ exchange at $13 per share. Although less than

the $14 to $16 per share debut for which the company had hoped, the IPO set the stage for aggressive expansion for the previously low-profile company. Management had identified 500 potential sites for new Hastings stores in small- to medium-sized markets.

Following the IPO, Hastings immediately began opening new units, providing evidence that the company's future would be filled with frenetic expansion activity. Five new stores were opened in a five-week period, giving the company 129 stores in 18 states by late 1998. Another 20 stores were slated to open in 1999, as the company extended the boundaries of its operating territory. In May 1999, Hastings launched a new electronic-commerce Web site on the Internet featuring more than ten million new and used multimedia products. The launch of www.gohastings.com, which was supported by a national advertising campaign, and the company's expansion plans suggested Hastings's future financial growth would far eclipse the rate of growth achieved during the company's first 30 years of business. Marmaduke, it appeared, was intent on transforming Hastings from a regional competitor into a national force. Whether Hastings could successfully make this leap was to be determined in the decade ahead, as the company pursued small markets with a large inventory of entertainment products.

Principal Subsidiaries

Hastings Properties, Inc.; Hastings Internet, Inc.; Hastings College Stores, Inc.

Further Reading

Albright, Max, "Amarillo, Texas-Based Book-Music Store Chain Plans Public Stock Offering," *Knight-Ridder/Tribune Business News,* May 14, 1998.

"Anderson News To Acquire Western Merchandisers," *Publishers Weekly,* June 20, 1994, p. 23.

Christman, Ed, "Anderson News to Western Confab: Embrace Change," *Billboard,* October 22, 1994, p. 55.

Garrett, Lynn, "The Small-Town Strategy," *Publishers Weekly,* August 25, 1997, p. 29.

"Hastings To Launch New www.gohastings.com E-Commerce Internet Web Site," *PR Newswire,* April 1, 1999, p. 2538.

Scally, Robert, "Hastings Hits Growth Spurt, Plans 50 Units by End of '99," *Discount Store News,* November 23, 1998, p. 4.

—Jeffrey L. Covell

Hennes & Mauritz AB

Box 1421
SE-111 84 Stockholm
Sweden
+46 08-796 55 00
Fax +46 08-796 57 03
Web site: http://www.hm.com

Public Company
Incorporated: 1947 as Hennes
Employees: 17,000
Sales: SKr 26.6 billion (US $3.15 billion) (1998)
Stock Exchanges: Stockholm
NAIC: 452110 Department Stores; 454110 Mail-Order
    Houses

With more than 550 stores in 12 countries across Europe, Hennes & Mauritz AB (H&M) has quickly become one of the world's most successful clothing retailers. Each year, the Sweden-based retail chain sells more than 300 million primarily company-designed garments and accessories, including cosmetics, worth some SKr 26.6 billion (US$3.15 billion). The company has been so successful at exporting its low-price, high-quality clothing fashions that more than 80 percent of its sales are realized outside of Sweden; in fact, since the mid-1990s, the company's largest single market has been Germany, where the company's 150 stores represent some 30 percent of total sales. H&M has also been expanding beyond Sweden with its catalog sales, operated under the name H&M Rowells, which remains limited to the Scandinavian market in the 1990s.

H&M's steady growth—which has seen its sales double in the four years between 1994 and 1998—can be expected to continue, with new store openings averaging some 60 per year. The company has only just begun to tap its growth potential. In Germany, the company represents less than two percent of the total retail clothing market; H&M remains similarly limited in England, where the company's market share is less than 0.5 percent.

H&M's expansion has barely touched such major clothing markets as France, Italy, and Spain. The company has been moving to fill out its southern European map, however. In 1998 the company entered France with six stores in Paris. Spain was added to the list in 1999, with the proposed opening of three stores. H&M is also making its first forays into the United States, a market already somewhat crowded with retailers marketing a similar concept—fashionable, low-priced, quality clothing targeted especially at 25- to 35-year-olds but extended also to include children and mature shoppers. Plans to open the company's first U.S. stores were announced in April 1999. In Europe, the company's chief competition remains the Spain-based Zara chain, the U.S.-based Gap chain, and, to a more limited extent, Italy's Benetton.

H&M operates under the strategy of "Fashion and quality at the best price." H&M stores are closely guided from the company's Stockholm headquarters to achieve a uniform concept—it is said that a sweater featured in a window display in London will be featured in exactly the same way in Reykjavik and all other H&M stores. Such control over its image has enabled H&M to build a consistent brand appeal throughout the wholly company-owned chain. H&M's low-debt, cash-rich position enables it to respond quickly to developing trends. New clothing products are introduced on a near-daily basis—breaking the traditional seasonal stock rotation found in the retail clothing industry. Clothing items rarely remain on H&M's shelves for more than a month; this rotation encourages repeat shopping.

H&M also controls the fashions featured in its stores: almost all of its clothing sales fall under the company's own range of brand designs. The company employs a staff of more than 50 designers, who create the designs for such H&M brands as Hennes (which means "hers" in Swedish), Woman Collection, and LOGG, for women; Uptown; LOGG, and Contemporary for men; Rocky, Rocky Girl, and Impuls for teenagers; and Baby Baby, LOGG, Rocky, and C-Dept for children. The company also sells cosmetics under the H&M Cosmetics, FOB (Face of Beauty), ResQ, Steele, Magnum, and Basic Spa brand names. H&M does not manufacture its own clothing but instead works with some 1,600 suppliers, principally in Europe and Asia, under strict quality and other human resource standards.

Company Perspectives:

H&M's business concept is "Fashion and quality at the best price." H&M has a design and buying department which creates H&M's collections, making it possible to offer the latest fashions. H&M can ensure the best price by: having few middlemen; buying large volumes; having depth and breadth of knowledge within every aspect of textile production; buying the right goods from the right market; being cost-conscious at every stage; efficient distribution. A number of measures have been introduced to secure and raise the quality of the goods, and by tightening the quality standards, H&M has also succeeded in developing and improving its suppliers. H&M also has the resources to carry out careful and effective quality controls. In addition to good quality products, the quality concept also requires that the garments are manufactured without the use of environmentally hazardous chemicals or harmful substances and that they are produced under good working conditions.

H&M continues to be majority controlled by the founding Persson family, who own some 70 percent of the company's stock. In 1998, however, chief architect of the company's expansion Stefan Persson was named the company's executive chairman. In his stead as managing director, the company has placed Fabian Mansson, former buying director.

Forming a Fashion Empire in the 1940s

H&M was founded as Hennes in 1947 by Erling Persson. A former salesman and founder of another company, Pennspecialisten, in Västerås, Sweden, Persson had discovered a new retail clothing store concept during a trip to the United States. Persson decided to import this retail concept—that of high turnover produced by low prices—to Sweden. From the first Hennes store, which featured exclusively women's clothing, opened in Västerås, Hennes expanded throughout Sweden, covering much of the country through the 1960s.

Hennes also began to export its low-price clothing concept, beginning with neighbor Norway in 1964, and joined by Denmark in 1967. By the end of the 1960s, Hennes looked to extend its range beyond women's clothing. The company also sought further expansion in Stockholm. These two goals were fulfilled with the purchase, in 1968, of Mauritz Widforss, a hunting and gun shop on Stockholm's Sergelgatan. As part of the purchase, Hennes also received a large stock of men's—primarily sportswear—clothing items.

These were quickly added to the company's retail offering; the company's name was changed to Hennes & Mauritz to reflect its expanded product range. At the same time, Hennes & Mauritz added a line of children's clothing to its stores, so that, by 1970, the company offered clothing for much of the family (two more segments, teenagers and babies, were added in 1976 and 1978, respectively). The Mauritz addition did more than add its name and expand the company's clothing range. It helped transform the company's product offering itself. The

introduction of sportswear led the company to develop clothing that better reflected the spirit of the times, as a new generation of youth clamored for clothing that allowed them to express their individuality. H&M began to develop the casual, down-to-earth yet fashionable image that proved a success in its later expansion.

Seeking further growth, the company made a new acquisition in 1973, buying up fellow Swedish company Beklädnadskompaniet. In the next year, as H&M prepared further foreign growth, the company went public with a listing on the Stockholm stock exchange. The Persson family, however, retained the largest share of the company stock, leaving control securely in the family's hands.

During the 1970s, H&M began to look beyond its Scandinavian base. In 1976 the company entered the British market—to mixed results. While H&M's British growth long remained limited, reaching just 25 in the late 1990s, the company posted better results on the European continent. At home, the company acquired the Rowells mail-order company, which became the base for H&M Rowells, the company's mail-order subsidiary.

The next move for H&M was to Switzerland, where the company's stores quickly became a mainstay in that country's major cities. Switzerland became one of H&M's principal foreign markets. In 1980 H&M launched its first German store. The H&M concept somewhat revolutionized the German clothing retail market, which was described as having remained rather stodgy. H&M's informality also raised some ripples in Germany, as employees were more than encouraged to drop the formal "Sie" form in their conversations with other employees. Nevertheless, the H&M concept caught on well with the German consumer at a time when few other retail brands existed on the German retail scene.

"Global Fashion" for the 1990s

A new generation took the lead of H&M when Erling Persson turned over the company's managing director position to his son Stefan Persson. Under the younger Persson, H&M continued its international expansion, while retaining tight control of the H&M image. H&M continued to expand its presence in its existing markets throughout the 1980s, steadily opening new stores. By the 1990s, H&M would grow to become one of the largest retailers in Sweden and that country's fifth largest company.

In the late 1980s, H&M attempted to diversify its brand line by opening the Galne Gunnar (Crazy Gunnar) chain of cut-price stores. After expanding the chain to 18 stores in Sweden, the company decided to abandon the concept after ten years, redeveloping the existing Galne Gunnar stores as H&M stores. Sticking with the H&M name appeared to be the most profitable future for the company. Growth of the H&M chain, particularly in foreign expansion, stepped up dramatically in the 1990s.

The time was ripe for what Stefan Persson described as "global fashion." Persson had been quick to recognize the emergence of fashions and trends—born of MTV, Hollywood, Madison Avenue advertising, and the Internet—that transcended national borders to become fads among youth and other age groups across the world. H&M, with its emphasis on uniformity among its stores, was well-positioned to appeal to this new generation of consumers. As a nod perhaps to the times, the company also created a new line of clothes, under the BiB (Big is Beautiful) brand name.

The company's international expansion stepped up in earnest. After opening in the Netherlands in 1989, the company moved into Belgium (1992), Austria (1994), and Luxembourg (1996). By 1994, the company's sales had topped SKr 13.5 billion; more than 70 percent of sales came from beyond Sweden. That same year the company's German stores overtook Sweden to become H&M's largest single market. By the end of the decade, Germany would represent more than double the company's Swedish sales—despite H&M's barely two percent of the German market.

International expansion continued in the second half of the 1990s, as the company opened some 60 or more stores per year. Finland was the next market to be tapped, in 1997; the following year, France became the company's new frontier. In 1998 six H&M stores appeared in France, primarily in Paris and surrounding areas. Some analysts wondered whether H&M's low-priced fashion concept would appeal to the more snobbish French clothing shopper, and questioned whether the company's success among Northern European countries would translate to the southern European markets.

Indeed, H&M had remained notably absent from Italy and Spain, two of the most important European retail clothing markets—perhaps the company had sought to avoid head-to-head battles with similar concept brands Zara, of Spain, and Benetton, of Italy. Nonetheless, in April 1999, the company announced its intention to enter the Spanish market by the end of the year, with two or three as a start. At the same time, the company announced its intention to reinvigorate its struggling British operation, with calls for opening a large number of new stores and to update a number of its existing locations.

Throughout its history, H&M had remained entirely in its European base. In 1999, however, the company judged the time auspicious for a U.S. entry, with the first stores expected to open in early 2000. It remained to be seen if the company could successfully re-import the formula of low-priced, quality fashions that had provided the inspiration for its own beginnings more than 50 years before.

Principal Subsidiaries

H&M Rowells.

Further Reading

"Fashion Guru," *Financial Times,* May 17, 1999.

Fitchett, Joseph, "Will Cheap Chic Win Over Stylish French?," *International Herald Tribune,* March 13, 1998.

"Hennes & Mauritz: Knickers to the Market," *Economist,* February 28, 1998.

Karacs, Imre, "The Button-Up Menswear Boss Who Couldn't," *Independent,* August 7, 1998, p. 15.

Watkins, Simon, "Invasion of the Retail Giants," *European,* October 30, 1997, p. 26.

—M. L. Cohen

Hildebrandt International

200 Cottontail Lane
Somerset, New Jersey 08873
U.S.A.
(732) 560-8888
(800) 223-0937
Fax: (732) 560-2566
Web site: http://www.hildebrandt.com

Private Company
Incorporated: 1975 as Hildebrandt Inc.
Employees: 37
Sales: Not Available
NAIC: 541611 Administrative Management & General
   Management Consulting Services

Formed by a 1999 merger between Hildebrandt Inc. and Hodgart Consulting, Hildebrandt International is the world's largest company providing consulting services for law firms, government and corporate law departments, and also accounting firms and other professional services firms. It has advised most large law firms in the United States and the United Kingdom, and many others as well, on strategic planning, mergers, firm finances, retirement systems, lawyer burnout, information technology, and other management issues. In addition to its main offices in New Jersey and London, the combined company maintains offices in Chicago; Naples, Florida; San Francisco; New York City; and plans one for Germany.

Origins and Early Years of Hildebrandt Inc.

Bradford W. Hildebrandt, the founder of Hildebrandt Inc., was born in 1941. In 1975 he started his own consulting firm Hildebrandt Inc. to advise law firms on how to improve their management practices. The firm's cofounder was Jack Kaufman, who had earned a University of Wisconsin B.A. degree and an LL.B. at Case Western Reserve University. He had worked ten years as a Cleveland law firm administrator. Kaufman served as Hildebrandt Inc.'s president, while Bradford Hildebrandt was chairman.

In 1975 Bradford Hildebrandt published *Financial Management for Law Firms,* which covered various accounting options, record keeping, cash management, compensation and employee benefits, retirement planning, and partnership agreements. In his book, Hildebrandt thanked ''all of the partners of Reavis & McGrath who have over the last five years given me a great deal of assistance and who have in many ways made this book possible.'' He also thanked Jack Kaufman, president elect of the Association of Legal Administrators, a group founded by Hildebrandt. In his first book and throughout his career, Hildebrandt stressed the importance of using good financial principles that ''can easily become the catalyst that divides a firm or, conversely, can help provide a stabilizing, objective force within the firm.'' In addition, in those early days of the first personal computers, Hildebrandt emphasized, ''Today, it is economically feasible for even the smallest firms to consider utilizing computer technology.'' Effective use of technology remained a key service provided to Hildebrandt clients throughout its history.

The increasing size and business orientation of law firms influenced the origins of Hildebrandt Inc. Before World War II, there were few large law firms. But the postwar American economic boom fueled the need for more attorneys. Plus, court rulings starting in the 1960s opened up new kinds of litigation, as described in several books on the so-called ''litigation explosion.'' In the 1970s a U.S. Supreme Court decision resulted in more advertising by lawyers and other professionals. Some law firms increased their hiring of top attorneys from competing firms after Steven Brill in 1979 began publishing *The American Lawyer,* which examined salaries and other internal law firm practices. Some attorneys complained that the law was becoming just another profit-oriented business and was losing its professional nature. In any case, sound management became more important as firms expanded far beyond their earlier size, say from 50 to 250 or even 500 or more attorneys.

Naturally, different firms tried different management practices. Author Laurel Sorenson in 1984 wrote, ''Phones are jangling coast-to-coast as lawyers trade tips on the latest management and personnel practices: part-time positions, flextime, maternity and paternity leaves, extended leaves of other sorts and sabbaticals.'' More attorneys wanted to balance a career with family life and other outside interests. "It's a difficult adjustment, but the order is clearly changing," said Hildebrandt Inc. President Jack Kaufman in the July 1984 *ABA Journal*.

With law firms growing rapidly, Bradford Hildebrandt and Jack Kaufman in 1984 published *The Successful Law Firm* to help large law firms deal with substantial issues such as mergers, partner compensation, and long-term planning. A February 1984 review in the *ABA Journal* stated, "If your law firm is considering employing a management consultant, this book would be a good starting place before your decision to hire, not because it tells you how to hire a consultant, but because it outlines the approach a consultant will take in the analysis."

The consulting firm's 1989 assistance to merger negotiations between the 92-lawyer firm Cole & Deitz and Chicago's Winston & Strawn illustrated Hildebrandt's services. Bradford Hildebrandt's previous experience with both firms helped bring them together. He had worked with the 300-lawyer Chicago firm for three years and helped it decide to build a strong New York office. Hildebrandt also had helped reorganize Cole & Deitz. No personality clashes blocked the merger between the two firms, which had similar practices. It was just a matter of Hildebrandt helping the firms resolve tax and retirement issues before the merger could move ahead.

Corporate law departments also hired Hildebrandt consultants. For example, CBS hired Hildebrandt in 1988 to conduct an efficiency study of its in-house law department, which had already decreased from 75 attorneys in 1985 to 42 in 1988. Two earlier consultant studies of CBS as a whole had been completed, but George Vrandenburg, vice-president and general counsel for CBS, wanted the Hildebrandt analysis of just the law department because "you can always get some independent views and maybe learn something," according to the May 10–16, 1988 *Manhattan Lawyer*.

Hildebrandt consultants advised clients not only on attorney matters but also on paralegals and staff needs. For example, in the second half of the 1980s law firms found it increasingly difficult to recruit skilled legal secretaries. Although secretarial salaries had increased, more women became attorneys and paralegals. Law firms tried different tactics to find and retain secretaries, including better pay, more flexible schedules, increased training, supervisory positions, and career options.

In the 1980s Hildebrandt Inc. expanded along with its client base. In 1989 Hildebrandt Inc. opened its eighth office in Houston, Texas. It was started by Allen L. Cleveland, formerly an attorney with the Houston law firm of Fulbright & Jaworski.

Hildebrandt in the 1990s

The decade started with more growth; in 1990 Hildebrandt Inc. started its first overseas office in London, but the firm closed that office in 1993 and also closed its Houston and Dallas offices in the 1990s. With the economic downturn around 1990, many law firms faced bad times. The November 30, 1990 *New York Times* said "trendmeister" Bradford Hildebrandt previously "spread the gospel of growth. More recently, he has amassed millions of frequent-flier miles evangelizing a creed of leanness-is-meanness, spreading apocalyptic visions of smaller profits or worse to firms that fail to tighten their money belts."

In 1991 Hildebrandt Inc. surveyed the 500 largest law firms to see how they had responded to the economic challenges. Of the 105 firms that responded, 60 percent reported asking partners to leave in the previous 18 months, more than 93 percent said they had fired associates during that same period, and the large majority said they planned to fire even more associates in the near future. The American Bar Association president said he was surprised at Hildebrandt's findings, especially the fact that so many partners had been dismissed.

Obviously many in the legal community paid attention to Hildebrandt's views. "Mr. Hildebrandt makes his name in the press—as oracle, soothsayer, trendmeister," said writer David Margolick in 1990. "In legal periodicals, his name appears more often than some bylines."

In the early 1990s Hildebrandt Inc. recommended that the New York law firm of Shea & Gould end its operations. Earlier the firm, on Hildebrandt's advice, fired more than 70 individuals, including 20 partners. Power struggles and internal conflict, however, led to Shea & Gould's demise on January 27, 1994.

In 1994 Hildebrandt Inc. formed alliances with two firms. First, Hildebrandt and the accounting firm Ernst & Young agreed to work together without merging. Hildebrandt sent clients to the accounting firm for assistance on litigation support and employee compensation and benefits. On the other hand, Ernst & Young referred its legal clients to Hildebrandt since it had closed its own inhouse legal consulting department two years earlier.

Second, Hildebrandt signed an agreement with Synergetix Systems to help its technology consultants provide law firms and other clients with improved systems integration and maintenance. The fact that some large law firms used hundreds of computers showed the importance of Hildebrandt's technology consulting. Curt Meltzer, the head of Hildebrandt Inc.'s technology division, recommended that law firms with at least 30 lawyers hire a full-time information systems director.

Hildebrandt consultants dealt with not only organizational issues, but also psychological factors. For example, Steven Berglas, a clinical psychologist with Harvard Medical School and Hildebrandt Inc., worked with business leaders to overcome their anxiety and fears of losing touch with advanced technology and new expectations in the marketplace, including new rules on sexual harassment. Interviewed in the September 8, 1997 *Fortune*, Berglas said, "Many people at all levels of companies now are, in effect, living in a foreign country: They don't know what the rules are anymore." Berglas, the author of *The Success Syndrome: Hitting Bottom When You Reach the Top*, included hundreds of executives among his clients.

An example of the law firm mergers with which Hildebrandt dealt occurred in 1998. The consulting firm helped unite the San Francisco firm Thelen, Marrin, Johnson & Bridges, with about 200 lawyers, and Manhattan's Reid & Priest, a 150-lawyer firm, to become Thelen Reid and Priest. In the April 6, 1998 *New York Times,* Bradford Hildebrandt said, "We are in the beginning of an enormous consolidation of the legal industry, much like what happened to the accounting firms 10 years ago . . . it is going much faster than anytime before."

In 1998 Hildebrandt also worked with one of the nation's most famous, or infamous, law firms—the Rose Law Firm of Little Rock, Arkansas, well known from its association with the Clinton administration and the Whitewater scandal. In March 1998 the firm's partners held a special meeting at which Hildebrandt's Don Akins presented them with his 75-page report based on interviews and surveys. Akins advised the firm either to change its leadership and compensation methods or to dissolve the partnership that had been started in 1820 by U. M. Rose. The Rose Law Firm, which had declined from 56 to 44 lawyers by March 1998, decided to fight to stay alive. They accepted Akins's counsel to change their loose democratic management system, which had allowed little accountability and thus permitted partner Webster Hubbell's embezzlement and conviction, to one run firmly by Ronald M. Clark, the chief operating officer. Whether or not these changes helped in the long run remained to be seen.

In the 1990s Hildebrandt Inc. ran The Hildebrandt Institute, described in its literature as "the unparalleled leadership skills training program" for law firm leaders. Headed by Carl A. Leonard in San Francisco, institute workshops in three years "trained over 600 managing partners, practice group leaders, marketing partners, and executive directors, throughout the United States, Canada, and Europe to rave reviews." Leading attorneys, consultants, psychologists, and others from within and outside the legal profession taught classes on lawyer morale and burnout, information technology, marketing, and practice management. One-day workshops cost $1,750, and two-day workshops cost $2,750.

Hodgart Consulting and Its 1999 Merger with Hildebrandt Inc.

In 1990 Alan W. Hodgart founded Hodgart Consulting in London to provide management consulting services to law firms and other professionals. With an M.A. from the University of Cambridge and other studies at the University of Melbourne, Hodgart worked several years with management consulting giant McKinsey before starting his own firm. By 1999 his firm had served large law firms, accounting firms, and chartered surveyors in the European Union, the United Kingdom, Eastern Europe, Australia, and other parts of the world. His clients included Eversheds, Frere Cholmeley Bischoff (before half of that firm merged with Eversheds), Simmons & Simmons, Lawrence Graham, DJ Freeman, Watson Farley & Williams, Taylor Joynson Garrett, and Bird Semple.

In the early 1990s Hildebrandt Inc. rejected a merger with Hodgart Consulting because of cultural differences. Then in 1996 Hodgart allied with the Pennsylvania consulting firm Altman Weil Pensa, said to be Hildebrandt's major competitor. The Hodgart-Altman complete merger failed, however, in 1998. Altman was disappointed that so little work was available for European inhouse law departments; such clients in the United States provided about 25 percent of its work. Unlike Altman, Hodgart wanted to expand its consulting to other professionals aside from lawyers, especially with the increasing prospects of multidisciplinary partnerships (MDPs) being formed.

In 1998 Hildebrandt and Hodgart still were competitors. Hildebrandt was expanding its presence in Europe, while Hodgart was planning to go head to head with Hildebrandt in the United States. "Our game plan was to take them [Hildebrandt] on at the strategy end, which we thought was, not weak, but it's their weaker area," said Alan Hodgart in the *Illinois Legal Times*. "We were looking at putting together a small firm in New York, pinching some consultants from elsewhere, and trying to set up a four- or five-consultant office in New York." Some clients had hired both consulting firms for advice.

Everything changed in late 1998 when by chance Alan Hodgart ran into Bradford Hildebrandt at London's Savoy Hotel. The next night the two men met again. In an hour they agreed to merge, effective May 1, 1999. They planned to keep their existing offices and open a New York office in early 1999, and they discussed opening a German office. The merged firm, including Hodgart's nine consultants, featured a professional staff of 36. Bradford Hildebrandt chaired Hildebrandt International, and Alan Hodgart headed it strategic planning practice and served as one of its 11 directors.

In the May 1999 *Illinois Legal Times,* Joel Henning, the head of Hildebrandt's Chicago office, said that by 1999, "What changed are the people in Alan Hodgart's organization. We now find his entire organization to be really compatible with ours. That wasn't the case a number of years ago."

The possibility of mergers between London and New York law firms stimulated the merger of the two legal consulting firms. Bradford Hildebrandt, for example, already had flown back and forth across the Atlantic to advise his firm's clients on such consolidation. "Everyone is talking about it," said Bradford in the March 18, 1999 *Wall Street Journal,* but at that point it had not yet happened. Since several American and Canadian law firms had merged, several global alliances of law firms had operated since the late 1980s, and consolidations among multinational corporations were becoming more common, many expected the imminent merger of some American and European law firms.

Both Hildebrandt Inc. and Hodgart Consulting agreed that MDPs presented new opportunities for consultants. The American Corporate Counsel Association approved such innovative partnerships in February 1999. C. Randel Lewis, Hildebrandt International's managing director, said in the April 1999 *Worldlaw Business,* "We are very interested in the rise of the MDP. We want to be the principal advisers in that area."

The 1999 merger also was designed to deal with increased competition. The Big Five accounting firms, particularly PricewaterhouseCoopers and Arthur Andersen, were providing legal services through affiliated law firms as well as advising law firms on management issues. Each accounting firm had more than 1,500 lawyers working internationally. Major business consulting firms, such as McKinsey, Bain & Company, and the Boston Consulting Group, had not worked much with law firms because most were relatively small, but it was believed that that might change as law firms grew larger from consolidation and internal hiring.

Globalization impacted corporations, law firms, and the consultants who served them. The Internet and electronic commerce was changing business practices worldwide. Some critics argued that business consultants could be a waste of time and money or even hurt their corporate clients. So Hildebrandt International faced many challenges and new opportunities as the new millennium approached.

Further Reading

Barker, Emily, "Thomas Gelbmann Takes Dorsey & Whitney High Tech," *American Lawyer,* May 1991, p. 12.

Barrett, Paul M., "Drive To Go Global Spurs Law-Firm Merger Talk," *Wall Street Journal,* March 18, 1999, p. B1.

Carter, Terry, "From Bum's Rush to Bum Rap: Rose Law Firm Rebuilds After Improper Shredding—of Its Reputation," *ABA Journal,* July 1998.

Clarke, Caroline V., "Secretary Sweepstakes," *American Lawyer,* January–February 1990, p. 32.

"Consultants Merge for Transatlantic Service," *Worldlaw Business,* April 1999, pp. 1–2.

"Death of a Law Firm," *International Financial Law Review,* March 1994, p. 2.

Fisher, Anne, "Why Are You So Paranoid," *Fortune,* September 8, 1997, p. 171.

Flaherty, Kelly, "Hildebrandt To Merge with U.K.-Based Consulting Firm," *The Recorder,* April 1, 1999.

Fung, Vigor, and Amy Dockser, "Two Large Canadian Law Firms Plan Merger That Upsets Provincial Tradition," *Wall Street Journal* (Eastern edition), October 10, 1988, p. 1.

Hildebrandt, Bradford W., *Financial Management for Law Firms,* New York: Law Journal Press, 1975.

Hildebrandt, Bradford W., and Jack Kaufman, *The Successful Law Firm,* New York: Prentice Hall Law & Business, 1988.

"Hildebrandt, Meet Hodgart," *Illinois Legal Times,* May 1999.

Jacobs, Deborah L., "Efficiency Study Has In-Housers at CBS Fearing Further Cuts," *Manhattan Lawyer,* May 10–16, 1988, p. 3.

Margolick, David, "At the Bar," *New York Times,* November 30, 1990, p. B5(L).

O'Shea, James, and Charles Madigan, *Dangerous Company: The Consulting Powerhouses and the Businesses They Save and Ruin,* New York: Times Business, 1997.

"Practicing What They Preach," *Legal Week,* April 15, 1999, pp. 10–11.

Robinson, Tony, "Cole & Deitz, Chicago Firm Ironing Out Merger Details," *Manhattan Lawyer,* April 18–24, 1989, p. 5.

—David M. Walden

Honda Motor Company Limited

1-1, 2-chome
Minami-Aoyama,
Minato-Ku,
Tokyo 107-8556
Japan
81-3-3423-1111
Fax: 81-3-3423-0217

U.S. Headquarters
American Honda Motor Co.
1919 Torrance Boulevard
Torrance, California 90501-2746
U.S.A
(310) 783-2000
Fax: (310) 783-3900
Web site: http://www.honda.com

Public Company
Incorporated: 1948
Employees: 109,400
Sales: US$52.4 billion (1999)
Stock Exchanges: Tokyo Osaka Niigata Nagoya Kyoto
   Fukuoka Supporo Hiroshima New York
Ticker Symbol: HMC
NAIC: 336991 Motorcycle, Bicycle & Parts Manufac-
   turing; 336211 Motor Vehicle Body Manufacturing;
   336999 Other Engine Equipment Manufacturing;
   335312 Motor & Generator Manufacturing; 333618
   Outboard Motors Manufacturing

Honda Motor Company Limited is perhaps best known as an automaker—it is the third largest automaker in Japan—but the company has its roots in motorcycles, and is the world's top motorcycle manufacturer. Its best market is in the United States, where the majority of its sales are generated. Honda's automobile product line accounts for approximately 90 percent of its sales, and includes well-known U.S. top-sellers such as the Accord, Legend, Civic, Prelude, and the luxury Acura. The Accord is the second most purchased car in the United States, although it actually ranks first on the country's list of most stolen (and thus, "in demand") vehicles. Honda also produces motorcycles such as the Super Cub, Foresight, and Shadow 750. Furthermore, the company's power products division makes other items that bolster annual sales, such as agricultural and industrial-use machinery, portable generators, outboard motors, and all-terrain vehicles.

The Early Years

Any description of Honda Motor Company's history and success must take into account the contrasting inclinations of its founders—Soichiro Honda and his partner, Takeo Fujisawa. Soichiro Honda's achievements as a mechanical engineer are said to have matched those of Henry Ford. Working in his Japanese machine shop in 1938, Honda concentrated his early efforts on casting a perfect piston ring. He soon succeeded in casting a ring that met his standards, and attempted to sell it to the Toyota Corporation.

Toyota rejected Honda's first batch of piston rings, but two years later the company finally placed a large order. At that time, however, Honda ironically found himself facing a major obstacle that came as a result of the order's large size—a shortage of cement. Because Japan was preparing for war, Honda could not secure the cement and materials needed to construct a factory to mass-produce piston rings. Furthermore, he could not produce the quantity of piston rings necessary using his facility at that time. Undaunted, Honda learned how to make his own cement and soon constructed the new facility.

Honda's new factories survived the bombing attacks during World War II, but were unfortunately later destroyed by an earthquake. At that time, Honda sold his piston ring operation to Toyota and went on to manufacture motorbikes instead. He had designed his first bike in the early postwar years when gasoline was very scarce and the need for a low fuel-consuming vehicle was great. After the destruction of his piston ring manufacturing facilities, he decided to attempt selling his motorbike on a larger scale.

To form a company, Honda joined efforts with investor Takeo Fujisawa, whom he had known throughout the 1940s. In 1949 Fujisawa provided the capital, as well as financial and marketing strategies, to start the new company. Honda's motivation for establishing the company—unlike Fujisawa's—was not purely commercial, but was instead to provide himself with a secure financial base so that he might pursue other ambitions such as motorcycle racing.

Innovations in the 1950s

In 1950, after his first motorcycle had been introduced in Japan, Honda stunned the engineering world by doubling the horsepower of the conventional four-stroke engine. With this technological innovation, the company was poised for success. By 1951 demand was brisk, yet production was slow. It was primarily due to design advantages that Honda became one of four or five industry leaders. By 1954 Honda had achieved a 15 percent share of the motorcycle market.

Still, the two owners of the company had different priorities. For Fujisawa, the engine innovation meant increased sales and easier access to financing. For Honda, the higher horsepower engine opened the possibility of more successfully pursuing his motorcycle racing ambitions. Indeed, winning provided the ultimate confirmation of his design abilities. Success came quickly, and by the end of the 1950s Honda had won all of the most prestigious motorcycle racing prizes in the world.

Throughout the decade, however, Fujisawa attempted to turn Honda's attention away from racing and instead toward the more mundane tasks of running a successful business venture. By 1956, as the technological innovations gained from racing began to pay off in vastly more efficient engines, Fujisawa prompted Honda to adapt this technology for a commercial motorcycle— with a particular segment of Japanese society in mind. At that time, most motorcyclists in Japan were male and the machines they used were primarily an alternative form of transportation to trains and buses. There were, however, a large number of small commercial establishments in Japan that still delivered goods and ran errands on bicycles. The finances of these small enterprises were usually controlled by Japanese housewives who resisted buying conventional motorcycles because they were expensive, dangerous, and difficult to handle. Fujisawa suggested to Honda that with his knowledge of racing, he might be able to design a safe and inexpensive motorcycle that could be driven with only one hand (to facilitate carrying packages).

In 1958 the Honda 50cc Super Cub was introduced. It featured an automatic clutch, three-speed transmission, automatic starter, and the safe, friendly look of a bicycle. Its inexpensive price was due almost entirely to its high-horsepower, yet lightweight 50cc engine. Overwhelmed by demand, the company arranged for an infusion of capital in order to build a new plant with a 30,000 unit per month capacity. By the end of 1959 Honda had climbed into first place among Japanese motorcycle manufacturers, with sales of $55 million. The company's total sales that year of 285,000 units included 168,000 Super Cubs.

Expansion into the United States in the 1960s

The success of the Super Cub in Japan prompted Honda to consider expanding its target market to other geographic regions. The company had already experimented with local southeast Asian markets in 1957 and 1958, however, with little success. The European market, while larger, was heavily dominated by its own name brand manufacturers, and their popular mopeds dominated the low price, low horsepower market. Thus, Fujisawa decided to focus Honda's attention on the U.S. market.

Prior to 1960, the image of the motorcyclist in the United States was that of an unsavory teenager who belonged to a group of unruly characters known by names such as "Hell's Angels" and "Satan's Slaves." In general, the U.S. public regarded motorcyclists as troublemakers who wore leather jackets. In the 1960s, however, Honda Motor Company worked to successfully transform that image, and at the same time establish the company as the leading motorcycle manufacturer in the world.

In 1959 Honda established a U.S. subsidiary—American Honda Motor Company, Inc.—an action which was in sharp contrast to other foreign manufacturers who relied on distributors. Honda's strategy was to create a market of customers who had never given a thought to owning a motorcycle. The company started its enterprise in America by producing the smallest, most lightweight motorcycles available. With a three speed transmission, an automatic clutch, five horsepower (an American cycle had only two and a half), an electric starter, and a step-through frame for female riders, Honda sold its unit for $250 retail compared to $1,000—$1,500 for the American machines. Even at that early date, American Honda was probably superior to its competitors in the area of productivity.

Honda followed a policy of developing the U.S. market one region at a time. The company started on the West Coast and moved eastward over a period of five years. During 1960, 2,500 machines were sold in the United States. In 1961, 125 distributors were established, and $150,000 was spent on regional advertising. Honda's success in creating a demand for lightweight motorcycles was impressive. Its U.S. sales skyrocketed from $500,000 in 1960 to $77 million in 1965.

Honda's advertising campaign, which was directed at young families, included the slogan, "You meet the nicest people on a Honda." This was a deliberate attempt to disassociate its motorcycles from the image many Americans had of motorcyclists. The slogan's creation was an interesting story itself. In the spring of 1963 an undergraduate advertising major at the University of California, Los Angeles (UCLA) submitted, in fulfillment of a course assignment, an advertising campaign for Honda. Its theme was: "You meet the nicest people on a Honda." Encouraged by his instructor, the student submitted his work to a friend at Grey Advertising. Consequently, the

"Nicest People" campaign became the impetus behind Honda's sales, and as a result, by 1964 nearly one out of every two motorcycles sold in the United States was a Honda.

Transitions into Automobile Manufacture

As a result of the growing number of medium-income consumers, banks and other consumer credit companies began to finance the purchase of motorcycles. This facilitated a shift away from dealer credit, which had been the traditional purchasing mechanism. Seizing the opportunity created by a soaring demand for its products, the company set into motion a risky plan. Late in 1964 Honda announced that soon thereafter it would cease to ship motorcycles on a consignment basis and would require cash on delivery. Meanwhile, management prepared itself for a dealership revolt. Instead, while nearly every dealer either questioned or complained about the decision, not one relinquished its franchise. Therefore, through this one decision Honda was able to transfer the financial authority (and, the power that goes with it) from the dealer to the manufacturer. Within three years this method became the basic pattern of the industry and the Honda motorcycle had the largest market share of any company in the world.

Meanwhile, as Honda was becoming the world's leading motorcycle manufacturer, in 1967 it diversified and also began to produce cars and trucks. In addition, the company started to manufacture portable generators, power tillers, lawn mowers, pumps, and outboard motors. In 1967 and 1968 the company introduced two lightweight passenger cars which performed poorly in both the Japanese and U.S. markets. It was not until 1973 and the introduction of the Honda Civic that the company became a real presence on the international automobile market. The world was in the grip of the oil crisis, and the energy-efficient Japanese compacts suddenly found a worldwide market.

Three years later, in 1976, as sales of the Honda Civic surpassed the one million mark, the company introduced an upscale, higher priced model named the Accord. Sales of the Accord grew rapidly, not only in Japan, but especially in the United States. In 1982, as a result of the burgeoning U.S. market for Japanese cars, production of the Accord was started at Honda's Marysville, Ohio, manufacturing plant. Meanwhile, Honda's total motorcycle production had reached some 3.5 million units per year, with one-third being produced or sold outside of Japan.

As the Accord became more and more popular with middle-class Americans looking for high-quality, reliable, and affordable cars, management was convinced that the company could succeed in entering the luxury car market. In 1986, Honda introduced the Acura, which immediately garnered large sales throughout Japan and the United States. By the end of the 1980s, Honda had developed into one of the leading car manufacturers in the world.

Stumbling Blocks in the Early 1990s

Honda's success continued into the new decade. The Accord was the most popular and bestselling car in the United States from 1990 to 1992. U.S. sales were astronomical, with two cars sold in the United States for every one sold in Japan. When Honda began selling cars in the late 1960s, no one could have predicted that Honda would ever surpass Chrysler Corporation to become the third largest seller of cars in the United States. It happened, however, in 1993. Furthermore, in addition to car sales, the company's motorcycle unit even broke new ground: in 1992 Honda organized the first ever joint venture to make motorcycles in China. Many industry analysts predicted that the agreement would give Honda an initial foothold in what could become the world's largest and most lucrative motorcycle market.

Yet Honda's success in an arena as competitive as the automotive industry could not continue indefinitely. With increasing sales of Pontiac's Grand Am, Ford's Taurus, and Toyota's Camry, sales of Honda's Accord slipped 35 percent in 1993. In the luxury car market, Acura's sales decreased 17 percent as well, battered by competition from Toyota's Lexus and Nissan's Infinity. Honda even lost a significant portion of its share of the Japanese market. Exacerbating its loss of market share was the widely publicized scandal that high-ranking Honda managers accepted payoffs as high as $100,000 from dealers who wanted Honda franchises and certain types of special treatment.

With over 40 percent of its worldwide sales located in the United States, Honda started to fight back on American soil. After Soichiro Honda died in 1991, the company initiated a comprehensive reorganization. Led by Nobuhiko Kawamoto, the company's president and chief executive officer, Honda reorganized its Japanese, European, and North American units into autonomous operations to improve cost effectiveness. In order to introduce more Americans into company management, Honda arranged for 50 employees from its Ohio plant to spend two to three years working in Japan. The company also expanded its sales training in the United States, and introduced dealer incentives of up to $1,000 per car in order to move some of its inventory. Finally, Honda introduced its first four-wheel drive vehicle, to compete with already established models such as Isuzu's Rodeo.

Although Honda trimmed its overhead, incorporated more Americans into the management of the company, and introduced new models, none of these changes altered one salient fact—namely, that the worldwide car industry was saturated and would remain extremely competitive for both the short and long term. Ironically, Honda would have to endure the same squeeze that U.S. car manufacturers had felt during the 1970s and 1980s, when Japanese competition almost forced them out of business.

The End of the Century and Beyond

In order to compete in the tough automobile industry environment, Honda focused much of its attention on research and development in 1993 and 1994. As a payoff, the company received a substantial amount of positive press related to its efforts. First, in 1993 it was noted that Honda's power product engines were the first to meet new California emission regulations. Later that year, Honda's experiments with alternative power sources for automobiles led the company to win the world's largest Solar Car race—the World Solar Challenge—with its Honda Dream. The following year, the company began selling the CUV-ES electric scooter on a limited basis, and

Honda's BP90 outboard motor received the IMTEC Innovation Award.

In 1995 Honda followed these feats with the introduction of the first gasoline-powered vehicle to meet Ultra Low Emission Vehicle (ULEV) standards. Around the same time, a new version of the Civic was introduced, featuring a three-stage VTEC engine and Multi Matic characteristic. By then, cumulative world production for the Civic had reached ten million units, and cumulative world production of all Honda automobiles had surpassed the 30 million unit mark. Late that year, Honda introduced another vehicle to its product line—the sport utility vehicle CR-V.

Honda also attempted to bolster U.S. sales through efforts to engineer and manufacture some of its U.S. products in that country, using American labor. In 1996, the Acura CL—which had been developed and produced in the United States—went on sale. That same year, the Valkyrie—a U.S.-made large-size custom motorcycle—was introduced. Honda won the World Solar Challenge once again in 1996.

The next year brought with it Honda's creation and application of a new 360-degree universally inclinable ultra-small four-stroke engine, as well as the manufacture of more automobiles with low emissions characteristics. Also in 1997, the company reached the cumulative production milestone of 100 million units for its motorcycle line, and of 30 million units for its power product line. Honda's sales continued to rebound, and the growth led the company to open production facilities in many new locations around the world. For instance, in 1997 alone, new production lines of different Honda products were started in India, Vietnam, Turkey, Indonesia, and Brazil. In 1998 Honda once again signed a joint venture agreement in China—this time to produce and sell cars.

Soon thereafter, Honda made headlines when its U.S. workforce began publicly voicing a potential desire to join unions. Up to that point, Honda had been a unionless enterprise, surrounded in the United States by most other U.S.-based car companies who were supported by unions such as the United Auto Workers (UAW) and the Teamsters Union. In fact, no other Japanese-owned automobile company had ever approved and instituted a union structure before. Among some of the complaints against the company by workers were working conditions, retirement plans, and special treatment of temporary workers. Nevertheless, many Honda employees quoted in U.S. media at the time seemed to voice the opinion that there was no significant need for Honda workers to become unionized.

In 1999 Honda poised itself to introduce to the U.S. market a new low-emission, fuel-efficient automobile made out of an aluminum and plastic mix. The new car, named the Insight, was powered by both gasoline fuel and electricity, and was estimated to achieve an amazing 84 miles per gallon of gasoline. Honda was not the first carmaker to come up with such a vehicle; Toyota had previously introduced a similar car to the market in Japan—the Prius. But Honda's late 1999 introduction of the Insight in the United States was set to beat Toyota's original plans for a year 2000 entry into the U.S. market.

As the end of the century approached, Honda was doing quite well but still had weaknesses to surmount. It had come to be known as one of the most efficient car companies in the world. Its strengths were in its research and development know-how, its high level of technological advances, and its global reach—Honda was selling markedly more units abroad than in its own country. Yet the company was beginning to rely more and more on its U.S. sales, which by the end of the decade accounted for nearly 85 percent of Honda's profits. Furthermore, there was too much reliance on the success of the company's Civic and Accord models, which could pose trouble in the future if production glitches occurred in either line. It would be Honda's ability to effectively deal with those potential problem areas that would determine its success in the 21st century.

Principal Subsidiaries

Honda Research and Development Co., Ltd.; Honda Engineering Co., Ltd.; Honda International Sales Corp.; Honda SF Corp.; Honda Minami Tokyo Co., Ltd.; Honda Motor Service Co., Ltd.; ACT Trading Corp.; American Honda Motor Co.; Honda of America Mfg., Inc.; Honda Research of America, Inc.; Honda Motor (China) Co., Ltd.; Press Giken Co., Ltd. (98.2%); Seiki Giken Co., Ltd. (98%); Honda and Co., Ltd. (86.6%); Honda Sogo Tatemono, Ltd. (70%).

Further Reading

Clark, Tanya, "How Honda Thrives," *Industry Week,* October 5, 1998.
"Handicapping Honda," *Business Week Online,* July 5, 1999.
"Honda Vs. the Giants," *Business Week Online,* July 5, 1999.
"Honda's Yoshino: 'Traditionally, We Build Small and Grow Big'," *Business Week Online,* July 5, 1999.
Kerwin, Kathleen, "We Just Kind of Sneak Up on You," *Business Week Online,* July 5, 1999.
Miller, Karen Lowry, "How Not to Buy a Car Company," *Business Week Online,* July 5, 1999.
"Newest Honda Claims 84 Miles Per Gallon," *Philadelphia Inquirer,* July 7, 1999.
Ramsey, Douglas K., *The Corporate Warriors: Six Classic Cases in American Business,* Boston: Houghton Mifflin, 1987.
Sakiya, Tetuus, *Honda Motor: The Men, The Management, The Machine,* Tokyo: Kodonsha International, 1982.
Taylor, Alex, "The Dangers of Running Too Lean," *Fortune,* June 14, 1993.
Thornton, Emily, Kathleen Kerwin, and Keith Naughton, "Honda: Can the Company Go It Alone?" *Business Week Online,* July 5, 1999.
"Unions Square Off over Honda Plant," *Detroit Free Press,* May 13, 1999.

—Thomas Derdak
—updated by Laura E. Whiteley

Hovnanian Enterprises, Inc.

10 Highway 35
Red Bank, New Jersey 07701
U.S.A.
(732) 747-7800
Fax: (732) 747-7159
Web site: http://www.khov.com

Public Company
Incorporated: 1959 as Hovnanian Brothers, Inc.
Employees: 1,200
Sales: $941.9 million (1998)
Stock Exchanges: American
Ticker Symbol: HOV
NAIC: 23321 Single Family Housing Construction;
    23332 Commercial & Institutional Building
    Construction; 522292 Real Estate Credit; 52413
    Reinsurance Carriers

New Jersey-based Hovnanian Enterprises, Inc. designs, constructs, and markets condominium apartments and attached townhouses (mainly for first-time buyers) and moderately priced townhouses with garages and single-family detached homes (primarily to first- and second-time move-up buyers and to active adult buyers). The company also provides mortgage loans and title insurance, both to its home buyers and to third parties. The company was active in six states, Washington, D.C., and Poland in 1998. Founded by Kevork S. Hovnanian in 1959, the enterprise was still under his control 40 years later.

Low-Cost Private Builder: 1959–83

Born and raised in Iraq, Kevork Hovnanian was an ethnic Armenian in charge of Iraq's largest roadpaving company when the king of Iraq was overthrown in 1958 by left-wing revolutionaries who nationalized the firm. Hovnanian escaped to the United States the following year, and was soon followed by his three brothers and two sisters.

In America, the Hovnanian siblings were able to secure a loan of $20,000 from one of the brother's in-laws to start a

business of their own. Together they decided to get into the building business, erecting a few houses on speculation in Toms River, New Jersey. When these homes were sold at a profit, Kevork Hovnanian was in the home-building business to stay, as president of newly founded Hovnanian Brothers, Inc.

By 1964, however, Hovnanian had switched from custom-built homes to condominiums, which were still a rarity in the region. Discussing the reason for the change in a 1986 interview with Thomas J. Lueck of the *New York Times*, Hovnanian recalled that he couldn't estimate the costs of custom-built homes properly, which "irritated me no end."

The Hovnanian brothers' early houses, which sold rapidly, were small and inexpensive: 950 square feet of floor space for $18,000 to $19,000. Between 1966 and 1969 Jirair Hovnanian, another brother who had left Iraq earlier, joined the firm, which was reincorporated as K. Hovnanian Enterprises in 1967. Jirair then left to form his own New Jersey-based home-building company, J.S. Hovnanian and Sons Inc. The other brothers also left in 1969 to found their own building companies.

The 1970s brought expanded markets, as Hovnanian Enterprises entered the Florida market in 1970, Texas and Georgia in 1973, and Pennsylvania in 1976. Revenues during this time were around $9.5 million, and Hovnanian soon found himself overextended financially. He had to stretch out his loans, which he would pay off entirely by the end of 1980. The founder's son, Ara, a graduate of the University of Pennsylvania's Wharton School, joined the firm as executive vice-president in 1979.

That year, the company had net income of about $500,000 on revenues of $25.2 million. During this time, Hovnanian Enterprises made a decision to mine the "baby boom" market by building smaller, more affordable houses as its main product. The firm's approach to keeping prices down involved high volume, rapid sales, and rapid delivery. To expedite its mortgage processing procedures, the firm acquired R.E. Scott Co., a mortgage brokerage concern, in 1982. In order to hold down costs further, it also purchased Najarian & Associates, an engineering company, the same year.

For the fiscal year ended February 1983, Hovnanian Enterprises built 1,250 single-family attached condominiums and townhouses and had revenues of $70.2 million. These were impressive results, given a lingering recession brought on by high interest rates that devastated the market for new housing. Net income fell from the previous year's peak of $3 million, however.

Hovnanian Enterprises sold 466 of its homes in New Jersey in 1983, most of them built on 63 acres off Route 1 in North Brunswick. This development, Society Hill North, was followed by another Society Hill development in neighboring East Brunswick. The starting price of $51,000 for a 1,133-square-foot condominium unit with two bedrooms and a bath was $10,000 below any other new house in the area. Society Hill also offered one- and two-bedroom townhouses for $60,000 to $63,000, as well as a two-bedroom, 2½-bath townhouse model with 1,048 square feet of space for $73,500. No garages, community buildings, swimming pools, or special financing deals were offered for these homes. In other markets, such as Florida and Georgia, Hovnanian was building new homes for as little as $38,000.

Hovnanian Enterprises was selling cheap by keeping its costs down through careful planning. A meticulous site-selection process, for example, even allowed for the calculation of how much earth would have to be moved. The company limited the number of models it offered in order to standardize construction. Models offered no variation in wall height, for example; all walls were built of identical lengths of board. This method allowed Hovnanian to assign carpenters and other subcontractors several projects at once, with corresponding gains in speed and efficiency.

Hovnanian Enterprises spared no effort in lining up sales, spending as much as $3,000 to $4,000 per home on marketing and advertising. "Get the sales first, and with the sales you'll get volume and a profit," was what Hovnanian told Howard Rudnitsky of *Forbes* in 1983. Prospective customers willing to buy into Society Hill before actual construction of the model homes received discounts of a few thousand dollars.

In one well-publicized effort, Hovnanian built a model home within the Empire State Building to help advertise its new development in Florida. The company also offered each home buyer a "Family Plan" certificate worth $1,000 on the purchase, within 24 hours, of another Hovnanian-built home, transferrable to anyone in the buyer's immediate family. Work on a Hovnanian project normally did not begin until firm contracts had been signed for at least half of the units to be made available.

Boom and Bust: 1983–90

Hovnanian Enterprises circumvented the credit crunch of the early 1980s when Drexel Burnham Lambert underwrote a pub-

lic debt issue, even though the company was still privately owned. This financing enabled the firm to raise $23 million by selling 12-year debentures, which in turn enabled it to borrow $45 million on a two-year revolving loan. When the company went public in 1983, most of the shares remained in the hands of the founder and other family members.

In early 1984 Hovnanian Enterprises had 15 communities under development—nine of them in Florida and New Jersey—consisting of almost 6,000 units priced from $31,450 to $81,450. With the national economy booming again, New Jersey sales surged. In Piscataway, for example, prospective homebuyers set up tents and sleeping bags three days before the opening of a new development. By opening day, some 700 mostly young, first-time buyers were lined up to make down payments on the 370 condominiums and townhouses selling for $75,000 to $93,000, even though no models were available for inspection. Although Florida sales were flat, Hovnanian recorded revenues of $163.9 million in 1985 and record net income of $6.6 million.

Hovnanian Enterprises also extended its reach to Westchester County, New York, offering 91 condominiums in Peekskill, New York, in April 1986 to more than 400 lined-up customers, some of whom had camped out in a neighboring parking lot for five days. The demand for the company's housing was so great that it began holding lotteries for its townhouse condos. The typical Hovnanian condominium remained a duplex with two or three bedrooms and two bathrooms, but no garage, no basement, and no kitchen fixtures or curtains. Revenues reached $228.2 million and net income $11.5 million in 1986. The company's revolving-credit line had reached $150 million by 1987.

Hovnanian Enterprises extended its geographic reach in 1986 by acquiring a controlling share of New Fortis Corp., a builder in North Carolina and Atlanta, for $1.5 million in stock. Hovnanian also began extended its reach into southern New Hampshire. In 1989 Hovnanian ranked 18th among the nation's top 100 home builders and first among builders of attached for-sale homes.

The national housing market peaked that year, however, and by the end of 1990 had contracted by one-third. Hovnanian, which had reported revenues of $410.8 million in 1990, lost $15.2 million on revenues of only $275.4 million in 1991. All markets except New Jersey were unprofitable during this time.

In December 1990 Hovnanian announced it would take a $19-million writedown on unsold properties in New Hampshire, New York, and Florida, auctioning the condominiums at bargain prices. "We expanded at the market's peak and paid top dollar for the land," Ara Hovnanian—who became company president in 1988—later conceded to Dan B. Levine of *Business for Central New Jersey*. He added, "We also hired people who were familiar neither with those markets nor with us." In New Jersey, the firm withdrew from the condo market to concentrate on building and selling higher-priced houses in the central part of the state.

New Jersey also became the center for a legal dispute in which Hovnanian became involved in the early 1990s. Specifically, Hovnanian Enterprises was one of several New Jersey builders that filed lawsuits against makers and suppliers of a fire-resistant-treated roofing plywood sheeting. This material had been found to decompose after only a few years, and the company sued on behalf of its 32 New Jersey developments after a section of crumbling roof in a Lawrence condominium collapsed under two workers, injuring one of them. A settlement announced in 1992 allowed 11,000 owners of Hovnanian-built homes in the state to pay only an estimated $200 to $400 each to cover the $2,000 cost of replacing their roofs. Plywood treaters, chemical suppliers, architects, and lumber companies bore most of the cost of the $50-million settlement.

Mixed Fortunes in the 1990s

By fiscal 1992, Hovnanian Enterprises was profitable again. The 1990–91 recession had improved its competitive position by weakening or eliminating many smaller, privately held builders, and allowing the company to acquire options on land in New Jersey and North Carolina at greatly reduced prices. The company was now marketing a new line of townhouses with amenities such as garages, basements, family rooms, and cathedral ceilings designed to look more like single-family homes than condominiums. These dwellings were starting at prices of about $85,000 in New Jersey.

In 1993 Hovnanian Enterprises launched its first large development of single-family detached homes for affluent buyers. Based in Monmouth County, New Jersey, the four- and five-bedroom homes, on three-quarter-acre lots and each accompanied by three-car garages, were priced at from $349,950 to $429,950. That year 72 percent of Hovnanian-built houses were single-family detached houses selling for about $500,000, compared to the eight percent these dwelling represented in 1989. In 1994 the company opened the first phase of an Ocean County, New Jersey, development for buyers aged 55 or older. This project was composed of condominiums, townhouses, and detached houses at introductory prices of $95,000 to $190,000. By this time Hovnanian was the tenth-largest homebuilder in the United States, as well as the largest in New Jersey.

Like many companies in many industries during this time, Ara Hovnanian embraced the total quality management concept in order to improve company performance on every measurable scale. Mark Hodges, the executive charged with implementing this task, later told *Professional Builder* magazine's William H. Lurz that "when we started in 1993, our relationships with customers were abysmal" and "our buying process was 'one notch above root canal [surgery],' according to one buyer we interviewed." Imposing a stringent measurement and reporting methodology on each of the 150 process-improvement teams operating within the company, this new quality management program was said to have achieved a bottom-line return of $1.2 million to the company in fiscal 1996. *Professional Builder* extended the company a National Housing Quality Gold Award in 1997 for this effort.

Hovnanian Enterprises entered the California market in 1994 by acquiring Stonebrook Homes, a residential developer that had build several communities in San Diego and Riverside counties. By that time the firm also was active in the Philadelphia area. The mid-1990s also brought slowed sales and higher interest rates, however, and the company lost $10.4 million in the eight-month period ending in October 1994. The following year Hovnanian laid off ten percent of its work force and instituted other restructuring moves in order to combat downward market trends.

Hovnanian's revenues and net income soon rebounded. By late 1997 the company was operating in 100 communities in seven states, and by early 1998 it was building the first townhouse project along the Hudson River in a decade, along the water's edge in West New York, New Jersey, across from midtown Manhattan. Much farther afield, the company also began homebuilding in Poland in 1997.

With sales of $784 million and $942 million in 1997 and 1998, respectively, Hovnanian Enterprises had rebounded nicely as it moved toward the 21st century. Moreover, the company's long-term debt of $301 million was $100 million below the peak at the end of 1995. Kevork Hovnanian yielded the position of chief executive officer to his son in 1997, while continuing as chairman of the board. In early 1999 he held nearly 40 percent of the company's Class A stock and more than three-fourths of the Class B shares. Ara Hovnanian held ten percent of the company's Class A shares and 15.6 percent of its Class B shares.

Principal Subsidiaries

K. Hovnanian Mortgage; K. Hovnanian Investent Properties.

Further Reading

Bledsoe, Lysbeth, "Diversification: Builder Hovnanian Changes with the Times," *Burlington County Times,* April 26, 1992, Bus. Sec.
Garbarine, Rachelle, "A Builder for Young Buyers Returns to an Older Market," *New York Times,* July 8, 1994, p. B6.
——, "Builder Cuts Sizes and Prices of Homes," *New York Times,* April 9, 1993, p. A17.
——, "Town House Project Is Rising on Hudson Shore," *New York Times,* January 23, 1998, p. B8.
Levine, Dan B., "K. Hovnanian Now Has a Global Vision," *Business for Central New Jersey,* January 25, 1995, pp. 1+.
Lueck, Thomas J., "The Few-Frills Condominium," *New York Times,* June 23, 1986, pp. D1, D14.
Lurz, William H., "K. Hovnanian Shows How to Turn a Big Ship Around," *Professional Builder,* October 1997 Supplement, pp. 16–19.
McLeister, Dan, "Hovnanian Shatters Cycle Time," *Professional Builder,* October 1998, pp. 14–15.
Oser, Alan S., "In Middlesex, Young People Can Afford a New Home," *New York Times,* May 22, 1983, Sec. 8, p. 7.
Peterson, Iver, "How 3 Embattled Builders Survive," *New York Times,* January 10, 1991, pp. D1, D5.
——, "A Plywood Used in Many Homes Is Found to Decay in a Few Years," *New York Times,* April 11, 1990, pp. A1, B2.
Roman, Monica, "Hovnanian Is Putting Its House in Order," *Business Week,* April 27, 1992, p. 72.
Rudnitsky, Howard, "Small Is Profitable," *Forbes,* July 18, 1983, pp. 66–67.
Troxell, Thomas N., Jr., "Affordability Leader," *Barron's,* February 20, 1984, pp. 65–66.
——, "Building Blocks," *Barron's,* January 5, 1987, pp. 37, 39.
——, " 'We Want to Be the Big Potato,' " *Barron's,* September 2, 1985, p. 42.

—Robert Halasz

Interface, Inc.

2859 Paces Ferry Road
Suite 2000
Atlanta, Georgia 30330
U.S.A.
(770) 437-6800
Fax: (770) 437-6809
Web site: http://www.interfaceinc.com

Public Company
Incorporated: 1973 as Carpets International of Georgia,
   Inc. *Employees:* 7,300
Sales: $1.28 billion (1998)
Stock Exchanges: NASDAQ
Ticker Symbol: IFSIA
NAIC: 31411 Carpet & Rug Mills; 31321 Broadwoven
   Fabric Mills; 325131 Inorganic Dye & Pigment
   Manufacturing

Originally a manufacturer and distributor of carpet tile, Interface, Inc., has developed into an international presence in the commercial and institutional interiors industry. Carpet tiles, uniform floor covering modules that are easier to maintain and replace than broadloom carpet, continue to underlie Interface's business, proving popular in office design because of their flexibility in redecoration and easy removal and replacement for rewiring and other repair work. These modular carpet systems—marketed under the brand names Interface Flooring Systems and Bentley in the United States, and Heuga in Europe—are used primarily in commercial and institutional settings. Interface is also the leading producer of interior fabrics for open plan office furniture systems in the United States. The fabrics for these systems, which are usually enclosed, customized work stations, are produced by the company's Guilford of Maine, Inc., subsidiary. Interface is also involved in specialty chemical production. The company's most important chemical is Intersept, an antimicrobial chemical agent used in some carpet manufacturing. Intersept is produced by another subsidiary, Rockland React-Rite, Inc. Foreign sales account for about one-third of Interface's revenue, and the company has 25 production and distribution facilities worldwide, as well as sales and marketing outposts in 110 different countries. Interface currently controls about 40 percent of the international carpet tile market.

Early History

Interface, Inc., was founded in 1973 by Ray C. Anderson, who would remain the company's chairman and chief executive officer into the late 1990s. Before founding Interface, Anderson had been working as a research manager for Milliken & Co., a privately owned textile firm. On behalf of Milliken, Anderson was sent abroad to research the technology for manufacturing carpet tiles in preparation for Milliken's prospective entry into that field. While visiting Carpets International plc (CI), a large British company specializing in carpet, Anderson was introduced to a process called ''fusion bonding.'' Anderson immediately recognized the potential of this process for producing carpet tiles, as well as the huge market for carpet tile in the United States that had not yet been tapped. In 1973 he quit his job with Milliken & Co. in order to start his own business.

Interface first appeared as a joint venture with CI, called Carpets International of Georgia, Inc. (CI-Georgia). Of the initial seed money for the company, $750,000 (half of the total) came from CI, the rest from Anderson and various backers mostly from his hometown of West Point, Georgia. The new company produced its first piece of carpet on New Year's Eve, 1973. On its first day of operation, CI-Georgia had only 15 employees, including Anderson. The company's first year of operation was a financial disaster. It lost $400,000 on sales of just over $800,000. Skyrocketing prices for petrochemicals, an important raw material in the carpet industry, were a large part of the problem. These price increases were the result of the 1973 oil embargo, and the recession that ensued.

On the other hand, the company's association with an established firm like CI gave it several advantages. The most important of these was access to advanced technology. CI was able to provide cutting technology superior to that of companies like Milliken, saving the company ten percent on the cost of yarn. Other technology was made available that enabled CI-Georgia

Company Perspectives:

Interface will be the first name in commercial and institutional interiors worldwide through its commitment to people, product and place. We will strive to create an organization wherein all people are accorded unconditional respect and dignity, one that allows each person to continuously learn and develop. We will focus on product through constant emphasis on quality and engineering which we will combine with superior attention to our customers' needs. We will honor the places where we do business by endeavoring to become the first name in industrial ecology, a corporation that cherishes nature and restores the environment. Interface will lead by example and validate by results, leaving the world a better place than when we began.

to develop special bonding equipment. This equipment made it possible to install carpet tiles without glue, bonding the four-ply carpet fibers to a fiberglass backing. These contributions, along with the beginning of the office building boom, helped CI-Georgia triple its sales to $2.4 million by the end of 1975. The company also turned its first profit that year.

During the second half of the 1970s there was tremendous growth in the white-collar segment of the U.S. economy. About 800,000 office jobs per year were created between 1975 and 1980, causing huge demand for office furnishing. It was during this period that modular carpet systems became extremely popular among office managers and interior designers. Carpet tiles allowed designers to install floor coverings that were pleasing to the eye, while at the same time were easy to remove and replace, whether for cleaning, redecorating, or accessing wiring beneath the floor. By 1978, Interface's sales had reached $11 million.

In the early 1980s CI began to face fierce competition from a flood of broadloom carpet being imported into the United Kingdom. Meanwhile, the American joint venture continued to grow, with sales swelling to $57 million in 1982. As CI continued to flounder, the American firm took over ten percent of CI's equity in the company, and changed its name to Interface Flooring Systems, Inc. The two companies continued to move in opposite directions. While Interface's sales leaped again in 1983, to $80 million, CI teetered on the edge of bankruptcy. In order to avert receivership for CI, Interface concocted a plan to provide a $4 million loan convertible to 41.3 percent future equity in CI. The agreement also gave Interface the option to purchase another 8.8 percent of CI shares for about $2.3 million through 1987, the year the loan was due. Interface also went public for the first time in 1983, selling its shares over-the-counter. The company raised $14.4 million in its initial offering.

Growth through Acquisitions in the 1980s

Interface purchased CI's carpet tile division for $8.4 million in 1984, giving Interface entry into the European market for the first time. This transaction gave Interface ownership of CI's Illingworth and Debron brands of carpet. Around the same time,

Interface acquired Carintusa Inc. from CI, for $440,000. Carintusa, the sole U.S. distributor of woven English-broadloom carpet manufactured by CI, was based in Los Angeles. In the same period, Interface also acquired Chemmar Associates, Inc., merging it with its Interface Research Corp. subsidiary. Chemmar was the licensor of Intersept, the antimicrobial agent developed for hospital carpets. Aided by these acquisitions, Interface's sales climbed to $107 million for 1984. By that time, after only 11 years of existence, Interface already controlled about 30 percent of the growing U.S. carpet tile market. This figure put the company in a virtual tie for the lead in market share with Milliken & Co., Anderson's former employers.

In 1985 Interface exercised its option to convert its CI promissory note, acquiring 41.3 percent of CI. The company's overseas business began to pick up around this time as well, particularly in oil-rich Middle Eastern countries. As the 1980s progressed, Interface began to diversify beyond carpets into related industries. The company purchased Guilford Industries for $97 million in 1986. Guilford was a textile company that specialized in fabrics for office furniture systems, including cubicle dividers, walls, and ceilings. This acquisition gave Interface the ability to market complete office furnishing packages, an idea that proved to be appealing to designers both domestically and abroad. Interface also began to expand its specialty chemical operations that year. Two Georgia-based companies, Rockland Corp. and React-Rite, Inc., were acquired on the last day of 1986, for a combined total of about $4 million. With the addition of these two companies, Interface improved its ability in polymer chemistry, essential to the further development of its Intersept program.

Interface swallowed up what was left of CI in 1987. CI's remaining debt was then paid off, and its broadloom carpet business sold. By this time, CI's name had been changed to Debron Investments Plc. For 1987, Interface reported sales of $267 million, nearly double the previous year's figure. During that year, the company's name was changed to Interface, Inc., and Interface Flooring Systems, Inc., was retained as the name of the company's North American carpet tile subsidiary. Interface became the undisputed world leader in carpet tiles in 1988, with the acquisition of Heuga Holdings B.V., a Dutch company with sales of more than $200 million. Heuga was one of the world's oldest manufacturers of carpet tiles. Interface had been trying to acquire the company since about 1983, when it was first put up for sale by the 13 children of Heuga's founder. At that time, Interface was not able to complete a deal. The company that did buy Heuga was subsequently acquired by Ausimont N.V., a firm that was not interested in the carpet tile business. From Ausimont, Interface purchased not only Heuga but Pandel, Inc., another wholly owned subsidiary. Heuga contributed manufacturing facilities in the Netherlands, the United Kingdom, Canada, and Australia. Pandel's U.S. plant produced carpet tile backing and mats. That company recorded sales of $10 million in 1987. The acquisition of Heuga expanded Interface's international business enormously, gaining the company contracts with a number of major British firms, as well as such prominent Japanese companies as Hitachi, Tokyo Marine, and Nomura Securities. It also helped Interface further diversify into residential carpet tile sales, which had accounted for about a quarter of Heuga's European business. With the addition of

Heuga, the company's revenues jumped dramatically once again, reaching $582 million.

In early 1990 Interface acquired the assets of Steil, Inc., based in Grand Rapids, Michigan. Steil had for several years been the exclusive U.S. distributor of Guilford's open line panel and upholstery fabrics. Later that year, the company invested in Prince Street Technologies, Ltd., a producer of upper-end broadloom carpet. Prince Street, based in Georgia, received a loan from Interface in exchange for the right to acquire an equity interest. Interface generated $623 million in revenue in 1990.

More than Carpet in the 1990s

Sales shrank for the first time in the company's history in 1991, largely due to the recession in the global economy. In that year, Interface generated net income of $8.9 million on sales of $582 million. During 1991, Interface Service Management, Inc. (ISM), was formed in conjunction with ISS International Service System, Inc., a Danish firm specializing in facility maintenance. The creation of ISM enabled Interface to provide its customers with a more integrated interior system in which all of its furnishing needs could be supplied by one source. In Europe the company launched a similar project, in which independent service contractors were licensed to provide maintenance services. These contractors operated under the name IMAGE (Interface Maintenance Advisory Group of Europe). Interface also reorganized its corporate structure in late 1991. The company's operations in Asia and the Pacific Islands were unified under a new holding company, Interface Asia-Pacific, Inc. Interface Europe, Inc., was also formed, merging Interface International, Inc., which had controlled operations in the United Kingdom, with the holding company that owned Heuga and its various European subsidiaries.

By 1992, Interface's antimicrobial chemical Intersept was being used in over a dozen product categories, including paints, wall coverings, ceiling tiles, carpet, fabrics, and coating materials. The marketing of Intersept was assisted by the formation of The Envirosense Consortium, a group of companies that used Intersept in the manufacture of a variety of products. The Envirosense program was initiated as a response to increasing cases of and concern over building-related illnesses and other health concerns associated with indoor work atmospheres. Interface's sales rebounded somewhat in 1992. Sales for the year were $594 million. Net income increased by over 37 percent, to $12.3 million.

In January 1993 Interface announced that it had acquired the low-profile access flooring system of Servoplan, S.A., of France. The acquisition, through the company's U.S. and French subsidiaries, included all patents, know-how, and production equipment relating to this flooring system. Interface had previously marketed the Servoplan system in North America alone, and the positive response of its customers led the company to seek worldwide control of the system's manufacture and distribution. At the time of the acquisition, Anderson indicated that the system would be sold under the name Intercell.

The following month, Interface announced another acquisition. The company's Guilford of Maine subsidiary had acquired the fabric division assets of Stevens Linen Associates, Inc., a leading producer of panel and upholstery fabric for office furniture systems. Another acquisition occurred in June 1993, when Interface bought Bentley Mills, Inc., a manufacturer of designer-oriented broadloom carpet used for commercial and institutional settings.

New Directions for the Mid-1990s and Beyond

In the mid-1990s, Interface's chairman and CEO Ray C. Anderson emerged as an outspoken advocate of sustainability, a concept that included environmental and social responsibility. Under the influence of Anderson's crusading efforts on behalf of sustainability, the company shifted strategy, aiming to redirect its industrial practices without sacrificing its business goals. Anderson, who served as co-chair of the President's Council on Sustainable Development, wrote a book entitled *Mid-Course Correction,* in which he discussed his own awakening to environmental concerns and commitment to changing a business not traditionally allied with the environmentalists. Anderson was called the "Eco CEO" by *Metropolis* magazine.

In 1996, Charlie Eitel was named president and chief operating officer of Interface. This allowed Anderson, who remained chairman and CEO, to pursue the ecological issues that had become so important to him. Under Eitel, the company began leveraging its market share with a sales approach he called "mass customization," which facilitated rapid delivery of a wide variety of patterns, in colors selected by the customers. The owned and aligned providers of carpet and installation and other services became known collectively as the Re:Source Solutions Provider Network, and Interface began bundling installation, maintenance, reclamation, and other services with carpet sales, promoting this strategy with the slogan "This Carpet Comes Installed." Carpet adhesives and other chemical applications began to be sold under the IMAGE brand name. Intercell became part of Interface Architectural Resources, a larger effort to integrate wiring and heating, ventilation, and air conditioning under the comprehensive facility solutions that Interface offered. Under Eitel, Interface branched out into a seemingly unrelated activity: motivational seminars. These sessions originated as "Why?" conferences for promoting social bonds with designers and other customers, and the positive response to these conferences led to the formation of "one world learning," a wholly owned subsidiary dedicated to fostering organizational development through activities and discussion.

In an attempt to penetrate the health care and education markets, which generally rejected carpet in favor of hard surface floorcovering, Interface introduced Solenium in 1999. Made from PTT (polytrimethylene terepthalate), a polymer developed by Shell Labs, Solenium was a dense, lightweight material that, according to the company, combined the design, comfort, sound absorption of carpet with the practicality of hard flooring. Solenium incorporated Intersept, the company's patented antimicrobial preservative.

In its quarter-century of activity, Interface had grown into a billion dollar corporation, named by *Fortune* as one of the "Most Admired Companies in America" and the "100 Best Companies to Work For." With the exception of the recession year of 1991, the company was able to increase its sales every year since its founding. In the first decade of the new century, Interface would likely be able to continue this pattern of expansion, primarily by introducing its products to a wider range of commercial customers in Asia and continental Europe. In addition, Interface's specialty chemical operations seemed poised for continued growth, as public attention to occupational health increased, and the potential hazards of higher technology in the office environment, came under closer scrutiny.

Principal Subsidiaries

Interface Flooring Systems, Inc.; Interface Europe, Inc.; Interface Asia-Pacific, Inc.; Guilford of Maine, Inc.; Rockland React-Rite, Inc.; Interface Research Corporation.

Further Reading

Anderson, Ray, *Mid-Course Correction: Toward a Sustainable Enterprise, The Interface Model,* Atlanta: Peregrinzilla Press, 1998.
"Interface's Premium: The Tiles That Bind," *Financial World,* August 7, 1984, pp. 81–82.
Kinkead, Gwen, "Green CEO," *Fortune,* May 24, 1999, pp. 190–200.
Lappen, Alyssa A., "Carpet Tile King," *Forbes,* April 17, 1989, pp. 60–64.
Lee, Shelley A., "Magic Carpet Ride," *Business Atlanta,* October 1992, pp. 111–19.
Neuwirth, Robert, "The Eco CEO," *Metropolis,* July 1998, pp. 69–73, 103–04.

—Mark Swartz

IXC Communications, Inc.

1122 Capital of Texas Highway South
Austin, Texas 78746-6426
U.S.A.
(512) 328-1112
Fax: (512) 328-0624
Web site: http://www.ixc-comm.com

Public Company
Incorporated: 1985 as Communications Transmission Inc.
Employees: 1,567
Sales: $648.8 million (1998)
Stock Exchanges: NASDAQ
Ticker Symbol: IIXC
NAIC: 51333 Telecommunications Resellers; 51221 Wired
    Telecommunications Carriers; 513112 Radio Stations;
    514191 On-Line Information Services

IXC Communications, Inc., is among five "new-age car-riers" (a group including Frontier Corporation, Level 3 Com-munications Inc., Qwest Communications, and The Williams Companies Inc.) that own and operate coast-to-coast digital communications networks, selling phone line service to corpo-rate users and other telecom companies. IXC's two principal products in the late 1990s were private telephone lines (trans-mitting voice and data over dedicated circuits between two points) and long distance switched services (processing and routing long-distance calls). The private line segment of its business became increasingly important to the company in the late 1990s, as IXC sought to take advantage of the growing demand for Internet and electronic data services. In 1999, IXC announced its intention to merge with Cincinnati Bell in a $3.2 billion deal that all concerned hoped would result in the creation of an integrated data communications powerhouse, according to a company press release.

1980s Origins

On January 1, 1984, the long distance telecommunications industry was changed forever upon AT&T's divestiture of its 22 Bell System operating companies, a move resulting from an antitrust suit filed against AT&T by the U.S. Department of Justice. Ultimately, the Baby Bells were grouped together into seven Regional Bell Operating Companies that provided local telephone service and local access service to long distance carriers. As a result of this legislative assistance, smaller long distance carriers emerged as alternatives to AT&T, Sprint, and MCI, prompting an explosion in business communications ser-vices in 1984.

One such new company was Communications Transmission Inc. (CTI) of Austin, Texas, formed in 1985 when the Times Mirror Company spun off its microwave communications enter-prise to a group of investors, among them cable television executive Ralph Swett, for about $175 million. Involved in providing digital microwave and fiber optic communications to long-distance telephone companies and other corporate clients, CTI quickly moved to expand through acquisition, purchasing Michigan-based ALC Communications Corp. for $30 million in 1988. By 1990, CTI was a cross-country network serving more than 90 cities. It was also in financial trouble. On sales of $426 million for 1989, CTI reported a net loss of $18.4 million. In 1990, the company defaulted on several loan agreements, hav-ing failed to turn the ALC subsidiary around and struggling unsuccessfully to keep up with shifts in the telecommunications industry, resulting in the loss of some important clients, includ-ing Western Union.

Efforts to restructure the company, led by Swett, resulted in the 1992 formation of IXC Communications. The arrangement also involved partnering with the Electra Communication Cor-poration (ECC), another Texas fiber optic transmission system. Under the reorganization, ECC became a wholly owned subsid-iary of IXC. By 1994, management at IXC had begun the planning stages of a new nationwide fiber optic network, fi-nanced in part by private loans secured by Swett.

Business Services in the Mid-1990s

Up until the mid-1990s, IXC's revenues had been garnered from private line services. In late 1995, however, the company expanded into the business of selling long distance switched services. IXC sold these on a per-call basis, with payments due monthly after services were rendered. Eventually, IXC also became a recognized provider of network transmission capacity to national and regional long distance carriers that elected to purchase capacity rather than invest in upgrading or replacing their older fiber networks. Revenues for the company at year-end 1995 were $91 million.

Also during this time, IXC began a fiber expansion program, anticipating great developments in the $100 billion-plus long distance industry, and the exponential growth in packetized (''packet-switched'') services, or broadband communications systems, including ATM (Asynchronous Transfer Mode), Frame Relay, and Internet-related applications. IXC, as well as the other so-called next-generation carriers—Frontier Corp., Qwest Communications, Level 3 Communications, and Williams Network—differed from the traditional carriers in that they constructed their networks around a packet-switched, data-friendly model rather than the slower circuit-switched, voice-centric models.

In 1996, the Telecommunications Act of 1996 began allowing for greater competition in the long distance business. Partly as a result of this legislation, IXC put in place its own nationwide ATM/Frame Relay network, launching the first broadband services product offering in early 1997. Regional and local Internet service providers began to purchase capacity from IXC. By leasing, selling, and swapping fiber capacity, IXC was able to significantly cut the costs involved in constructing its network. By the end of 1996, IXC had tripled its revenues from 1992, earning a total of $203 million. IXC was taken public in 1996, trading on the Nasdaq exchange under the symbol IIXC.

Acquisitions, Joint Ventures, and ''Swap'' Agreements

The stage was thus set for growth at IXC. In 1997, IXC acquired Network Long Distance, Inc., a Virginia-based long distance reseller. Also that year, IXC entered an agreement to share network capacity with Vyxx, a telecom unit of Williams Companies, which provided IXC with greater network access in the South. In turn, Vyxx received access to an IXC line between New York and Los Angeles. The agreement, part of the company's ''capacity swap'' growth strategy, saved IXC's network expansion budget an estimated $100 million. IXC also began the next stage of its growth strategy by entering the retail market and concentrating on gaining small- to medium-sized businesses as clients. Toward that end, the company purchased Telecom One of Chicago, which served business customers in 32 states.

In September 1997, Ben Scott was named the company's president and CEO. Scott had been among the veterans of the cellular industry who had helped shape the evolution of wireless communications. He came to IXC from his post as president and CEO of PrimeCo Personal Communications, a joint venture among Bell Atlantic, US West, and AirTouch, where he was responsible for the largest wireless business launch in telecommunications history.

Under Scott, expansion was not limited to the United States. IXC formed a joint venture of its own with Telenor AS, the Norwegian national telephone company. The venture, called Storm Telecommunications Ltd., was formed to provide telecommunication services to carriers and resellers in nine European countries. The company also acquired a minority interest in the Mexican long distance markets through an indirect joint venture in Marca-Tel S.A. de C.V. Marca-Tel held a long distance concession in Mexico that reached over 80 percent of the population.

IXC also became a member of InterconnX, a consortium of ATM/Frame Relay network companies, to further extend its data networking reach. By the end of 1997, IXC's facilities, in addition to its coast-to-coast digital communications network, included seven long distance switches and 15 Frame Relay-ATM switches to capitalize on the growing demand for Internet and electronic data transfer services. IXC's revenues stood at $420 million, double that of the previous year, and the company had over 100 long distance resellers as customers.

Industry Milestones and Influential People

By April 1998, IXC completed a major industry milestone: the first new coast-to-coast fiber-optic network in the United States in more than a decade, joining Los Angeles with New York City. The company commemorated the lighting of the network by hosting a special event from New York City's Waldorf-Astoria Hotel, demonstrating the network's nationwide capabilities as it linked simultaneous events in Austin, Texas, and Los Angeles via videoconference.

IXC also announced a four-year, $156 million agreement with Excel Communications, Inc. to provide private line and switched network services. Excel, a Dallas-based firm with more than 3,000 employees, was the fifth largest long distance carrier in the United States at the time. IXC continued to grow through acquisition, adding several Internet service provider (ISP) companies, including SmartNAP (a web hosting company in Austin, Texas); The Data Place, Inc. (an Internet systems integrater in Newark, Delaware); and ntr.net, of Louisville, Kentucky, which had sophisticated back-office capability, such as online ordering processing and web-enabled billing.

The company's retail arm, comprised of Telecom One and Network Long Distance, was organized as Eclipse Communications, Inc., a wholly owned subsidiary of IXC offering a comprehensive set of communications services to business customers around the United States, including Internet-related data services. By this time, IXC was providing a solid national Internet access service and was meeting the growing demand of its reseller customers for expanded Internet offerings. Through the knowledgeable sales professionals of Eclipse, IXC could provide cost-effective communication services with flexible, customized billing to small and medium businesses. The company's Internet services were headed up by senior vice-president Dominick DeAngelo, previously head of Sprint's Internet division. Bringing DeAngelo on board the executive team, according to some analysts, meant that IXC was serious about providing its resellers the whole range of Internet-related services, including hosting, security packages, and other services. Also joining the IXC executive management team was former AT&T executive David Hughart, who became president of IXC's retail business division. Hughart was put in charge of expanding Eclipse.

By September 1998, total revenues rose 40 percent to $498.8 million. The increase was attributable to increased private line revenues and increased wholesale billable minutes. At the same time, higher net losses reflected $4.5 million in merger-related costs alone, as well as increased headcount.

On November 8, 1998, IXC was selected by Bell Atlantic to help extend the latter's nationwide ATM cell relay service. Being part of IXC's digital fiber network would mean that Bell Atlantic could provide its business customers with cost-effective, high-speed communications beyond its local access borders in the East Coast region.

1999 and Beyond

By December 1998, the company's business included three major services: private line services (long-haul transmission of voice and data over dedicated circuits under the long-term bulk contracts), long distance switched services (billing based on actual minutes of use, including origination and termination fees), and broadband services (Frame Relay, ATM, and IP transport).

During this time, IXC further enhanced its coast-to-coast, next-generation Internet backbone by dividing it among eight regions, containing a central traffic aggregation point (core site). This network, named Gemini2000, would be the first next-generation carrier to support both commercial and research community traffic, plus offer high-speed communications 100 to 1,000 times faster than other ISPs. The Gemini name was chosen because the NASA missions of Gemini 6 and Gemini 7 achieved the first rendezvous in orbit between two spacecraft on December 15, 1965, orbiting the earth in parallel six inches apart. IXC wanted to reflect the duality of diversity and change, critical in a new Internet for the next millennium. By December 31, the company had the New York, Washington D.C., and San Francisco Core Sites online and activated. Other Core Site facilities were planned for Atlanta, Chicago, Dallas and Newark, Delaware and Austin, Texas.

In July 1999, a future-shaping event took place at IXC, when the company agreed to a merger with Cincinnati Bell, one of the country's leading local communications providers. In preparation for big changes at the company, a new IXC management team was brought on board; Scott resigned as chairman of the board and was replaced by Richard Irwin, and Stanley W. Katz replaced James Guthrie as chief financial officer.

The merger with Cincinnati Bell was expected to be completed in the year 2000, barring any complications in obtaining the necessary regulatory approval. Together the two companies hoped to become the next century's most powerful data communications company, with more than one million customers, 5,000 employees in 35 locations, and a communications network of about 13,000 miles, coast to coast, in the United States.

Principal Subsidiaries

Applied Theory (34%); Data Place, Inc.; Eclipse Telecommunications, Inc.; IXC Communications Services, Inc.; Marca-Tel S.A. de C.V. (Mexico; 24.5%); Network Evolutions, Inc.; ntr.net Corporation; PSINet, Inc. (16.3%); Storm Communications Ltd. (Europe; 40%); Telecom One, Inc.; UniDial Direct (20%).

Further Reading

Biagi, Susan, "A Trio of Acquisitions," *Telephony,* June 29, 1998.

Carter, Wayne, "IXC Pares Network Cost," *Telephony,* June 30, 1997, p. 78.

——, "Telco Trade Fiber Routes; IXC/Metromedia Deal to Boost Both Networks," *Telephony,* March 9, 1998, p. 8.

"IXC and Excel Sign $156 Million Network Services Agreement," *Business Wire,* April 17, 1998.

"IXC and UniDial Communications Join Forces to Build a Direct Sales Force," *Business Wire,* January 24, 1998.

"IXC Company Overview," Austin, Texas: IXC Communications, Inc., 1997, 2 p.

"IXC Expands IP and Internet Service Offerings through Acquisition of Network Evolutions, Inc." *Business Wire,* April 8, 1998, p. 1.

"IXC Fiber-Optic Network Pact," *Wall Street Journal,* December 21, 1998, p. B10.

"IXC Names Former AT&T Executive Hughart to Lead Rapidly Expanding Retail Business," *Business Wire,* July 14, 1998.

"IXC Sells Preferred Stock," *Wall Street Journal,* April 2, 1997, p. B7.

"IXC Signs $12 Million Agreement with Adelphia and Hyperion, *Business Wire,* October 14, 1998, p. 1.

Jaynes, Daryl, "Dispute May be Settled with Stock Acquisition," *Austin Business Journal,* December 18–24, 1998, p. 6.

Ladendorf, Kirk, "Communications Transmission Losses Mount," *Austin American-Statesman,* April 19, 1990, p. F2.

——, "CTI Believes It Will Emerge from Default," *Austin American-Statesman,* April 5, 1990, p. F1.

——, "IXC of Texas Adds Companies to Bolster Internet-Related Sales," *Austin American-Statesman,* June 24, 1998, p. 1.

Meyers, Jason, "Wireless-to-Wireline Migration: PrimeCo CEO Ben Scott Heads to Fiber Network Reseller," *Telephony,* October 6, 1997, p. 16.

"PSI Net Shareholders Are Set to Approve Agreement With IXC," *Wall Street Journal,* January 23, 1998, p. B16.

"Williams Cos.' Vyxx Unit Will Swap Network Access," *Wall Street Journal,* January 10, 1997, p. B4.

"Williams, IXC in Joint Project," *Wall Street Journal,* October 13, 1998, p. C15.

—Kim L. Messeri

Jefferson-Pilot Corporation

100 North Greene Street
P.O. Box 21008
Greensboro, North Carolina 27420
U.S.A.
(336) 691-3000
Fax: (336) 691-3938

Public Company
Incorporated: 1907 as Jefferson Standard Life Insurance
Employees: 2,200
Sales: $2.6 billion
Stock Exchanges: New York Midwest Pacific
Ticker Symbol: JP
NAIC: 524113 Direct Life Insurance Carriers; 524114
Direct Health & Medical Insurance Carriers; 524126
Direct Property & Casualty Insurance Carriers;
513112 Radio Stations; 51312 Television
Broadcasting

Jefferson-Pilot Corporation is a major U.S. provider of life insurance, annuities, pension plans, and mutual funds for individuals and groups. The company also sells commercial casualty and title insurance and invests in various broadcasting ventures. Active primarily in the southern and southwestern United States, Jefferson-Pilot possesses a rich history characterized by shrewd, conservative growth.

In the Beginning: Jefferson Standard Life

Jefferson Standard Life Insurance was founded on August 7, 1907, in Raleigh, North Carolina. Although it set up operations in a relatively modest second-story office in the state's capital city, Jefferson Standard began with half a million dollars in capital. In fact, it was heralded as the largest corporation ever to have been established in North Carolina. The company was patriotically named after Thomas Jefferson, the third U.S. president and the framer of the Declaration of Independence. "A Jefferson Standard Policy is a Declaration of Independence for the Family," was Jefferson Standard's official slogan.

Jefferson Standard enjoyed immediate acceptance by the local community. Only 111 life insurance companies existed in the entire country when it opened its doors (compared to about 2,000 in the early 1990s), and people were eager to take advantage of the promise of security proffered by the fledgling insurance industry. After only five months of operation, Jefferson Standard had about $1 million of insurance in force and was finding strong demand in other parts of North Carolina and even outside of the state.

Jefferson Standard's quick start was orchestrated by brothers P. D. and Charles W. Gold, members of a prominent newspaper family from Wilson, North Carolina. The Golds had inherited an entrepreneurial bent from their father and had access to a pool of capital to back their ideas. In addition to their desire to create a new enterprise, the Golds were driven by another force. The Civil War had ended and Reconstruction was ongoing; the Golds wanted to make their contribution to the New South. Recognizing that large financial institutions, including insurance companies, in the North were draining vital development capital from the South, the Golds wanted to form an institution that could fund local industrial growth.

The Golds and 22 like-minded associates began Jefferson Standard with the intent of developing it into a regional insurance powerhouse. Charles Gold's daughter came up with the name of the company, and P. D. Gold crafted a logo that would serve the organization for decades to come. However, these developments were incidental to the primary mission of Jefferson Standard's founders—to create a regional insurance company, operated with uncompromising ethics, that could withstand national fiscal upheavals and enhance the economic stability of North Carolina. Evidencing this goal and foreshadowing the philosophy that would dominate Jefferson Standard's future was this quote from the board minutes of 1910: "The future . . . is fraught with difficulties. The way to profit is long, the task is arduous, and the cost is great."

The Julian Price Years: 1912–46

Eager to expand its reach and increase its capital strength, Jefferson Standard completed mergers with two other companies in 1912. It absorbed Security Life and Annuity Company

---

Company Perspectives:

Jefferson-Pilot's business strategy is to achieve nationwide growth through aggressive market penetration, partnering with independent agents, and effective consolidation of acquisitions. From a base as a strong regional life insurer, Jefferson-Pilot has grown into a major national presence in personal financial services.

---

and Greensboro Life Insurance Company, subsequently transferring its headquarters to Greensboro. The year 1912 also marked the beginning of an era of expanding prosperity for Jefferson Standard under the direction of Julian Price, who had worked for Greensboro Life before the merger. Although he was not named president of Jefferson Standard until 1919, when the last of the aging Gold brothers stepped down, Price played a pivotal role in the company's progression throughout the 1910s and until his death in 1946.

The 1912 mergers brought Jefferson Standard's total base of assets to a stunning $3.6 million and its total insurance in force to more than $37 million. Having established a firm footing and acquired a sizable sales force, the company stepped up its marketing efforts and worked at creating a more sophisticated investment program for its flourishing reserve of capital. In fact, the company realized stunning growth after the mergers, swelling its assets to almost $10 million by 1919 and boosting total insurance sales to more than $81 million. "The record is a success unparalleled in the history of southern life insurance companies, and one beyond our most sanguine expectations," reported the board of directors during that period.

Much of Jefferson's success in its early years stemmed from the devotion and persistence of its sales force. It was that group that actually went out to the farms and met with small-town business owners to educate them about the concept of life insurance and to sell them on the Jefferson Standard name. The agents often were not paid in cash, having to barter for their commissions instead. According to company annals, one salesman, after being paid with a bull yearling, fattened up his commission and sold the bull for twice its value the following year.

By the late 1910s, Price was pushing hard for faster growth—and he got it. Notwithstanding setbacks experienced during World War I, Jefferson Standard realized its greatest year ever in 1918, when it boosted sales more than 50 percent and extended its operations into a total of 14 southern states. The following year Price replaced George A. Grimsley as president of the company, gaining unfettered command of the organization. He quickly set Jefferson Standard on a course of expansion that would make it a national leader in the insurance industry and would make him one of the most respected CEOs in the United States. Noted as an articulate man of vision, Price combined top-notch skills in sales and finance with the deep sense of ethics originally prescribed by the company's founders.

Jefferson Standard, under Price, was still dedicated to its goal of building the South. It sought an aggressive lending strategy throughout the region, providing much-needed capital to farmers and industrialists. It also extended its sales activities throughout the Midwest and West during the 1920s in an effort to boost its reserves and generate new capital for regional investments. The company even authored a widely distributed book entitled *A Pattern for Southern Progress*. At one point Price, as part of a marketing effort, Price had an artist superimpose a rendering of a cow on a U.S. map; the cow was being fed in the South and milked in the North, signifying the loss of southern capital to northern financial institutions.

As if to stake its claim on the future of the life insurance industry, Jefferson Standard erected a 17-story "skyscraper" in the early 1920s. Although the project was considered bold and nervy, particularly in a town of only 19,000 people, the marble-laden complex was completed in 1923 and was completely paid for before its doors were opened. When the company moved into its new headquarters it boasted a record $200 million worth of insurance policies in force. Before the Great Depression hit, moreover, the company had boosted that figure to a striking $300 million and was unfurling a national sales force at a rate that awed many of its competitors.

Jefferson Standard was battered during the Depression. Many of its debtors defaulted, and its investments and sales soured. Nevertheless, it did emerge relatively unscathed in comparison to most of its industry counterparts, the result of its conservative fiscal strategy and the determination of its managers. Price, in particular, was credited with guiding the company through that trying era. Although some people, including some coworkers, castigated Price's cantankerous and outspoken personality, his assertiveness and grit helped the company weather financial adversity and stay its course through the 1930s and even through World War II.

Moreover, Price relished his reputation as a polite, though scrappy, man of principle and vision. He was admired and respected within his family, community, and industry. Shortly before his death in a car accident in 1946, the Greensboro newspaper, *The Democrat*, devoted almost an entire issue to Price. The paper offered some ideology and homespun common sense espoused by Price and also gave some insight into his unconventional character. For example, Price reportedly didn't own a home until he was 60 years old, choosing instead to rent: "Fools build houses. Wise men live in them," he believed. Other bits of Price wisdom were recorded for posterity: "Stay out of debt. If you don't owe any money, you're able to look a man in the eye and tell him to go to Hell," and "I like a fellow with his shoulders back and his head up. A fellow who looks like he is going somewhere, even if he isn't."

Steady, Quiet Growth: 1946–67

Price was succeeded as president of Jefferson Standard by his son, Ralph Clay Price, in 1946. However, Ralph Clay Price served for only four years before the board of directors essentially forced him out of his leadership role and selected Howard Holderness as president. Holderness had been with Jefferson Standard since the mid-1920s, first working there during the summers and then assuming a full-time job in 1925. His qualifications were impeccable. His father had helped found the company before sending his son to earn his Masters in Business Administration at Harvard. Holderness left Jefferson in 1945 and formed his own successful company before returning as president of Jefferson Standard.

Holderness was the antithesis of Julian Price. A soft-spoken, easy-going man, Holderness never gave direct orders and prided himself on not interfering with his fellow managers' duties. Although his style was different, the results were just as successful. One year after taking the helm at Jefferson, Holderness announced that the company had achieved $1 billion worth of life insurance in force. From there, the company embarked on a journey of steady and rapid expansion that propelled it to the forefront of the insurance industry.

By its 50th anniversary, Jefferson Standard had achieved total insurance in force of $1.5 billion. Just a few years later, in 1960, that figure had risen to $2 billion. In 1967, the same year in which Holderness retired as president, Jefferson Standard reached a record $3 billion of insurance in force and was approaching $1 billion in assets. By the late 1960s, in fact, Jefferson was providing insurance services to more than one million U.S. policyholders in 32 states, the District of Columbia, and Puerto Rico. Furthermore, the company had managed to retain its prized reputation as a fiscally sound enterprise, garnering the admiration of life insurance industry leaders nationwide.

Although Jefferson Standard was known to the general public as a life insurance company as it entered the 1970s, it was also active in several media ventures. Its interest in newspapers and broadcast companies could be traced back to the Gold and Price families, both of which owned newspapers at the time that the company was founded. Price, having become fascinated with newspapers, had authorized a sizable loan to a local Greensboro newspaper in 1923. Recognizing the lack of capital available to aspiring newspaper publishers, Price advanced money to several start-up newspapers that went on to become major publications during the mid-1900s. Jefferson Standard also purchased an interest in several radio stations and studios. The media division operated under a philosophy of ''showmanship and citizenship'' congruent with the purpose of the overall organization. Although the company continued to focus on insurance, its media holdings were a profitable arm of its operations in the mid-1900s and particularly into the 1980s and early 1990s.

Faster Growth, Greater Diversification: 1967–92

W. Roger Soles took the reins from Holderness in 1967 after 20 years of service to the company. Like Holderness, Soles was known as a soft-spoken, intuitive man with a knack for finance. However, he also possessed the visionary traits that had made Price so successful as the company's leader. The 46-year-old Soles displayed his intent to achieve a new vision for Jefferson Standard immediately after assuming leadership. To take advantage of tax laws and changing financial markets, Soles reorganized the organization into a holding company, under the name Jefferson-Pilot Corporation, to reflect the integration of a major subsidiary, Pilot Life. Soles believed that the holding company structure would allow Jefferson-Pilot to achieve faster growth and greater diversification in evolving U.S. financial markets.

Soles was correct. Under his leadership, Jefferson-Pilot experienced two decades of expansion unparalleled in its history.

Soles brought a new emphasis on marketing to the organization and carried Jefferson-Pilot into the computer age by implementing vast automated systems. He also became a leader in the insurance industry, serving as the first chairman of the American Council of Life Insurers (ACLI), considered the highest management office in the industry. Jefferson-Pilot entered a variety of new business and consumer markets during the 1970s, including tax sheltered annuities, retirement and pension programs, and numerous investment and financial planning services. The company also restructured its sales force and developed new pay incentives for its agents.

By 1976, Jefferson-Pilot had more than $5 billion of insurance in force, reflecting rapid growth since Soles' selection as president. The company continued to expand in the late 1970s, boosting its insurance in force to $6 billion by 1978. Sales growth was augmented by increased investments in media ventures; Jefferson-Pilot began to actually acquire newspaper and broadcasting companies, rather than investing as a sideline. Despite its rampant increase in insurance and media revenues, however, Jefferson-Pilot's profit opportunities were diminished by widespread trends that were affecting the entire U.S. insurance industry. Specifically, rising interest rates and inflation in the late 1970s, combined with growing state and federal tax and regulatory pressures, crimped industry earnings.

While the overall life insurance industry suffered a general downturn during the late 1970s and early 1980s, Jefferson-Pilot sustained moderate growth and remained financially healthy in comparison to most of its competitors. During the 1980s, the company's operations continued to grow at a steady rate, though its growth lagged that of many of its life insurance company peers. Indeed, many insurers were able to reap huge investment gains during the 1980s by placing their reserves in real estate, junk bonds, and other high-risk vehicles that paid fantastic returns. Jefferson-Pilot, in contrast, maintained its staid, conservative strategy of investing in low-risk, long-term, wealth-building instruments.

By 1989, Jefferson-Pilot had increased its life insurance in force to $37 billion, more than six times the amount of in-force insurance just ten years earlier. Although this growth belied the lack of a corresponding rise in profits from life insurance sales, Jefferson-Pilot was able to bolster its bottom line during the decade by expanding into an array of complementary markets. While it earned about $109 million in net income during 1989 from life insurance, for example, it captured an additional $28 million from its casualty and title insurance activities, communications subsidiaries, and miscellaneous investment gains.

More important than Jefferson-Pilot's steady revenue and profit gains during the 1980s was its successful strategy of conservatively investing its reserves. By the early 1990s, the company's balance sheet contrasted sharply to the sea of red ink that swamped many of its competitors. Indeed, as new tax laws and an economic recession battered financial markets during the late 1980s and early 1990s, many insurers were teetering on the edge of bankruptcy or were, in fact, insolvent. ''Jefferson-Pilot's got one of the best balance sheets in the business,'' said Myron Picoult, industry analyst, in the August 1992 issue of *Business-North Carolina,* adding ''What they did was absolutely correct in terms of maintaining the integrity of their balance sheet, given the environment of the 1980s.''

Despite Soles' success at keeping the company focused on long-term growth during the 1980s, he came under attack in the early 1990s from Louise Price Parsons, the daughter of Ralph Clay Price and a major shareholder in the company. Parsons and her husband petitioned the board to remove Soles as president of the company, citing, among other things, the company's slow profit growth in comparison to a few more successful insurers in the region.

While the Parsons did not succeed in their two-year effort to remove Soles, they were able to reach a settlement with the company that mandated that the board implement certain corporate governance principles. During his last two years as president, Soles oversaw healthy income and profit gains; revenues rose to $1.20 billion in 1992 as net income rose an impressive 48 percent in three years to $195 million. In early 1993, Soles retired at the age of 71 and was followed by several other senior managers who had reached retirement age.

1990s and Beyond: Becoming a National Force

Soles was replaced in 1993 by David A. Stonecipher, who came from the Life Insurance Company of Georgia. The aggressive Stonecipher set about transforming Jefferson-Pilot from a respected, regionally known company to a nationally recognized insurance power. Whereas Soles had been extremely conservative, amassing enormous cash reserves, Stonecipher proved more of a risk-taker. In 1995, he initiated a rapid-growth phase by purchasing the insurance in force from Kentucky Central Life and Alexander Hamilton Life. Two years later, Stonecipher made an even larger buy when he acquired the life insurance division of Chubb Corporation, which was renamed Jefferson-Pilot Financial Life Insurance Company. Altogether, the three acquisitions cost $1.5 billion.

Despite the large price tags, Stonecipher's spending accomplished what he had set out to do. Jefferson-Pilot rapidly ascended the ranks of life insurance companies, moving from the nation's 65th-largest in 1993 to the nation's 15th-largest in 1997. The company's total assets doubled, jumping to $23 billion, and its life insurance in force soared to $160 billion. The acquisitions also served to increase Jefferson-Pilot's presence throughout the United States. While the company had traditionally sold its products through approximately 1,000 of its own agents, by 1997, more than 17,000 independent agents were offering Jefferson-Pilot insurance in all 50 states.

The Chubb acquisition was important in another way, as well. It enhanced Jefferson-Pilot's already-strong position in the universal life insurance market. Chubb had a variable universal life product, which appealed to a more financially upscale market than Jefferson-Pilot's traditional universal policies. By the end of 1998, Jefferson-Pilot was the nation's third largest provider of universal life insurance policies. Variable policies made up one-third of the company's total life insurance production.

While Stonecipher was making acquisitions that added to the company's core business segments, he was simultaneously shedding those that no longer fit. Jefferson-Pilot Data Services and Jefferson-Pilot Fire & Casualty were both sold in 1995. In 1998, the company announced that it also planned to sell off its group medical insurance business. "In group medical insurance, Jefferson Pilot was a relatively small competitor in a market increasingly dominated by large managed-care companies, and it was a line of business that exposed our earnings to significant potential volatility," Stonecipher wrote in the company's 1998 annual report. He added, "Thus, group medical insurance simply no longer fit our definition of an attractive core business, and exiting it frees substantial capital for investment elsewhere."

Jefferson-Pilot closed out 1998 with record numbers: $2.6 billion in revenues and $418 million in net income. The company's insurance division accounted for approximately 90 percent of its total revenues. The remainder came from its radio and television broadcasting operations and from earnings on investments. With a strong capital position and the aggressive leadership of Stonecipher, Jefferson-Pilot was poised to continue growing in the coming years. The company planned to further expand through acquisitions that offered added distribution potential and products that extended and enhanced the Jefferson-Pilot product line. Growth was also expected in the existing subsidiaries in the form of new product introductions and new, innovative distribution channels.

Principal Subsidiaries

Alexander Hamilton Life Insurance Company of America; Jefferson-Pilot Communications Company; Jefferson-Pilot Financial Insurance Company; Jefferson–Pilot LifeAmerica Insurance Company; Jefferson-Pilot Life Insurance Company; JP Investment Management Company.

Further Reading

Bailey, David, "Where There's a Will, There's a Way: After Inheriting 290,000 Shares of Jefferson Pilot Stock, an Heiress Sets Out to Make Its CEO Play by Her Rules," *Business-North Carolina*, August 1992, Sec. 1, p. 12.

Catanoso, Justin, "Insurer Continues Toward Lofty Goal," *Greensboro News & Record*, February 25, 1997, p. A1.

Coleman, Kathleen, "The Pilot at JP Communications," *Business Journal-Charlotte*, November 13, 1989, Sec. 1, p. 8.

Fox, James F., *75 Years: 1907 to 1982; Jefferson Standard Life Insurance Company*, Greensboro, N.C.: Jefferson-Pilot Corp., 1982.

"Greensboro's Home to Major Insurance Companies," *Greensboro News & Record*, September 16, 1990, p. 40.

"The Jefferson Standard Story," *Jeffersonian*, August 1982, pp. 14–17.

Marshall, Kyle, "JP Reaches Outside for Next CEO," *News & Observer*, August 12, 1992, Bus. Sec.

Still, John T., "Jefferson-Pilot and Parsons Group Settle Litigation," *PR Newswire*, April 5, 1993.

Weidner, David, "Unchartered Waters," *Greensboro News & Record*, March 9, 1997, p. E1.

—Dave Mote
—updated by Shawna Brynildssen

PERSONAL WEIGHT MANAGEMENT

Jenny Craig, Inc.

11355 North Torrey Pines Road
La Jolla, California 92037
U.S.A.
(619) 812-7000
(800) 388-6213
Fax: (619) 812-2700
Web site: http://www.jennycraig.com

Public Company
Incorporated: 1983
Employees: 4,100
Sales: $352.24 million (1998)
Stock Exchanges: New York
Ticker Symbol: JC
NAIC: 812191 Diet & Weight Reducing Centers; 311999
   All Other Miscellaneous Food Manufacturing

Through its chain of weight management centers, Jenny Craig, Inc. markets a meal plan, based on the purchase of its own prepared foods, and provides advisory and motivational services to its customers. The chain experienced rapid growth during the 1980s, and in 1998 it was operating 643 company owned and 138 franchised centers in 45 states, as well as in Australia, New Zealand, Canada, and Puerto Rico. However, by the late 1990s, the company was also showing signs of slower sales, reporting a 22 percent decrease in service revenues from U.S. company-owned operations between 1997 and 1998. Moreover, revenues had fallen from $401 million in 1996 to $352 million in 1998. The company was responding to the declines by leveraging the Jenny Craig name: expanding its conventional marketing venues to include e-commerce, and by extending its product line to include cookbooks and exercise equipment.

Company Origins

Co-founder Jenny Craig developed an interest in the fitness industry in the 1960s, through her efforts to lose weight following a pregnancy. She operated a gym in her hometown of New Orleans, before joining the staff at the Body Contour fitness center in 1970. Body Contour was headed by Sid Craig, who maintained a 50 percent interest in the company. Jenny and Sid married in 1979, and together they helped turn the struggling company into a thriving business that was reporting $35 million in sales by 1982.

That year, the Craigs sold Body Contour to a subsidiary of Nutri/System Inc. With the $3.5 million they made from the sale, the Craigs formed Jenny Craig, Inc. in 1983. Initially barred from entering the U.S. diet industry by a noncompetition clause, the company opened its first weight loss center in Australia. By 1985, 69 Jenny Craig Weight Loss Centers were in operation in Australia, and the company became one of the biggest players in that country's diet industry. That year, the Craigs returned to the United States, opening 13 centers in the Los Angeles area, which were soon followed by six additional facilities in Chicago.

U.S. Expansion in the 1980s

By 1987, the company had established 46 centers in the United States and 114 in foreign countries; of these 160 units, 45 were franchised operations. Seeking capital from outside investors, the Craigs considered taking their company public but were discouraged by a weak market for initial public offerings. Instead, Michael Tennenbaum, vice-chairman of investment banking at Bear Stearns Companies, Inc., stepped in. Tennenbaum brought together a group of investors that included his partners at Bear Stearns, the New York Life Insurance Co., and TA Associates, an investment and venture capital firm, among others. Together they invested $50 million in Jenny Craig, and two bank loans contributed another $50 million to the company's recapitalization. The successful expansion left the Craig family with a $108 million dividend.

Marketing was integral to Jenny Craig's success. In the early 1990s, ten percent of sales went into commercial advertising each year, and franchises were required to spend the higher of ten percent of sales or $1,000 a week on advertising for their centers. The company's television campaigns featured celebrities, such as actors Elliot Gould and Susan Ruttan, who had

Company Perspectives:

In response to the needs of today's hectic, fast-paced world, Jenny Craig, Inc. offers a comprehensive weight management program that takes a practical, non-dieting approach to losing weight to help clients develop a healthy relationship with food, build an active lifestyle, and create a more balanced approach to living.

achieved success with the Jenny Craig program. Moreover, ads provided a toll free number which automatically connected callers to the center nearest to them. In 1991, the company also began a direct mail campaign based on its extensive database of two million current and former clients.

The Jenny Craig program was designed by its staff of registered dieticians and psychologists and approved by an advisory board consisting of health and nutrition research experts. The three principal tenets of the program were behavior education, proper nutrition, and exercise. Central to the program was Jenny's Cuisine, portion and calorie controlled foods that participants were required to purchase. Jenny's Cuisine was created by suppliers in compliance with standards set by a board of dieticians; suppliers included Overhill Farms, Magic Pantry Foods, Truitt Bros., Campbell Soup Company, Carnation, and Vitex Foods. The program made available 60 different breakfast, lunch, dinner, dessert, and snack food items, including apple cinnamon oatmeal, teriyaki beef, and chocolate mousse. Menus were updated to include microwaveable entrees and canned foods in 1986. The company's gross revenues from food sales increased from 60 percent in 1986 to 91 percent in 1993.

Another important part of the Jenny Craig program was its twice-weekly meetings. New clients met with a counselor, who would monitor their progress and sell them installments of Jenny's Cuisine. At subsequent group meetings, participants attended classes covering such subjects as "dining out," "asserting yourself," and "dieting as a team." In 1989, video cassette programs were introduced into counseling classes to ensure consistency at all centers. After viewing video cassettes, participants engaged in discussion facilitated by their counselor.

A Public Offering and a Challenging Marketplace

In 1991, under improved market conditions, Jenny Craig was taken public, issuing 3.5 million shares at $21 per share. The offering generated $73.5 million in capital, which was used to satisfy the company's bank loans and its debt to the investment group. During this time, the Craigs sold another 1.65 million of their own shares for $36 million, and the banks and investors garnered $11.5 million for the 550,000 shares they sold. As a result, the Craigs retained 59 percent of the company, while banks and investors controlled 20 percent and the public claimed 29 percent.

Sid Craig's expectations for company revenues to grow by 15 to 20 percent a year through expansion proved unrealistic. After a period of remarkable growth in the weight loss industry

as a whole during the 1980s, public attention focused on the potential health risks involved in dieting during the early 1990s, and enrollment at diet centers dropped. In 1990, Jenny Craig and its rival Nutri/System Inc. were named as defendants in a class action lawsuit alleging that weight loss programs, like those promoted by the companies, had resulted in cases of gallbladder disease. Moreover, Jenny Craig was named in 11 other personal injury cases during this time. The disputes were settled, and the alleged link between gallbladder problems and the Jenny Craig program was never proven. However, the cases prompted a Federal Trade Commission investigation into the validity of the claims for successful weight loss made by Jenny Craig and other companies in the diet industry.

The company soon terminated its operations in the United Kingdom, due to their lack of profitability, and, in 1992, a secondary offering of public stock was postponed indefinitely, due to weak market conditions and a decline in profits linked to a failed promotional campaign. Nevertheless, Jenny Craig continued the expansion of its diet center chain, opening 89 new centers and repurchasing 41 franchises.

During 1993, the ongoing FTC investigations into the advertising and promotional practices of the diet industry generated more negative publicity. Specifically, the FTC questioned whether advertising was leading consumers to mistakenly believe that maintaining weight loss after finishing the diet program would be easy. Moreover, medical journals and newspapers reported that "yo-yo dieting"—the repeated gain and loss of weight—caused more health problems than simply remaining slightly overweight.

Jenny Craig and four other major commercial weight loss companies—Weight Watchers, Nutri/System, Diet Center, and Physician's Weight Loss Center—petitioned for standard advertising rules for the industry, but the petition was rejected.

When Nutri/System reported severe financial setbacks in April 1993 and was forced to close its headquarters and 283 of its centers, Jenny Craig immediately began an advertising campaign offering Nutri/System clients the opportunity to continue their weight loss programs at Jenny Craig at no additional service fee. In its open letter to Nutri/System clients, Jenny Craig emphasized its financial strength as a "debt-free, $500 million New York Stock Exchange Company with ten years of proven success." However, neither Jenny Craig nor Weight Watchers International, which had launched a similar campaign, saw a significant increase in enrollments.

Increased competition in the industry, largely by "do-it-yourself" diet companies, also began to cut into Jenny Craig's market by emphasizing the high costs of membership in diet center programs. Typical Jenny Craig clients—women wanting to lose 30 or more pounds—could spend over $1,000 as clients of Jenny Craig, paying an initial start-up fee and about $70 a week for meals. Other companies, such as Just Help Yourself, began offering self-administered diet plans, marketing themselves as cheaper, more convenient alternatives to diet centers.

Despite the shrinking market, the Craigs continued to expand. In 1993, Jenny Craig added 100 new centers and bought back 48 franchises, bringing its total outlets to 794. The company also introduced a program for those living in areas beyond the reach of its centers, allowing customers to order products by telephone and receive direct shipments.

Some shareholders disagreed with the company's expansion policy. Stock purchased at $21 per share in 1991 had sunk below $15 the following year. In October 1993, three shareholders filed a suit against the company, alleging that the expansion was designed to bolster sales figures, overshadowing the company's financial difficulties. While Jenny Craig's total revenues for the year ended June 30, 1993 were $490.5 million, up six percent from 1992, average revenues for each company-owned center had declined ten percent from the previous year. Moreover, although the company's Southern California centers remained profitable, these outlets had experienced a 26 percent decline in revenues.

A Change at the Top in the Mid-1990s

When Ronald E. Gerevas, chief operating officer and president, departed unexpectedly in November 1993, Jenny Craig stock dropped to $11.75 a share. Gerevas' replacement, Albert J. DiMarco, left after just four months; William R. Lewis, a former business associate of DiMarco who had just been appointed chief financial officer the month before, left with DiMarco. By this time, confidence in the company was declining, and its stock was trading at about $6.25 per share, less then one-third of its original price. In April 1994, hoping that new management would help restore investor confidence, the company appointed C. Joseph LaBonté as president and CEO, and Ellen Destray was made chief operating officer. Sid Craig remained as the company's chairperson.

Jenny Craig introduced modifications to its original program in 1994. A wider variety of meetings were offered, and clients were allowed to choose the classes most pertinent to their lifestyle. The company's video programs were also updated and made available for home use. Perhaps most importantly, the program was modified to reflect current trends in popular psychology that suggested that overeating was a result of emotional distress. Accordingly, Jenny Craig encouraged clients to discover, address, and overcome individual emotional issues that might impede the success of their dieting. Nonetheless, the company continued to struggle with declining membership into the late 1990s.

The late 1990s brought new challenges for Jenny Craig, some in the form of litigation against the company both by consumer groups and the U.S. government. In May 1997, as a result of an earlier charge of deceptive advertising against the company, the FTC imposed restrictions requiring Jenny Craig to stipulate in its advertising: ''For many dieters weight loss is temporary.'' Furthermore, testimonials of those who had been very successful under the plan had to be accompanied by a disclaimer: ''This result is not typical. You may be less successful.'' In addition to these provisions, Jenny Craig was also forced to publish the average weight loss its customers experienced and to provide scientific data supporting future claims.

Next, in September 1997 the Federal Food and Drug Administration recalled a popular diet drug composed of either dexfenfluramine (sold as Redux) or fenfluramine and phentermine (fen-phen). Data indicated that fen-phen damaged the heart valves of some people who used the drug. This decision affected Jenny Craig, as the company had begun using physicians outside its organization to write prescriptions for fen-phen and had incorporated the drug into the weight-loss program. Also during this time, the company faced litigation on the part of some former employees in Boston, men who alleged sex discrimination in the workplace.

In February 1999 Jenny Craig joined a coalition of weight-loss organizations in issuing guidelines to give consumers regarding program effectiveness, safety, and costs. This effort, it was hoped, would forestall further efforts at regulating the weight-loss industry. These full disclosure guidelines required weight-loss organizations to give consumers information about the qualifications of their staffs, health risks associated with obesity, health risks of rapid weight loss, and the full costs of their program, including the price of the food.

The weight-loss industry in general and Jenny Craig in particular experienced financial setbacks during this time. Net income between 1994 and 1998 was a roller coaster ride for Jenny Craig, with postings of $36.7 million in 1994, to $11.7 million in 1995, a rebound of $22.9 million in 1996, and a decline to $2.12 million in 1998. The company reported that its membership rate had stalled, and its number of outlets had fallen to 675.

1999 and Beyond

Jenny Craig reacted to uneven profits on several fronts. On December 9, 1998 the company announced the appointment of a new president, Philip Voluck, who would continue to serve as chief operating officer, a position he had gained six months earlier, coming to the company with considerable experience at ex-rival Nutri/System. Founder Jenny Craig continued to serve as vice-chairman of the company, while her husband Sid Craig remained chairman and CEO. In March 1999 the company announced its plans to refocus its mission into one of self-improvement rather than weight-loss. The new program included two new product lines: a new Advanced Nutrients line of food supplements, sold exclusively via the Internet, and a new Jenny Craig line of exercise equipment. At the same time, the company refocused its food program, and the resultant ABC program was simpler to use and gave clients more choices. Subsequent program variations included a less costly plan for clients, under which they were able to purchase supplements rather than meals.

Personal struggles also ensued for Jenny Craig herself as company spokesperson. According to her own account in *People* magazine, in April 1995 Craig awakened one evening, startled by the television, and her sudden movement snapped her lower jaw tight over her upper jaw. The resultant injury to the muscles of her jaws deteriorated her ability to speak. Craig's daughter took over as company spokesperson as Craig sought medical treatment from one expert after another. Finally, three years later, a California surgeon reconstructed her jaw and placed her on a rigorous therapy program. No stranger to rigorous exercise routines, Jenny Craig reported success and hoped she could start the new century with fully restored ability to speak. Similarly, Jenny Craig management hoped that its efforts to refocus the company's mission would help it withstand the uncertainty facing the weight-loss industry.

Principal Subsidiaries

Jenny Craig Weight Loss Centres, Inc.; Jenny Craig International, Inc.; Jenny Craig Australia Holdings, Inc.; Jenny Craig Weight Loss Centres Pty. Ltd. (Australia); Jenny Craig Distributing Pty. Ltd. (Australia); Jenny Craig Management, Inc.; Jenny Craig Operations, Inc.; Jenny Craig Products, Inc. JCCH1, Inc.; JCCH2, Inc.; JCH, Inc.; Jenny Craig Weight Loss Centres (Canada) Company; Jenny Craig (Canada) Holdings, LLC.

Further Reading

Barret, Amy, "How Can Jenny Craig Keep on Gaining?," *Business Week,* April 12, 1993, p. 52.

Berman, Phyllis, "Fat City," *Forbes,* February 17, 1992, pp. 72–73.

Bird, Laura, "Jenny Craig Kicks Off a Database Program," *Adweek's Marketing Week,* January 7, 1991, p. 8.

"Craigs Again Take Control of Jenny Craig," *San Diego Business Journal,* October 13, 1997, p. 47.

Goldman, Kevin, "Ads Dished up for Nutri/System Dieters," *Wall Street Journal,* May 7, 1993, p. B8.

Holden, Benjamin A., "Financial Officer Quits Jenny Craig After Brief Tenure," *Wall Street Journal,* March 10, 1994, p. B10.

Hyten, Todd, "Ex-Jenny Craig Male Workers Allege Discrimination," *Boston Business Journal,* October 14, 1994, p. 5.

Leon, Hortense, "Doctors, Pharmacies Say Fen-Phen Recall No Problem," *South Florida Business Journal,* September 19, 1997, p. 5.

Lippert, Barbara, "Weighty Matters," *Adweek,* January 10, 1994, p. 28.

Melton, Marissa, "Guaranteed: Lose 1 Pound in 90 Days," *U.S. News & World Report,* February, 22, 1999, p. 67.

Pollack, Judann, "Fed Up with Promoting Diets, Weight-Loss Rivals Branch Out," *Advertising Age,* March 29, 1999, pp. 3–4.

Rizzo, Monica, "Painful Silence," *People,* May 3, 1999, pp. 79–81.

Rundle, Rhonda L., "Jenny Craig Inc. Delays Planned Stock Offering," *Wall Street Journal,* May 28, 1992, p. A8.

Saddler, Jeanne, "Three Diet Firms Settle False-Ad Case; Two Others Vow to Fight FTC Charges," *Wall Street Journal,* October 1993, p. B5.

Valeriano, Lourdes Lee, "Diet Programs Hope Broader Services Fatten Profits," *Wall Street Journal,* August 5, 1993, p. B4.

—Elaine Belsito
—updated by Shannon and Terry Hughes

Journal Register Company

50 West State Street
Trenton, New Jersey 08608-1298
U.S.A.
(609) 396-2200
Fax: (609) 396-2292
Web site: http://www.journalregister.com

Public Company
Incorporated: 1990
Employees: 5,500
Sales: $426.8 million (1998)
Stock Exchanges: New York
Ticker Symbol: JRC
NAIC: 51111 Newspaper Publishers; 551112 Offices of
Other Holding Companies

The Journal Register Company (JRC) owns and operates 24 daily newspapers and 185 nondaily publications in seven geographic areas: Connecticut, Philadelphia, Ohio, St. Louis, central New England, and the Capital-Saratoga and Mid-Hudson, New York, regions. Its flagship newspaper is the *New Haven Register,* first published in Connecticut in 1755. Between 1993 and 1998 JRC completed 13 strategic acquisitions that involved 12 daily newspapers, 117 nondaily publications, and three commercial printing companies. The company followed a strategy of increasing the cash flow and profitability of the newspapers it acquired. More than half of the company's daily newspapers have been published for more than 100 years. Its acquisitions were guided by a geographic cluster strategy, which enabled JRC to become the number-one provider of local news and sports and advertising in the majority of markets it served. Geographic clustering was a key element of a strategy that had four major points: to expand advertising revenues and leadership, grow by acquisition, capture synergies from geographic clustering, and implement consistent operating policies and standards in its acquired properties. As a result of the high levels of debt incurred by its predecessor corporation, Ingersoll Publications Co., in the 1980s, approximately three-fourths of the common shares of the JRC are controlled by the investment firm E.M. Warburg, Pincus & Co.

Background and Early History: 1980s

The Journal Register Company was established in 1990 from the remnants of Ralph Ingersoll II's collapsed newspaper empire. During the 1980s Ingersoll had assembled a family of newspapers through his company, Ingersoll Publications Co., using high-risk junk bonds to finance his acquisitions. He overpaid for some papers and amassed a large amount of debt. When the stock market experienced a severe downturn in 1987, the 1980s way of financing acquisitions came to an end. One of Ingersoll's last acquisitions was the historic *New Haven Register* of New Haven, Connecticut, which had been published since 1755.

In July 1990 investment firm E.M. Warburg, Pincus & Co., which was Ingersoll's partner and financier, bought him out of the U.S. newspaper market, with Ingersoll gaining ownership of Warburg, Pincus's European newspaper properties. Robert Jelenic, who was president of the U.S. newspaper companies at Ingersoll Publications, became CEO of the newly incorporated Journal Register Company. After JRC went public in 1997, Warburg, Pincus remained a majority shareholder with a 72 percent ownership interest.

Acquisitions Guided by Geographic Clustering Strategy in the 1990s

When the JRC was formed in 1990, it already owned newspapers in Philadelphia, Ohio, St. Louis, central New England, and the Capital-Saratoga region of New York, in addition to the *New Haven Register.* For the next decade JRC would acquire more publications in those regions as part of its geographic clustering strategy, through which the company hoped to enjoy operating synergies.

In 1993 JRC took over the *Times Herald* of Norristown, Pennsylvania, a western Philadelphia suburb, adding to its stable of four daily and nine weekly newspapers in the Philadelphia region. The *Times Herald* was a historic newspaper that was founded in June 1799 as the *Norristown Gazette.* Six months later it published George Washington's obituary.

The JRC immediately reduced the *Times Herald's* sales and marketing staff by about 25 or 30 people. Responding to charges that the JRC "ran roughshod over the staff," Jelenic said, "In our opinion the *Times Herald* was overstaffed." He asserted that each JRC acquisition is evaluated on a case-by-case basis and that JRC did not have a policy of reducing staff in every case. In any event, the Philadelphia Newspaper Guild staged a one-day strike in September 1993 to protest cuts in jobs, benefits, and pay that were imposed by the JRC. Although its acquisition agreement did not require it to do so, the JRC agreed to negotiate with the union.

Additional newspapers were acquired in Connecticut in 1993 and 1994, including the dailies *Torrington Register Citizen* and the *Bristol Press,* along with *Thomaston Express.* For 1994 JRC reported net income of $20.7 million on combined revenues of $300.2 million. For the next five years the company's revenues and net income would grow steadily, except for 1997 when it incurred a one-time charge related to its initial public offering (IPO), which reduced net income from the previous year.

JRC's largest acquisition in 1995 involved 42 nondaily publications in Connecticut and Rhode Island and one commercial printing plant in Connecticut, which was acquired from Capital Cities/ABC Inc. for $31 million. JRC also paid $11 million for the *Herald* of New Britain, Connecticut and $5.5 million for the *Middletown (Ct.) Press* in separate transactions. For 1995 JRC reported net income of $26.8 million on combined revenues of $339.0 million. The company's total debt was $689.3 million, compared with $306 million in assets, and interest and other nonoperating expenses were a record $64 million.

In 1996 JRC paid $18 million for the *Taunton (Mass.) Daily Gazette.* By the end of 1996 JRC's debt level was still at $655 million. Revenues were up to $351 million, and net income rose to $28.1 million.

Initial Public Offering in 1997 Set Stage for Aggressive Acquisitions Program

On May 8, 1997, the company's common stock began trading on the New York Stock Exchange for $14 a share. The IPO raised $130 million, which would be used mainly for acquisitions. Jelenic was quoted as saying, "We went public so we could acquire. That was the main reason." Of the $130 million, about $34.5 million was used to repay obligations to Warburg, Pincus. At the time it went public, JRC owned and operated 18 daily newspapers and 118 nondaily publications in five geographic regions: Connecticut, Ohio, Philadelphia, St. Louis, and central New England.

In December 1997 JRC announced three major acquisitions. It added to its St. Louis cluster with the purchase of the *Ladue News* of Ladue, Missouri, which served the suburbs of St.

Louis. JRC also expanded its presence in Philadelphia by acquiring the Intercounty Newspaper Group for $12.8 million. The acquisition included 17 weekly newspapers published in the Philadelphia, central New Jersey, and south New Jersey regions. Also included in the sale were two printing plants located in State College and Bristol, Pennsylvania. A third acquisition involved HVM LLC of New Milford, Connecticut, for $3.8 million. The acquisition added another eight weekly newspapers, two shoppers, and three monthly magazines.

For 1997 JRC reported combined revenues of $359.4 million. Net income fell to $23.0 million as a result of a one-time pretax charge of $31.9 million related to management bonuses and incentive plans in connection with the IPO. For 1997 Jelenic received $11 million in executive compensation, including a one-time $10.5 million bonus and a salary of $825,000. It was nearly nine times more than the $1.35 million he earned in 1997. In 1996 he received about $1 million in salary and bonus, comparable with salaries of some of the newspaper industry's biggest players.

The Future of Journal Register Company: Will the Size of Acquisitions Keep Growing?

In its biggest acquisition to date, JRC acquired five daily newspapers, including the *Delaware County Daily Times,* and 20 nondaily publications in Pennsylvania, New York, and Ohio for $300 million in cash from the Goodson Newspaper Group of Lawrenceville, New Jersey. The acquisition resulted in JRC having a combined circulation of more than 197,000 daily and 600,000 Sunday publications in suburban Philadelphia.

The price of the acquisition was estimated to be 14 times the newspapers' 1997 cash flow, a substantial premium considering recent newspaper deals were accomplished at ten to 12 times cash flow. Jelenic predicted, however, that the acquisition cost would be less than 11 times 1999 cash flow after the company improved the newspapers' cash flow and cut expenses by integrating them into JRC's clusters.

At the same time JRC started a new geographic cluster around Kingston, New York, with the acquisition of Taconic Media in Dutchess County, New York. Taconic owned seven weeklies with a combined circulation of 321,600 in Dutchess County.

As a result of the Goodson acquisition, combined revenues rose significantly in 1998 to $426.8 million. Net income nearly doubled to $41.1 million, but JRC's debt level rose to $765 million. Operating as a pubic company since 1997, JRC's management and strategy seem firmly in place to guide the company toward future growth and increased profitability, as long as its combined revenues allow it to service its relatively high level of debt.

Principal Operating Units

New Haven Register; The Herald; The Bristol Press; The Register Citizen; The Middletown Press; Daily Times; Daily Local News; The Mercury; The Times Herald; The Phoenix; The Trentonian; The News-Herald; The Morning Journal; The Times Reporter; The Independent; The Telegraph; Ladue

News; The Herald News; Taunton Daily Gazette; The Call; The Times; The Record; The Saratogian; The Oneida Daily Dispatch; Daily Freeman.

Further Reading

Downing, Neil, "Newspaper Company Discloses Financial Data in Advance of Stock Issue," *Knight-Ridder/Tribune Business News,* March 20, 1997.

Garneau, George, "Agreement to Buy: Journal Register Co. Agrees to Buy Connecticut and Rhode Island Newspapers from Capital Cities/ABC," *Editor and Publisher,* March 18, 1995, p. 35.

——, "Takeover Sparks Union Anger," *Editor and Publisher,* October 16, 1993, p. 13.

Gelles, Jeff, "Trenton, N.J.-Based Chain to Buy Two Philadelphia Suburban Dailies," *Knight-Ridder/Tribune Business News,* May 19, 1998.

Giobbe, Dorothy, "Quick Turnaround: Dean Singleton's Abrupt Sale of a Connecticut Daily to Journal Register Co. Was Reportedly Done Against the Wishes of the Family That Sold Him the Newspaper," *Editor and Publisher,* September 30, 1995, p. 9.

"Journal Register Co. Acquires Missouri Newspaper," *Knight-Ridder/Tribune Business News,* December 16, 1997.

"Journal Register Posts Net Gain," *Editor and Publisher,* February 13, 1999, p. 53.

Kasrel, Deni, "Journal Register Expands Area Newspaper Holdings," *Philadelphia Business Journal,* December 12, 1997, p. 3.

"More Strong Postings," *Editor and Publisher,* May 1, 1999, p. 16.

Neuwirth, Robert, "Goodson Liquidates as Buyers Cluster," *Editor and Publisher,* May 23, 1998, p. 11.

——, "Merger Mania Hits Garden State," *Editor and Publisher,* November 29, 1997, p. 9.

"New Haven Register Launches Audiotex Service," *Editor and Publisher,* April 29, 1995, p. 45.

"New Jersey-Based Journal Register Co. Plans IPO," *Knight-Ridder/Tribune Business News,* March 19, 1997.

Perrucci, Dori, "Journal Register Acquires Newspapers in 4 States," *Mediaweek,* May 25, 1998, p. 6.

Sullivan, John, "From Rags to Riches," *Editor and Publisher,* August 30, 1997, p. 12.

"Trenton, N.J.-Based Journal Register Co. Executives Receive Big Bonuses," *Knight-Ridder/Tribune Business News,* April 1, 1998.

—David Bianco

Kia Motors Corporation

15-21 Yoido-dong
Youngdeungpo-ku
Seoul 150-706
South Korea
82 2 7881114
Fax: 2 7840746
Web site: http://www.kia.co.kr

51% Owned by Hyundai Group
Founded: 1944
Employees: 18,098
Sales: $3.9 billion (1997)
NAIC: 336111 Automobile Manufacturing

Until its merger with Hyundai in 1998, Kia Motors Corporation was the second largest manufacturer of automobiles and trucks in South Korea. In addition to the core Korea market, Kia exports vehicles to Europe, North America, and several Asian countries. The company started out as one of Korea's giant *chaebols* (groups of companies), but was operating as an independent, publicly traded company in the early 1990s. It entered the world's largest potential market, the United States, in 1992 with the formation of subsidiary Kia Motors America. However, the Asian financial crisis forced Kia into receivership, until Hyundai bailed it out in 1998, obtaining 51 percent share of ownership.

Origins in the Politics of South Korea

Kia (Korean for "arise from Asia") was formed in 1944, shortly before North Korea invaded the South. The company would eventually succeed, first as a diversified manufacturer of bicycles and industrial products, and later as a manufacturer of trucks and automobiles. However, during the late 1940s and 1950s commercial expansion was effectively thwarted by the Korean War. By the end of the war in 1953, in fact, South Korea's industrial base lay in ruins. Throughout the 1950s and early 1960s, Korea's recovery was slow. The Rhee (Rhee Syngman) government resorted to favoritism and corruption to maintain power and became increasingly authoritative. Student revolts in the 1960s forced Rhee Syngman into exile, and the ruling party that finally emerged from the ensuing political fray was headed by military leader Park Chung-hee.

Park ruled Korea in characteristic military style. His regime during the 1960s and 1970s was marked by increasing centralization of power, both political and industrial. Importantly, though, his government was obsessed with economic growth and development. So while Park was widely criticized for his authoritarian style, his government is credited with laying the foundation for South Korea's economic renaissance. Between 1960 and 1980, in fact, South Korea's annual exports surged from a negligible $33 million to more than $17 billion.

Kia Motors benefitted from the economic revolution, growing from a small bicycle manufacturer to a global supplier of automobiles. Kia started out producing steel tubing and bicycle parts before building its own line of bicycles in the 1950s. It eventually parlayed that know-how into its own line of motorcycles, and later turned to truck production.

A key dynamic influencing Kia's (and South Korea's) gains during the 1960s and 1970s was the *chaebol* (a business group consisting of large companies that are owned or managed by relatives of one or two "royal" families). Park decided that the best way to develop South Korea's economy was to identify key industries and then select specific companies to serve those sectors. The government would work with the companies, providing protection and financial assistance as part of a series of five-year national economic growth plans. By concentrating power in the hands of a few giant, family-held companies, Park reasoned, impediments to success would be minimized and cost-efficiencies would result. The Kia *chaebol* was selected by Park to concentrate on trucks and various industrial goods such as machine tools. The company sold its first truck in 1962.

Kia grew quickly during the 1960s and 1970s through a combination of hard work and government assistance. Between 1962 and 1966, during the first of Park's five-year plans for the Korean vehicle industry, Kia acted much like an import processor. The company imported many of the parts used to build its trucks from foreign producers and assembled them locally. Kia was protected by the Motor Vehicle Industry Protection Law of 1962, which forbade the importation of already-assembled vehicles or major components. During Park's second phase (1967 to 1971), Kia increasingly developed its own parts using knowledge it gained from its outside suppliers. During the 1970s, Kia gradually weaned itself from extreme dependence on imports and started to develop proprietary technology that would eventually allow it to compete as an exporter of completed vehicles.

Becoming an Auto Maker in the 1970s

In accordance with Park's "Long-Term Plan for Motor Vehicle Industry Promotion" of 1973, Kia began manufacturing automobiles in 1974. Although that move represented new territory for the truck and tool manufacturer, another South Korean company—Hyundai—had preceded Kia's entry into the truck industry by about 15 years. In addition, Hyundai pioneered Korea's car industry with production of the Pony, Korea's first completely domestic passenger car, in 1968. Hyundai led Kia in automobile production throughout the 1970s and into the mid-1990s. However, the two companies did not directly compete in their home country because the government set car prices according to engine size. Kia's domestic car and truck business proved successful and allowed Kia to become the second largest domestic vehicle manufacturer and the tenth largest *chaebol* in the country by the 1980s. Hyundai was ranked second, and its giant Hyundai Motors division eventually became one of the 200 largest companies in the world.

Despite Korea's economic gains, Park's government had many enemies, and Park was assassinated in 1979. His successor, Chun Doo Hwan, was also a military leader. His economic goals were similar to those articulated by Park, and he sustained Park's basic long-term economic plan. For the 1980s, that scheme entailed Korea's transformation into an exporting, rather than importing, nation. To that end, Chun's government continued to support *chaebols* like Hyundai and Kia while blocking foreign competitors from entering the South Korean market on a significant scale.

In 1981 the Chun government decided that South Korea's automobile industry was growing too quickly. It chose to limit the number of domestic vehicle producers to the five in operation at that time, and to freeze the particular areas of production. Thus only three companies, including Kia, were allowed to

manufacture cars, and only Kia was allowed to build lightweight trucks.

Overseas Expansion in the 1980s

Chun's overall economic strategy was generally successful, despite citizens' growing displeasure with South Korea's authoritative, centralized political and economic structure. While Kia enjoyed a relative dearth of competition in its core domestic market, it also launched an aggressive and successful export campaign during the 1980s that penetrated Japan and Europe, among other regions. By the mid-1980s Kia was selling about 300,000 cars annually, still mostly in South Korea. A major breakthrough for Kia occurred in 1987, however, when it started shipping automobiles to the largest single international car market, the United States. Kia reached an agreement to supply Ford with its Festiva model. The Festiva was a "microcar" aimed at the low-end buyer. Kia planned to ship about 70,000 units annually for Ford and a like number of the cars to other countries. Kia's sales topped US $2.4 billion in 1987 as its work force swelled to about 23,500.

Kia's arrangement with Ford reflected its strategy, first evident in the mid-1980s, to gradually assume Japan's role as the leading supplier of low-end economy cars. By the mid-1980s, in fact, it was clear to Kia executives that Japan was reducing its emphasis on low-priced cars and focusing on higher-priced, high-profit vehicles. Rival Hyundai had also observed the trend, as evidenced by its 1986 jump into the North American car market. Kia planned to use its low-cost production advantages to fill the void. Kia's greatest edge in comparison to U.S., European, and Japanese automakers was labor. Indeed, until the late 1980s Kia paid its workers a mere fraction of what their foreign counterparts earned. The savings were mirrored in cars like the Festiva, which enjoyed steady demand as a result of their extremely low prices. Over a period of about five years, Kia shipped 350,000 Festivas to Ford.

In addition to its low labor costs, Kia continued to benefit throughout the 1980s from rigid trade barriers imposed by its home country. Overseas producers had previously paid little attention to the restrictions because of the comparatively small size of the Korean market. By the late 1980s, however, foreign governments were pressuring South Korea to open its markets. The inequity was undeniable. In 1988, for instance, a total of 305 foreign cars were sold in South Korea. During the same year the country exported more than half a million automobiles, most of which were made by Hyundai and Kia. The government lifted some barriers in 1988 and 1989, but imposed less obvious restrictions. Nevertheless, foreign producers made inroads in the South Korean market during the early 1990s.

Labor Problems and the End of Chaebols in the 1990s

Besides proliferating domestic competition, Kia also suffered during the late 1980s and early 1990s from labor problems. Fed up with low pay and poor working conditions, South Korea's workers rebelled during the period. Union strikes forced many companies, including Kia, to significantly raise wages. The labor uprising was actually just one part of a much larger movement begun in the 1980s to dismantle South Korea's political and economic framework. Since the mid-1980s, in particular, the government had been working to decentralize. A corollary of that effort was the diminished dominance of the *chaebols*. In the late 1980s the Chun government was voted out and replaced by a more liberal administration. Privatization and increased competition ensued. By the early 1990s Kia jettisoned its own *chaebol* structure and became an independent, publicly traded company, although it continued to benefit from government ties and protected domestic markets.

Following a string of setbacks in the late 1980s and early 1990s, Kia experienced some major breakthroughs. One development was its 1992 introduction of the Sephia, a compact four-door sedan, to the domestic market. The car quickly became the best selling automobile in South Korea. The success of the car was a great relief to Kia, which was simultaneously preparing to enter the U.S. market with its own cars and dealers. Partly in preparation for that project, Kia invested heavily during the early 1990s to vastly expand its production capacity. By 1992 its debt load ballooned to more than $2 billion; by 1994 the company's debt had surged to $3.3 billion.

Kia bet heavily on its ability to market its Sephia and another new model, the Sportage, in international markets. The introduction was well-timed because car sales in many regions were booming in 1994. The big draw for Kia products was the low price. Kia claimed that products such as the Sephia were of comparable performance and quality to vehicles offered by other manufacturers, and Kia marketed them at a much lower cost.

By the time Kia entered the United States with its own nameplate in 1993, it was already selling its cars in about 80 foreign countries and building a total of more than 500,000 cars annually. The company hoped to achieve unprecedented global growth during the mid- and late-1990s. Kia increased production capacity from 650,000 in 1993 to 930,000 in 1994 and planned to boost that figure to 1.5 million by 1997. Kia's global strategy was multi-faceted. In addition to European and U.S. operations, for example, it aggressively chased the blooming Chinese market. To that end, Kia opened the Yanbian Industrial Technology Training Institute in China to train expatriates in production techniques. Kia planned to eventually build a network along China's east coast.

Kia's U.S. foray in the mid-1990s was conducted through the newly formed Kia Motors America. Heading that division was automotive industry veteran Gregory Warner. Warner planned to bring Kia into the U.S. market slowly, starting with selected dealerships in California and expanding into 11 western states. His initial goal was to sell 30,000 to 50,000 units annually.

In 1994 Kia's diversified operations generated about $6.8 billion in revenues. Most of that amount was attributable to shipments of automobiles and related parts, although about 16 percent came from truck sales. The revenue figure marked a significant increase over the $4.5 billion reported in 1993 and the $2.5 billion in 1990. Kia's profitability, however, was extremely weak. Net income fluctuated around a paltry $20 million throughout the early 1990s before bobbing up to $27 million in 1994. Kia's stock plummeted that year, and the company defended its stressed balance sheet by emphasizing anticipated profits from its popular new models. Kia entered the mid-1990s as the 20th largest

car maker in the world and the seventh biggest corporation in South Korea. However, by July 1997 the Asian financial crisis would devastate both South Korea and Kia.

The Mid-1990s: Troubled Times

The financial woes of both South Korea and Kia were tied to the still-present *chaebol* structure. These 64 family-controlled organizations had over the years expanded and diversified into many different fields. The expansion and diversification was accompanied by huge debts exhorted from lending institutions afraid to jeopardize the business of these huge companies. Rather than risk family control by allowing outside equity purchases, the *chaebols* secured their loans with their own subsidiaries. These procedures allowed rapid capital expansion but reduced South Korean competitiveness. Most *chaebols* owned companies so diverse and so subject to price swings that usually only one or two subsidiaries were profitable at a given time. Moreover, the country was experiencing problems with labor and productivity. With the introduction of democracy in 1987, wages began a decade long climb of nearly 15 percent per year. At the same time, job security expectations weakened productivity. Even though the South Korea auto industry nearly matched Detroit with plant and production resources per worker, South Korea produced fewer than half the number of cars manufactured in Detroit.

Moreover, even before the Asian financial crisis, South Korean industry had been hurt by falling semiconductor prices and poor exports of chemicals and steel. Once the financial crisis arrived, the network of interdependencies rippled through the South Korean economy, causing large-scale collapse. While Kia's portion of that collapse stemmed in part from the foundering of Kia's steel subsidiary, Kia's fairly stable automobile industry was crippled nonetheless. By July 1997, Kia was $5.7 billion in debt and had experienced negative net income for three years in a row. Total revenues fell from $8 billion to $4 billion, and Kia was up for sale. Although numerous foreign investors considered bids for the company, the *chaebol* system prevailed, as the Hyundai Group purchased 51 percent interest of Kia. That same year Ford Motor Co. divested itself of its 17 percent interest in Kia.

Problems lingered for South Korea and Kia. South Korea's domestic auto market declined by 50 percent and exports were growing by only two percent in 1999. Efforts by the South Korean government to eliminate the *chaebol* structure remained largely ineffective. The government did, however, effectively require more stringent reporting of financial data, outlawed the practice of using subsidiaries for securing loans, and insisted that companies reduce their debt/equity ratio below 200 percent. It also prodded the *chaebols* to sell subsidiaries to foreign investors. Still, the *chaebols* could circumvent most government provisions which were difficult to police. In 1999 South Korean policy still protected redundant labor practices, and the government continued to block the attempts some companies made to downsize.

The Late 1990s and Beyond

In the late 1990s Hyundai and Kia announced an austerity program of selling off subsidiaries, consolidating manufacturing, and reducing the number of models produced. Hyundai announced it would streamline its subsidiaries from 79 to 26 and concentrate instead on five core businesses. Yet, by 1999 Hyundai had actually eliminated only four subsidiaries and had sold eight. Meanwhile, the company had expanded by its purchase of the majority of Kia, as well as acquiring an oil refinery, a computer chip business, and two fund managers. Meanwhile, Kia was strapped by a no-strike, no-lay-offs clause in its labor contract that would require production of 800,000 units per year. Kia sold 460,000 units in 1998.

All was not dire for Hyundai/Kia, though. The combine was working to streamline its operations. New marketing plans called for Kia to focus on the young and stylish consumer, while Hyundai would target an older, more mature consumer. By July 1999 Kia reported rebounding sales with an expected net profit of $655 million by the end of the year. It also reported reducing its debt-equity ratio from 370 percent to 170 percent. In addition, Kia Motors America reported record U.S. sales in 1999 for the Sephia and Sportage models, despite a July 1999 recall of 32,653 Sephia compact sedans to replace ailing emissions systems. In fact, by mid-1999, Kia's auto sales were up 59.3 percent in the United States, and the company planned to enhance its three model lineup (the Sephia, the Sportage five-door, and the Sportage three-door) with at least three new models, including a four-door subcompact, a Sportage with V-6 engine, and a minivan called the Sedona. As Kia closed the century, its future remained unpredictable, though indications of an upswing in the Asian economy were apparent. Certainly, the company hoped Kia would again "rise from Asia" as its Korean name indicates.

Principal Subsidiaries

Kia Motors America.

Further Reading

Burstiner, March, "Kia Drives into Town with Nine Bay Area Dealerships," *San Francisco Business Times,* April 15, 1994, p. 3.

Butler, Steven, "Korean Car Makers May Be Up for Grabs," *U. S. News and World Reports,* May 18, 1998.

Darlin, Damon, "The Keep-it-Simple Strategy," *Forbes,* August 16, 1993, p. 98.

Garrett, Jerry, "Seoul Survivors," *Car and Driver,* August 1999, p. 41.

Harrison, Leah, "Dealers Hope Service, Low Cost Will Drive Kia Sales," *Puget Sound Business Journal,* November 19, 1993, p. 3.

Hart-Landensberg, Martin, *The Rush to Development: Economic Change and Political Struggle in South Korea,* New York: Monthly Review Press, 1993.

"Kia Motors in Positive Mood on Rising Sales," *South China Morning Post* (Web Edition), July 14, 1999, pp. 1–2.

"Kia Recalls 32,653 1996–97 Sephia Sedans," *Rueters,* July 15, 1999.

Luebke, Cathy, and Vince Maietta, "Kia Sephia Isn't Too Good to Be True," *Business Journal,* May 27, 1994, p. 26.

Nakarmi, Laxmi, and Larry Armstrong, "Ford, Toyota, Volkswagen, Fiat, Kia. . . . Kia?," *Business Week,* December 12, 1994, p. 58.

"Nation-Builders," *Economist,* July 10, 1999, pp. 53–58.

Nauman, Matt, "South Korea Import Tries to Crack Compact Car Market," *Knight-Ridder/Tribune Business News,* April 12, 1994.

Onishi, Norimitsu, "Korea's Kia Motors Enters U.S. Market with Sephia," *Knight-Ridder/Tribune Business,* September 22, 1993.

Shin, Yoo Keun, Richard Steer, and Gerardo R. Ungson, *The Chaebol,* New York: Harper & Row, 1989.

Whitehair, John, "Korea's Kia Arrives in Area," *San Bernardino County Sun,* August 6, 1994, p. B8.

—Dave Mote
—updated by Shannon and Terry Hughes

Kreditanstalt für Wiederaufbau

Palmengartenstrasse 5-9
D-60325 Frankfurt am Main
Germany
(49) (69) 74 31-0
Fax: (49) (69) 74 31 29 44
Web site: http://www.kfw.de

Government-Owned Company
Incorporated: 1948
Employees: 1,827
Operating Revenues: DM 315 billion (1998)
NAIC: 52111 Monetary Authorities—Central Bank

The Kreditanstalt für Wiederaufbau (KfW) is a promotional bank serving the German domestic economy, and a development bank for the developing countries. Some 80 percent of its DM 1 billion in equity capital is owned by the German Federal government, and 20 percent by the German Länder (equivalent to U.S. states) governments. On behalf of the Federal Republic of Germany, the KfW finances investments for approximately 1,600 projects to develop social and economic infrastructure, industry, and environmental protection in over 100 countries along with advice. The KfW raises the funds for its programs in the domestic capital market, and—through its wholly-owned subsidiary KfW International Finance Inc. in the United States—in foreign capital markets. Governed by the German Banking Act, loans taken out and bonds and notes issued by KfW, as well as loans to third parties guaranteed by KfW, are considered equivalent to obligations of the Federal Republic of Germany itself. With a 1998 balance-sheet total of DM 315 billion and DM 10.6 billion in capital and reserves, the KfW ranks among Germany's largest banks. Headquartered in Frankfurt am Main, the bank also has a branch office in Berlin.

The KfW's "Investment Finance" program provides purpose-tied, long-term loans that finance projects at favorable fixed interest rates for German small and medium-sized enterprises; the energy, steel, and coal industries; communal infrastructure and housing projects; and in particular for environmental protection and innovation. The "General Export and Project Finance" program provides long-term loans to German firms in manufacturing; raw materials extraction; telecommunications; and the energy sector, for the export of capital goods. "Special Export and Project Finance" is awarded to projects in the shipping, air transport and land-based transport industries, including seaports and airports. The KfW also administers subsidies for ship and aircraft export in the German federal budget. In addition, the KfW helps launch projects at home and abroad in which Germany has considerable interest, primarily in developing and newly industrialized countries as well as in Central and Eastern Europe.

Financing Germany's Reconstruction: 1948–53

As its name Kreditanstalt für Wiederaufbau (reconstruction loan corporation) suggests, the KfW was founded to finance urgent reconstruction projects after World War II. It became well known as the financial institution which allocated Marshall Plan funds in Germany. After World War II had ended, the American and British military governments discussed the possible structure of a new banking and monetary system in Germany. While the Americans preferred the idea of decentralizing the German banking system by creating a "Bank of German States" with central banks on the state level, the British military government insisted on establishing a central financial institution for the German reconstruction.

Finally in the summer of 1947, after almost a year of negotiations, they agreed on a compromise which included the establishment of a central "Loan Corporation" to finance reconstruction projects. In June 1948 all the parties agreed on the main principles for this institution, and the Anglo-American military government assigned the German authorities the task of setting it up. In October 1948, the "KfW Law" was passed by the German Economic Council and went into effect on November 18, 1948. In January 1949—the year in which two separate German states were founded—the KfW started its business operations as a corporation under public law directly answerable to the federal government.

It took the young Federal Republic of Germany, founded in 1949, about five years to rebuild the country after World War II.

Company Perspectives:

As a bank the KfW has a public mission. Although it is not an institution with political responsibilities, its mission is to serve the public interest in the country which it serves through banking means. Its public mandate cannot be rigidly defined for in the course of its fifty-year history the KfW repeatedly had to—and did—adapt rapidly and flexibly to the frequently changing political and economic requirements with an efficient decision-making procedure not subject to a long, bureaucratic chain of command. Again and again its experience and qualifications as a multipurpose institution have enabled it to perform complex and large-scale financing operations in the public interest—as well as customized administrative tasks—efficiently, cost-effectively and discreetly. This achievement has been based on a corporate ethos characterized by close and harmonious cooperation with its partners and a spirit of mutual understanding—understanding on the part of the politicians and ministries for the bank's possibilities and limitations, and understanding on the part of the bank for the needs and constraints of the politicians and ministries.

The German economy grew at about eight percent per year. The KfW contributed to this effort significantly, mainly by channeling funds from the Allied forces into industries that were key in attracting economic growth and by long-term export financing.

KfW's first chairman, Marshall Aid advisor Dr. Otto Schniewind, calculated in 1948 that about DM 8.3 billion was needed to fund urgent reconstruction projects, but finding sources of funding proved extremely difficult. Foreign capital markets were out of reach, the new German Deutschmark had lost 14 percent of its value in only six months, and it was feared that massive government deficit spending would have weakened trust in the new currency. KfW's first attempt, in the fall of 1949, to raise money on the limited German capital market by issuing long-term bonds failed miserably. In the end, the KfW was left with the counterpart funds from the Allies, including GARIOA and the Marshall Fund money. GARIOA counterparts were food and commodity imports financed by the U.S. defense budget before the Marshall Aid program, announced by U.S. secretary of state George C. Marshall in June 1947, was actually carried out. However, those sources were usually connected with far-reaching ideas on the part of the givers about how they were to be used.

In the reconstruction years, the KfW allocated about half of its credit volume directly to companies, while the other half was issued through the borrower's "house bank." Tens of thousands of individual farmers received individual loans as blanket credit lines from two specially designated banks for farmers. However, upon request of the Allies, counterpart funds were granted only by the German federal government, which also evaluated the applicants and even scheduled individual loans.

Between 1949 and 1953, the KfW concentrated on providing financing for sectors crucial to economic reconstruction which needed a large amount of financing and industries with limited access to funds, such as the highly regulated energy and housing sectors. More than half of the KfW's credit volume in those years went into coal mining, power generation, and steel, which helped manage the rising demand for energy and raw material by other industries. A total of DM 1.1 billion was provided mainly for larger manufacturing companies in the chemical, cement, and other raw materials industries and for export-intensive machinery building and mechanical and electrical engineering firms. About DM 286 million went into the ship-building industry. By 1953 the KfW had channeled DM 623 million into residential construction. Another DM 500 million—about 20 percent of KfW's total credit volume in those years—was directed into the farming and food industries. The KfW also transmitted about DM 705 million, raised by the Confederation of German Industry, to help the basic goods sector finance its investment needs in 1951.

Securing Sustainable Growth: 1954–60

By 1954, the KfW had basically fulfilled its mission to allocate financial aid for German reconstruction. However, the German government did not want to dissolve an organization that had gained a great deal of expertise on the support of economic development that was politically desirable. KfW board member Dr. Herbert Martini, who had assisted Schniedewind in carrying out Marshall Aid programs and authored a big part of the KfW Law, showed brilliant strategic foresight and initiative in opening new sources of funding and new tasks for the KfW. He convinced older, skeptical KfW board members as well as politicians in Bonn that the KfW could be developed into a multi-purpose financial institution that acted in the public interest of Germany.

After the London Debt Agreement of February 27, 1953 had established the amount of international debt owed of Germany to the United States, the European Recovery Program (ERP) special fund was set up by the German government. Administered by the former Ministry for the Marshall Plan, which was now called Ministry for Economic Cooperation, the ERP special fund soon became KFW's foremost source of capital, totaling over DM 4.6 billion between 1954 and 1960. Between 1958 and 1960 the KfW also raised almost DM 1 billion by establishing long-term bonds and new medium-term fixed-rate notes shortly called KOs—the abbreviation for "Kassenobligationen"—on the German capital market.

Most of the funds provided through the KfW in the second half of the 1950s were aimed at supporting structurally weak regions such as the Saarland (which joined the Federal Republic after French occupation ended in 1957), the regions bordering East Germany, and isolated West Berlin. Beginning in 1954, the KfW administered the "Berlin Contract Financing" program fueled by the ERP special fund which offered investment loans for West German companies who contracted with suppliers in West Berlin. Beginning in 1960 the KfW offered liquidity assistance to commercial banks in West Berlin. The KfW opened its Berlin office in 1960 to carry out those programs, and by the end of the year the loans issued reached a total of DM 728 million. Almost DM 500 million was earmarked by the KfW for environmental protection projects, primarily sewage disposal and water purification. Another DM 664 million was channeled through the KfW by the European Coal and Steel Community (ECSC) granted to promote the German coal, iron, and steel industries between 1954 and 1960.

Export financing was another important field of activity which the KfW had begun in the early 1950s. At that time, commercial banks only offered short-term loans to German exporters. The federal government ordered the KfW to finance middle- and long-term German export risks—in particular industrial plants and equipment—for up to 24 months. To secure its own share of this risky but potentially promising business, the private banking sector formed the Ausfuhrkredit Aktiengesellschaft (AKA) in spring 1952. The AKA took over the DM 600 million rediscount facility, 14 specialists, and all the contracts previously managed by the KfW. However, it soon became clear that the AKA was refusing to back exports to politically unstable countries such as Turkey and Yugoslavia, and was not interested in financing export risks for more than four years. Realizing the need for longer-term export financing, the KfW offered AKA-follow-up loans with practically no risk to exporters. The so-called Hermes credit programs were backed financially by the German government and managed by the Hermes Kreditversicherungs AG, one of the world's leading Export Credit Agencies. In the following years, the KfW was able to raise significant funds for export financing to developing countries, mainly from public insurance companies and also—after the Deutschmark became freely convertible in 1958—from free capital markets. Up until 1959, export financing was granted to German suppliers. From 1959 on the German government also offered credits to foreign buyers tied to German exports through the KfW, the so-called "Hermes guarantees." In 1960 KfW's DM 265 million for export financing was granted for exports of power stations and industrial plant to such countries as Pakistan, Mexico, Chile, Spain, and Greece, with 58 percent of the total issued as buyer loans.

By the end of the 1950s, the KfW had transformed itself from an interim distribution agency for postwar reconstruction funds into a financial institution supporting the German economy in gaining and sustaining a leading position in the world markets. Owned jointly by the federal and Länder governments, its new long-term funding basis was established through the ERP special fund as well as through KfW bonds in the capital market. While the KfW operated with some 50 employees in 1949, that number increased to about 150 in 1951 and reached about 180 in 1960. At the same time, KfW's balance sheet total rose from under DM 1 billion in 1949 to about DM 5 billion in 1954—at that time the largest of any German credit institution, according to Heinrich Harries. In 1960 KfW's assets/liabilities totaled about 7.5 billion.

New Tasks as a Development Bank: 1961–70

In 1959 Schniedewind was succeeded by the institution's first spokesman of the management board, Dr. Hermann Josef Abs. The excellent banker and prewar chairman of the Deutsche Bank with a strong ability to influence political leaders had headed the German delegation in the London Debt Agreement negotiations. Martini succeeded retiring spokesman of the KfW's board of management Otto Neubaur. He drew on his experience at the former economics ministry and the Berlin

stock exchange, helping develop a solid foundation for the further success of the KfW.

On August 16, 1961, when the Wall was being erected in Berlin, the KfW Law was amended to add a new task to the bank's agenda in addition to investment and export financing: financing projects in foreign countries, development aid projects in particular. At the same time the KfW's capital structure was altered. The federal government took over 80 percent of KfW's equity capital which was increased from DM 1 million to DM 1 billion, while the Länder, now including the Saarland and Berlin, held 20 percent. For this transaction the German government converted DM 90 million worth of loan claims on ERP special funds into capital stock. DM 850 million was guaranteed by the federal and Länder governments should the money ever be needed to pay the KfW's liabilities. This way, neither party needed to draw on budget resources.

In the 1960s the KfW made a massive entrance into the international arena. As early as in 1958 the KfW had granted loans to foreign countries such as Iceland, Sudan, and India to enable them to pay German exporters quickly. A legendary program was the secret "Operation Business Partner" under which the KfW channeled about DM 630 million covert loans to Israel between 1961 and 1965 on behalf of the German government. The program arose after the Israeli prime minister, David Ben Gurion, met German Chancellor Adenauer at the Waldorf Astoria Hotel in New York City in March 1960 and requested financial help. Following German official diplomatic recognition of Israel in 1965, Israel was given official capital aid. In 1966 a general agreement between the German federal government and the KfW regulated the KfW involvement in bilateral capital aid projects between Germany and developing countries. The agreement stated that "it was the government which . . . assumed the blanket refinancing and the credit risk of capital aid," according to Heinrich Harries in *Financing The Future*. Harries added, "For its part the KfW had to maintain its autonomous profile as a credit institution [and] could decide on its own whether to grant a loan for its own account or on behalf of the federal government."

One of KfW's international credit programs was aimed at securing raw material supplies for the German economy, which was traditionally highly dependant on imports. In 1960 the KfW granted its first financing loan of DM 208 million to the Lamco iron ore project in Liberia. Other loans were given to mining companies in South Africa. A special five-year mineral oil promotion program was launched in 1964. For larger international projects in which more than one party had a stake, the KfW worked with other financial institutions, pooling resources and distributing the risk. In 1961 the KfW became involved for the first time in a co-financing project with the World Bank and the International Development Organization (IDA) in the Roseires dam project in Sudan, organizing a mixed financing loan amounting to DM 175 million. In another co-financing project in Bolivia, KfW became partners with the Inter-American Development Bank and the United States Agency for International Development (AID) in 1962. Four years later the bank co-financed textile projects in Cameron and Chad with the Deutsche Gesellschaft für wirtschaftliche Zusammenarbeit (DEG), a German economic development organization, and the European Investment Bank (EIB). Two particularly noteworthy commercial German mixed financing projects were the UNINSA steelworks in Spain and the Atucha I nuclear power station in Argentina to which the KfW contributed DM 450 million and DM 175 million, respectively.

The change of ministers in Bonn under four chancellors in the space of a decade resulted in a high turnover rate on the KfW's board of directors. However, new tasks meant growth. Its staff rose from over 200 in 1961 to more than 400 in 1966, and reached over 500 in 1970. The balance sheet total grew steadily during that decade, from about DM 11 billion in 1961 to approximately DM 23 billion in 1970. In 1961 the KfW granted about DM 2.6 billion to domestic and international organizations. At the end of the decade KfW's financial commitments totaled more than DM 3.5 billion. The bank's financial resources during the 1960s were comprised of DM 6.5 billion from the German government—with about three-quarters of that coming from the ERP special funds—and DM 4.9 billion raised on the capital market from the issue of long-term bonds and bearer debt securities.

Funding German Business and Fundraising on Wall Street: 1971–89

The KfW started the 1970s with a fundamental restructuring program. First of all, its main focus was re-directed towards the domestic economy. The collapse of the Bretton Woods international monetary system based on fixed interest rates in the early 1970s, as well as extensively increasing oil prices caused by the newly formed OPEC cartel, created difficult domestic and international market conditions for the German economy. To serve German industry better, new departments were set up which specialized in promotional programs for particular industry sectors which also included the proven export financing and commodity loan programs. KfW's international activities, including development aid and other financial cooperation projects, were served by departments organized by country or geographical region. On the personnel side, Martini resigned as spokesman of the board of management in 1971. In 1974 Helmut Schmidt—then German finance minister and later German chancellor—became chairman of the board of directors at KfW.

In order to promote domestic investment the KfW developed its own low-interest loan programs which were not funded by the German government as in the reconstruction years, but by funds raised on the capital market. The share of the ERP special fund in KfW's total financial funding for the promotion of domestic projects dropped from 32 percent in 1971 to 15 percent in 1989. The new programs were targeted at small and mid-sized businesses which, because of their small size, did not traditionally have access to the international capital markets to satisfy their financial needs. The KfW offered long-term investment loans with favorable interest rates to this clientele through its so-called "M-programs" by refinancing the other bank loans that borrowers had to apply and be approved for. The M-programs encouraged investments aimed at energy saving, environmental protection, and innovation; their annual volume grew from DM 500 million in 1971 to DM 6 billion in 1989. Another program introduced in 1971, the ERP equity participation program, helped strengthen the equity capital base of small and medium sized businesses. It was supported by the German economics ministry, as was a cyclical stimulation program

launched jointly with the federal government in 1981 to encourage the development of new energy technologies with a budget of DM 5.4 billion. In 1978 the KfW granted its first loan in a foreign currency; in succeeding years a growing part of its business was conducted in foreign currencies.

Besides KfW's activities for small and mid-sized businesses, the bank also supported large German companies by co-financing certain projects of high importance: a conveyor belt built by Krupp for the transportation of phosphates stretching over 100 kilometers through the Spanish Sahara; the Bosporus bridge in Istanbul which connected Asia with Europe; the Atucha II nuclear power station in Argentina to which KfW contributed loans worth DM 1 billion; and the Channel Tunnel connecting the Great Britain with Europe. International capital aid and financial cooperation (FC) projects were more and more directed towards social infrastructure.

A particularly noteworthy international aid project received financial support from the KfW in fall 1975 when Poland was granted a loan of DM 1 billion to facilitate the migration of ethnic Germans to the Federal Republic. A major project which served commercial goals was the Airbus project. The Airbus, a civilian jumbo jet developed in the 1960s by a consortium of European aircraft manufacturers, had to break into the competitive world market dominated by North American firms such as Boeing, Douglas, and Lockheed. In 1976 the KfW granted Airbus-loans to airlines in Korea, India, and South Africa. Two years later the KfW co-financed a major deal with Eastern Airlines—the first Airbus order from a United States airline.

In order to sustain its ambitious programs, the KfW was constantly looking for new sources of funding. One of those new sources came in the form of partners from Arabia who had been able to accumulate significant wealth during oil crises between 1973 and 1982. In 1975 the KfW raised its first loans against borrowers notes from the Saudi Arabian Monetary Agency (SAMA), mainly due to the personal effort of management board member Alfred Becker. In the mid-1980s the KfW took another crucial step towards new fundraising opportunities when it applied for an international credit rating. For its domestic six percent DM bond, backed by the institutional liability of the Federal Republic of Germany, KfW was rated "Triple-A," the highest rating possible, by the agencies Moody's and Standard & Poor's in 1986. In the year of KfW's 40th anniversary it issued its first foreign currency bonds: a $200 million Eurobond and CHF 100 million private placement. The same year the KfW was admitted by the Securities and Exchange Commission as the first German financial institution to issue bonds on the United States capital market. KfW International Finance Inc. headquartered in Wilmington, Delaware, started doing business in 1988 by issuing the first bonds worth $500 million on Wall Street. As a result of these efforts, the KfW raised funds worth DM 17.4 billion on the capital markets in 1989, compared with DM 2.4 billion in 1971.

The substantial growth in business experienced by the KfW during the 1970s and 1980s was reflected in its balance sheet total which increased from DM 25 billion in 1971 to DM 199 billion in 1989. KfW's financial commitments reached DM 20 billion in 1988. According to Harries, the promotion of domestic trade and industry grew by no less than 800 percent during that period of time; the volume of FC projects doubled; and the volume of export financing grew fivefold. In 1973 the number of KfW employees exceeded 600 for the first time and reached 920 by 1989.

Reunification and Global Challenges: 1990 and Beyond

In the 1990s the KfW, a child of World War II, had to deal with the war's ultimate aftermath. After the fall of the Berlin Wall in 1989, a large portion of the financing offers was directed at projects aimed at rebuilding the eastern German economy. As early as March 1990 the KfW opened an office in Berlin again after its previous one had been closed at the end of 1974. During that year the bank launched various programs: a start-up program for companies owned nationally by the German Democratic Republic (GDR); an environmental program; a program for mid-sized East German firms; a municipal loan program for the new East German Länder; and a housing modernization program. By the end of 1990 the KfW's financial commitments to the new East German Länder reached DM 4.2 billion, and over two-thirds of all investment loans channeled into the domestic economy went there.

However, the biggest deal in the history of the KfW was made when the German government agreed to spend DM 7.8 billion in subsidies on the construction of new homes in the Soviet Union for officers of the USSR army leaving eastern Germany. Over half a million Soviet soldiers and civilians stationed in the GDR in 1989 had to be transferred back to the Soviet Union by the end of 1994. In December 1992 German Chancellor Kohl agreed to spend additional DM 550 million to co-finance this ambitious project. More than 45,000 dwellings, together with the necessary technical and social infrastructure (from power stations to playgrounds), were built in the Soviet Union in only four years. Other KfW programs were launched to give former members of the Soviet army a civilian professional training, and to enhance living conditions for ethnic Germans in the former USSR. In 1992 the KfW also started coordinating Germany's economic consultation activities for Central and Eastern European countries. In the following years coordination agencies were opened in Moscow, Kiev, and Minsk. In 1996 the KfW granted a DM 1 billion loan to the Russian foreign trade bank for financing projects of mutual interest.

In 1994 the KfW merged with Staatsbank Berlin, the central bank of the former GDR. Effective October 1, 1994, the federal finance minister transferred the assets and liabilities of the Staatsbank Berlin to the KfW. After the merger the bank's equity capital was raised to DM 7.23 billion and its staff grew to 1,615. KfW's sectoral business was reorganized and an advisory council for promotional measures in the new Länder set up. With the year 1998 two amendments of the German Banking Act went into effect which placed the KfW on a level with the federal government as a borrower, and the government became legally liable for funds raised by the KfW and for associated derivatives business.

In 1992, 90 percent of the KfW's financial commitments resulted from self-refinanced programs. In 1998 the American subsidiary KfW International Finance, issued Euro-bonds for $1 billion while the parent company at home issued global bonds worth DM 4 billion—the largest issue in the bank's history. In 1998 KfW's commitments for domestic economic promotion totaled DM 48.8 billion; DM 13.1 billion were committed to export and project financing; DM 2.7 billion were budgeted for developing countries; and DM 400 million were set aside to finance advisory and other services. Total commitments reached DM 65 billion in 1998, compared with DM 28 billion in 1989. KfW's balance sheet totaled DM 315 billion in 1998, and the bank's net income was DM 452 billion. Of the DM 69.6 billion in funds raised in 1998, less than one-tenth came from public budgets. A big challenge KfW faced in 1999 was the conversion of its business to the new EURO currency.

Principal Subsidiaries

KfW International Finance Inc. (United States).

Further Reading

"FOCUS-Gulf Air Secures $350 Mln Loan for Plane Buy," *Reuters*, June 13, 1999.

"Germany's KfW to Fund Indian Renewable Energy Projects," *AsiaPulse News,* March 19, 1999.

Harries, Heinrich, *Financing the Future: KfW—The German Bank with a Public Mission,* Frankfurt am Main: Fritz Knapp Verlag, 1998.

Kemp, Peter, "A Growing Emphasis on Environment," *MEED Middle East Economic Digest,* September 5, 1997, p. 12.

"KFW: Policy Push as the Price of Support," *MEED Middle East Economic Digest,* November 4, 1994, p. 10.

"KfW spürt Investitionsboom," *Die Welt,* May 6, 1999.

—Evelyn Hauser

LABOR READY
TEMPORARY LABOR - ON DEMAND

Labor Ready, Inc.

1016 South 28th Street
Tacoma, Washington 98409
U.S.A.
(253) 383-9101
Fax: (253) 383-9311
Web site: http://www.laborready.com

Public Company
Incorporated: 1985
Employees: 1,238
Sales: $606.9 million (1998)
Stock Exchanges: New York
Ticker Symbol: LRW
NAIC: 56132 Temporary Help Services

The fastest growing temporary staffing company in the world, Labor Ready, Inc. supplies temporary manual laborers to construction, light industrial, and small business customers in the United States, Canada, and Puerto Rico. Unlike many other temporary help firms, Labor Ready focuses exclusively on providing manual laborers to its customers, a segment of the market without any national competitors during the late 1990s. The process of recruiting laborers and matching them with customers in need of temporary, unskilled workers is conducted by the company's network of dispatch offices, which has increased from one outlet in 1989 to more than 650 within a decade. To its client companies, Labor Ready promises "Satisfaction Guaranteed," and to its legions of day laborers, the company offers a policy of "Work Today, Paid Today." Labor Ready provides basic equipment to workers, free of charge, and pays workers at the end of each day, either with a check or a voucher to be redeemed at a cash dispensing machine, installed in every dispatch office.

Founded in 1989

When Glenn A. Welstad founded Labor Ready, he was beginning a second career. In 1969 he and two business partners had started Northwest Management Corporation, a restaurant holding company that occupied Welstad's attention for the next 15 years. When Welstad sold his stake in the company, Northwest Management controlled eight Hardee's restaurants and more than a dozen pizza and Mexican restaurants scattered throughout a five-state territory. His expansion of the company, he believed, represented his life's work, but within five years his assessment changed. "Stepping into retirement at age 40," Welstad later wrote, "led to boredom and the realization that my finances were not as originally thought." Consequently, Welstad decided, in 1989, to try his luck as an entrepreneur again. It was a decision that aside from alleviating boredom also turned Welstad into a multimillionaire and Labor Ready into one of the notable business success stories of the 1990s.

As he had with Northwest Management, Welstad enlisted the help of two associates to start Labor Ready in 1989, using a $50,000 bankroll to get the company started. The company started with an office in Kent, Washington, where Welstad provided day laborers for companies in need of temporary assistance. Welstad entered the market by signing a contract with Action Temporary Services, but by 1991 the business relationship had turned litigious. Welstad attempted to sever the ties connecting the two companies, which led to a number of lawsuits filed by each party. Welstad eventually gained his independence and Action Temporary Services eventually fell on hard times, filing for bankruptcy in 1994. Against the backdrop of legal salvos, however, Labor Ready was quietly building a foundation for what later promised to be a $1 billion business. Unknown to many at the time, and perhaps even to himself, Welstad governed a company in 1991 that possessed a formula capable of realizing enormous success. The fuel that would ignite the company's potential was expansion on a national scale, but in 1991 Labor Ready comprised only eight offices—dispatch centers that served as matchmakers for the unemployed and the construction, light industrial, and small business clients that needed temporary help. When expansion on a national scale began in earnest, the efficiency and strategy bred under Welstad's leadership unleashed the prolific financial strength of Labor Ready.

Before stock analysts and industry experts began trumpeting the success of Labor Ready, the company was a regional sup-

Company Perspectives:

Labor Ready, Inc. is the nation's leading provider of temporary manual labor to the light industrial and small business markets. Based in Tacoma, Washington, Labor Ready was founded in 1989 by Chairman, CEO, and President Glenn Welstad. Labor Ready operates 650 offices in 46 states, Puerto Rico, and Canada. Labor Ready currently provides workers for over 195,000 customers, up from 70,000 in 1997. The "Work Today, Cash Today" mission gives Labor Ready a competitive advantage when attracting workers for temporary manual labor. If a customer decides to hire a Labor Ready worker for a full time position, no fee is charged to either party. Labor Ready filled more than 4.8 million work orders, issued over 6.5 million paychecks, and processed 533,000 W-2's in 1998.

plier of manual labor, providing its services in a modern, efficient, yet old-fashioned way. Labor Ready offices operated much like union halls. To get daily employment, prospective workers arrived at a Labor Ready office by 5:30 in the morning. If the applicant had never sought employment through Labor Ready before, he or she was interviewed by a branch office employee and the applicant's skills were stored on a computer database. Background checks and drug screening were performed on a voluntary basis, necessary only when the applicant desired to work for a company with such requirements. If the skills matched the needs of the client company, Labor Ready dispatched the applicant to the work site and charged the client company generally 30 percent more than the worker's hourly wage. In return, the Labor Ready office provided the recruitment of the daily laborer and the financial and administrative services associated with the day laborer's employment, including payroll and workers' compensation premiums. The day laborer received, if needed, the basic equipment needed for the work, such as hard hats, boots, back braces, eye protection, and gloves, free of charge, and transportation to the work site for a small fee. Perhaps most important to the Labor Ready laborer was the company's policy of "Work Today, Paid Today." At the end of a day's work, Labor Ready provided its workers with a check, an enticing service that kept Labor Ready offices generally inundated with hopeful workers each morning.

The type of labor performed by Ready Labor-provided workers was generally strenuous, sometimes dirty work, the type of manual labor required of a blue-collar worker of the lowest rank. Accordingly, many of the applicants who gathered in Labor Ready offices each morning represented the fringe of society, those who found steady employment difficult to obtain because of substance abuse problems or criminal records. There were others, however, without glaring employment liabilities, individuals who, for various reasons, needed the employment assistance provided by Labor Ready and were attracted by the "Work Today, Paid Today" policy. Within this large, itinerant labor pool were people who had just moved to a new area without employment contacts, those who preferred the variety of a different job each day, and others who used Labor Ready to gain the experience needed to secure a full-time job.

At the heart of Labor Ready's operations was the company's network of dispatch offices, each managed by a branch manager who was assisted by several support personnel. Each office was responsible for its own sales and marketing, customer relations, accounts receivable collection, budget controls, and recruitment of day laborers, giving the company a highly decentralized structure. Profitability hinged on the efficiency of each dispatch office and its ability to minimize workers' compensation claims. Safety classes were held to reduce injuries, while operational efficiency was honed over time as the company expanded the number of its branch offices.

The characteristic that set Labor Ready apart from other competitors was the exclusive market niche it occupied. There were other companies that supplied manual laborers on a regional basis and there were temporary staffing companies that provided white collar employees nationally, but as Labor Ready embarked on a decade of prodigious expansion, there were no national companies concentrating exclusively on supplying temporary manual laborers. Further, this market niche—the industrial segment of the temporary staffing market place—registered explosive growth during the 1990s, expanding as Labor Ready itself expanded. Between 1991 and 1997, the industrial temporary staffing industry grew from a $5-billion-a-year business to a $13-billion-a-year business. Labor Ready moved headlong into this fast-growing market segment, positioning itself as the only national competitor. Between 1991 and 1997, the company increased its number of dispatch offices from eight to 316, fueling annual revenue growth from less than $10 million to $335 million.

Mid-1990s Expansion

The company's rapid expansion did not gather speed until the mid-1990s. By the end of 1994, there were 51 dispatch offices, including four in Canada, but Welstad had not yet penetrated any markets in the Northeast and the Atlantic, and it maintained only a small presence in the Southeast with one branch office. To accelerate expansion, the company experimented with franchising the Labor Ready concept in 1994, licensing one franchisee in Minnesota who eventually opened five branch offices, but the company's franchising efforts stopped there, prompting Welstad to search for an alternative method to finance expansion. The logical alternative was an offering of stock to investors, which Labor Ready did in June 1996. Prior to the company's initial public offering (IPO), it had increased the number of its branch offices to 106 by the end of 1995, a year during which the first Labor Ready office was established in the Northeast. With the proceeds gained from the IPO, expansion plans became decidedly more ambitious. The company operated 200 branch offices by the end of 1996, including outlets in the Atlantic region for the first time, and by the end of 1997, the total had swelled to 316.

By this point in its history, Labor Ready had developed considerable skill in opening branch offices, using a process that had become standardized over time to blanket a market and achieve predictable results. Each new office cost approximately $50,000 to establish, generally taking no more than six months to realize a profit. On average, a Labor Ready office required $12,000 in business per week to show a profit. In 1997 a Labor Ready office averaged $27,000 in revenue per week, spurring

Welstad to accelerate his expansion plans for the future. His expansion efforts in 1998, which included the establishment of 170 new Labor Ready offices, produced even greater results than the company-owned branches produced in 1997. In 1998 Labor Ready outlets averaged $31,000 in business per week, helping the company to record astounding financial totals for the year. Companywide revenue was up 81 percent to $607 million. Net income recorded a more prolific leap, increasing 184 percent to $19.8 million.

Along with the robust financial and physical growth recorded in 1998, Labor Ready also celebrated the introduction of a new service for its day laborers during the year, a service Welstad heralded as "a wonderful recruiting tool." Beginning in April 1998, the company installed cash dispensing machines (CDMs) in its dispatch offices, which gave its workers the choice of receiving cash at the end of the day's work instead of a check. Instead of "Work Today, Paid Today," the company could proclaim "Work Today, Cash Today," by distributing vouchers that could be redeemed at a Labor Ready CDM. For the workers, more than half of whom lacked a bank account, the approximately $1.50 fee charged by the CDM was a welcome alternative to the check-cashing fee charged by banks to individuals without bank accounts, which was generally $3 per transaction. For Labor Ready, the financial benefits of installing CDMs were also attractive. The company saved money by not having to process checks and it generated revenue from the CDMs as the recipient of the transaction fee charged to the worker. By the end of 1998, Labor Ready had collected $3.6 million in CDM fees.

$1 Billion in Revenue by 2000

By this point in the company's history, few could ignore the aggressive expansion and the impressive financial results achieved by Welstad. In five years, the number of Labor Ready offices had increased from 51 to 486, as annual revenues increased from $38 million to $606 million. "They're going in after a market niche with almost no competition on a [national] scale," one analyst remarked in 1998. Welstad, well aware of the enviable position his company occupied, was intent on tightening Labor Ready's grip on markets, both large and small, nationwide. He announced, at the end of 1998, that Labor Ready would open 200 offices in the United States in each of the next two years, giving the company a projected 875 offices and $1 billion in revenues by the end of 2000. Welstad intended to saturate every viable market in the country, an objective the company's time-tested business formula appeared capable of fulfilling.

Labor Ready celebrated the beginning of its tenth anniversary by completing the most prodigious expansion in it history. During the first four months of 1999, the company opened 166 new dispatch offices, nearly reaching its goal of opening 200 offices during the first half of the year. "The faster we can get offices opening and running early in the year," Welstad explained, "the greater the opportunity for better sales in the third and fourth quarters, traditionally the company's busiest time of the year." With this record-setting work completed, the company marshaled its forces for the addition of more than 200 new offices in the ensuing year, well positioned for reaching $1 billion in revenues by the beginning of the 21st century.

Further Reading

Beel, Susan, "These Temps Might Not Type But Some Will Do Windows," *San Diego Business Journal*, December 24, 1990, p. 14.

Fagerstrom, Scott, "The News Tribune, Tacoma, Wash., Market Summary Column," *Knight-Ridder/Tribune Business News*, May 7, 1996, p. 5070290.

Gorham, John, "Employer of Last Resort," *Forbes*, March 23, 1998, p. 48.

Keenan, Charles, "Temp Agency Uses Diebold To Pay Daily in Cash," *American Banker*, March 3, 1998, p. 21.

"Labor Ready Celebrates Its 10th Anniversary," *PR Newswire*, March 17, 1999, p. 6691.

"Labor Ready Helps Texas Businesses Meet Daily Work Needs," *Knight-Ridder/Tribune Business News*, February 8, 1998, p. 208B0904.

Maharry, Mike, "Tacoma, Wash.-Based Labor Ready Reports Record Earnings," *Knight-Ridder/Tribune Business News*, October 23, 1997, p. 1023B0946.

"Tacoma, Wash., Temp Firm Founder Named Entrepreneur of the Year," *Knight-Ridder/Tribune Business News*, June 26, 1998, p. OKRB98177773.

"Washington-Based Temp Agency Focuses on Manual Labor in Southwest Florida," *Knight-Ridder/Tribune Business News*, February 12, 1998, p. 212B1208.

—Jeffrey L. Covell

Lands' End, Inc.

1 Lands' End Lane
Dodgeville, Wisconsin 53595
U.S.A.
(608) 935-9341
(800) 356-4444
Fax: (608) 935-4260
Web site: http://www.landsend.com

Public Company
Incorporated: 1963 as Lands' End Yacht Stores
Employees: 4,900
Sales: $1.37 billion (1999)
Stock Exchanges: New York
Ticker Symbol: LE
NAIC: 44811 Men's Clothing Stores; 44812 Women's
Clothing Stores; 44813 Children's & Infants' Clothing
Stores; 44815 Clothing Accessories Stores; 44819
Other Clothing Stores; 45411 Electronic Shopping &
Mail-Order Houses

Lands' End, Inc. is perhaps best known as a marketer of traditionally styled, casual clothing, available through catalogs known for their folksy, chatty style. The company's emphasis on quality merchandise and customer service has made it a leader in the mail-order marketing field. Based in rural Wisconsin, Lands' End has grown steadily since its inception as a seller of sailing equipment for racing boats. By the late 1990s, the company was marketing clothing for children and products for the home, in addition to its tailored clothing for men and women, as well as overseeing a popular Website, where customers could view merchandise and place orders.

1960s Origins

Lands' End got its start in 1963 when Gary Comer, a successful advertising copywriter with Young & Rubicam, who had long pursued a love of sailing in his spare time, decided to pursue his long-standing dream of opening his own business. Comer quit his job of ten years, and with $30,000 in initial funds started a company that made sails and sold other marine hardware. The company set up shop in a storefront at 2317 North Elston Avenue, along the Chicago River in the city's old tannery district.

In 1964, Comer produced a catalog offering Lands' End's goods through the mail. The first booklet, entitled "The Racing Sailors' Equipment Guide," was printed in black-and-white, had 84 pages, and featured a variety of technical-looking sailing implements on its cover. A printer's error, however, resulted in the company's name being rendered "Lands' End," with the apostrophe in the wrong place. Since Comer couldn't afford to have the piece reprinted, he decided to simply change the name of the business to correspond with the brochure.

Lands' End began filling orders from its basement. The company shipped out orders the day they were received, and unconditionally guaranteed all that it sold. In a subsequent catalog, Comer put his copywriting skills to work in an innovative, customer-friendly format. The text in the Lands' End publications, rather than being dry, technical, and brief, had a casual, engaging, informative, and sympathetic air. Customers were put at ease reading it and came to feel that they had developed a personal relationship with the company that had produced the catalog and the items that filled it. Comer is credited with originating the concept of the "magalogue," in which pictured items for sale are surrounded and cushioned by appealing text and illustrations.

Lands' End's customers began to look to the company for more than just technical sailing gear, and many felt comfortable writing to the company to ask about purchasing foul weather gear and duffel bags. In response, Lands' End added a small clothing section to the catalog, featuring rainsuits, canvas luggage, shoes, sweaters, and some other clothing. The catalog's name was accordingly altered to simply the "Lands' End Catalogue." Items sold in the clothing portion of the catalog soon became the company's most profitable offerings.

Shifting Focus in the 1970s

Throughout the 1960s, Lands' End continued to sell sailing equipment and related items through its catalog. In 1970, Lands' End's mail order business had grown large enough to

Company Perspectives:

The Lands' End Principles of Doing Business: Principle 1. *We do everything we can to make our products better. We improve material, and add back features and construction details that others have taken out over the years. We never reduce the quality of a product to make it cheaper.* Principle 2. *We price our products fairly and honestly. We do not, have not, and will not participate in the common retailing practice of inflating mark-ups to set up a future phony "sale."* Principle 3. *We accept any return for any reason, at any time. Our products are guaranteed. No fine print. No arguments. We mean exactly what we say: GUARANTEED. PERIOD.* Principle 4. *We ship faster than anyone we know of. We ship items in stock the day after we receive the order. At the height of the last Christmas season the longest time an order was in the house was 36 hours, excepting monograms which took another 12 hours.* Principle 5. *We believe that what is best for our customer is best for all of us. Everyone here understands that concept. Our sales and service people are trained to know our products, and to be friendly and helpful. They are urged to take all the time necessary to take care of you. We even pay for your call, for whatever reason you call.* Principle 6. *We are able to sell at lower prices because we have eliminated middlemen; because we don't buy branded merchandise with high protected mark-ups; and because we have placed our contracts with manufacturers who have proven that they are cost conscious and efficient.* Principle 7. *We are able to sell at lower prices because we operate efficiently. Our people are hard working, intelligent, and share in the success of the company.* Principle 8. *We are able to sell at lower prices because we support no fancy emporiums with their high overhead. Our main location is in the middle of a 40-acre cornfield in rural Wisconsin.*

merit computerization of its inventory and sales operations. Lands' End made its first foray into the world of manufacturing something other than sailing equipment in 1973, when the company began to make its own duffle bags. The next year, Lands' End also began to market its own brand of rainsuit, a two-piece outfit worn by sailors in foul weather. In 1975, the company came out with its first all-color catalog, which featured 30 pages of sailing equipment and two full pages of clothing. By the following year, the company had decided to shift its emphasis to the sale of clothing and canvas luggage, and the quotient of non-nautical equipment had risen to include eight pages displaying duffel bags, and three pages of clothing, including a men's chamois-cloth shirt.

In the spring of 1977, Lands' End issued its first catalog that paid serious attention to clothing, with 13 out of 40 pages dedicated to dry goods. In addition, the company introduced its own line of soft luggage, called Square Rigger. Following these innovations, sales for the year reached $3.6 million. After 1977, Lands' End phased out the sailing equipment aspect of its operation altogether, retaining the rugged, reliable, and traditional nature that sailing implied, and applying it to a broader variety of clothing. In 1978, the company introduced its first button-down Oxford-cloth shirt, heralding the move to offerings of solid, conservative, basic clothing upon which it would build its future.

Lands' End also began to shift its operations from its Chicago base to a small town in rural Wisconsin called Dodgeville. Comer chose this location for his growing enterprise because, as he noted in a piece of promotional literature, "I fell in love with the gently rolling hills and woods and cornfields and being able to see the changing seasons." In addition to the intangible spiritual benefits of life on the land, the move enabled Lands' End to ultimately locate the bulk of its operations in the middle of a cornfield in rural Wisconsin, an area in which costs were extremely low. The company began this shift when it moved its Chicago warehouse to an empty garage in Dodgeville in 1978.

Lands' End's operations were also shifting in another significant way during this time, as the company moved from filling orders by mail to filling orders by phone. The company had brought its first toll-free 800-number on line, and operators were standing by to take customer calls by the middle of 1978. With this shift, the company had incorporated another point of contact with the customer into its operation, and it stressed politeness and customer service in its operators, a continuation of the message it strove to portray in its catalog. Calls were answered within a ring and a half, and operators were permitted to chat with customers for as long as it took to make a sale.

Lands' End continued the process of transferring operations to Dodgeville in 1979, when it opened an office in a pre-existing strip mall, while it broke ground for an office building and an accompanying 33,000-square-foot warehouse in a Dodgeville industrial park. The following year, the company moved into its new space on "Lands' End Lane." By this time, the clothing section of its catalog had grown further, and the 800-number service had been expanded to accommodate customers 24 hours a day. Interested in gaining more control over the quality of the clothes it sold, the company began to recruit employees who were knowledgeable about fabric and the manufacture of clothing.

In addition to its new facilities in Dodgeville, Lands' End also opened an outlet store in Chicago, just one block from its original location, to sell the goods that made up excess inventory if catalog sales of a particular item were not as brisk as expected. Further physical expansion took place the following year, in 1981, when Lands' End began work on a 40,000-square-foot addition to its warehouse in Wisconsin. The company also broke ground on a plant to manufacture its own line of soft luggage in West Union, Iowa.

Marketing Tactics in the 1980s

To further support its burgeoning sales and reputation, Lands' End embarked on a national advertising campaign in 1981. The purpose of this effort was to make customers aware of the Lands' End business philosophy, and associate its name with service, value, and quality. The company used the expression "direct merchant" to describe its relationship, as a manufacturer and distributor, with the customer.

In the next year, Lands' End followed up this effort with a significant investment in computerization, as the company introduced on-line customer sales and ordering to speed up processes. Efficient use of computers was a keystone of Lands' End's program for success, and soon computer systems enabled operators to provide customers with a wealth of information at the touch of a finger.

In addition, Lands' End continued to expand its warehouse facilities as it started construction on an additional 126,000-square-foot warehouse across the street from its original Dodgeville facilities. Moving into this facility in 1983 required the unloading of 8,000 boxes of goods so that the company's new automated sorting system could be made operational. By this time, a nationwide boom in mail-order shopping was beginning to take off, and Lands' End saw its sales and earnings start to grow.

In an effort to exploit Americans' increasing willingness to shop by phone using their credit cards, Lands' End introduced a line of fancier clothing for men and women in 1983, under the name Charter Club. Instead of cotton and wool, these products were manufactured from Italian silks and other luxury fabrics. This line soon had its own catalog of offerings.

In 1984, Lands' End passed another landmark on the way to becoming a full-fledged manufacturer when its logo was registered as a U.S. trademark. By the following year, demand for Lands' End goods had increased to the point where the company was able to begin issuing monthly as opposed to seasonal catalogs. In addition, Lands' End broke ground on yet another warehouse addition.

In 1986, Lands' End discontinued its Charter Club line of dressier clothing, despite the fact that it was profitable, in an effort to maintain the company's culture and focus on solid, traditional, no-nonsense clothes. "When they started shooting photographs of models in London, I said, 'That's it, enough'," Comer later told *Fortune*. His conception of the company was more straightforward. "I picked things that I liked, and over the years people interested in the same sorts of things gathered around," he said, explaining Lands' End's growth.

By 1986, growth had brought Lands' End profits of more than $14 million on sales topping $200 million. At that point, after several years of phenomenal advances, the company sold stock to the public for the first time, offering 1.4 million shares at $30 a piece. In the following year, shares of Lands' End began to be traded on the New York Stock Exchange, as the company racked up earnings of about $15 million.

Also in 1987, in response to customer requests, Lands' End introduced a line of children's clothing. Within a year it had yielded sales of almost $15 million. By 1988, Lands' End had built up a loyal core of catalog shoppers. The company shipped nine million booklets a month, full of homey straight talk about classic casual clothing, for a total of 80 million pieces mailed a year. To take the orders generated by this promotional literature, Lands' End also spent heavily on technology to improve its customer service, adding new sorting, packaging, and sewing equipment (for alterations). In addition, the company broke ground on an additional phone center in a town about 30 miles from Dodgeville, Cross Plains, Wisconsin. With this facility, Lands' End planned to add 100 new employees to its payroll.

At the end of the year, the company also opened a small retail outlet in Dodgeville to sell its clothes. Although Lands' End had no intention of branching out from the mail order

business into conventional retail, the company had discovered that people felt so at home with the places and people depicted in the Lands' End catalog that they frequently got in their cars and drove to Dodgeville on vacation to see the place for themselves. After customers began wandering into Lands' End's corporate offices looking to buy turtlenecks and sweatshirts, the company opened a small store to serve them. Additional Lands' End outlet stores followed, offering overstock items to the public.

Challenges in the Late 1980s and Early 1990s

After a blockbuster year in 1988, Lands' End's revenues had nearly doubled in the span since its first stock offering, rising to $456 million for the fiscal year ending in January 1989. Two months later, however, the company was forced to announce its sharpest drop in earnings ever. Although sales had continued to grow, costs had grown at a much steeper rate. Confident that sales would continue strongly after 1988, the company had amassed a large inventory of merchandise. When sales slowed, it was forced to send out a large number of additional catalogs in an attempt to win new customers. This campaign proved to be extremely costly, adding about $2 million to the company's promotional budget. This cost promised to rise further as the post office implemented a 17 percent hike in third class mailing rates.

In addition, Lands' End found itself hurt by the stodgy reputation of its merchandise, as competition in the catalog sales field heated up. In particular, the company lost ground to Eddie Bauer, a marketer of rugged outdoor gear, as well as to L.L. Bean. Lands' End needed to update and freshen its offerings without alienating old customers who appreciated the company's solid, traditional goods.

The company's outdated offerings continued to damage its profitability throughout the start of 1990, and it posted a two-thirds drop in profits in the first quarter of that year. Concerned that Lands' End and its rival L.L. Bean might have grown so large that they had glutted the market for their type of merchandise, industry watchers predicted further declines at the company.

In response to its falling profits, Lands' End began to increase the amount of new merchandise in its catalog. Whereas the previous two years' catalogs had offered first eight and then 11.5 percent new items, as much as 18 percent of the products in 1990's catalogs were new introductions. Among the additions were sunglasses, children's swimsuits, and clothing and bedding for infants. The company also began to market "Mom Packs," combinations of merchandise packed together to be presented as Mother's Day gifts. In addition, Lands' End introduced three new specialty catalogs: Buttondowns and Beyond, which featured tailored clothing for men; Coming Home with Lands' End, with products for the bed and bath; and in August 1990, a separate catalog just for children called Kids. Also in 1992, the company created its corporate sales unit. This unit distributed five catalogs per year to corporations that regularly purchased gifts for clients and employees.

Lands' End also began its first attempt to expand its market beyond the borders of the United States. In typical company style, Lands' End encouraged its customers to become part of this new push, asking them to send in the names of their relatives who lived overseas. The company first began to mail a catalog to potential customers in the United Kingdom, and eventually opened a U.K. phone center and distribution facility in the fall of 1993. By the late 1990s, the company was publishing catalogs for 175 countries, with prices converted to the English pound, the German mark, and the Japanese yen. Moreover, it introduced three international subsidiaries, Lands' End Japan, K.K., Lands' End Direct Merchants UK Limited, and Lands' End GmbH in Germany.

The Late 1990s and Beyond

During this time, the saturation of the catalog sales market had a major effect upon Lands' End's profitability. Although sales continued to increase, gross profit margins dropped. The 1990s saw the company acquire and then divest two subsidiaries—Territory Ahead, Inc. and MontBell America, Inc.—as well as liquidate Willis & Geiger, its outdoor clothing and accessories division. Lands' End made further reductions in early 1999, restructuring the company and eliminating ten percent of its salaried jobs and closing three of its 19 outlet stores. These efforts streamlined the company to help it maintain its competitive edge. Management changes also ensued. In 1998 President and CEO Michael J. Smith resigned and was replaced by David F. Dyer. Company founder Gary C. Comer remained as chairman of the board.

Lands' End faced the future armed with several new retailing concepts to enhance its operations. In 1997 the company opened its first Inlet Store, described by its designers as "a catalog come to life." The Inlet Store prototype, in Richfield, Minnesota, featured a central area decorated in warm, residential tones, designed to overcome resistance some customers had to catalog shopping. In a comfortable homelike atmosphere, the "catalog-in-a-store" provided sales and sizing assistance, returns, alterations, and monogramming services. Along the perimeter of the Inlet Store were Lands' End overstocked and discontinued items. After the prototype's successful launch, the company began converting its existing outlet stores to Inlet Stores.

Lands' End also hoped to enhance its operations via the Internet, and it launched a Website for that purpose. In 1998 management reported that the Internet was still an insignificant but potentially valuable portion of their $1.2 billion business, serving as another venue for already-established customers. Visitors to the Lands' End site could peruse and purchase from an online catalog that allowed various views of an article of clothing, additional information about the clothing, and side-by-side views of various articles of clothing. The online shopping experience, in contrast to the company's phone order rules against "upselling," offered the customer the opportunity to add accessories to their purchases. The Internet site was continuously updated, while discontinued and out-of-stock items were quickly removed from the site. From Lands' End perspective, the online site represented a savings in catalog distribution costs, rather than a means of increasing client base.

However, a 1999 innovation drew media attention, when Lands' End became one of the first to provide 3-D apparel modeling for women. At www.landsend.com, online shoppers could key in their personal measurements, and their own personal 3-D apparel model would appear onscreen, helping the customer better determine whether the clothing suited him. *Computerworld* magazine characterized the 3-D process as "cool" and fun, noting that "according to retail experts, it's seen as one of the most promising ways to convert online browsers to online buyers." Oxford Express was another new feature of the Lands' End Website in 1999. With this feature, customers could select sizes, fabrics, styles, collars, and cuffs, and a depiction of the shirt appeared on screen, ready to order. Still, Lands' End expected the major portion of its business to be conducted through traditional catalog sales well into the next century.

Prospects for the newly restructured Lands' End remained strong as it headed into the next century. Its strong reputation for quality and its steady course of business growth ensured that it was rigged for competitive sailing in increasingly competitive seas.

Principal Subsidiaries

Lands' End Japan, K. K.; Lands' End Direct Merchants UK Limited; Lands' End GmbH (Germany).

Principal Operating Units

Core Business; Specialty Business; International Operations.

Further Reading

Berg, Eric N., "Standout in the Land of Catalogues," *New York Times,* December 8, 1988.

Bremner, Brian, "Lands' End Looks a Bit Frayed at the Edges," *Business Week,* March 19, 1990.

Caminiti, Susan, "A Mail-Order Romance: Lands' End Courts Unseen Customers," *Fortune,* March 13, 1989.

Higgins, Kevin T., "Opportunity Calls," *Marketing Management,* Winter 1997, pp. 4–8.

King, Julia, "3-D Images May Spur Web Buys," *Computerworld,* May 24, 1999, p. 1.

"Lands' End to Restructure, Cut Jobs and Close Stores," *Direct Marketing,* February 1999, p. 8.

Schwadel, Francine, "Lands' End Stumbles as Fashion Shifts Away from Retailer's Traditional Fare," *Wall Street Journal,* April 27, 1990.

Wagner, Mitch, "From the Top—Michael J. Smith, President and CEO, Lands' End," *Internetweek,* September 14, 1998, p. 22.

Wilson, Marianne, "Lands' End Captures Catalog Experience," *Chain Store Age,* March 1997, pp. 140–41.

—Elizabeth Rourke
—updated by Shannon and Terry Hughes

Larry H. Miller Group

5650 South State Street
Murray, Utah 84107
U.S.A.
(801) 264-3100
Fax: (801) 264-3198
Web site: http://www.lhmauto.com

Private Company
Founded: 1979 as Larry H. Miller Toyota
Employees: 3,500
Sales: $1.4 billion (1997 est.)
NAIC: 551112 Ofices of Other Holding Companies;
44111 New Car Dealers; 44112 Used Car Dealers;
711211 Sports Teams & Clubs; 51312 Television
Broadcasting; 532112 Passenger Car Leasing; 23311
Land Subdivision & Land Development; 44819 Other
Clothing Stores; 53112 Lessors of Nonresidential
Buildings

The Larry H. Miller Group is a diversified operation that includes 36 auto dealerships in seven states: Utah, Idaho, Arizona, Oklahoma, New Mexico, Oregon, and Colorado. Those Toyota, Honda, Subaru, Dodge, Chevrolet, Cadillac, Jeep, Eagle, Chrysler, Plymouth, Lexus, Oldsmobile, Ford, Mazda, Pontiac, Mitsubishi, Acura, Buick, and Geo dealerships, the origin and heart of this complex group of companies, rank the Miller Group as the tenth largest car dealership in the nation. From 1979 to 1999, Larry Miller, the company's founder, had sold about 420,000 cars. Through his group of companies, Miller also owned the Utah Jazz team in the National Basketball Association, the Utah Starzz of the Women's National Basketball Association, and Salt Lake City's Delta Center, the home of the Jazz and Starzz, which also is used for concerts, other entertainment, and business conferences. Miller's additional business holdings include KJZZ-TV and the Jordan Commons office/entertainment complex in Salt Lake City and 28 Fanzz sports apparel stores in five states.

Miller's Background

Born in 1955, Larry H. Miller grew up in Salt Lake City, the son of an oil refinery worker and a homemaker. Even in the sixth grade, Miller demonstrated his entrepreneurial bent by using money from his paper route to acquire more marbles, baseball cards, stamps, pennies, and pigeons than any other kid on his block.

After he graduated from West High School in 1962, he worked as a framer in his uncle's construction company. But in November 1963, with the end of the building season, Miller found a job at American Auto Parts as a driver and apprentice counterman. In 1968 he took another position as a parts manager at Peck & Shaw Toyota in Murray, a Salt Lake City suburb.

In the meantime, Miller honed his skills as an outstanding softball pitcher for Salt Lake City adult teams. To play in a fast-pitch league, he moved to Denver, where he became the parts manager of the Stevenson Toyota dealership. In three years Miller turned around that dealership's parts operation from one of the poorest in sales to become Toyota's national leader. It became the first Toyota dealership in the nation to sell $1 million in parts and then $2 million in one year. "Larry did a phenomenal job," said Gene Osborn, a partner in the Denver dealership, in the May 2, 1999 *Salt Lake Tribune,* adding that "He was intense and committed to his job."

In his mid-thirties, Miller worked 90 hours a week as the operations manager of five Denver Toyota dealerships, but bigger opportunities soon arose for the ambitious man with a growing family.

The Early Car Dealerships: Late 1970s

In 1979 Miller was looking for something new after Gene Osborn left to start a solo dealership. While in Salt Lake City to attend a wedding, Miller visited Hugh Gardner, a friend who was a partner in Universal Toyota in Murray. After years of asking Gardner if he would sell his dealership, Miller was surprised when Gardner finally consented. On April 6, 1979 Miller paid Gardner $20,000 in earnest money. He also used the rest of his own savings and a $200,000 bank loan to pay

Gardner, then agreed to pay the balance of the $3.5 million price in $17,000 monthly payments for ten years. Deep in debt, Miller risked much in 1979 when he began buying his first dealership. ''If I'd stopped to think about it, it would have scared me and I probably would not have done it,'' recalled Miller in the May 2, 1999 *Salt Lake Tribune.*

In any case, the new car entrepreneur did not rest on his laurels. Later in 1979 he purchased a second dealership in Spokane, Washington, but later sold it. In 1980 he bought an undercapitalized dealership in Phoenix that turned out to be his best-selling operation. In 1983 Miller paid about $2 million for Gordon Wilson Chevrolet in Murray, and by 1984 he owned six dealerships.

According to the Utah Division of Corporations, on December 30, 1986 the new Larry H. Miller Corporation was created as a Utah corporation. It consolidated Cottonwood Chrysler-Plymouth, Inc; Miller Imports Ltd.; Larry H. Miller Hyundai; Larry H. Miller Leasing; and Larry H. Miller Toyota.

In October 1990 the Larry H. Miller Lexus dealership was officially dedicated at 5701 South State Street in Salt Lake City. The new $2.8 million, 16,000-square-foot dealership offered two cars made by the Toyota division: the smaller, less expensive ES 250, and the upscale LS 400 that competed with Mercedes Benz, Jaguar, BMW, and the Nissan Infinity.

By 1990 Miller owned 16 dealerships in Utah, Colorado, New Mexico, and Arizona, and was ranked as Utah's largest car dealer and the seventeenth largest in the nation. He employed 1,500 in the four states. In 1989 he sold 21,953 cars and recorded gross revenues of $310.77 million.

Such fast-paced growth required some changes, however. ''We made a major change in our management style about two years ago,'' said Miller in the November 1990 *Utah Holiday.* ''For the first eight years, we managed primarily on a basis that we would be successful if we continued to market and merchandise aggressively, and continued to grow and control expenses reasonably well. The last two years taught us we couldn't do that. We've made a lot of adjustments and started to utilize very stringent cost control methods.'' Because of the tough times, Miller said there had ''been a certain number of casualties . . . And I don't think there's any question that there are too many dealers.''

Ownership of the Utah Jazz: Mid-1980s

Meanwhile, the professional basketball team Miller would eventually buy struggled on the court and at the box office. Original owner Sam Battistone in 1974 had started the New Orleans Jazz and named the club for the birthplace of jazz music. Although the team had star ''Pistol'' Pete Maravich, in five seasons in New Orleans it failed to win even half its games.

Battistone moved the franchise to Salt Lake City, where in its initial 1979–1980 season it continued its losing ways. But colorful Frank Layden, who became head coach in 1981, helped to turn things around eventually. Key players drafted during this period were Mark Eaton, the center from UCLA, in 1982; Thurl Bailey from North Carolina State in 1983; and little-known guard John Stockton from Gonzaga University in 1984. The

Utah Jazz in the 1983–1984 season achieved their first winning record and for the first time went to the NBA playoffs.

In spite of the winning season, by 1985 Sam Battistone had lost $17 million after 11 seasons of owning the Jazz. Larry Miller was concerned about the persistent rumors the Jazz might leave small-market Salt Lake City for greener pastures. In 1985, as a successful car dealer, he was asked if he would like to be one of several investors each putting up $200,000 to support the team and become limited partners.

Miller declined because he felt that piecemeal approach would not work, but he negotiated another deal. On April 11, 1985 he purchased half of the Utah Jazz for $8 million from Sam Battistone. Then 14 months later he paid about $14 million for the second half of the Jazz franchise. Of course, he borrowed much of that money, thus assuming major debts for the second time in his career.

Miller's first season as the Jazz owner, 1985–1986, was also the first for Karl Malone, drafted in 1985 after playing at Louisiana Tech. Initially, Malone knew little about Utah and was disappointed with the draft result. Writer Clay Latimer wrote, ''When Karl Malone arrived in Salt Lake City in 1985, he couldn't make a free throw, hit a jumper, decipher a game plan, and he lacked the emotional resources and ruthlessness to make himself into a first-rank power forward, according to his plentiful critics. The Utah Jazz, meanwhile, was a burlesque of an NBA franchise.''

Jazz coach Frank Layden saw Malone's potential, which eventually earned him the nickname of ''The Mailman'' for delivering what the team needed. By his third season, Malone averaged more than 25 points per game. With guard John Stockton wracking up record numbers of assists, Jazz fans loved to hear the phrase ''Stockton to Malone'' again and again.

After putting together a winning combination, Frank Layden early in the 1988–1989 season resigned as the Jazz coach to become its president. Assistant Coach Jerry Sloan, a former NBA star, took over as head coach.

The Delta Center and Other Ventures in the 1990s

With his car dealerships and Jazz ownership a success, Larry Miller decided to go into debt for a third time—to build a new sports and entertainment arena called the Delta Center. The Salt Palace simply was not large enough to hold a sufficient number of Jazz fans. So in 1990 Miller invested $5 million of his own money and borrowed $66 million to build the new sports/entertainment center that seated more than 19,000.

Jay Francis, senior vice-president for marketing, negotiated with Smith's Food & Drug Centers and Franklin Quest (later renamed Franklin Covey) before the Jazz sold Delta Air Lines the rights to use its name on the new facility. Owner Larry Miller disliked such commercialization of sports but realized it was an economic necessity as the cost of players' salaries and operating expenses escalated faster than ticket prices.

Francis also played a crucial role in selling the Delta Center's 56 luxury suites. Originally, in 1990 and 1991, one could buy a suite for $50,000 to $95,000 a year. But like everything else in the NBA, including season tickets and players' salaries, the cost of the suites increased to between $78,000 and $130,000 in 1999.

On October 9, 1991 the Delta Center was dedicated, and the Utah Jazz played their first game in the new arena that fall. On October 22, 1991 the Delta Center held its first rock concert when the group Oingo Boingo came to Salt Lake City. President J. C. O'Neil of United Concerts, in the September 19, 1991 *Salt Lake Tribune,* said the new building's seating capacity, along with better power sources and improved access for those with disabilities, made such concerts possible. Another feature was the Sony Jumbotron Video System, a four-sided 9-by-12-foot screen that showed both live performances and instant replay, more important for sports teams. Scott Williams, the Delta Center's general manager, reported that its designers took good ideas from other sports arenas and that it closely resembled Milwaukee's Bradley Center.

Although the Delta Center hosted mainly sports and entertainment, large business meetings also have been held there. For example, Dexter Yager, a major Amway distributor, held annual conventions in the Delta Center, attracting thousands of people who booked most of the city's hotels.

In January 1993 Miller finally realized that his business success had cost him a lot of time away from his wife Gail and their children. In line with his Mormon beliefs, Miller found more time for his children and grandchildren as the decade progressed, while still promoting his businesses.

A popular speaker, Miller once spoke at a college symposium for 11 hours straight. He even said in the November 1996 *HomeCourt* magazine, a Jazz publication, that he did not sell cars or own the Jazz for a living. "What I do for a living is talk."

After five years of owning the Golden Eagles, a professional hockey team in Salt Lake City, in 1994 Miller sold the team that had lost about $1 million each year. The franchise left the city and became the Detroit Vipers.

To promote his businesses, including the Utah Jazz, his car dealerships, the Delta Center, KJZZ-TV, Pro Image retail stores, and Salt Lake City's Thrifty Car Rental, in 1995 Miller started his own in-house advertising agency called LHM Advertising. Working out of the Jazz headquarters in the Delta Center, Jay Francis, the Jazz marketing vice-president who managed the new ad agency, said it used direct mail and telephoning to market the businesses, in addition to more traditional methods like radio, billboard, and TV advertising.

In 1996 the NBA Board of Governors approved the formation of the Women's National Basketball Association (WNBA), and Salt Lake City was chosen as one of the eight cities to sponsor charter teams. Larry Miller's Utah Starzz thus helped make women's basketball history.

In June 1999 the WNBA's 12 teams started the league's third season. After a rocky start, the league was maturing. For example, its teams enjoyed an average attendance of 10,000 fans per game in the 1998 season, far more than had been expected.

The retail division of the Utah Jazz had started in March 1987 when the Jazz purchased four ProImage shops that sold sports apparel and other gifts and souvenirs. In 1996 the Jazz ended any association with ProImage and changed the name of their stores to Fanzz. By March 1999, 28 Fanzz stores, including 15 stores in Idaho, California, Colorado, and New Mexico, sold items with the Jazz logo, as well as hats, shirts, and other items promoting the Utah Starzz, Utah's college teams, professional teams in other cities, and two teams not owned by Larry Miller—the Utah Grizzlies professional hockey team and the Salt Lake Buzz minor league baseball team. Although retail sales were a minor part of Larry Miller's businesses, the Fanzz stores were profitable. Shauna Smith pointed out in 1999 that, "Few NBA teams have ventured into the retail business. Teams like the Phoenix Suns, Detroit Pistons, and Orlando Magic are involved in the business, but no team comes even close to the retail involvement of the Utah Jazz."

In 1999 the financial world considered the Utah Jazz to be one of the NBA's best managed franchises. In March, Morgan Stanley along with First Security Bank of Utah helped refinance the $50 million that Larry Miller still owed on the Delta Center. Investors were encouraged by the Jazz's strong fan base, aided by the team's *HomeCourt* magazine started in 1998 and increased season ticket sales. Investors also knew that the Utah Jazz had gone to the NBA finals two years in a row in the late 1990s and consistently for many years participated in the playoffs, thus making them one of the NBA's best teams. Standard & Poor Corporate Rating Service gave the March 1999 refinancing a "low-A" grade, the highest it had ever given for a sports or entertainment deal. In addition to Miller's Delta Center debts, in 1999 he also owed about $92 million for buildings and land used by his car dealerships.

After opening his first Sandy car dealership a few years earlier, Larry Miller sought ways to promote business and entertainment in the Salt Lake City suburb. He and other car dealers invested in a huge AutoMall in Sandy. In addition, in 1997 Miller purchased and then demolished the old Jordan High School on 9400 South State Street in Sandy. At a West High School assembly, Miller told the students that in 1962, his senior year at West High, the school lost the state basketball championship to Jordan High School. "It has been a burr under my saddle," added Miller jokingly in the January 17, 1998 *Salt Lake Tribune.* "So, I bought the old Jordan High and tore that sucker down. It took 35 years, but we got even."

Then Miller began construction of a new office and entertainment building called the Jordan Commons. It was planned to include 270,000 feet of office space, a 35,000-square-foot Mexican restaurant, and a 16-screen multiplex theater. By January 1999 the ten-story complex was half completed. Miller had invested $20 million in the Jordan Commons by May 1999 and was looking at spending about another $90 million to finish that project.

In late 1998, also in Sandy, Miller began construction of a two-story Larry H. Miller Entrepreneurship Training Center in partnership with Salt Lake Community College. Miller planned to give the $7 million building, land, and accompanying parking lot to the college. Sterling Francom, director of the college's entrepreneurship program that started in 1990, said in the November 12, 1998 *Deseret News* that the new facility would "be able to accommodate upwards of 5,000 to 7,000 people annually through the training program. . . . There's no other place in the country that will have such a thing as this."

"I have to consider myself fortunate," said Larry Miller in the November 1990 *Utah Holiday*. "It's proof the American dream is alive and well." To encourage others to take the risks necessary to fulfill their dreams of owning their own business, Miller supported Salt Lake Community College and other programs with not only funding but also his time. For example, he taught a graduate class on entrepreneurship at the Brigham Young University School of Management.

In 1999 Miller's companies were overseen by two men. Richard Nelson served as president of the Larry H. Miller Group of Automotive Companies. Dennis Haslam, who had founded the law firm of Winder and Haslam, had served since 1997 as the president of the Larry H. Miller Group of Sports and Entertainment Companies.

Although Miller took numerous risks trying new business ventures, his management style also included long-term relationships. For example, he helped veterans John Stockton and Karl Malone start their own dealerships in the late 1990s. Three of his vice-presidents by 1999 had served a combined 54 years with the Utah Jazz: David Allred, vice-president, public relations; Jay Francis, senior vice-president, marketing; and Grant Harrison, vice-president, promotions and game operations. Jazz President and Utah Starzz Coach Frank Layden also spent many years with the Jazz. "Hot Rod" Hundley was the voice of the Jazz on both radio and TV for about 25 years. Such continuity, somewhat rare among other professional teams and businesses, might have seemed old-fashioned, but it was part of Miller's formula for continued success.

Principal Subsidiaries

Larry H. Miller Corporation-Colorado Inc.; Larry H. Miller of Colorado Springs Inc.; Larry H. Miller Subaru Ltd.; Larry H. Miller Arena Corporation; Heritage Imports Inc.; Larry H. Miller Corporation-New Mexico; Larry H. Miller Corporation-Oklahoma; Jazz Basketball Investors Inc.

Principal Divisions

LHM Advertising; Fanzz; Larry H. Miller Leasing; Larry H. Miller Toyota; First Western Heritage Leasing; Prestige Leasing; Larry H. Miller Real Estate; Larry H. Miller Chevrolet; Larry H. Miller Chrysler Plymouth-Jeep Eagle; Landcar Management.

Further Reading

Buttars, Lori, "Delta Center To House Rock Concerts in Addition to Jazz," *Salt Lake Tribune,* September 19, 1991, p. B6.

Cates, Karl, "Larry's World: An Interview with Larry H. Miller," *Deseret News* (Web Edition), April 28, 1994.

——, "Long Live the Jazz," *Deseret News,* May 12, 1996, pp. A1, A8.

——, "Unknowns Suit Up for the Jazz," *Salt Lake Tribune,* May 14, 1999, pp. A1, A15.

Free, Cathy, "Life with Larry: Off the Court and Showroom Floor, Miller Is Your Basic Family Man," *Salt Lake Tribune,* June 10, 1990, pp. B1–B2.

Horowitz, Alan S., "Off the Court: Jazz Greats in the Business Arena," *Utah Business,* November 1996, pp. 38–42.

Hundley, Rod, with Tom McEachin, *Hot Rod Hundley: "You Gotta Love It, Baby,"* Champaign, Ill.: Sports Publishing, 1998.

Kratz, Gregory, "Encouraging Entrepreneurship," *Deseret News* (Web Edition), November 12, 1998.

Lewis, Michael C., *To the Brink: Stockton, Malone, and the Utah Jazz's Climb to the Edge of Glory,* New York: Simon & Schuster, 1998.

Ryan, Kevin, "Driven To Succeed," *Utah Holiday,* November 1990, pp. 50–54, 62.

Sahm, Phil, "Miller Built Empire on Calculated Risks," *Salt Lake Tribune,* May 2, 1999, pp. D1, D10.

Smith, Shauna, "Fanzz Stores Are Big Hit," *HomeCourt,* March 1999, pp. 56–57.

Sorensen, Dan, "A Man of Parts," *HomeCourt,* November 1996, pp. 19–21, 64.

Swensen, Jason, "Miller Complex Halfway Complete," *Deseret News* (Web Edition), January 20, 1999.

—David M. Walden

LeBoeuf, Lamb, Greene & MacRae, L.L.P.

125 West 55th Street
New York City, New York 10019-5389
U.S.A.
(212) 424-8000
Fax: (212) 424-8500
Web site: http://www.llgm.com

Private Partnership
Founded: 1929 as LeBoeuf & Winston
Employees: 1,725
Sales: $225.5 million (1997)
NAIC: 54111 Offices of Lawyers

One of the world's largest law firms, LeBoeuf, Lamb, Greene & MacRae, L.L.P., maintains 15 offices across the United States. The firm represents over 2,500 corporate clients of various sizes in over 50 nations, and operates seven overseas offices, including locations in Kazakstan, Uzbekistan, and Kyrgyz, as well as an associated office in Sao Paulo. From its beginnings in 1929, LeBoeuf has been known for its representation of energy and public utility firms, and since 1965 it has been preeminent in serving insurance companies. The firm's major clients include ITT, Niagra Mohawk Power Corporation, Lloyd's of London, the Equitable Life Assurance Society, and Alcoa.

Origins and Early Decades

Randall J. LeBoeuf, Jr., the firm's founder, was born in Albany, New York, in 1897. After serving in World War I, he began practicing law in his father's office in Albany in 1920. In 1925 he began a two-year period as assistant attorney general for New York in charge of legal matters surrounding water utility companies. While still in solo practice in 1929, LeBoeuf became general counsel to Niagra Hudson Power Company and the Aluminum Company of America (ALCOA). As his workload increased, LeBoeuf recruited his friend Bill Winston from another Albany law firm to form the partnership LeBoeuf & Winston on October 7, 1929, just before the stock market collapsed. Within six months, the new partnership had moved to

New York City, where it shared offices with Niagra Hudson Power at 15 Broad Street.

The LeBoeuf law firm began with clients in the utilities and energy industry, but in a few years those early clients needed help in areas other than just water rights law. So in 1934 Horace Lamb joined the expanding young partnership to enhance its expertise in a wider variety of legal matters. Characterized as an aggressive litigator, Lamb came to the firm after working for the Antitrust Division of the U.S. Department of Justice as well as in private practice. Lamb would soon become a name partner at the firm.

Business continued in the 1940s, and the 1950s brought new clients and partners to the still modest-sized law firm. In 1952 Adrian C. Leiby, a former clerk to U.S. Supreme Court Justice Harlan Fiske Stone, left his position at the firm of DeForest & Durr to join LeBoeuf, which was renamed LeBoeuf, Lamb & Leiby. Leiby brought with him 20 years of experience in corporate securities and finances.

Anticipating the creation of the Atomic Energy Commission to regulate the new civilian use of fission plants, LeBoeuf opened its first branch office in 1952 in Washington, D.C. to help utilities license nuclear plants. According to a firm chronology, the new branch also did a "modest amount of secret, but routine work for the CIA," the U.S. intelligence agency created in the late 1940s at the start of the Cold War.

Cameron F. MacRae, Jr., left the rival law firm of Whitman Ransom in 1958 to join LeBoeuf. With 20 years experience as one of the nation's top public utility lawyers, the new lateral hire brought several important clients with him. The following year, the firm took a major step forward when company founder Randall LeBoeuf became the special assistant attorney general representing New York in a water rights dispute over the amount of Great Lakes water that could be diverted through the Chicago Drainage Canal. This conflict pitted the lakes states against those next to the Mississippi River. This drawn out battle helped the firm enjoy high profits for over a decade as it represented New York.

From 1961 to 1965 LeBoeuf represented seven large utility companies that filed 42 antitrust lawsuits against large electrical equipment manufacturers, including General Electric, Westinghouse, and Allis Chalmers. To handle these major cases, LeBoeuf in 1961 laterally hired Taylor Briggs to enhance the firm's litigation department, and we eventually go on to serve as the company's chairperson, though not a name partner. At the time, the firm included 24 lawyers, half of whom were partners. In 1962 the growing partnership moved to larger offices at the Chase Manhattan Bank headquarters in New York.

In 1965 Lloyd's of London chose LeBoeuf as its new general counsel in the United States. This appointment led to the law firm representing other major insurance companies, including Aetna, All State, Chubb, Cigna, Crown Life, Liberty Mutual Insurance, Metropolitan Life, Transamerica Life, Mutual Life Insurance Company of New York, and others. By helping such insurance corporations deal with the ever-changing laws and regulations of 50 states and the federal government, as well as with litigation, restructuring, antitrust suits, and other matters, LeBoeuf became the nation's preeminent firm in the insurance industry.

Growth in the 1970s and 1980s

In the 1970s, the firm lost its three os its name partners, who died in successive years: Randall LeBoeuf in 1975, Adrian Leiby in 1976, and Horace Lamb in 1977. Cameron MacRae, who had been formally installed as presiding partner in 1970, remained at the firm, which had become known as LeBoeuf, Lamb, Leiby & MacRae.

The company moved to grow through acquisition in the 1970s. In 1978 it acquired the New York law partnership of Reed, McCarthy and Giordano, founded in 1910. The attorneys brought over to the firm in the takeover would help found LeBoeuf's municipal bond practice. Also during this time, LeBoeuf named its first female partner, attorney Sheila Marshall, who had begun with the firm as a legal secretary to founder Randall LeBoeuf. By 1978 the firm numbered 106 lawyers in New York and Washington, D.C. offices. Later in the year LeBoeuf opened its first foreign office in London, mainly to oversee the business generated by client Lloyd's of London.

Like many other law firms, LeBoeuf grew rapidly in the 1980s. In 1981 the firm moved west, opening an office in Salt Lake City, only the second "outside" firm to break into Utah. By offering high salaries and opportunities to work on high-profile cases, outside law firms attracted some of the best local attorneys. By 1994 LeBoeuf's Utah office employed 14 attorneys who represented local clients as well as some in other states, such as the Los Angeles Department of Water and Power. The Salt Lake City's local managing partner, Ralph Mabey, handled several notable cases during this time, including representing the airline pilots of TWA, the creditors in the bankruptcy case of Federated Department Stores and Allied Stores, and also Bonneville Pacific in a controversial bankruptcy case.

Further intrastate expansion continued, as in 1987 the law firm started a one-attorney office in Jacksonville, Florida, its first branch in the South and the first started by a New York firm in that city. LeBoeuf began its Florida operations with two insurance clients, Metropolitan Security Life and Guarantee Security Life. The following year, LeBoeuf represented the National Farmers Union Acquisition Company, when it acquired the Loyalty Life Insurance Company, a subsidiary of Continental Insurance Company. By 1990 the Jacksonville office had grown to maintain a staff 11 lawyers.

Other branch offices were established in the 1980s, including sites in Boston, Albany, Newark, San Francisco, Los Angeles, Hartford, Harrisburg, and Brussels, Belgium. In 1987 LeBoeuf opened an office in Raleigh, North Carolina, merging with the local law firm of Moore, Ragsdale, Liggett, Ray & Foley. The branch had only a six-year history, however, closing in 1993 following conflicts with the New York headquarters, as well as reported low morale and a high rate of associate turnover. The resultant new firm of Ragsdale, Liggett & Foley, formed by former LeBoeuf attorneys, planned to maintain a correspondent relationship as needed with LeBoeuf.

This period of expansion was not without its challenges. *The American Lawyer* noted, for example, that from 1986 to 1988 Leboeuf increased its work force of attorneys by 29 percent, from 281 to 362, while its profits per partner increased only 12 percent. Moreover, according to *The Guide to New York Law Firms,* one legal consultant criticized the firm's management, alleging that LeBoeuf was "not well-managed . . . and takes in marginal people. It is not picking off good laterals." Other critics pointed to LeBoeuf's financial performance or maintained that such rapid growth had resulted in internal strife at the work place. With the growth of legal specialization, such developments were not surprising.

The growth of many law firms, including LeBoeuf, was fueled by several trends or changes. First, the U.S. Supreme Court ruled in the 1970s that restrictions on professional advertising were unconstitutional, paving the way for more competition in the industry. Also, in 1979 *The American Lawyer* magazine was introduced, which featured articles on internal practices at law firms as well as financial and salary rankings, information not generally made public until that time. With increased demand for legal services, given a good economy and ever more litigation, law firms were hiring more associates and competing for lateral hires of experienced lawyers from rival firms. For many, the days of lifetime employment at one firm became an outmoded concept.

Practice in the 1990s

In 1991 LeBoeuf established an office in Moscow headed by James I. Mandel, making it one of just five American law firms to operate there. Having doubled in size between 1982 and 1992, LeBoeuf soon needed larger and more efficient office space. In July 1992 the firm moved from its Madison Avenue facilities into new headquarters at 125 West 55th Street, signing a 20-year lease for eight floors as well as space in the basement and ground floor of the 23-story building.

In fall 1993 the law firm opened its Denver office, which was soon enhanced by the addition of prominent Denver bankruptcy attorney Carl Eklund and four associates, who were recruited laterally. Eklund brought to LeBoeuf his major client, America West Airlines, whose bankruptcy reorganization he had managed since 1991. Later in 1994 six prominent trial lawyers also joined LeBoeuf's Denver office, bringing the Denver total to 29 lawyers, and making Denver the fifth largest of LeBoeuf's 16 branch offices.

In 1993 the Aluminum Company of America (Alcoa) announced that it planned to shut down its own litigation staff of six attorneys and give its national litigation duties to the newly formed Pittsburgh office of LeBoeuf. LeBoeuf had become Alcoa's product liability counsel for cases in New York and New Jersey in 1982. The Alcoa-LeBoeuf deal was unusual for two reasons. First, it contradicted a trend in which corporations were hiring more inhouse attorneys. Alcoa had started hiring its own litigation attorneys about ten years before, and had saved money for about six years before its legal business necessitated outside hirings and thus dramatically increased expenses. By giving all litigation to LeBoeuf, Alcoa expected significant savings, important because the firm lost $1.1 billion in 1992. The move was also unique in that the two firms agreed on a flat annual fee, rather than the more typical practice of hourly billing.

In 1994 the firm changed its name to LeBoeuf, Lamb, Greene & MacRae. Name partner Donald Greene had been with the firm since 1965 and was named to replace Briggs as chairperson in 1989. Under Greene, the firm began seeking to create a truly multinational practice, commencing to hire British lawyers to work in its London office. By the end of 1995 about a dozen London attorneys had joined LeBoeuf's London office and plans were to increase that number to 50.

In the United States, the firm was kept busy with events in California. In December 1994, Orange County, California, declared Chapter 9 bankruptcy, having lost $1.64 billion in bad investments. In June 1996, the county filed five lawsuits in U.S. Bankruptcy Court against those it claimed had known of the imminent financial distress and had done nothing to stop it. LeBoeuf—along with Rauscher Pierce Refsnes, Standard & Poor's, Morgan Stanley, and the Student Loan Marketing Association—was among those sued, having been employed by the county as bond counsel. In all, the county was asking for about $7 billion, $500 million of that total from LeBoeuf. LeBoeuf was also named in a related suit during this time brought by the North Orange County Community College.

In early 1998 LeBoeuf, without admitting guilt, settled its two lawsuits before either went to trial, agreeing to pay the community college $10.2 million and Orange County $45 million. As the college was a party to the Orange County suit, it agreed to cede $2 million as its share of the $45 million county suit. LeBoeuf's total cost thus came to around $53.2 million, one of the largest settlements against a law firm in the nation's history.

Also during this time, LeBoeuf was expanding into Texas. In January 1998 four attorneys, including the managing partner, of the Houston law firm Hutcheson & Grundy left to establish the Houston office of LeBoeuf, Lamb, Greene & MacRae. The 44 remaining partners voted to dissolve Hutcheson & Grundy due to its inability to win corporate clients. LeBoeuf was the third New York law firm to open a Houston office. Representing PanEnergy Corporation, Texas Utilities Company, and PG&E Corporation in various acquisitions had created a significant Houston base of operations for LeBoeuf in Houston. The Houston office planned to employ about 50 attorneys within a couple years as it focused on energy, insurance, and Latin American project financing.

Based on its 1997 gross revenue of $225.5 million, the LeBoeuf law firm was ranked by *The American Lawyer* as the USA's 26th largest law firm in the United States. That publication, in cooperation with London's *Legal Business,* listed LeBoeuf as number 33 based on 1997 revenue and number 20 based on number of attorneys (736) in its first ranking of the world's largest law firms.

As the new century approached, LeBoeuf met the same challenges facing other megafirms. Globalization of the economy was stimulating the internal growth of law firms as well as prompting many to form alliances or joint ventures with other firms abroad. New currencies, such as Europe's "euro," and new trade agreements including the North American Free Trade Agreement, were changing the way international business would be conducted in the next century. Competition was generated not just from other law firms but also from accounting firms that were hiring their own attorneys. Moreover, as more women and minorities became attorneys, law firms faced new management challenges. Many were having to offer either part-time or more flexible scheduling for their work force as well as programs to combat sexual harassment in the work place. Finally, with rapid developments in technology, increasing numbers of attorneys were performing more of their duties from offices in their homes. Dealing with such internal changes, as well as meeting the expectations of clients and government regulations, gave LeBoeuf's leaders plenty to ponder.

Further Reading

Boselovic, Len, "Alcoa Hires Outside Lawyers," *Pittsburgh Post-Gazette,* August 20, 1993, p. B2.

Cherovsky, Erwin, "LeBoeuf, Lamb, Leiby & MacRae," *The Guide to New York Law Firms,* New York: St. Martin's Press, 1991, pp. 118–121.

Campbell, Ronald, and Chris Knap, "O.C. Sues Its Former Advisers," *Orange County Register,* June 12, 1996, p. A1.

Campbell, Ronald, "Bond Lawyers Settle with O.C.," *Orange County Register,* April 15, 1998, p. B1.

Conner, Chance, "Top Lawyers Quit Patton, Boggs," *Denver Post,* September 29, 1994, p. C1.

Day, Janet, "Bankruptcy Attorney Eklund Joins LeBoeuf," *Denver Post,* February 1, 1994, p. C1.

DeMarco, Anthony, "LeBoeuf, Lamb Leases New Law Space with Vision," *Facilities Design & Management,* June 1994, p. 42.

Funk, Marianne, "Local Opportunities Blossom as National Law Firms Branch Out," *Deseret News,* April 3, 1994, pp. M1–M2.

Hirsch, Jane, "Ellis Zahra: He's Constantly Challenged by the Law," *Jacksonville Business Journal,* April 20, 1990, p. 8.

Holzinger, Albert G., "Bulletin Boards' Global Reach," *Nation's Business,* February 1995, p. 33.

The LeBoeuf Story, New York: LeBoeuf, Lamb, Greene & MacRae, self-produced historical video, 1994.

Livingston, Skip, "N.Y. Law Firm Wins Top Local Attorney in First Foray in South," *Jacksonville Business Journal,* November 23, 1987, p. 4.

Mollenkamp, Carrick, "Tracing the Roots of LeBoeuf Split," *Triangle Business Journal* (Raleigh, N.C.), December 6, 1993, p. 1.

Olson, Thomas, "Alcoa Moves to Trim Legal Staff, Hire NYC Firm," *Pittsburgh Business Times Journal,* July 26, 1993, p. 1.

Perin, Monica, "Hutcheson Dissolves in Departures' Wake," *Houston Business Journal,* January 16, 1998, p. 1.

—David M. Walden

Lindal Cedar Homes, Inc.

4300 South 104th Place
Seattle, Washington 98178
U.S.A.
(206) 725-0900
(800) 426-0536
Fax: (206) 725-1615
Web site: http://www.lindal.com

Public Company
Incorporated: 1966
Employees: 190
Sales: $37.7 million (1998)
Stock Exchanges: NASDAQ
Ticker Symbol: LNDL
NAIC: 321992 Prefabricated Wood Building
    Manufacturing

The largest and oldest manufacturer of premanufactured cedar houses in the world, Lindal Cedar Homes, Inc. sells year-round cedar homes and sunrooms. The company's precut homes are sold in kits containing nearly every component necessary to build a house, excluding mechanical items, flooring, cabinetry, and bathroom fixtures. During the late 1990s, the kits were sold by 170 independent dealers located in the United States and in foreign markets. A family-operated enterprise throughout its history, Lindal Cedar Homes maintains operations in Surrey, British Columbia, where the company obtains the cedar for its kits, and in the Pacific Northwest region surrounding its headquarters in Seattle.

Origins

Company founder and family patriarch Walter Lindal entered the precut housing business immediately after World War II. During the war years, Lindal served as an ordnance specialist, testing captured enemy weapons at military bases in the United States and Canada. Lindal's military experience exposed him to the prefabrication building methods used to house troops and proved to be the inspiration for his professional career. When he was discharged from the Canadian army in 1945, Lindal settled in Toronto and started his own business producing modest, prefabricated frame vacation homes that resembled log cabins. To add to what little experience he had—consisting only of observing the construction of army barracks and working for an uncle involved in the lumber business prior to the war—Lindal studied architecture at the University of Ottawa on a part-time basis. With this background Lindal opened shop, entering an industry that would later regard him as a pioneer.

Aside from the normal challenges a fledgling entrepreneur faced, Lindal had to contend with an obstacle of his own making. By his admission, he had selected one of the most difficult markets in which to sell log-cabin-style housing. In Toronto, brick was the construction material of choice, its prevalence making Lindal's sales efforts a daunting task. Further, Lindal's material of choice—cedar—was not abundantly available, particularly the grades of wood he needed. Despite these inherent problems with the location of his company, Lindal managed to create a burgeoning and stable business. By the beginning of the 1960s, he had four plants in operation producing the primary material components for his cabins. At this point, however, the problems with his location could no longer be surmounted. High transportation costs in the area limited Lindal's shipping radius to approximately 300 miles. Beyond that boundary, the shipping charges priced his log cabins out of the market. In order to expand his business further, Lindal needed to move, so he, his wife, and his children (the future senior executives of the company) packed up and headed west.

Lindal arrived in Vancouver, British Columbia, in 1962, ready to re-establish his business in an environment conducive to growth. Vancouver proved to be an ideal location. There was an abundant supply of red cedar in British Columbia and the long-haul freight costs were low, providing Lindal with the material and the room to expand his business. Expansion was on his mind and his expectations for the company were growing, leading him to invest in a new sawmill in British Columbia, where the company would obtain the bulk of its timber for the remainder of the century. Lindal established a longstanding presence in Canada, but the lure of fast-growing markets in the United States prompted another relocation of his company's

Company Perspectives:

We use only the highest quality building materials—starting with Western red cedar. The enduring beauty of our fine-grained wood can't be imitated with inferior materials. Our guaranteed supply of kiln dried timber ensures that you will be provided with the best in the industry. With the finest materials and the most stunning home designs on the market today, Lindal's trademark post and beam construction allows for soaring cathedral ceilings, exposed beams, and large expanses of glass—creating a truly remarkable design you'll be proud to call home. Plus, our new Select building system combines more design possibilities than ever before at an exceptional value for our renowned quality. What's more, our international team of local Lindal dealers are there to assist you from the design to the completion of your new home.

sales and administrative offices. In 1966 he moved his family again, establishing a permanent headquarters in Seattle. In 1971, he took his company public.

Marketing Strategy Matures in the 1970s

Shortly after Lindal Cedar Homes completed its initial public offering of stock, Lindal began to think on a grander scale. As the decade progressed, he began manufacturing and marketing housing kits to serve as primary residences rather than as vacation cabins, making a transition from the company's origins as a log-cabin producer toward a more upscale producer of premium-priced homes. Customers were offered the opportunity to design their future homes according to their particular desires, the diversity and complexity of which increased as technology advanced. Concurrent with this foray into a much larger, much more lucrative market, considerable effort was devoted to cultivating a network of dealers. The dealers, the liaison between the customer and Lindal Cedar Homes, sold the kits, helped secure financing, and assisted the customer in custom designing a home. The specifications decided upon by the customer were then sent via the dealer to Lindal Cedar Homes' manufacturing facilities. In building this dealer base, the company strove to secure agreements that restricted dealers to selling Lindal Cedar Homes exclusively, which created a partnership between the two parties that represented an integral facet of the company's success.

As Lindal Cedar Homes repositioned itself in the mainstream market, Lindal's children began taking their places as the next generation of management. "Dad," Lindal's son Robert explained, "wanted us all in the business, and he wanted us to grow with it." Robert Lindal, like his two brothers, Douglas and Martin, and his sister, Bonnie, started working for the company during summer vacations from high school. As the Lindal children grew older, each gravitated toward his or her particular interest on a full-time basis, with Robert attracted by the operational aspect of the business, Douglas by sales, Bonnie by marketing, and Martin by administration. Robert, appointed chief executive officer in 1981, rose to the greatest prominence

within the organization, but his siblings played essential supporting roles, helping the company realize the greatest success in its history during the 1980s. With the combination of shrewd marketing and the strength of an efficient and loyal dealer base, Lindal Cedar Homes more than tripled its revenue volume between 1983 and 1987. By 1987 the company was collecting $35 million in sales a year, while its net income, which had totaled $190,000 in 1983, had swelled to more than $2 million. Although the financial totals recorded at the end of 1987 represented prodigious increases, the celebrations in Seattle would cease a short time later. At the peak of its performance, the company stumbled profoundly. The remainder of the 1980s would be spent trying to cure the pernicious problems before they caused irreparable harm to the company.

Diversification in the 1980s

With annual sales escalating at an encouraging rate, the Lindals decided it was time to diversify the company's interests and extend its reach into other markets. It was a move few industry pundits questioned at the time—a strategically sound maneuver made while the company was recording the greatest financial growth in its history—but the results were unquestionably disappointing. First, in 1986, the Lindal Cedar Home board of directors decided to begin producing oak and maple flooring to be used for the company's home packages and to sell to the outside market. "We had a vacant plant, we had equipment, we had the kilns," explained Robert Lindal, rationalizing the foray into flooring. "It looked like a good way to build volume with comparatively little investment." It was a natural, logical extension of the company's business, much like the other attempt to diversify in 1986 through the acquisition of WindowVisions, Inc. For years, WindowVisions had been making window frames for Lindal Cedar Homes. Its acquisition by the Lindals presented management with an opportunity to vertically integrate company operations, "to get control of the supply and at the same time expand the market," explained Robert Lindal. Making hardwood floors and pine window frames proved to be ill-advised ventures, however, quickly hobbling Lindal Cedar Homes' progress.

Shortly after the company delved into it, the flooring business began to rack up losses. The company's entry into flooring occurred at roughly the same time industry capacity increased significantly, which forced prices down and eroded profit margins. WindowVisions, which to Robert Lindal and those around him "seemed like a good fit," also recorded mounting losses, as the Lindals found themselves stewarding a company they did not have the experience to manage. As a result of the losses, Lindal Cedar Homes' earnings fell from $.94 per share in 1987 to $.37 per share in 1989, punctuating a decline that "seemed to last forever," according to Robert Lindal. A reaction to the company's miscues came relatively quickly and the financial slide was arrested, despite Robert Lindal's impression that the financial malaise dragged on for years. WindowVisions was trimmed to a quarter of its original size, with its production restricted primarily to meeting Lindal Cedar Homes' needs. While the window business was being reduced to a more manageable size (downsizing began in May 1989), the Lindals also turned their attention to the floundering flooring business and took a more drastic approach. In January 1990, the entire hardwood flooring business was shut down, its failure a painful lesson in the danger of diversification. Although the mistakes made in 1986 had caused companywide profits to plummet, the debacle lasted less than two years, representing a damaging yet brief hiccough in 40 years of otherwise strident success. By the beginning of the 1990s, Lindal Cedar Homes had fully recovered.

The 1990s: A Mixed Picture

Entering the 1990s, Lindal Cedar Homes ranked as the largest maker and distributor of custom cedar houses in the world. Internationally, the company had achieved great strides by negotiating agreements with dealers overseas. By 1990 the company had a network of independent dealers in Spain, the United Kingdom, West Germany, Greece, Korea, Japan, and New Zealand—350 dealers in all, counting those in the United States and abroad. The dealers exclusively sold Lindal kits and worked with customers to facilitate the home's construction. Lindal Home Cedar dealers helped customers find a contractor to build the home, arranged financing, and explained applicable local building codes. Additionally, customers were given the opportunity to custom design their homes within certain parameters. In 1990 the company introduced new technology that broadened the customer's design choices and expedited the completion of his or her order. Called "Lindal-sketch," the computer-aided design system allowed dealers to produce floor plans and home designs for individual customers. "Once major decisions have been made," explained Douglas Lindal, executive vice-president, "a customer can leave the distributor's office with a floor plan acceptable to a bank for mortgage appraisal and accurate enough to get bids from contractors." After a customer completed design decisions, the dealer sent a floppy disk to the company's headquarters, where the data was fed into another computer that created the necessary working drawings.

Armed with new design technology and supported by its expansive dealer base, Lindal Cedar Homes neared its 50th anniversary exuding the vibrancy that had characterized the company during the mid-1980s. Orders for its sunrooms, which were sold in both the remodeling and new home markets, were up 50 percent, representing one of the promising areas of growth for the company during the 1990s. On a general trend, the custom-home market derived its greatest growth from what company officials described as "move-up buyers," affluent, 30- to 60-year-old professionals with household incomes in excess of $50,000. The changing demographics of Lindal Cedar Homes' customers was welcome news, continuing the company's climb toward increasingly upscale markets, a characteristic of its development from the 1970s forward. As the wealth of the company's typical customer increased, the designs of the homes offered by Lindal Cedar Homes changed to cater to the new tastes. Nearly half of the company's customers opted for traditional-style homes with natural-stained red cedar, but the demand for less rustic-looking homes was on the upswing, fueled by the increasing affluence of customers. Clapboard sid-

ing, round log, plank siding, and color-stained exteriors were becoming increasingly popular choices, prompting the company to supplement its range of selections. "We are going after different looks and reaching out beyond the appeal of natural cedar," explained Bonnie Lindal McLennaghan, vice-president of publications. "Home buyers can have anything they want from Lindal."

Following the completion of the company's first half-century of business, the encouraging growth prospects of the 1990s began to fade. During the latter half of the 1990s, as Lindal Cedar Homes hotly pursued further penetration into the upscale segment of the market, the company fell victim to shortages of its primary raw material—western red cedar—which forced prices upward. For decades, the threat of reductions in cedar supply had loomed over the company, but it always managed to obtain sufficient supplies to feed the demands of its business and withstand fluctuations in lumber prices. In 1997, however, high raw material prices persisted, severely hampering profitability. "In more than 50 years of operation," Robert Lindal noted at the time in a press release, "this is one of the most difficult periods we've experienced, and this wood-pricing cycle is one of the longest we've ever seen." For the first time since 1981, Lindal Cedar Homes lost money in 1997, registering a net loss of 452,000. In the wake of the disappointing loss, the company focused on improving operations and efficiencies while it waited for market prices to stabilize.

By the end of the 1990s, Lindal Cedar Home's outlook was more sanguine than it had been at the end of 1997. Although 1998 ended as another unprofitable year, lower wood costs in early 1999 fanned a modicum of optimism. Sales increased 44 percent in the first fiscal quarter of 1999 and profitability improved, aided in part by an 11 percent reduction in general and administrative costs. Further encouraging news arrived during the company's second quarter of business when new home orders increased 28 percent, although sustained profitability continued to elude Lindal Cedar Homes as it planned for the next decade. The first years of the 21st century promised to test the company's ability to withstand the cyclical pressures of its business—a test the oldest and largest manufacturer of cedar homes was amply qualified to pass.

Further Reading

Bady, Susan, "The Growing Market for Factory-Built Housing," *Professional Builder,* August 1990, p. 100.

"Lindal Cedar Homes Reports First Quarter Revenues Rose 44%; Improved Productivity and Lower Wood Costs Reduce Seasonal Loss," *PR Newswire,* May 6, 1999, p. 4718.

Phalon, Richard, "The Dangers of Diversifying," *Forbes,* July 23, 1990, p. 60.

Prinzing, Debra, "Lindal Cedar Homes Aren't Just Rustic Cabins Now," *Puget Sound Business Journal,* September 10, 1990, p. 22.

—Jeffrey L. Covell

Logan's Roadhouse, Inc.

565 Marriott Drive, Suite 490
Nashville, Tennessee 37214
U.S.A.
(615) 885-9056
Fax: (615) 885-9058

Wholly Owned Subsidiary of CBRL Group
Incorporated: 1991
Employees: 5,100
Sales: $101 million (1998)
NAIC: 72211 Full-Service Restaurants

Logan's Roadhouse, Inc. is a chain of more than 40 company-owned and five franchised full-service restaurants located in Tennessee, Kentucky, Indiana, Alabama, Georgia, Virginia, West Virginia, Florida, Louisiana, Ohio, Texas, Oklahoma, and the Carolinas. The restaurants have a casual "honky-tonk" décor and atmosphere, complete with wooden planked floors, a jukebox full of country music, and open, gas-fired mesquite grills. Buckets of unshelled peanuts on each table—which patrons shell onto the floor—are the restaurant's trademark. Logan's menu is standard steakhouse fare: steak, ribs, burgers, and grilled chicken and seafood, along with appetizers, salads, sides, and desserts. The restaurants' moderate prices—an average of $8.75 for lunch and $12.00 for dinner—appeal primarily to a middle-of-the-road, mainstream customer base. By offering selections that range in price from the more budget-minded to the higher end, however, the restaurant attracts a wide spectrum of casual dining patrons.

1991: The First Logan's

The initial Logan's Roadhouse was established in Lexington, Kentucky, in 1991 in a building that had previously housed a Western Sizzlin' steakhouse. Its founders were Dave Wachtel, a restauranteur from Nashville who had earlier served as the CEO for the Shoney's chain, and his partner Charles Mc-Whorter. Striving for a unique casual dining experience that combined reasonably priced, quality food with a fun atmosphere, Wachtel and McWhorter came up with the concept for Logan's—a restaurant that would have the look and feel of the American roadhouses of the 1940s and 1950s. The duo fleshed out their concept with atmospheric touches, such as hand-painted murals, wooden floors, a Wurlitzer jukebox playing foreground music, and a menu of American steakhouse staples. Soon, Logan's atmosphere, in combination with its down-to-earth fare and affordable prices, proved to be a formula for success. Whereas Western Sizzlin', the previous occupant of the site, had been doing approximately $9,000 in weekly sales, Logan's averaged around $50,000. With reaffirmed confidence in the Logan's concept, Wachtel and McWhorter began planning for expansion. One of their first moves was to contact Edwin (Ted) Moats, Jr., a successful restaurateur in his own right.

A 1970 graduate of Vanderbilt University, Moats had begun his career as staff assistant to the president of the First American National Bank in Nashville. Working in business development and commercial lending gave him the opportunity to analyze what worked and what did not for various businesses. One of his most successful accounts was Shoney's—a large, Nashville-headquartered restaurant chain founded by Ray Danner and formerly headed by Wachtel. While handling the Shoney's account, Moats developed a strong relationship with Danner, who was to serve as his mentor throughout the coming two decades. Moats entered the restaurant business himself in 1978 when he took over a Captain D's seafood restaurant, rapidly turning it into one of the chain's most profitable units. Together with a partner, Moats successfully took on several more Captain D's, and by the time Wachtel and McWhorter approached him, had proven himself to be both a shrewd financial analyst and a skillful restaurant operator.

Moats began serving as a consultant to Logan's in January of 1992. His first move was to visit the restaurant quietly and inconspicuously, as a regular patron. Noting that some customers were waiting as long as two hours for a table, Moats suggested enlarging the kitchen to handle more volume and adding more seating to cut down on the wait. He also proposed beefing up the menu to include more choices. Within months of implementing the recommendations, Logan's weekly sales had increased by 60 percent—and Moats had agreed to become the

---

Company Perspectives:

Our mission is to be a growing restaurant company that achieves superior financial results by consistently exceeding our guests' expectations. Our commitment to and our strong belief in the training, development, and retention of performance-oriented team members will drive our success. We are passionate about providing the "Logan's Roadhouse Experience" to each of our guests:

Great food, great drinks, great prices
Friendly, enthusiastic people
Fun, casual, upbeat atmosphere
Great value

---

company's president. Shortly thereafter, Wachtel and Mc-Whorter relinquished active leadership roles, leaving Moats to pilot the fledgling company on his own.

1992–95: Adding Links to the Chain

For the first two years of Moats's leadership, Logan's grew at a conservative pace. Aware that a too rapid expansion could sabotage an otherwise successful concept, Moats opened only one additional restaurant in 1992—in the Hickory Hollow area of Nashville, Tennessee. The following year was likewise slow-paced; at the end of 1993, there were only three Logan's in operation. In the next two years, however, the company picked up steam; by the end of 1995, there were nine Logan's Roadhouses located in Kentucky and Tennessee.

Part of the reason for the company's modest growth rate during its first three years was the painstaking care Moats's management team took in selecting good sites. Logan's strategy was to locate in middle-sized cities with populations of 175,000 to 500,000. If a city looked promising, Moats analyzed the existing restaurant dynamic to see how competitors were faring. "If newcomers are taking business from the tired, older concepts, that's OK," Moats was quoted as saying in a May 12, 1997 article in *Nation's Restaurant News*. "But if the new concepts are competing, that's a sign of saturation." Favoring high-traffic areas, Logan's frequently located near malls, on major thoroughfares, and in college towns.

Moats's diligence was not limited to choosing locations; he was meticulous about virtually *every* aspect of his new venture. Applying wisdom he had picked up from Shoney's Ray Danner, as well as findings from his own restaurant experience and research, he developed a handful of key principles that he used to drive the budding chain: quality, consistency, attention to detail, and low employee turnover. In a May 1997 interview with the *Tennessean,* Moats credited his mentor, Danner, with teaching him the importance of details. "How does our grill look? How does our deli case look? Is the music at the right level?" Moats asked, demonstrating the breadth of his attention to minutiae. "What are the restrooms like? Is the parking lot litter-free? What's the attitude of our employees?"

Moats's last example, employee attitude, was especially important to him. In an industry notorious for its high work force turnover, he set out to improve employee retention and thereby improve overall consistency. Focusing on employee quality of life, Moats structured a work schedule that was somewhat atypical in the restaurant business. Each Logan's location employed six full-time managers, working five-day, 45- to 50-hour weeks, as opposed to the six-day, 60-hour week commonly required in other restaurants. As a result, the company was able to maintain a substantially lower-than-average rate of management turnover: nine percent in 1995, as compared with an industry standard of about 30 percent. Logan's also was able to keep turnover of hourly employees lower than the industry norm—120 percent as compared with the typical 200 percent.

Moats's tactics paid off. Between fiscal 1993 and 1994, sales climbed from $8.8 million to $15 million, and net income more than tripled. At the mid-year point in 1995, Logan's eateries posted revenues of $13.26 million—more than double the total sales for the first half of 1994. Net earnings also were up: $770,000 for the six-month period, as compared with $464,000 for the previous year's corresponding time frame.

1995: Going Public

In July of 1995, Logan's went public in an initial public offering (IPO) that generated more than $13 million in net proceeds. Trading on the Nasdaq market under the ticker RDHS, Logan's stock debuted at $13.50, climbing almost immediately to $17.50 and exceeding the company's expectations. Moats offered his interpretation of the rapid jump-up in Logan's stock in a September 1995 interview with *Nation's Restaurant News*. "We've been on a good run for several years as a private company," he said. "And we hit the market at a time when investors are looking for a company with good growth potential. Restaurant stocks showing that potential are the ones that are coming back."

Logan's added another six sites in 1996, bringing its total to 15 and spreading out from its Tennessee–Kentucky base into Alabama, Georgia, and Indiana. Year-end sales were $41 million, with net earnings of $4.1 million. The company's strong performance continued to attract investor attention and generate activity in the market. In April of 1996, a secondary public offering netted approximately $20 million, and two months later, Logan's issued a three-for-two stock split. Between its 1995 IPO and the end of 1996, the company's stock price had increased by well more than 100 percent, positioning it as the leader of the casual dining category in stock appreciation. Logan's banner year was recognized by *Business Week,* who ranked it number nine in its 1996 list of 100 Hot Growth Companies.

Also in 1996, the company signed its first franchise agreement, with a franchisee who agreed to develop locations in Arkansas, Oklahoma, and Texas over a five-year period. Under the terms of the contract, the franchisee paid an initial $30,000 fee and agreed to monthly royalties of three percent of gross sales. The company's first two franchised restaurants opened in May and November of 1996, in two Oklahoma locations. Viewing franchising as a good auxiliary growth tactic, Moats began looking at similar opportunities. His strategy was to hand-pick developers who would agree to grow franchises in regions falling just outside the company's identified growth area—which was the southern Midwest and the Southeast.

1997: Rapid Growth

During 1997, Logan's added nine new restaurants, increasing their growth rate and exceeding their own goals for the year. Eight of the new restaurants were located in markets new to the company. By the end of the year, there were 24 company-owned and three franchised Logan's Roadhouses operating in Alabama, Georgia, Indiana, Kentucky, Louisiana, Tennessee, West Virginia, and Oklahoma. Five more restaurants were under construction. The company also had signed its second franchise agreement, covering the areas of North Carolina, South Carolina, and Augusta, Georgia.

Each Logan's location was serving approximately 6,800 patrons per week. With average check prices of around $10.00 per person, each restaurant was grossing roughly $3.5 million annually. According to a May 1997 article in the *Tennessean,* that number compared favorably with Logan's competition. The *Tennessean* reported an annual gross of $2.5 million per location for the O'Charley's and Lone Star chains and approximately $3.1 million for Outback Steakhouse.

The company's performance earned accolades from both business and restaurant industry authorities. In the spring of 1997, *Nation's Restaurant News* designated Logan's as one of the country's nine "hottest concepts," based on its originality in menu, atmosphere, service, and consumer appeal. The following November, *Forbes* magazine named Logan's number 17 of the "200 Best Small Companies in America." In addition, for the second year in a row, the company was included on *Business Week's* annual list of the top 100 small U.S. businesses.

Logan's closed out 1997 with total revenues of $66.5 million—an increase of 62 percent over 1996. Net income increased almost 60 percent, to $6.6 million from the previous year's $4.1 million. Despite strong financial performance and positive reviews, however, Logan's stock was suffering at the year end. It closed at $15.50—a 34 percent drop from 1996's close at $23.50. In the 1997 annual report, Moats wrote that the decline was partially attributable to "the general softness in the restaurant industry that has led to disappointing results for many of our industry peers during the last two years."

1998–99: Joining Forces with Cracker Barrel

Logan's had been ratcheting up its expansion rate since 1995, adding six new sites in 1996 and nine in 1997. The year 1998 brought a far greater acceleration in growth. By December of that year, Logan's was operating 41 company-owned and four franchised restaurants in 12 states. The added locations pushed annual sales up to $101 million—an increase of more than 50 percent from the prior year. Net income for 1998 also showed improvement, climbing 27 percent to an $8.4 million total.

Having proven itself capable of succeeding in multiple markets and showing opportunity for significant further growth, Lo-

gan's had become an attractive candidate for an acquisition. This potential came to fruition in December of 1998 when Logan's announced that it was to be purchased by CBRL Group. CBRL, another Tennessee-based restaurant developer, was the parent company of Cracker Barrel Old Country Store, Inc., a 380-unit chain with locations in more than 35 states. Like Logan's, the Cracker Barrel restaurants were fashioned to resemble establishments from a bygone age. Whereas Logan's modeled itself after the American roadhouses of the 1940s and 1950s, however, Cracker Barrel stepped even further into the past—to the old country stores common at the turn of the century.

Cracker Barrel had only recently reorganized its corporate structure, creating CBRL Group as a holding company to facilitate the acquisition of new restaurant concepts. Its first acquisition after the reorganization was the Florida-based Carmine Giardini's Gourmet Markets. Logan's was to be the second concept added to the CBRL stable. Under the terms of the deal, CBRL agreed to buy all outstanding shares of Logan's stock at a $24.00 per share price, or approximately $179 million total. Logan's would continue to function as a separate corporate entity and to maintain its own unique character. "As with our other concepts, we intend to operate Logan's Roadhouse as a separate company," said CBRL Chairman and CEO Dan Evins in a December 11, 1998 press release. Logan's shareholders approved the agreement by an overwhelming majority on February 5, 1999, and the acquisition was completed two weeks later.

Looking Ahead

CBRL and Logan's entered the spring of 1999 working to interface their management and accounting operations. Logan's change in ownership was not expected to significantly alter its course of expansion. In a 1997 interview with *Nation's Restaurant News,* Moats had predicted that there would be up to 60 corporate-owned Logan's by the year 2000. At the beginning of March 1999, there were already 45 such sites, and CBRL had solid plans for continued growth. In a March 12, 1999 SEC filing, the company said it planned to open 13 new Logan's in fiscal 1999 and an additional 11 sites in fiscal 2000—easily enough to make Moats's prediction a reality.

Further Reading

Bernstein, Charles, "At Steak: Newcomers Chase the Leader, Outback," *Restaurants and Institutions,* March 15, 1997, http://www.rimag.com/06/steakhse.htm

Harris, Nicole, "The Well-Done Steakhouse," *Business Week,* May 27, 1996.

Hartman, Stacey, "Logan's Roadhouse Satisfies Diners, Investors," *Tennessean,* May 8, 1997, p. 1E.

Hayes, Jack, "Edwin W. Moats, Jr.: Making Logan's Roadhouse One of the Hottest Stops on the Casual-Dining Map," *Nation's Restaurant News,* January 27, 1997, p. 150.

Papiernik, Richard, "Logan's Run: Roadhouse Follows Nasdaq Debut with Sales Spurt," *Nation's Restaurant News,* September 11, 1995, p. 11.

Smyth, Whit, "Logan's Roadhouse Offers a Wagonful of Food and Good Times," *Nation's Restaurant News,* May 12, 1997, p. 126.

—Shawna Brynildssen

LONDON FOG®

London Fog Industries, Inc.

1332 Londontown Boulevard
Eldersburg, Maryland 21783-5399
U.S.A.
(410) 795-5900
Fax: (410) 795-5900

Private Company
Incorporated: 1922 as Londontown Clothing Company
Employees: 1,465
Sales: $335.6 million (1998)
NAIC: 315228 Men's & Boys' Cut & Sew Other
Outerwear Manufacturing; 315239 Women's & Girls'
Cut & Sew Other Outerwear Manufacturing; 44819
Other Clothing Stores

London Fog Industries, Inc. is a major designer and distributor of raincoats and outerwear. Its own brands include London Fog, Towne, W by London Fog, Pacific Trail, Black Dot, and Inside Edge, which are made in Asia and Columbia. It also produces sportswear and outerwear under license for Sperry Top-Sider and Docker's. London Fog brands are sold in department and specialty stores and in its own chains of Weather Stores, Weather Clothing Company, and London Fog outlet stores. London Fog licenses stores in China and its subsidiary, Pacific Trail, Inc., licenses stores in Japan. A group of investment firms control the private company.

A Clothing Manufacturer: 1922–53

Israel Myers was 16 years old in 1923 when he went to work as a part-time stenographer at the Londontown Clothing Company. Londontown, which had been founded in Baltimore, Maryland, a year earlier, made finely tailored men's clothing and topcoats. The relationship between Myers and Londontown would last more than 40 years, but it almost did not survive the Depression.

Londontown failed in 1930, but Myers bought the name and the physical assets in 1931, and kept the company making

men's clothing. In the process he become president and chairman. As he told the *Baltimore News American* in 1971, "If I [had] had a good job offer, I probably would have taken it. But there were no jobs available, [and] I had worked hard and saved my money."

When the United States entered World War II, Myers accepted a Navy contract to make rubber-based waterproof coats for enlisted men, even though he knew nothing about the procedure for doing so. When the war ended, Myers changed the name of his company to Londontown Manufacturing Company and continued to make raincoats. At that time, raincoats were considered by manufacturers and consumers as anything that would keep the water off, and Myers obviously saw possibilities.

He wanted to make the raincoats a fashionable part of the wardrobe, and to do that, he had to find a material that would be both waterproof and comfortable. When that proved impossible with conventional fabrics, he tried a new synthetic polyester developed by E.I. du Pont de Nemours & Co. The friction from his sewing machines, however, melted the fibers. Finally, Du Pont and Reeves Brothers, Inc., a fabric maker, created a cotton and Dacron material that did not melt during the sewing process, was water-repellent, and remained so even when put through a washing machine.

Raincoat Innovations: 1954–65

The company designed its new line of men's raincoats after the World War I "trench coats," with epaulets, sleeve straps, and a belt. Myers reluctantly agreed to use the name London Fog, having originally rejected it because he did not think it sellable. Saks Fifth Avenue was the first store to offer the raincoats, introducing London Fog in a *New York Times* ad on March 7, 1954. The ad described the coat as "The perfect answer to everything a man can ask for in a raincoat. Remarkably lightweight and wrinkle-free . . . it actually resists creasing even after packing." The 100 coats sold out immediately, even though the $29.75 price was more than double that of other men's raincoats.

The following week, the *New York Times* called London Fog the perfect name. The "Advertising and Marketing Fields" column in the March 13, 1954 edition stated: "Every once in a while a name comes along for a product that is exactly right. It describes the product exactly and does a selling job that even the legendary 10,000 words cannot do. Such a one is London Fog."

Londontown quickly followed up this first wash-and-wear raincoat for men with a second innovation. After watching women customers buy London Fog coats for themselves, John Wanamaker's, the leading Philadelphia department store, asked Londontown to make a raincoat for women. Using the same design but adding two darts at the chest and moving the buttons to the left side, Londontown introduced the first line of women's raincoats in 1955, and Wanamaker's quickly sold all 90 produced.

During the 1950s and mid-1960s, Londontown appeared particularly attuned to what customers needed. It designed the first full, removable liner. With a simple zip, what had been winter raincoats could be used year-round. Londontown patented a process to keep buttons from falling off and an inner barrier to keep shoulders drier. Several of its innovations became commonplace, such as including replacement buttons and sewing washing instructions to the inside of its coats.

In 1961 Myers took Londontown public and soon began signing foreign licensing agreements. In 1966 the company was listed on the New York Stock Exchange.

Changes Occur: 1968–75

Jonathan P. Myers, Israel's son, assumed the presidency of Londontown in 1969, the year after coat sales fell by a quarter. Blaming the problems on the company's lack of attention to women's changing clothing styles, he spent the next five years working to gain back women customers. While maintaining its tradition for classic coats, the company began producing raincoats designed specifically for women.

The design of women's coats was not the only area in which Jon Myers made changes. He acquired Star Sportwear Manufacturing Company of Lynn, Massachusetts, a prominent maker of men's leather and suede garments, opened the first London Fog outlet store, and introduced the Clipper Mist label of well-made men's and women's rainwear, priced less expensively than the London Fog line. Clipper Mist, incidentally, was one of the names rejected by his father in 1954. By 1975, about two-thirds of all mid-priced and better raincoats sold in the United States carried the London Fog label.

Londontown also moved heavily into licensing agreements with U.S. companies, averaging nearly a license agreement a year between 1968 and 1983. Customers were able to buy London Fog accessories and clothing ranging from umbrellas and rainhats to sweaters, dress slacks, belts and billfolds, handbags, luggage, briefcases, sport shirts, flannel shirts, girl's and boy's outerwear, and even sunglasses.

Part of Interco Corp.: 1976–88

In 1976 Londontown had sales of $71 million and agreed to be bought by Interco Inc. of Saint Louis in a stock swap worth about $33.3 million. Interco was the parent company of Ethan Allen furniture and Florsheim shoes, among others.

Jon Myers remained president until 1980, when he was named chairman and CEO. Mark Lieberman, who had joined the company in 1978, became president and, in 1981, assumed the CEO position. Among his first moves was to merge the Clipper Mist and Startown subsidiaries, which began operating as Star Sportwear Manufacturing Corp.

During the 1980s, domestic rainwear companies came under greater pressure from cheaper imported raincoats. In 1983 Londontown introduced its London Towne brand, a less expensive line of raincoats, made overseas. The company hired actress Stephanie Powers for a television ad campaign, which saw sales "explode," according to Lieberman.

At the same time, department stores and other retailers wanted more diversity in their rainwear departments. Customers with more disposable income wanted both a classic raincoat and lines offering a wider variety of fabrics and colors. During 1983 and 1984, Londontown sold more than half its merchandise in fashion rainwear, according to a January 22, 1985 *WWD* article.

In 1985 Londontown bought Milford Sportwear, Inc., its licensee for men's knit shirts. By 1987, the company had 3,000 workers and was the world's largest manufacturer of raincoats and outerwear, with six domestic manufacturing plants.

In July 1988 Interco announced that it would sell its clothing manufacturing group in a restructuring undertaken to fight a takeover bid. Near the end of December, Londontown CEO and president, Lieberman, along with four other top executives, organized as Eldersberg Acquisition Corp. and acquired Londontown Corp. for $178 million, taking it private in a leveraged buyout. Total financing came to $311 million. Sales for the year ending February 28, 1989 were about $231 million, more than triple the $71 million in sales for 1976, the year Interco bought Londontown.

New Management and a New Image: 1989–90

The new owners laid off some workers in a cost reduction necessitated by the huge debt Londontown had, but increased budgets for advertising, design, and marketing. The strategy was to emphasize the company's lines of women's and fashion-oriented raincoats and outerwear and styles to attract younger customers.

In June 1989 Londontown went public, using proceeds from the sale of $75 million in junk bonds to pay part of the debt from the buyout. Sales for the year increased to $265.1 million, with the company selling more jackets and outerwear than raincoats, and women's apparel accounted for 52 percent of overall sales.

Fifteen years earlier, in 1975, rainwear had represented 85 percent of sales, with 65 percent in men's categories.

New Owners: 1990–92

In June 1990 management sold a 90 percent interest in Londontown Holdings, the company's parent, to Merrill Lynch Capital Partners, Inc., which paid a reported $275 million. That amount included assumption of about $180 million in debt. Merrill Lynch gained three seats on Londontown's 11-member board, but Lieberman and Londontown's other officers remained responsible for day-to-day operations.

Lieberman moved more aggressively into wool coats for women. "People need coats for the rain and the cold, no matter what the retail cycle is," he told *Women's Wear Daily* in 1990. "Our high name recognition—98 percent of consumers recognize the London Fog brand—pretty much insures that we will get a substantial share of the markets in which we sell."

In 1992 the company began selling London Fog raincoats in the United Kingdom and continued to expand beyond rainwear. It introduced Gold Fog, a line of high-priced, fashion outerwear including a gold lamé jacket and a cotton velvet jacket with gold studs and fox fur trim. It also expanded its lower-priced Towne by London Fog line of rainwear and hired actress Stephanie Powers again for a $4 million national television campaign.

The company had sales for the year of $318 million, but a loss of $262,000. The company was still the largest raincoat maker in the United States, but its share of the rainwear market had dropped to around 60 percent.

New Leadership: 1993–94

The following year, 1993, Lieberman created London Fog Corp., a holding company, with Londontown Corp. as its sole subsidiary. He retired in June, selling his interest in the company.

Three months later, in September, Arnold Cohen, from catalog clothing company J Crew, was hired to be the new president and CEO. Over the 11 months of his tenure at Londontown he made several major changes. He moved company headquarters from Maryland to Darien, Connecticut, near his home, laid off 1,000 people, closed five plants, and shifted almost all manufacturing overseas. He also mounted a big marketing campaign, started to push the company into children's sportswear, and increased the use of new fabrics and styles, including, finally, microfibers, which were by then dominating the outerwear market.

One of his most critical undertakings was to prohibit stores from marking down London Fog coats until the second week of December. This move greatly angered retailers whose best raincoat business traditionally occurred during their Columbus Day, Veterans Day, and Thanksgiving promotions. Many were further incensed because London Fog was selling its coats at discount at its 100 outlet stores. Department store orders dropped significantly.

In April 1994 Cohen merged London Fog Corp. with Seattle-based Pacific Trail, Inc., which had been making ski jackets and other outerwear since 1945, and was owned by GKH Partners. The merger gave GKH a 36 percent share of London Fog. Around this time, the company's name was changed to London Fog Industries.

New Leadership: 1994–95

London Fog's debt stood at $425 million. It had poor relations with its large retailers and was barely breaking even on cash flow. In August 1994 Cohen was ousted and James Milligan, a seasoned troubleshooter, was named CEO and charged with rescuing the company.

Milligan relaxed the ban on discounts, and although he did not eliminate it completely, he helped repair relations with the department stores. He also moved the company back to Eldersburg, Maryland and went after the discount and chain store customer, with five separate labels. The company ended the fiscal year with a loss of $125 million in operations alone, not counting debt payments.

New Leadership: 1995–96

With the company not able to make all of its debt payments, Merrill Lynch and GKH brought in turnaround specialist Robert A. Gregory from Gitano Group to head the company. In March 1995 Gregory negotiated a debt restructuring, avoiding bankruptcy. He stretched out loan payments and had the banks forgive one-third of the $317 million debt in exchange for control of the company. Merrill Lynch and GKH gave the banks 88 percent of London Fog's preferred stock and 80 percent of the common stock. As CEO, Gregory closed the children's clothing divisions and established a mission to refocus London Fog and Pacific Trail on making and selling outerwear. He also invested $2 million in the sole remaining manufacturing plant, in Baltimore.

In 1996 the company relaunched its FOG (Functional Outerwear Gear) label as a new line of performance outerwear for men and women in their 20s. Marketed as "functionality with a fashion twist," the line included light outer shells in a variety of styles, insulated vests, and jackets made from fleece, goose down, and nylon.

November saw the introduction of a new retail venture, with the opening of two Weather Stores. Located at Union Station in Washington, D.C. and in the Pittsburgh (PA) Airport, the stores sold London Fog raincoats and weather-related accessories and were aimed at the travel-oriented customer.

In his first year with London Fog, Gregory reduced the operating loss to $13 million, and in his second year produced a profit, the first for the company since 1991. But the price paid for the ongoing recovery included the closing of the last London Fog manufacturing plant.

Leadership Continuation: 1997–98

Gregory expanded the company's retail concepts during 1997, opening seven London Fog superstores of 25,000 square feet. Featuring all the London Fog merchandise and accessories, the stores were located in strip malls in New York and Ohio. In addition, the company operated some 120 outlet stores. That same year London Fog signed licensing agreements with the Stride Rite Corp. to produce Sperry Top-Sider casual and performance outerwear. The company also introduced a new proprietary insulation technology called nrg 2000, which had been developed by Thermore Technologies of Milan. London Fog claimed nrg 2000 was lighter, less bulky, and more flexible than Thinsulate and Thermoloft, products by 3M that London Fog (and most other outerwear manufacturers) had been using. For the fiscal year ending February 28, 1998, London Fog had annual sales of $335.6 million and earnings of $155.7 million.

During 1998, Gregory again restructured London Fog's long-term debt, giving eight million shares of newly issued stock to several dozen creditors. He discontinued the FOG label, folding its activewear styles into the core London Fog line, and introduced a new label, W for London Fog. This line offered rainwear in luxury fabrics lined with Thermostat 37, another new proprietary climate-control insulation. He also signed a new distribution license in China, opening some 25 in-store shops in major department stores in Beijing, Shanghai, and other major cities, and entered the shoe business, teaming up with Atsco Footwear Inc to introduce London Fog brand foul-weather shoes and boots in department stores.

Meanwhile, Pacific Trail, under the presidency of Bill Dragon, Jr., was having sales of nearly $100 million. The subsidiary designed and distributed women's outerwear and women's and men's performance outerwear for skiing and snowboarding under the Inside Edge and Black Dot labels. It also produced Dockers men's and women's outerwear under license for Levi Strauss & Co. and had Pacific Trail stores in Japan, selling men's and boys' clothing.

At the end of 1998, Gregory introduced a new chain of stores called Weatherwear Clothing, selling casual outerwear and sportswear, including khakis, polo jackets, and shirts. Some of the company's superstores were converted into Weatherwear Clothing shops.

1999 to the Present

Having completed the final year of his four-year contract, Gregory resigned in March 1999, as did President C. William Crain. Bill Dragon, Jr., who headed Pacific Trail, was named president and CEO of London Fog Industries. Crediting Gregory and Crain with having stopped the bleeding, Dragon told the *Baltimore Sun,* "There was a need to put more emphasis on outerwear as opposed to rainwear. Today, we're in a much better financial position."

Dragon indicated he wanted to stay true to the London Fog brand and improve internal sourcing and customer service functions. But financial problems still existed for the venerable raincoat and outerwear maker. The company remained highly leveraged, with outstanding debt of $224.4 million, and Gregory's hoped-for public offering had not yet materialized. Relatively warm weather also contributed to a dismal outerwear market. Only time would tell whether Dragon's experience at

Pacific Trail would be enough to continue London Fog's rebuilding.

Principal Subsidiaries

Pacific Trail, Inc.

Further Reading

Brill, Eileen B., "Rainwear Firms Forecast a Sunny Spring," *WWD,* January 22, 1985, p. 11.

Clark, Kim, "London Fog Reaches Debt Accord," *Baltimore Sun,* June 6, 1995, p. 11C.

D'Innocenzio, Anne, "Londontown Pins Growth to Fashion," *WWD,* February 25, 1992, p. 9.

Friedman, Arthur, "The Air Clears at London Fog," *WWD,* January 6, 1998, p. 8.

——, "Pacific Trail Reaches a Peak," *Daily News Record,* July 28, 1998, p. 10.

——, "Turnaround Executives Leave London Fog After Four Years," *WWD,* March 12, 1999, p. 2.

"Future Dim for London Fog Makers," *Washington Times,* November 10, 1993, p. B7.

Glenn, Karen A., "Fog's Future Still Murky," *Baltimore Business Journal,* March 19, 1999, p. 1.

Hetrick, Ross, "Fresh Air at London Fog," *Baltimore Sun,* September 25, 1994, p. 1D.

Lockwood, Lisa, "London Fog: A Name That Weathers," *Daily News Record,* November 15, 1983, p. 20.

"London Fog at 75," Eldersburg, Md.: London Fog Industries, 1997.

"London Fog Seeks To Advertise," *FTC Watch,* May 23, 1994.

"Londontown Corp. Will Move Part of Its Workforce," *U.P.I.,* October 26, 1987.

Macintosh, Jeane, "Londontown Seeks To Reduce Debt," *WWD,* January 23, 1990, p. 16.

Malone, Scott, "London Fog Getting into the Shoe Business," *Footwear News,* January 12, 1998, p. 2.

"Mark Lieberman Steps Down From Top Posts at London Fog," *WWD,* May 3, 1993, p. 9.

Mirabella, Lorraine, "Designer Named London Fog CEO," *Baltimore Sun,* March 12, 1999, p. 1C.

Pogoda, Dianne M., "Londontown: After the Buyout," *WWD,* March 21, 1989, p. 55.

——, "Londontown Refinanced and Ready To Grow," *WWD,* August 21, 1990, p. 6.

Schechter, Dara, "Londontown To Make Public Offering," *WWD,* June 13, 1989, p. 9.

Schechter, Dara, and Debra Michals, "Londontown's Senior Management To Buy Rainwear Firm for $178M," *Daily News Record,* December 20, 1988, p. 5.

Somerville, Sean, "Forecast Improves for London Fog," *Baltimore Sun,* April 27, 1997, p. 1D.

Strom, Stephanie, "London Fog: Out of the Drizzle and Into the Rain," *New York Times,* November 20, 1994, p. C5.

Taylor, Hal, "Interco Asks FTC To Allow It To Set Prices," *Daily News Record,* August 14, 1987, p. 11.

Underwood, Elaine, "London Fog Tries To Corner Weather with Traveler-Oriented Store Chain," *Brandweek,* November 4, 1996, p. 8.

"Weather Where," *WWD,* December 15, 1998, p. 9.

Wilson, Eric, "London Fog Is Rolling on the Comeback Trail," *WWD,* August 12, 1997, p. 24.

—Ellen D. Wernick

Excellence in Imaging

Lunar Corporation

313 West Beltline Highway
Madison, Wisconsin 53713
U.S.A.
(608) 274-2663
Fax: (608) 274-5374
Web site: http://lunarcorp.com

Public Company
Incorporated: 1995
Employees: 320
Sales: $80 million (1998)
Stock Exchanges: NASDAQ
Ticker Symbol: LUNR
NAIC: 334517 Irradiation Apparatus Manufacturing

Lunar Corporation is one of the leading designers and manufacturers of bone densitometers, a highly sophisticated, state-of-the-art machine that measures bone density in humans. Densitometers are used primarily as a diagnostic tool for identifying osteoporosis and various other types of bone diseases. The company's most profitable product is the DPX-IQ axial densitometer, with more than 5,000 of the DPX sold and shipped by the end of fiscal 1998. Also the most popular and widely used densitometer in the world, the product's software is compatible with the Windows95 operating system. The more affordable DPX-MD enables a physician to provide affordable axial densitometry to patients in the outpatient setting. Lunar Corporation's EXPERT-XL is the only Imaging Densitometer available around the globe, providing the only reliable vertebral morphometry anywhere. The company's Achilles+ is an ultrasound device that measures the bone in a patient's heel to diagnose the risk of osteoporosis bone fracture. This product is used extensively for diagnosing the risk of fracture in younger women ages 45 to 65. The ORCA mini C-arm is the company's mobile fluoroscopic C-arm, which provides high-quality diagnostic images of an individual's extremities for orthopedic surgical treatment. Although the company's revenues decreased from 1997 to 1998, management is convinced that the cause was its flawed distribution network in burgeoning new markets rather than the quality of its products or effectiveness of its customer service.

Early History

The founder of Lunar Corporation is Richard B. Mazess, Ph.D., a well-known and highly respected researcher at the University of Wisconsin at Madison. Mazess had been teaching and conducting research for a number of years at the main campus of the University of Wisconsin when he became interested in bone densitometry. He was one of the leading researchers on the pioneering effort that led to the development of the first bone densitometer for commercial use in 1972. At the time and previous to it, bone densitometry was an extremely new and untested area. In fact, there were only a few prototype bone densitometers in the world at the time, and those were all employed for research purposes in teaching hospitals or medical research centers primarily within the United States. Recognizing the need for such a sophisticated diagnostic tool to assist medical personnel in their treatment of bone diseases, and specifically in the field of osteoporosis, Mazess and his colleagues at the university made a commitment to developing a commercially viable densitometer that could be used for many different applications. With the creation of the first commercially viable bone densitometer in the early 1970s, Mazess and his group of researchers thought that their job was essentially over.

Yet the academician soon realized that the creation of a bone densitometer was not nearly enough to guarantee its success in the marketplace. Mazess was disappointed that no large medical supplies or manufacturing firm elected to develop and produce his densitometer for commercial use and, for a number of years, the revolutionary machine went unnoticed and unused. Nearly eight years following its first introduction, Mazess and his fellow academicians at the university decided to form their own company to facilitate the further development, production, and sale of their product to researchers and medical personnel around the world. As a result, Lunar Corporation was incorporated in 1980 and opened its doors for business in the same year.

Growth and Expansion in the 1980s and 1990s

From its beginning, Lunar Corporation was an unqualified success. With Mazess assuming the position of president of the company, there was a concerted effort to develop and produce as many densitometers within as short a time as possible. From 1980 to 1994 Lunar Corporation shipped almost 1,000 of its radionuclide densitometers to hospitals and medical research facilities throughout the United States. As a result, sales increased and the company's number of employees expanded rapidly.

Mazess, an academic himself, clearly recognized the necessity of a research and development department that included some of the most talented people in the field of densitometry. From the time that the research and development department was established, Mazess was adamant about providing it with the money needed for new and improved densitometers. In fact, Mazess insisted on earmarking approximately 25 percent of the company's annual revenues for research and development, which in retrospect has turned out to be one of his best decisions, since the firm's scientists and engineers not only set the standard for bone measurement excellence, but also garnered numerous patents during the 1980s and 1990s. One of the company's most important innovations was the development of the dual energy x-ray absorptiometry in 1988. This machine, the first of its kind developed specially for the commercial market, enabled medical personnel and researchers to conduct highly precise bone measurements with low radiation doses and at higher speeds. The result was a machine that enhanced the company's reputation for innovative design, while at the same time expanding its customer base and increasing revenues.

In the autumn of 1993 company management reached an agreement with Esaote Biomedica, a designer and manufacturer of magnetic resonance imagers based in Genoa, Italy, to market and distribute the ARTOSCAN magnetic resonance imager in the United States. The ARTOSCAN provided high-resolution images of a small field-of-view. The machine's design enables medical personnel to scan large patients at a fraction of the cost of magnetic resonance imagers designed for the entire body. Thus large athletes, such as football and baseball players, could be accommodated by the machine. Soon, with the engineers and designers at Lunar Corporation adding their own improvements to the machine, football teams and baseball teams across the United States started placing orders for the machine.

In 1994 the company introduced the dual-energy x-ray absorptiometer, otherwise known as the EXPERT-XL Imaging Densitometer. The only imaging densitometer in the world, it can perform highly reliable vertebral morphometry, which enables the operators to clearly identify spinal problems. As the engineers and scientists at Lunar Corporation improved the machine over the years, it has developed into the world's fastest axial densitometer and has received approval and clearance

from the United States Food and Drug Administration for lateral spine, orthopedic, and total body applications. In addition, it has one of the clearest, near radiographic image systems of any machine of its kind. In 1997 Lunar Corporation brought out the PIXI, a peripheral densitometer that quickly became known as the fastest in the world, providing extremely precise bone measurements in approximately five seconds. The only peripheral densitometer that provides precise measurements for the heel and forearm, within a short time the machine was one of the company's best sellers.

Another of the company's most successful product introductions includes the Achilles +, an ultrasonometer that enables medical personnel to achieve precise measurements of spine and hip fractures. The device employs ultrasound to measure bone of the heel and also allows for measuring a patient's risk of osteoporotic fracture. In addition, it can measure and monitor bone changes due to either therapy or the progression of a disease. By the end of fiscal 1998, the company had sold more than 2,800 of the machines to customers around the world. In 1997 Lunar Corporation started to sell the ORCA mini C-arm, a very compact, readily mobile fluoroscopic C-arm that provides extremely high-quality images of the extremities for orthopedic surgical applications. Easy to use, the ORCA mini C-arm had gained a small portion of its market by the end of 1998, but company management regards the device as one its most promising products.

The world's most sophisticated and innovative densitometer was introduced by Lunar Corporation also in 1998. Named the PRODIGY, this new densitometer used low dosage, pencil beam precision, and fan beam speed. Another product, the E-SCAN, was introduced at the same time. The E-SCAN is a brand new magnetic resonance imaging device that not only incorporates all of the new technological developments in the field, but also is a cost-effective system to which health care professionals are attracted. In 1999 the company launched the ORCA-DX, the only fluoroscopic mini C-arm in the world that is able to provide health care professionals and researchers with precise bone density measurements.

Strategic Partnerships and Innovative Marketing During the 1990s

As Lunar Corporation grew, and as its research and development department developed one of the best reputations in the electromedical equipment industry, Mazess and his management team implemented a strategic partnership plan for the decade of the 1990s and beyond. Financial figures during the middle and late 1990s were not as good as the early years of the decade. Some of this was due to the Asian currency crisis, which dramatically affected the company's new marketing efforts around the Pacific Rim. In fact, during fiscal 1998, Lunar Corporation sales in the region fell a precipitous 42 percent, and there seems no likelihood for a quick market recovery. In addition, company management had evaluated its distribution network, especially in new efforts directed toward overseas markets, and came to the conclusion that a more sophisticated and professional approach was required to make progress.

For the foregoing reasons, Lunar Corporation reached an agreement with Henry Schein Medical (Caligor) of Pelham

Manor, New York and McKesson General Medical (MGM) located in Richmond, Virginia. The contract with these two firms provided Lunar Corporation with more than 700 sales representatives and gave them non-exclusive rights to sell a number of the company's products. In fact, this one agreement alone enabled Lunar Corporation to market its product line to more than 140,000 primary care physicians working in the United States. In 1998 the company reached an agreement with Philips Medical Systems, one of the largest and most respected medical equipment manufacturers throughout the world. This Dutch-based firm agreed to market Lunar Corporation's ORCA mini surgical C-arm.

At the same time, the company entered into an agreement with Office of the Future Research and Development Consortium, a group of major medical device manufacturers that assists doctors in redesigning their offices to more efficiently use high-technology medical equipment. Management at Lunar also made it a priority to continue cultivating potentially lucrative relationships with hospitals and hospital purchasing groups such as Premier, Voluntary Hospital of America, Inc., and Health Services Corporation of America. Finally, the company made a major effort in developing and expanding its international presence by reaching distribution agreements with firms throughout South America, Eastern Europe, and around the shores of the Mediterranean. To develop its presence within the Western European market, Lunar Corporation opened a new office in France.

As Lunar Corporation continues to design and develop innovative bone densitometers, there is little doubt that profits will increase as the firm garners a worldwide reputation. Company management is astute enough to recognize that, even though it has a good product line, the only way to sell its products is to establish a comprehensive sales and distribution network.

Further Reading

Bak, David, "Magnetic Resonance Becomes Roadmap for Cancer Surgeons," *Design News,* June 10, 1996, p. 78.
Britt, Philip J., "New Technology Takes the Film Out of Chest X-rays," *American Medical News,* January 4, 1999, p. 21.
Chamberlain, Gary, "Medical Images To Move on the Internet Using Java," *Design News,* March 1, 1999, p. 24.
Field, Karen Auguston, "Portable Radiotherapy Machine Revolutionizes Cancer Treatment," *Design News,* March 1, 1999, p. 120.
Hensley, Scott, "With FDA Backing, X-ray Going Digital," *Modern Healthcare,* December 8, 1997.
Modic, Elizabeth Engler, "Anatomy Lessons in Medical Device Machining," *Tooling and Production,* April 1997, p. 77.
Tereske, John, "Striking a Balance: While Maintaining Its Innovative Edge, Today's Medical-Electronics Equipment Must Also Be Low-Cost and Highly Productive," *Industry News,* May 6, 1996, p. 34.

—Thomas Derdak

Malaysian Airlines System Berhad

33rd Floor, Bangunan MAS
Jalan Sultan Ismail
50250 Kuala Lumpur
Malaysia
(603) 2610555
Fax: (603) 2633178
Web site: http://www.malaysia-airlines.com

Public Company
Incorporated: 1937 as Malayan Airways Limited
Employees: 17,688
Sales: M$7.47 billion (US$1.93 billion) (1998)
Stock Exchanges: Kuala Lumpur Singapore
Ticker Symbol: MASM
NAIC: 481111 Scheduled Passenger Air Transportation

Malaysian Airlines System Berhad is the holding company for Malaysia's national airline carrier, one of Asia's fastest growing airlines. Through several other subsidiaries, the company manufactures aircraft parts, offers trucking and cargo transportation services, caters food, provides laundry and dry-cleaning services for airlines and other industrial institutions, and oversees a travel agency. Company Chairman Tajudin Ramli owns a significant share in Malaysian Airlines System (MAS), and the Malaysian government retains a strong voice in MAS affairs.

1930s Origins

The history of Malaysian Airlines dates back to 1937, when the Straits Steamship Co. of Singapore joined forces with two British companies—Ocean Steamship Co. and Imperial Airways—and won approval from Singapore's government to operate an airline in the region. Malayan Airways Limited was registered on October 21, 1937.

Getting clearance and getting planes in the air, however, proved to be two different things for Malayan Airways Ltd. Operations did not begin until 1947, well after the Japanese occupation had come to an end, when a twin-engined Airspeed Consul lifted off from Subang International Airport in Kuala Lumpur, linking that city with Singapore, Ipoh, and Penang in the north of the country. In 1947 the fledgling airline added a 21-seater DC-3 to its fleet of three Airspeed Consuls. By the end of the year the airline was flying to Jakarta (then called Batavia), Palembang, Bangkok, Medan, and Saigon (later called Ho Chi Minh City). Jointly controlled by the intercontinental carriers BOAC and Qantas, Malayan Airways was for a time run by Keith Hamilton, who would later become head of Qantas.

1960s Independence

Following Malaysia's political establishment in September 1963—the new country comprised the former states of Malaya and Singapore, and the one-time colonies of North Borneo, Sabah, and Sarawak—Malayan Airways became Malaysian Airways and was reorganized to focus on connecting the new country's disparate regions. Expansion brought more aircraft into the fleet after Borneo Airways was purchased and folded into Malaysian Airways in 1965. This brought four Dakota jets and two Scottish Aviation Twin Pioneer aircraft to the carrier's stable of aircraft.

More organizational changes for the airline occurred in 1966, a year after Singapore seceded from Malaysia to become a sovereign state on its own. That year, the governments of Singapore and Malaysia jointly bought a controlling stake in the airline and renamed it Malaysia-Singapore Airlines Ltd.(MSA). Powerful Boeing jets then entered the fleet and enabled flights to reach a number of far-flung Asian destinations. However, differences between Kuala Lumpur and Singapore over the future direction of MSA prompted a split in 1972. Lee Kuan Yew, prime minister of Singapore, desired a truly national carrier for his country, the aim being to fly a small fleet of Boeing 707s displaying the yellow and blue colors of Singapore Airlines.

Malaysia likewise chose to go its own way. In October 1972, Malaysian Airline Systems (MAS) was established. (The acronym MAS means gold in the Malaysian language.) Each of its aircraft would henceforth sport a winged tiger logo, a stylized form of the traditional Kelantan ''wau'' or Malaysian kite.

The split was crucial to the future fortunes of MAS. From 1972, the airline continued to see itself as a regional carrier, connecting a myriad of remote destinations in Peninsular Malaysia, including Sabah and Sarawak. Singapore Airlines, on the other hand, was committed from its inception to becoming an international success. By 1975, Singapore Airlines was flying to Seoul, Hong Kong, and Taipei. A year later, that airline was carrying passengers to Paris, Dubai, and New Zealand.

Unlike Singapore, Malaysia looked to focus on exploiting its vast reserves of natural resources—petroleum and petroleum products, natural gas, timber products, and rubber. The country's government would choose much later than Singapore had to attempt competing with Western companies in manufacturing and high-tech markets.

Thus, maintaining a successful regional airline carrier was judged the best strategy for Malaysia during the 1970s. The company slowly built up its regional services to Jakarta and Medan in Indonesia. Later the destinations of Bangkok, Hong Kong, Manila, and Singapore were added. "Malaysia felt that MAS was not serving the needs of Malaysians," explained Abdullah Mat Zaid, director of corporate planning at MAS.

Expanding as a regional airline was not without incident for MAS. In 1978, the company's low-wage policy met with a setback. Kuala Lumpur had set out rules limiting union activity at the national air carrier as a means of keeping wages and costs down, and a bitter and disruptive labor dispute occurred in 1978. Events surrounding a strike at the national airline prompted the government to intervene and cite MAS workers as being engaged in illegal activity. Several union officials were subsequently arrested.

Growth in the 1980s–90s

An economic boom in Malaysia during the 1980s helped spur growth at Malaysian Airlines. By the end of the decade, MAS was flying to 47 overseas destinations. These included eight European cities: London, Zurich, Paris, Frankfurt, Istanbul, Vienna, Amsterdam, and Brussels. MAS also flew at this time to six Australian cities—Brisbane, Adelaide, Darwin, Perth, Melbourne, and Sydney—as well as to Auckland, New Zealand. Besides flights to such Asian hubs as Hong Kong, Tokyo, and Peking, MAS also connected with Los Angeles and Honolulu. By 1992, MAS had added scheduled flights to Athens, Madrid, and Rome, and plans were in motion to reach at least one destination in Eastern Europe. Moreover, a new service to South Africa and Brazil was scheduled for 1993. The airline would also look to reach one city on the eastern seaboard of the United States.

MAS also chose during the early 1990s to expand by teaming up with other airlines to make additional destinations available for its customers. For example, Iran Air connected Kuala Lumpur with Tehran, and Royal Jordanian connected MAS flights with Amman. In addition, joint services to Chile and Argentina were discussed in late 1991.

The impetus for this expansion came from Malaysia's burgeoning economy. Between 1986 and 1991, the country's export-oriented economy posted an average real growth of nine percent. Changes to Malaysia's foreign investment rules during the mid-1980s were designed to help speed a shift from an economy previously dependent on natural resources to a finely tuned industrialized economy. At the same time, a number of large Asian and Western corporations such as Sanyo, NEC, Toshiba, and Philips established branch plants in Malaysia. The extra traffic of company officials flying back and forth from their headquarters to Malaysia, and the transportation of their high-tech goods, spurred on ticket sales for the airline. The number of business passengers MAS accommodated was underscored by gross foreign investments in Malaysia that rose 30 percent in 1991 to M$10.7 billion ($5 billion).

The 1980s–90s Tourist Trade

As the country's export trade thundered ahead in the late 1980s, so did the domestic passenger traffic in and out of Malaysia, and naturally tourism also provided a springboard to expansion for MAS. By the late 1980s Malaysia began to go after the prized Western tourist, a market already well exploited by neighboring Thailand and the Philippines. Nearly 5.5 million travelers visited Malaysia in 1991. Although the country, and its airline, were hit by the effects of the Gulf War and global recessionary conditions, tourism contributed M$5 billion—or $2.4 billion—to the country's trade balance in 1991. The bulk of these tourists came from neighboring Brunei, Indonesia, the Philippines, Singapore, and Thailand. Kuala Lumpur's plans to build a number of luxury golf courses in the country were expected to help secure growing numbers of Japanese tourists.

Getting into the package tour business also helped MAS encourage increased passenger traffic. Malaysia Airlines Golden Holiday packages and Malaysia Stopover packages were established in 1984. These encouraged European and Australian travelers in transit between the two continents to take a rest break in Malaysia before carrying on to their final destination. To further stimulate tourism, a joint campaign was run by the Malaysian government and MAS to declare 1990 Visit Malaysia Year. During the year, some 7.4 million tourists flew into and out of the country, as compared with the 4.8 million tourists who visited Malaysia in the previous year.

Another source of new traffic for the airline was the growing number of foreign students attending educational institutions in Malaysia. In September 1989 the International School of Kuala

Lumpur registered 700 students; a year later, the school had doubled its enrollment. By the same token, young Malaysians were studying in Europe and North America. In Canada, where many Malaysian students attended universities, it was felt in early 1992 that this new traffic source might warrant regular service between the two countries.

Canada's own national airline, Air Canada, which was suffering from economic recession and increasing global competition, was slow to grant Malaysian Airlines landing rights. The Canadian government felt that allowing MAS to land in Vancouver would encroach on territory commanded by Canadian Airlines International Ltd., while Toronto International Airport was considered the preserve of Air Canada. Malaysia's case at the time was not helped by Ottawa having a year earlier announced the cancellation of Singapore Airline's landing rights in Toronto. Even so, Kuala Lumpur officials reasoned that Canada was out-of-step in trying to protect its national airline carriers. The global airline industry as a whole was going the opposite way, towards increased deregulation and competitiveness. Malaysia was prepared to wait for Canada to accept its growing economic might and grant reciprocal landing rights.

Intercontinental traffic for the airline was encouraged by the purchase of Boeing 747 wide-body jets. By 1991, the airline had four of them, and three more were added a year later with an average of two more due for delivery each year until 1995. In 1992, a tightening labor supply in Malaysia, in part the result of its increasingly prosperous economy, was cited by international corporations as the prime obstacle standing in the way of future expansion plans. Manpower shortages were especially acute at the middle management and technical levels. All of these circumstances would impact on MAS's passenger and cargo traffic figures as the country's economy moved from the farm to the factory and beyond.

Amid this backdrop, the Malaysian government in 1992 forecast that passenger traffic on the country's combined airways—international and regional—would grow by ten percent annually in the five years before 1997. International freight volume in the same period was expected to rise by 13 percent annually.

Officials in Kuala Lumpur announced in 1992 that they had plans to build a new international airport in Sapang, adding that all other airports in the country were expected to cope with the increased passenger demand of the 1990s without the need for expansion. Government forecasts in 1992 pointed to 9.5 million passengers to be carried by MAS that year, a figure expected to jump to approximately 15 million by 1995.

Cargo was also identified as an expanding source of revenue for the airline in the 1990s. In recognition of this potential, MAS in 1992 introduced MASkargo in order to begin providing a full cargo service to the United States and Europe. A DC-10-30 jet was fitted to carry up to 60 tons of cargo per flight. Further plans were announced to purchase an additional Boeing 747-400 freighter to carry 45 tons of extra cargo per flight. In 1992 MASkargo also opened a fully automated cargo handling center in Penang. The new facility complemented the expanded MAS Cargo Center at Subang Airport, which provided semi-automated and computerized facilities including elevating transfer vehicles and electronic scissor lifts fitted with computerized scales. Expansion at the cargo center brought MASkargo's total warehouse storage space to 150,000 square meters.

The ambitious expansion plans taxed the carrier's profits, which were nearly halved, from M$206 to M$120, between 1991 and 1992. Turnover increased 23 percent in 1992, however, reaching M$3.6 billion. Correspondingly, employment at MAS rose from 17,575 workers in 1992 to 20,370 in 1993. Demand for flight crews was so great that the carrier contracted for 35 percent of these positions with overseas personnel, mostly Australian. Fifteen hundred of the employees worked in the airline's unique flight kitchen, which served 22 airlines. All 17,000 meals a day were *hallal,* that is, observing Muslim dietary restrictions that prohibited pork.

During this time, MAS hired *Star Wars* producer George Lucas's special effects unit to create a stunning sci-fi television commercial. The spot, which aired around the world, was commissioned to present MAS as a modern, world-class airline and featured a huge kite-shaped space station. The cost was estimated at between $2 and $4 million dollars.

In 1993, MAS bought a 24.9 percent interest in U.S. charter operator World Airways. The company also leased five of its MD-11 aircraft. Operations personnel, in high demand at MAS, were also made available.

1994: Ramli Buys a Stake in the Airline

In 1994 Malaysian entrepreneur Tajudin Ramli bought a 32 percent controlling interest for M$2 billion ($745 million) worth of stock. The government retained an 11 percent interest. Tajudin, who had earlier put together a mini-aviation empire in preparation of competing with MAS, was saddled with an overlarge fleet and diminishing profits. Although sales rose to $M4.1 billion ($1.6 billion) in the fiscal year ending March 3, 1994, profits fell from M$145.4 million ($56.4 million) to M$7.7 million ($2.9 million). The carrier was still receiving large shipments of new aircraft, including Boeing 747s, and sales of its used aircraft were slow. (Some of MAS's new A330 aircraft were delivered late, resulting in penalty payments from Airbus.)

Tajudin immediately set out to trim the fat. He introduced a more businesslike attitude and required better reporting from the company's managers. Aircraft utilization was increased. The carrier signed code-share agreements on transpacific routes and promoted its Kuala-Lumpur-Los Angeles route to attract more business passengers.

Virgin Atlantic Airways teamed with MAS in 1995 to operate joint London-Kuala Lumpur flights. The service proved convenient for Virgin's Australia-bound passengers. Planes stayed just as full after the number of flights was increased from eight to 14 a week, although the two carriers faced very formidable competition from the British Airways/Qantas alliance, which operated the only single-plane service between London and Australia.

MAS recorded its highest ever pretax profit in 1996–97 of M$349.4 million ($120 million). The company continued to buy new planes and relocated to Kuala Lumpur's new Sepang International Airport, a move expected to further enhance its reputation. However, the new airport's opening was plagued with lost baggage, computer malfunctions, and other annoyances.

Depreciating Malaysian currency brought MAS debt up to M$12 billion by 1998. Debt servicing helped MAS lose M$260 million ($62 million) in 1997–98. In response, the carrier deferred new aircraft purchases, sold old planes, and slashed underperforming routes. A new restructuring plan put forth by Tajudin, whose hands were tied by the government when it came to cutting jobs, was rejected on the grounds it would rescue Tajudin at the expense of minority shareholders. Foreign airlines with an eye towards global expansion (such as Thai Airways and British Airways) seemed interested in investing in the troubled carrier, however.

Principal Subsidiaries

Syarikat Pengangkutan Senai Sdn Bhd; Pengangkutan Kargo Udara MAS Sdn Bhd; Abacus Distribution Systems (Malaysia) Sdn Bhd; MAS Hotels and Boutiques Sdn Bhd; Airfoil Services Sdn Bhd; Aircraft Engine Repair and Overhaul (Malaysia) Sdn Bhd; Aerokleen Services Sdn Bhd; MAS Academy Sdn Bhd; MAS Catering Sdn Bhd; MAS Engineering Services Sdn Bhd; MAS Golden Boutiques Sdn Bhd; MAS Golden Holidays Sdn Bhd; MAS Wings of Gold Sdn Bhd; MAS Properties Sdn Bhd; MASKARGO Sdn Bhd.

Further Reading

Abdullah Mat Zaid, "Malaysia Airlines' Corporate Vision and Service Quality Strategy," *Managing Service Quality*, Vol. 4, No. 6, 1994, pp. 11–15.
——, "Measuring and Monitoring Service Quality at Malaysia Airlines," *Managing Service Quality*, Vol. 5, No. 2, 1995, pp. 25–27.
Daneels, Jenny, "Operator Gears Up to Be High Flier," *Asian Business,* October 1997.
Donville, Christopher, "Malaysian Airlines Spreads Its Wings Internationally," *Globe and Mail,* July 7, 1992.
Feldman, Joan, "Malay Makeover," *Air Transport World,* June 1995, pp. 37–42.
Forward, David C., "Critical MAS," *Airways,* January 1999, pp. 45–51.
Hill, Leonard, "Asia's Newest 'Dragon'," *Air Transport World,* September 1993, pp. 66–74.
Hoon, Lim Siong, "Make or Break for Tajudin and MAS," *Asiamoney,* July/August 1994, pp. 35–37.
Jayasankaran, S., "Unhappy Landings," *Far Eastern Economic Review,* July 23, 1998, pp. 52–53.
Malaysia—A Special Study by Corporate Location, London: Century House Information Ltd., 1991.
Mecham, Michael, "MAS Profits Slide, But Worst May Be Over," *Aviation Week and Space Technology,* June 6, 1994, pp. 33–36.
——, "777 Wins Key Round of Asian Face-Off," *Aviation Week and Space Technology,* January 15, 1996, p. 34.
"Nation Can Afford to Pick and Choose among Investors," *Globe and Mail,* July 7, 1992.
"Operator Gears Up to be High Flier," *Asian Business,* October 1997, pp. 10–12.
Shifrin, Carole, "Virgin Atlantic, Malaysia Team to Gain Global Strength," *Aviation Week and Space Technology,* January 23, 1995, pp. 43–44.
Tsuruoka, Doug, "Flying High," *Far Eastern Economic Review,* January 13, 1994, pp. 77–78.
——, "Go Fly a Kite," *Far Eastern Economic Review,* September 30, 1993, p. 70.
Vandyk, Anthony, "Going Technical," *Air Transport World,* May 1991, pp. 80–81.
Vatikiotis, Michael, "Financial Headwinds: Malaysian Carrier's Expansion Hits Profits," *Far Eastern Economic Review,* June 1992, pp. 65–68.

—Etan Vlessing
—updated by Frederick C. Ingram

Matthews International Corporation

2 NorthShore Center
Pittsburgh, Pennsylvania 15212-5851
U.S.A.
(412) 442-8200
Fax: (412) 442-8290
Web site: http://www.matthewsbronze.com

Public Company
Incorporated: 1972
Employees: 1,600
Sales: $211 million (1998)
Stock Exchanges: NASDAQ
Ticker Symbol: MATW
NAIC: 323122 Prepress Services; 339943 Marking
   Device Manufacturing; 333293 Printing Machinery &
   Equipment Manufacturing

Matthews International Corporation is one of the most prominent designers and manufacturers of custom-made identification products. The company has three core businesses, including: custom-made bronze products, graphic imaging, and marking products. Matthews Bronze comprises approximately 50 percent of the firm's revenues and focuses primarily on the design and manufacture of cast bronze products used as memorials in cemeteries. These products include flush bronze memorials, crypt letters, cremation urns, flower vases, and monuments. One of the most famous of the company's bronze memorials marks the grave of Elvis Presley. Matthews Bronze is also the leading American producer of cremation equipment, as well as the number one builder of mausoleums in the United States. The Graphic Imaging business, which comprises approximately 35 percent of company revenues, provides pre-press services, printing plates, and imaging systems to the packing industry. The company's printing plates are used by firms within the packaging industry to print corrugated boxes, for example, with lettering and graphics that assist in selling the packaged product. The company's Marking Products business, comprising about 15 percent of its revenues, designs and manufacturers equipment used to mark and identify such items as industrial products and packaging containers. For most of its long history, Matthews International has been known for its bronze memorial products, but during the middle and late 1990s management has made a concerted effort to strengthen its product base by expanding the Graphics Imaging business through a strategic acquisitions program.

Early History

The founder of the company, John Dixon Matthews, was born and lived most of his early life in Sheffield, England. Although Matthews was not formally educated, he was talented with his hands, and at an early age became an apprentice to learn the intricacies of the engraving profession. The young man learned his trade quickly and soon was designing and making such items as branding irons, stamps for wooden crates, and ornate engravings for small businesses that desired unique signs of identification. As his apprenticeship ended, Matthews decided that the best opportunity for advancement, and for making more money, was to establish his own engraving firm. The likelihood of his achieving this goal in England was minimal, however, due to the fact that there were many highly skilled engraving firms engaged in intense competition with each other. As a result, Matthews traveled to the United States to establish his own company.

From the time Matthews opened the door of his company for business, it was a thriving concern. Having established his firm in Pittsburgh, Pennsylvania, a growing metropolis with a burgeoning population, the young man was inundated with requests for identification products. Throughout the first 40 years of his business, from 1850 to 1890, his company focused on manufacturing and distributing various products such as branding irons for cattle ranches in the Great Plains and Southern States, ornate engravings that were used in the decoration of public buildings, military stamping dies used by the U.S. Army, especially during the period of the Civil War and immediately afterward, and stamps for crates, packaging, and different sorts of large bundles. As the company grew and prospered, revenues continued to increase at a steady pace. When John Dixon Matthews passed away during the waning years of the 19th century, his company was on the verge of a major transformation.

During the 1890s, the company established the Bronze Tablet Department, specifically intended to design and prepare patterns for bronze plaques and other items that later would be cast by other firms. Historically, bronze had been used since 2,500 BC when metalsmiths living in the eastern part of the Mediterranean discovered that an addition of very small amounts of tin to molten copper produced bronze. These metal smiths soon learned that this new alloy was castable, allowing it to be widely used in casting and creating swords, helmets, and breastplates for war, as well as for statues and decorative articles such as jewelry. As the skills of metalsmiths developed, they found that cast bronze was ideal for artistic expression, since the metal was malleable, easily cast for detail, easy to work with, and exhibits an attractive natural color. As the centuries rolled onward, hollow casting was discovered and used by many artists to produce bronze statues honoring those men who had become heros to their nation. Although the use of bronze in art had declined dramatically and was not widespread either in Europe or the United States during the 19th century, the Bronze Tablet Department at Matthews Company was convinced there was a growing market for such items. Thus, as the company finished and detailed the castings done by other suppliers and shipped them to customers around the United States, its reputation for quality bronze workmanship began to grow. By the start of the 20th century, the company had garnered a national reputation for its identification work using bronze.

Growth and Expansion in the Early 20th Century

The company's success continued during the early decades of the 20th century, and revenues steadily increased. Yet in 1927 the company developed a product that not only changed the direction of its business but affected the history of what has become known as "Memorialization." Throughout the ages people from around the world memorialized the dead by constructing ornate tombs that identified the person as someone of importance. Ground burial and mausoleum entombment were the traditionally preferred methods of disposition and, since the rise of Christianity, cemeteries were created for resting places of the deceased and as a place for the living to seek consolation and peace. Memorialization primarily consisted of stone memorials with the date of birth, date of death, and name of the deceased.

American cemeteries, especially during the 19th and early 20th centuries, were filled with and characterized by memorials of stone carving and sculpture, with an occasional enhancement of bronze from time to time. Memorials encompassed all budgets and a wide variety of tastes, from large, ornate, exquisitely decorated private family mausoleums built for wealthier people to simple and plain upright monuments carved with the person's birth and death dates and the first and last names of the deceased. One of the most important developments in the history of memorialization occurred in 1906, when Dr. Hubert Eaton designed and built Forest Lawn Cemetery in California. A turning point in memorialization, Eaton combined stone, bronze, and marble to create a revolution in funerary sculpture. Within a few short years, Forest Lawn had become one of the most famous cemeteries in the United States, known for its works of memorialization in a variety of materials.

In 1927 the employees at Matthews Tablet Department were approached by a family that wanted to exhibit its affection and respect for a deceased member by commissioning an entirely bronze memorial. Matthews accepted the commission and cast the very first flush bronze memorial for a gravesite in Oaklawn Cemetery in Jacksonville, Florida. The first flush bronze memorial designed, cast, and installed in a cemetery within the United States, the piece immediately revolutionized memorialization in American cemeteries. Soon Matthews had garnered a reputation as the preeminent designer and manufacturer of flush bronze memorials for use in cemeteries, and people from across the United States began placing orders with the company.

Developments in Bronze Memorialization from the Mid-20th Century Through the Present

As the company grew, its expertise in bronze memorials grew apace. The men working at Matthews Bronze were recognized as the best in the business for casting bronze for freestanding memorial sculptures. Much more preferable than stone or wood, the durability and lightness of bronze allowed Matthews Bronze a freedom of conception and design that was virtually impossible in stone and other materials. As a natural outgrowth of its work in the field of bronze memorialization, the most important development for the company during the 1940s, 1950s, and 1960s accompanied the rise of interest in the process of cremation. Cremation goes back to the prehistoric period and developed a large following in the major world cultures of Ancient Greece, the Roman Empire, India, and Japan. Burning the body released it from its corporeal, earthly form and purified the soul on its journey to the realm of the spiritual world. The first documented case of cremation in the United States was reported in 1792, but it was not until the late 19th century that the number of cremations began to increase. By 1913, there were more than 50 crematories located throughout the United States and, during the 1950s and 1960s, the number grew rapidly.

For Matthews, the rise in the interest in cremation meant that people wanted permanent placements of the remains of their deceased loved ones, and memorializations assisted in preserving the memories of love, devotion, and respect. People were no longer limited in their choices for cremation memorialization, as in the days of the Ancient Greeks and Roman Empire, because of the wide array of memorialization options that Matthews offered to satisfy an individual's taste, including outdoor Cremorials, unique and distinctive columbarium estates, elegant and uniquely designed handcrafted urns, attractive niches, and highly personalized memorial plaques that could be set in gardens or parks. By the end of the 1960s, Matthews Bronze was the leading designer and manufacturer of cremation memorializations throughout the United States.

Starting in 1961, the company has designed and cast some of the most notable bronze memorials in the United States. One of the company's high-profile projects includes hand-crafting and casting the plaques used in the Major League Baseball Hall of Fame. Matthews Bronze cast the metal plaque situated on the top of Pike's Peak to commemorate the 100th anniversary of the composition of "America the Beautiful." The company cast bronze memorialization tributes for some of the most popular celebrities in America, including Lucille Ball, Jack Benny, Humphrey Bogart, Nat King Cole, Sammy Davis, Jr., Alan Ladd, Michael Landon, Liberace, Groucho Marx, and Selena. Many people regard Matthews Bronze as having made a memorial for the most famous singer in the world—Elvis Presley. His bronze memorial, which is situated on the southern end of his estate at Graceland in Memphis, Tennessee, is considered to be the most visited piece of work ever cast by Matthews Bronze, with more than 700,000 people visiting the site annually. Another one of Matthews Bronze creations includes the very famous identification plaque cast for the 1984 Summer Olympics in Los Angeles, California.

The company also has done a significant number of bronze memorials for American veterans of wars dating from World War I to the Gulf War in the early 1990s. One of the company's most recent bronze memorials included the installation of a tribute to the men and women of the 14th Quartermaster Detachment Unit at the U.S. Army Reserve Center in Greensburg, Pennsylvania, which suffered the most casualties of any unit in the entire Allied Force throughout the duration of the hostilities between the United Nations and Iraq. The memorial includes the boots, a rifle, and helmet of a fallen soldier, life-sized American soldiers cast in bronze reflecting on the fate of their fallen comrade-in-arms, and an imposing bronze eagle, which symbolizes the bravery and honor of American soldiers in battle.

During the 1990s, in addition to its hold on the market for bronze memorializations, Matthews decided to expand its presence in the Graphics Imaging market. Seven acquisitions were made in 1998 alone, the most important including an interest in O.N.E. Color Communications L.L.C., a digital graphics firm located in California, and S + T Gesellschaft fur Reprotechnik mbH, a well-respected manufacturer of photopolymer printing plates in Germany. The overseas acquisition, in combination with the bronze casting work done for the Sultan of Brunei and the Saudi Arabia Monetary Authority, provided the company with approximately ten percent of its total revenues for the 1998 fiscal year.

Matthews International Corporation is clearly the undisputed leader in the bronze memorialization market, and its dominance is likely to continue for years to come. Nonetheless, management at the company has been astute enough to realize that there is wisdom in a certain amount of diversity when the markets experience a downturn, and so it has implemented a long-term strategic plan to enhance the position of its graphics imaging business, as well as its marking products business, both of which are showing signs of growth and expansion.

Further Reading

Brown, Monique R., "Preparing for the Hereafter," *Black Enterprise,* March 1999, p. 129.
Ellis, Junius, "This Talented Value Hunter Aims for Profits of 51% from Four Obscure Stocks," *Money,* April 1996, p. 183.
"Ink Jet System," *Beverage World,* January 15, 1999, p. 72.
Lenderman, Maxim, "Customers Call, Coders Respond," *Beverage World,* June 1996, p. 86.
"Matthews International Corporation," *Wall Street Journal,* April 28, 1998, p. B26(E).
Nix-Ennen, Steven, "Ink-Jet Printers Cut Through the Dust," *Packaging Digest,* October 1998, p. 86.

—Thomas Derdak

Maui Land & Pineapple Company, Inc.

120 Kane Street
Kahului, Hawaii 96732
U.S.A.
(808) 877-3351
Fax: (808) 871-0953
Web site: http://www.mauiland.com

Public Company
Incorporated: 1969
Employees: 2,030
Sales: $143.7 million (1998)
Stock Exchanges: American
Ticker Symbol: MLP
NAIC: 311421 Fruit & Vegetable Canning; 23311 Land
   Subdivision & Land Development

One of Hawaii's oldest and largest corporations, Maui Land & Pineapple Company, Inc. (Maui Pine) grows and cans pineapple and develops and operates resort and commercial property. Maui Pine conducted its business through two primary operating subsidiaries, Maui Pineapple Company, Ltd. and Kapalua Land Company, Ltd. The pineapple operations, situated on roughly 7,900 acres owned by the company, represented the company's original business, whose roots indirectly stretched to the first appearance of pineapple in Hawaii in 1813. The real estate-related business of Maui Pine emerged during the 1960s, when the company began developing residential, commercial, and resort properties. During the late 1990s, Maui Pine developed and managed property at the Kapalua Resort, located on 1,500 acres bordering the ocean. The company also operated retail properties, including Kaahumanu Center, Napili Plaza, and other nonresort property.

Origins

The history of Maui Pine incorporated the history of the Baldwins, a family of New England Congregational missionaries who arrived on the Hawaiian Islands in 1836. Displaying considerably more prowess as land barons than as proselytizers, the Baldwins became one of the Big Five families who controlled Hawaii in the century before World War II, establishing a far-reaching business empire with holdings in agriculture, ranching, coffee, canning, and other activities. Their grasp on the Hawaiian economy was comprehensive, maintained by a labyrinthine network of businesses whose development spanned generations of Baldwins. One of these businesses spawned from the varied interests of the Baldwins was Maui Pine's earliest direct predecessor, the Keahua Ranch Co., which was incorporated in December 1909 to control a portion of the family's pineapple operations. In 1929 the Keahua Ranch Co. was renamed the Haleakala Pineapple Co., Ltd., three years before the pineapple operations of Haleakala and Maui Agricultural Company were consolidated to create Maui Pineapple Company, Ltd. J. Walter Cameron, a descendant of the Baldwin family, was appointed manager of the new company, presiding over its development for the next 30 years until a flurry of corporate maneuvers created the Maui Pine that existed during the 1990s. In August 1962, Alexander & Baldwin, a principal Baldwin family concern, merged three of its pineapple operations, Baldwin Packers, Ltd., Maui Pineapple Company, Ltd., and the old Haleakala Pineapple Company, to create what four months later became the Maui Pineapple Company, Ltd. J. Walter Cameron was named president of the Alexander & Baldwin subsidiary, joined by his son, Colin Campbell Cameron, who was appointed general manager.

It was the younger Cameron who exerted the greatest influence over Maui Pine during the 20th century. A Maui native, Colin Cameron earned a master's degree in business administration at Harvard College, leaving the institution in 1953 to return to the pineapple operations on Maui. Two years after the formation of Maui Pineapple Company, Colin Cameron was promoted to general manager and executive vice-president when his father retired from day-to-day control over the company and became its chairman. Although the Camerons held prominent titles at Maui Pineapple, the fortunes of the company were not entirely under their control. Alexander & Baldwin held sway as the parent company of Maui Pineapple, having the final say in the decision-making affecting its subsidiary. It was a relationship that became strained during the 1960s and irrevocably damaged in 1967 when Alexander & Baldwin's new president, Stanley Powell Jr., delivered an ultimatum. Powell wanted to centralize all management decisions in Honolulu, which, in Colin Cameron's view, put him in an untenable position. Cameron believed the pineapple operations could not flourish if they were managed from afar. Further, he had tired of competing for attention with Alexander & Baldwin's other subsidiaries, which included sugar and shipping operations that were much larger and made much more money than Maui Pineapple. In response, Colin Cameron resigned in 1967, the same year his father retired as chairman. Both remained on the company's board of directors, however, and would return shortly to submit a proposal to Alexander & Baldwin.

1969: A New Beginning

In 1969 the Camerons made their bid for independence. They approached Alexander & Baldwin about purchasing Maui Pineapple Company and reached an agreement in July for a $20 million buyout of the enterprise. In September the Camerons changed the name of the company to Maui Land & Pineapple Company, Inc. Three months later, they took Maui Pine public. With J. Walter Cameron serving as chairman and Colin Cameron serving as president and chief executive officer, Maui Pine took its first steps unfettered by Alexander & Baldwin, beginning a new era as the 1970s began.

As the company set out on its own, it drew support from two primary business areas. One side of Maui Pine represented the most recent addition to the Cameron family's business activities, its importance reflected by the inclusion of the word "land" in Maui Pine's corporate title. During the 1960s, Colin Cameron had spearheaded resort planning and development activities that had operated under the control of Maui Pineapple Company. Following the Camerons' purchase of Maui Pineapple Company, these real estate activities were organized into a new subsidiary incorporated in 1970 as Honolua Plantation Land Company, Inc. Through Honolua Plantation, which counted Colin Cameron as its president, Maui Pine began building residential housing projects, beginning with a 174-unit, low- and moderate-cost housing project called Napilihau that began construction in 1972. By the time the Napilihau units were ready for occupancy in 1974, the Camerons had formed another real estate development subsidiary named Kapalua Land Company, Ltd. Following the 1974 incorporation of Kapalua Land, the Honolua Plantation subsidiary was responsible for the management and development of nonresort lands, while Kapalua Land oversaw the duties of resort development. Kapalua Land's resort development activities during the 1970s included the construction of an 18-hole golf course, condominium complexes, and the 196-room Kapalua Bay Hotel, which opened in 1978. The other side of Maui Pine's business was its pineapple operations, representing the thread that connected the Cameron family-controlled company to the 1909 founding of the Keahua Ranch Co. In 1977 the pineapple operations were separated into their own subsidiary called Maui Pineapple Company, Ltd.

J. Walter Cameron's death in 1976 left Colin Cameron as the patriarch of the family and principal leader of Maui Pine. His father's legacy—a half century of stewarding the fortunes of the company's pineapple operations—would stand in contrast to his own, as Colin Cameron devoted the bulk of his energies to the development of Maui Pine's real estate activities, particu-

larly during the late 1980s. The Kapalua Land subsidiary served as the hub of activity, presiding over the development of The Ironwoods, a 40-unit condominium project that was completed in 1980, and The Ridge, a 161-unit condominium project, also completed in 1980. The subsidiary also completed its second golf course, The Village Course, in 1980. Financial pressure, attributable to the more than $50 million of debt that weighed Maui Pine down in 1984, forced Cameron to sell what was regarded as his masterpiece, the Kapalua Bay Hotel, in 1985. Despite the divestiture, Cameron, serving as chairman and acting president of Kapalua Land after the sale of the company's signature hotel property, pressed ahead with other real estate development projects. In 1985 the company acquired the Kaahumanu Shopping Center and broke ground the following year on the Pineapple Hill at Kapalua project, a single-family residential project. The Pineapple Hill at Kapalua development, comprising 99 lots, was completed in 1987 and was followed by the development of Kapalua Place, an eight-lot, single-family residential project, completed in 1989.

Late 1980s: Controversy and Despair

Against the backdrop of commercial and residential development projects, Cameron was busy working on what could rightly be called his dream project. At roughly the same time as Maui Pine's formation, Cameron and his father had begun planning a large-scale hotel project that became known as the Kapalua project. They conducted an archeological survey on an area in West Maui, later deciding on a beachfront plot known as the Honokahua site. Years of planning went into the project, time spent designing the hotel, having the zoning code changed to permit the construction of the hotel, and securing the financial backing to fund the project. By 1986, the final hurdles before beginning construction had been cleared. Ritz-Carlton had agreed to serve as the hotel operator and financing had been obtained from Japanese investors. There was one nagging problem, however. The Honokahua site was discovered to be an ancient Hawaiian burial ground, the magnitude of which was not fully realized until late in the project's development. A thorough excavation of the site had unearthed 700 burials by 1988, including a variety of artifacts that were estimated to be 3,500 years old. By 1989, construction of the $100 million, 450-room Ritz-Carlton was a year behind schedule and Cameron found himself at the center of protests and heated debate. Kapalua Land was at risk of losing the financial backing for the project and suffering the departure of its Ritz-Carlton partners.

While Cameron's hotel project sat motionless, mired in controversy, Maui Pine could at least fall back on it pineapple operations, which had recorded consecutive years of profitability that stretched from 1977 to the end of the 1980s. The company's Maui Pineapple Company subsidiary ranked as the largest producer of private-label pineapple in the United States, providing a steady stream of income that tempered the frustration stemming from the hobbled Kapalua hotel project. As Maui Pine exited the 1980s, however, its pineapple operations suffered a devastating setback that later resulted in the worst year ever recorded by Maui Pine or any of it predecessors. The first sign of trouble surfaced in 1989, at the same time the Kapalua project was a year behind its construction schedule. The source of the trouble was Thailand, which had begun gearing up for large-scale pineapple production in the late 1980s. As a pineapple-producing region, Thailand possessed ideal characteristics, including excellent growing conditions and laborers willing to work for low wages. The number of canning businesses in the country proliferated as a result, concurrent with increased production by Maui Pine and other U.S.-owned pineapple canning businesses. In 1989 the abundance of pineapple produced and canned led to an oversupply in global markets, resulting in Maui Pineapple Company's $3.9 million operating loss for the year, a year after the subsidiary had registered profits totaling $7.2 million.

By 1993, the situation had become disastrous. After ordering its workers to let 20,000 tons of pineapple rot in the fields rather than try to move the fruit onto the glutted world market, Maui Pineapple Company recorded $16.2 million in operating loss. Maui Pine, unable to offset the loss with its real estate activities, registered a net loss of $11 million on revenues of $131 million.

While the company reeled from its mounting pineapple losses, the ill-fated Kapalua project regained its footing, giving Maui Pine executives at least one positive development to which they could point during the early 1990s. The site of the resort had been relocated away from the burial ground and the hotel was slated to open in 1992. Unfortunately for Cameron, the grand opening of the long-planned-for hotel was a celebration that, tragically, he missed. In June 1992 Cameron was found unconscious in the ocean near his home on Maui, having died of a heart attack while swimming. The Ritz-Carlton hotel opened four months later.

Cameron's sudden death prematurely ushered in a new era of leadership. Mary Cameron Sanford, Colin Cameron's sister, was appointed chairman and Maui Pineapple Company's president, Joseph H. Hartley, was promoted to president and chief executive officer of Maui Pine. Together, the pair had to contend with the worst crisis in the company's history. The first order of business was to arrest the financial slide experienced by the company's pineapple business and to resolve the difficulties stemming from the market glut. Pineapple harvesting and canning were trimmed by 25 percent in response to the surfeit of pineapple available and extensive efforts to reduce costs were initiated. Capital improvement spending was cut drastically, slashed from $8.2 million to $1.5 million over the course of the next two years. Executive salaries were reduced, wages were frozen, and employees were laid off. The company ended its 20-year practice of hiring offshore workers during the harvest season and a long-standing arrangement with Wailuku Agribusiness to farm 40,000 tons of pineapple for Maui Pine was abandoned. By 1995, the sweeping measures had begun to yield positive results, aided substantially by the U.S. International Trade Commission's ruling that Thai pineapple canneries were guilty of selling their product in the United States at prices lower than the cost of production. As a result of the ruling, duties were imposed that averaged roughly 25 percent of Thai pineapple sale prices, which buoyed the market sufficiently to enable Maui Pine to raise its prices 23 percent.

A drought in 1996 inflicted another blow to Maui Pine's pineapple business, but after the temporary setback the company recorded encouraging success with its pineapple operations during the late 1990s. Pineapple sales registered their greatest upswing at the end of the decade, when, in sharp contrast to the early 1990s, there was a worldwide shortage of pineapple. At the decade's conclusion, a new generation of management took the helm at Maui Pine. Mary Sanford was appointed director emeritus, making room for the ascension of the next line of Camerons, Richard H. Cameron, Colin Cameron's son, who was selected as chairman in March 1999. As Richard Cameron faced the challenge of shepherding the family business into the next century, Maui Pine's legacy of perseverance bolstered belief in its ability to contend with the difficulties of the future.

Principal Subsidiaries

Maui Pineapple Company, Ltd.; Kapalua Land Company, Ltd.

Further Reading

Bartlett, Tony, ''Kapalua Expands Resort with Hotel, Golf Course, More Acreage: Secluded Location Will House 550-Room Ritz-Carlton,'' *Travel Weekly,* December 13, 1990, p. 66.
Chang, Diane, ''Paradise Lost,'' *Hawaii Business,* December 1991, p. 68.
Ishikawa, Lisa, ''Greener Acres?,'' *Hawaii Business,* May 1994, p. 12.
Jokiel, Lucy, ''Colin Cameron's Toughest Decision,'' *Hawaii Business,* May 1989, p. 16.
Ma, Lybia, ''Still on Track; the Group Dubbed 'Most Likely to Succeed' in 1987 Is Still Running Hard,'' *Hawaii Business,* May 1990, p. 77.
''Passing the Baton,'' *Hawaii Business,* May 1993, p. 9.

—Jeffrey L. Covell

Mazel Stores, Inc.

31000 Aurora Road
Solon, Ohio 44139
U.S.A.
(440) 248-5200
Fax: (440) 349-4056
Web site: http://www.mazelstores.com

Public Company
Incorporated: 1975 as The Mazel Company
Employees: 1,181
Sales: $237.1 million (1998)
Stock Exchanges: NASDAQ
Ticker Symbol: MAZL
NAIC: 45299 All Other General Merchandise Stores;
   42199 Other Miscellaneous Durable Goods
   Wholesalers; 42299 Other Miscellaneous Nondurable
   Goods Wholesalers

Mazel Stores, Inc. is a retailer and wholesaler of consumer closeout items. Its wholesale operation, which is the largest for closeout merchandise in the United States, buys in bulk from manufacturers, wholesalers, and retailers who have overstocked, discontinued product lines, or are liquidating their assets. From its headquarters and distribution facility in Solon, Ohio, Mazel buys merchandise from more than 700 suppliers throughout the world at costs considerably lower than traditional wholesale prices. The company then resells this merchandise to more than 2,000 wholesale customers, including major regional and national retailers, as well as smaller retailers, manufacturers, wholesalers, and distributors.

The company also markets merchandise through its own chain of retail stores, which operate under the names "Odd Job" and "Odd Job Trading." There are more than 45 of these stores located in New York, New Jersey, Connecticut, and Pennsylvania. They offer brand-name closeout merchandise—which includes housewares, stationery, books, party goods, health and beauty aids, food, toys, hardware, electronics, and garden supplies—at prices substantially below traditional retail.

Wholesale Beginnings in 1975

Mazel Stores, Inc. began as The Mazel Company in 1975. Founded by entrepreneurs Reuven Dessler, Jacob Koval, and a number of other investors, the operation was at that time strictly wholesale. With an eye for "deals," Dessler and Koval capitalized on the potential closeout bargains inherent in supplier overruns, overstocks, and bankruptcies. By making rapid purchasing decisions, purchasing vendors' entire product offerings, and taking possession of merchandise more quickly than many of its competitors, Mazel essentially made things easier for vendors and minimized disruption to their business caused by excess stock. Soon, the company had established relationships with several key vendors who offered their closeout merchandise to Mazel first.

After more than five years' wholesale success, Dessler and Koval attempted to implement the complementary wholesale/ retail structure that was to characterize the Mazel Stores of the 1990s. In 1981 the company initiated "Just Closeouts," a chain of retail outlets in Ohio.

After a brief period of success, however, Just Closeouts did not prove profitable. In 1993 the business faltered and never recovered, losing a total of $2.2 million for the company by October of 1995. That year, Mazel shed the loss-making 11 stores for approximately $1.8 million in cash and a contingent note for up to $500,000, realizing a $1.6 million loss on the divestiture.

The early 1990s also marked changes in the ownership structure for The Mazel Company. A new corporate entity, Mazel Company L.P., was formed by Dessler, Koval, and a group of investors in a private investment fund. Mazel Company L.P. acquired The Mazel Company and Just Closeouts in a recapitalization transaction. The new company was capitalized with $13.5 million of equity: $9 million contributed by the private investment fund and $4.5 million contributed by Dessler and Koval. Under the new arrangement, Dessler continued to serve as the company's president and Koval acted as its vice-president.

Mid-1990s: Retail Revisited

In 1995 Mazel hired two key members of its management team. Brady Churches, named president of retail operations on

Company Perspectives:

Already the largest wholesaler of closeout merchandise in the United States, our goal is to establish the retail side of our business, Odd Job, as the leading closeout retailer in the Northeast and Mid-Atlantic markets. The key to our success—we buy quality, brand-name merchandise at substantial discounts and sell these goods far below the original retail price, bringing exceptional value to our customers.

August 14, 1995, had served previously in various managerial positions for Consolidated Stores Corporation, another national retailer and wholesaler of closeout merchandise. During Churches's time at Consolidated, the company had grown from one store to approximately 800. Mazel's second new leader—Jerry Sommers, who was brought in as executive vice-president of retail—was also a veteran of Consolidated Stores.

With its new management team in place, Mazel was ready to try its hand at retail again. In late 1995, through a complicated reshuffling of corporate interests, Mazel's main investor, ZS Fund, acquired all the stock and equity interests of one of the company's key customers—Odd Job Trading Corp. Odd Job, which consisted of 12 retail stores and a warehouse and distribution facility, was owned by its co-founders, Howard Snyder and Israel Horowitz, and the Mazel Stores' corporate predecessor, The Mazel Company. The Odd Job stores, most of which had opened in the late 1980s and early 1990s, were located in New York and New Jersey.

At the end of fiscal 1995, Mazel's wholesale operations had grown to $77.3 million—a 6.9 percent annual growth rate over the previous five years. This wholesale income made up 77 percent of Mazel's total sales, with retail sales making up the remainder.

1996: Restructuring and IPO

In March of 1996 two more New York retail stores were added to the Odd Job collection. Formerly operated under the name "The CloseOut Store," these outlets were purchased from Melen Trading Corp., an entity partially owned by Snyder, Horowitz, and the owners of the then-defunct The Mazel Company. The absorption of these two stores gave ZS Fund 14 retail outlets in all. The company also implemented a new merchandising approach. By increasing the number of brand-name products offered, Mazel targeted brand-loyal customers in hopes that they would shop Odd Job for their desired products before shopping traditional retail. In concurrence with the new merchandising approach, Mazel launched a marketing campaign that promoted its brand-name products.

By the end of the year, Mazel was operating 23 stores, which ranged in size from 6,500 to 25,000 square feet. To support this current growth and planned future expansion, the company increased the size of its Englewood, New Jersey warehouse from 140,000 to 253,000 square feet and broke ground on a 100,000-square-foot addition to its Solon, Ohio facility.

The fall of 1996 marked a number of major changes for Mazel. In preparation for a planned initial public offering (IPO), the company underwent yet another reshuffling. Mazel Company L.P. acquired the Odd Jobs holdings from ZS Fund for $1.4 million. Mazel Stores, Inc., a new entity, was then formed as a wholly owned subsidiary of Mazel Company L.P.—and all of Mazel Company L.P.'s assets were transferred to Mazel Stores, Inc. Although Mazel Stores' ownership was essentially identical to that of Mazel Company L.P., the restructuring was accompanied by changes in management. Formerly president and vice-president, Dessler and Koval assumed the positions of chairman of the board/CEO and executive vice-president of wholesale operations, respectively. Brady Churches stepped into the role of company president, and Jerry Sommers assumed a director's position, with responsibility for all retail division purchasing.

Restructured and poised for growth, the company made an initial public offering of 2,574,000 shares in November 1996. With shares priced at $16.00, Mazel netted approximately $37.3 million after expenses—leaving it debt-free and ready to move forward. Year-end 1996 sales for Mazel were $179.8 million. The shift to a retail focus was evident in the 1996 financials. Retail operations generated 47 percent of the year's total income, whereas in 1995 retail accounted for only 23 percent of the total.

1997–1998: Building the Retail Base

Rapid retail expansion was the theme for 1997. The company's goal was to open nine new Odd Job stores by fiscal year end; management wasted no time in working toward that goal. By the end of its first fiscal quarter, in April, the company had signed leases for five new store locations: two in New York, two in New Jersey, and one in Connecticut, a new territory for Odd Job. Perhaps more significant, on April 25 Mazel announced its first strategic partnership—with Value City Department Stores, a 95-store chain with locations in the Midwest and East. Under the terms of the joint venture, Mazel agreed to acquire and operate the toy and sporting goods and health and beauty aids departments in 90 of the Value City stores.

At the midpoint of Mazel's fiscal year, three new Odd Job stores were operating and leases had been signed for four more locations. The company also had assumed operational control of the identified departments for Value City stores. Bringing to bear its expertise in the closeout market, Mazel altered the merchandise mix in these departments to include approximately 70 percent closeout products. Historically, Value City had carried approximately only 20 percent closeout merchandise.

Just before Thanksgiving 1997, the company met its goal of opening nine new stores. Extended lease negotiations delayed the scheduled openings for four of the stores, however, resulting in loss of potential revenues, higher inventory costs, and lower retail profits. In addition, the Value City joint venture got off to a slower start than the company had anticipated. These setbacks, and their associated losses, created a slight dip in financial results. Third quarter net income was $1.6 million, compared with $2.1 million for the previous year's third quarter, and Mazel's stock dropped to $11 per share in November, from a 52-week high of more than $29 the previous month.

Mazel regained momentum during the fourth quarter of 1997, closing the year with sales of $208.3 million, a 16 percent increase over 1996. The expansion of the retail base again was reflected in the proportions of the retail and wholesale income streams for the year. Retail operations brought in 54 percent of the total sales, while wholesale operations accounted for 46 percent—an almost perfect reversal of the previous year's proportions.

The company's shift in orientation from wholesale to retail continued to play out through 1998. Seven new stores were opened by the end of the first fiscal quarter. An additional four stores opened in the second quarter brought the total store count up to 43 by midyear 1998. Retail at that point accounted for 65 percent of total sales mix.

Although Mazel's retail sales grew during this time frame, its wholesale dropped off slightly because of the loss of its largest customer, MacFrugal's Bargains Close-Outs Inc. MacFrugal's, which was bought by a competitor late in 1997, had contributed approximately 30 percent of Mazel's 1997 wholesale revenues. In the company's 1998 second quarter report, Dessler wrote, ''Our wholesale operation remains focused on making new inroads. We have worked hard to develop other sales opportunities and are very encouraged by sales to non-traditional closeout businesses.''

In the fall of 1998 Mazel relocated its Englewood, New Jersey, warehouse to a larger, 350,000-square-foot facility in South Plainfield, New Jersey, in preparation for further expansion. The company also added a new executive vice-president and general manager—Thomas Kiley, previously affiliated with discount retailing operations McCrory Corporation and Jamesway Corporation.

Mazel had opened 15 new stores by October 31, 1998, bringing the total to 47. This growth resulted in record sales of $60.3 million for the third quarter—an increase of 23 percent over the previous year's third quarter. Retail, which accounted for 60 percent of the total sales, grew by 39 percent. In addition, the wholesale division rebounded from its shaky second quarter, growing by almost six percent as new customers and increased sales to existing customers made up for the loss of MacFrugal's. The warehouse relocation, however, took its toll on the company's bottom line. Net income for the first nine months of 1998 was $1.8 million—down substantially from 1997's nine-month net of $5.1 million. In a November 1998 press release, Dessler stated, ''We have accomplished many of our strategic infrastructure goals for 1998 and are well positioned for the holiday season. While these projects have adversely impacted our near

term financial results, we remain focused on long-term growth for our shareholders.''

In the final quarter of 1998 wholesale proceeds again took a hit, dropping 27 percent. Retail revenue, however, grew by 32 percent. The resulting net sales were $74.6 million—11 percent higher than in the fourth quarter of 1997. The year-end sales total for Mazel was $237.1 million, compared with $208.3 million for fiscal 1997. The retail division accounted for 66 percent of the year's total sales.

Staying the Course for the Future

Since the acquisition of the Odd Job chain in 1995, Mazel has remained true to its vision of becoming the leading closeout retailer in the Northeast and Mid-Atlantic regions. With plans to open 17 new stores in 1999, the company expected to exceed its goal of having 60 stores by the year 2000. ''Our growth vehicle continues to be the expansion of our Odd Job retail operation,'' said Dessler in a March 1999 press release. This projected growth was expected to result in retail sales accounting for an increasingly large share of total sales. As such, future earnings were likely to become more seasonal—with holiday sales in the second half of the year providing the bulk of the full year's revenues.

In an effort to bolster sagging wholesale revenues, in 1999 Mazel entered into an agreement with Value America, an online retailer of consumer products, technology, and office supplies. Under the agreement, Mazel would serve as a closeout product source, with associated customer fulfillment services in Value America's e-commerce operation. The company also planned to explore other e-commerce sales opportunities for its wholesale division.

Principal Subsidiaries

Odd Job Trading Corp.

Further Reading

Hevesi, Dennis, ''Restoring a Remnant of 1950s Glitz,'' *New York Times,* July 19, 1998, Sec. 11.
Livingston, Sandra, ''Mazel Stores Appeals to Analysts,'' *Cleveland Plain Dealer,* in ''Mazel History,'' at http://www.mazelstores.com/mazel_corp/history.html.
Much, Marilyn, ''Closeouts,'' *Investor's Business Daily,* January 8, 1997, p. A4.

—Shawna Brynildssen

Meadowcraft, Inc.

1401 Meadowcraft Road
Birmingham, Alabama 35215
U.S.A.
(205) 853-2220
(888) 539-3726
Fax: (205) 856-0847
Web site: http://www.meadowcraft.com

Public Company
Incorporated: 1985
Employees: 772
Sales: $162.2 million (1998)
Stock Exchanges: New York
Ticker Symbol: MWI
NAIC: 337124 Metal Household Furniture Manufacturing

Meadowcraft, Inc. is a leading domestic maker of casual outdoor furniture and the largest manufacturer of outdoor wrought-iron furniture in the United States. Other Meadowcraft products, all of which are designed and distributed by the company, include a variety of wrought-iron indoor furniture and both indoor and outdoor wrought-iron accessories, outdoor cushions, umbrellas, and wrought-iron garden products. Meadowcraft's customers are mass merchandisers and specialty stores, retailer Wal-Mart perhaps the most notable, primarily in the United States.

Origins of the Iron Works

Meadowcraft traces its history to the early 20th-century founding of the Birmingham Ornamental Iron Co., in Birmingham, Alabama, by B. M. Meadow. The fledgling operation began fashioning such ornamental iron products as decorative fencing and gates for Birmingham residences and businesses. Over the years, the company diversified its iron product offerings and its customer base, producing a variety of iron products for local business facilities.

During World War II, Birmingham Ornamental Iron (BOI) began manufacturing a line of metal furniture, in part to offset seasonal drops in revenues it experienced given its dependence on the construction industry. They found a ready, if unlikely, customer in electronics giant Philco, which had been diversifying its interests during the war. From 1946 to 1948 Philco marketed and sold Meadowcraft furniture, named for the founder of BOI, but dropped the line when demand for Philco electronics products resumed following the war.

Following the loss of Philco as a customer for its furniture, BOI resumed its focus on the construction industry, producing stairs, railings, grillwork, metal signs, and a variety of metal products for use in local industrial facilities, including regional plants for Ford Motor Co. and the Container Corp., as well as in the construction of Prudential Life Insurance Co. offices and the Georgia Tech library.

By the early 1950s, the company's furniture line was languishing and facing steep financial losses. Moreover, BOI had warehoused thousands of tons of metal for use in its furniture; further losses would ensue if that inventory had to be sold as scrap. The problem was met by the company's vice-president, general manager, and treasurer William McTyeire Jr. McTyeire, an engineering grad and enthusiastic salesperson as well, decided to turn the furniture operations around.

Meadowcraft Furniture Takes Off: 1950s–60s

McTyeire installed a policy of commitment to quality in design and manufacture, as well as to dealer satisfaction. Among the qualities recommending Meadowcraft furniture were its ten-year rust-free guarantee and its availability in popular styles and colors. Moreover, to ensure a high quality product, the company invested in the latest and best manufacturing equipment. Maintaining that "the dealer is always right," McTyeire once reportedly accepted a return shipment of wrought iron furniture made by a competitor, from a dissatisfied dealer who mistook the furniture for Meadowcraft. Rather than returning the shipment to the dealer, McTyeire saw to it that the pieces were refurbished and returned to the dealer, with an explanation, at no charge. Of course, that dealer was duly impressed with Meadowcraft as were many other dealers over the years.

McTyeire also spearheaded direct mail selling efforts aimed at leading furniture retailers across the country. The company spent

Company Perspectives:

Why should I buy wrought iron and select Meadowcraft? There are many advantages to wrought iron manufactured by Meadowcraft: primed (undercoated) using an Electrostatic process, which provides superior protection against the elements; powder coat finish; wind will not blow furniture around; fully welded frames; traditional in style; comfortable with or without cushions; cool to sit on, even on the hottest of days; terrific accessories at great values; the look in outdoor furniture that has remained popular for over 50 years; easiest of all outdoor furniture to keep clean.

heavily on advertising in general, overseeing print and radio promotions. Moreover, the company began offering Meadowcraft furniture for use on the sets of the country's most popular television programs. In the mid-1950s, the company received an important commission from television stars Desi Arnaz and Lucille Ball, who ordered over 500 pieces of Meadowcraft furniture for use at their new Palm Springs resort hotel.

By the late 1950s, the company was ranked third in the United States in wrought iron furniture sales and was first in the South. The iron works' sales surpassed $3 million in 1957, over one-third of which was generated by its Meadowcraft furniture line. Still, the iron works' primary business was in manufacturing the miscellaneous and ornamental metal products.

A New Identity in the 1980s

By 1967, when the company was employing a work force of 259 and the founder's descendant Evelyn Meadow was serving as chairman, BOI had grown into a collection of consolidated furniture and housewares makers, still based in Birmingham. In 1985, these manufacturers were incorporated as Meadowcraft, with Samuel R. Blount as the new concern's chairman.

The popularity of Meadowcraft furniture was rekindled during this time, when retail giant Wal-Mart began offering outdoor furniture at its stores, including the company's lines of chairs, tables, and benches. The Meadowcraft products proved popular and regularly sold out.

When Bill McCanna took over the presidency of Meadowcraft in 1991, his focus was on quality-control particularly as it pertained to designing, producing, and shipping on a reliable, timely, and cost-effective basis. McCanna, who came to Meadowcraft after two decades of running manufacturing plants for Fortune 500 companies, made modernizing the firm's distribution his first order of business. At the time, the company had been overseeing about ten warehouses scattered around Birmingham, with crews wandering around them searching for the furniture needed to fill orders. A new, better organized system would be in place by mid-decade.

Meadowcraft had net income of $2.2 million in fiscal 1991 (the year ended April 28, 1991) on $50.1 million in sales. In the early 1990s Meadowcraft's factory closeout sale at Wal-Mart's flagship store in Bentonville, Arkansas, reportedly sold more wrought-iron furniture in 32 days than the Wal-Mart chain

sometimes sold during an entire outdoor-furniture selling season. For Wal-Mart ''it was a real eye-opener,'' according to Blount, and impelled the giant chain to increase its orders from Meadowcraft.

Meadowcraft added indoor wrought-iron furniture to its products in the early 1990s. The company reported net income of $2.8 million in 1993 on net sales of $73.1 million. This increased to $6.4 million on net sales of $96.2 million in 1994 and $10 million on net sales of $120.8 million in 1995.

In 1994 Meadowcraft added a 660,000-square-foot manufacturing and distribution facility to its existing operation in Wadley, Alabama. The company also completed a 500,000-square-foot distribution center on Birmingham's Carson Road in early 1995 and a 160,000-square-foot addition to that center later in the year. This facility was adjacent to the company's newest expansion, a 350,000-square-foot factory near company offices off Pinson Valley Parkway. A smaller factory/warehouse at the company's Selma, Alabama, plant was also under construction in 1995. The $30-million Pinson Valley plant, located in Valley East Industrial Park, was completed in late 1995. The company also was leasing a 240,000-square-foot plant and corporate headquarters on Meadowcraft Road and a 340,000-square-foot distribution center on Goodrich Drive. Both were about a half-mile from the Carson Road/Pinson Valley facilities.

McCanna told a reporter in 1995, ''We've probably added more square footage of manufacturing space over the past few years than any other company in Alabama.'' The expansion came in the face of caution among analysts about the furniture industry, but McCanna maintained that Meadowcraft's improved sales had come across the board. By this time, the company's outdoor furniture brands included Meadowcraft, Plantation Patterns, Arlington House, and Salterini. The new Interior Images line of upscale, iron indoor furniture for specialty stores also had shown strong sales, and Meadowcraft was about to introduce a lower-priced line of indoor furniture for mass-market merchants. The firm also was making bedframes, tables, plant stands, kitchen racks, and other home accessories. In fiscal 1997 it added wrought-iron garden products as well.

Expansion: 1996–1998

Meadowcraft's net income grew to $7.9 million on net sales of $117.4 million in 1996 and $15.9 million on net sales of $141.9 million the following year. The company was a partnership 90-percent owned by Blount and other family members and ten-percent owned by McCanna in 1997, prior to making its initial public offering of common stock in November 1997. More than 3.2 million shares—about 17 percent of the company—were sold at $13 a share, raising $39 million, of which $32.7 million was paid to Blount and McCanna, who retained 73 percent and eight percent of the company, respectively. The remainder of the amount was earmarked for capital investments. Another 500,000 shares were sold shortly after.

Meadowcraft began production in March 1998 at a new, 600,000-square-foot manufacturing/office/distribution center north of San Luis, Arizona, that became the largest manufacturing complex in Yuma County. A 175,000-square-foot plant across the border in San Luis, Mexico, purchased in October

1997, was turning out welded patio chairs, umbrella tables, and poolside tables. This unfinished furniture was then shipped to the Arizona plant to undergo a primer-coat process in order to reduce corrosion, followed by an electrostatic dry-paint process. A gas furnace then fused the paint to the metal. These new facilities were intended to reduce transportation costs for Meadowcraft's West Coast customers.

Meadowcraft begin production in early 1998 of outdoor tubular-steel furniture in an idle Alabama manufacturing facility whose conversion was completed in December 1997. That year the company also added to its Carson Road complex in Birmingham by completing a 520,000-square-foot manufacturing/distribution/office facility. In addition, it was expanding its Selma and Wadley facilities by about 70,000 and 10,000 square feet, respectively. Work on a second Pinson Valley warehouse also was underway in 1998.

Meadowcraft's net sales grew to $162.2 million in 1998 and its net income to $22.3 million. By this time it was commanding 23 percent of the $1.5 billion outdoor furniture market, according to McCanna. Advertising remained an important component of company success; Meadowcraft's products were being promoted by Paul Harvey on his daily news-and-commentary radio show.

With Meadowcraft's sales increasing so rapidly, production was at a record pace. A *Birmingham News* reporter who visited the new Carson Road plant in early 1998 described it as "a scene from America's industrial heyday." Whereas before 1991, workers had, artisan-style, labored over a particular chair, table, or bench from start to finish, the new plant was built in such a manner that the job would be broken down into segments, with workers organized into teams. The new factory was expected to turn out two million piece of wrought-iron furniture in 1998.

Meadowcraft was working closely with its mass-market clients, building enough inventory between June and January to supply them for the February-through-May rush period for outdoor furniture. Orders were arriving electronically in selling season by means of a computer line. Computerized inventory tracking and shipping systems enabled line supervisors to ensure that all goods were sent out exactly as ordered. During the peak of spring selling season as many as 150 trucks and trailers arrived at the loading docks. "They have as sophisticated of an operation as I have seen," said a securities analyst, who observed of Meadowcraft's main customer, "Wal-Mart has put people out of business [for not meeting delivery dates]. They can make your life hell."

The Late 1990s and Beyond

Meadowcraft, in mid-1998, was offering consumers a wide variety of products in three markets: the outdoor mass market under the Plantation Patterns brand name; the outdoor specialty market under the Meadowcraft, Arlington House, and Salterini brand names; and the indoor specialty and mass markets under the Interior Images by Salterini and Home Collection from Plantation Patterns brand names, respectively.

Outdoor products sold through mass merchandisers under the Plantation Patterns name included dining groups composed of action chairs, stack chairs, dining tables, bistro groups, and accent tables; accessories such as chaises, gliders, bakers' racks, and tea carts; cushions and umbrellas; and garden products. Outdoor products for the specialty market were similar. The company's outdoor furniture products came in a variety of styles and colors and were being sold at different prices to appeal to a range of consumers. The indoor collections, all in wrought iron, included occasional tables, dining groups and beds, and accent pieces. The garden products included shepherds' hooks, trellises, arbors, and plant stands.

Meadowcraft was serving the outdoor mass market, including national chains, discount retailers, mass merchants, and home centers; the outdoor specialty market, including furniture stores, specialty stores, and garden shops; and the indoor market, including specialty furniture stores, mass merchandisers, and department stores. In fiscal 1998, the company sold products to more than 1,500 mass and specialty accounts, including nine of the top ten U.S. discount retailers/mass merchants and home centers. Typically, by early fall of each year, Meadowcraft received estimated requirements from customers for about 70 percent of the sales that it would produce and ship during the following selling season.

In 1998, Meadowcraft was ranked first in terms of earnings and sales in *Business Week* magazine's June roster of "100 Hot Growth Companies." As the company name was becoming well-known nationally, Meadowcraft chair and controlling stockholder, Samuel Blount, made moves to acquire all outstanding shares of Meadowcraft under the umbrella of his MWI Acquisition Co. in 1999. Also that year, Bill McCanna retired as the company's president and was replaced by Timothy Le Roy, formerly the company's vice-president of sales and marketing. Despite shifts in ownership and leadership on the horizon, the company had a longstanding reputation for quality and was well positioned to control a large share of the outdoor furniture market.

Principal Subsidiaries

Meadowcraft (UK) Limited; Meadowcraft de Mexico, S.A. de C.V.

Further Reading

Diel, Stan, "Meadowcraft Goes Public; Shares on NYSE," *Birmingham News,* November 26, 1997, p. 1C.

Hubbard, Russell, "Wrought-Iron Chain Link," *Birmingham News,* February 1, 1998, pp. 1D, 3D.

Milazzo, Don, "Furniture Maker Expanding," *Birmingham Business Journal,* July 10, 1995, p. 10.

Normington, Mick, "Meadowcraft Expands with 400 New Workers," *Birmingham News,* September 8, 1995, pp. 1B, 5B.

Scott, L.E., "New Firms for Yuma County," *Arizona Business Gazette,* April 8, 1998, p. 1.

"Business and Industry: Success Story," *South,* August 1, 1957, pp. 14–16.

Thomas, Larry, "Wrought-Iron Producer Meadowcraft to Go Public," *Furniture Today,* August 18, 1997, pp. 2, 57.

—Robert Halasz

Meredith Corporation

1716 Locust Street
Des Moines, Iowa 50309-3023
U.S.A.
(515) 284-3000
(800) 284-4236
Fax: (515) 284-2700
Web site: http://www.meredith.com

Public Company
Incorporated: 1902
Employees: 2,559
Sales: $1 billion (1998)
Stock Exchanges: New York
Ticker Symbol: MDP
NAIC: 51112 Periodical Publishers; 51113 Book
    Publishers; 51312 Television Broadcasting

Meredith Corporation is a leading media company, focused primarily on magazines and broadcasting. The company is best known for publishing two of America's most popular magazines: *Better Homes and Gardens,* with a circulation of 7.6 million, and *Ladies' Home Journal,* with a circulation of 4.5 million. About 85 percent of the diversified media company's revenues comes from its magazine business, which publishes 21 subscription magazines, more than 40 special interest publications, and a number of custom publications. The company also publishes close to 300 books, including the best-selling, red-and-white checkerboard-covered *Better Homes and Gardens Cookbook* and a line of do-it-yourself titles it produces in conjunction with the Home Depot chain of stores. In addition, the company owns and operates 11 television stations, primarily in smaller markets such as Flint, Michigan and Ocala, Florida. As of 1999 the company was in the process of buying Atlanta's CBS affiliate KGNX-TV, giving Meredith an entry into the nation's tenth largest television market. Meredith's diverse media projects focus for the most part on home and family. It maintains a database of some 60 million customer names, the largest such database among U.S. media companies. Approximately one-third of the U.S. population, or 65 million people, read a Meredith magazine each year.

Early History

The seeds that started the Meredith Corporation were given to Edwin Thomas (E. T.) Meredith as a wedding present. On E. T. Meredith's wedding day, his grandfather gave him several gold pieces, the controlling interest in his newspaper, and a note that said, "Sink or swim." After returning his grandfather's newspaper to profitability, Meredith sold it for a profit and began publishing a service-oriented farm magazine called *Successful Farming* in 1902. The magazine grew quickly, from a starting circulation of 500 to more than half a million subscribers by 1914. The company had grown proportionally, from five employees in 1902 to almost 200 in 1912. In 1999 the company had more than 2,500 employees and still occupied the same building that was established as company headquarters in 1912. The building went through some expansion as well, including an $18 million renovation completed in 1980.

After serving a year as Woodrow Wilson's Secretary of Agriculture, E. T. Meredith returned to his company in 1920 and decided to publish more magazines. In 1922 the company purchased one magazine, *Dairy Farmer,* and launched another, *Fruit, Garden and Home.* Meredith tried to make *Dairy Farmer* a national success for five years before merging it with *Successful Farming.* Unable to make a profit until 1927, *Fruit, Garden and Home,* a magazine similar to *Successful Farming* for the home and family, had start-up difficulties as well. At first, advertisers paid $450 per black-and-white page in *Fruit, Garden and Home,* as opposed to *Successful Farming's* rate of $1,800 per black-and-white page. After a name change in 1924 to *Better Homes & Gardens,* the magazine's fortunes turned around, allowing it to command $1,800 per black-and-white page of advertising by 1925.

By the time of E. T. Meredith's death in 1928, the year he was considered a candidate for the presidency, *Better Homes and Gardens* and *Successful Farming* had reached a combined circulation of 2.5 million. After World War II, *Better Homes and Gardens* had surpassed *McCall's, Good Housekeeping,* and *Ladies' Home Journal* to become the leading monthly magazine. Holding a circulation of about eight million for more than two decades, *Better Homes and Gardens* remained a powerful magazine into the 1990s, when it ranked third largest in the

United States, behind only *Reader's Digest* and *National Geographic.*

Meredith capitalized on the success of *Better Homes and Gardens* magazine and began publishing the *Better Homes and Gardens Cook Book* in 1930. Magazine subscribers received complimentary copies of the first edition, and book sales grew rapidly. The cookbook became one of the best-selling hardback books in America, with more than 29 million copies sold by its eleventh edition in 1995. The company has since used the *Better Homes and Gardens* name to further its profits, using it to sell special interest publications starting in 1937, to open a real estate service in 1978, and to offer garden tools at 2,000 Wal-Mart stores starting in 1994.

Diversification in the Postwar Years

To raise the capital necessary to diversify its interests, the company began offering stock to the public in 1946. Over the next ten years, Meredith bought three television stations and opened a commercial printing business. By 1965, the company was listed on the New York Stock Exchange. By 1969, the company had formed a printing partnership with the Burda family of West Germany, which would grow into one of the largest printing businesses in the United States.

In 1978 Meredith began a franchise-operated real estate business under the *Better Homes and Gardens* name. "It's a natural extension of the product franchise," Meredith chairperson Robert Burnett told *Advertising Age.* By 1985, the business challenged established realtors like Century 21 and Coldwell Banker, according to *Advertising Age.* The real estate business had grown to include about 700 firms, which owned and operated about 1,300 offices and had 24,000 sales associates by 1994. Company headquarters supplied the franchisees with marketing, management, and sales training information.

Growth in the 1980s

Although Meredith was publicly owned, it had a long history of only cautiously seeking investors. In 1985, however, it turned into "a very different kind of company," Paine Webber analyst J. Kendrick Noble told *Advertising Age.* At that time, Meredith began welcoming interest in its operations. Meredith started sponsoring art exhibits in New York and giving presentations to security analysts. The change occurred to fuel a growth strategy, which helped make it a Fortune 500 company.

At the beginning of the 1980s, Meredith's interests included a printing business, a fulfillment system, a real estate franchise, four television stations, and three magazines: *Better Homes and Gardens, Metropolitan Home,* and *Successful Farming.* The company expanded quickly during the 1980s, entering the video market with Meredith Video Publishing, purchasing three television stations, launching seven new magazines, publishing a Korean edition of *Better Homes and Gardens* magazine (an Australian edition had been published since 1978), and purchasing *Ladies' Home Journal,* the sixth largest women's service magazine when ranked by circulation at the time of the purchase in 1986. Despite its acquisitions and expansion, however, the company soon floundered. In 1992 Meredith had a net loss of $6.3 million.

In response, management decided to streamline Meredith, ridding the company of ancillary businesses. To soften the blow of a nationwide advertising slump it felt in its magazines and television stations, Meredith sold its 50 percent interest in the Meredith/Burda printing partnership to R. R. Donnelley & Sons Company of Chicago in 1990. Given the high costs of remaining competitive in the printing business, Meredith president Jack Rehm felt the sale was smart, telling *Business Record* that "we had to make a choice to either get bigger or else to get out. We felt we could better use our resources in our other businesses and depart the printing business." To further streamline, Meredith sold its fulfillment business to Neodata of Boulder, Colorado, in 1991, and two television stations were sold off in 1993. Moreover, the company's work force was cut by seven percent, to 2,000, between 1992 and 1994.

Meredith's cuts and investments allowed it to focus on what it did best. E. T. Meredith III told *Business Week* in 1994, "We're going back to what we were: a successful magazine and broadcasting company." Meredith planned to add three or four magazines per year. Realizing that advertising profits might never be as high as they were during the lucrative 1980s, the company earmarked $400 million for additional TV and magazine acquisitions, according to *Business Week.* In addition, the company developed customized marketing programs, which could create tailored packages of Meredith's magazine and book publishing, real estate service, and television stations for advertisers' specific needs. By 1994, company profits had started to climb again, jumping 23 percent over 1993 to $22.9 million on revenues of $799 million.

Meredith's streamlining helped the company take advantage of its unique niche, the home and family. Meredith sold its chic magazine, *Metropolitan Home,* to Hachette Filipacchi Magazines, the publishers of *Elle,* and introduced several new titles that targeted different domestic topics, such as *Country Home, Country America, WOOD, Midwest Living,* and *Better Homes and Gardens American Patchwork & Quilting.* Meredith's new magazines met with significant success, with growing circulations of 200,000 to one million. Shari Wall, senior vice-president at J. Walter Thompson in Chicago, noted Meredith's fortuitous position in the market, telling *Business Week* that "their thrust of family and home is the hot thing for the 1990s." Meredith, too, eagerly publicized its area of focus. The company launched an advertising campaign for its magazine group in 1993, which asserted, "If it has to do with home and family, it has to be in Meredith." The campaign featured black-and-white pictures of real families having fun together.

Although Meredith promoted itself aggressively to advertisers, it relied most heavily on its subscribers, who fueled the company's rebound. Circulation for most of the company's magazines was up in 1993, but company president Jack Rehm told the *New York Times* that "the reason we have succeeded with so many magazine titles in the last several years is that we are able to get readers to really pay for the magazines. We must count much more on the reader to generate the revenue stream than the advertiser. Historically, that has not been true, and magazines who were overly dependent on advertising were the ones who really suffered." In 1993 Meredith's magazine subscription and newsstand revenues accounted for 32.2 percent of the company revenues, or $257.45 million, and magazine advertising revenues made up 29.6 percent, with $236.81 million.

Meredith's *Better Homes and Gardens* magazine proved a good example of the company's success in managing large publications. *Better Homes and Gardens* led the shelter magazine industry in ad revenues and pages in 1988, offering its advertisers an audience four times the size of its next competitor, according to *Marketing and Media Decisions*. A four-color page cost $103,480 in *Better Homes and Gardens;* in *Architectural Digest, Better Homes and Gardens'* closest competitor in shelter magazines, a similar advertisement cost $28,490. According to some analysts, *Better Homes and Gardens'* fortunes can be traced to the trend toward home and hearth that started in the late 1980s and early 1990s; the magazine benefited because it bridged the home and women's service categories.

Meredith took a conservative approach to changing its flagship magazine, refusing to bow to the shifting winds of publishing fashion. For example, when faced with "single, disenfranchised dropouts" at advertising agencies in the 1960s who were "insulted that we would continue to publish [*Better Homes and Gardens*] when [they] didn't think it should exist," Burnett told *Advertising Age,* "it was tempting to say, 'We've got to change *Better Homes and Gardens* and get with it.' " Meredith remained committed, however, to the magazine's focus on home and family.

To keep the magazine contemporary, Meredith continually made subtle changes, rather than doing major redesigns every five years like other magazines. According to Burnett, in an article in *Advertising Age,* rapid change was likely to alienate readers; Burnett commented that "the worst thing that could happen is for your best friend to show up with a changed personality; it's a shock and a negative." The magazine's enhancements for 1994 included the addition of puzzles and games for parents and their children. The company's strategy paid off, as *Better Homes and Gardens* continued to be a leader in its category.

In 1994 Meredith's several large circulation magazines and book clubs generated a subscriber database of 63 million, the largest database in the United States. Meredith began exploiting this database for profit in 1992, as the company's marketing department began using the database to give editors valuable feedback on their magazine's readership, as well as to cross-promote books and magazine spin-offs, target direct mail programs for advertisers, research new markets, and test new products. The company also used the database to aid in the launch of a new magazine called *Crayola Kids,* to insert specialized ads in

targeted magazines for an auto advertiser, and to put in targeted editorials in *Better Homes and Gardens* issues. The database also helped to turn around the fortunes of Meredith's book division. Despite its more than 30 years of experience in database marketing, during which it had also used rented lists, Meredith did not consider itself a very sophisticated user of its own resource. Clem Svede, vice-president and director of consumer marketing, noted in *Direct* that "when someone asks how our database is doing, we say 'We think we're at the top of our class—but we're only in the first grade.' "

In 1993 the company faced a challenge in the form of a natural disaster. Massive flooding in the Midwest that year, particularly in Iowa, reached the company's Des Moines headquarters, ruining the company's mainframe computer system. As a result, the company was forced to install a new desktop publishing network about eight months earlier than planned. Under the guidance of Robert Furstenau, director of production and technology for Meredith's magazines, the company converted to the new system in about two days. Meredith immediately purchased $400,000 worth of Macintosh computers and peripheral equipment, installed them in a rented space, and flew in software specialists from around the country to give 103 editorial employees two weeks of training information in a few hours. Despite the chaotic atmosphere, no deadlines were missed, and in the long run the desktop system has reduced the company's prepress production costs. Furstenau told the *Des Moines Register* that the flood "has got to be one of the better things that has happened to magazine production at Meredith in a long time."

Changes in the Late 1990s

The company had floundered in the early 1990s, with erratic earnings, a rather staid image, and thin operating margins well below the publishing industry average. Yet it had great assets, particularly in its under-exploited customer database and in its *Better Homes and Gardens* brand name recognition. In 1994 the company announced ambitious plans to launch new magazine titles, buy more television stations, swing lucrative licensing deals, and expand its book publishing division. The book division ultimately did not pay off, and in 1995 the company sold its book club to Book of the Month Club and reduced its commitment to book publishing. But in other areas Meredith was right on track. It managed to launch new magazine titles with great skill, primarily because it learned to target audiences using its existing customer database. Although other media companies such as Hearst and Time Warner also had massive databases, Meredith's was singular in that its customers were very similar, described in a December 4, 1994 *Forbes* article as "nesters—people who are interested in their homes and in spending money to make them better." Thus it was not too difficult for Meredith to cull the list and find, for example, people with older homes: a good market for its *Traditional Home* magazine and the related *Renovation Style.* Other new titles in the mid-1990s were *American Patchwork & Quilting* and *homegarden.* The company managed to hold costs for new magazines down to $2 million to $3 million, considered impressively low in the publishing industry, and most turned a profit within two to three years. The company also embarked on a successful licensing deal in 1994, letting mass-marketer Wal-Mart open Better Homes and Gardens Garden Centers in more than 2,000 stores. These sold gardening equipment marked with the Better Homes and Gardens name, as well as the magazine itself and other Meredith gardening titles. The deal with Wal-Mart led to minimum royalties of $3 million for each of the first three years and $5 million for the next two years. Meredith also brokered the Better Homes and Gardens name by publishing small booklets for sale at checkout counters, with titles like *Garden, Deck & Landscape Planner.* The company had 40 such books by 1995 and printed a total of 35 million copies. By the mid-1990s, such brand extensions were leading to impressive earnings: the company told *Forbes* in 1995 that it derived $1.05 in income from brand extensions for every dollar of revenue the magazine *Better Homes and Gardens* earned.

In its broadcasting segment, Meredith also performed as planned. By 1996, the company had seven stations, and these contributed more than 40 percent of the firm's profit. In 1997 the company purchased three more television stations, picking them up for $435 million from First Media Television. This acquisition gave Meredith stations in Orlando, Florida, Greeneville, South Carolina, and Bend, Oregon. They were small markets, but increased Meredith's share of the nation's television market from five percent to eight percent. By 1998, Meredith owned 11 stations, and these accounted for about 18 percent of the company's total revenue. Its stations were all in small markets, yet most of them were predicted to be strong growth areas. In late 1998 Meredith negotiated to buy its first station in a top ten market, Atlanta's WGNX. Not only was Atlanta a major market, but it was one of the country's fastest growing TV markets.

By 1999, Meredith seemed to be in very good shape. Its big advantage was that its core product—home-related publications and products—was more and more the ''in'' thing. The number of people aged 45 to 54 was increasing as the baby-boomers aged, and this demographic tended to spend the most on home-related goods. The old-fashioned appeal of *Better Homes and Gardens* and the other Meredith publications seemed likely to be back in style with a vengeance in the coming decade. The company had managed to shed unprofitable businesses such as its real estate venture and much of its book publishing and concentrate on what it knew best. In addition, Meredith was able to make useful cross-connections between its publishing and broadcasting sectors, for example, launching a syndicated ''Better Homes and Gardens'' television show. Financially, the company was in record shape, with sales topping $1 billion for the first time in fiscal 1998.

Principal Subsidiaries

Meredith Cable, Inc. (70%); Meredith Video Publishing Corporation; Meredith International, Ltd.

Further Reading

Carmody, Deirdre, ''A Focus on Home, Hearth and Profit,'' *New York Times,* October 4, 1993, p. C7.
Chase, Brett, ''Meredith Leaves Printing Behind, Looks to Future,'' *Business Record,* January 13, 1992, p. 2.
Cyr, Diane, ''Database Magic at Meredith,'' *Direct: The Magazine of Direct Marketing Management,* February 1994.
Ebert, Larry Kai, ''Meredith at 75: Multi-Media Expansion,'' *Advertising Age,* October 31, 1977, pp. 3, 78, 80.
Kasler, Dale, ''Meredith Veteran Named New Better Homes Editor,'' *Des Moines Register,* April 6, 1993.
——, ''Meredith Will Launch 'Big' Gardening Magazine,'' *Des Moines Register,* July 4, 1994, p. 3.
——, ''The Talk of the Industry: Flood a Boon for Meredith,'' *Des Moines Register,* September 13, 1993.
Levin, Gary, ''Meredith: Growing Up with an '800-lb. Gorilla','' *Advertising Age,* March 11, 1985.
Melcher, Richard A., ''Homes, Gardens—And a Tidy Turnaround,'' *Business Week,* August 22, 1994, pp. 55–56.
Podems, Ruth, ''Serving Families for 77 Years,'' *Target Marketing,* September 1989, pp. 18–24.
Williams, Scott, ''Realtor Links Up with Chain,'' *Seattle Times,* July 15, 1992, p. B4.

—Sara Pendergast
—updated by A. Woodward

Merit Medical Systems, Inc.

1600 West Merit Parkway
South Jordan, Utah 84095
U.S.A.
(801) 253-1600
Fax: (801) 253-1651
Web site: http://www.merit.com

Public Company
Incorporated: 1987
Employees: 956
Sales: $68.4 million (1998)
Stock Exchanges: NASDAQ
NAIC: 339112 Surgical & Medical Instrument
　　Manufacturing; 339113 Surgical Appliance &
　　Supplies Manufacturing

Merit Medical Systems, Inc. designs, manufactures, and sells disposable medical equipment used in diagnosing and treating cardiovascular disease. Billing itself as the world's leading producer of angioplasty inflation devices that open blocked arteries, Merit sells over 750 products approved by the Food and Drug Administration, including disposable syringes, catheters, guide wires, pressure monitoring items, needles, and products to safely handle blood wastes from angiography. The company's 72-percent-owned subsidiary, Sentir, Inc., produces silicon sensors, and that company's injection molding equipment is also used by Merit to manufacture items for non-competing medical device companies, including C. R. Bard, Baxter Healthcare, Boston Scientific, B. Braun, Medtronic, and SciMed Life. Although Merit sells its products primarily to American hospitals, the company also has customers in over 60 countries. In addition to its main office and manufacturing plant in South Jordan, Utah, a suburb of Salt Lake City, it also operates manufacturing plants in Galway, Ireland, and Angleton, Texas, as well as a distribution center in Maastricht, The Netherlands. A young company, Merit has grown rapidly, with over 50 patents and three acquisitions under its belt in 1999.

Getting Started in the 1980s

Merit Medical Systems was founded by Fred P. Lampropoulos and Kent W. Stanger. Lampropoulos had grown up in Salt Lake City and eventually worked for stock brokerage firms, including Dean Witter, helping corporations raise capital. One of the companies he helped was Salt Lake City's Utah Medical Products, and he eventually became that company's chairman and chief executive officer, where he served from 1983 to 1987.

During this time, Utah Medical Products was a relatively small firm with one product and about $8 million in annual sales. There, Lampropoulos met Stanger, an accountant from Bountiful, Utah, who had previously been employed as the controller at American Laser. In June 1987 Lampropoulos and Stanger left Utah Medical Products to found their own company, incorporating Merit Medical Systems under Utah laws. Lampropoulos became Merit Medical's president/CEO and board chairman, while Stanger was the new company's chief financial officer and secretary-treasurer. In 1999 both founders remained in those positions at Merit Medical.

Two others also left Utah Medical Products to help start Merit Medical. Darla R. Gill, who had served as a manager at Utah Medical from 1984 to 1988, became a vice-president and director of Merit Medical in early 1988. She left the company in 1993 to start her own firm, Salt Lake City's Momentum Medical Corporation, which was engaged in the manufacture of home health products. William Padilla, another early leader, had worked for Utah Medical from 1985 to 1987, when he left to become a Merit Medical director and vice-president in charge of the firm's injection molding operations.

The groundwork for Merit Medical's line of business had been laid by pioneering medical efforts in the 1960s and 1970s. In 1967, Rene Favaloro had developed a treatment for blocked arteries through bypass surgery. Ten years later, Andreas R. Gruentzig invented angioplasty as an alternative to bypass surgery. This development opened a market for such products as tubing and inflation products used in heart surgeries.

In May 1988 Merit Medical began selling control syringes, its first products. In November 1989 it introduced its IntelliSystem inflation devices. Two years later it began offering Medallion specialty syringes, Sherlock high pressure tubing, and its Monarch, Basix, and Limited inflation products.

Demand for the company's products proved high, and Merit Medical quickly gained about a 50 percent share of the world market for inflation products designed to help diagnose and treat cardiovascular disease caused by blocked arteries (atherosclerosis) from the buildup of cholesterol and plaque. Such blockages annually caused about 1.5 million heart attacks, as well as an estimated 500,000 strokes resulting in brain damage.

Merit Medical's initial business plan outlined the values and strategies needed to reach its technical, manufacturing, distribution, financial, and personnel goals. From the beginning, the company focused on building strong long-term relationships among its management and workers. Toward that end, a work atmosphere was developed in which open communication was encouraged between all levels of employees. Perks like reserved parking spaces for upper management were done away with, as the only special parking permits available were for car pooling vehicles.

Meeting Goals and Facing Litigation in the Early 1990s

The company's initial business plan also stated that it would not rely on venture capitalists but would as quickly as possible become a public corporation. By 1990 the firm's annual sales had reached $4.4 million, up from $1.4 million the year before. Moreover, Merit had by 1990 reported a net income ($140,987), after three years of losses. In 1991, Merit Medical was able to go public. Its initial public offering (IPO) under the NASDAQ ticker MMSI raised $6 million, shares having been offered at $4 each.

Another original goal was to become a vertically integrated company that handled its own product design, manufacturing, marketing, and distribution. Again, the company was able to reach this goal quickly, replacing its initial dealer network with its own direct sales force in the United States in 1990. Merit's sales force—which by 1992 included 27 direct salespersons, including regional and national managers—was thoroughly trained in the uses of Merit's product line. Having its own sales personnel helped the company increase its sales and profit margins and improve communication with its customers. At the same time, feedback from cardiologists and radiologists helped the company refine its products and develop new ones.

Merit also intended early on to sell its products overseas. Initially, this goal was addressed through independent dealers, primarily in Japan, Canada, and Germany. Sales in those three nations accounted for about ten percent of the company's total sales in 1991. Soon, the firm had hired its own international sales director to work with dealers, as well as to expand the company's presence in New Zealand, Australia, Brazil, Switzerland, Mexico, and the United Kingdom. In 1994 the World Trade Association of Utah recognized the young company's progress in this area by naming it the International Company of the Year. Moreover, Merit made *Inc.* magazine's list of the 100 fastest growing companies.

Merit's product development was enhanced by the September 1991 formation of Sentir, Inc., founded by Fred Lampropoulos and headquartered in Santa Clara, California. According to the company prospectus, Sentir was created "to develop micro-machining technology and to develop and market silicon sensors, including sensors which are similar to those presently purchased by the Company." Sentir supplied Merit with the product, representing an important step towards Merit's vertical integration. In 1994 Merit Medical purchased 72 percent of Sentir for $177,000, Lampropoulos' entire interest in Sentir.

Merit's rapid growth in the early 1990s required new facilities. Initially its offices and manufacturing were based in several small buildings in an industrial park at 79 West 4500 South in Murray, a Salt Lake City suburb. By the summer of 1992 the company employed 237 individuals and leased about 44,000 square feet in Murray. In the mid-1990s the company moved its operations to a new site on 45 acres in South Jordan, Utah. That was adequate for awhile, but later in the decade Merit again leased some of its original properties in Murray to handle its expansion.

The company's expansion was not without its challenges. In the early 1990s, Utah Medical Products sued Merit, alleging that the upstart company had stolen patented technology for use in their IntelliSystem and Monarch angioplasty inflation devices. In 1992 Merit and Utah Medical settled this matter out of court, with Merit receiving a nonexclusive license to Utah Medical Products' angioplasty patents, in exchange for paying a one-time licensing fee of $600,000. Merit also agreed to pay Utah Medical a 5.75 percent continuing royalty, not to exceed $450,000, on annual sales of products using the protected patents. This litigation cost Merit Medical an estimated $520,000 in legal fees.

Then, in 1994, Merit stockholder David D. Bennett filed another lawsuit over the origins of Merit Medical. Maintaining that he represented other stockholders in this class action suit, Bennett charged Merit and its founder Fred Lampropoulos with committing fraud in the company's initial stock prospectus, which claimed that no Merit products competed with those of Utah Medical Products at the time. According to Bennett, the 1992 settlement between the two firms proved that Merit Medical "owed its entire corporate existence to cannibalizing Utah Medical personnel, customers and technology." As a result Merit's stock price declined from nearly $32 to less than $6 per share. Merit won this contest in 1998 when the court decided to dismiss the case and granted Merit a summary judgment. However, Bennett would continue to appeal the decision.

Enhancing Facilities and Product Lines

In early 1995 Merit Medical opened a new facility in Galway, Ireland, to expand the firm's manufacturing, distribution, and research capabilities. In 1997 Merit Medical acquired Universal Medical Instrument Corporation, a small New York firm that produced vascular access items. With this acquisition and its own research capabilities, the company was able to introduce a new line of angiographic needles, specialty guide wires, and a thrombolytic catheter.

In 1998 Merit Medical introduced three significant products with considerable financial potential. First was the Tomcat guide wire, which guided a balloon angioplasty catheter through a blood vessel and then penetrated the blocked heart artery. Second, a new Fountain Infusion Catheter was introduced for use by doctors in delivering clot-dissolving drugs to peripheral arteries and veins, thus restoring normal circulation. Third was the Squirt Infusion System, which resembled a squirt gun.

Used with the Fountain catheters, the Squirt Infusion System allowed a doctor to use just one hand to pump drugs into the patient, thus freeing up his other hand to guide the position of the catheter. Moreover, doctors could also use the Squirt technology to irrigate wounds resulting from bites, knives, ulcers, burns, and other causes. Since it involved no needles or catheters, this system proved less frightening to children, who made up about 30 percent of the estimated ten million persons a year who sought help for skin injuries.

The trademarked Squirt system marked Merit Medical Systems' initial entry into hospital emergency rooms. However, President/CEO Fred Lampropoulos was quick to point out in a press release that "There are other, secondary markets to which the Squirt Wound Irrigation System could be marketed, including urgent care facilities, burn units, nursing homes, long-term care facilities, family practice, pediatrics, internal medicine, the operation room and orthopedics."

With such successful products on the market, Merit worked to consolidate some of its manufacturing operations, closing its New York plant and transferring its guide wire and catheter production to Salt Lake City and Ireland. These moves saved the company about $250,000 annually. At the same time, Merit improved its European distribution by moving customer service and warehousing from Ireland to Maastricht, The Netherlands, which decreased shipping time overseas and also provided more space for production in Ireland.

The Late 1990s and Beyond

In 1998, Merit recorded the highest sales and net income figures in its history. Sales reached $68.4 million, up from $60.6 million in 1997, while net income reached $2.5 million after a slump to $797,532 the year before. Merit's finances continued to grow in the first half of 1999. At the end of its second quarter ending June 30, 1999, the company reported quarterly revenues of $19 million, up from $18 million the previous year, and a net income increase of 28 percent over the second quarter of 1998.

During this time, Merit signed contracts with two corporate purchasers. In 1998 Tenet Healthcare Corporation, based in Santa Barbara, California, signed a national contract giving its network of hospitals access to Merit systems. Then in 1999 Merit signed a three-year deal with the Mid-Atlantic Group Network of Shared Services Inc. (MAGNET) based in Mechanicsburg, Pennsylvania. MAGNET included eight group purchasing organizations; Merit Medical expected to receive about $10 million in annual sales from the MAGNET contract.

Moreover, in July 1999 Merit announced a plan to purchase Mallinckrodt's Angleton, Texas, plant, which manufactured catheters used in cardiology and radiology. Merit expected this acquisition to add about $10 million in annual revenue and provide additional capability needed to prepare for a challenging future.

In a December 1998 interview in the *Wall Street Corporate Reporter,* Lampropoulos explained his optimism about Merit Medical's future. He noted that given Utah's concentration of medical device companies, the company benefitted from "a good availability of mechanical and electrical engineers"—a crucial factor in the firm's research and development. New products, such as very small catheters used in the hands and feet, were in the development stages at Merit.

In pitching Merit as a good investment opportunity, Lampropoulos gave a thumbnail sketch of Merit's position in the industry: "we have proven we can develop all of the appropriate aspects of a business including new products, their manufacture and distribution. We have built a critical mass so that we go forward, we will have the economies of scale that pertain to gross margins and pre-tax and after-tax profits. We have put core technologies into place that we can then build new products onto." At the same time, Merit did face competition from rivals that were larger and had more resources, including Maxxim Medical, Pfizer, and St. Jude Medical.

At the end of the decade, analysts were cautiously optimistic about Merit Medical's future. While some noted that Merit's effort to focus on higher margin, primary care products sold to its current customers would result in increased sales, others pointed out that much of the company's business remained concentrated in low-margin, price-sensitive items. In any case, the huge demand for diagnostic and therapeutic procedures to help patients with heart disease and other cardiovascular problems continued to fuel the need for Merit Medical Systems' products.

Principal Subsidiaries

Merit Holdings, Inc.; Merit Medical International, Inc.; Sentir, Inc. (72%).

Further Reading

"First Informed Investors Atlanta Health Care Stocks Forum to be Broadcast by Vcall Over the Internet," *Business Wire,* February 24, 1999, p. 1.

Lampropoulos, Fred P., "Interventional Cardiology and Radiology: Accessory Devices for Angioplasty Procedures," *Wall Street Corporate Reporter,* December 14–20, 1998.

"Merit Medical Will Buy Catheter Manufacturing," *Salt Lake Tribune,* July 22, 1999, p. D5.

Parker, Stephanie, "Merit Medical and Utah Medical Settle Patent Litigation," *Business Wire,* March 16, 1992, p. 1.

Rattle, Barbara, "Class Action Suit Accuses Merit Medical and Founder of Fraud, Misrepresentation," *Enterprise* (Salt Lake City), February 14, 1994, p. 1.

—David M. Walden

Micron Technology, Inc.

8000 South Federal Way
P.O. Box 6
Boise, Idaho 83707-0006
U.S.A.
(208) 368-4000
Fax: (208) 368-4435
Web site: http://www.micron.com

Public Company
Incorporated: 1978
Employees: 16,000
Sales: $3 billion (1998)
Stock Exchanges: New York
Ticker Symbol: MU
NAIC: 334113 Computer Terminal Manufacturing;
334413 Semiconductor & Related Device
Manufacturing; 33429 Other Communications
Equipment Manufacturing; 334419 Other Electronic
Component Manufacturing

Micron Technology, Inc., is a holding company for subsidiaries engaged in the design and production of computers, semiconductors, and other related products. One of the few U.S. manufacturers to remain in the market for DRAM (dynamic random access memory) chips, Micron competed against formidable foreign competition during the 1980s, when the global semiconductor market rapidly expanded into a $20 billion industry by the 1990s. Having grown from a small operation in the basement of a dentist's office in Boise, Idaho, into an internationally recognized and respected manufacturer of memory chips, Micron entered the mid-1990s exhibiting robust growth, confounding those convinced that a comparably small player could not effectively compete in a market dominated by powerful foreign competitors.

Early Struggles

During the summer months of 1978, three design engineers left the employ of Mostek Corporation, a pioneer in the design and production of semiconductors, to join Inmos Ltd., a British-financed competitor. On the surface, the emigration of three employees to Inmos appeared insignificant—an unremarkable switch of employers by a small number of employees—but at Mostek tempers flared. These three engineers, Ward Parkinson, Dennis Wilson, and Douglas Pittman, were not the first employees to leave Mostek for better offers from Inmos. One former Mostek employee, in fact, had co-founded Inmos, and Mostek's management wanted to stanch the flow of additional employee departures, particularly if those employees were moving to Inmos. A legal battle ensued, with Mostek filing a suit against Inmos that called for a permanent injunction to stop further raids on its personnel. Mostek also attempted to enjoin Inmos from starting operations, but both of these demands were dismissed, including charges that the three engineers took trade secrets from Mostek to Inmos.

Caught in the middle of these accusations, the three engineers made the summer's squabble moot in October, when, led by Ward Parkinson, they decided to leave Inmos and start their own design and consulting company, Micron Technology. Incorporated that month, five days after Parkinson left Inmos, the company established modest operations in the basement of a dentist's office in Boise, Idaho, performing essentially the same work for the same people as they had before the summer began. All three had been working on a 64-kilobit (K) random access memory (RAM) program while at Mostek, and now, after the dispute between Inmos and Mostek, the three contracted to design a 64K chip for Mostek, Micron's first and, it appeared, only customer.

The company had been formed with the intent of serving only Mostek; Parkinson told *Electronic News,* a trade publication, ''We are not looking for other customers.'' However, the idea of working for Mostek on an exclusive basis was short-lived, falling apart the following year when United Technologies acquired Mostek. United Technologies canceled the contract with Micron, leaving the fledgling company, entirely dependent on Mostek for revenue, without any customers. The three design engineers, later joined by Parkinson's twin brother, Joseph L. Parkinson, a Wall Street lawyer and eventual leader of Micron, decided to continue designing the 64K chip on their own and began looking for investors to finance their endeavor.

The first of Micron's many struggles, the loss of the contract with Mostek tested the company's commitment to manufacture semiconductor chips in a market dominated by leviathan Japanese electronic companies. Success in the memory chip market was essentially determined by size; the smaller the size of the chip and the greater the size of its memory capabilities, the greater the manufacturer's profits and market share. In this race for smaller chips and greater memory, a race predicated on technology, the Japanese were well ahead, rivaled only by large American companies based typically in California's Silicon Valley, the U.S. bastion for semiconductor research and production. Industry pundits and, more important, loan officers and venture capitalists strongly believed no new U.S. memory chip manufacturer could enter the market as late as 1979 and hope to succeed—certainly not a tiny company based in Boise, Idaho. Consequently, Micron's entreaties for financing were met with disdain. As Ward Parkinson later related to *Forbes*, his typical response from investors "wasn't 'no,' it was 'Hell, no'."

However, as was often true throughout its history, Micron's weaknesses were its strengths, or, more precisely, the company drew from characteristics regarded as weaknesses and used them to its advantage. With its decision to enter the memory chip manufacturing arena, Micron immediately inherited three weaknesses: its size, its location, and the late date of its entry into the memory chip market, all of which were adversely affecting its ability to secure financing. To solve this formidable problem, Micron drew upon one of its weaknesses, its location, and canvassed wealthy Idaho residents for an interest in Micron. There, at home, the company found success, enlisting the support of a machine shop operator, Ron Yanke, a wealthy sheep rancher, Tom Nicholson, and Allen Noble, a wealthy potato farmer—all Boise residents. Next came Micron's wealthiest supporter, John R. Simplot, a billionaire potato farmer and the largest supplier of potatoes to McDonalds. McDonalds in turn invested $1 million in Micron in 1980 and later poured tens of millions of dollars into Micron. With this distinctly Idahoan cadre of investors, Micron began operations, starting with $9 million in an industry that conventionally required at least a $100 million start-up investment.

Micron's location also served it well in other important areas that gave the company a much-needed boost in its transformation from a design and consulting firm to a manufacturer of memory chips. Land in Idaho was considerably cheaper than in Japan or in the Silicon Valley, which helped to reduce start-up costs. Labor was cheaper, and Idaho's hydroelectric power rates were roughly a third of those incurred by California memory chip manufacturers. With these advantages, Micron required less initial capital investment. In addition, its small size forced the company to closely examine the production methods currently employed by other manufacturers with the hope of identifying inefficiencies in conventional processes. This bare-boned approach to all aspects of the memory chip business enabled Micron to operate in an industry dominated by much larger and perhaps more complacent competitors, a cost-cutting approach that enabled the company to construct its first factory for $20 million, roughly one-quarter of the typical cost for a semiconductor manufacturing facility.

However, Micron could not control all aspects of the memory chip business. As Micron was effecting its transformation, Japanese electronic companies, such as Hitachi, NEC, and Fujitsu, had gained an early lead in the market for 64K DRAM chips, a key component of computers, video games, and telecommunications systems. By 1981, Japanese companies had secured 70 percent of the global market for 64K DRAM chips, without having to contend with any serious challenge from U.S. manufacturers. Finally, two U.S. companies, Texas Instruments and Motorola, began volume production of 64K chips the following year, whereas other American contenders, Intel, National Semiconductor, and Mostek did not begin production until late 1982. Before the year was through, however, the two strongest U.S. entries, Texas Instruments and Motorola, did not prove to be serious forces in the global market—Motorola's chip, derogatorily known as the "postage stamp," was large and, consequently, expensive to manufacture, and Texas Instruments' chip suffered from temporary production problems in late 1982. For Micron, these developments were unfavorable because they strengthened Japan's grip on the market and kept worldwide attention, the attention of potential Micron customers, focused on Asia.

1982–84: Making Progress

As it turned out, what Micron lacked in financial backing and timeliness of product entry, it made up for in product quality and innovation. Micron shipped over one million chips in 1982, not by itself a noteworthy achievement when compared to the production totals of its competitors, but notable in the quality and size of its chips. With bigger, easier-to-read memory cells than competing chips, Micron's chips were more reliable and were also remarkably small, 40 percent smaller than Motorola's chip and 15 percent smaller than Hitachi's chip. In early 1983, Micron achieved a dramatic breakthrough when it further reduced the size of its chips, thus garnering the attention of semiconductor engineers and customers worldwide. Micron's 1982 chip measured 33,000 square mils (one mil equals $\frac{1}{1000}$ of an inch), whereas the new chip measured 22,000 square mils, roughly half the size of Japan's leading chips and a third smaller than Texas Instruments' chip. As the size of Micron's chips decreased, so did the company's manufacturing costs, giving the company a significant advantage over its competitors and a springboard toward viability in the global semiconductor market.

The financial rewards of this innovation in memory chip production arrived the following year, in 1984, the same year Micron became a publicly held corporation. For the year, Micron earned $29 million in after-tax profit on revenues of $84 million, a profit-to-revenue ratio that ranked among the highest recorded by electronics companies worldwide. Micron used part of the proceeds from its success with its 64K chip to begin development of the industry's next benchmark semiconductor chip, the 256K chip, which the company began shipping in small quantities by the end of the year.

1985: Illegal Practices by Competitors

However, earlier in the year, significant developments in the semiconductor industry had occurred that promised to radically change the industry's future and Micron's position in it. In September of that year, when worldwide demand for chips exceeded supply, Micron drastically reduced the price of its chips, selling each for $1.95, well below the international list price of $3.40. It was a move to strengthen the company's position in the memory chip market at the expense of profit margins, a temporary maneuver to increase its customer base and undercut its competitors. At the same time, several major U.S. manufacturers, such as Intel and AMD, retreated from the fierce competition of the Japanese companies and into the high-performance, specialty chip market, where competition was less intense. Micron had decided to stay in the conventional chip market, and its price reduction was an indication of its intent; however, its strategy was not without precedent, a strategy the Japanese had been employing for a year.

For Micron, its price reduction was a way of increasing business, but the ploy was only temporary because undercutting competitors' prices impinged on profits, leaving Micron without money it sorely needed. For the Japanese companies, however, price reductions could be adopted as a long-term strategy because their large reservoirs of cash could withstand significant reductions in profits. This the Japanese companies did, dropping their prices, and forcing U.S. competitors to exit the market for memory chips. National Semiconductor suspended plans to market a 256K chip in 1985, Intel announced it was closing all of its RAM production during the fall, and United Technologies closed Mostek's operations the same year.

The effect of this aggressive pricing strategy was disastrous for Micron. In 1985, the price of 64K chips plummeted from approximately $4 to 25 cents, and the price of 256K chips fell from $20 at the beginning of the year to $2.50 by its conclusion. Micron's earnings aped this pattern, falling from $28.9 million in 1984 to $154,000 in 1985. For Micron the worst was yet to come. The company had to cope without half of its work force, which was laid off in the spring of 1985, and without one of its two production lines, which also fell victim to the pernicious downward swing of memory chip prices. In 1986, the company lost $33.9 million and generated $48.8 million in revenue, significantly less than 1985's total of $75.8 million.

Micron responded by formally accusing the Japanese semiconductor industry in 1985 of creating the collapse of the U.S. industry by illegally flooding the U.S. market with products sold below manufacturing costs, a practice commonly known as "dumping," and, several months later, in the fall, filed a $300 million antitrust lawsuit against six Japanese electronics companies. The result of these and other, repeated dumping charges against the Japanese led to the signing of the Semiconductor Trade Agreement between the United States and Japan in 1986, which established fair prices for Japanese memory chips and, according to Micron's management, enabled the company to effect a recovery.

1988–95: Market Fluctuations

Before the recovery, Micron recorded another dismal year, equally poor as 1986. The company lost $22.9 million in 1987, although total sales climbed to $91.1 million, but in 1988 both revenues and earnings recorded substantial leaps: revenues soared to $300.5 million and earnings jumped to $97.9 million, giving credence to the company's accusations of dumping. Now once again recording profits, Micron moved forward, still operating in a highly competitive market dominated by Japanese companies, something the Semiconductor Trade Agreement had not altered. Sales climbed to $446.4 million in 1989 and earnings increased modestly to $106.1 million. The following year demonstrated the volatility of the semiconductor market when the arrival of a nationwide recession caused sales to fall to $333 million and earnings to plummet to $4.9 million.

In 1991, Micron entered the personal computer market with the establishment of a new subsidiary, Edge Technology, Inc. Edge was created to manufacture personal computers at competitive prices. It was hoped that steady revenues from the PC division would help lessen the effect of fluctuation in the memory chip market. A year later, Edge Technology changed its name to Micron Computer, Inc.

During the recessive early 1990s, revenues recorded modest gains, rising to $425.3 million in 1991, then reaching $506.3 million the following year, but earnings remained deleteriously low, rising to only $6.6 million by 1992. That year, Micron canceled its plans to develop microprocessors and decentralized its operations, dividing the company into five subsidiary companies with Micron Technology, Inc., serving as the parent company and Micron Semiconductor, Inc., as the core operating unit.

In 1993, the semiconductor market once again demonstrated its volatility, but this time in a most agreeable manner, particularly for Micron shareholders. Revenues increased 63 percent, bringing the year's total to $828.3 million, but the most remarkable increase—a 1,470 percent increase—was recorded in Micron's profits, which soared to $104.1 million, nearly reaching the total generated before the recession in 1989. With profits on the upswing and global demand for semiconductors outstripping supply, Micron initiated a phase of rapid growth. The semiconductor division began a $60 million expansion, projected to increase output by 20 to 25 percent. Micron Computer likewise kicked off an expansion project, which would add a 100,000 square foot manufacturing facility in Idaho and 1,200 new employees. The company's stock rose sharply, achieving a 200 percent increase during 1993.

Still, the semiconductor market was booming. In response to growing demand for memory chips, in 1994 Micron announced plans to build a new $1.3 billion manufacturing complex in Utah. That same year, the company acquired PC manufacturer ZEOS, merging it with its Micron Computer and Micron Custom Manufacturing subsidiaries to become Micron Electronics. The new subsidiary hit the ground running; within two years, Micron

Electronics had doubled the capacity of its Idaho operation, and added two new facilities in North Carolina and Malaysia.

1996–98: Oversupply and Shrinking Profits

After three highly profitable years, Micron again fell victim to the vagaries of the market. Beginning in late 1995, a glut of memory chips started a price spiral that was to severely damage Micron's profits. During the company's fiscal 1996, chip prices fell 75 percent, shaving $250 million off the company's record profits of the previous year. Faced with thinning margins and resulting shareholder unease, Micron suspended construction on its Utah fabrication plant.

The next two years proved to be no better. Chip prices dropped another 40 percent in 1997 and 60 percent again the following year, leaving Micron with a 1998 year-end loss of $233.7 million. Despite financial woes, the company expanded its operations in late 1998 with the acquisition of Texas Instruments' memory division. Management was banking on the belief that memory chip prices would rebound—and that when they did, the newly bulked-up Micron would be prepared. "The additional wafer fabs, joint-venture relationships, Singapore assembly and test operation, royalty-free patent cross-license, and favorable TI financing create an opportunity to further reduce our cost of manufacturing and position us as one of the world's largest DRAM producers," Micron president and CEO Steve Appleton said in the company's 1998 annual report.

In 1998, Micron attributed 46 percent of its revenues to memory chip sales and 48 percent to its Micron Electronics division's sales of PC systems. By the middle of the company's fiscal 1999, however, sales of computer systems had dropped off, making up only 36 percent of total sales. Sales of memory chips made up more than 60 percent of total revenue. As Micron charted its future, then, much appeared to depend upon the volatile memory chip market. To offset this dependence somewhat, the company was planning further diversification efforts, which focused on businesses that either enabled memory technology or served to promote consumption of semiconductor memory.

Principal Subsidiaries

Micron Semiconductor Products, Inc.; Micron Technology Italia, S.r.l.; Micron Europe Limited (U.K.); Micron Semiconductor GmBH (Germany); Micron Technology Japan K.K.; Micron Technology Asia Pacific, Inc. (Taiwan); Micron Technology Texas, LLC; Micron Electronics, Inc. (64%); Micron Communications, Inc.

Further Reading

Brammer, Rhonda, "Back in the Chips?," *Barron's,* February 3, 1986, p. 16.

Chakravarty, Subrata N., "We've Heard All That Before," *Forbes,* December 31, 1984, p. 34.

Connelly, Joanne, "Micron Asks Dumping Duties on Korean Memories," *Electronic News,* April 27, 1992, p. 4.

Davis, Dwight B., "Micron's Formula: Be the First to Make Money," *Electronic Business,* March 1993, p. 59.

Fisher, Lawrence M., "The Rescue of a U.S. Chip Company," *New York Times,* April 6, 1988, p. D1.

Gianturco, Michael, "The Semiconductor Double Take," *Forbes,* April 2, 1990, p. 170.

Gilder, George, "Idaho's New Breed of RAMs," *Forbes,* March 14, 1983, p. 130.

Greenburg, Adam, and Brooke Crothers, "Micron, NEC Sign Memory Deal," *Electronic News,* June 8, 1992, p. 37.

Hardie, Crista, "Micron Cuts Back," *Electronic News,* March 4, 1996.

Hershberger, Steven, "3 Engineers Exit Inmos, Form Firm," *Electronic News,* October 23, 1978, p. 1.

"Micron Splits into 5 Operating Firms, Shifts Execs, Drops Processor Effort," *Electronic News,* August 10, 1992, p. 23.

"Micron Technology Is Making Its Initial Public Offering," *Wall Street Journal,* June 4, 1984, p. 40.

Miller, Michael W., "Fallen Star: Precipitous Decline of Memory Chip Firm Shakes the Industry," *Wall Street Journal,* January 17, 1986, p. 1.

Pulliam, Susan, "Micron Probably Will Escape Serious Damage Even If Computer Sales Ease, Its Backers Say," *Wall Street Journal,* May 19, 1994, p. C2.

Waldman, Peter, "Micron, a Critic of Japan, Explored Takeover by Firm There, Sources Say," *Wall Street Journal,* March 23, 1987, p. 5.

——, "Micron Technology Says Japanese Firms Still Violate Chip Pact," *Wall Street Journal,* March 19, 1987, p. 4.

Wrubel, Robert, "Micron Technology: Finally, Good News," *Financial World,* March 2, 1993, p. 15.

—Jeffrey L. Covell
—updated by Shawna Brynildssen

Monsanto Company

800 North Lindbergh Boulevard
St. Louis, Missouri 63167
U.S.A.
(314) 694-1000
Fax: (314) 694-6572
Web site: http://www.monsanto.com

Public Company
Incorporated: 1933 as Monsanto Chemical Company
Employees: 21,900
Sales: $8.64 billion (1998)
Stock Exchanges: New York Amsterdam Brussels
    Chicago
Frankfurt Geneva London Paris Tokyo Zürich
Ticker Symbol: MTC
NAIC: 325412 Pharmaceutical Preparations; 325311
    Medicinal & Botanical Manufacturing

An agricultural and pharmaceutical stalwart, Monsanto Company is a leading producer of herbicides, prescription drugs, and genetically engineered seeds. Originally a chemical company, Monsanto sold its chemical business in 1997 to build a presence in biotechnology, scoring much-publicized success in developing soybeans able to resist the affects of its market-leading herbicide, Roundup. The company also produced NutraSweet, the dominant sugar substitute in the United States. A sprawling global corporation, Monsanto operated sales offices, manufacturing plants, and research facilities in more than 100 countries.

Early 20th-Century Origins

Monsanto traces its roots to John Francisco Queeny, a purchaser for a wholesale drug house at the turn of the century, who formed the Monsanto Chemical Works in St. Louis, Missouri, in order to produce the artificial sweetener saccharin. By 1905 John Queeny's company was also producing caffeine and vanillin and was beginning to turn a profit. In 1908 Queeny felt

confident enough about his firm's future to leave his part-time job with another drug house to work full time as Monsanto's president. The company continued to grow, with sales surpassing the $1 million mark for the first time in 1915.

While prior to World War I America relied heavily on foreign supplies of chemicals, the increasing likelihood of U.S. intervention meant that the country would soon need its own domestic producer of chemicals. Looking back on the significance of the war for Monsanto, Queeny's son Edgar remarked, "There was no choice other than to improvise, to invent and to find new ways of doing all the old things. The old dependence on Europe was, almost overnight, a thing of the past." Monsanto was forced to rely on its own knowledge and nascent technical ability. Among other problems, Monsanto researchers discovered that pages describing German chemical processes had been ripped out of library books. Monsanto developed several strategic products, including phenol as an antiseptic, in addition to acetylsalicyclic acid, or aspirin.

With the purchase of an Illinois acid company in 1918, Monsanto began to widen the scope of its factory operations. A postwar depression during the early 1920s affected profits, but by the time John Queeny turned over the company to Edgar in 1928 the financial situation was much brighter. Monsanto had gone public, a move that paved the way for future expansion. At this time, the company had 55 shareholders and 1,000 employees and owned a small company in Britain.

Under Edgar Queeny's direction Monsanto, now the Monsanto Chemical Company, began to substantially expand and enter into an era of prolonged growth. Acquisitions expanded Monsanto's product line to include the new field of plastics and the manufacture of phosphorus.

By the time the United States entered World War II in 1941, the domestic chemical industry had attained far greater independence from Europe. Monsanto, strengthened by its several acquisitions, was also prepared to produce such strategic materials as phosphates and inorganic chemicals. Most important was the company's acquisition of a research and development laboratory called Thomas and Hochwalt. The well-known Dayton, Ohio, firm strengthened Monsanto at the time and provided the basis for some of its future achievements in chemical technology. One of its most important discoveries was styrene monomer, a key ingredient in synthetic rubber and a crucial product for the armed forces during the war.

Expansion and New Leadership in the Postwar Period

Largely unknown by the public, Monsanto experienced difficulties in attempting to market consumer goods. However, attempts to refine a low quality detergent led to developments in grass fertilizer, an important consumer product since the postwar housing boom had created a strong market of homeowners eager to perfect their lawns. In the mid-1950s Monsanto began to produce urethane foam, which was flexible and easy to use; it later became crucial in making automobile interiors. In 1955 Monsanto acquired Lion Oil, increasing its assets by more than 50 percent. Stockholders during this time numbered 43,000.

Having finally outgrown its headquarters in downtown St. Louis, Monsanto moved to the suburban community of Creve Coeur in 1957. Three years later Edgar Queeny turned over the chair of Monsanto to Charles Thomas, one of the founders of the research and development laboratory so important to Monsanto. Charlie Sommer, who had joined the company in 1929, became president. Under their combined leadership Monsanto saw several important developments, including the establishment of the Agricultural Chemicals division, created to consolidate Monsanto's diverse agrichemical product lines. Monsanto's European expansion continued, with Brussels becoming the permanent overseas headquarters in 1962.

In 1964 Monsanto changed its name to Monsanto Company in acknowledgment of its diverse product line. The company consisted of eight divisions, including petroleum, fibers, building materials, and packaging.

According to Monsanto historian Dan Forrestal, ''Leadership during the 1960s and early 1970s came principally from . . . executives whose Monsanto roots ran deep.'' In 1964 Edward O'Neal became chairperson. O'Neal, who had come to Monsanto in 1935 with the acquisition of the Swann Corporation, was the first chair in company history who had not first held the post of president. Another company leader was Edward J. Bock, who had joined Monsanto in 1941 as an engineer. He rose through the ranks to become a member of the board of directors in 1965 and president in 1968. Edgar Queeny, who left no heirs, died in 1968.

Although Bock had a reputation for being a committed company executive, several factors contributed to his volatile term as president. High overhead costs and a sluggish national economy led to a dramatic 29 percent decrease in earnings in 1969. Sales were up the following year, but Bock's implementation of the 1971 reorganization caused a significant amount of friction among members of the board and senior management. In spite of the fact that this move, in which Monsanto separated the management of raw materials from the company's subsidiaries, was widely praised by security analysts, Bock resigned from the presidency in February 1972. After a nine-month search, John W. Hanley, a former executive with Procter and Gamble, was chosen as president. Hanley also took over as chairperson in 1975.

Under Hanley, Monsanto more than doubled its sales and earnings between 1972 and 1983. Toward the end of his tenure, Hanley put into effect a promise he had made to himself and to Monsanto when he accepted the position of president, namely, that his successor would be chosen from Monsanto's ranks. Hanley and his staff chose approximately 20 young executives as potential company leaders and began preparing them for the head position at Monsanto. Among them was Richard J. Mahoney. When Hanley joined Monsanto, Mahoney was a young sales director in agricultural products. In 1983 Hanley turned the leadership of the company over to Mahoney. Wall Street immediately approved this decision with an increase in Monsanto's share prices.

Legal Challenges in the 1970s–80s

During this time, public concern over the environment began to escalate. Ralph Nader's activities and Rachel Carson's book *Silent Spring* had been influential in increasing the U.S. public's awareness of activities within the chemical industry in the 1960s, and Monsanto responded in several ways to the pressure. In 1964 the company introduced biodegradable detergents, and in 1976, Monsanto announced plans to phase out production of polychlorinated biphenyl (PCB).

In 1979 a lawsuit was filed against Monsanto and other manufacturers of agent orange, a defoliant used during the Vietnam War. Agent orange contained a highly toxic chemical known as dioxin, and the suit claimed that hundreds of veterans had suffered permanent damage because of the chemical. In 1984 Monsanto and seven other manufacturers agreed to a $180 million settlement just before the trial began. With the announcement of a settlement Monsanto's share price, depressed because of the uncertainty over the outcome of the trial, rose substantially.

Also in 1984, Monsanto lost a $10 million antitrust suit to Spray-Rite, a former distributor of Monsanto agricultural herbicides. The U.S. Supreme Court upheld the suit and award, finding that Monsanto had acted to fix retail prices with other herbicide manufacturers.

In August 1985, Monsanto purchased G. D. Searle, the ''NutraSweet'' firm. NutraSweet, an artificial sweetener, had generated $700 million in sales that year, and Searle could offer Monsanto an experienced marketing and a sales staff as well as real profit potential. Since the late 1970s the company had sold nearly 60 low margin businesses and, with two important agriculture product patents expiring in 1988, a major new cash source was more than welcome. What Monsanto didn't count on, however, was the controversy surrounding Searle's intrauterine birth control device called the Copper-7.

Soon after the acquisition, disclosures about hundreds of lawsuits over Searle's IUD surfaced and turned Monsanto's takeover into a public relations disaster. The disclosures, which inevitably led to comparisons with those about A. H. Robins, the Dalkan Shield manufacturer that eventually declared Chapter 11 bankruptcy, raised questions as to how carefully Monsanto management had considered the acquisition. In early 1986 Searle discontinued IUD sales in the United States. By 1988 Monsanto's new subsidiary faced an estimated 500 lawsuits against the Copper-7 IUD. As the parent company, Monsanto was well insulated from its subsidiary's liabilities by the legal "corporate veil."

Toward the end of the 1980s, Monsanto faced continued challenges from a variety of sources, including government and public concern over hazardous wastes, fuel and feedstock costs, and import competition. At the end of the 99th Congress, then President Ronald Reagan signed a $8.5 billion, five-year cleanup superfund reauthorization act. Built into the financing was a surcharge on the chemical industry created through the tax reform bill. Biotechnology regulations were just being formulated, and Monsanto, which already had types of genetically engineered bacteria ready for testing, was poised to be an active participant in that field.

In keeping with its strategy to become a leader in the health field, Monsanto and the Washington University Medical School entered into a five-year research contract in 1984. Two-thirds of the research was to be directed into areas with obviously commercial applications, while one-third of the research was to be devoted to theoretical work. One particularly promising discovery involved the application of the bovine growth factor, a way to greatly increase milk production.

In the burgeoning low-calorie sweetener market, challengers to NutraSweet were putting pressure on Monsanto. Pfizer Inc., a pharmaceutical company, was preparing to market its product, called alitame, which it claimed was far sweeter than NutraSweet and better suited for baking.

In an interview with *Business Week,* senior vice-president for research and development Howard Schneiderman commented, "To maintain our markets—and not become another steel industry—we must spend on research and development." Monsanto, which has committed eight percent of its operating budget to research and development, far above the industry average, hoped to emerge in the 1990s as one of the leaders in the fields of biotechnology and pharmaceuticals that are only now emerging from their nascent stage.

By the end of the 1980s, Monsanto had restructured itself and become a producer of specialty chemicals, with a focus on biotechnology products. Monsanto enjoyed consecutive record years in 1988 and 1989—sales were $8.3 billion and $8.7 billion, respectively. In 1988 the Food and Drug Administration approved Cytotec, a drug that prevents gastric ulcers in high-risk cases. Sales of Cytotec in the United States reached $39 million in 1989.

The Monsanto Chemical Co. unit prospered with products like Saflex, a type of nylon carpet fiber. The NutraSweet Company held its own in 1989, contributing $180 million in earnings, with growth in the carbonated beverage segment. Almost 500 new products containing NutraSweet were introduced in 1989, for a total of 3,000 products.

Monsanto continued to invest heavily in research and development, with seven percent of sales allotted for this area. The investment began to pay off when the research and development department developed an all-natural fat substitute called Simplesse. The FDA declared in early 1990 that the product was "generally recognized as safe" for use in frozen desserts. That year, the NutraSweet Company introduced Simple Pleasures frozen dairy dessert. Monsanto hoped to see Simplesse used eventually in salad dressings, yogurt, and mayonnaise.

Despite these successes, Monsanto remained frustrated by delays in obtaining FDA approval for bovine somatotropin (BST), a chemical used to increase milk production in cows. Opponents to BST said it would upset the balance of supply and demand for milk, but Monsanto countered that BST would provide high-quality food supplies to consumers worldwide.

The final year of the 1980s also marked Monsanto's listing for the first time on the Tokyo Stock Exchange. Monsanto officials expected the listing to improve opportunities for licensing and joint venture agreements.

Early 1990s Transitional Period

Monsanto had expected to celebrate 1990 as its fifth consecutive year of increased earnings, but numerous factors—the increased price of oil due to the Persian Gulf War, a recession in key industries in the United States, and droughts in California and Europe—prevented the company from achieving this goal. Net income was $546 million, a dramatic drop from the record of $679 the previous year. Nonetheless, subsidiary Searle, which had experienced considerable public relations scandals and headaches in the 1980s, had a record financial year in 1990. The subsidiary had established itself in the global pharmaceutical market and was beginning to emerge as an industry leader. The Monsanto Chemical Co., meanwhile, was a $4 billion business that made up the largest percentage of Monsanto's sales.

Monsanto continued to work at upholding "The Monsanto Pledge," a 1988 declaration to reduce emissions of toxic substances. By its own estimates, the company devoted $285 million annually to environmental expenditures. Furthermore, Monsanto and the Environmental Protection Agency agreed to a cleanup program at the company's detergent and phosphate plant in Richmond County, Georgia.

The company restructured during the early 1990s to help cut losses during a difficult economic time. Net income in 1991 was only $296 million, $250 million less than the previous year. Despite this showing, 1991 was a good year for some of Monsanto's newest products. Bovine somatotropin finally gained FDA approval and was sold in Mexico and Brazil, and Monsanto received the go-ahead to use the fat substitute, Simplesse, in a full range of food products, including yogurt, cheese and cheese spreads, and other low-fat spreads. In addition, the herbicide Dimension was approved in 1991, and scientists at Monsanto tested genetically improved plants in field trials.

Furthermore, Monsanto expanded internationally, opening an office in Shanghai and a plant in Beijing, China. The company also hoped to expand in Thailand, and entered into a joint venture in Japan with Mitsubishi Chemical Co.

Monsanto's sales in 1992 hit $7.8 million. However, as net income dropped 130 percent from 1991 due to several one-time aftertax charges, the company prepared itself for challenging times. The patent on NutraSweet brand sweetener expired in 1992, and in preparation for increased competition, Monsanto launched new products, such as the NutraSweet Spoonful, which came in tabletop serving jars, like sugar. The company also devoted ongoing research and development to Sweetener 2000, a high-intensity product.

In 1992, Monsanto denied that it planned to sell G. D. Searle and Co., pointing out that Searle was a profitable subsidiary that launched many new products. However, to decrease losses, Monsanto did sell Fisher Controls International Inc., a subsidiary that manufactures process control equipment. Profits from the sale were used to buy the Ortho lawn-and-garden business from Chevron Chemical Co.

Monsanto Reinvents Itself in the 1990s

Monsanto expected to see growth in its agricultural, chemical, and biotechnological divisions. In 1993, Monsanto and NTGargiulo joined forces to produce a genetically altered tomato. As the decade progressed, biotechnology played an increasingly important role, eventually emerging as the focal point of the company's operations. The foray into biotechnology, begun in the mid-1980s with a $150-million investment in a genetic engineering lab in Chesterfield, Missouri, had been faithfully supported by further investments in the ensuing years. Monsanto's efforts finally yielded tangible success in 1993, when BST was approved for commercial sale after a frustratingly slow FDA approval process. In the coming years, the development of further biotech products moved to the forefront of Monsanto's activities, ushering in a period of profound change. Fittingly, the sweeping, strategic alterations to the company's focus were preceded by a change in leadership, making the last decade of the 20th century one of the most dynamic eras in Monsanto's history.

Toward the end of 1994, Mahoney announced his retirement, effective the following year in March 1995. As part of the same announcement, Mahoney revealed that Robert B. Shapiro, Monsanto's president and chief operating officer, would be elected by Monsanto's board of directors as his successor. Shapiro, who had joined Searle in 1979 before being named executive vice-president of Monsanto in 1990, did not waver from exerting his influence over the company he now found himself presiding over. At the time of his promotion, Shapiro inherited a company that ranked as the largest domestic acrylic manufacturer in the world, generating $3 billion of its $7.9 billion in total revenues from chemical-related sales. This dominant side of the company's business, representing the foundation upon which it had been built, was eliminated under Shapiro's stewardship, replaced by a resolute commitment to biotech.

Between the mid-1980s and the mid-1990s, Monsanto had spent approximately $1 billion on developing its biotech business. Although biotech was regarded as a commercially unproven market by some industry analysts, Shapiro pressed forward with the research and development of biotech products, and by the beginning of 1996 he was ready to launch the company's first biotech product line. Monsanto began marketing herbicide-tolerant soybeans, genetically engineered to resist Roundup, and insect-resistant cotton, beginning with two million acres of both crops. By the fall of 1996, there were early indications that the first harvests of genetically engineered crops were performing better than expected. News of the encouraging results prompted Shapiro to make a startling announcement in October 1996, when he revealed that the company was considering divesting its chemical business as part of a major reorganization into a life-sciences company.

By the end of 1996, when Shapiro announced he would spin-off the chemical operations as a separate company, Monsanto faced a future without its core business, a $3 billion contributor to the company's annual revenue volume. Without the chemical operations, Monsanto would be reduced to an approximately $5-billion company deriving half its sales from agricultural products and the rest from pharmaceuticals and food ingredients, but Shapiro did not intend to leave it as such. He foresaw an aggressive push into biotech products, a move that industry pundits generally perceived as astute. "It would be a gamble if they didn't do it," commented one analyst in reference to the proposed divestiture. "Monsanto is trying to transform itself into a high-growth agricultural and life sciences company. Low-growth cyclical chemical operations do not fit that bill." Spurring Shapiro toward this sweeping reinvention of Monsanto were enticing forecasts for the market growth of plant biotech products. A $450 million business in 1995, the market for plant biotech products was expected to reach $2 billion by 2000 and $6 billion by 2005. Shapiro wanted to dominate this fast-growing market as it matured by shaping Monsanto into what he described as the main provider of "agricultural biotechnology."

As preparations were underway for the spin-off of Monsanto's chemical operations into a new, publicly owned company named Solutia Inc., Shapiro was busy filling the void created by the departure of the company's core business. A flurry of acquisitions completed between 1995 and 1997 greatly increased Monsanto's presence in life sciences, quickly compensating for the revenue lost from the spin-off of Solutia. Among the largest acquisitions were Calgene, Inc., a leader in plant biotech, which was acquired in a two-part transaction in 1995 and 1997, and a 40 percent interest in Dekalb Genetics Corp., the second-largest seed-corn company in the United States. In 1998, the company acquired the rest of DeKalb, paying $2.3 billion for the Illinois-based company.

By the end of the 1990s, Monsanto bore only partial resemblance to the company that entered the decade. The acquisition campaign that added dozens of biotechnology companies to its portfolio had created a new, dominant force in the promising life sciences field, placing Monsanto in a position to reap massive rewards in the years ahead. For example, a rootworm-resistant strain under development had the potential to save $1 billion worth of damages to corn crops per year. The company's pharmaceutical business also faced a promising future, highlighted by the introduction of a new arthritis medication named Celebrex in 1999. During its first year, Celebrex registered a record number of prescriptions. As Monsanto entered the 21st century, however, there were two uncertainties that loomed as potentially serious obstacles blocking its future success. The acquisition campaign of the mid- and late-1990s had greatly increased the company's debt, forcing Monsanto to desperately search for cash. Secondly, there was growing opposition to genetically altered crops at the decade's conclusion, prompting the United Kingdom to ban the yields from such crops for a year. A great part of the company's future success depended on the resolution of these two issues.

Principal Subsidiaries

Calgene Inc.; Asgrow Seed Co.; DEKALB Genetics Corp.; DEKALB Swine Breeders Inc.; Nutrasweet Co.; Monsanto Agricultural Co.; G. D. Searle & Co.

Further Reading

Crisafulli, Patricia, "Monsanto, EPA Resolve Superfund Cleanup," *Journal of Commerce,* April 12, 1991, p. 13A.

Desloge, Rick, "Is a Divided Monsanto a Target for Purchase?," *St. Louis Business Journal,* December 30, 1996, p. 3.

Donlon, J. P., "After Restructuring, What?" *Chief Executive (U.S.),* March–April, 1988, p. 50.

Ellis, James E., "Monsanto and the Copper-7: A 'Corporate Veil' Begins to Fray," *Business Week,* September 26, 1988, p. 50.

Forrestal, Dan J., *Faith, Hope, and $5,000: The Story of Monsanto: The Trials and Triumphs of the First 75 Years,* New York: Simon and Schuster, 1977.

"The Green Gene Giant," *The Economist,* April 26, 1997, p. 66.

Henkoff, Ronald, "Monsanto: Learning from Its Mistakes," *Fortune,* January 27, 1992, p. 81.

Jaffe, Thomas, "How Do You Top This?," *Forbes,* June 1, 1998.

Kiesche, Elizabeth S., "Monsanto Cultivates Lawn and Garden Line with Ortho Buy," *Chemical Week,* January 20, 1993, p. 7.

Steyer, Robert, "Going It Alone," *Knight-Ridder/Tribune Business News,* October 19, 1998.

Stringer, Judy, "Monsanto Poised to Reap BioTech Harvest," *Chemical Week,* November 6, 1996, p. 51.

—Marinell Landa
—updated by Jeffrey L. Covell

Morgan, Lewis & Bockius LLP

1701 Market Street
Philadelphia, Pennsylvania
U.S.A.
(215) 963-5000
Fax: (215) 963-5299
Web site: http://www.mlb.com

Private Partnership
Founded: 1873 as Morgan & Lewis
Employees: 2,300
Sales: $320 million 1998
NAIC: 54111 Offices of Lawyers

Morgan, Lewis & Bockius LLP is one of the world's largest law firms, with over 200 attorneys in each of its offices in Philadelphia (its headquarters), New York, and Washington, D.C. Other offices operate in Los Angeles; Miami; Pittsburgh; Harrisburg, Pennsylvania; and Princeton, New Jersey. Overseas branches are located in London, Brussels, Frankfurt, Tokyo, Singapore, and Jakarta (an associated office). Morgan Lewis attorneys practice in just about every legal specialty, from personal and family law to corporate law fields such as antitrust, taxation, and intellectual property. They also represent clients worldwide, from Latin America to Asia and Europe.

Origins in the Gilded Age

According to company literature, Francis Draper Lewis wrote in his diary on March 11, 1873 that he "moved table into Morgan's office." Thus began the legal partnership between Lewis and Charles Eldridge Morgan, Jr. Born in Boston, Lewis graduated from Amherst College in 1869 and Harvard Law School two years later. Morgan, who hailed from Philadelphia, graduated from the University of Pennsylvania in 1864 and then fought in the Civil War. He "read law" before being admitted to the bar in 1868, as in those days most lawyers achieved their profession by way of apprenticeship rather than law school.

Morgan and Lewis established their office in Philadelphia and soon achieved a thriving business representing local banks, businesses, and utility companies. In 1883, a third partner joined the firm; Morris Rex Bockius, also native to the Philadelphia area, had recently graduated from the University of Pennsylvania and its law school when he joined Morgan and Lewis as an associate.

The firm's early clients included the Girard National Bank, the Germantown Hospital, and the Germantown Trust Company. Its first major client was the United Gas Improvement Company, later known as UGI, the nation's largest gas and electric company. Morgan Lewis had represented UGI from its inception in 1882, and in the ensuing decades Morgan Lewis and UGI maintained a close relationship. For example, partners at the law firm often accepted posts as UGI inhouse attorneys or corporate officers, as happened in the long-term relationship between the New York law firm Milbank, Tweed, Hadley & McCloy with Chase Manhattan Bank. After generating some political controversy, Morgan Lewis was eventually replaced as UGI's legal counsel in 1962.

Early Twentieth-Century Practice

In 1898 Bockius became a partner, and in 1908 the firm adopted the permanent name of Morgan, Lewis & Bockius (MLB). Bockius was not a litigator but worked closely with business leaders to help them deal with new government laws and regulations. Through Bockius's initiatives, the law firm gained important new clients, including the *Philadelphia Bulletin,* the city's largest daily newspaper, in 1909; Provident Life and Trust Company in 1908; Fidelity Trust Company and British glass manufacturer Pilkington Brothers in 1912; Scott Paper Company in 1915; Baldwin Locomotive Works in 1917; Victor Talking Machine Company in 1920; Drexel & Co. in 1921; and the newly reorganized Philadelphia-Girard National Bank in 1926.

By the 1920s, founders Morgan and Lewis had retreated from the business, and Bockius was left to guide the firm. Under Bockius, MLB continued to strengthen its ties with important corporate clients. In 1922 MLB began representing the Reading Company, owner of the well-known Reading Railroad of *Monopoly* game fame. The railway had been founded in 1833 to carry anthracite coal and grew to operate 63 coal mines and serve 22 million passengers at its Philadelphia terminal. MLB handled thousands of claims, most of them filed against Reading by railroad employees, under the 1908 Federal Employers' Liability Act, which gave employees the right to sue in federal court for job-related injuries. MLB also represented Reading subsidiary the Philadelphia & Reading Coal & Iron Company, the world's largest anthracite mining operation in the late 1800s. The law firm handled the coal company's bankruptcy reorganization beginning in 1937 and later handled related litigation. Morris Bockius, the last of the firm's founding attorneys and perhaps its greatest contributor in terms of bringing in new business, died in 1939.

The firm, which by early decree would remain forever known as Morgan, Lewis & Bockius, continued to garner business during World War II and the postwar economic boom in the United States. Prominent attorneys during this time included William Clarke Mason, who had joined the firm in 1922 bringing with him his client, the Reading Company, and thus a business relationship that would serve the firm well for years. British glassmaker Pilkington and industry giant Scott paper became perhaps the firms most important clients in the 1950s.

1960s–70s Diversifications

The 1960s brought radical changes to the social climate of the United States and, in turn, to MLB. In its early years, MLB was comprised of a largely homogenous work force consisting of white men of Christian faith, and although the firm had hired its first Jewish associate early in the 20th century, that attorney had never become a partner. In the 1960s, however, the firm began making more concerted efforts to widen the scope of its representation. The firm's first Jewish partner was recruited in 1961, and two years later MLB hired its first woman attorney. In 1970 MLB hired its first black male associate, and later, in 1984, the first African-American woman to serve as associate at MLB was recruited.

Also during this time, the firm began to shed much of the collegiality and intimate ties with clients that had characterized its business in earlier decades. Increasing size, specialization, and competition with other law firms necessitated a new approach, and the pervading sense of "brotherhood" at the firm was supplanted by a larger, more diverse work force and more formal business arrangements.

In fact, in the 1970s most law firms became increasingly business-oriented and competitive following a U.S. Supreme Court decision ruling that restrictions on professional advertising were unconstitutional. In addition, 1979 saw the introduction of *American Lawyer,* which provided comparative information on lawyer salaries and other data regarding the nation's major firms. After that, top lawyers began seeking greener pastures as lateral hiring or the "raiding" of other firms became more common. What Dilks, in his history of MLB, called "cradle to grave" law practice became a thing of the past.

During the 1970s, as the pace of technological change increased dramatically, the firm went from using manual to electric typewriters and then in the late 1970s to computers. By this time, MLB had offices in Philadelphia, New York, Harrisburg, Pennsylvania, and Washington, D.C. In 1976 the firm entered the West Coast market by opening new facilities in Los Angeles, and the following year, a Miami office was added.

Expansion in the 1980s

Meanwhile, the firm also expanded its international practice, which had been sporadic before that time. In 1972, MLB organized an international division with a small office in Paris at which it worked in conjunction with another law firm. By 1981 MLB had become one of the first firms to start a multinational practice in London.

In 1986, the Japanese government began allowing foreign lawyers to practice in Japan under very strict conditions. Two years later, MLB opened its own office in Tokyo. Like the London office, the Tokyo office proved successful from the beginning. In 1989 MLB opened its Brussels and Frankfurt offices, following the 1986 Single European Act that foresaw open markets for the 12 nations of the European Community.

In the United States, one of the firm's major victories occurred in the 1980s when it represented Kansas City Southern Industries, Inc. and its railroad subsidiary. In 1983 the state of South Dakota sued Kansas City Southern over some disputed rights to property and in 1988 won a jury verdict that required KCS to pay $844.2 million, more than the company's net worth. Over years of litigation, MLB attorneys got that decision reversed, and the U.S. Supreme Court denied any appeal.

Also during this time, MLB worked on behalf of long-time client Scott Paper Company to install new laws in Pennsylvania aimed at averting hostile takeovers of businesses. Through this work, MLB gained Strawbridge & Clothier, a family-owned department store, as a client, defending this company from a hostile takeover in 1986. Other MLB clients in the 1980s included the U.S. Department of Transportation, which tried in vain to prevent the nation's air controllers' strike of 1981. MLB also represented the Major League Baseball Player Relations Committee, Inc., starting in 1982.

Developments in the 1990s

By the early 1990s, MLB was Philadelphia's largest law firm and the eighth largest law firm in the United States. MLB then moved from eighth to fourth in 1994 when it announced a major addition to its work force. The firm would acquire a total of 105 more attorneys, including 55 who would join the New York office from their former firm of Lord Day, as well as 50 lawyers from Newman, Bouknight & Edgar, who were merged into the Washington, D.C. office. The Lord Day firm contributed its expertise in personal law and corporate tax, securities, and litigation, while the Newman Bouknight attorneys specialized in energy and utilities law.

MLB was growing in several geographic as well as practice areas. Like other law firms, it recruited lateral hires, associates, and new law school graduates to meet the rising demand for attorneys, and in 1996 it opened branch offices in Pittsburgh and Singapore, as well as an associated office in Jakarta. Meanwhile the firm's Latin American operations, based in New York and Miami, represented major corporate clients in Mexico and throughout South America.

MLB's New York office continued to experience rapid growth, primarily through recruiting from such local law firms as Shearman & Sterling and acquiring the 20-attorney New York practice of Zalkin Rodin & Goodman, specialists in bankruptcy. By early 1999 Morgan Lewis had about 265 lawyers in New York, which made it the Big Apple's 19th largest law firm.

Expansion at its home base in Philadelphia soon prompted MLB to move into larger facilities there, as the firm signed a long-term lease to be the only tenant of a 40-year-old building at 6 Penn Center, which the firm called 1701 Market. The thoroughly renovated structure gave the firm more flexible space for teams of lawyers and paralegals to work on projects, the major advantage over its previous home at One Logan Square.

To keep abreast of high-tech trends, MLB launched its own Web site and also teamed up with West Group to create the "first online searchable database of interpretations of the Hart-Scott-Rodino Antitrust Improvements Act (HSR Act)." Private and public attorneys and others could search the trademarked HSRScan database using West Group's Westlaw search engine. This free resource described on Morgan Lewis' Web site included the text of the 1976 federal HSR Act, associated regulations, over 1,000 letters to the Federal Trade Commission, and FTC commentary illustrating how the law has been interpreted over the years. One project manager from West Group asserted that "Morgan Lewis is at the leading edge of law firms providing compelling content through their Web sites."

Based on its 1997 gross revenues of $359 million, MLB was ranked eighth among U.S. law firms by *American Lawyer.* In its first ranking of the world's largest law firms, the magazine listed MLB as 12th based on 1997 revenues and tenth based on number of attorneys, which numbered 901 at the time.

Having doubled in size in roughly ten years, MLB did experience some growing pains. Perhaps the most notable of these involved one of its partners in the late 1990s. Attorney Allen W. Stewart, a partner at MLB with controlling interests in two Pennsylvania insurance companies, reportedly looted the companies' finances, setting them up for collapse and causing what was thought to be among the largest insurance losses in the state's history. In late 1997 Stewart was convicted of fraud,

money laundering, and racketeering; this led to a 15-year prison sentence for Stewart and some unwelcome press coverage for MLB. Moreover, another challenge to MLB arose when the Pennsylvania Insurance Department sued MLB for being partly liable for the $124 million the state paid out because of the two collapsed insurance firms. In February 1998 a settlement was announced in which the law firm agreed to pay $35 million. Francis Milone, MLB's managing partner, maintained that the firm had done nothing wrong but did want to avoid costly future litigation.

At the end of the 1990s, MLB faced some challenges in the form of frequent law firm consolidations, increasing competition from large accounting firms providing legal services, and more demands from lawyers for more flexible schedules. Nevertheless, MLB had wide range, geographically and in its areas of expertise, and was known among the world's leading law firms, which boded well for the firm as it entered the next century.

Further Reading

Dilks, Park B., Jr., *Morgan, Lewis & Bockius: A Law Firm and Its Times 1873–1993*, Philadelphia: Morgan, Lewis & Bockius, 1994.

George, John, "Two Deals Make Morgan Lewis Nation's No. 4 Law Firm," *Philadelphia Business Journal,* November 11, 1994, p. 3B.

Goldstein, Matthew, "NY Law Gets Outsider Spin: Out-of-State Firms Grab Biz," *Crain's New York Business,* February 1, 1999, p. 3.

Starkman, Dean, "Morgan Lewis to Pay $35 Million to Settle Insurer-Looting Case," *Wall Street Journal,* February 24, 1998, p. B5.

Steward, Allen W., "Former Morgan Lewis Partner is Sentenced to 15 Years in Prison," *Wall Street Journal,* August 13, 1998, p. B10.

Walsh, Thomas J., "Real Estate Market Fuels Law Firm Recruitment," *Philadelphia Business Journal,* August 28, 1998, p. 3.

Yingling, Bill, "Morgan Lewis Lease Marks Shift for City Office Market," *Philadelphia Business Journal,* September 20, 1996, p. 13.

—David M. Walden

Mountain States Mortgage Centers, Inc.

1333 East 9400 South
Sandy, Utah 84093
U.S.A.
(801) 576-1000
Fax: (801) 572-8431
Web site: http://www.mortgagespan.com

Private Company
Incorporated: 1983
Employees: 120
Sales: $540 million (1998)
NAIC: 522292 Real Estate Credit; 52239 Other Activities
Related to Credit Intermediation

Mountain States Mortgage Centers is a large mortgage banking firm that originates and services residential mortgage loans for new homes, refinancings, debt consolidation, construction, home improvement, and home equity. Registered to operate in most states and the District of Columbia, Mountain States has over 100 different programs to help its customers. The company also administers the MortgageSpan division that allows individuals to work out of their homes as self-employed loan originators and recruit others to do the same, thus qualifying as a multilevel marketing (MLM) means of direct sales.

1980s Origins

Jerilyn R. (J. R.) Bills, the founder of Mountain States Mortgage, was born in San Diego and moved with her family to Salt Lake City. She first worked in the mortgage industry while attending college in pursuit of an art degree. "After about six months, I came to the stunning realization that I loved this business, and I wanted to make a career out of it," said Bills in the *Broker Agent Magazine*. So in 1972 Bills left college. Over the next decade she worked for several companies, learning what she could to eventually start her own firm.

Bills started Mountain States for two reasons. "I was disappointed with the [existing] service. It was taking from six to eight weeks to get a loan approved, and I found it difficult to make changes from within the industry." Moreover, Bills remarked, "It had always been my goal to become self-employed and financially secure, so I decided to strike out on my own."

Mountain States Mortgage Centers, Inc. was incorporated on January 26, 1983, with total authorized capital of $50,000. The company's incorporators and initial board of directors were comprised of J.R. Bills, based in Salt Lake City, her friend and associate Joseph C. Knudson, and his mother Dorothy R. Knudson, the latter two hailing from Hildale, Utah, a small town on the Utah-Arizona border. When the company was started, Bills had already built relationships with some realtors; her connections in the field helped her gain $2 million in mortgage applications in the first two weeks of business. The company began in a small office in Salt Lake City. By 1989 the firm was employing a work force of 60, and it moved to a 25,000-square-foot building in the Salt Lake City suburb of Sandy.

In December 1989 Mountain States Mortgage directors Dorothy R. Knudson and Joseph Knudson, joined by Joseph's brother Alan E. Knudson, incorporated their own Utah firm called West Star Financial Corporation, thus laying the foundation for an eventual split from J. R. Bills and Mountain States. Alan Knudson, a University of Utah grad, had begun at Mountain States in 1984 as a loan officer and manager of the Sandy branch and had risen to become vice-president. In the early 1990s, J.R. Bills bought out the Knudsons' shares of Mountain States, becoming the company's sole stockholder. Still, Mountain States and West Star reportedly worked out of the same building in Sandy, before West Star eventually left to merge with the VanderFord Company, another Nevada corporation headed by the Knudson family.

Expansion under Bills in the 1990s

The split between the original directors of Mountain States Mortgage Centers occurred during a period of general expansion at Mountain States. To help manage the business, Bills hired Larry Jentzsch, formerly the senior vice-president of finance and administration at Utah's Megahertz Corporation. A notice in the November/December 1993 issue of *Utah Business* listed Mountain States as "one of the nation's largest GNMA loan producers," referring to federally guaranteed loans, either FHA or VA loans, through the Government National Mortgage Association (Ginnie Mae). Mountain States' net income increased 125 percent from 1992 to 1993, when it reportedly closed 14,000 loans worth over $822 million.

Bills' management style was distinguished by her commitment to good customer service and fair treatment in the work place, including efforts to incorporate nonsexist language in all business dealings. In a brief profile in the *Deseret News* on November 14, 1993, Bills described her business methodology as one of "timeline management and motivational goal setting." Though it was processing loans in more than 40 U.S. States, the company also opted to stick close to its roots in Utah. One attempt to expand with facilities across state borders, specifically an office in Phoenix, was described by Bills as "a miserable failure and a good lesson." She affirmed that "Now everything originates and is managed from Utah."

In January 1994 Bills announced that Mountain States had paid $1.8 million cash for a building on seven acres of land in Sandy, Utah. Once the facility was remodeled, it would become the site for processing loan applications, and overseeing the transfer of investor money to contractors, while the company's main office would continue to oversee the collection of loan payments.

Bills expected further growth in the mid-1990s. "Our servicing department is at $2 billion right now," she remarked in an October 1994 profile in *Deseret News,* adding "but we expect it to be at $30 billion in about three years." About 90 percent of Mountain States Mortgage's business at the time came from loans on existing homes; national economic recovery would soon further stimulate Mountain States Mortgage's expansion. In 1990–1991 mortgage rates ran about ten percent. By 1993, housing had become more affordable than it had been since the mid-1970s, with mortgage rates declining to below eight percent.

New Directions: The MortgageSpan Program

Geographic expansion continued to interest Mountain States. Moreover, Bills had observed how more people were working out of home offices, facilitated by the explosive growth of the Internet. "Who says loan originators have to come to the office?" questioned Bills in the *Broker Agent Magazine.* While Mountain State Mortgage Center's business was throughout the United States, the public continued to perceive it as a lending company for the western United States. To correct this perception, and to take advantage of a growing home-based work force, in 1997 the company created MortgageSpan, which would, according to company literature "convey widespread lending abilities and assist the company in attaining its goals nationally."

Specifically, MortgageSpan helped established real estate agents, or even anyone new to the business, become a self-employed independent loan originator (ILO). For $299, an ILO received a start-up kit with a reference manual, training workbook and video, a computerized mortgage data analyzer, and a diskette with ads and other resources. The ILO also paid $69 per month to have MortgageSpan staff process and underwrite loans, provide further training, and to gain support from the program's national advertisements and a monthly newsletter on the mortgage industry. "The days of operating a mortgage business based solely on traditional practices are gone," Bills observed in the October 1998 *Salt Lake City Enterprise.* "In order to stay competitive, mortgage companies must find new ways to cut costs and increase value for their customers. With our new division, we'll be able to do both," she stated.

Soon MortgageSpan was signing up about 100 new loan originators every month, with the goal of having about 1,000 ILOs after one year of operation. ILOs made money by networking with their family, friends, and acquaintances to offer them loans. If they closed six $150,000 loans a month, they received a 0.4 percent commission of $600 per loan. Moreover, ILOs also could receive volume bonuses on their own sales. If independent loan originators referred someone who also became a MortgageSpan ILO, they received $100 plus $5 for every month that the new recruit stayed in the program. In addition, ILOs who coached and managed their enrollees were paid a percentage on the loans they closed.

Although not all succeeded, some MortgageSpan ILO's did quite well. The MortgageSpan program did compete with another multilevel marketing operation—Primerica Financial Services— that trained its representatives to offer term insurance, mutual funds, and consolidated loans available for refinancing mortgages. Like MortgageSpan, Primerica Financial Services paid its representatives a percentage for sales of those they recruited.

In November 1998 *Utah Business* magazine ranked Mountain States Mortgage as Utah's largest company under female ownership, based on its gross revenues of $540 million. Utah was at the time one of the ten fastest-growing states for women-owned businesses, according to the National Foundation for Women Business Owners. Bills and Mountain States Mortgage had participated in a major trend for women in the 1980s and 1990s of starting their own companies, some small and some large. Such entrepreneurs decided to quit trying to break through the so-called "glass ceiling" in which male corporate executives prevented competent women from reaching the top. Instead, they were jumping ship and founding their own businesses at twice the rate of the general population.

In 1999 Mountain States Mortgage Centers continued to be led by President/CEO and sole owner J. R. Bills. Other officers included Vice-President and Chief Financial Officer Gene G. Jensen, as well as Vice-President Linda Malin. Bills' daughters were also involved in the business, closing loans and managing the documents departments. As it headed into the next century, Mountain States Mortgage Centers looked to incorporate new technologies associated with data storage and the Internet, while also extending its geographic reach through its MortgageSpan program. Likely, the company would also adhere to its policy of inclusiveness, as stated by Bills in a real estate trade magazine: "We believe everyone should be able to own their own home, and we rarely decline a loan."

Principal Divisions

Mountain States Mortgage Servicing, L.L.C.; MortgageSpan L.L.C.; Mortgage Servicing Associates, Inc.; Collier Corporation.

Further Reading

"Executive Focus: Jerilyn R. 'JR' Bills, President, Founder Chief Executive Officer & Sole Owner Mountain State Mortgage Center Inc.," *Deseret News* (Web Edition), November 14, 1993.

Jones, Lara, "Mtn. States Mortgage to Boost Staff to 1,200 over Three Years," *Enterprise* (Salt Lake City), January 24, 1994, p. 1.

Kemeny, John, "The Online Mortgage Company Manual," *Mortgage Banking,* June 1999, pp. 103–06.

"Loan Originators Needed," *Income Opportunities,* January/February 1999, p. 48.

"Mountain States Mortgage Launches New Division," *Enterprise* (Salt Lake City), October 19, 1998, p. 6.

Newbold, Gail Andersen, "These Women Mean Business! A Roundtable on the Challenges and Successes of Utah's Women in Business," *Utah Business,* November 1998, pp. 20–25.

Pusey, Roger, "Mortgage Center Offers Speed, Service," *Deseret News* (Web Edition), October 2, 1994.

Spiers, Joseph, "Here Comes the Best Housing Market in a Decade," *Fortune,* May 3, 1993, p. 21.

—David M. Walden

Mrs. Baird's Bakeries

7301 South Freeway
Fort, Worth, Texas 76134
U.S.A.
(817) 293-6230
Fax: (817) 615-3090
Web site: http://www.mrsbairds.com

Wholly-Owned Subsidiary of Grupo Industrial Bimbo
   S.A. de C.V.
Founded: 1908
Employees: 3,400
Sales: $307 million (1997)
NAIC: 311812 Commercial Bakeries

For more than 90 years Texans have enjoyed the products of Mrs. Baird's Bakeries, a company that offers several varieties of bread and bread products, including hot dog and hamburger buns, rolls, bagels, and tortillas. The company produces baked sweet goods for breakfast as well as for desert. Old-fashioned baking methods are still employed: dough is allowed to rise naturally and long rolls of bread dough are hand-twisted into loaves of bread. Mrs. Baird's Bakeries prides itself on ''Quality, Freshness, and Service.'' Established in 1908, Mrs. Baird's was family-owned and -operated until Grupo Industrial Bimbo, a large Mexican baking company, acquired the company in 1998.

A Modest Start

Mrs. Ninnie Baird began her bakery out of necessity in 1908 when her husband's poor health prevented him from working on a regular basis. She already had a reputation among her Fort Worth, Texas, neighbors as an excellent baker, so it did not take long for Ninnie Baird to establish a business. She started baking bread at home in her wood-fired stove in batches of four loaves and delivered the bread to her customers on foot. After her husband died in 1911 the business became more of a family affair. The four Baird sons—Dewey, Hoyt, Roland, and C.B.—helped Ninnie to bake and deliver the bread while her older daughters did the household chores and cared for younger siblings. The business expanded to include pies and cakes which were sold door-to-door in the neighborhood along with loaves of bread. As the area where the family sold their products grew the Baird boys began to make their deliveries on bicycle. Later, Baird's daughter, Bess, obtained employment as a secretary to provide financial support for expansion of the family business.

In 1915 Mrs. Baird's Bakery upgraded business operations to accommodate growing customer demand. The family purchased a commercial oven from an area hotel for $75.00—$25 in cash and $50 in bread and rolls. The baking equipment, which had a capacity to bake 40 loaves of bread in one batch, was moved to a small wooden building behind the family home. To deliver Mrs. Baird's products farther and faster, the family's horse (Ned) and buggy was turned into a sales wagon; 14 year-old Hoyt Baird became responsible for the daily delivery route a year later. By 1917 the family had acquired an automobile which they converted into a delivery vehicle. The family business was advertised on the doors of the car, encouraging people to, ''Eat More Mrs. Baird's Bread.'' Also, Baird developed a weekly credit system for her regular customers as well as a system of exchange. Under the system, a customer could purchase 24 tickets at a cost of one dollar and exchange each ticket for a one-pound loaf of bread as needed.

Baird's efforts to expand her customer base propelled the company into wholesale operations. One of three wholesale accounts she secured at this time, Sandegard's Grocery, prospered and opened 14 additional stores. Mrs. Baird's Bakery also prospered as the company's products were distributed to all new Sandegard Grocery stores. In 1918, the family decided to change from a primarily retail business to a strictly wholesale business. An $8,800 investment in a larger baking facility included a new gas-fired oven capable of baking 400 loaves of bread at one time. A second truck was purchased to accommodate the growing number of sales routes which then covered the city of Fort Worth. Over the next decade, business demanded that the facility be expanded nine times. By 1928, the company would open a second bakery in Dallas.

Mid-Century: Fluctuation and Growth

The following decades provided a number of challenges for Mrs. Baird's Bakeries. Business declined sharply during the

Great Depression, requiring salary cutbacks for all employees, though everyone was provided with bread. By 1938 business had rebounded and two more baking plants were opened. A new facility in Fort Worth was used for baking bread, while the older facility continued to be used for baking sweet goods only. The other new facility was located in Houston. The company acquired four new ovens to be divided between the two new bakeries. The facilities also featured plate glass windows which allowed passers-by to view the bakers' handicraft.

Wars at mid-century presented a different set of challenges for the Baird family. World War II brought shortages in sugar and labor, and Mrs. Baird's responded by scaling back its product line. The family decided to produce and sell only the basic baked goods: white and wheat breads, and hamburger and hot dog buns. By 1949 business had endured well enough to move the Dallas bakery to a new location and to open a new bakery in Abilene. Then the war in Korea created a shortage of labor. The problem was resolved by hiring people with hearing disabilities, who had been disqualified for service in the armed forces. Clayton Baird found that communication through sign language was beneficial in the noisy atmosphere of a large baking plant.

Baird continued to be involved in the family business while her children and grandchildren bore responsibility for daily business activities. As chairman of the board she kept tabs on the overall operations and was active in making the major decisions of the company, such as when and where to open a new plant. In the 1950s, as old age overcame Baird's health, board meetings were often held in her home. Though in her 80s, Baird insisted on overseeing the expansion of the company's distribution throughout the state of Texas. In 1959 and 1960 bakeries were acquired in Victoria, Lubbock, Waco, and Austin with the involvement of four grandsons, Bill, Vernon, Allen, and Clayton, who were learning all aspects of the family business at that time.

After Baird's death at 92 years of age in 1961, the company continued to be a strictly family-owned and operated enterprise. Three of Baird's sons, C.B., Dewey and Hoyt, continued to be involved in the company. In 1969 a third generation took the lead when Ninnie Baird's grandson Vernon Baird became president and CEO, a position he held until 1978 when Allen Baird, another grandson, took charge. Capitalizing on its status as a long-time, family-owned and -operated bakery in Texas, television and print media advertisements featured members of the Baird family.

As the sales and distribution network expanded throughout the state of Texas, new technology and specialized facilities assisted day-to-day operations. In the 1960s Mrs. Baird's was a pioneer among family-owned businesses in the use of computer and information technology including hand-held computers for in-store inventory at delivery. Also, the company purchased a pie plant in Abilene in 1969 and construction was completed on a cake plant in South Fort Worth in 1972. In 1976 a bread plant was acquired in San Antonio, the last densely populated area of Texas for the company to initiate production.

Technological Transformation in the 1980s

Daily production procedures were modernized with and through plant expansion. In 1985 the company built a new, 153,600 square-foot plant in Houston which was equipped with state-of-the-art technology, capable of baking 150 loaves of bread and 780 buns per minute. Though technology facilitated large-scale production, the Baird family continued to use old methods of preparation to preserve the quality of their bread. The bread dough was still allowed to rise naturally, rather than using technology, particularly chemicals, to speed the process. Bakers continued to twist the dough by hand. Two long pieces of dough were entwined into one loaf, which was left to rise again before it was sent to the oven for baking.

Technology at a new, 165,000-square-foot plant, built at company headquarters in 1992, included an automated dry handling system to accurately weigh ingredients, sift them and feed them into a mixer. This was a complicated process to automate, given that as many as 17 minor ingredients may be part of one recipe and each ingredient was assigned a separate feeder. A computer controls the six-hour operation, from weighing ingredients to packaging the bread, and each of the plant's six mixers has a computer monitor which keeps operators informed of the status of each batch of bread dough.

Mrs. Baird's was the first baking company in the United States to implement an automatic trough storage-and-retrieval system for bread dough as computerization and robotics streamlined the 'sponge-and-dough process.' With elements of artificial intelligence integrated into the system, one-ton troughs automatically transferred dough mixtures by shuttle along a guided rail system. A 'sponge' of yeast, yeast food, flour, and water was blended in a mixer and moved to the temperature and humidity controlled fermentation room. A computer monitored the three-and-a-half to four-hour fermentation process and automatically transferred one of the 32 sponge troughs from a compartment in the fermentation room to a mixing bowl on one of the plant's production lines. While the trough was shuttled along the rail system, bars punched the 1,000 pound sponge to allow gas to escape. The trough emptied the sponge into a mixing bowl, where flour, sugar, dry milk, and other ingredients were added to complete the bread dough mixture. The trough then returned to an empty compartment in the storage rack. When the bread dough was ready, one of four dough troughs transferred the dough to a divider where the dough was cut into smaller pieces for kneading. As the troughs shuttled to different areas of the bakery, infrared scanners identified obstacles on the rail line as much as six feet away and stopped the trough automatically if necessary.

Implementation of the storage-and-retrieval system allowed Mrs. Baird's to become more flexible in production output, which was aligned with sales demand. The four story high "open-rack" set-up in the fermentation room allowed different varieties of bread to be prepared at one time. Rather than a "first-in, first out" system of production, robotics enabled "just-in-time" production, to bring fresher products to grocery store shelves with less waste. Technology also created uniformity in the quality of the company's products. The new $21 million facility went into full production for more than 150 varieties of bread and cake products in June 1992.

With expanded production capacity, Mrs. Baird's was ready to expand distribution as well. In January 1994 then company Chairman Allen Baird announced that Mrs. Baird's had entered into a joint venture agreement with Grupo Industrial Bimbo (GIB), the largest bakery in Mexico with more than 11,000 delivery routes, over 350,000 accounts served on a daily basis, and 350 distribution centers, including plants in Guatemala, Chile, Venezuela, and El Salvador. The new company, named QFS Foods, widened the distribution of baked goods for the two companies and provided a wider variety along the distribution routes as well. Increased capital resources as well as a broader product line would facilitate distribution on a national level. Business at QFS Foods was conducted as Mrs. Baird's Bakeries, using Mrs. Baird's brand name and marketing team. Allen Baird was named chairman of the new company.

Upheaval and Renewal: 1995–97

In January 1995, the U. S. Justice Department began an investigation of four baking companies operating in Texas, including Mrs. Baird's Bakeries, for fixing the price of white bread. A competitor of Mrs. Baird's sought immunity in exchange for cooperation with federal investigators. Georgia-based Flowers Industries, Inc. admitted that executives at both companies had exchanged information about whether they intended to increase the price of bread. Mrs. Baird's contended that the practice was not illegal since companies often gathered information on their competitors' activities. The prosecution disputed the argument, saying that exchanging 'price letters' meant for grocers was a cunning manner in which the two companies might fix the price of bread.

The prosecution argued that Mrs. Baird's had sought to fix the price of a loaf of white bread at over 76 cents in the years 1977 to 1993. A memorandum sent by Vernon Baird in April 1990 implicated the company on charges of price-fixing and bid-rigging. The memorandum ordered employees not to discuss pricing or any factors which affected pricing with competitors. A five-year stature of limitations on price-fixing would have prevented conviction, but a company executive testified that he had no memory of the memorandum and he never changed from his ''old-fashioned'' methods.

In February 1996 a jury acquitted Mrs. Baird's of three charges of price-fixing and bid-rigging, acquitted then-president Carroll Baird, but convicted the company on one charge of price-fixing in small towns in eastern Texas. A few months after the conviction Mrs. Baird's was given five years probation, fined the maximum $10 million, and ordered to perform 2,500 hours of community service. Company executives continued to deny its practices were illegal but agreed to halt a federal appeal in exchange for amnesty. Mrs. Baird's also agreed to assist in future investigations of anti-competitive activities.

The price-fixing conviction prompted civil suits against Mrs. Baird's totaling $100 million. The class action suits were filed by companies and public agencies said to have been damaged by Mrs. Baird's business practices. In response, Mrs. Baird's filed for bankruptcy protection under Chapter XI of the U.S. Bankruptcy Code in March 1996; the petition claimed assets of $95 million and liabilities of $14 million. The strategy worked for Mrs. Baird's, which settled the lawsuits for $18 million. Mrs. Baird's settled with the State of Texas for $600,000. The deal freed the company from previous and related claims, and did not involve an admission of guilt.

Federal antitrust investigations prompted the company to reorganize. For the first time in the company's history, the position of president and CEO was filled by someone who was not a member of the Baird family. In May 1995 Carroll Baird, grandson of Ninnie Baird, was replaced as the head of Mrs. Baird's Bakeries by Larry Wheeler from the Pillsbury Company. The company then restructured into three regional divisions, North Texas, South Texas, and Houston. The Board of Directors, formerly composed of 19 members of the Baird family, was reconfigured to 16 members including three elected members from outside the family.

New leadership also reflected a shift in focus from relying on the company's tradition of a low-key sales and service strategy in daily customer relations to a consumer and marketing orientation. Equipment upgrades improved output while a new pricing formula increased profits and improved cash flow. Mrs. Baird's successfully introduced chocolate donuts, tortillas, and bagels into its product line. The company's entry into the trendy $10 million Texas market for bagels was timely, and Mrs. Baird's tortillas quickly became the second most popular brand in Texas.

Building on the success of its new products in 1996, Mrs. Baird's sought new ways to market its products. In March 1997 the company introduced its ''Fresh Ideas'' campaign to reach a more health conscious public by showing how Mrs. Baird's products were suited to a healthy lifestyle. Press packets sent to Texas food and lifestyle editors included monthly articles and healthy recipes. The company also introduced a 98 percent fat-free, ''Dark 'N Grainy'' bread.

Appealing to a younger audience, Mrs. Baird's became the official bread of the North Texas Soccer Association (NTSA). The company also teamed up with the Reebok athletic shoe and sportswear manufacturer to support the organization of some 8,000 teenagers through joint store/celebrity promotions. The two companies offered NTSA teams an opportunity to win shoes, uniforms, soccer balls, and league fees in the ''Kick, Score, Win'' contest by collecting proof-of-purchase seals from Reebok and Mrs. Baird's products.

Mrs. Baird's expanded production and distribution in the 1990s. At a cost of $8 million, the San Antonio plant was enlarged 21,000 square-feet to accommodate another production line. With $5 million invested in baking equipment, the level of production doubled from 60 to 120 loaves per minute and from 300 to 600 buns per minute. New distribution routes served states bordering Texas, parts of Oklahoma, New Mexico, and Louisiana. In July 1997 a distribution agreement with CPC Baking Business of Bay Shore, New York, accepted Mrs. Baird's as the exclusive distributor of CPC products in Mrs. Baird's product service area.

At the End of a Century

After 90 years as a family owned and operated business, the Baird family made the arduous decision that its status needed to change. In 1997 executives at Mrs. Baird's Bakeries explored the possibility of taking the company public with a stock offering in order to increase liquid assets. Instead they ended up inviting Grupo Industrial Bimbo to purchase the company. In March 1998 GIB agreed to the acquisition, and an agreement was signed the following May. GIB, a publicly traded company founded in 1965 in Mexico City, was Mexico's largest baker and food company. In July 1998 GIB appointed Juan Muldoon, former head of its Chile operations, as president of Mrs. Baird's. Baird family members maintained high level positions within the company and remained on the board of directors. GIB then moved its U.S. headquarters from Carrollton, Texas, to Mrs. Baird's headquarters in Fort Worth and placed Mrs. Baird's under its U.S. division, Bimbo Bakeries USA.

Under GIB, national expansion of Mrs. Baird's continued. The company expanded into the Oklahoma market with 11 new delivery routes in September 1998. Television and radio promotions coincided with entry into that market. The company planned an ambitious strategy for national expansion as well as expansion of its product line for 1999.

Further Reading

"Bad News, Baird's," *Texas Monthly,* August 1996, p. 52.

"Bimbo Flies North of the Border," *Bakery Production and Marketing,* September 1994, p. 118.

"Bimbo Gains U.S. Foothold in Mrs. Baird's," *Milling and Baking News,* May 26, 1998, p. 1.

"Bimbo Names New President and Other Executives to Mrs. Baird's," *Milling and Baking News,* July 21, 1998, p. 10.

Bowen, Bill, "Mrs. Baird's Joint Venture Reflects Nationwide Trend," *Dallas Business Journal,* February 4, 1994, p. 7.

"Grupo Industrial Bimbo Agrees to Acquire Mrs. Baird's Bakeries," *PR Newswire,* March 24, 1998.

"A Guilty Verdict for Mrs. Baird's," *New York Times,* February 15, 1996, p. D5.

Halkias, Maria, "Mrs. Baird's Must Help with Investigation," *Dallas Morning News,* August 27, 1997, p. D1.

Krumrei, Doug, "Mrs. Baird's New Campaigns Get the Good Word Out," *Bakery Production and Marketing,* March 15, 1997, p. 14.

Krumrei, Doug, "The New Mrs. Baird's," *Bakery Production and Marketing,* April 15, 1997, p. 22.

Lahvic, Ray, "Bimbo and Mrs. Baird's Form Joint Venture," *Bakery Production and Marketing,* March 24, 1994, p. 84.

"Lawsuit by State of Texas is Settled for $600,000," *Wall Street Journal,* September 19, 1996, p. B2.

Leach, Mark S., "Baird's Agrees to Federal Amnesty," *Fort Worth Star-Telegram,* August 27, 1997, p. C1.

Malovany, Dan, "Relax! Sponge and Dough Made Simple," *Bakery Production and Marketing,* January 24, 1993, p. 11.

"Mrs. Baird's Bakeries is Fined $10 Million," *New York Times,* May 31, 1996, p. D3.

Rice, Judy, "Automating Bakery Logistics: Keebler, Archway and Mrs. Baird's Offer Real-Life Examples of Successful Projects," *Food Processing,* August 1993, p. 60.

"Vernon Baird, Baking Industry Leader, Passes Away," *Bakery Production and Marketing,* February 24, 1992, p. 16.

Wren, Worth, Jr., and Mitchell Schnurman, "Mexico's Top Baker Buying Mrs. Baird," *Fort Worth Star-Telegram,* March 25, 1998, p. A1.

Wren, Worth, Jr., "Baird's Ponders Option to Go Public," *Fort Worth Star-Telegram,* September 19, 1997, p. C1.

——, "Grupo Bimbo's Bear Witnesses Signing of Mrs. Baird's Deal," *Fort Worth Star-Telegram,* May 19, 1998, p. C1.

—Mary Tradii

Nathan's Famous, Inc.

1400 Old Country Road, Suite 400
Westbury, New York 11590
U.S.A.
(516) 338-8500
Fax: (516) 338-7220

Public Company
Founded: 1916
Employees: 690
Sales: $28.9 million (1998)
Stock Exchanges: NASDAQ
Ticker Symbol: NATH
NAIC: 722211 Limited-Service Restaurants

Nathan's Famous, Inc. is a chain of fast food restaurants, perhaps best known since its inception for its hot dogs. Since its inception, Nathan's signature product has been its hot dog, but other menu items include hamburgers, chicken strips, salads, and french fries. There are approximately 190 company-owned and franchised Nathan's outlets in 17 states, Israel, and Aruba. Whereas some Nathan's outlets are traditionally formatted restaurants, many of them are smaller and more compact—such as carts, kiosks, and snack bars. These smaller outlets often are located in nontraditional sites such as airports, schools, entertainment venues, military facilities, and convenience and department stores. Aside from the company's owned and franchised outlets, Nathan's branded products are sold through more than 500 points of distribution in 33 states and three countries. The company also is engaged in several co-branding ventures with other fast food outlets, including Burger King, TCBY, Pizza Hut, and Baskin Robbins. Under the co-branding agreements, Nathan's products are sold in its partner restaurants as a complement to their own product lines. Nathan's also owns Kenny Rogers Roasters, a 100-unit chain of chicken restaurants in the United States and Asia, and has entered into an agreement to acquire Miami Subs Corp., a chain of 194 restaurants.

Early 20th Century: Nickel Hot Dogs and Innovative Marketing

In 1915 Coney Island—a seaside resort area in Brooklyn, New York—was one of the world's largest and finest amuse-ment areas. With three amusement parks, beaches, arcades, sideshows, shooting galleries, restaurants, and saloons, the long narrow strip of land at Brooklyn's south end was a destination spot for visitors looking for fun. One of the many thousands who visited Coney Island in the summer of 1915 was Nathan Handwerker, a Polish immigrant who worked in a restaurant in downtown Manhattan. While visiting, Handwerker saw a "help wanted" sign in one of Coney Island's most popular restaurants—a large beer garden called Feltman's Restaurant. Deciding to leave Manhattan and settle in Coney Island, Handwerker took the job at Feltman's.

Handwerker's new job was to slice rolls for a kind of sandwich Feltman had invented. The sandwich, consisting of boiled tubes of spiced meat on a roll, was the hot dog—and Feltman sold them by the thousands for ten cents each. Two of Handwerker's co-workers were a pianist and a singing waiter who performed together: Jimmy Durante and Eddie Cantor. Although both Durante and Cantor later were to become well-known and successful, at the time they could not even afford the price of Feltman's hot dogs. They suggested that Handwerker start his own hot dog stand and undercut Feltman by selling the sandwiches for a nickel each.

In 1916 Handwerker and his wife, Ida, did just that. With a savings of $300, the Handwerkers bought an 8-foot by 25-foot space at the corner of Surf and Stillwell Avenues, one block from the beach. Nathan installed walk-up counters in the building and hung up big red signs that advertised his five-cent hot dogs. Ida, meanwhile, developed a spicy recipe that used all beef and lots of garlic. The Handwerkers added roast beef sandwiches, hamburgers, and french fries to the menu, and "Nathan's Famous Frankfurter & Soft Drink Stand" was launched.

Things did not go exactly as planned, however. Rather than the new stand's lower price drawing customers away from Feltman's, it instead made them suspicious about the quality of Nathan's food. Because his price was so much lower, many assumed that he must be using inferior meat. This problem was exacerbated by an already shaky public opinion of hot dogs in general. When Feltman had first started selling them, it was rumored that they were made of dog or horse meat. Although those rumors had for the most part died away, the eating public was still skeptical. Handwerker, however, believed in the quality of his product—and he came up with an ingenious way to convince others of it. He hired people to dress up as doctors, complete with lab coats and stethoscopes, and stand in front of his restaurant, eating hot dogs. Handwerker reasoned that the sight of medical professionals munching on Nathan's hot dogs would allay customers' health fears and give his restaurant the stamp of approval. To drive the point home, he posted a new sign reading, "If doctors eat our hot dogs, you know they're good!"

Another of Handwerker's innovative promotional tactics was to become deeply embedded in Coney Island culture: the Nathan's Fourth of July Hot Dog Eating Contest. The 12-minute contest to see who could eat the most hot dogs began the first year Nathan's opened. Quickly becoming an annual favorite, it drew attention, headlines, and crowds of customers.

1920s–40s: Nathan's and the Nickel Empire

If there was any question that Nathan's hot dog business was sustainable, those doubts were put to rest in the early 1920s when the New York subway system was extended to reach Coney Island. Up until then, the resort area had been patronized primarily by visitors who had private transportation—that is, those of the middle and upper classes. The subway access, however, brought in a whole new set of customers, many of whom recently had immigrated and were extremely poor. Jumping at the new opportunity afforded them, these New Yorkers fled the miserably hot city in droves each weekend for a visit to the seaside. The Coney Island crowds swelled dramatically— from approximately 500,000 visitors per day to more than a million per day. Because the subway ride to the resort cost only five cents, the Island came to be called the "Nickel Empire."

Nathan's was perfectly positioned to profit from the influx of new visitors. Its already good location at the corner of Surf and Stillwell became even better when the city built the Coney Island subway station directly across the street. Every weekend, thousands of visitors disembarked right in front of Nathan's counter. In addition, Handwerker's lower-priced hot dogs proved to be very appealing to the new cost-conscious crowd. Business picked up rapidly, and soon there were 50 employees working in the Nathan's stand. Hungry Coney Island visitors lined up at the 20-foot lunch counter until they overflowed into the street, and Nathan's sold an average of 75,000 hot dogs every summer weekend. In addition, the restaurant sold hundreds of gallons of root beer, Coca-Cola, and malted milk shakes.

During the 1920s and 1930s, while Coney Island remained a thriving hot spot, Nathan's Famous became truly famous. Poli-

ticians, sports figures, and celebrities often were photographed eating Handwerker's hot dogs during visits to the popular resort. Nathan's famous hot dogs became closely associated with Coney Island and New York—a "must-have" for any visitor to the city. As his business grew, Handwerker turned his original small lunch stand into a 30,000-square-foot restaurant.

1950s–80s: Ownership Changes

Despite their success, the Handwerkers did not attempt to expand their hot dog empire for four decades, preferring to feed the New York masses from their original Coney Island location. "Coney Island was his life," Handwerker's son, Murray, said of his father in a February 1996 interview with *Nation's Restaurant News*. "He spent almost all his time at that one store and around Coney Island." In the mid-1950s, however, Handwerker's family convinced him to open another Nathan's hot dog stand on Long Island, which had become a popular residential spot after World War II. Once started, Nathan's continued expanding at a leisurely pace, focusing mainly on properties in Brooklyn and Queens. In 1968 the small chain of eateries went public.

In the early 1970s Nathan Handwerker went into semi-retirement and his son, Murray, became the company's president. Under Murray's leadership, Nathan's began establishing restaurants in other states, including New Jersey and Connecticut. The company also grew through a series of franchise agreements in various states. By the late 1980s, Nathan's had approximately 40 restaurants.

After almost 20 years of growth as a publicly held company, Nathan's Famous went private again in early 1987, when a New York investment firm, Equicor Group Ltd., purchased all of the company's shares for $8.50 per share—a total price of around $19.5 million. The years immediately following Nathan's purchase by Equicor were rocky ones, as bad management and rising overhead led to a record loss. At the beginning of the 1990s, just when it looked as though the new owners were going to sink Nathan's, sweeping changes in management left the company in the capable hands of a new CEO and president— Wayne Norbitz.

1990–96: New Tactics

Under Norbitz's leadership, one of the company's first initiatives was to cut operating expenses dramatically. Another was an aggressive franchise drive, which enabled the chain to grow without risking its own capital. The changes were effective, and Nathan's again became profitable. In 1993 the company went public for the second time in its 77-year history. The capital raised—$15 million—enabled Nathan's to pursue further growth, opening a dozen more restaurants at various locations in the New York region.

Business in the new restaurants was uneven, however, with some locations falling short of sales expectations. Norbitz became increasingly convinced that for Nathan's to thrive, it needed to rethink its whole strategy. He felt that the company's strongest asset was its brand equity and that, therefore, its strategy should capitalize on that asset. He and his management team began to look for ways they could do just that. "Nathan's distinguished history and reputation for quality foods have enabled us to develop and maintain a strong brand identity, particularly in markets where we are best known," the company's 1994 annual report read. "The Company has used the strength of this brand equity as a cornerstone of its expansion strategy."

One of the main tenets of Nathan's new expansion strategy was to focus on captive market settings, such as airports, malls, department stores, and entertainment venues. Because space was extremely limited in these types of settings, the company began moving away from the larger, more traditional restaurant concept. Instead, it developed a line of carts, kiosks, and countertop modules—small, flexible units designed to allow for rapid and low-cost start-ups in an extremely wide range of settings. Then it began looking for likely locations— nontraditional venues where substantial traffic already existed—and forging alliances with the companies who owned those locations. Some of the company's first such alliances were with Caldor, a chain of discount department stores, Home Depot, a chain of home improvement stores, and Unocal, a chain of gas stations. By 1994, Caldor was Nathan's largest franchisee, with 57 Nathan's Famous outlets opened in their department stores. Nathan's also had ten outlets in airports, 19 in highway travel plazas, and six in gas stations by the end of 1994. Other strategic alliances included institutional food service operators, who began offering Nathan's products in stadiums, university campuses, and convention centers.

Another key tenet of the company's expansion strategy was the addition of a supermarket retail income stream. Through a licensing agreement with SMG Inc., a specialty meat packaging and distribution company, Nathan's hot dogs became available in grocery stores and supermarkets in the New York area in the early 1990s. By the mid-1990s, they were the largest selling brand in the New York supermarkets, earning Nathan's in excess of $1 million annually. In 1996 the company signed another license agreement with Gold's Pure Food Products Co Inc. to distribute Nathan's mustard and salsa in New York area stores.

By the end of 1996, Nathan's was operating 205 outlets, most of which were smaller units in nontraditional settings. Through aggressively seeking new franchise partners, the company had established a presence on eight college campuses, six racetracks, and 34 airports and travel plazas. One could also find Nathan's in convenience stores, convention centers, hotels, and bowling alleys as the company continued to tap new markets. Nathan's also initiated a co-branding strategy in 1996, bundling its products with such nationally knowns as Kentucky Fried Chicken, Pizza Hut, Burger King, and TCBY Yogurt to appeal to a broader customer base within the captive market settings.

1997–99: New Markets

In 1997 Nathan's took its brand equity marketing a step further, with a new "branded product program." The program allowed food vendors to purchase Nathan's products and offer them on their menus without paying licensing or franchise fees—a desirable option for many vendors. "In a time when consumers have clearly made their preference for branded products known, the prospect of replacing the sale of non-branded hot dogs with Nathan's has an enormous appeal," Norbitz wrote in the company's 1997 annual report.

The branded product initiative proved to be a vehicle for rapid growth. Attracted by the low-capital, low-hassle terms of the program, more than 250 new outlets had begun offering Nathan's products by the end of 1998. Including these new outlets, the number of total outlets offering Nathan's products at the close of fiscal 1998 was 491, as compared with 230 outlets at the end of the previous year.

Nathan's made another rapid jump-up in size in 1999, this time by acquiring the Kenny Rogers Roasters chain of restaurants. Roasters, which consisted of approximately 70 U.S. locations and 30 Asian locations, came under Nathan's ownership in April of 1999, for a purchase price of $1.25 million. Nathan's planned to continue to operate the Roasters chain as a wholly owned, separate subsidiary. Also in 1999, the company entered into an agreement to purchase Miami Subs Corp., a chain of 194 owned and franchised restaurants.

Future Plans

As it readied to move into the year 2000, Nathan's held out great hope for its Branded Product program, believing that there was a vast, yet untapped opportunity for growth in that area. The company also expected to continue its expansion strategy of locating in nontraditional settings and targeting captive markets. Nathan's was also pursuing new opportunities in supermarket retailing by preparing to break into the home meal replacement market—a $47 billion industry projected to grow around nine percent yearly. Nathan's planned to offer about 60 home meal replacement items in supermarkets, including mashed potatoes, creamed spinach, chicken strips, and, of course, hot dogs.

Principal Subsidiaries

N.F. Roasters Corp.; Nathan's Famous Svc. Inc.; Nathan's Famous Systems, Inc.

Further Reading

Connors, Anthony, "Why Nathan's Famous," *New York Daily News,* May 12, 1998.
Grimes, William, "A Man, a Plan, a Hot Dog: Birth of a Nathan's," *New York Times,* January 25, 1998.
Hamstra, Mark, "Nathan Handwerker," *Nation's Restaurant News,* February 1996, p. 76.
Steinberg, Carol, "Changes at Nathan's Go Beyond the Menu," *New York Times,* June 28, 1998.

—Shawna Brynildssen

National Football League

280 Park Avenue
New York, New York 10017
U.S.A.
(212) 450-2000
Fax: (212) 681-7573
Web site: http://www.nfl.com

Not-for-Profit Organization
Incorporated: 1920 as American Professional Football
   Conference
Employees: 400
Sales: $2.44 billion (1998)
NAIC: 711211 Sports Teams & Clubs

The governing body for the most popular spectator sport in the United States, the National Football League (NFL) serves as a trade association for 30 U.S.-based franchised teams and operates an American football league in Europe under the name NFL Europe League. The owners of the franchised teams operated their teams much like stand-alone businesses, but shared approximately 75 percent of their revenue with other franchises. The NFL negotiated television and radio broadcast rights for the teams and maintained the right to market team names and logos through licensing agreements.

Origins

American football evolved as a hybrid of soccer and rugby during the early 1870s, gaining distinction from its two influences in 1876 when the first rules for the sport were written. By the 1890s, the new version of football was a popular activity at local athletic clubs, particularly in Pennsylvania where intense rivalry between two clubs led to the first payment to a player. In 1892 William ''Pudge'' Heffelfinger was paid $500 by the Allegheny Athletic Association to play one game against rival Pittsburgh Athletic Club, marking the advent of professionalism in American football. Five years later, the Latrobe Athletic Association football team comprised entirely professional players, becoming the first team to field professionals for a full season. Other purely professional football clubs were organized in the ensuing years, as the epicenter of football activity moved from Pennsylvania to Ohio. Ohio was home to at least seven professional teams during the first decade of the 20th century, but the growth of football in Ohio and elsewhere bred a host of problems, each attributable to the professionalism that spurred the sport's growth. As the number of professional teams proliferated and competition became more heated, the salaries paid to players escalated rapidly. The lure of these rising salaries prompted players to switch continually from one team to another, going wherever the highest bid beckoned. In the search for talent, football clubs began scouting college players, hiring some while the players were still enrolled in school. The outbreak of these problems created confusion within the sport, compounded by the widely varying schedules each team maintained. By the end of the 1910s, there was need for order and discipline, for the establishment of a uniform set of rules and conduct that would govern the sport. The strongest cries for organization and structure emanated from the stronghold of professional football in Ohio, where the foundation for the NFL was laid.

Several attempts to organize a professional football league had been made early in the century, but each had failed until an attempt to form a league took root in 1920. In August the first organizational meeting for what later became the NFL was held in Canton, Ohio, at the Jordan and Hupmobile automobile showroom. In attendance were representatives of the Akron Pros, the Canton Bulldogs (arguably the best professional team in the country) the Cleveland Indians, and the Dayton Triangles. Their meeting marked the establishment of the American Professional Football Conference, which one month later at a second meeting was renamed the American Professional Football Association (APFA). At the second meeting, also held in Canton, the participants of the first meeting were joined by representatives of teams from three other states, including Indiana's Muncie Flyers, the Rochester Jeffersons from New York, and the Racine Cardinals from Illinois.

1920s: The NFL Takes Shape

By the end of the APFA's first year, there were 14 teams within the league, but the scheduling of games, both the overall number of games and the number of games contested between APFA teams, was left for each team to decide on its own. The league did not begin to exert control over its constituents until its second year of operation when a new president, Joe Carr of the Columbus Panhandles, was elected at the APFA meeting in April 1921. Carr, who presided over the league for the ensuing 18 years, became the NFL's first architect, establishing the framework that gave the league control over affiliated teams. He made his mark early in his tenure, drafting a league constitution during his first year in office. Carr also developed bylaws, assigned teams territorial rights, restricted player movements, and developed membership criteria for team franchises. Carr's inaugural year also included the debut of league standings, which enabled the designation of a league champion— previously an issue of considerable debate. In 1922, by which time membership within the league had increased to 22 teams, the APFA was renamed the National Football League.

Carr continued to give shape and structure to the NFL during the 1920s, making alterations that would endure for decades. He instituted the first roster limit (16) in 1925, and in 1927 resolved a fundamental weakness of the league by eliminating the financially weaker teams and consolidating the more talented players into a reduced number of financially stronger teams. Carr's most critical changes occurred during the 1930s, when the nation sank into a deep economic depression. The pernicious economic environment whittled the number of league teams to eight in 1932, the lowest during the 20th century, but amid the despair the NFL achieved important strides. In 1932 the first tie for first place occurred, prompting the need for the first NFL play-off game. The following year, Carr labored to give the NFL its own identity. Since its inception, the NFL generally had followed the rules of college football, but in 1933 Carr began developing separate rules that addressed the needs and style of the professional game. Some of these changes were born from the first championship game in 1932, which had to be held indoors because of freezing temperatures and heavy snow. The alterations included hashmarks and goal posts fixed on the goal line rather than the end-line, both of which were innovations required because of the limited space available for the 1932 championship game. Further, the forward pass was legalized from any point behind the line of scrimmage. Organizationally, the league was divided into two divisions in 1933, the Western and Eastern divisions, with the winners of each scheduled to meet in an annual championship game. The NFL also took charge of an annual draft of college players, instituted for the first time in 1936, the same year all member teams played the same amount of games in one year for the first time. The decade ended with Carr's death and the first television broadcast of a NFL game. In 1939 NBC aired a game between the Brooklyn Dodgers and the Philadelphia Eagles, at a time when there were 1,000 television sets in New York.

By the end of the 1930s, the NFL played a vital role in the sport of football, lending cohesion and legitimacy to what was becoming a national pastime. From the legacy of Carr's achievements, the NFL gained the structure to support its increasing influence over the game during the postwar period, when football developed into a multibillion-dollar business. One of the chief factors igniting such growth was the increasing fees paid by broadcasters to air NFL games. The value of radio and television deals increased in part because of the expansion

of the NFL. From its early strength in Ohio, football, in terms of its popularity, moved eastward into the large cities following Carr's consolidation of the league in 1927. In 1946 the NFL became national in scope for the first time when the Cleveland Rams moved to Los Angeles. In 1950 the Los Angeles Rams became the first team to have all of their home and away games televised, an arrangement other teams secured as the 1950s progressed. Following the promulgation of a congressional bill legalizing single-network television contracts by professional sports leagues in 1961, the NFL reached a single-network agreement with CBS in 1962 for broadcasting all regular season games. The NFL-CBS contract, valued at $4.6 million annually, marked the beginning of an ever-increasing bidding war waged by the networks to secure the rights for NFL games. Two years later, CBS paid $14.1 million for broadcasting rights.

The exponentially increasing television deals were indicative of the growing popularity of football. By the mid-1960s, football was the country's favorite sport, eclipsing baseball (41 percent to 38 percent, according to a survey) for the first time. To take advantage of the widespread interest in the sport, the NFL developed ancillary businesses for the modern, lucrative era of football. In 1963 the league formed NFL Properties, Inc. to serve as the licensing arm of the NFL. The following year, the league purchased Ed Sabol's Blair Motion Pictures, renaming it NFL Films. Football's growth in popularity and its attendant revenue-generating potential also spawned the organization of competing leagues, nothing new to the NFL. Since its inception, the league had butted against rival leagues, including four leagues—each named the American Football League— between 1920 and 1940. By the 1960s, however, a new version of the American Football League (AFL) had taken root and proved to be a meddlesome entity with which the NFL was force to contend. Rivalry between the two leagues was litigious, resulting in an antitrust suit filed by the AFL against the NFL during the early 1960s. The legal battle dragged on for nearly four years, with the courts ultimately ruling against the AFL, but the ruling did not signal the end of the AFL. The rival league continued to flourish, securing a $36 million, five-year deal with NBC for television rights beginning in 1965. The resilience of the AFL led to a series of secret meetings between two team owners from the two leagues in 1966. Their discussions centered on a potential merger between the AFL and NFL, which was announced in mid-1966. Under the terms of the agreement, the merger created an expanded league comprising 24 teams, although the two leagues maintained separate schedules until they officially merged in 1970 to form one league with two conferences. In the interim, the two leagues played a World Championship Game, beginning in January 1967, the first of what later became known as the Super Bowl.

Rozelle Leads PostWar Growth

Overseeing the merger between the AFL and the NFL was Pete Rozelle, who held the title of NFL commissioner. Rozelle was selected as commissioner in 1960 and held the same title after the merger. Rozelle's tenure, which stretched until 1989, was as influential on the development of the NFL as Carr's effect on the league. When Rozelle took control, he inherited a fragmented league in which the team owners maintained substantial control. The league governed the game, but the team owners operated their franchises essentially like stand-alone businesses. Operating as such, the teams negotiated individually with broadcasters for the rights to air games, a state of affairs Rozelle disliked. He perceived a sporting event's greatest strength as representing a piece of programming and, to give the sport its greatest bargaining power when negotiating with broadcasters, he realized that the franchises needed to cease operating as fiefdoms and combine their strength under the NFL. To accomplish this, Rozelle convinced the owners to share their broadcasting revenue evenly among all franchises and to give the NFL control over negotiating broadcasting rights. Rozelle accomplished this diplomatic feat during the early 1960s, fueling the dramatic rise in broadcasting rights during the early part of the decade. Broadcasters, in the wake of Rozelle's shrewd maneuver, found themselves, in the words of one broadcasting executive, with "about as much clout as the Dalai Lama has dealing with the Chinese army."

Rozelle transformed football into big business, taking a league that along with its franchises generated less than $20 million annually in 1960 and developing it into a multibillion-a-year business by the end of his stewardship as commissioner. He did so by acting as a skilled promoter of the game, which again was a product of his emphasis on football as a piece of programming. With the millions of dollars the networks were paying for the rights to the NFL, they were obliged to promote the game themselves to ensure the success of their investment. Together with Roone Arledge, the head of ABC Sports, Rozelle created Monday Night Football, which debuted on ABC in 1970 and developed into one of the longest-running shows in the history of television. Rozelle also expanded, moving into new markets—a new term in the sports world—with the establishment of a franchise in New Orleans in 1967 and in Tampa Bay and Seattle in 1976. The NFL expanded internationally as well, playing its first game outside North America in 1976, when a preseason match was played in Korakuen Stadium in Tokyo.

Among the list of achievements during Rozelle's 29-year career as commissioner, the NFL also suffered its low points. Two players' strikes in 1982 and 1987 marred the league's otherwise strident progress. A litigious relationship with a rival league, the United States Football League (USFL), also diverted the league's attention, resulting in a $1.7 billion antitrust lawsuit filed against the league. The jury rejected all of the USFL's television-related claims in 1986, however. The 1980s also bore witness to a contentious battle between the NFL and the owner of the Oakland Raiders, Al Davis, formerly head of the AFL. Davis, who wanted to move his team to Los Angeles, prevailed, despite repeated attempts by the NFL to stop the team's reloca-

tion. In addition, television ratings for the NFL dipped during the mid-1980s amid escalating expenses arising from increasing player salaries. Integral to the league's ability to withstand the turbulence was the willingness of broadcasters to pay increasing amounts for the right to air NFL games, upon which Rozelle had predicated the league's success. Toward this end, the league demonstrated encouraging vibrancy by the end of the 1980s. When Rozelle retired in 1989, a new four-year contract was signed with the three major networks, ABC, CBS, NBC, and two cable networks, ESPN and TNT, valued at $3.6 billion, the largest in television history.

Rozelle's successor, Paul Tagliabue, took charge of the league in 1989, becoming the seventh chief executive to lead the NFL. Under Tagliabue's control, the NFL expanded during the 1990s, both domestically and abroad. In 1991 the NFL decided to expand to 30 franchises, leading to the debut of the Jacksonville Jaguars and the Carolina Panthers in 1994. The league also launched the World League of American Football in 1991, after years of staging preseason games at international venues. When the new league began playing Europe, the NFL became the first sports league to operate on a weekly basis on two continents. Initially, the World League faltered, taking a two-year hiatus before resuming operation as the NFL Europe League in 1998. Although the NFL continued to contend with rising player salaries—a perennial problem predating the league's existence—broadcasters consistently demonstrated a willingness to keep pace with the league's rising expenses by paying vast sums for broadcasting rights. In 1998, as the NFL prepared for the century ahead, the market value of its programming showed no signs of weakening in the least. In a record-setting, eight-year deal with ABC, FOX, CBS, and ESPN, the networks paid a staggering $17.6 billion for the broadcast rights to NFL games. Clearly, the strength of NFL programming was sufficient to ensure the league's continued success into the next millennium.

Principal Divisions

NFL Enterprises; NFL Properties; NFL Charities.

Further Reading

"League's 1991 Sales Show No Recession," *Sporting Goods Business,* December 1991, p. 14.
Lewis, Michael, "High Commissioner—Pete Rozelle," *Time,* December 7, 1998, p. 188.
"NFL Sacks Itself," *Fortune,* January 21, 1985, p. 10.

—Jeffrey L. Covell

National Record Mart, Inc.

507 Forest Avenue
Carnegie, Pennsylvania 15106
U.S.A.
(412) 276-6200
Fax: (412) 276-6201
Web site: http://www.nrmmusic.com

Public Company
Incorporated: 1937
Employees: 1,305
Sales: $129.9 million (1999)
Stock Exchanges: NASDAQ
Ticker Symbol: NRMI
NAIC: 45122 Prerecorded Tape, Compact Disc & Record
   Stores

With origins in the late 1930s, National Record Mart, Inc. (NRM) was the first music-store chain in the United States and is the nation's fourth largest specialty retailer of prerecorded music. NRM owns about 175 stores in 30 states, most of which are in the eastern half of the country. The company operates within five different store concepts: National Record Mart stores (targeting 12- to 24-year-olds and usually located in shopping malls), Waves (appealing to an adult market and positioned in upscale specialty stores), Music Oasis (the largest of the company's stores, either located in strip malls or freestanding, and appealing to a broad range of price-oriented consumers), Vibes (targeting college students and located on campuses), and Music X (''alternative music'' stores based in malls). NRM also sells music online through two Web sites, where online shoppers can purchase new and used music products, download songs, and create customized CDs. The company is run by Chairman and CEO William Teitelbaum, who owns a 32 percent share in the company.

From Jitterbug Records to National Record Mart

National Record Mart began when Hyman Shapiro and his sons Sam and Howard decided to meet public demand for a store selling prerecorded music, a relatively new concept at the time. In 1937, the Shapiros opened their first music store, a tiny storeroom in downtown Pittsburgh called Jitterbug Records. The store sold used jukebox records—78 rpm ''shallac'' records—priced at one for a dime or two for 25 cents. The company had relatively little competition during this time, as prerecorded music was marketed through music sections in variety and department stores.

By 1941, the Shapiros had begun marketing new records in its original store as well as in two new stores, all three of which were renamed National Record Mart. Growth on a grander scale ensued during the postwar economic boom, and the stores began offering the 45 rpm records popular with American youth, in addition to the then-standard 33 rpm record albums. Hyman Shapiro's youngest son, Jason, became involved in the family business during this time, as did another key figure in the company's development. Around 1951, the company hired a teenaged Frank Fischer to wash windows and floors part-time at a Pittsburgh store location; after studying music at a local college, and following a stint in the armed forces, Fischer became a National Record Mart store manager and would eventually move through the ranks to become company president.

By the 1960s, the chain of National Record Mart stores totalled 20, all located in and around Pittsburgh. As the enclosed shopping mall came to replace downtown shopping districts as the preferred consumer outlet, new National Record Mart stores were more frequently established in malls. The company also kept pace with new technology in the industry; the development of stereo and quadrophonic sound meant enhanced product lines at National Record Mart stores.

In the 1970s, the retail chain expanded beyond Pennsylvania's borders, establishing locations in malls in Roanoake, Virginia, Buffalo, New York, and Chicago. By mid-decade, company founder Hymen Shapiro had retired, handing control of his company over to his three sons, who oversaw expansion to a total of 38 stores. In 1978, the Shapiros opened the company's first entertainment superstore, Oasis Records and Tapes, the name reflecting the growing importance of cassette tapes in the industry.

Still, the company remained a closely-held family operation into the 1980s, and expansion was slow and careful, with annual sales of about $40 million. The music-store chain had grown to 76 stores by 1986, when the Shapiro brothers were ready to retire. That year, the Shapiros sold the company to a group of investors, including the sons and daughters of the Shapiro brothers, headed by William A. Teitelbaum for about $10 million.

New Ownership in the 1980s

The 33-year-old Teitelbaum had little music experience at the time of the sale. A New York native and former polo player, Teitelbaum began his career in the finance department of L.F. Rothschild and later became a partner at Bear Stearns and Company, a financial services holding company. Teitelbaum was also the chairman and sole shareholder of the investment firm Remsen Partners, Ltd., and the sole director of Vista Properties Inc.

When he purchased National Record Mart, Teitelbaum admitted that he could not name a single artist on the alternative top ten list. ''I had to slowly learn the industry,'' he explained in the *Pittsburgh Business Times,* adding ''I had to make the change from looking at a green computer screen to understanding people.'' Nevertheless, Teitelbaum felt the time was right to enter the prerecorded music industry, which was on the brink of a transformation. Breakthroughs in digital technology were about to make magnetic media a thing of the past. Teitelbaum predicted that music-lovers would soon discard their records and tapes in favor of compact discs (CDs), which offered superior sound.

Teitelbaum's first attempt into the music industry in 1981 had failed. At that time he had tried to buy the CBS music library when it went up for sale. CBS was asking $100 million for the intellectual rights to all of its recordings, and the new owner would collect royalties every time the recordings were played. However, Teitelbaum could not persuade Bear Stearns to purchase the music library. So, in 1986, Teitelbaum and a group of investors purchased National Record Mart.

Plans for growing the company included aggressive expansion efforts to double the company's store total to 200; acquisition of small and mid-sized chains; aggressive advertising campaigns; and the introduction of a new concept store called Waves, which would eschew record albums in favor of CDs and cassette tapes. As the company celebrated its 50th anniversary, under new ownership but the constant leadership of President Frank Fischer, National Record Mart was ranked as the tenth-largest music retailer in the country by *Billboard* magazine. A new company logo, using the acronym NRM, was implemented, in an effort to eradicate the increasingly dated ''record'' from the company's name.

Despite high expectations, Teitelbaum's first few years with National Record Mart were not easy. The heavy debt the company assumed during the leveraged buyout, and its expensive plans for expansion, almost pulled it under. In 1991, industry experts predicted National Record Mart would file for Chapter 11 protection. However, Teitelbaum was determined to save the company. He sold off 20 stores to W.H. Smith's music chain, The Wall, for about $12 million.

The sale generated enough money for National Record Mart to go public. In June 1993, the company sold 1.7 million shares, which generated $10 million in capital that was used to pay off $3 million in debt. A few months later, the company switched bankers from Equibank to Barclay's of London, which gave National Record Mart a new $17 million revolving line of credit. With the profits from the initial offering and the new line of credit, the company was able to purchase the nine-unit Leonard Smith music chain, increasing the number of stores to 118.

The music industry considered Teitelbaum's turnaround of National Record Mart one of the most successful in the history of the industry. The National Association of Recording Merchandisers nominated National Record Mart for ''Retailer of the Year.'' While the company did not win the coveted title, Teitelbaum presented each of his managers with a ''retailer of the year'' trophy for his or her outstanding effort.

Teitelbaum's turnaround of National Record Mart did not last long, however, as changes in the industry put a strain on the company. Specifically, large discounters, such as Circuit City, Wal-Mart, Kmart, and Best Buy, began selling prerecorded music at prices lower than the specialty store chains could offer. Many of National Record Mart's competitors filed for Chapter 11 protection during this time. Nevertheless, in 1996, Teitelbaum described the prerecorded music industry as challenging and remained optimistic. He assembled a new management team and hoped to profit from the folding of many competitors.

Teitelbaum also capitalized on changing demographics; as the baby boomers aged, the company shifted its focus away from teenagers and onto older, wealthier shoppers, aged 24 to 54. In 1996, the company refurbished its Waves Music stores, which targeted adult shoppers, to feature dome-shaped listening centers and interactive ''Intranet'' kiosks that allowed customers to download news and information about their favorite performers from the World Wide Web. Finally, Teitelbaum tried to attract patronage with exceptional customer service, something customers would not necessarily receive when they shopped at the superstores.

Some industry experts criticized Teitelbaum's plans for failing to focus on increasing the number of stores in the chain. Competitors such as Musicland, Camelot, Transworld, and The Wiz were expanding aggressively in an effort to generate sales. Teitelbaum quoted Muhammad Ali, saying he planned to ''Let the other guy punch himself out.'' He added that while he did plan to expand the company, he would do so at a conservative, reduced rate. He planned to save money by purchasing existing stores instead of building new ones. He insisted that the company grow slowly and ''absorb the body blows'' of its competitors.

This strategy proved foresighted, and it worked—for a while. While its competitors began to fold, NRM went from being the nation's ninth-largest prerecorded music retailer to its sixth-largest, just by avoiding bankruptcy. Then, however, the competition became tougher, and NRM struggled. Large bookstore chains, such as Borders and Barnes and Noble, began selling prerecorded music, and in 1996, NRM lost more than $3.8 million on sales of $99.08 million. The following year, the company lost more than $1.1 million on sales of $99.43 million. Even though NRM was floundering, it had assumed less debt than its competitors.

During this time, NRM, backed by an unidentified investment firm, put in a bid for $80 million to purchase the 296-chain Wherehouse Entertainment. Industry experts doubted whether NRM—a company only one-quarter of Wherehouse's size—could raise the funds needed to buy the chain, which was operating under Chapter 11 protection at the time. The deal eventually fell through.

By 1997, the tables had turned and many in the industry believed NRM would be purchased by Wherehouse, which had emerged from Chapter 11 well-positioned with a great deal of cash. Industry trade publications speculated that the two companies would merge. In 1998, Teitelbaum confirmed that Cerberus Partners, Ltd., the New York Investment branch of a Bahamas-based company that owned the majority of Wherehouse, had purchased about 134,000 shares—more than three percent—of NRM's stock. Teitelbaum remained chairman and CEO of the company. He turned the role of the president over to Larry Mundorf, until the latter's resignation a year later at which time he assumed the presidency as well.

New Technologies and Products for a New Century

NRM entered into the online music business in 1998 when it launched two Web sites: http://www. wavesmusic.com and http://www. nrmmusic.com. Teitelbaum hoped the sites would prove superior to those offered by such competitors as K-Tel International, a music publisher and record producer based in Plymouth, Maine. Online shoppers accessing NRM's Web sites could initially select from over 25,000 titles. They could use the sites as "trading posts" to purchase and sell used products, download songs, and create customized CDs from more than 28,000 selections. NRM's sites also allowed dealers to sell overstocked CDs at reduced rates instead of shipping the CDs back to the manufacturer. The company received a percentage of the sales generated from these CDs.

Teitelbaum hoped the Web sites would open a new market for NRM, and he believed the Web sites could effectively compete with music mail-order companies rather than with the company's own retail stores. Around the same time, NRM signed letters to purchase 23 more stores, most of which were operating under the name Tempo Music. This purchase gave the company access to new markets in Hawaii and California and added $14 million in annual sales to the coffers.

In an attempt to diversify the offerings of its online service, NRM formed a partnership with Titan Sport, better known as the World Wrestling Federation (WWF), in March 1999. The partnership made NRM's Web site the exclusive sale source for certain limited edition WWF products. NRM's Web site was advertised on the WWF's site (wwf.com) as well as during WWF television programs. The company's partnership with the WWF increased customer hits on its Web site by 50 percent.

By mid-1999, NRM was maintaining about 175 stores in 30 states and had reported a modest increase in sales. The company had learned from its many ups and downs that to stay afloat in the prerecorded music industry, it had to adapt to industry and technological changes, which were often sudden and unpredictable. While NRM has proven it can survive in tumultuous times, the outlook for the specialty prerecorded music-store chains remained uncertain as the company moved into a new century.

Principal Divisions

NRM Music; Waves Music; Music Oasis; Vibes Music; Music X.

Further Reading

Allan, William, "National Record Mart Booming," *Pittsburgh Press,* August 13, 1985.

Christman, Ed, and Don Jeffrey, "National Record Mart Enters Agreement to Purchase Smith Chain," *Billboard,* November 27, 1993, p. 3.

Christman, Ed, and Jeff Clark-Meads, "National Record Mart Selling 20 Stores to W.H. Smith," *Billboard,* February 8, 1992, p. 4.

Christman, Ed, "Growth in Off(er)ing at Record Mart; Retailer Plans New Stores, Tests Video," *Billboard,* August 21, 1993, p. 45.

——, "National Record Mart Completes Turnaround," *Billboard,* August 7, 1993, p. 42.

——, "National Record Mart Makes $80 Million Bid on Debt-Ridden Wherehouse Chain," *Billboard,* February 3, 1996.

——, "National Record Mart Marks 60 Years, Latest Gains," *Billboard,* August 16, 1997, p. 49.

——, "National Record Mart to Stay Out of Retail Wars," *Billboard,* July 29, 1995, p. 81.

——, "NRM Selling 20 Stores to W.H. Smith," *Billboard,* February 8, 1992, p. 4.

Conley, Keri, "National Record Mart's Chief Writes a New Score," *Pittsburgh Business Times,* January 30, 1995, p. 6.

Fitzpatrick, Dan, "NRM Wants to Play Dirge for Competitors; Money Woes of Music Retailing May Help Local Firm Rise Above it All," *Pittsburgh Business Times,* January 2, 1998, p. 3.

Jeffrey, Don, "National Record Mart Posts Gains," *Billboard,* August 20, 1994, p. 72.

——, "National Record Mart's Fiscal Year Shows Mixed Picture," *Billboard,* May 6, 1995, p. 49.

Lindman, Teresa F., "Carnegie, PA-Based Music Retailer Signs Deal with Wrestling Federation," *Knight-Ridder/Tribune Business News,* April 13, 1999.

"National Record Mart Agrees to Acquire up to 23 Stores, Expands Stock Repurchase Program," *Business Wire,* September 24, 1998, p.1114.

"National Record Mart Inks Deal with World Wrestling Federation to be Exclusive Music Retailer for 'wwf.com.' " *PR Newswire,* April 13, 1999.

Ranii, David, "National Record Mart Moves Feet to Sound of Growth," *Pittsburgh Press,* November 22, 1987, pp. D22, D28.

Tascarella, Patty, "Competitor Buys Into NRM; Is Takeover Next?," *Pittsburgh Business Times,* May 8, 1998, p. 1.

——, "National Record Mart Embraces the Web; Retailer Plans to Maintain Recent Acquisition Mode," *Pittsburgh Business Times,* December 4, 1998, p. 3.

——, "National Record Mart Mum on Competitor, Takeover Talks," *Pittsburgh Business Times,* May 13, 1995, p. 1.

—Tracey Vasil Biscontini

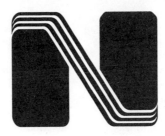

Nebraska Public Power District

1414 15th Street
Columbus, Nebraska 68602
U.S.A.
(402) 563-5690
(800) 282-6773
Fax: (402) 563-5653
Web site: http://www.nppd.com

Private Company
Founded: 1940 as the Nebraska Public Power System
Employees: 2,100
Sales: $494 million (1998)
NAIC: 221112 Fossil Fuel Electric Power Generation;
 221111 Hydroelectric Power Generation; 221113
 Nuclear Electric Power Generation

The Nebraska Public Power District (NPPD) generates and distributes electricity to about one million Nebraskans in 91 of the state's 93 counties, including customers in more than 205 retail communities, 69 wholesale communities, and 25 rural cooperatives and public power districts. About 60 percent of its power comes from coal plants, with 20 percent from hydroelectric plants, and 20 percent from its one nuclear power plant. NPPD and other public power districts make Nebraska the only state served entirely by public power.

Conversion to Public Power in the Early 20th Century

Nebraska and the other Great Plains states were the last settled by American pioneers. During much of the 1800s it was called the "Great American Desert" and simply bypassed. Even after farmers began moving there after the Civil War, many suffered from drought, temperature extremes, and loneliness. For many years few Nebraskans had access to modern technology, including electrical power.

In the late 1800s Nebraskans began irrigating, but by the early 20th century they realized the limits of getting water from the North and South Platte Rivers. This increased demand for irrigation water and electrical power eventually led to the creation of public power in Nebraska.

Before 1930 few Nebraskans realized the state's potential for hydroelectric power, with plants in the Platte River Basin producing only 10,446 horsepower. But successful power production owned by Nebraska municipalities in the 1920s influenced many to favor publicly owned power over private utilities. With the support of Nebraska's U.S. Senator George Norris, a 1932 federal law allowed the Reconstruction Finance Corporation to provide loans to public entities for irrigation and hydroelectric projects.

In 1933 the Nebraska legislature passed a law allowing the creation of public power/irrigation districts if 15 percent of an area's voters signed a petition submitted to the Nebraska Department of Roads and Irrigation. Although private utilities opposed this law, it opened the door to start public corporations to increase access to water and electricity, both in short supply in many areas of Nebraska during the Great Depression.

Residents in Columbus, Nebraska organized first with the 1933 formation of the Loup River Public Power District. With federal money, construction of a hydroelectric plant began on the Loup River in 1934 and by 1937 the plant was operational. Its sole purpose was to produce electricity.

Meanwhile, the North Platte-based Platte Valley Public Power and Irrigation District was organized in 1933 to produce both power and irrigation water. Construction began in 1934 and was completed in 1936. The new Sutherland Reservoir held about 175,000 acre-feet of water. This effort, often called the Sutherland project, served those in Keith, Dawson, Lincoln, Buffalo, and Hall counties.

The third public power district in Nebraska faced more difficulties than did the first two. To serve Adams, Gosper, Phelps, and Kearney counties, the Central Nebraska Public Power and Irrigation District based in Hastings was organized in late 1933, but it had to resubmit its plans before the federal Public Works Administration finally approved it in 1935. Construction of the Kingsley Dam on the North Platte River near Ogallala started in

---

Company Perspectives:

As we enter a new era of deregulation and competition, we are presented with a unique opportunity to provide even more services to Nebraskans. However, to compete successfully in the years ahead, we must develop stronger name recognition, higher awareness levels and increase our identity across the state as Nebraska Public Power District, Nebraska's Energy Leader.

1938; power was first generated in 1941; and the project finally was completed a year or two later. Much more expensive than the first two projects, the Central Nebraska project cost $38 million. The new dam produced 233 million kilowatt-hours annually. According to Olson's state history, the Kingsley Dam was "the second largest earthen dam in the world." It measured three miles long, 162 feet high, and 1,100 feet wide at the bottom. It also created Lake McConaughy with its 105-mile shoreline, one of Nebraska's major recreational spots.

In the late 1930s Nebraska's hydroelectric power districts tried in vain to buy private utility companies to increase their production and marketing. So in August 1939 the Nebraska Legislature created Consumers Public Power District. Over the next two years it purchased for about $44.5 million most remaining private power firms using revenue bonds.

In 1940 the Loup River, Platte Valley, and Central Nebraska public power districts signed a joint agreement that created the Nebraska Public Power System (NPPS) that combined their production and revenues under one management board comprised of the general managers of the three power districts. Central in 1949 withdrew from NPPS to focus on irrigation; it sold its hydro generation to NPPS.

In the 1930s rural Nebraska began to organize rural power districts that used federal funds from the Rural Electrification Administration, created by President Franklin Roosevelt with support from Senator Norris. From just 5.8 percent of Nebraska's farms having electricity in 1929, by the early 1950s about 78 percent enjoyed that benefit supplied by about 30 rural power districts.

To represent the increasing number of public power agencies across the nation, including thousands of municipal-owned systems, the federal Tennessee Valley Authority, and area-wide entities like those in Nebraska, in 1940 the American Public Power Association (APPA) was founded. Since that time, it has provided research, training, and counseling for public power agencies seeking support in their ongoing dealings with government and private utilities.

In 1945 the Omaha Public Power District was organized, and the following year it purchased the Nebraska Power Company, a subsidiary of American Power and Light and Electric Bond and Share Company (EBASCO). The Omaha district serving Douglas, Dodge, Sarpy, Saunders, and Washington counties had its own generating plants but sometimes bought power from the interconnected hydroelectric power districts.

Thus Nebraska became the only state in the nation where public power totally replaced private utility companies.

Some Americans criticized the public power movement, however, as a form of socialism or even communism. Omaha Senator J. P. O'Furey said public power districts would "set up a group of communistic super states that rival Soviet Russia for nefariousness," according to Donald E. Schaufelberger.

Post-World War II Developments

Economic expansion in Nebraska following World War II resulted in a doubling of power demands from 1948 to 1951. Demand again doubled from 1952 to 1957. As World War II veterans got married, raised families, and needed employment and new housing, increased power demands were not surprising. It was the Baby Boom era in American history.

To meet the demands for more power, the Consumers District proposed building its own generating facilities, but that conflicted with its distribution mission. Litigation resulted over Consumers' right to build energy producing plants. In 1956 the Nebraska Supreme Court ruled that Consumers could generate its own power, so Consumers moved ahead with its plans for a 100,000-kilowatt steam plant near Hallam, along with its 75,000-kilowatt Hallam Nuclear Power Facility built as an experimental plant for the former Atomic Energy Commission, later renamed the Nuclear Regulatory Commission. Once the AEC gained the information it needed, it decommissioned the nuclear part of what became known as the Sheldon Station. In 1961 the coal and gas-fired part of the Sheldon Station began generating power. It was upgraded in 1968 with a second generator and boiler that brought its capacity to 225,000 kilowatts.

From 1952 to 1956 many conflicts occurred between Nebraska's power districts. The state legislature in 1965 tried to merge some generation and transmission facilities by passing legislation, but that effort failed when the legislation was thrown out by the courts. After these merger efforts mandated by state law failed, negotiations began in the 1960s to find ways of voluntarily merging the power districts.

NPPD in the 1970s and 1980s

In the late 1960s negotiations began that culminated in the creation of the Nebraska Public Power District in 1970. The first step was finalized on June 1, 1967 when Loup River Public Power District and the Consumers Public Power District made an important trade. Loup took over Consumers' retail distribution properties in Nance, Platte, Colfax, and Boone counties, while Consumers replaced Loup as the partner of the Platte Valley Public Power and Irrigation District in operating the Nebraska Public Power System.

The second and final step began July 5, 1968 when the directors of both Consumers and Platte agreed to merge. A joint statement from both districts read, "We have long been aware that the State would be better served by one centrally directed power district providing large scale generation and transmission." Completed on January 1, 1970, NPPS and Platte were merged into Consumers, with the new utility named the Nebraska Public Power District. It served 85 of Nebraska's 93 counties and parts of two other counties. Nebraska's other counties received electricity from the Omaha Public Power District.

NPPD ended the waste, duplication, and legal conflicts that had occurred when Consumers and NPPS had built separate facilities to serve their customers living in the same area. ''In one short month, the management and directorate of NPPD have swept aside many of the petty irritations of the past, and cleared the way to concentrate on its paramount consideration of providing the best and least expensive electrical service that is humanly possible . . . ,'' stated a *Nebraska State Journal* editorial on February 2, 1970.

NPPD's creation united some 1,400 employees under one management team. In 1970 NPPD's combined assets of generating, transmitting, and irrigating properties totaled nearly $588 million. By 1983 NPPD's assets reached about $1.7 billion.

In 1974 NPPD began operating its largest plant, the Cooper Nuclear Station (CNS) next to the Missouri River near Brownville in southeastern Nebraska. Located on a 1,351-acre site, NPPD's only nuclear reactor used uranium fission to produce steam to turn the plant's electrical power producing turbines. Used uranium fuel rods were stored on site, while the federal government made plans to eventually store such high-radiation wastes in a permanent facility elsewhere.

The Cooper plant produced 801 megawatts of electricity. Half that output was sold to Iowa's MidAmerican Energy Company, and the Lincoln Electric System purchased 12.5 percent. NPPD and other utilities used the rest of the nuclear plant's power.

By 1983 NPPD employed about 2,000 individuals and provided them an annual payroll of nearly $47 million. It owned or controlled 33 plants with a generating capacity of more than 2.7 million kilowatts, including the state's largest coal plant, the 1,300-megawatt Gerald Gentleman Station at the Sutherland Reservoir. It also owned more than 6,000 miles of transmission lines. NPPD purchased some hydroelectric power from the Western Area Power Administration and also was interconnected as a member of the Mid-Continent Area Power Pool in eight upper Midwestern states.

In the late 1980s NPPD's major project was building a $700 million, 500,000-volt transmission line called the MANDAN Project linking the Canadian province of Manitoba with the Dakotas and Nebraska. Instead of building new generating plants, the 600-mile line allowed northern areas with surplus power in summer months to send that power south and vice-versa.

Challenges in the 1990s

After several fines for violating federal safety regulations of its nuclear plant, NPPD replaced its management in 1994. In 1996, however, the Nuclear Regulatory Commission (NRC) threatened to fine NPPD $50,000 for another violation. An NRC inspector in November 1995 found that the plant's main steam tunnel blowout panels had been improperly modified in 1985 and had not been approved by the NRC. The panels were designed to relieve steam pressure to maintain the integrity of the nuclear reactor's primary containment area. This level III violation (level I being the most serious) was corrected in the fall of 1995 after it was first reported, which helped the NRC cancel the fine.

In 1995 NPPD hired William R. Mayben of Mercer Island, Washington as its new president and CEO. A professional electrical engineer, Mayben had worked since 1962 for Seattle's R. W. Beck, a consulting firm specializing in public power. Mayben often had consulted with NPPD on its projects, since he had worked at Beck's office in Columbus, Nebraska from 1968 to 1980. In 1987 Mayben became Beck's CEO.

Electrical utilities across the nation faced new challenges in the 1990s from government deregulation. The federal government in 1992 passed a law permitting competition in purchasing wholesale electricity. California became the first state to take this option when it passed energy deregulation legislation in 1996. By December 1998, 12 states had passed laws giving consumers retail power choices. The idea was to increase competition by ending the virtual monopoly enjoyed by private and public power companies in their respective areas.

Since Nebraskans paid average electrical rates about 20 percent lower than average private utilities, many opposed deregulation or said public power could compete, if required, against private power. Others argued that it would be wise to sell public power facilities to private investors, thus gaining money for government through the sale of assets as well as through taxes on private utilities. Public power entities paid no federal or state taxes.

In any case, private utilities prepared to compete against public power in Nebraska. For example, UtiliCorp United, a $1.5 billion private electricity and natural gas firm in Kansas City, Missouri, sought to expand into new markets like Nebraska. ''The 1990s are a time of change,'' said Dave Penn, the APPA's deputy executive director, in the March 10, 1996 *Omaha World-Herald.* ''I caution people to not be blind to the fact that retail [electrical] competition is developing, but don't go off the cliff with the herd thinking it's inevitable.''

In 1996 the Nebraska legislature created a 41-member advisory group to study the energy deregulation controversy. ''This is going to be the historic opportunity to shape the industry for a long time to come,'' said Nebraska State Senator Chris Beutler, chair of the Natural Resources Committee, in the October 4, 1996 *Omaha World-Herald.* Regardless of what states decided, new 1996 rules from the Federal Energy Regulatory Commission facilitated competition by requiring both public and investor-owned utilities to allow competitors to use their transmission lines and gain information about their transmission capabilities.

In the late 1990s the NPPD took several major steps to improve its technical and financial operations. For example, on April 11, 1996 the NPPD energized its new 345-kilovolt transmission line that ran 98 miles between substations near Hastings and Lincoln. This new line eased a bottleneck that had blocked the district's ability to transfer power to the eastern half of its territory, where most of its load was located. Unlike similar projects that often took three years just for gain permits, this project from conception to completion took three years. During public meetings, NPPD dealt with concerns such as private property loss, damage to crops, and health risks from electromagnetic fields (EMFs), a controversy often discussed in media reports.

In 1996 the Nebraska Power Association and its member utilities, including NPPD, began a $300,000 study of wind power. Monitors collected data on wind speeds, direction, and turbulence. Based on that research, NPPD in 1998 worked with other agencies to build its first two wind turbines located near Springview, Nebraska. These variations on the old windmill already had operated for several years in other areas. For example, dozens of wind turbines were located near Palm Springs, California. But electrical deregulation and increased competition threatened such alternative power sources as wind turbines, unless improved technology could bring their costs below the costs of fossil fuels, hydroelectricity, and nuclear energy.

In the 1990s NPPD also burned old tires as an alternative energy source at its Sheldon Power Station near Hallam in Lancaster County. Beginning in 1991, NPPD contracted with Controlled Materials and Equipment Transportation (CMET) to buy chopped tires for $20 a ton, about the same cost as a ton of coal. The Sheldon plant burned about 600,000 old tires annually. The plant burned 98 percent coal and two percent tires but was allowed by government permit to burn up to five percent tires. The Lincoln-Lancaster County Health Department monitored emissions from the Sheldon plant, which turned out to be well under regulatory limits.

Every year Nebraskans threw away about 1.6 million old tires. The state government banned whole tires from landfills as of September 1, 1995 and extended that ban to tire scraps starting on September 1, 1996. CMET lost money, however, when it charged just $20 a ton, so it requested government subsidies. NPPD said it would pay no more than that amount. Otherwise, it would have to raise power rates for its consumers.

In the late 1990s NPPD improved its customer service by consolidating its offices and using more automated technology, which increased flexibility in paying bills and gaining information and help when needed. Nebraska Public Power District's President/CEO William R. Mayben and Board Chairman Ralph E. Holzfaster, with the help of their other executives and direc-

tors and the New York City law firm of O'Melveny & Myers, dealt with other complex issues, ranging from environmental quality and dealing with radioactive wastes from the Cooper nuclear plant. In addition, in the late 1990s NPPD examined its options to offer many new electrical-related services to its clients. Such diversification was seen as a way to prepare for deregulation and increased future competition.

Although public power in Nebraska and other states had proved successful in terms of serving customers with low-cost energy, in 1999 its future appeared uncertain, in large part because of energy deregulaton. Some public power leaders thought it was time to sell publicly owned facilities and move on to a privatized system. Even if that happened, the Nebraska Public Power District would retain its legacy of one of the nation's most significant electrical power utilities.

Further Reading

Anderson, Julie, "A Recycling Problem Tire Shredder Wants To Cut New Deal," *Omaha World-Herald,* October 4, 1996, p. 1.

Gentleman, Gerald, "Public Power in Nebraska," typescript available from Nebraska Public Power District, 1977.

Heinzl, Toni, "NPPD Faces $50,000 Fine for Violation at Cooper Plant," *Omaha World-Herald,* April 19, 1996, p. 13SF.

Hendee, David, and Leslie Boellstorff, "Public Power: Should the State Pull the Plug? Panel To Study Impact, Options of Deregulation," *Omaha World-Herald,* March 10, 1996, p. 1A.

Hirsh, Richard F., *Technology and Transformation in the American Electric Utility Industry,* New York: Cambridge University Press, 1989.

"Nebraska Districts Merged," *Public Power,* December 1969, pp. 11, 26–27.

Olson, James C., *History of Nebraska,* Lincoln: University of Nebraska Press, 1955.

Oswald, Bob, and Bill Eisinger, "Partnership Build NPPD's 345-kV Line," *Transmission & Distribution World,* October 1996, p. 28.

Reinemer, Vic, "Public Power's Roots," *Public Power,* September-October 1982, pp. 22–23, 25–26.

Schaufelberger, Donald E., *Nebraska Public Power District: A Vision Fulfilled,* The Newcomen Society of the United States, 1984.

—David M. Walden

Next plc

Desford Road
Enderby
Leicester LE9 5AT
United Kingdom
(44) 1162 866411
Fax: (44) 1162 848998
Web site: http://www.next.co.uk

Public Company
Incorporated: 1864 as J. Hepworth & Son
Employees: 19,000
Sales: £1.24 billion (US $1.9 billion) (1999)
Stock Exchanges: London
Ticker Symbol: Next
NAIC: 44812 Women's Clothing Stores; 44811 Men's Clothing Stores; 44813 Children's & Infants' Clothing Stores; 45411 Electronic Shopping & Mail-Order Houses; 442299 All Other Home Furnishings Stores

Next plc designs, manufactures, and distributes clothing and home furnishing and accessory items to nearly 330 Next retail stores and through the company's Next Directory mail order sales catalog. Almost all of Next company-owned stores are located in England and Ireland. After ending a brief international expansion—in 1999 the company closed its seven company-owned foreign stores, including its five U.S. retail stores—Next has shifted its international strategy to brand expansion focused on franchising. Next operates franchises in some 20 international markets, especially in the Middle Eastern and Far East Asian markets. The difficult economic climate in the Asian markets in the late 1990s has curtailed the Next franchise expansion, however; after building to 43 franchised locations by 1998, the company entered 1999 with just 35 franchise stores.

At home, Next operations are divided into two complementary activities: retail stores and catalog sales. At the beginning of 1999, the company operated nearly 330 Next retail stores

throughout England and Ireland, with total retail sales space of some 1.35 million square feet. Average store size is 3,500 square feet. Next, however, has been phasing out or extending its smaller stores—some of which are as small as 500 square feet—in favor of a larger multidepartment store concept with an average selling space of 14,000 square feet. Next retail operations provided more than £821 million of the company's total sales in 1998, while representing more than two-thirds of operating profits.

Once a separate division of the company with its own product offering, the Next Directory catalog sales operations have been dovetailed with those of its retail stores activities so that, in the late 1990s, the two divisions offer the same product lines under the company's "One Brand—Two Methods of Shopping" strategy. Next Directory offers a shop-at-home concept with fast delivery turnaround times of as little as one-day delivery. The hardbound catalog, which in ten years of existence has become something of a British shopping mainstay, is delivered to nearly 900,000 active customers, providing nearly £270 million of the company's 1998 total sales.

Next pursues a strategy of selling almost exclusively company-designed clothing, accessories, and other merchandise under the Next and other brand names. In this way, the Next product offerings of womenswear, menswear, childrenswear, and home furnishings are available only through the Next retail and catalog channels. Targeted at an age range between 20 and 46, with a focus on the 25–35 age group, the Next product range features high-quality, contemporary but not trendy styling, priced at levels affordable to the company's targeted middle-class market. The company employs its own design staff to keep an eye on seasonal trends and to create each year's clothing offerings accordingly.

Manufacturing is done primarily on a contractor basis, guided in part by the company's Hong Kong office. Next also operates several specialized warehouses ranging in size from 300,000 square feet to more than 600,000 square feet. Distribution to retail stores and to some Next Directory customers is handled by third party operators.

In addition to its retail store and catalog sales operations, Next offers financial services, particularly Next brand credit financing. Another growing division of the company is its Club 24 customer service subsidiary, which, under the Ventura name, operates call centers providing customer service and other services. Ventura's participation in the company topped £100 million in 1998.

Next Plc has been guided by chief executive officer David Jones since 1988. The company trades on the London Stock Exchange.

From Tailor to Trendy in the 1980s

By the time of Next plc's formation in 1981, the company had already been clothing England for more than a century. The company's origins were with the operations of J. Hepworth & Son, Gentleman's Tailors, founded in Leeds in 1864. Over the next 50 years, Hepworth & Son would expand, forming a nationwide retail chain of principally men's clothing. The company would long remain a mainstay of the United Kingdom's high street shopping districts.

Hepworth & Son's continued expansion led the company to go public in 1948. By the late 1970s, however, Hepworth & Son had begun to suffer from old-age pains and, especially, from its conservative image. Led by chairman Terence Conran, however, Hepworth & Son made a bold move to remake itself completely at the start of the 1980s.

In 1981 the company acquired the Kendalls retail store chain. The Kendalls chain, with some 80 locations, catered to the womenswear market, complementing the Hepworth & Son menswear line. If Kendalls also complemented Hepworth & Son's somewhat stuffy image, the acquisition would serve as a strong stepping stone for the company's move to transform itself into a full-line clothing retailer.

With the Kendalls acquisition, Conran brought in a new chief executive, George Davies, and gave Davies instructions to reinvent the Kendalls chain. While remaining in the womenswear segment, Davies turned the company toward sales of company-designed and branded merchandise. This merchandise would be sold under a new name and retail store concept, Next, at the former Kendalls locations.

The first year of Next brand operations would see a turnover of more than £82 million. By the end of 1982, more than 70 Kendalls locations had been converted to the Next concept. The Next sales would provide steady growth to Hepworth & Son's annual sales, which reached £108 million by 1984. That year saw the launch of a new Next brand range, men's clothing, as the Next for Men retail store concept took over many of the Hepworth & Son retail locations. By the end of 1984, the company, still called Hepworth & Son, operated 52 Next for Men shops.

In that same year, Hepworth & Son extended the Next retail concept to open the first multidepartment Next retail store. Featuring the company's lines of menswear and womenswear, the new Next concept, which opened first in Edinburgh, also included a shoes department and a café. The success of the Next concept continued to see the replacement of much of the remaining Hepworth & Son retail stores with Next for Men signage; at the same time, the company extended the Next name into entirely new locations. By the end of 1985, the company operated some 130 Next for Men stores.

The company also expanded with a new product category—and retail format—in 1985 with the launch of the Next Interiors concept. Featuring home furnishings under the Next brand names, the Next Interiors line also would be incorporated in the company's growing numbers of multidepartment stores. The first Next store to feature all of the company's product lines would open in 1985 in Regent Street, London. In that year the company also made a new acquisition, of rival clothing retailer Lord John.

Hepworth & Son had all but been replaced by the Next name. In 1986 this change was made official with the adoption of a new company name, Next Plc. One of the new Next company's first acts was to make a new acquisition, that of the mail order business Grattan Plc. With this acquisition, the company began to prepare its entry into the catalog sales channel; the Next Directory would be launched—to great success—in 1988.

Meanwhile, Next had undergone an aggressive expansion. Apart from boosting the number of retail locations—which reached some 750, primarily single-department stores by 1986—Davies led the company on a diversification binge that would see the company's revenues explode from £190 million in 1986 to more than £1.1 billion in 1988. By then, the Next empire would encompass not only the Grattan mail order business, but also the Salsburys and Zales jewelry chains, acquired by Next through parent Combined English Stores Group in 1987; newsstand operations, added with the acquisition of Dillons-Preedy, also in 1987; and an investment in the nascent British Sky Broadcasting Company.

The rise in sales brought about by the company's increased operations did not, however, translate to a corresponding boom in profits. Despite turnover of more than £1 billion, Next would see only some £81 in net profits in 1988. Profitability for the diversified company proved only temporary; hit by rising costs, a heavy debt load, and increasing competition from a new field of smaller, trendy shops (emulating in part the Next concept), Next would see its profits slump into losses in 1989.

Focusing in the 1990s

A boardroom battle ensued, costing George Davies his job. The CEO position was filled by David Jones, who had held that position for Next's Grattan subsidiary. Jones led Next through a streamlining operation, bringing the company back to its core clothing and home furnishings sales by the early 1990s. The company's noncore operations were sold off, starting with its jewelry store holdings to the Ratners Group in 1988, and ending with the sale of the Grattan mail order subsidiary to the German mail order specialist Otto Versand in 1991. In that same year, Next wrote off its British Sky Broadcasting investment.

The streamlining would prove costly for the company. By 1991, with turnover cut back to £878 million, the company posted a net loss of £445 million. Meanwhile, as Next shed its noncore activities, it also began streamlining its remaining operations. Whereas previously Next had manufactured much of its own range, it now began closing factories and outsourcing its production needs to third parties. The company's restructuring also would see the closing of nearly half of the existing Next stores as the company dropped money-losing locations and moved to convert the Next brand from several store signs to a single, multidepartment format.

By 1992, the company was back in the black; the trimmed-down operation, now with some 310 remaining stores, saw its sales cut back to £462 million, with a profit of £11 million. To solidify its position, Next embarked on a new strategic drive of "One Brand, Two Methods of Shopping." Whereas the company's Next Directory sales had featured product offerings different from those offered by the Next retail store chain, the two sales operations now were brought together to present the same Next brand products to the company's customers.

Next could then turn to new expansion activities. Until the 1990s, the company's focus had remained entirely on the United Kingdom and Ireland. The company now sought to export the Next brand overseas. For this, the company would use multiple approaches. For entry into the Asian, Eastern European, and Middle Eastern markets, the company chose a franchising approach, partnering with local businesses with knowledge of their markets. In the United States, Next entered a joint venture partnership to import the Next brand. The first Next store opened in Boston in 1993, followed by four more U.S. stores by the mid-1990s. Finally, for the company's entry on the European continent, the company chose to launch the Next brand in France, opening a company-owned store there. Another Next store would follow in Belgium.

Next also was seeking to branch out from the Next retail brand. In 1994 the company bought into a joint venture with Intimate Brands to operate that company's U.K.-based chain of Bath & Body Works shops. Next also moved beyond retail, taking over operations of the Ventura customer-service and call-center service provider.

By 1995, Next's annual sales had topped £650 million, for a net profit of more than £80 million. While the total number of company-owned stores had remained at slightly more than 300 retail stores, the company had engaged on a program of phasing out many of its smaller stores in favor of the larger, multidepartment Next concept. This was heightened as more and more stores began including the company's Next Interiors line in addition to its men's, women's, and children's clothing.

Next's sales would boast strong growth in the second half of the 1990s, jumping to more than £1.1 billion by year-end 1998. In that year, however, the company renounced its North American expansion effort, which had been less than successful. The company's five U.S.-based stores, as well as its stores in France and Belgium, were closed in April 1999. Regrouped around its U.K.-based retail and catalog sales operations, while focusing its international expansion around the Next brand franchise, Next looked toward the next century of retail sales.

Principal Subsidiaries

Next Retail Limited; The Next Directory; Next Financial Services; Club 24 Limited; Ventura; Clydesdale Financial Services Limited; Callscan Limited; Callscan Australia (Pty) Limited; Next (Asia) Limited; Next Distribution Limited.

Further Reading

"Next Brings the Flavor of England to N.Y. Area," *Women's Wear Daily,* August 27, 1997.
"Next Has a Knack for Hits," *Women's Wear Daily,* September 28, 1995.
Next Factfile, Leicester: Next Plc, 1997.

—M.L. Cohen

Norfolk Southern Corporation

Three Commercial Place
Norfolk, Virginia 23510
U.S.A.
(757) 629-2600
Fax: (757) 664-5069
Web site: http://www.nscorp.com

Public Company
Incorporated: 1980
Employees: 35,000
Sales: $4.2 billion (1998)
Stock Exchanges: New York
Ticker Symbol: NSC
NAIC: 482111 Line-Haul Railroads; 551112 Offices of
    Other Holding Companies

Norfolk Southern Corporation (NS) is a holding company that owns and operates one of the nation's biggest railroad systems, the Norfolk Southern Railway Company. Its lines run through 22 states, mostly in the South and East, and extend into Ontario, Canada, covering approximately 21,600 miles of rail. About one-third of its rail was acquired in a takeover of lines formerly owned by Conrail. Norfolk Southern also operates a coal, natural gas, and timber company through its subsidiary, Pocahontas Land Corporation. Most of Norfolk Southern's revenues come from the transportation of coal, coke, and iron ore. The railway's predecessors date back to the 1830s.

19th Century Roots

Norfolk and Western Railway Company was the result of numerous mergers. It started as a ten-mile line, City Point Railroad, which served two small Virginia towns beginning in 1838. William Mahone orchestrated the company's first mergers. He was elected president of a successor, the Norfolk and Petersburg Railroad (N&P) in 1860. He joined the company in 1853 as chief engineer and was the innovator of a roadbed through swampland that continues to hold up under the huge tonnages of coal traffic. After the Civil War, N&P linked up with South Side Railroad and Virginia & Tennessee Railroad, forming Atlantic, Mississippi & Ohio Railroad (AM&O). In 1870 this line extended from Norfolk to Bristol, Virginia. The combined railroads were damaged during the war and reconstruction was slow and expensive. One-half of the railroads in the South failed between 1873 and 1880. Mahone borrowed heavily and three years after the crash and financial panic of 1873, the company was put into receivership by its creditors. A private Philadelphia banking firm—E.W. Clark and Company—purchased the AM&O in 1881, changing its name to Norfolk and Western Railroad Company.

A partner in the firm, Frederick Kimball, took charge of Norfolk and Western, merging it with the Shenandoah Valley Railroad. Kimball's interest in minerals led to lines being built with access to coal deposits, although at this time the railroad was mainly an agricultural line, cotton being its primary freight. Four years later, the coal handled by Norfolk passed the one-million-ton mark. Within a decade, coal would account for the line's greatest traffic.

Henry Fink became president when the company emerged from bankruptcy in 1896 as Norfolk and Western Railway Company (NW). For the next three decades, NW expanded aggressively. Building through West Virginia, north to Ohio and south to North Carolina, NW established its trademark route. Between 1895 and 1905 railroads across the nation consolidated and improved operations. In 1904 Lucius Johnson became president of NW.

War Years

During World War I, traffic was heavy and equipment condition and upkeep suffered from material shortages. Government control of the railroads took place in 1917 and was relinquished in 1920. For the next ten years, NW consolidated its strength as a coal carrier. The early 1920s saw increased Interstate Commerce Commission (ICC) involvement in the industry and increased union activity. The drive for greater efficiency and reduced costs, as well as the company's coal revenues, helped NW through the Great Depression, but unprofitable branch lines were abandoned and equipment purchases were delayed.

Company Perspectives:

Norfolk Southern's mission is to enhance the value of stockholders' investment over time by providing quality freight transportation services and undertaking any other related businesses in which our resources, particularly our people, give the company an advantage.

With the start of World War II, NW rebounded. Traffic volume reached a peak in 1944. Robert H. Smith assumed the presidency in 1946. Between 1945 and 1950, $14 million was spent on improvements. During this same time, diesel locomotives were becoming an indelible presence in the industry. Although NW had great investments in coal-burning power and steam engines, the greater economy and efficiency of diesel were decisive; the company ordered its first diesel engines in 1955.

Mergers Through the 1980s

The 1950s were marked by union battles, the abandonment of steam power, and a decline in coal traffic, but growth nonetheless. Stuart Saunders became president in 1958. A lawyer, he stepped up the company's mergers through complicated transactions, beginning with Virginian Railway in 1959. In 1964 NW acquired two railways: Wabash, Nickel Plate, Pittsburgh & West Virginia and Akron, Canton & Youngstown. With this, NW became a Midwestern presence, providing service between the Atlantic, the Great Lakes, and the Mississippi River. Saunders expected expansion to reduce the company's reliance on coal as a revenue source.

Following the flurry of merger activity in the 1960s, the ICC authorized rights to NW in 1971 for portions of the tracks of the Atchison, Topeka & Santa Fe Railway. NW began merger talks with Southern Railway in 1979. The year before the consummation of the NW-Southern merger in 1982, NW acquired the Illinois Terminal Railroad.

Like NW, Southern Railway was the result of many railroad lines combined and reorganized—nearly 150 lines. The earliest of these lines was the South Carolina Canal & Rail Road Company, a nine-mile line chartered in 1827. It was the first regularly scheduled passenger train in the United States in 1830. It was also the first to carry U.S. troops and mail. Within three years, it was 136 miles long, the longest in the world.

Prior to the Civil War, rail expansion crossed the South. By 1857 Charleston, South Carolina and Memphis, Tennessee were linked by rail, but growth was stopped by the Civil War. With the devastation of the southern economy and railroads by the war, rebuilding of the industry was slow. Repairs and reorganization took place during the postwar period, and new railroads were built along the Ohio and Mississippi rivers.

Southern Railway (SR) was formed in 1894, when the Richmond & Danville merged with the East Tennessee, Virginia & Georgia Railroad. The company's first president was Samuel Spencer. Its line spread over 4,400 miles, two-thirds of which SR owned. The Alabama Great Southern Railway, and the

Georgia Southern and Florida were also under SR's control. Over the span of Spencer's 12-year presidency, SR acquired many more lines and equipment, and revenues went from $17 million to more than $153 million. The company shifted from dependency on tobacco and cotton to more involvement with the South's industrial development. By 1916 SR had an 8,000-mile line over 13 states, establishing its territory for the next half century.

Fairfax Harrison became president in 1913. World War I traffic was substantial but was offset by inflation, and the postwar boom period helped pay for repairs and equipment replacement delayed by the war. In 1922 SR invested $77 million in improvements. The stock market crash of 1929 came two months after SR moved into lavish new headquarters. Many U.S. railroads were forced into bankruptcy in the early 1930s. SR operated at a loss for the first time in 1931 and began amassing debts. The company did not show a profit again until 1936.

Under Ernest Norris, SR recovered, paying its debts to the Reconstruction Finance Corporation in 1941. That same year SR purchased its first diesel equipment, and World War II began. Wartime traffic led to increased efficiency and safety. By 1951 SR owned a fleet of almost 850 diesel-electric units that drove nearly 92 percent of its freight service and 86 percent of its passenger service. SR became the first U.S. railroad to convert entirely to diesel-powered locomotives in 1953, closing the era of the steam locomotive.

SR prospered as a result of dieselization. The southern economy led the nation in growth in the late 1950s. SR took advantage of this growth by acquiring railroads and gaining access to developing industrial areas beginning with the 1952 purchase of the Louisiana-Southern Railway. In 1957 it acquired the Atlantic & North Carolina Railroad and in 1961 the Interstate Railroad, which brought SR to new coal fields in southwest Virginia. In 1963 the Central of Georgia merged with SR.

W. Graham Claytor became president in 1967, instituting the streamlined management and tough budgets that saw the company through the 1974 recession. An unrelated company called Norfolk Southern Railway was acquired in 1974, adding 622 miles of line in an area marked for economic growth. At this time, SR was thriving. There was a 70 percent increase in revenue between 1974 and 1978. In 1979 Harold Hall became president and later ushered the company through its merger with Norfolk and Western. SR was considered one of the best managed railroads in the industry. In 1980 the company enjoyed its fifth consecutive year of record profits.

At the time of the merger, both NW and SR were among the most profitable firms in the industry. Between 1971 and 1981, net income at NW had increased fivefold. At SR it had tripled. Prior to merging, both railroads had added many miles and much time to their transportation routes to avoid using each other's tracks; the amount of overlap was small but affected operations significantly. In some cases three days of transportation time was added just to circumvent ten miles of track operated by the other system. SR operated a 10,000-mile line between Washington, D.C., New Orleans, Louisiana, Cincinnati, Ohio, and St. Louis, Missouri. NW had a 7,000 mile line between Norfolk and Kansas City.

In 1980 Chessie System Inc. and Seaboard Coast Line Industries, Inc. merged, forming CSX Corporation. This provided some impetus for the Norfolk Southern merger. Equally compelling was the complementary territories and corporate objectives of NW and SR. Norfolk Southern, incorporated in 1980 and completing its acquisition of the railroads in 1982, became the lowest cost, highest profit corporation in the industry. Merging also made NS the nation's fourth largest system in terms of track line. Robert Claytor, who had been president of NW, became the first chairman of Norfolk Southern Corporation. Huge assets and conservative investments kept NS sound in 1982, when the steel and coal businesses slowed, but NW's revenues dipped as a result. It was expected that SR's merchandise traffic would help offset NW's coal business if it slowed, and vice versa. Both slumped, however, in the early 1980s.

Acquisitions in the 1980s

With an eye toward becoming the country's first integrated transportation company, NS moved to purchase North American Van Lines, Inc. (NAVL) in 1984. The acquisition was completed in 1985. NAVL was known mostly for its household moving, which, however, constituted only one-third of its revenues. Other services offered include commercial transport, moving general commodities from manufacturer to distributor, and transporting high-value products such as computers. NAVL was founded in Ohio in 1933, moved to Indiana in 1947, and was purchased by Pepsico in 1968. The purchase of NAVL by NS for $369 million put the recent industry deregulation policy of the ICC to the test. NS became the dominant railroad in trucking, developing a transportation system that provided both motor carrier and rail service.

In the mid-1980s, NS aggressively pursued the purchase of Consolidated Rail Corporation (Conrail) from the U.S. government. Conrail was founded in 1976 from six bankrupt northwestern railroads and subsequently became profitable. The purchase would have made NS the nation's largest railroad, but after several years of negotiations, it fell through. The unsuccessful bid to take over Conrail, however, resulted in 1986 in a profitable cooperation between the two companies, including an interchange agreement that allowed NS and Conrail to offer competitive services over the same areas.

In the mid-1980s NS's principal revenue-producing commodities, aside from fuel, were paper, chemicals, and automobiles. In 1985 NS had revenues of $3.8 billion and was the most profitable railroad in the nation. In 1987 Arnold McKinnon succeeded Robert Claytor as CEO and chairman and Harold Hall became vice-chairman.

The company further profited from its investments in Santa Fe Southern Pacific and Piedmont Aviation, both of which it sold later at huge profits. By 1988 coal and merchandise traffic began to increase after a long slump. McKinnon worked on cutting costs and smoothing the way for increased intermodal traffic, traffic that shifts easily between railroad and highway. Only six percent of NS's business in 1988, intermodal traffic posed great growth potential.

With the recession in 1989, automobile and steel industries suffered, as did housing and, therefore, lumber shipments and coal. The decline in industrial freight shipments hit railroads hard. NS's revenues were down by about three percent because of traffic declines early in 1989. At the same time fuel prices and insurance costs rose.

Growth in the 1990s

Although heavy freight and merchandise revenues remained lower in 1990, increased shipments of coal, coke, and iron ore helped the company offset losses. Profits dipped in 1990, the result of higher fuel costs and the expense of employee layoffs and early retirements. At the end of 1990, NS restructured its rail operations, changing Southern Railway's name to Norfolk Southern Railway Company and transferring ownership of Norfolk and Western to it. The company spent $20 million in the early 1990s to improve its routes for double-stacked containers and vied with the trucking industry for freight. NS entered a joint venture with Conrail in 1993 to run a hybrid truck and rail service. It used vehicles called Road-Railers, which could convert quickly from truck to rail car, and ran these on a network that joined Chicago, Atlanta, and Harrisburg, Pennsylvania. NS also acquired more varied business in its home southern territory as auto companies built new plants. Toyota expanded a plant in Georgetown, Kentucky, and BMW built a new factory in Greer, South Carolina, in the early 1990s, giving NS a lucrative new product—automobiles—to ship.

NS was a remarkably stable and profitable company despite the downturn in coal exports, and it was known for its low costs and efficient management. Much of its profits came from running the easy downhill route from the coal mines in the Appalachians down to the port of Hampton Roads, Virginia, where waiting tankers took its freight abroad. One snag on its profitability, however, was its trucking unit, North American Van Lines, which continued to do poorly. The company sought to sell off two of its trucking unit's divisions in 1993, after trucking operations came in with a loss of close to $40 million in 1992. The rest of its trucking operations was sold off in 1998.

Meanwhile, NS began merger talks with its old friend Conrail. Conrail controlled 12,200 miles of rail, particularly in the industrial Northeast and Midwest. Heavy traffic between Chicago and Philadelphia and from East St. Louis to Boston gave the firm much of its profits. When Conrail and NS began to talk in 1994, Conrail was valued at around $4 billion. Negotiations between the two companies broke down in the summer of 1994, however, apparently because Conrail wanted a price substantially higher than that market value. After talks between the companies broke off, Conrail's CEO James Hagen told *Forbes* magazine in a November 21, 1994 interview, ''We don't need a merger.'' Yet two years later, in November 1996, Conrail was on the verge of accepting a merger offer from rival railroad CSX. NS topped CSX's bid, offering $9 billion for the company that had been too expensive at more than $4 billion in 1994. In March 1997 a new deal was cemented, involving all three companies: CSX bought Conrail for $10.3 billion and then sold half of Conrail's routes (58 percent of the company) to NS for $5.9 billion. This led to what one analyst, transportation curator of the Smithsonian Institution William Withuhn called ''the most complicated merger in history,'' according to a *Wall Street Journal* article from June 10, 1998. Norfolk Southern and CSX had to divide up the thousands of miles of Conrail track, despite daunting physical and administrative problems. The two companies spent more than a billion dollars each expanding tracks, terminals, and equipment, and had other headaches such as working their computer systems into Conrail's. The breakup of Conrail was carefully plotted, yet myriad problems led to delays. By January 1999 NS was paying out approximately $1 million every day in interest costs on the roughly $6 billion it had borrowed for its share of Conrail. Finally, the merger was physically complete on June 1, 1999 when Conrail's rail lines went into use by its respective owners. The many expenses incurred by the merger were expected to dampen income for that year, but to NS it seemed a wise long-term investment. The company was now about evenly matched with CSX, splitting the eastern United States between them, just as two other railroads dominated the West. NS was convinced it would be a stronger company with Conrail's addition, as the expanded mileage opened many more markets to it.

Principal Subsidiaries

Lambert's Point Docks Inc.; Norfolk Southern Railway Company; Pocahontas Land Corp.; Triple Crown Services Co.

Further Reading

"All Steamed Up Over Conrail," *Business Week,* November 4, 1996, p. 54.

Davis, Burke, *The Southern Railway: Road of the Innovators,* Chapel Hill: University of North Carolina Press, 1985.

Dinsmore, Christopher, "Norfolk Southern, CSX Announce Date for Conrail Breakup," *Knight-Ridder/Tribune Business News,* January 20, 1999, p. OKRB9902010E.

——, "Norfolk, Va.-Based Railroad Company Looks Forward to Conrail Takeover," *Knight-Ridder/Tribune Business News,* May 13, 1999, p. OKRB991331C2.

Gilbert, Nick, "The Road Not Taken," *Financial World,* March 14, 1995, p. 28.

Machalaba, Daniel, "Conrail Carve-Up Turns Toward Its Real Uphill Climb," *Wall Street Journal,* June 10, 1998, p. B4.

——, "Conrail Faces Labor Unrest After Walkout," *Wall Street Journal,* August 17, 1998, p. B4.

——, "Norfolk Southern Charts New Course as Coal Profits Slip," *Wall Street Journal,* April 27, 1993, p. B4.

——, "Norfolk Southern Corp. Seeks Buyers for 2 of Its Trucking Unit's Divisions," *Wall Street Journal,* June 28, 1993, p. A9C.

Norman, James R., "Choose Your Partners!," *Forbes,* November 21, 1994, pp. 88–89.

"Our Corporate History," Norfolk, Virginia: Norfolk Southern Corporation.

Striplin, E.F. Pat, *The Norfolk & Western: A History,* Norfolk, Va.: The Norfolk & Western Railway Company, 1981.

Weber, Joseph, "Highballing Toward Two Big Railroads?," *Business Week,* March 17, 1997, pp. 32–33.

—Carol I. Keeley
—updated by A. Woodward

Olsten Corporation

175 Broad Hollow Road
Melville, New York 11747-8905
U.S.A.
(516) 844-7800
(800) WORK NOW
Fax: (516) 844-7011
Web site: http://www.olsten.com

Public Company
Incorporated: 1950
Employees: 700,850
Sales: $4.6 billion (1998)
Stock Exchanges: New York
Ticker Symbol: OLS
NAIC: 56131 Employment Placement Agencies; 56132
Temporary Help Services

The third largest temporary employment provider in the world, Olsten Corporation recruits, screens, and places individuals for temporary work assignments with employers. In 1999 Olsten Corp. provided roughly 700,000 temporary employees for an estimated 600,000 clients through a network of 1,500 offices. Aside from its commercial business, which supplied temporary personnel for a variety of corporate and light industrial positions, the company provided temporary staffing services to information technology and health care industries, its two areas of specialization. During the 1990s, Olsten Corp. completed a number of acquisitions in the health care industry that made it the largest supplier of temporary health care personnel in North America.

1950 Founding

William Olsten was regarded as one of the pioneers in the temporary help industry, opening his first office—housed in one small room—in New York City in 1950. Ambitious and a risk-taker, Olsten demonstrated an intuitive sense of timing as a temporary help supplier, foreseeing changes in the labor market and anticipating the skills employers were seeking from their work force. He consistently positioned his company to take advantage of emerging trends in the workplace, a skill that enabled his modest, one-office business to flourish from the start. As the 1950s began, office workers were in short supply, their ranks depleted by a postwar transition that saw many women give up the clerical jobs they had performed during the war and return home. Olsten, with the help of his brother-in-law, took to the streets and canvassed suburban New York City to recruit women for temporary office work. Within eight years, Olsten had expanded his business to five offices, first by establishing offices in the outer boroughs of New York City and then moving into other major urban markets such as Boston and Philadelphia. As a tool to promote his business and to recruit temporary workers, Olsten created what he called the "Temp-Mobile," a Volkswagen bus that traveled from neighborhood to neighborhood. Olsten began using his Temp-Mobile in 1957 and later replaced it with a radio-equipped van that shuttled temporary workers from suburbia to their assignments in New York City.

The 1960s witnessed the maturation of the Olsten enterprise, as it evolved from a relatively small, five-office staffing firm into a rapidly expanding, diversified, publicly held corporation. Market conditions propelled the company forward, as the concept of employing temporary workers cemented itself in the mindset of corporate America. Olsten capitalized on the changing business practices and advancing technologies of the decade, demonstrating a strong desire to develop his company into a national force. Looking for a way to accelerate expansion, Olsten began franchising his business concept in 1962. In 1965 the company opened its first Canadian office, establishing a branch in Toronto. By this point, the company had tripled in size, comprising 20 offices scattered throughout nine states, and had deepened its penetration into the temporary worker industry, as Olsten increased the services his company provided to employers. To the company's selection of secretarial and clerical workers, Olsten added other professions, such as those related to engineering work. A change in the company's corporate title to "Olsten Corporation" in 1967 was followed in 1968 by the debut of the newly named company as a publicly traded corporation, the same year corporate headquarters were moved to Westbury, New York. In a display of his company's new-found might, Olsten finished the decade by completing two acquisitions that diversified Olsten Corp. and foreshadowed its involvement in a new, significantly important area. In 1969 Olsten acquired a medical laboratory named Rush Laboratories and purchased another medical laboratory, Path-Tek Laboratories, the following year.

Expansion and Diversification in the 1970s and 1980s

The foray into the medical field represented a significant event in Olsten Corp.'s history, introducing the company into a market segment that was the central focus of its activity during the 1990s. The acquisition of the two medical laboratories led to Olsten Corp.'s entry into the market for temporary workers in the health care industry, inaugurated by the creation of Olsten Health Care Services in 1971. By creating a subsidiary to provide temporary medical staffing services, Olsten had seized upon a way to insulate his company from the cyclicality of its commercial business. As the demand for temporary workers in the corporate world dipped and rose, the company's medical staffing business would serve as a stabilizer, enabling Olsten Corp. to generate revenue at a more consistent level. The entry into health care services also represented another example of Olsten's foresight, positioning his company in what would become a significant and lucrative market for temporary staffing services. During the first half of the 1970s, however, Olsten Corp.'s medical services business was little more than a sideline venture; its prominence within the corporation was still two decades away. In the interim, the company's commercial business was recording explosive growth, as Olsten developed his business into a national chain. Between 1965 and 1975, the number of offices increased from 20 to 150, flooding principal markets throughout the United States. Although there were several areas beyond the company's reach by the end of the 1970s, expansion during the 1980s ensured that every state in the country could claim at least one Olsten Corp. office within its borders.

The reliance on temporary employees by businesses big and small increased during the 1980s, fueled by the flexibility it gave employers as they contended with the fluctuating productivity demands of their businesses. Temporary staffing firms recruited and screened potential employees, identifying their particular skills and matching those skills with the specific demands of the employer. Olsten Corp. had decades of experience in appraising prospective temporary employees, developing its own system

called the Olsten Profiler in 1972 that was trademarked the following year. In 1986 the company computerized the Olsten Profiler, improving its efficiency and accuracy further.

Expansion during the 1980s doubled the size of the company from its stature in 1975, establishing offices throughout the nation. With the opening of offices in Hawaii, Alaska, and Puerto Rico in 1987, the company had offices in all 50 states, the District of Columbia, Puerto Rico, and Canada, ranking it as the third largest temporary staffing firm in the United States. The company had developed well beyond its original business of providing clerical workers to embrace a variety of positions. In 1987 Olsten Corp.'s more than 400 offices placed 240,000 temporary workers in positions for 80,000 clients, providing workers with skills in office services, office automation, accounting, legal support, records management, marketing, technical and light industrial services, as well as nursing, home health care, and therapy. By the end of the 1980s, there were more than 525 Olsten Corp. offices in operation.

Focus on Health Care in the 1990s

The end of the 1980s marked a turning point in the history of Olsten Corp., ushering in a decade of dynamic change. Olsten retired in 1990, vacating his posts as chairman and chief executive officer during the company's 40th anniversary. Behind him, Olsten left a business capable of generating nearly $1 billion in sales per year, a company with a far-reaching grasp on the commercial temporary staffing market and a promising involvement in the health care temporary staffing market. Olsten's successor was Frank Liguori, a Brooklyn-born butcher's son who had been president of the company since 1986. Liguori, an accountant by training, took the helm of Olsten Corp. and initiated dramatic changes, immediately steering the company toward a greatly increased presence in the health care industry. Olsten had not neglected the company's involvement in health care—opening its first Medicare-certified office in 1983—but Liguori pushed the business headlong into health care, taking the legacy left by Olsten to another level. One of the first steps taken in this direction was the acquisition of Upjohn Co.'s Upjohn Health Care Services subsidiary, purchased in December 1990. Upjohn Health Care Services had collected $182 million in sales in 1989 by providing home health care and supplemental staffing to hospitals, nursing homes, and other health care organizations. The acquisition, which lifted Olsten Corp.'s sales beyond $1 billion, added 200 offices to Liguori's portfolio of health care properties and made health care a contributor of 30 percent of Olsten Corp.'s revenue volume.

Liguori was merely getting started when he acquired Upjohn Health Care Services. His efforts during the 1990s reflected an emphasis on the global expansion of Olsten Corp.'s commercial business and on the development of an information technology business, but progress on both these fronts paled in comparison with the strides gained in the health care industry. In May 1993, Liguori made headlines when he proposed to pay $449 million worth of Olsten Corp. stock for Lifetime Corp., a supplier of home health care personnel with an enormous $886 million in annual sales. His offer drew criticism from industry analysts for several reasons. Lifetime was saddled with debt and had demonstrated erratic profitability, recording nearly $18 million in earnings in 1990 and $5 million two years later. The company, by its own admission, also suffered from what it referred to as "operational inefficiencies" and overstaffing, but Liguori brushed the problems aside, remarking, "One man's operating problems are the next man's opportunity." Perhaps the most alarming aspect of the deal was the amount Liguori had proposed to pay. Earlier in 1993, Lifetime had been trading at roughly $16 per share when another company, Abbey Healthcare, attempted to purchase it for $23.50 per share. Abbey Healthcare later raised its offer to $27.50 per share, a bid Liguori preempted by offering $33 per share, which critics believed was too high. Despite the widespread belief that the acquisition was ill advised, Liguori pressed forward and completed the deal, gaining shareholder approval on a transaction that doubled the size of Olsten Corp. overnight.

Aside from substantially increasing Olsten Corp.'s annual revenue volume, there were other, equally profound, effects stemming from the Lifetime acquisition. Olsten Corp. was transformed from a company whose foundation rested on commercial temporary staffing into a company whose sideline involvement in health care had become its future—"something of a flip-flop," according to Liguori. After the acquisition of Lifetime, Olsten Corp. derived 55 percent of its business from health care and 45 percent from its former mainstay commercial temporary staffing business, ranking as the largest supplier of staffing services to the home health care market in the country. Industry pundits watched Olsten Corp. closely, waiting to see if Liguori had made a mistake or acquired the means to create a formidable temporary staffing firm with a two-pronged strategy.

Olsten Corp.'s commercial business also saw its scope increased during the first years of Liguori's tenure. During the 1980s, the company had solidified its position in the United States, establishing offices in every state. During the 1990s, Liguori set his sights on the rest of the world, beginning a concerted attack on international markets. The company's progress overseas was achieved through a series of acquisitions. In 1993 Olsten Corp. purchased Office Angels, a staffing service firm headquartered in the United Kingdom. The following year, the company acquired a stake in a Mexican staffing agency, which subsequently was renamed Olsten STAFF S.A. In 1995 the company moved in several directions, acquiring operations in Argentina, Norway, Denmark, and Germany.

By the end of 1995, systemwide sales for Olsten Corp., including franchises, exceeded $3 billion, only four years after the company had reached the $1 billion mark. Much of the financial growth was attributable to the acquisition of Lifetime and the increasing use of temporary employees by employers, but some of the revenue growth was derived from Liguori's foray into a new business area. In 1995, one year after moving company headquarters to Melville, New York, Liguori acquired IMI Systems Inc., an international information technology services company. With $47 million in sales in 1994, IMI was recording growth in excess of 40 percent per year, making leaping strides in a fast-growing industry. IMI served a clientele consisting of a large number of Fortune 100 companies, including banks, utilities, and telecommunications concerns. For these clients, IMI designed, developed, and maintained information systems, providing its comprehensive services on either an individual or project-oriented basis. The company, which Liguori planned to use as the foundation for the further development of information

technology services business, was supported by a network of 12 offices, including two branches in Europe.

After the acquisition of IMI, Liguori moved ahead with further acquisitions during the latter half of the 1990s, behaving "like a Monopoly player on amphetamines," according to a reporter from *Chief Executive* magazine. Despite the characterization, there was no implication that he was being too aggressive. Liguori had few critics following the IMI acquisition, having silenced his earlier detractors by successfully assimilating Lifetime into Olsten Corp. "The ongoing shift to lower-cost health care settings, such as the home, and the dramatic growth in business and industry temporary staffing needs should result in continued revenue growth acceleration for Olsten," explained one analyst, typifying the industry's assessment of Liguori's progress. Amid such praise, Liguori completed two acquisitions in 1996, purchasing Co-Counsel, a leading provider of legal staffing services, and Quantum Health Resources, a provider of alternate-site therapies and infusion support services. Also in 1996, CIGNA selected Olsten Kimberly QualityCare as sole-source provider of home health care services for nearly ten million managed care participants nationwide, the type of full-service partnerships with large clients that Liguori was seeking. The following year, further expansion occurred, particularly overseas, where the company established staffing services outlets in Chile, France, and Spain.

Olsten Corp. entered the late 1990s with glowing prospects, its rapid growth during the decade heralded as a success story and its leader hailed as an astute and ambitious manager. Both assessments quickly changed during the late 1990s, however, as Olsten Corp. faltered and Liguori bore the brunt of the damage. The company became embroiled in a series of federal investigations claiming Medicaid fraud charges that eventually led to a $102 million settlement to end the Department of Justice's litigation. Concurrently, the company's profits declined by 50 percent in 1998, in large part because of cutbacks in Medicare payments. In response to the internal turmoil, Olsten Corp.'s stock fell to roughly $7 per share, far below the $32-per-share price of two years earlier. To add insult to injury, *Fortune* magazine reported that the nation's leading business leaders ranked Olsten Corp. as one of the "least admired" companies in the United States. For Liguori, the situation could not be bleaker. In February 1999 he surprised industry analysts by submitting his resignation. The responsibility for restoring the company's image and its financial results fell to Edward Blechschmidt.

Blechschmidt had joined Olsten Corp. in 1996 as the company's president. Although he was regarded as Liguori's heir apparent at the time, few thought he would assume control over the company three years later. During his first few months in office, Blechschmidt presided over the closure of 60 offices in markets deemed to be oversaturated. Although opinions differed concerning the company's prospects as it prepared for the 21st century, there was justifiable confidence in the future growth of Olsten Corp.'s commercial temporary staffing business. Sales at Olsten Staffing Services increased 20 percent in 1998, rising to $3.55 billion. Whether or not the company could restore its health care business following the federal investigations was a question to be answered in the decade ahead.

Principal Subsidiaries

Co-Counsel, Inc.; IMI Systems, Inc.; Olsten Financial Staffing; Olsten Health Services; Olsten Staffing Services; Olsten STAFF S.A.

Further Reading

Croghan, Lore, "Escaping the Cycle: Expanding a Home Health Care Sideline Helps a Provider of Temps Avoid Cyclical Downturns," *Financial World,* July 18, 1995, p. 55.

Goldstein, Matthew, "New Olsten CEO May Ease Stock's Low-Grade Fever," *Crain's New York Business,* February 22, 1999, p. 4.

Hollis, Kerissa, "Interview with a Headhunter," *Memphis Business Journal,* October 10, 1994, p. 1A.

Long, Jeff, "Bill Olsten: Temp Help Pioneer," *Management World,* November-December 1987, p. 22.

Lutz, Sandy, "Newly Expanded Olsten Seeking Hospital Partners," *Modern Healthcare,* August 16, 1993, p. 30.

McCarthy, Joseph L., "Riding the Boom in Staffing Services," *Chief Executive,* December 1995, p. 20.

"Olsten Becomes a Force in Personnel Field," *LI Business News,* December 17, 1990, p. 18.

"Olsten Corp. Marks Its 40th Anniversary," *LI Business News,* March 12, 1990, p. 38.

"Olsten Purchases Upjohn Subsidiary," *LI Business News,* September 24, 1990, p. 6.

Phalon, Richard, "Olsten's New Tail," *Forbes,* July 19, 1993, p. 101.

Rosenberg, Hilary, "Olsten Corp.'s Frank Liguori: Coping with a Skills Shortage," *Institutional Investor,* July 1994, p. 29.

Strugactch, Warren, "Olsten Focuses on Healing Itself," *LI Business News,* May 7, 1999, p. 5A.

—Jeffrey L. Covell

Owosso Corporation

The Triad Building
2200 Renaissance Boulevard, Suite 150
King of Prussia, Pennsylvania 19406
U.S.A.
(610) 275-4500
Fax: (610) 275-5122
Web site: http://www.owosso.com

Public Company
Incorporated: 1973
Employees: 1,800
Sales: $160 million (1998)
Stock Exchanges: NASDAQ
Ticker Symbol: OWOS
NAIC: 335312 Motor & Generator Manufacturing;
333111 Farm Machinery & Equipment
Manufacturing; 335314 Relay & Industrial Control
Manufacturing; 336312 Carburetor, Piston, Piston
Ring & Valve Manufacturing; 33633 Motor Vehicle
Steering & Suspension Components (Except Spring)
Manufacturing; 336212 Truck Trailer Manufacturing

Owosso Corporation, through its subsidiaries, produces engineered component products, including motors, timers, heat transfer coils, and replacement camshaft bearings. These products are sold primarily to original equipment manufacturers (OEMs), who use them in the manufacture of various end products. End markets served by Owosso's components include commercial products, refrigeration systems, process equipment, construction, health care, and automotive. Owosso also manufactures all-aluminum trailers through its Sooner Trailer Manufacturing subsidiary. The majority of Sooner's products are horse and livestock trailers, but the company also makes trailers for automobiles, boats, and general cargo. Approximately 20 percent of Owosso's total sales derive from Sooner products.

Building a Business: 1973–89

In January 1973, three investors—George Lemmon, John Northway, and Ronald Hendee—formed Owosso Corporation in order to purchase an Owosso, Michigan-based division of The Singer Company. The division, Motor Products-Owosso, was a maker of factional horsepower D/C motors used in a variety of end products.

At the time, Lemmon was living in Philadelphia and working in Manhattan for the investment bank of Wood, Struthers & Winthrop. When The Singer Company retained Wood, Struthers & Winthrop to sell off several of its smaller subsidiaries—including its Owosso operation—Lemmon traveled to Michigan to arrange the sale. Once there, he was impressed with both the business and the plant's manager, John Northway. Although several buyers were interested in the $4 million Owosso business, Lemmon and Northway decided to purchase it themselves. They brought Hendee on board as a third investor and completed the deal in six weeks, paying $1.3 million. Lemmon became the CEO of the newly formed company, with Northway remaining in charge of its day-to-day operations.

After seven successful years, Lemmon and Northway were ready to try their hands at another acquisition. In 1980, Owosso purchased the Longview, Texas-based Snow Coil, Inc. Snow Coil manufactured heat-transfer coils that were used in heating and cooling applications, including commercial refrigeration truck, bus, and van heating and air conditioning. Also in 1980, Lemmon's and Northway's third investor, Ronald Hendee, decided to sell his stake in the company. Lemmon and Northway offered Hendee's stock to John Reese, one of Lemmon's colleagues at Wood, Struthers & Winthrop, who accepted.

Owosso's next major expansion came in 1984, with the acquisitions of Airmax, Inc. and Cramer Company. Airmax was a manufacturer of heating and cooling components, and Cramer manufactured subfractional horsepower motors and timers used primarily in the appliance industry. The following year Owosso diversified further, stepping away from motors and HVAC components and into the agricultural marketplace. The company purchased Parker Industries, an Iowa-based manufacturer of grain transportation and weighing equipment. Parker's products included grain wagons and auger carts, which were typically used by large-scale corn, soybean, and wheat farmers to transport grain. Parker also manufactured weigh wagons, which were used by seed companies to monitor harvest yields.

Company Perspectives:

Owosso's mission is to be a world-class, diversified manufacturing company with an intense customer-driven strategy, and an organization with an attitude of continuous improvement in all areas of the business. Owosso's goal is to generate consistent, predictable earnings growth in order to provide maximum value to its customers, employees, suppliers and shareholders.

In 1986, Owosso was back to what it knew best: motors. The company added to its line of subfractional horsepower motors and timers with the purchase of Bristol Company, which was consolidated into Cramer Company the following year.

Owosso added a new product and a new end market to its portfolio in 1987, when it purchased the Dura-Bond Bearing Company. Dura-Bond, located in Carson City, Nevada, manufactured replacement camshaft bearings for internal combustion gas engines. Replacement bearings were used in the automotive aftermarket—to rebuild cast-iron engines in automobiles, trucks, and farming equipment. Unlike most of Owosso's other products, Dura-Bond's bearings were not marketed to OEMs; rather, they were sold primarily to large brand-name distributors and engine rebuilders.

Acquisitions and IPO: Early 1990s

As Owosso moved into the 1990s, it continued to grow through acquisitions. In 1991, the company purchased its second agricultural-market company: DewEze Manufacturing, Inc. DewEze was a Kansas-based maker of flatbed hay bale handlers—that is, hydraulic lifts that mounted on a pickup truck chassis and hoisted up to 5,000 pounds of hay onto the pickup bed. The company had little competition in this niche market; only two other U.S. companies manufactured similar products. Another key DewEze product was a hay bale processor, which sliced large hay bales into pieces to be used for livestock feed.

Owosso again strengthened its presence in the agricultural market in 1994 with the $17 million purchase of Sooner Trailer Manufacturing Co. Located in Duncan, Oklahoma, Sooner manufactured aluminum trailers for horses, livestock, automobiles, boats, and general cargo. The majority of its revenues came from the sale of horse trailers, which ranged from two-horse bumper hitch trailers to multi-horse goose neck trailers complete with living quarters.

In October 1994, Owosso went public, selling 1,865 shares and generating more than $20 million. Lemmon and other major shareholders retained control of the company, holding more than 63 percent of the shares. At the time of its IPO, Owosso's various subsidiaries were divided into two business segments: Engineered Component Products and Specialized Equipment. The company's Engineered Component Products segment included the Cramer, Snowmax, Dura-Bond, and Motor Products-Owosso businesses. Its Specialized Equipment segment consisted of Sooner, Parker, and DewEze. Altogether, the companies employed some 1,300 workers and had total combined sales of approximately $74 million. Because its subsidiaries were both diversified and geographically far-flung, Owosso's corporate management maintained a decentralized, hands-off approach. The 11-person staff in the company's Pennsylvania headquarters handled financing, employee benefits, and management information systems for its seven subsidiaries. Aside from those functions, each onsite manager was responsible and accountable for running his or her own business. Owosso's senior vice-president, John Wert, Jr., described the company's management style as "decentralized and attentive without being obtrusive" in an August 1995 interview with the *Philadelphia Inquirer*.

Second Generation Leadership: 1995–96

In 1995, Lemmon's son, George Lemmon, Jr., took over as Owosso's CEO. Although he was only in his early 30s, Lemmon, Jr., had almost 20 years of industry experience. He had begun working summers in his father's companies when he was in his teens and joined Owosso's management team in the early 1990s. Thus, he had a broad understanding of all aspects of the business, from manufacturing to management. Lemmon, Sr., remained active in the company, serving as chairman of the board of directors.

The year 1995 was also marked by two acquisitions, one for each operating segment. The first of the two, Great Bend Manufacturing, Inc., was a maker of front-end loaders for farming tractors. Owosso paid $4.3 million for the company, which had 1994 sales of $13.4 million. Great Bend's previous owner, Max Bennett, stayed on as president under the new ownership. Owosso's second 1995 acquisition was Stature Electric, Inc., a maker of integral horsepower motors located in Watertown, New York. Stature's motors were used primarily in the health care market to power wheelchairs and scooters. Also in 1995, Owosso incorporated Motor Products-Ohio, a manufacturing facility that operated as a division of the company's flagship business, Motor Products-Owosso.

Another two companies were added to the growing list of Owosso subsidiaries in 1996. In August the company acquired Snyder Industries, Inc., of Seattle, Washington, for $1.3 million. Snyder manufactured valve seats, valve seat inserts, and valve seat booster shims used to remanufacture automobile engines. In early 1997, Snyder's operations were consolidated into Owosso's Dura-Bond subsidiary, whose products, like Snyders, were used in the automotive aftermarket. In October 1996, Owosso purchased Koepke & Associates, a manufacturers' representative firm located in Northfield, Illinois. Renamed Owosso Motor Group, Inc., the firm served as a central sales organization for Owosso's motor companies, providing a more unified and focused sales presence.

Owosso's sales for 1996 were $128.2 million, an increase of almost 19 percent over 1995's sales of $108 million. Fifty-six percent of the total sales were generated by the Engineered Component Products subsidiaries, with the Specialized Equipment businesses making up the remainder. Despite its increase in sales, the company's bottom line for 1996 was disappointing. From a net of $6.4 million in 1995, profits fell to $848,000 in 1996. In a December 1996 interview with *The Philadelphia Inquirer*, a company representative said that while Owosso's total sales had increased due to acquisitions, its core businesses had suffered from lower sales and margins, higher taxes, and an inventory reduction program. The company also said it planned to take a more active role in managing its subsidiaries' operations in the coming years, striving for greater integration of the businesses.

Integration and Focus: 1997–98

True to its word, Owosso spent 1997 and 1998 reworking its management style in order to become less of a holding company and more of an integrated manufacturing company. In a 1997 strategic planning session, the company's management identified its core competencies as operational excellence, information technology, and management process. They then set about establishing a long-term growth plan built around those competencies. One of the main tenets of the plan was a tighter focus on engineered component products. Owosso believed that by devoting its energies more exclusively to this business segment, it could eliminate operational inefficiencies, provide greater value to its customers, and become more competitive in its various markets.

One of the company's first steps toward realizing this goal was to exit its agricultural equipment businesses—Parker Industries, Great Bend Manufacturing, and DewEze. In the spring of 1998, the company announced its intention to sell the three subsidiaries, which together had accounted for almost 24 percent of Owosso's 1997 sales. It was the first time Owosso had ever sold a financially successful subsidiary for strategic purposes. In a March 30, 1998 press release, George Lemmon, Jr., stated that the divestitures marked a "significant new strategic direction" for Owosso. He also noted that the capital derived from the sales would allow the company to pursue acquisitions in its Engineered Component Products segment.

Two such acquisitions were announced in April 1998. The first was Astro Air Inc., a Jacksonville, Texas, manufacturer of fin and tube heat exchange coils. Astro Air's products were used primarily in HVAC systems for large trucks, buses, and off-road vehicles. Owosso's second 1998 acquisition was M.H. Rhodes Inc., a maker of mechanical timers and photoelectric controls used mainly in the appliance industry. The Rhodes business was an ideal complement to Owosso's Cramer subsidiary, which manufactured both motors and timers used in appliances. Upon completing the acquisition, Owosso merged its Cramer operations into Rhodes' manufacturing facility located in Avon, Connecticut.

Owosso also made substantial investments in its Stature Electric business in 1998. Stature was at that point the company's fastest growing subsidiary, with sales that had increased by 45 percent since 1996. To accommodate this growth, Owosso initiated an expansion project that would add 30,000 square feet of manufacturing space and $4 million in new equipment to the Stature facility by the end of 1999.

Growth on Dual Fronts: 1999 and Beyond

At the end of 1998, Owosso had net sales of $160 million. The company's Sooner Trailer business contributed more than 21 percent of the total sales, followed by Stature, Motor Products-Owosso, and Snomax. Net income for 1998 was $702,000, which translated into a net per-share loss of $.06 for the year. Owosso's poor bottom line was due largely to charges associated with the Astro Air and M.H. Rhodes acquisitions and the subsequent consolidation of the Rhodes and Cramer subsidiaries.

The company's goal for the future was annual growth of 15 to 20 percent, split evenly between internal initiatives and acquisitions. The company's corporate acquisition team was continuing to seek acquisition candidates that would fit into its engineered components business segment. Likely candidates were profitable manufacturing operations that opened new end markets or broadened the ones already served. Internal growth was to be achieved through a continued effort to eliminate inefficiencies and reduce costs throughout the entire manufacturing process and supply chain, from raw materials to finished product. Owosso believed that by streamlining operations, it could enhance its service and value to customers, providing them with a "product package" that included consistently on-time delivery, shared data, and jointly engineered products. By providing a superior product surrounded by value-added services, the company hoped to sharpen its competitive edge and capture substantial market share in each of its niche markets.

Principal Subsidiaries

Astro Air, Inc.; Dura-Bond Bearing Company; M.H. Rhodes, Inc.; Motor Products-Owosso Corporation; Motor Products-Ohio Corporation; Owosso Motor Group, Inc.; Snowmax, Incorporated; Sooner Trailer Manufacturing Co.; Stature Electric, Inc.

Principal Operating Units

Engineered Component Products; Specialized Equipment.

Further Reading

Binzen, Peter, "W. Conshohocken Firm Succeeds by Trying Not to Interfere," *Philadelphia Inquirer,* August 21, 1995, p. C3.
Natarajan, Prabha, "No Grass Under these Young Feet: Three CEOs Strike Gold before 40," *Philadelphia Business Journal,* August 2, 1999.

—Shawna Brynildssen

Pathé SA

5, boulevard Malesherbes
75008 Paris
France
(33) 1 49 24 40 83
Fax: (33) 1 49 24 40 89
Web site: http://www.pathe.com

Private Company
Incorporated: 1896 as Pathé Frères
Employees: 1,400
Sales: FFr 1.18 billion (US $374 million) (1998)
NAIC: 51211 Motion Picture & Video Production; 51212
    Motion Picture & Video Distribution; 512131 Motion
    Picture Theaters (Except Drive-Ins); 51321 Cable
    Networks; 51111 Newspaper Publishers

One of the most illustrious names in motion picture history, Pathé remains one of France's leading forces in film production and distribution. Led by Jerome Seydoux, whose younger brother Nicolas has long served as the head of another illustrious French name in cinema, Gaumont, Pathé operates its own network of some 300 movie theaters and multiplexes in France and Holland; produces and distributes films for cinema and for television; owns its own cable television and satellite television networks (the theme channel Voyage and a 51 percent share of AB Sports); owns the daily newspaper *Liberation*; and, in 1998 purchased a share of the Olympiques Lyonnaise soccer team.

Until 1999, Pathé also possessed a 17 percent share in BSkyB Television, one of the leading European satellite broadcasters, jointly owned by Rupert Murdoch, and a 20 percent share of CanalSatellite, the leading satellite television provider in France. These two holdings represented the largest part of Pathé's revenues, which reached FFr 1.18 billion for the company's 1998 year. In June 1999, however, Vivendi—in the process of reinventing itself as a major force in European communications—announced that it had taken control of Pathé and was merging the two companies' holdings with that of CanalPlus, parent of CanalSatellite and controlled at 34 percent by Vivendi. The merger agreement would group Pathé's satel-

lite television holdings under Vivendi, while giving Seydoux full control of Pathé's film production, distribution, theme channels, and other communications holdings. Seydoux, who previously led the breakup of former Pathé parent Chargeurs International and who continues to control both companies, has chosen to keep Pathé off the public market.

Founding French Motion Picture History

Born in 1863, Charles Pathé became one of the first to recognize the potential of a new generation of inventions in the 1890s. Originally from the French Alsace region, Pathé had come to the Parisian suburb of Vincennes with his family in the 1860s. The Pathés owned a small delicatessen; Pathé's older brother Jacques would remain close to the family trade, operating a butcher's shop in Saint Sauveur. Charles Pathé came to work with Jacques, and proved so successful at building his brother's trade that Jacques gave him a gift of a thousand francs. Pathé looked toward founding his own business: a traveling butcher's serving France's fairs and markets.

Instead, Pathé traveled to Buenos Aires aboard a ship of the young company Chargeurs. In Argentina, Pathé attempted to sell laundry machines. A bout of yellow fever, which killed his partner, would send Pathé back to France soon after. By 1891, Pathé was back in Vincennes, now operating a family-owned bistro. A falling-out with his parents would set Pathé, now broke and newly married, on his own.

In 1894, however, Pathé would find his calling. A new invention—the phonograph, created by Thomas Edison—was making the rounds of the country's fairs and markets. Pathé quickly recognized the phonograph's potential. After borrowing 700 francs, Pathé bought his own phonograph and began traveling the market circuit. Pathé's traveling days were brief, however. In 1895 Pathé opened his own phonograph shop, not only selling the machines but also establishing studios for recording and selling rolls of music. The following year, Pathé added another Edison invention, the kinetoscope, which was then making a successful tour of the country's fairs.

By 1896, Pathé had convinced his brothers to join him in his growing business, and Pathé Frères was born. Brother Emile would take charge of the company's phonograph operations, and

Charles Pathé would launch the company into motion pictures. Pathé was joined in this by Henri Joly, who, with Pathé's backing, invented a so-called "chronophotographique" camera-projector, one of the first of the true "motion picture" devices. Despite a falling out with Joly, Pathé would retain possession of the latter's machine. By then, the Lumière brothers had already realized the first film—its success would encourage Pathé to enter not only the filmmaking business, but also film distribution. Pathé soon recognized the potential of renting films, rather than selling them outright. This activity would later lead the company into establishing its own film houses.

The new entertainment form would quickly capture the attention of Parisian high society—and, after a devastating fire caused by the projection equipment, would as quickly fall out of favor. Facing financial ruin, Pathé was forced to accept the capital of leading industrialist Claude Grivolas. The company's name was changed to Compagnie Générale de Cinématographes, Phonographes et Pellicules. The company merged with another leading motion picture equipment maker, Continsouza et Bunzli, and Pathé acquired the rights to the Lumière projection machine. Pathé quickly improved the device and by 1898 was marketing his own "reinforced" projector, which would soon establish itself as the leading projector in the world.

By the turn of the century, Pathé provided not only the projectors, cameras, and motion pictures, but also its own raw film stock, breaking the monopoly then held by Eastman Kodak. In 1906 the company established its film laboratories in Joinville. The company also was making a name worldwide for its motion pictures—in particular, a Pathé innovation, that of filming current events. The Pathé Journal, the first newsreel, would long remain a fixture in the world's cinema programs. Many of Pathé's actors also would become world-renowned stars. Meanwhile, the company had introduced the first films in color—hand-painted frame by frame at the Pathé laboratories.

Changing Hands in the 1930s

Pathé, meanwhile, had begun to expand internationally, establishing branch offices in major cities around the world. During the First World War, the company moved its headquarters to the United States, where Pathé could continue its activities. By the end of the war, however, Charles Pathé had decided to rein in his growing empire, concentrating operations once again at the company's Joinville location. At this time, the Pathé brothers decided to break up the company into its two operations, with Emile taking over the phonograph business and Charles taking the lead of the film business.

Pathé would transform the company, now known as Société Pathé Cinéma, in the next decade. A decision to abandon manufacture of motion picture apparatus caused a national uproar. At the same time, Pathé shut down its U.S. and British branches, concentrating film and film stock production in France. By the end of the decade, the company would no longer operate under Charles Pathé's control.

In 1927, after more than two decades of an often bitter rivalry, Pathé and Eastman Kodak agreed to merge their film stock manufacturing activities to form Kodak-Pathé. This unit was absorbed formally as a subsidiary to the Eastman Kodak Company in 1931. By then, Pathé's cinema operations already

had been taken by Bernard Natan, who had succeeded in buying up a majority of Pathé's shares. Charles Pathé remained on the company's board; one year later, in 1930, however, after disagreements with Natan over the company's direction, Pathé stepped down from the board, ending his association with the company he had founded. Charles Pathé would die in 1957.

Meanwhile, Pathé struggled into the Depression Era. The company's revenues were slipping; box office receipts were plunging. Pathé also was facing competition from the bustling Hollywood film industry and the arrival of the first "talkies," which quickly came to dominate the motion picture market. In addition, Natan had led the company into a series of financial investments and other activities that were doubtful at best. Charges of corruption brought an end to Natan's reign over the company in 1935, when Natan was arrested for embezzlement. By the end of the decade, Pathé was forced to declare bankruptcy.

The company passed into the hands of a consortium of banks and the French finance ministry, before being taken over by Adrien Ramauge in 1943 and having its name changed to Société Nouvelle Pathé Cinema. Under Ramauge, Pathé once again would combine its motion picture operations with the Pathé phonograph operations, which soon after merged with Marconi, and branched out into manufacture of televisions and phonographs under the Pathé-Marconi brand. In the film business, Pathé would score one of its greatest successes, with the release of 1945's *Les Enfants du Paradis* (Children of Paradise).

The Postwar Years

At the end of the Second World War, the world's cinema market had dramatically changed. The French film industry had seen its facilities devastated and its markets restricted. In the meantime, Hollywood—where many of Europe's film professionals had fled to escape the Nazis—had successfully imposed itself as the world's leading film production center, a position it would retain through the end of the century.

Pathé itself would never quite regain its position as a moving force in motion picture—and phonographic—development. Nonetheless, the company continued to play a leading role in French cinema. If French cinema could not rival Hollywood in box office figures, it nonetheless underwent a revival in the 1950s and 1960s, bringing international acclaim to a *Nouvelle Vague* generation of directors, actors, and films. Pathé, meanwhile, was attracting the financial interests of the Rivaud Group, which succeeded in taking majority control of the company by the end of the 1960s.

Film distribution also was becoming more and more important to Pathé's revenues. In the mid-1960s, the company's only true domestic rival was fellow film pioneer Gaumont. The two companies would end that rivalry before the end of the decade by forming a distribution alliance for the direction of the companies' combined 250 theaters. This alliance, in the form of a "grouping of economic interests" (GIE) would give Pathé and Gaumont a de facto monopoly over France's screens: by 1974, the Pathé-Gaumont GIE operated nearly 450 theater screens, a number that would top 600 before the end of the decade. By then, a new name had appeared on the French film scene—Nicolas Seydoux, one of the heirs to the prominent Schlumberger family fortune, had succeeded in acquiring majority control of Gaumont.

The Société Nouvelle Pathé Cinema became simply Pathé Cinéma in 1979. By then, however, the company's film production had sunk to a low point in the company's history, while the exploitation of theaters had risen to become its primary revenue source. Those revenues soon were threatened when the Pathé-Gaumont GIE was dismantled by the newly elected Socialist government of 1983. Pathé responded by building a federation of its own theaters with those of a number of independents. The company then reached a cooperation agreement with the Eveline family, then holder of more than 100 theaters in the Paris area. This cooperation would once again allow Pathé to claim the leadership of the French film distribution market.

The defection of the Eveline family to rival distributor UGC in 1989 would, however, end this leadership. The company also was suffering from a malaise in the French film market, as box office receipts slumped dramatically into the new decade. Meanwhile, Pathé had become the object of a series of takeover bids, including moves by the Italian financier Paretti, that finally would see the company lose its independence.

In 1990 Pathé became a subsidiary of Chargeurs International. Led by Jerome Seydoux, older brother of Gaumont chief Nicolas, Chargeurs had been developing an audiovisual portfolio, including strong shareholdings in the proposed British Sky Broadcasting satellite television effort and the emerging subscriber-based CanalPlus television network. Seydoux quickly reorganized Pathé's operations. The Pathé-Marconi television and phonographic manufacturing was sold off as EMI France. Pathé's remaining operations were split into two divisions: Cinema, which operated the company's network of theaters, by then expanded to included a strong presence in the Dutch theater market; and Television, which provided programming for the French and international television broadcasting markets.

Return to Roots in the 1990s

In 1993 Pathé became the first to introduce a new cinema concept to the French theater market—that of the multiplex theater. The multiscreen theater concept caught on quickly with the French theatergoing public, and Pathé began converting a number of its theaters to the new format. Seydoux also stepped up Pathé's film production and financing activities—an effort that would meet with mixed results. The Chargeurs subsidiary recorded a number of flops—including the expensive *Pirates* and *Showgirls*—into the middle of the decade.

In 1996 Jerome Seydoux announced his intention to break up Chargeurs International into two separate, publicly quoted entities. Chargeurs would continue as operator of the group's manufacturing interests. The group's audiovisual activities, including its theater networks, film and television production, and holdings in the successfully launched BSkyB satellite network and the emerging CanalSatellite broadcasting service, were split off into the newly formed Pathé SA.

Jerome Seydoux continued to hold majority interests in Chargeurs. Seydoux, however, left leadership of Chargeurs to his long-time righthand man, Eduardo Malone. Seydoux, while remaining a vice-president of Chargeurs, took the CEO title of Pathé. The independent Pathé recorded nearly FFr 2.3 billion by the end of 1997. The largest part of these revenues, however, came from the company's nearly 22 percent holding in the BSkyB and CanalSatellite networks.

Through the end of the decade, Seydoux continued to build Pathé's theater network, with an ambitious program of new and converted multiplexes bringing the company's network to more than 300 theaters. Seydoux also began developing Pathé's holdings beyond France and The Netherlands, announcing new theaters for the Italian market in 1999. Pathé recorded success with the production of *The Fifth Element*, the most expensive French (and European) film ever made, which became a worldwide hit in 1997. The company continued to struggle with its film production and distribution arm, however, with flops (including the controversial remake of *Lolita*) contributing to a drop in revenues, down to FFr 2.18 billion in 1998.

Meanwhile, the company's satellite television holdings had begun to attract interest from outside investors. In 1998 French financier Vincent Bolloré announced that he had bought up some ten percent of Pathé's shares. Seydoux was forced to fight off the takeover attempt by looking for a white knight investor. In June 1999, Pathé announced its agreement to be purchased by the French Vivendi, pursuing its own multimedia development—particularly in the satellite television arena. Under the agreement, which also included television network and Vivendi holding CanalPlus, Vivendi would take over Pathé's stake in BSkyB; Pathé's CanalSatellite holdings were placed under control of CanalPlus.

The remaining Pathé operations included the theater network; its satellite television holdings, which included the specialist channels Voyage and a 51 percent stake in AB Sports; ownership of the daily newspaper, *Liberation*; and a share in the soccer team Olympiques Lyonnaise, purchased by Pathé in 1998. Jerome Seydoux would take full control of Pathé's operations; the company's listing was removed from the Paris stock exchange to continue its development as a private company. The French film industry was now more or less firmly in the control of the Seydoux family, with Nicolas Seydoux leading Gaumont and Jerome Seydoux holding Pathé. A combination of the family's interests into a single Gaumont-Pathé entity appeared inevitable—despite the continued denials of interests by both Seydoux brothers.

Principal Operating Units

AB Sports (51%); Voyage; Liberation; Olympiques Lyonnaise.

Further Reading

Chabert, Patrick, "Trois frères à Cannes," *Les Echoes,* May 12, 1999, p. 78.
Esquirou, Martine, "Jerome Seydoux reste present dans le cinema et le textile," *Les Echoes,* June 8, 1999, p. 16.
——, "Le Groupe Vivendi absorbe Pathé pour prendre pied dans BSkyB," *Les Echoes,* June 8, 1999, p. 16.
Horsman, Mathew, "Chargeurs Split Fuels Media Rumours," *Independent,* February 28, 1996, p. 15.
Kermabon, Jacques, ed., *Pathé: Premier Empire du Cinema,* Paris: Editions du Centre Pompidou, 1994.
"Vivendi To Get BSkyB in Pathé Merger," *Reuters,* June 7, 1999.

—M.L. Cohen

Pentech International, Inc.

195 Carter Drive
Edison, New Jersey 08817
U.S.A.
(732) 287-6640
Fax: (732) 287-6610

Public Company
Incorporated: 1984
Employees: 208
Sales: $57.5 million (1998)
Stock Exchanges: NASDAQ
Ticker Symbol: PNTK
NAIC: 339941 Pen & Mechanical Pencil Manufacturing;
    339942 Lead Pencil & Art Good Manufacturing;
    42212 Stationery & Office Supplies Wholesalers

Pentech International, Inc. manufactures and sells pens, pencils, markers, art supplies, school supplies, and other stationery products. Its products are sold under the Pentech name or under other licensed trademark brands. For example, the company has licensing agreements with entities such as Walt Disney, Lucasfilm, Coca-Cola, the NFL, the NHL, and the NBA, to produce writing implements bearing the logos or characters associated with those groups. Pentech's products are sold through most mass-marketing retail channels, such as Wal-Mart, Kmart, Target, Walgreen, and other office supply chains. Although the company distributes its products throughout the world, approximately 95 percent of the company's sales come from within the United States.

The Early Years

Although Pentech International, Inc. was not founded until 1984, the company's beginnings can actually be traced back to more than 40 years earlier. In 1941, at the age of ten, Norman Melnick began working for his uncle in the pen-making business. He learned a lot about the business in these early years and began experimenting with innovations of his own. Fifteen years later, Melnick found his place in history when he invented the first commercially available dry ink for ballpoint pens.

Almost 25 years passed, and Melnick continued to work in the business. In 1980 he purchased Magic Marker, which was the manufacturer and distributor of a line of felt-tip coloring pens. The pens, known as "markers," came in many different colors and were a huge hit among children. That year, however, the company was having difficulties. Melnick acquired Magic Marker and made efforts to nurse the ailing company back into health.

Three years later, however, Melnick sold Magic Marker and began formulating plans to start his own company with his son, David Melnick. Together, the two created Pentech International, Inc. in 1984. Their new company designed and sold writing and drawing instruments, as well as other art supplies and stationery items.

Pentech began inking distribution deals with major retail chains around the United States, and soon its products were found nationwide in well-known stores such as discount retailers Wal-Mart, Kmart, and Target; drug stores such as Walgreen, CVS, and Eckerd; and office supply stores such as Office Max and Staples.

Pentech was soon quite successful, and by 1987 had grown to the point that the Melnicks were justified in making the decision to take the company public. Two years later the company created a subsidiary called Sawdust Pencil Company to manufacture Pentech's line of pencil products.

Growth in the Early 1990s

Pentech also brought in revenue and expanded its product line through licensing agreements, in which it obtained the rights to use another company's logo or trademark characters on its pens, pencils, and markers. One such deal was formed in 1991 with Walt Disney, who agreed to let Pentech manufacture and market products featuring many different Disney cartoon characters.

The company diversified its product line greatly in 1993. At that time, the company formed a new division to handle—

surprisingly—the manufacture of a line of cosmetics products. A few years earlier Pentech had taken on extra business for a while and had used its pencil-making machinery to produce private label eye pencils under the Cara-Bella brand name. The enterprise proved to be profitable, and Pentech began to believe that it could churn out even more revenue if it created an entire line of products to sell on its own. The new product line was named Fun Cosmetics and was planned to be targeted mainly at the teenage market.

Shortly following the company's foray into the land of cosmetics, Pentech inked another licensing agreement—this time with the National Basketball Association (NBA). The agreement called for Pentech to create, produce, and sell items from its writing implements product line featuring the team logos of different NBA franchises. The agreement gave the NBA increased exposure, while also giving Pentech access to a portion of the near $3 billion in sales of NBA-licensed merchandise during the 1993–1994 season. Pentech soon developed its NBA line into an entire Pro Sports line, which eventually came to include National Hockey League (NHL) and National Football League (NFL) licensed products.

Also in 1994, Pentech created and began to sell the Color Club product line for kids. Color Club was a group of art supply activity sets with numerous different themes. For example, there were sets based on dinosaurs and endangered animals and sets with washable markers and stick-on decals. Furthermore, customers could actually enroll in the Pentech Color Club, which entitled members to an art supply kit and a monthly newsletter in exchange for three proofs of purchase and a $2.95 shipping fee.

Meanwhile, by mid-1995 Pentech was implementing marketing plans for its Fun Cosmetics line. The Pentech cosmetics division worked closely with *Teen* magazine's in-house advertising staff to develop a print advertisement campaign, into which more than $1 million was funneled during late 1995 and early 1996. After the product line was test-marketed in Wal-Mart for two months and later shipped to other retailers, the print advertisements began running in *Teen* and *Sassy* magazines in December 1995. In the October 10, 1995 issue of *Brandweek,* Pentech cosmetics marketing director Kristin Penta supported the company's decision to focus mainly on the teenage market: "Teens are where the spending power is . . . Teens make or influence purchases of more than $200 billion a year, by some estimates." According to the U.S. Census Bureau, the teenage demographic was projected to increase dramatically to 31 million by 2010.

Shortly thereafter, the Melnicks made another move that surprised some outsiders when they brought in John Linster as the new Pentech president and CEO. Since its inception, Pentech had been a family-run business. On November 15, 1995, however, the company announced the hiring of Linster, who had worked previously for office supplies manufacturing company Avery Dennison. At Avery Dennison, Linster had worked in the area of new product development and had helped create a division that dramatically increased the company's annual sales. Thus Pentech's founders hoped that Linster's experience would help propel their company forward into an era of new growth.

The Mid-1990s and Beyond

In 1996 Pentech's sales were slipping and the company posted large overall annual losses that were attributed to a lawsuit settlement paid to Paradise Creations. Paradise had sued Pentech for patent infringement with relation to an erasable marker product and had won the case.

Still experiencing financial woes in 1997, Pentech began a reorganization that included a reaffirmed focus on its roots as a writing instrument developer and manufacturer. This decision was based in part on the fact that in 1997 95 percent of Pentech's business came from sales of its writing instruments, with the other five percent stemming from sales of cosmetics. The cosmetics line, although doing well, was not contributing enough to Pentech's earnings to make it a worthwhile keeper. Therefore, the company divested the cosmetics division and also reduced its core product line dramatically. This second move helped Pentech capitalize on its most profitable lines while avoiding the manufacture of the less profitable. Fun Cosmetics was spun off and began publicly trading its own stock in mid-March of 1998. Linster also was let go, and David Melnick assumed the role of CEO in 1998.

Meanwhile, Pentech had sued the law firm that had handled its defense in the Paradise Creations patent infringement case. In the new lawsuit, Pentech accused its former New York-based law firm, Cooper and Dunham, of malpractice when the unfavorable judgment was received in the Paradise case. In April 1998 Pentech won its malpractice case and was awarded a $1.3 million settlement.

Even though the company's sales slipped by about 1.5 percent from 1996 to 1997, in 1997 the company posted earnings of around $600,000 on its overall sales of $60.8 million. This was a welcome improvement after the previous year's losses and signaled that the company might be back on track again.

The following year, unfortunately, Pentech's sales slipped once again, this time to $57.5 million for the 1998 fiscal year. The decrease resulted in a $3.5 million loss for the year. One contributing factor to the lackluster sales activity was a significant decrease in sales of the company's licensed products—especially that of its NBA products. The NBA experienced a lockout in late 1998; therefore, fan support of the league—and subsequent purchases of NBA products—was at a low.

In March of 1999 Pentech made a move to increase its exposure and sales potential by announcing its intent to develop a web site and engage in e-commerce. According to David Melnick in a company press release, "We intend to leverage the power of our Color Club brand and become a leading marketer of children's activity products in the World Wide Web." The company planned to have the new web site up and running by July 1999.

As the end of the 20th century approached, Pentech announced that it was predicting a turnaround of its sales and earnings declines from the previous few years. The company cited the increasingly strong sales of its popular Color Club line since its inception as a high point during the downturn. Furthermore, Pentech focused on aggressively producing and marketing the line to meet consumer demand and to increase Color

Club sales. Pentech's ability to capitalize on its strong products, while refraining from diverting too much attention to its weaker lines, would determine the company's potential for profitability in the future.

Principal Subsidiaries

Sawdust Pencil Company.

Further Reading

Curan, Catherine, "Fun Cosmetics Begins Public Trading This Week," *Women's Wear Daily,* March 20, 1998, p. 8.

"Fun for Teenagers: Pentech's Color Effect," *Women's Wear Daily,* August 25, 1995, p. 8.

Gerena, Charles, "New Product Parade," *Equities,* December 1994, p. 42.

Marcial, G. G., "This Penmaker's Ink Is All Black," *Business Week,* July 24, 1989, p. 62.

"New Blood," *Business News New Jersey,* November 29, 1995, p. 5.

Parks, Liz, "Will Consumers Just Want To Have Fun?," *Drug Store News,* January 22, 1996, p. 21.

"Pentech Creates Outsourcing Subsidiary," *Employee Benefit Plan Review,* January 1997, p. 59.

"Pentech International, Inc.," *Wall Street Journal—Eastern Edition,* December 30, 1996, p. B2.

"Pentech Settles Suit Against Ex-law Firm Over a Patent Case," *Wall Street Journal—Eastern Edition,* April 9, 1998, p. B9.

"Results To Miss Forecasts; Top Executive Leaves Firm," *Wall Street Journal—Eastern Edition,* March 31, 1998, p. B4.

Symons, Allene, "Kids' Arts and Crafts on the Grow," *Drug Store News,* November 17, 1997, p. 59.

Weisz, Pam, "Teens Get Fun Choice," *Brandweek,* October 9, 1995, p. 8.

—Laura E. Whiteley

Perot Systems Corporation

12404 Park Central Drive
Dallas, Texas 75251
U.S.A.
(972) 340-5000
Fax: (972) 340-6788
Web site: http://www.perotsystems.com

Public Company
Incorporated: 1988
Employees: 6,000
Sales: $993.6 million (1998)
Stock Exchanges: New York
Ticker Symbol: PER
NAIC: 541511 Custom Computer Programming Services;
    541512 Computer Systems Design Services; 51421
    Data Processing Services; 541519 Other Computer
    Related Services

Perot Systems Corporation, based in Dallas and chaired by Texas billionaire H. Ross Perot, is a worldwide leader in information technology services and business solutions. The company helps businesses create and manage their technology networks, with services including consulting, systems integration and operation, and software development. The company works primarily in the energy, financial services, healthcare, and travel industries. Major competitors include Perot's former company, Electronic Data Systems (EDS), which in 1984 became a wholly owned subsidiary of General Motors Corporation and then was spun off 12 years later.

Pre-Perot Systems— *The Navy, IBM, and EDS: 1952–87*

At the age of 19, a young Texan named H. Ross Perot received a much desired appointment to the U.S. Naval Academy. Although he valued his time in the military, he found it too restrictive and decided against building a career in the Navy.

In 1952, while still in the Navy, he was recruited to be a salesman by International Business Machines (IBM). Initially he found their business style comfortable, but became frustrated after a time.

In January 1962 Perot already had fulfilled his entire annual sales quota because of a recent change in IBM's commission structure. Not satisfied with the administrative job then offered him by IBM, he recognized an unmet need among IBM's many computer customers. Most companies had few knowledgeable personnel to operate their new computer equipment. Perot wanted to offer skilled electronic data processing management services to these companies. He presented his ideas to IBM executives, but they were not interested.

Perot left the company and, on June 27, 1962 (his 32nd birthday) incorporated Electronic Data Systems (EDS) in Dallas, a company that would develop a business concept later termed "facilities management." Perot spent the first five months canvassing the East Coast and the Midwest to find a first customer for his computer services company. He had bought wholesale computer time on an IBM 7070 computer installed at Southwestern Life Insurance in Dallas during the latter company's idle hours (EDS would not acquire its own computer until 1965). Once he sold this time at retail, he was in business. Collins Radio in Cedar Rapids, Iowa, became EDS's first customer and launched a new industry called information services. The company grew rapidly and employed many of Perot's former colleagues at IBM.

On June 27, 1984, although the company never had a contract with an automobile manufacturer, EDS became a wholly owned subsidiary of General Motors Corporation (GM). GM needed EDS to coordinate and manage its huge, unwieldy data processing system and to cut its $6 billion annual data processing costs. Roger B. Smith, GM's chairman of the board, thought Perot's management style would be an asset to his giant corporation. The $2.5 billion purchase price was the largest ever paid for a computer services business. GM agreed to maintain EDS as a separate entity, keep key personnel, and issue a special class of common stock that would be tied to EDS's performance. Perot retained managerial control of EDS and served on

Company Perspectives:

We listen attentively to our customers and to team members working directly with our customers. Every member of our team, including our CEO, is available 24 hours a day, seven days a week, to go anywhere, anytime, to serve our customers.

GM's board of directors. Problems surfaced within a year when the differences in management style between Perot and Smith became evident. By 1986 the differences had become intolerable; GM paid Perot $700 million for his GM and EDS stock and asked him to depart and not hire any GM or EDS employees for at least a year.

Perot Systems: 1988–99

In June 1988, a year-and-a-half to the day later, Perot founded Perot Systems with eight EDS veterans, including former EDS leader Morton Meyerson. Almost immediately, the company landed a ten-year contract to cut costs for the U.S. Postal Service. However, because the GM separation agreement prohibited Perot from competing with EDS for profit until December 1989, Perot Systems worked for free for another 18 months. Lobbying pressure from GM resulted in Perot Systems losing the Postal Service contract, but generated enough publicity for the beset new company that Perot Systems was deluged with new contracts. The new company began to sink quickly, though, and not just because it was working without getting paid. Perot's anti-NAFTA political speeches just as Perot Systems was working on ventures with Volkswagen de Mexico and Multibanco Mercantil Probursa alienated Mexicans and the deals fell through.

Rapid changes in technology and deregulation created new challenges for the company's customers in the energy industry. Its work in the early 1990s with European utility companies provided unique insights into the requirements for deregulation of the industry in the United States. The company worked with regulated utilities, nonregulated and new market entrants, and entirely new market entities, providing solutions to address market restructuring and compliance and provide solutions for settlements and clearing systems, integrated supply chain management, trading and risk management, and transaction management systems.

In 1992 Perot stepped down as leader of the new company to devote more time to his unsuccessful first campaign for the White House, turning the company over to former EDS leader Morton Meyerson. Meyerson, who became CEO, moved the company away from computer outsourcing in an effort not to go head-to-head against EDS, which had since split away from GM and was rapidly becoming the number one company in that field in the world. Instead, Perot Systems would begin focusing on higher-margin consulting services. In 1994 the company acquired the Custom Development Division of Platinum Software, a financial software firm.

James Cannavino, former number two executive at IBM, joined the company in 1995, becoming president. He helped leverage a seven-year contract with Tenet Health Care, marking an early outsourcing of computer operations in the healthcare industry. That year, the company reincorporated in Delaware and added products and services in manufacturing equipment for the first time.

In its battle with EDS, Perot Systems also targeted small to mid-sized clients, including First National Bank of Tucumcari in New Mexico, North Side Bank and Trust Co. in Cincinnati, and Southside State Bank in Tyler, Texas, all of whom joined the company's client list in 1996. Also that year, the company acquired four companies, among which were Technical Resource Connection, an object-oriented programming company, and CommSys, a telecommunications billing system developer. The company brought in $600 million in revenues for the year.

In February 1997 Perot Systems acquired Benton International, Inc., a consulting organization that pioneered the concept of electronic funds payments and that consulted to the largest financial institutions in the world. Benton, which got its start developing electronic funds transfer systems, evolved into broad expertise in alternate channel strategy and implementation, including such elements of electronic commerce as smart cards, credit/debit cards, and related networking infrastructures. With its acknowledged expertise in electronic commerce, Benton represented a strategic fit for Perot Systems' growing Global Financial Services (GFS) group, which was focusing on serving leading banking institutions such as Swiss Bank Corporation, NationsBank, and Barclays Bank. Benton, which was established in 1978 by Jack Benton, retained its name and operated as a subsidiary. The acquisition also brought nearly 50 employees, a veritable "Who's Who" list of clients, and offices in Tampa, Florida; New York; Buenos Aires, Argentina; Bogota, Colombia; and London.

The following month, Perot Systems purchased a controlling stake (70 percent) from SwissAir Corp. in Icarus Consulting AG, a Zurich- and Frankfurt-based management consulting firm that served the travel and transportation industries in Europe, including major European air carriers, forwarders, hotels, the German railway system, and the German Navy. Founded in 1988, Icarus had been owned 55 percent and 45 percent by SAir Group, the holding company of SwissAir, and Icarus's management, respectively. Perot Systems also obtained a fixed option to purchase the remaining 30 percent from SAir Group over a three-year period. As an example of its work, Icarus conceived and implemented a new air cargo system that combined the services of SwissAir and Sabena Airlines. Under the unique arrangement, Sabena essentially sold its airline cargo space to SwissCargo, the SAir Group's cargo arm, giving up marketing and operational costs in exchange for a guaranteed revenue stream. SwissCargo gained added capacity and market share and was able to utilize its existing sales infrastructure much more efficiently. The acquisition further expanded Perot Systems' insertion into European markets, which accounted for 40 percent of the company's revenue by that time.

In June the company acquired Syllogic B.V., a leading technology company specializing in systems management, data warehousing, and data mining applications and services, based in the Netherlands. The acquisition expanded Perot Systems' data warehousing and data mining skills in Europe. The company, which kept its name, was founded in 1991 and brought 125 employees in offices in the United States, Ireland, and the United Kingdom.

Nets Inc., the struggling Internet commerce company launched by Lotus founder Jim Manzi, was acquired by Perot Systems in June 1997. The acquisition brought 58 employees to the company and greatly accelerated Perot Systems' strategy to deliver business-to-business electronic commerce systems, services, and online market ventures.

In a major step to expand its Health Care Group's strategic consulting capabilities, in July the company acquired Stamos Associates Inc. (SAI), a 30-member healthcare consulting firm founded by Dr. Peter S. Stamos, former chief of staff to U.S. Senator Bill Bradley. The acquisition of the consulting firm, which specialized in the design and implementation of innovative healthcare business strategies for integrated delivery systems, hospitals, physicians, and insurers, brought additional clients throughout the United States, Australia, Canada, Sweden, the United Kingdom, and Malaysia.

Also in 1997, Cannavino stepped down from his position as president and CEO amidst rising costs and falling earnings. Meyerson took over in the interim while the company looked for a new leader. When Perot retook the helm without pay in November, Meyerson resigned as chairman. Immediately, Perot got busy shaking things up, revoking health benefits for same-sex partners, cutting expenses, reinstating drug testing, and pushing recruitment from the military. The company's revenues reached $781.6 million, with a net income of $11.2 million, and added to its arsenal of products and services: computer software products and services in the fields of accounting communications systems and facilities management, and telecommunications and Internet products and services.

Throughout 1997 and 1998, Perot Systems forged strategic alliances with a plethora of diverse companies, providing IT services and solutions to each. These companies included The Bank of Ireland in the financial services industry; AT&T and WinStar in the telecommunications industry; National Car Rental and Eastern Pacific Airlines in the travel industry; and Physicians Online, The International Committee of the Red Cross, and Integrated Health Services in the healthcare industry.

In August 1998 the company filed to go public. Up to that point, Perot owned more than 40 percent of the company, and Meyerson owned ten percent. The company ranked 358th in the *Forbes* Private 500 list that year, with total revenue growing to $993.6 million (up 27 percent) and net income jumping to $40.5 million (up 261 percent). On February 1, 1999, the company's stock began trading on the New York Stock Exchange.

Principal Subsidiaries

Benton International, Incorporated; Deutsche Perot Systems GmbH; HCL Perot Systems N.V.; HCL Perot Systems Private Limited (India); HCL Perot Systems Pte. Limited (Singapore); HCL Perot Systems (Mauritius) Pvt. Ltd.; HPS America, Inc.; HPS Europe Limited; Icarus Consulting A.G.; Icarus Consulting GmbH; Perot Systems A.G.; Perot Systems Asia Pacific Pte Ltd.; Perot Systems B.V.; Perot Systems (Canada) Corporation; Perot Systems Communication Services, Inc.; Perot Systems Europe (Energy Services) Limited; Perot Systems Europe Limited; Perot Systems Field Services Corporation; Perot Systems Financial Services Corporation; Perot Systems Holdings Pte Ltd.; Perot Systems Investments B.V.; Perot Systems (Japan) Ltd.; Perot Systems Monaco S.A.M.; Perot Systems Realty Corporation; Perot Systems S.A.; Persys Ireland Limited; PSC Government Services Corporation; PSC Health Care, Inc.; PS Information Resource (Ireland) Limited; RothWell International, Inc.; Stamos Associates Inc.; Syllogic Ireland Limited; Syllogic B.V.; Syllogic Limited; The Technical Resource Connection, Inc.

Further Reading

Appleby, Chuck, "Tenet's Computer Compact," *Hospitals & Health Networks,* October 20, 1995, p. 52.

Bishop, Amanda, "Perot Systems Settles on Site," *Dallas Business Journal,* August 28, 1998, p. 1.

Bounds, Jeff, "Perot Plans New 'Command Center,' " *Dallas Business Journal,* August 29, 1997, p. 1.

Burlingham, Bo, and Curtis Hartman, "Cowboy Capitalist," *Inc.,* January 1989, p. 54.

Chambers, Larry, "Better Participant Savings Is Perot Systems' Immediate Goal," *Pension World,* July 1994, p. 12.

Champy, James, "Taking Sales to New Heights," *Sales & Marketing Management,* July 1998, p. 26.

Colodny, Mark M., "Ross Perot on His Good Luck," *Fortune,* June 3, 1991, p. 211.

Demery, Paul, "Perot Systems Corp.," *LI Business News,* May 6, 1991, p. 14.

Epper, Karen, "NationsBank Sidelines Perot As Its Outsourcer," *American Banker,* April 11, 1995, p. 1.

Feldman, Amy, "Ross Perot Plans Initial Public Offering for Company," *Knight-Ridder/Tribune Business News,* August 6, 1998, p. OKRB9821809E.

Gabor, Andrea, "Mark Ross Perot: How He'll Make His Next Billion," *U.S. News & World Report,* June 20, 1988, p. 24.

Garrison, Trey, "Perot Systems Plans Move North," *Dallas Business Journal,* March 6, 1998, p. 1.

Goldstein, Alan, "Dallas-Based Perot Systems Lines Up Public Offering, Magazine Reports," *Knight-Ridder/Tribune Business News,* August 2, 1998, p. OKRB98214138.

Hoffman, Thomas, "Perot Takes the Wheel at National," *Computerworld,* October 20, 1997, p. 3.

Iida, Jeanne, "How 4-Day Snafu at NationsBank Disrupted Some Retail Operations," *American Banker,* February 2, 1993, p. 1.

Jordahl, Gregory, "Oh No, Perot!," *Insurance Review,* April 1991, p. 34.

King, Julia, "Ryder Had to Teach Perot the Truck Business," *Computerworld,* October 12, 1998, p. 37.

Kutler, Jeffrey, "Bank Tech Guru Plans an Active Role at Perot," *American Banker,* May 13, 1997, p. 17.

Marjanovic, Steven, "Perot Systems Seeks to Raise $115M in IPO," *American Banker,* August 10, 1998, p. 30.

Mead, Wendy S., "Citicorp Hires Perot Systems to Run Travel Payment Service," *American Banker,* November 5, 1996, p. 19.

Mullich, Joe, "TRAIN Brings Perot Systems Up to Speed; Growth Caused Integration Concerns," *PC Week,* March 31, 1997, p. 29.

Power, Carol, "Perot Systems Wins Contest to Acquire Bankrupt Firm's Intellectual Talent," *American Banker,* June 10, 1997, p. 17.

Scrupski, Susan, "A Mystery Wrapped in an Enigma," *Datamation,* March 1, 1995, p. 32.

Seligman, Daniel, ''Moving Pianos in the Grand Canyon, Betting on an Astronaut, Target Practice in Pittsburgh,'' *Fortune,* July 4, 1988, p. 147.

Seymann, Marilyn R., Steven P. Williams, and Carl A. Faulkner, ''Client/Server Core Systems for Banks Proliferating,'' *American Banker,* April 5, 1995, p. 14.

Sheets, Kenneth R., ''The Story Continues,'' *U.S. News & World Report,* October 10, 1988, p. 51.

Sullivan, Deidre, ''Side Bank and Trust Co.,'' *American Banker,* August 24, 1994, p. 15.

Tracey, Brian, ''Perot and Swiss Bank Wrap Up a Unique Outsourcing Deal,'' *American Banker,* January 18, 1996, p. 11.

Tucker, Tracey, ''Swiss Bank-Perot Deal Seen As Boon to Both,'' *American Banker,* September 12, 1995, p. 22.

Weston, Rusty, ''Back to the World,'' *PC Week,* April 29, 1996, p. E1.

—Daryl F. Mallett

Petco Animal Supplies, Inc.

9125 Rehco Road
San Diego, California 92121
U.S.A.
(619) 453-7845
Fax: (619) 677-3095
Web site: http://www.petco.com

Public Company
Incorporated: 1965
Employees: 9,300
Sales: $839.6 million (1999)
Stock Exchanges: NASDAQ
Ticker Symbol: PETC
NAIC: 45391 Pet & Pet Supplies Stores

The second largest pet food and supplies retailer, Petco Animal Supplies, Inc. operates a chain of superstores that sell a broad selection of pet merchandise. By the end of the 1990s, Petco operated 482 stores in 37 states and the District of Columbia. Trailing PETsMART—the only other publicly held, national pet merchandise chain—Petco positioned itself as a premium retailer, deriving the bulk of its sales from premium pet brands such as IAMS and Science Diet. The company's stores averaged 15,000 square feet and stocked roughly 10,000 items. An aggressive acquisition campaign during the middle and late 1990s led to financial problems for the chain, but by the end of the 1990s it was showing signs of recovery.

Birth of the Petco Superstore

Petco had been operating as a retailer of pet food and supplies for nearly 30 years before the company launched its bid to become the dominant national player in its industry. Founded in 1965, the company competed during its first decades as one of the hundreds of regional pet merchandisers scattered across the country who found it difficult to operate under the shadow of the all-powerful supermarkets. In the battle to lure pet owners into their stores, the supermarkets prevailed comfortably, accounting for 95 percent of all the pet food sold in the country.

Their dominance came at the expense of specialized retailers like Petco, but beginning in the mid-1980s the stifling grip maintained by the supermarkets started to weaken. The cause for the change was part of a pervasive transformation of the retail industry as whole, a trend that saw massive "warehouse" discount stores and "superstores" secure a substantial foothold in the retail sector. Along with the growing prominence of these new retail formats, the diversity of pet products—particularly food—increased, providing a lucrative niche for the specialized retailers to exploit. Supermarkets had held sway by stocking their shelves with popular brands such as Alpo, Kal Kan, and Purina, but beginning in the mid-1980s new premium brands of pet food were introduced into the market. Premium brands such as IAMS, Science Diet, and Nutro that offered higher levels of nutrition than the supermarket brands became increasingly popular among pet owners, and specialized pet products stores were the only retailers to carry such brands. The changing dynamics of the pet products industry led to the decreasing strength of the supermarkets and the growing prominence of retailers like Petco. Between the mid-1980s and the mid-1990s, the percentage of pet food sold in supermarkets slipped from 95 percent to 50 percent, with specialized pet products retailers, warehouse clubs, and mass merchandisers accounting for the change. The conditions were prime for Petco's growth and expansion into a national chain. In the reshaping of the pet products industry, the nearly 30-year-old regional retailer played a leading role.

Petco did not begin to transform into a national force until after its 1994 initial public offering (IPO) of stock, but the individual who spearheaded the mid-1990s expansion arrived as the decade began. Brian K. Devine joined Petco in August 1990, bringing with him 20 years of retail experience. Prior to his arrival at Petco, Devine had served as president for Krause's Sofa Factory, a furniture retailer and manufacturer, but the bulk of his professional experience came from his association with Toys 'R' Us, a retailer of children's toys. From 1970 to 1988 Devine served in various capacities for the specialty retailer, including as senior vice-president in charge of growth, development, and operations and as the chain's director of stores. His background in specialty retailing contributed to the personality of Petco as a national retailer, distinguishing it from its main rival, but the company did not take on this personality until it fully embraced the superstore concept. The transition from operating traditional stores to superstores had begun by the early 1990s, when there were nearly 200 Petco stores of various sizes in operation. The majority of the stores consisted of Petco's traditional units, which measured roughly 3,500 square feet. The company had discovered, however, that it could achieve greater customer traffic, sales volume, and profitability with a larger format: Petco's prototype superstore. Petco's superstores were five times larger than the company's traditional units, stocking a full range of pet food and supplies, as well as fish aquarium systems, reptiles, and other small animals—selections generally not available at the traditional stores. By the end of 1991, the company had established 37 superstores, recording sufficient success with the new format to convince executives to direct expansion efforts toward the establishment of additional superstores. Although Petco officials had not abandoned the traditional concept and would continue to operate smaller units that were profitable, the first half of the 1990s would see an increasing number of Petco superstores and a decline in the number of traditional stores.

By the end of 1992, there were 208 Petco stores in operation, 76 of which were superstores. The following year, the number of superstores exceeded the number of traditional stores for the first time, with the 239-unit chain comprising 132 superstores and 107 traditional stores. By this point, the success of the superstore concept encouraged the company to expand more rapidly and give the superstore concept a national reach. To expand at a greater rate and to take advantage of market conditions primed for a company with Petco's characteristics, Devine, who was named chairman of the corporation in January 1994, decided to take the company public. Petco's IPO was completed in March 1994, giving the company the financial resources to step up its expansion, something Devine intended to do through acquisitions of smaller pet merchandise chains.

Mid-1990s Expansion

Over the course of the ensuing year-and-a-half, Petco completed 12 acquisitions representing 100 stores located in 16 states, converting the purchased units to its superstore format. Petco's superstores carried a merchandise assortment of more than 10,000 items, which was far more than the 400 items generally stocked by supermarkets. Inside the stores, the shelves were stocked with premium cat and dog food, grooming products, toys, and a broad assortment of pet-related items whose diversity was intended to stimulate impulse purchases. Confronted with crab-and-tuna-flavored cat treats, peanut butter-flavored dog biscuits, orthopedic dog beds, bird beak conditioners, pet greeting cards, and numerous other pet-related items, customers responded by

generally buying more than they originally intended. It was a marketing strategy one Petco employee summarized by saying, "They'll come in to just buy dog food and end up buying toys and treats." Petco customers admitted as much, their buying habits typified by one customer who explained, "I usually pick up something that I didn't intend to buy. I even look at the dog stuff and I don't have a dog."

Aside from tantalizing its customers with a vast array of pet products, Petco devoted considerable effort to ways in which products were presented to customers. One of the signature traits of the chain was its practice of incorporating the merchandising ideas of other retailers, including competitors big and small and retailers outside the pet products industry. The company's senior vice-president of merchandising and distribution traveled worldwide searching for innovative ideas from his visits to other stores. For example, the idea for a brochure stand that began appearing in Petco superstores was first seen by a Petco executive in a hardware store in Europe. The inspiration for a pet bar stocked with pet treats similar to a salad bar for humans was taken from a chain of pet stores in Boston. The result was the adoption of market-proven merchandising techniques and the elimination through assimilation of merchandising advantages held by competitors.

The rewards for capturing the spending dollars of pet owners were vast, estimated at $20 billion by the mid-1990s. Vying for a share of the annual, pet owner expenditures were legions of small, independent pet shops, supermarkets, mass merchandisers, and convenience stores. Petco perceived itself to be competition with all such pet products retailers, but the most obvious rival was the only other publicly held, national pet merchandise chain, Phoenix-based PETsMART Inc. Industry pundits preferred to view the two sprawling chains as waging a battle against one another for national supremacy, but Petco officials emphasized the distinctions separating the two companies and downplayed the drama of two industry heavyweights competing head to head. "There's a giant difference," Devine explained. "They're [PETsMART] catering more toward the grocery store user and the mass-market customer. We're catering more to the specialty retail customer. We both sort of picked our niches." The niches occupied by the two companies were reflective of the different professional backgrounds of the leaders who controlled each company. Devine's years at Toys 'R' Us influenced his decision to position Petco as a specialty retailer, whereas PETsMART's president and chief executive officer, Mark Hansen, used his experience as a grocery store veteran to pattern PETsMART after the supermarket model of high turnover and lower profitability. Accordingly, PETsMART focused on stocking less expensive merchandise in larger, 26,000-square-foot stores. Petco, on the other hand, based its strategy on retailing more expensive merchandise in smaller, 15,000-square-foot stores.

The contrasting philosophies of PETsMART and Petco also affected each company's real estate strategy, which was part of the reason Devine did not perceive the success of Petco as being dependent on the demise of PETsMART. Generally, the two chains were not side-by-side competitors; instead, each moved into distinct areas, pursuing different demographics. Typically, PETsMART located its superstores in what were referred to as "power centers" alongside other superstores and warehouse stores like Home Depot, Costco, and Staples, hoping to draw customers from outside their immediate neighborhoods. Petco, in contrast, established its stores within neighborhoods, positioning its premium outlets in local shopping centers anchored by supermarkets, where the company's target customer—accounting for 70 percent of its customer base—frequented. "The educated woman is our best customer," explained Devine. "She's the best premium food customer. We try to place our stores where they shop on a regular basis. We try to go with the upscale grocer if possible."

Difficulties in the Late 1990s

With Petco and PETsMART occupying separate turfs and together controlling only five percent of a $20 billion market, there was substantial room for expansion as the two companies faced the late 1990s. Devine foresaw the expansion of Petco to 1,250 stores, roughly four times the size of the chain by the end of 1996, but as the company pursued its ambitious goal it faltered, sparking criticism that it had been over-zealous in its growth plans. Problems surfaced after the company registered an aggressive year of expansion in 1997, when 104 stores were added to the chain, with the majority of the new units coming from the acquisition of the 81-store PetCare chain, which operated in nine midwestern and southern states. The process of efficiently incorporating the new stores into the company's fold and continuing to transform from a 3,000-square-foot format to a superstore format proved to be difficult. As a result of the acquisitions that increased the company's store count to more than 430 units and extended its presence into 31 states, crippling financial losses were incurred. During the first half of 1998, Petco racked up more than $8 million in net losses. The company's stock, which had swelled to more than $30 per share in 1997, plunged to nearly $5 per share. One stock analyst offered his opinion, explaining, "The company has had problems because, frankly, they expanded their business too much, too fast. The company's costs got a little out of line of what they should have been." To make matters worse, the company also faced three class action shareholder lawsuits charging management with securities violations and fraud. The acquisition of nearly 20 retail chains since the 1994 IPO caused considerable strain on the once vibrant chain, but the late 1990s witnessed the recovery of the company that touted itself as the "premier specialty retailer of pet food and supplies in the United States."

By the early months of 1999, Petco began to display signs of vitality. The company had eased back on its acquisition campaign and focused on invigorating the profitability of its existing stores. The stores acquired in 1997 that had precipitated the company's downfall were expected to begin producing as well as the other units by the end of 1999. Analysts, who previously had warily distanced themselves from the company, began to view Petco's prospects more positively. The cause for their more sanguine outlook derived from the company's emphasis on producing returns to shareholders and its new growth strategy. Petco operated 476 stores in 37 states and planned to add to its store count, but expansion in the years ahead was expected to come from the construction of new stores rather than through acquisitions, thereby avoiding the pitfalls of converting stores to the Petco format. In 1999 the company planned to build 40 new stores. As Petco pushed ahead with its plans, its future success depended on producing consistent earnings growth, something that eluded the company during the 1990s. A perennially growing market and a tighter control on profitability, however, engendered optimism for the 21st century.

Principal Subsidiaries

International Pet Supplies and Distribution, Inc.; Pet Nosh Consolidated Co., Inc.; Petco Southwest, Inc.; Pet Concepts International; PM Management Incorporated; Petco Southwest, L.P.

Further Reading

Allen, Mike, "Dog Days Hound Petco in Wake of Stock Drop," *San Diego Business Journal,* October 12, 1998, p. 4.

Buttita, Bob, "Petco Set To Acquire 81 Pet Care Superstore Outlets," *Pet Product News,* November 1997, p. 4.

Chadwell, John, "Power Brokers," *Pet Product News,* July 1996, p. 62.

Creno, Glen, "Pet Superstore Chains Gear Up for All Out War," *Knight-Ridder/Tribune Business News,* March 22, 1997, p. 322B1211.

Rooney, Brian, "Pet Food Retailer Booms into National Chain," *Business Journal,* May 30, 1988, p. 5.

Sahm, Phil, "Petco Plans To Open 4 Utah Stores," *Knight-Ridder/Tribune Business News,* April 7, 1999, p. OKRB990970EA.

Scally, Robert, "The Clever Copy Cat," *Discount Store News,* December 8, 1997, p. 71.

—Jeffrey L. Covell

Piercing Pagoda, Inc.

3910 Adler Place
Bethlehem, Pennsylvania 18017
U.S.A.
(610) 691-0437
Fax: (610) 694-9077
Web site: http://www.pagoda.com

Public Company
Incorporated: 1973
Employees: 3,837
Sales: $222.1 million (1998)
Stock Exchanges: NASDAQ
Ticker Symbol: PGDA
NAIC: 44831 Jewelry Stores

A fast-growing jewelry retailer, Piercing Pagoda, Inc. sells moderately priced gold and silver jewelry through a vast network of mall-based kiosks and conventional stores. In 1999 there were 940 outlets in 47 states and Puerto Rico operating under the names Piercing Pagoda, Gold Plumb, and Silver & Gold Connection. Typically, Gold Plumb and Silver & Gold Connection outlets were established in malls where a Piercing Pagoda unit already was in operation. Although merchandise selection varied slightly within the three formats, all of the company's retail locations offered a range of 14-karat and ten-karat gold jewelry, including chains, bracelets, earrings, charms, and rings. The average price of the jewelry was roughly $25. The company pierced ears free of charge with the purchase of earrings and attracted repeat customers by offering membership in a buy-five-get-one-free jewelry club. Through two acquisitions in 1997, Piercing Pagoda eliminated all national rivals, leaving only relatively small, regional companies as its competitors. In late 1998 and early 1999 the company began introducing diamond jewelry in its stores, following the mid-1998 launch of a new, all-diamond kiosk concept called Diamond Isle.

1972: The First Kiosk

The founders of Piercing Pagoda, Bernard and Bertha Cohen, started the company relatively late in life. Bernard

Cohen was in his mid-50s when he and his wife opened their first jewelry kiosk in May 1972 in Plymouth Meeting Mall, located in suburban Philadelphia. To Bernard Cohen, a businessman who had traveled extensively with his wife and developed a particular affection for Japan, the Plymouth Meeting Mall kiosk resembled a Japanese pagoda. Based on this similarity the business attained its name, but the essence of Piercing Pagoda—a retailer of jewelry that pierced customers' ears at small stands—drew its inspiration from Bertha Cohen, whose family had operated a number of jewelry stores in Bethlehem, Pennsylvania. As a way of promoting sales of its diamond earrings, Bertha Cohen's family—the Finkelsteins—began piercing ears in boothlike structures. From this example, the Cohens took their cue, offering customers fast, convenient ear piercing and inexpensive jewelry, but the important difference was the location of the Cohens' kiosk. Situated in the walkways of the shopping mall, a permanent feature amid pedestrian traffic flow, Piercing Pagoda benefited enormously from the efforts of its more traditional neighbors. The retail occupants of the mall spent time and money to attract customers, and Piercing Pagoda enjoyed the fruits of their labors and investment without any comparable expense of its own. The Cohens had struck upon a concept with promising potential—though far from the magnitude Piercing Pagoda would later exude—and began expanding it by franchising Piercing Pagoda kiosks.

The opportunity to operate a Piercing Pagoda franchise introduced Richard H. Penske, the son of a printer and a Lehigh University graduate, to Bernard Cohen. Cohen's foray into franchising ended within a year of its introduction, however, proving to be an intolerable way of operating the business. Cohen preferred to operate the kiosks as company-owned properties, and he hired Penske to help him in his expansion of the concept. As the sprawl of suburbia extended outward from large metropolitan areas during the 1970s and 1980s, fertile ground was created for the establishment of more malls. As more malls opened, the Piercing Pagoda chain flourished, opening an increasing number of kiosks that stayed true to the formula developed early in the company's history. The company remained free of debt as it expanded and it did not stray into offering other merchandise, such as precious gems or costume jewelry. The company did expand beyond selling only gold earrings, however, offering its customers gold chains and bracelets beginning

382

Company Perspectives:

Our easy-to-shop environment and competitive everyday low pricing attracts both destination customers and impulse shoppers. We differentiate our merchandise selection from other jewelry retailers by focusing on basic styles of lower priced 14 karat and 10 karat gold jewelry, comprised primarily of chains, bracelets, earrings, charms and rings. We believe that, by offering a broad assortment of basic styles, we provide our customers with a wide variety of choices while limiting merchandising risks associated with fashion trends. A large portion of merchandise is common to all stores, and the remaining products are selected based on the characteristics and local preferences of a particular store's customer base. We also maintain a balance between new merchandise and proven successful styles.

in 1979 and later fleshing out its merchandise selection to include gold charms and rings. The company also opened jewelry kiosks that operated under different names, beginning with the opening of the first Gold Plumb kiosk in 1981, but the fundamental aspects of the company remained unaltered as it grew into an extensive chain.

1986 Change in Ownership Spurs Expansion

For Penske, who had assisted his mentor in the expansion of Piercing Pagoda and witnessed its retail prowess, ownership of the concept gradually became his aim. By 1986, when there were more than 200 company-owned kiosks in operation, Penske was ready to make his bid for the company. He borrowed heavily to accomplish his goal, accumulating nearly $17 million of debt to buy out the Cohens' interest in Piercing Pagoda. Although he refused to divulge exactly how much he paid the Cohens for control of the company, he did concede it was approximately half the total he borrowed.

Under Penske's guidance, the Piercing Pagoda name gained national prominence, evoking the fears of competitors and grabbing the attention of Wall Street, but neither reaction was educed during his first years of control. Strapped for cash, Penske was unable to expand—his ultimate desire—in any significant magnitude for nearly a decade, forcing him to exert his new-found influence in other ways. Penske worked on fine-tuning the Piercing Pagoda concept. He bided his time by improving the operations he already controlled, succeeding in increasing sales, improving profitability, and procuring the proper inventory for the kiosks. Penske also assembled an executive team to build upon the sturdy foundation he was creating. By 1994, the foundation was firmly set and the company's finances were in order. The time had come for aggressive expansion.

To help him in his expansion of the concept, Penske, like Cohen before him, solicited the aid of an assistant and hired John F. Eureyecko in 1992. Seven years Penske's junior, Eureyecko brought with him 18 years of experience as an executive with Triangle Building Supplies and Lumber Co.—experience that related to a different product, to be sure, but the

differences between lumber and jewelry were minimal, in Eureyecko's mind. "A lot of the elements of success are the same with any business, regardless of the product," he explained. With Penske and Eureyecko leading the way, the company prepared for its initial public offering (IPO) of stock, slated for October 1994. The chain, before the IPO, comprised 279 kiosks, each offering a selection of 14-karat and ten-karat gold earrings, chains, charms, bracelets, and rings, as well as a selection of silver jewelry. Prices ranged between $11 and $64, governed by an everyday low price policy implemented in 1992, with the average Piercing Pagoda product selling for $24. The kiosks averaged 153 square feet and typically generated in excess of $200,000 in sales a year, producing $58.7 million for the company in 1993.

Piercing Pagoda completed its IPO on October 24, 1994, raising $15.7 million in net proceeds. The stock debuted on the NASDAQ exchange at $11 per share. With the money gained from the IPO, Penske and Eureyecko not only planned to increase the number of kiosks under their control, but also envisioned diversifying the company's expansion on several fronts. They were considering the acquisition of competing companies and were intent on experimenting with complementary retail concepts. They anticipated introducing mall carts to sell silver jewelry during holiday seasons and they considered opening kiosks in locations other than mall concourses, such as in resort locations and airline terminals. Perhaps most ambitious, the company planned to open small conventional stores in malls, units referred to as "in-line" stores. In each of these potential areas of expansion, the company followed through with its plans. In the years ahead, acquisitions were completed, silver-selling mall carts debuted, kiosks were established in resort locations and airline terminals, and in-line stores were opened, representing what some pundits believed was the company's most promising avenue of growth.

The first in-line store opened in 1995, located in Deptford Mall, near Philadelphia. Other Piercing Pagoda in-line stores were added to the company's portfolio of operations, their inclusion regarded as significant because they allowed the company to establish a presence in malls where kiosks were not permitted. Moreover, the in-line stores, typically 600 square feet, allowed Piercing Pagoda to offer a larger selection of merchandise, which included higher priced items not available at the company-owned kiosks. The more upscale in-line stores, decorated in cherry woods and tapestries, resembled traditional jewelry salons, an environment conducive to attracting an older customer than those who frequented the company's kiosks.

By the end of 1995, there were 366 Piercing Pagoda and Plumb Gold units in operation, but the company had yet to attract widespread attention. Wall Street and participants in the jewelry industry did not raise their collective eyebrows until Piercing Pagoda embarked on the acquisition trail, a direction the company started pursuing in 1996. In 1996 the company acquired bankrupt Earring Tree, gaining 51 kiosks and 17 conventional mall stores, which accelerated the expansion of the in-line store concept. The company opened its 500th store in 1996, ending the year by nearly reaching 600 stores, which included an in-line store located in the El Conquistador Resort in Puerto Rico that opened in December. Annual sales began to rush upward by this point, reaching $121.5 million by the end of the company's 1996 fiscal year in March. By the following year, widespread attention was focused on the rapidly growing company.

1997: All National Competition Eliminated

Much of the attention attracted in 1997 stemmed from two acquisitions completed during the year, purchases that swelled the ranks of its stores and, most important, eliminated all national rivals. In January 1997 Piercing Pagoda acquired the second largest kiosk jewelry chain in the United States, Gemstone Jewelry, Inc., for roughly $8 million. The addition of Gemstone, whose kiosks were similar in size and merchandise selection to Piercing Pagoda kiosks, gave the company 93 new kiosks. Three months later, Piercing Pagoda acquired the third largest kiosk jewelry chain in the nation, The Silver & Gold Trading Company, Inc., for approximately $8.2 million. The purchase added 43 kiosks, comparable in size and merchandise to Piercing Pagoda kiosks, and marked the addition of a new format for the company: kiosks that sold their merchandise under the Silver & Gold Connection.

With the acquisition of the only national kiosk jewelry chains, Piercing Pagoda faced only isolated competition from two regional chains, Piercing Ear and Touch of Gold, each of which operated no more than 20 units. Penske, who controlled more than 700 stores, stood as a veritable giant in his market niche. "There's absolutely no one else around that's close to us," he said. Analysts, who had watched the company's stock increase in value from $11 per share to in excess of $30 per share, surveyed Piercing Pagoda's market and arrived at the same conclusion. "They've basically created a barrier to entry," one analyst remarked. "No one can come in and acquire a chain of any size. They would have to start from scratch." The absence of any serious competition did not dull Penske's appetite for further expansion, however. "We have the potential," he announced in 1997, "to double in size again in another five years." The company, in 1997, operated in approximately 500 malls, less than half of the 1,200 malls in the country. Further, the company's expansion was not limited to mall-based locations, evidenced by the debut of the company's first street location in Old San Juan, Puerto Rico, in January 1998.

To help pay for its acquisition and to gain the financial resources to expand, Piercing Pagoda completed a secondary sale of stock in June 1997, raising nearly $15 million in net proceeds. With cash at its disposal, Piercing Pagoda opened approximately 150 stores between March 1998 and March 1999, giving the company a total of more than 940 stores. The increase included the largest acquisition in the company's history, the July 1998 purchase of 104 units from Nevada-based Sedgwick Sales, Inc., which controlled a number of differently named kiosk chains. With efforts under way to remerchandise the acquired units, the company launched another new format in mid-1998 called Diamond Isle, a Newark, Delaware kiosk that sold diamond jewelry exclusively. The success of the kiosk prompted Penske to introduce a selection of diamond jewelry into 180 Piercing Pagoda units during late 1998 and early 1999.

With the addition of diamond jewelry and an all-diamond concept, Piercing Pagoda faced a future tantalizingly rich with directions in which to pursue growth. As Penske prepared for the beginning of the 21st century, he planned to ease back on expansion and concentrate on operating performance. Between 60 and 80 new stores were planned for fiscal 2000, including the establishment of a handful of Diamond Isle kiosks. With these short-term objectives directing the company progress at the end of the 1990s, Piercing Pagoda pushed ahead, holding sway as the unrivaled heavyweight in its industry niche.

Further Reading

Frischknecht, Donna, "Growing by Diversifying," *SuperSellers,* May 1998, p. 14.

Kletter, Melanie, "Pagoda Tops 900 with Buy," *WWD,* July 6, 1998, p. 19.

McDonald, Duff, "Piercing Pagoda," *Money,* December 1998, p. 68.

McLean, Bethany, "Going for Gold," *Fortune,* November 25, 1996, p. 218.

"Pagoda Promotion," *WWD,* July 29, 1996, p. 23.

"Piercing Pagoda Plans New Units in Growth Move," *WWD,* October 24, 1994, p. 11.

Sabatini, Patricia, "Stock Increases Steadily for Bethlehem, Pa.-Based Mall Kiosk Jewelry Retailer," *Knight-Ridder/Tribune Business News,* July 16, 1998.

—Jeffrey L. Covell

Pillsbury Madison & Sutro LLP

235 Montgomery Street
San Francisco, California 94104
U.S.A.
(415) 983-1000
Fax: (415) 983-1200
Web site: http://www.pillsburylaw.com

Private Partnership
Founded: 1874
Employees: 1,300 (est.)
Sales: $215.5 million (1997)
NAIC: 54111 Offices of Lawyers

Pillsbury Madison & Sutro LLP ranks as the nation's 33rd largest law firm, according to the June 1999 *Corporate Legal Times,* and in 1999 became the nation's first large law firm to be headed by a woman. In addition to several offices in California, the firm also operates offices in Hong Kong, Tokyo, New York City, and Washington, D.C. Its attorneys work in 14 practice areas: creditor's rights and bankruptcy; commerce and technology; corporate securities, banking, and emerging companies; environmental and land use; tax; real estate and construction; executive compensation; estate and probate; intellectual property; international transactions and project finance; labor and employment; life sciences and biotechnology; political law; and class actions and complex litigation. About half of the firm's attorneys are litigators, and Chevron Corporation, the firm's major client, provides about ten percent of its annual billings. The firm still represents such traditional clients as oil firms and banks but in the late 20th century began dealing in high-tech fields such as software and biotechnology. Pillsbury Madison & Sutro also represents Internet companies and maintains an award-winning Web site of its own.

Late 19th-Century Origins

The history of Pillsbury Madison & Sutro can be traced to the legal practice of Evans S. Pillsbury, already a well-established attorney when he opened an office in San Francisco in 1874. The following year, Pillsbury took on a partner, William E. Green, and the practice became known as Pillsbury & Green. A subsequent partner, David Titus, replaced Green around 1879, and the firm changed names again, to Pillsbury & Titus. Notable among Pillsbury's early clients was the San Francisco-based banking and express company Wells Fargo.

In 1883 Pillsbury resigned his partnership with Titus to join two other San Francisco lawyers in the formation of the firm Wallace, Pillsbury & Blanding. Blanding was a prominent attorney who had helped incorporate Los Angeles-based Pacific Coast Oil Company, which would later become known as Chevron. This marked the beginning of the firm's involvement in the nation's oil industry, an association that would continue into the late 20th century.

By the mid-1890s, Blanding had retired, and Wallace had left to serve on the Superior Court of San Francisco. In 1895 Pillsbury's practice was joined by associates Alfred Sutro and Frank D. Madison; three years later Horace D. Pillsbury, the founder's son, also came on board. The firm then became known as E.S. Pillsbury and Pillsbury, Madison & Sutro and was by this time a thriving and well-respected business with associates who held sway with large corporate and political figures.

Early 20th Century Expansion

A brief venture abroad occurred in 1901, when Oscar Sutro started a separate partnership in the Philippines called Pillsbury & Sutro. At this new office, Sutro drafted the Philippine legal code and reportedly befriended the islands' governor general and future President of the United States, William Howard Taft. Following this work Sutro returned to California in 1905, and the firm's name was shortened to Pillsbury, Madison & Sutro. The next year the infamous San Francisco earthquake completely destroyed the firm's office and records. Nevertheless, the firm continued operating and in fact found much business involving local insurance companies, some of whom who were refusing to honor policies following the earthquake and subsequent fires.

Specifically, in 1906 Pillsbury Madison & Sutro won a landmark case by representing the California Wine Association and forcing fire insurance companies to pay for fire damage

Company Perspectives:

The law firm of Pillsbury Madison & Sutro delivers cutting-edge, strategic services to our clients to help them achieve their goals. We are a hard working, energetic, skilled team of professionals—attorneys and staff—deeply committed to serving our clients. We conduct ourselves according to the highest standards of ethics, collegiality and mutual respect and recognize that our rewards depend on helping our clients achieve their goals. We have a clear and compelling view of what we want to achieve. That view is the basis for our strategic plan, which is regularly refined and updated with input from our clients, our people and our markets. We are accountable for the business we manage, and we give all of our professionals relevant, timely performance information that permits them to gauge their individual and collective success in serving our clients. We are proud of our achievements. We enjoy our work and find fulfillment in doing it well. We celebrate our success.

from the earthquake. According to a Pillsbury historical timeline, this case proved pivotal for all San Franciscans with fire insurance seeking to recover damages from their insurance companies.

The 1920s brought a new generation of attorneys to the forefront as E. S. Pillsbury retired to Santa Barbara, California, and Oscar Sutro left law to serve as vice-president of Standard Oil. Large corporations continued to provide the bulk of the firm's business, and the firm continued to grow, boasting a work force of 26 lawyers by 1931.

At the onset of World War II, Pillsbury's roster had grown to include 40 attorneys, but this force was severely depleted by the war, as 26 of the men, four of whom were partners, left to serve their country. During this time, business at home was handled by the 14 attorneys who stayed behind as well as local law professors. One attorney at Pillsbury Madison & Sutro, John Marshall, became the chief counsel for the Petroleum Administration for War.

Postwar Developments

In the postwar boom, as retail and housing facilities were cropping up at a rapid pace, Pillsbury Madison & Sutro expanded its focus to include cases generated by the finance and construction industries. In 1952 the firm represented the lender of all financing involved in building the Stonestown Shopping Center, the largest in the Bay Area and one of the largest in the nation. In 1960 the law firm drafted California's first condominium law while representing Haas and Hanie Corporation, which built Nob Hill, the state's first high-rise condominium.

Moreover, the firm's interests were by no means limited to California or construction. In 1954, after the Central Intelligence Agency had helped install Shah Pahlevi in Iran, Pillsbury Madison & Sutro helped create a new international consortium to produce and refine Iran's oil and give Western powers access to Iranian oil. This Iranian consortium would prove pivotal in establishing the United States as a major influence in the oil industry and political life of the Middle East.

Still, the representation of large corporations continued to be a mainstay at Pillsbury Madison & Sutro. In the mid-1950s, attorney John A. Sutro, a descendant of co-founder Oscar Sutro, successfully represented Pacific Telephone & Telegraph in a case involving the fees charged by municipalities to the phone company for occupying city streets with telephone lines and underground cables. In 1957 Pillsbury Madison & Sutro helped Standard Oil of California in its negotiations with Southern Pacific in the ''largest fuel supply contract in the world at the time,'' according to the firm's timeline. Other important clients included various oil and financial corporations and Ford Motor Co., which hired the firm to represent it in a 1960 discrimination suit filed by a dealership. By 1979 the firm had opened two new offices, one in San Jose, California and the other in Washington, D.C.

The Progressive 1980s

In 1980 Pillsbury Madison & Sutro lawyers helped make financial history when they were hired by Genentech in that company's bid to go public. Founded in 1976 by a professor at the University of California at San Francisco Medical Center, Genentech pioneered the new field of genetic engineering or biotechnology when it showed that gene-splicing was commercially viable. Pillsbury Madison & Sutro represented Blyth Eastman Paine Webber Inc., a New York investment banking firm and the main underwriter of Genentech in its initial public offering. That IPO, in just one minute, sold one million shares of common stock for $35 million, the fastest public offering in history at the time. The Genentech IPO marked Pillsbury Madison and Sutro's entry into one of the major growth industries of the late 20th century, and the firm would go on to represent such high-tech companies as LSI Logic Corporation and others. To support high-tech firms interested in investing in Russia, Pillsbury Madison in 1989 chaired a group of advisors of the first Soviet-American venture capital fund.

While keeping pace with the ever-changing corporate climate, Pillsbury Madison & Sutro was also progressive in its internal operations: in the late 1980s it had more female attorneys on staff than any other firm in the country, and nine of its partners were women. During this time, the firm opened two new offices in California to reach its 1988 goal of becoming the premiere law firm in the state. In 1988 it opened its San Diego office, followed by a Sacramento office in 1989.

The growth of Pillsbury Madison & Sutro and other U.S. law firms in the 1970s and 1980s was fueled by several events. The U.S. Supreme Court ruled that restrictions on advertising for professional services were unconstitutional, helping all professions to become more business-oriented and competitive. Moreover, Steven Brill in 1979 founded the publication *The American Lawyer* to look at law firms' finances and other internal operations. The comparative data published therein sparked a greater knowledge of the business and promoted lateral hiring of experienced attorneys from rival firms. Finally, the growth of new industries and the merger-and-acquisition craze of the 1980s also stimulated the legal industry.

Challenges in the 1990s

In 1991 law firms across the nation suffered along with the rest of the nation in an economic downturn. Moreover, many corporations began hiring their own inhouse attorneys for about half what outside counsel charged. "At our firm today," said Pillsbury Madison Sutro attorney T. Neal McNamara at a 1991 *American Lawyer* seminar, "our clients are among our major competitors. Not only were they one of the root causes of our recession, they're exacerbating it." During this difficult time, Pillsbury merged with the firm of Lillick and McHose, a deal described in company literature as "the largest merger of law firms in history to date." The well-known Pillsbury company name was retained through the merger.

In the 1990s Pillsbury Madison & Sutro continued its historic representation of oil firms. In 1992 the firm represented Chevron in its lawsuit against Penzoil and oversaw a Chevron-Penzoil restructuring deal worth $1.17 billion. In 1998 it helped Chevron Products negotiate a joint venture with Texaco to form Fuel and Marine Marketing LLC with offices in over 40 nations.

Also important to its business during this time were telecommunications corporations. In 1992 Pillsbury helped its long-term client Pacific Telesis Group spin off its wireless services to form an independent firm made up of four units: PacTel Cellular, PacTel Paging, PacTel Teletrac, and PacTel International Operations. In 1994 the firm represented Netcom Online Communications when it became the nation's first company solely providing Internet access to go public. In 1996 Pillsbury again represented Pacific Telesis in its $16.7 billion merger with SBC Communications, the first unification of "Baby Bell" companies. The firm also advised Tele-Communications, Inc. (TCI) when it acquired Viacom's cable systems for about $2.15 billion and in 1996 assisted AirTouch in its acquisition of the remaining 40 percent ownership of Cellular Communications. In 1997 Pillsbury Madison & Sutro represented Octel Communications when that company was purchased by Lucent Technologies for $1.8 billion. Other clients in the 1990s included BankAmerica Corporation, AT&T, the San Francisco Giants, Quaker State, and Healthsouth Corporation.

The scope of Pillsbury's expertise was broadened in 1996, when it merged the operations of the law firm Cushman Darby & Cushman, an intellectual property firm based in Washington, D.C., into its own in 1996. That year, a team of Pillsbury lawyers helped client Haworth Inc. win a $211 million judgment from a rival firm, Steelcase Inc. The decision of the U.S. District Court for Western Michigan ended an 11-year battle over Haworth patented designs used to build electrified office panels, the building blocks of modern workstation cubicles. In a press release, the law firm stated the court "victory represents the second-largest award in patent litigation history."

In 1997 Pillsbury signed a lease to consolidate its three existing offices in the San Francisco area to one headquarters in the 50 Fremont Building. "50 Fremont provides an excellent platform for the law firm of the 21st century," said Pillsbury Chairman Al Pepin in the December 22, 1997 *PR Newswire*. The consolidation was planned for completion early in the year 2000.

The American Lawyer ranked the Pillsbury law firm, with 1997 gross revenues of $215.5 million, as one of 11 San Francisco firms in the nation's top 100 firms. *American Lawyer* and London's *Legal Business,* in their first rankings of the world's largest law firms, placed Pillsbury as number 39 based on 1997 revenues and number 41 based on its number of lawyers, which stood at 555.

In December 1998 Pillsbury opened an office in Carmel Valley about 20 miles north of its downtown San Diego, California, office, in response to more high-tech and life-sciences clients located along the coast north of the city who wanted attorneys located nearby. A similar move was made in early 1999 when the law firm opened its tenth office in Tysons Corner, Virginia, about 15 miles from its Washington, D.C. office. "The Northern Virginia area is a rapidly growing center of high-tech and biosciences business," said Jorge del Calvo, the Pillsbury partner in charge of its Internet group, in the February 18, 1999 publication *Recorder*. Pillsbury and other law firms dealing with biotechnology and other high-tech businesses in the late 1990s began hiring more attorneys with Ph.D. degrees and other academic credentials.

Management Changes

In late 1998 Pillsbury Madison & Sutro elected Mary Cranston as the new chair of its managing board, effective January 1, 1999. A graduate of Stanford Law School and head of the firm's litigation group, Cranston became the first woman to lead a major law firm. "The fact that I am the first female chair of a major US firm shows that there is a glass ceiling," said Cranston in the February 1999 *International Financial Law Review*. She went on to suggest that "There have been many women coming out of law school for some time. This will ultimately be resolved as more women take up positions as legal counsel. Then we will have an old girls' network to match the old boys' network."

According to *American Lawyer,* seven of the nation's top ten law firms with the highest percentage of women partners were in San Francisco. The highest percentage of women equity partners was still only 27.5 percent, and the average at the 100 largest law firms was just 13.1 percent. Thus, one journalist in the April 11, 1999 *San Francisco Chronicle* concluded that "The real story is that the numbers are still pitifully low."

At the same time Cranston was chosen, the firm elected Marina Park to a new position of firmwide managing partner. Park, a graduate of the University of Michigan School of Law and head of its Silicone Valley office, would split with Cranston the duties of the outgoing chair, Alfred Pepin, Jr. Park said in the December 9, 1998 *Recorder* that she and Cranston "have a shared vision for the firm's future.... We look forward to helping the firm shed its stodgy image—which was never accurate." Toward that end, one of Cranston's first decisions was to open up corporate communications by sharing information from the law firm's managing board. Prior to that time, only partners were apprised of board discussions, but Cranston soon began distributing summaries of board meetings to everyone in the firm.

Cranston and the other leaders of Pillsbury Madison & Sutro faced plenty of challenges in 1999. As a profile in the March 1999 *American Lawyer* pointed out, Pillsbury was badly in need of a turnaround "after years of sliding profits, plunging morale, and an exodus of more than 40 partners in the last two years." The article noted that Pillsbury, "once the gold standard for West Coast firms . . . has in recent years looked like a devalued currency." Despite such criticism, however, Pillsbury Madison & Sutro remained a top law firm nationwide, and the company's executives and board were optimistic that under the new leadership of Cranston and a new strategic plan, the firm would recover from its profit slide to compete on a global scale.

Further Reading

Beck, Susan, "There's Something About Mary," *American Lawyer,* March 1999, pp. 65–66.

Ford, Chris, "The Biotech Beyond," *California Law Business,* June 7, 1999, pp. 12–15.

Gawalt, Gerald W., *The New High Priests: Lawyers in Post-Civil War America,* Westport, Conn.: Greenwood Press, 1984.

Holding, Reynolds, "Women in Law: Status Report on the Glass Ceiling," *San Francisco Chronicle,* April 11, 1999.

"LaSalle Partners Consolidates Pillsbury Madison & Sutro LLP Headquarters to 50 Fremont in San Francisco," *PR Newswire,* December 22, 1997, p. 1.

McClintock, Pamela, "Pillsbury's New Leaders Seek to Revitalize the Firm," *San Francisco Daily Journal,* December 11, 1998, p. 1.

——, "Turning Pillsbury on its Stodgy Old Head," *Recorder,* May 18, 1999, p. 1.

Stewart, James B., "Genentech: Pillsbury, Madison & Sutro," in *The Partners: Inside America's Most Powerful Law Firms,* New York: Simon and Schuster, 1983, pp. 114–51.

—David M. Walden

PricewaterhouseCoopers

1251 Avenue of the Americas
New York, New York 10020
U.S.A.
(212) 536-2000
(888) 846-7076
Fax: (212) 536-3035
Web site: http://www.pwcglobal.com

Private Company
Incorporated: 1898 as Lybrand, Ross Bros. &
    Montgomery; 1865 as Price and Waterhouse
Employees: 140,000
Sales: $15.3 billion (1998)
NAIC: 541211 Offices of Certified Public Accountants

The international partnership of PricewaterhouseCoopers is the largest accounting and business consultancy firm in the world. With approximately 140,000 employees in 150 countries in 1999, the company offers auditing services, tax and legal advice, financial advice, business process outsourcing, and management consulting services. The partnership was created in 1998 from the merger of two Big Six accounting firms: Price Waterhouse and Coopers & Lybrand.

History of Coopers & Lybrand

Accounting practices were necessitated by the increasingly complex and sophisticated needs of businesses during the early 19th-century Industrial Revolution. Accounting as a profession emerged over several decades in the United States, and by 1898, the year in which Coopers & Lybrand was founded, there was not yet a single school of accounting. Furthermore, the only texts available were British and these often failed to address American problems and practices.

Accountants therefore received their training on the job, initially as bookkeepers, the most able and talented ones trained by their supervisor in accounting practices and procedures. This was the route taken by the four American founders of Coopers & Lybrand: William M. Lybrand, brothers T. Edward Ross and Adam A. Ross, and Robert H. Montgomery. All had worked in the same firm of Heins, Lybrand & Co. in Philadelphia and had received the same training; all four would be active in establishing accounting as a profession. The Ross brothers, Adam and Edward, were pioneer members in 1897 of the Pennsylvania Association of Public Accountants, one of the few professional associations for accountants in the country. During this time, a British accounting firm known as Cooper Bros. & Co., founded by William Cooper, was celebrating its 44th anniversary. Nearly 60 years later, the American and the British firms would merge into Coopers & Lybrand International.

The four American employees of the Heins office pooled their resources, and on January 1, 1898 they opened a two-room, two-desk business in Philadelphia. Until 1973, the company would be known as Lybrand, Ross Bros. & Montgomery. Hours were extremely long, almost always beyond the official nine hours per day, Monday through Friday. For many years, young men hired by the firm would receive $7 a day and were expected to work evenings and be on call during weekends.

From the start, the firm had a reputation for high professional standards, which the four partners attributed to the example of their former chief, John Heins. Also from the start, clients were plentiful. Outside of his regular accounting duties, Adam A. Ross, who as an apprentice in Heins's office had taken part in the first regular audit of a bank by a public accountant in Philadelphia's history, lobbied for state legislation mandating certification for public accountants, a cause that his brother and partner, T. Edward Ross, would also espouse. Partners in the firm also gave lectures in accountancy in the evenings and were hard at work persuading the University of Pennsylvania to establish a night school in accountancy, which finally happened in 1902. Robert Montgomery undertook the first U.S. textbook on accountancy, published in 1905, while also that year Lybrand contributed several articles to the new *Journal of Accountancy,* establishing the principles of the accounting profession. That was just the beginning of the many contributions the four partners would make over the years to the professionalization of their field.

Barely two years after the firm of Lybrand, Ross Bros. & Montgomery was founded, it was already necessary to move

Company Perspectives:

PricewaterhouseCoopers is the world's largest professional services organization. Drawing on the knowledge and skills of 155,000 in 150 countries, we help our clients solve complex business problems and measurably enhance their ability to build value, manage risk and improve performance.

into larger facilities in Philadelphia. By 1902, the firm's first branch office was established in New York City, followed by another in Pittsburgh in 1908. In its initial forays into tax consulting, the company assisted in the drafting of the first federal income tax law in 1913, and a member of the firm, Walter Staub, wrote a seminal essay, *Income Tax Guide,* explaining the pending tax legislation. In 1917 Montgomery published the classic (and continuously updated until 1929) *Income Tax Procedure 1917.* When the author established a tax practice in the New York office in 1918, he was immediately besieged by anxious customers.

In 1919, Lybrand, Ross Bros. & Montgomery decided to expand their company into the District of Columbia. During the year and a half in which the United States participated in World War I, Montgomery served on Bernard Baruch's War Industries Board in Washington and also on the Board of Appraisers of the War Department; other firm members served on the Liberty Loan committee and engaged in other war efforts.

By the end of the war, the professionalization of accountancy and its indispensability to the country's economic structure, were established. The greatly expanded firm of Lybrand, Ross Bros. & Montgomery, pacesetters in the accounting profession, were demanding college degrees of their job applicants. Because of the paucity of accounting schools at universities and colleges, the firm was willing to take on college graduates with little or no background in accounting, subjecting them, once hired, to a rigorous two-year night school program of training. Accounting being an exclusively male profession during this time, the company hired only men.

During the 1920s, the firm experienced rapid expansion. Branches were established in the center of the vital automobile industry, Detroit, in 1920, and as far away as Seattle. In 1924, when the firm merged with the accounting company of Klink, Bean & Co., offices opened in Los Angeles and San Francisco. Also that year, an office was established in Berlin, Germany, followed by a Paris office in 1926 and a London office in 1929, the year of the stock market crash. This would mark the beginning of the firm's globalization that would eventually result in branches in over 120 countries worldwide.

The Great Depression was both bane and blessing to the accounting firm of Lybrand, Ross Bros. & Montgomery. The greatly expanded firm, employing hundreds of staff, was faced with shrinking business opportunities as financial institutions and corporations collapsed and went bankrupt. On the other hand, throughout the country and more importantly, on Capitol Hill, the crash was blamed on the lack of independent auditing

of the stock exchange. With a new president installed in 1933, Congress established the Securities and Exchange Commission, the regulatory agency for public corporations and the stock exchange, which resulted in a plethora of auditing activities for the firm. The company also became involved in New Deal projects, serving, for instance, as independent auditors for the Tennessee Valley Authority after 1944. Throughout the Depression years, expansion of the company continued, with branch offices opening up in Illinois, Texas, and Kentucky. In 1935 Robert Montgomery became the president of the prestigious American Institute of Accountants.

During World War II over 400 employees of Lybrand, Ross Bros. & Montgomery served in the Armed Forces. These accountants in uniform, along with 18 administrative assistants, received entertaining newsletters from the company wherever they were stationed; in the end, six members of the firm lost their lives in the conflict. Remarkably, the London and Paris branches of the firm stayed open for business throughout the war, with only the Berlin office having closed down in 1938.

By its 50th anniversary in 1948, the company employed nearly 1,200 staff members and 56 partners. The professionalization of accountancy by then was complete, the role of accountants in business and government unquestioned. The company's evolution in the postwar years therefore would be marked by an enormous expansion in the company's array of services and the continued internationalization of the firm.

Lybrand, Ross Bros. & Montgomery emerged from the war one of the largest accounting firms in the United States. Times were changing, however, and no accounting firm could afford to restrict itself to traditional auditing and accounting services. In 1952 the firm entered a new arena when it started a management consulting service for its clients in the banking and big business world. This was the first of what would become a wide array of consulting services as well as information services and special software packages with the advent of personal computers. While these services by no means supplanted traditional auditing and accounting, they had a significant impact on the firm. By 1974 the firm was the first to establish a career track in accounting for those with computer expertise.

The year 1957 marked the establishment of the European Common Market. Soon thereafter, a merger resulted in Coopers & Lybrand International, consisting initially of the firm's Canadian and British branch firms. While all foreign branches of the firm would bear the name Coopers & Lybrand, the company in the United States retained its original name, Lybrand, Ross Bros. & Montgomery, until 1973. That year, the firm's management decided in favor of adopting a single name for the entire global network of branch companies, which by then were located on all five continents. While the firms, in over 120 countries, remained autonomous, they shared common goals and policies.

Since 1971, Coopers & Lybrand headquarters have remained in the hub of the financial and business world, New York City, with an important office and political action committee located in Washington, D.C. By 1977 Coopers & Lybrand was ranked the third largest accounting company in the United States and was still among the Big Six accounting firms by

1993. In 1981, Coopers & Lybrand became the first U.S. accounting firm to establish a foothold in China. The following year, the company played an important role in the breakup of the $115 billion telephone monopoly, AT&T. Despite the severity of the 1990s recession, Coopers & Lybrand did well—with a 2.5 percent growth in revenue in 1991, the worst year of the recession—partly due to its rapid adaptation to the changing needs of business and a lack of dependency on the domestic marketplace. With the fall of communism in Eastern Europe, Coopers & Lybrand opened offices in Hungary, Poland, Czechoslovakia, Berlin, and Russia, and remained one of the few U.S. firms to do business in Eastern Europe.

History of Price Waterhouse

Price Waterhouse was founded in London in 1850 by Samuel Lowell Price, who wanted to take advantage of England's recent parliamentary laws requiring the examination of a company's financial statements and records. The public accounting profession was growing so rapidly during these years that in 1865 Price took on a partner, Edwin Waterhouse, to help with the expanding business. During the late 1860s and 1870s, while primarily working on arbitrations, bankruptcies, and liquidations, Price and Waterhouse also developed a practice of introducing borrowers to prospective lenders. At this time, many privately owned businesses were converted to public companies and, consequently, reports on earnings signed by reputable accountants soon became an indispensable ingredient in any firm's prospectus.

As the 19th century drew to a close, the firm of Price Waterhouse had garnered a reputation in Britain as one of the leaders of auditing, accounting, and financial consulting services. And, as many of its European clients established operations in the United States, Price Waterhouse sent its own representatives to evaluate the business ventures and opportunities they were financing in order to protect investments and shareholders' interests. Although Price had died in 1887, business in the former colonies was so significant that Waterhouse made the commitment to establish a permanent U.S. presence. On September 1, 1890, the company opened an office at 45 Broadway Avenue in New York City.

A talented member of the London staff, Lewis D. Jones, was the first office manager in New York. Faced with developing clients over an enormous territory that included North, Central, and South America, and serving the needs of diverse industries such as brewing, mining, steel, railroad, leather, and packing, Jones soon required an assistant. Another member of the firm from London, William J. Caesar, arrived and opened a Chicago office the following year. Caesar's aggressive style and management ability soon earned him the leadership of the U.S. operation.

At the turn of the century Arthur Lowes Dickinson succeeded Caesar; it was Dickinson who made the U.S. office uniquely American in both outlook and operation. Rather than continuing the practice of bringing accountants from Britain to serve clients in the United States, Dickinson focused on hiring native talent. Dickinson also encouraged his employees to develop their professional creativity. This quest to break new ground in accounting methods and procedures led to the firm's creation of consolidated financial statements. After Price Waterhouse consolidated the accounts of U.S. Steel, the method gained industrywide acceptance.

The financial report for U.S. Steel was the very first to include supporting statements and time schedules that reflected significant balance sheet accounts, such as inventories and long-term debt, and to provide information on assets, operating funds, payroll statistics, and additional facts of interest to stockholders. By this method of fair disclosure, Price Waterhouse set the standard for financial reporting at the beginning of the 20th century. Price Waterhouse was also the first to provide client shareholders with quarterly financial data and, in 1903, while the firm conducted its first municipal audit, it also pioneered efforts to survey the accounting and audit systems of government organizations. These accomplishments drew attention to accountancy and the role of public accountants in a rapidly developing industrialized economy.

As a young accountant working on Price Waterhouse's audit of Eastman Kodak, George O. May so attracted the attention of George Eastman that Eastman offered him a job. May refused and 20-odd years later, while Eastman was visiting May's office, Eastman remarked, "What a mistake you would have made had you accepted." May, whom many people regard as the father of the accounting profession in the United States, assumed leadership of Price Waterhouse in 1910.

May opened many new offices throughout the United States, and developed new services for clients. In 1913, immediately after Congress enacted a federal income tax, May initiated a tax practice. He also encouraged the firm to provide services for emerging industries, such as the motion picture and automobile industries. It was under May's stewardship that the firm was contracted to handle the balloting of the Academy Awards in 1935 to assure the honesty of the voting process.

Primarily remembered for his devotion to public service, May campaigned relentlessly during the 1920s for Congress to enact laws stipulating that publicly traded companies adopt standard auditing methods and accounting procedures. May secured the New York Stock Exchange as a client of Price Waterhouse, and his work there in the late 1920s and early 1930s led to the formulation and passage of the Securities Exchange Act of 1934. He retired in 1940 and devoted the remainder of his life to writing about the accounting profession.

During the 1940s, the firm faced its first major crisis. A highly profitable drug wholesaler, McKesson & Robbin, Inc., was the victim of an embezzlement scheme carried out by a senior executive and the man's three brothers. The scheme, extremely complex and carefully conceived, eluded detection by the independent auditors from Price Waterhouse. Although a subsequent investigation indicated that the firm's auditing procedures were in strict compliance with the law and the industry's professional standards, the inability of the auditors to discover the embezzlement was of concern to both the firm and the industry at large.

When senior partner John C. Scobie, a Scotsman with a reputation for being scrupulously honest, became head of the firm, he implemented new auditing procedures which were designed to provide auditors with more access to a client's operations. Scobie's plan was to improve the auditor's ability to evaluate whether accounting data reflected the actual performance of any given company; this, in turn, would enable auditors to provide advice to clients on the many operational factors that influence financial results.

After World War II, overseas expansion and investment by companies previously maintaining a national or even regional profile led to the demand for Price Waterhouse to develop a stronger international organization. During this period, the first U.S. senior partner, Percival F. Brundage, and a native New Zealander, John B. Inglis, acted as co-leaders of the firm. Their strategy was twofold: to initiate broader national and international approaches to serving the needs of clients and to build and improve the firm's operational structure.

In concert with the British arm of the organization, the Price Waterhouse International Firm—which promoted uniform accounting standards for all Price Waterhouse offices around the world—was established in late 1945. A management consulting service, MCS, otherwise known as the systems department, was founded in 1946 as part of the evolution of manual accounting systems the firm had been developing for various clients throughout the years. The importance of electronic data became increasingly obvious during the war, and the leadership at Price Waterhouse was quick to recognize the advent of the computer age. Full-time auditors and data processing professionals were hired to design charts for account and pro forma financial statements, develop accounting and various financial systems, and provide advice on productivity improvements. During these years, Price Waterhouse was called upon more and more to recommend the kinds of systems used to organize and produce financial and management information.

When Brundage resigned as senior partner in 1954 to accept a position in the Eisenhower Administration, John Inglis took over sole command and guided the firm into an era of specialization. Since clients more frequently needed nonauditing services, Inglis created four specialized divisions, including accounting research, international tax, SEC review, and an international department. Following the comprehensive revision of the U.S. tax code in 1954, the tax department developed into one of the most important of the firm. The firm's success was indisputable—in 1959 its gross income was nearly $28.5 million.

Inglis retired in 1960 and was replaced by Herman W. Bevis, a brilliant theoretician and writer, who garnered a reputation for leading the debates on the controversial issues of the day, such as deferred taxation and investment tax credits. He led Price Waterhouse through an enormous period of expansion. Within the United States, federal, state and local governments became important clients of the firm's services. In the international arena, Price Waterhouse was sought after by many companies to supply information on foreign business practices, taxes, and government regulations, and to help assess the comparability of financial statements. The firm also helped companies such as Toyota and Sony secure capital from U.S. financial markets by making sure their financial statements were in full compliance with the requirements of the Securities and Exchange Commission.

From its earliest days, Price Waterhouse's elite image had helped the firm bring in blue-chip corporations. Oil and steel industry giants had always been high profile clients, and over the years their presence prompted more and more blue-chip companies to want to share in the prestige of the firm. By the time John C. Biegler became U.S. chairman in 1969, Price Waterhouse counted almost 100 of the *Fortune* 500 as clients.

Yet Biegler's appointment came at a time of dramatic changes not only for Price Waterhouse but for the accounting profession itself. The expanding economy the firm knew since World War II had suddenly vanished, and a creeping inflation and slow national growth ushered in recession. Dramatic drops in the stock market and futures exchanges during 1970 led to a decade of financial instability. Moreover, many of the Big Eight accounting firms were served with lawsuits from disgruntled owners of failed businesses. These problems led directly to an increased competition for clients among all the accounting firms. As a result, Price Waterhouse could no longer rely on its reputation and high-quality work to secure accounts. In order to compete more effectively for clients, the firm was forced to develop aggressive hard-sell marketing techniques, expand the scope and range of its services, and reduce fees.

When Joseph E. Connor replaced Biegler to lead the firm in 1978, he succeeded in implementing a specific market-driven strategy which had immediate payoffs. Connor developed ''industry services groups'' which were comprised of specialists with extensive knowledge and experience in various industries. This strategy helped bring in new clients. Expanding services in the firm's traditional areas of tax, audit and management consulting also helped retain many previous clients.

Notwithstanding the success of his strategy, in 1984 Connor met with chairman Charlie Steel and discussed a merger with Deloitte Haskins & Sells, another of the Big Eight accounting firms, widely known in accounting circles as the 'auditors' auditor.'' The intention behind the merger was to create an organization of such proportions that no other accounting firm could ever again gain a competitive advantage. A letter of intent was signed on October 11, 1984, and, conditional upon the approval of the partners, the merger would take place on January 1, 1985. Yet despite Connor and Steele's confidence in the benefits of such a union, when the balloting was finished the U.S. partners of Price Waterhouse approved while the influential British part of the firm vetoed the merger. For both men, it was a personal and professional defeat. Steel was forced to resign in 1986, while Connor remained as chairman of the U.S. firm until he was replaced in 1988 by Shaun F. O'Malley.

The failure of the proposed merger between Price Waterhouse and Deloitte had raised the possibility of creating a giant accounting firm, and many of the Big Eight partners discussed little else besides potential mergers. After Ernst & Whinney merged with Arthur Young on June 22, 1989, to create Ernst & Young, within weeks four other firms announced plans to merge: Deloitte Haskins & Sells with Touche Ross, and Price Waterhouse with Arthur Andersen.

The proposed merger between Price Waterhouse and Andersen seemed doomed from the start. The Andersen people thought the new firm should be named Arthur Andersen while the Price Waterhouse people thought it should be named Price

Waterhouse; Andersen thought it would be acquiring an auditing practice while Price Waterhouse thought it was acquiring a consulting practice, but neither firm wanted to give the impression that its services were "acquired" by the other; and finally, O'Malley and Andersen's chairman, Larry Weinbach, were new in their positions and just starting to implement development and marketing strategies for their own respective firms. O'Malley and Weinbach agreed to halt merger negotiations after three months.

The year 1990 did not begin auspiciously for Price Waterhouse. In May, a federal judge ordered Price Waterhouse to offer a partnership and nearly $400,000 in back pay to Ann B. Hopkins, who claimed that she had been denied a promotion to partner on grounds of sexual discrimination. In November of the same year, a British bank, Standard Charter PLC, sued the firm for negligence in failing to provide an accurate financial accounting during the acquisition of United Bank of Arizona in 1987. Financial analysts interpreted this latter action as another setback for the accounting industry in the United States: more than $3 billion in damage claims had already been brought against accounting firms by regulatory agencies during the collapse of many savings and loan associations.

Entering the 1990s, Price Waterhouse was expanding its services to clients. The firm offered accounting, tax, and consulting products and services in relation to information systems technology, corporate finance, financial services, petroleum, public utilities, retailing, entertainment, and other industries. With the highest partner earnings and more blue-chip clients—including IBM, USX, J.P. Morgan, Westinghouse, and Shell Oil—than any of the other Big Six U.S. accounting firms, the partners at Price Waterhouse were not worried about the firm's future. However, as its blue-chip client base showed signs of shrinking, and with its sterling image tarnished by two aborted merger attempts, Price Waterhouse would have to fight vigorously for smaller clients and market itself aggressively to survive in the modern world of consulting services.

The 1990s

Both Coopers & Lybrand and Price Waterhouse gradually increased their emphasis on consulting in the 1990s. Auditing was proving risky and expensive, as the Big Six were being held liable for the failure of companies they audited and induced into paying huge settlements. In 1992 Coopers & Lybrand settled a suit brought against it by the investors of MiniScribe, a disk-drive maker that went bankrupt. Fighting against claims that they should have caught the company's fraud, Coopers & Lybrand eventually agreed to pay investors $92 million. In another fraud-related case, the firm made large payments in 1996 to settle claims regarding failed companies in the media empire of the deceased Robert Maxwell. The accounting firm was fined by regulators in 1999 for their failure to detect Maxwell's fraudulent transfer of $650 million from a company pension fund to himself. Among other payments was Coopers & Lybrand's expensive settlement related to their auditing of Phar-Mor pharmacies, bankrupt in the mid-1990s.

Price Waterhouse had their own legal troubles in the 1990s. A protracted battle over the company's audit of Bank of Credit and Commerce International ended in 1995 with a payment of $200 million, significantly less than the $11 billion sought by the creditors of the collapsed bank. In addition to hefty settlements, the suits led to soaring insurance costs for the accounting firms. By the mid-1990s, many insurers refused to even cover the auditing practices of the Big Six firms, forcing Coopers & Lybrand and Price Waterhouse to set aside money to cover themselves.

Several factors led to growth in fee income for Coopers & Lybrand and Price Waterhouse in the mid-1990s. An economic recovery in the United States helped raise fee income by five percent for the Big Six in 1994. In addition, Coopers & Lybrand expanded its presence in Russia; in Moscow alone the firm employed 250 people by 1995. Price Waterhouse also grew in Russia and Eastern Europe, counting almost 1,000 employees there by 1994. The most important factor in their growth was successful expansion of consulting services in the United States. Both companies focused on providing services to certain industries, becoming specialists in those areas. Coopers & Lybrand primarily advised clients in pharmaceutical, insurance, and telecommunications industries, whereas Price Waterhouse specialized in banking, media and entertainment, and oil and gas industries.

The 1998 Merger

Price Waterhouse made yet another attempt at a merger in 1997 and came to an agreement with Coopers & Lybrand. Although the merger was voted in by the 3,250 Price Waterhouse partners and the 5,250 Coopers & Lybrand partners, the merger met some opposition from the companies' clients and financial regulators. Christopher Pearce, finance director of Rentokil and chairman of a group representing FTSE 100 companies' finance directors, told the *Economist* that the mergers will "reduce the choice for auditing services and increase the conflicts of interest."

These concerns and those of financial regulators looking at conflicts of interest between consulting and auditing branches of the companies did not stand in the way of the merger, which was completed in 1998. The combination of the fourth and sixth largest of the Big Six firms resulted in a new industry leader in terms of size and revenues, with approximately 13,000 employees and revenues estimated at $12 billion. In the area of management consulting, the merger created little overlap because the two founding firms specialized in separate industries. It resulted in combined revenue of $1.6 billion, making the new PricewaterhouseCoopers second only to Arthur Andersen in consulting income. Nicholas G. Moore, chairman of Coopers & Lybrand International, became the chairman of PricewaterhouseCoopers, and James J. Schiro, chief executive officer of Price Waterhouse, became the CEO of PricewaterhouseCoopers.

Revenues for the newly forged company were $15.3 billion in 1998. The company continued to grow, acquiring several European consulting firms in the first half of 1999, including the France-based SV&GM Group, the Italian consulting firm Galgan & Merli, and Belgium-based KPMG Consulting. To support its rapid growth, the PricewaterhouseCoopers launched a brand positioning ad campaign in 1999 designed to attract new employees.

Further Reading

"Accountancy Mergers: Double Entries," *Economist,* December 13, 1997.

"Accounting: The Big Five?" *Economist,* September 20, 1997.

Allen, David Grayson, and Kathleen McDermott, *Accounting for Success: A History of Price Waterhouse in America, 1890–1990,* Cambridge, Mass.: Harvard Business School Press, 1993.

Bedrosian, Linc, "The Art of Accounting: CPAs Move Beyond Bean Counting to Assume Greater Roles," *BusinessWest,* March, 1993, p. 13.

Boys, Peter, "What's in a Name: Update (Names of Accounting Firms)," *Accountancy,* March 1990, p. 132.

Cassidy, Tina, "Brain Drain at Coopers," *Boston Business Journal,* February 8, 1993, p. 1.

"Coopers & Lybrand: Foundation for Tomorrow," New York: Coopers & Lybrand, 1991.

"Coopers & Lybrand International," *New York Times,* January 14, 1993, p. C6.

"Coopers in TV Land," *CPA Journal,* March 1993, p. 8.

The Early History of Coopers & Lybrand, 1898–1948, New York: Garland, 1984.

Elliott, Stuart, "Coopers & Lybrand (Accounts)," *New York Times,* November 25, 1992, pp. C17, D18.

Felsenthal, Edward, "Coopers Wins Suit," *Wall Street Journal,* March 2, 1993, pp. B10–11.

"Finance and Economics: Disciplinary Measures," *Economist,* June 8, 1999.

"A Glimmer of Hope," *Economist,* April 1, 1995.

Lawyer, Gail, "Largest Accounting Firms in the Metro Area (Metropolitan Washington Area)," *Washington Business Journal,* March 19, 1993, p. 30.

O'Malley, Shaun F., *Price Waterhouse: 100 Years of Service in the United States,* New York: Newcomen Society, 1990, pp. 1–28.

"The Price Was Right? Price Waterhouse and BCCI," *Economist,* June 10, 1995.

Stevens, Mark, *The Big Eight,* New York: MacMillan, 1981.

——, *The Big Six,* New York: Simon and Schuster, 1991.

Woo, Junda, "Big Six Accounting Firms Join Forces for Legal Change (Firms Want Protection from Shareholders of Client Companies)," *Wall Street Journal,* September 1, 1992, p. B7.

—Sina Dubovoj and Thomas Derdak
—updated by Susan Windisch Brown

PROGRESSIVE®

The Progressive Corporation

6300 Wilson Mills Road
Mayfield Village, Ohio 44143
U.S.A.
(440) 461-5000
Fax: (440) 446-7436
Web site: http://www.progressive.com

Public Company
Incorporated: 1956 as Progressive Casualty Insurance
    Company
Employees: 15,735
Sales: $5.29 billion (1998)
Stock Exchanges: New York
Ticker Symbol: PGR
NAIC: 524126 Direct Property & Casualty Insurance
    Carriers; 524128 Other Direct Insurance (Except Life,
    Health & Medical) Carriers; 551112 Offices of Other
    Holding Companies

By practically any measure, The Progressive Corporation ranks among the United States' most successful property and casualty insurers. The holding company's primary subsidiary, Progressive Casualty Insurance Co., got its start by insuring "nonstandard" or high-risk drivers. The firm's profits have consistently outperformed the industry: from 1970 to 1992, Progressive averaged a three percent annual profit margin on underwriting insurance, whereas its competitors averaged a seven percent annual loss. In the more profitable 1990s its underwriting profit margin increased to 8.4 percent in 1998. Total revenues increased fourfold from $1.39 billion in 1989 to $5.29 billion in 1998. In 1992, Progressive became the nation's largest provider of automobile insurance through independent agents. In 1993, Progressive became the largest automobile insurer in its home state of Ohio. By 1999 it was the fifth largest auto insurer in the United States and was set on becoming the largest. Although a publicly traded company, Progressive remained a family-run enterprise in the late 1990s; Peter B. Lewis, son of one of the co-founders, was chief executive officer, president, and chairman of the board. His youn-

ger brother, Daniel R. Lewis, was process leader of Progressive's largest business, the Agency Business Unit.

Innovative Auto Insurance: 1930s and 1940s

The Progressive insurance organization was created in 1937 when Peter and Daniel's father, Joe, joined fellow Cleveland attorney Jack Green for a state-sponsored investigation of a group of door-to-door insurance salesmen. In the course of that operation, the partners discovered a profitable and (unlike the subjects of their investigation) legal niche in the insurance business. To fill that niche, the two graduates of Western Reserve University School of Law first obtained insurance licenses. Using $10,000 borrowed from Lewis's mother-in-law, they acquired five small auto service companies and called their new venture Progressive Mutual Insurance Company.

Lewis and Green established innovation as a hallmark of their enterprise at the outset. Before World War II, insurers customarily set premiums according to noncompetitive rate tables and required prepayment of policies. Progressive targeted blue-collar drivers with an inexpensive $25 policy, a monthly payment plan, and an industry first—the "one-and-one" policy. In the event of an accident, this coverage would pay up to $1000 to repair either the insured's or the other driver's car, at the policyholder's discretion. By virtue of its establishment in a garage, Progressive also offered its clients another unique convenience—drive-in claims services.

Lewis and Green wrote less than $10,000 in premiums that first year, and by 1939, Progressive's original capital had dwindled to less than $1,500. A Chicago consultant advised the partners to get out of insurance, but they struggled on through the early 1940s. Peter B. Lewis would later observe that "World War II saved Progressive. People finally had jobs and money, so they could afford cars and insurance, but gas was rationed so they couldn't drive and didn't have many accidents." The booming, car-crazy, postwar economy further accelerated Progressive's business: premium revenues reached $480,000 by 1946. The era saw Progressive expand into the related areas of fire, theft, and collision insurance, as well as some financing services.

Company Perspectives:

We seek to be an excellent, innovative, growing and enduring business by cost-effectively and profitably reducing the human trauma and economic costs of auto accidents and other mishaps, and by building a recognized, trusted, admired, business-generating brand.

Innovation, Expansion, and Reorganization: 1950s

A new market opened up in the 1950s as many leading insurers began to segment their clients according to age, driving record, and other quantitative categories. They then insured only the statistically best candidates, known in the industry as "standard risks." Progressive Casualty Insurance Company was created in 1956 to capture the growing "nonstandard" pool of drivers that didn't make it into the preferred category. The new subsidiary wrote $83,000 in premiums during its first year in operation.

Founder Joe Lewis had died just one year earlier, and his son Peter B. Lewis joined the firm after graduating from Princeton University. The younger Lewis helped lead Progressive's expansion outside Ohio's boundaries after 1960. The company began writing policies in Michigan, Florida, Tennessee, Kentucky, Georgia, and Mississippi, and, within three years, extra-Ohio premiums topped $5 million annually. The Progressive Corporation, an insurance holding company, was formed in 1965 upon Jack Green's retirement. It brought Progressive Casualty and three related insurance agencies under the Lewis family's control through a leveraged buyout. The new company's premium revenue totaled about $7.4 million during its first year of incorporation, which was also Peter Lewis' first year as president and chief executive officer.

In nearly 35 years at its helm, Peter Lewis has left his personal imprint on Progressive. The avid art collector and patron started a corporate collection and commissioned a new artist to illustrate the company's annual report each year. By 1987, the corporate collection constituted over 1,000 pieces of award-winning contemporary art. Lewis was characterized as "a brilliant and unusual man" in a 1990 *Financial World* profile, and he has been credited with the managerial savvy that kept Progressive in the vanguard of auto insurance. Lewis established high employment standards early in his career. Progressive recruited employees at the country's top business schools on the assumption that only the best students are accepted at, and matriculated from, these institutions. Lewis prided himself on the "ruthless discipline" expected of his executives. In 1990, he told *Financial World* that "There are 15 people who used to work for us who we asked to leave who became presidents of other insurance companies."

Crisis and then Unchecked Growth: 1970s

Lewis took Progressive public in 1971 with the sale of 110,000 shares. That same year, the company formed a subsidiary, Progressive American Insurance Co., in Miami, Florida. Progressive and the property/casualty industry in general got a

"wake-up call" in the mid-1970s, when years of consolidation, acquisition of major companies by noninsurance conglomerates, and depletion of reserves brought on the worst years since the Depression. During this crisis, Lewis set forth one of the company's most important goals: to always achieve an underwriting profit. That standard, measured in the insurance industry as the combined operating ratio, soon became one of Progressive's hallmarks. Most auto insurance companies were satisfied with a combined operating ratio of 100 or more—meaning that claims and expenses paid equaled or exceeded premiums collected. They made money not from selling insurance, but from profitable investments. Progressive insisted on keeping its combined ratio under 100 and making an operating profit before investments. Since the 1960s, the auto insurance industry overall has consistently recorded losses on underwriting activities, while Progressive has done so very infrequently.

As one of the few nonstandard or high-risk insurance companies, Progressive grew virtually unchallenged in the late 1970s. From 1975 to 1978, premium income nearly quadrupled, from $38 million to $112 million, as standard auto insurers turned away and dropped their riskier customers. By 1979, the company wrote policies in 31 states. Ohio accounted for one-third of premiums.

One of the keys to Progressive's impressive results was its exacting actuarial standards. In the 1950s the company began to invest far more heavily than its competitors in collecting and analyzing accident data. Progressive's actuaries sought out the best of the bad risks and devised more accurate pricing policies. For example, actuaries at Progressive found that, of motorists arrested for driving while under the influence of alcohol, those with children were least likely to drive drunk again. These select customers were still charged higher-than-normal rates, but Progressive's "high-risk" premiums remained lower than those of its competitors.

Revenue Growth in the 1980s

These pricing policies helped the company's premium volume increase to $157.3 million by 1980. As business around the country increased, Progressive established regional offices in Sacramento, Tampa, Richmond, Colorado Springs, Austin, Omaha, and Toronto in the late 1970s and early 1980s. In 1986, the company wrote over $830 million in premiums, over five times as much as it had at the beginning of the decade.

After the 1987 stock market crash, Lewis ousted his investment team and brought Alfred Lerner, chairman of Equitable Bancorp, MNC Financial Inc., and MBNA Corp., on as chairman and director of investments. Upon his hiring, Lewis compared Lerner's investment expertise to basketball great Michael Jordan's athletic prowess. Lewis asked Lerner to invest $75 million in Progressive to ensure the newcomer's vested interest in his new employer's financial performance.

The insurer celebrated its 50th anniversary in 1987 with its first $1 billion year and a listing on the New York Stock Exchange. Lewis told the *Cleveland Plain Dealer* that "We feel humble here because this could happen only in America."

Over the course of his five-year tenure at Progressive, Lerner appeared to have invested the firm's funds profitably. Then, late in 1992, the investor converted his $75 million bond into $244.5 million in Progressive stock and sold half of his holdings. Lewis resumed the responsibilities of the chair and control of the firm's investment strategy early in 1993, asserting that he simply had "the desire, time and comfort level necessary to re-assume responsibility for the financial side of the business," in a February 1993 *Cleveland Plain Dealer* article.

The insurance industry overall suffered consumer backlash that took the form of rate legislation in the late 1980s. The most notorious law, California's Proposition 103, mandated 20 percent cuts in auto insurance premiums and refunds to many customers after its 1988 adoption. That year, $305 million, or 28 percent, of Progressive's business was in California. By 1993, Progressive had reduced its revenues from the state to $50 million and created a $150 million reserve to pay for rate rollbacks to 260,000 current and former policyholders. That year, Lewis reached an agreement with John Garamendi, California's insurance commissioner, to refund $51.2 million, or 18 percent of premiums paid on policies written between November 1988 and November 1989. The remaining $100 million in the contingency fund went to Progressive's coffers.

Competition in the nonstandard segment also heated up in the late 1980s, as Allstate, Integon, American Premier (formerly Penn Central Corp.), and small local rivals followed Progressive's lead into this "risky business." Progressive responded to these challenges and instituted several operational changes, including a five-year, $28 million overhaul of its information system and a new Immediate Response claims service accessible using a toll-free, 24-hour hotline. A television advertising campaign emphasized not only the speed, but the compassion, that Progressive's policyholders could expect by recounting an incident when a Progressive claims representative actually arrived at an accident site before the police.

However, Progressive and its talented leader were not infallible. In 1986, the company began insuring long-haul truck and bus fleets. This segment grew from nothing to $175 million in premiums within two years. However, trucking companies wielded strong buying power, and insurance industry rivals' price cuts soon siphoned off Progressive's long-haul business. By 1992, the experiment had lost $84 million—an amount unheard of and unacceptable at Progressive—and was eliminated.

Remarkable Growth After Difficult Start: 1990s

The combination of rollbacks in California, the misstep into transportation insurance, and drastically lower net income in 1991 (profits dropped from $93.4 million in 1990 to $32.9 million in 1991) created a "mini-crisis" that soured Wall Street on Progressive. The stock's price inched up just six percent in 1991, compared to its 35 percent increase the previous year. In response, Lewis reduced employment at Progressive the next year by 19 percent, or 1,300 workers. Lewis softened the blow for the remaining 5,600 employees by instituting a profit-sharing program, but admitted to *Fortune* magazine that the money-saving decision "destroyed morale." However, Progressive was able to cut costs enough to actually reduce premium rates in 18 states during 1993. After 1991's rather dismal results, profits nearly tripled to $153.8 million in 1992 and rose to $267.3 million the following year.

Standard and preferred policies only constituted 4.5 percent of Progressive's private passenger auto premiums in 1993, but in 1993 and 1994 the company established pilot programs in Texas, Florida, Ohio, Illinois, and Virginia to break into that market. In 1997 it began selling policies in the preferred auto insurance market in California, competing against the state's big three auto insurers Farmers Insurance Group, State Farm Insurance Cos., and Allstate Insurance Co. Following the passage of Proposition 103 in 1988, Progressive had backed away from the California market, laying off 800 workers at its Rancho Cordova office. Now the company intended to compete more aggressively in the state, adding five more offices to the six it already operated there. After net premiums grew from $1.45 billion in 1992 to $3.44 billion in 1996, Progressive was the sixth largest U.S. auto insurer and the 13th largest in California.

Progressive continued its tradition of innovative services in 1994, when it introduced its 1-800-AUTO-PRO service. Consumers could call the number any time of the day or night to receive a quote on their auto insurance from Progressive. During the same call, they could also receive comparison rates for up to three other leading auto insurers, a move designed to help consumers more easily comparison shop and make more informed buying decisions.

In 1996 the company announced its interest in taking into account personal credit histories, which reflected a customer's financial responsibility and how he chose to pay his bills, when setting their auto insurance rates in California, something which Progressive was able to do in other states. Progressive had found that people with better credit ratings tended to cost the company less money, and therefore should be charged lower rates. The proposal would have to be approved by the state's insurance commissioner. Critics charged that it would discriminate against certain groups of people, including low-income individuals such as minorities and college students. According to Progressive, using a consumer's financial responsibility as a factor in setting their insurance rates was not reflective of that person's income, race, or gender.

In 1998 the company's underwriting profit margin increased from 6.6 percent in 1997 to 8.4 percent, while the industry average was .3 percent. With Personal Lines net premiums written of $4.9 billion, Progressive was the fifth largest U.S. auto insurer. Auto premiums accounted for 93 percent of Progressive's total net premiums written, which reached $5.3 billion in 1998. Brand-building efforts included sponsoring the 1999 Super Bowl XXXIII half-time show and introducing new commercials featuring E.T. as Progressive's spokesperson.

At the beginning of 1999 Progressive created a second CEO position, perhaps to ensure an orderly management succession when 65-year-old Peter B. Lewis decided to retire. Charles Chokel, who had managed the company's $5.6 billion investment portfolio for the past six years as chief financial officer, assumed the new position of CEO in charge of investments and capital management. Lewis remained chairman and CEO in charge of insurance operations as well as president.

Throughout the 1990s Progressive's stated goal was to be the number three auto insurer in the United States. To reach that goal the company would have to increase its premiums to an annual rate of about $10 billion. The company's recent brand-building efforts were aimed at making Progressive the number one consumer choice for auto insurance. The company had offered quotes over the Internet through its own Web site (www.progressive.com) since 1997 and was the first auto insurer to sell policies online. To achieve its goal of being the most widely available auto insurance, Progressive also began offering its quotes over other Web services, such as InsWeb (www.insweb.com) and Quotesmith (www.quotesmith.com). By 1997 it was selling auto insurance to every driver in as many ways as possible: through independent agents, over the telephone, and on the Internet.

Progressive's unique Immediate Response claims service, competitive prices, cost-cutting measures, and other efforts had resulted in a decade of solid growth. For the next decade the company was poised to grow as aggressively as its plans called for and prosper in a very competitive business environment.

Principal Subsidiaries

Airy Insurance Center, Inc.; Allied Insurance Agency, Inc.; Auto Insurance Solutions, Inc.; Classic Insurance Co.; Express Quote Services, Inc.; Gold Key Insurance Agency; Greenberg Financial Insurance Services, Inc.; Insurance Confirmation Services, Inc.; Lakeside Insurance Agency, Inc.; Midland Financial Group, Inc.; Mountain Laurel Assurance Co.; Mountainside Insurance Agency, Inc.; National Continental Insurance Co.; Pacific Motor Club; Paloverde Insurance Company of Arizona; PCIC Canada Holdings, Ltd.; Progressive Adjusting Company, Inc.; Progressive American Insurance Co.; Progressive Casualty Insurance Co.; Progressive Insurance Agency, Inc.; Progressive Investment Company, Inc.; Progressive Max Insurance Co.; Progressive Mountain Insurance Co.; Progressive Northern Insurance Co.; Progressive Northwestern Insurance Co.; Progressive Partners, Inc.; Progressive Preferred Insurance Co.; Progressive Premium Budget, Inc.; Progressive Risk Management Services, Inc.; Progressive Southeastern Insurance Co.; Richmond Transport Corp.; Tampa Insurance Services, Inc.; Progressive Agency, Inc.; Transportation Recoveries, Inc.; United Financial Casualty Co.; Village Transport Corp.; Wilson Mills Land Co.; Bayside Underwriters Insurance Agency Inc.; Garden Sun Insurance Services Inc.; Halcyon Insurance Co.; Marathon Insurance Co.; Ohana Insurance Company of Hawaii Inc.; Paragon Insurance Company of NY; Progressive Casualty Investment Company; Progressive NY Agency Inc.; Progressive American Life; Progressive Bayside Insurance Company; Progressive Casualty Insurance Company of Canada; Progressive County Mutual Insurance Company; Progressive Gulf Insurance Company; Progressive Life Insurance Ltd.; Progressive Premier Insurance Company of Illinois; Progressive Specialty Insurance Company; Progressive Universal Insurance Company of Illinois; Pro-West Insurance Company; The Paradyme Corporation; United Financial Adjusting Company.

Further Reading

Adams, David. "Ohio-Based Progressive Corp. to Sponsor Super Bowl Halftime Show," *Knight-Ridder/Tribune Business News*, January 28, 1999.

Bowler, William R., "High Risk's Reward: Progressive Corp. Writes Good Profits on Bad Drivers," *Barron's*, September 17, 1979, pp. 56–57.

David, Gregory, "Chastened?," *Financial World*, January 4, 1994, pp. 38–40.

Dumaine, Brain, "Times Are Good? Create a Crisis," *Fortune*, June 28, 1993, pp. 123–30.

Flaum, David, "Ohio's Progressive Corp. Acquires Midland Financial of Memphis, Tenn.," *Knight-Ridder/Tribune Business News*, March 11, 1997.

Gleisser, Marcus, "Progressive Insurance Profits Hit $1 Billion," *Cleveland Plain Dealer*, February 6, 1988, p. 5B.

Greene, Jay, "Progressive Switches Control of Investments," *Cleveland Plain Dealer*, February 12, 1993, p. 1E.

Haggerty, Alfred G. "Progressive Set to Rebate $51.2 Million in California," *National Underwriter Property & Casualty-Risk & Benefits Management*, June 22, 1992, p. 2.

Hann, Leslie Western, "Auto Insurer Progressive Corp.," *Best's Review—Property-Casualty Insurance Edition*, February 1999, p. 84.

——, "Hard Choices Ensure Success," *Cleveland Plain Dealer*, June 7, 1993, p. 17G.

Johnson, Kelly. "Aggressive Progressive Impressive in Auto Insurance," *Sacramento Business Journal*, July 21, 1997, p. 4.

——, "Progressive's Latest Proposal Sparks Interest, Outrage," *Sacramento Business Journal*, October 31, 1997, p. 8.

King, Julia, "Re-Engineering Puts Progressive on the Spot," *Computerworld*, July 15, 1991, p. 58.

Loomis, Carol J. "Sex, Reefer? And Auto Insurance!," *Fortune*, August 7, 1995, p. 76.

McGough, Robert, "Like to Drink and Drive?," *Financial World*, November 27, 1990, pp. 26–28.

Mendes, Joshua, "Progressive: The Prince of Smart Pricing," *Fortune*, March 23, 1992, pp. 107–08.

Phillips, Stephen, "Bad Risks Are this Car Insurer's Best Friends," *Business Week*, November 12, 1990, p. 122.

Serres, Christopher, "Progressive Creates Second CEO Position," *Crain's Cleveland Business*, January 4, 1999, p. 1.

——, "Progressive's Promoted Takes His Place: CEO Chokel Offers Stark Contrast to Eccentric Lewis," *Crain's Cleveland Business*, January 11, 1999, p. 3.

Shingler, Dan, "Progressive's Attitude Now Matches Name," *Crain's Cleveland Business*, October 17, 1994, p. 1.

—April Dougal Gasbarre
—updated by David Bianco

Res-Care, Inc.

10140 Linn Station Road
Louisville, Kentucky 40223
U.S.A.
(502) 394-2100
Fax: (502) 394-2206
Web site: http://www.rescare.com

Public Company
Incorporated: 1974
Employees: 18,500
Sales: $522.7 million (1998)
Stock Exchanges: NASDAQ
Ticker Symbol: RSCR
NAIC: 62431 Vocational Rehabilitation Services; 62321
   Residential Mental Retardation Facilities; 62399 Other
   Residential Care Facilities

Res-Care, Inc. is the United States' largest provider of residential, training, educational, and support services for persons with special needs, serving more than 20,000 people in 30 states and Puerto Rico. The company has two main operating divisions. The Division for Persons with Disabilities offers a full range of residential support services, vocational training, and other services to individuals with mental retardation and other developmental disabilities. The Division for Youth Services provides educational, training, and treatment programs for at-risk youth and young adults. The Division for Youth Services provides these services as a private contractor in the federal Job Corps program and through two subsidiary operations: Youthtrack, Inc. and Alternative Youth Services, Inc.

Job Corps Beginnings in 1974

Res-Care was founded in 1974 by James R. Fornear. Fornear had served previously as a center director for the Job Corps program, a U.S. Department of Labor-administered program that provides educational and training programs for unemployed and disadvantaged youth. Fornear used his experience with the program and his desire to work with at-risk youth to establish Res-Care as a private contractor for the Job Corps. The company was awarded its first government contract in 1976, to operate the Whitney Young Job Corps Center in Shelby County, Kentucky. In the following two years, Fornear acquired additional Job Corps operations in Crystal Springs and Gulfport, Mississippi.

After four years of success in the Job Corps program, Res-Care stepped into a new service sector by establishing the Higgins Learning Center near Morganfield, Kentucky. This center, developed to serve persons with mental retardation, marked a broadening and diversification of Res-Care's services. This diversification—to serve disabled persons in addition to at-risk youth—was the inception of the company's modern-day service duality.

For Res-Care, the 1980s were characterized by growth in both Job Corps contracts and services for persons with disabilities. In 1983 the company was awarded a contract for the Job Corps Center in Miami, Florida, a program serving 300 students. That same year, Res-Care began to operate small community-based group homes for persons with developmental disabilities in both Florida and Indiana. These state-licensed, Res-Care-staffed group homes typically consisted of six to eight individuals living together in a house located in a residential neighborhood. More group homes and Job Corps programs were in the offing for Res-Care, and by 1989 the company had expanded to serve persons in Kentucky, Indiana, Florida, West Virginia, and New York.

In 1989 Fornear recruited Ron Geary to become Res-Care's president and CEO. Geary had a wide range of professional experience, having served as president of the Cincinnati Bible College and as Secretary of Revenue for the state of Kentucky, as well as practicing in the areas of law and accounting. The somewhat unusual combination of Geary's managerial expertise and Fornear's know-how in the service industries proved to be synergistic.

Res-Care continued to grow at a moderate pace for the next few years. In 1990 the company began operating Job Corps centers in Puerto Rico. Two years later, it opened facilities for

---

developmentally disabled persons in both Colorado and Nebraska. Res-Care's Colorado operation was its first "supported-living" program. The supported living program differed from the group home concept in that it allowed services to be provided on a more individualized basis. Instead of six to eight persons living in a group home, supported-living consumers were able to live either singly or in much smaller groups of two or three. Res-Care offered a broad spectrum of services to its supported-living consumers—from 24-hour staffing to only a few hours of service weekly—depending upon need.

At the close of 1992, Res-Care issued an initial public offering (IPO) and began trading on the Nasdaq exchange. Using the capital raised in its IPO, the company ramped up its expansion pace substantially, and the next five years were to be busy ones. During that time frame, the company established facilities for developmentally disabled persons in California, Texas, New Mexico, Kansas, Oklahoma, Tennessee, Illinois, and Ohio, in addition to acquiring a new Job Corps contract in Edison, New Jersey. It also moved its headquarters into a new 50,000-square-foot office building on Linn Station Road in Louisville, in November of 1995.

Youth Division Expansions in the Mid-1990s

While Res-Care's Division for Persons with Disabilities was moving into new territory geographically, its Division for Youth Services was preparing to move into a completely new type of service. In late 1995 the company created a subsidiary called Youthtrack, Inc., to serve delinquent youth. Based in Denver, Colorado, Youthtrack offered programs to young people, both male and female, who had either been sentenced or were awaiting sentencing for criminal activity. Through Youthtrack, Res-Care offered a menu of services, including secure residential treatment; short-term, intensive training; detention programming; aftercare programs for released delinquent youth; and an array of specialized services such as substance abuse programming, vocational and life skills training, gender-specific programming, and offense-specific programming. Youthtrack soon grew to be the largest private provider of services to youth in the Colorado juvenile justice system, eventually expanding into Utah and Puerto Rico as well.

The following year saw further expansion for Res-Care's Division for Youth Services, with the creation of another subsidiary, Alternative Youth Services, Inc. (AYS). The goal in creating AYS was to serve at-risk and special-needs youth who were not viable candidates for the Job Corps or Youthtrack

programs. AYS targeted youth who had behavioral and emotional disorders and who, in some cases, had been diagnosed with mental retardation or other learning disabilities. The initial AYS facility was the Georgia Center for Youth, a residential treatment center and alternative school. The new subsidiary grew in 1997 through a series of acquisitions and management agreements. In the course of that year, AYS signed a long-term agreement to manage two foster care programs in Ohio and Kentucky, acquired a collection of ten group homes in Kentucky, and acquired an outdoor therapeutic program and emergency treatment shelter in Tennessee. Altogether, AYS's acquisitions were projected to serve more than 750 new consumers and generate more than $7 million in revenue.

In the fall of 1997 Res-Care more than doubled the scope of its Job Corps operations by acquiring Teledyne Economic Development, of Allegheny, Pennsylvania. Teledyne, which operated five Job Corps centers in Pennsylvania, Virginia, Oklahoma, and Arizona, had annual revenues of approximately $40 million. The addition of Teledyne made Res-Care one of the three largest private contractors in the Job Corps programs, with 12 Job Corps centers serving 4,500 individuals. In an October 3, 1997 press release, Geary called the Teledyne acquisition "perhaps the most exciting transaction in the history of Res-Care."

New Service Delivery Systems in 1997

The year 1997 also brought expansion in Res-Care's Division for Persons with Disabilities, in the form of 11 new acquisitions, entry into four new states, and the capacity to serve 1,751 new consumers. Among the division's 11 new acquisitions, three provided entry into new markets. The first came in January of 1997, when the company acquired a partnership interest in Premier Rehabilitation Centers, a Chicago-based, privately owned provider of services to persons with acquired brain injury and related neurological disorders. Although Res-Care previously had serviced a small number of consumers with acquired brain injury (ABI) through its existing programs, the Premier acquisition marked its first operation dedicated to this specific disability.

A second strategic acquisition was completed in July of 1997. With the purchase of Communications Network Consultants, of Lenoir, North Carolina, Res-Care began providing "periodic services." This delivery method allowed the company to provide services to consumers in their own homes on an as-needed basis—a departure from the traditional residential delivery method, in which all consumers lived in a home owned and staffed by the company. Subsequent to the acquisition of Communications Network Consultants, Res-Care began to introduce the periodic service delivery model throughout the company.

In late 1997 the Division for Persons with Disabilities made its third key acquisition: Other Options, a Maryland-based non-profit service agency designed to serve persons with developmental disabilities and behavioral challenges. The acquisition of Other Options positioned Res-Care as a niche provider for a segment of the population often refused service by other community-based providers. The Other Options' program model focused on generating community support for these often difficult to serve consumers, rather than trying to make these consumers conform to the community's expectations. By the end of 1997, Res-Care was implementing this model in three states, with plans for further expansion.

In the years between 1992 and 1997, Res-Care had grown from serving 1,378 persons in six states and Puerto Rico to serving more than 14,000 persons in 24 states and Puerto Rico. This growth in capacity was paralleled by a steady growth in revenues. For the five years 1992 through 1996, the company showed a 26 percent annual compounded growth rate in net income—and in 1997 posted a record 36 percent increase.

Record Growth in 1998

Res-Care kicked off 1998 with January acquisitions in both the Division for Persons with Disabilities and the Division for Youth Services. On January 6, the Disability division announced completion of the acquisition of Creative Networks, LLC. The purchase of this agency, a privately owned provider of supported living services, gave Res-Care 1,600 new consumers located in the Phoenix, Flagstaff, and Prescott, Arizona areas. A week later, the company's Alternative Youth Services subsidiary announced its purchase of Arizona Youth Associates, which included ten group homes in the Phoenix and Mesa areas, a 35-student alternative school, and an outpatient counseling program serving 200 youth.

The spring of 1998 was filled with further acquisitions. In March, Res-Care purchased the Louisville-based Normal Life, Inc., one of the nation's largest privately owned providers of services to mentally retarded and developmentally disabled persons. Normal Life had annual revenue of approximately $68 million and served 1,300 consumers in California, Florida, Georgia, Indiana, Kentucky, Louisiana, and Texas. Res-Care added another $11 million in revenue and 1,100 consumers with the purchase of Southern Home Care, a provider of home- and community-based services for persons with developmental disabilities in Georgia and South Carolina. The company also expanded its acquired brain injury unit with the acquisition of Iowa-based Victorian Acres, a provider of supported living services to persons with ABI.

Res-Care's Division for Youth Services moved into Utah for the first time with the late-March purchase of Family Preservation Institute, a juvenile services provider that offered community-based residential and day programs to 40 consumers in Brigham City. On the heels of the Utah acquisition, the youth division was awarded a Job Corps contract for the Earle C. Clements Job Corps Center in Morganfield, Kentucky. With a service capacity of 2,000 students and $60 million in revenue, the Kentucky operation was the nation's largest Job Corps center—and an important contract for Res-Care. "This award is perhaps the most significant event in our 24 years in the federal Job Corps program," Res-Care President Ron Geary said in an April 2, 1998 press release.

Acquisitions in May included the Prescott, Arizona-based Schumacher Consulting, Inc. and the Ohio-based Four Star Residential—both agencies service developmentally disabled persons—and the New Summit School, a private school in Jackson, Mississippi serving youth with special learning needs. Together, the three acquisitions added a projected $1.9 million

in revenue and 400 new Res-Care consumers. May also brought two new contracts for the company's Division for Youth Services, totaling a projected $1.8 million in revenue. Fueled by its growth, Res-Care finished the month of May with a 3-for-2 stock split, turning its 12.5 million outstanding shares into 18.7 million.

After a brief summer lull, Res-Care's steady growth recommenced. In late August the Division for Youth Services' AYS subsidiary announced the acquisition of Copper Canyon Academy, a 200-student charter school in Glendale, Arizona. At the same time, AYS announced a new long-term management agreement with a Fort Wayne, Indiana foster care program. This was followed in early September by a one-year, $1.6 million contract with the U.S. Department of the Interior to provide support services at two Job Corps centers in Kentucky and West Virginia.

Res-Care's acquired brain injury division made another expansion in mid-October 1998, with the merger of Tangram Rehabilitation Network, Inc., located in San Marcos, Texas. Tangram, which began operating as part of Res-Care's ABI unit, served 125 ABI patients and generated revenues of approximately $14 million at the time. Three smaller acquisitions followed in November. Bumpershoot Enterprises, of Riverside, California, and Texas Living Centers, of Garland, Texas—both service providers for mentally retarded and developmentally disabled persons—were added to Res-Care's Division for Persons with Disabilities. Subsequently, the Division for Youth Services acquired Gator Human Services, a not-for-profit delinquent youth services provider with programs in seven Florida communities. The three acquisitions together were expected to bring in an additional $8.2 million in income.

Res-Care closed out 1998 on a high note by winning two substantial Job Corps contracts in December—and adding a projected total of more than $50 million. Altogether in 1998, the company made 27 acquisitions and new contracts, which were expected to generate $178.1 million in annual revenues and serve more than 8,100 new consumers. The hectic growth pace paid off in the year-end financials. Net revenues for 1998 increased a record 71 percent—to $522.7 million from $306.1 million in 1997. Net income increased by 50 percent, and earnings per share were up 31 percent.

1999 and Beyond

As Res-Care entered the last year of the century, it continued the pattern of acquisitions that had proven successful through the 1990s. Between January and March of 1999, the company announced the acquisition of four providers of services to disabled persons. The companies—located in Hickory, North Carolina, Tampa, Florida, Loomis, California, and Rome, Georgia—together were projected to add an additional $12.5 million in revenues and more than 500 new consumers.

In early April 1999, however, the company made perhaps its most significant announcement in its history: a planned merger with PeopleServe, Inc., one of the nation's largest privately owned agencies serving developmentally disabled persons. PeopleServe, headquartered in Dublin, Ohio, served approximately 4,300 persons in 12 states and Washington, DC, and had 1998 revenues of $184 million. Once merged, the companies were projected to have revenues in excess of $800 million; serve 26,000 persons in 32 states, Washington, DC, and Puerto Rico; and employ approximately 25,300 people. The $170 million transaction was expected to be complete by the end of 1999.

''There are growing pressures to expand the availability of services for person with developmental disabilities, evidenced by long waiting lists in most states and the aging boomer generation of caregivers,'' Res-Care's president, Ron Geary, said in an April 5, 1999 press release. ''The merger will solidify our position as the leading provider of these services and will position us to achieve our goal of annualized revenues in excess of $1 billion during the calendar year 2000.''

Principal Subsidiaries

Alternative Youth Services, Inc.; Youthtrack, Inc.

Principal Divisions

Division for Person with Disabilities; Division for Youth Services.

Further Reading

Benmour, Eric, ''Res-Care Headquarters Gains 46 Jobs as Company Expands,'' *Business First of Louisville,* January 26, 1998.
''Human Touch a Priority as Res-Care Grows,'' *Louisville Courier-Journal,* July 28, 1996.
''Louisville Firm Buys Allegheny Teledyne Division,'' *Pittsburgh Business Times,* September 17, 1997.
''Res-Care Subsidiary Offers Youth Services,'' *Business First of Louisville,* March 4, 1996.

—Shawna Brynildssen

Ritz-Carlton Hotel Company L.L.C.

3414 Peachtree Road NE, Suite 300
Atlanta, Georgia 30326
U.S.A.
(404) 237-5500
Fax: (404) 261-0119
Web site: http://www.ritzcarlton.com

Wholly Owned Subsidiary of Marriott International, Inc.
Incorporated: 1983
Employees: 15,000
Sales: $970.6 million
NAIC: 72111 Hotels (Except Casino Hotels) & Motels

The Ritz-Carlton Hotel Company L.L.C. operates a chain of 36 hotels worldwide. The chain banks on the lustrous image of its name and strives to make each of its locations uniquely luxurious. Its hotels are top-rated, including several that earned five stars and five diamonds in domestic rankings. Aside from its 20 hotels across the United States, Ritz-Carlton has locations in Sydney, Australia, Shanghai, China, Bali, Indonesia, Seoul, Korea and other Asian locations, several in Europe and the Middle East, and others in the Caribbean. As of 1999 the chain was in the midst of plans to expand abroad and domestically. Founded in 1983 when William Johnson bought the rights to the famous Ritz-Carlton name, the chain is owned by hotel giant Marriott International.

Early History

The history of the current Ritz-Carlton Hotel Company properly begins in the 19th century, with the exploits of legendary hotelier Cesar Ritz. The ambitious child of a poor herdsman, Ritz was born in 1850 in the small mountain village of Niederwald, Switzerland. One of 13 children, Ritz left home at the age of 16 to work in the dining room of a hotel in the adjacent town of Brieg. After a few months on the job he was fired, according to his employer, for not possessing even an "aptitude," much less a "flair," for the hotel business. Hired as a waiter in the restaurant of another hotel, Ritz soon was fired once again.

Undismayed, Ritz traveled to Paris, where he worked emptying slops for small hotels. Fired from two more jobs, he finally landed a position at a chic restaurant near the Madeleine and worked his way up from bus boy to manager. At the age of 19 he was asked to become a partner by the owner of the restaurant, yet Ritz politely refused the offer. His ambition was still unsatisfied, but now that he knew what he wanted, he rolled up his aprons and sauntered down the street to the most elegant and famous restaurant of the day, Voisin, an international meeting place for royalty and gourmets. Starting at the bottom as an assistant waiter, Ritz learned how to carve a roast and press duck, how to decant wine, and how to serve food in ways that pleased both the eye and the palate.

It was at Voisin that Ritz developed his instincts for high-quality food and service, and his personal touch began to attract influential customers such as Sarah Bernhardt, Alexandre Dumas the younger, and the Rothschilds. When Germany invaded France and laid siege to Paris in 1871, a food scarcity led the city zoo to butcher its two elephants; Voisin's purchased the trunks of the animals. When Ritz served them in high style, *trompe sauce chasseur* became a gourmet's rage and Ritz himself an overnight sensation in Parisian culinary circles.

A short time later, Ritz left Paris and worked for three years in resort restaurants and fashionable hotels in Nice, San Remo, Rome, Baden-Baden, and Vienna. Good luck now came his way. Ritz was the restaurant manager at Rigi-Kulm, an Alpine hotel renowned for its location and cuisine, when he was informed one cold winter day that the heating plant had broken down and, at almost the same moment, that a group of 40 wealthy Americans were to arrive soon for lunch. Ritz ordered lunch to be served in the drawing room instead of the dining room—it looked warmer because of the large red curtains that framed the room. He directed the waiters to pour alcohol into large copper pots and then set them afire, and bricks were placed in the ovens. The room was warm when the Americans arrived, and each of them was given a brick wrapped in flannel to warm their feet. By the end of the meal, which started with a peppery hot consomme and ended with flaming crepes suzette, the guests were gushing with praise for the young manager.

Reports of Ritz's modest miracle of quick thinking and resourcefulness spread among hotelmen throughout Europe and

Company Perspectives:

Since the early years of the 20th century, the name Ritz-Carlton has been synonymous with the luxury hotel, conjuring images of opulent yet elegant furnishings based on designs from Versailles and Fontainebleau, haute cuisine in the best French tradition, and meticulous attention to the needs and comforts of its clientele. The Ritz-Carlton Hotel Company is known in the hotel industry for its unwavering commitment to the tradition of impeccable service and luxurious ambiance introduced by the man who made the Ritz name famous, Cesar Ritz.

the United States. When the owner of a large hotel in Lucerne heard the story, he immediately hired Ritz to act as his general manager. The hotel had been losing money steadily for some time, but the 27-year-old former peasant revived the hotel in two years. Here he developed and refined the hotel service and methods that made his name famous. "People like to be served, but invisibly," Ritz once said. It was Ritz who originated the phrase, "The customer is always right." Ritz remembered who preferred Turkish cigarettes, who loved gardenias in their room, and who ate chutney during breakfast. If a diner did not like the way his meat was prepared, it was immediately whisked away without any questions asked. For Ritz, no detail was too small and no request too big if it meant satisfying a customer.

In 1892 Ritz journeyed to London to manage the Hotel Savoy, an elegant hotel in the midst of a financial crisis. Ritz brought along his lifelong associate, Auguste Escoffier, a chef whom he had met during one of his jobs in Europe. With Ritz devoting his attention to a myriad of details, sometimes roving from room to room remaking beds to assure his guests the most comfortable night's sleep in London, at other times arranging lavish entertainment for important customers, and with Escoffier whipping up gourmet dishes in the kitchen, the Savoy soon became the toast of London's high society. When Alfred Beit, a diamond mogul from South Africa, asked Ritz to arrange a party for him, Ritz flooded the Savoy's main dining room and transformed it into a miniature Venice, with dinner served to guests as they lounged in gondolas serenaded by native gondoliers. At another party, with Cecil Rhodes, James Gordon Bennett, Lord Randolph Churchill, and Gilbert and Sullivan attending, Ritz arranged for Caruso to sing for their evening pleasure. After three years, the Savoy's stock rebounded from a few shillings to 20 pounds a share.

When a quarrel broke out one day between Ritz and the directors of the Savoy, Ritz left the hotel never to return again. Ritz's friends reacted immediately with more than 200 telegrams sent to show him their support. The Prince of Wales, a close friend who was later to become King Edward VII, wired the statement, "Where Ritz goes, we follow." With such support from wealthy and influential friends, Ritz decided to pursue a dream he had had for years—to open a hotel of his own that would be the epitome of elegance.

The Ritz Hotel, built in Paris on the Place Vendome, opened for business in 1898. The lobby was small to discourage idlers,

and only 225 rooms were constructed for its guests, but furnishings were exquisite and service meticulous to the last detail. Ritz designed a garden to encourage conversation over coffee and tea; he painted the hotel's walls instead of papering them because it was easier to keep clean; he borrowed the overall color scheme for the hotel from a painting by Van Dyck; and, highly innovative for the time, Ritz equipped many of the rooms with private baths. Ritz also established the traditional apparel for hotel personnel: a black tie for the maitre d'hotel, a white tie for the waiter, and brass buttons for the bellhop's uniform. On opening day people came from miles around Paris to walk through the hotel's corridors. And anybody who was anyone during the early years of the 20th century—from J. P. Morgan to Lily Langtry—either lunched or dined at some time in the Hotel Ritz.

Ritz prepared an elaborate reception and elegant dinner in 1902 in honor of the coronation of his good friend Edward VII. All the arrangements had been finalized when a telegram informed Ritz that Edward was grievously ill and required an operation. With a heavy heart the great hotelier attended to the details of cancellation and then, exhausted from his exertions, collapsed. He revived and redoubled his efforts to please patrons of the hotel, but suffered a physical and mental breakdown in 1911. Never fully regaining his renowned verve and energy for work, for seven years Ritz was a figurehead at his own hotel. In October 1918, as he lay dying, Ritz thought he saw his wife at the bedside and asked her to take care of their daughter. Ritz and his wife had no daughter—the "daughter" was the way both of them referred to Ritz's dream hotel in Paris.

Ritz-Carlton Chain in the Early 20th Century

Near the turn of the century, Ritz had arranged to build and operate the Carlton Hotel in London and, shortly thereafter, opened the Ritz Hotel in Piccadilly. At this time, he also organized a group of hoteliers and financiers and created the tricontinental Ritz-Carlton Management Corporation. The purpose of the group was to lease the Ritz-Carlton name, crest, and stationery to interested parties willing to establish a hotel of their own and abide by the service and culinary standards set by Ritz himself. Under the terms of this agreement, one of the most famous of all the Ritz-Carlton Hotels opened in New York in 1910.

The New York Ritz-Carlton was built for $5 million, and its equipment and furnishings cost $750,000 more. Robert Goelet, a businessman, paid $5,000 for use of the Ritz-Carlton name and nurtured the hotel like one of his children. Soft rugs, gilded mirrors, glittering chandeliers, oversized bathtubs, and vials of perfume under the seats of the elevators welcomed and rewarded its rich guests. The hotel immediately became renowned for its superb cuisine—Chef M. Diat created Vichyssoise in its kitchen in 1912. On every floor two waiters were stationed day and night to attend the needs of customers who preferred to eat in their rooms. The hotel was a mecca for the world's richest and most famous people and, for New York society, was host to a seemingly endless stream of balls, cotillions, and receptions. For one coming-out party, its ballroom was decorated with $10,000 worth of eucalyptus trees; at another, live monkeys helped transform the ballroom into a tropical jungle. Joffre, Foch, Clemenceau, Leopold I of Belgium, the Duke of

Windsor, Mrs. George W. Vanderbilt, and Charlie Chaplin were all served at the Ritz-Carlton. The New York Ritz-Carlton remained faithful to Cesar Ritz's imperatives—pamper your guests with lavish surroundings and meticulous service.

During the 1920s, the Ritz-Carlton Management Company leased the use of its name to a number of financiers that wanted to build hotels and also were willing to abide by the standards set down by Cesar Ritz. During this decade the Philadelphia Ritz-Carlton, Montreal Ritz-Carlton, Atlantic City Ritz-Carlton, and Boston Ritz-Carlton opened for business. All of these hotels, in their individual manner, carried on the tradition of fashionable sophistication so important to the Ritz name. Yet those who had known Cesar Ritz would say that none of the hotels ever captured the rococo elegance of the Paris Ritz on the Place Vendome.

After Cesar Ritz and one of his sons died in 1918, it was assumed that the remaining son, Charles, would take the place of his father and continue managing the Paris and London hotels under the Ritz-Carlton name. But Charles was more inclined to travel, and even before the death of his father he journeyed to the United States and worked in a New London, Connecticut hotel. His jobs over the next several years ranged from working as a night manager at the New York Ritz-Carlton to selling Swiss music boxes to department stores. The rather leisurely pace of Charles Ritz's business activities provided him the time to pursue what interested him most—fly fishing. In 1928 his mother made a pilgrimage across the Atlantic to persuade him to return to Paris and work at his father's hotel. He yielded to his mother's urging, but once in Paris he found that all the top management spots at the hotel were filled, so he worked in the local office of a New York stockbroker. Rather than being disappointed with not working for the hotel, Charles was able to continue developing his expertise in fly fishing. In fact, he had already launched a secondary career as a designer of fishing rods.

After the crash of the New York Stock Market in 1929, the hotels that bore the Ritz-Carlton name in Europe and America suffered from the onset of a worldwide depression. Although the hotels were able to weather the financial hardship, many of them began to lose the elegant luster they so earnestly and carefully cultivated before the depression. Many millionaires who frequented Ritz-Carlton dining rooms in search of new gustatory delights were no longer millionaires; indeed, the New York Ritz-Carlton even changed its luncheon and dinner menus from French into English hoping that it would result in more customers. The owner and manager of the Boston Ritz-Carlton, realizing he was almost at the point of insolvency, went from room to room turning on the lights in its empty rooms to impress his wealthy father before the old man arrived to discuss terms of a loan for the hotel.

The difficulties luxury hotels experienced during the depression were compounded by World War II. When leisure travel between Europe and America was common in the 1920s and 1930s, many wealthy individuals stayed and dined at Ritz-Carlton hotels. This traffic ceased altogether when the war started in Europe in 1939 and, not surprisingly, Ritz-Carlton hotels suffered as a result. When World War II was at its height, many Ritz-Carlton dining areas and ballrooms on both sides of the Atlantic were used as meeting rooms for military personnel.

Hotels for Businessmen After World War II

Many of the Ritz-Carlton hotels did not survive the combined effects of the depression and World War II. Even though the Paris Ritz celebrated it 50th birthday in 1948 amid diplomats and millionaires drinking champagne, the Philadelphia Ritz-Carlton and Montreal Ritz-Carlton had closed their doors. In 1950, when the New York Ritz-Carlton announced that it would close to make way for a 25-story office building, its former guests protested. The only Ritz-Carlton hotel left in North America was the Boston Ritz-Carlton, and its survival was questionable.

The London Ritz-Carlton and the Paris Ritz prospered during the 1950s and 1960s by gradually adapting to a new breed of guest—the international businessman. When Charles Ritz became chairman of the board of the Ritz-Carlton Management Company in 1953, most of the old wealth and aristocracy were gone. By 1968, 70 percent of the guests staying at the Paris Ritz were American businessmen on expense accounts. With his success in Paris, Ritz was asked to serve as a consultant to the firm of Cabot, Cabot, and Forbes, purchasers of the Boston Ritz-Carlton in 1964. He also served as consultant to the Ritz-Carlton in London.

The Ritz-Carlton Management Company leased its name to financiers in both Lisbon and Madrid, stipulating that the hotels meet acceptable standards. Although Charles Ritz owned only one percent of the stock in the company, with the remainder held by British and Continental investors, he was the guardian of the hotel's standards; during the late 1960s, the company sued the Ritz in Rome over use of the name because the hotel did not measure up to those standards.

The hotels operating under the Ritz name in Europe prospered throughout the 1970s, primarily due to the ever increasing presence of international business travelers with corporate expense accounts and a surge in travel by the nouveau riche. Indeed, the company's continued commitment to and cultivation of attentive service to a new generation of guests had the effect of raising revenues for almost all the European operations. The week before Charles Ritz died in July 1976, he was still issuing orders to improve the luxury and elegance that symbolized the Paris hotel.

Revitalized Under Johnson in the 1980s

In 1983 William B. Johnson, a real estate mogul and developer from Atlanta, purchased the rights to the name and the aging Ritz-Carlton in Boston for approximately $70 million. Having already constructed more than 100 Waffle House restaurants and numerous Holiday Inns, Johnson turned his attention to the Boston Ritz-Carlton and spent $22 million to restore the hotel to its original condition. He then established a headquarters for his company in Atlanta, the Ritz-Carlton Hotel Company, and began to arrange financing for new hotels around the country, mostly through partnerships between Johnson and other parties.

Bumps in the 1990s

By 1990, Johnson's Ritz-Carlton Hotel Company operated and managed 28 Ritz-Carlton hotels. Johnson directly owned the hotels in Boston, Buckhead, Georgia, and Naples, Florida;

financing for the remainder of the hotels was through partnerships, including those in Australia, Hawaii, and Cancun. The only Ritz-Carlton Hotel that Johnson did not operate was in Chicago. Built by Four Seasons before Johnson purchased rights to the name, the Chicago Ritz-Carlton also was managed by the rival hotel.

The company won the Malcolm Baldridge National Quality Award in 1992. Chosen by the U.S. Department of Commerce, the Ritz-Carlton Hotel Company was the first hotel company awarded the highly prestigious prize. With 24-hour room service, twice-a-day maid service, complete gymnasium facilities, and menus that continued the tradition of culinary excellence first established by Cesar Ritz, Johnson's company was well prepared for competing with Four Seasons and other hotel groups in the luxury hotel market.

But although the chain was doing extremely well on quality and service, finances were a different matter. The company had expanded aggressively, opening or acquiring eight hotels in 1990 alone, with six the next year and many more planned. By 1992 the company had full or part ownership in 13 of the chain's hotels, and the others were owned by private investors. These investors included financier Willard G. Rouse III, Ford Motor Company's real estate division, Prudential Realty Group, and John F. McDonnell, of McDonnell Douglas. Presumably those who had put money into new Ritz-Carltons were not as happy as some of the pampered guests. The hotel industry as a whole was still suffering from the effects of late 1980s recession, and many hotels were stuck with empty rooms. The Ritz-Carlton was no exception. The Buckhead Ritz-Carlton in Atlanta, which Johnson himself owned, was said to require an occupancy rate of virtually 100 percent every night of the year to make enough money to cover its debt. The splashy Mauna-Lani Ritz-Carlton in Hawaii was also in debt, having run approximately $13 million over its estimated construction costs, and its occupancy rate for 1991 was only 44 percent. Teachers Insurancy and Annuity Association, a backer of several Ritz-Carltons, sued in 1992 to recover payment on $80 million it had lent the owners of the Tyson Corners (Virginia) Ritz-Carlton and had trouble collecting on its loan to a Kansas City Ritz-Carlton as well. Sources quoted in a July 6, 1992 *Business Week* article claimed the Ritz-Carlton Hotel Company was more than $1 billion in debt. The company president, Horst Schulze, admitted only that the company was in default on a loan for $70 million and that it was seeking to restructure other debts. The company insisted that the hotels would get over any stumbling blocks caused by the economic downturn and that its money problems were only short-term.

But bad news continued to dog the luxury chain. When its Aspen, Colorado hotel opened in October, 1992, it was shadowed by lawsuits from investors and dire reports that the 257-room hotel would have to achieve at least 60 percent occupancy just to break even, in a town where 50 percent occupancy was the average. The Hong Kong Ritz-Carlton was completed in August, 1992 but stood empty for months, in receivership, with no prospective buyer. By 1994, a *Wall Street Journal* report (April 22, 1994) quoted sources who claimed that out of the 30 Ritz-Carltons open at the time, all but six or seven were losing money. This was contested by Ritz-Carlton's President Schulze. He allowed that 30 percent of the chain's hotels were unprofitable.

Many Ritz-Carltons were in cities that could not really support such a luxury hotel. For example, in Kansas City, the average room rate was $67. The Kansas City Ritz-Carlton charged on average $115, and according to a local hotel consultant, this was still $70 less than the hotel needed to make a profit. The company's distinctive quest for service often led to exorbitant costs, spending lavishly on harpists, flowers, even champagne-stocked limousines for guests turned away on an overbooked night. The Ritz-Carlton Hotel Company continued to take on average five percent of its hotel's gross revenues, whether the hotel made money or not, and some investors seemed to think the management company did not really care whether the hotels were profitable, as long as the brand image was maintained.

In 1995 the sprawling hotel chain Marriott International bought a 49 percent stake in Ritz-Carlton. The larger company believed it could increase sales and profit margins at the Ritz and that things would eventually look up for the troubled chain. The cost of Marriott's initial investment was estimated to be more than $150 million. The next year, Marriott spent $331 million to take over the Ritz-Carlton Atlanta and buy a majority interest in two of the other Ritz-Carltons owned outright by William Johnson. In 1998 Ritz-Carlton announced plans to move its headquarters out of Atlanta and into the Washington, D.C. area. This would put it close to Marriott's headquarters in Bethesda, Maryland. In the late 1990s, the Ritz-Carlton chain was still moving ahead with expansion plans, constructing hotels in the Phillippines, Mexico, Jamaica, and Egypt, and domestically in Miami, Florida, Houston, Texas, Las Vegas, and New Orleans. Despite the tarnishing reports of economic difficulties, the poshness of the Ritz-Carlton name was still maintained, and the chain took many honors, winning 39 separate five- and four-star awards from Mobil Travel and AAA in 1998 for service, quality, and facilities.

Further Reading

Beirne, Mike, "Collins Checks into New Ritz Digs," *Brandweek,* January 4, 1999, p. 33.

Carey, Susan, "This No-Frills (at Present) Hotel Won't Leave a Light on for You," *Wall Street Journal,* February 24, 1993, p. B1.

Cleary, Mike, "Ritz-Carlton May Move Atlanta Headquarters to D.C., Not Virginia," *Knight-Ridder/Tribune Business News,* August 5, 1998, p. OKRB982170F4.

Durbin, Fran, "Ritz-Carlton Commissions Study To Examine Meetings Market," *Travel Weekly,* April 18, 1994, p. 56.

Gutner, Toddi, "Puttin' on the Ritz," *Forbes 400,* October 19, 1992, p. 22.

Hirsch, James S., "Of Luxury and Losses: Many Ritz Hotels Are in the Red," *Wall Street Journal,* April 22, 1994, p. B1, B4.

Kent, George, "The Word for Elegance," *Readers Digest,* 1948, pp. 147–50.

McDowell, Edwin, "Ritz-Carlton's Keys to Good Service," *New York Times,* March 31, 1993, p. D1, D5.

Shaw, Russell, "Ritz Buyer Touts Deal's Benefits," *Hotel & Motel Management,* April 3, 1995, p. 1.

Touby, Laurel, "Too Many Rooms at the Inn for Ritz-Carlton," *Business Week,* July 6, 1992, pp. 74–76.

"Why the Ritz Caters to a Business Elite," *Business Week,* August 17, 1968, pp. 56–62.

—Thomas Derdak
—updated by A. Woodward

Rolls-Royce Allison

2355 S. Tibbs
P.O. Box 420
Indianapolis, Indiana 46241
U.S.A.
(317) 230-2000
Fax: (317) 230-4020
Web site: http://www.rolls-royce.com

Wholly Owned Subsidiary of Rolls-Royce plc
Incorporated: 1915 as Allison Speedway Team Company
Employees: 5,100
Sales: $1.2 billion (1998)
NAIC: 33361 Engine, Turbine & Power Transmission
    Equipment Manufacturing

Rolls-Royce Allison, owned by the London-headquartered Rolls-Royce plc, designs, manufactures, and services gas turbine engines for both military and commercial aerospace applications. Rolls-Royce Allison serves as the lead organization for three of Rolls-Royce's 13 business units: Corporate and Regional Airlines; Helicopters; and Defense North America. The company has four facilities in Indianapolis, comprising more than 3.5 million square feet, and one facility in Evansville, Indiana. A subsidiary of Rolls-Royce Allison, the Allison Advanced Development Company, is co-located with Allison's Indianapolis facilities and focuses on research and development of defense-related products for the U.S. government.

The Early Days: Race Cars and Army Business

Rolls-Royce Allison has its roots in one of Indiana's most beloved institutions: auto racing. The company's founder, James A. Allison, was one of the three original developers of the Indianapolis Motor Speedway, home of the famed Indy 500. Allison and his cohorts set out to build the world's finest racetrack—one that would be used for testing by automobile manufacturers, thus turning Indianapolis into a major auto manufacturing hub. When the track was completed in 1909 and the auto racing began, Allison developed his own race team, featuring a young driver named Eddie Rickenbacker.

It is perhaps not surprising, given his evident love of all things car-related, that Allison's next venture would be an auto machine shop. This shop, the forerunner to Rolls-Royce Allison, opened in 1915 to redesign and refit domestic and foreign cars for racing. Named the Allison Speedway Team Co., it employed 20 of the most skilled mechanics and engineers that Allison could locate. It was not long before the shop's pioneering inventiveness in piston engine design and manufacturing garnered a reputation.

When the United States entered World War I in 1917 its reputation for innovation landed the company, by then called Allison Engineering Company, a subcontract to do engineering work for the military. As the United States prepared to enter the battle, the Army had encountered difficulties with its newly designed "Liberty" aircraft engine, an engine that incorporated design elements from several automotive engines. Tapping Allison's prowess with high-performance automotive engines, the Army commissioned the company to revamp the prototype Liberty engines. Allison came through, improving the engine design with new crankshaft bearings, better propeller reduction gearing, and a new type of supercharger.

Late 1920s Through the Early 1950s: New Owners and Wartime Contracts

James Allison died in 1928, and his company was purchased by his former racecar driver, Eddie Rickenbacker. Rickenbacker had left racing in 1917 to join the Army and had distinguished himself as a fighter pilot during World War I, earning the prestigious title "Ace of Aces." Upon his return from the war, he had established a short-lived car manufacturing company, the Rickenbacker Motor Company, which closed after only six years of operation. In 1927, the year before he acquired Allison, Rickenbacker had made a substantially higher-profile acquisition: he had purchased the Indianapolis Motor Speedway. Although he would remain in control of the Speedway until after World War II, his tenure as Allison Engineering's leader was brief; in 1929 he sold the company to Fisher Brothers Investment Trust of Detroit.

Fisher Brothers did not hang on to the engine maker long, either. In just a few months, the Detroit firm turned the company over to the automotive giant, General Motors Corp. Under

---

Company Perspectives:

Our mission is to unleash the collective talents, dedication and integrity of Allison's employees and partners to relentlessly outperform customer expectations with world-class, cost-effective products and services delivering optimum stakeholder value.

General Motors' ownership, Allison Engineering became the Allison Division.

In the years between GM's purchase of Allison and America's entry into World War II, the Allison Division grew steadily. By 1941, the company had three Indianapolis plants, which employed more than 12,000 workers. When the United States joined the war, the size and the nature of Allison's business made it a prime candidate to help meet burgeoning defense needs. The Allison Division contributed to the war effort by designing and manufacturing the V-1710 aircraft engine—a 12-cylinder, 1200 shp liquid-cooled, V-1710 engine that powered such famous wartime fighters as the Flying Tigers P-40, the Lockheed P-38, and the P-51 Mustang.

Postwar, Allison continued to break new ground in engine design. During the late 1940s and early 1950s, the company designed and produced some of the earliest "turbojet" engines—engines in which air from the atmosphere was compressed for combustion by a turbine-driven compressor. One of the turbojets Allison produced during this period was the T56. This 2500 shp turboprop was later to become a 5000 shp engine that would remain in production for 40 years.

1960s–80s: Division Switching

Between 1963 and 1983, the Allison Division felt the impact of a series of corporate reshufflings. In 1963 the company became a part of General Motors' Power Products and Defense Operations Group. In 1970 Allison again was repositioned, merging with Detroit Diesel to form the Detroit Diesel Allison Division. This newly formed division developed and manufactured turbine and diesel engines, generators, and transmissions. The division's aerospace segment made various types of engines for a number of applications—including small turboshaft engines for helicopters and other aircraft, large turboprop engines for military and civilian transports, jet engines for military attack planes, industrial turbine engines for power generation and oil pipeline uses, and turbines for the marine industry.

In 1983 General Motors separated Allison from Detroit Diesel, making it an independent division—the Allison Gas Turbine Division. Throughout the remainder of the decade and into the 1990s, the division made deeper inroads into the military engine market. One of the most significant of these inroads came in when the U.S. Navy chose Allison's 6000 shp class turboshaft T406 engine to power its innovative V-22 Osprey. The V-22 was a tiltrotor aircraft—a unique, flexible hybrid of helicopter and jet. The craft could take off and land like a helicopter, then convert in the air to a high-speed turboprop airplane, capable of high altitude flight. Each V-22, which

received final Defense Department approval for production in April of 1997, carried two Allison T406 engines.

A second important military contract teamed Allison with a division of AlliedSignal Aerospace Company to design and produce an engine for the Army's RAH-66 Comanche reconnaissance and attack helicopter. The Comanche, which was still in the design and test stages, was scheduled to go into full-rate production in 2006. Allison and AlliedSignal designed the T800 turboshaft engine for the new aircraft. In addition to designing military engines, Allison was working on two new engines for civilian aircraft as well: the AE 2100 turboprop and the AE 3007 turbofan, based on the military version of the T406.

1993–95: Flying Solo

In the early 1990s General Motors decided to focus its attentions more completely on the automobile business and, therefore, to shed its non-auto divisions, including Allison. The company, which employed approximately 4,700 employees and had sales of $700 million, went up for bid in April of 1992. Through the spring and summer of 1992, GM received—and rejected—three offers for Allison, including one from General Electric Co. Subsequently, however, a bid for $310 million was accepted from a New York investment firm. The firm, Clayton Dubilier & Rice, specialized in buying detached divisions of large industrial companies and positioning them to stand alone. Under the terms of the buyout, Clayton Dubilier & Rice would hold between 80 and 90 percent of the company's ownership. Allison's senior management would have ten percent; the remainder of shares was to be offered later to other key employees.

The deal was finalized in December of 1993, ending Allison's 64-year affiliation with General Motors. Although the company had a new name—Allison Engine Company—the faces on its management team were familiar. The CEO, F. Blake Wallace, had been with the company for 11 years, serving as the general manager at the Allison division and as a GM vice-president. Three other long-term Allison managers—Wilson Burns, Frank Verkamp, and Mike Hudson—were made executive vice-presidents. Wallace was pleased with the outcome of the sale negotiations and the fact that the company was to retain much of its essence. "It is very satisfying after two years of difficult transition, to come out where the company is whole, has been kept from being dismembered or sold to a competitor who would take our work elsewhere," he was quoted as saying in a March 1994 *Indiana Business Magazine* article. "We pretty well kept the team together, kept the strategy together. I like that extremely well."

The transition was not without its casualties, however. Immediately after completing the purchase from General Motors, Allison terminated employment for almost 500 of its hourly workers, many of whom worked on a component line that had supplied other GM divisions.

1995–97: Joining Forces with Rolls-Royce

Allison Engine Company's tenure as an independent business was brief. In 1995, after holding it for little more than a year, Clayton Dubilier & Rice sold the company to Britain's Rolls-Royce plc for $525 million. Rolls-Royce—which, despite the shared name, was not affiliated with the luxury carmaker—was the third largest producer of aircraft engines in the world. It also manufactured power generation systems and marine propulsion and oil and gas engines in its smaller Industrial Power division.

Having already done business under at least six different monikers, Allison once again was renamed and was absorbed into Rolls-Royce's Aerospace division. At the time of the Allison purchase, the two companies established the Allison Advanced Development Company (AADC) as a wholly owned subsidiary of Rolls-Royce Allison. The AADC was formed to perform defense-related research, design, and development work for U.S. government agencies. It was structured specifically to adhere to Department of Defense security requirements and occupied secure facilities that were separate from its parent company's operations.

The following year, Rolls-Royce put plans for its newly purchased subsidiary into action when it awarded Allison new production work. In September of 1996, Rolls-Royce Allison announced that it would begin producing Adour F405 engines, which were used in the U.S. Navy's T-45 Goshawk training planes. Rolls Royce's Bristol, England plant, which was producing all of its Adour engines at the time, would continue to produce the engines for British military applications. Allison also announced that it had been assigned the production of turbine blades, gears, and other parts for Rolls-Royce's RB211 engine—work that previously had been slated for outsourcing. According to a September 27, 1996 article in the *Indianapolis Star/News,* Allison management felt that being awarded the new work represented a "vote of confidence" by Rolls-Royce.

Production of the RB211 components was scheduled to begin in 1997, with work on the Adour engines to start the following year. Rolls-Royce Allison, which had a work force of approximately 4,300, anticipated that the new production work would result in the addition of between 700 and 850 new jobs over the course of four years.

Rolls-Royce Allison received another shot in the arm in 1997, when it received two major contracts from Lockheed Martin and AMR Eagle, a commuter service affiliate of American Airlines. The order from Lockheed Martin, valued at $500 million, was for Allison's AE 2100D2 turboprop engine, which would be used to power Lockheed's new C-27J Spartan aircraft. The AMR Eagle order, valued at more than $275 million, was for Allison AE 3007A1 engines to be used in 42 EMB-145 Embraer regional jets.

1998: Top-Down Changes

The year 1998 ushered in structural changes for Rolls-Royce—which ultimately meant shakeups in Rolls-Royce Allison as well. Rolls-Royce reorganized its entire business into 13 market-based units, with each unit having an increased autonomy to oversee everything from development to marketing. Rolls-Royce Allison became the home of three of these new units: Corporate and Regional Airlines, Helicopters, and Defense North America. The Helicopters division was charged with responsibility for all Rolls-Royce helicopter products, both civilian and military. Defense North America would work with all North American military and military-related customers, including the U.S. and Canadian military agencies. The Corporate and Regional Airlines unit would supply engines to be used in commuter airlines and company-owned aircraft.

Under the new arrangement, Allison's president and CEO, S. Michael Hudson, had the responsibility of running the Helicopter and Defense North America units, and John Ferrie, the company's executive vice-president of business operations, assumed control of the Corporate and Regional Airlines unit. Other changes were afoot as well. Since purchasing Allison in 1995, Rolls had been concerned with the subsidiary's level of efficiency—and management's efforts to improve productivity had failed to completely eradicate the problem. The parent company's new plan addressed the efficiency issue by calling for major changes in the way Rolls-Royce Allison operated. The parent company's goals included consolidating factory operations into a much smaller physical area, freeing up approximately half of the manufacturing facility's square footage. The vacated space would then be used to house operations that were performed offsite in rented facilities. Another major change struck at the very core of Allison's manufacturing methods. Rolls planned to implement a "cell" system of manufacturing, in which teams of employees performed multiple tasks.

Rolls-Royce Allison's reaction to the planned upheavals was generally positive. According to a July 2, 1998 article in the *Indianapolis Star/News,* employees felt that the restructuring proved Rolls was committed to retaining Allison. "Employees always wondered were we going to be integrated or set up for another sale," Lee Rhyant, Allison's vice-president of production operations, was quoted as saying. He called the restructuring a "comfort zone."

Looking Ahead

At the beginning of 1999, Rolls-Royce Allison had 5,100 employees and sales of $1.2 billion—with sales of $1.3 billion projected for the coming year. Company management anticipated that if the previous year's Rolls-mandated changes went well and operational efficiency was improved, there was potential for growth. One of the most significant growth possibilities in the company's near future was the building of a worldwide training center in Indianapolis. The training center would be used by Rolls-Royce employees, customers, and vendors who produced, operated, and serviced Rolls' aircraft engines. Talks between Rolls-Royce and its Allison subsidiary were still in the preliminary stages.

Principal Subsidiaries

Allison Advanced Development Company.

Further Reading

Johnson, J. Douglas, "Allison Takes Off," *Indiana Business Magazine,* March, 1994, pp. 8–13.

Koenig, Bill, "Allison Engine To Add Up to 850 Jobs," *Indianapolis Star/News,* September 27, 1996.

——, "Allison Gas Turbine Deal Unveiled," *Indianapolis Star,* September 16, 1993.

——, "It's an Engine for Growth," *Indianapolis Star/News,* July 2, 1998.

O'Malley, Chris, "Allison Engine Begins Life Anew," *Indianapolis News,* December 2, 1993.

—updated by Shawna Brynildssen

Sabratek Corporation

8111 North St. Louis Avenue
Skokie, Illinois 60076
U.S.A.
(847) 720-2400
Web site: http://www.sabratek.com

Public Company
Incorporated: 1989
Employees: 382
Sales: $67 million (1998)
Stock Exchanges: NASDAQ
Ticker Symbol: SBTK
NAIC: 334510 Electromedical & Electrotherapeutic
   Apparatus Manufacturing

Sabratek Corporation designs and manufactures therapeutic and diagnostic medical systems and products for the alternative site health care market. The company believes that all of its current and future products will facilitate the creation of a "virtual" hospital room, where a wide range of care that was provided previously within the acute care and intensive ward setting will soon be provided by alternative site providers. With this purpose as its overall strategy, the company makes such items as multitherapy infusion devices, prefilled flush syringe products, portable diagnostic devices, ambulatory patient monitors, and it also provides remote programming software and other capabilities that allow for care givers to deliver high-quality, cost-effective health care services in alternative sites. One of Sabratek's most important products in the creation of a virtual hospital room is MediVIEW, a remote programming, monitoring, and data gathering software system that enables health care providers to monitor a patient's clinical status from remote locations over regular telephone lines. Since 1996, the company has focused on forming strategic partnerships and alliances that enhance its own position in the highly competitive stationary and ambulatory pump products market. Although Abbot Laboratories and Baxter International, Inc. are just two of the larger firms with which Sabratek competes, company management is confident that its products point in the direction where health care services are going in the future.

Early History

One of the founders and the driving force behind Sabratek is K. Shan Padda, one of the more accomplished men of his generation, and one of the most unusual. Padda was born into an East Asian family that immigrated to the United States. Padda's father and mother had always been interested in providing a good education for their children, and Padda received the best that his parents could afford. But the one thing that made Padda stand out from his fellow students and other people his own age was his ambition and business savvy, which is an unusual combination in such a young person. By the time Padda was 25 years of age, he already had launched two highly successful business ventures, arranging for their financing and managing them for the short term.

As with most young men, however, Padda was bored with a lack of challenge. The two businesses that he had started were apparently so easy for him that he quickly sold both of them as soon as they were financially stable and viable firms. Then, seemingly out of character, he traveled around the Pacific Rim for an entire year, visiting China, Malaysia, Thailand, and other Southeast Asian countries. Many people who knew him professionally speculated as to the reason why he had embarked on such a long and faraway holiday. Some financial analysts surmised that he was storing up his energy to begin another start-up venture when he returned to the United States. Others thought Padda was searching for business opportunities in the areas where he was traveling. But the truth, as it turned out, was much more simple and straightforward. Upon his return, the young man reiterated why he sold his first two companies and gave boredom as the reason for his lengthy vacation. Padda had grown bored with what he had been doing up to that time and, consequently, he decided to take a break.

When he set foot back in the United States, he immediately reevaluated what he had been doing previously and what he would do different the next time around. Padda was certain that he was not interested in starting a software company or a medical device company, for example. Not knowing what to do, he felt anxious about his future. Yet the young man was supremely confident in his ability to listen to people and what they needed and to be creative and flexible enough to provide efficient solutions that would meet those needs. Most important,

Company Perspectives:

Our corporate logo, the desert cactus, is the perfect representation of Sabratek's vision and what it means for our customers, our employees and our stockholders. The cactus thrives by successfully adapting in a difficult and changing environment and by making the most of its resources. And, in doing so, it produces a beautiful and useful result. A similar result for health care has been the focus of Sabratek's efforts since we began manufacturing technologically advanced medical devices. . . . Our goal is a model of seamless, innovative efficiency that expands health care access while maintaining and even improving the quality of care. This model provides health care systems with the necessary resources and efficiencies to adapt and thrive in today's challenging health care environment.

when he started a new business this time, Padda wanted whatever it was to help people.

As sometimes happens in life, Padda met Doron Levitas, another entrepreneur searching for an idea to which he could commit. Levitas and Padda entered into discussions about the state of health care in the United States, and how much it cost, and soon decided to provide a viable solution to the problem of long-term health care. The two men had listened to people within the health care industry and learned that approximately 70 percent of all medical costs are due to labor. The problem with which they were faced came down to the following question: How is it possible to maintain quality health care service while reducing the amount of labor involved in providing that service at the same time?

To find an answer, Padda and Levitas devoted the entire first year of their partnership to interviewing a host of CEOs, nurses, doctors, hospital administrators, people at HMOs, insurance companies, and numerous other health care providers. They asked the interviewees to explain to them exactly what they needed, regardless of the cost. The answers surprised the two men. They were told that the services already provided within a hospital setting were ideal, but that costs for such services were skyrocketing out of control, consequently, many hospitals were forced to reduce the amount of health care services provided to their patients. If alternative site health care could be provided to patients, which essentially recreated all of the services and functions of a hospital, yet was able to maintain a high level of medical personnel contact with patients, monitor patient compliance with prescribed therapies, and determine future variations in treatment and therapies to combat the patient's disease, then costs could be reduced without affecting the quality of health care provided.

Growth and Expansion in the 1990s

Padda and his partner took these suggestions to heart and began to create a company that addressed the rising costs of health care in the United States by promoting the concept of the "virtual hospital room." Incorporating Sabratek Corporation in 1989, the two ambitious entrepreneurs found themselves with

one of the most formidable challenges any businessman has ever faced, namely, devising a strategy to change the way health care is delivered in the United States. Managed care companies, employers, government agencies, indemnity insurers, and the medical profession itself were all employing a number of different strategies to contain health care expenditures. Yet their overriding concern was to maintain the high quality of health care services provided to patients, which led to a general reluctance or suspicion about the alternative site health care industry.

Sabratek Corporation appeared on the scene at precisely the moment when the alternative site health care industry was just beginning to grow. The delivery of respiratory therapy, pharmaceutical therapies, intravenous infusion, physical therapy, and skilled nursing services in outpatient centers, in long-term care facilities, and in the home had grown substantially during the entire decade of the 1980s. Between 1980 and 1990, the expenditure for alternative site health care services had grown from $11 billion to $24 billion, indicating that alternative site settings were more and more accepted as critical components in cost-effective medical care strategies. One of the most important ingredients of this movement was the development of highly sophisticated medical technology that facilitated the provision of quality health care services outside the hospital setting. With such technology, the medical profession discovered that diseases that ordinarily necessitated traditional acute care hospital settings, such as neurological conditions, infectious diseases, AIDS-related symptoms, digestive disorders, and various forms of cancer, were able to be treated in alternative site settings, most notably the patient's own home.

Padda and Levitas recognized that infusion therapy was one of the most important components of providing alternative site health care services and, therefore, began to develop and manufacture sophisticated infusion pumps as the core of Sabratek's business. Infusion therapy involves a patient being administered and receiving fluid intravenously at a regulated volume and rate. Employed in a wide range of applications, including pain management, the delivery of antibiotics, chemotherapy, and nutrition therapy just to name a few, infusion therapy soon became one of the fastest growing components of the alternative site health care industry. Since all of these therapies require highly specialized infusion pumps to provide patients with extremely precise dosages of the fluid needed, Sabratek Corporation developed its own stationary multitherapy infusion pump for use in a wide variety of infusion therapies. The pump incorporated preprogramming capabilities, multiple language capabilities, remote communications capacities, and a relatively easy-to-learn format. Using this infusion pump as its flagship product, Sabratek Corporation was able to sell millions worth within the first year of its introduction.

Additional products were developed and manufactured by Sabratek Corporation at a rapid pace, including: MediVIEW, a remote programming, monitoring, and reporting software system that operates over regular telephone lines; PumpMaster, a portable device designed to provide diagnostic tests on the company's own infusion pumps; Stat-Site System, a portable, hand-held system that provides immediate diagnostic blood testing; Ambulatory Patient Monitor 2000, a monitor that measures a patient's temperature, pulse rate, heart rate, respiratory rate, and other vital signs; and Virtual Hospital Room Communicator, a miniature computer with eight communications ports that a care giver uses to plug in a host of different mechanical devices to monitor a patient's health.

At the same time, the company was forming strategic partnerships and collaborations that enhanced its market position. In November of 1998 Sabratek entered into a software licensing and marketing agreement with Healthmagic, Inc., a firm that develops information management tools by employing intranet technology so that medical personnel can access essential information regarding a patient regardless of the location. Other partnerships included an agreement with Unitron Medical Communications, the developer of MOON, a unique clinical patient information management network; an agreement with GDS, a medical device company that specializes in point-of-care diagnostic testing equipment; and a collaboration with Healthcare, L.L.C., a firm that provides consulting services for supply chain management of integrated health care delivery networks. In addition to these strategic partnerships, Sabratek acquired CMS Healthcare, a company that provides utilization management services.

The company faces daunting competition from such behemoths as Smiths Industries, plc, Abbott Laboratories, Baxter International, and McGaw Inc., but the leadership of Padda and Levitas is astute enough to develop Sabratek into a player within the field of alternative site medical equipment. The company's sales figures jumped 55 percent in 1998 over the previous year, which indicates that the two ambitious and talented entrepreneurs know how to build a viable business.

Principal Subsidiaries

CMS Healthcare, Inc.

Further Reading

Borzo, Greg, ''Computer Screens (Pattern Recognition Systems Used for Diagnosis),'' *American Medical News,* September 7, 1998.

Chase, Marilyn, ''Home Monitors Help Battle Hypertension, But Are They Reliable,'' *Wall Street Journal,* February 22, 1999, p. B1(E).

Gross, Daniel, ''IPO Infusion Pumps Maker of Drug Delivery System,'' *Crain's Chicago Business,* September 16, 1996, p. 31.

''Keeping Tabs on Blood Pressure,'' *Supermarket News,* February 1999, p. 42.

Murray, Charles, ''Portable Instrument Speeds Blood-Gas Analysis at the Bedside,'' *Design News,* June 10, 1996, p. 83.

Sakurai, Jennifer M., ''A Company's Devices Aim To Change the Nature of Health-Care Delivery,'' *Medical Device and Diagnostic Industry,* December 1998, p. 16.

—Thomas Derdak

ScanSource, Inc.

6 Logue Court, Suite G
Greenville, South Carolina 29615
U.S.A.
(864) 288-2432
(800) 944-2439
Fax: (864) 288-1165
Web site: http://www.scansource.com

Public Company
Incorporated: 1992 as ScanSource, Inc.
Employees: 229
Sales: $182.80 million (1998)
Stock Exchanges: NASDAQ
Ticker Symbol: SCSC
NAIC: 334119 Other Computer Peripheral Equipment
    Manufacturing

ScanSource, Inc. supplies value-added resellers with bar code scanners and printers, magnetic stripe readers, and other tools for electronic inventory management. ScanSource maintains sales personnel in South Carolina, California, New Jersey, Georgia, Washington, and Canada and has a 100,000 + -square-foot distribution center in Memphis, Tennessee and a 20,000-square-foot facility in Toronto. Its offerings include more than 14,000 products from 60 manufacturers.

Origins

ScanSource, Inc. was formed at the end of 1992 to service resellers of point-of-sale (POS) and auto identification (AutoID) equipment. This labor-saving technology allowed the transfer of data without manual input of each character and included such devices as bar code and label printers, laser scanners, and magnetic stripe readers. AutoID technology was spreading pervasively into many other uses aside from inventory control, materials handling, distribution, shipping, and warehouse management. Scientific researchers were discovering its uses as well. POS products included terminals, receipt printers, pole displays, cash drawers, and peripheral equipment. ScanSource was known as the only AutoID and POS distributor that did not sell to end users.

Gates/FA Distributing Inc. provided logistical support for the joint venture with one of its former CEOs, Steve Owings, who also had led the PC maker Argent Technologies, Inc. (Both companies were located in Greenville, South Carolina.)

By 1991, large retail chains were devotees of bar code scanners and printers. Although smaller businesses were beginning to use them in PC-based applications, these types of devices typically were not carried by microcomputer resellers. Cash register companies had been supplying this market. ScanSource's backers felt that therein lay an excellent opportunity to capture a large share of the $2.5 billion bar coding market.

The company started with 19 employees. Demand increased steadily from the beginning. Within a few months, ScanSource was representing about 20 vendors, including AutoID market leader Symbol Technologies Inc., Fargo Electronics Inc., and Star Micronics America. Business continued to pour in as retail inventory management grew more complex. At the same time, AutoID and POS equipment were becoming more standardized, less dependent upon proprietary technology. This was expected to spur growth in the AutoID segment at an annual rate of 14 percent through the end of the century. The AutoID market was valued at $2.2 billion; the POS equipment market was valued at $2.6 billion.

In May 1993, ScanSource bought Marietta, Georgia-based Alpha Data Systems Inc., a ten-year-old company. The transaction introduced a national client list to ScanSource. The purchase of the equipment distribution portion of MicroBiz Corp. of Spring Valley, New York soon followed. The transaction was valued at approximately $650,000. MicroBiz, a $4-million-a-year company, developed PC-based POS software for small retail stores.

ScanSource ended its first fiscal year in June 1993, having lost $243,242 on sales of $2.4 million in its first seven months. The next six months, however, saw a profit of $64,597 on sales of $6.5 million, and fiscal year 1993–94 ended with sales of $16.1 million and a $352,000 profit.

Company Perspectives:

ScanSource, Inc. is an international value-added distributor of specialty technologies, including automatic identification (Auto ID) and point-of-sale (POS) products, and—through Catalyst Telecom—business telephone systems (telephony) and computer telephony integration (CTI). Auto ID products distributed by ScanSource include bar code scanners and printers, portable data collection terminals, wireless networks, magnetic stripe readers and other related equipment. POS products sold by the Company include personal computer-based terminals, receipt printers, cash drawers, keyboards and related peripherals. Telephony and CTI products sold by the Company include key, hybrid and PBX phone systems as well as voice mail, peripherals, fax on demand, interactive voice response and other messaging solutions.

Serving only the value-added reseller (VAR), ScanSource is committed to growing specialty technology markets by strengthening and enlarging the VAR channel. ScanSource's commitment to VARs includes offering a broad product selection, competitive pricing, fast delivery, system integration, technical support, sales training, customer financing and qualified leads.

—ScanSource, Inc., ''Corporate Overview,''
1998 Annual Report

An initial public offering in March 1994 raised $4.6 million in capital. The stock was a lively seller and within a couple of months the share price had nearly tripled from $5 to $14. Gates/FA owned a 12.5 percent stake, while Stephen Owings owned 15 percent. Fast growth was part of the plan. Company founders expected to reach $100 million in sales within five years.

Dropping Gates/FA in July 1994

With Arrow Electronics Inc.'s impending acquisition of Gates/FA, ScanSource cut ties to its partner in July 1994. Arrow also had begun to compete in the POS market. ScanSource was compensated $1.4 million to make up for losing its warehouse partner.

ScanSource found an operational replacement for Gates/FA in MicroAge Inc. The firm's warehouse and MIS agreement began in the fall of 1994. MicroAge, however, did not provide financing support. MicroAge's warehouse facilities were located in Cincinnati.

Several new product lines enhanced ScanSource revenues in 1995: Epson America receipt printers, Zebra Technologies bar code label printers, and Micro-Touch POS touch screen monitors. PC-based POS units continued to rise in popularity in small retail applications. At the same time, the Windows operating system reached new levels of acceptance, prompting upgrading throughout the market. ScanSource competed against 50 other distributors in the POS market, including a dozen specializing in products for small business. Besides peripherals such as pole displays, cash drawers, and scanners, ScanSource also offered specialized software suited to various retail applications.

ScanSource revenues reached $90 million in 1996, when it had 101 employees. The company, which had an exclusive relationship with IBM, was well positioned when the computer maker unveiled its new PC-based SureOne POS system in February 1996. ScanSource expected to sell 10,000 units per year with an end price of about $3,000 each. IBM's new integrated system contrasted with the typical set-up patched together by resellers and was backed by more marketing savvy.

A leading data collection technology company, Intermec Corporation, tapped ScanSource to service its value-added resellers (VARs) in February 1997. Intermec cited ScanSource's experience with this particular market as a deciding factor in choosing the company. At this time, ScanSource already had a state-of-the-art shipping facility in Memphis, Tennessee, as well as regional sales offices in Canada and the United States.

ScanSource created its Professional Services Group to focus on hand-held, wireless data collection devices. Clients for these products required extra support through the installation process. ScanSource used special events to grow its market. The Solutions USA show, co-sponsored by Globelle, introduced hundreds of resellers to new products from dozens of vendors. Transition Marketing, Inc. was created in fiscal 1996 by ScanSource and Globelle Corporation to sponsor such trade shows. (Globelle later sold back its shares in the venture.) ScanSource also cooperated with vendors in advertising through trade periodicals, direct mail, and other promotional avenues.

In 1997 ScanSource acquired another PC-oriented distributor, POS ProVisions of Canada, for $4.3 million worth of stock. ProVisions had 15 employees and garnered $12 million in annual sales.

New Ventures in the Late 1990s

ScanSource created Catalyst Telecom in 1997 to distribute business telephone and computer telephony integration (CTI) products. Telephony products included business telephone systems and fax and data applications. ScanSource worked with Lucent Technologies to bring this to fruition, marketing Lucent's telephone handsets, cables, and voice mail equipment. ScanSource bought telephony company ProCom Supply the same year. In 1998 the company added The CTI Authority, Inc., a maker of computer-based voice messaging devices, which had sales of $8 million a year.

In its 1996–97 fiscal year, ScanSource had $2.5 million in profits on revenues of $93.9 million. It aimed to double sales in 1999 as the POS, AutoID, and telephony markets moved further away from direct sales. Employees numbered 131 in August 1997.

As PC-based applications began to become important in commercial security systems, ScanSource planned to enter that market as well, most likely through acquisition. An additional stock offering raised $26 million in capital that could be used toward this purpose. (The offering, delayed because of low share prices, had originally aimed for $32.5 million.) Scan-

Source also was considering expanding into the Canadian CTI market.

Lucent began to require ScanSource subsidiary Catalyst and other distributors to stock more parts for its switches to facilitate their timely delivery, rather than waiting for orders to be placed to begin building them. Having the distributors complete the assembly allowed the switches to be shipped in a matter of days versus up to six weeks.

ScanSource continued using road shows to recruit PC-oriented VARs to its line of POS, AutoID, and CTI products. TechTeach '99 featured educational seminars from some of the top vendors, such as IBM, Lucent, and Symbol, designed to help resellers enter new markets. PC VARs accounted for approximately half of ScanSource's 9,300 clients. The rest were specialty technology VARs.

In 1998 ScanSource launched Catalyst Commerce and the Internet Fulfillment Group to allow customers to place orders over the Internet. They also could check inventories and get delivery tracking information on-line.

In 1999 ScanSource boasted of sales growth in more than two dozen continuous quarters, a compound annual growth rate of 80 percent between 1994 and 1997. Operating income increased at a 92 percent compound annual rate during the same time period.

Both ScanSource and Catalyst Telecom achieved ISO 9002 certification in 1999. The process was completed in just eight months. The ISO 9000-series documents internationally accepted standards of quality management and assurance.

Sales increased by 65 percent to $76.9 million in the third quarter of 1998–99, compared with one year earlier. ScanSource's new ventures—business telephones, Catalyst Commerce, CTI, and Canada—performed as well as its core bar code and POS business, according to Mike Baur, company president.

Principal Subsidiaries

Transition Marketing, Inc. (58%).

Principal Divisions

Catalyst Telecom; Catalyst Commerce; Professional Services Group.

Further Reading

Bennett, Jeff, "ScanSource May Go on Acquisition Hunt," *Greenville (South Carolina) News,* December 4, 1997, p. 6D.

Campbell, Scott, "Lucent's Distributors Promise Faster Delivery of Switches," *Computer Reseller News,* January 4, 1999.

Hausman, Eric, "Mobile Solutions on Upswing," *Computer Reseller News,* May 19, 1997, pp. 47–48.

Longwell, John, "Gates F/A To Distribute Bar-Coding Hardware—Enters into Joint Venture with Ex-CEO," *Computer Reseller News,* January 11, 1993, p. 131.

——, "IBM Aims PC POS System at Channel," *Computer Reseller News,* January 22, 1996.

——, "Specialty Distributors Add Markets," *Computer Reseller News,* May 10, 1993, p. 115.

Moltzen, Edward F., "ScanSource Launches VAR Seminars," *Computer Reseller News,* March 8, 1999, p. 32.

Pereira, Pedro, "Scanning the Field: Distributor Eyes New Markets," *Computer Reseller News,* March 2, 1998, pp. 57–58.

Rushing, R.W., "ScanSource Targets Point-of-Sale Niche," *Computer Reseller News,* May 23, 1994, p. 44.

"Scanning a New Venture," *Computer Reseller News,* August 16, 1993, p. 63.

Terdoslavich, William, "POS Specialists Mine Growth Niche," *Computer Reseller News,* October 20, 1997, pp. 34–35.

Thompson, Samantha, "ScanSource Goes Public, Stock Climbs," *Greenville (South Carolina) News,* March 24, 1994, p. 7D.

——, "ScanSource Pulls Plug on Offering," *Greenville (South Carolina) News,* March 25, 1997, p. 8D.

—Frederick C. Ingram

SCB Computer Technology, Inc.

1365 West Brierbrook Road
Memphis, Tennessee 38138
U.S.A.
(901) 754-6577
Fax: (901) 754-8463
Web site: http://www.scb.com

Public Company
Incorporated: 1976 as Seltmann, Cobb & Bryant, Inc.
Employees: 1,100
Sales: $109.5 million (1998)
Stock Exchanges: NASDAQ
Ticker Symbol: SCBI
NAIC: 541511 Custom Computer Programming Services

SCB Computer Technology, Inc. is a provider of numerous information technology (IT) services to clients such as state and local government agencies, *Fortune* 500 companies, and other large organizations. SCB offers its services in five main areas: IT consulting, outsourcing, professional staffing services, telecommunications consulting, and Year 2000 compliance consulting. Headquartered in Memphis, Tennessee, SCB also operates regional offices out of Atlanta, Georgia; Dallas, Texas; Nashville, Tennessee; Long Island, New York; and Phoenix, Arizona. The company has also opened an Emerging Technology Center in Memphis, and has plans in the works to open additional such centers throughout the country.

The Early Years

SCB Computer Technology, Inc. was actually incorporated in 1984, but the company's beginnings date back eight years earlier. In 1976, three employees at Deloitte & Touche in Memphis—Ben Bryant, Scott Cobb, and Lyle Seltmann—founded a company of their own and named it Seltmann, Cobb & Bryant, Inc. The company was formed to provide IT services to other area businesses, which up to that point had been forced to do that type of work in-house.

The three men had varied backgrounds prior to their meeting at Deloitte & Touche, not all of which included extensive training in computer programming and technology. For example, while Cobb began college with the knowledge that he wanted to enter the fields of mathematics or engineering, Bryant graduated from Memphis State University in 1968 with an accounting degree—but ironically did not want to become an accountant. Therefore, on a whim he took an aptitude test for McDonnell Douglas Corp., and began working there as a computer programmer—with no previous experience in the field. Seven years later, he returned to Memphis to work as a consultant at Deloitte & Touche, which led to his meeting up with Cobb and Seltmann. They all shared an interest in computer technology, but had no idea what the field actually had in store for them in the years to come.

In its first year, Seltmann, Cobb & Bryant, Inc. operated with just four employees, including the three founders. The enterprise achieved around $179,000 in revenues that first year, and the three men decided to stick it out and work to achieve further growth.

Eight years later, in 1984, Seltmann, Cobb & Bryant, Inc. was reorganized and incorporated as SCB Computer Technology, Inc. At that time, Cobb assumed the roles of chairman of the board and president, and Bryant began acting as CEO, vice-chairman of the board, and treasurer, finally putting his accounting degree to work. Seltmann later became a strategic planning advisor for the company.

For the next ten years, the company continued to operate as a privately held entity, gradually increasing both its annual revenues and its client list. Most of its growth, however, came from the recruitment of new clients and the provision of additional IT services to existing clients. It soon became clear that if the company was going to grow substantially, it needed the revenue that would come from a public offering of stock.

Growth Through Acquisitions in the Mid-1990s

By 1994 SCB's annual revenue had grown to $28.6 million, but the company posted a loss of $15,000 for the year. The following year, sales increased to $39.2 million, this time with

Company Perspectives:

SCB is following a course for the future that encompasses three key strategic directives: acquisitions, strategic alliances, and internal development. This combination provides a strong foundation to achieve future success.

earnings of $1.6 million. At that time, the decision was made to enter the public arena. In February 1996 SCB went public, issuing its stock at just over $5 per share. Cobb turned over his presidency to Bryant, but remained the company's chairman of the board.

The public offering allowed SCB to increase the amount and scope of the services it offered, while also providing funds for the company to begin expanding through acquisitions. In September of that year, SCB purchased Delta Software Systems, Inc., a provider of IT consulting and application development services. Delta had been founded in 1982 as a programming and consulting firm for IBM, and had expanded its services throughout the rest of the decade. After the acquisition, Delta became a subsidiary of SCB.

Meanwhile, three SCB employees had become the targets of a federal grand jury investigation involving the company's billing procedures during a job that was completed for the Tennessee Valley Authority (TVA) in early 1996. Cobb was named in the investigation, along with Executive Vice-President Steve White and an unnamed SCB administrative assistant. The Securities and Exchange Commission (SEC) also began conducting an informal investigation into the matter. On May 31, 1996, SCB paid the TVA around $40,000 in relation to the possible billing errors, although the matter had not yet been settled.

SCB attained 1996 earnings of almost $2 million on sales of $56 million. It was at that time that the company achieved a heap of recognition from the media. First came Cobb's Entrepreneur of the Year Award from the *Memphis Business Journal.* Then SCB was recognized in the November 1996 issue of *Forbes* magazine as one of the country's "200 Best Small Companies," ranking 131st. Soon thereafter, *Business Week* ranked SCB 69th on its list of "Hot Growth Companies" for 1997.

In 1997 SCB completed two more acquisitions. In February, the company purchased Technology Management Resources, Inc., another IT consulting company. Technology Management Resources had been formed in 1991 to provide consulting for special state and local government divisions, including areas such as child support enforcement, welfare, the courts, and human services. The second 1997 acquisition came in June, when SCB purchased Partners Resources, Inc. and Partners Capital Group, which collectively came to be known as The Partners Group. The Partners Group was created in 1986 as a computer leasing company and service provider to the Unisys, Hewlett-Packard, Tandem, and Open Systems user groups. Both Technology Management Resources and The Partners Group were added to SCB's subsidiary holdings. SCB's annual revenues rose to $64.1 million for the year.

The company negotiated another merger deal in May 1998 with Proven Technology, Inc. Proven Technology was a systems integration services company, and was also added to SCB's subsidiary portfolio.

2000 and Beyond

As SCB approached the millennium, it was experiencing an extreme growth spurt. Sales for 1998 skyrocketed to $109.5 million, and by that point the company was operating out of five regional offices in addition to its Memphis headquarters.

In January of that year, the city of Memphis placed on the Top 20 List of "entrepreneurial hot spots" in the United States. SCB not only helped Memphis achieve the notice, but the company also benefited from the city's recognition and the business environment surrounding it. In the January 26, 1998 issue of *Memphis Business Journal,* SCB Director of Marketing Rick Nunn described the potential benefits for his company when he stated, "We do have more firms here now that are demanding high tech employees." He explained that SCB specialized in providing many such companies with skilled technical employees through its Professional Staffing Services division, and was therefore able to capitalize on the situation. That year, SCB was again recognized by *Forbes,* this time being ranked 44th in the magazine's list of "200 Best Small Companies" of 1998.

The company also gave something back to the community in which it was headquartered when it contributed to the University of Memphis's Global Information Technology Center project. Spearheaded by Professor Prashant Palvia, the center was developed to research practical applications for global IT, while also providing education, information, and resources to businesses. In 1998 SCB and Bryant himself pledged the equivalent of $1 million to get the center up and running.

SCB's immense growth and success in the end of the decade was a direct result of a headline-making problem in the late 1990s, the "Year 2000" problem. Better known as "Y2K" or the "millennium bug," the problem resulted from many computer systems' inability to properly interpret lines of code containing the two-digit date "00" as 2000 instead of 1900. By 1998, Y2K was stirring up quite a bit of concern throughout the world, as people predicted the crash of a computerized world at the turn of the millennium. SCB benefited from the problem in that one of the company's main offerings was Y2K conversion. In other words, in the late 1990s, SCB gained contracts and was paid millions by numerous clients to convert the code within their computers to read the dates properly after the new century rolled in.

By mid-1998, it was predicted that less than 60 percent of corporate America had completed even the preliminary steps in Y2K conversion. According to James Overstreet in the September 11, 1998 issue of the *Triangle Business Journal,* "It's an alarming study that illustrates just how lackadaisical corporate America has been when it comes to dealing with Y2K." SCB and its competitors, therefore, had just about all the work they could handle. In fact, as the turn of the century neared, the biggest problem facing SCB was not a shortage of available work, but a difficulty in finding enough qualified technicians to carry out the task. In the July 14, 1997 issue of *Memphis Business Journal,* SCB's Rick Nunn confirmed: "We are definitely facing a shortage in the workplace. Everything else still has to go on. Other types of businesses can put jobs on the back-burner, but not this one."

Therefore, as the company's revenues and client list rapidly expanded, so did its employee count. The company even resorted to enticing retired government employees who were familiar with the old computer language still used in many present systems to return to the workplace. Furthermore, as the problem neared and demand for conversion increased, the price tag for the work soared. For example, in 1994 many SCB conversion programmers were earning around $35 per hour; in 1998, the same work was being done for $100 per hour or more.

Up to its ears in Y2K contracts, in 1999 SCB began formulating plans to build a new $10 million, 75,000-square-foot headquarters building near its already existing corporate offices. SCB predicted that the expansion would create over 150 new jobs with a median income of around $80,000, in addition to giving the company more space to house its blossoming enterprise. The company obviously predicted future growth as the new century neared; its ability to facilitate such growth, even when its Y2K conversion services were no longer needed, would undoubtedly determine the company's future.

Principal Subsidiaries

Delta Software Systems, Inc.; Technology Management Resources, Inc.; The Partners Group, Inc.; Proven Technology, Inc.

Principal Divisions

Professional Staffing Services.

Further Reading

"Alabama Y2K Job for SCB," *Memphis Business Journal,* July 31, 1998, p. 18.

Bort, Julie, "How to Climb Your Way to City Hall," *VARBusiness,* March 30, 1998, p. 147.

Farrar, John, "Beware the 'Y2K,' the Year 2000 bug," *Memphis Business Journal,* July 14, 1997, p. 33.

——, "Record Revenues and Profits Rolling in for SCB," *Memphis Business Journal,* October 6, 1997, p. 42.

"Local High-Tech Firm on 'Hot Growth' List," *Memphis Business Journal,* June 2, 1997, p. 7.

"Newcomer Brings Hope for High-Tech," *Memphis Business Journal,* July 17, 1998, p. 54.

"Officers of Memphis, Tenn. Computer Company Targets," *Commercial Appeal,* November 20, 1997.

Overstreet, James, "Corporate America Not Ready for Y2K," *Triangle Business Journal,* September 11, 1998, p. 12Y.

——, "SCB Took Off from Enthusiasm for Technology, Programming," *Memphis Business Journal,* October 2, 1998, p. 47.

"Politics Wins with Politicians," *VARBusiness,* March 30, 1998, p. 152.

Roman, Leigh Ann, "SCB Finds 'Forbes' Dream in Wake of Entrepreneur of the Year Award," *Memphis Business Journal,* October 28, 1996, p. 1.

Rosenstein, Ann, "Memphis-Area Largest Announced Expansions in 1998," *Memphis Business Journal,* September 18, 1998, p. 28.

Rosewater, Leslie, "SCB Moving Forward After Weathering Investigation," *Memphis Business Journal,* September 2, 1996, p. 8.

"SCB Recognizes Opportunity Early in Information Technology Field," *Memphis Business Journal,* March 11, 1996, p. 17.

"SCB Wins Deals in Arkansas," *Computer Reseller News,* October 19, 1998, p. 108.

Scott, Jonathan, "SCB Plans New Headquarters, 150 New Positions," *Memphis Business Journal,* July 10, 1998, p. 1.

Sewell, Tim, "U of M's Global Tech Center Gets a Big Hand from SCB," *Memphis Business Journal,* January 26, 1998, p. 34.

"200 Best Small Companies," *Forbes,* November 2, 1998, p. 250.

Yochum, Dave, and Jonathan Scott, "Memphis in Top 20 Nationally As Hot Spot for Entrepreneurs," *Memphis Business Journal,* January 26, 1998, p. 1.

—Laura E. Whiteley

Schindler

Schindler Holding AG

Seestrasse 55
CH-6052 Ebikon
Switzerland
(41) (41) 632-8550
Fax: (41) (41) 445-3134
Web site: http://www.schindler.com

Public Company
Incorporated: 1874 as Schindler & Villiger
Employees: 38,574
Sales: CHF 6.55 billion (1998)
Stock Exchanges: Zürich Berlin Frankfurt/Main
Ticker Symbol: SCHN
NAIC: 333922 Conveyor & Conveying Equipment
   Manufacturing; 335312 Motor & Generator
   Manufacturing; 333999 All Other Miscellaneous
   General Purpose Machinery Manufacturing; 42143
   Computer & Computer Peripheral Equipment &
   Software Wholesalers; 551112 Offices of Other
   Holding Companies

Through its numerous subsidiaries, Schindler Holding AG is Europe's top supplier of elevators and escalators and ranks second in the world in that capacity. Managed and majority-owned by fourth-generation descendants of its founding family, the group operates about 100 subsidiaries and affiliated companies around the world with nearly 40,000 employees and generates about $4.4 billion in sales annually. As the "electronic heart" of the group, Schindler Elettronica S.A., in Locarno, Switzerland, develops and manufactures high technology control systems, power converters, electronic equipment and accessories, and other elevator components. The Schindler drive systems plant, Schindler S.A., in Zaragoza, Northern Spain, produces drives for elevators, while another main Schindler subsidiary, Etablissements Henri Peignen S.A., near Paris, develops and produces elevator doors—the most sensitive part of an elevator. Elevator Car System in France specializes in the mass production of elevator cars, push-button boards, and door

drives. As a second line of business, the Schindler Group holds the majority share of ALSO Holding AG, Switzerland's leading wholesale distributor of computers, peripheral equipment, and software, with annual sales of $700 million.

The First 50 Years: 1874–1924

In 1874, a mechanical engineering workshop was built in Lucerne, Switzerland. Newly established by two Swiss men, Robert Schindler and Eduard Villiger, the partnership of Schindler & Villiger produced lifting equipment and other machinery. Nine years later the business moved to a new and bigger factory. In 1892 partner Eduard Villiger left the firm, which continued operations under a new name: Robert Schindler, Machinery Manufacturer. Schindler's most important customers during its first years were large hotels and production plants, first in Lucerne and later throughout Switzerland.

In 1901 Robert Schindler sold the business to his brother Alfred Schindler, who became the new sole proprietor and changed the firm's name accordingly. Five years later, a new business partner, Fritz Geilfuss, joined the company and it became a partnership, Schindler & Cie. Around the same time, the company's first subsidiary, Schindler & Cie. o.H.G., was established in Berlin, Germany. Over the following years, the Schindler company expanded into more and more European countries. It established Schindler & Houplin in France, purchased the Severin Senator GmbH in Berlin, Germany, and opened new sales and branch offices in Switzerland, Argentina, Turkey, Algeria, Romania, Russia, Belgium, Italy, Spain, Egypt, Poland, and Chile. In 1923 a new production facility was established in Mulhouse, France.

While elevators manufactured by Schindler & Villiger in 1883 were water driven, the first hydraulic models for lifting freight were shipped from the factory in 1890. They were followed two years later by the first belt-driven electric elevator. In 1899 Schindler elevators were equipped with worm gears and controlled by a pull rope. The first electric passenger elevator with automatic push-button control left the factory in 1902. In 1915 Schindler began manufacturing elevator motors; cranes were added to its product range in 1920.

419

Becoming Europe's Leader: 1925–69

In 1925 Adolf Sigg became Alfred Schindler's new business partner after Fritz Geilfuss died in an accident. That same year, after the company's iron foundry (which had produced munitions during World War I) was spun off, the firm was renamed Kommanditaktiengesellschaft Schindler & Cie., Aufzüge und Maschinenfabrik. The subsidiary in Mulhouse was renamed as well, becoming the Société Schindler & Cie. By 1931 Schindler had expanded into Croatia, Greece, Lithuania, Bulgaria, Yugoslavia, Morocco, Egypt, Colombia, Ecuador, South Africa, and even China. The company was incorporated as Aufzüge und Elektromotorenfabrik, Schindler & Cie. A.G. in 1932. When Alfred Schindler died in 1937, his son Alfred F. Schindler took over management of the company. Although World War II slowed the company's growth as Word War I had earlier—elevators and escalators were not first-priority goods for the war and defense production—Schindler continued to expand internationally. New subsidiaries were opened in Locarno, Johannesburg, Caracas, and London. Testing facilities were added to the modernized and expanded factory in Lucerne, and a brand new factory was built in Ebikon, Switzerland, between 1954 and 1957. By 1959, Schindler had established itself as Europe's number one elevator maker. In 1960 the Schindler company employed about 9,100 people worldwide. Between 1967 and 1969 Schindler acquired a share in the Dutch firm Westdijk and in the Austrian Wertheim-Werke.

While its geographic scope widened, Schindler's product line expanded as well. In 1925 Schindler had produced the world's first elevators that had a speed of 1.5 meters per second and were equipped with automatic floor leveling and cascade control. The first Schindler escalator was introduced in 1936. The same year after Schindler engineers modernized Europe's fastest and highest passenger elevator in Bürgenstock-Hammetschwand, Switzerland, it had a running speed of 2.7 meters per second. Improvements continued, and just before the outbreak of World War II in Europe Schindler built an elevator for the overhead cable car of the city of Zürich. It was the fastest passenger elevator in Europe and could travel at 4.2 meters per second. In 1955 the company introduced the first programmed control system called ''Supermatic,'' and one year later it marketed its first elevator with electronically controlled alternating current drive.

Worldwide Growth and Reorganization: 1970–89

With the establishment of the Schindler Holding AG in 1970, a basic corporate structure was in place that would endure for the next 20 years. In 1974, the firm's 100th anniversary year, the Schindler empire consisted of 56 subsidiaries in Western Europe, Latin America, and South Africa, employing 22,270 people, and generating operating revenues of CHF 46 million.

In 1979 Schindler extended its reach to include the United States. The company acquired the Haughton Elevator Division from Reliance Electric Cleveland and transformed it into the Schindler Haughton Elevator Corporation based in Toledo, Ohio. In 1985 all of Schindler's North American subsidiaries were unified as one entity—the Schindler Elevator Corporation. The same year Schindler pioneered double-decker elevators in the Scotia Place building in Toronto, Canada, a 68-story high-rise.

Over the following 15 years the company entered a period of unprecedented growth. In 1980 Schindler pioneered a new chapter in economic relationships with the People's Republic of China when it established China Schindler Elevator Co. in Beijing, China's first industrial joint venture with a western company. A second joint venture in China followed in 1988, when the Suzhou Elevator Company, with 1,000 employees and an output of 950 elevators per year, was set up in the Jiangsu province. A Schindler subsidiary was established in Australia in 1981, followed by the acquisition of Precision Elevator Pty. Ltd., an Australian elevator company. A participation, licensing, and agency agreement was reached between Schindler and Bharat Bijlee Ltd., India's second-largest elevator manufacturer in 1986. A year later Schindler purchased a majority share of Nippon Elevator Industry Co. Ltd. based in Tokyo, Japan. In 1989 Schindler took over two elevator companies in New Zealand.

In addition to the worldwide growth of its core business, Schindler diversified into other fields. With the acquisition of a majority share in FFA Flug- und Fahrzeugwerke AG Altenrhein, Schindler strengthened its rolling stock production arm, managed by the new Schindler Waggon Altenrhein AG. When Schindler acquired a majority share in ALSO Holding AG, a Swiss personal computer wholesaler, in 1988, industry analysts wondered whether the company was spreading its resources too thin. However, once ALSO was restructured and downsized, it began to thrive.

In 1985 a new generation of management took over the Schindler group. Alfred N. Schindler—an MBA graduate of the renowned Wharton School of Finance in Pennsylvania, as well as a graduate of the University of Bern Law School—together with Luc Bonnard and Dr. Uli Sigg were elected at the general shareholder meeting as the new executive directors. Among their first actions was to develop new ways to reduce overcapacities in Europe and increase production efficiency. Component manufacturing for the whole Schindler group was streamlined, standardized, and concentrated in six factory sites: Ebikon and Locarno in Switzerland; Mulhouse and Melun in France; Zaragoza in Spain; and Berlin, Germany.

In the late 1980s, Schindler made its biggest deal to date in the United States, signing a contract with the Westinghouse Electric Corporation to take over Westinghouse's entire North American elevator and escalator business, worth a total of half a billion dollars in annual sales and with resources of 5,500 employees. The takeover was effective on January 1, 1989 and was followed by a complete reorganization of Schindler's North American business. Westinghouse's business units in Canada were integrated into Schindler's Canadian subsidiary, Schindler

Elevator Corporation located in Pickering, Ontario. In the United States, the installation businesses of the two companies were merged, manufacturing was concentrated in Gettysburg and Sidney, three other factories were closed down, and a brand-new one built in Clinton, North Carolina.

New Group Strategy for the 1990s

In 1990 Schindler's top managers developed a new group strategy, with the intention of transforming the group from an engineering company to a service provider. At the end of the year, Uli Sigg, who had initiated Schindler's early China strategy and the ALSO takeover, left the group. The newly developed management structure which came into effect in 1991 was set up to better manage the group's rapid growth. Under this structure, a new executive committee of the board would be mainly responsible for strategic planning, while the management committee would be in charge of the day-to-day business. At Schindler's annual meeting in 1995, Alfred N. Schindler was elected CEO.

In January 1991 a major fire broke out in the Ebikon factory, causing damage valued at several million Swiss Francs. Fortunately, nobody was injured. Three years after the incident, the Ebikon plant ceased component production. That production was transferred to Schindler's factory in Zaragoza, Spain. In 1991 Schindler was chosen exclusive supplier for infrastructure installations at the World Exhibition EXPO '92 in Seville, Spain. A total of 213 pieces of Schindler equipment were in service from April until October 1992, among them 79 elevators and 33 escalators. 8,000 Schindler customers attended the show. In spring of 1994 the new Schindler 300 elevator car range was launched and received several design prizes. However, the high-priced innovation hit the market just as prices collapsed in Europe, cutting Schindler's profits in half.

In September 1991 the first escalator left Schindler's brand-new factory in Clinton, North Carolina. Over the next two years, Schindler came to command a market share of over 20 percent and thus became the number one escalator maker in the world. In 1995 a new Schindler-owned factory for the production of aluminum escalator steps was opened in Suzhou, China. Schindler's computer wholesale business, ALSO, obtained a majority interest in the Swiss computer trading and services firm MPC SA in Lausanne. Two state-of-the-art logistics centers were built in Emmen, near Lucerne, and in the Southern German Straubing. Schindler's rolling stock units were concentrated under the umbrella of Schindler Waggon AG.

In 1995, the Total Cycle Time Program was introduced which, a year later, was transformed into the far-reaching Schindler Program for Radical Innovative New Thinking (SPRINT). Both programs were initiated to bring about a significant improvement in Schindler's productivity, by redesigning processes and introducing new efficiency standards, such as cutting production time by an ambitious 50 percent and striving for error-free production.

Schindler's international acquisition activity in the first half of the 1990s concentrated on expanding into Middle and Eastern Europe, strengthening its interests in various foreign ventures, and making the group's presence more visible by giving its name a higher profile. After the reunification of Germany, Schindler established a joint venture between its subsidiary in Berlin and a Dresden elevator company formerly owned by the East German government. Later Schindler took over 11 other companies in the former German Democratic Republic. In 1990, a new joint venture was also set up in the USSR. Schindler held a 51 percent share in Schindler Mosmontash Lift based in Moscow. Another joint venture was set up with a Hungarian partner in Budapest. The length of Schindler's contract for the Chinese Suzhou joint venture was extended to 50 years in 1991, and Schindler's stake in the project was increased to 55 percent in 1993. New joint ventures were established in Latvia and Lithuania after those countries had separated from the Soviet Union. In the early 1990s Schindler acquired a Turkish elevator manufacturer, Türkeli Ticaret S.A. based in Istanbul, and a majority interest in the Czech elevator firm Vytahy CSFR A.S., based in Prague. The group's subsidiaries in Great Britain and France were transformed into holding companies, subsidiaries in Ireland and Australia were now completely owned by Schindler, and all of them carried the group's name. In 1995 Schindler increased its interest in the Beijing-based China Schindler Elevator Co. to over 60 percent.

Stronger than Ever: 1996–99

The second half of the 1990s saw a flood of Schindler innovations. In 1996, an "intelligent" hall call destination control system known as Miconic 10 was launched, which—according to Schindler—was able to increase the capacity of elevator groups by up to 50 percent and significantly cut down overall travel time. With the new system, instead of pushing "up" or "down" buttons, elevator users entered their destination on a decimal keypad before entering the elevator.

The "SchindlerMobile"—launched in April 1997—was a new type of passenger elevator. Its self-propelled car could operate without a machine room, suspension ropes, or hoistway walls, while its wheels moved up and down self-supporting aluminum columns. Preassembled at the factory, "SchindlerMobile" could be installed with the help of a crane in just three days. In the same year Schindler launched the first elevator which could be ordered via the Internet: "Schindler 001," a simple, standardized elevator for residential buildings. In the escalator field Schindler introduced "Schindler 9300," a new modular system manufactured in Vienna for European customers, in Clinton for the North American customers, and in China for the Asian market. "SMART MRL 001," another elevator with no machine room was introduced in 1998. It too could be ordered via the Internet by European customers. For the North American Market Schindler offered a new hydraulic elevator called the Schindler 321A and Networx, a communication system for Schindler customers that allowed them to track the progress of their orders, monitor the condition and maintenance status of their Schindler installations, calculate prices, and place orders online. Installation and maintenance mechanics were able to retrieve information on the jobs and download drawings through Networx.

Despite a downturn in the industry, Schindler's market position improved. As the Swiss construction market was about to collapse, the company managed to increase exports by no less than 82 percent to CHF 240 million. The escalator factory in

Clinton, North Carolina, was named one of *Industry Week* magazine's "America's Ten Best Plants" in 1996 and was expanded again that same year. Schindler became world market leader in the marine business as well, as Schindler elevators were installed on the *Carnival Destiny* and the *Grand Princess*—both the world's largest cruise liners at the time of their launchings. In 1997 Schindler's escalator service division, including its subsidiary Millar Escalators, was granted a contract by Sears, Roebuck and Co. to maintain about 2,000 elevators and escalators in the retail chains' 820 U.S. stores.

Computer subsidiary ALSO exceeded the CHF 1 billion mark for the first time in 1998; as a result, its office and distribution facilities in Switzerland and Germany were expanded. During this time, the Schindler group also took over the German Haushahn Group, an elevator and elevator component manufacturer headquartered in Stuttgart with DM 400 million in annual sales and about 1,750 employees.

In 1999, Schindler's celebrated its 125th anniversary, presenting 1998 financial results that were cause enough for celebration. Net profits had reached CHF 244.9 million, a 71.5 percent increase over 1997, in part due to Schindler's earlier divestment of its rolling stock business. The company's operating revenues totaled CHF 6.6 billion, a 6.3 percent increase over 1997. During this time, about 60 percent of Schindler's invoiced sales were realized in Europe, 24 percent in the Americas, and 16 percent in Asia, Africa, and Australia. Schindler's elevator and escalator business made up 80 percent of operating revenues and enjoyed a 12 percent growth rate in North and South America. Finally, the Suzhou Schindler Elevator Company was the number one elevator maker in China in mid-1998, according to *AsiaInfo Services*. Schindler's 25 percent share of the world market for escalators enabled the company to outperform even its chief rival Otis Elevator, which led the world elevator market. At the same time, Schindler held an 18-percent share of the escalator market, and computer wholesaler ALSO realized impressive growth as well, contributing

one-fifth of Schindler's total operating revenues. Despite an uncertain economic climate in Japan, Southeast Asia, Russia, and Brazil, the company expected net profits to continue to grow modestly in 1999. In a maturing and increasingly competitive market, Schindler reported that it would concentrate on information technology, training, achieving cost leadership in all important market segments, and on being "the reliable and user-friendly service company of choice" in the elevator and computer wholesale businesses.

Principal Subsidiaries

Schindler Aufzüge AG (Switzerland); Schindler Elettronica S.A. (Switzerland); Schindler Aufzüge und Fahrtreppen AG (Austria, 96.9%); Elevator Car System (France, 99.9%); Etablissements Henri Peignen S.A. (France, 99.9%); Schindler Holding Deutschland GmbH (Germany); Schindler S.p.A. (Italy); Schindler S.A. (Spain, 99.1%); ALSO Holding AG (Switzerland, 69.7%); Elevadores Schindler do Brasil S.A. (Brazil); Schindler Elevator Corporation (United States); Millar Elevator Industries, Inc. (United States); China-Schindler Elevator Co. Ltd. (China, 62.7%); Schindler Lifts (Hong Kong) Ltd.

Further Reading

Marsh, Peter, and William Hall, "Schindler Starting to Push the Right Financial Buttons," *Financial Times,* April 3, 1998, p. 32.

"Parametric Technology Corporation Receives $2.0 Million Order for Software and Services from Schindler Elevator Corporation," *Business Wire,* September 24, 1998.

Rennardson, I., "Schindler Holding Ltd.," *Merrill Lynch Capital Markets,* April 16, 1999.

Sraeel, Holly, "Profile: Alfred N. Schindler," *Buildings,* January 1991, p. 52.

Taninecz, George, "Schindler Elevator Corp.," *Industry Week,* October 21, 1996, p. 54.

—Evelyn Hauser

▯ SCHOLASTIC

Scholastic Corporation

555 Broadway
New York, New York 10012-3999
U.S.A.
(212) 343-6100
Fax: (212) 343-6928
Web site: http://www.scholastic.com

Public Company
Incorporated: 1920
Employees: 4,500
Sales: $1.058 billion (1998)
Stock Exchanges: New York
Ticker Symbol: SCHL
NAIC: 51112 Periodical Publishers; 51113 Book
Publishers; 51121 Software Publishers; 51211 Motion
Picture & Video Production; 551112 Offices of Other
Holding Companies

The Scholastic Corporation is one of the leading publishers and distributors of books, magazines, and other educational materials for children in the United States. In addition to printed materials, the company also produces educational software and videos and is involved in movies and children's television programming. Scholastic began as a newsletter for Pennsylvania high school students in the early 1920s, then struggled throughout its first three decades, finally gaining steady profits in the post-World War II years when it expanded its offerings and channels of distribution.

Scholastic was founded in 1920 by Maurice R. Robinson, whose experience in journalism was enhanced during his tenure as a staff member on the Dartmouth College student newspaper. Upon graduation from Dartmouth, Robinson returned to his hometown of Wilkinsburg, a suburb of Pittsburgh, and took a job at the Pittsburgh Chamber of Commerce. There he came across statistics indicating that the high school student population was expected to increase steadily throughout the decade, and he decided that a newspaper dedicated to students' interests

would be a good prospect. The first edition of *The Western Pennsylvania Scholastic* provided articles on topics of general interest to students and was published on October 22, 1920. Robinson designed the four-page paper from a desk in his mother's sewing room, and he sold it for five cents a copy.

The following year, Robinson arranged for office space in Pittsburgh and hired a clerk to serve as office manager and assistant editor. To finance the publication of *The Western Pennsylvania Scholastic,* Robinson continued to work at various jobs in public relations. Although the paper did not turn a profit during the 1921–22 school year, its circulation reached 4,000.

Expansion But No Profits in the 1920s

In 1922 Robinson decided to widen the scope of his student newspaper. Over the summer he distributed a brochure describing his proposed publication, the *Scholastic,* to those present at the National Education Association convention in Boston. The publication's new format was to resemble that of a magazine and would include articles relevant to classroom work in English, social studies, science, and foreign languages. Preparing for increased business, Robinson hired a circulation manager and incorporated his venture as the Scholastic Publishing Company. The first issue of the *Scholastic,* which billed itself as "The National High School Bi-Weekly," was published on September 16, 1922 and sold for 15 cents per copy.

To stimulate circulation, sell advertising space, and generate copy of interest to students across the nation, Robinson assembled an advisory board of high school teachers and administrators and a staff to sell ads and push subscriptions to teachers and their students. Moreover, he began selling shares of Scholastic stock to raise funds. In 1924 Scholastic began to sponsor the Scholastic Creative Writing Awards as well as a contest to provide cover designs by high school art students, programs that proved extremely popular. As a result of these activities, circulation of the *Scholastic* reached 33,000 by the spring of 1925, a figure that would nearly double by the end of the decade. Despite the publication's popularity, Scholastic continued to struggle financially, never realizing a profit in the 1920s. Moreover, its seasonal distribution generated no income during the summer months.

In the early months of 1929, Robinson acquired a weekly social studies periodical, *The World Review,* for which he paid with Scholastic stock. When the stock market crashed in October, he was able to sell this property to a competitor, giving his company a much-needed infusion of cash. Shortly thereafter, Scholastic acquired the children's magazine *St. Nicholas,* and the company's name was changed to Scholastic-St. Nicholas Corporation.

Added Publications But Financial Problems Persisted in the 1930s and 1940s

Continued financial strains brought on by the Great Depression, however, prompted Robinson to seek the economic resources of another publishing firm. During the 1931–32 school year, Scholastic entered into a joint venture with competitor American Education Press, in which Scholastic gained control of four publications: *The Magazine World, World News, Current Literature,* and *Looseleaf Current Topics.* Temporarily bolstered by increased business, Scholastic opened offices on East 44th Street in New York and launched another new publication, *Scholastic Coach.*

In April 1932 Scholastic bought out American Education Press and, two months later, the company's name was changed to Scholastic Corporation, as plans were made to sell *St. Nicholas* before the end of the year. By the fall of 1932, circulation of the company's publications had dropped sharply and salary cuts for all staff members at Scholastic were necessary. Focusing on the potential of its original publication, the *Scholastic,* Robinson cut costs by doing away with its expensive cover art and printing the entire magazine on less expensive paper. Hoping to increase revenues, he also put the *Scholastic* on a weekly publication schedule.

Scholastic reported slight gains in circulation in 1934 and 1935, and the following year the company reported its first annual profit ever, $2,400. A magazine for junior high school readers, entitled *Junior Scholastic,* was introduced during this time, and the company's underpaid staff received salary increases. By the spring of 1938, however, the circulation of the mainstay *Scholastic* (which eventually became known as *Senior Scholastic* to distinguish it from its junior counterpart) had dropped precipitously, and projections for the success of *Junior Scholastic* proved overly optimistic. Consequently, Robinson was forced to suspend payment of his staff for a month. The

losses were attributed, in part, to the fact that many Scholastic publications came under the scrutiny of disapproving parents and politicians during this time. Facing charges that the material was unsuitable for young people, some schools were forced to ban Scholastic magazines. In two widely publicized cases, in Washington, D.C. in 1936 and in Topeka, Kansas in 1938, *Senior Scholastic* was accused of promoting communism.

In the early 1940s Scholastic's two principal stockholders, hoping to recoup their investment, sought a buyer for the company. When no suitable offers were forthcoming, they brought in an outside management consultant to evaluate Scholastic's operations. The study was completed in 1941 and recommended that the company either be liquidated or that Robinson be replaced as its head. Instead, however, Scholastic's backers agreed to finance the company on a long-term basis, provided some economizing measures were taken.

At the onset of World War II, Scholastic introduced a new magazine devoted to current events. *World Week,* first published in September 1942, was promoted as ''The New All Social Studies Classroom Magazine Graded to Meet Your Wartime Teaching Requirements.'' When wartime rationing of paper went into effect on January 1, 1943, however, Scholastic was forced to produce thinner publications and turn down subscribers.

After the war, Scholastic moved to expand its circulation and the number of titles it offered. In 1946 *Scholastic Teacher, Practical English,* and *Prep* were introduced. Two years later, *Literary Cavalcade* for high school English classes was added to the fold as was the Teen Age Book Club, a joint endeavor with Pocket Books formed to market newly available paperback books to young people in school. It marked Scholastic's entry into the highly successful book club business, which grew over the next 50 years to include 11 book clubs serving preschool through junior high school students. To boost circulation, company executives divided up their sales territory into 180 ''Scholastic Districts,'' hiring part-time sales staff, referred to as Resident Representatives, to work on commission in each district. By 1951, Scholastic was able to pay a dividend on its stock for the first time.

Political Controversies Continued To Affect Scholastic's Reputation in the 1950s

Problems concerning the political views reflected in Scholastic publications resurfaced in the late 1940s and 1950s. In 1948 the city of Birmingham, Alabama, issued a ban on *Senior Scholastic,* finding articles advocating racial equality unacceptable; this ban was lifted three years later. Perhaps the most widespread controversy surrounding Scholastic publications developed when Senator Joseph McCarthy and others serving on the House Committee on Un-American Activities began a program of accusing American citizens of communist affiliations. In 1952 a Scholastic editor was ordered to explain his involvement 20 years prior with a short-lived youth magazine under suspicion of promoting Communist sympathies. While he did so satisfactorily and was exonerated, several similar charges were leveled against Scholastic over the next few years.

By the end of the decade, Scholastic had added several new publications to its roster, including *Practical Home Economics,* acquired in 1952, and *JAC/Junior American Citizen,* which was renamed *Newstime.* Student book clubs were proving successful, and Scholastic added two new book clubs, the Arrow Book Club for younger students grades 4–6 and the Campus Book Club. The growth of Scholastic's student book club operations created the need for a warehouse to hold goods for shipping. In 1959 the company completed construction of such a facility in Englewood Cliffs, New Jersey.

Explored New Markets in the 1960s

During the 1960s, Scholastic explored new markets, introducing two book clubs for young children, Lucky and See-Saw, and adding 13 new periodicals to its line. Furthermore, the company began publishing various instructional materials and books, including a series of books adapted for different age levels intended to develop reading skills and introduce young people to the short story and poetry. In 1962 the World Affairs Multi-Text series was offered for use in social studies classes, and a series of arithmetic booklets were promoted for individual study at home.

The company expanded internationally during the 1960s after opening its first international subsidiary, Scholastic Canada, in 1957. Scholastic United Kingdom and Scholastic New Zealand were established in 1964, followed by Scholastic Australia in 1968.

In 1965 Scholastic introduced its hardcover book publishing division, the Four Winds Press. This unit eventually became central to Scholastic's Library and Trade Division, which marketed publications to libraries and book wholesalers and distributed a new line of Scholastic/Folkways Records, the company's first audio offerings. By 1968, a series of short films, entitled *Toute la Bande,* had been designed for instruction in the French language. That same year the company opened a book distribution facility in Jefferson City, Missouri that would become its national distribution center with 2,000 employees and 1.5 million square feet of warehouse and office space.

Financial Growth as a Public Company in the 1970s

The company continued to expand its audiovisual offerings in the early 1970s, introducing Enrichment Records; Art & Man Filmstrips, which supplemented a Scholastic periodical published under the direction of the National Gallery of Art; Bill Russell's Basketball Films; Clifford Filmstrips; and Margaret Court Instructional Films.

Another area of concentration at Scholastic during this time reflected the country's increased awareness of the need for remedial reading instruction at all age levels. For those students regarded as slow learners, Scholastic offered several textbook programs and magazines, some of which featured easy-to-read articles and stories that would appeal to older students. In addition to exploiting a new and growing market, such material helped offset the declining popularity of *Senior Scholastic.*

Scholastic stock was first offered to the public through the New York Stock Exchange in 1969, and the 1970s began a period of steady financial growth at Scholastic. With the scope and complexity of its operations expanding, the company underwent several corporate reorganizations in the 1970s. In 1971 a School Division was created to oversee operations involving the company's book clubs and magazines. This division was headed by M. Richard Robinson, Jr., son of the company's founder, and four years later Robinson took over as president of the company, initiating another period of reorganization. Richard "Dick" Robinson would continue to lead the company for the next several decades after being named chief executive officer (CEO) in 1975 and chairman in 1982.

Foundations Laid for Diversification into New Media in the 1980s

Scholastic Productions was formed in 1978 to provide the company with the capability of producing children's television series, feature films, home videos, and multimedia products based on its popular book characters. Renamed Scholastic Entertainment in 1998, the division would be an important source of revenue during the 1990s. In 1982 the New Media division was launched to focus on educational software.

By 1980, budget cuts and declining school enrollment rates posed a challenge to Scholastic. Unable to raise prices to meet the rapidly increasing costs of publishing books and periodicals, the company saw its revenues decline. To offset this trend, the company decided to invest more than $5 million to enter the highly competitive textbook market, building on the instructional materials it first offered in 1961. Within two years, however, the venture had failed to provide the expected returns, and the company resumed its focus on supplementary educational materials.

The company entered the book fair business by acquiring California School Book Fairs in 1981. Book fairs were typically run by parents and teachers in schools and offered Scholastic another distribution channel. They proved so successful that Scholastic went national by acquiring Great American Book Fairs in 1983. By the 1990s Scholastic Book Fairs was the largest children's book fair operation in the United States.

During the 1980s Scholastic also explored the burgeoning market for educational material related to computers, introducing *Electronic Learning* and *Teaching and Computers* magazine to help teachers with new technologies in the classroom. The company also launched its first consumer magazine, *Family Computing,* a line of software for children entitled Wizware, and a magazine on disk, called *Microzine.*

By May 1984, however, these new ventures had resulted in losses of $13.8 million, and the company's stock price plummeted. When new management and reorganizations failed to alleviate the financial burden, Robinson decided to take Scholastic private. In 1986 he reestablished control over the company by creating SI Holdings Inc., which maintained a 51 percent share of the company's stock. In July 1987, SI Holdings paid $84 million for the remaining Scholastic shares.

In 1986 two important children's book series were launched that would provide Scholastic with revenues over the next decade not only from book sales, but also from related merchandise and television programming. One was *The Magic School*

Bus series, written by Joanna Cole and illustrated by Bruce Degen. By the late 1990s it had ten original titles with more than 2.4 million copies in print. It also ran as a successful children's television series on Public Broadcasting Stations (PBS). The other series was *The Baby-sitters Book Club* book series, written by Ann Martin for young girls ages eight to 12. By the late 1990s it had 335 titles and more than 172 million copies in print, with 12 new titles published each year. It resulted in a television series, home videos, CD-ROMs, and consumer products, as well as its own Web site and fan club. *The Baby-sitters Club Movie* was released in 1995 and then on video in 1996.

Growth Outpaced Book Industry in the 1990s

Once the company was back on solid financial ground, it again went public, offering $90 million worth of stock in February 1992. Scholastic went public with shares selling for $26. A year later the stock was trading at $36 a share. In July 1992 R.L. Stine's popular *Goosebumps* series debuted. For 1992–93 (fiscal 1993 ending May 31, 1993), Scholastic reported revenues of $552 million and net income of $28 million. Book publishing contributed 66 percent of revenue and 91 percent of net income. Sales of the company's 28 school magazines were growing at a slower pace. The company's payroll grew 20 percent to 3,700 employees at a time when many other media companies were downsizing.

In 1993–94 Scholastic was moving toward multimedia and interactive products as well as television programming. It spent $20 million to develop its first animated television series, *The Magic School Bus,* which debuted on PBS in fall 1994. In September 1993 the company started Scholastic Network, an educational online computer service available on America Online (AOL).

At this time book clubs were Scholastic's largest distribution channel, accounting for approximately half of its domestic book publishing revenue of $428 million. By 1995 trade distribution had surpassed book clubs as Scholastic's largest distribution channel, due largely to the popularity of *Goosebumps,* which helped Scholastic realize a 21 percent jump in domestic book publishing sales to $516.8 million in 1994–95. Scholastic was releasing one *Goosebumps* title a month, usually with a first printing of 600,000 copies. Overall revenues reached $749.8 million, and net income increased 17.3 percent, from $32.9 million to $38.6 million.

The company also was focused on building its educational publishing, with several states adopting its new instructional programs. The multimedia (books, videos, and software) *Scholastic Science Place* program for grades K-2 generated sales of $19 million. It was expanded to cover grades K-6 and was supplemented by *Scholastic Math Place,* launched in April 1994; in 1995 Scholastic introduced *Scholastic Literacy Place* in English and Spanish-language versions. This elementary language arts core curriculum program was adopted by many major school districts and endorsed for use by U.S. Department of Defense Schools.

Movie and television projects were becoming a growing part of Scholastic. Scholastic licensed some 40 consumer products related to *The Magic School Bus* series, ranging from clothing to toys, to partners such as Hasbro and Sega. The company co-produced the movie, *The Indian in the Cupboard,* which was released by Paramount in the summer of 1995, as was *The Baby-sitters Club Movie.* The *Goosebumps* series was launched on Fox television in the fall of 1995. As a result, the company's best-performing division of 1995–96 was Scholastic Productions, whose sales rose 104 percent to $39.8 million. Overall the company reported a 24 percent increase in revenues to $928.6 million. Net income declined to $31.9 million in fiscal 1996; it was affected by an after-tax charge of $14.9 million due to a change in accounting standards and other factors.

Between 1992 and 1996 Scholastic had enjoyed tremendous sales and income growth, with sales increasing 439 percent and net income rising 147 percent. By 1996–97 the growth had slowed, and the company found it necessary to make staff reductions and eliminate some operations to achieve a profitable fiscal 1998. Net income for fiscal 1997 (ending May 31) was only $361,000 on sales of $966 million.

The company undertook several cost-cutting and restructuring measures. More than 400 positions were eliminated as part of a $25 million cost-cutting program. In addition, the company closed unprofitable magazines and its French operation, improved productivity at its Jefferson City, Missouri, distribution facility, and began subleasing 40,000 square feet of office space in New York City. It also consolidated four instructional units into one division.

For 1996–97 declining sales from the *Goosebumps* series resulted in a decrease in retail sales. With 103 *Goosebumps* titles in the market and 200 million copies in print, Scholastic was trying to lessen its dependence on the series. It recently had launched two new series, *Animorphs* and *Dear America.* Licensing revenues from *Goosebumps* made Scholastic Productions highly profitable. Fox Network ordered another 24 episodes for 1997–98. For 1998, 13 episodes of *The Magic School Bus* series would be completed for a total of 52 shows. *Animorphs* was being adapted for television, with 13 shows set to air on Nickelodeon during 1998.

In September 1996 Scholastic acquired the New York-based Lectorum Publications, the largest U.S. distributor of Spanish-language books to schools and libraries. In January 1997 it acquired Red House Books Ltd., a British children's book distributor and book club operator, making Scholastic the largest children's book publisher and distributor in the United Kingdom. Scholastic also was exploring emerging markets through its subsidiaries in Mexico, India, and Hong Kong.

After announcing it would extend its agreement with Parachute Press to publish and manage licensing of *Goosebumps,* Scholastic became involved in a legal dispute with Parachute Press. In another legal matter, three class action suits relating to the sharp downturn in the company's stock in 1997 were consolidated into one lawsuit. The plaintiffs charged that the company made misleading statements about its earnings before announcing on February 20, 1997 that it would have a huge loss in the third quarter. Following the announcement, the company's stock lost about half its market value, falling from around $69 a share to between $30 and $36 a share.

Faced with a need to improve profitability, Scholastic rebounded in fiscal 1998. Net income rose to a respectable $23.6 million. Book publishing revenues rose substantially from $645.9 million to $728.5 million, and revenues from international operations increased from $178.9 million to $195.9 million. For the first time Scholastic surpassed the $1 billion mark in revenue with $1.058 billion, a 9.5 percent increase over fiscal 1997.

In January 1998 Scholastic sold its SOHO Group (Small Office and Home Office) of business publications for $20 million. The sale included *Home Office Computing* and *Small Business Computing,* along with an online site and a custom publishing division. Scholastic's management deemed these to be noncore assets.

Later in 1998 Scholastic purchased the assets of Pages Book Fairs, the second largest book fair operator, for $10.5 million. With the acquisition Scholastic planned to increase the number of parent-teacher-run book fairs as early as fall 1998. It also acquired The Electronic Bookshelf (EBS) in April 1998. EBS is a technology-based reading motivation, management, and assessment system designed for use in schools. It utilized computer-based tests on popular, high-quality books and provided a method of recognizing and rewarding students for reading achievement.

The company showed continued revenue growth and profitability in early 1999. It introduced two new products to improve literacy, *Scholastic READ 180* and *Scholastic Reading Counts!.* Scholastic improved its marketing muscle with the January 1999 acquisition of QED (Quality Education Data) from Peterson's, an International Thomson Publishing company.

Scholastic's future growth will be fueled by the so-called Millennial Generation, some 70 million children under the age of 18. This demographic surpasses even the 65 million members of the Baby Boom generation born after World War II. As a result, educational spending by government was growing significantly for the first time since the 1960s. Parents also were spending more for their children's educational materials, while children themselves were spending money on entertainment. Scholastic was positioned to reach these children in school, on the Internet, through television and movies, and at home.

Principal Subsidiaries

Scholastic Inc.; Scholastic Entertainment, Inc.; Scholastic Book Clubs, Inc.; SE Distribution Inc.; Lectorum Publications, Inc.; The Electronic Bookshelf, Inc.; Red House Book Clubs Ltd. (England); Scholastic Canada Ltd.; Scholastic Publications Ltd. (England); Scholastic Australia Pty. Ltd.; Scholastic New Zealand Ltd.; Scholastic Mexico S.A. de C.V.

Further Reading

Block, Valerie, "A Hard Lesson: Scholastic Recovers After Horror Story," *Crain's New York Business,* October 19, 1998, p. 1.

Cassidy, Neil, "Scholastic Sheds Biz Books," *Folio: The Magazine for Magazine Management,* January 1998, p. 13.

Kelly, Keith J., "New York Publishers Scholastic Corp. Sells Two Computer Magazines," *Knight-Ridder/Tribune Business News,* December 15, 1997.

Kindel, Stephen, "When Girls Put Down Their Barbies: Hit Products, Great Demographics and Education Reform Make Staid Scholastic a Hot Publisher," *Financial World,* April 13, 1993, p. 52.

Lippert, Jack, *Scholastic: A Publishing Adventure,* New York: Scholastic Book Services, 1979.

"Milestones: A Concise Look at Scholastic Inc.'s History," at http://www.scholastic.com/aboutscholastic/info/milestones.htm.

Milliot, Jim, "Big Drop at Retail Hurts Scholastic in Fiscal '97," *Publishers Weekly,* September 8, 1997, p. 11.

——, "Scholastic Has Small Profit on 4% Sales Gain, to $966 Million," *Publishers Weekly,* July 21, 1997, p. 108.

——, "Scholastic Plans Consolidation After 'Overexpansion,'" *Publishers Weekly,* May 5, 1997, p. 10.

——, "Scholastic Sales Up 24% But Charges Hurt Earnings," *Publishers Weekly,* July 29, 1996, p. 11.

——, "Scholastic Says Its Turnaround Is on Track," *Publishers Weekly,* December 22, 1997, p. 15.

"Scholastic Acquires Assets of Pages Book Fairs for $10.5 Million," company press release, June 25, 1998, at http://www.scholastic.com/aboutscholastic/invrel/press/980625.htm

"Scholastic Acquires *The Electronic Bookshelf,*" company press release, April 20, 1998, at http://www.scholastic.com/aboutscholastic/invrel/press/98april20.htm

"Scholastic Agrees To Buy Red House," company press release, November 19, 1996, at http://www.scholastic.com/aboutscholastic/invrel/press/96nov19.htm

"Scholastic Inc. Acquires QED, One of the Country's Leading Education Technology Market Research and Database Firms," company press release, January 21, 1999, at http://www.scholastic.com/aboutscholastic/invrel/press/1.21.99.htm

"Scholastic Slapped with More Suits," *Publishers Weekly,* June 16, 1997, p. 19.

—Elizabeth Rourke
—updated by David Bianco

sea containers
Sea Containers Services Limited

Sea Containers Ltd.

41 Cedar Avenue
P.O. Box HM 1179
Hamilton HM EX
Bermuda
(441) 295-2444
Fax: (441) 292-8666
Web site: http://www.seacontainers.com

Sea Containers House
20 Upper Ground
London SE 1 9PF
United Kingdom
0171-805-5000
Fax: 0171-805-5900

Public Company
Founded: 1965
Employees: 8,000
Sales: $1.267 billion (1998)
Stock Exchanges: New York Pacific London
Ticker Symbol: SCRA; SCRB
NAIC: 483212 Inland Water Passenger Transportation;
483211 Inland Water Freight Transportation; 48832
Marine Cargo Handling; 332439 Other Metal Container Manufacturing; 72111 Hotels (Except Casino
Hotels) & Motels; 72211 Full-Service Restaurants

Sea Containers Ltd. (SCL) operates in more than 80 countries through three main businesses. In mid-1999 its passenger transport division operated 21 ferry routes, ranging from cross-Channel to between Wall Street, Manhattan, and Brooklyn; high-speed passenger trains between London and Scotland; and three ports in England. The leisure division owned or managed 23 luxury hotels on five continents, five tourist trains, two restaurants, and a river cruise ship. These properties included New York's ''21'' Club, the venerable Orient Express train, and the Copacabana Palace Hotel in Rio de Janeiro. The company's largest business, marine container leasing, was conducted pri-

marily through GE SeaCo SRL, a 50/50 joint venture with GE Capital Corporation. SCL also made and repaired marine containers and held several patents. Other company activities included property development, fruit farming, and publishing. Registered in Bermuda, the company was based in London and owned primarily by U.S. stockholders. With its ferries and leisure divisions accounting for 60 percent of its revenue, Sea Containers announced in 1999 that it was considering a name change to more accurately reflect its business.

The First Years: 1965–75

James B. Sherwood founded Sea Containers Inc. in 1965, with initial capital of $100,000. Born in Pennsylvania, Sherwood grew up in Lexington, Kentucky and earned a degree in economics at Yale. He learned about shipping first in the U.S. Navy, spending three years as a cargo officer, and then working for U.S. Lines and CTI for six years.

The company leased cargo containers to ocean carriers and shippers. Initially providing standard steel dry cargo containers, the company soon began offering refrigerated boxes (reefers), tanks, and other specialized types of containers. It also bought and operated its own fleet of small containerships. These were particularly useful in the Mideast for transporting cargo from bigger ships that could not get into the crowded ports. The fleet and the specialization contributed to nine years of earnings increases, despite a global recession and reduced international trade. During this period, Sea Containers established two subsidiaries, Sea Containers Atlantic, based in Bermuda, and Sea Containers Pacific, out of Hong Kong. For 1975, when world trade dropped by six percent, the company's earnings grew by 60 percent on sales of $45 million. Most of its competitors in the fast-growing business saw earnings drop sharply, or even experienced losses. ''We have a larger percentage of our fleet fully paid for, or nearly so, and this enabled us to take lower charter rates and still have a positive cash flow from our tonnage,'' Sherwood explained in a 1976 *Forbes* article.

But Sherwood had more interests than his shipping business. That year he wrote and published *James Sherwood's Discriminating Guide to London,* a gourmet dining and shopping guide.

Pairing Shares: 1976–83

In 1976 world trade began growing again and the U.S. Congress returned to exploring how to tax reinvested foreign earnings, such as those from ships flying under foreign flags. Sea Containers Inc. made its Bermuda subsidiary an independent company, to lease ships, containers, and cranes in Europe, the Mideast, South America, and Africa. The new company's shares became a dividend for owners of Sea Containers and were listed on the New York Stock Exchange on a "paired" basis along with the parent. Under the law, a shareholder had to buy or sell equal amounts of stock in both companies at once, and stocks actually were printed back-to-back, giving rise to the term "stapled stock." As a result of this maneuver, New York-based Sea Container's growth would be much slower, whereas Sea Container Atlantic's earnings were not subject to U.S. corporate taxes. Sea Containers and Sea Containers Atlantic were not the only U.S. companies with this arrangement. Four others, including Santa Anita Consolidated Inc., the California racetrack, traded as "stapled shares."

While arranging this reorganization and overseeing shipping and leasing operations that brought in $56.5 million in revenue for the year, Sherwood started what he called his "frivolous ventures," buying the luxurious Hotel Cipriani in Venice. Acquired mainly as a tax loss, the hotel turned a profit within two years and laid the foundation for what would become the company's leisure business.

During the rest of the decade, the container leasing business boomed. In 1977 Sea Container's revenues were up more than 50 percent to $90 million, with $26 million in profits. The following year, the company earned nearly $32 million on revenues of $163 million.

Sherwood and his wife Shirley began collecting vintage railroad sleeper and parlor cars in 1978. Four years later, with 35 restored antique railroad cars (and some 250 recreated silk-shaded lamps, bud vases, dinner plates, and other artifacts), they reinaugurated the Venice Simplon Orient Express. The trains ran from London to Venice, taking 24 hours to complete the 926-mile trip.

Also in 1982, the two paired companies changed their names and clarified, respectively, their business focus. The New York company, the original Sea Containers, became SeaCo Inc., the owner of the Orient Express train, property, and hotel interests, including a hotel in Florence, Italy, and the Lodge in Vail, Colorado. Bermuda-based Sea Containers Atlantic, which became Sea Containers Ltd., concentrated on the shipping business.

Two Separate Companies: 1984–88

In 1984 the two companies unstapled, having saved about $65 million in U.S. taxes since the arrangement began in 1976, according to a 1984 Forbes article. Again the IRS provided the impetus, as it moved to force all such pairs to separate by 1987. Under the restructuring, SeaCo Inc. got out of the container and ship leasing business all together, selling most of those assets to Sea Containers Ltd. Sherwood, however, remained president of both companies.

Although registered in Bermuda, Sea Containers Ltd. operated out of London. It took advantage of the privatization occurring under the Thatcher government to purchase Sealink U.K. Ltd., the ferry subsidiary of the government-owned rail service. The $86.9 million price bought the company 37 ships on 24 routes to Ireland and Europe, ferry services on Lake Windermere and the Thames River, and facilities at ten harbors.

In 1985 Sea Containers bid unsuccessfully on a cross-Channel link with the Channel Expressway, a twin-bore road tunnel and a separate rail tunnel. The same year the company began joint marketing of commercial ship designs that could be converted quickly to auxiliary helicopter carriers in wartime. The idea was born in 1982 during the Falklands war, when containerships, with their strong main decks, proved able to support helicopters.

Meanwhile, SeaCo changed its name to Orient-Express Hotels Inc., hoping that name would help give it more prominence. By 1986, the company was strapped for cash, due to its inability to sell its containerships quickly at the price Sherwood wanted and the drop in the number of American tourists booking at its European luxury hotels or riding the Orient Express.

Sea Containers experienced its first loss ever in 1986, primarily because of overcapacity in the industry and the failure of several large shipping companies. Taking the traditional route of closing money-losing ferry and freight routes, laying off workers, and selling off surplus containers and ships, Sherwood got the company back on track. Over the next two years, he bought more of the specialty type containers, refurbished ferries, bought Hoverspeed (U.K.)—a cross-Channel ferry competitor, announced plans to launch an express train service from Thailand through Malaysia to Singapore, and began building residential housing on real estate around the company's U.K. ports.

By 1988, the industry's excess capacity had vanished through consolidation. The freshness of produce was becoming increasingly important to consumers, particularly in the United States, and companies such as Dole, United Brands, and Del Monte wanted refrigerated and tank containers for their bananas and other fruits. With those reefers and other specialty boxes making up 70 percent of its container fleet, Sea Containers had little trouble leasing its inventory. But the number three container lessor in the world was about to run into a storm.

A Restructured Sea Containers: 1989–94

In 1989 Swedish shipper Stena AB bought an eight percent stake in the company. That move initiated a year-long takeover battle, with lawsuits and a stock buyback. Sea Containers ended up selling its Sealinks ferry operations to Stena and its dry cargo and tank containers to Tiphook PLC, partners in the takeover bid. The price of the deal, $1.14 billion.

The slimmed-down Sea Containers, although now the world's sixth largest container leasing company, remained the biggest in terms of refrigerated and specialized containers. It also kept its extensive hotel, property, and container manufacturing interests. Sherwood quickly began rebuilding the company's dry freight container fleet.

He also caused a big flap on June 23, 1990, when the Hoverspeed SeaCat ''Hoverspeed Great Britain'' broke the trans-Atlantic speed record for passenger ships and won the prestigious Hales Trophy, the Blue Riband of the Atlantic. Many traditionalists were upset at the idea that a twin-hulled ferry would hold an award associated with luxury liners such as *Normandie* and *United States.* But Hoverspeed held the trophy for eight years, until its record of three days, seven hours, 54 minutes, with an average speed of 37 knots, was broken.

With the SeaCat, the company began operating the world's first car-carrying high-speed catamarans across the Channel between Dover and Calais. The Hoverspeed Great Britain was soon joined by other SeaCats in the company's ferry fleet, replacing Hoverspeed's hovercraft, and by 1993, there were six SeaCat routes, including one between Argentina and Uruguay and one in Australia. Revenge may have been sweet, as Stena AB laid off workers in 1991 because of mounting losses in the U.K. ferry operations it bought from Sea Containers.

Although Sea Containers also was experiencing losses in its ferry operations, the company continued to make acquisitions—including new SeaCats, the Copacabana Palace in Rio, and, at a price of $55 million, the Windsor Court Hotel in New Orleans. That purchase brought to 11 the number of hotels managed or owned by Orient Express Hotels Inc. To finance its acquisitions and capital expenditures, such as berths for the SeaCats, Sea Containers carried some $649 million in long-term debt in 1991.

Among the company's other forward-looking activities was the work going on in its container factories, including materials to reduce the weight of containers and new refrigerants to comply with new international regulations that would take effect in 1995. With factories in Britain, Singapore, and Brazil, Sea Containers was a major container manufacturer, producing some 60 different types of containers. The company was willing to build specialty containers on speculation to test customer reaction and was the first to develop refrigerated tank containers. Other products included open-top, flat-rack, and ventilation containers. In 1993 it had about 46 percent of the specialty leasing market.

During 1992, in what may have been a defense against another takeover attempt, Sea Containers announced a dual capitalization proposal. It would issue two classes of common shares, with Class A paying higher cash dividends but allotted fewer voting rights. The proposal would allow the company to increase the number of shares it was authorized to issue, giving it greater financial flexibility.

Continuing to expand, the company explored but eventually backed out of running a car ferry between Seattle and Victoria. More successfully, in 1993, it launched the Eastern & Oriental Express from Singapore to Bangkok, a 41-hour, 1,207-mile route. The train included three dining cars, two bar cars, an observation car, five service or baggage cars, and 11 sleeping cars, with everything air-conditioned. The undertaking cost Sea Containers some $25 million. Shirley Sherwood explained to Andrew Ranard of the *International Herald Tribune,* ''We would like to give [people] the chance to see the countryside, the life that seems to happen along the track—the villages, rice paddies, the water buffalo.''

The year 1994 was a busy year for the company. It saw the opening of the Chunnel, the tunnel under the English Channel. Sea Containers had prepared for a drop in ferry traffic by shifting some of its ferries to routes in the Southern Hemisphere. That same year, the company bought Orient-Express Hotels Inc. in a stock exchange. The two companies were together again, but what had once been the subsidiary, Sea Containers Atlantic, was now the parent.

Continuing To Diversify: 1995–97

During the second half of the decade, Sea Containers expanded its leisure properties with the purchase of the ''21'' Club in New York City and the launch of its river cruise ship, the Road to Mandalay, operating in Myanmar. It also bought up luxury hotels, including a share in Charleston Place, in historic Charleston, South Carolina; Reid's Hotel on the island of Madeira; La Samanna beach resort in St. Martin, French West Indies; and Hotel da Lapa in Lisbon. Orient-Express Hotels managed these and also took over management of non-Sea Container properties, including the Hotel de la Cite in Carcassonne, France and the Bora Bora Lagoon Resort in the South Pacific Society Islands.

The passenger transport division also grew. In 1996 the company was awarded the InterCity East Coast rail franchise in the final privatization effort by the John Major government. Sea Containers renamed the line, which ran from London to Scotland and included the ''Flying Scotsman'' train, the Great North Eastern Railway Ltd. The following year the company signed an agreement to buy two Italian-built tilting trains for the line, to come into service in 2000. New ferry services opened between Scotland and Northern Ireland and between Liverpool and Dublin and, in 1997, the company launched its SuperSeaCat on the Dover-Calais ferry route. The new ship, a monohull vessel that could carry 774 passengers and 175 cars, was slightly faster than the two-hulled SeaCats that carried up to 600 passengers. At $30 million a ship, they were also less expensive to build than other large single-hulled ferries. That year, the company's combined profits from passenger transport and leisure activities for the first time exceeded those from container leasing.

But the company was not ignoring its container business, introducing a new patented SeaCell unit that was as wide as two-pallet containers and could be easily moved in ordinary container ships, unlike other two-pallet wide dry cargo units. In 1997 the company created a new means of financing its container fleet. ''The ability to securitize container debt in the commercial paper market enables the company to increase its container leasing business significantly without many of the constraints normally imposed by banks,'' the company explained in a *Journal of Commerce* article. What Sea Containers did was to create negotiable commercial paper, like a bond or stock, that was secured by cargo containers. The cost of the new notes was less than the interest paid to banks for lines of credit and enabled the company to reduce its long-term debt by a full percent a year, a savings of at least $2 million annually.

1998 to the Present

The company's big news in 1998 was the formation of a 50/50 joint venture with GE Capital Corporation. This new entity, GE SeaCo SRL, combined the container fleets of Sea Containers and Genstar, becoming one of the largest marine container operating lessors in the world. Sea Containers continued to operate its own leasing business in countries in which GE Capital did not want to operate.

On the ferry side, the company bought 50 percent of Holyman Sally Ltd., taking over management of its United Kingdom-to-Belgium passenger and car ferry services, and became a majority shareholder in Neptun Maritime Oyj, the leading cruise ferry operator in the Baltic. In 1999 the company entered the U.S. ferry market, buying Express Navigation Inc. for $5 million and taking over ferry service between ports in New Jersey, Wall Street in Manhattan, and Brooklyn. The number of tourist trains grew to five, with the acquisition of Regency Rail Cruises in the United Kingdom and the assumption of the management of the Great South Pacific Express, a luxury train in Queensland, Australia. Orient-Express Hotels bought a third hotel in Portugal, two in Peru, and one each in Virginia and Maryland. This brought to 23 the number of owned and managed hotels.

New ferry routes and new hotels, combined with falling lease rates for marine containers, pointed the direction of the company. Sherwood reiterated it at Sea Container's 1999 annual meeting: "For several years our strategy has been to transform the company from what was primarily a marine container asset leasing business into a company which is largely passenger transportation and leisure based." To underscore the changing focus, he also announced that a name change would be proposed before the end of the year.

Principal Subsidiaries

Orient-Express Hotels Inc.; Sea Containers Ferries Ltd.; Hoverspeed Ltd.; GE SeaCo SRL.

Further Reading

Batchelor, Charles, "Tilting Trains Service Set to Start in 2000," *Financial Times* (London), September 10, 1997, p. 10.

Beman, Lewis, et. al., "Orient Express," *Fortune,* June 5, 1978, p. 22.

Berss, Dorman Marcia, "Kicked While He Was Down," *Forbes,* January 30, 1984, p. 104.

"Blue Riband of the Atlantic Exhibition," Hoverspeed press release, October 22, 1998.

"Britain Is Selling Ferry Line," *New York Times,* July 19, 1984, p. D15.

"The Chunnel's Railpolitik," *Economist* (U.S. Edition), December 14, 1985, p. 54.

Gadsden, James, "What the Credit Analyst Should Know About Securitization," *Business Credit,* March 1998, p. 54.

Heins, John, "Back on Course," *Forbes,* October 31, 1988, p. 66.

Jacobs, Jon, "Catamaran Sets Speed Record," *Journal of Commerce,* June 26, 1990, p. 1B.

Jones, John A., "Sea Containers Breaks Seasonal Loss as Traffic Picks Up," *Investor's Business Daily,* May 24, 1993, p. 38.

Lague, Louise, "All Aboard, Sports!," *People,* June 28, 1982, p. 37.

Lueck, Thomas J., "Big Ferry Operator to Enter New York Market," *New York Times,* January 30, 1999, p. B5.

"Orient Express Hotels: Nostalgia Can Cost You Dear," *Economist* (U.S. Edition), December 6, 1986, p. 86.

Porter, Janet, "Sea Containers Quick to Rebuild Box Fleet," *Journal of Commerce,* September 30, 1991, p. 1A.

Ranard, Andrew, "Train as Museum: Orient Express Reaches the Orient at Last," *International Herald Tribune,* May 21, 1993.

"Sea Containers Completes Sale of Container and Ferry Assets for $1.14 Billion," *PR Newswire,* April 9, 1990.

Sea Containers Ltd., "Sea Containers Ltd. Expects Substantial Increase," press release, June 9, 1999.

"Sea Containers Proposes To Offer Dual Capitalization," *Journal of Commerce,* March 27, 1992, p. 5B.

"Sea Containers Reaches Approximately 96% in its Exchange Offer for the Common Stock of Orient-Express Hotels," *Business Wire,* July 1, 1994.

"SeaCo Launches Two SuperSeaCats," *Travel Trade Gazette UK & Ireland,* June 25, 1997, p. 43.

"SeaCo Inc. and Sea Containers Ltd. To De-Pair," *PR Newswire,* January 12, 1984.

"Siamese Shares," *Forbes,* September 1, 1980, p. 59.

Stetkiewica, Christian, "Sea Ups Convertible Offer To Satisfy Strong Demand," *Investment Dealers' Digest,* July 29, 1991, p. 18.

"The Terrible Worry . . . ," *Forbes,* July 15, 1976, p. 33.

Tirschwell, Peter, "Box Lessor Floats New Financing Tool," *Journal of Commerce,* January 23, 1997, p. 1B.

" '21' Club Sold to London-Based Corporation," *Associated Press,* September 14, 1995.

"Westland, Shipbuilders Plan Convertible Helicopter Carrier," *Aviation Week and Space Technology,* January 14, 1985, p. 104.

—Ellen D. Wernick

Second Harvest

116 S. Michigan Avenue
Suite #4
Chicago, Illinois 60603-6001
U.S.A.
(312) 263-2303
Fax: (312) 263-5626
Web site: http://www.secondharvest.org

Non-Profit Company
Incorporated: 1979
Employees: 55
Sales: $400 million (1998 est.)
NAIC: 624210 Food Banks

Second Harvest is the largest not-for-profit domestic hunger-relief organization in the United States. The organization provides food to people that are unable to purchase it themselves by raising money for and distributing food and other grocery products through an extensive and comprehensive network of food banks across the United States. In addition, the organization sees its mission as partly educational in raising the American public's level of awareness about the nature of hunger in the United States. Second Harvest works closely with over 50,000 local hunger-relief agencies and organizations, including soup kitchens, day care centers, grassroots youth programs in urban areas, senior centers, homeless shelters, women's shelters, and food pantries. The organization has arranged to secure surplus food from food growers, distributors, retail grocery stores, and food processors, including such corporate giants as General Mills, Kraft, Nabisco, Pillsbury, Proctor & Gamble, and Kellogg. Approximately 26 million Americans were assisted by the Second Harvest food network in 1998, including households with working individuals, women, children, and the elderly. More than one billion pounds of food and grocery products were distributed through its network during the same year. What might be the most impressive accomplishment of Second Harvest is that the organization distributes 34 pounds of food and grocery products for every dollar that it receives as a donation.

Early History

The creation of Second Harvest arose out of an idea put into practice by John Van Hengel. A successful businessman who lived and worked most of his life in Phoenix, Arizona, Van Hengel wanted to give something back to the community after he decided to retire. Not quite sure what to devote his energy to, he volunteered at a local soup kitchen operating in one of the poorer areas of Phoenix. Van Hengel soon noticed that the soup kitchen was not only overcrowded, but that there was a need for much larger quantities of food and produce. Having been well connected in the Phoenix business community for years, Van Hengel began to solicit food donations from many of the businesspeople that he had come to know. Initially, much of the food that he solicited would have otherwise gone to waste, but within a short period of time the soup kitchen was overwhelmed with food and grocery product donations. As a good entrepreneur does when he sees an opportunity, Van Hengel established a warehouse facility where he began to stock the donations, and then distribute them to charitable agencies and organizations throughout the Phoenix area that were feeding needy people. Thus the first food bank was developed by Van Hengel during the late 1960s, and the concept has been refined and replicated across the United States ever since.

During the early 1970s, people from around the nation heard about Van Hengel's charitable work in Phoenix, and began to take notice of the food bank concept. Within a few short years, food banks modeled on Van Hengel's warehouse facility were started in larger cities throughout the country, including New York, Los Angeles, Denver, Chicago, Atlanta, Minneapolis, Boston, Philadelphia, and San Francisco. All of these food banks provided similar services to the community, relying primarily on the corporate sector and retail groceries in the local area to donate food products so that disadvantaged people could eat a more nutritious and well-balanced meal.

It was in 1976, however, that the food bank concept was given the added impetus to make it a national program. The 1976 Tax Reform Act significantly altered the tax structure for most for-profit corporations by making it financially advantageous for large and small companies alike to donate their products to charities. The pharmaceutical industry was espe-

Company Perspectives:

Feed hungry people by soliciting and judiciously distributing food and grocery products through a nationwide network of certified affiliate food banks, and educate the public about the nature of and solutions to the problems of hunger. In carrying out its mission, Second Harvest and the National Network of Food Banks are committed to standards of performance represented by the following values in which we believe: Integrity: We will be open and honest in all relationships, dealings and transactions. We will strive to earn and convey trust through openness and honesty. Stewardship of Resources: We will keep faith with the public trust through the efficient and compassionate use of resources entrusted to us. We will strive to be mindful that the mission is accomplished through the generosity of others. Accountability: We will set clear standards for the benchmark against which to measure competence, efficiency and effectiveness of mission. We will embrace a twofold responsibility through accountability: first, for policy, decisions and actions; and second, for complete, accurate and clear record keeping and report information. Service: We will commit to provide excellent service. We will continually strive to study, understand and meet the changing needs with competence and compassion.

cially affected by the Tax Reform Act, since companies that manufactured drugs were then able to donate large quantities of expired items—their effectiveness still intact—in accordance with rules established by the Food and Drug Administration. Food processors and food product companies were also able to contribute large amounts of food for charitable causes and take a tax deduction. The result of the 1976 Tax Reform Act was far-reaching, therefore, since food banks like the one Van Hengel had started were now able to procure donated food products much more easily.

Just as important as the Tax Reform Act was the large grant that Van Hengel received from the federal government to establish a comprehensive network of food banks throughout the country. For nearly ten years, Van Hengel had worked assiduously to develop an efficient and effective food bank facility in Phoenix. By the late 1970s, his work had not only been replicated by other groups across the nation, but state and federal government representatives had noticed Van Hengel's ability to provide a genuine service that assisted people who were themselves unable to purchase enough food to eat. As Van Hengel laid the foundation for a national network of food banks, and began to devise a strategic plan for expanding his activities, many of the people who were working closely with him suggested that he form his own not-for-profit charitable organization to develop the food bank concept. The federal government agreed, and was more than happy to provide additional funding for building the capacities of a new organization devoted to eradicating hunger in America. Second Harvest was formally incorporated in 1979 as a charitable organization, and rapidly developed into a clearinghouse for food and grocery product contributions from national and multinational corporations

based in the United States. As a good businessman, Van Hengel developed and quickly implemented a comprehensive list of standards that he thought all food banks should follow, including detailed recommendations for quality control, the establishment of storage facilities, and the responsibilities of management. This list of recommendations was enthusiastically received by almost everyone associated with the food bank concept, and served as the national guideline for those groups who wanted to establish a food bank.

Addressing the Problem of Hunger During the 1980s

By the end of 1982, the large source of funding that had been previously provided by the federal government was discontinued. Representatives of the government had fulfilled their pledge to help the food bank concept expand across the United States and, by the time federal funding for the program was curtailed, the goal had been attained. As a result, Second Harvest, as well as other food bank programs, were forced to search for funding from alternative sources. Management at the nonprofit organization decided to pursue the corporate sector as a possibility for funding Second Harvest programs, and began to look for a firm within the food products industry.

With a little bit of luck, and not a little persistence, the people at Second Harvest were able to convince Pillsbury Corporation to help them implement the vision of food for the poor in the United States. Pillsbury, of course, was one of the nation's leading producers of grocery items, including Green Giant frozen foods, Pillsbury brand-name refrigerated dough products, Hungry Jack canned and frozen meat products, Progresso soup, and many other types of products for the international consumer market, as well as a major supplier of baking goods to the food service and commercial baking industries. During the early 1980s, Second Harvest and Pillsbury Corporation formed a unique partnership to support Production Alliance, a revolutionary program in which Pillsbury agreed to be the first firm among the top food products companies to produce high-quality food items exclusively for donation to Second Harvest and its network of food banks that fed hungry people. Up until that time, food banks throughout the country, including Second Harvest, had been forced to rely upon surplus, slightly damaged, or discontinued food products as the primary source of contributions for their food supply to the hungry. In a groundbreaking agreement, Pillsbury agreed to use a philanthropic budget and its available production capacity to make high-quality, top-of-the-line food products for donation to Second Harvest and the organizations and agencies working within its food bank network. In just a short time, Pillsbury's participation as the initial corporate partner in support of the Production Alliance spurred numerous other major firms in the food industry to follow suit.

By the time Second Harvest relocated its headquarters from Phoenix, Arizona, to Chicago, Illinois, in 1984, there were food banks in almost every major city across the United States, many of which were providing very good services to the hungry due to the Production Alliance program and the growing number of corporate partnerships that resulted in larger and larger high-quality food donations. Since food banks were sprouting up throughout the country, the network expansion that Second Harvest had achieved on its own began to slow down, and management decided to shift its focus to improving the organization's programs that were currently operating. Along with this shift in focus, management also implemented a comprehensive internal evaluation process that led to an increased efficiency in the activities of the Second Harvest food bank network, and that ultimately resulted in greater amounts of food distributed through the network to people in need. As the decade of the 1980s drew to a close, Second Harvest had transformed itself from a largely untrained volunteer organization to a sophisticated, highly professional agency whose reputation continued to grow as it was able to collect and distribute ever-increasing amounts of donated food products to feed the hungry.

The 1990s and Beyond

When Second Harvest was established in 1979, the people working as volunteers sorting the canned goods at food banks or serving meals at the local soup kitchens all felt that their services would not be needed when the U.S. economy improved. Unfortunately, this was not what happened. Even though the economy expanded during the 1980s and 1990s, unemployment rates continued to increase, with over 13 percent of the U.S. population living at or below the poverty line. According to statistics collected by the Census Bureau, poverty was on the increase due to the reduction of government sponsored support programs and safety nets, and the new economy which did not welcome unskilled workers.

For the reasons outlined above, the people who founded Second Harvest and those from a second generation who now work there took it upon themselves to address the growing problem of hunger in the United States. One of their most successful partnerships has been with corporations in the dairy industry. In the mid-1990s, the company formed a partnership with Dean Foods, with the corporation becoming one of the first private-label donors to the Second Harvest food bank network.

Another high-profile firm that agreed to a partnership was Land O'Lakes. The company soon began making ongoing donations that included everything from financial support to sour cream to butter. Kraft joined in partnership as well, making a $200,000 donation in order to ship fresh foods to organizations working within the Second Harvest food bank network. Other large corporate donations during the mid-1990s arrived from General Mills, Borden, and Nabisco.

At the end of the 20th century, Second Harvest had developed into the largest charitable hunger-relief organization in the United States. The organization distributed over one billion pounds of grocery products and other kinds of donated foods in 1998 through a network of over 200 food banks. For more than 26 million hungry people—American men, women, and children—the food that Second Harvest provided was what kept them alive.

Further Reading

Balu, Rekha, "Food Industry's Efficiency Poses Dilemma for Charity," *Wall Street Journal,* December 18, 1998, p. B4.
"The Dairy Industry Delivers," *Dairy Foods,* February 1998, p. 22.
Harper, Roseanne, "Gooding's Chefs' Demo Is Recipe for Aid to Poor," *Supermarket News,* February 28, 1998, p.13.
McDonald, Barbara, "Kraft, Chains Aid Second Harvest for Hungry," *Supermarket News,* December 21, 1998, p. 31.
"Second Harvest Recognizes Burger King As Special Donor," *Nation's Restaurant News,* October 12, 1998, p. 90.
Seligman, Dan, "Is Philanthropy Irrational?," *Forbes,* June 1, 1998, p. 94.
Stark, Ellen, "Which Charities Merit Your Money," *Money,* November 1996, p. 100.
"Your Money Goes Far at These A+ Charities," *Money,* December 15, 1997, p. 27.

—Thomas Derdak

Seminis, Inc.

1905 Lirio Avenue
Saticoy, California 93004-4206
U.S.A.
(805) 647-1572
(800) 927-4769
Fax: (805) 647-8963
Web site: http://www.seminis.com

68% Owned Subsidiary of Savia S.A. de C.V.
Incorporated: 1995
Employees: 3,000
Sales: $428.42 million (1998)
Stock Exchanges: NASDAQ
Ticker Symbol: SMNS
NAIC: 115114 Postharvest Crop Activities (Except
   Cotton Ginning); 54171 Research & Development in
   the Physical, Engineering & Life Sciences

Seminis, Inc. is the world's largest producer of vegetable and fruit seeds, best known under the brand names of Asgrow, Petoseed, and Royal Sluis. The California-based company develops vegetable and fruit hybrids and varieties with desirable traits that result in advantages such as higher crop yields, superior disease resistance, and tolerance to environmental stress. The company also maintains biotechnology research laboratories, principally in California, France, and the Netherlands, in which it reinvests some 12 percent of the money generated by sales. Seminis is 68 percent-owned by the Mexican agricultural leader Savia S.A. de C.V., formerly known as Empresas La Moderna or ELM. The remaining stock was made public on the NASDAQ exchange in June 1999.

Seminis's Predecessor Companies

Seminis was founded in 1995 by the merger of Asgrow Seed Co. with Petoseed Co. Inc. and Royal Sluis. Asgrow had been acquired by Empresas La Moderna from the Upjohn Co. the previous year, a purchase that consisted of a product line of more than 16 major species of vegetable seeds, principally peas, beans, processing tomatoes, cucumbers, and lettuce seeds, and agronomic (field crop) seeds for corn, soybeans, sorghum, sunflowers, and other varieties. Asgrow had revenues of $306 million in 1994.

The business that developed into Asgrow was founded as the Everett B. Clark Seed Co. in 1856 on a half acre in Orange, Connecticut. In 1927 Arthur B. Clark, the founder's son, merged the company with two others to form Associated Seed Growers, Inc. for the development, production, and wholesale distribution of vegetable seed in the United States. In 1956, when it celebrated its centennial, the company had its headquarters in New Haven, Connecticut, and its eastern breeding station in Orange, but 90 percent of its output was being grown west of the Rocky Mountains, mainly in California and southern Idaho. Associated Seed had six other breeder stations and, with four million acres planted each year, was the largest breeder and grower of vegetable seed in the world. Its biggest customers were vegetable freezers and canners.

Commonly called Asgrow, Associated Seed officially took as its name Asgrow Seed Co. in 1959. By 1962 it was operating 28 retail farm-supply stores in the United States and had subsidiaries in Argentina, Canada, Germany, Italy, and Mexico. Asgrow's research, which since 1870 had resulted in more than 300 new strains of vegetables, had as its focal point a research center in Twin Falls, Idaho. In 1965 (the fiscal year ended June 30, 1965) agricultural chemicals and lawn- and garden-care products were almost as important to Asgrow as seeds, accounting for 45 percent of the company's record revenues of $24.4 million. The company was sold to Upjohn in 1968. In 1967, its last full year as an independent company, Asgrow had net sales of $27.5 million and net income of $1 million.

Asgrow, at the time of its acquisition by ELM, had about 1,100 employees around the world and was producing and marketing more than 600 varieties of more than 20 different species of crops. It had 23 agronomic research stations and 14 vegetable research facilities, including 23 in the United States and other Latin American and European nations. Of its $306 million in annual sales, 68 percent was derived from North America and 24 percent from Europe.

In October 1995 ELM also purchased the Petoseed and Royal Sluis brands from Chicago-based George J. Ball Inc. in a stock exchange valued at $320 million. ELM took ownership of 60 percent of the new company, called Seminis, with an option to increase its share over the next few years. ELM raised its stake in Seminis in January 1998 to 92 percent.

Seminis based itself at Petoseed's headquarters in Saticoy, California. Petroseed had originated from the partnership of Howard Peto and Vic Hollar, who bought a Colorado company, R.H. James Seed Co., in 1950. They renamed the business Peto-Hollar and opened a unit in Ventura, California, for the production of tomato seeds. This partnership was dissolved in 1953, and the California branch became Petoseed. Head offices were established in Saticoy in 1958.

At this time much of the basic research into new vegetable hybrids was being performed at universities with government money, but federal budget cuts subsequently opened up an opportunity for private companies such as Petoseed, which developed tomatoes, peppers, squash, and onions with such desirable traits as resistance to disease and insects. It became the world's leading tomato seed company and in 1995 was producing more than 20 major species of vegetable seeds, including peppers, onions, tomatoes, melons, cauliflower, and cucumbers, in about 110 countries. Its research facilities, stretching from Chile to as far east as Thailand, were designing hybrid vegetables with each country's climate and diet in mind.

Royal Sluis, a financially troubled Dutch company founded in 1870, had been acquired by George J. Ball in July 1994. Royal Sluis accounted for nearly half of Petoseed's revenues of $229.6 million in 1995.

Focusing on Genetic Engineering in the 1990s

The combined company ranked itself among the leading vegetable and agronomic seed producers in the world, with 22 percent of the global market, annual revenues of $535 million, and 1,500 employees. In vegetable seed, Seminis claimed to be number one. Among its holdings was the world's largest privately held collection of vegetable and fruit germplasms. Approximately 63 percent of Seminis's sales in 1995 were from vegetable seeds, with the balance agronomic. About one-half of its seed sales were in Canada, Mexico, and the United States, and about 45 percent in Europe. The company was providing commercial growers and food processors with an extensive selection of proprietary hybrid seeds capable of growing under different climate and soil conditions and meeting the individual needs of its customers around the world.

The company was, in 1996, employing genetic engineering in tomatoes, peppers, melons, cucumbers, carrots, and other crops. That year Seminis Vegetable Seeds Inc., a wholly owned subsidiary, established research headquarters at Petoseed's Woodland, California, research site. This subsidiary was coordinating research by 500 employees at 36 stations around the world and marketing five seed brands in 110 countries.

In its first year of operation, Seminis (through the vegetable-seeds subsidiary) marketed its first genetically engineered product, a tomato used in sauces, pastes, and other processed products. Developed by researchers of Petoseed, Zeneca Plant Science of London (a unit of British chemicals giant Zeneca Group PLC), and England's University of Nottingham, this tomato had been genetically modified to maintain its natural pectin level as it ripened, reducing spoilage after harvesting. Processed products from this new tomato variety became available in United Kingdom supermarkets in 1996. The tomatoes, grown and processed in Mexico and the United States, had received U.S. Department of Agriculture approval.

Seminis, through ELM, formed a partnership with Monsanto Co. in 1996 that enabled it to acquire access to Monsanto's patented genetic technology and gene library in order to create a broad range of disease- and insect-resistant and otherwise enhanced fruits and vegetables. The agreement gave ELM and its Seminis subsidiaries access to all Monsanto's genes at no initial cost, with revenues derived from commercialized products to be shared with Monsanto. Ed Green, Seminis Vegetable's director of plant biotechnology, told Leo Smith of the *Los Angeles Times,* ''This radically improves the ability of SVS to develop and commercialize new products.... Monsanto has done a good job developing a number of new traits in biotechnology—like insect resistance, herbicide resistance, increased sugar and others—which are going to be easy for us to test and move into products.''

In January 1997 Monsanto acquired Asgrow Agronomics, Seminis's less-profitable corn- and soybean-seed division based in Michigan, for $240 million. Seminis was now focused solely on vegetable and fruit seeds. Excluding the agronomic business sold to Monsanto, Seminis had sales of $385 million in 1996, with Europe representing 43 percent and North America 36 percent. Its sales slumped to $383 million in 1997 but advanced to $428.4 million in 1998 (the fiscal year ended September 30, 1998). Operating income dropped from $64 million in 1996 to $47 million in 1997. In 1998 Monsanto sold the vegetable-seed division of Agroceres, a Brazilian company, to Seminis Vegetable Seeds, which thereby gained three seed production units, two research stations, and 160 employees. In order to accommodate its increased staff, Seminis Vegetable Seeds, in 1997, purchased a 32-acre parcel in an Oxnard, California, business park. It was planning to build a 300,000-square-foot facility on the site for its corporate office and its Saticoy processing and distribution facility.

The Late 1990s and Beyond

Seminis, as of 1997, oversaw the Asgrow and Petoseed/Royal Sluis businesses, as well as its own distinct operations. Asgrow's principal markets were in North America and Europe, targeting commercial fresh-market vegetable producers and commercial vegetable food processors. Petoseed/Royal Sluis had its own research and development stations in the United States, the Netherlands, and France, its own subsidiaries and joint ventures, and its own networks of independent dealers and commercial food processors. The Asgrow, Petoseed, and Royal Sluis brands had separate breeding, product development, marketing, and sales teams. The Seminis brands—principally Bruinsma and Genecorp—also had these separate teams for operation on a regional or specialized basis.

In all, Seminis was maintaining 39 research and development centers in 1997, of which 20 were in the Americas, 17 in Europe, and Africa, and two in Asia. Significant programs were being maintained for more than 20 major vegetable species, yielding over 1,300 different varieties, plus ten minor species. Seminis' breeding strategy was to create fruit and vegetable hybrids and varieties that were economic to produce, had high field and marketable yields, possessed superior disease resistance, environmental tolerance and nutritional traits, and had superior external appearance and processing characteristics. New product introduction generated 24 percent of total sales in 1997.

Seminis's biotechnology programs, principally in laboratories in California, the Netherlands, and France, conducted DNA research to examine the organization and functions of plant genes in order to enable researchers to clone these genes for their reintroduction into germplasm that would be transformed into viable plants for breeding. At plant-pathology laboratories in the United States, France, Italy, the Netherlands, and Spain, Seminis scientists were targeting more than 90 different diseases that had the greatest impact on commercial vegetable production. As a result, the company was leading its industry with the widest range of disease-resistant hybrids requiring reduced or no chemical applications.

Seminis ensured distribution of quality products throughout the world by maintaining production capabilities for each variety in two locations in each hemisphere. This enabled the company to capitalize on low labor costs in certain locations by producing labor-intensive products in those areas. In the United States, seeds were being produced in Arizona, California, Idaho, Oregon, and Washington through contract production. Internationally, seeds were being produced through subsidiaries in Chile, China, France, Guatemala, Hungary, Russia, South Africa, and Thailand, and through exclusive agents using Seminis technology in Australia, Denmark, India, the Netherlands, New Zealand, and Tanzania. The four biggest production facilities were (in order of size) in Warden, Washington; Filer, Idaho; Erkhuizen, the Netherlands; and Nampa, Idaho.

Seminis marketed its five major brands worldwide both directly and through dealers. Its North American sales were mainly in the Asgrow and Petoseed brands, with Asgrow sold both directly and through dealers and Petoseed primarily through dealers. Royal Sluis was the company's dominant brand in northern Europe. All three were strong brands in southern Europe. Petoseed was the top brand in the dealer-oriented Middle East.

Asgrow and Petoseed also had strong sales in South America, where Seminis used both the direct and dealer approach. Bruinsma was sold primarily in northern Europe and the Middle East, and Genecorp was sold in the United States.

Seminis maintained, in 1997, a market share of 42 percent in South America, 38 percent in North America, and 22 percent in Europe. In the United States, it was supplying the seeds producing more than 40 percent of the commercial fruits and vegetables grown.

In 1999, ELM, now known as Savia following a merger with financial services company Segcoam, spun off a large portion of Seminis in a public stock offering in which 13 million shares were offered on the NASDAQ exchange for $15 per share. The proceeds Savia garnered were used to help pay down its own liabilities which had grown considerably following aggressive acquisitions. With a presence in more than 120 countries, Seminis was becoming an increasingly international operation as it moved into a new century.

Further Reading

Baker, David R., ''Seeding Global Market,'' *Los Angeles Times* (Ventura County edition), December 17, 1995, pp. 1+.
''The Commercial Whirl,'' *New Yorker,* October 20, 1956, pp. 26–27.
Graebner, Lynn, ''Petoseed's Woodland Gains Clout Via Mergers,'' *The Business Journal Serving Greater Sacramento,* February 12, 1996, p. 6.
——, ''Woodland Enjoys Fruits of Seed Firm's Input,'' *The Business Journal Serving Greater Sacramento,* August 12, 1996, p. 8.
Hrebicek, Valerie, ''Asgrow Seed Grows and Grows,'' *Investment Dealers' Digest,* September 20, 1965, pp. 21–22.
Lehr, John A., ''Tomatoes Ripe for Distribution,'' *Thousand Oaks Star & News Chronicle,* July 6, 1995, p. B8.
Mathews, Carol, ''Asgrow Has Long History of Success,'' *Investment Dealers' Digest,* November 19, 1962, pp. 21–22.
''Seeds of Latin Revolution Are Sown,'' *New York Times,* September 16, 1962, Sec. 3, pp. 1, 14.
Smith, Leo, ''Valley and Ventura County,'' *Los Angeles Times* (Ventura County edition), June 9, 1998, p. 13B.
——, ''Ventura County Review,'' *Los Angeles Times* (Ventura County edition), October 8, 1996, p. 7C.
''Yes, the UK Has Biotech Tomatoes,'' *Applied Genetics News,* 1998.

—Robert Halasz

SGI

2011 North Shoreline Boulevard
Mountain View, California 94039
U.S.A.
(650) 960-1980
Fax: (650) 932-0661
Web site: http://www.sgi.com

Public Company
Incorporated: 1982 as Silicon Graphics Inc.
Employees: 10,286
Sales: $3.1 billion (1998)
Stock Exchanges: New York
Ticker Symbol: SGI
NAIC: 334111 Computers Manufacturing; 334119 Other
   Computer Peripheral Equipment Manufacturing;
   51121 Software Publishers

Known for 17 years as Silicon Graphics Inc., SGI is one of the leading manufacturers of graphics computer systems, workstations, and supercomputers. Its history may be described as an exemplary, perhaps even archetypal, Silicon Valley success story, until lower-priced competitors and inept production methods resulted in heavy losses in the late 1990s. Founded by a high school dropout turned college professor, Silicon Graphics capitalized on pioneering technology in 3-D computer graphics to create products used in a wide variety of professions, including engineering, chemistry, and film production. The company combined technological prowess with shrewd management to produce explosive growth; within a decade of its founding, it had entered the *Fortune* 500.

The story of Silicon Graphics began in 1979, when James Clark, an electrical engineering professor at Stanford University, assembled a team of six graduate students to study the possibilities of computer graphics. Within two years, Clark's team developed a powerful semiconductor chip, which they called the Geometry Engine, that would allow small computers to produce sophisticated three-dimensional graphics simula-

tions previously the domain of large mainframes. Clark patented the Geometry Engine, and in 1982 he and his team left Stanford to found Silicon Graphics.

Established Lucrative Niche, 1980s

In 1983 the company released its first products: the IRIS 1000 graphics terminal and an accompanying software interface known as the IRIS Graphics Library. The next year Silicon Graphics released its first workstation, the IRIS 1400, and followed it in 1985 with the IRIS 2400, a workstation with a window manager. These early entries in the IRIS series targeted the middle range of the graphics workstations market—those selling for $45,000 to $100,000—and accounted for over 50 percent of all 3-D graphics workstations sold by 1988. Sales increased steeply and consistently, reaching $153 million in 1988. Within its first six years, Silicon Graphics had established a secure and lucrative niche for itself in the computer industry.

Silicon Graphics succeeded in its early years in large part because it had introduced a useful product that had drawn relatively little attention from any of its potential rivals. 3-D graphics simulations were extremely useful to mechanical engineers who wanted to assess their designs without having to build prototypes, as well as to chemists who used 3-D modeling to study molecules. Such workstations as the IRIS series provided power at a relatively affordable price and major workstation manufacturers, including Hewlett-Packard, Apollo Computer, and Sun Microsystems, were slow to focus their energies on 3-D graphics, leaving Silicon Graphics without much direct competition.

Observers also credited James Clark's technical skill and entrepreneurial sense for the company's success. The path to Silicon Valley glory was a circuitous one for Clark, who dropped out of high school in Plainview, Texas, after he was suspended for setting off a smoke bomb on a school bus. After a hitch in the Navy, he went back to school, enrolling as an undergraduate at Tulane University. He went on to earn an M.S. in physics from the University of New Orleans and a Ph.D. in computer science from the University of Utah, where he first became interested in computer graphics. Clark then committed himself to an academic career, holding teaching posts at the University of California at Santa Cruz, the New York Institute of Technology, and the University of California at Berkeley before coming to Stanford. Along the way, however, he became disenchanted with academia. "I had always seen myself as a senior professor at a university," he once told the *Business Journal—San Jose,* "but I think I learned that my strength is making things that work, rather than writing papers. Universities encourage writing a lot of papers." Hence, he departed Stanford and founded Silicon Graphics in 1982.

Once he established the company, Clark displayed the good sense to find his proper role within the operating structure and stick to it. Soon after Silicon Graphics was born, Clark brought in Edward McCracken, a veteran Hewlett-Packard executive, to run the company as president and CEO while he remained chairperson. Clark concentrated on serving as the company's technology guru, leaving McCracken to take care of the business operations. According to McCracken, this role best suited Clark's temperament: "Jim's not a day-to-day person. He works in his own time frame," he told the *Business Journal—San Jose.* McCracken continued, "He takes complex things and makes it simple. It might take a month, a day, or a year. He gets in these moods for a while where he's almost unavailable. He's most effective when he's in that mood." Clark also used this division of labor to devote more time to outside interests that included ballet, classical music, art, and stunt flying.

A useful blend of high technology and business sense enabled Silicon Graphics to move forward from its early successes. In 1987 it became the first computer company to make use of MIPS Computer Systems' innovative reduced instruction-set chip, or RISC, when it incorporated RISC architecture into its new IRIS 4D/60 workstation. Within several years, most workstations would use RISCs. The company received a boost the next year when IBM agreed to buy Silicon Graphics' IRIS graphics card for use in its own RS/6000 graphics workstations and to take out a license for the IRIS Graphics Library—a big first step toward making the IRIS Graphics Library the industry standard.

Lower-Priced Workstations Broadened Customer Base, Late 1980s

Also in 1988, Silicon Graphics introduced amid much fanfare a new line of entry level graphics workstations, which it called Eclipse. Although it dominated the more expensive end of the graphics workstation market, the company needed to broaden its customer base if it expected to maintain sales

growth. The Eclipse was designed to bring 3-D graphics to people who had previously regarded IRIS workstations as unaffordable. Eclipse lacked the speed and processing power of more expensive machines, but initial versions sold for less than $20,000—as little as one-fifth of the cost of higher-end machines. Eclipse scored a major success soon after its release when Chrysler announced that it would buy a large number of the machines to go with the IRIS workstations that it was already using to help design its automobiles.

Although Eclipse put Silicon Graphics into more direct competition with its rival workstation manufacturers, who began to chip in with their own low-end 3-D workstations, it also succeeded in expanding the company's customer base. In 1990 sales volume topped $420 million. The move into the lower priced, high-volume end of the market worked well enough for Silicon Graphics that in 1991 the company released an even less expensive product line—the IRIS Indigo, a 3-D graphics workstation so compact that the company called it the first personal computer to use RISC architecture. The Indigo offered many features found on more expensive models, as well as digital audio and video processing capability, and the base model sold for less than $10,000.

During this time, Silicon Graphics scored several major coups on the business side. In 1991 the company granted a license to software giant Microsoft for the IRIS Graphics Library. Microsoft intended to use the IRIS Graphics Library in its New Technology operating system for personal computers. Also in 1991, Compaq Computer agreed to acquire a 13 percent stake in Silicon Graphics for $135 million, giving Silicon Graphics a much-desired infusion of capital. Furthermore, Compaq agreed to invest $50 million in a joint workstation development project with Silicon Graphics. Together, these moves provided software developers with greater incentive to write programs for Silicon Graphics machines and also broadened the company's customer base even further.

In 1992 Silicon Graphics agreed to acquire MIPS Computer Systems, which had run into financial difficulties, in a stock swap valued at $230.8 million. The cost of assimilating MIPS forced Silicon Graphics to post a loss of $118.4 million that year, but it also secured the company's long-term supply of MIPS's RISC microprocessors, which had become a crucial piece of technology. The merger with MIPS was "endorsed" by a consortium of eight international high-tech companies, which announced plans to buy 1.5 million shares of Silicon Graphics. It turned out to be a successful merger. By mid-1993 the company was able to ship the new R4400 microprocessor, and MIPS employees who survived layoffs seemed productively integrated into the Silicon Graphics organization.

In January 1993 Silicon Graphics announced a new computer that would use RISC architecture to achieve supercomputer power at relatively affordable prices. The Power Challenge, as it was called, would link multiple RISCs in a single machine to provide unprecedented processing capability in a computer of that price. Whereas traditional supercomputers like those made by IBM and Cray Research typically sold for millions of dollars, the Power Challenge would sell for between $120,000 and $900,000. The new product was announced over a year in advance of its anticipated shipping date to give targeted customers, such as government agencies and universities previously unable to afford supercomputers, time to include it in their budgets. Observers pegged Power Challenge as a sudden move into the faltering field of supercomputer manufacturing, but in fact the company's ever more powerful workstations were approaching the level of supercomputers anyway, and the company had already established contacts with customers at whom the Power Challenge would be aimed.

Silicon Graphics Workstations Used in Film Industry, 1990s

In April 1993 Silicon Graphics and Industrial Light and Magic, the famed special effects division of Lucasfilm, announced that they had joined forces to create a high-tech entertainment special effects laboratory. The joint venture was called Joint Environment for Digital Imaging—the acronym JEDI recalled the Jedi Knights of Lucasfilm's (George Lucas's) *Star Wars* trilogy—and grew out of the fact that Industrial Light and Magic had been using Silicon Graphics workstations since 1987. The liquid metal cyborg featured in the film *Terminator 2,* the dinosaurs in *Jurassic Park,* special effects in *The Hunt for Red October* and *The Abyss,* and animation in *Beauty and the Beast* were all created on Silicon Graphics computers. For Lucas and Industrial Light and Magic, JEDI was expected to yield both financial and aesthetic benefits: digital manipulation of images cost about one-tenth as much as models and drawings, and, according to Lucas, would ''change motion pictures from a photographic process to more of a painterly process,'' enabling greater authorial control over a film's appearance. For its part, Silicon Graphics hoped that alliance with an entertainment industry partner would help push the leading edge of its technological development forward.

The entertainment industry was a growing interest of James Clark's at the time. In 1995 Silicon Graphics teamed up with DreamWorks SKG—the entertainment entity formed by Steven Spielberg, Jeffrey Katzenberg, and David Geffen—to form DreamWorks Digital Studio for the creation of animation, feature films, and other products. Silicon Graphics also acquired Alias Research and Wavefront Technologies for $500 million in 1995, which positioned Silicon Graphics in the software business. Alias specialized in 3-D animation software that was widely used in the entertainment industry and in industrial design. It had developed new ways to simulate wind, fire, skin, and other special effects, and it also had an animation tool used by Nintendo in its video games. WaveFront Technologies developed industrial visualization software.

Silicon Graphics was facing fierce competition in the 3-D graphics and imaging markets from Apple Computer Inc., which was introducing QuickDraw 3D, and Microsoft Corporation, which had recently acquired SoftImage and its line of simulation software. In addition Steve Jobs, founder of Apple and NeXT, had recently purchased animation producer Pixar and teamed with Walt Disney Studios on *Toy Story,* a full-length animation film created entirely with computers.

Major Acquisitions Continued, 1996–97

In 1996 Silicon Graphics acquired financially troubled supercomputer maker Cray Research Inc. for $767 million. Although lower end workstations accounted for more than half of Silicon Graphics' revenues, its high-end workstations were facing increasing competition from lower-priced PCs. The Cray acquisition was intended to help Silicon Graphics dominate the high end of computing where workstation prices started at $10,000 and ran as high as $1 million. Together, Cray and Silicon Graphics would have accounted for 43 percent of the $1.9 billion scientific and engineering market in 1995, and analysts predicted the two companies could generate $4 billion in combined revenues.

In 1997 Silicon Graphics acquired ParaGraph International Inc., a leading vendor of Virtual Reality Modeling Language (VRML) for Web graphic tools. Silicon Graphics created a new software business unit, Cosmo Software, to manage and develop areas such as VRML, 3-D, audio, and video software for multiple platforms.

Operating Losses Became a Problem, 1997–98

After posting a profit of $78.6 million on revenues of $3.66 billion for fiscal 1997 (ending June 30), Silicon Graphics experienced mounting losses in fiscal 1998. During the first quarter the company lost $55.5 million on revenues of $768 million, and CEO Ed McCracken and Executive Vice-President Gary Lauer resigned.

Silicon Graphics' losses were caused by several factors. More than half of Silicon Graphics' sales came from shrinking markets such as Unix workstations and supercomputers, whose sales were being undercut by less expensive machines running industry standard Windows NT on Intel processors. Silicon Graphics also had a poor operations record, with numerous product delays, production shortfalls, and a lack of controls.

Richard Belluzzo was brought in from Hewlett-Packard, where he was second in command, to take over as CEO and president, effective January 1, 1998. He immediately took steps to turn the company around and address its most immediate problems. Costs were trimmed in a corporate restructuring that involved laying off 700 to 1,000 employees, nearly ten percent of Silicon Graphics' workforce. Two factories that manufactured printed circuit boards were sold, and Silicon Graphics' operating structure was simplified by reducing its 26 profit-and-loss centers to five product groups.

Belluzzo recognized that Silicon Graphics would have to take steps to meet the competition its higher-end proprietary workstations were experiencing from industry standard machines running on Windows NT. Silicon Graphics entered into a strategic alliance with Microsoft to produce a low-priced Visual Workstation for Windows NT that would cost around $3,400 for introduction in fiscal 1999.

Belluzzo also divested some of Silicon Graphics' non-core business assets. In July 1998 a previously planned spinoff of MIPS Technologies Inc. was completed, raising more than $70 million for Silicon Graphics, which retained an 85 percent interest in MIPS. Also sold were a number of applications software research groups, and the company terminated its investment in its Cosmo software business.

Fiscal 1998 (ending June 30) was a poor year for Silicon Graphics due to market conditions, poor operational execution, and missed opportunities. The company reported a net loss of $460 million on declining revenues of $3.1 billion. Restructuring and other one-time charges amounted to $206 million.

In October 1998 Silicon Graphics entered into a joint venture with Real 3D Inc. of Orlando, Florida, to codevelop and market advanced computer graphics technology worldwide. Silicon Graphics took a ten percent stake in Real 3D for an estimated $30 million. Real 3D, which was spun off by Lockheed Martin Corporation in 1996, had been a smaller-scale competitor to Silicon Graphics in providing graphics systems for higher priced computer workstations. As part of the venture the two companies agreed to a royalty-sharing licensing agreement and gave up their longstanding patent infringement litigation.

For the first six months of fiscal 1999 Silicon Graphics posted a net loss of $87 million on revenues of $1.6 billion. Belluzzo's plan to turn Silicon Graphics around included driving sales up through the introduction of lower-priced visual workstations and finding new applications for its high-end supercomputers. His plan to revamp Silicon Graphics' operations included outsourcing production of Silicon Graphics' computers and cutting the company's operating budget by $200 million. He was also attempting to change Silicon Graphics' corporate culture through a "Get Serious" campaign.

In April 1999 Silicon Graphics Inc. changed its name to SGI as part of a new worldwide corporate identity strategy that reflected the breadth and depth of the company's products and services. The strategy included three sub-brands: SGI servers and workstations, Silicon Graphics visual workstations, and Cray supercomputers. The three sub-brands consolidated previously ill-defined product lines. It was hoped that the new branding strategy would reposition SGI and its products and services in the marketplace.

Still, SGI faced several obstacles in its search for profitability. Rival computers were offering vastly improved performance as sales of Cray supercomputers were plummeting at a 40 percent annual rate. Entering the Windows NT market would require more rapid production cycles, something SGI had not shown it could accomplish. As a competitor in the Windows NT market, SGI would also be subject to delays associated with the introduction of new versions of Windows NT and Intel processors. Given SGI's operating results for the first half of fiscal 1999, Belluzzo and SGI appeared to have their work cut out for them.

Principal Subsidiaries

Silicon Graphics Ltd. (United Kingdom); Nihon Silicon Graphics K.K. (Japan); Silicon Graphics Ltd. (Hong Kong, People's Republic of China); Cray Research, Inc.; MIPS Technologies Inc.

Principal Divisions

Consumer Products Division; Strategic Software Division; Visual Systems Group; Alias/Wavefront; Supercomputing Group.

Further Reading

Burnett, Richard, "Orlando, Fla., High-Tech Firm Teams with Mountain View, Calif., Company," *Knight-Ridder/Tribune Business News*, October 7, 1998.
Burrows, Peter, and Andy Reinhardt, "What Makes Rick Run?" *Business Week*, February 1, 1999, p. 62.
DeTar, Jim, "MIPS Goes Public," *Electronic News (1991)*, July 6, 1998, p. 1.
Fisher, Susan E., "Cloudy Forecast Seen for SGI/MIPS Merger," *PC Week*, June 15, 1992, p. 154.
Goldberg, Michael, "SGI + Cray = Scientific Powerhouse," *Computerworld*, March 4, 1996, p. 32.
Hof, Robert, "Is Silicon Graphics Busting Out of Its Niche?," *Business Week*, April 22, 1991.
Hof, Robert, and Jeffrey Rothfeder, "This Machine Just Might Eclipse Apollo and Sun," *Business Week*, October 10, 1988.
Hostetler, Michele, "Cray Deal Boosts SGI to Top of the Supercomputer Heap," *Business Journal*, March 4, 1996, p. 4.
Johnson, Bradley, "Silicon Graphics Rethinks Entire Brand," *Business Marketing*, May 1998, p. 42.
"Jurassic Pact: Silicon Graphics," *Economist*, March 2, 1996, p. 58.
Koland, Cordell, "Graphics Firm Leader Combines Technical, Managerial Skill," *Business Journal—San Jose*, December 14, 1987.
Lee, Yvonne L., and Pardhu Vadlamudi, "Acquisitions Move SGI into Software," *InfoWorld*, February 20, 1995, p. 34.
Levin, Carol, "Animation's Next Frontier," *PC Magazine*, April 25, 1995, p. 29.
Moylan, Martin J., "Wall Street Remains Wary of Silicon Graphics, Cray Merger," *Knight-Ridder/Tribune Business News*, February 23, 1997.
Nash, Jim, "A Merger Success: SGI-MIPS," *Business Journal*, April 5, 1993, p. 1.
Niccolai, James, and Dana Gardner, "SGI Plans to Cut Jobs and Shift Focus to NT," *InfoWorld*, November 3, 1997, p. 10.
"SGI Acquisition Bolsters Web Graphics Tools," *PC Week*, May 19, 1997, p. 28.
"SGI Launches New Worldwide Corporate Identity Strategy," http://www.sgi.com/newsroom/press—releases/1999/april/brand.html.
"SGI to Merge with Alias, Wavefront," *Design News*, April 10, 1995, p. 20.
"Silicon Graphics Inc.," *Advanced Imaging*, January 1998, p. 8.
Simons, John, "Ghosts in the Machine: SGI Tries to Regain Its Former Luster—But Challenges Abound," *U.S. News & World Report*, November 11, 1996, p. 60.
Stedman, Craig, "Shareholders Approve MIPS-SGI Deal; Advisory Board Set with RISC Partners," *Electronic News (1991)*, June 29, 1992, p. 6.
Taninecz, George, "Cinema Without Celluloid," *Industry Week*, June 19, 1995, p. 47.
Tedesco, Richard, "SGI, Cray in $780 Million Merger," *Broadcasting & Cable*, March 4, 1996, p. 46.
Vijayan, Jaikumar, "SGI Results Worse Than Expected; McCracken out, Layoffs Planned," *Computerworld*, November 3, 1997, p. 4.
Yamada, Ken, "Silicon Graphics Aims to Be Supercomputer Contrarian," *Wall Street Journal*, January 27, 1993.

—Douglas Sun
—updated by David Bianco

Sodexho Alliance SA

3, avenue Newton
78180 Montigny-le-Bretonneux
France
(33) 1 30 85 75 00
Fax: (33) 1 30 43 09 58
Web site: http://www.sodexho.com

Public Company
Incorporated: 1966 as Sodexho SA
Employees: 250,000
Sales: FFr 41.1 billion (US $6.9 billion) (1998)
Stock Exchanges: Paris
Ticker Symbol: Sodexho
NAIC: 72231 Food Service Contractors

Sodexho Alliance SA is the worldwide leader in food and management services. In an aggressive acquisition and expansion drive during the 1990s, the Marseilles, France-based services giant has seen its payroll explode to 250,000 employees and its revenues jump from FFr 11 billion in 1993 to FFr 41 billion in 1998. The company currently operates in some 66 countries, through nearly 19,000 operating units. More than 84 percent of the company's sales are achieved outside of France. The United States is the company's single largest market, contributing more than one-third of the company's annual sales, through the company's subsidiaries and through its 49 percent share of Sodexho Marriot Services Inc., the US $4 billion food and other services giant created in 1998 through the merger of Marriot Inc.'s and Sodexho's North American food services operations. Other principal markets include France (19 percent of annual sales); United Kingdom and Ireland (22 percent); and the rest of Europe, including Eastern Europe (18 percent). Both the Asian and Latin American regions contribute five percent to Sodexho Alliance's annual sales.

Sodexho Alliance's operations fall under three primary categories. In Food and Management Services, Sodexho Alliance has built the leading worldwide position, overtaking chief rival Compass, of the United Kingdom. The company's core business, Food and Management Services, supplies clients in the corporate, administration, public and private school, health care, university, and other markets, including prisons and other detention centers. This division's Prestige group offers fine dining and conference and related services to the hotel and restaurant industries, museums, cultural centers, and conference centers. Sodexho's Food and Management Services division also has built more than 25 years of experience as a provider of services to remote locations, such as offshore oil platforms and other industrial sites. Food and Management Services contribute some 97 percent of Sodexho Alliance's annual sales. Of this figure, some 53 percent of the company's sales are contributed by the business and industry sector; the health care and education markets contribute 21 percent and 19 percent, respectively, and remote site management activities fill out this segment with four percent of total company sales.

The company's two other main activities are its Sodexho Pass service vouchers and cards operations and the company's River and Harbor Cruise division. Sodexho Pass holds the number two global position in the management and distribution of service vouchers and cards, for such products as dining and groceries, gasoline purchases, school supplies, toys, pharmacy and other medical services, and many others. The company distributes more than one billion vouchers and cards per year through a client base numbering nearly 90,000. Sodexho Pass represents two percent of Sodexho Alliance's annual sales. The company's River and Harbor Cruise division, contributing the remaining one percent of the company's total sales, is the world's largest operator in this market segment, with a fleet of more than 40 boats operating in New York, Boston, the United Kingdom, and France. The company's River and Harbor Cruise subsidiaries include Spirit Cruises in New York, Catamaran Cruisers in the United Kingdom, and Bateaux Parisiens in Paris.

After a number of strategic acquisitions, including the 1995 acquisition of the United Kingdom's Gardner Merchant, which doubled the company's size at that time, Sodexho Alliance captured the lead of the North American food and management services market with the merger of its North American operations with those of hotelier Marriot International. The merger created Sodexho Marriot Services, Inc., with 100,000 employ-

Company Perspectives:

Our purpose: Our company is a community that includes our clients and customers, our employees and our shareholders. Our purpose is to exceed their expectations. To achieve this mission, we focus on responsible growth in sales and earnings, while contributing to the economic health of the countries where we provide our services. Our mission: To create and offer services that contribute to a more pleasant way of life for people, whenever and wherever they come together. Our goal: To be the benchmark wherever we offer our services, in every country, in every region, in every city, and for every client. Our core values: Service spirit. Team spirit. Progress.

ees and annual sales of more than US $4 billion. Sodexho Marriot Services is listed on the New York Stock Exchange under the symbol SDH.

Sodexho Alliance continues to thrive under the active leadership of chairman, chief executive, and founder Pierre Bellon. The company's stock trades on the Paris stock exchange, joining the prestigious CAC 40 listing in 1998.

Founding a Food Services Giant in the 1960s

Pierre Bellon founded the food services company Sodexho SA in Marseilles in 1966 with FFr 100,000. Bellon did not enter the food services industry without experience, however. Since the turn of the century, the Bellon family had been a prominent name among the cruise ship and luxury liner industries. Bellon sought to bring the family's expertise onshore. Sodexho was created with the original mission to supply food services to collective organizations, such as businesses, schools, and hospitals.

Bellon's ambitions quickly looked beyond France. In 1971 the company was awarded its first nondomestic contract, across the border in Belgium, providing food services for hospitals in that country. The company would continue to expand its activity throughout Europe over the next decade. Sodexho also would begin to diversify its activities, while remaining focused on its core food services operations. In 1975 the company added a new service, providing food and other management services to large construction sites and offshore drilling platforms under its Remote Site Management division set up for that purpose. Early contracts saw the company enter Africa and then the Middle East.

A new piece in the Sodexho puzzle was added in 1978, when the company began its service vouchers operations. These vouchers, which would provide prepaid coupons—and, later, so-called smart cards—ranging from restaurant dining to gasoline purchases to medical prescriptions fulfillments, were first introduced in Belgium and Germany. The voucher operation proved so successful that the company quickly rolled out its Sodexho Pass subsidiary services throughout much of its growing operations. Another area of expansion combined the Bellon family's past experience with Sodexho's expertise: the com-

pany launched its own series of river boats and harbor cruise ships, serving such waterways as Paris's Seine River.

By the start of the 1980s, Sodexho had determined to launch the company on a truly global scale. Although its operations had remained in large part limited to the French and western European markets, in 1980 the company launched its first subsidiaries in the North and South American markets. Sodexho would make particular inroads in the Chilean and Brazilian markets; in the United States, too, the company established a strong presence.

To finance its continued expansion activities—which would bring the company on the acquisition trail in the mid-1980s—Sodexho went public in 1983, selling shares on the Paris stock exchange. Bellon, however, retained the controlling share of the company he founded. Beyond maintaining Sodexho's independence, Bellon now sought to impose Sodexho as one of the world's leading food services and management services businesses.

In the mid-1980s, the company began making the series of acquisitions that would lead it to worldwide leadership in its industry. The company's initial acquisition, that of Boston-based Seiler, a vending machine and restaurant business, was made in 1985. This was followed soon after by the purchase of Food Dimensions, based in San Francisco, and complemented by several other U.S. acquisitions. These businesses later were regrouped as Sodexho USA and included the company's Spirit Cruises subsidiary, which brought Sodexho's river and harbor cruise ship operations to such U.S. markets as New York, Boston, and Seattle.

Going Global in the 1990s

The late 1980s saw a crash in the hotel and hospitality industries, which, coupled with a worldwide recession in the early 1990s, would bring a number of food services companies on the market. With its traditionally low-debt, independent position, Sodexho would continue to accelerate its growth by acquisitions. Not all of its attempts were successful, however. After gaining a 20 percent share of Wagon Lits, Sodexho nonetheless lost a bitter battle for full control of that major European services provider to rival French company Accor. Sole consolation for Sodexho was its benefit from the resultant rise in the value—and sale—of its Wagon Lits shares, which added an additional FFr 400 million to its profit sheet in 1993.

Despite the loss of Wagon Lits, Sodexho was far from abandoning its dream of vastly increasing its size. Bellon recognized that increasing competition in the industry, the heavy debt load of many of Sodexho's competitors, and the need for some groups to restructure their operations would bring still more acquisition opportunities among the world's leading food and management services companies. Sodexho's next attempt to acquire an improved position in the industry came with negotiations to acquire Britain's Gardner Merchant, the restaurant and food services arm of the Forte group. Sodexho abandoned that attempt, however, when Bellon decided the purchase price would be too high.

In the meantime, Sodexho continued to strengthen its position in North America—in particular, taking, in 1994, a 20 percent position in Corrections Corporation of America. At the same time, the company was stepping up its international presence with entries into a number of new markets, including Japan, Russia, Africa, and much of Eastern Europe; in total, Sodexho added 25 new markets in less than three years, bringing its international presence to more than 60 countries.

Sodexho's next big growth chance came again in 1995. Once again, Gardner Merchant, which was in the process of detaching itself from the Forte group, came into Sodexho's view. This time the marriage was consummated: for a purchase of some UK £500 million, Sodexho doubled its size, adding Gardner Merchant's FFr 10 billion per year in annual sales to Sodexho's own FFr 11.2 billion, and creating one of the world's leading food and other services firms with more than 100,000 employees. As icing on the cake, Sodexho acquired in that same year the Swedish management services sector leader Partena. The double acquisition placed Sodexho as the world leader in the food and management services industry.

With nearly FFr 25 billion in 1995 annual sales, Sodexho barely took any time to integrate its new acquisitions before completing a new significant merger, of Brazil's Cardàpio, the third largest service voucher provider in the world's leading market for service vouchers. Also in 1996, the company merged its Sodexho USA operations with the U.S. operations of its Gardner Merchant subsidiary, creating the fourth largest food service provider in the United States.

After acquiring Universal Odgen Services, the leading U.S.-based remote site services provider, Sodexho changed its name to Sodexho Alliance in 1997. Sodexho Alliance would end the year with nearly FFr 29.5 billion in sales. One year later, the company would take a new leap in revenues. In March 1998 Sodexho agreed to a merger with Marriot Management Services, the food and management services wing of the Marriot hotels group. Sodexho's and Marriot's North American service operations were merged together to form Sodexho Marriott Services, Inc., the U.S. market leader. The merged company, in which Sodexho retained nearly 49 percent, was listed on the New York Stock Exchange.

Buoyed by the merger, which swelled Sodexho's annual sales to more than FFr 41 billion by the end of its 1998 year,

Sodexho also was granted a listing on the prestigious CAC index on the Paris bourse. Back in Europe, Sodexho continued to cement its position, through organic growth, but also through acquisitions, including the early 1999 acquisition of Spain's GR Servicios Hoteleros, which gave Sodexho the leadership position in that country's catering market. As the company pledged to continue its expansion, both through acquisition and internal growth, Sodexho also was preparing to branch out into the still larger global services market. Under the leadership of Pierre Bellon, Sodexho appeared likely to achieve a strong position in that market—without sacrificing its treasured independence.

Principal Subsidiaries

Bateaux Parisiens (France); Bay State Cruise Company (US); Cardàpio (Brazil); Catamaran Cruisers (UK); Gardner Merchant (UK); Kelvin Aberdeen (UK); Luncheon Tickets SA (Argentina); Partena AB (Sweden); Siges (France); Socorest (Congo); Sodex Corporation (Japan); Sodexho Gardner Merchant (Australia); Sodexho Marriott Services Inc. (US; 48.5%); Sodexho Prestige (France); Spirit Cruises (US); Van Hecke (Netherlands).

Principal Operating Units

Sodexho Food and Management Services; Sodexho Pass; River and Harbor Cruises.

Further Reading

Cheveilley, Philippe, "Sodexho Alliance se donne trois ans pour digérer son mariage américain," *Les Echoes,* December 17, 1998, p. 19.

——, "Sodexho prêt pour une acquisition majeure," *Les Echoes,* December 16, 1994, p. 12.

Gasquet, Pierre, and Besses-Boumard, Pascale, "Sodexho-Compass: le match très serré des deux géants mondiaux de la restauration collective," *Les Echoes,* January 1, 1999, p. 24.

Thiault, Beatrice, "Sodexho et Marriott fusionnent leurs activités de restauration," *L'Hôtellerie,* October 9, 1997.

——, "Une année de forte expansion," *L'Hôtellerie,* December 25, 1997.

—M.L. Cohen

SOTHEBY'S

Sotheby's Holdings, Inc.

1334 York Avenue
New York, New York 10021
U.S.A.
(212) 606-7000
Fax: (212) 606-7107
Web site: http://www.sothebys.com

Public Company
Founded: 1744
Employees: 1,921
Sales: $447.1 million (1998)
Stock Exchanges: New York London
Ticker Symbol: BID
NAIC: 7389 Business Services Not Elsewhere Classified

Sotheby's Holdings, Inc. is the holding company for Sotheby's, one of the world's premier fine arts auction houses. The company got its start in the mid-18th century, focusing on the British book market, and later in the century branched out into other markets. Sotheby's began to expand beyond its British base in the 1940s, and it had established a significant worldwide presence at the time of the art boom in the 1980s, which pushed its sales totals up dramatically. After the bottom fell out of that market, the company found new categories of collectibles to sell. Fine arts still account for about half of auction sales, and 80 percent of the lots Sotheby's sells now are valued below $5,000.

18th-Century Origins

The history of Sotheby's may be traced to 1744, when the English bookseller Samuel Baker held his first auction. During this time, book collectors had become increasingly interested in enhancing their holdings by purchasing works from the libraries of collectors who had died. Baker's first auction, in March 1744, featured 457 books previously belonging to Sir John Stanley. Baker sold the contents of Stanley's library for £826. Following this event, Baker and his associates became the premier auctioneers of British libraries. Baker auctioned the

book collections of several famous clients, including Prince Talleyrand, John Wilkes, John Bright, the Marquess of Landsdowne, the Dukes of York, Buckingham, and Devonshire, and the Earls of Pembroke, Sunderland, and Hopetoun. One client, Richard Rawlinson, had amassed so many books that the only room left for him to sleep in was the hallway of his living quarters. Upon Rawlinson's death, it took Baker 50 days to disperse the collection.

In 1767, Baker took on a partner in his business, an accomplished auctioneer named George Leigh, who was noted for using props, such as a snuff box and an ivory gavel, in conducting sales of books. When Baker died in 1778, his estate was divided between Leigh and Baker's nephew John Sotheby.

Under the leadership of John Sotheby, the auction house expanded its activities beyond books for the first time, including the sale of prints, medals, coins, and rare antiquities. The company's staff also expanded, and, in 1842, Sotheby's senior accountant, John Wilkinson, was permitted to purchase a 25 percent share in the partnership. In 1861, the last member of the Sotheby family died, and Wilkinson took over as the company's leader. Three years later, Wilkinson promoted another long-time employee, Edward Grose Hodge, and changed the enterprise's name to Sotheby, Wilkinson, and Hodge, the name it would carry for the next 60 years.

In the late 19th century, Sotheby's dominated the book trade of London. Key to this success were the activities of Bernard Quaritch, a book dealer who purchased the property of such prominent figures of the day as Disraeli and Gladstone, both British prime ministers, and other leading cultural and political figures. Quaritch maintained a high profile, bringing free publicity and renown to Sotheby's and helping the company to maintain its preeminent spot in the industry.

In 1878, Thomas Hodge, the son of Edward Grose Hodge, joined the firm, and in 1896, as the previous generation retired, the younger Hodge became the sole active partner in the business. Over the course of his career, Hodge developed a rich store of knowledge about the antiquities that Sotheby's sold. In addition to his concern for old things, Hodge was notorious for his attachment to old ways; for example, he loathed the telephone and insisted that all of his letters be handwritten, not typed.

New Directions in a New Century

When Edward Hodge died in 1907, his son sold three additional shares in the Sotheby's partnership. These were purchased by Montague Barlow, a lawyer and Member of Parliament; Felix Warre, a banker; and Geoffrey Hobson, an official in the British Foreign Service. The new partners undertook as one of their first major projects the sale of the Huth library. This property, which had taken 50 years and two generations to amass, took 12 sales over 11 years to disperse, netting £300,000.

In 1917, Sotheby, Wilkinson, and Hodge moved its business offices from Wellington Street in London, to 34/35 New Bond Street. At the time of the move, company employees carefully detached a black basalt bust of the lion-goddess Sekhmet, carved in ancient Egypt around 1320 B.C., from its place of honor in Sotheby's offices and installed it over the front entrance of the firm's new premises. The statue had come to the company in the 1800s as part of a collection of Egyptian artifacts and was sold for £40. When the object's buyer never appeared to collect it, the orphaned goddess' was adopted by Sotheby's and became its muse, giving the company the oldest privately owned monument in London.

In the wake of World War I, a way of life for many of Britain's old landed families began to come to an end. As a result of the break-up of Britain's vast country estates, Sotheby's began to receive commissions to auction the contents of many country houses. At the suggestion of a young company employee, Sotheby's began to hold these sales on the premises of the estates. The first such sale was at Kinmel Park in Wales, where the sole surviving member of the manor's family lived alone in a house with 57 bedrooms. Sotheby's continued to hold on-site estate sales throughout the 1920s and 1930s.

During this time, Sotheby's began to see the bulk of its business shift away from books and literary property, in favor of paintings and other works of art. Nevertheless, Sotheby's did continue to conduct major sales of libraries. The Britwell collection took 21 separate sales to disperse and set a new record for the sums fetched by a library at auction. In addition, the company presided over the sale of Yates Thompson's collection of illuminated manuscripts, Anton Mensing's collection of early printed books, and the unpublished papers, containing three million words, of Sir Isaac Newton.

In 1937, Sotheby's conducted its most notable house sale of the prewar era, when it dispersed the contents of 148 Piccadilly, formerly owned by the Rothschild family. The BBC broadcasted the auction live, and £125,000 was netted from the sale, an enormous sum for the time. Within two years of this sale, however, Britain had entered World War II, and the war-time economy naturally brought changes to Sotheby's activities.

After the war, Sotheby's experienced a boom in operations. In 1946, the company sold £1.5 million worth of goods, a figure that would not be equaled for the next eight years. As British regulations governing monetary exchanges were relaxed, Sotheby's was allowed to expand its operations beyond Great Britain for the first time in the late 1940s. With this new freedom, the company sought to become a dominant player in the international auction business.

American Expansion in the Mid-1950s

A key step in this strategy was taken in 1955, when Sotheby's inaugurated American operations, opening an office in New York. With this move, along with gains in other areas, the company's receipts climbed to £1.7 million in that year. The most striking development in Sotheby's business in the late 1950s was the rapid increase in popularity and price of Impressionist and Modern art. In 1957, Sotheby's held its first auction devoted exclusively to these works, when it sold the Weinberg collection in London.

On October 15 of the following year, Sotheby's sold the famed Goldschmidt Collection. This group of seven paintings was sold at an evening auction, a black tie event attended by many celebrities and covered extensively by the press. In just 21 minutes, the works were sold for £781,000, the largest amount ever attained in a fine arts sale. The Paul Cézanne painting entitled *Garçon au Gilet Rouge* was sold to Paul Mellon for £220,000, more than seven times higher a price than any other modern painting had ever fetched. The auctioneer, Sotheby's president Peter Wilson, responded famously to this bid by asking, "What, will no one offer any more?" At the end of the Goldschmidt sale, the audience of 1,400 stood on their chairs and cheered for an extended period of time. With this event, an international boom in art sales was launched.

In June 1959, another major sale strengthened the market for art works, when Rubens' altarpiece *The Adoration of the Magi,* painted in 1634 for a Flemish convent, sold for £275,000, following two minutes of bidding. The painting was offered for sale by the Duke of Westminster, whose family had owned it since 1806. Because it measured 8 feet by 12 feet, Sotheby's had to winch the work into its West Gallery through a hole made in the floor and then break down two walls to get it into the main gallery for sale.

On the day after the Rubens sale, Sotheby's set another record, when it sold the Westminster Tiara for £110,000, twice as much as any other piece of jewelry had ever fetched. This diamond crown featured two enormous pearl-shaped diamonds, known as the Arcot Diamonds, surrounded by 1,240 smaller stones. It was purchased by Harry Winson, who reset the stones in different pieces of jewelry. By the end of 1959, with contributions from these two landmark sales, Sotheby's annual sales had reached £6 million.

Throughout the late 1950s and the early 1960s, the main thrust of Sotheby's growth was in markets outside the United Kingdom. In 1964, the company dramatically enhanced its foreign operations when it purchased Parke-Bernet in New York, the largest American fine art auction house. With this acquisition, Sotheby's became Sotheby Parke Bernet. The American arm of the firm reaped its most handsome profits from the sale of Impressionist and Modern pictures in the mid-1960s. In October 1965, for instance, Cézanne's *Maison à l'Estaque* brought a record $800,000.

With these strong returns from its American branch, Sotheby's increased its international presence in the late 1960s. In 1967, the company opened offices in Houston, Los Angeles, and Paris. The following year, operations in Toronto, Florence, and Melbourne were inaugurated, and, in 1969, Sotheby's added Edinburgh, Zürich, Munich, and Johannesburg. The company's Swiss location soon became a center of European jewelry sales.

More Expansion in the 1970s

In the 1970s, Sotheby's continued to expand its reach. In 1971, the company opened a second London showroom, in the section of the city known as Belgravia. This facility specialized in art from the Victorian and Edwardian eras. In 1973, Sotheby's moved overseas again, opening an office and showroom in Hong Kong, which soon handled the sale of the Chow collection of Ming and Qing porcelain. In the following year, the company expanded its European holdings, purchasing Mak van Waay, a Dutch seller of fine art. From this base, Sotheby's began to conduct annual sales of Flemish and Dutch Old Master paintings and drawings. Also in 1974, Sotheby's opened offices in Stockholm, Milan, Brussels, and Dublin. In January of the following year, Sotheby's expanded into that area of Europe controlled by the French customs service, signing an agreement to conduct auctions in Monaco. In this way, the company was better able to circumvent the French government's state control of all auctions. The company's first Monaco sale, held in the Winter Casino, was an auction of furniture and silver owned by Baron Guy de Rothschild. In 1976, Sotheby's expanded its Swiss operations to include winter jewel auctions held in the resort of St. Moritz. In May 1976, the company successfully auctioned the renowned Pink Diamond, for a record price of $1.09 million.

The following year, Sotheby's turned its attention to its home base, undertaking a significant expansion in Britain and Ireland. The company opened a salesroom outside London, in Billingshurst, Sussex, and also began to conduct auctions in Scotland. Eventually, Sotheby's grew to include eleven offices and ten further representatives throughout Great Britain.

In the spring of 1977, Sotheby's decided to sell shares in the partnership to the public for the first time. The company's initial stock offering proved highly popular, and the price of shares had soon more than doubled. In the wake of this move, Sotheby's pushed on with its international expansion. At the end of the 1970s, the company opened a third Swiss office in Geneva. In 1979, Sotheby's also opened an office in Spain, which was inaugurated in May 1979, with the house sale of El Quexigal, a former residence of the Hohenlohe princes. The company had also opened offices in Rome and Hamburg by the end of the decade.

Bidding for Control in the 1980s

In 1980, Peter Wilson, Sotheby's long-time leader, stepped down from his post and was followed by a number of other executives in quick succession. In 1982, the company's chief expert on Chinese art was appointed head of Sotheby's International outside the United States. The following year, the company faced a major threat in the wave of corporate takeovers that swept the financial world in the early 1980s, when two investors amassed a large number of Sotheby's shares and attempted a hostile takeover of the company. It was rescued by A. Alfred Taubman, an American businessman and patron of the arts, who formed Sotheby's Holdings, Inc., to purchase Sotheby Parke Bernet Group plc. With the approval of the company's leaders, Taubman purchased all of Sotheby's on November 9, 1983.

The sale and purchase of Sotheby's itself came as the business of selling things in general entered a boom period. The company set records for prices of art works sold at auction in 1983 and 1984 and recorded its highest annual totals of sales in 1984 and 1985. The dramatic growth rate continued throughout the following two years, and, in 1987, Sotheby's reported an 85 percent annual increase in auction sales, as the company passed the $1 billion mark for the first time. In that year, the company sold the Duchess of Windsor's jewels for £31 million and Van Gogh's *Irises* for $53.9 million, an astounding figure that was later revealed to have been enhanced by the auction house's offer of a loan to the buyer.

Sotheby's Holdings executed an initial public offering in 1988. The firm's fantastic success continued, as annual sales rose to $1.81 billion, a three-fold increase over the last five years. The company auctioned off a part of the Andy Warhol estate and also conducted sales in the Soviet Union and China for the first time. The following year, Sotheby's moved further afield, opening offices in Tokyo and Budapest and conducting an auction in Vienna.

By the end of 1989, the company's sales had doubled again over just two years, with strong returns from contemporary and impressionist art. There seemed to be no end in sight to the boom, and, in July 1990, Sotheby's annual sales reached $3.2 billion.

Challenges in the 1990s

By the start of 1991, however, the bubble had burst. A severe worldwide economic downturn, as well as anxiety surrounding the Persian Gulf War, brought an end to the auction returns of the late 1980s. The company's contemporary, modern, and impressionistic art sales were hurt particularly badly. By December 1991, annual sales had dropped to $1.1 billion. Sotheby's annual sales figures remained in the $1 billion range for the next few years.

Taubman, whose vast financial empire was crumbling, sold some of his Sotheby's shares in the spring of 1992. *Forbes* estimated Taubman's wealth fell from over $2 billion to about $400 million between 1989 and 1994. Fortunately, he had $40 million a year in Sotheby's income to sustain him during this period. Michael Ainslie, who had served as CEO since 1984, left the firm in 1993 after becoming enriched by bonuses and stock options. He was succeeded by Diana Dwyer "Dede" Brooks, who had first joined Sotheby's in 1979.

Brooks set about cutting costs and reorganizing management. She also, in January 1993, increased its buyer's premium, which helped to improve its profits. By 1994, improving prices in some areas, such as jewelry, began to indicate a slow recovery in the market. Given its illustrious history, wide range of operations, and expertise in the field of fine arts, Sotheby's was well situated to take advantage of any upturns in the art market.

However, Christie's, led by Christopher Davidge, was making impressive gains in market share. In 1995, although Christie's did secure several important collections, Sotheby's landed a Picasso that sold for nearly $30 million and edged out its rival yet again.

Robert Lacey's history of Sotheby's suggests that this was a difficult transition period. Three of the firm's top experts left the field around the same time. Moreover, when Brooks attempted to conduct an important auction herself, it failed. Sotheby's posted just under $1.6 billion in 1996 auction sales, and Christie's outsold them by the slimmest of margins, giving Christie's its first lead in 42 years. Although Sotheby's posted more profits, it was a historic marker of defeat.

To bolster sales, the definition of what was appropriate for the firm to auction was enlarged to include baseball cards, celebrity memorabilia, and even an abandoned lunar rover, permanently fixed on the moon. Thus, the company's customer base broadened. In 1993, the firm reached an agreement with Disney to auction simulated "celluloids" as souvenirs of its films. Although no longer part of the filmmaking process, these reconstructed frames proved popular to collectors and attracted bids of up to $20,000 each.

Journalists continued to report on the perceived competition between Sotheby's and rival Christie's. Christie's was holding impressive sales during this time, including a single modern art collection which landed $206.5 million. Moreover, Christie's posted a turnover of $2.02 billion for the year 1997, passing Sotheby's for a second year running. Still, Sotheby's profits were $18 million better, perhaps because Sotheby's kept a better eye on costs than its rival. It exercised an option to buy its New York headquarters building, thereby saving millions each year in rent. Plans were in the works to more than double the height of the building to create an art marketplace of unprecedented scale.

Then, a February 1998 auction of the personal effects of the Duke and Duchess of Windsor was a tremendous success which garnered enormous media attention. A piece of the Windsors' wedding cake in its original box fetched nearly $30,000. Dede Brooks reportedly performed masterfully, redeeming her earlier attempts. The sale attracted 1,095 buyers—more than half new to Sotheby's.

January 1999 marked the debut of sothebys.com, a web site offering information on art collections, auctions, and catalogs. Shortly thereafter, Sotheby's opened its refurbished Grosvenor Galleries in London specifically to handle new categories of collectibles such as pop memorabilia. While critics in the art world worried that the reputation of Sotheby's might suffer from over-commercialization, the company benefited in the form of a boost in sales, and industry analysts attributed much of Sotheby's turnaround to CEO Brooks. As it moved into the 20th century, Sotheby's was well-positioned to appeal to a broader customer base. Moreover, it could always count on the auctioneer's old allies, death and taxes.

Principal Subsidiaries

Sotheby's, Inc.; Sotheby's Financial Services, Inc.; SPTC, Inc.; SFS Holdings, Inc.; York Avenue Development, Inc.; Fine Art Insurance Ltd. (Bermuda); Oatshare Limited (United Kingdom); Sotheby's (United Kingdom).

Further Reading

Brown, Christie, "Revenge of the Philistines," *Forbes,* December 6, 1993.
Bruce, James, "Sotheby's Eyes the Future," *Australian Business Monthly,* February 1993, pp. 84–86.
Dalby, Stewart, "The Shock of the New," *Director,* November 1998, pp. 70–73.
Decker, Andrew, "The Thrilla' in Chinchilla," *Forbes,* December 15, 1997, pp. 282–84.
Dobrzynski, Judith H., "A Bigger Canvas for Sotheby's," *Business Week,* May 21, 1990, pp. 134–36.
Du Bois, Peter, C., "Study in Black and White: Christie's Sale Sparkles, Sotheby's Bombs," *Barron's,* November 16, 1992, pp. 18, 44.
Ebony, David, "Spring Auction Rollercoaster: Art Auctions," *Art in America,* July 1993.
Gregg, Gail, "Masterpiece Management," *Working Woman,* September 1995, pp. 48–52, 75.
Hughes, Robert, "Auctions in the Pits," *Time,* May 16, 1994.
Lacey, Robert, *Sotheby's: Bidding for Class,* Boston: Little, Brown, 1998.
Meyers, William, "What if They Held an Auction and Nobody Came?," *Institutional Investor,* August 1990, pp. 62–64.
Morais, Richard C., "Blood and Monet," *Forbes,* November 25, 1991, pp. 149–50.
Rees, Jon, "Art Nous," *Marketing Week,* October 13, 1995, pp. 35–36.
Robinson, Walter, "Sizzle or Fizzle?," *Art in America,* January 1993.
Sivv, Michael, "Pricier Art Could Brighten Sotheby's Picture by 69%," *Money,* January 1994.
"Sotheby's Makes a Bold Bid," *Money,* December 1998, p. 62.

—Elizabeth Rourke
—updated by Frederick C. Ingram

STERIS®

STERIS Corporation

5960 Heisley Road
Mentor, Ohio 44060
U.S.A.
(440) 354-2600
(800) 548-4873
Fax: (440) 354-7043
Web site: http://www.steris.com

Public Company
Incorporated: 1987
Employees: 4,500
Sales: $719.7 million (1998)
Stock Exchanges: New York
Ticker Symbol: STE
NAIC: 339112 Surgical & Medical Instrument
Manufacturing; 42199 Other Miscellaneous Durable
Goods Wholesalers

STERIS Corporation develops, manufactures, and markets infection prevention, contamination prevention, microbial reduction, and surgical support systems, products, services, and technologies. It has a worldwide, diversified customer base in the areas of health care, science, research, food, and general industry. Infection prevention products—such as low- and high-temperature sterilization systems and washing, as well as decontamination products—make up the bulk of STERIS' business, with surgical support products, such as surgical tables, examination lights, and other accessories, making up the second largest segment of annual revenues. Other products and services include scientific and industrial contamination prevention systems and contract sterilization and microbial reduction services to manufacturers of pre-packaged consumer and medical products. The company has manufacturing facilities in 13 states and in Germany, Finland, Sweden and Canada. Its products are sold and distributed through a network of 950 field sales and service representatives in North America and operations or support personnel in more than 15 other countries.

Early Success

Although STERIS Corporation was formed in 1987, it had its real beginning two years earlier in 1985. That year, an innovative researcher named Dr. Ray Kralovic left his employer, the Pittsburgh-based American Sterilizer Co., to develop his own technique for sterilizing surgical instruments used in minimally invasive surgeries such as endoscopy and arthroscopy. Traditionally, surgical equipment had been sterilized in a lengthy process that involved high temperatures and strong disinfectants. However, the delicate heat-sensitive instruments used in minimally invasive procedures could not withstand the intensive sterilization process used on the more durable instruments. Kralovic's idea was to develop a rapid, low-temperature sterilization system that could be safely used on heat-sensitive equipment.

Kralovic first approached Primus Venture Partners, a Cleveland venture capital firm. Primus was unwilling to take on the concept, but suggested that Kralovic contact Bill Sanford, a health care consultant with a reputation for buying and selling medical technology. Kralovic was able to convince Sanford of the new sterilization system's potential for success, and STERIS was formed with a venture capital investment of $1.2 million. Sanford became the new company's CEO.

A year later, STERIS introduced what was to become its most successful product: the STERIS System 1. The System 1 was a complete low-temperature sterilization system that could be used at or near the site of the surgical procedure. The system included a tabletop computer-controlled central unit, a single-use sterilizing solution, and various sizes of containers and trays. The patented sterilizing solution contained a chemical biocide that killed microorganisms, along with an anti-corrosion formula that protected the instruments themselves. The whole sterilization process took fewer than 30 minutes, so healthcare professionals were able to sterilize and safely use the same surgical instruments several times per day. The efficient System 1 was well received, and as the trend toward minimally invasive surgeries continued to pick up steam, STERIS' sales grew. In June 1992, the company made an initial public offering, which was followed by a secondary offering nine months later.

More innovative products followed the System 1. In 1993, STERIS entered into a joint venture with Indianapolis-based Ecomed, Inc., a manufacturer of hazardous waste disposal equipment. Together, Ecomed and STERIS developed the EcoCycle 10, a biohazard disposal system that ground up and decontaminated disposable medical equipment, such as syringes. The following year, the company acquired Medical & Environmental Designs, Inc., a St. Louis company with an FDA-approved system for collecting and disposing of fluid biohazardous wastes.

Meanwhile, the System 1 was rapidly growing in popularity. Between the company's fiscal 1993 and 1994 years, sales climbed 70 percent to $45.8 million, and stock prices doubled. Because every one-time sale of a System 1 ensured continued sales of STERIS 20, the patented sterilizing solution, STERIS had a built-in stream of recurring revenue. By 1995, the company's revenues were almost evenly split between capital equipment sales and recurring sales of consumables, such as chemicals and other accessories.

Mid-1990s Amsco Acquisition: A Giant Step

In December 1995, STERIS made the surprising announcement that it planned to acquire Pittsburgh-based Amsco International. What made this acquisition so unusual was that, with more than 2,000 employees and $400 million in sales, Amsco was at least five times the size of STERIS. The 100-year-old Amsco was the nation's leading manufacturer of steam and gas sterilizers, surgical tables and lights, and related infection prevention products. Despite its strong market position, however, the company was plagued with FDA regulatory problems, diminishing sales numbers, and a too-rapid turnover in management. Amsco needed a boost—and STERIS needed to diversify its product line. "When we began STERIS 10 years ago, we knew we would always have to have a broader and deeper product line," said STERIS CEO Bill Sanford in an article in the *Akron Beacon Journal.* "Amsco was a leader in some of the more traditional technologies, and the product lines were very complementary, with no overlap," he explained. The acquisition, which was completed in May 1996, added some 300 items to STERIS' product line. It also positioned the company as an industry leader in both the large-scale, heat-based sterilization systems traditionally used in hospitals and the smaller, low-temperature systems it pioneered, which were often used in outpatient and clinic settings.

After the Amsco addition, STERIS had 35,000 customers and major manufacturing operations in the United States, Ger-

many, Finland, and Canada. As anticipated, revenues rose sharply—up to $587.8 million for the fiscal year ending March 31, 1997, a 544 percent increase from the previous year's $91.2 million. However, after various acquisition costs, including $81.3 million to close Amsco's Pittsburgh headquarters, STERIS was left with a net loss of $30.6 million for the year.

The Amsco buy also had negative short-term effects on the company's stock. Analysts and investors predicted that Amsco's bulk and baggage would drag down STERIS' pace of growth. When the acquisition was announced in December 1995, the company's stock dropped 22 percent in a single day. The worries continued in the months both before and after the deal closed. STERIS stock fluctuated throughout 1996, slowly gaining momentum only to drop sharply again in January 1997, when the company posted earnings below analysts' expectations.

Further Expansion: 1996–97

Despite wobbly stock prices and Wall Street naysayers, STERIS proceeded undaunted to pursue an aggressive growth strategy. In September 1996, the company acquired Surgicot, Inc., a developer of sterility assurance technologies and products. Three months later, the company bought Calgon Vestal Laboratories, the infection and contamination control division of Bristol-Myers Squibb. With about 400 employees and annual sales of more than $50 million, Calgon Vestal was a market leader in developing and manufacturing instrument decontamination products, high-risk and routine skin care products, hard surface disinfectants, and surgical scrubs.

After a six-month lull, STERIS re-entered the acquisitions game in mid-1997. In July, the company purchased Joslyn Sterilizer Corporation, a Rochester, New York, manufacturer of steam and low-temperature gas sterilizers. Two months later, it purchased the New Jersey-based Isomedix Inc. for $130 million. With facilities in the United States, Canada, and Puerto Rico, Isomedix provided contract sterilization services to manufacturers of prepackaged medical equipment and consumer products. Its sterilization methods included irradiation, fumigation, and electron beam sterilization.

Shortly after it was acquired, STERIS' new Isomedix division made news. On December 3, 1997, the U.S. Food and Drug Administration approved the company's use of irradiation on red meat to reduce bacterial contamination and help protect consumers from food-borne illnesses. FDA approval of the petition, which Isomedix had prepared and submitted in 1994, opened up new business opportunities for STERIS. The company organized a Food Safety Initiative business unit to direct growth in the newly opened arena, and in a December 3, 1997 interview with the Meat Industry Insights News Service said that it planned to offer "a broad range of technologies, systems, products, and services to the food industry."

STERIS ended its fiscal year on March 31, 1998 with net revenues of $720 million, a 22 percent increase from the previous year. The total revenues were evenly divided between sales of capital equipment and sales of recurring consumables, accessories, and services. The company posted net income of $65.5 million for the year, a vast improvement over the previous year's $30.6 million loss.

1998: Gaining Momentum

In early June 1998, STERIS announced FDA approval of its new STERIS System 2S, a point-of-use steam sterilization system. Designed primarily for use in non-acute markets, the System 2S was marketed as a compact, cost-efficient alternative to the large and expensive steam sterilization systems typically used in hospital settings. The System 2S provided the same level of sterilization as these traditional steam sterilizers, but was faster, more flexible, and significantly less expensive—and therefore a sensible option for outpatient, ambulatory, and urgent care centers. Upon its FDA approval, STERIS immediately began marketing the System 2S in both domestic and international markets.

Three months after adding the System 2S to its line of sterilizers, STERIS took on a whole new product line when it acquired the Medina, Ohio-based Hausted, Inc. Hausted, a privately held company, developed and manufactured specialized mobile systems for surgical and diagnostic patient positioning and transport. Although a departure from the existing product portfolio, the Hausted line served as a complement to STERIS' line of surgical support systems and services acquired from Amsco.

STERIS released results for the first half of its fiscal year on October 27, 1998. Net revenues for the six months were $364.9 million—an 11 percent increase from the same time period in the previous year. Net income and net income per share also showed improvements.

In the following quarter, the company expanded its contract sterilization business with the acquisition of Royal Sterilization Systems of Arizona. Royal Sterilization, located in Nogales, Arizona, provided contract sterilization and microbial reduction services to producers of medical devices in the Southwestern U.S. and in Mexico. STERIS also laid the groundwork for technological innovation and enhancement of its surgical products line by forming a strategic alliance with Computer Motion, Inc., of Goleta, California. Computer Motion had recently received FDA approval for its HERMES Control Center, a voice-controlled system that would allow surgeons to control operating room equipment using spoken commands.

Under the STERIS-Computer Motion agreement, the HERMES system was to be integrated with STERIS' line of surgical tables, lights, and cameras. Computer Motion agreed to develop customized software and hardware for STERIS' products; STERIS, in exchange, agreed to purchase the software and hardware on an OEM basis and to market it as a value-added option. "We believe that voice control will play a significant role in the operating room of the future," said Paul Zamecnik, president of STERIS' Product Systems group in a December 10, 1998 press release. He added, "Our agreement with Computer Motion reflects our intent to take a leadership position in the application of this technology."

STERIS had spent a rocky few years on the stock market, beginning when its 1995 Amsco acquisition announcement was met with skepticism. The year 1998 was no exception. Despite the fact that the company drew positive recommendations from Wall Street pundits, stock prices continued to fluctuate. After starting the year at around $25, STERIS' stock climbed to a high of more than $35 in mid-July—only to drop back to the mid-$20 range in December 1998. In November 1998, the company announced that its shares would begin trading on the New York Stock Exchange. STERIS management hoped that the increased international exposure gained by listing on the New York exchange would prove to be a boost.

1999 and Beyond

In late January 1999, STERIS released very positive results for its fiscal third quarter. Net revenues were $205 million—a ten percent increase from the previous year's third quarter and the highest for any quarter in the company's history. The quarter's net income of $23 million was even more encouraging—up 26 percent from the previous year's $23 million. For the nine months ending December 31, 1998, STERIS showed a net income of $56.1 million, a 24 percent increase from the previous year's corresponding nine-month period.

STERIS entered 1999 with more than 4,500 employees; more than 20 sales offices in 17 countries; and 20 production and manufacturing facilities in Canada, Finland, Germany, Sweden, and the United States. In the 11 years since the introduction of the System 1, the company had gone from offering one product plus accessories to more than 2,500 products in 24 major categories.

Despite its diversified product portfolio, however, STERIS' flagship product, System 1, remained central to total sales. At the beginning of 1999, the company had sold more than 16,000 System 1 units to more than 3,700 facilities. The company estimated the potential global market for these units to be at 100,000, with the expected increase of minimally invasive and outpatient surgeries around the world. As sales of the System 1 grew, STERIS experienced a corresponding increase in sales of the accompanying sterilant, STERIS 20. "Customer demand for STERIS 20 Sterilant Concentrate has increased every quarter since STERIS System 1, our site-of-use low temperature sterile processing system, was introduced in 1989," said Sanford in a March 26, 1999 press release, adding "The current rate of growth in STERIS 20 sales is well in excess of our overall business growth, and we expect to continue." At the end of 1998, the company reported that sales of the concentrate— priced at around $5.00 per container—were at 2.6 million for the previous quarter.

The already-high sales of STERIS 20, in tandem with the expected growth in System 1 sales, led STERIS to make plans for expanding its sterilant production capabilities. In late March 1999, the company announced that it would add STERIS 20 production capabilities to an existing chemical facility in St. Louis. In addition, the company planned to establish a new sterilant production facility in Auburn, Australia. The two projected expansions would together more than triple the company's production capacity.

In addition to the expansion of production facilities, STERIS also planned to grow through further acquisitions. During the quarter ending December 31, 1998, the company increased its line of credit from $215 million to $400 million, and in a January 26, 1999 press release, Sanford noted that the credit increase was for "business expansion purposes." Possible markets for expansion included dental, extended care, home care, and other human health care areas, along with the company's traditional hospital and outpatient markets. STERIS was also planning to aggressively grow its Food Safety Initiative operations, which it established with the 1997 acquisition of Isomedix.

Principal Operating Units

Anti-Microbial and Routine Skin Care Products; Biohazardous Waste Management Systems; Cleaning/Decontamination Systems; Contract Sterilization; Environmental Decontamination Products; Food Safety Products; High Temperature Sterile Processing Systems; Low Temperature Sterile Processing Systems; Microbial Reduction Services; Patient Positioning and Transport Systems; Pure Water Systems; Sterilands and Supplies; Sterility Assurance Products; Surgical Lights; Surgical Tables.

Further Reading

McEnaney, Maura, "STERIS Corp. Is on the Way, Way Up," *Akron Beacon Journal,* June 23, 1996.

Russell, John, "Sterilization Company Cleans Up in Market," *Akron Beacon Journal,* June 22, 1997.

"STERIS Corp. Expands with Isomedix Purchase," *Akron Beacon Journal,* August 14, 1997.

"STERIS Corporation Announces FDA Clearance of System 2S Sterile Processing System," *PR Newswire,* June, 9, 1998.

"STERIS Says Approval of Meat Irradiation will Increase Food Safety," *Meat Industry Insights* Internet News Service, December 3, 1997.

"STERIS to Acquire Amsco in $660 Million Deal," *CNN Financial Network,* December 18, 1995.

"STERIS to Pay $76 Million for Bristol-Myers Unit," *New York Times,* November 28, 1996.

—Shawna Brynildssen

Stryker Corporation

2725 Fairfield Road
Kalamazoo, Michigan 49002
U.S.A.
(616) 385-2600
Fax: (616) 385-1062
Web site: http://www.strykercorp.com

Public Company
Incorporated: 1946
Employees: 10,974
Sales: $1.1 billion (1998)
Stock Exchanges: New York
Ticker Symbol: SYK
NAIC: 339112 Surgical & Medical Instrument
Manufacturing; 339113 Surgical Appliance &
Supplies Manufacturing; 339111 Laboratory
Apparatus & Furniture Manufacturing; 621399 Offices
of All Other Miscellaneous Health Practitioners

Stryker Corporation develops and manufactures specialty surgical and medical products for health care markets around the world. The company's product lines include various powered surgical instruments, orthopedic implants, trauma systems for use in bone repair, endoscopic systems, and patient care and handling equipment such as stretchers and hospital beds. Stryker also provides outpatient rehabilitative physical therapy through its Physiotherapy Associates Inc. subsidiary, and is engaged in clinical testing of a patented bone growth protein through its Stryker Biotech subsidiary. The company is broken into ten discrete operating divisions: Howmedica Osteonics; Stryker Endoscopy; Stryker Instruments; Stryker Medical; Physiotherapy Associates; Stryker Pacific; Stryker Europe; Matsumoto Medical Instruments; Stryker Americas; and Stryker Biotech. Each division operates as its own entity and produces its own line of health-related products or services.

1940–77: Innovations in Patient Care

Stryker Corporation was founded by Dr. Homer Stryker, an innovative orthopedic surgeon from Michigan. Stryker, born in 1894, started his medical career as a general practitioner in his hometown of Kalamazoo. After spending eight years in general practice, however, he decided to enter the field of orthopedics. He spent three years in an orthopedic residency at the University of Michigan Medical School at Ann Arbor before returning to Kalamazoo in 1940 to practice his new specialty. He was 45 years old.

As an orthopedist, Stryker discovered that some of the medical products used in his field were less effective than they could be—in terms of both caregiver efficiency and meeting patient needs. While this was, no doubt, a common complaint of many physicians, Stryker's response was somewhat atypical. He began designing new devices to replace those that he found inefficient. His first such device was the Wedge Turning Frame, a mobile hospital bed with a frame that pivoted from side to side. This turning frame, which came to be known in the industry as the ''Stryker Frame,'' allowed doctors to position injured patients as needed while still keeping them immobile. When his invention proved to be successful, Stryker formed the Orthopedic Frame Company, the predecessor to Stryker Corporation, to manufacture and sell the beds.

Stryker continued to pursue his medical career while at the same time overseeing his small company. As before, he found various aspects of patient care that needed improvement, and, as before, he designed and built solutions. One of his next inventions was the Cast Cutter, a motorized saw that cut through patients' casts without cutting the skin underneath. As his company grew and began to manufacture a more diverse line of medical devices, Stryker insisted that each product either improve the efficiency of the caregiver or reduce the cost of providing treatment. In 1946, the name of the company was changed to Stryker Corporation.

Stryker's son, Lee, became president of the company in 1955, and continued to run it in much the same fashion as had his father. Stryker worked to improve and market the company's line of hospital beds and stretchers, which made up almost 70 percent of its total sales. He also focused on the development of a series of innovative medical devices, including the first medical pulsed irrigation system and the first flume evacuator for bone cement. As Stryker grew the company's product line and sales presence, he maintained a very centralized form of management, keeping a close hold on all decision making.

In the mid-1970s, one of his top-down decisions had very negative results. After tinkering with his salespeople's compensation arrangement, switching them from commission to salary, Stryker found himself with virtually no sales force at all. While it was still in the middle of this sales force crisis, the company was dealt an even worse blow. Lee Stryker was killed in a plane crash in July 1976.

It was into this turbulent atmosphere that Stryker's new CEO, John W. Brown, entered in 1977. Brown, a 43-year-old native of Tennessee, had previously been in charge of a subsidiary of Bristol-Meyers Squibb that manufactured surgical instruments. When he was first offered the Stryker position in 1976, he declined. He was happy at Squibb, satisfied with his progress and thoroughly entrenched in the corporate culture. The Stryker board was persistent, however, offering Brown a second chance at the CEO position in 1977. That time he accepted, although apprehensively.

1977–83: John Brown's Company

Brown had definite ideas about what Stryker needed, and he moved quickly to realize them. One of his first moves was to rebuild the decimated sales force, changing the compensation structure back to commission. He also set up a formal budget, worked to trim operating costs, and established a procedure for managerial goal-setting. After instituting more formal management controls, Brown turned his focus to Stryker's product line. In addition to expanding its line of surgical power tools, Brown added a new category to the company's product line with the 1979 acquisition of Osteonics Corp. The three-year-old Osteonics was a maker of hip implants for joint replacement surgeries.

Also in 1979, the Stryker family decided to sell some of their stock in the company, and Stryker was taken public. It was at this time that Brown announced an ambitious goal for the company: a 20 percent annual growth rate from then on. He chose this goal because he had been told that emerging growth companies had growth rates of no less than 20 percent. Brown did not soft-pedal his expectations, referring to his 20 percent growth goal as ''the law'' and demanding that each and every employee do his or her part to achieve it.

Overall, Brown's early years at Stryker were not smooth ones. His style of management and straightforward attitude clashed with many of the existing executives, and his changes were not always met with enthusiastic acceptance. Rocky transition notwithstanding, Brown delivered on his promises; Stryker consistently showed no less than 20 percent annual growth. In 1981, it

was named to the *Forbes* list of the Best 200 Small Companies in America, where it would remain for ten years straight.

1983–85: Sweeping Changes

While Stryker was struggling through its own personal transitions, the health care industry itself was undergoing even greater upheavals. Since the passing of the Medicaid and Medicare bills in the mid-1960s, health care costs had skyrocketed. Between 1970 and 1980, U.S. annual medical care expenditures had more than tripled, triggering a social and governmental backlash. Concerned with excessive spending under the Medicaid and Medicare plans, the federal government began looking for ways to control those costs. In 1983, the Reagan administration instituted a new payment system for hospital patients on Medicare, which was designed to reduce unnecessary treatments and hospitalizations. Under this system, the Prospective Payment System, hospitals were reimbursed for the cost of care determined by diagnosis rather than by length of hospitalization or actual services performed.

The Prospective Payment System took its toll on hospitals and on patients. Many treatments and procedures that had formerly required hospital admission became outpatient procedures. Hospital admissions dropped, patient stays became much shorter, and health care providers had to look for ways to contain their own costs. Unfortunately for Stryker, fewer hospital admissions meant the need for fewer hospital beds, the company's main source of revenue. To offset this slowdown, Brown led Stryker into new product areas that would be less affected by health care cost controls.

One such area was biotechnology. In 1985, Stryker entered into a long-term collaborative research program with Creative BioMolecules, Inc. The purpose of the collaboration was to develop an implant that utilized an osteogenic protein. The protein, OP-1, occurred naturally in humans and helped to promote natural bone growth and healing. Using DNA engineering, Stryker and Creative were able to produce this protein and began testing its use in animals. Early trials indicated that OP-1 stimulated the formation of new bone when it was implanted in bony areas that were not healing properly. A year later, Stryker again added to its product portfolio with the acquisition of Syn-Optics, Inc. Syn-Optics specialized in endoscopic systems—medical video cameras, light sources, powered instruments, and disposable materials used in minimally invasive surgical procedures. Unlike the hospital bed market, the demand for endoscopic equipment was growing rapidly. Endoscopic procedures, which were usually done on an outpatient basis, were increasingly replacing traditional, more invasive procedures for a wide range of diagnostic and surgical applications. Stryker's newly acquired endoscopy business soon became one of its fastest growing divisions.

As the company's product line grew more diverse, Brown made a radical departure from Stryker's traditional management style. He completely decentralized the company, breaking it into several fully autonomous operating divisions. Each division head became responsible for setting the division's goals, establishing its manufacturing operations, and managing its sales and marketing efforts. Brown believed that in a business operating in diverse markets, decentralization was a natural choice. "Decentralization allows each division to run like its own business, and make quicker decisions about product and strategy," he said in a November 1994 interview with *Sales & Marketing Management.* "We want each autonomous division to enjoy all the thrills of success and all the anxieties of failure. There's nothing like running your own business," he observed.

1986–97: New Products, New Divisions

One byproduct of Stryker's decentralization was a closer relationship between sales staff and customers. Whereas previously sales reps had been responsible for selling the whole gamut of Stryker's products, the decentralization allowed them to narrow their focus. They became better acquainted with a smaller product portfolio and thus better able to understand and respond to their customers' needs. From these closer customer relationships, salespeople began to garner ideas for new products and for ways to improve existing ones. Stryker responded to this influx of product ideas by sinking more money into research and development. Between 1986 and 1991, the company almost quadrupled its research and development (R&D) budget, and doubled its product line.

The 1990s ushered in a flurry of acquisitions for Stryker. In 1992, the company acquired Dimso S.A., a French maker of spinal implant systems used for patients with degenerative spinal diseases and spinal injuries. Another acquisition followed in 1994, when Stryker bought a majority interest in Matsumoto Medical Instruments, Inc. Matsumoto was one of the largest distributors of medical devices in Japan. Also in 1994, the company purchased a product line called Steri-Shield from a private company. Steri-Shield was a personal protection system that helped protect operating room personnel from infectious diseases. Stryker entered the market for orthopedic trauma treatment systems in 1996 with the acquisition of Osteo AG. The Switzerland-based Osteo was a maker of equipment used to set bone fractures.

At the same time Stryker was expanding via acquisition, its existing businesses were meeting Brown's goal of growing by 20 percent each year. The company's revenues steadily ratcheted up, increasing from sales of $280.6 million in 1990 to $980.1 million in 1997. Net earnings followed suit, from $33.5 million in 1990 to $125.3 million in 1997. Its consistent success won high favor from Wall Street pundits, industry analysts, and even a U.S. president. In 1992, President George Bush paid a visit to Kalamazoo to recognize Stryker for its achievements. "Stryker is celebrated across the nation and around the world for the quality of your work and the excellence of the management, the way it's handled," Bush said in an address to Stryker employees. "You're leaders in an innovative industry that makes our country proud."

1998 and Beyond: Becoming a Big Player

Near the end of 1998, Stryker acquired Howmedica, the orthopedic division of Pfizer, Inc., for $1.65 billion. Howmedica developed and manufactured specialty medical products used to treat musculoskeletal disorders. Its main products included hip and knee implants, bone cement, and trauma systems for bone repair. Through its subsidiary, Leibinger, Howmedica also manufactured products and instruments used in craniofacial surgery.

Howmedica was integrated with Stryker's Osteonics division, which was renamed Howmedica Osteonics.

The purchase of Howmedica was highly significant in that it transformed Stryker from a small player into a very large one. Brown's decision to make this jump had much to do with the changing face of the health care marketplace. For the past several years, a trend toward consolidation had been sweeping the industry. Increasingly, independent hospitals and surgery centers were being absorbed into large health care conglomerates. As a result, purchasing power was often centralized—and physician preference became less significant than economies of scale. Stryker, who had built its sales approach on personal relationships with individual decision-makers, realized that it could not compete effectively as a small company any longer. "Larger institutions and buying groups are demanding everhigher quality at ever-lower cost, and they prefer to deal with clearly identified market leaders," Brown wrote in his 1998 letter to shareholders, adding "In this environment, only companies that offer scale and superior efficiency will succeed."

As Stryker wound down its sixth decade in business, it remained true to its growth goal. Although the purchase of Howmedica broke its 21-year streak of 20 percent net earnings increases, the company expected to return to its historical growth rate as early as the year 2000. Its long-term growth strategy centered around the global marketing of diversified product lines with an orthopedic core. With well-developed markets in the United States and Asia, Stryker planned to improve its position in Europe, Australia, and the rest of the world. It also planned to continue aggressively developing and marketing new, innovative products within its key markets, as well as improving and expanding its existing lines.

Principal Divisions

Howmedica Osteonics; Physiotherapy Associates; Stryker Biotech; Stryker Canada; Stryker Endoscopy; Stryker Europe; Stryker Instruments; Stryker Japan; Stryker Latin America; Stryker Leibinger; Stryker Medical; Stryker Pacific; Stryker Trauma.

Further Reading

"Bigger Niche at Stryker," *New York Times,* December 16, 1980.

Brewer, Geoffrey, "20 Percent—or Else," *Sales & Marketing Management,* November 1994, p. 66.

Gowrie, David, "Giving Back the Ability to Walk," *Hackensack (New Jersey) Record,* October 28, 1998.

Jones, John A., "Stryker Keeps Moving with Strong Research Commitment," *Investor's Business Daily,* January 20, 1992.

Kramer, Farrell, "Stryker Becomes a Synonym for Consistency," *Investor's Daily,* July 6, 1990.

Rogers, Doug, "Stryker Skillfully Handles a Steady Run of New Products," *Investor's Daily,* March 21, 1991.

Sawaya, Zina, "Focus Through Decentralization," *Forbes,* November 11, 1999, p. 242.

Seebacher, Noreen, "Stryker Products: Just What the Doctor Ordered," *Detroit News,* May 6, 1991.

Stavro, Barry, "The Hipbone's Connected to the Bottom Line," *Forbes,* December 3, 1984.

Stroud, Michael, "Stryker: Another Play on Endoscopy Boom," *Investor's Business Daily,* October 25, 1991.

—Shawna Brynildssen

Syms Corporation

Syms Way
Secaucus, New Jersey 07094
U.S.A.
(201) 902-9600
(800) 477-7967
Fax: (201) 902-9278
Web site: http://www.symsclothing.com

Public Company
Incorporated: 1983
Employees: 2,511
Sales: $343.9 million (1999)
Stock Exchanges: New York
Ticker Symbol: SYM
NAIC: 44814 Family Clothing Stores

Syms Corporation operates a chain of off-price apparel stores under the Syms name, selling men's clothing and haberdashery; women's clothing, separates, and accessories; children's wear; and luggage, domestic goods, and fragrances. There were 44 Syms stores at the end of 1998, most of them east of the Mississippi, and especially concentrated in the New York City area, where the company began. Geared to the quality-minded but price-conscious middle-income buyer, Syms is unusual among discounters in stocking a large quantity of high-end apparel. It has copyrighted its long-standing slogan, "An educated consumer is our best customer." A 1998 *Consumer Reports* survey rated Syms the best of seven off-price clothing store chains.

Apparel Discounter and Manhattan "Real Estate Legend" Launches Business in 1959

Sy Merns was a radio sportscaster in the early 1950s when he left this field to join his older brother George's discount clothing store—inherited from their father—on Greenwich Street in lower Manhattan. As Sy's daughter Marcy described the situation in her 1992 book *Mind Your Own Business and Keep It in the*

Family, Sy Merns labored for six years to come up with $6,000—the agreed-on amount for 20 percent of the business. At the end of this period, however, George said 20 percent of the store was now worth much more, so Sy left, about 1959, to open, with a partner, a rival clothing store around the corner in 2,000 square feet of space, an enterprise that he named "Sy Merns." Since "Merns Mart" was the name of George's store, he went to court and forced his brother to change the name. Sy then abbreviated the name of his store to "Syms" and, eventually, took it as his legal surname—apparently in 1986.

Syms bought brand-name menswear irregulars at less than wholesale prices and, after removing the labels at the manufacturer's insistence, sold the merchandise at about 40 percent below retail, offering the widest selection possible. By 1967 there were five Syms stores, all in the rapidly developing low-rent area on the western fringe of Manhattan's financial district. Three of them were scheduled for demolition, two to make way for the giant World Trade Center. With a lease running through May 1968, Merns was refusing to vacate another of the five so that U.S. Steel Corp. could construct a 50-story office building unless he received a payment in six figures. According to his daughter, he "prevailed and became a real estate legend." Merns bought out his partner in 1968.

Syms opened a small Miami store in 1969, which moved to a larger location in Hallendale, Florida, in 1975. A small Buffalo store opened in 1970. By 1974 the single remaining Manhattan location was on Park Place, still on the western fringe of the financial district but now occupying 36,000 square feet. The company had opened its first suburban store in Bergen County, New Jersey, and in 1974 it opened another one, in Roslyn, Long Island. In 1978 it opened its first store in the Washington, D.C. metropolitan area, in Falls Church, Virginia.

Syms did not advertise its wares until 1971, when accountants told the boss that the money saved by not doing so would be lost to taxes anyway. As a former broadcaster, Merns announced his own commercials. The company broadcast its first television commercial, with Merns again as its representative, in 1974, the same year it adopted the "educated consumer is our best consumer" slogan that would become increasingly familiar to New Yorkers. It began selling women's clothing in 1971.

456

Syms had net income of $4 million on net sales of $72.1 million in 1979. The following year, when it had eight units, the enterprise purchased A. Sulka & Co., a prestigious retailer of men's haberdashery, established in 1895, with a store on Fifth Avenue in midtown Manhattan and another in London. There was also a second New York City store and a San Francisco one. In 1983 Sulka acquired a Paris operation. Leased Sulka departments were placed in Philadelphia, Houston, and Chicago department stores in 1983, 1984, and 1985, respectively. A Sulka store on Manhattan's Park Avenue became the chain's flagship in 1985, and a Troy, Michigan outlet was added in 1988. The Sulka chain was sold in 1989.

More Stores, Bigger Profits in the 1980s

There were ten Syms stores in the fall of 1982. By now manufacturer's labels appeared in all the clothing—women's as well as men's—accompanied by a tag listing both the nationally advertised price and the sharply discounted Syms price. Sy Syms, appearing in his own television spots and writing his own copy, would deliver messages such as, "If a garment doesn't have a recognizable name on it, it's not advisable to buy it." He was receiving goods from hundreds of manufacturers, one of whom told Walter McQuade of *Fortune*, "You have to bite the bullet and get rid of mistakes. I called Sy and dickered. . . . A soft touch he's not, but he doesn't gouge. He keeps his commitments." And Syms—free of debt—paid promptly out of cash flow, sometimes within ten days. In 1981 the chain sold more than 150,000 men's suits with more than 200 well-known brand names.

In a 1985 *Forbes* article, however, Richard Behar wrote that Syms was "sometimes hoodwinking its 'educated consumers' and sometimes selling them inferior-grade garments that can be mistaken for top-of-the-line goods." Behar reported that, for example, although Syms was the largest customer in the United States for "leftover" Givenchy suits, these were "visibly of lower overall quality than the Givenchys that are sold in department stores." He added that Syms had agreed to remove the Givenchy label before the customer was allowed to take the suit out of the store. "On balance," Behar concluded, "it seems clear that a good deal of Syms' merchandise is, in fact, manufactured specifically for it and is not 'leftover' in the accepted sense of the word."

This challenge to Syms's credibility did not go unanswered. Interviewed by Jay Palmer of *Barron's* in 1988, the founder's feisty eldest child—by now second in command to her father—insisted, "Despite what you have read elsewhere, the suit that you buy from Syms is made by the same people from the same fabric and the same patterns at the same factory and with the same workmanship as the suit with the same label sold at much higher prices in other stores. We are talking fabrics, not finished suits, when Syms buys from the suit maker. . . . We always ask them to make the suits up into the more conservative, lower-priced lines because that is what does best at Syms. Critics who look at our suits and compare them elsewhere don't compare like with like."

Syms, like other off-price retailers, saved its customers money by not putting up a front. There were no mannequins to display the merchandise, the dressing rooms had no separate stalls and were dimly lit, alterations, gift wrapping, and deliveries were extra, only Syms's own credit card was accepted, and the stretched-thin sales staff received no commissions. Syms maintained it held no sales, but its stores frequently announced "dividends," especially on rainy and snowy days, and certain women's garments were marked down every ten days until sold. Some 64 percent of Syms's $179.2 million in 1983 sales was generated by men's tailored clothes and haberdashery and 32 percent by women's dresses, suits, separates, and accessories. A small portion of the merchandise, mostly sweaters, jackets, and shirts, was being sold under the company's own "S" private label, but by 1987 brand or designer names were on all garments in Syms stores.

Syms made its initial public offering in 1983, clearing nearly $30 million in selling shares of its stock. Sy Syms, according to Behar, pocketed about $25 million and also retained control of 80 percent of the stock. To the 11 existing Syms stores, the company added, in 1984, new ones in two Chicago suburbs—Niles and Addison—and a Philadelphia suburb—Cherry Hill, New Jersey. By this time the Hallendale, Florida store had moved to Fort Lauderdale, the Buffalo store had moved to nearby Williamsville, two outlets were in Boston suburbs, a second New Jersey store had opened in Woodbridge, and Westchester County, New York also had a Syms store.

Expansion continued at a rapid pace in subsequent years. A second Philadelphia-area store opened in 1985 in King of Prussia, Pennsylvania. New Syms stores were established in 1986 in Monroeville, Pennsylvania and Secaucus, New Jersey. In 1987 the chain opened stores in Norcross, Georgia, Southfield, Michigan, Brentwood, Missouri, and North Randall, Ohio, and in 1988 in Hurst, Texas (outside Dallas), and in Charlotte and Henrietta, New York. The company moved its headquarters and warehouse from Lyndhurst, New Jersey, to Secaucus in 1987. That year was Syms's tenth consecutive year of record sales and net income. Its operating margin before taxes—once, at 14 percent, the highest of any U.S. retailer—remained at a comfortable 12.5 percent. The chain, in 1988, no longer was cutting out famous-name labels before buyers left the stores, but it continued its policy of not mentioning manufacturers' names in its advertising.

Sticking to Its Formula in the 1990s

Syms moved its Roslyn store to Westbury in 1989 and opened new stores in Baltimore, Houston, and Tampa in 1990. In the recessionary fiscal year ended February 28, 1991, profits slipped for the first time since 1977. The chain—which in 1992 owned, rather than leased, 18 of its stores, compared with only one in 1983—found itself overstocked with merchandise and was forced to slash its prices. Almost a dozen new Syms stores opened during the next few years, but revenues remained stagnant and net income dropped in 1994 to the lowest level since 1982. Industry observers noted that retailers like Syms were facing increased competition from other off-price stores, discounters, and department stores.

With company stock selling in late 1995 for only $8 a share, compared to $15 a share in its initial public offering a dozen years earlier, Sy Syms explored the possibility of taking his company private but ultimately rejected the idea because of the need to take on a major debt load. In the fiscal year ended March 1, 1997, Syms recorded its highest profit level in seven years. The company opened a second Manhattan outlet in midtown, on high-rent Park Avenue, in late 1996. Despite the location, a retail consultant, Alan Millstein, told Beth Fitzgerald of the *Newark Star-Ledger* that Syms "runs the homeliest looking stores in retailing," adding that even the new Park Avenue store "looks like a used airplane hangar—but it's jammed full of people."

Its momentum restored, Syms announced in April 1997 plans to open 19 new stores over the next four years, including four in Los Angeles and two each in San Francisco, Seattle, and Toronto, thereby entering the West Coast and Canada for the first time. The Atlanta, Baltimore, Detroit, Houston, and Miami metropolitan areas, plus the Princeton, New Jersey area, were slated to receive second units. For Atlanta, Detroit, and Miami, this was accomplished in 1998. A Syms opened in Boston in 1998, and similar downtown outlets were scheduled for Chicago in 1999 and Washington, D.C. In April 1999 Syms opened its 12th store in the metropolitan New York City area, in Lawrenceville, New Jersey. The chain's stores were averaging 40,000 square feet in size and holding some 8,000 suits on average.

Marcy Syms, president since 1983 and chief operating officer since 1984, succeeded her father as chief executive officer in January 1998. She vowed not to make any major changes, retaining the chain's large selection of merchandise and its no-frills ambience, telling Jean Palmieri of *DNR/Daily News Record,* "We see no need to fool around with a successful formula." Two younger brothers were serving as vice-presidents. At 71, Sy Syms retained the position of chairman and continued to come into the office every day. He owned about 41 percent of the company's shares of stock at this time, and members of his family held another 11 percent.

In the year ended February 28, 1998, the company registered record net income of $23 million, sending its stock price to the $15-a-share level. The fiscal year ended February 27, 1999 was not as rosy for Syms as the previous one. Net sales fell $9 million, to $343.9 million, and net income dropped $5.5 million, to $17.5 million. Men's tailored clothes and haberdashery accounted for 53 percent of sales; women's dresses, suits, separates, and accessories, for 31 percent; shoes, eight percent; children's wear, six percent; and luggage, domestics, and fragrances, two percent. The company blamed the downturn on an

undersupply of the lower-priced brands that its customers were seeking. Syms's stock dropped back to the $8-a-share level. The chain continued its record, however, of never losing money in a quarter, much less a year. Always conservatively financed, it had a long-term debt of only $400,000 in early 1998.

Principal Subsidiaries

Generic Products Inc.; The Rothschild's Haberdashery Ltd.; SYL, Inc.; Syms Advertising, Inc.

Further Reading

Behar, Richard, "Hi, This Is Sy Syms," *Forbes,* September 9, 1985, pp. 30–32.

Fitzgerald, Beth, "Syms Stays Ahead of the Retail Pack by Meeting Customer Expectations," *Newark Star-Ledger,* April 9, 1997, pp. 37–38.

Furman, Phyllis, "Sy, Marcy Outrun Apparel Downturn," *Crain's New York Business,* January 27, 1992, pp. 1, 41.

Gellers, Stan, "Syms Schools Consumers on Better Suits," *DNR/Daily News Record,* April 23, 1997, pp. 2, 14.

——, "Syms Set To Embark on Major Expansion," *DNR/Daily News Record,* April 25, 1997, cover, p. 1.

Kaplan, Don, "Syms Steps Out on Park Avenue," *DNR/Daily News Record,* November 22, 1996, p. 3.

——, "Syms Sticking to Its 'Values,' " *DNR/Daily News Record,* December 12, 1994, pp. 10–11.

Lasseter, Diana G., "Sy Syms Wants To Take Syms Private," *BUSINESS News New Jersey,* October 4, 1995, p. 8.

Lipowicz, Alice, "Retail's Slow Summer Tests Syms' Fiber," *Crain's New York Business,* October 5, 1998, p. 40.

"Marcy Syms Discusses How Retail and Her Family Business Are Entering a New Era," *BUSINESS News New Jersey,* November 29, 1995, p. 25.

McQuade, Walter, "The Man Who Makes Millions on Mistakes," *Fortune,* September 6, 1982, pp. 106–08, 110, 112, 116.

Palmer, Jay, "Fancy Labels, Plain Prices," *Barron's,* September 26, 1988, pp. 18, 20, 47.

Palmieri, Jean E., "It's Marcy's Turn To Educate the Consumers," *DNR/Daily News Record,* April 29, 1998, pp. 4–5.

Prial, Frank J., "Small Haberdashery Upsets U.S. Steel's Skyscraper Project," *Wall Street Journal,* September 18, 1967, pp. 1, 21.

Syms, Marcy, *Mind Your Own Business and Keep It in the Family,* New York: Mastermedia Limited, 1992.

—Robert Halasz

Components for a Modern World

Technitrol, Inc.

1210 Northbrook Drive, Suite 385
Trevose, Pennsylvania 19053
U.S.A.
(215) 355-2900
Fax: (215) 355-7397
Web site: http://www.technitrol.com

Public Company
Incorporated: 1947
Employees: 21,400
Sales: 448.5 million (1998)
Stock Exchanges: New York
Ticker Symbol: TNL
NAIC: 334419 Other Electronic Component
Manufacturing

A fast-growing supplier to the data communications, telecommunications, housing, and automobile industries, Technitrol, Inc. manufactures electronic components and metallurgical products at 28 locations in 15 countries. Technitrol's electronic components, which include delay lines and pulse transformers, are used by manufacturers to modify or filter electrical signals. The company's metallurgical components include electrical contacts and assemblies and contact materials used in circuit breakers, wiring devices, and a variety of electrical products and appliances. During the 1990s, Technitrol expanded aggressively overseas to become a leading supplier to data communications and telecommunications manufacturers.

Post-World War II Origins

Technitrol was founded in 1947 by four engineering graduates of the University of Pennsylvania's Moore School of Engineering, each a participant in the development of the ENIAC, the world's first electronic computer. Their pioneering work in the design and development of computer equipment was carried over into their early development of Technitrol, which itself became a pioneer in the computer and electronics industries. Technitrol held the first patent for a magnetic disk drive, which later became the prevalent storage medium for modern computers. The company never manufactured magnetic disk drives, however, deciding the start-up costs involved in such an endeavor were too high. Instead, Technitrol licensed the patent to companies such as IBM, Sperry Rand, RCA, and General Electric, and opted to manufacture other, less capital-intensive products it had developed, products that could be used in the computer industry and by other industries. The company pioneered the development of mercury delay lines and magnetic drums for computer-memory storage, discovering, as it delved into the development of computer equipment during the late 1940s, that there was a dearth of suitable electronic components available on the market. Forced to make its own electronic components, Technitrol's management realized other companies faced a similar problem. Consequently, company executives resolved to market the electronic components developed by their engineers to other manufacturers, a decision that broadened the company's customer base considerably—widening its scope from those companies involved in the nascent computer industry to the scores of manufacturers involved in the more broadly defined electronics industry.

Positioned as an electronic components developer and manufacturer, Technitrol achieved early success in 1952 by producing its proprietary pulse transformers, the manufacture of which required less start-up investment than magnetic disk drives. IBM figured as an early and important customer for Technitrol's pulse transformers and its delay lines, providing sure financial footing as the company developed into an electronic components maker. Development into a premier electronic components manufacturer was pursued through internal expansion and through acquisitions. In 1958 Technitrol purchased L&O Research and Development Corporation, which bolstered the company's capabilities to produce electronic equipment and provided expertise in the development of complex electromechanical and electro-optical devices—a facet of Technitrol's equipment division. In 1961 growth was pursued internally, manifested in the formation of Technitrol Engineering Corporation, a subsidiary established to provide engineering services to industrial and government customers.

By the mid-1960s, Technitrol comprised an equipment division, strengthened by the acquisition of L&O, and a compo-

459

nents division, which designed, developed, and manufactured pulse transformers, delay lines, and other electromagnetic devices. Manufacturing activity for both divisions was conducted adjacent to the company's headquarters, located in suburban Philadelphia, and supported by a third manufacturing facility in Durham, North Carolina, which opened in 1965. Sales offices were operating in Philadelphia and Los Angeles. The composition of the company in the mid-1960s offered a limited view of Technitrol's future, however. By resting its fortunes on the electronics industry—a business whose development was spurred and transformed by advances in technology—Technitrol was forced to rethink its business strategy often, creating a company in constant transition. The changes provoked by advancing technology were continuous, but they were sometimes punctuated definitively, representing turning points in Technitrol's history. The first such momentous period occurred during the early 1970s, when Technitrol was forced to tailor its operations and strategy to accord with the changing needs of its customers.

Early 1970s Diversification

From its founding to the beginning of the 1970s, Technitrol had depended heavily on the demand for its pulse transformers, a breakthrough invention during the company's early years, but no longer a technological marvel years after its development. Advances in core memory technology, Technitrol's management believed, left the company too dependent on its existing product lines, so a diversification program was launched during the early 1970s. The acquisitions were orchestrated by longtime Technitrol employee, Roy E. Hock. Hock, who had joined the company in the mid-1950s, controlled Technitrol from the mid-1970s until the mid-1990s, becoming its most prominent personality during the 20th century.

During his 18 years of service to Technitrol before being named president in 1973, Hock had held the titles of engineering manager, systems division manager, director, and vice-president. As vice-president of the company, Hock served as "the author of our acquisition program," according to Technitrol's chairman in an address to shareholders in the company's 1973 annual report. The acquisitions spearheaded by Hock included companies that would remain integral facets of Technitrol's operations into the 1990s. Foremost among these acquisitions were John Chatillon & Sons Inc. and Advanced Metallurgy, Inc. (AMI), both acquired in 1972. Founded in 1835, Chatillon manufactured mechanical scales for commer-

cial and industrial markets and precision springs and spring assemblies for the scale, aircraft instrument, and controls industries, marketing its products through a worldwide network of distributors. AMI manufactured electrical contacts, typically used in circuit breakers, which were sold to customers such as Westinghouse and General Electric. Other subsidiaries operated by Technitrol—the products of the company's diversification—included Electric Apparatus Company, a manufacturer of small (one horsepower) to large (600 horsepower) electrical motors, and Eastern Data Processing, a subsidiary created in 1968 to provide payroll checks, personnel records, and other data processing services to businesses in the region surrounding Technitrol's headquarters. The addition of these businesses, particularly Chatillon and AMI, contributed to a 125 percent increase in sales between 1972 and 1973, from $4.7 million to $10.6 million, and caused profits to quadruple from $107,000 to $466,000. With the announcement of these record-setting financial totals, the Hock era of leadership began.

A decade after Hock took control, Technitrol's annual revenues hovered slightly below $40 million, one tenth of the total the company generated at the end of the 1990s. The exponential leap in sales was achieved primarily through acquisitions, acquisitions that propelled the company toward a change in its business focus. The "strategic repositioning," as company officials called it, that reshaped Technitrol officially began in 1994, but meaningful progress began at the decade's start, as the company sought to bolster and to tailor its operations for success in the 1990s and beyond.

Entering the 1990s, the company was collecting slightly more than $90 million in sales a year, a total produced by AMI, Chatillon, and Chace Precision Metals, Inc., a Technitrol subsidiary that manufactured thermostatic and clad metals used by manufacturers of components and controls serving the automotive, appliance, electronics, and electrical equipment industries. The company's business, divided into a Components & Transformer Division and a Products Division, was conducted in three business segments: Electronic Products, Electrical Products, and Mechanical Products. The operations involved in two of these business segments were expanded through acquisitions during the early 1990s. In 1991 Technitrol acquired Lloyd Instruments, Ltd., a manufacturer and marketer of equipment used in material testing applications, which became part of the company's Electronic Products business segment. Comprising Lloyd Instruments and certain operations belonging to Chatillon, the Electronic Products segment produced electronic scales, material testing instruments, currency and document counting and dispensing equipment, and electronic components. Technitrol's Electrical Products segment included the company's manufacture of electrical contacts and assemblies, undertaken by AMI. In 1992 the contributions of AMI to this segment were augmented by the acquisition of Doduco Corporation, which manufactured electrical contacts in Cedar Knolls, New Jersey. The company's third segment, Mechanical Products, included the force measuring and weighing instruments and metal laminate material manufactured by Chatillon and Chace.

New Strategy Executed in the Mid-1990s

Annual sales, after the acquisition of Lloyd Instruments and Doduco, amounted to $98 million in 1992, having been held in check during the previous two years primarily because of recessive economic conditions. Although financial growth had been achieved haltingly during the early 1990s, robust gains occurred consistently after 1993, when Technitrol edged past the $100-million-in-sales mark for the first time in its history. The catalyst spurring the company's growth was the sweeping change in business strategy begun in 1994. Organizationally, the company underwent dramatic changes in 1994. The Mechanical Products segment was eliminated, reorganized as the End User/Finished Products segment, which included Lloyd Instruments and Chatillon. The Electrical Products segment became the Metallurgical Products segment, comprising the operations of AMI and Chace. Other striking changes occurred as well, sparked by the strategy devised in 1993, and carried out through acquisitions from 1994 forward. The number of Technitrol employees skyrocketed from 1,000 prior to the benchmark year to more than 21,000 four years into the company's "strategic repositioning." Annual sales, during this four-year span, quadrupled, an increasing percentage of which were garnered from international operations. Fittingly, for a campaign executed by absorbing other companies, the transformation and aggrandizement of Technitrol began with an acquisition, completed in January 1994.

In January 1994 Technitrol acquired Fil-Mag Group from FEE Technology, which included FEE Fil-Mag Taiwan, FEE Fil-Mag Singapore, and Fery Electronics, Inc. Fil-Mag, with manufacturing operations in Taiwan and the Philippines, manufactured delay lines, pulse transformers, and filters. The products were used in a variety of computer and telecommunications applications, which became the focus of Technitrol's strategic repositioning in the years ahead. Data communications and telecommunications were the growing markets of the 1990s, and Technitrol had decided to position itself as an important supplier to such markets in the years ahead.

The acquisition of Fil-Mag was followed in 1995 by other important developments, in what represented a symbolically significant year for Technitrol. After 20 years of leadership, Hock retired, paving the way for a new generation of leadership. James M. Papada, III, a long-time director of Technitrol who had performed legal work for the company during the early years of Hock's presidential tenure, took over as chairman, and Thomas J. Flakoll, the company's president and chief operating officer, earned promotion to chief executive officer. As management changed hands, the company took another important step toward becoming a global supplier to the data communications and telecommunications markets by acquiring Pulse Engineering, Inc., a San Diego-based designer, producer, and marketer of electronic components and modules used by manufacturers of local area networks (LANs) and telecommunications systems. Acquired for approximately $60 million, Pulse's strength was in international markets, where the company maintained an extensive presence through manufacturing operations in Hong Kong, the People's Republic of China, and Ireland. Primarily because of the Pulse acquisition, the sales recorded by Technitrol's Electronic Components segment in 1995 increased more than 65 percent to $68.4 million and profits swelled 130 percent to $10.7 million. In addition, Technitrol's work force tripled in size during the year.

In the wake of the Pulse acquisition, a "new" Pulse organization was formed, comprising the combination of Pulse, Fil-Mag, and the Electronic Components segment, which represented one of the world's largest suppliers of magnetic components to data communications and telecommunications industries. Having broadened the geographic scope of its electronic components operations, Technitrol next moved to accomplish the same for its metallurgical business. In 1992 the company had acquired the U.S.-based operations of Doduco, and in 1996 it acquired the company's European operations, which included Doduco GmbH, with operations in Pforzheim, Sinsheim, and Huchenfeld, Germany, and Doduco Espana, located in Madrid. By the end of 1996, Technitrol's advances on the international front were evident on the company's balance sheet. International sales had increased from 17 percent of total sales to 31 percent of total sales within two years, driven by the growth of the company's European operations, which accounted for six percent of sales in 1994 and 25 percent of sales in 1996.

Technitrol's 50th anniversary in 1997 saw the company continue to build upon its core strength in magnetic components and steer away from businesses deemed outside its scope. Late in the year, the company acquired the magnetic components business of Northern Telecom Ltd., which included manufacturing facilities in Malaysia and Thailand and design offices in Ottawa, Canada. Earlier in the year, management decided to abandon its involvement with test and measurement products, leading to the June divestiture of Chatillon and Lloyd Instruments.

With the sale of Chatillon and Lloyd Instruments, Technitrol's operations were focused on two business segments: electronic components and metallurgical components. On the electronic side, the company was represented by its Pulse organization, while the company's metallurgical business was consolidated in 1998 by integrating AMI, Chace Precision Metals, and Doduco to form a single global subsidiary named AMI Doduco. Each division expanded geographically in 1998 through acquisitions. In July, the company acquired FEE Technology, S.A., a magnetic components manufacturer based in France and supported by operations in Bangkok, Warsaw, and Frankfurt. With sales of approximately $36 million, FEE Technology designed its products for telecommunications and power conversion equipment. Once acquired, the French company became part of the Pulse subsidiary. On the same day Technitrol acquired FEE Technology, it also acquired Metales y Contactos, S.A. de C.V., a Mexico City-based designer and manufacturer of precious and semi-precious metal contacts used in automobiles and other durable goods. The acquisition of Metales y Contactos was indicative of Technitrol's desire to expand its metallurgical business throughout Latin America. The Mexican company was organized as part of the AMI Doduco subsidiary. Late in the year, the purchase of GTI Corporation, a manufacturer of electronic components, added to the breadth and depth of Pulse's operations.

As Technitrol entered 1999, concerns surfaced regarding the company's future leadership. In early January, Flakoll resigned to pursue other interests, leaving the company without a president or a chief executive officer. Meanwhile, as a search for a replacement was conducted by Technitrol's board of directors, Papada filled the leadership vacuum on a temporary basis and directed his energies toward integrating 1998's acquisitions into Technitrol. In April, the board of directors ended their executive search and appointed Papada president and chief executive officer. Concurrent with the decision, the responsibilities of a chairman and chief executive officer were combined, leaving Papada fully in charge of the company's future. Papada's immediate objectives were to assimilate FEE Technology, Metales y Contactos, and GTI Corp. into the Technitrol family, which was expected to be completed by the third fiscal quarter of 1999, while long-term plans called for the continued expansion via acquisition of the company's electronic components and metallurgical businesses.

Principal Subsidiaries

AMI Doduco (PA), Inc.; AMI Doduco (NJ), Inc.; AMI Doduco (PR), Inc.; AMI Doduco (NC), Inc.; AMI Doduco (Mexico), S. de R.L. de C.V.; AMI Doduco Espana, S.L. (Spain); AMI Doduco GmbH (Germany); Dongguan Pulse Electronics Co., Ltd.; FEE GmbH (Germany); FEE S.A. (France); Pulse Canada Ltd.; Pulse Components Ltd. (Hong Kong); Pulse Electronics (Singapore) Pte. Ltd.; Pulse Engineering, Inc.; Pulse Engineering Distribution Ltd. (Ireland); Pulse Philippines, Inc.; Pulse Production (Malaysia) Sdn. Bhd.; Pulse Production (Thailand) Ltd.; Pulse Taiwan Corporation; Technitrol Delaware, Inc.; Technitrol Singapore Holdings Pte. Ltd.; TNL Singapore Components Holdings Pte. Ltd.; Valor East Electronics Ltd. (Hong Kong); Valor Europe Ltd. (United Kingdom); Valor GTI Electronics (Shenzhen) Co. Ltd. (People's Republic of China).

Principal Operating Units

Pulse; AMI Doduco.

Further Reading

"Aberdeen American News, S.D., Farm & Business Briefs Column," *Knight-Ridder/Tribune Business News,* April 12, 1994.

Ahles, Andrea, "Trevose, Pa., Computer Components Maker Continues Past CEO's Strategy," *Knight-Ridder/Tribune Business News,* January 26, 1999.

Armstrong, Michael W., "Technitrol Planning To Buy Chief Competitor for $24M," *Philadelphia Business Journal,* May 2, 1988, p. 4.

Key, Peter, "Merger Target Sues To Close Deal," *Philadelphia Business Journal,* September 25, 1998, p. 1.

——, "Technitrol Blames Report," *Philadelphia Business Journal,* August 7, 1998, p. 3.

"Technitrol Inc.," *Philadelphia Business Journal,* November 13, 1989, p. 20.

"Technitrol Inc.—TNL," *CDA-Investnet Insiders' Chronicle,* June 10, 1996, p. 16.

—Jeffrey L. Covell

Tetra Tech, Inc.

670 N. Rosemead Boulevard
Pasadena, California 91107
U.S.A.
(626) 351-4664
Fax: (626) 351-5291
Web site: http://www.tetratech.com

Public Company
Incorporated: 1966
Employees: 3,800
Sales: $382.93 million
Stock Exchanges: NASDAQ
Ticker Symbol: WATR
NAIC: 54133 Engineering Services; 54169 Other
Scientific & Technical Consulting Services; 54161
Management Consulting Services; 54138 Testing
Laboratories; 513322 Cellular & Other Wireless
Telecommunications

Tetra Tech, Inc. is a leading specialist in the field of environmental restoration and hazardous waste cleanup. The company also develops telecommunications systems and designs and builds infrastructure related to its environmental projects. One of the company's primary customers is the United States government, particularly the Environmental Protection Agency and the Air Force. Other work is performed for state government agencies, foreign countries, and private businesses. The company has grown dramatically since the early 1990s through a series of acquisitions. Tetra Tech and its subsidiaries have over 110 offices worldwide.

1960s Beginnings

Tetra Tech was founded in 1966 by a group of engineers that included Henri Hodara, Dr. Bernard Le Mehaute, and Nicholas Boratynski, the latter of whom was chosen to be the company's first president. The new company's purpose was to perform engineering services for marine and energy related projects. This work included designing ports, harbors, marinas, and other coastal and waterways structures, as well as performing water quality control engineering and the management of gas and oil exploration projects. Other early work reportedly involved research for the Department of Defense, calculating the effects of an offshore nuclear explosion.

During the company's early years its income grew steadily, with annual revenues topping $5 million by 1973. In December of that year Tetra Tech purchased Hydro Products, Inc., a manufacturer of underwater television systems, nuclear reactor inspection camera systems and remote-controlled deep-sea vehicles. Sales of Hydro's products soon accounted for half of Tetra Tech's income. By 1976 the combined companies' annual sales had grown to $18 million.

In January 1977 Tetra Tech offered 500,000 shares of common stock on the over-the-counter market, which in May was listed on the American Stock Exchange. The company had created several subsidiaries by this time including Tetra Tech International, headquartered in Arlington, Virginia, and Hydro Products International. The company's overseas work ranged from surveying and clearing shipping channels in Oman to designing a harbor in Korea. Other international business included selling underwater vehicles and television equipment to oil exploration companies. A major customer was the government of Saudi Arabia.

Tetra Tech's work in the United States in the late 1970s included developing methods of predicting flood levels and frequency for the Flood Insurance Administration, a study of the causes of acid rain for the Electric Power Research Institute, and performing environmental impact studies for the Alaskan gas pipeline. Much work was being done for the U.S. Navy as well, including studies on facets of submarine warfare and the installation of Hydro Products equipment on the Sealab underwater research station. The company had opened almost two dozen offices by this time, mostly in the United States. Although revenues and the company's contract backlog continued to grow, various complications were dragging down profits. These included the loss of a deep-sea exploration prototype and problems receiving payments from Saudi Arabia. Tetra Tech posted its first annual loss in 1979, but steps were quickly taken to decrease risk and the company was back in the black by the end of 1980.

Company Perspectives:

Tetra Tech provides services to protect and improve the quality of life through responsible resource management, sound infrastructure, and rapid communications ability. The company continuously adapts its services to provide for society's changing needs and to meet customer expectations. The three business areas in which the company provides capabilities to its customers are critical to sustaining quality of life and in offering expanding horizons for its services in the future.

Sale to Honeywell in 1982

In 1982 the company was purchased by Honeywell, Inc. for $33.3 million, while Tetra Tech International (TTI) was sold to a separate group at this time. Stories later surfaced about TTI's work for the government of Oman, which included virtually running the Musandam peninsula portion of the country. This rugged area was isolated from the rest of Oman and was close to American enemy Iran. TTI president James Critchfield had worked for the CIA prior to 1974, and while TTI's work officially involved improvement of water distribution, intelligence-gathering activities were also suspected.

Under the parentage of Honeywell in the 1980s, one newly emerging Tetra Tech business was data systems, and in 1984 the company signed a three-year, $30 million contract with the Navy to install hundreds of computer systems on ships and command centers. During the mid-1980s the company's gas exploration and products divisions were gradually phased out, while the engineering business was growing steadily. In 1988 Honeywell sold Tetra Tech's engineering division, and its name, to a consortium consisting of company employees and a Los Angeles investment firm, Riordan Venture Management. The company's data systems division was meanwhile retained by Honeywell, and company co-founder Henri Hodara stayed behind to head this operation. The new, independent Tetra Tech would now be run by Dr. Li-San Hwang, who had been with the company since 1967.

Hwang had fled with his family from Communist China to Taiwan as a child and had emigrated to the United States in the early 1960s to study engineering. He began his career with Tetra Tech as the company's lowest-paid employee, but quickly rose through the ranks and was named director of engineering in 1972, vice-president in 1974, and later senior vice-president of operations. Following the company's acquisition by Honeywell he had been instrumental in shifting Tetra Tech's focus from coastal engineering to environmental engineering and hazardous waste management. When Tetra Tech split off from Honeywell, Hwang oversaw its growth in these fields and would later coordinate a string of acquisitions that increased the company's size dramatically.

The first of these came in 1988 when GeoTrans, Inc. was purchased. GeoTrans specialized in investigating and containing groundwater pollution at hazardous waste sites. Tetra Tech was moving more and more into the field of hazardous waste

cleanup and soon signed several large contracts with the U.S. Navy to perform studies on the waste problems of bases that were being closed. The company's business was steadily growing under the leadership of Hwang, with Tetra Tech also signing environmental restoration contracts with the states of Oregon and California, among others.

1991: Tetra Tech Goes Public Again

In December 1991 the company went public yet again, offering 1.4 million shares of stock on the NASDAQ exchange. The sale was a success, and the stock's price began to climb. The company was soon signing more major contracts, including one with the U.S. Air Force worth $125 million over five years, and another for $60 million with the Army Corps of Engineers. Both of these involved investigating and resolving environmental problems at a variety of contaminated sites around the United States. Tetra Tech also utilized the cash generated by its stock sale to acquire more subsidiaries. In December 1993 the company purchased Simons, Li & Associates, Inc., a California-based water resources engineering firm that specialized in urban drainage, flood control, bridge waterway design, and other types of civil engineering. Simons, Li did business in the United States and abroad, generating annual revenues of $3.3 million. Tetra Tech's own revenues had leapt from $51.5 million in 1991 to $74.5 million in 1993.

The year 1994 saw the acquisition of Simon Hydro-Search Inc., a Denver company specializing in water resource management. The $6 million deal further strengthened Tetra Tech's capabilities in this area. Several years later Hydro-Search was merged into GeoTrans to form HSI-GeoTrans, Inc. Another large contract was signed with the U.S. Air Force in August 1994, one worth up to $100 million over five years. Tetra Tech was to provide environmental assessment, planning, restoration, and compliance at 15 Air Mobility Command bases and installations. Revenues for 1994 reached another peak, topping $96.5 million.

The company's business at this time continued to consist mainly of environmental restoration and hazardous waste cleanup. Tetra Tech's work typically involved making an assessment of a particular situation and defining goals and priorities for the cleanup process. The company was less involved in the actual cleanup work than in the planning end, though it did see some projects through to closure. Tetra Tech also provided analysis of risks for new construction projects with the goal of minimizing future environmental problems. Other work included the creation of integrated resource management programs for military bases.

1995: Acquisition of EMI

In September 1995 Tetra Tech purchased PRC Environmental Management, Inc., familiarly known as EMI. EMI provided hazardous waste management and cleanup for a wide range of U.S. and international clients. Its annual revenues of $100 million and order backlog of $500 million made it nearly the equal of Tetra Tech in size. EMI was integrated directly into Tetra Tech's operations. The acquisition gave the company a much stronger national and international profile, adding over 30 regional offices in the United States alone.

The EMI purchase was closely followed by the acquisition of KCM, Inc., a water quality engineering firm. KCM, based in the Pacific Northwest, had been founded in 1943 and, with its subsidiary CMI, provided a variety of services that ranged from waste and surface water management to transportation projects and building design. KCM had annual revenues of $22 million. The year 1995 was another record year for Tetra Tech, with revenues bolstered by both newly signed contracts and the income of new subsidiaries. Sales topped $120 million, with a net income of over $7.5 million.

In early 1996 Tetra Tech announced that its various companies were in the process of signing contracts with federal and state government agencies worth nearly $800 million. Two-thirds of the company's business at this time came from the federal government. A pair of acquisitions were completed during the year, those of IWA Engineers, Inc. and FLO Engineering, Inc. IWA specialized in design of water and wastewater plants, and also did work for such entertainment business clients as Knott's Berry Farm and Universal Studios. FLO, a Colorado-based firm, was involved in studies of the environment in harsh or mountainous areas. Much of its work was done for the U.S. Bureau of Reclamation.

Acquisitions continued to come fast and furious in 1997, as did the signing of major contracts. In March Tetra Tech announced a $230 million, ten-year deal to perform a variety of tasks at Environmental Protection Agency Superfund sites in the Midwest. Also that month, the company acquired SCM Consultants, Inc. The Kennewick, Washington-based SCM was a designer of various water and wastewater systems, as well as related infrastructure and other types of facilities including schools and penal institutions. SCM had annual revenues of $6 million.

Two months later Tetra Tech purchased Whalen & Company, a wireless telecommunications development firm that operated worldwide. The $66 million Whalen acquisition was the start of a new direction for Tetra Tech, a venture into the growing business of telecommunications. The fields of hazardous waste and water management were expanding less rapidly than they had during the 1980s and early 1990s, and the company was seeking to reduce its reliance on the federal government. Telecommunications were an important aspect of many of the projects the company took on, and development of cell phone transmission towers and other telecommunications facilities were also easy to incorporate into the company's business.

Another wireless firm, CommSite Development Corporation, was purchased in July 1997. CommSite's activities included site acquisition and construction management for the telecommunications industry. Late in 1997 Halliburton NUS Corp. joined the Tetra Tech family and was renamed Tetra Tech NUS. NUS provided environmental and waste management services to private industry and government agencies, and was noted for its ability to successfully manage difficult projects.

The company purchased three new businesses in 1998: CDC Engineering; McNamee, Porter & Seeley, Inc.; and Sentrex Cen-Comm Communications Systems, Inc. The first two were wastewater and engineering service companies, while Sentrex concentrated on television and data networking services. Sentrex, headquartered in Toronto, was Canada's largest pro-vider of such services, with annual revenues of $28 million. Tetra Tech also formed a new division, the Infrastructure Southwest Group, by merging CDC into IWA, FLO, and Simons, Li & Associates. Annual sales for 1998 reached $382.9 million, more than triple the figure of just three years earlier.

In February 1999 Tetra Tech purchased environmental consulting and engineering firm McCulley, Frick & Gilman. In June two additional companies came aboard, D.E.A. Construction Co. of Denver and Baha Communications of Las Vegas. D.E.A., with revenues of $13 million, provided network infrastructure engineering and construction services. Baha, which had $6 million in sales, specialized in the construction and maintenance of communications infrastructure. Tetra Tech also announced the signing of several major contracts, including one for $75 million to perform environmental cleanup and maintenance at Tinker Air Force Base in Oklahoma City. Others were a $100 million deal with the Department of Energy to facilitate safe storage of nuclear weapons, and a $35 million-plus arrangement with the EPA to implement provisions of the Resource Conservation and Recovery Act.

As it neared the end of the 1990s, Tetra Tech was still growing under CEO Li-San Hwang through acquisitions and the negotiation of numerous major contracts. Its reliance on the federal government remained high, but through its newly purchased telecommunications and infrastructure services companies it was branching out into new territory. Since going public in 1991 the company had seen annual revenues grow by more than sevenfold, and its backlog of orders was also at an all-time high. The company appeared well positioned to maintain its status as a leading environmental and hazardous waste services provider, and its future in the telecommunications and infrastructure businesses looked promising.

Principal Subsidiaries

KCM Inc.; Tetra Tech EM, Inc.; HSI GeoTrans, Inc.; GeoTrans Wireless; McNamee, Porter, & Seeley, Inc.; SCM Consultants, Inc.; Whalen & Company, Inc.; McCulley, Frick & Gilman, Inc.; Sentrex Communications Company; Tetra Tech NUS, Inc.; D.E.A. Construction Co.; Baha Communications, Inc.

Principal Divisions

Infrastructure Southwest Group; Integration Technologies.

Further Reading

Dickey, Christopher, "Va. Firm Has Big Role in Oman—Ex CIA Man's Company Guides Ministries on Gulf Peninsula," *Washington Post,* March 24, 1986.

Hughes, Amy, "Tetra Tech: Co. Defends Its Merger Accounting," *Dow Jones News Service,* February 23, 1999.

Mencke, Claire, "Revitalized: Tetra Tech Sees its Business Up from the Ashes in Months," *Investor's Business Daily,* July 21, 1995, p. A5.

Palazzo, Anthony, "Tetra Tech Keeps Its Head Above Water by Shifting with Currents," *Dow Jones Online News,* January 8, 1998.

Turner, Nick, "Leaders & Success: Tetra Tech Inc.'s Li-San Hwang," *Investor's Business Daily,* November 21, 1997, p. A1.

—Frank Uhle

Thomas Industries Inc.

4360 Brownsboro Road, Suite 300
P.O. Box 35120
Louisville, Kentucky 40232
U.S.A.
(502) 893-4600
Fax: (502) 895-6618
Web site: http://www.thomasind.com

Public Company
Incorporated: 1953
Employees: 3,200
Sales: $177.2 million (1998)
Stock Exchanges: New York
Ticker Symbol: TII
NAIC: 333912 Air & Gas Compressor Manufacturing;
   333911 Pump & Pumping Equipment Manufacturing

Thomas Industries Inc. manufactures compressors and vacuum pumps for Original Equipment Manufacturers (OEM) applications. The largest OEM markets for the company's compressors and pumps are in the medical, information technology, automotive, and environmental industries. Until the late 1990s, Thomas was also known as a leading producer of consumer, commercial, and industrial lighting fixtures. In 1998, through a joint venture with competitor The Glenlyte Group Incorporated, its lighting business was spun off into a new company—Glenlyte Thomas Group LLC—which subsequently became the third largest lighting fixture manufacturer in North America, with an estimated 13 percent domestic market share. Headquartered in Louisville, Kentucky, Thomas Industries has more than 25 manufacturing and distribution facilities located in the United States, Europe, and Asia.

20th-Century Predecessors

Thomas Industries was formed in a 1953 merger of two companies—a lighting fixture manufacturer and the maker of electrical spraying machines—both of which came into being in the late 1920s. The unlikely marriage of these two product lines was the cornerstone of what would become the company's two core businesses: lighting fixtures and air compressors/pumps.

The lighting fixture side of Thomas Industries traces its history back to Milwaukee, Wisconsin, and two brothers: Henrik and Ole Moe. The Moe Brothers, together with a number of other entrepreneurs, owned the Moe-Bridges Co., a lighting fixture manufacturer formed in 1919. As a result of friction among the Moe-Bridges management, however, the Moe brothers were frozen out of the company in the late 1920s by the majority owners. Deciding to stay with the industry they knew, the Moes formed another lighting fixture company called Moe Brothers Manufacturing. Henrik's two sons joined the business in the early 1930s, and in 1938, the company moved its operations from Milwaukee to Fort Atkinson, Wisconsin.

While the Moe brothers were building their lighting fixture business, the Electric Sprayit Company—the forerunner to Thomas Industries' compressor and pump division—was also testing its wings. In 1928, the Electric Sprayit Company was formed in Chicago "to manufacture, buy, and sell electrical spraying machines, blowers, air compressors, mechanical, and mercantile devices." In a curious twist of fate, in 1934 the Electric Sprayit Company acquired Moe-Bridges, the company that had forced out the Moe brothers, and moved from Chicago into the Moe-Bridges plant in Milwaukee. In 1939, Electric Sprayit moved its operations again, this time to Sheboygan, Wisconsin.

During World War II, both companies stopped making their standard product lines in order to produce materials for the war effort. At the close of the war, in 1946, Moe Brothers received a large contract from Sears to produce household pressure cookers. Although the company had not previously manufactured pressure cookers, the large stamping presses they had obtained for the war gave them the production capabilities for the job. The brothers planned to use sales revenues from the pressure cooker contract to return to the lighting fixture business. Unfortunately, Sears rescinded the company's contract due to a product malfunction. In the aftermath of the contract loss, pressured by the bank to repay existing debt, the Moe brothers decided to sell the company.

Moe Brothers was purchased in 1948 by a Louisville investment group headed by Lee Thomas. Thomas, the former president of Ekco Products in Chicago, had recently purchased a small saw business in Louisville and was looking for further investment opportunities. His new purchase was renamed Moe Light, and a national advertising campaign was launched to promote residential lighting fixtures. Two years later, Moe Light expanded by opening a new residential lighting factory in Kentucky and acquiring the Los Angeles-based Star Lighting Fixture Company.

1950s Founding of Thomas Industries

In 1953, Moe Light Inc. and the Electric Sprayit Company merged, under the name of Thomas Industries. At that time, Electric Sprayit Company's Sheboygan, Wisconsin, plant produced paint spraying equipment, specialized lighting for the government, and ordinance items. Two years after the merger, Thomas Industries began to diversify further, acquiring a power saw manufacturer and a Detroit-based bathroom cabinetry manufacturer. That same year, Thomas opened a new 114,000-square foot residential lighting fixture plant in Hopkinsville, Kentucky and moved its corporate headquarters from Wisconsin to Louisville, Kentucky. 1955 also marked Thomas Industries' move from a privately owned company to a publicly owned one, with the company's initial public offering.

The remainder of the 1950s were characterized by growth in the form of more acquisitions. The year 1957 saw the addition of the Radiant Glass Company of Fort Smith, Arkansas, a producer of street lighting globes and opalware glass for lighting fixtures. The Radiant Glass Company took over production of the blown glass components for Thomas's lighting fixtures, which had previously been purchased from outside providers. A 1958 acquisition added the Benjamin Electric Manufacturing Company to the Thomas Industries stable. Located in Des Plaines, Illinois, Benjamin Electric was a manufacturer of commercial lighting fixtures. The final acquisition of the decade came in 1959, when the company purchased C&M Products Co., Ltd., of Toronto. Thomas proceeded to use the new foothold to introduce its U.S. products into the growing Canadian market.

In 1961, Lee Thomas stepped down from his position as president of Thomas Industries and was elected to serve as chairman of the board of directors, as well as CEO. Thomas was replaced by the company's former executive vice-president, John Beam. Although this change in leadership was significant, it was perhaps less significant than another change that occurred that same year—a change in the design of the compressor units used in the Sprayit products. In 1961, these units were reconfigured to accommodate other continuous-air source applications. This redesign was the inception of the modern-day Thomas Industries' OEM product line.

Thomas Industries expanded yet again in 1962 and 1963. In 1962, the company acquired the Thomas Products Company of Johnson City, Tennessee, a manufacturer of paint rollers, roller pans, and roller covers. Thomas management felt that the line of paint-related products would complement the Sprayit line of paint sprayers and compressors. In 1963, the company opened a new 250,000-square foot lighting fixture plant in Sparta, Tennessee, to replace the Benjamin Electric facility in Illinois, which was then closed. An existing 50,000-square foot Star Lighting plant in Los Angeles was also replaced by a new facility more than twice the size of the original.

1960s: Restructuring and Further Growth

By 1963, Thomas Industries was sprawling, both in terms of product lines and geographic distribution. To better order and manage the business, the company was split into five operating divisions. Its Residential Lighting Division, which consisted of the former Moe Lighting and Star Lighting lines, included dimmers, recessed, hand-blown glass, and illuminated signs. The company's Commercial and Industrial Lighting Division consisted of Benjamin Electric products, such as air-handling fixtures, dimming systems, electronic signaling devices, and contract metalworking and porcelainizing. The Special Products Division included what would become the company's OEM lines—Sprayit paint sprayers, compressors, and pumps— as well as the Wright power blade and chain saws and Thomas paint rollers, covers, and pans. The final two divisions were more geographic in nature. The Pacific Division handled residential, commercial, and industrial lighting fixtures in the nine western states, Hawaii, and Alaska; and C&M Products oversaw the Canadian market.

The company moved into new territory in the lighting field in 1967, when it acquired Sandel Manufacturing, of Chicago, a producer of portable lamps, and the Phil-Mar Corporation, of Cleveland, a producer of ceramic lamps. This same year, Thomas opened a new residential lighting plant in Beaver Dam, Kentucky, and sold off the Wright Saw operation. The Wright plant was used to accommodate expansion of the Sprayit line of paint spraying equipment. In the fall of 1967, the expanding Thomas Industries' stock was listed on the New York Stock Exchange.

The pattern of expansion and diversification continued through the remainder of the 1960s and into the early 1970s. A 1968 purchase added a Princeton, Indiana, paintbrush plant, whose operations were absorbed by Thomas's paint roller operation in Johnson City, Tennessee. An acquisition in the following year brought Jet Line Products, of Matthews, North Carolina, into the fold. Jet Line's product line included electrical conduit fishing equipment and built-in vacuum cleaning systems. In 1971, the company diversified further by acquiring Harris & Mallow Products, Inc., a maker of decorative wall clocks and weather instruments.

Thomas Industries had expanded well beyond the two-facility operation it began as 18 years earlier. By the end of 1971, the company had more than 2,308,300 square feet of production space in 13 plants. The company employed more than 3,700 persons and had sales of $82 million. The 1970s were to be characterized by a similarly rapid growth rate for Thomas.

New Products and Distribution Channels

Thomas's next two acquisitions were Portland Willamette Company, a major manufacturer of firescreens and fireplace accessories, and House of Mosaics, a small producer of styrene and fiberglass lamps. These 1972 buys were followed in 1973 by the purchase of Abbott Industries, a producer of children's lamps, and Spring Steel Fasteners, Inc. Both Abbott Industries and House of Mosaics served to broaden Thomas's Residential Lighting Division, while Spring Steel Fasteners, which produced products for the electrical and construction industry, added to the Commercial and Industrial Lighting Division.

In 1974, Thomas engineers unveiled a series of new products that was to contribute much to the company's overall growth and to the direction it would take in coming years. These products, stemming from the company's existing line of compressors, included new OEM applications for compressors. Products for the automotive and copying equipment manufacturing industries were especially key to this new phase of growth. To accommodate the expansion of the compressor line, Thomas built a second, 126,000-square foot plant in Sheboygan, Wisconsin.

Also in 1974, Thomas acquired its second clock manufacturer: Colonial Manufacturing Company, a 76-year-old company with production facilities in Zeeland and Grand Rapids, Michigan. The largest maker of grandfather clocks in the world, Colonial also produced wall and mantel clocks. The following year, Thomas purchased All Wood Products Company, located in Hudson, North Carolina. All Wood Products was a manufacturer of wood components for the lamp and furniture industries.

In response to the growing do-it-yourself home improvement market, Thomas launched a new distribution and marketing effort in 1975. The initiative targeted these do-it-yourselfers via mass merchandisers and home building centers. By the end of 1975, the company's fleet of delivery trucks was distributing products to more than 1,500 customers throughout the nation.

Five more companies were added to the ever-diversifying Thomas Industries collection in 1977 and 1978. The first, Oliver-MacLeod Limited, of Ontario, was a manufacturer of insulated chimneys and fireplaces. The second, Fastway Fasteners, of Ohio, manufactured metal and plastic fasteners—a complement to Thomas's 1973 Spring Steel Fasteners acquisition. Los Angeles-based Builders Brass Works Corporation was a manufacturer of builder trim hardware and door control products; and Contempra Industries, of New Jersey produced food preparation appliances, such as yogurt makers, crepe makers, and outdoor grills. In 1978, Thomas acquired Pouliot Designs Corporation, a manufacturer of artificial plants, floral arrangements, and fiberglass planters. In the last major change of the decade, the company sold off its Phil-Mar ceramic lamp division that same year.

The 1980s began with a divestiture, a closing, and two moves. All Wood Products, which Thomas had acquired in 1975, was sold in 1980. Shortly thereafter, the All Illuminating Glass operation, formerly the Radiant Glass Company, was closed. Radiant Glass, purchased in 1957, had been one of Thomas Industries' earliest acquisitions. The company also reshuffled some of its facility locations in 1980. The clock-making Colonial Manufacturing left Grand Rapids to relocate in Kentwood, Michigan, and Abbott Industries moved its operations into an existing plant in Brownsville, Tennessee.

Two more acquisitions of lighting fixture manufacturers followed in 1984: Capri Lighting and Gardco Manufacturing, both of California. Then in 1985, Thomas initiated an asset redeployment program, designed to shed less profitable divisions and reinvest in areas that offered better growth potential. As part of this new program, the company sold off its two clock divisions—Colonial Manufacturing and Harris & Mallow Products—and Contempra Industries, the maker of small, niche kitchen appliances. Following these divestitures, Thomas purchased Emco Lighting, of Milan, Illinois, and entered into a joint venture with a German company, ASF-Gesellschaft Fur Elektrotechnische GmbH & Co KG. Two years later, the German company was completely absorbed by Thomas.

The company's decision to realign its investments set the stage for the next phase of the company: an intensified focus on what are today the company's two main businesses—OEM air pumps and compressors and lighting.

Late 1980s and 1990s: Reorganization and Focus

As the 1980s drew to a close, Thomas repositioned itself to move into the coming decade. Along with a change in leadership brought on by the 1987 retirement of Chairman Lee Thomas came a reorganization of the corporate structure. This new structure tightened Thomas's focus, replacing the five divisions established in the mid-1960s with two key divisions: Lighting and Specialty Products. This reorganization was followed closely by an expansion of the company's compressor and vacuum pumps business, with the acquisition of the Louisiana-based FL Pneumotive and a second German company, Helmut Brey, GmbH.

The next several years were devoted to the dual goals of building the core businesses and divesting of companies that no longer "fit"—that is, those that fell outside the parameters of the two identified growth areas. In 1988, the company sold its interests in North American Decorative Products and Pouliot Designs, companies that were not part of the core businesses. Between 1992 and 1994, the Fastway Fasteners, Oliver-MacLeod, Portland Willamette, and Builders Brass Works divisions were also sold. The divestiture of these four companies further streamlined Thomas and gave it the capital necessary to make more targeted acquisitions.

One of the most significant acquisitions, and the company's largest to date, occurred in 1989 when Thomas purchased Day-Brite Lighting for $90 million. Day-Brite, which manufactured commercial and industrial fluorescent lighting, also owned two separate, specialty product lines: McPhilben, which produced exits and electrical signage, and Omega, which produced architectural specification downlighting. Further growth for the lighting division came with the introduction of a patented, totally electronic fluorescent ballast. This product gave Thomas the distinction of being the only U.S. manufacturer of both electronic ballasts and fluorescent fixtures. In 1997 and 1998, the company grew its Canadian operations by purchasing two niche market manufacturers: ZED, of Quebec, and Horizon/Lite Energy of Ontario.

As the lighting division expanded, Thomas made concurrent efforts to grow the air compressors and pumps operation. In 1990, the German pump and compressor maker, Wilhelm Sauer GmbH, was acquired. One of the most significant expansions for this division came in 1996, however, with the acquisition of Welch Vacuum Technology. Welch, a leading supplier of vacuum pumps for laboratory and chemical equipment applications, served as Thomas's entry into this growing OEM market. During these years of market expansion, the company was also broadening its geographic reach. In 1990, the compressors and pumps division opened a sales office in Japan, which was followed in 1992 by a sales office in Brazil. The company established its Asia Pacific headquarters in Hong Kong in 1997 and this same year initiated manufacturing operations in Mexico and the Czech Republic.

In 1998, Thomas made the most significant change in its corporate history when it merged its lighting division with major competitor, The Glenlyte Group. The joint venture, named Glenlyte Thomas Group LLC, gave Thomas a 32 percent interest, with Glenlyte carrying the remaining 68 percent. The pooling of the companies made the newly formed Glenlyte Thomas the third largest lighting fixture manufacturer in North America, with a domestic market share of approximately 13 percent. The companies each maintained their own brand identifications and organized two separate sales forces to support the two distinct product lines.

By 1998, 50 years after Lee Thomas bought the Moe brothers' stock, Thomas Industries had grown into a major player in its two targeted businesses. The air compressors and pumps division had annual sales of more than two million units into more than 60 countries. Over 40 percent of the $177.2 million total sales were non-domestic. The company had operations in Europe, Asia, and the United States, and sales offices in Germany, the United Kingdom, Japan, Taiwan, China, and the United States.

The lighting division maintained nine manufacturing locations, seven divisions across the United States, and 14 major product lines. The company served markets in residential, office,

educational, retail, healthcare, hospitality, industry, and municipal. Under the structure of the new joint venture with Glenlyte, sales income from Thomas's lighting division was not included in Thomas Industries' 1998 net sales, and therefore could not be meaningfully compared to those of the previous year.

Looking Ahead

Essentially, the merger of Thomas's lighting division with The Glenlyte Group served to further separate the company's two core businesses. With Glenlyte Thomas operating under its own auspices, Thomas planned to devote its energies to growth efforts in the area of OEM air compressors and pumps. The company's 1998 annual report noted that, ''Thomas Industries, formerly a two-core business, has now become a company focused on significantly growing its already world-class compressor and vacuum pump business.''

Strategies for growth in this division included enhanced research and development initiatives, toward the twin goals of developing new products and finding new applications for products. The company also planned to focus on identified growth markets, such as medical, laboratory and chemical equipment, automotive, and specific consumer products. Finally, patterning its future on its successful past, Thomas anticipated expanding into new markets via strategic partnerships, joint ventures, and acquisitions.

Principal Subsidiaries

Welch Vacuum Technology Inc.

Principal Divisions

North American Compressor and Vacuum Pump Group; European Compressor and Vacuum Pump Group.

Further Reading

Benmour, Eric, '''We've Got Some Nice Things Goin' On': Thomas Industries Expects Record Pace to Continue in 1998,'' *Business First of Louisville*, April 13, 1998.
''Glenlyte Group and Thomas Industries Agree to Create Powerful New Joint Venture,'' *Business Wire*, April 29, 1998.
Thomas Industries Inc.: A Complete History through 1998, Louisville: Thomas Industries Inc., 1998.
''Thomas Industries, Glenlyte Complete Joint Venture,'' *Business First of Louisville*, August 31, 1998.

—Shawna Brynildssen

Torstar Corporation

One Yonge Street
Toronto, Ontario
M5E 1P9
Canada
(416) 869-4010
Fax: (416) 869-4183
Web site: www.torstar.com

Public Company
Incorporated: 1958
Employees: 5,965
Sales: $1.33 billion (Canadian) (1998)
Stock Exchanges: Toronto Montreal
Ticker Symbol: TORSF
NAIC: 51111 Newspaper Publishers; 51113 Book Publishers; 551112 Offices of Other Holding Companies

The Torstar Corporation is a diversified publisher based in Toronto, with three major business segments: newspapers, book publishing, and children's supplementary educational publishing. Its newspaper operations include publication of the *Toronto Star,* which has the largest circulation of any daily newspaper in Canada. It also publishes four daily newspapers in southern Ontario, which were acquired in 1999, and more than 50 community newspapers throughout Canada, along with some miscellaneous monthly tabloids. Through a strategic alliance with Sing Tao Holdings Ltd., Torstar publishes the *Sing Tao Daily,* the largest Chinese-language daily newspaper in Canada with editions in Toronto, Vancouver, Calgary, and Montreal. Torstar's book publishing consists of its subsidiary Harlequin Enterprises, the world's largest publisher of series romance fiction. Torstar's children's supplementary educational publishing operations include several publishers acquired in the late 1990s: Frank Schaffer Publications, Tom Snyder Productions, Delta Education, and Brighter Vision Learning Adventures. For 1998 newspapers accounted for 48 percent of Torstar's revenue, book publishing 39 percent, and supplementary educational publishing 12 percent.

Early History

Torstar Corporation was incorporated on February 6, 1958, to acquire the *Toronto Daily Star,* which was first published in 1892. Until 1975 the company's principal activity was publication of the *Toronto Star,* along with other interests in commercial printing and community newspaper publishing. In 1975 Torstar began to acquire interests in domestic and international book publishing as well as supplementary educational products.

Acquisition of Harlequin Enterprises in 1981

In 1981 Torstar acquired Harlequin Enterprises. Harlequin was founded by Canadian publishing executive Richard Bonnycastle in 1949. At first the small firm published a variety of American and British paperbacks, including mysteries, Westerns, classics, and cookbooks. In 1957 Harlequin began purchasing the rights to works of romance fiction published by the British firm of Mills & Boon, which had been publishing romance fiction since 1909. By 1964 Harlequin was publishing romance fiction exclusively.

After Harlequin became a publicly held company in 1968, it began to adopt a unique marketing strategy for book publishing, namely, a packaged consumer goods strategy. It became the first book publisher to use television advertising in North America. Instead of concentrating on bookstores, Harlequin sold its books where women shopped: supermarkets, drugstores, and department stores.

This strategy enabled Harlequin to grow at an annual rate of 25 percent throughout the 1970s. The Harlequin name became accepted as a guarantee of quality, and the company could introduce many new authors each year and still achieve high levels of sales based on its reputation.

In 1971 Harlequin purchased Mills & Boon, an acquisition that included the talents of more than 100 British authors. From 1972 to 1984 overseas acquisitions, joint venture partnerships, and licensing arrangements put Harlequin books in 100 markets. Sales soared from $3 million (Canadian) in 1970 to more than $165 million (Canadian) over the next three decades.

Harlequin's highly successful North American direct mail operation was the final element in the company's best-selling marketing strategy. Direct mail services were introduced subsequently in the United Kingdom, Australia, Holland, France, and Scandinavia.

When Harlequin became a wholly owned subsidiary of Torstar in 1981, it was well established as the world's leading series romance publisher. In 1984 Harlequin acquired Simon & Schuster's Silhouette imprint, one of its most spirited competitors. Under two specially created imprints, Worldwide Mysteries and Gold Eagle Books, Harlequin entered the mystery and male action adventure markets. Harlequin's Steeple Hill imprint became a leader in the inspirational romance market. Harlequin's Web site (www.romance.net) was launched in February 1996.

In 1998 Harlequin sold more than 165 million books worldwide. It published more than 70 titles in 14 series each month. More than 800 Harlequin titles hit the stands each month around the world in more than 100 international markets in more than 23 different languages. The company had editorial offices in 16 countries. Approximately one in every six mass market paperbacks sold in North America was either a Harlequin or Silhouette novel.

In 1999 Torstar began to implement a strategy to develop a major worldwide Internet presence in electronic commerce for Harlequin. In June Harlequin signed an agreement to partner with Women.com Networks, a leading Internet network for women, to integrate Harlequin into the Women.com Network. Harlequin's strategy was to build a strong community-of-interest Web site that would attract romance readers who were online, a market that was projected to grow to 20 million romance readers online by 2002.

Newspaper Publishing Beginnings in 1958

Torstar was first incorporated in 1958 to take over the operations of the *Toronto Daily Star,* later called the *Toronto Star.* It has the largest circulation of any daily newspaper in Canada. In 1999 Torstar added four daily newspapers in southern Ontario, which it acquired from Quebecor Inc. Through its subsidiary, Metroland Printing, Publishing and Distributing Ltd., the company also published more than 50 community newspapers throughout Canada, along with some miscellaneous monthly tabloids. In June 1999 Metroland completed the purchase of Eedy Publications, which added ten weekly newspapers and a printing plant in western Canada.

The *Sunday Star* was launched in October 1977 to compete with the *Sunday Sun.* In 1991 the *Star* began publishing *eye,* a weekly arts and entertainment publication, which was distributed free every Thursday to some 2,200 outlets in the greater Toronto area, with a circulation of 106,000 copies a week.

In 1993 the *Star* completed construction of a new production facility, The Toronto Star Press Centre, on 32 acres of company-owned property on the outskirts of metropolitan Toronto. Since July 1993 the *Star* has been entirely printed and distributed from the Press Centre. In addition to expanding printing capacity, the Press Centre allowed for the use of full color throughout the newspaper. In 1998 Torstar expanded the color capacity of the *Star* from 28 pages to 48 pages.

The new ventures group of the *Star* began by launching two projects, the *For Rent Magazine,* with a circulation of 100,000 copies per month, and a redesigned *Real Estate News,* which the *Star* printed through an arrangement with the Toronto Real Estate Board. Its weekly circulation was more than 100,000 copies. In 1998 the new ventures group acquired a 50 percent interest in the Canadian operations of Sing Tao's media group. *Sing Tao Daily* was the largest Chinese-language newspaper in Canada, with editions in Toronto, Vancouver, Calgary, and Montreal. The group also was involved in printing, outdoor advertising, radio broadcasting, direct mail catalogs, and magazines.

In 1998 the *Toronto Star* was engaged in an all-out newspaper war with the existing dailies and the *National Post,* which was launched by the Hollinger/Southam group in the fall of 1998. The *Star* unveiled its most expensive consumer marketing campaign. The multimedia campaign, "The Toronto Star: It's Where You Live," appeared on television and radio, billboards and buses, and in a variety of print media.

With 51 percent of the market, the *Star* was the number one newspaper in the Toronto market. To bolster its position, it hired more than 40 new editors and writers during 1998. Its marketing campaign was aided by the recent expansion of color pages from 28 to 48 pages out of a total of 96 pages in the newspaper. While advertising linage in the *Star* was relatively flat for 1998, ad revenues increased $14 million (Canadian), due to linage price increases.

In October 1998 Torstar initiated a hostile takeover of Sun Media, which published seven daily newspapers in major Canadian cities, including the *Toronto Sun.* Torstar initially offered $748 million (Canadian), or $16 per share. By December Torstar had raised its bid to more than $19 per share, or approximately $900 million (Canadian). Torstar allowed its bid to lapse when Quebecor Inc. tendered a higher offer. Torstar subsequently entered into a binding agreement with Quebecor in December 1998 to purchase the *Hamilton Spectator,* the *Record* (Kitchener-Waterloo), the *Cambridge Reporter,* and the *Guelph Mercury,* four broadsheets that belonged to Sun Media, which Quebecor was in the process of acquiring. The agreement would allow Torstar to expand its presence in southern Ontario and increase Torstar's total average weekly circulation to 4.67 million copies, or 14.2 percent of the total for daily newspapers in Canada.

The acquisition was completed in March 1999 for about $335 million (Canadian) after Quebecor acquired Sun Media in December. At the same time, Torstar announced the formation of the Torstar Daily Newspaper Group, which included the four acquired broadsheets and the *Toronto Star.* The five newspapers began sharing stories, photographs, and graphics in the newly formed Torstar News Service. The *Toronto Star* would handle the advertising for the other four newspapers for national and multimarket advertisers. With 21 percent of the Canadian population and 25 percent of its disposable income, southern Ontario was becoming a more unified market for advertisers. The Torstar Daily Newspaper Group was the third largest newspaper group in Canada behind number one Southam Inc. and number two Quebecor.

Multimedia in the 1990s

A multimedia division was established in the 1990s to explore business opportunities in electronic publishing. Torstar's Web site, www.torstar.com, offered content from most of its newspapers on the Internet. The online version of the *Toronto Star* was launched on March 30, 1996 (www.thestar.com).

Throughout 1998 new content and services were added to the Torstar site, including a chat service, online games, television listings, food and money guides, technology news, cartoons, and links to the *Star's* weather, horoscopes, stock quotes, and sports sections.

The multimedia division also helped Harlequin launch its Web site (www.romance.net) in February 1996. The site included advanced technology that allowed Harlequin to market books and merchandise via the Internet.

In September 1997 Toronto Star CitySearch was launched by a partnership between Torstar and the Canadian subsidiary of CitySearch U.S.A. The new online service provided information about restaurants, entertainment, retail establishments, community events, and other services for the greater Toronto area. The original partnership was terminated in August 1998 and succeeded by a new partnership, toronto.com, among Torstar, CitySearch, and Tele-Direct Inc. Tele-Direct Inc subsequently became Bell Actimedia. Torstar held a 45 percent ownership interest in toronto.com (www.toronto.com), an online information service with more than 250,000 business listings and more than 2,000 information sites from Toronto-area businesses.

The multimedia division was also responsible for Toronto Star Television (TSTV), a 24-hour direct-response teleshopping channel that primarily featured infomercials along with news, weather, and sports headlines. Launched in October 1997, TSTV was reaching 1.4 million homes in greater Toronto by 1999.

Children's Supplementary Education Publishing (CSEP) Formed in the 1990s

Torstar's CSEP division provides a broad range of high quality educational materials to teachers, children, and parents. It consisted of four operating subsidiaries that were acquired in the 1990s.

Frank Schaffer Publications (FSP), based in Torrance, California, was acquired in 1994. Subsequent acquisitions, Warren Publishing House in 1995 and the Judy Group in 1997, were combined with FSP to make it a leading publisher of print and manipulative educational materials, such as teacher resource books, activity books, puzzles, charts, and posters for children from preschool age to the eighth grade.

Tom Snyder Productions (TSP), based in Watertown, Massachusetts, was acquired in 1996. TSP published a broad array of software titles in the areas of social studies, math, and science for the elementary and middle school markets. TSP was founded originally by Tom Snyder, a former science and social studies teacher, in 1980. The company was established to help teachers create great learning experiences for their

students. Snyder developed more than 100 CD-ROM, videodisc, videotape, and audio tape products for schools, and TSP became a leading developer and publisher of educational software for K-12 classrooms. In addition, TSP developed a reputation as an innovative producer of animation, including the animated television series *Science Court,* shown on ABC, and *Dr. Katz: Professional Therapist,* shown on HBO's Comedy Central.

Delta Education provided K-8 educators with hands-on science and math materials and programs. Based in Nashua, New Hampshire and originally established in the 1970s, Delta Education was acquired by Torstar in 1996. In 1997 Delta took a major step into curriculum program publishing with the acquisition of FOSS (Full Option Science System). FOSS was developed at the Lawrence Hall of Science at the University of California with funding from the National Science Foundation. It is a widely recognized activity-based full science curriculum for grades K-6.

Brighter Vision Learning Adventures was launched by Torstar in 1997. It is an educational continuity program targeted to parents of children ages 2 to 6. It was developed by educators to support the early childhood education process. Brighter Vision Retail was also launched in 1997 to create and distribute high quality education products for children and parents in convenient shopping locations. The first international CSEP operation, Brighter Vision Education, was launched in the United Kingdom in 1996.

Another 1997 CSEP acquisition, Troll Communications, was sold in April 1999 to Willis Stein Partners, L.P., a Chicago-based investment firm, for $69 million. Torstar realized a loss of approximately $100 million (Canadian) on the sale. Troll was a leading publisher of children's books and operated school book clubs and book fairs as well as direct mail programs for children, teachers, and schools, but it had two consecutive years of poor financial performance.

Following its failed attempt to acquire Sun Media, Torstar reaffirmed its commitment to its Children's Supplementary Educational Publishing Division. Torstar had announced previously that it would sell CSEP to finance the planned Sun Media acquisition.

Other Interests in the Late 1990s: ITI Education Corporation

In May 1998 Torstar increased its interest in ITI Education Corporation by three million shares, giving it a 26 percent ownership interest. ITI's Information Technology Institute was Canada's leading postgraduate information technology (IT) educational institution, with five campuses in Canada and plans for two new schools in both Canada and the United States for 1999. It was Canada's largest single source of IT graduates, and in 1995 ITI became the first Canadian education corporation to be publicly traded on a Canadian stock exchange. By the end of 1998, Torstar purchased another one million shares of ITI Education Corporation for about $7 million (Canadian), giving Torstar a 39 percent ownership interest in ITI.

Outlook

Torstar experienced solid growth during the 1990s, with operating profits doubling from $84 million (Canadian) in 1995 to $177 million (Canadian) in 1998. Total revenues grew at a steady pace from $1 billion (Canadian) in 1995 to $1.33 billion (Canadian) in 1998, with the strongest growth in the newspaper segment. Substantial investment in children's supplementary educational publishing boosted revenues in that segment from $36 million (Canadian) in 1995 to $164 million (Canadian) in 1998. Net income grew from $64 million (Canadian) in 1995 to $260 million (Canadian) in 1997. Three properties that were sold off in 1997 and 1998 resulted in a $99 million loss from discontinued operations, which resulted in a net loss of $5 million for 1998.

Future prospects for Torstar's newspaper, book publishing, and children's publishing are mixed. Newspaper revenue traditionally correlates with economic activity and media spending, and the economic outlook was uncertain for 1999 based on the momentum of the *Star* at the end of 1998. The *Star* may also face higher labor costs as its largest union attempts to include the newspaper carriers, who previously had been considered self-employed independent contractors.

Torstar sees a bright future for its book publishing subsidiary, Harlequin, which dominates series romance fiction. Its continued success will be dependent on being able to offer high quality editorial product, just as its profitability will remain dependent on its operating efficiencies. Strong results also were expected for the individual units of the company's CSEP segment.

Principal Subsidiaries

Toronto Star Newspapers Ltd. (Canada); Harlequin Enterprises Ltd. (Canada); Metroland Printing, Publishing and Distributing Ltd. (Canada); TDNG Inc. (Canada); Frank Schaffer Publications, Inc.; Tom Snyder Productions, Inc.; Delta Education, Inc.; Brighter Vision; Brighter Vision Education (United Kingdom).

Principal Divisions

Torstar Daily Newspaper Group; Children's Supplementary Educational Publishing Division; Multimedia Division.

Further Reading

"Building a Legend: The Harlequin Story," at http://www.harlequin enterprises.com/history.html

Fox, Bill, "The Battle for Hearts and Minds," *Time International,* May 24, 1999, p. 34.

"Galloway Is Sole CEO at Torstar," *Publishers Weekly,* July 4, 1994, p. 15.

"Harlequin Acquires Educ. Publisher," *Publishers Weekly,* October 9, 1995, p. 10.

"Harlequin Enterprises Limited," at http://www.torstar.com/corporate/ book.html

Neuwirth, Robert, "Torstar Ends Sun Media Bid, But Gets Four Papers," *Editor & Publisher,* December 19, 1998, p. 10.

"The Sun Says No Thanks," *Maclean's,* November 23, 1998, p. 101.

"Supplementary Education," at http://www.torstar.com/corporate/ education.html

"Torstar Acquires 10 Community Newspapers," company press release, June 30, 1999, at http://www.torstar.com/corporate/news_ june3099.html

"Torstar Announces Purchase of Broadsheet Papers," company press release, March 1, 1999, at http://www.torstar.com/corporate/news_ mar0199.html

"Torstar Announces Sale of Troll Communications," company press release, February 22, 1999, at http://www.torstar.com/corporate/ news_feb2299.html

"Torstar Announces Strategic Alliance with Women.com," company news release, June 29, 1999, at http://www.harlequinenterprises .com/press_index.html

"Torstar Completes Sale of Troll Communications," company press release, April 1, 1999, at http://www.torstar.com/corporate/news_ apr0199.html

"Torstar Corporation," at http://www.torstar.com/corporate/

"Torstar Daily Newspaper Group," at http://www.torstar.com/ corporate/paper.html

"Torstar Increases Bid for Sun Media by $2.75 Per Share to $19.34," company press release, December 7, 1998, at http://www.torstar .com/corporate/news_dec798.html

"Torstar Increases ITI Education Ownership," company press release, December 31, 1998, at http://www.torstar.com/corporate/news_ dec3198.html

"Torstar Offers $486M for Sun Media," *Editor & Publisher,* October 31, 1998, p. 14.

"Torstar Offers $748 Million for Sun Media Corporation," company press release, October 28, 1998, at http://www.torstar.com/ corporate/news_oct2898.html

"Torstar Sheds Kid Book Unit," *Editor & Publisher,* February 27, 1999, p. 21.

"Torstar To Acquire Four Sun Media Broadsheets from Quebecor," company press release, December 21, 1998, at http://www .torstar.com/corporate/news_dec2198.html

"Torstar To Retain Most of its Children's Supplementary Educational Publishing Businesses," company press release, December 21, 1998, at http://www.torstar.com/corporate/news_dec21b98.html

"A Week of Major Changes," *Maclean's,* November 9, 1998, p. 2.

Wilson-Smith, Anthony, "Chain Reaction: The Launch of a New National Daily Starts an Industry Upheaval," *Maclean's,* November 9, 1998, p. 44.

—David Bianco

Toymax International, Inc.

125 East Bethpage Road
Plainview, New York 11803
U.S.A.
(516) 391-9898
Fax: (516) 391-9151
Web site: http://www.toymax.com

Public Company
Incorporated: 1990 as Toymax Inc.
Employees: 65
Sales: $99.33 million (1998)
Stock Exchanges: NASDAQ
Ticker Symbol: TMAX
NAIC: 339932 Game, Toy & Children's Vehicle
    Manufacturing; 42192 Toy & Hobby Goods &
    Supplies Wholesalers; 31134 Nonchocolate
    Confectionery Manufacturing; 551112 Offices of
    Other Holding Companies

Toymax International, Inc., through its wholly owned subsidiaries and divisions, makes children's toys, leisure products, and novelty candy. Its toys, which are known for being high-tech and interactive, include Laser Challenge, Creepy Crawlers, Mighty Mo's Wireless Infrared Remote Vehicles, R.A.D Robot, and a line of products featuring the pop music group The Spice Girls. Toymax's Go Fly a Kite division specializes in kites, windsocks, banners, and flags. Another holding, Florida-based Monogram International, Inc., makes gift, novelty, and souvenir merchandise. Much of Monogram's business is built around producing trademarked items for Disney, Warner Brothers, and Coca-Cola. Toymax's Candy Planet division produces novelty and themed candy items.

The Toymax Beginning: Carrying On a Legacy

The founder and president of Toymax International, Steve Lebensfeld, cut his teeth on the toy industry. As the son of a toy manufacturer, the young Lebensfeld got to spend hours of free time at his father's New York factory, which produced blackboards, magnetic letters, and other educational toys. The result was an enduring love for both toys and the business of making them. Before he was 20, Lebensfeld had designed his first toy: an indoor basketball hoop that hung on the back of a door. Shortly after graduating from college, he started his own toy company called Hot Items and, a few years later, founded another business, HG Toys Hong Kong.

In 1987, teaming up with some associates from HG Toys, Lebensfeld co-founded a third company: Toy Biz. Toy Biz met with early success when it obtained the exclusive license to produce action figures based on Marvel Comics and DC Comics. This new line of action figures, which included Batman, Superman, and Spiderman, rapidly made Toy Biz the largest action figure company in the industry.

In 1990, Lebensfeld sold Toy Biz to a group of investors and went on to co-found Toymax, Inc. that same year. His partners in the Toymax venture were David Chu, Harvey Goldberg, and Ken Price, all seasoned veterans of the toy industry. Goldberg and Price had worked with Lebensfeld at Toy Biz as sales and marketing representatives. Chu owned a toy factory in southern China and had served as a supplier for some of Lebensfeld's previous companies. The four founders, who had been working together in various capacities since the early 1980s, brought to the table a wide range of skills. Together, they set out to develop cutting-edge, highly interactive toys. "We realized that we had to be something else at Toymax," Lebensfeld said in a July 1998 interview with the Associated Press, explaining "We had to use technology and licensing, but not the way everyone else was using them."

The company was set up so that Chu's manufacturing plant in China, Jauntiway Investments Limited, produced the majority of Toymax's product. A second Chu-owned company, Tai Nam Industrial Company Limited, served as its purchasing agent. Toymax focused on selling in international markets right from the start. Concurrent with the establishment of the New York-based Toymax, the founders established its Asian counterpart, Toymax (H.K.) Limited, to sell products to international retailers and distributors.

Company Perspectives:

Our mission is to create, design, and develop innovative toys that promote fun and creative play for kids of all ages. We continue to develop great new products that define their niches. Our toys come alive in the hands of a child; this success has been achieved through the vision, dedication, and hard work of our management team and staff.

The company's first big hit was a 1992 reintroduction of Creepy Crawlers, a classic toy activity set that had been popular in the 1960s. Creepy Crawlers—which consisted of a molding compound called "Plasti-Goop," creature- and insect-shaped molds, with a toy oven—allowed kids to make their own brightly colored plastic bugs. The retro toy proved to have enormous appeal to baby boomer parents, many of whom remembered playing with Creepy Crawlers in their own childhoods. Toymax capitalized on the popularity of its Creepy Crawlers by introducing a series of ancillary products, including multi-colored and textured Plasti-Goop and licensed character set molds featuring Batman, Spiderman, the Power Rangers, and Looney Tunes characters. The following year, Toymax took the basic idea behind Creepy Crawlers and put a feminine spin on it, introducing the Dollymaker. The Dollymaker allowed children to mold and bake their own dolls and doll outfits from "Glamour Goop."

1996–97: New Products, New Markets

The year 1996 saw the introduction of some of Toymax's most innovative and best selling toys. One of them, the Metal Molder Die Cast Factory, was the first of its kind on the retail market. The Metal Molder allowed children to die-cast metal figures and vehicles using molds, metal alloy beads, and an electric oven. However, it was another new Toymax product that drew the most attention: Laser Challenge. Laser Challenge, Toymax's first foray into action toys, was developed to capitalize on the popularity of indoor laser tag. It used an advanced infrared light technology to allow for long firing distances and outdoor play. Laser Challenge won accolades right away, receiving honors in 1996 from *Family Fun Magazine* and the National Association of Parenting Publications Awards. The game won consumer interest as well, fast becoming Toymax's leading brand and one of the top selling toys in the United States.

The company made its first real move toward diversification in the fall of 1996 when it formed a new subsidiary—Craft Expressions, Inc.—to target the adult crafts market. The first two Craft Expressions products utilized Toymax's earlier expertise in making and selling molding kits. Creative Castings Sandstone Casting Kit allowed users to design molded sandstone sculptures, while Liquid Ceramics let them mold and bake a special ceramic compound.

Throughout 1996 and 1997, Toymax adhered to its early strategy of continually freshening existing product lines by introducing new accessories and versions. In 1997, the company introduced the girl's version of its Metal Molder set. The new product, called Precious Metals, allowed users to melt and mold metal alloy beads into pieces of jewelry that could then be decorated. Toymax also introduced an enhanced version of its popular Laser Challenge game, called Laser Challenge Pro. Extensions of other lines included new mold packs for both Creepy Crawlers and Metal Molder sets with designs based on the hit movie *Jurassic Park*, as well as a Classic Chevrolet mold pack for the Metal Molder.

Toymax closed out its fiscal year in March 1997 with sales of $54.7 million and net income of $3.3 million. The Laser Challenge alone accounted for more than 48 percent of the total sales. In October 1997, the company made an initial public offering of approximately 2.7 million shares. The IPO generated $22.9 million, giving Toymax the capital it needed to diversify and expand. Concurrent with its IPO, Toymax reorganized its corporate structure, forming Toymax International, Inc. as a parent company for Toymax Inc., Toymax (H.K.) Limited, and three other Toymax satellite operations incorporated in Canada, Bermuda, and the United Kingdom.

1998: Accelerated Growth

In its 1997 prospectus, Toymax listed five key tenets of its growth strategy: to extend the product lines of existing core brands; to expand into new core product categories; to expand into traditional spring toys; to develop and penetrate new markets; and to continue to license recognized brand names and characters. The two years following the company's IPO saw rapid progress along all five identified growth fronts.

In early 1998, Toymax entered the rapid-growth market for handheld electronics when it signed an exclusive agreement to distribute Nintendo licensed Mini Classics in the United States and Canada. The Nintendo Mini Classics were small, key-chain sized versions of some of Nintendo's best-known games, including Super Mario Brothers and Donkey Kong. Early in the summer of 1998, Toymax obtained another major licensing agreement, this one to produce and distribute a line of products based on the wildly popular singing group, The Spice Girls. The product line included collectible figures; a line of youth electronics including microphones, cassette players, and radios; and role-play and dress-up sets that allowed girls to doll up like their favorite Spice Girls. To promote its new Spice Girls line, Toymax shot a television commercial featuring four mini-Spice lookalikes chosen from an open audition in New York. Around 6,000 young girls showed up for the try-outs.

Among 1998's other new products were a walking, talking, radio-controlled robot named R.A.D.; a line of wireless infrared remote vehicles called Mighty Mo's; and the Arcadia Electronic Skeet Shoot. The Arcadia Electronic Skeet Shoot and R.A.D. Robot were especially hot sellers during the 1998 holiday season; according to a December 23, 1998 *USA Today* article, both FAO Schwarz and Toys R Us reported that the two Toymax products were being "snatched off store shelves as soon as they're stocked." Toymax was completely sold out of its R.A.D. inventory before Christmas arrived that year.

In addition to its successful line of new products, Toymax continued to push its Laser Challenge line. New versions of the toy included a deluxe set and a water set, which splashed players when they were hit by the laser beam. "Laser Challenge is our evergreen product," Lebensfeld was quoted as saying in a February 13, 1998 *Newsday* article, adding "We intend to expand that business, but we also want to be in more aisles of the store."

1999: New Subsidiaries

On January 6, 1999, Toymax made its first acquisition, purchasing Go Fly a Kite, a Connecticut-based manufacturer and distributor of kites, windsocks, banners, mini-flags, and WindWheels. The acquisition was strategic in several ways. Perhaps most significantly, Go Fly a Kite was a leader in a largely spring and summer business. This provided Toymax with the perfect seasonal complement to its existing business, which was heavily concentrated in the winter holiday months. In addition, the acquisition opened up new channels of distribution. Go Fly a Kite's products were largely sold in specialty retail stores, whereas Toymax's distribution had traditionally been dominated by mass market toy retailers. The combination of the two distribution networks gave Toymax a broader retail base for both its existing and newly acquired product lines.

A bit later in January, Toymax announced that it would expand its product line to include educational toys. The company's first step into educational toy territory was a licensing agreement with Knowledge Adventure, a leading maker of educational software. Under the agreement, Toymax began developing a line of hand-held and tabletop electronic games based on Knowledge Adventure's best-selling JumpStart Learning System and Blaster Learning System software.

Further diversification came a month later when Toymax formed a new division called Candy Planet. Candy Planet aimed to enter the growing candy market with a line of confections based on the popular wrestlers of the World Wrestling Federation. The new line was to include WWF themed gummi treats, lollipops, gum, and sour candies, as well as interactive candy products such as key chain gum dispensers and gumball machines. Like its licensing agreement with Knowledge Adventure, the formation of Candy Planet gave Toymax a foothold in another year-round market, helping to offset the seasonality of its core toy business.

The company continued with an aggressive diversification strategy, acquiring Monogram International, Inc. in May 1999. The Florida-based Monogram was one of the leading U.S. manufacturers of gift, novelty, and souvenir products, with annual sales of approximately $22 million. Like Lebensfeld's previous company, Toy Biz, Monogram had made a name for itself via licensing agreements with major entertainment companies. Its most significant licensing relationship was with the Walt Disney Company, with whom it had been associated for more than 25 years. Monogram also held licenses from Warner Bros. Consumer Products, Coca-Cola, and Crayola. Lebensfeld

called Monogram "another key building block" in Toymax's strategy to diversify. "This acquisition is important to us because it provides tremendous opportunities to expand our portfolio of licensed product and distribution channels and allows us to cross-sell to retailers our toy, candy and kite lines," he said in a May 27, 1999 press release.

Toymax grouped its three new divisions—Go Fly a Kite, Candy Planet, and Monogram—together under a new entity, Toymax Enterprises. The company hired Barry Shapiro, a 32-year veteran of the toy industry and the former president and CEO of Just Toys, Inc., to oversee the newly created Toymax Enterprises. Shapiro was charged with integrating the operations of the new businesses and any other future acquisitions.

Future Fun and Games

As Toymax prepared to move into the new millennium, it was holding fast to the five tenets of its growth strategy, seeking ways to expand its business beyond its original niche and encompass the full range of the leisure industry. The company planned to grow through further acquisitions as well as internal expansion. Likely acquisition targets included companies with more year-round, or "evergreen," products, strong and diverse distribution networks, and appeal to broad demographic markets. Toymax also expected to continue building on the strength of its core product lines, as well as developing new and innovative products for future introduction. It had especially ambitious plans for its Monogram subsidiary. According to a June 7, 1999 article in Florida's *St. Petersburg Times,* Toymax anticipated increasing Monogram's business two-and-one-half times over the course of the coming three years.

Principal Subsidiaries

Toymax Inc.; Toymax Enterprises Inc.; Toymax (H.K.) Limited (Hong Kong).

Principal Divisions

Candy Planet; Go Fly a Kite; Monogram International.

Further Reading

Applegate, Jane, "Succeeding at the Toy Game," *Triangle Business Journal,* December 26, 1997, p 10.
"From Spice Girls to Laser Challenge to Robots, Toymax Has Holiday Toys for the Girls and Boys on Your List," *Washington Times,* December 18, 1998.
Martorana, Jamie, "Diversity Name of Game for Toymax," *Newsday,* May 31, 1999, p. 1
Stapleton, Tara, "Toymax' IPO Move Is Not Child's Play," *Newsday,* November 17, 1997, p. C5.
"Toymax President Creates Hottest Toys, but Is Still a Big Kid," *Augusta Chronicle,* July 25, 1998.

—Shawna Brynildssen

Transaction Systems Architects, Inc.

224 South 108th Avenue
Omaha, Nebraska 68154
U.S.A.
(402) 334-5101
Fax: (402) 390-8077
Web site: http://www.tsainc.com

Public Company
Incorporated: 1975 as Applied Communications Inc.
Employees: 1,372
Sales: $289.8 million (1998)
Stock Exchanges: NASDAQ
Ticker Symbol: TSAI
NAIC: 51121 Software Publishers; 541511 Custom
    Computer Programming Services; 334113 Computer
    Terminal Manufacturing; 334111 Electronic Computer
    Manufacturing; 334119 Other Computer Peripheral
    Equipment Manufacturing

A fast-growing company in an expanding market, Transaction Systems Architects, Inc. (TSA) develops software for processing card-based transactions. The company's customers included more than 100 of the world's 500 largest banks and 19 of the 100 largest retailers in the United States. TSA's electronic funds transfer software was used in transactions involving automated teller machines, point-of-sale terminals, wire transfers, home banking, and credit and debit cards. Roughly three-quarters of the company's revenue during the late 1990s was derived from software designed to run on Tandem computers, the popular hardware among financial institutions. For years, all of TSA's software was exclusively programmed for Tandem computers, but in the mid-1990s the company began to diversify its product line to lessen its dependence on Tandem's platform. Diversification was achieved through acquisitions, giving the company greater market reach and positioning it in burgeoning markets, such as home banking. Annual revenues swelled during the expansion, rising from approximately $70 million in 1992 to nearly $300 million six years later. TSA's customers processed 16 billion transactions a year during the late 1990s, a total that represented only two percent of the estimated transactions completed worldwide. More than half of the company's revenues was derived from outside the United States.

Origins

TSA's corporate roots stretched to the origins of one of its subsidiaries, Nebraska-born Applied Communications Inc. Applied Communications was founded in 1975 by computer programmer James Cody and two colleagues. The entrepreneurs had developed electronic funds transfer software for banks, marking their entry into a nascent yet soon-to-burgeon industry. Point-of-sale (POS) systems that enabled card-based, electronic payments were introduced in the early 1980s to accommodate consumer preferences for using credit and debit cards instead of cash or checks. Prior to the development of automated POS systems, card-based transactions generally were processed manually, using paper-based systems to obtain authorization from card-issuing banks. As the volume of credit and debit card transactions increased, however, a more sophisticated method of authorization was needed. Card-issuing banks, with the backing of VISA and MasterCard, offered financial incentives to promote the development and use of POS-related technologies, which spawned the creation of electronic payment systems that improved accuracy, reduced costs, increased efficiency, and reduced credit card abuse and fraud. Cody and his partners were early developers in this field, entering when the technology was raw and the use of such technology was a relatively novel alternative, rather than obligatory, as electronic-based systems later would be. Although Applied Communications was marketing a product whose time was yet to come, the company did well early on, with its software making enough of an impression on bankers to overcome the less than reassuring appearance of Cody, who on one sales visit sold the company's software while wearing mismatched shoes.

By the time electronic-based systems had started to become commonplace, Applied Communications was prepared to take advantage of a market that had caught up to its pioneering technology. The company went public in 1983 to gain the financial resources to expand and began doing so aggressively, particularly overseas. Until 1982, Applied Communications had never made an effort to cultivate international business and,

Company Perspectives:

At TSA we're a business just taking root—a business tied to the world's growing demand for anytime, anywhere access to money and information. In coming years electronic transactions are projected to grow at a faster pace than those made by cash and check, increasing the need for the proven, reliable products in the TSA portfolio. The TSA product set extends from ATM processing solutions to products that address emerging technologies like the Internet and smart cards, while operating on a variety of hardware platforms and offering Year 2000 compatibility. The employees of TSA stand behind their products with a simple philosophy—meet customers' needs on time, on budget, with no surprises. While simple, it provides a guiding set of principles that continue to earn TSA a high customer-retention rate, and additional business from existing customers. ACI Worldwide, TSA's distribution and support division, delivers product and services to customers in 70 countries. Opportunities await as the acceptance of technology fuels the spread of electronic payments around the globe. TSA "stores acorns" by basing our financial model on volume-sensitive pricing, monthly licensing fees and maintaining a healthy backlog of contracted, but not yet recognized revenue. The result is an organization that's just getting started—an organization designed to take long-term advantage of the shift to electronic payments and tap the potential in a vital and growing industry.

consequently, collected only a fraction of its revenues from foreign sales. Although the company had not made itself known to the global marketplace, overseas businesses had heard of Applied Communications. The company's marketing staff began receiving a growing number of unsolicited inquiries about its software in 1982, prompting an organized pursuit of overseas business and the establishment of an international distribution unit, ACI Ltd. (ACIL). Much of Applied Communications' growth during the decade was derived from the concerted, international effort to market its software for automated teller machines (ATMs) and POS systems, contributing to a more than sixfold increase in the company's work force between 1982 and 1989. Applied Communications was awarded the President's "E" Award for excellence in exporting in 1987 and by 1989 was selling its software in 29 countries. By the end of the decade, international sales accounted for more than half of the company's revenue.

Ownership Changes During the 1980s and 1990s

Midway through the company's decade-long expansion overseas, Applied Communications became the target of a much larger suitor. The demand for the technology conceived and developed by Applied Communications had exponentially increased since the company's founding, repositioning the software developer from the fringe of the mainstream market to the center of attention. US West was interested in Applied Communications' expertise, and it purchased the company in 1986. Life as a subsidiary of a much larger parent gave the company voluminous financial support, but freedom was the expense. US West, not surprisingly, was pursuing its own objectives and

enlisted the assistance of Applied Communications to achieve those objectives, directing the company to develop telephone company systems. The redirection of Applied Communications' focus ran counter to the company's original focus, an alteration that a third company, Tandem Computers Inc., found disturbing. The reason for Tandem's anxiety, and the company's eventual intervention into the relationship between US West and Applied Communications, hinged on one of the fundamental aspects of Applied Communications' success. Early in its corporate life, Applied Communications had allied itself to Tandem's technology, programming its software to run on the computer manufacturer's hardware, which was used by an overwhelming majority of banks. Under US West's ownership, however, Applied Communications' focus had strayed, provoking Tandem to respond. "We didn't see [Applied Communications] flourishing under US West ownership," explained a Tandem official, "so we decided to acquire them to protect our joint customer base." The acquisition, completed in 1991, gave Tandem control of Applied Communications and ACIL for slightly less than $60 million.

The change in ownership returned Applied Communications' focus to the banking industry. Virtually all of the company's software was designed to run exclusively on the computers made by its new parent company, but despite the strong synergy between the two companies, Tandem professed no desire to own Applied Communications on a long-term basis. By 1993, after two-and-a-half years of control, Tandem decided to sell Applied Communications, explaining that its subsidiary was sufficiently profitable to operate on its own. Under the terms of the agreement, Tandem sold Applied Communications and ACIL, which had moved to London in 1992, to the subsidiary's senior management.

Independence in 1993 Sparks Expansion

Leading the group of senior executives who purchased Applied Communications was William E. Fisher, the individual who guided the company during its new-found independence. Fisher, who received his MBA from the University of Nebraska, had joined Applied Communications in 1987 and held a number of different titles, including president of financial systems, senior vice-president of software and services, executive vice-president, and chief operating officer. When Tandem bought the company from US West in 1991, Fisher was named chairman and chief executive officer, the same offices to which he was appointed when a new company was formed to facilitate the management-led buyout from Tandem. Transaction Systems Architects, Inc. (TSA) was formed in November 1993 and the acquisition of Applied Communications and ACIL occurred the following month, completed on the last day of 1993.

During its last full year as a Tandem subsidiary, Applied Communications had generated more than $70 million in revenue, ranking it as the world's largest supplier of electronic funds transfer software programmed for Tandem computers. In the years ahead, however, the company's business would be far less dependent on the success of Tandem ATM and POS hardware. "As we look forward," Fisher said, "we know our future is open systems." Independence provided Fisher with the opportunity to develop software for other platforms, such as Microsoft Corp.'s NT operating system, as well as Unix and IBM operating systems. Although the company continued to regard its software partnership with Tandem as its mainstay business and continued to develop software for its long-time associate, the ability to diversify its product line to run on other vendors' computers opened numerable avenues for growth. It was Fisher's task to take advantage of these opportunities during the fast-paced growth of the middle and late 1990s.

After seven years of operating under the corporate umbrella of a parent company, TSA did not wait long to express its independence. Four days after the buyout from Tandem was completed, Fisher acquired U.S. Software Inc. (USSI), headquartered near Omaha, Nebraska, in Crater Lake, Iowa. Founded three years before TSA acquired it, USSI provided software solutions to the financial and payment card industries, developing its software products at a facility in Victoria, Texas. TSA's purchase of USSI signaled the beginning of an acquisition campaign that diversified TSA's product line and expertise beyond the capabilities of its core subsidiary, Applied Communications. The middle and late 1990s witnessed the rapid growth of electronic commerce around the globe, as card-based transactions proliferated and new areas of opportunities, such as home banking, emerged. To keep pace with technological advances surrounding it, TSA sought to accelerate its own technological development through the fastest means possible: by acquiring companies with expertise in emerging areas of growth. The company's motto was "it's an electronic world, we move the money," underscoring its intention to involve itself in as many as possible of the billions of card-based transactions that were completed annually.

Before TSA began to strategically position itself through acquisitions, the company filed for an initial public offering (IPO) in January 1995. The IPO of 2.75 million shares at $15 per share was completed the following month, giving the company the means to reduce its debt. Six months later, in August, TSA returned to Wall Street for additional cash from investors, completing a second sale of stock that netted the company $22 million. Fisher explained: "We had a strong IPO, and our underwriters thought we could have sold more shares. We decided to go back to the market in order to strengthen up our balance sheet a bit, as well as have some cash for acquisitions."

Financially invigorated after two stock offerings, the company turned its attention to the expanding markets and emerging industries in the "electronic world." Fisher was looking for acquisition candidates that could extend TSA's market reach and found one in late 1995. In October 1995 TSA acquired a German software firm named M.R. GmbH. Three more acquisitions—TXN Solution Integrators, Grapevine Systems, Inc., and Open Systems Solutions, Inc.—followed in 1996. By this point, more than 60 percent of the largest U.S. banks and nearly 25 percent of the 500 largest banks worldwide used software designed by TSA. Revenues had more than doubled from the total generated under the auspices of Tandem, yet the majority of the company's business was derived from its BASE24 product line, programmed for Tandem computers. Applied Communications, responsible for the BASE24 software, still represented TSA's mainstay business, but the acquisitions were giving the company expertise in complementary and promising areas. One of these new market niches centered on "smart" cards, or plastic cards programmed with a particular monetary value that could be used at ATMs and elsewhere like a debit card. TSA established a name for itself in the smart card market with two acquisitions, the August 1998

purchase of Smart Card Integrators Ltd., a London-based technology developer for systems such as Modex and Visa Cash, and the November 1998 acquisition of Media Integration BV, a Dutch smart card systems developer. Also in 1998, the company strengthened its presence in the market for home banking software, convinced that the practice of paying bills and transferring money from a consumer's home computer would develop into a widespread trend.

By the end of the 1990s, TSA stood as a strategically diversified, global company, marketing its products in 68 countries. For the immediate future, revenues were projected to increase 25 percent annually and earnings were expected to increase 35 percent. Based on this forecast, there was justifiable optimism for the company's success during the early 21st century, optimism expressed not only by TSA executives but also by stock analysts. "These guys don't get a lot of press," remarked one analyst in reference to TSA, "but they are a really well-positioned company." Despite rising revenues and earnings, however, the company's stock was not performing as well as some analysts believed it should, prompting several industry pundits to characterize TSA as a "sleeper" yet to be discovered by the investing public. "The company hasn't been given credit for the type of business it runs," explained an analyst at Lehman Brothers. Considering that the company was a direct beneficiary of lucrative trends in electronic commerce, the secrecy of its success appeared to be nearing its end.

Principal Subsidiaries

Applied Communications Inc.; Crystal Clear Technology; Grapevine Systems, Inc.; USSI Inc.

Further Reading

"Developer of ATM Technology Grows with New Products, Acquisitions," *Knight-Ridder/Tribune Business News,* February 24, 1998, p. 224B0935.

"Exporting Pays Off," *Business America,* July 3, 1989, p. 14.

Iida, Jeanne, "Tandem To Sell Software Unit to Its Senior Management," *American Banker,* November 16, 1993, p. 17.

Jennings, Robert, "Transaction Systems Architects Files for 2.75M-Share IPO To Retire Debt," *American Banker,* January 18, 1995, p. 19.

Marjanovic, Steven, "A Software Sleeper May Awaken in '99," *American Banker,* December 7, 1998, p. 32.

McLean, Bethany, "Cashing in on Plastic," *Fortune,* November 25, 1996, p. 218.

Norris, Melinda, "Omaha, Neb., ATM Technology Firm To Buy Milwaukee ATM Services Company," *Knight-Ridder/Tribune Business News,* December 3, 1998, p. OKRB983370FB.

"Tandem To Buy Rest of ACI," *Supermarket News,* December 6, 1993, p. 21.

Tracey, Brian, "Transaction Systems Raises $60M with Second Public Offering of Year," *American Banker,* August 14, 1995, p. 16.

——, "Transaction Systems of Omaha, Neb., Acquires Two Companies," *Knight-Ridder/Tribune Business News,* September 3, 1998, p. OKRB982460FE.

"Transaction Systems Buying Intranet Inc.," *American Banker,* April 29, 1998, p. 15.

"Transaction Systems Closes on Dutch Deal," *American Banker,* December 4, 1998, p. 23.

—Jeffrey L. Covell

Tree of Life, Inc.

1750 Tree Boulevard
St. Augustine, Florida 32086-0410
U.S.A.
(904) 824-4699
(800) 260-2424
Fax: (904) 825-2013
Web site: http://treeoflife.com

Wholly Owned Subsidiary of Koninklijke Bols Wessanen, N.V.
Founded: 1972
Employees: 2,000
Sales: $916.6 million (1998)
NAIC: 42221 Durgs & Druggists' Sundries Wholesalers; 42249 Other Grocery & Related Products Wholesalers

Tree of Life, Inc. is the world's leading marketer and distributor of natural and specialty foods, serving, in 1999, more than 10,000 retailers in the United States, Canada, and the Caribbean. It had an inventory of more than 25,000 products, a fleet of more than 165 trucks (the industry's largest), and more than 1.3 million square feet of warehouse space. More than 1,000 items were being marketed under the company's own brand names. Tree of Life's distribution and transportation network allowed it to present any new product from coast to coast in a single day. The company also was offering retailers marketing and merchandising expertise, including unique in-store training programs. Gourmet Award Foods was the name of the company's specialty foods group. Tree of Life was a wholly owned subsidiary of Wessanen U.S.A., the American subsidiary of Koninklijke Bols Wessanen, N.V., a Dutch company with more than two centuries of experience in the food industry.

Development and Growth in the 1970s and 1980s

Tree of Life was founded by Irwin Carasso in St. Augustine, Florida in the early 1970s as a natural foods retailer. It soon developed into a successful regional wholesale distribution company. The rapid growth of the natural foods industry in the 1980s enabled Tree of Life to establish operations in key markets across the country. Carasso sold Tree of Life in 1982 to Wilson Financial Corp., a company based in Jacksonville, Florida and controlled by Jacksonville financier J. Steven Wilson. Annual sales had reached $40 million by 1985, when the company was sold to Koninklijke Wessanen (which became Koninklijke Bols Wessanen in 1993). The sale included another Wilson Financial unit, American Natural Snacks Inc., which was making items such as roasted nuts and carob- or yogurt-coated pretzels in St. Augustine.

The growth of Tree of Life was piecemeal. For example, it purchased Midwest Natural Foods Distributor, an Ann Arbor, Michigan company with distribution outlets throughout the country by the late 1980s. This company was moved to Bloomington, Indiana and combined with another division to form Tree of Life's Midwest unit. Customers included health food and specialty food stores, some grocery store chains carrying natural foods, and some food cooperatives. Gourmet Award Foods, a specialty foods distributor supplying ethnic and fancy food products from around the world, was created in 1988 from specialty foods distributors Tree of Life had added earlier. Consumer demand was a significant factor in the growth of both the natural products and specialty foods businesses, because shoppers in supermarkets increasingly were demanding niche products.

Further Growth in the 1990s

Tree of Life's sales reached $370 million in 1991 and $410 million in 1992 (of which Gourmet Award Foods' share came to $60 million). By late 1993 it was operating nationwide, with ten distribution centers stretching from Miami to Seattle. Aside from American Natural Snacks, the company now included Atlanta area-based Swan Gardens, which was manufacturing a soy-based cheese substitute. Tree of Life had outgrown its 85,000-square-foot distribution center near its corporate headquarters and was planning a new 70,000-square-foot facility in St. Augustine. With 280 staffers, the company was the second largest employer in St. Johns County.

Tree of Life's sales reached $540 million in 1995, and it held a 30 percent share of the natural foods market in the United

States that year, making it the largest distributor of natural foods and health supplements in the nation. In 1996 Tree of Life made its tenth acquisition since being purchased by Wessanen, adding McLane America, Inc., the Salt Lake City-based specialty foods distribution subsidiary of McLane Co., Inc. With annual sales of about $60 million, McLane America was supplying supermarkets west of the Mississippi with gourmet, ethnic, and health food items. The operation was attached to Gourmet Award Foods, and its Salt Lake City facility added to Gourmet Award's distribution centers in Albany, New York, St. Paul, Minnesota, and Dallas, Texas. Tree of Life was now supplying 12,000 different natural/organic foods and food supplements to more than 5,000 retailers in the United States, Canada, and the Caribbean.

Tree of Life strengthened its national distribution network by acquiring Specialty Food Distributors, Inc. of Plant City, Florida in 1997 and Ray's Food Service, Inc. of Portland, Oregon in 1998. The latter, with annual sales of $80 million, was the leading marketer and distributor of specialty foods in the Pacific Northwest. This enterprise was combined with Tree of Life's Northwest division to form Tree of Life/Gourmet Award Foods Northwest, allowing it to offer a full assortment of natural and specialty foods products and services and one-stop shopping to all natural foods stores and supermarkets in the region.

Tree of Life introduced a new proprietary-branded vitamin and supplement line in 1998. By 1999 it had raised its market share in natural foods to 35 percent. About 60 percent of its business, however, now was being generated by specialty foods, compared with 40 percent a few years earlier. The specialty foods category, which had grown both autonomously and by acquisitions, was more attractive to the company because it offered higher profit margins than natural foods. In all, sales reached 1.81 billion guilders ($916.6 million) in 1998, and operating income came to 61.7 million guilders ($31.3 million). These figures compared with 1.47 billion guilders ($724.9 million) and 53.1 million guilders ($26.2 million), respectively, in 1997.

Tree of Life announced in February 1999 the acquisition of Wine & Schultz, Inc., a specialty foods distributor based in Louisville, Kentucky, servicing Illinois, Indiana, Kentucky, Ohio, and Tennessee and providing sales, marketing, and distribution services to supermarket retailers throughout the region. The operation was added to Tree of Life/Gourmet Award Foods' Midwest division in Bloomington, which Norman Wine, the company's president, joined as director of specialty food marketing. In the same month parent Koninklijke Wessanen announced the acquisition, for Tree of Life, of the North American-based Specialty Foods Group of Hagemeyer N.V., a

Dutch company. The purchase consisted of the marketing and distribution companies Liberty Richter in New Jersey, MBC Foods in Milwaukee, Fine Distributing in Atlanta and Fort Lauderdale, Florida, and Ashley Koffman in Calgary and Toronto, Canada. Annual sales of these companies came to more than $300 million.

Tree of Life in 1999

Tree of Life's national system of distribution centers and the industry's largest tractor-trailer fleet were strategically positioned to serve every major metropolitan market in the United States with next-day delivery. This same distribution and transportation network allowed the company to present any new product from coast to coast in a single day. It also allowed Tree of Life's retail customers to efficiently coordinate product introductions and promotions at all levels, from local to national. Electronic communication was making it possible for retailers to utilize on-line ordering systems such as MSI, Telzon, POS, and EDI. They also had instant access to the company's real-time pricing, catalogs, and promotions.

Tree of Life had 11 distribution centers in 1999. Its warehouse technology included radio-frequency picking and smart conveyors to expedite the fulfillment processes. The company offered to deliver daily or weekly to stores, using electronic routing and dispatching.

Tree of Life's inventory of more than 25,000 products offered a broad assortment of premium imported, kosher, fat-free, natural, and organic foods; ethnic specialties; personal care items; vitamins and herbal supplements; and frozen and refrigerated items. The foods it was carrying ranged from Mexican salsas to Mandarin oranges, pasta to peanut butter, cookies to crackers. The more than 1,000 items in Tree of Life's family of proprietary products included fat-free, reduced-fat, and all-natural and all-organic products; foods for consumers with allergy and dietary restrictions; frozen entrees and side dishes; instant single-serve products; and gourmet and ethnic specialties.

Tree of Life and Gourmet Award Foods also were offering marketing and distribution services in 1999. These were available to small and large retailers alike, from natural foods stores and gourmet grocers to supermarket chains and major drugstores. Retail services included shelf management, back door check-in, ordering/receiving services, and store/department set design. Marketing and merchandising expertise were offered in the areas of product assortment, monthly merchandising guides, co-op advertising, product demos, and category management.

Tree of Life's retail service programs offered to write and receive orders, maintain store shelves, set up and break down promotional displays, add new departments or reset existing ones, and even to help design a new store from the ground up. The company also offered a series of unique in-store training programs to help maximize retail merchandising efforts and improve the overall performance of the retailer's staff. A monthly merchandising guide was being circulated to all customers, packed with exclusive purchasing opportunities and merchandising tips, in-depth information on new products, and emerging consumer trends. Other merchandising programs ranged from co-op advertising and product demonstrations to national promotions, endcaps, and impulse displays. Gourmet Award Foods was holding an annual international food festival for retailers and vendors.

Principal Operating Units

American Natural Snacks; Gourmet Award Foods Midwest; Gourmet Award Foods Northeast; Gourmet Award Foods Southeast; Gourmet Award Foods Southwest; Swan Gardens; Tree of Life/Gourmet Award Foods Northwest; Tree of Life/ Gourmet Award Foods West; Tree of Life Midwest; Tree of Life Northeast; Tree of Life Southeast; Tree of Life Southwest.

Further Reading

Horak, Kathy, ''Tree of Life Buys Land for $3 Million Expansion,'' *Business Journal-Jacksonville,* November 26, 1993, p. 3.
Orgel, David, ''McLane To Sell Unit to Tree of Life,'' *SN/Supermarket News,* February 26, 1996, p. 4.
Zelade, Richard, ''Healthy Merger,'' *International Business,* May 1996, p. 56.

—Robert Halasz

Tuscarora Inc.

800 Fifth Avenue
New Brighton, Pennsylvania 15066
U.S.A.
(724) 843-8200
Fax: (724) 847-2140
Web site: http://www.tuscarora.com

Public Company
Incorporated: 1962 as Tuscarora Plastics, Inc.
Employees: 1,826
Sales: $232.9 million (1998)
Stock Exchanges: NASDAQ
Ticker Symbol: TUSC
NAIC: 32614 Polystyrene Foam Product Manufacturing

Tuscarora Inc. is the largest manufacturer in the United States of custom molded products made from expanded foam plastic materials. It designs and manufactures interior protective packaging and material handling products and components for industrial and consumer products. In addition to custom molded and die-cut plastic foams, it uses thermoformed plastic, corrugated paperboard, and wood in its products. Tuscarora's principal markets are the high-technology consumer electronics, automotive, and major appliance industries. In 1998 it had manufacturing facilities in the United Kingdom and Mexico as well as the United States.

Three Decades of Growth

The company was founded as Tuscarora Plastics in 1962 by John P. O'Leary, Sr., and Thomas Woolaway, utilizing German technology brought to the United States by Koppers Co. to expand polystyrene into a bubble that could be molded to shape, with the air inside providing insulation. Tuscarora Plastics took the process a step further when it used the air inside the bubble for a shock absorber as well. O'Leary, formerly a Westinghouse Electric Corp. purchasing agent, did not know much about polystyrene foam, but he recognized it as having a potentially large market as a packaging material. Corporate headquarters and the company's first plant were located in New Brighton, Pennsylvania, outside Pittsburgh. The company was named for an Indian tribe that at times lived in what is now western Pennsylvania.

Tuscarora Plastics grew in large part by acquiring similar small businesses making plastic foam packaging. The company was producing polystyrene foam at a dozen locations by 1980. Its net sales, which came to $29 million in 1981, grew from $45.2 million in 1985 (the year ended August 31, 1985) to $55.3 million in 1987, the last year before it became a public company. Its net income rose from $2 million to $2.8 million over this span. In the latter year it had 18 facilities in 14 states, all east of the Mississippi. Tuscarora needed a far-flung network of manufacturing plants because its facilities were limited to serving a market area within a 200- or 300-mile radius. The company made its initial public offering in July 1988, raising about $5.6 million by selling about 15 percent of the outstanding stock at $15.50 a share.

Tuscarora Plastics enjoyed its 19th consecutive year of profit in 1988. By then nearly every television set assembled in the United States was being packed with the company's protective polystyrene foam. It was also molding and fabricating polyethylene and co-polymer resins for use as thermal insulation for refrigeration equipment and other industrial products, such as insulation for coolers, and foam polypropylene components for automobile bumper cores (the company's own technology development). A 1988 Parker Hunter Securities research report quoted in a 1989 issue of the *Pittsburgh Business Times & Journal* stated, "Once a customer has selected Tuscarora to produce its packaging components, Tuscarora will usually have that business as long as the customer's model is in production."

Tuscarora Plastics was also growing by acquisition: in 1989 it purchased Plastronic Packaging Corp. and Preferred Plastic Co., the latest of about 25 or 30 small companies acquired since its inception. In about half of the most recent cases of acquisition, Tuscarora continued to run the acquired facility, while in the other half it consolidated operations. Making a name for itself in the industry, the company was included on the *Forbes* magazine 1990 list of the 200 best small companies in the United States, based on its five-year average return on equity.

New Products and Markets in the 1990s

O'Leary retired at the end of 1989 and was succeeded as president and chief executive officer by John P. O'Leary, Jr., who had been with the company since graduating from the University of Pennsylvania's Wharton School in 1971. Thomas Woolaway assumed the role of chief operating officer. Interviewed by *Wall Street Transcript* in 1990, the younger O'Leary said that most of Tuscarora's manufacturing equipment was being purchased in Germany and that much of its technology for the development of new materials had come from Japan. He added that "We service virtually all the major Japanese assembly plants both in consumer electronics and automotive.... Also, there has been continuing pressure for offshore manufacturers to bring their production into the United States. That's probably been our single biggest growth area in the last three years." In addition, he said that the company intended to introduce a new manufacturing process in foam sheet thermoforming for hard plastics.

Given the increasing number of environmental concerns during this time, O'Leary usually spent some time defending Tuscarora against charges that its output was degrading the environment. Speaking to *Wall Street Transcript,* he conceded that "plastics have a bit of a blemish in that they are part of the solid waste stream" but added that all plastics were recyclable to one degree or another. Interviewed by Mark Houser of Greensburg, Pennsylvania's *Tribune Review* in 1995, he indicated that the problem was best addressed by the free market. "The producer's motivation to have as little packaging as possible was already in place long before the environmental concerns came along," he maintained. "Packaging costs money but does not add value to his product, so his boss is telling him not to use any more than he has to. My ability to sell my product to him is the ability to sell as little of it as possible."

During the Persian Gulf War Tuscarora Plastics shipped the sensitive nosecones of Patriot air-defense missiles in large expandable polystyrene bead-shape packages. The short-term gains from this military order were more than counteracted, however, by a recession that slowed demand by Tuscarora's customers for shape packaging and stalled new product development and adoptions. Net sales dropped from $85.5 million in 1990 to $84.4 million in 1991. Earnings also fell from 1990's record. In 1991 the company's products were being sold to 1,300 customers in more than 35 states, Canada, and Mexico.

Tuscarora Plastics, which shortened its name to Tuscarora Inc. in 1992, resumed its growth that year, purchased two more companies, expanded its customer base to about five more states, and secured a new plant in Las Cruces, New Mexico—its first industrial facility west of the Mississippi. Most of the new clients were Fortune 500 firms. During 1993 and 1994 Tuscarora purchased four more companies, including two corrugated-cardboard packagers and a foam packager in Ciudad Juarez, Mexico, that was manufacturing cushioning materials for consumer electronics produced in the assembly plants springing up across the border from El Paso, Texas.

The production of custom-molded foam to protect consumer products in shipment remained Tuscarora's main business. In 1993, however, IBM—Tuscarora's biggest customer at the time—converted its orders from high-grade resilient polypropylene and polyethylene packaging to more common-grade polystyrene in order to cut expenses. Accordingly, the company was striving more than ever to develop alternative packaging materials. The company's Tuscarora Container Systems, for example, began producing lightweight aluminum shipping containers with hinges allowing a unit to fold to nearly one-tenth of the original size, then be shipped back for reuse. Moreover, the company's Thermo Forming department was forming warmed plastic sheeting into a shape suitable for shipping products, such as cases for scientific instruments.

Tuscarora's sales of nonfoam products and integrated materials—packaging made of wood, thermoformed plastics, corrugated cardboard, molded pulp paper, collapsible aluminum shipping crates, or combinations of those materials—accounted for 13 percent of all sales in 1994. In 1995 O'Leary told Houser, "This year we will have almost $40 million in sales of products that for all intents and purposes we didn't manufacture five years ago."

Tuscarora entered the British market in February 1995 by purchasing M.Y. Trondex Ltd. of Northampton, England. The following June it opened a plant in Spennymoor and by that October had acquired EPS Moulders Ltd. of Livingston, Scotland. With the 1997 acquisition of Arrowtip Group, a foam-packing producer with operations in London and Norwich, England, Tuscarora brought its annual sales to $30 million in the United Kingdom, where it was the largest producer of plastics packaging.

In 1996 Tuscarora had record net sales of $182.6 million and record net income of $9.7 million. By May 1997 the company had further extended its operations to west of the Mississippi by acquiring two manufacturers in Colorado Springs, Colorado, and a plant in Storm Lake, Iowa, with another scheduled to open during the year in Brenham, Texas. Also, during 1997, the company acquired two California companies and announced plans to build a second manufacturing plant in Mexico. This plant, in Tijuana, opened in 1998.

Tuscarora's largest customer during this time was Sony Electronics Inc., a Pennsylvania-based producer of high-definition and large thin-screened television sets. Tuscarora added new molding presses to its New Brighton plant to accommodate orders for the larger and flatter televisions. The company anticipated such products becoming a major factor in its future because the federal government had ordered all broadcasters to transmit digitally by 2006. In the high-technology area, Tuscarora had a license for E-PAC, a design-for-assembly technology, utilizing foam plastic shapes, developed by Hewlett-Packard Co. in Germany. E-PAC was intended to reduce both material cost and assembly time by bundling delicate electronic components into a lightweight, protective carrier placed inside an exterior housing.

1998 and Beyond

Tuscarora had record net sales of $232.9 million in 1998. Its lackluster net income of $8 million—the lowest since 1994—came after a pretax restructuring charge of $3.5 million. The long-term debt (excluding the current portion) rose to a record $61.2 million at the end of 1998.

Tuscarora's interior protective packaging products, made from foam plastic materials and integrated materials, were being used to protect a wide range of finished consumer and industrial goods during shipment in order to reduce or eliminate damage as a result of shock, vibration, or wide temperature fluctuations. Material handling products generally served the same purposes and functions but were being used primarily in intraplant and interplant movement of parts and components rather than shipment of finished goods. They were usually more durable than the interior protective packaging products and usually reusable. Most of these were foam plastic shapes manufactured at Tuscarora's custom molding facilities.

Tuscarora was also manufacturing foam plastic shapes used as components in automobiles, watercraft, and recreational vehicles; as thermal insulation components used by appliance manufacturers in such products as refrigerators, freezers, and air conditioners; and as insulation by the construction industry. Components such as garage-door panels and motor-vehicle trim were being made from thermoformed materials. Of Tuscarora's net sales during 1998, interior protective packaging and material handling products accounted for about 86 percent, with component products responsible for the remainder.

At Tuscarora's integrated-material facilities, foam plastics were being combined with other materials such as corrugated paperboard to produce protective packaging products with superior properties and/or lower costs compared to products made from a single material. Thermoformed interior protective packaging products were being used where the shock absorbency or thermal insulating properties of foam plastic were not required, generally to hold finished goods in place inside an exterior container during shipment and handling. In 1998, about 19 percent of Tuscarora's net sales came from products manufactured by its integrated-materials facilities and about six percent from its thermoforming facilities.

Four major markets accounted for two-thirds of Tuscarora's sales in 1998: high technology (21 percent); consumer electronics (18 percent); automotive (15 percent); and major appliances (13 percent). The company was serving more than 3,500 customers, of which none accounted for more than five percent of sales and the ten largest for about 26 percent.

Virtually all of Tuscarora's products were being custom designed at seven design and testing centers equipped with computer-aided design and manufacturing systems. After a shape was approved by the customer, aluminum production molds were being made and then shipped to a custom molding facility, generally the one nearest the customer. There were 33 manufacturing facilities in 1998, including four in the United Kingdom and two in Mexico.

Principal Subsidiaries

Alpine Packaging, Inc.; Tuscarora International, Inc.; Tuscarora Investment Corporation; Tuscarora Limited.

Principal Divisions

Eastern U.S. & U.K.; Midwestern Division; Southern Division; Western Division.

Further Reading

Antonelli, Cesca, "Tuscarora Molds a Fragmented Market in England," *Pittsburgh Business Times & Journal,* August 11, 1997, p. 5.
——, "Tuscarora Wants to Double Its Size in Next Four Years," *Pittsburgh Business Times & Journal,* May 19, 1997, p. 3.
Cotter, Wes, "Tuscarora Starts New Ventures in Westinghouse Space," *Pittsburgh Business Times & Journal,* May 18, 1992, p. 3.
Gaynor, Pamela, "Ready to Roam?," *Pittsburgh Post-Gazette,* July 12, 1996, p. C5.
Houser, Mark, "Packaging Company Molding New Markets," *Tribune Review* (Greensburg, Penn.), March 12, 1995, pp. H1 +.
Klein, Barbara, "The Big Time Without the Glitz," *Pennsylvania Business & Technology,* April 1992, p. 23.
Leaversuch, Robert D., "The War That Was: Pains and Gains for Processors," *Modern Plastics,* April 1991, p. 14.
Rhodes, Gary, "Tuscarora Sees Growth Following Sale of Stock," *Pittsburgh Business Times & Journal,* April 10, 1989, Sec. 2, p. 2.
Robertson, Scott, "Tuscarora Plastics Molds Plan for Future," *Allegheny Business News,* January 8, 1992, pp. 1 +.
Tascarella, Patty, "Local Manufacturer Keeps the Future of High-Tech Appliances Under Wraps," *Pittsburgh Business Times & Journal,* December 4, 1998, p. 26.
"Tuscarora Plastics, Inc.," *Wall Street Transcript,* May 7, 1990.
Willis, Rod, "Tuscarora Plastics Stays Hungry," *Financier,* August 1991, pp. 54–55.

—Robert Halasz

Unicom

Unicom Corporation

One First National Plaza
Chicago, Illinois 60690
U.S.A.
(312) 394-7399
(800) 950-2377
Fax: (312) 394-7251
Web site: http://www.ceco.com

Public Company
Incorporated: 1907 as The Commonwealth Edison Co.,
  Inc.
Employees: 16,700
Sales: $7.15 billion
Stock Exchanges: New York Chicago Pacific
Ticker Symbol: UCM
NAIC: 221122 Electric Power Distribution; 221113
  Nuclear Electric Power Generation; 221112 Fossil
  Fuel Electric Power Generation; 551112 Offices of
  Other Holding Companies

Unicom Corporation was created in 1994 as a holding company for The Commonwealth Edison Co., Inc. (ComEd), which is responsible for the production, transmission, and distribution of electricity to more than three million wholesale and retail customers in northern Illinois. The company serves 70 percent of the state's population, including Chicago and its greater metropolitan area. ComEd uses nuclear-generated power to supply the majority of its electricity, to a greater extent than any other investor-owned electric company in the United States. Other Unicom subsidiaries generate cool air for business districts, manufacture power generators, and perform energy-related consulting.

19th-Century Origins

Samuel Insull helped make Commonwealth Edison an industry giant and in fact laid the foundations of the electrical power industry. Insull popularized mass production and selling at the lowest possible cost, developed modern public relations, and devised methods for marketing securities in a way that led to the large public corporations of the later 20th century.

At the age of 21 Insull possessed outstanding financial acumen and unwavering ambition to succeed in business. In the early 1880s, he traveled from his home in London to the United States to take his position as Thomas Edison's personal secretary. Insull gained from his employer vast financial responsibilities and decision-making power, while quadrupling sales at Edison Electric Light Company's main factory and selling central power plants to cities across the country.

Edison's company was renamed Edison General Electric Company in 1889, and soon thereafter it merged with Thomson-Houston Electric Company, forming General Electric Company. At the time, Insull was offered a $36,000-a-year executive position at General Electric (GE), but instead he took a $12,000-a-year position as president of Chicago Edison Company. The 32-year-old Insull borrowed $250,000 from the newspaper tycoon Marshall Field, purchased a large share of the company's stock, and then went to work selling electricity.

There were almost four dozen electric companies competing for Chicago's electricity business when Insull came on the scene. At the time, less than one percent of Chicago's homes used electric lamps. Insull's goal was to grow—exponentially. Expansion spelled greater volume, which meant lower unit costs of production, which meant greater profit. More income meant more investment, and more growth, and so on.

Insull formed a 25-person sales department and, according to Forrest McDonald's biography *Insull,* told them to "sell at the lowest possible price." Insull was not lowering prices to compete. He maintained that competition was "economically wrong" and was instead lowering prices in an attempt to wipe out competition all together. Insull quietly bought exclusive rights to electric equipment manufactured by General Electric and most other U.S. manufacturers to thwart competition. In his first 42 months in Chicago, Insull increased Chicago Edison's sales almost five times. He also expanded Chicago Edison by buying out competitors.

Company Perspectives:

As a leading generator and provider of energy, we recognize that excellence in Nuclear and Fossil Operations and maintenance of our high standards of system reliability are imperative. The competitive market further compels us to focus on our customers, improving their satisfaction and our corporate reputation. We must continue to aggressively reduce our operating costs to meet the mandated rate reduction and provide value to our shareholders. New systems have been put in place to allow for profitability-based decision-making throughout the organization, from the operation of ComEd's generating facilities to improved purchasing functions. All of our strategic initiatives are designed to work toward the most important goal of all: ensuring that customers choose ComEd when they have a choice. We will invest to build shareholder value, tailor our business to profitably deliver what the marketplace wants and maximize our competitiveness.

Local politicians soon caught wind of Edison's success. Accustomed to receiving kickbacks from companies doing business in Chicago, a group of politicians reportedly devised a plan to extort $1 million from Chicago Edison. They formed a dummy company, called Commonwealth Electric Company, and gave it a 50-year franchise to provide the city's electricity. The founders of Commonwealth planned to force Insull to buy their company for $1 million or be frozen out of the market. They did not realize, however, that Insull owned the rights to the equipment it would take to run this company. Insull therefore was able to buy Commonwealth with its 50-year electricity franchise for the city of Chicago for just $50,000.

In 1907 Insull merged Commonwealth Electric Company and Chicago Edison Company to form Commonwealth Edison, a company whose sales exceeded the combined sales of New York Edison, Brooklyn Edison, and Boston Edison. After the merger, Insull formed a holding company called Middle West Utilities (MWU) to own small interests in Com Ed and other investor-owned utilities. MWU itself was also a publicly traded company. Insull controlled MWU, and by 1912 MWU, in turn, controlled utilities in 13 states through relatively small shareholdings. Insull wanted nothing less than a monopoly wherever he operated, and in order to achieve this, he was willing to sacrifice a degree of control. Therefore, Insull agreed that his exclusive franchises with municipalities should be regulated by a state commission.

Growth in the Early 1900s

In 1906 Insull's customers numbered 50,000; in 1909, that number had reached 100,000. ComEd's growth was both rapid and smart. Insull diversified customers, spreading the demand for power as much as possible. For instance, he obtained major contracts with Chicago electric streetcar companies, which drew the most power when residential customers were at work and not at home using electric lamps and appliances. He went after big industry, offering huge subsidies to induce these daytime users away from using small, private power stations. Insull

termed this approach to business "massing production" and was succeeding at it before Henry Ford gained fame as a mass producer of the automobile.

Taking an idea he learned from the English electricity business, Insull charged a dual rate for power: a higher rate for the first several hours of electrical usage, and a progressively lower rate thereafter. This covered the costs of adding equipment for new customers and encouraged greater use. He also kept cutting rates. The company, from early on, regularly paid out an eight cent dividend to shareholders.

Insull approached generating electricity with the same zeal he showed for selling electricity. He ignored the apparent limits of the day's technology, pushing his engineers to build generators that were several times larger than any other generators in existence. Historical accounts suggest that Insull was progressive in his dealings with workers, not out of personal convictions but rather to ensure the effective and continuous operation of ComEd's facilities. Insull hired women and minorities, gave his employees relatively generous benefits, and maintained a cooperative relationship with labor leaders.

Insull was ahead of his time in yet another significant way—he was a master at public relations. He established an advertising department as early as 1901, and his rate cuts were well timed and well publicized. Moreover, he published and distributed a free tabloid, *Electric City,* which shaped a positive public opinion of electricity, and, of course, the electric company itself. Insull began publishing annual reports 15 years before they became standard.

During World War I Insull was a fervent supporter of England. He personally spent $250,000 attempting to sway public opinion in favor of the U.S. entry into the war, after which Insull worked to raise money for the war effort. After World War I, Insull was able to capitalize on the high profile he had cultivated during the war to promote the interests of ComEd.

The postwar period was a time of immense growth in demand for the electric industry. In 1923, the year the electric refrigerator became available to residential customers, ComEd added over 75,000 new customers to its service area, its largest annual increase up to that time. ComEd proved to be the only major steam-power electric company in the nation that neither raised its rates nor cut its dividends during the postwar period, though money for expansion was scarce. Insull exploited an idea he got from Pacific Gas & Electric, launching a hugely successful customer ownership drive. From 1919 to 1921 the number of ComEd shareholders who lived in Illinois grew from 50,000 to 500,000. Insull's name was equated with trust by small investors.

Weathering the Depression

The phenomenal control Insull had been able to exercise over his empire's destiny began to crumble around 1926; he made several less-than-wise, if not illegal, financial moves over the next few years. After the October 1929 stock market crash, Insull, who believed the Great Depression would be short, continued to spend great sums of money, on both the company and his many philanthropic endeavors. During that time, he was perhaps most recognized for his contribution to the Chicago

Civic Opera. ComEd continued to grow and its stock continued to rise.

Much of this growth, however, was deceptive. Assets and earnings were inflated, and in 1931 utility stock prices plunged. MWU's stock dropped from $570 to $1.25 per share. Insull had financed much of MWU's growth by using other utility properties as collateral. In 1932 banks took over MWU, and Insull was forced to resign, claiming a personal loss of nearly $15 million. Eventually he was tried for fraud and embezzlement. Though Insull was not found guilty, he had left the power industry for good.

ComEd itself, however, weathered the Depression relatively well, and business carried on. Modern conveniences such as the air conditioner and the electric water heater came on the scene in the 1930s and continued to stimulate increased demand for electricity.

During World War II reserve capacity attracted war industries to the Chicago area; in 1943 about 40 percent of the company's yearly output was tied to war production. In 1947 the city of Chicago conducted a study of ComEd's service and found the company was significantly overcharging, especially residential and commercial customers. The utility's initial franchise with the city was soon to expire, and a battle involving politicians, the utility, and customers ensued.

As a utility overseen by a regulatory commission, ComEd was allowed a reasonable rate of return, but there was a great deal of debate over what "reasonable" meant. In comparing utilities in the nation's 23 largest cities, ComEd was found to spend twice as much on advertising as any other utility. Critics questioned whether customers should pay higher rates to support advertising of a monopoly. Moreover, they wondered, would legal fees be passed on to customers if the city were to take ComEd to court? Although these and other criticisms were addressed in the report, in the media, and by members of the city council, a powerful faction in the city council supported ComEd, and the city ultimately signed a 42-year franchise that did little to address these criticisms. Some observers believed that neither the franchise agreement nor the state regulatory body, the Illinois Commerce Commission (ICC), clearly defined "reasonable rate of return." It was left up to ComEd, although the ICC did set a maximum rate.

ComEd's customers did not feel the sting of this arrangement until many years down the road, when Edison's nuclear program ran into decades of cost overruns. In the short term the company flourished, and customers benefited. By 1951 ComEd had assets of $1 billion. In 1953 the Public Service Company of Northern Illinois—which had been created in 1950 by the merger of Western United Gas & Electric Company and Illinois Northern Utilities Company—merged with ComEd. The following year, ComEd created the Northern Illinois Gas Company to own and operate its gas properties. In 1955 the company began using an electronic computer for billing, and by 1959 ComEd was reaching two million customers.

Rate reductions averaged more than $36 million a year between 1962 and 1967; the utility's operating revenues rose from $492 million in 1962 to $658.7 million in 1966. In 1966 ComEd absorbed the Central Illinois Electric and Gas Company, basi-

cally establishing an integrated electric system for all of northern Illinois, and further capitalizing on economies of scale.

1960s–70s: The Pros and Cons of Nuclear Power

In 1960 ComEd began operating the nation's first privately financed commercial nuclear power station, a 200,000-kilowatt facility called Dresden I near Morris, Illinois. ComEd was leading the national charge toward nuclear power. J. Harris Ward became ComEd's chairman the next year. He linked the company's growth to nuclear power and committed large sums of capital investment to this program.

The utility's ambitious plans called for 40 percent of its entire generating capacity to be supplied by seven nuclear-fueled plants by 1973. By 1969, however, the company's nuclear program was experiencing technical difficulties, falling behind schedule, and suffering rapidly escalating costs. ComEd was forced to begin building a $160 million coal-fired unit at its Powerton plant in Pekin, Illinois. "The delays forced us to double-build," Ward told a reporter in the September 15, 1969 issue of *Forbes*. This adjustment in ComEd's nuclear program was only one in a long line of costly setbacks.

The company's commitment to nuclear-generated power was due, in part, to nuclear power's potential as a cleaner fuel. The problems associated with burning fossil fuels came to a head in 1970 when the Chicago Department of Environmental Control named ComEd the worst polluter in Chicago, accusing the electric company's fossil-fuel plants of causing more sulfur pollution than all other companies in the city combined. Thomas G. Ayers, president of ComEd, began bringing in low-sulfur coal from Montana, cutting sulfur emissions by 60 percent by 1973. In 1973 he was elected chairman and CEO of ComEd. By 1972 ComEd was using nuclear power to generate 22 percent of its capacity, more than any other investor-owned utility in the nation. In the interest of assuring a uranium supply, ComEd acquired Cotter Corporation, a uranium mining and milling company in 1974.

In 1971 planning began on a joint proposal with the Tennessee Valley Authority to build and operate the United States' first commercial fast breeder reactor. This kind of power plant would produce more fuel than it used. It would also produce more highly radioactive waste than its predecessors. The project was approved by the Atomic Energy Commission in 1972, and though that breeder reactor was completed and more followed, the problems of disposing of the high-level nuclear waste continued. Nevertheless, in 1973 the company, for the third time in its history, received the industry's Edison award for its leadership in the development of the breeder reactor.

During the 1970s the ComEd faced soaring operating and expansion costs, exacerbated by problems of getting rate increases and plant construction clearances. The widely publicized nuclear accident at Three Mile Island, Pennsylvania, in 1979 heightened attention of both the public and regulators, and ComEd sent teams of nuclear experts to assist and study the situation. In 1980, in the middle of ComEd's $4.5 billion construction of six new nuclear plants, earnings per share sank to their lowest level since 1965. As heavy industry in the area stopped growing, ComEd's sales slowed drastically.

New Leadership in the 1980s

Into this bleak picture stepped ComEd's newly appointed CEO, James O'Connor. Beginning in 1980, the ICC granted the utility a series of large rate increases. ComEd began to rebound, and by December 1984, O'Connor was predicting that rates would increase about 2.5 percent a year for three years, level off in 1988, and then stabilize.

In 1986, as ComEd struggled to finance the $7.1 billion building program for the last three of 12 nuclear plants, problems with the company's Braidwood nuclear plant increased its construction cost more than 40 percent. This meant that ComEd would need a 4.8 percent annual increase for 11 years to cover the cost. Many observers felt that ComEd should have canceled or postponed some of its plants in the early 1980s, due to underestimated construction costs and overestimated demand.

As a result of overbuilding in its nuclear program, ComEd's generating capacity exceeded average peak demand by 33 percent in 1990 (most utilities maintain a 15 percent surplus). Thus, while many major utilities around the nation were found to be spending $15 to $51 on conservation per customer, ComEd was spending 39¢ per customer, according to a study by a committee of the Chicago City Council.

Rate Rollbacks and Refunds in the 1990s

In 1990 the company's net income fell to $128 million, or 22 cents per share, from the previous year's $693 million, or $2.83 per share, largely because of court-ordered refunds and rate rollbacks. Also in 1990, at a time when customers were growing increasingly unhappy with paying some of the nation's highest rates, the utility's franchise term with the city of Chicago was due to expire. A coalition of community and environmental groups had formed in 1988 to pressure the city to stir up public debate over the city's electricity options. These amounted to a renegotiated franchise or municipal acquisition. Meanwhile, ComEd waged an advertising campaign to tout the quality of its service.

In the summer of 1990, two major substation fires caused 60,000 customers to lose power for up to three days. The city postponed its decision on the franchise issue to allow more time to study the utility's reliability. Negotiations on a new franchise concluded in 1991, and ComEd was granted a 29-year contract.

The company's costs were still high, and with a series of lawsuits on the verge of settlement ComEd cut its dividend in 1992 by a whopping 47 percent. A year later the company agreed to the biggest refund in utility industry history. Over the next 12 months ComEd would pay back $1.34 billion to its customers, primarily because it had passed the costs of building unnecessary nuclear plants on to them. A rate reduction of $339 million was also effected.

In 1994 ComEd became part of a newly created holding company, Unicom Corporation. The company had recently been granted legislative approval to create an unregulated energy subsidiary, and the new corporate structure was intended to facilitate this. A subsidiary, Unicom Thermal, was also formed to develop new types of cooling systems to take advantage of laws mandating reductions in ozone-depleting cooling agents.

Other subsidiaries would become involved in energy consulting and the manufacture of power generators, though revenues from these operations were small.

Troubles with the company's nuclear power plants continued to bring down profits, and in 1995 a 16 percent reduction in the work force was announced. Moreover, ComEd was being fined regularly by the Nuclear Regulatory Commission for incidents ranging from workers planting a small quantity of radioactive material in a coworker's pocket, to an employee being allowed to work while visibly drunk. By the mid-1990s only half of the company's reactors were typically online, with the Zion plant the most seriously troubled. Other problems arose when the company announced the possibility of "rolling blackouts" when peak energy demands exceeded production capacity. Critics pointed out that the company was still charging one of the highest rates for power in the country, yet was openly resisting buying extra electricity during the peak summer cooling season to keep its customers supplied with power.

In January 1998 ComEd finally moved to permanently close its Zion plant, and the following month CEO O'Connor stepped down. His successor was 52-year old John W. Rowe, former CEO of New England Electric System and a lawyer with a strong background in nuclear power issues. Rowe's challenge was not only to bring up the company's ailing bottom line but to develop a strategy for the impending power industry deregulation that Illinois legislators had enacted. This would finally open up the power marketplace to all comers, with business customers available in 1999 and residential users to follow in 2002. Rowe's strategy, which he had developed in his years with New England Electric, was to focus more on delivery of power than production, opening the door to purchasing energy from outside providers. To that end he sold 16 of ComEd's non-nuclear plants for $4.8 billion in early 1999, while the company also sought approval of a $3.4 billion bond issue. He also announced the company's intention to purchase more energy industry service companies, such as heating and air conditioning contractors. Perhaps his boldest gesture was to publicly admit that ComEd's long-time nuclear power strategy had been a mistake.

As the company sought to turn its fortunes around, the failures of its nuclear power strategy still needed to be dealt with definitively. The moves to develop new energy businesses and implement cost-cutting were the first steps in preparing it for the level playing field deregulation would bring. While it was uncertain how that scenario would play out, ComEd's well-established infrastructure and long history of energy production gave it a decided head start on the competition.

Principal Subsidiaries

The Commonwealth Edison Co., Inc.; Unicom Enterprises, Inc.; Unicom Resources, Inc.

Further Reading

Crown, Judith, "Why O'Connor is Turning Off the Lights: Faced with Nuclear Dereg Turmoil it was Time to Exit," *Crain's Chicago Business*, October 13, 1998, p. 1.

Daniels, Steve, "Cash in Hand, ComEd Gets Ready to Shop: Set to Buy Energy Service Providers in Growth Bid," *Crain's Chicago Business,* March 29, 1999, p. 4.

Knowles, Francine, "Shareholders OK Edison Restructuring," *Chicago Sun-Times,* May 11, 1994, p. 63.

Lashinsky, Adam, "A ComEd Peace Treaty," *Crain's Chicago Business,* September 27, 1993, p. 1.

McDonald, Forrest, *Insull,* Chicago: University of Chicago Press, 1962.

Munson, Richard, *The Power Makers,* Emmaus, Penn.: Rodale Press, 1985.

Oloroso, Arsenio, Jr., and Judith Crown, "Rowe's Strategy: Power Up ComEd—Rowe's Formula: Cost-Cutting, Asset Sales, Mini-Mergers," *Crain's Chicago Business,* June 15, 1998, p. 1.

Samuels, Gary, "Burying the Hatchet," *Forbes,* December 5, 1994, p. 56.

Snyder, David, "In a Sound Bite: A Cultural Revolution Begins at ComEd," *Crain's Chicago Business,* July 20, 1998, p. 11.

—Carole Healy
—updated by Frank Uhle

USANA, Inc.

3838 West Parkway Boulevard
Salt Lake City, Utah 84120
U.S.A.
(801) 954-7100
Fax: (801) 954-7300
Web site: http://www.usana.com

Public Company
Incorporated: 1992
Employees: 455
Sales: $121.6 million (1998)
Stock Exchanges: NASDAQ
Ticker Symbol: USNA
NAIC: 325411 Medicinal & Botanical Manufacturing;
   325412 Pharmaceutical Preparation Manufacturing;
   32562 Toilet Preparation Manufacturing

Although still a young company, USANA, Inc. contributes significantly to the rapidly growing natural products industry. USANA primarily produces nutritional supplements but also sells lines of skin care, personal care, and weight management items. Like many companies in its industry, USANA uses network or multilevel marketing (MLM), whereby self-employed representatives sell the products to customers or buy the products for their own use. USANA is part of a booming herbalism and natural products industry in Utah, among the key areas in this relatively new field. The company's success relies on expanding consumer demand, advanced nutritional science, modern marketing, and one-on-one direct sales, an old method that in the late 20th century was proving surprisingly effective, both in the United States and overseas.

1970s Origins as Gull Laboratories

USANA's founder, Dr. Myron Wentz, received his Ph.D. in microbiology with an emphasis in immunology from the University of Utah. He served as the microbiology director of three hospitals in Peoria, Illinois, from 1969 to 1973. In 1973 he started Gull Laboratories in Salt Lake City to use advanced cell culture techniques to make commercial tests to diagnose viral diseases. In company literature Wentz later recalled the origins of Gull and USANA: "My objective in virology at Gull Laboratories was to produce complete, not-defective viral antigens. . . . After spending all of those years in the laboratory, maybe I smelled too many vapors, fumes or touched too many chemicals; I was continually sick. I pulled my nose out of virology just long enough to get a taste of nutrition. . . . I started eating right, but what I learned in the laboratory made me realize . . . that supplementation was necessary."

Wentz began taking a multivitamin, what he believed was the best multivitamin on the market. Then one day he read the label and was decidedly unimpressed with the supplement's ingredients. "If we were to nutrient our cells in culture like this, Gull Laboratories wouldn't be here today," said Wentz, adding "We wouldn't have gotten off the ground. I believe it was that day that I made the commitment that I was going to nutrient myself and my family with the kind of nutrition that I use to grow cells in culture."

Wentz credited Dr. Michael Colgan as "the individual who convinced me of the importance of producing [USANA's first] products." After giving a talk at the National Nutritional Foods Association, Colgan spoke with Wentz privately and a few days later visited the Gull headquarters in Salt Lake City. Once he saw Wentz's approach to nutrition at the cellular level, Colgan reportedly remarked, "The potential for this is far greater than personal health for you and your family. I know everything that is going on in the nutritional industry, I have been in this field for 20 years. This will be a major boon to human nutrition. You must market these products."

Thus in 1990 USANA was born as the Gull Health Products Division, to test and manufacture herbal and other natural products. In 1992 Wentz incorporated USANA, Inc., as a wholly-owned subsidiary of his Gull Laboratories. In 1993 he spun off USANA as an independent firm.

Early Developments in the 1990s

By the summer of 1994 the company had begun its own publication for its distributors, *USANA Magazine,* in which Wentz announced that he had sold his controlling interest in

Company Perspectives:

USANA's mission is to create opportunity, independence, and personal growth for our distributors and their customers by providing the most effective wellness and weight management program available anywhere.

Gull Laboratories to Fresenius, a German health care firm with annual sales of over $1 billion. After six months of working on the sale, Wentz said he was looking forward to focusing on USANA's research programs, particularly those concerning products to help reverse the effects of coronary heart disease and stroke, the number one and three main causes of death in the United States, respectively. With $22.7 million from selling Gull, USANA's finances were considerably strengthened, and new research could begin.

To reach his goals, Wentz planned to enlarge USANA's cell culture research at Moscow's Cardiology Research Center. In 1994 he also announced an agreement to contract with the Linus Pauling Institute, where independent tests would show, Wentz was certain, that USANA products were superior to others on the market, particularly as regarded their antioxidant capabilities.

USANA grew rapidly in its first few years, as its nutritional supplements gained popularity in the United States and Canada. From 1993 sales in the United States of $3.9 million, the company reported an increase to $7.3 million in 1994. In 1995 U.S. sales reached $21.5 million, and Canadian sales accounted for an additional $3 million. Based in Ontario, the subsidiary USANA Canada, Inc., had been incorporated in February 1995.

By early 1996 USANA had joined the Direct Selling Association (DSA), a trade group for firms in network marketing and other kinds of direct sales. The DSA governing board took a year to look at USANA to make sure it complied with the DSA's ethical standards. At the same time, USANA produced new sales tools for its distributors. Actor and USANA distributor Gordon Jump hosted a new video called *Real Health, Real Wealth.* Moreover, Dr. Denis Waitley, a well-known motivational speaker, also became a USANA distributor and narrated an audiotape, *How to Survive and Thrive.*

Product Lines and Leadership in the 1990s

In 1998 USANA offered a wide variety of nutritional and personal care products. Its two "Essentials" to supplement adult diets were Mega Antioxidant tablets and Chelated Mineral tablets, which, taken together, promised to "work interactively, in conjunction with a healthy diet, to provide your body with the proper combination of nutrients needed for optimum performance from all of the body's cells." In addition to these Essentials, the company offered several Optimizers, including Proflavanol, a grape seed extract that reportedly mimicked the antioxidant advantages of French wines; Poly C concentrated tablets of Vitamin C; CalMag Plus, with Vitamin D3, calcium, and magnesium; Melatonin KL, with the hormone melatonin and extracts from the Polynesian kava plant, for better sleep

patterns; Nutrimeal, a drink mix powder with carbohydrates and proteins; and several others. Children's nutrition was addressed through a child-strength blend of vitamins, minerals, and antioxidants called Kid's Choo-Ables.

USANA also sold a LEAN Team line of weight management products, including Nutrimeal LEAN drink mix, available in chocolate and vanilla; LEAN Team energy bars; and Lean Team Entrees, food mix made with soy protein, available in vegetarian chili and vegetarian pasta varieties.

USANA's Personal Care Products featured cleansers, moisturizers, shampoo, hair conditioner, and a sunscreen. Its Dental Care System included a specially designed toothbrush, floss, tongue scraper, mouthwash, toothpaste, and a fluoride gel to prevent cavities. Finally, the company also marketed a water distiller that used steam distillation and carbon filtration to provide purer drinking water.

According to the firm's 1997 annual report, USANA received about 82 percent of its sales from nutritional products. The company's best selling items were its two "Essentials," which accounted for 41 percent of total sales, and Proflavanol, which held 22 percent.

In the late 1990s, USANA founder Wentz remained as president, CEO, and chairman of the board. As the sole owner of Gull Holdings, Ltd., an Isle of Man company, he owned 60.7 percent of USANA's common stock. Other USANA officers included Dallin Larsen, who served as vice-president of sales, and Jeb McCandless, vice-president and chief operating officer, who, having a B.A. in zoology, an M.S. in pathology, and an MBA degree, was responsible for all scientific activities, customer relations, and legal/regulatory issues. The founder's son, David A. Wentz, joined the business in 1992 and served as director and vice-president of strategic development.

Financial Growth and International Expansion

In 1995 Wentz announced that USANA would build a new facility at 2700 South Bangerter Highway in Salt Lake City. Located on a 16-acre site, the new building with about 95,000 square feet tripled the size of the firm's laboratory space, which allowed it to consolidate its cell culture research at one location instead of at other locations as far away as Moscow.

The year 1997 was pivotal in extending USANA's global reach, with the formation of three new wholly-owned subsidiaries. USANA New Zealand Limited was incorporated on March 18 of that year, followed by USANA Australia Pty. Ltd., incorporated on March 25, and the USANA Trading Co., Inc., a foreign sales corporation, in September.

The following year USANA began operations in the United Kingdom, making 17 of its products available through distributors in England, Northern Ireland, Scotland, and Wales. Moreover, the company purchased a 23,800-square-foot building in Milton Keynes, about one hour's drive north of London, for administration, distributor relations, and shipping/warehousing.

"We plan to address the UK market with the same successful approach we used to enter the Australia-New Zealand market," said Myron Wentz in a September 1998 press release. He observed, "International expansion is an integral part of our growth strategy. The United Kingdom is intrinsically an important market and . . . a base from which to build a presence in Europe."

For its independent distributors worldwide, USANA started new programs and incentives, including the option to purchase company stock through sales commission deductions. Also available for sale to distributors were proprietary telephone and credit card services. Thus, like several other multilevel marketing firms including Amway Corporation, USANA began selling services beyond their original core products.

In 1997 USANA also started its Preferred Customer Program for those who wanted to purchase USANA products at wholesale prices but not become distributors. They were required to purchase at least $20 worth of USANA products every four weeks. By the end of 1997 some 9,000 persons had become Preferred Customers.

Improved health and financial well-being drew an increasing number of distributors to USANA. By September 26, 1998, the end of USANA's third quarter, about 110,000 persons were listed as current distributors, up from 82,000 one year earlier. USANA defined a current distributor as one who had made at least one purchase in the last 12 months. The company paid 46 percent of its 1997 revenues to its distributors in various commissions and bonuses.

In its 1997 annual report, USANA maintained that it was particularly well-positioned to compete in the network marketing industry not only due to its popular products but because of its compensation plan, which made available to USANA distributors weekly commissions and bonuses, unlike many other network marketing firms that paid monthly.

Not surprisingly, many of USANA's main competitors also used the multilevel marketing approach: the Amway Corporation (Nutrilite supplements and personal care products), Avon Products (personal care products), NuSkin (personal care products), Herbalife International (nutritional supplements), Nature's Sunshine (herbal supplements), and Rexall Showcase International (nutritional products). Other competitors included Murdock Madaus Schwabe, Sunrider Corporation, and Weider Nutrition.

The Future of Holistic Health

USANA's success in the 1990s reflected a growing trend worldwide of people choosing to emphasize disease prevention, as well as self-care rather than dependence on health professionals. By exercising, eating healthy foods, using nutritional supplements, and avoiding dangerous substances such as tobacco and alcohol, more tried to gain optimum physical and emotional health in a holistic, integrated approach.

The growing use of supplements had prompted the federal government in 1994 to pass the Dietary Supplement Health and Education Act, which prohibited the Food and Drug Administration from regulating vitamins, minerals, and nutritional and herbal products, unless such supplements proved dangerous,

were mislabeled, or made specific claims that they prevented or treated particular diseases. In 1998 the Federal Trade Commission issued guidelines to help companies know the limits of what they could and could not say about their products.

Due to the rapidly rising costs of orthodox medical care, a growing number of health insurance companies in the 1990s began covering alternative health methods, including chiropractic, homeopathy, massage therapy, acupuncture, and the use of herbs and supplements. For example, the American Western Life Insurance Company of Foster City, California, introduced The Wellness Plan, a holistic approach to bodily health.

In addition, more doctors were apparently recognizing the benefits of supplements and had started examining or even embracing the growing alternative health movement. By 1998, over half of the nation's medical schools taught a course on alternative healing or at least included basic principles of non-Western methods in required classes.

Through scientific research in the formulation of its products, USANA sought to bridge the gap between the medical establishment and the alternative health field. Its distributors presented their ideas at holistic health fairs, which included all kinds of practitioners, from herbalists to spiritual healers. USANA also published clinical studies of nutritional ingredients to educate its distributors and customers.

USANA continued to prosper under the leadership of its founder Wentz. The April 13, 1998 *Investor's Business Daily* listed USANA as the nation's fifth-ranked cosmetics/personal care products firm, based on earnings per share. In June of that year, COO Jeb McCandless stated in a press release that "USANA sales have surpassed the $100 million annual run rate with only 27 core products." Soon thereafter, the company was able to announce a two-for-one stock split of its common stock. More good news was on the horizon, as the following year the company extended its reach to the Asian market, with operations in Hong Kong. With no long-term debt, USANA seemed poised for even more growth in the new century.

Principal Subsidiaries

USANA Australia Pty Ltd.; USANA New Zealand Limited; USANA Trading Company, Inc.; USANA Canada, Inc.

Further Reading

Brown, Caryne, "Door-to-Door Selling Grows Up," *Black Enterprise,* December 1992, p. 76.

Carton, Barbara, "Health Insurers Embrace Eye-of-Newt Therapy," *Wall Street Journal,* January 30, 1995, p. B1.

Duffy, James A., "Nation's Doctors Opening Doors for Alternative Medicine," *Salt Lake Tribune,* November 11, 1998, pp. A1, A8.

Grugal, Robin M., "USANA Sees Growing Network of Vitamin Fans, Distributors," *Investor's Business Daily,* June 1, 1998.

"Guidelines to Govern Dietary Supplements," *Salt Lake Tribune,* November 24, 1998, p. C7.

Miller, Leslie, "Wellness Plans Insure an Alternative," *USA Today,* August 16, 1994, p. 6D.

—David M. Walden

VARIG S.A. (Viação Aérea Rio-Grandense)

Rua 18 de Novembro #800
90240-040 Porto Alegre/R S
Brazil
(051) 358-7063
Fax: (051) 358-7001
Web site: http://www.varig.com.br

Public Company
Incorporated: 1927
Employees: 17,741
Sales: R $3.62 billion (1998)
Stock Exchanges: Sao Paulo Rio de Janeiro
Ticker Symbol: RG; VRG
NAIC: 481111 Scheduled Passenger Air Transportation

An estimated 11 million passengers a year fly VARIG S.A. to 36 cities within Brazil and 32 cities abroad. Domestic and European routes each accounted for slightly less than 30 percent of passenger traffic; North American destinations accounted for about 17 percent. Asian and Latin American routes each accounted for about a sixth share. North American routes accounted for nearly 40 percent of cargo traffic, versus 32 percent for Europe.

Origins

VARIG was founded by a German immigrant, Otto Meyer, when he obtained a license to operate Brazil's first registered commercial aircraft, a nine-passenger Atlantico, in 1927. That same year, Meyer saw the need for administrative assistance. He hired a secretary, Ruben Berta, and later described his new employee as "an energetic young man of 19 who attached little importance to the salary I could afford . . . I invited him to hang up his hat and coat and get the typewriter going."

Meyer and Berta worked together to develop the fledgling airline, headquartered at the time in Porto Alegre, a coastal town in southern Brazil. It was Berta who ultimately would exert the most influence on VARIG's future, with his vision of a company owned by its employees.

When Brazil joined the Allies of World War II in 1941, Meyer withdrew from the company and Berta assumed the presidency of VARIG. After the war, Berta restructured VARIG's ownership based on the message in a papal letter by progressive Roman Catholic Pope Louis XIII. (Brazil is the largest Catholic nation in the world, with more than 90 percent of its population belonging to the church.) Pope Louis XIII's Rerum Novarum (Of New Things) of May 15, 1891 called for a commitment to collective bargaining and fair pay on the part of employers while suggesting that workers would exert greater efforts for their employers if they held ownership interests. This dictum inspired Berta to develop a plan for mutual ownership of VARIG by its employees.

Postwar Employee Ownership

Berta established an employee foundation in 1945, with the approval of VARIG shareholders, to oversee conversion to shared ownership. The foundation (which was named for Berta after his death in 1966) reported in 1992 that approximately 80 percent of VARIG's stock was held by employees and less than 20 percent of its shares were traded on the open market.

In addition to acting as an umbrella foundation for VARIG and its subsidiaries, the Berta Foundation was the financial base for employee perquisites not generally available through government programs. Those include, but are not limited to, free medical and dental treatment, low interest loans, subsidized meals, and vacation retreats, primarily for the benefit of employees living in Brazil. Those working at overseas offices (there are 25 offices in North America alone) received medical, dental, and life insurance coverage from the Berta Foundation, along with a matched savings plan and a pension plan that began paying benefits to employees as early as age 55. Oversees workers also had the opportunity to use the foundation's services and facilities while in Brazil.

Erik de Carvalho, who succeeded Berta in 1966, was at VARIG's helm to oversee several of the company's acquisitions, beginning with an air charter company, Rotatur, in 1969. But it was not until the 1970s, with the acquisition of VARIG Agropecuaria, an agricultural enterprise that started in the State of

Maranhao in 1973, that VARIG took its first step away from air transport. VARIG Agropecuaria consisted of a 45,000-acre complex devoted to raising poultry and livestock and to farming. The company also acquired the Tropical Hotel chain consisting of six properties, each located in or near Brazil resort areas. The five-star Manaus Tropical Hotel, for example, is located in Manaus, a city not only steeped in history, but natural beauty as well—the Rio Negro meets the Amazon River in Manaus.

Although VARIG has diversified through various nonairline acquisitions, it continues to dominate the Latin American airline industry. VARIG strengthened its South American operations with the addition of Cruzeiro do Sul Airlines in 1975 and Rio Sul Airlines, which operates only in southern Brazil. But VARIG's air ventures outside of South America have given it a stability not available to companies limited by government regulation to national air service. VARIG's most significant international connection was the establishment of services to the United States, which started with twice-a-week flights on VARIG's Super G Constellation planes from New York to Rio on August 2, 1955. Routes to Miami and Los Angeles were added in 1961, followed by routes to Chicago in 1990. The U.S. connection proved to be VARIG's ace-in-the-hole during Brazil's economic upheaval of the 1980s.

VARIG continued to expand operations in the early 1990s, adding Toronto to its list of destinations and establishing three Los Angeles/Japan flights. The company also flew to 12 European destinations, four African cities, two cities in Japan, and all of the principal cities of Latin America. In addition, no doubt responding to the strong Asian economy, VARIG planned to begin a Rio/Johannesburg/Bangkok/Hong Kong cargo route in January of 1993, giving VARIG coverage extending eastward from Tokyo to Hong Kong.

VARIG's growth included continuous upgrading of its equipment. The 1992 VARIG/Cruzeiro fleet included ten Boeing B-747s, ten DC-10-30s, ten B-767s, two McDonnell Douglas MD-11s, 41 Boeing B-737s, and 14 B-727s. Because the company was consistently able to meet or exceed the stringent safety guidelines of both the Deparmento Aeronatical Civil of Brazil and its U.S. counterpart, the Federal Aviation Administration, its fleet maintenance earned a reputation that was literally worth money. VARIG was awarded contracts to service Brazil's military aircraft at the company's industrial maintenance complex in the Rio de Janeiro International Airport.

In 1991 VARIG carried 6,519,255 passengers on its domestic and international routes and logged 16,402,000 passenger-kilometers. The figures, however, were lower than in previous years due to the effects of the Persian Gulf War, deregulation, and fluctuating economic conditions.

Those changes did not prevent VARIG from maintaining its status as the leading Latin American airline in kilometers flown, hours flown, cargo transportation, passenger-kilometers, route systems, and number of employees, but it did lead to a reorganization after the death of President Helio Smidt. When Rubel Thomas succeeded Smidt, he restructured the company's upper management with an eye toward more direct decision-making. He sought to increase competitiveness by streamlining costs while updating the air fleet—not a small feat, with a devalued currency and the need to buy aircraft from U.S. and European suppliers.

Deregulation in the 1980s

The impact of the Gulf War on VARIG was minimal compared with the combined effect of deregulation and economic factors. Inflation, which in Brazil has been as high as 1,500 percent a year, had a significant influence on the air carrier's strength in the late 1980s and early 1990s. World prices for major Brazilian exports such as sugar cane, rubber, coffee, and oranges fluctuated during this time period. These price changes, along with droughts and floods within the country during the 1980s, wreaked havoc on the Brazilian economy. The country attained the unenviable position of being one of the world's largest debtor nations. In addition, Rio de Janeiro was losing stature as a tourist destination because of high crime rates and the conspicuous problem of homeless children.

In 1986 the government mounted a stabilization campaign that hinged on changing its status from that of a mostly agricultural nation to a more industrialized economy. Among the recovery strategies instituted by President Fernando Collor de Mello was a plan to deregulate Brazil's airline industry, much the way President Ronald Reagan did in the United States in the 1980s.

In October of 1990, Brazilian trucking magnate Wagner Canhedo used US $43 million of his own money along with other financing to purchase Brazil's second largest airline, VASP, from the State of Sao Paulo. The transaction took place at the end of a three-year period in which Brazil's three major airlines—VARIG, VASP, and Transbrasil—posted a combined loss of US $1.5 billion. Canhedo planned to use VASP to challenge VARIG's domestic leadership. He quickly increased VASP's fleet by 50 percent.

VARIG President Thomas noted the benefits of the privatization of VASP, telling a reporter in 1991 that while VASP was a state-owned entity, the company was "not much concerned about competing in the market, because the state would cover it." That, he said, hurt private companies like VARIG and Transbrasil that did not have such resources.

VASP stepped up competition within the first 18 months of its privatization, snagging a larger share of Brazil's cargo market, mostly from Transbrasil. VARIG, which had 51 percent of the market in 1990, lost two percent of its business during that period. VASP and Transbrasil also announced intentions to challenge VARIG in the international market with a possible joint venture. The cargo market itself was expanding, as Brazil became more industrialized and began shipping a more equitable amount of products to North America.

Transbrasil received approval for routes to Orlando, Miami, Washington, D.C., and New York. VASP announced intentions to begin passenger service to Tokyo with connections in Los Angeles and San Francisco, a move that would open the door for the company to begin cargo operations, as well as tap into demand for passenger service by Brazil's substantial Japanese population. Up until 1991, VARIG—then the nation's flag carrier—had held a state-chartered monopoly on such activity. The Brazil market also became more open to U.S. airlines such as Pan Am. VARIG responded to international competition by increasing the number of flights flown on its routes to the United States, Canada, and Europe.

Deregulation allowed both new and established airlines to expand existing fleets, thereby increasing capacity not as a result of demand, but in anticipation of it. That led to speculation on the part of some airline officials that the resultant fare wars would, rather than create a more dynamic market, force some airlines out of business.

But those concerns did not stop others from entering the field. In late 1991 the president of Lider Taxi Aereo of South America, Capt. Jose Afonso Assumpcao, convinced international investors to back his plan to create Air Brasil, a domestic service linking three of Brazil's major cities: Rio de Janeiro, Sao Paulo, and Belo Horizonte. He planned to use the British Aerospace jet, 146-200. It was the first new airline the country had seen in many years. Until then, strict government regulation prevented such new growth.

Air Brasil's limited service was strategic: to parallel but not directly compete with the Ponte Aerea (Air Bridge), a Rio/Sao Paulo shuttle operation shared by VARIG, Transbrasil, and VASP. Around the same time, VARIG's President Thomas announced that the 30-year-old Lockheed Electra turboprops used for the Air Bridge would be replaced with the larger Boeing 737s, sparking questions about safety in traveling to and from airports that are hemmed in by mountains and other obstacles. VARIG responded by increasing minimum experience requirements for pilots and suggesting that the runways be inspected more often.

Officials of the nation's pilots union remained skeptical on safety issues, despite successful trial runs by VARIG from the Santos Dumont airport (where pilots must negotiate a runway with a mountain at one end and a bridge at the other) to the Congonhas airport, located in Sao Paulo's downtown area.

New routes, new competition, and new aircraft increased the effect of ongoing air fare wars. Some airline executives voiced concerns about stringent federal controls that prevented them from matching fare increases to the rate of inflation. Continued government regulation of air fares—allowing for rate decreases but not necessarily increases—made it more difficult for airlines to remain competitive while still turning a profit.

More Challenges in the 1990s

By 1991, the VARIG Group consisted of 23 companies, which boasted combined sales figures of US $2.5 billion. It lost $614 million from 1991 to 1993, however. The company took advantage of a weak aircraft market to renegotiate terms with its creditors; in 1993 its annual leases amounted to $500 million for 50 planes.

In a major restructuring, VARIG also cut more than 2,500 jobs and closed ticket offices. The carrier was losing money on international passenger operations, but earning a profit domestically. To spur business, VARIG entered a marketing agreement with Delta Air Lines.

The carrier's share of international traffic to and from Brazil fell to less than 40 percent in the mid-1990s. Other sectors slipped as well. A new ad campaign was launched to update VARIG's image. The planes began sporting a new paint scheme and logo, which added the word "Brasil" to make VARIG aircraft more identifiable overseas. It also launched its "Smiles" frequent flyer program that encouraged passengers to recommend particular flight personnel for special bonuses of their own.

After a short stint by Willy Engels, the VARIG board appointed Fernando Pinto president of the airline in January 1996. At the time, the carrier was $2.5 billion in debt, about half of it aircraft debt. Pinto, son of a VARIG pilot, had led the company's regional subsidiary, Rio Sul, through a period of fantastic growth.

VARIG aimed to recapture the international business traveler. It increased the number of business class seats and made them roomier. Sony personal inflight entertainment systems were part of the prescription to win back customers.

Pinto went right to work improving the company's bottom line. It conducted well-timed sale/leaseback agreements on aircraft that saved the company millions. Pinto dismissed 5,000 employees, mostly administrative ones. At the same time, he was challenged to raise motivation levels. He bemoaned the carrier's once great reputation for service. Pinto also preached cost control throughout the organization and sought to instill a European-styled accountability in individual employees. VARIG succeeded in raising on-time performance to 95 percent.

By October 1997 VARIG had dropped its brief alliance with Delta and instead teamed with United Airlines before becoming a member of the global Star Alliance, which also included SAS, Lufthansa, Thai International, and Air Canada. In 1998 VARIG entered into a joint venture with General Electric to make GE VARIG Engines.

The carrier continued to be burdened by enormous interest charges. In January 1999 the Brazilian currency was sharply devalued; fortunately, VARIG earned a significant portion of its revenues in U.S. dollars.

Principal Subsidiaries

Companhia Tropical de Hotéis; Companhia Tropical de Hotéis da Amazonia; Serviços Auxiliares de Transporte Aereo S.A. (SATA); Serviços Aereos Gerionais S.A. (RIO-SUL); Nordeste Linhas Aereas S.A.

Further Reading

Fannin, Rebecca A., "Varig Marketing Overhaul Arrives Via Y&R Brazil," *Advertising Age,* November 18, 1998.

Feldman, Joan M., "Making Alliances Work," *Air Transport World,* June 1998, pp. 27–35.

Fotos, Christopher P., "Brazilian Reforms to Give Airlines New Era of Freedom," *Aviation Week & Space Technology,* November 11, 1991, pp. 36–37.

Kolcum, Edward H., "Brazil's VARIG Foresees Steady Growth in Domestic, International Air Traffic," *Aviation Week and Space Technology,* August 31, 1987.

Lima, Edvaldo Pereira, "Advancing Through Crossfires," *Air Transport World,* June 1991, pp. 49–51.

——, "Rift Over Rules in Rio," *Air Transport World,* February 1992, pp. 106–07.

——, "Varig's 10-Years War," *Air Transport World,* June 1997, pp. 46–50.

Malkin, Richard, "Logistics with a Samba Beat," *Distribution,* September 1995, p. 102.

O'Connor, Anthony, "Latin Savior," *Airfinance Journal,* November 1996, pp. 16–20.

"Varig Fends Off Eximbank Feud," *Airfinance Journal,* May 1994, p. 14.

"Varig Officials See Mixed Blessing in Liberalization of Civil Aviation," *Aviation Week & Space Technology,* November 11, 1991, pp. 49–50.

—Peg McNichol
—updated by Frederick C. Ingram

Weider Nutrition International, Inc.

2002 South 5070 West
Salt Lake City, Utah 84104-4726
U.S.A.
(801) 975-5000
Fax: (801) 972-2223
Web site: http://www.weider.com

Public Subsidiary of Weider Health and Fitness Inc.
Founded: 1989
Employees: 625
Sales: $250.5 million (1998)
Stock Exchanges: New York
Ticker Symbol: WNI
NAIC: 325411 Medicinal & Botanical Manufacturing;
312111 Soft Drink Manufacturing; 312112 Bottled
Water Manufacturing

One of the companies founded by Joe Weider to promote health and physical fitness, Weider Nutrition International, Inc., is a leader in the nutritional supplement and natural products industry. The company manufactures both its own branded items, such as Mega Mass powdered drink mix, Fat Burner supplements, and Tiger's Milk energy bars, and also private-label botanical capsules and tablets and sports beverages. Such products had for years been sold mainly to bodybuilders and weight lifters, but in the 1990s Weider began making supplements for endurance athletes and the general public. Unlike many firms that use multilevel marketing, Weider sells its products in some 38,000 outlets, including mass retail/discount stores such as Wal-Mart and Costco and in health food stores such as the General Nutrition Center chain. Weider products are distributed in 42 nations. The firm enjoys a growing demand for health products in general and increased instances of research showing the usefulness of such items. However, those trends are also attracting more competitors to the supplement and herbal industry. Weider Health and Fitness, a subsidiary of Canada's M.L.E. Holding Company Ltd., owns about 65 percent of Weider Nutrition International.

Company Origins

The history of Weider Nutrition International begins with that of founder Joe Weider. He was born in 1923 in Montreal, Canada, and dropped out of school at age 12 to support his family. He was a skinny adolescent and hated being pushed around by stronger kids. So one day Weider decided to start a work-out program, building his own weight set from junk yard parts. Weider also became interested in nutrition and even drank the cream at the top of milk bottles to ingest more calories during this time. The hard work eventually paid off, and Weider won some body building contests. By age 17 he had begun publishing his own newsletter, called *Your Physique.*

The newsletter was a success, and after it hit both American and Canadian newsstands, Joe Weider moved to Jersey City, New Jersey, where he continued to build his newsletter business and also started a mail-order venture to sell nutritional supplements and bodybuilding equipment.

After serving in the Canadian military in World War II, Ben Weider joined his brother's business operations. Together they organized body building contests and soon formed the International Federation of Bodybuilders (IFBB) that eventually expanded to 137 nations.

By 1950 Joe Weider was publishing 16 magazines, including *American Manhood and Fury* and *True Adventure,* under the parentage of American News Company, and by the early 1950s he had become a millionaire. From the early days, Weider used his magazines to advertise supplements and fitness equipment.

In 1955 new owners took over American News and did not have enough resources to continue distributing Weider publications. Weider pared down his operations by cutting back his mail-order business and eliminating all but one magazine called *Muscle Builder.* In spite of the restructuring, Weider struggled financially for several years.

To turn things around, Weider moved to Los Angeles in the late 1960s to take advantage of the growing number of bodybuilders and health/fitness devotees in that region. However, many continued to believe misperceptions that body-building caused high blood pressure and other health problems; some critics even contended that bodybuilding led to narcissism or homosexuality.

Reaching a Broader Audience in the 1970s–80s

The Weider brothers used several methods to improve the marginal image of bodybuilding and promote their related fitness and supplement business. In 1971 they established the Mr. Olympia contest through the IFBB, using experts to judge bodybuilders' qualifications. At the same time, they discouraged such odd show tactics as demonstrations of bodybuilders biting through metal, which had helped create a bad reputation for bodybuilding.

Joe Weider in 1972 paid for Austrian bodybuilder Arnold Schwarzenegger to come to Los Angeles, where the two helped each other. Schwarzenegger wrote articles about diet and training in *Muscle Builder*, while Weider reportedly helped the bodybuilder pursue an acting career. Weider also emphasized that women could benefit from bodybuilding. He featured women on the cover of his glossy *Muscle & Fitness* and in 1981 began publishing *Shape* magazine for the female audience.

Meanwhile, Weider increased marketing for diet supplements, including Muscle Builder protein mix, Anabolic MegaPaks, a pancake mix called Performance Foods, and Carbo Energizer Chewables. In 1985 the Federal Trade Commission decided that some Weider nutritional products had labels with unproven claims and thus ordered Weider to reimburse unhappy customers. However, that did not slow down sales among athletes who used Weider products to build muscle tissue.

Growth in the Early 1990s

The Weider Nutrition Group, formed in 1989 as a subsidiary of Weider Health and Fitness based in Woodland Hills, California, soon moved its operations to Salt Lake City to make its own products. Weider Health and Fitness had previously put its name on products made by other companies, but opted to purchase the Salt Lake City-based Great American Foods, which made powdered supplements, in order to enter the nutrition business. The company also bought Schiff Vitamins, a New Jersey company that sold $14 million of vitamins annually. Schiff was also moved to Salt Lake City, where it eventually expanded to a $60 million business.

''The Utah environment was perfect for our expansion,'' recalled Weider Chief Operating Officer Robert K. Reynolds in the August 10, 1997 *Deseret News.* The supervisor of Weider's initial manufacturing said, ''We liked the work ethic, the family values, the character of the community . . . and we liked the fact that it was about 800 miles to Seattle, Denver, northern California and southern California—all of them trend-setter areas that consume more of our products per capita than any other.'' Weider perhaps also appreciated Utah's right-to-work law, which meant that the firm could operate without unions.

In December 1993 the Weider Nutrition Group purchased the Excel brand of herbal supplements from Las Vegas-based Key Products, Inc. Weider planned to extend Excel's distribu-

tion from its regular health food markets into mass retail and sporting goods stores.

In early 1994 Weider acquired Exceed Sports Nutritionals from Columbus, Ohio-based Ross Laboratories, which had marketed its energy drink, liquid sports meal, high carbohydrate drink, and energy bar mainly to long-distance runners and cyclists. Weider President/CEO Richard Bizzaro said in the February 1994 *Sporting Goods Business* that, ''Bringing in Exceed is intended to further expand our customer base'' beyond Weider's usual customers—the body builders and weight lifters. ''The key for us is to switch from focused bodybuilding to the mainstream, and we plan on more acquisitions in the future which will focus on sports-related and health food brands. . . . When the average person starts taking a supplement, that's when the market will pop,'' said Bizzaro.

In 1994 Congress passed a new law supported by Weider and other nutritional products firms. Sponsored by Utah's Senator Orrin Hatch, the Dietary Supplement Health and Education Act was passed to prevent the Food and Drug Administration from overregulating the health products industry. Later that year, Weider Nutrition honored Senator Hatch for his work on the Dietary Supplement Health and Education Act. Arnold Schwarzenegger came to Salt Lake City to present Hatch with Weider's first annual award for major health contributions. The Hollywood actor and Republican Party supporter joked about liberal Democrats wanting to increase regulations on supplements: ''Imagine what would have happened if it [proposed tougher FDA regulations] had gone through. You take 10 milligrams too much of vitamin C, and you have the FBI knocking on your door.'' As reported in the November 4, 1994 *Deseret News,* Schwarzenegger continued the joke: ''I can imagine the conversation in prison. What are you in here for? 'Murder.' What about you? 'Zinc'.''

Meanwhile, Joe Weider was receiving honors for his work in the fitness industry. The Periodical Book Association in 1983 gave him the Publisher of the Year Award. Other honors included a Distinguished Citizen Award from the Boy Scouts of America in 1991, the United States Sports Academy's Dwight D. Eisenhower Fitness Award in 1992, and the Lifetime Achievement Award from the California governor's Council on Physical Fitness in 1995.

The Late 1990s

To reach more of a mainstream audience, Weider Nutrition in 1996 spent about $2.5 million on an advertising campaign for its Prime Time herbal supplements. To encourage men in their forties and fifties to use the supplements for health maintenance, the company hired actor Robert Urich as the spokesman for Prime Time, and Winner Communications filmed the spots showing Urich in vigorous health. However, Urich soon found out that he had cancer, and though it kept Urich's picture on Prime Time containers, Weider postponed using the television ads pending Urich's remission. Without the planned TV spots, Prime Time's initial sales were slower than expected.

In February 1997 Weider Nutrition announced its acquisition of Science Foods, Inc., a 12-year-old company based in Las Vegas, Nevada. Science Foods produced sports beverages for bodybuilders and health club members. Weider said that it would expand the Las Vegas plant to meet consumer demands and that Science Foods would continue to operate under its own name.

In preparation to go public, Weider Nutrition International, Inc. was formed in 1996 as a subsidiary of Weider Health and Fitness. The Weider Nutrition Group then became a subsidiary of Weider Nutrition International. Weider Nutrition went public on May 1, 1997, listing on the New York Stock Exchange under the ticker symbol WNI. In a press release, WNI's President/CEO Richard Bizzaro said, "The timing of the listing is fitting as we are closing out our strongest year yet." The IPO resulted in Weider selling 6,440,000 shares at $11 each, with about $63.9 million raised in net proceeds. The firm used those funds to reduce debt from acquisitions and to pay a dividend to Weider Publications, another subsidiary of Weider Health and Fitness.

In June 1998 Weider Nutrition International dedicated its new headquarters and manufacturing plant at 2002 South 5070 West, in Salt Lake City. To help company founder Joe Weider mark the event, actor Arnold Schwarzenegger spoke to the audience. Located on a 35-acre site, the new building was named the 1997 "Project of the Year" by the Utah Chapter of the Associated General Contractors of America. The $18 million facility built by Camco Construction was part of Utah's booming economy in the late 1990s.

The new 418,000-square-foot plant, which could produce one million sports bars daily and 250 million capsules and tablets monthly, effectively doubled Weider Nutrition's manufacturing capacity, a crucial factor in the firm's efforts to supply its mass retailers, such as Wal-Mart and American Stores. It continued to use its nearby plant at 1960 South 4250 West; the combined facilities totaled 600,000 square feet. Weider operated other plants in England, Spain, Canada, Nevada, South Carolina, and California.

In 1998 Weider's largest customers were retailers General Nutrition Center, Wal-Mart, and Costco, with about 16 percent, 13 percent, and 12 percent, respectively, of net sales. Others selling Weider Nutrition products included Sam's Club, Walgreens, CVS, Thrifty/Payless, Albertsons, American Stores, REI, Kmart, Wild Oats, Sports Authority, and Bally's Health and Fitness. Some 38,000 retail stores sold Weider products, and the firm made private-label products for such companies as Nu Skin and SlimFast.

The Weider product line included its trademarked Cold-Free lozenges introduced in 1996. Made of zinc nitrate, the lozenges were sold under the Great American Nutrition name to help relieve symptoms of the common cold. Zinc products from Weider and other firms became more popular after a study in the July 1996 *Annals of Internal Medicine* indicated that zinc helped prevent the spread of cold viruses. In 1997 Weider expanded its Cold-Free line to include new cherry-flavored candy lozenges and an oral spray in a two-ounce bottle. The company also made other products to fight colds, such as Vitamin C and echinacea supplements.

To help customers lose weight, Weider Nutrition offered its PhenCal 106 product made with natural amino acids. Dr. Kenneth Blum, a Texas biologist, helped Weider Nutrition with this particular product. Blum's participation illustrated the increas-

ing reliance on professionals and scientific standards in the supplement industry.

For the fiscal year ended May 31, 1998, Weider Nutrition recorded net sales of $250.5 million, up 14.6 percent from 1997 net sales of $218.6 million. Net income rose from $4.3 million in 1997 to $14 million in 1998.

During this time, Weider announced it would spend about $4 million on a new campaign to advertise products for those over 50 years old. In the first half of 1999 the firm would promote its Schiff Pain Free dietary supplements and also its new Schiff Joint Free and Joint Free Plus drink mixes designed to increase joint flexibility. Described in the November 30, 1998 *Brandweek* as "the largest dedicated product effort in the company's history," the ad campaign included TV spots on *The Roseanne Show, Hollywood Squares, Wheel of Fortune, Judge Judy, Jeopardy,* and *Live with Regis and Kathie Lee,* plus print ads in *Shape* and *Men's Fitness.* The firm also announced its 1999 plans to reformulate and repackage its line of Schiff Women's Health products.

In July 1998, the company acquired 100 percent of the outstanding shares of the Hamburg, Germany-based firm of Haleko Hanseatisches Lebensmittel Kontor GmbH. Weider borrowed $25.2 million cash from General Electric Capital Corporation (GECC) to purchase Haleko. The purchase price also included 200,000 shares of Weider's Class A common stock and $8 million contingent upon future financial performance. In addition, Weider assumed $16 million of Haleko's debt and estimated capital costs for the acquisition were about $5 million. Weider Nutrition planned to combine Haleko with its United Kingdom subsidiary, Weider Nutrition Group Ltd. Haleko recorded sales of about $65 million in 1998, which made it the largest sports nutrition company in Europe. The new acquisition manufactured powder, tablet, and capsule supplements—sold under such brand names as Multipower, Multaben, and Champ—to 20,000 European retail stores, and also marketed Venice Beach sportswear in European health clubs.

The 1998 major league baseball season helped boost sales of one Weider Nutrition product. St. Louis Cardinals slugger Mark McGwire in September of that year hit a new world record of 62 home runs. Some critics in the media commented on McGwire's use of androstenedione (andro), a controversial nutritional supplement that reportedly helped build muscles by increasing the body's production of testosterone. The Olympic games, the National Football League, professional tennis, and the National Collegiate Athletic Association had banned andro, but major league baseball had not. Still, the U.S. Food and Drug Administration had reported no harm from andro. Weider Nutrition had introduced Androstene, its brand of andro, seven months before McGuire broke the home run record. In any case, intense media coverage of McGuire helped Weider Nutrition double its andro sales in just two weeks after the andro story came out in late August 1998.

Weider Nutrition was just one of many supplement or herbal firms in Utah at this time. Some even referred to Utah's Interstate 15 as the "herbal highway," said Loren Israelsen, executive director of the Utah Natural Products Alliance, in the September 1998 *Utah Business.* "I think there are probably

40–50 companies. . . . It is growing dramatically here in Utah. In fact, Utah has been recognized in recent years as the (supplement) center in the United States.'' Other Utah firms in this industry included Nature's Sunshine, Nature's Herbs, Nature's Way, Nu Skin, USANA, and Nutraceutical.

Although press releases claimed that Weider Nutrition International was the ''largest supplier of health, fitness and wellness products in the world,'' other health products firms were reporting higher annual sales, including Nu Skin ($890.5 million in 1997), California-based Sunrider (estimated $700 million in 1998), and Nature's Sunshine ($281 million in 1998). Weider also faced another large competitor with the merger of multilevel marketing firm Rexall Sundown with Twinlab. Still, with increased interest in achieving optimum health, particularly among the country's baby-boom and older populations, Weider Nutrition seemed well-positioned to compete in the next century.

Principal Subsidiaries

Weider Nutrition Group Inc.; Weider Nutrition Group Ltd. (United Kingdom).

Further Reading

Bittar, Christine, ''Weider Puts $4M on 50-Plus Line,'' *Brandweek,* November 30, 1998, p. 4.

Boulton, Guy, ''Famous Muscleman Stumps for Muscle Products,'' *Salt Lake Tribune,* June 12, 1998, pp. B4, B8.

Campbell, Joel, ''Nature's Own,'' *Deseret News* (Web Edition), June 28, 1998.

Carricaburu, Lisa, ''The Changing Nature of Supplements,'' *Salt Lake Tribune,* December 20, 1998, pp. E1, E4.

——, ''Utah's Natural-Products Firms Blossom from Need,'' *Salt Lake Tribune,* August 16, 1998, pp. E1, E2.

Davidson, Lee, ''Time's Up for Hatch's Foe, 'Terminator' Says,'' *Deseret News* (Web Edition), November 4, 1994.

Horowitz, Alan S., ''Bulking Up With Weider Nutrition International,'' *Utah Business,* September 1997, pp. 58–59.

Knudson, Max B., ''Home-Run King Adds Muscle to S.L. Nutrition Firm's Ads,'' *Deseret News* (Web Edition), September 10, 1998.

McEvoy, Christopher, ''Weider Acquires Exceed and Excel,'' *Sporting Goods Business,* February 1994, p. 42.

Mehegan, Sean, ''The Urich Factor,'' *Brandweek,* January 20, 1997, p. 24.

Repanshek, Kurt, ''Powders, Pills + Profits: What Supplements Are Doing for Our Bodies and the Economy,'' *Utah Business,* September 1998, pp. 38–40.

Spangler, Jerry, ''From Quackery to Credibility,'' *Deseret News* (Web Edition), October 12, 1997.

——, ''In Business for Health,'' *Deseret News* (Web Edition), August 10, 1997.

Strauss, Gary, ''Joe Weider, Once a Scrawny Kid, Builds Fitness Company with Plenty of Muscle,'' *Salt Lake Tribune,* May 20, 1998, p. E6, reprint of article in *USA Today.*

Thomson, Linda, ''S.L.-Based Weider Goes Public,'' *Deseret News* (Web Edition), May 2, 1997.

—David M. Walden

West Coast Entertainment Corporation

West Coast Video®

Route 413 and Double Woods Road
Langhorne, Pennsylvania 19047
U.S.A.
(215) 968-4318
Fax: (215) 968-5164
Web site: http://www. westcoastvideo.com

Public Company
Founded: 1983
Employees: 2,640
Sales: $123.8 million (1998)
Stock Exchanges: NASDAQ
Ticker Symbol: WCEC
NAIC: 53223 Video Tape & Disc Rental; 45122
   Prerecorded Tape, Compact Disc & Record Stores

West Coast Entertainment Corporation owns and operates about 286 video stores and about 217 more franchises, most under the name West Coast Video, located primarily in the Northeast and Midwest United States, although some are located in Canada, Peru, and Curaco. West Coast Video stores rent and sell new and used videos, video games, and DVDs (digital versatile discs). The company also operates an electronic commerce site, www.westcoastvideo.com, which offers customers over 150,000 new and used video titles along with industry news, features, and film trivia. Customers can use an online store locator to find a map and directions to the closest West Coast Video store. Once the world's largest video chain, West Coast Video trailed industry giants Blockbuster and Hollywood Entertainment in the late 1990s. West Coast was founded by millionaire Elliot Stone, who also owns Sorbee International (a sugarless candy company) and Medical Products Laboratories (a Philadelphia firm that sells prescription drugs and dental supplies to dentists). The Company's sales for 1998 were $123.8, with net income reported at $3.6 million.

A Bright Idea in 1983

Company founder and millionaire Elliot Stone had a reputation for fixing what irked him. In 1978, when Stone was working at family-owned Medical Products Laboratories, which serviced dentists with prescription drugs and dental supplies, he noticed that the lollipops dentists gave out to kids were high in sugar. "It seemed a little silly to me for a dentist to be giving sugary candy to a kid who just had a cavity or two filled," Stone said in the *Philadelphia Business Journal.* Soon after, Stone founded Sorbee International, a sugar-free candy company.

West Coast Video was created along the same lines. Stone first conceived of the company in 1983 when he and wife had trouble finding the tape they wanted in a video store. "I looked around and I saw all these people in the same situation we were in, and walking out because they couldn't find the movie they wanted. I thought, 'I could run a video store better than this'," Stone explained in the *Philadelphia Business Journal.* A few months later, he invested about $300,000 in his first video store, located in Northeast Philadelphia.

Stone reportedly chose the name West Coast Video to evoke the sense of a glitzy West Coast retail chain. Stone stocked the store with over 6,000 tapes and computerized the inventory and customer list. He made sure there were enough copies of new releases and placed an empty tape box on display for each copy of a video, while the videos themselves were stored behind the counter. Within four months, Stone opened three more stores, and the West Coast Video chain was launched.

Stone hired Richard J. Abt as executive vice-president of the company, and together the men planned to open more stores and over 100 franchises. Initially, franchisers had to pay around $85,000 to open a West Coast Video store, $12,000 of which was a franchise fee to West Coast. The remaining sum paid for tapes, building improvements, and links to the computer systems. Franchisers then paid seven percent of gross sales to West Coast each year.

Acquisitions and Expansions in 1988

The company rapidly expanded its video-store chain, and by 1988 West Coast Video had grown to 215 video stores and franchises. In September 1988, the company purchased National Video, adding 455 more stores to its portfolio. With the addition of National Video stores, West Coast could boast a total of 660 stores and revenues of about $110 million. The acquisition made West Coast the largest video store chain in the world.

However, competition in the field soon heated up, as rival Blockbuster Video oversaw some 1,500 stores by 1990. Moreover, Blockbuster's stores were larger and in prime locations. West Coast tried to compete by keeping its operating costs lower with smaller stores and less overhead. The company tried to generate additional business by promoting its stock of lesser-known "B" titles, movies shown on cable or offered for the first time to West Coast Video stores. To bolster customer service, flash cards were inserted in each video box with a synopsis of the movie, its rating, and its stars. West Coast also used posters to highlight the lesser-known titles.

Bankruptcy and Reorganization in the Early 1990s

By 1992, changes in the industry had begun to take their toll on West Coast. Larger video-store chains were buying more stores and consolidating the industry. Moreover, video sales in general had declined, following economic recession and the increasing popularity of "Pay Per View" movie viewing services. Still, West Coast attributed most of its financial problems to $6.6 million in loans it made on behalf of Red Lion Entertainment, a limited partner in West Coast that owned and operated 70 video stores before filing for bankruptcy.

Recovery from these challenges did not ensue, and in March 1992 West Coast filed for Chapter 11 bankruptcy. At the time, the company reported $3.6 million in assets and $9 million in debt. The West Coast bankruptcy worried some industry analysts, who feared it was a reflection of the health of the industry as a whole. Some predicted that Blockbuster would buy out West Coast stores and further consolidate the industry. West Coast franchisers in general were concerned that the company would not be able to continue its services; some even withheld payments. West Coast remained in Chapter 11 protection for nine months.

Nevertheless, Stone maintained his faith in West Coast and insisted he could turn the company around. He unveiled a plan to reorganize West Coast, which called for a new company to purchase West Coast's fixed assets and franchise agreements. Stone unveiled a plan to acquire 20 new or converted stores a year for two years and twice that number of stores by 1995. Under Stone's plan, all new West Coast stores would have a new "ultra store" format. The stores would be bigger than most West Coast stores—about 5,000 square feet—and built with

adjustable interior fixtures, so the layout could be changed easily. New stores would be free-standing to ensure customers easy access and lots of parking.

Stone agreed to pledge $1 million of his personal stock from Sorbee International to fund his plan. He persuaded creditors to accept 25 cents on every dollar West Coast owed, instead of the expected ten cents, if they agreed not to take legal action against the company. CoreStates Financial Corporation, one of West Coast's largest creditors, would receive ten percent of the reorganized company's stock.

In the six months following its filing for Chapter 11, West Coast generated a positive cash flow of $600,000. In 1993, West Coast changed its name from West Coast Video to West Coast Entertainment Corporation to reflect its diversification into areas other than video stores.

One such diversification was GamePower Headquarters, which the company opened in 1994 in Newtown Square, Pennsylvania. GamePower was the first store to combine the rental, sale, and trade of entertainment software. GamePower's strategy was unique in comparison with that of most toy stores, which sold entertainment software in unopened packages, in that GamePower customers could try out the software before buying or renting it. Employees supplied customers with coins that activated terminals for three or four minutes per coin. GamePower's rental costs were lower than Blockbuster's, and customers renting software earned credits toward the purchase of new software. GamePower also sold the hardware that customers needed to play the games at home.

Moreover, West Coast video store franchises were given the opportunity to incorporate the GamePower concept into their stores. Each franchise that incorporated GamePower would operate under the name West Coast Video Plus and was guaranteed an exclusive territory. In addition to franchises, GamePower Headquarters stores were built in shopping centers, strip mall centers, and downtown shopping districts.

While GamePower and West Coast Entertainment Corporation shared a common ownership and the same upper-level management, they operated as two separate companies. GamePower traded under the name Interactive Electronics Corporation.

New Leadership and New Challenges in the Mid-1990s

In 1995, Ralph Standley and his son Kyle purchased the West Coast Video franchises and took over the name. The Standleys owned and operated the small-but-ambitious Giant Video Corporation, which had recently acquired five small video chains for a total of 105 stores with revenues of $50 million. Under the direction of the Standleys, the franchiser West Coast video went public in 1996 with an initial public offering of 5.4 million shares at $13 a share. Net proceeds from the initial offering were about $163 million and were used to redeem outstanding notes and reduce bank debt.

However, 1997 marked the beginning of new troubles for West Coast. A planned acquisition of more than 170 stores in Canada and Australia fell through, and the company's stock plummeted when it failed to meet earning expectations. In fact the company was eventually delisted from the Nasdaq

National Market because it was unable to maintain the $1 minimum bid price.

An industry shift to revenue sharing gave industry giants Blockbuster and Hollywood Entertainment a significant advantage over West Coast and other small, regional video chains. Before revenue sharing, video stores bought videocassettes of new movies for about $65 to $75 each. With revenue sharing, video stores could purchase videocassettes for only $8 to $12 each if they agreed to share the rental revenues. This enabled large chains to line their shelves with many copies of each new release, giving customers a much better chance of renting the movie of their choice. Because of its small size, West Coast was unable to take part in revenue sharing at first, though it eventually was allowed to share revenues on some titles.

Striving to offer the latest in movie-viewing technology during this time, West Coast entered into an agreement with Warner Home Video and Toshiba to introduce digital video technology to its customers in New York and northern New Jersey. West Coast customers could rent DVD players for private demonstrations on their home systems. West Coast stores stocked their shelves with DVD software and related hardware.

The company also executed an expense reduction program in 1998 to reduce operating and administrative expenses by $4 million over the next year. West Coast planned to close 25 stores and reduce corporate personnel and administrative expenses. As a result of the store closings, West Coast endured a one-time charge of $6 million.

In 1998, West Coast launched a television advertising campaign consisting of two 60-second spots. One spot featured a parachute-less sky diver and the other a comical paint ball warrior. Both adventurers were caught in hunter's headlights while viewers heard the voice over, "Need a new release? West Coast Video." Both spots won the 1998 Addy Award for television from the Philadelphia Advertising Council.

Around the same time, West Coast entered into a partnership with Microsoft to offer free rentals of a "Discover Microsoft Windows 98" video. West Coast customers could also rent free copies of the educational and entertaining McGruff the Crime Dog videos.

E-Commerce in 1999

In May 1999, West Coast launched an online e-commerce site at www.westcoastvideo.com. To launch the web site, West Coast entered into partnerships with *American Cinematography Magazine, Videoscope Magazine,* and KidFlix.com. Customers accessing the site could search for their favorite movies by title, actor, director, film theme, or content. An "Advanced Search Feature" even allowed customers to search for movies by character names, original works on which movies were based, or film locations. West Coast offered more than 150,000 new and used videocassettes and DVDs on its web site. Customers could access movie news and information about new releases on the site. West Coast strove to make its site superior to the rival Hollywood Entertainment web site at reel.com.

Through a deal with America Online (AOL), West Coast created a strong marketing presence in AOL's Digital Cities, a group of web sites designed for specific cities. Standley estimated that the web site would generate a positive cash flow within two years. While the outlook for the web site was good—over 10,000 people visited the site in one week—industry experts claimed that the future of the company was still uncertain. Industry trends toward consolidation, they speculated, might eventually involve the sale of West Coast to a larger video-store chain.

Further Reading

Alaimo, Dan, "West Coast, Giant Video Set to Splice," *Supermarket News,* July 10, 1995, p. 38.

Calkins, Laurel, "West Coast Video Enterprises," *Houston Business Journal,* April 8, 1991, p. 18.

Davis, Jessica, "West Coast Entertainment Alters Name to Point to Widened Focus," *Philadelphia Business Journal,* September 10, 1993, p. 6.

Davis, Jessica, "West Coast Video to Unveil Interactive Electronic Games," *Philadelphia Business Journal,* November 12, 1993, p. 4.

Elson, Joel, "New West Coast Selector to Match Tastes, Genres," *Supermarket News,* May 4, 1992, p. 112.

——, "West Coast 'B' Titles Get Flash Cards," *Supermarket News,* March 2, 1992, p. 36.

"GamePower HG Expands," *Television Digest,* August 1, 1994, p. 16.

Jeffrey, Don, "Giant Video Buys Its Way Into Big Time," *Billboard,* June 3, 1995, p. 4.

Luebke, Cathy, "West Coast Video Plans to Set up at Least 20 Valley Outlets," *The Business Journal,* September 24, 1990, p. 2.

McConville, James, A., "West Coast Video Paves Game Path," *HFD—The Weekly Home Furnishings Guide,* August 1, 1994, p. 71.

McDonald, Owen, "'Industry-Wide Phenomenon' Hobbles West Coast Revenue," *Video Store,* June 22, 1997, p. 1.

McDonald, Owen, "West Coast Hopes Revenue-Sharing Will Boost Profits," *Video Store,* September 20, 1998, p. 1.

——, "West Coast Posts First Net Loss as Public Company," *Video Store,* September 21, 1997, p. 1.

"Microsoft and West Coast Video to Offer Consumers Free Rental Program," *PR Newswire,* October 1, 1998.

Millstein, Marc, "West Coast Bankruptcy May Bode Ill for Video," *Supermarket News,* March 9, 1992, p. 19.

——, "West Coast Video Files Bankruptcy," *Supermarket News,* March 2, 1992, p. 54.

Paige, Earl, and Craig Rosen, "West Coast Video Seeks Bankruptcy Protection," *Billboard,* March 7, 1992, p. 3.

Paige, Earl, "West Coast Video Plans Expansion: Roars out of Bankruptcy with Franchise Strategy," *Billboard,* December 19, 1992, p. 6.

Reagan, Kellie, "West Coast Blames Down Numbers on Lack of Revenue-Sharing Deals," *Video Store,* January 17, 1999, p. 8.

——, "West Coast Launches Online Retail Store Offering 150,000 Titles," *Video Store,* January 24, 1999, p. 8.

Rogan, Ed, "Lights, Cameras . . . Success; Video Latest Venture for Entrepreneurs," *Philadelphia Business Journal,* p. 1.

Wallace, David, "Creditors OK West Coast Video Reorganization Plan," *Philadelphia Business Journal,* November 2, 1992, p. 5.

——, "West Coast Video's Stone Has Personal Take in Its Recovery," *Philadelphia Business Journal,* August 10, 1992, p. 6.

"West Coast Entertainment Launches First Major TV Campaign," *PR Newswire,* June 4, 1998.

—Tracey Vasil Biscontini

Westin Hotels and Resorts Worldwide

2001 Sixth Avenue
Seattle, Washington 98121
U.S.A.
(206) 443-5000
Fax: (206) 443-5169

Division of Starwood Hotels & Resorts Worldwide, Inc.
Incorporated: 1930 as Western Hotels Inc.
Employees: 45,000
Sales: $2.4 billion (1996)
NAIC: 72111 Hotels (Except Casino Hotels) & Motels

Westin Hotels and Resorts Worldwide is the oldest hotel management company in North America and one of the most admired. Throughout its history, the company has pioneered many hotel innovations adopted by the industry worldwide. Westin operates more than 110 hotels in 23 countries.

Setting the Stage

In the late 1920s, hotel ownership in the Pacific Northwest included several key figures. Severt W. Thurston arrived in Seattle in 1903 to pursue a career as a vaudeville acrobat. According to legend, Thurston's brief career behind the stage lights came to an ignoble end when, as the top man on a human pyramid, he was thrown off balance and into the orchestra pit by one of his human supports whose sobriety was in question. Thurston quickly left show business and took a job as a porter in a local hotel. The hotel owner's son, Harold E. Maltby, became friends with Thurston and, eventually, they decided to enter the hotel business, forming the Maltby-Thurston Corporation in 1910.

At roughly the same time the Maltby-Thurston partnership was created, Nebraska native Frank A. Dupar was working in Seattle as a plumber. After several years, Dupar became the owner of Palmer Supply Co., a wholesale plumbing and supply firm, and promoted apartment houses and hotels in the area with his younger brother Harold. The Dupars initially contracted to lay the plumbing for hotels and apartments, obtaining the materials from their supply business, but then, as their work earned the esteem of the local building community, they began contracting for the construction of entire hotels. Ownership of one particular hotel, the Cascadian, fell into their hands as a result of the stock market crash in 1929. A majority of the investors who were to supply equity funds for the hotel were stripped of their assets by the collapse of the stock market, so the Dupars hired a stock promoter to sell enough shares in the hotel to meet costs, and the two brothers found themselves owning the 130-room hotel.

The following year, in 1930, Frank Dupar and Severt Thurston were seated at different tables in a coffee shop in a small town east of Seattle called Yakima. Both hotel owners were in the area looking to expand their hotel business. As competitors, Dupar and Thurston recognized each other and ended up sitting together. In the course of their discussion in the coffee shop, they talked of the advantages of pooling their efforts toward expansion and decided to include two other hotel owners in their proposed union who were also vying for expansion in Yakima, Adolph and Peter Schmidt. The Schmidts, forced to close their beer distillery, the Olympia Brewing Company, in accordance with prohibition laws, owned five hotels in the Puget Sound area. A meeting was arranged and, as a protective measure from the depressed economic climate pervading U.S. business at the time, the three groups of owners decided to unite their hotels under a single management umbrella. The joint venture, called Western Hotels Inc., was formed as a management corporation. Rather than owning the hotels, Western Hotels signed management agreements with local hotel owners and provided accounting, advertising, and referral services to the owners, as well as the hotel's personnel, whose salary was paid by the owners. As recompense, Western received one percent of the gross receipts from each of the hotels it managed. And so, with Peter Schmidt as the chairperson, Severt W. Thurston as president, Harold E. Maltby and Adolph Schmidt as vice-presidents, and Harold E. Dupar as treasurer, the odd combination of a former vaudeville acrobat, a plumber, and two displaced brewers formed the foundation of what would later become Westin Hotels & Resorts.

More Than Managing in the 1930s

In its first year of operation, Western Hotels operated 18 hotels containing 3,137 rooms. All of the hotels were located in Washington, with the exception of one in Boise, Idaho. The following year, in 1931, Western assumed the management of its first property outside U.S. borders by adding Vancouver, British Columbia's Georgia Hotel to its consortium of hotels. That year, Western concluded a pivotal deal with the Multnomah Hotel in Portland, Oregon. The Multnomah, a prestigious 500-room hotel, was suffering severe losses during the early 1930s, losing up to $20,000 a month. For the first time, Maltby, Thurston, Dupar, and the Schmidts entered into a joint purchase of the property. Under Western management, the lobby and the rooms were refurbished, and the failing hotel began producing profits within 90 days.

News of its success with the Multnomah earned Western the reputation as a management team that could produce profits for properties even during the harsh economic times of the Great Depression. Capitalizing on this reputation, the company assumed managerial control of six additional hotels by the end of the decade, one of which, the Baronof in Juneau, extended Western's presence into Alaska. Western's dramatic turnaround of the Multnomah also showed those in charge of the company that success could sometimes be achieved quickly. Often, Western managed a hotel for only a short time, reviving a floundering property, then withdrawing its control. The company maintained this fluid method of managerial control well into the future, constantly acquiring new contracts to replace those that were dissolved. Contracts were terminated with six of Western's original 18 hotels by the end of the decade, and more than half of the properties managed by the company in the 1930s would operate in the 1940s without Western's assistance.

Growing During and After WWII

In its first decade of business, Western achieved considerable success in the Pacific Northwest. With the exception of the three hotels in Idaho, Oregon, and Alaska, all of Western's hotel concerns were located in Washington. As the company entered the 1940s, it sought to expand its interests outside of the region and, in 1941, an opportunity arose in California. Conrad Hilton owned the Sir Francis Drake, a 438-room hotel in San Francisco, but when Hilton settled a local strike, the city's businessmen became enraged, causing the hotel's clientele to shrink, so

Hilton decided to sell the hotel. He sold it to a local industrialist and financier, E.B. Degolia. When Degolia attempted to get a mortgage for the property, his insurance company suggested he hire a professional hotel management firm to operate the hotel. The insurance company recommended Western, and DeGolia began negotiations with Thurston and Dupar (the Schmidts had returned to brewing beer when prohibition was repealed in 1933). Thurston and Dupar agreed to manage the hotel, provided they receive an equity share in the hotel. DeGolia agreed and, by the end of the year, Western had assumed managerial control over the Sir Francis. Additional California properties came under control of Western later in the decade. In 1949 Western gained the stewardship of the Maurice Hotel in San Francisco and the Mayfair Hotel in Los Angeles.

As the expansion of the 1940s increased Western's territory of operations to Los Angeles in the south and Utah to the east, issues of lasting importance were being discussed among the company's senior management. In 1941 managers at a meeting in Seattle began to precisely describe the role of Western in relation to the hotels it managed. Virtual autonomy of the various hotels was decided as the best stance to assume. Managers were to be given full responsibility and authority in their particular hotel, guided generally by the operating policies of Western. Western's influence over the hotels was to be downplayed in all publicity, with the hope that the individual hotels would not be perceived as units of a hotel chain—a modern, corporate concept many found distasteful.

By 1946, however, Western had begun a gradual shift toward assuming a more prominent image within its hotels. During another manager's meeting in Portland, Oregon, the first such meeting since the gathering in Seattle five years earlier, Western's strategists decided to hire an advertising firm and to produce an employee handbook and publication. The company also decided to affix its logo on stationery, matchbooks, soap wrappers, and other items.

The decision to adopt a more visible role was consistent with several innovative services Western introduced that hinted of a larger administrative structure than an individual hotel would likely possess. In 1946 the company issued the first guest credit cards, enabling patrons of Western hotels to charge their rooms, food, and beverage bills to a single account. The introduction of the paper cards was followed the next year by the establishment of "Hoteltype," the industry's first reservations system. Before the implementation of Hoteltype, reservations were booked by mail, telegram, or telephone, and often resulted in lost or forgotten reservations. The new teletype machines, however, enabled instantaneous confirmation of reservation requests.

The 1940s also witnessed the emergence of Western's "specialty rooms," as management discovered the profits that could be garnered by devoting more energy and investing more money in their hotels' coffee shops, lounges, and dining facilities. During Western's early years, little attention had been paid to providing a place for hotel guests to eat and drink inside the hotel, but, as the years progressed, and after a survey of its hotels, Western discovered that the greatest earnings per square foot were gleaned from the coffee shops and cocktail lounges and the smallest profits were produced by the more formal dining rooms. Greater care was given to providing livelier and more intimate eating and drinking facilities, as Western created an assortment of distinctive motifs for each hotel. Cocktail lounges and dining areas were decorated in motifs replicating various geographical locations and historical periods. With names such as the ''Matador Room,'' ''The Outrigger,'' and the ''Hitching Post,'' the lounges and dining rooms experienced increased revenues and were greatly augmented when Idaho and Washington legalized the sale of liquor by the drink in 1949.

Western continued to expand in the 1950s, adding 22 hotels located throughout California, Arizona, Colorado, Montana, and Washington. In 1956 the company began managing the massive, 1,200-room Hawaiian Village in Honolulu and, by the end of the decade, had assumed control of four hotels in Guatemala. As the number of Western hotels proliferated, further guest service innovations made their debut. In 1952 Western's ''Family Plan'' was introduced, allowing children under the age of 14 to stay without charge in their parents' rooms. Seven years later, the company made a long-standing promise to honor confirmed reservations, paying for the room if the guest had to be relocated to another hotel. That year, Western also made available the hotel industry's first 24-hour room service.

New Leadership for the Space Age

In the late 1950s and early 1960s, new management took the reins of Western from the company's founders. The core of this new leadership, Lynn P. Himmelman, Edward E. Carlson, and Gordon M. Bass, was drawn from inside the Western organization, establishing Western's tradition of promoting from within. The early working years of these men paralleled the modest beginnings of their predecessors, Thurston and Dupar. Himmelman, a fourth generation hotelier whose father was an early investor in the Maltby-Thurston Corporation, started his hotel career as a room clerk at the Multnomah. After serving as the manager of Seattle's Benjamin Franklin Hotel in 1946, he became Western's executive vice-president in 1960 and chief executive officer ten years later. Carlson, who would eventually become chair and chief executive officer of United Airlines parent UAL, Inc., started as a page boy at the Benjamin Franklin in 1929, then became the hotel's elevator operator and bellhop. In 1946 he accepted a position as Thurston's assistant and steadily rose through the ranks, becoming Western's president in 1960. Bass also got his start at the Benjamin Franklin, working as a cashier for Himmelman's father. After managing the Multnomah, he was named vice-president of Western in 1951, executive vice-president in 1965, and president in 1971.

With this infusion of new management, Western experienced a fantastic surge in growth in the 1960s, adding 57 hotels to its management contracts, 36 of which were located outside of the United States. The company had become a genuine international concern, with hotels in Mexico, Guatemala, Venezuela, Ecuador, Australia, Japan, and Hong Kong. To better reflect this dramatic entry into foreign countries, Western changed its name in 1963 to ''Western International Hotels.''

As Western's business expanded internationally, it also entered into a new arena within the hotel industry—building its own hotels. Its first such venture was the construction of the 332-room Bayshore Inn in Vancouver, British Columbia. This was followed by the construction of Calgary, Alberta's Calgary

Inn, in 1964, the 800-room Century Plaza in Los Angeles two years later, and Colorado Springs' Antlers Plaza in 1967. Building projects for the decade ended in 1969 with the construction of the Washington Plaza in Seattle. These projects proved successful, evidenced by the vigorous construction Western embarked upon in the next decade. Of the 30 hotels added to Western's management group in the 1970s, more than half were built by Western.

Megamerger in the 1970s

Physical growth translated into fiscal growth over the next few years. From 1965 to 1970, the company's gross revenues doubled from $45 million to $90 million, and its net earnings jumped from $750,000 to $3 million. This success had not gone unnoticed. During the late 1960s, United Airlines had been searching for an entry into the hotel business to complement its international transportation service. Airlines had just recently begun to seek control of hotels as a solution to the sometimes limited, sometimes overcrowded accommodation facilities offered by the various destination cities the airlines served. For United, Western's chain of international hotels seemed a perfect match; 78 percent of Western's hotel rooms were located in cities served by United. To facilitate its proposed diversification into the hotel industry, United formed a holding company, UAL, Inc., in 1969, and began negotiations with Western. Carlson, Western's chairman and chief executive officer, foresaw the additional opportunities an affiliation with United would create. In 1970 negotiations were concluded and United and Western merged, with Western operating as an autonomous, wholly owned subsidiary, keeping its management and headquarters in Seattle. Five months after the merger, Carlson became president and chief executive officer of UAL, Inc. and Lynn Himmelman became chief executive officer of Western.

Although Western had aggressively expanded almost throughout its history, its expansion during the 1970s was unique. Instead of managing hotels with 300 or 400 rooms, Western assumed control of much larger hotels, many of which were constructed by Western, such as the 1,500-room Hotel Bonaventure in Los Angeles. Although the company continued to manage smaller hotels, it had begun to focus on the massive hotel complexes that were becoming popular in the industry. Expansion also took the Western name to new areas of the world during the company's fifth decade of operation. In 1970 a 525-room hotel was opened in Bangkok and, a year later, a hotel of similar size was opened in Singapore, both of which were constructed by Western. Two other Western-built hotels brought the company into South Africa and Norway, with the opening of Johannesburg's Carlton in 1972 and the Hotel Scandinavia three years later in Oslo.

Westin in the 1980s and 1990s

In 1981 Western changed its name to Westin Hotels, and then four years later to Westin Hotels & Resorts. The company continued to aggressively pursue additional management contracts during the early 1980s to counterbalance the termination of contracts with hotels no longer deemed profitable. By the late 1980s, however, Westin's capability to expand or even to plan for the future was in doubt. United Airlines' strategy to develop a vertically integrated travel empire, which had begun with its merger with Westin, had proved unsuccessful and, by 1987, United was looking to divest the hotel chain. An interested party, the Aoki Corporation of Japan, began negotiations with United and, in 1988, Aoki Corp.—a diversified international corporation with major lines of business in engineering, construction, and hotels—purchased Westin for $1.53 billion. The acquisition proved mutually beneficial; Aoki Corp. constructed the hotels, and Westin assumed the management of the new buildings. Three years after the acquisition, Westin became the operating company for all the hotels owned by Aoki Corp., including Caesar Park Hotels, the Hotel Vier Jahreszeiten in Hamburg, Germany, and The Algonquin Hotel in New York.

Westin planned to double its size during the 1990s and intended to aggressively pursue international properties, especially in Europe where the company's presence was limited. Asia was another prime focus. A massive restructuring in 1991 consolidated Aoki's hotel assets with the Westin operating company. It also created four new regional divisions: North America, South America, Asia/Pacific, and Europe.

It was soon apparent, however, that the boom years of the 1980s were over. The industry as a whole was left with excess capacity, particularly in the United States. Westin adopted the Total Quality Management system to make itself more competitive. Westin also was innovative in cutting costs. Its bar code-based Automated Uniform Distribution System halved associated labor costs at one hotel.

To differentiate itself, in January 1993 Westin launched the Service Express program as well as Westin Royal Vacations. Service Express was a kind of in-room telephone concierge service. Westin redesigned its front counters to make them less imposing to guests than the traditional check-in desk. It trademarked the title "Director of Romance" for its wedding specialists.

Starwood: Mid-1990s

By 1993 Aoki was planning to sell Westin North America. The parent company felt it alone did not have the resources to expand those operations. A group led by Starwood Capital and Goldman, Sachs bought the chain for $537 million in cash and debt in late 1994. Juergen Bartels was brought on as CEO and the company went on a buying spree, acquiring 22 hotels in one 12-month period. Bartels also invested heavily in marketing, launching Westin's first TV ads, which soon blossomed into a $25 million national campaign. Improved sales validated this strategic vision.

In the mid-1990s Westin pondered developing a limited service corporate-type brand extension similar to Courtyard by Marriott. It also was conceptualizing a combination hotel/health club chain for suburban markets.

In September 1997 Starwood Lodging Trust announced that it would buy Westin from the group (including Starwood Capital) that bought it in 1994. Starwood Lodging paid $1.6 billion in stock, cash, and assumed debt for the "flagship" brand of four-star resorts.

Westin was one of the few groups building resorts in the late 1990s. It opened nine new properties in 1999 "from Texas to Taiwan." The Rio Mar Beach Resort in Puerto Rico and Westin La Cantera Resort at San Antonio, Texas together cost about $280 million to build. They were dwarfed, though, by Westin's new flagship property: the $1.2 billion *America World City: The Westin Flagship.* The ship, scheduled to be launched in 1999, would be the largest in the world and would carry 6,200 passengers and 2,400 crew members.

Further Reading

Blalock, Cecilia, "Industry Pays for Its Excesses," *Hotel and Motel Management,* April 27, 1992.

Copeland, Sid, *The Story of Western International Hotels,* Seattle: Western International Hotels, 1976.

Del Rosso, Laura, "Westin Moves into Area with Management of Former Doubletree," *Travel Weekly,* April 27, 1992, p. C14.

Ellis, James E., "The Allegis Experiment Turns into a Bonanza," *Business Week,* November 9, 1987, pp. 123, 126.

Jaquette, Leslee, "Westin Implements Corporate Restructuring," *Hotel and Motel Management,* November 4, 1991.

——, "Westin Shapes 'Green' Goals," *Hotel and Motel Management,* November 4, 1991.

——, "Westin Uses 'PODS' Approach," *Hotel and Motel Management,* April 27, 1992.

Koss, Laura, "Westin Hotels Expands Guest Services," *Hotel and Motel Management,* February 1, 1993.

——, "Westin Looking Ahead as Purchase Looms," *Hotel and Motel Management,* October 4, 1993.

Rismond, Maureen, "Magnan Heads Banquet Table He Once Waited On," *Puget Sound Business Journal,* January 29, 1990, pp. A4–A5.

Vinocur, Barry, "Stellar Deal?," *Barron's,* July 21, 1997.

Watkins, Ed, "It's All About Marketing," *Lodging Hospitality,* June 1996.

Wolff, Carlo, "Capitalizing on the Resort Community," *Lodging Hospitality,* February 1997.

——, "Keeping the Boom on Course," *Lodging Hospitality,* January 1997.

—Jeffrey Covell
—updated by Frederick C. Ingram

World Duty Free Americas, Inc.

63 Copps Hill Road
Ridgefield, Connecticut 06877
U.S.A.
(203) 431-6057
Fax: (203) 438-1356
Web site: http://www.dutyfreeint.com

Wholly Owned Subsidiary of BAA PLC
Incorporated: 1983
Employees: 2,000
Sales: $563.6 million (1998)
NAIC: 45399 All Other Miscellaneous Store Retailers

World Duty Free Americas, Inc. operates one of the largest chains of duty free stores in the world. The company sells merchandise through approximately 200 shops, located primarily near U.S. border crossings and in airports. Its most popular products are perfumes, tobacco, and liquor, for the most part of premium brands. Customers save substantially buying goods free of excise taxes. The company is also the leading supplier of goods to foreign diplomats, and it supplies ships engaged in international travel. Formerly known as Duty Free International, the company became a subsidiary of the British airport operator BAA in 1997.

Beginning of the Chain in the 1980s

The duty free, or tax free, industry emerged following World War II. As international travel became increasingly popular during the late 1940s and 1950s, an international system was developed allowing travelers to purchase foreign goods free of all duties, sales taxes, and excise taxes. Under the system, customers typically were able to save between 20 and 60 percent on their purchases, making duty free goods extremely attractive. As a result of the duty free system, however, many countries began imposing additional fees or limits on the total value of merchandise travelers brought back to their home countries.

David Couri and John Bernstein, two duty free industry veterans, started Duty Free International in 1983. Couri had gained exposure to the business during his youth, as his father had founded a duty free company (the first, in fact, to offer goods other than liquor and cigarettes). As a teenager, Couri worked part-time in his family's duty free shop in New York's Kennedy Airport. In 1963 Couri graduated from Syracuse University with a degree in economics and then served two years in the Army before taking a sales job. After several years in the floor covering business, Couri saw the chance to strike out on his own. On his way to Japan from Kennedy International Airport, he noticed that there was no duty free shop in the Northwest Airlines terminal. By 1972, Couri had obtained a permit to open a duty free concession in the terminal, thus launching DFI International, Inc.

Bernstein also was exposed to the duty free business as a youth. At Samuel Meisel & Company, Inc., a Maryland-based duty free wholesaler, Bernstein worked summers in one of the company's two duty free shops in Washington, D.C., which catered to foreign diplomats. After receiving a B.A. in political science from Johns Hopkins in 1957, Bernstein went to work full-time on the sales staff at Meisel. He was running the company 25 years later. By this time, Couri's venture had expanded into a six-store chain at Kennedy International Airport.

In 1983 Couri and Bernstein joined forces to start Duty Free International. They were aware that duty free sales along the Canada/U.S. border had been growing at a rate of ten to 15 percent annually, but they felt that the existing shops were failing to capitalize on the full potential of the market. "We looked at these 'Canadian border' stores," Couri recalled in the August 19, 1991 issue of *Forbes,* "and many of them were dilapidated." Couri and Bernstein used some of their own money and borrowed heavily from banks to finance the $4.7 million buyout of 19 border stores and one airport shop in Maine, New York, and Vermont. They then spent an additional $4 million to revitalize the lagging outlets. As a result, sales volume at the stores doubled almost immediately. Amazingly, the fledgling business paid off most of its acquisition debt after only two years of operation.

Encouraged by their early success, Couri and Bernstein quickly acquired 11 more shops in small towns along the Canadian border. After considerable renovation, these stores were generating healthy profits by the mid-1980s. The border stores offered Duty Free an excellent opportunity to break into the industry quickly. Although those establishments lacked the prestige of airport shops and did not have access to a steady stream of well-heeled business travelers and tourists, border shops proved easier to open, since obtaining a concession license in an airport usually involved an expensive and complicated bidding process.

In 1986 Couri and Bernstein expanded the scope of Duty Free by purchasing Bernstein's old employer, Meisel. Meisel gave the company a dominant position in the niche market for merchandise sold to foreign diplomats. Indeed, embassies and consulates in Washington, D.C. and New York bought liquors and fine wines by the case from Meisel to avoid hefty taxes on those items. Duty Free also continued to buy border properties and to seek licenses for airport shops. By 1988, just five years after its inception, Duty Free International was racking up $69 million in annual sales and generating earnings of nearly $6 million. By 1989, the chain included several stores on the eastern U.S./Canadian border that operated under the name AMMEX Tax & Duty Free Shops and generated 46 percent of company sales. Several high-volume airport shops made up about 30 percent of revenues, and the Meisel division represented the remainder of receipts.

As a Public Company in the 1990s

In the late 1980s, however, the company's plans for further expansion were stalled by a lack of investment capital. To obtain more cash for growth, Couri and Bernstein tried to take their company public in 1987. Indeed, all of the details for a Duty Free public stock offering had been worked out by October of that year. But the morning of the pricing meeting, during which traders and underwriters hammer out the per-share price of the stock, Couri turned on the radio and learned that stock prices were slipping precipitously. Less than a week later, on a day known as "Black Monday," the market crashed, dashing any hopes of a successful offering for Duty Free.

Nevertheless, Couri (who became chief executive of Duty Free while Bernstein served as chairperson) rallied back to the market in 1989 with a stock sale that generated $22.6 million. Rather than have the money wired into the company's account, Couri requested a check for the full amount. He placed a framed copy of the check on his office wall next to a letter of apology from the underwriter of the failed 1987 issue. The fresh injection of capital, combined with funds from successive offerings, bankrolled a period of rapid growth for Duty Free International, which continued into the early 1990s. The company's earnings increased more than 100 percent in 1989, to about $10 million, as sales spiraled upward to $86 million. In anticipation of even faster growth, Couri and Bernstein moved Duty Free into a new, 100,000-square-foot, $5.5 million headquarters building.

The strategy behind Duty Free's strong performance during the 1980s and early 1990s was relatively simple. It grew by acquiring underperforming duty free shops and improving their performance with sound management. The company also offered a more profitable product mix than many of its competitors, following the example set by Couri's father; aside from cigarettes and other highly taxed merchandise, Duty Free emphasized the sale of luxury items, such as leather goods, perfume, and cosmetics, all of which offered relatively high profit

margins. Moreover, the company augmented border store acquisitions with lucrative airport shops. As the company swelled in size, economies of scale were achieved through bulk purchases and consolidated distribution and marketing operations.

In addition to solid management techniques that allowed Duty Free to gain on its industry peers, the company benefited from favorable economic and demographic trends, particularly during the early 1990s. During that period, the value of the U.S. dollar dropped, making domestic goods a relative bargain for most foreigners. A $41 carton of cigarettes, for example, could be had at a Duty Free shop for just $15, and a bottle of American scotch whiskey that sold for $26 dollars in Canada cost less than half that when purchased duty free. As a result, the "capture rate," or number of border crossers that would stop at a duty free shop, increased from two percent in 1983 to ten percent in 1989, and then to 13 percent in 1991. Furthermore, the average sale at Duty Free's border stores climbed nearly 20 percent between 1989 and 1991, to $31.5 million. Similarly, airport store performance improved. Japanese travelers, for example, purchased an average of $125 worth of goods apiece when they visited the shops.

Duty Free's sales reached $105 million during 1990, about $15 million of which was netted as income, and Duty Free's stock price soared fivefold after its initial offering to about $29 by early 1991. During that year, moreover, Duty Free's revenues rose dramatically to $187 million as a result of new acquisitions and higher sales at existing stores. In an effort to sustain the explosive growth rate, Couri and Bernstein began searching for ways to diversify Duty Free and extend its geographic presence. In 1992 Duty Free purchased UETA Inc., a chain of duty free shops along the U.S./Mexican border that had 1991 sales of $150 million. Duty Free also launched multimillion-dollar advertising campaigns in Canada and Mexico and added stores along the western U.S./Canada border. By the early 1990s, Duty Free was accounting for 90 percent of all duty free sales made along the U.S./Canada border.

In large part as a result of the pivotal UETA merger, Duty Free's sales rose to $362 million in 1992, while net earnings surged to more than $30 million. The company continued to branch out along the Canadian and Mexican borders during 1992 and 1993, eventually amassing a force of 60 stores in the North and 28 shops in Texas, Arizona, and California. Duty Free also expanded its airport operations to include 85 retail and duty free shops in 14 international airports across the United States and Canada and in Puerto Rico. Sales from its shops continued to be augmented by Duty Free's Meisel division.

By 1993, Duty Free had organized its sprawling operations into three succinct divisions: airport, border, and diplomatic and wholesale. Under the name Fenton Hill American Limited, the airport division operated traditional duty free stores, as well as several specialty shops aimed at foreign buyers of perfume, cosmetics, sports clothing, and jewelry. Its America-To-Go stores, for example, emphasized uniquely American products, such as regional foods and housewares. Moreover, Fenton Hill oversaw the operations of several premium brand boutiques, such as Chanel, Elizabeth Arden, and Christian Dior.

Duty Free's border division was separated into north and south operations. Stores in the North operated under the

AMMEX Tax & Duty Free name and were located along the Canadian/U.S. border from Maine to the state of Washington. Several of those stores also offered gas stations, convenience stores, and currency exchanges. Shops in the South, located along the Mexican/U.S. border, all operated under the UETA name. They also offered a full line of luxury items in addition to popular tobacco and alcohol products.

Duty Free's diplomatic and wholesale division operated through three subsidiaries: Samuel Meisel & Company, Inc.; Lipschutz Bros., Inc.; and Carisam International Corp. Aside from handling Duty Free's warehousing and distribution tasks, these subsidiaries provided upscale merchandise to diplomats primarily in the New York City and Washington, D.C. areas. The division also provided merchandise to cruise and merchant ships departing from Baltimore, Philadelphia, New York, Seattle, Los Angeles, and Miami.

Economic downturns and new government regulations in Canada caused sales from Duty Free's important north border division to drop in 1992 and 1993, reflecting the sensitivity of the duty free industry to outside economic and political influences. Nevertheless, Duty Free's diversification strategy paid off during this time, as gains in sales were realized in shops along the southern border. In fact, by 1993, UETA revenues had surpassed sales in the once dominant AMMEX stores near Canada. As a result, Duty Free was turning its attention toward greater expansion near Mexico. Sluggish sales in the north also were offset by steady gains in the diplomatic and wholesale division, particularly in the lucrative airport division—those two segments made up about 40 percent of company revenues in 1993.

Despite an overall sales slowdown from its border operations, Duty Free revenues increased four percent in 1993, reaching $376 million. Net income slipped to a still healthy $27 million. During this time, Couri continued to penetrate new marketing channels and to diversify regionally. In 1993, for example, Duty Free entered into an agreement with McDonald's Corporation to form Chicago Aviation Partners, a joint venture designed to develop concessions at Chicago's O'Hare International Airport.

Early in 1994, Duty Free purchased Inflight Sales Group Limited, a New York-based concessionaire that sold merchandise on more than 20 airlines. Inflight would provide more than $100 million in additional annual revenues to the Duty Free organization, and the buyout ensured Duty Free's status as the largest provider of duty free merchandise in the world at that time. With operational efficiency, a light debt load, and dominance in its core market segments, Duty Free expected continued success throughout the 1990s.

Changes in the Mid-1990s

Yet by the third quarter of 1994, the company was experiencing difficulty. Duty Free took a $53.7 million charge against its third quarter earnings to restructure. The company's costs had gotten beyond it, and Duty Free shut 23 of its stores and slashed its work force from 2,000 to 1,800 at the end of 1994. Sales for the year were more than $376 million, with earnings of $27.4 million, but administrative and other expenses were rising, eating into profits. By the middle of the next year, Duty

Free had suffered a severe decline in earnings due to the devaluation of the Mexican peso and poor sales along the Canadian border. Its Mexican border operations accounted for almost a third of total sales, and an even larger percentage of profits, so problems with its southern operations affected the company greatly. Moody's Investor Service had to downgrade Duty Free's debt, though Moody's at the same time affirmed that other aspects of the company, particularly its Inflight Services subsidiary, still showed strong earnings potential.

By the close of 1996, Duty Free had better news to report. Earnings at the third quarter mark were up more than 34 percent from the previous year. Total sales rose more than eight percent, and sales at its airport stores gained almost 20 percent. The numbers at this point looked good, yet it was not long before Duty Free succumbed to a merger, and let itself be bought by Britain's BAA PLC for $674 million. BAA, formerly the British Airport Authority, was a private company built out of a former British government agency. It operated seven airports in the United Kingdom, as well as the Pittsburgh and Indianapolis International Airports in the United States. With sales of more than $2 billion in the mid-1990s, BAA was a smart retailer. It conducted extensive market research to determine what international travelers were most likely to buy. It tailored its airport displays to feature, for example, the whiskey the Taiwanese preferred before Taiwan-bound flights, and it switched to Wedgewood china to snag travelers returning to Japan. When BAA took over management of the Pittsburgh International Airport, it also showed its shrewd marketing skills. The company ordered airport merchants to charge the same amount for goods and food inside the airport as outside. Travelers had frequently felt cheated by prices for coffee and soft drinks that were typically twice as much at the terminal as at a restaurant in the city. Under BAA's management, prices were made to match what consumers were used to paying and, as a result, sales volume increased dramatically. BAA had been eyeing a U.S. expansion for several years and also wanted to keep pace with some of its competitors in the duty free industry, who were consolidating in the late 1990s. The cash-rich company made the offer for Duty Free in July 1997, and the deal was completed only a month later. BAA folded Duty Free into its airport operations and renamed the now private company World Duty Free Americas, Inc. The new parent company did not publish separate financial information about its subsidiary, but BAA itself seemed to flourish after the acquisition. Airport traffic increased in the late 1990s, rising almost eight percent for 1998. BAA's marketing worked well to snare customers, so more traffic translated to rising sales. World Duty Free International continued to operate its in-flight sales division, its Canadian border and Mexican border subsidiaries, its nearly 200 airport stores, and its diplomatic and wholesale division.

Principal Subsidiaries

Fenton Hill American Ltd; AMMEX Tax & Duty Free Shops; UETA Inc.; Samuel Meisel & Company, Inc.; DFI Inflight Inc.

Further Reading

"BAA of Britain Will Buy Duty Free International," *New York Times*, July 4, 1997, p. D15.

Banks, Howard, "Tomorrow, the World," *Forbes,* December 18, 1995, pp. 178–79.

"British Airport Operator's Profit Is Up," *Wall Street Journal,* June 2, 1999, p. A12.

Cutro, Dyan C., "Duty Free International Reports Fourth Quarter and Fiscal Year 1993 Sales and Earnings," *Business Wire,* February 25, 1993.

——, "Duty Free International To Acquire Inflight Sales Group," *Business Wire,* March 30, 1994.

"Duty Free Sets Major Realignment," *WWD,* November 4, 1994, p. 5.

Frank, Robert, "BAA of Britain Signs Accord for Duty Free," *Wall Street Journal,* July 7, 1997, p. A6.

Higgins, Carol B., "When Government Taxes Sin, Firm's Duty Is Clear," *Intercorp,* July 21, 1989, p. 16.

Lehren, Andrew W., "Partnership of N.Y., Chicago Firms Undergoes Biggest Changes," *Philadelphia Business,* June 17, 1994, p. 13.

Lynch, Mickey, "Duty Free Restructures UETA Inc.," *Daily Record,* June 25, 1992, p. 3.

Lyons, James, "Border Merchants," *Forbes,* August 19, 1991, pp. 56–57.

"Moody's Cuts Rating on Duty Free," *WWD,* April 12, 1995, p. 18.

Myers, Randy, "Behind Clinton's Take Hike Plan, Duty Free Finds a Silver Lining," *Warfield's Business Record,* April 23, 1993, p. 3.

Roberts, Dan, "Doing Their Duty at Duty Free Shops," *Central New York Business Journal,* January 1988, p. 20.

Shopping Opportunities for the International Traveler, Ridgefield, Conn.: Duty Free International, Inc., 1993.

Williams, Elisa, "Duty Free Warehouse Makes Way for Growth," *Washington Times,* September 18, 1990, p. C1.

—Dave Mote
—updated by A. Woodward

INDEX TO COMPANIES

Index to Companies

Listings in this index are arranged in alphabetical order under the company name. Company names beginning with a letter or proper name such as Eli Lilly & Co. will be found under the first letter of the company name. Definite articles (The, Le, La) are ignored for alphabetical purposes as are forms of incorporation that precede the company name (AB, NV). Company names printed in bold type have full, historical essays on the page numbers appearing in bold. Updates to entries that appeared in earlier volumes are signified by the notation **(upd.)**. Company names in light type are references within an essay to that company, not full historical essays. This index is cumulative with volume numbers printed in bold type.

Financial Security Assurance Inc., **III** 765; **25** 497

Financial Services Corp., **III** 306–07

Financial Services Corporation of Michigan, **11** 163

Financial Systems, Inc., **11** 111

Financial Technologies International, **17** 497

Financiera Aceptaciones, **19** 189

Financière Crédit Suisse-First Boston, **II** 268, 402–04

Financiere de Suez, **II** 295

Financière Saint Dominique, **9** 151–52

FinansSkandic A.B., **II** 352–53

Finast. *See* First National Supermarkets, Inc.

Fincantieri, **I** 466–67

Find-A-Home Service, Inc., **21** 96

Findomestic, **21** 101

Findus, **II** 547; **25** 85

Fine Art Developments Ltd., **15** 340

Fine Fare, **II** 465, 609, 628–29

Fine Fragrances, **22** 213

Finelettrica, **I** 465–66

Finevest Services Inc., **15** 526

Fingerhut Companies, Inc., **I** 613; **V** 148; **9** 218–20; **15** 401; **18** 133

Fininvest Group, **IV** 587–88

The Finish Line, Inc., 29 186–88

FinishMaster, Inc., **17** 310–11; **24** **159–61**

Finland Wood Co., **IV** 275

Finlay Enterprises, Inc., 16 206–08

Finlay Forest Industries, **IV** 297

Finmare, **I** 465, 467

Finmeccanica S.p.A., **II** 86; **13** 28; **23** 83

Finnair Oy, **I** 120; **6** 87–89; **25 157–60** **(upd.)**

Finnforest Oy, **IV** 316

Finnigan Corporation, **11** 513

Finnish Cable Works, **II** 69; **17** 352

Finnish Fiberboard Ltd., **IV** 302

Oy Finnish Peroxides Ab, **IV** 300

Finnish Rubber Works, **II** 69; **17** 352

Oy Finnlines Ltd., **IV** 276

Finsa, **II** 196

FinSer Capital Corporation, **17** 262

Finservizi SpA, **II** 192

Finsider, **I** 465–66; **IV** 125

Firan Motor Coach, Inc., **17** 83

Fire Association of Philadelphia, **III** 342–43

Firearms Training Systems, Inc., 27 **156–58**

Fireman's Fund Insurance Company, **I** 418; **II** 398, 457; **III** 214, **250–52**, 263; **10** 62

Firemen's Insurance Co. of Newark, **III** 241–42

Firestone Tire and Rubber Co., **III** 440, 697; **V** 234–35; **8** 80; **9** 247; **15** 355; **17** 182; **18** 320; **20** 259–62; **21** 73–74

Firma Hamburger Kaffee-Import-Geschäft Emil Tengelmann. *See* Tengelmann Group.

The First, **10** 340

First Acadiana National Bank, **11** 107

First Alert, Inc., 28 133–35

First American Bank Corporation, **8** 188

First American Media, Inc., **24** 199

First American National Bank, **19** 378

First American National Bank-Eastern, **11** 111

First Analysis Securities Corporation, **22** 5

First and Merchants, **10** 426

First Atlanta Corporation, **16** 523

First Atlantic Capital, Ltd., **28** 340, 342

First Bancard, Inc., **11** 106

First BanCorporation, **13** 467

First Bank and Trust of Mechanicsburg, **II** 342

First Bank of Savannah, **16** 522

First Bank of the United States, **II** 213, 253

First Bank System Inc., **11** 130; **12** **164–66**; **13** 347–48; **24** 393

First Boston Corp., **II** 208, 257, 267–69, 402–04, 406–07, 426, 434, 441; **9** 378, 386; **12** 439; **13** 152, 342; **21** 145–46. *See also* CSFB.

First Brands Corporation, 8 180–82; 16 44

First Capital Financial, **8** 229

First Carolina Investors Inc., **17** 357

First Chicago Corporation, II 284–87

First Chicago Venture Capital, **24** 516

First City Bank of Rosemead, **II** 348

First Colony Farms, **II** 584

First Colony Life Insurance, **I** 334–35; **10** 290

First Commerce Bancshares, Inc., 15 **161–63**

First Commerce Corporation, 11 105–07

First Commercial Savings and Loan, **10** 340

First Consumers National Bank, **10** 491; **27** 429

First Dallas, Ltd., **II** 415

First Data Corp., **10** 63; **18** 516–18, 537; **24** 393

First Data Management Company of Oklahoma City, **11** 112

First Delaware Life Insurance Co., **III** 254

First Deposit Corp., **III** 218–19

First Empire State Corporation, 11 **108–10**

First Engine and Boiler Insurance Co. Ltd., **III** 406

First Executive Corporation, III 253–55

First Federal Savings & Loan Assoc., **IV** 343; **9** 173

First Federal Savings and Loan Association of Crisp County, **10** 92

First Federal Savings and Loan Association of Hamburg, **10** 91

First Federal Savings and Loan Association of Fort Myers, **9** 476

First Federal Savings and Loan Association of Kalamazoo, **9** 482

First Federal Savings Bank of Brunswick, **10** 92

First Fidelity Bank, N.A., New Jersey, 9 **221–23**

First Fidelity Bank of Rockville, **13** 440

First Financial Management **Corporation,** **11** 111–13; **18** 542; **25** 183

First Florida Banks, **9** 59

First Hawaiian, Inc., 11 114–16

First Health, **III** 373

FIRST HEALTH Strategies, **11** 113

First Healthcare, **14** 242

First Heights, fsa, **8** 437

First Hospital Corp., **15** 122

First Industrial Corp., **II** 41

First Insurance Agency, Inc., **17** 527

First Insurance Co. of Hawaii, **III** 191, 242

First International Trust, **IV** 91

First Interstate Bancorp, **II** 228, **288–90**; **8** 295; **9** 334; **17** 546

First Investment Advisors, **11** 106

First Investors Management Corp., **11** 106

First Jersey National Bank, **II** 334

First Liberty Financial Corporation, **11** 457

First Line Insurance Services, Inc., **8** 436

First Madison Bank, **14** 192

First Maryland Bancorp, **16** 14

First Mid America, **II** 445; **22** 406

First Mississippi Corporation, 8 183–86. *See also* ChemFirst, Inc.

First Mississippi National, **14** 41

First National Bank, **10** 298; **13** 467

First National Bank (Revere), **II** 208

First National Bank and Trust Company, **22** 4

First National Bank and Trust Company of Kalamazoo, **8** 187–88

First National Bank and Trust of Oklahoma City, **II** 289

First National Bank in Albuquerque, **11** 119

First National Bank of Akron, **9** 475

First National Bank of Allentown, **11** 296

First National Bank of Atlanta, **16** 522

First National Bank of Azusa, **II** 382

First National Bank of Boston, **II** 207–08, 402; **12** 310; **13** 446

First National Bank of Carrollton, **9** 475

First National Bank of Chicago, **II** 242, 257, 284–87; **III** 96–97; **IV** 135–36

First National Bank of Commerce, **11** 106

First National Bank of Harrington, Delaware. *See* J.C. Penny National Bank.

First National Bank of Hartford, **13** 466

First National Bank of Hawaii, **11** 114

First National Bank of Highland, **11** 109

First National Bank of Houma, **21** 522

The First National Bank of Lafayette, **11** 107

The First National Bank of Lake Charles, **11** 107

First National Bank of Lake City, **II** 336; **10** 425

First National Bank of Mexico, New York, **II** 231

First National Bank of Minneapolis, **22** 426–27

First National Bank of New York, **II** 254, 330

First National Bank of Raleigh, **II** 336

First National Bank of Salt Lake, **11** 118

First National Bank of Seattle, **8** 469–70

First National Bank of York, **II** 317

First National Bankshares, Inc., **21** 524

First National Boston Corp., **II** 208

First National Casualty Co., **III** 203

First National City Bank, **9** 124; **16** 13

First National City Bank of New York, **II** 254; **9** 124

First National City Corp., **III** 220–21

First National Holding Corporation, **16** 522

First National Insurance Co., **III** 352

First National Life Insurance Co., **III** 218

First National Supermarkets, Inc., **II** 641–42; **9** 452

First Nationwide Bank, 8 30; **14 191–93**

First Nationwide Financial Corp., **I** 167; **11** 139

First Nationwide Holdings Inc., **28** 246

First New England Bankshares Corp., **13** 467

PG&E Corporation, 26 370–73 **(upd.)**; **27** 131. *See also* Portland General Electric.

PGH Bricks and Pipes, **III** 735

Phaostron Instruments and Electronic Co., **18** 497–98

Phar-Mor Inc., 12 209, **390–92**, 477; **18** 507; **21** 459; **22** 157

Pharma Plus Drugmarts, **II** 649–50

Pharmacia & Upjohn Inc., 25 22, **374–78 (upd.)**. *See also* Upjohn Company.

Pharmacia A.B., I 211, **664–65**

Pharmaco Dynamics Research, Inc., **10** 106–07

Pharmacom Systems Ltd., **II** 652

Pharmacy Corporation of America, **16** 57

PharmaKinetics Laboratories, Inc., **10** 106

Pharmanex, Inc., **27** 352

Pharmaprix Ltd., **II** 663

Pharmazell GmbH, **IV** 324

Pharmedix, **11** 207

Pharos, **9** 381

Phelan & Collender, **III** 442

Phelan Faust Paint, **8** 553

Phelps Dodge Corporation, IV 33, **176–79**, 216; **7** 261–63, 288; **19** 375; **28** **352–57 (upd.)**

Phenix Bank, **II** 312

Phenix Cheese Corp., **II** 533

Phenix Insurance Co., **III** 240

Phenix Mills Ltd., **II** 662

PHF Life Insurance Co., **III** 263; **IV** 623

PHH Corporation, V 496–97; **6** 357; **22** 55

Phibro Corporation, **II** 447–48; **IV** 80; **13** 447–48; **21** 67

Philadelphia and Reading Corp., **I** 440; **II** 329; **6** 377; **25** 165

Philadelphia Carpet Company, **9** 465

Philadelphia Coke Company, **6** 487

Philadelphia Company, **6** 484, 493

Philadelphia Drug Exchange, **I** 692

Philadelphia Electric Company, V **695–97**; **6** 450

Philadelphia Life, **I** 527

Philadelphia Smelting and Refining Co., **IV** 31

Philco Corp., **I** 167, 531; **II** 86; **III** 604; **13** 402

Philip Environmental Inc., 16 414–16

Philip Morris Companies Inc., I 23, 269; **II** 530–34; **V** 397, 404, **405–07**, 409, 417; **6** 52; **7** 272, 274, 276, 548; **8** 53; **9** 180; **12** 337, 372; **13** 138, 517; **15** 64, 72–73, 137; **18** 72, **416–19 (upd.)**; **19** 112, 369; **20** 23; **22** 73, 338; **23** 427; **26** 249, 251; **29** 46–47

Philip Smith Theatrical Enterprises. *See* GC Companies, Inc.

Philipp Abm. Cohen, **IV** 139

Philipp Brothers Chemicals, Inc., **II** 447; **IV** 79–0; **25** 82

Philipp Holzmann AG, II 279, 386; **14** 169; **16** 284, 286; **17 374–77**

Philippine Aerospace Development Corporation, **27** 475

Philippine Airlines, Inc., I 107; **6 106–08**, 122–23; **23 379–82 (upd.)**; **27** 464

Philippine American Life Insurance Co., **III** 195

Philippine Sinter Corp., **IV** 125

Philips, **V** 339; **6** 101; **10** 269; **22** 194

Philips Electronics N.V., 8 153; **9** 75; **10** 16; **12** 475, 549; **13** 396, **400–03 (upd.)**; **14** 446; **23** 389; **26** 334; **27** 190–92

Philips Electronics North America Corp., 13 396–99; **26** 334

N.V. Philips Gloeilampenfabrieken, **I** 107, 330; **II** 25, 56, 58, **78–80**, 99, 102, 117, 119; **III** 479, 654–55; **IV** 680; **12** 454. *See also* Philips Electronics N.V.

Philips Medical Systems, **29** 299

Phillip Hawkins, **III** 169; **6** 285

Phillip Securities, **16** 14

Phillippe of California, **8** 16

Phillips & Drew, **II** 379

Phillips & Jacobs, Inc., **14** 486

Phillips Cables, **III** 433

Phillips Carbon Black, **IV** 421

Phillips Colleges, **22** 442

Phillips Manufacturing Company, **8** 464

Phillips Petroleum Company, I 377; **II** 15, 408; **III** 752; **IV** 71, 290, 366, 405, 412, 414, 445, 453, 498, **521–23**, 567, 570–71, 575; **10** 84, 440; **11** 522; **13** 356, 485; **17** 422; **19** 176; **24** 521

Phillips Sheet and Tin Plate Co., **IV** 236

Phillips-Van Heusen Corporation, 24 **382–85**

PHLCorp., **11** 261

PHM Corp., **8** 461

Phoenicia Glass, **25** 266–67

Phoenix Assurance Co., **III** 242, 257, 369, 370–74

Phoenix Financial Services, **11** 115

Phoenix Fire Office, **III** 234

Phoenix Insurance Co., **III** 389; **IV** 711

Phoenix Microsystems Inc., **13** 8

Phoenix Mutual Life Insurance, **16** 207

Phoenix Oil and Transport Co., **IV** 90

Phoenix State Bank and Trust Co., **II** 213

Phoenix Technologies Ltd., **13** 482

Phoenix-Rheinrohr AG, **IV** 222

Phone America of Carolina, **8** 311

Phonogram, **23** 389

Photocircuits Corp., **18** 291–93

PHP Healthcare Corporation, 22 423–25

Phuket Air Catering Company Ltd., **6** 123–24; **27** 464

Physician Corporation of America, **24** 231

Physician Sales & Service, Inc., 14 **387–89**

Physician's Weight Loss Center, **10** 383

Physicians Formula Cosmetics, **8** 512

Physicians Placement, **13** 49

Physio-Control International Corp., 18 **420–23**

Physiotherapy Associates Inc., **29** 453

Piaget, **27** 487, 489

Piaggio & C. S.p.A., 17 24; **20 426–29**

PIC International Group PLC, 24 **386–88 (upd.)**

Pic 'N' Save, **17** 298–99

PIC Realty Corp., **III** 339

Picard Surgeles, **27** 93

Picault, **19** 50

Piccadilly Cafeterias, Inc., 19 299–302

Pick, **III** 98

Pick-N-Pay, **II** 642; **9** 452

Pickands Mather, **13** 158

Picker International Corporation, **II** 25; **8** 352

Pickfords Ltd., **6** 412–14

Pickland Mather & Co., **IV** 409

PickOmatic Systems, **8** 135

Pickwick, **I** 613

Pickwick Dress Co., **III** 54

Pickwick International, **9** 360

Piclands Mather, **7** 308

Pico Ski Area Management Company, **28** 21

Picture Classified Network, **IV** 597

PictureTel Corp., 10 455–57; **27 363–66 (upd.)**

Piece Goods Shops, **16** 198

Piedmont Airlines, Inc., **6** 132; **12** 490; **28** 507

Piedmont Coca-Cola Bottling Partnership, **10** 223

Piedmont Concrete, **III** 739

Piedmont Natural Gas Company, Inc., 27 367–69

Piedmont Pulp and Paper Co. *See* Westvaco Corporation.

Pier 1 Imports, Inc., 12 179, 200, **393–95**

Pierburg GmbH, **9** 445–46

Pierce, **IV** 478

Pierce Brothers, **6** 295

Pierce Leahy Corporation, 24 389–92

Pierce National Life, **22** 314

Pierce Steam Heating Co., **III** 663

Piercing Pagoda, Inc., 29 382–84

Pierre Foods, **29** 203

Pierre Frozen Foods Inc., **13** 270–72

Pierson, Heldring, and Pierson, **II** 185

Pietrafesa Corporation, **29** 208

Pietro's Pizza Parlors, **II** 480–81; **26** 56–57

Piezo Electric Product, Inc., **16** 239

Pig Improvement Co., **II** 500

Piggly Wiggly Southern, Inc., II 571, 624; **13** 251–52, **404–06**; **18** 6, 8; **21** 455; **22** 127; **26** 47; **27** 245

Pignone, **IV** 420

Pike Adding Machine, **III** 165

Pike Corporation of America, **I** 570; **8** 191

Pikrose and Co. Ltd., **IV** 136

Pilgrim Curtain Co., **III** 213

Pilgrim's Pride Corporation, 7 432–33; **23 383–85 (upd.)**

Pilkington plc, I 429; **II** 475; **III** 56, 641–42, 676–77, 714–15, **724–27**; **16** 7, 9, 120–21; **22** 434

Pillar Holdings, **IV** 191

Pilliod Furniture, Inc., **12** 300

Pillowtex Corporation, 19 303–05

Pillsbury Company, II 133, 414, 493–94, 511, **555–57**, 575, 613–15; **7** 106, 128, 277, 469, 547; **8** 53–54; **10** 147, 176; **11** 23; **12** 80, 510; **13 407–09 (upd.)**, 516; **14** 212, 214; **15** 64; **16** 71; **17** 70–71, 434; **22** 59, 426; **24** 140–41; **25** 179, 241; **27** 196, 287; **29** 433

Pillsbury Madison & Sutro LLP, 29 **385–88**

Pilot, **I** 531

Pilot Freight Carriers, **27** 474

Pilot Insurance Agency, **III** 204

Pinal-Dome Oil, **IV** 569; **24** 520

Pinault-Printemps-Redoute S.A., 15 386; **19 306–09 (upd.)**; **22** 362; **27** 513

Pincus & Co., **7** 305

Pine Tree Casting. *See* Sturm, Ruger & Company, Inc.

Pinecliff Publishing Company, **10** 357

Pinelands, Inc., **9** 119; **26** 33

Pineville Kraft Corp., **IV** 276

Pinewood Studios, **II** 157

Pininfarina, **I** 188

INDEX TO INDUSTRIES

Index to Industries

CONSTRUCTION

CONTAINERS

DRUGS/PHARMACEUTICALS

ENTERTAINMENT & LEISURE

FINANCIAL SERVICES: BANKS

FINANCIAL SERVICES: NON-BANKS

FOOD PRODUCTS

HEALTH & PERSONAL CARE PRODUCTS

HEALTH CARE SERVICES

HOTELS

PAPER & FORESTRY

PERSONAL SERVICES

PETROLEUM

PUBLISHING & PRINTING

RUBBER & TIRE

TELECOMMUNICATIONS

Multimedia, Inc., 11
National Broadcasting Company, Inc., 28 (upd.)
NetCom Systems AB, 26
Nevada Bell Telephone Company, 14
New Valley Corporation, 17
Nextel Communications, Inc., 27 (upd.)
Nippon Telegraph and Telephone Corporation, V
Norstan, Inc., 16
Northern Telecom Limited, V
NYNEX Corporation, V
Octel Communications Corp., 14
Ohio Bell Telephone Company, 14
Österreichische Post- und Telegraphenverwaltung, V
Pacific Telecom, Inc., 6
Pacific Telesis Group, V
Paging Network Inc., 11
PictureTel Corp., 10; 27 (upd.)
Posti- ja Telelaitos, 6
Qualcomm Inc., 20
QVC Network Inc., 9
Rochester Telephone Corporation, 6
Saga Communications, Inc., 27
Schweizerische Post-, Telefon- und Telegrafen-Betriebe, V
Scientific-Atlanta, Inc., 6
Sinclair Broadcast Group, Inc., 25
Società Finanziaria Telefonica per Azioni, V
Southern New England Telecommunications Corporation, 6
Southwestern Bell Corporation, V
Sprint Communications Company, L.P., 9
StrataCom, Inc., 16
Swedish Telecom, V
SynOptics Communications, Inc., 10
Telecom Australia, 6
Telecom Eireann, 7
Telefonaktiebolaget LM Ericsson, V
Telefónica de España, S.A., V
Telefonos de Mexico S.A. de C.V., 14
Telephone and Data Systems, Inc., 9
Télévision Française 1, 23
Tellabs, Inc., 11
U.S. Satellite Broadcasting Company, Inc., 20
U S West, Inc., V; 25 (upd.)
United States Cellular Corporation, 9
United Telecommunications, Inc., V
United Video Satellite Group, 18
Vodafone Group plc, 11
Watkins-Johnson Company, 15
Westwood One, Inc., 23
Wisconsin Bell, Inc., 14

TEXTILES & APPAREL

Adidas AG, 14
Albany International Corp., 8
Algo Group Inc., 24
American Safety Razor Company, 20
Amoskeag Company, 8
Angelica Corporation, 15
AR Accessories Group, Inc., 23
Aris Industries, Inc., 16
Authentic Fitness Corp., 20
Banana Republic Inc., 25
Benetton Group S.p.A., 10
Birkenstock Footprint Sandals, Inc., 12
Blair Corporation, 25
Brazos Sportswear, Inc., 23
Brooks Brothers Inc., 22
Brown Group, Inc., V; 20 (upd.)
Bugle Boy Industries, Inc., 18
Burberrys Ltd., 17
Burlington Industries, Inc., V; 17 (upd.)

Calvin Klein, Inc., 22
Canstar Sports Inc., 16
Cato Corporation, 14
Chargeurs International, 21 (upd.)
Charming Shoppes, Inc., 8
Cherokee Inc., 18
Chic by H.I.S, Inc., 20
Christian Dior S.A., 19
Claire's Stores, Inc., 17
Coach Leatherware, 10
Coats Viyella Plc, V
Collins & Aikman Corporation, 13
Columbia Sportswear Company, 19
Concord Fabrics, Inc., 16
Cone Mills Corporation, 8
Courtaulds plc, V; 17 (upd.)
Crown Crafts, Inc., 16
Crystal Brands, Inc., 9
Culp, Inc., 29
Cygne Designs, Inc., 25
Danskin, Inc., 12
Deckers Outdoor Corporation, 22
Delta Woodside Industries, Inc., 8
Designer Holdings Ltd., 20
The Dixie Group, Inc., 20
Dominion Textile Inc., 12
Donna Karan Company, 15
Donnkenny, Inc., 17
Dyersburg Corporation, 21
Edison Brothers Stores, Inc., 9
Esprit de Corp., 8; 29 (upd.)
Fab Industries, Inc., 27
Fabri-Centers of America Inc., 16
Fieldcrest Cannon, Inc., 9
Fila Holding S.p.A., 20
Fossil, Inc., 17
Frederick's of Hollywood Inc., 16
Fruit of the Loom, Inc., 8; 25 (upd.)
Fubu, 29
G&K Services, Inc., 16
G-III Apparel Group, Ltd., 22
Galey & Lord, Inc., 20
Garan, Inc., 16
Gianni Versace SpA, 22
The Gitano Group, Inc. 8
Greenwood Mills, Inc., 14
Groupe DMC (Dollfus Mieg & Cie), 27
Groupe Yves Saint Laurent, 23
Guccio Gucci, S.p.A., 15
Guess, Inc., 15
Guilford Mills Inc., 8
Gymboree Corporation, 15
Haggar Corporation, 19
Hampton Industries, Inc., 20
Hartmarx Corporation, 8
The Hartstone Group plc, 14
Healthtex, Inc., 17
Helly Hansen ASA, 25
Hermès S.A., 14
Hyde Athletic Industries, Inc., 17
Interface, Inc., 8; 29 (upd.)
Irwin Toy Limited, 14
Items International Airwalk Inc., 17
J. Crew Group Inc., 12
Jockey International, Inc., 12
Johnston Industries, Inc., 15
Jordache Enterprises, Inc., 23
JPS Textile Group, Inc., 28
Kellwood Company, 8
Kenneth Cole Productions, Inc., 25
Kinney Shoe Corp., 14
L.A. Gear, Inc., 8
L.L. Bean, Inc., 10
LaCrosse Footwear, Inc., 18
Laura Ashley Holdings plc, 13
Lee Apparel Company, Inc., 8
The Leslie Fay Companies, Inc., 8
Levi Strauss & Co., V; 16 (upd.)

Liz Claiborne, Inc., 8
London Fog Industries, Inc., 29
Lost Arrow Inc., 22
Maidenform Worldwide Inc., 20
Malden Mills Industries, Inc., 16
Marzotto S.p.A., 20
Milliken & Co., V; 17 (upd.)
Mitsubishi Rayon Co., Ltd., V
Mossimo, Inc., 27
Mothercare UK Ltd., 17
Movie Star Inc., 17
Nautica Enterprises, Inc., 18
New Balance Athletic Shoe, Inc., 25
Nike, Inc., V; 8 (upd.)
The North Face, Inc., 18
Oakley, Inc., 18
OshKosh B'Gosh, Inc., 9
Oxford Industries, Inc., 8
Pacific Sunwear of California, Inc., 28
Pentland Group plc, 20
Pillowtex Corporation, 19
Pluma, Inc., 27
Polo/Ralph Lauren Corporation, 12
Quaker Fabric Corp., 19
Quiksilver, Inc., 18
R.G. Barry Corp., 17
Recreational Equipment, Inc., 18
Reebok International Ltd., V; 9 (upd.); 26 (upd.)
Rollerblade, Inc., 15
Russell Corporation, 8
St. John Knits, Inc., 14
Shelby Williams Industries, Inc., 14
Springs Industries, Inc., V; 19 (upd.)
Starter Corp., 12
Stone Manufacturing Company, 14
Stride Rite Corporation, 8
Sun Sportswear, Inc., 17
Teijin Limited, V
Thomaston Mills, Inc., 27
The Timberland Company, 13
Tommy Hilfiger Corporation, 20
Toray Industries, Inc., V
Tultex Corporation, 13
Unifi, Inc., 12
United Merchants & Manufacturers, Inc., 13
Unitika Ltd., V
Vans, Inc., 16
Varsity Spirit Corp., 15
VF Corporation, V; 17 (upd.)
Walton Monroe Mills, Inc., 8
The Warnaco Group Inc., 12
Wellman, Inc., 8
West Point-Pepperell, Inc., 8
WestPoint Stevens Inc., 16
Williamson-Dickie Manufacturing Company, 14
Wolverine World Wide Inc., 16

TOBACCO

American Brands, Inc., V
B.A.T. Industries PLC, 22 (upd.)
Brooke Group Ltd., 15
Brown and Williamson Tobacco Corporation, 14
Culbro Corporation, 15
Dibrell Brothers, Incorporated, 12
DIMON Inc., 27
800-JR Cigar, Inc., 27
Gallaher Limited, V; 19 (upd.)
Imasco Limited, V
Japan Tobacco Incorporated, V
Philip Morris Companies Inc., V; 18 (upd.)
RJR Nabisco Holdings Corp., V
Rothmans International p.l.c., V
Rothmans UK Holdings Limited, 19 (upd.)

WASTE SERVICES

NOTES ON CONTRIBUTORS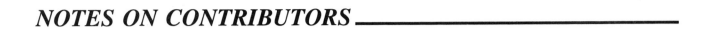

Notes on Contributors

BIANCO, David. Freelance writer, editor, and publishing consultant.

BISCONTINI, Tracey Vasil. Pennsylvania-based freelance writer, editor, and columnist.

BRENNAN, Gerald. Freelance writer based in San Francisco.

BROWN, Susan Windisch. Freelance writer and editor.

BRYNILDSSEN, Shawna. Freelance writer and editor based in Bloomington, Indiana.

COHEN, M. L. Novelist and freelance writer living in Paris.

COVELL, Jeffrey L. Freelance writer and corporate history contractor.

DERDAK, Thomas. Freelance writer and adjunct professor of philosophy at Loyola University of Chicago.

HALASZ, Robert. Former editor in chief of *World Progress* and *Funk & Wagnalls New Encyclopedia Yearbook*; author, *The U.S. Marines* (Millbrook Press, 1993).

HAUSER, Evelyn. Freelance writer and marketing specialist based in Northern California.

HUGHES, Shannon and Terry. Indiana-based educators and freelance writers.

INGRAM, Frederick C. South Carolina-based business writer who has contributed to *GSA Business, Appalachian Trailway News,* the *Encyclopedia of Business,* the *Encyclopedia of Global Industries,* the *Encyclopedia of Consumer Brands,* and other regional and trade publications.

KNIGHT, Judson. Freelance writer based in Atlanta.

LEMIEUX, Gloria A. Freelance writer and editor living in Nashua, New Hampshire.

MALLETT, Daryl F. Freelance writer and editor; actor; contributing editor and series editor at The Borgo Press; series editor of SFRA Press's *Studies in Science Fiction, Fantasy and Horror;* associate editor of Gryphon Publications and for *Other Worlds Magazine;* founder and owner of Angel Enterprises, Jacob's Ladder Books, and Dustbunny Productions.

MARTIN, Rachel. Denver-based freelance writer.

MESSERI, Kim L. Austin-based freelance editor, researcher, and writer specializing in the high-tech and hospitality industries.

ROTHBURD, Carrie. Freelance technical writer and editor, specializing in corporate profiles, academic texts, and academic journal articles.

SWARTZ, Mark. Writer and editor living in Chicago.

TRADII, Mary. Freelance writer based in Denver, Colorado.

UHLE, Frank. Ann Arbor-based freelance writer; movie projectionist, disc jockey, and staff member of *Psychotronic Video* magazine.

WALDEN, David M. Freelance writer and historian in Salt Lake City; adjunct history instructor at Salt Lake City Community College.

WERNICK, Ellen. Freelance writer and editor.

WHITELEY, Laura. Memphis-based freelance writer and editor.

WOODWARD, A. Freelance writer and editor.